my BusinessCourse

Financial Accounting
for Undergraduates

Fifth Edition

James S. Wallace
The Peter F. Drucker and Masatoshi Ito
Graduate School of Management
Claremont Graduate University

Karen K. Nelson
M. J. Neeley School of Business
Texas Christian University

Theodore E. Christensen
Terry College of Business
University of Georgia

Cambridge
BUSINESS PUBLISHERS

FINANCIAL ACCOUNTING FOR UNDERGRADUATES, Fifth Edition, by James Wallace, Karen Nelson, and Theodore Christensen.

ISBN 978-1-61853-441-5

Bookstores & Faculty: To order this book, contact the company via email **customerservice@cambridgepub.com** or call 800-619-6473.

Students & Retail Customers: To order this book, please visit the book's Website and order directly online.

Printed in the United States of America.
10 9 8 7 6 5 4 3 2 1

About the Authors

JAMES S. WALLACE is an Associate Professor at The Peter F. Drucker and Masatoshi Ito Graduate School of Management at The Claremont Graduate University. He received his B.A. from the University of California, Santa Barbara, his M.B.A. from the University of California, Davis, and his Ph.D. from the University of Washington. Professor Wallace also holds a CPA certification from the state of California. He previously served on the faculty of the University of California, Irvine and has served as a visiting professor at the University of California, San Diego. Professor Wallace's work has appeared in leading academic journals including the *Journal of Accounting and Economics*, the *Journal of Corporate Finance*, and *Information Systems Research*, along with leading applied journals such as the *Journal of Applied Corporate Finance*, the *Journal of Accountancy*, *Issues in Accounting Education* and *Accounting Horizons*. Prior to his career in academics, Professor Wallace worked in public accounting and in industry with a Fortune 500 company. He has done consulting work with numerous companies in multiple industries.

Karen K. Nelson is the M. J. Neeley Professor of Accounting in the M. J. Neeley School of Business at Texas Christian University. She earned her Ph.D. from the University of Michigan and a bachelor's degree (summa cum laude) from the University of Colorado. Prior to joining TCU, Professor Nelson served on the faculty at Stanford University and Rice University, and as a Visiting Professor at the University of Michigan. A Certified Public Accountant in Colorado, she is a past member of the Standing Advisory Group of the Public Company Accounting Oversight Board.

Professor Nelson's research focuses on financial reporting and disclosure issues, including the role of regulators, auditors, and private securities litigation in monitoring financial reporting quality. She has held research seminars at numerous conferences and business schools in the U.S. and abroad. Her research is published in several leading academic journals including *The Accounting Review*, *Journal of Accounting and Economics*, *Journal of Accounting Research*, and the *Review of Accounting Studies*, and has been featured in the popular financial press. She is an Associate Editor at the *Journal of Accounting and Economics* and was previously on the Editorial Board at *The Accounting Review*. She is also an author of an intermediate financial accounting textbook and has taught financial accounting and reporting at the undergraduate, MBA, and Ph.D. levels. Professor Nelson is the recipient of numerous awards for teaching excellence at the MBA level and was recently named a Top 50 Undergraduate Business Professor by Poets & Quants.

THEODORE E. CHRISTENSEN is director and Terry Distinguished Chair of Business in the J. M. Tull School of Accounting at the University of Georgia. Prior to coming to UGA, he was on the faculty at Brigham Young University and at Case Western Reserve University. He was a visiting professor at the University of Michigan, the University of Utah, and Santa Clara University. He received a B.S. degree in accounting at San Jose State University, a M.Acc. degree in tax at Brigham Young University, and a Ph.D. in accounting from the University of Georgia. Professor Christensen has authored and coauthored articles published in many journals including *The Accounting Review*, *Journal of Accounting and Economics*, *Journal of Accounting Research*, *Review of Accounting Studies*, *Contemporary Accounting Research*, and *Accounting Organizations and Society*. He is also the author of an advanced financial accounting textbook. Professor Christensen has taught financial accounting at all levels, financial statement analysis, business valuation, both introductory and intermediate managerial accounting, and corporate taxation. He is the recipient of numerous awards for both teaching and research. He has been active in serving on various committees of the American Accounting Association and is a CPA.

Preface

"THE MOST COMPELLING VALUE PROPOSITION OFFERED IN THE FINANCIAL ACCOUNTING MARKET!"

That has been our goal since this product's inception, and we have made that value proposition even more compelling with the Fifth Edition of Financial Accounting for Undergraduates. We created this product to satisfy the needs of students taking their first financial accounting course by providing a **high-quality**, **contemporary**, and **engaging** textbook and online learning system at an **affordable** price. With a suggested retail price of **$85** for the paperback, full-color textbook that **includes access** to **myBusinessCourse** (MBC), we challenge faculty to find a better overall value for their students.

Read on to learn why Financial Accounting for Undergraduates has become a best-seller, and why you should use it in your introductory financial accounting class.

PEDAGOGY THAT ENCOURAGES STUDENT SUCCESS

Financial accounting can be challenging — especially for students lacking business experience or previous exposure to business courses. To help students succeed in the course, we use a number of pedagogical devices throughout the textbook, and we provide a wealth of resources through our online learning and homework system, **myBusinessCourse** (MBC).

The Past/Present/Future feature puts each chapter in context.

PAST	PRESENT	FUTURE
Chapter 2 explained how we analyze and record transactions (the first two steps in the *accounting cycle*), including the system of debits	This chapter completes our examination of the final three steps in the five-step accounting cycle: adjust, report, and close	Chapter 4 examines the balance sheet and income statement more closely and introduces techniques for analyzing and interpreting

Road Maps outline each chapter and provide a quick reference table that summarizes the print and digital resources for that chapter.

Road Map

LO	Learning Objective	Page	eLecture	Guided Example	Assignments
LO1	Describe the nature of liabilities and discuss various current liabilities.	10-3	E10-1	YT10.1	SS1, SS2, SS4, E1A, E2A, E3A, E4A, E5A, E6A, E7A, E1B, E2B, E3B, E4B, E5B, E6B, E7B, P1A, P2A, P3A, P4A, P5A, P6A, P1B, P2B, P3B, P4B, P5B, P6B
LO2	Illustrate the accounting for long-term liabilities.	10-9	E10-2	YT10.2	SS8, SE2, SE8, SE9, SE10, E8A, E9A, E10A, E11A, E14A, E15A, E16A, E17A, E18A, E19A, E21A, E8B, E9B, E10B, E11B, E14B, E15B, E16B, E17B, E18B, E19B, E21B, P7A, P7B
LO3	Define contingent liabilities and explain the rules for their accounting and disclosure in the	10-19	E10-3	YT10.3	SS3, SS5, SE1, SE3, E1A, E7A, E7B, E12A, E12B, P6A, P6B

Your Turns provide hands-on practice after each major concept to ensure mastery of a topic before proceeding to the next concept.

The following inventory information is gathered from the accounting records of Tucker Enterprises:

YOUR TURN! 6.2

Beginning inventory	4,000 units at $ 5 each
Purchases	6,000 units at $ 7 each
Sales	9,000 units at $10 each

Calculate (a) ending inventory, (b) cost of goods sold, and (c) the gross profit using each of the following methods (i) FIFO, (ii) LIFO, and (iii) weighted-average cost.

MBC

The solution is on page 6-50.

iv

© Cambridge Business Publishers

On December 2, WebWork obtained a two-year bank loan for $36,000, signing a note payable. Annual interest of 10 percent is due each November 30.

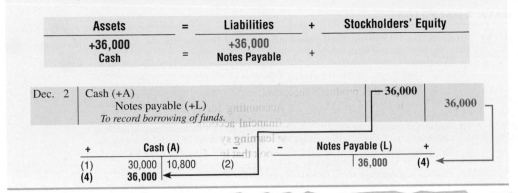

Assets	=	Liabilities	+	Stockholders' Equity
+36,000	=	**+36,000**	+	
Cash	=	Notes Payable	+	

Dec. 2 | Cash (+A) | | 36,000 | |
| | Notes payable (+L) | | | 36,000 |
| | *To record borrowing of funds.* | | | |

+	Cash (A)	−		−	Notes Payable (L)	+
(1)	30,000	10,800	(2)		36,000	(4)
(4)	**36,000**					

Hint: In contrast to the percentage of net sales method, the accounts receivable aging method takes into account the beginning balance of the Allowance for Doubtful Accounts.

A.K.A. The Allowance for Doubtful Accounts is also often referred to as the Allowance for Uncollectible Accounts.

DATA ANALYTICS & EXCEL SKILL DEVELOPMENT FOR CAREER READINESS

The basics of accounting haven't changed much in hundreds of years, but businesses have experienced significant change in the last decade due to the increased use of new technologies ranging from data analytics and Blockchain to machine learning and artificial intelligence. Technology is rapidly altering how accounting is performed and what can be done with the data once they are collected. In response to the changing demands of the business world, the AACSB has incorporated data analytics requirements within its educational framework. More recently, the AICPA and NASBA have underscored the importance of data analytics by making it a significant element in the CPA Evolution Model Curriculum. The consensus suggests that today's business students need an understanding and working knowledge of data analytics and data visualization to compete for the best jobs.

In addition to data analytics skills, employers expect prospective employees to be proficient with Excel. In recognition of the increasing importance of data analytics and the need for Excel proficiency, the Fifth Edition includes several new features to enhance students' career readiness.

■   We include Data Analytics boxes throughout the text to expose students to techniques that are used by businesses in areas related to the topic being discussed. The following box appears in the chapter on inventory.

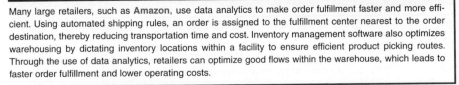

DATA ANALYTICS Data Analytics Can Make Order Fulfillment Faster and More Efficient

Many large retailers, such as **Amazon**, use data analytics to make order fulfillment faster and more efficient. Using automated shipping rules, an order is assigned to the fulfillment center nearest to the order destination, thereby reducing transportation time and cost. Inventory management software also optimizes warehousing by dictating inventory locations within a facility to ensure efficient product picking routes. Through the use of data analytics, retailers can optimize good flows within the warehouse, which leads to faster order fulfillment and lower operating costs.

■ Each chapter includes assignments that require students to use **Excel** and **Tableau** to hone data analysis and data visualization skills.

DATA ANALYTICS

Data Analytics

DA12-1. Preparing and Interpreting Excel Visualizations Created from Income and Cash Flow Data The Excel file associated with this exercise includes data extracted from Form 10-K reports for **CVS Health Corporation** (CVS) and **Walgreens Boots Alliance** (Walgreens Boots) for six years. In this exercise, we analyze changes to and the relations between net income and operating cash flows over a six-year period.

Required

1. Download Excel file DA12-1 found in myBusinessCourse.
2. Prepare a line chart for the six-year period for each company showing net income and operating cash flows. *Hint:* Highlight your data; click on Insert, Select line chart. There should be a separate line for net income and a separate line for operating cash flows. If necessary, edit the chart by opening the Chart Design tab and clicking Select Data. There should be two series.
3. Use the visualizations to answer the following questions.
   a. In what year(s) does net income exceed operating cash flows for CVS?
   b. In what year(s) do operating cash flows exceed net income for Walgreens Boots?

■ **Appendix F** at the end of the book provides an overview of data analytics, data visualization, and best practices for the effective display of data.

DATA ANALYTICS

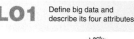

Data analytics can broadly be defined as the process of examining sets of data with the goal of discovering useful information from patterns found in the data. Increasingly, this process is aided by computers running programs ranging from basic spreadsheet software, such as **Microsoft Excel** and **Google Sheets**, to specialized software, such as **Tableau** or **Power BI**. This technology can reveal trends and insights that would otherwise be lost in the overwhelming amount of data.

LO1 Define big data and describe its four attributes.

eLecture

MBC

Big Data

The concept of data analytics is intertwined with the concept of **big data**. Although no precise definition exists for big data, a commonly accepted definition is that big data is a collection of data that is both extremely large and also extremely complex, thus making its analysis beyond the scope of traditional tools. Important attributes of big data, commonly referred to as

■ MBC now contains a series of short videos that demonstrate the basic functions of Excel. These videos can be accessed within MBC as part of your MBC course.

ENVIRONMENTAL, SOCIAL, AND GOVERNANCE (ESG)

Increasingly, companies have found that "doing good" leads to a more successful, profitable enterprise. Today's students are very engaged in the ESG movement, and we have incorporated ESG boxes and assignments to help students understand how corporate reporting on ESG is being embraced by forward-thinking enterprises as part of their long-term business models.

ENVIRONMENTAL, SOCIAL, AND GOVERNANCE   **Financing Green Investment**

Being a "green" company takes a lot of green—money that is. **Walmart** created their Green Financing Framework to finance investments that will enable the company to meet its environmental objectives. Their Framework is designed to meet the best practice guidelines of the International Capital Markets Association (ICMA) Green Bond Principles. In September 2021, Walmart launched its inaugural $2 billion green bond offering to fund current and future projects to advance the company's sustainability goals (see **Exhibit 10-3**). The bonds fund investment in renewable energy, high performance buildings, sustainable transport, zero waste projects, water stewardship, and habitat restoration and conservation.

BEST BUY

EYK6-8. Environmental, Social, and Governance Problem The Environmental, Social, and Governance (ESG) highlight in this chapter discussed how **Best Buy** is working to make sure its supply chain complies with the company's high ethical standards. One of the ways this is done is for Best Buy's Global Sourcing team to work with their Social and Environmental Responsibility team.

Go to the Best Buy website and its page on Environmental Sustainability (https://corporate. bestbuy.com/sustainability/ and locate Best Buy's Fiscal Year 2020 ESG Report. Open the report

TECHNOLOGY THAT IMPROVES LEARNING AND COMPLEMENTS FACULTY INSTRUCTION

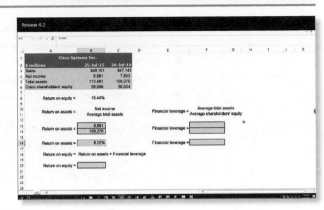

my BusinessCourse is an online learning and assessment program intended to complement your textbook and faculty instruction. Access to **my-BusinessCourse** is FREE ONLY with the purchase of a new textbook, but can access be purchased separately.

MBC is ideal for faculty seeking opportunities to augment their course with an online component. MBC is also a turnkey solution for online courses. The following are some of the features of MBC.

Increase Student Readiness

- **eLectures** cover each chapter's learning objectives and concepts. Consistent with the text and created by the authors, these videos are ideal for remediation and online instruction.
- **Guided Examples** are narrated video demonstrations created by the authors that show students how to solve select problems from the textbook.
- Immediate feedback with **auto-graded homework**.
- **Test Bank** questions that can be incorporated into your assignments.
- Instructor **gradebook** with immediate grade results.

Make Instruction Needs-Based

- Identify where your students are struggling and customize your instruction to address their needs.
- Gauge how your entire class or individual students are performing by viewing the easy-to-use gradebook.
- Ensure your students are getting the additional reinforcement and direction they need between class meetings.

> In two recent surveys of students who used MBC, **95%** responded that MBC helped them learn accounting.*

Provide Instruction and Practice 24/7

- Assign homework from your Cambridge Business Publishers' textbook and have MBC grade it for you automatically.
- With our eLectures, your students can revisit accounting topics as often as they like or until they master the topic.
- Guided Examples show students how to solve select problems.
- Make homework due before class to ensure students enter your classroom prepared.
- For an additional fee, upgrade MBC to include the eBook and you have all the tools needed for an online course.

> In the same two surveys, over **86%** of the students who responded said they would encourage their professor to continue using MBC in future terms.*

Integrate with LMS

my BusinessCourse integrates with many learning management systems, including **Canvas**, **Blackboard**, **Moodle**, **D2L**, **Schoology**, and **Sakai**. Your gradebooks sync automatically.

NEW TO THIS EDITION

- **Data Analytics:** we have expanded Data Analytics coverage in this edition.
  - ○ New Data Analytics boxes have been incorporated throughout the text. These boxes describe how Data Analytics is being used in business.
  - ○ New Data Analytics assignments using Excel have been included in each chapter.
  - ○ Appendix F on Data Analytics has been significantly expanded and includes assignments that utilize Tableau.

---

* These statistics are based on the results of two surveys in which 2,330 students participated.

- **Environmental, Social, and Governance Reporting (ESG):** Increasingly, companies have found that "doing good" leads to a more successful, profitable enterprise. A new introduction to ESG reporting is included in Chapter 1, and ESG boxes are incorporated throughout the text to help students understand how ESG is being embraced by forward-thinking enterprises as part of their long-term business models. New ESG reporting assignments have also been added to every chapter to reinforce the concepts presented.
- **Chapter 12** on the statement of cash flow has been revised to be more intuitive for students.
- New **graphics and illustrations** have been incorporated to convey key concepts.
- **Updated financial data** throughout the text and assignments where real data is used.
- **Expanded the number** of guided example videos and assignments included in MBC.
- MBC now includes short videos that show students how to use various features and functions in **Excel**.
- The focus companies for five chapters have been changed:
  - **Salesforce** replaces Krispy Kreme in Chapter 3
  - **Nike** replaced Best Buy in Chapter 6
  - **Luckin Coffee** is new to Chapter 7
  - **Tesla** replaces MGM Resorts International in Chapter 8
  - **Lululemon** replaces Facebook in Chapter 9

SUPPLEMENT PACKAGE

For Instructors

*my*BusinessCourse: A web-based learning and assessment program intended to complement your textbook and classroom instruction.

Solutions Manual: Created by the authors, the *Solutions Manual* contains complete solutions to all the assignment material in the text.

PowerPoint: The PowerPoint slides outline key elements of each chapter.

Test Bank: The Test Bank includes multiple-choice items, exercises, and problems.

Excel Templates: We provide Excel spreadsheets for select assignments. These spreadsheets will save time in data entry and allow students to dedicate additional time to learning the material. The assignments accompanied by Excel spreadsheets are identified by the Excel icon.

Website: All instructor materials are accessible via the book's Website (password protected) along with other useful links and marketing information: www.cambridgepub.com

For Students

*my*BusinessCourse: A web-based learning and assessment program intended to complement your textbook and faculty instruction. This easy-to-use program grades homework automatically and provides you with additional help when your instructor is not available. Assignments with the MBC in the margin are available in myBusinessCourse. Access is free with new copies of this textbook (look for page containing the access code towards the front of the book). If you buy a used copy of the book, you can purchase access at www.mybusinesscourse.com.

Excel Templates: We provide Excel spreadsheets for select assignments that can be downloaded from myBusinessCourse. These spreadsheets will save time in data entry and allow students to dedicate additional time to learning the material. The assignments accompanied by Excel spreadsheets are identified by the Excel icon.

Website: Updates and other useful links are available to students free of charge on the book's Website.

ACKNOWLEDGEMENTS

All five editions of this book benefited greatly from the valuable feedback of focus group attendees, reviewers, students, and colleagues. We are extremely grateful to them for their help in making this project a success.

Markus Ahrens	David Ambrosini	James Bannister	Sara Barritt	James Benjamin	Jim Borden
James Aitken	Matthew Anderson	Richard Barnhart	Melody Barta	Debbie Benson	Lydia Botsford
Dave Alldredge	Adam Baker	Gerhard Barone	Nancy Batch	Christine Betts	Salem Boumediene
Bam Alling	Felicia Baldwin	Robyn Barrett	Vernon Bell	Swati Bhandarkar	Amy Bourne

Robert Bowen
Scott Boylan
Rada Brooks
Marilyn Brooks-Lewis
Stephen Brown
Amy Browning
Helen Brubeck
Patricia Burnett
Ian Burt
Sandra Byrd
Jeffrey Byrne
Jennifer Cainas
Michael Calegari
Mike Campbell
John Capka
Tommy Carnes
Jackie Casey
Melissa Chadd
Christy Chauvin
Betty Chavis
Alan Cherry
Catherine Chiang
Gerald Childs
Alice Chu
Lawrence Chui
Leslie Cohen
Erin Cornelsen
Nancy Coster
John Coulter
Rachel Cox
Timothy Creel
Cheryl Crespi
Jim Crumbacher
Richard Culp
Dori Danko
Emmanuel Danso
Lois Darga
Judy Daulton
Annette Davis
Harold Davis
Patricia Davis
Regina Derzon
Rosemond Desir
Glenn Dickerson
Vicky Dominguez
Pamela Donahue
Doris Donovan
Tom Downen
Chan Du
Peggy Eaton
Jeanne Eibes
Lisa Eiler
Jerrilyn Eisenhauer

Ahmed El-Zayaty
James Emig
Li Li Eng
Cole Engel
Michael Fagan
Connie Fajardo
Alan Falcon
Lucile Faurel
Kevin Feeney
Bud Fennema
Cathy Finger
Julie Finnegan
Linda Flaming
Gary Ford
David Forester
Jackie Franklin
Mitchell Franklin
Carolyn Galantine
Rena E. Galloway
Dennis George
Julie Gilbert
Lisa Gillespie
Brian Gilligan
Julie Gittelman
Alan Glazer
Hubert Glover
David Golub
Julie Goodin
Marina Grau
Lisa Gray
Thomas Guarino
Wendy Gunn
Bruce Gunning
Joo Ha
James Halstead
Lorna Hardin
David Harr
Bob Hartman
Rosemary Hayward
Haihong He
Joshua Herbold
Merrily Hoffman
Cynthia Hollenbach
Steven Hornik
Jana Hosmer
Marsha Huber
William Huffman
Carol Hughes
Kathy Hurley
Richard Hurley
Helen Hurwitz
Laura Ilcisin
Rajeshwari Iyer

Stephen Jablonsky
Sharon Jackson
Shirin Jahanian
Marianne James
Ching-Lih Jan
Mark Jasonowicz
Bill Jefferson
Catherine Jeppson
Gene Johnson
Randy Johnston
Jane Jollineau
Thomas Kam
Kathryn Kapka
Jocelyn Kauffunger
Tom Kelley
Sara Kern
Suzanne Kiess
Christine Kloezeman
Aaron Knape
Becky Knickel
Dennis Knutson
John Koeplin
Paul Koulakov
Elida Kraja
Mary-Jo Kranacher
Lynn Krausse
Christopher Kwak
Steven LaFave
Luke Lammer
Benjamin Lansford
Cathy Larson
Doug Larson
Greg Lauer
Gary Laycock
Ron Lazer
Joan Lee
Charles LeFlar
Zawadi Lemayian
Jennifer LeSure
Elliott Levy
Christine Li
Siyi Li
Zining Li
Lihong Liang
Emily Lindsay
Sara Linton
John Long
Suzanne Lozano
Debbie Luna
Heather Lynch
Nancy Lynch
Susan Lynn
David Manifold

Jeff Mankin
William J. Mann
Joe Manzo
Ariel Markelevich
Thomas Marsh
Dawn Massey
Michele Matherly
Clarice McCoy
Molly McFadden-May
Florence McGovern
Michele McGowan
Allison McLeod
Jeff McMillan
Michelle McNeil-Brown
Casey McNellis
Cathryn Meegan
Lindsay Meermans
Sara Melendy
Jean Meyer
Michael Meyer
Linda Miller
Jill Mitchell
April Mohr
Michelle Moshier
Sheila Muller
Johnna Murray
Patricia Naranjo
Tammie Neeley
Pam Neely
Joshua Neil
Bruce Neumann
Monica Newman
Joseph Nicassio
Micki Nickla
Tracie Nobles
Hossein Noorian
Lisa Novak
Sarah Nutter
Barbara Nyden
Cynthia Nye
Joanne Orabone
Roshelle Overton
Ken O'Brien
Kalpana Pai
Abbie Gail Parham
Keith Patterson
Paige Paulsen
Sy Pearlman
Mary Pearson
Ron Pearson
Aaron Pennington
Kimberly Perkins

Ryan Peterson
Julie Petherbridge
Kathy Petroni
Marietta Peytcheva
Robert Picard
Gary Pieroni
Kendell Poch
April Poe
Ronald Premuroso
Jean Price
Allan Rabinowitz
Ann Randolph
Kathy Rankin
Melinda Ratliff
Paul Recupero
Aaron Reeves
Vernon Richardson
Cecile Roberti
Shani Robinson
Andrea Roerdink
Gregg Romans
Lydia Rosencrants
Mark Ross
John Rossi
Eric Rothenburg
Maria Roxas
Pinky Rusli
Ron Sabado
John Sanders
Roby Sawyers
Albert Schepanski
Arnold Schneider
Robert Schweikle
Steve Sefcik
Jamie Seitz
Perry Sellers
Randy Serrett
Cathy Sevigny
Tracy Sewell
Ray Shaffer
Vikram Sharma
Carol Shaver
Dennis Shea
Regina Shea
John Shon
Gregory Sinclair
Ken Sinclair
Bhaskar Singh
Eric Slayter
Gene Smith
Gerald Smith
Nancy Snow
Robin Soffer

Marilyn Stansbury
George Starbuck
Ronald Stone
Carolyn Strauch
Rick Street
Scott Stroher
Rob Stussie
John Suckow
John Susenburger
Stephanie Swaim
Aida Sy
Mary Sykes
Ted Takamura
Robert Tallo
Diane Tanner
Linda Tarrago
Randall Thomas
Robin Thomas
Dalton Tong
Sheri Trumpfheller
Jennifer Tseng
Anthony Tuan
Michael Tydlaska
Joan Van Hise
Marcia Viet
George Violette
Marcia Vorholt
Robert Walsh
Doris Warmflash
Brian Watkins
Randi Watts
Debra Webb
Andrea Weickgenannt
Patricia Wellmeyer
Donna Whitten
Monica Widdig
Gayle Williams
Idalene Williams
Paula Wilson
Michele Wiltsie
Douglas Woods
Justin Wood
Maef Woods
Daryl Woolley
Susan Wright
Kean Wu
Rong Yang
Kathryn Yarbrough
Robert Yu
Amy Yurko
Judith Zander
Jian Zhou

In addition, we are grateful to George Werthman, Lorraine Gleeson, Jocelyn Mousel, Debbie McQuade, Terry McQuade, and the entire team at Cambridge Business Publishers for their encouragement, enthusiasm, and guidance. Feedback is always welcome. Please feel free contact us with your suggestions or questions.

Jim Wallace   *Karen Nelson*   *Ted Christensen*

January 2022

Brief Contents

Contents

CHAPTER **6**

Accounting for Inventory 6-1

CHAPTER **7**

Internal Control and Cash 7-1

CHAPTER 8

Accounting for Receivables   8-1

CHAPTER 9

Accounting for Long-Lived and Intangible Assets   9-1

CHAPTER **10**
Accounting for Liabilities   10-1

CHAPTER **11**
Stockholders' Equity   11-1

CHAPTER **12**

Statement of Cash Flows **12-1**

CHAPTER **13**

Analysis and Interpretation of Financial Statements **13-1**

Chapter 1
Financial Accounting and Business Decisions

Road Map

Road Maps *summarize each chapter's resources and categorize them by learning objective.*

eLectures *are videos available in MBC that provide 3-5 minute reviews of each learning objective.*

Assignments *reinforce learning and can be completed by hand or within MBC.*

LO	Learning Objective	Page	eLecture	Guided Example	Assignments
LO1	Explain the three forms of business organizations.	1-3	E1-1	YT1.1	SE1, E1A, E1B, P1A, P1B
LO2	Describe business activities.	1-4	E1-2	YT1.2	SE5, SE10, E6A, E6B
LO3	Identify who uses accounting information.	1-5	E1-3	YT1.3 YT1.4	SE3, SE8, E3A, E14A, E3B, P8A, P8B
LO4	Explain the accounting process and generally accepted accounting principles.	1-8	E1-4	YT1.5	SE2, SE4, SE9, SE15, SE19, E2A, E5A, E15A, E2B, E5B, E15B
LO5	Describe the accounting equation and each financial statement.	1-11	E1-5	YT1.6	SE6, SE11, SE12, SE13, SE14, E4A, E7A, E9A, E10A, E11A, E12A, E19A, E4B, E7B, E8B, E9B, E10B, E11B, E12B, 19B, P2A, P3A, P4A, P5A, P6A, P7A, P9A, P10A, P2B, P3B, P4B, P5B, P6B, P7B, P9B, P10B
LO6	Explain additional disclosures that accompany financial statements.	1-18	E1-6	YT1.7	SE7, E13A, E13B, P9A, P9B
LO7	Describe careers in accounting.	1-20	E1-7		
LO8	Appendix 1A: Discuss FASB's conceptual framework.	1-23	E1-8		SE16, SE17, SE18, SE20, SE21, E16A, E17A, E18A, E19A, E20A, E16B, E17B, E18B, E19B, E20B, P11A, P11B

Learning Objectives *identify the key learning goals of the chapter.*

YourTurns *follow each learning objective and require students to apply what they have just learned.* Guided Example *videos accompany most of the YourTurns and demonstrate how to solve various types of problems. YourTurns are also assignable in MBC.*

It is often said that accounting is the language of business. Like all companies, **Columbia Sportswear Company** (Columbia.com), a maker of clothing for dedicated lovers of the greater outdoors, relies upon accounting for its success. It uses financial reports to judge its performance and that of its managers. It uses accounting controls to monitor its inventory. It uses accounting data to assess the amount and timing of dividend payments to shareholders.

This first chapter introduces many basic relations and principles underlying financial statements. It also identifies many key users of accounting information and discusses how that information is useful in businesses.

*A **Focus Company** introduces each chapter and illustrates the relevance of accounting in everyday business.*

PRESENT

This chapter explains business formation, the uses and users of accounting information, the types of activities companies pursue, and financial statements that report on those activities.

FUTURE

The next chapters more fully explain financial statements, including how they are prepared, constructed, analyzed, and interpreted.

Past/Present/Future *provides an overview of where the chapter fits within the context of the whole book.*

Chapter Organization charts visually depict the key topics and their sequence within the chapter.

FINANCIAL ACCOUNTING AND BUSINESS DECISIONS

Forms of Business Organizations	Business Activities	Accounting Information and Its Use	Information Dissemination	Other Annual Report Components	FASB Conceptual Framework (Appendix 1A)
• Sole proprietorship • Partnership • Corporation	• Financing • Investing • Operating	• External users • Internal users • Ethics and accounting	• Accounting process • Generally Accepted Accounting Principles • International Financial Reporting Standards • Financial statements	• Notes to financial statements • Independent auditor's report • Management's Discussion and Analysis	• Objectives • Elements • Characteristics • Recognition and Measurement

Learning Objectives are repeated at the start of the section covering that topic.

BUSINESS ORGANIZATION

LO1 — Explain the three forms of business organizations.

eLecture icons denote the availability of an instructional video in **myBusinessCourse** *(MBC). See the Preface for more information on MBC.*

Key Terms *are highlighted in bold, red font.*

The first decision every business faces is deciding what form of organization it will take. The three principal forms of business organization are the sole proprietorship, the partnership, and the corporation. Although each of these organizational forms is treated as an accounting entity, only the corporation is viewed under the law as a legal entity separate and distinct from its owners. A corporation has an unlimited life, which means that it will continue to exist indefinitely unless it is formally dissolved. The life of a sole proprietorship or partnership is limited by the participation of the existing owners. If an owner dies or withdraws, the business typically ends as well.

A **sole proprietorship** is a business owned by one person; it is the most common of the three forms of business organization. The primary advantage of the sole proprietorship is its ease of formation. As the only owner, the sole proprietor makes all of the decisions affecting the business. This organizational form also enjoys certain income tax advantages relative to a corporation in that the income of the business is not taxed; instead, its income is included as part of the owner's income that is reported to the taxation authorities.

A **partnership** is a voluntary association of two or more persons for the purpose of conducting a business. Partnerships and sole proprietorships differ principally with respect to the number of owners. Partnerships can be as small as two people or as large as the biggest accounting or legal firms, which have hundreds or even thousands of partners. Partnerships are also easy to establish. Because a partnership involves multiple owners, the partners should establish the rights and obligations of each partner to avoid any misunderstandings that might lead to disputes and lawsuits. An advantage of the partnership form over the sole proprietorship is the broader skill set that multiple partners can bring to a business. Partnerships also enjoy the same income tax advantage as sole proprietorships.

A **corporation** is a legal entity created under the laws of a state or the federal government. A corporation can have as few as one owner but most have many owners. The owners of a corporation receive shares of stock as evidence of their ownership interest in the business, and consequently, they are referred to as **stockholders** (or *shareholders*). Since corporations are a separate legal entity, they must pay income taxes on their profits. This leads to a situation of double taxation because the income of the corporation is taxed and stockholders also pay taxes on dividends they receive from the corporation. The corporation is the dominant organizational form in terms of the volume of business activity conducted in the United States and worldwide.

While most businesses start off as either a sole proprietorship or as a partnership, some outgrow these organizational forms and convert to the corporate form. For example, **Columbia**

Sportswear Company was incorporated in 1961 after beginning as a sole proprietorship in 1938. Two primary advantages of the corporate form of business are the relative ease of raising capital to grow the business and the protection afforded to stockholders against personal liability. A third advantage of the corporate form is the relative ease of selling ownership shares. For example, stock exchanges, such as the **New York Stock Exchange (NYSE)**, exist to enable stockholders to readily buy and sell their ownership shares. No such exchanges exist for sole proprietors or partners, and thus, selling an ownership interest in a sole proprietorship or a partnership is a more difficult, time-consuming event.

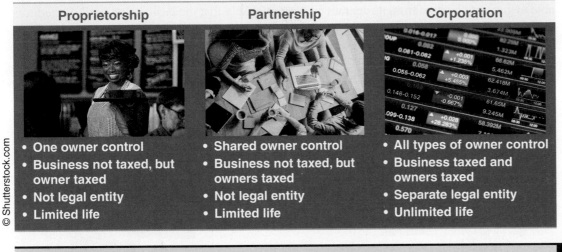

Proprietorship	Partnership	Corporation
• One owner control	• Shared owner control	• All types of owner control
• Business not taxed, but owner taxed	• Business not taxed, but owners taxed	• Business taxed and owners taxed
• Not legal entity	• Not legal entity	• Separate legal entity
• Limited life	• Limited life	• Unlimited life

© Shutterstock.com

Your Turn! boxes reinforce the material just presented with self-study questions. To aid learning, solutions are provided at the end of the chapter.

Identify three characteristics for each of the principal forms of business organizations.

1. Sole proprietorship
2. Partnership
3. Corporation

YOUR TURN! 1.1

The solution is on page 1-53.

ACTIVITIES OF A BUSINESS

Every business, regardless of its organizational form, its industry, or its size, is involved in three types of business activities—financing, investing, and operating.

LO2 Describe business activities.

Financing Activities

Before a company can begin operations, it must acquire money to support its operations. Employees need to be hired, buildings constructed, raw materials purchased, and machinery put in place. Companies can obtain the necessary funds to undertake these activities in several ways. These **financing activities** are generally categorized as either debt financing or equity financing.

Debt financing involves borrowing money from sources such as a bank by signing a note payable or directly from investors by issuing bonds payable. The individuals or financial institutions that lend money to companies are called their **creditors**. Debt financing involves an obligation to repay a creditor both the amount initially borrowed, called the **principal**, and interest for the use of the funds.

Equity financing involves selling shares of stock to investors. In contrast to creditors who lend money to a business and expect to receive that money back with interest, investors that purchase shares of stock are buying an ownership interest in the company. Investors hope that their stock will increase in value so that they can earn a profit when they sell their shares. The owners of a company's stock may also receive dividend payments when the company decides to distribute some of its profits.

eLecture

MBC

A.K.A. (Also Known As) identify commonly used alternative terms.

A.K.A. Land, buildings, and equipment is often referred to as property, plant, and equipment, or simply PP&E.

Investing Activities

Before a company can begin operations, it must purchase the long-term resources necessary to conduct its business, such as land, buildings, and equipment. **Investing activities** involve the acquisition and disposition of factories, office furniture, computer and data systems, delivery vehicles, and other items that will be used to carry out the company's business plans.

Companies can obtain the money needed to make these investments from either the financing activities discussed previously or from any excess cash accumulated from operating the business profitably.

Operating Activities

The day-to-day activities of producing and selling a product or providing a service are referred to as **operating activities**. Operating activities are critical for a business because if a company is unable to generate income from its operations it is very likely that the business will fail. If creditors and stockholders do not believe that a company will be able to generate a profit, they are unlikely to provide the financing needed to start, or maintain, its operations.

Exhibit 1-1 provides a summary of the three types of business activities. Arrows are pointing both toward, and away from, operating activities. This is because financing and investing activities are necessary to carry out a company's operating activities; however, if a company's operating activities generate excess cash, then the excess cash can be used to either finance additional investments, repay the company's creditors, or pay dividends to shareholders.

EXHIBIT 1-1   Business Activities

Investing Activities
(purchase factory, acquire land, buy equipment)

Operating Activities
(sell products, buy supplies, conduct marketing)

Financing Activities
(issue stock, obtain loans)

© Shutterstock.com

YOUR TURN! 1.2	Classify each of the following activities as a financing, investing, or operating activity.
The solution is on page 1-54.	1. Receiving a loan from a bank. 4. Purchasing merchandise for resale to customers. 2. Selling merchandise online. 5. Issuing shares of stock in exchange for cash. 3. Purchasing a delivery truck. 6. Paying employee salaries.

ACCOUNTING INFORMATION AND ITS USE

LO3 Identify who uses accounting information.

In today's society, many individuals and agencies are involved in the economic life of a business. The information needs of these parties are fulfilled, in part, by accounting information. The users of accounting information are classified by their relation to a business as either *external users* or *internal users*.

eLecture

MBC

External Users of Accounting

An important function of the accounting process is to accumulate and report accounting information that details a business's results of operations, cash flows, and financial position. By U.S. law, publicly owned businesses must publish financial statements annually and quarterly. The process of preparing these publicly available financial statements is referred to as **financial accounting**.

Financial accounting information serves a variety of users. Potential investors and investment professionals need financial data to compare prospective investments to determine which, if any, they should invest in, and at what price. Creditors must consider the financial strength of a business before lending it funds, and stockholders must evaluate whether to remain invested in a business, buy more shares, or sell their existing shares of stock. The financial statements issued by a company are the main source of financial information for these external users.

Because financial statements are often used to evaluate the management team running the business, their objectivity is sometimes called into question because the reports are prepared by the management team itself. To establish the validity of financial statements, most businesses have their financial data audited by an independent public accountant. Publicly owned businesses are required to have their financial statements audited. The independent public accountant, or independent auditor, examines the financial statements and recommends any changes or improvements that are warranted. The independent auditor then expresses a professional opinion as to whether the financial statements are fairly presented "in conformity with generally accepted accounting principles." External users have greater confidence in financial statements that have been audited by an independent, certified public accountant.

ACCOUNTING IN PRACTICE **The Big Four**

Independent auditors are licensed by the state in which they do their auditing work and are identified as **certified public accountants (CPAs)**. To qualify as a CPA, an individual must pass a rigorous examination that is administered nationally and must meet the educational and work experience requirements set by each state to ensure high standards of accounting and auditing performance. The four largest U.S. public accounting firms, referred to as the *Big Four*, have offices located throughout the world and employ thousands of auditors. These firms are **Deloitte & Touche, Ernst & Young, KPMG**, and **PricewaterhouseCoopers**.

Accounting In Practice boxes describe how accounting is used in real companies.

There are many other external users of a company's accounting information. For example, customers may want information to help them determine if a company like **Whirlpool** will be able to honor its product warranties. Labor unions require information when negotiating for pay raises with companies like **United Parcel Service**. **Exhibit 1-2** illustrates the kind of accounting information that is required by a company's external users.

Real Companies and Institutions are highlighted in bold, blue font.

EXHIBIT 1-2	Accounting Information Needs of External Users	
User Group		**Accounting Information Used to Answer Questions such as:**
Potential investors and current stockholders		How does the profitability of **Target** compare to that of **WalMart**? How does **Bank of America Corporation** compare with **Wells Fargo & Company** in terms of firm size?
Creditors and lenders		Will **Delta Airlines** be able to repay its creditors in a timely fashion? Is it safe to provide a bank loan to the **Federal Express Corporation**?
Taxation authorities and regulators		Is **Tesla Motors, Inc.** reporting the proper amount of taxable income? Is **Duke Energy**'s rate hike justified by its operating costs?

Internal Users of Accounting

A major function of accounting is to provide the internal management of a company with the data needed for decision making and the efficient management of the business. While managers have an interest in the information reported to external users, managers also require various other types of information, such as the cost of its products, estimates of the income to be earned from a sales campaign, cost comparisons of alternative courses of action, and long-range budgets. Because of the strategic nature of much of this information, it is usually only available to a company's top-level management. The process of generating and analyzing such data is referred to as **managerial accounting**. **Exhibit 1-3** illustrates the various types of accounting information that are required by a company's internal users.

EXHIBIT 1-3	Accounting Information Needs of Internal Users
User Group	**Accounting Information Used to Answer Questions such as:**
Marketing Department 	What is the optimal price to sell the **Samsung** Galaxy phone to maximize the company's sales revenue? Was Netflix's promotional campaign for *The Umbrella Academy* successful?
Management Team 	How much is the Olive Garden restaurant chain contributing to the overall profitability of its parent company, the **Darden Restaurant Group**? What is the projected profitability of the **General Motors'** Chevrolet brand for the coming year?
Finance Department 	Is there sufficient cash available for **Hewlett Packard** to buy back a large amount of its outstanding common stock? Will **General Electric** have sufficient cash flow to pay its short-term expenses?

© Shutterstock.com

YOUR TURN! 1.3

The solution is on page 1-54.

1. Are financial statements the primary output of managerial or financial accounting? Explain.
2. Identify at least two internal users and explain why they need accounting information.
3. Identify at least two external users and explain why they need accounting information.

Ethics and Accounting

Ethics deals with the values, rules, and justifications that govern one's way of life. Although fundamental ethical concepts such as right and wrong, good and evil, justice and morality are abstract, many issues in our daily lives have ethical dimensions. The way that we respond to these issues defines our ethical profile. In both our personal and professional lives, our goal is to act ethically and responsibly.

Ethical behavior has not always been the rule in business. Business history reveals unethical activities such as price gouging of customers, using inside information for personal gain, paying bribes to government officials for favors, ignoring health and safety regulations, selling arms and military equipment to aggressor governments, polluting the environment, and issuing misleading financial information. Well-known accounting scandals at such companies as **Wirecard AG**, **Wells Fargo**, and **Luckin Coffee** have again brought ethics to the forefront.

Increasingly, business managers recognize the importance and value of ethical behavior by their employees. It is now commonplace for businesses to develop a written code of ethics to help guide the behavior of employees. Similarly, professional organizations of accountants have written ethics codes. The **American Institute of Certified Public Accountants (AICPA)**, for example, has a professional code of ethics to guide the conduct of its member CPAs. Similarly, the **Institute of Management Accountants (IMA)** has written standards of ethical conduct for accountants employed in the private sector.

Unethical behavior that results in misleading financial statements has the potential to erode public confidence and trust in accounting information. In response to this decline in public confidence, the U.S. Congress passed the **Sarbanes-Oxley Act** in 2002 with the goal of restoring

A.K.A. The Sarbanes-Oxley Act of 2002 is often referred to as SarBox or SOX.

investor trust by reducing the likelihood of future accounting scandals. Among the many provisions of this legislation is a requirement that a company's top management certify in writing the accuracy of its reported financial statement information. These executives risk criminal prosecution for fraudulent certification. In addition, companies must report on the internal controls designed to help deter errors in the financial reporting process and to detect them should they occur.

FORENSIC ACCOUNTING   **Accountant as Detective—CSI in Real Life**

Law enforcement personnel are not the only people who perform criminal investigations. A branch of accounting known as **forensic accounting** is vitally important in many types of criminal investigations, from financial statement fraud, to money laundering, to massive investment frauds such as the one perpetrated by Bernard Madoff (who was sentenced to a 150-year prison term). Unlike law enforcement personnel, forensic accountants are involved both before and after the commission of a crime.

> **Forensic Accounting** *boxes highlight how financial accounting knowledge can help aid in the prevention of errors and fraud.*

Accountants face several unique ethical dilemmas, such as:

1. The output produced by accountants has financial implications for individuals, as well as businesses. These situations generate considerable pressure on the accountant to influence the reported results. The amount of income taxes to be paid by an individual or business, the amount of a bonus to be received by an employee, the price to be paid by a customer, and the amount of money to be distributed to a business's owners are examples of situations in which the financial implications can lead to efforts to influence the outcome. *Ethical behavior mandates that accountants ignore these pressures.*

2. Accountants have access to confidential, sensitive information. Tax returns, salary data, details of financial arrangements, planned acquisitions, and proposed price changes are examples of this type of information. *Ethical behavior mandates that accountants respect the confidentiality of information.*

3. A criticism of U.S. business practices is that they are too "bottom-line" (that is, short-term profit) oriented. This orientation can lead to unethical actions by management to increase reported short-term profits. Because accountants measure and report a firm's profit, they must be particularly concerned about these ethical breakdowns. Studies indicate that, over the long term, successful companies and ethical practices go hand in hand. *Both accountants and management must recognize the importance of a long-run perspective.*

As an accountant for the Madoff Corporation, you are responsible for measuring and reporting the company's net income. It appears that actual results are going to be less than was expected by Wall Street analysts. Your supervisor has asked that you report some of next period's sales revenue early so that the current period's net income will be in line with analyst expectations. You know that reporting revenue like this represents a violation of generally accepted accounting principles. Your supervisor states that you will not really be doing anything wrong because the sales revenues are real—the company will just be reporting the revenue earlier than accounting guidelines allow. What should you do?

> **YOUR TURN! 1.4**
>
> The solution is on page 1-54.

THE ACCOUNTING PROCESS

Accounting is *the process of measuring economic activity of an entity in monetary terms and communicating results to users.* The accounting process consists of two principal activities—measurement and communication.

    The measurement process must (1) identify the relevant economic activities of a business, (2) quantify these economic activities, and (3) record the resulting measures in a systematic manner. Measurement is done in monetary terms. In the United States, measurements are stated in U.S. dollars. In other countries, measurements are expressed in the local currency.

LO4 Explain the accounting process and generally accepted accounting principles.

eLecture

MBC

Because the purpose of accounting is to provide useful financial information, the communication process is extremely important. Accordingly, the accounting process (1) prepares financial reports to meet the needs of the user and (2) helps interpret the financial results for that user. To provide reports that serve users effectively, managers must be aware of how these users are likely to apply the reports. The needs of the various users differ; as such, there are different types of accounting reports. Managers employ various techniques to help users interpret the content of reports. These techniques include the way the report is formatted, the use of charts and graphs to highlight trends, and the calculation of ratios to emphasize important financial relations.

THINKING GLOBALLY

Companies measure their operating performance using the currency of their principal place of business. The **Johnson & Johnson Company**, a well-known maker of baby shampoo and Band-Aids, is headquartered in New Jersey, and reports its financial results using the U.S. dollar. On the other hand, **Moet Hennessy Louis Vuitton**, the luxury goods manufacturer, is headquartered in Paris, France, and reports its financial results using the euro. Some companies prepare "convenience translations" of their financial statements in the currency and language of other countries so that potential foreign investors can more readily understand the company's financial performance and condition.

Thinking Globally boxes emphasize the similarities and differences in business practices between companies in the U.S. and companies in other countries.

Generally Accepted Accounting Principles

It is important that financial statements be prepared under a set of rules that is understood by the users of those reports. Imagine if every business were free to determine exactly how it measured and communicated its financial health and operating performance. How would a user of this information be able to compare one company's results to another if each played by a different set of rules? Financial statement users who rely on accounting data expect that all companies will follow the same standards and procedures when preparing their statements. In the United States these standards and procedures are called **generally accepted accounting principles (GAAP)**.

A.K.A. Generally accepted accounting principles are often referred to as GAAP (pronounced like the clothing store "Gap").

Generally accepted accounting principles are guides to action that can (and do) change over time. Sometimes specific accounting principles must be altered or new principles formulated to fit a changing set of economic circumstances or changes in business practices.

Financial Accounting Oversight

The **Financial Accounting Standards Board (FASB)**, the American Institute of Certified Public Accountants (AICPA), and the **U.S. Securities and Exchange Commission (SEC)** are instrumental in the development of generally accepted accounting principles in the United States. As a federal agency, the SEC's primary focus is to regulate the interstate sale of stocks and bonds. The SEC requires companies under its jurisdiction to submit audited annual financial statements to the agency which it then makes available to the general public. The SEC has the power to set the accounting principles used by these companies, but the agency has largely delegated that standard-setting responsibility to the FASB.

The FASB is a nongovernmental entity whose pronouncements establish U.S. GAAP.[1] The FASB consists of seven members and follows a process that allows for input from interested parties as it considers a new or changed accounting principle (see the appendix to this chapter for additional information on the conceptual framework the FASB has developed to formulate accounting standards). A new or changed principle requires the support of a majority of the board members. More recently, the **Public Company Accounting Oversight Board (PCAOB)** was established. The PCAOB approves auditing standards, known as **generally accepted auditing**

---

[1] Paralleling the FASB structure, the **Governmental Accounting Standards Board (GASB)** was organized in 1984 to formulate generally accepted accounting principles for state and local governments.

standards (GAAS), and monitors the quality of financial statements and audits. **Exhibit 1-4** illustrates the structure of financial accounting oversight in the United States.

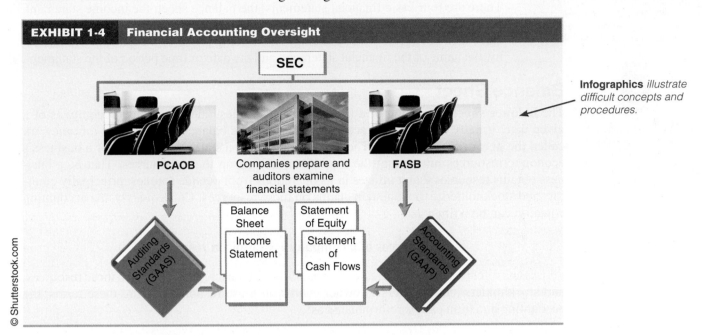

EXHIBIT 1-4   Financial Accounting Oversight

Infographics illustrate difficult concepts and procedures.

The FASB developed the Accounting Standards Codification as the single source of authoritative U.S. GAAP for non-governmental entities. The codification organizes GAAP into accounting topics and is easily researched through an online database maintained by the FASB. The purpose of the Accounting Standards Codification is to reduce the amount of time and effort required to research accounting standards, provide real-time updates as new standards are released, and present the single authoritative source of U.S. GAAP all in one location.

International Financial Reporting Standards

The past few decades have witnessed a steady acceptance of international financial reporting standards coinciding with the increasing globalization of business. The organization that has taken the lead in formulating international accounting principles is the **International Accounting Standards Board (IASB)**. The accounting standards formulated by the IASB are referred to as **International Financial Reporting Standards (IFRS)**. Approximately 120 nations or reporting jurisdictions either require or permit the use of IFRS. This includes the European Union, Australia, New Zealand, Israel, and Canada.

A.K.A. International financial reporting standards are often referred to as IFRS (pronounced "eye furs").

Match the items from column 1 with the correct item in column 2.

1. Accounting
2. Generally Accepted Accounting Principles (GAAP)
3. Public Company Accounting Oversight Board (PCAOB)
4. International Accounting Standards Board (IASB)

a. Guides to action for financial reporting
b. Responsible for formulating international accounting standards
c. The process of measuring economic activity of an entity in monetary terms and communicating the results to users
d. The organization empowered to approve auditing standards

YOUR TURN! 1.5

The solution is on page 1-54.

FINANCIAL STATEMENTS

LO5 Describe the accounting equation and each financial statement.

eLecture

MBC

A.K.A. The balance sheet is also referred to as the statement of financial position.

A.K.A. The accounting equation is also called the balance sheet equation.

There are four basic financial statements: the balance sheet, the income statement, the statement of stockholders' equity, and the statement of cash flows. Each financial statement begins with a heading. The heading provides the name of the company, the name of the financial statement, and the date or time period of the statement.

Balance Sheet

The **balance sheet** is a listing of a firm's assets, liabilities, and stockholders' equity as of a given date, usually the end of an accounting period. The balance sheet depicts a framework called the **accounting equation**. The accounting equation states that the sum of a business's economic resources must equal the sum of any claims on those resources. That is, a business obtains resources that it utilizes in its operations from outside sources, principally creditors and stockholders, who maintain claims on those resources. Consequently, the accounting equation can be written as:

Resources of a company = Claims on resources

Assets refer to a company's resources, liabilities refer to creditor claims on those resources, and stockholders' equity refers to owner claims on those resources. Using these terms, the accounting equation can be reformulated as:

Assets = Liabilities + Stockholders' equity

This equation states that the firm's assets equals the sum of its liabilities plus its stockholders' equity—see **Exhibit 1-5**. Throughout the accounting process, the accounting equation must always remain in balance.

Hints *help explain difficult concepts.*

Hint: Only resources that can be expressed in monetary terms are included among the assets reported on the balance sheet. There exist some assets that cannot be expressed in monetary terms, such as the value of a company's workforce, and, therefore, are not reported on a balance sheet.

EXHIBIT 1-5	**Accounting Equation for a Business**				
Economic Terms	Resources	=	Creditor claims on resources	+	Stockholder (owner) claims on resources
Accounting Terms	Assets	=	Liabilities	+	Stockholders' equity

Assets are the economic resources of a business that can be expressed in monetary terms. Assets take many forms. Cash is an asset, as are claims to receive cash payments from customers for goods or services provided, called accounts receivable. Other types of assets include inventory, supplies, land, buildings, and equipment. The key characteristic of any asset is that it represents a probable future economic benefit to a business.

Liabilities are the obligations or debts that a business must pay in cash or in goods and services at some future time as a consequence of past transactions or events. For example, a business can borrow money and sign a promissory note agreeing to repay the borrowed amount in six months. The business reports this obligation as a liability called notes payable. Similarly, if a business owes money to various suppliers for goods or services already provided, it is called accounts payable, or if it owes wages to its employees for work already performed, it is called wages payable. The business reports these obligations as liabilities on its balance sheet.

Stockholders' equity refers to the ownership (stockholder) claims on the assets of the business. Stockholders' equity represents a *residual claim* on a business's assets; that is, it is a claim on the assets of a business that remain after all liabilities to creditors have been satisfied.

For this reason, stockholders' equity is sometimes referred to as a business's **net assets**, where net assets equal the difference between total assets and total liabilities. In equation format,

$$\text{Assets} - \text{Liabilities} \quad = \quad \text{Stockholders' equity}$$

and,

$$\text{Net assets} \quad = \quad \text{Stockholders' equity}$$

Columbia's balance sheet is shown in **Exhibit 1-6** and reports the company's assets, liabilities, and stockholders' equity. (All Columbia Sportswear amounts are reported in thousands of dollars.) Columbia's assets totaled $2,836,571 at year-end 2020, with the largest asset being cash of $790,725. Total assets ($2,836,571) are equal to the sum of liabilities ($1,003,800) and stockholders' equity ($1,832,771). This equality must always exist as required by the accounting equation.

EXHIBIT 1-6	Columbia Sportswear Balance Sheet

Real financial data *for focus companies illustrate key concepts of each chapter.*

COLUMBIA SPORTSWEAR COMPANY
Balance Sheet
December 31, 2020
(In thousands)

Assets

Cash	$ 790,725
Investments	1,224
Accounts receivable	452,945
Inventories	556,530
Prepaid expenses and other current assets	54,197
Property, plant, and equipment, net	309,792
Other assets	671,158
Total assets	$2,836,571

Hint: Final totals in the financial statements are double underlined. Follow this format whenever asked to prepare a financial statement.

Liabilities and Stockholders' Equity

Liabilities

Accounts payable	$ 206,697
Income taxes payable	73,103
Other liabilities	724,000
Total liabilities	1,003,800

Stockholders' Equity

Common stock	20,165
Retained earnings	1,812,606
Total stockholders' equity	1,832,771
Total liabilities and stockholders' equity	$2,836,571

Columbia's balance sheet indicates that the company principally depends on stockholders' equity to finance its operations since liabilities totaled only $1,003,800 at 2020 year-end, or approximately 35 percent of total assets.

Concept →	Method →	Assessment	TAKEAWAY 1.1
What mix of financing does a company use?	The balance sheet provides information regarding the various forms of financing, both debt financing and equity financing. Compare the amount of liabilities appearing on the balance sheet to the amount of equity appearing on the balance sheet.	A higher ratio of liabilities to equity implies a higher use of creditor financing, and vice versa. Creditor financing is viewed by users as more risky.	*Takeaways summarize the key concepts before proceeding to the next topic.*

Income Statement

The **income statement** reports the results of operations for a business for a given time period, usually a quarter or a year. The income statement lists the revenues and expenses of the business. **Sales revenue** are increases to a company's resources from providing goods or services to customers. The amount of sales revenue earned is measured by the value of the assets received in exchange for the goods or services delivered.

Expenses are decreases in a company's resources from generating revenue. Expenses are generally measured by the value of the assets used up or exchanged as a result of a business's operating activities. Common examples of expenses include the cost of the items sold, referred to as cost of goods sold, selling expense, marketing expense, administrative expense, interest expense, and income tax. When total revenue exceeds total expenses, the resulting amount is called **net income**; when total expenses exceed total revenue, the resulting amount is called a **net loss**.

Columbia's income statement is presented in **Exhibit 1-7**. The statement begins with the business's name, statement title, and time period covered. For Columbia, total revenue in 2020 is reported to be $2,516,136 (remember amounts are rounded to the nearest $1,000). Next, Columbia subtracts a series of expenses totaling $2,408,123, yielding net income of $108,013.

EXHIBIT 1-7	Columbia Sportswear Income Statement

COLUMBIA SPORTSWEAR COMPANY
Income Statement
For Year Ended December 31, 2020
(In thousands)

Revenue	
Sales	$2,501,554
Other revenue	14,582
Total revenue	2,516,136
Expenses	
Cost of goods sold	1,277,665
Selling, general, and administrative expense	1,098,948
Income tax expense	31,510
Total expenses	2,408,123
Net income	$ 108,013

TAKEAWAY 1.2	Concept ⟶	Method ⟶	Assessment
	Is a company profitable?	The income statement reports a company's performance for a given period of time. Compare reported sales revenue to reported expenses.	Sales revenue in excess of expenses yields net income, implying a profitable company. If expenses exceed revenue, the company has a net loss.

Statement of Stockholders' Equity

The **statement of stockholders' equity** reports the events causing an increase or decrease in stockholders' equity during a given time period. The statement of stockholders' equity consists of two parts—contributed capital and earned capital. **Contributed capital** is a measure of the capital contributed by the stockholders of a company when they purchase ownership shares in the company. Ownership shares are called *common shares* or *common stock*. **Earned capital** is a measure of the capital that is earned by the company, reinvested in the business, and not distributed to its stockholders—that is, its *retained earnings*.

Retained earnings increase when operations produce net income and decrease when operations produce a net loss. Retained earnings also decrease when a company pays a dividend to its stockholders.

A company's retained earnings for a period is determined as follows (sometimes called the *statement of retained earnings*):

Retained earnings, beginning of period	$1,844,510
Add: Net income (loss)	108,013
Less: Dividends and other	(139,917)
Retained earnings, end of period	$1,812,606

Note: According to a survey of 500 companies, nearly 98% (489 out of 500) of the companies surveyed issue a Statement of Stockholders' Equity, while only 1% issue a separate Statement of Retained Earnings. Source: Accounting Trends & Techniques.

Columbia's statement of stockholders' equity appears in **Exhibit 1-8**. We focus here on Columbia's retained earnings from its statement of stockholders' equity to emphasize two important concepts: (1) the relation between the income statement and the balance sheet and (2) the components of retained earnings. Columbia's statement of stockholders' equity in **Exhibit 1-8** begins with its ending retained earnings from 2019 of $1,844,510. The beginning balance of retained earnings is then increased by its net income of $108,013 from 2020. (Can you find this amount on Columbia's income statement in **Exhibit 1-7**?) Next, earnings that were distributed as a dividend to Columbia's stockholders in 2020 ($139,917) are subtracted to yield an ending retained earnings balance of $1,812,606 as of December 31, 2020. (Can you find this amount on Columbia's balance sheet in **Exhibit 1-6**?)

EXHIBIT 1-8	Columbia Sportswear Statement of Stockholders' Equity

COLUMBIA SPORTSWEAR COMPANY
Statement of Stockholders' Equity
For Year Ended December 31, 2020

(In thousands)	Common Stock	Retained Earnings	Total
Balance, December 31, 2019	$ 4,937	$1,844,510	$1,849,447
Add: Common stock issued	20,164		20,164
Net income		108,013	108,013
Less: Common stock repurchased	(4,936)		(4,936)
Dividends and other		(139,917)	(139,917)
Balance, December 31, 2020	$20,165	$1,812,606	$1,832,771

Notice that in 2020 Columbia distributed more in dividends than they reported in income. This is possible because of the large balance in retained earnings at the beginning of the year. In other words, some of the dividends distributed in 2020 represent earnings retained from prior years.

Concept ➡	Method ➡	Assessment	TAKEAWAY 1.3
What portion of a company's current period net income is distributed to its stockholders, and what portion is retained?	The statement of stockholders' equity reports both a company's net income and the amount of dividends distributed to stockholders. Compare the company's dividends to its net income.	A higher ratio of dividends to net income implies that a company is distributing more of its net income to its stockholders, whereas a lower ratio implies it is retaining more of its income for purposes such as growing its business.	

Environmental, Social, and Governance boxes showcase how forward-thinking companies are embracing ESG as part of their long-term business models.

ENVIRONMENTAL, SOCIAL, AND GOVERNANCE	Reporting on Triple Bottom Line

Companies worldwide are focused on more than just the bottom line. Research shows that financial responsibility goes hand in hand with social responsibility. This is labeled a "virtuous cycle" because financial success provides the means to act in a socially responsible manner, and acting socially responsible

continued

continued from previous page

increases a company's financial performance. Financial statements are not well suited for measuring social performance. To aid in the pursuit of socially responsible behavior, accountants have developed a **triple bottom line** framework in which the single bottom line of financial performance on the income statement is supplemented with a social bottom line and an environmental bottom line. The triple bottom line standard for urban and community accounting has been ratified by the United Nations and has become widely used in public sector accounting.

Statement of Cash Flows

The **statement of cash flows** reports a business's cash inflows and cash outflows during a given period of time. The cash flows are grouped into the three business activities of operating, investing, and financing. Cash flow from operating activities includes the cash received from the sale of goods and services and the cash spent on operating expenses. Cash flow from investing activities includes cash payments and receipts from buying and selling certain assets that the business uses in its operations. Cash flow from financing activities includes the issuance and repurchase of the business's own shares and the amounts borrowed and repaid to creditors.

Columbia's statement of cash flows is in **Exhibit 1-9**. This statement shows that Columbia's cash balance increased during 2020 by $104,716 from $686,009 on December 31, 2019 to $790,725 on December 31, 2020. Columbia's operating activities provided $276,077 in cash while Columbia's investing activities used $27,171 and Columbia's financing activities used $144,190. Adding the changes in cash for the three types of activities produces the increase of $104,716. The statement of cash flows always concludes with a reconciliation of the cash balance from the beginning of the year to the end of the year. (Can you find the ending cash balance on Columbia's balance sheet in **Exhibit 1-6**?)

EXHIBIT 1-9	Columbia Sportswear Statement of Cash Flows

COLUMBIA SPORTSWEAR COMPANY
Statement of Cash Flows
For Year Ended December 31, 2020
(In thousands)

Cash flows from operating activities	$276,077
Cash flows from investing activities	(27,171)
Cash flows from financing activities	(144,190)
Net increase (decrease) in cash	104,716
Cash at beginning of year	686,009
Cash at end of year	$790,725

TAKEAWAY 1.4	Concept ⟶	Method ⟶	Assessment ⟶
	What are the major sources and uses of a company's cash?	The statement of cash flows reports a company's sources and uses of cash separated into three activities: operating, investing, and financing. Identify a company's sources and uses of cash as reported in the statement of cash flows.	Sources of cash are reported as positive numbers and uses of cash as negative numbers. Ideally, a company should have positive cash from operations that can be used for additional investment or to pay creditors or shareholders.

Relations Among the Financial Statements

The income statement, the statement of stockholders' equity, the balance sheet, and the statement of cash flows are linked to one another. That is, the financial statements *articulate*. To illustrate the linkages, refer to the financial statements of Columbia Sportswear in

Exhibit 1-10. Observe that Ⓐ, the company's net income (or net loss) for a period from the income statement is an input to the statement of stockholders' equity, and that Ⓑ, the ending common stock, retained earnings, and total equity from the statement of stockholders' equiy are inputs to the balance sheet. The statement of cash flows Ⓒ explains the change in the cash balance on the balance sheet for a period.

EXHIBIT 1-10	Financial Statements for Columbia Sportswear Company

Columbia Sportswear Company
Income Statement
For Year Ended December 31, 2020

Revenue	
Sales.	$2,501,554
Other revenue.	14,582
Total revenue	2,516,136
Expenses	
Cost of sales.	1,277,665
Selling, general, and administrative	1,098,948
Income tax expense	31,510
Total expenses	2,408,123
Net income	$ 108,013

Columbia Sportswear Company
Statement of Stockholders' Equity
For Year Ended December 31, 2020

	Common Stock	Retained Earnings	Total
Balance, December 31, 2019. .	$ 4,937	$1,844,510	$1,849,447
Add: Common stock issued . .	20,164		20,164
Net income		108,013	108,013
Less: Common stock repurchased.	(4,936)		(4,936)
Dividends and other. . . .		(139,917)	(139,917)
Balance, December 31, 2020. .	$20,165	$1,812,606	$1,832,771

Columbia Sportswear Company
Balance Sheet
December 31, 2020

Assets		Liabilities	
Cash	$ 790,725	Accounts payable	$ 206,697
Investments	1,224	Income taxes payable.	73,103
Accounts receivable	452,945	Other liabilities	724,000
Inventories	556,530	Total liabilities	1,003,800
Prepaid expenses and other current assets . . .	54,197	**Stockholders' Equity**	
Property, plant, and equipment, net	309,792	Common stock	20,165
Other assets.	671,158	Retained earnings	1,812,606
		Total stockholders' equity	1,832,771
Total assets	$2,836,571	Total liabilities and stockholders' equity . .	$2,836,571

Columbia Sportswear Company
Statement of Cash Flows
For Year Ended December 31, 2020

Cash flows from operating activities	$276,077
Cash flows from investing activities.	(27,171)
Cash flows from financing activities	(144,190)
Net increase in cash.	104,716
Cash at beginning of year.	686,009
Cash at end of year	$790,725

When financial statements are prepared, the sequence suggested by these relations is customarily followed; that is, (1) the income statement is prepared first, followed by (2) the statement of stockholders' equity, then (3) the balance sheet, and finally (4) the statement of cash flows.

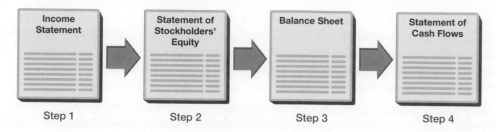

Three of these financial statements present information covering a specific period of time: the income statement, the statement of stockholders' equity, and the statement of cash flows. For this reason, these financial statements are referred to as **period-of-time statements**. In contrast, the balance sheet reports information as of a specific date. The balance sheet, therefore, is referred to as a **point-in-time statement**. (Illustrated in **Exhibit 1-11**.)

EXHIBIT 1-11   Financial Statement Links Across Time

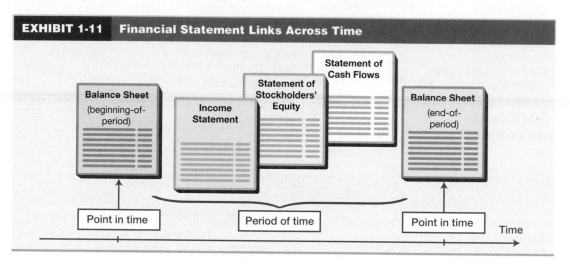

YOUR TURN! 1.6

The solution is on page 1-54.

MBC

Guided Example *icons denote the availability of a demonstration video in* **myBusinessCourse** *(MBC). See the Preface for more on MBC.*

Kanzu Corporation started business on January 1. The following information was compiled by Kanzu as of December 31.

Sales revenue	$20,000	Accounts payable	$ 4,000
Expenses	12,000	Notes payable	33,000
Dividends	3,000	Common stock	20,000
Cash	1,500	Retained earnings	?
Accounts receivable	2,500	Cash flow from operating activities	6,500
Inventory	3,000	Cash flow from investing activities	(55,000)
Equipment	15,000	Cash flow from financing activities	50,000
Building	40,000		

Prepare the company's year-end financial statements: an income statement, a statement of stockholders' equity, a balance sheet, and a statement of cash flows.

OTHER ANNUAL REPORT COMPONENTS

LO6 **Explain** additional disclosures that accompany financial statements.

eLecture

MBC

Columbia Sportswear Company, like all publicly traded companies in the United States, must file an **annual report** called a **Form 10-K** with the U.S. Securities and Exchange Commission (SEC). Some companies also send a less detailed version of their annual report to their stockholders. The four financial statements explained in this chapter are essential components of this report. Additional components of the annual report are the notes to the financial statements, the auditor's report, and the Management's Discussion and Analysis.

Notes to Financial Statements

Financial statement users need to know more than just the numbers reported in the financial statements. It is also important for the user to know assumptions and estimates that were used in preparing the statements, the measurement procedures that were followed, and the details behind certain summary numbers. The **notes to the financial statements**, which are quantitative as well as qualitative, provide a great deal more information than just the numbers alone. For example, notes usually contain a description regarding how the company determined the value of its inventory, a detailed chart to explain the property, plant, and equipment account, and a description of any pending lawsuits. No analysis of the annual report is complete without a careful reading of the notes to the financial statements. The following is a short excerpt from Columbia's notes:

> **Accounts receivable**   Accounts receivable have been reduced by an allowance for doubtful accounts. The Company maintains the allowance for estimated losses resulting from the inability of the Company's customers to make required payments.

Excerpts *from recent financial statements and notes are used to illustrate and reinforce concepts.*

The notes are considered a key part of the financial statements and, with the four basic financial statements, are audited by the company's independent auditor.

Independent Auditor's Report

The report of the independent auditor, commonly referred to as the **auditor's report**, describes the activities undertaken by a company's independent auditor and provides that auditor's opinion regarding whether the financial statements fairly present the results of the company's operations and financial health. The audit report will also communicate **critical audit matters (CAMs)**, which inform financial statement users of matters arising from the audit that required especially challenging, subjective, or complex audit judgment, and how the auditor responded to those matters. A short excerpt from the auditor's report included with Columbia Sportswear's annual report follows. **Deloitte & Touche**, which is Columbia's independent auditor, reports that the financial statements of Columbia are, in its opinion, fairly presented. The independent auditor has intentionally avoided using language such as the statements are "correctly presented" or are "exactly correct." As we will see in subsequent chapters, the financial statements are prepared only after the management team makes a number of assumptions, estimates, and accounting policy decisions. As a consequence, it is inappropriate to describe the statements as being right or wrong since the reported numbers are dependent on the accounting policies selected and the assumptions and estimates made by management.

> **Report of Independent Registered Public Accounting Firm**
> In our opinion, such financial statements present fairly, in all material respects, the financial position of the Company as of December 31, 2020 and 2019, and the results of its operations and its cash flows for each of the three years in the period ended December 31, 2020, in conformity with accounting principles generally accepted in the United States of America.
>
> *DELOITTE & TOUCHE LLP*

Management's Discussion and Analysis

In addition to the financial statements and notes, the SEC requires companies to provide other information, such as a description of its business, the properties it owns, and the risks it faces. Unlike the financial statements and notes, however, this information is not audited by the company's independent auditor. An important component of this other information is the **Management's Discussion and Analysis**, or MD&A, which contains management's interpretation of the company's recent performance and financial condition. This interpretation helps financial statement users gain context to help frame their own analysis and interpretation of the numbers that appear in the financial statements.

The MD&A is also where a company's management provides its view regarding what the future holds for its business. Discussions of future opportunities and risks are called "forward-looking" and are helpful to any financial statement user interested in learning about such things as potential new markets for the company's products or potential new competitors. Obviously these forward-looking statements are subjective in nature, and the financial statement user must do his or her own independent analysis.

The following is a short excerpt from Columbia's MD&A.

Business Outlook

The ongoing business disruption and uncertainty surrounding the COVID-19 pandemic make it difficult to predict our future results. Consistent with the seasonality and variability of our business, we anticipate 2021 profitability to be heavily concentrated in the second half of the year. Business uncertainties and risks surrounding the ongoing pandemic may further exacerbate this seasonality.

Factors that could significantly affect our full year 2021 financial results include:

- Lower consumer demand as a result of ongoing effects from the COVID-19 pandemic and/or related governmental actions and regulations;
- Growth, performance and profitability of our global DTC operations, including depressed consumer traffic in our retail stores and elevated DTC e-commerce growth trends;
- Our ability to staff and operate our distribution centers to fulfill DTC e-commerce demand while providing a safe working environment with adequate social distancing and other safety precautions;
- Port congestion and equipment and labor capacity of third-party logistics providers to service the demands of our business and the retail industry generally;
- Increasing consumer expectations and competitive pressure related to various aspects of our e-commerce business, including speed of product delivery, shipping charges, return privileges and other evolving expectations;
- Impairment of long-lived assets, operating lease right-of-use assets, intangible assets and/or goodwill;
- Unseasonable weather conditions or other unforeseen factors affecting consumer demand and the resulting effect on cancellations of advance wholesale and distributor orders, sales returns, customer accommodations, replenishment orders and reorders, DTC sales, changes in mix and volume of full price sales in relation to promotional and close-out product sales, and suppressed customer and end-consumer demand in subsequent seasons;
- Our ability to effectively manage our inventory, including liquidating excess inventory timely and profitably through close-out sales in our wholesale and DTC businesses;
- Difficult economic, geopolitical and competitive environments in certain key markets globally, coupled with increasing global economic uncertainty; and
- Economic and industry trends affecting consumer traffic and spending in brick and mortar retail channels, which have created uncertainty regarding the long-term financial health of certain of our wholesale customers, and, in certain cases, may require cancellation of customer shipments and/or increased credit exposure associated with any such shipments.

YOUR TURN! 1.7

The solution is on page 1-55.

Match each of the items in the left column with the appropriate annual report component where we would find that item in the right column.

1. An opinion regarding the fair presentation of financial statements.
2. Information regarding the procedures followed to value a company's assets.
3. A discussion of new markets that a company plans to enter.

a. Management Discussion and Analysis
b. Notes to the Financial Statements
c. Auditor's report

ENVIRONMENTAL, SOCIAL, AND GOVERNANCE REPORTING

The financial statements previously discussed are not the only reports that are published by companies. **Environmental, social, and governance (ESG) reporting** is an area of rapidly growing interest to various parties, including many of the same parties that are the intended audience of the financial statements.

ESG reporting includes a broad set of both quantitative and qualitative measures that may influence a company's business strategy, cash flows, financial position, and financial performance. For these reasons, it is important for business people to understand ESG reporting and how it intersects with traditional financial reporting. The importance of this issue, and the wide interest in the subject, has led the Financial Accounting Standards Board (FASB) to publish an educational paper on the "Intersection of Environmental, Social, and Governance Matters with Financial Accounting Standards." While the paper does not change or modify current generally accepted accounting principles (GAAP), it does highlight many areas where accountants need to consider ESG matters when addressing GAAP. An example of an ESG report for Columbia Sportswear can be found on this textbook's Website.

CAREERS IN ACCOUNTING

Job prospects after graduation are one of the primary considerations students have when selecting a major. The good news for accounting majors is that the present is very good and the future continues to look good. According to the Bureau of Labor Statistics, accounting jobs are expected to grow by 4 percent through 2029, assuring accounting majors will be in demand for the foreseeable future.

LO7   **Describe** careers in accounting.

eLecture

MBC

Accounting opportunities are present in multiple areas. **Exhibit 1-12** lists some typical job titles in (1) private accounting; (2) public accounting; and (3) government. Accountants working in the private sector work for a particular company, whereas accountants working in public accounting spend most of their time working for clients of their employer.

EXHIBIT 1-12	Careers in Accounting		
	Private Accounting	**Public Accounting**	**Government Accounting**
Typical Positions	Internal audit Tax Financial reporting Analyst Budgeting Cost accounting	Auditor Tax Consulting Strategy	Auditor Tax Budgeting Criminal investigation

Accounting professionals are not just in high demand, they are also held in high regard by the public. Accounting professionals often earn various certificates in order to further distinguish themselves. The most sought after certification is the Certified Public Accountant (CPA) certificate. This certification requires both education and professional experience, passing an examination, and the highest ethical standards. Three other important certifications are the Certified Management Accountant (CMA), the Certified Internal Auditor (CIA), and the Certified Fraud Examiner (CFE) certificates.

One of the reasons that accounting graduates find great opportunities upon graduation is because their accounting courses provide specific skills that can be applied immediately on the job. It is therefore quite apparent that when one compares the advantages and disadvantages of an accounting career, the positive job outlook and the high salaries are often listed. Accountants also have a great deal of mobility and upward advancement potential.

According to the U.S. Bureau of Labor Statistics, the 2019 median pay for the 1.4 million accounting jobs in their database was $71,550. **Exhibit 1-13** compares the 2021 salaries of starting accountants, accountants with a couple years of experience, and more senior accountants in both public accounting and in large corporations.

EXHIBIT 1-13	Accounting Salaries	
Area of Employment	**Position and Experience**	**Midpoint of Salary Range**
Corporate Accounting	Bookkeeper	$ 39,750
	Financial Reporting < 1 year	61,750
	Financial Reporting 1 to 3 years.	74,250
	Financial Reporting—Senior	85,000
	Financial Reporting—Manager.	116,750
	Internal Auditor—Senior.	90,500
	Internal Auditor—Manager	116,750
	Forensic Accountant.	95,500
	Business Intelligence Analyst—Manager . . .	123,500
	Corporate Controller.	178,750
	Chief Financial Officer	203,750
Public Accounting	Junior Accountant < 1 year.	49,000
	Senior Accountant	66,750
	Senior Manager	134,750

Source: Robert Half Accounting & Finance Salary Guide 2021

Data Analytics and Blockchain Technology

Accounting skills are not stagnant; rather they are constantly evolving. What was once done by hand is now done with the aid of specialized software. Programs like **QuickBooks** from **Intuit** have automated the basic accounting job of transaction recording, and programs like **Microsoft Excel** have greatly aided in the analysis of accounting data. While some industry observers had predicted these technological advances would replace the need for accountants, these applications have simply changed the way accountants perform their jobs. Newer technologies such as data analytics and blockchain are further changing the way accountants do their jobs. However, knowledge of these technologies and the related skills needed to use them are often lacking among current accountants. That was the key finding in a recently released joint report, *Building a Team to Capitalize on the Promise of Big Data*, by the human resource consulting firm Robert Half and the Institute of Management Accountants (IMA).

Data Analytics

Data analytics (DA) can broadly be defined as the process of examining sets of data with the goal of discovering useful information from patterns found in the data. Accountants employing data analytics can glean important insights from a company's financial data and identify areas where improvements can be made.

Blockchain was made famous as the underpinning technology used for digital currencies, such as **Bitcoin** and **Ethereum**. **Blockchain** is a distributed digital ledger that provides a secure means, for those that have permission, to view recorded transactions. This technology has wide-ranging implications for business and is expected to greatly affect the way accountants perform audits.

Understanding what data analytics and blockchain technology are and how they are used is the first step towards developing marketable skills in each area, so we have included examples of each at various points in the book and assignments in most chapters that require the use of data analytics tools, including **Excel** and **Tableau**. In addition, **Appendix F** at the end of this book provides a more detailed discussion of both topics.

Data Analytics

Columbia Sportswear is a global leader in outdoor and active lifestyle apparel and equipment, but until recently it failed badly in its supply chain management. Luckily, after implementing data analytics, things have turned around. According to an article reported in the Wall Street Journal:

← **Data Analytics** boxes describe how data analytics tools and techniques are used in companies.

> "The company says the [FusionOps] software, which tracks open purchase orders, product fill rate, sales, as well as where products are in the supply chain, helped boost the share of merchandise delivered on-time and in-full, considered a core metric among retailers, from 28% to 78%. The analytics include a diagnostic component, showing Columbia why products are late, such as a ship delay at a port...When TurboDown jackets "took off" in the U.S. in December and January, the FusionOps software automatically notified Columbia staff to order more. Such data enabled Columbia to increase supply to minimize out-of-stock issues, reducing the amount of apparel the company marked down as sales waned."

COMPREHENSIVE PROBLEM

You have been approached by Janet Jones about helping her assemble a set of December 31 year-end financial statements for her new business. Janet began the operations of her bakery shop on January 1. Janet decided that she did not want to risk any personal liability resulting from operating the business; consequently, she organized the bakery, called Sweet Pleasures, as a corporation.

GuidedExample

MBC

Required

Use the format of **Exhibits 1-6** through **1-9** to prepare an income statement, statement of stockholders' equity, balance sheet, and statement of cash flows for Sweet Pleasures as of December 31. Use the account titles and balances provided below. Be sure to use proper underlining and double underlining.

Sales of goods	$200,000	Dividends	$ 10,000
Cash	99,000	Bank loan payable	20,000
Rent expense	16,000	Accounts receivable	40,000
Interest payable	1,600	Cash received from operating activities	160,000
Cash received from issuance of common stock	50,000	Cash payments for operating activities	94,000
Insurance expense	20,000	Salary expense	40,000
Purchase of equipment	27,000	Cash received from borrowing from bank	20,000
Equipment	27,000	Interest expense	1,600
Common stock	50,000	Administrative expense	18,000
Cash dividends paid	10,000		

Solution

SWEET PLEASURES CORPORATION
Income Statement
For Year Ended December 31

Revenue		
Sales of goods		$200,000
Expenses		
Rent expense	$16,000	
Insurance expense	20,000	
Salary expense	40,000	
Administrative expense	18,000	
Interest expense	1,600	
Total expenses		95,600
Net income		$104,400

SWEET PLEASURES CORPORATION
Statement of Stockholders' Equity
For Year Ended December 31

	Common Stock	Retained Earnings	Total
Balance, January 1	$ 0	$ 0	$ 0
Add: Common stock issued	50,000		50,000
Net income		104,400	104,400
Less: Dividends		(10,000)	(10,000)
Balance, December 31	$50,000	$ 94,400	$144,400

SWEET PLEASURES CORPORATION
Balance Sheet
December 31

Assets		Liabilities	
Cash	$ 99,000	Bank loan payable	$ 20,000
Accounts receivable	40,000	Interest payable	1,600
Equipment	27,000	Total liabilities	21,600
		Stockholders' Equity	
		Common stock	50,000
		Retained earnings	94,400
		Total stockholders' equity	144,400
Total assets	$166,000	Total liabilities and stockholders' equity	$166,000

SWEET PLEASURES CORPORATION
Statement of Cash Flows
For Year Ended December 31

Cash flow from operating activities		
Cash received from operating activities	$160,000	
Cash payments for operating activities	(94,000)	
Cash provided by operating activities		$66,000
Cash flow from investing activities		
Purchase of equipment	(27,000)	
Cash used by investing activities		(27,000)
Cash flow from financing activities		
Borrowing from bank	20,000	
Issuance of common stock	50,000	
Cash dividends paid	(10,000)	
Cash provided by financing activities		60,000
Net increase of cash		99,000
Cash at January 1		0
Cash at December 31		$99,000

APPENDIX 1A: FASB's Conceptual Framework

LO8 Discuss FASB's conceptual framework.

MBC

The FASB has developed a conceptual framework, in coordination with the International Accounting Standards Board. The **conceptual framework** is a cohesive set of interrelated objectives and fundamentals for external financial reporting whose purpose is to guide the formulation of specific U.S. accounting principles. This framework, outlined in **Exhibit 1A-1**, consists of (1) financial reporting objectives, (2) financial statement elements, (3) qualitative characteristics of accounting information, and (4) recognition and measurement criteria for financial statements. A recurrent theme in the conceptual framework is the importance of providing information that is useful to financial statement users.

EXHIBIT 1A-1   **Summary of Conceptual Framework**

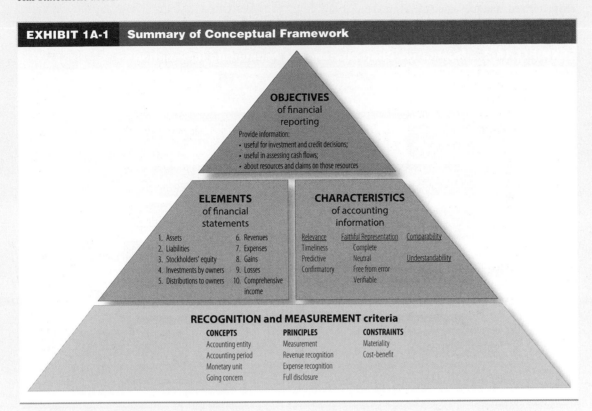

Financial Reporting Objectives

The **financial reporting objectives** focus on information useful to investors and creditors. Accordingly, financial statements have the principal objective of providing information that is (1) useful in making investment, credit, and similar decisions and (2) helpful in assessing the ability of enterprises to generate future cash flows. Financial statements should also (3) contain information about a company's economic resources, the claims on those resources, and the effects of events that change those resources and claims. This helps to identify a company's financial strengths and weaknesses, predict future performance, and evaluate earlier expectations.

Financial Statement Elements

The **financial statement elements** are the components of financial statements. These elements include assets, liabilities, stockholders' equity, investments by owners, distributions to owners, revenues, expenses, gains, losses, and comprehensive income.

Qualitative Characteristics

The **qualitative characteristics of accounting information** are depicted in **Exhibit 1A-2**. These qualities are intended to contribute to decision usefulness. The two primary qualities are **relevance** and **faithful representation**. To be relevant, accounting information must make a difference in a user's decisions. Relevant information must be timely and contribute to the predictive and evaluative decisions made by investors and creditors. Faithful representation has the characteristics of being complete, neutral, free from error, and verifiable.

Additional enhancing qualitative characteristics of accounting information are comparability and understandability. In order to enable users to most effectively compare financial results across companies, U.S. GAAP requires that companies disclose in the notes to financial statements the accounting policy choices they elected to use in the preparation of their financial statements. **Comparability** aids users to understand similarities and differences among items. Related to comparability is **consistency**, although they are not the same. Comparability relates to making comparisons among more than one item, whereas consistency relates to a single item and means the same accounting methods are used from one accounting period to the next. U.S. GAAP requires that when a firm changes a method of reporting its financial results that the financial impact of the method change be revealed in its notes to financial statements. **Understandability** is enhanced if information is classified, characterized, and presented clearly and concisely.

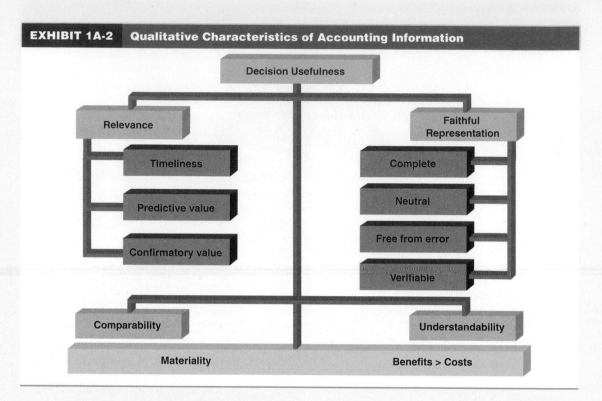

EXHIBIT 1A-2   Qualitative Characteristics of Accounting Information

Recognition and Measurement Criteria

The **recognition and measurement criteria** specify the conditions that must be satisfied before a particular asset, liability, revenue, or expense can be recorded in the financial records. An item under consideration must meet the definition of an element and be measurable, and information about the item must achieve the primary qualitative characteristics of accounting information. The recognition and measurement criteria consist of concepts, principles, and constraints.

Concepts

A fundamental concept in accounting is the entity. An **accounting entity** is an economic unit with identifiable boundaries for which we accumulate and report financial information. Before we can analyze and report activities, we must identify the particular entity. Each sole proprietorship, partnership, and corporation is an entity, and separate accounting records must be maintained for each unit. In accumulating financial information, we maintain a record of the activities of the accounting entity separately from the economic and personal activities of its owners. The operations of most businesses are virtually continuous. Yet, the economic life of a company can be divided into specific periods of time, known as the **accounting period**, which is typically one year or one quarter for purposes of preparing financial statements. Although the division of the total life of a business into segments is artificial, the concept of the accounting period is useful for financial reporting. The **monetary unit concept** specifies that a monetary unit (for example, the dollar in the United States and the euro in the European Union) is to be used to measure and record an entity's economic activity. Only items that can be expressed in these monetary units are included in the financial statements. When all assets, liabilities, and stockholders' equity are stated in monetary terms, they can be added or subtracted to prepare financial statements. Also, relations among financial statement components can be calculated and presented to help interpret the statements. In the absence of evidence to the contrary, a business is assumed to have an indefinite life. The **going concern concept** presumes that an enterprise will continue to operate indefinitely and will not be sold or otherwise liquidated.

Principles

Four principles frame financial accounting information: measurement, revenue recognition, expense recognition, and full disclosure. U.S. GAAP is a mixed measurement system. It is primarily founded on the **cost principle**, meaning assets and liabilities are initially recorded at the amount paid or obligated to pay. Historical acquisition cost is considered the proper initial measurement because, for example, at the time an asset is acquired, it represents the fair value of the asset as agreed upon by both the buyer and seller. However, the fair value principle is sometimes applied after acquisition, which is a "market-based" measurement system for assets and liabilities. In 2014, the FASB and IASB issued a joint **revenue recognition** standard with the intention of improving financial reporting by providing consistent principles for recognizing revenue regardless of the company's industry or geography. The rule replaces a patchwork of previous standards and is based on a five-step process that broadly considers when a performance obligation has been satisfied. This generally occurs when goods or services are transferred from the seller to the buyer. The amount of revenue recognized is the amount that reflects the consideration to which the seller expects to be entitled in exchange for those goods or services. The **expense recognition principle** states that net income is determined by linking any expenses incurred with the related earned sales revenues. Thus, expenses are recorded in the period that they help to generate the revenues.

Together, the revenue recognition principle and the expense recognition principle define the **accrual basis of accounting**. It is important to observe that recording revenues and expenses does not depend upon the receipt or payment of cash. The accrual basis of accounting is widely used. Under the **cash basis of accounting**, revenues are recorded when cash is received from operating activities and expenses are recorded when cash payments are made for operating activities. Net income, therefore, becomes the difference between operating cash receipts and operating cash payments. The cash basis is not considered generally accepted.

All information necessary for a user's understanding of financial statements should be disclosed in a company's annual report. The purpose of accounting is to provide useful information to those parties interested in a firm's performance and financial health. Sometimes, facts or conditions exist that, although not specifically part of the data in the accounting system, have considerable influence on a full understanding and interpretation of financial statements. To properly inform financial statement users, the **full disclosure principle** requires that a business disclose all significant financial facts and circumstances.

Constraints

Two factors constrain the qualitative characteristics of accounting information: materiality and cost-benefit. Applying accounting procedures requires effort and costs money. When amounts involved are too small to affect the financial picture, the application of theoretically correct accounting procedures is hardly worth its cost. The concept of **materiality** permits a firm to expense the cost of such assets as small tools, office equipment, and furniture when acquired because their cost is "immaterial" in amount. The **cost-benefit constraint** requires that the benefit derived from the information outweighs the cost of providing it.

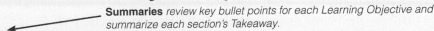

Summaries *review key bullet points for each Learning Objective and summarize each section's Takeaway.*

SUMMARY OF LEARNING OBJECTIVES

Explain the three forms of business organizations. (p. 1-3)   **LO1**

- There are three primary organizational forms that a business can take: proprietorship, partnership, and corporation.
- A sole proprietorship consists of a single owner. It is the most common form of business and the easiest to establish.
- A partnership is similar to a sole proprietorship except that there is more than one owner. Partnerships are also relatively easy to establish. An advantage of the partnership form over the sole proprietorship is the broader set of skills and resources that multiple partners can bring to an enterprise.
- A corporation is the most complex of the three organizational forms. The advantages of the corporate form of business include the ease of transferring ownership interests and the ease of raising funds. Another advantage is the limited liability protection it offers its owners. A disadvantage of the corporate form is the possibility of double taxation of the company's net income.

Describe business activities. (p. 1-4)   **LO2**

- Companies engage in three types of business activities: operating, investing, and financing.
- Operating activities consist of selling products or providing services to generate sales revenue and using economic resources to manufacture goods or provide services.

■ Investing activities consist of those activities needed to provide the infrastructure to run a company's operations. Also included in this activity category are investments of excess cash.

■ Financing activities consist of both debt financing and equity financing. Debt financing involves the procurement of a bank loan, whereas equity financing involves the sale of shares of stock to investors.

LO3   Identify who uses accounting information. (p. 1-5)

■ Accounting information is important to both internal and external users.

■ Financial accounting produces publicly available financial statements for external users including investors, creditors, taxation authorities, regulatory agencies, labor unions, and customers.

■ The process of generating and analyzing data for internal management use is referred to as managerial accounting.

■ Business leaders recognize the importance of ethical behavior.

LO4   Explain the accounting process and generally accepted accounting principles. (p. 1-8)

■ Accounting is the process of measuring the economic activities of an enterprise in monetary terms and communicating the results to interested parties.

■ The basic purpose of accounting is to provide financial information that is useful in making economic decisions.

■ The Financial Accounting Standards Board (FASB) is a private sector organization that has responsibility for formulating generally accepted accounting principles in the United States.

■ Generally accepted accounting principles (GAAP) are the standards and procedures that guide the preparation of financial statements.

■ The International Accounting Standards Board (IASB) has taken the lead role in formulating International Financial Reporting Standards (IFRS).

LO5   Describe the accounting equation and each financial statement. (p. 1-11)

■ The accounting equation, Assets = Liabilities + Stockholders' Equity, is the fundamental framework within which accounting analysis takes place.

  • Assets are the economic resources of a business that can be expressed in monetary terms.

  • Liabilities are the obligations that a business must pay in money or services in the future as a consequence of past transactions or events.

  • Stockholders' equity is the residual interest of the owners in the assets of a business.

■ The *income statement* presents a company's sales revenues and expenses for a period of time.

■ The *statement of stockholders' equity* reports the financial events causing a change in stockholders' equity during a period of time, and includes retained earnings and common stock.

■ The *balance sheet* presents a company's assets, liabilities, and stockholders' equity as of a given date.

■ The *statement of cash flows* reports a company's cash inflows and outflows during a period of time.

LO6   Explain additional disclosures that accompany financial statements. (p. 1-17)

In addition to the basic financial statements, the annual report includes notes to the financial statements, an independent auditor's report, and Management's Discussion and Analysis.

■ The notes to the financial statements provide both a quantitative and a qualitative description of a company's financial statements and explain the numbers reported in those financial statements.

■ The independent auditor's report provides a degree of assurance that a company's financial statements are presented fairly and can be relied upon for decision-making purposes.

■ The Management's Discussion and Analysis (MD&A) provides management with an opportunity to both analyze past performance and discuss future opportunities and concerns involving a company.

LO7   Describe careers in accounting. (p. 1-20)

■ Accounting graduates are in high demand and can anticipate bright employment prospects.

■ Accountants can find jobs in public accounting, private corporations, or the government.

LO8   Appendix 1A: Discuss FASB's conceptual framework. (p. 1-23)

■ The conceptual framework provides a guide to the formulation of U.S. generally accepted accounting principles.

■ The framework consists of interrelated objectives, elements, characteristics, and recognition and measurement criteria.

■ The financial reporting objectives focus on information useful to investors and creditors.

■ The financial statement elements are the components of financial statements.

■   The qualitative characteristics of accounting information are intended to contribute to decision usefulness.

■   The recognition and measurement criteria specify the conditions that must be satisfied before a particular asset, liability, revenue, or expense can be recorded in the financial records.

Concept ──────►	Method ──────────►	Assessment	SUMMARY
What mix of financing does a company use?	The balance sheet provides information regarding the various forms of financing, both debt financing and equity financing. Compare the amount of liabilities appearing on the balance sheet to the amount of equity appearing on the balance sheet.	A higher ratio of liabilities to equity implies a higher use of creditor financing, and vice versa. Creditor financing is viewed by users as more risky.	**TAKEAWAY 1.1**
Is a company profitable?	The income statement reports a company's performance for a given period of time. Compare reported sales revenue to reported expenses.	Sales revenue in excess of expenses yields net income, implying a profitable company. If expenses exceed revenue, the company has a net loss.	**TAKEAWAY 1.2**
What portion of a company's current period net income is distributed to its stockholders, and what portion is retained?	The statement of stockholders' equity reports both a company's net income and the amount of dividends distributed to stockholders. Compare the company's dividends to its net income.	A higher ratio of dividends to net income implies that a company is distributing more of its net income to its stockholders, whereas a lower ratio implies that it is retaining more of its income for purposes such as growing its business.	**TAKEAWAY 1.3**
What are the major sources and uses of a company's cash?	The statement of cash flows reports a company's sources and uses of cash separated into three activities: operating, investing, and financing. Identify a company's sources and uses of cash as reported in the statement of cash flows.	Sources of cash are reported as positive numbers and uses of cash as negative numbers. Ideally, a company should have positive cash from operations that can be used for additional investment or to pay creditors or shareholders.	**TAKEAWAY 1.4**

Key Terms are listed for each chapter with references to page numbers within the chapter.

KEY TERMS ◄────

Accounting (p. 1-8)	**Balance sheet** (p. 1-11)	**Cost principle** (p. 1-26)
Accounting entity (p. 1-25)	**Blockchain** (p. 1-21)	**Creditors** (p. 1-4)
Accounting equation (p. 1-11)	**Cash basis of**	**Critical audit matters**
Accounting period (p. 1-25)	**accounting** (p. 1-26)	**(CAMs)** (p. 1-18)
Accrual basis of	**Certified public accountants**	**Data analytics** (p. 1-21)
accounting (p. 1-26)	**(CPAs)** (p. 1-6)	**Debt financing** (p. 1-4)
American Institute of Certified	**Comparability** (p. 1-24)	**Earned capital** (p. 1-13)
Public Accountants	**Conceptual framework** (p. 1-23)	**Environmental, social,**
(AICPA) (p. 1-7)	**Consistency** (p. 1-24)	**and governance (ESG)**
Annual report (p. 1-17)	**Contributed capital** (p. 1-13)	**reporting** (p. 1-20)
Assets (p. 1-11)	**Corporation** (p. 1-3)	**Equity financing** (p. 1-4)
Auditor's report (p. 1-18)	**Cost-benefit constraint** (p. 1-26)	**Ethics** (p. 1-7)

Expense recognition (matching) principle (p. 1-26)
Expenses (p. 1-13)
Faithful representation (p. 1-24)
Financial accounting (p. 1-5)
Financial Accounting Standards Board (FASB) (p. 1-9)
Financial reporting objectives (p. 1-24)
Financial statement elements (p. 1-24)
Financing activities (p. 1-4)
Forensic accounting (p. 1-8)
Form 10-K (p. 1-17)
Full disclosure principle (p. 1-26)
Generally accepted accounting principles (GAAP) (p. 1-9)
Generally accepted auditing standards (GAAS) (p. 1-10)
Going concern concept (p. 1-25)
Governmental Accounting Standards Board (GASB) (p. 1-9)
Income statement (p. 1-13)
Institute of Management Accountants (IMA) (p. 1-7)

International Accounting Standards Board (IASB) (p. 1-10)
International Financial Reporting Standards (IFRS) (p. 1-10)
Investing activities (p. 1-4)
Liabilities (p. 1-11)
Management's Discussion and Analysis (p. 1-18)
Managerial accounting (p. 1-7)
Materiality (p. 1-26)
Monetary unit concept (p. 1-25)
Net assets (p. 1-12)
Net income (p. 1-13)
Net loss (p. 1-13)
New York Stock Exchange (NYSE) (p. 1-4)
Notes to the financial statements (p. 1-18)
Operating activities (p. 1-5)
Partnership (p. 1-3)
Period-of-time statements (p. 1-17)
Point-in-time statement (p. 1-17)

Principal (p. 1-4)
Public Company Accounting Oversight Board (PCAOB) (p. 1-9)
Qualitative characteristics of accounting information (p. 1-24)
Recognition and measurement criteria (p. 1-25)
Relevance (p. 1-24)
Retained earnings (p. 1-14)
Revenue recognition principle (p. 1-26)
Sales revenue (p. 1-13)
Sarbanes-Oxley Act (p. 1-8)
Sole proprietorship (p. 1-3)
Statement of cash flows (p. 1-15)
Statement of stockholders' equity (p. 1-13)
Stockholders (p. 1-3)
Stockholders' equity (p. 1-11)
Triple bottom line (p. 1-15)
Understandability (p. 1-25)
U.S. Securities and Exchange Commission (SEC) (p. 1-9)

Homework icons indicate which assignments are available in myBusinessCourse (MBC). This feature is only available when the instructor incorporates MBC in the course.

Self-Study Questions *in multiple-choice format with answers provided at the end of each chapter.*

Assignments with the ⬤ logo in the margin are available in BusinessCourse.
See the Preface of the book for details.

SELF-STUDY QUESTIONS

(Answers to Self-Study Questions are at the end of this chapter.)

LO1   1. **Which form of business organization is characterized by limited liability?**
     a.   Sole proprietorship   *c.*   Corporation
     b.   Partnership   *d.*   Both sole proprietorship and partnership

LO4   2. **Which of the following processes best defines accounting?**
     a.   Measuring economic activities   *c.*   Preventing fraud
     b.   Communicating results to interested parties   *d.*   Both *a* and *b*.

LO4   3. **Generally accepted accounting principles are:**
     a.   A set of guidelines to aid in the financial reporting process   *c.*   A set of standards for ethical conduct
     b.   A set of laws to prevent financial fraud   *d.*   A set of voluntary "best business practices"

LO3   4. **For which area of accounting are generally accepted accounting principles primarily relevant?**
     a.   Managerial accounting   *c.*   Tax accounting
     b.   Financial accounting   *d.*   Financial reporting to all regulatory agencies

LO2   5. **Which of the following is not one of the three types of business activities?**
     a.   Investing   *c.*   Marketing
     b.   Financing   *d.*   Operating

LO5   6. **If assets total $140,000 and liabilities total $50,000, how much are net assets?**
     a. $40,000   *c.* $140,000
     b. $90,000   *d.* $50,000

7. What are increases in resources that a firm earns by providing goods or services to its customers?   **LO5**

 a. Assets   *c.* Expenses

 b. Revenues   *d.* Liabilities

8. Which of the following items is not required to be included as part of a company's annual report?   **LO6**

 a. Notes to the financial statements   *c.* Detailed history of the company

 b. Management discussion and analysis   *d.* Auditor's report

9. Which of the following situations presents ethical challenges to accountants?   **LO3**

 a. Pressure by superiors to produce a "good"   *c.* An emphasis on short-term results
   number   *d.* All the above present ethical challenges to

 b. Avoiding the disclosure of confidential   accountants
   information

10. Match the following organizational attributes in the left column with the organizational form in the   **LO1**
right column that the attribute is most often associated with.

 1. Tax advantages   *a.* Sole proprietorship
 2. Unlimited liability   *b.* Partnership
 3. Shared control   *c.* Corporation
 4. Most complex to set up
 5. Easiest to raise a large amount of funds
 6. Single owner

11. The financial statements of People Company contain the following. How much is net income?   **LO5**

Accounts payable	$12,000
Revenues	27,000
Accounts receivable	10,000
Expenses	8,000
Cash	7,000

 a. $6,000   *c.* $19,000

 b. $11,000   *d.* $17,000

12. If Bing Company reports its year-end total liabilities to be $40,000, and its year-end stockholders'   **LO5**
equity to be $60,000, how much are Bing Company's year-end total assets?

 a. $15,000   *d.* Cannot be determined from the given

 b. $185,000   information

 c. $100,000

13. Puff Company began the year with a retained earnings balance of $50,000, reported net income for   **LO5**
the year of $45,000, and reported ending retained earnings of $60,000. How much dividends did
Puff Company report for the year?

 a. $135,000   *c.* $15,000

 b. $35,000   *d.* $30,000

QUESTIONS

 1. Define *accounting*. What is the basic purpose of accounting?

 2. What is the distinction between *financial* accounting and *managerial* accounting?

 3. Who are some of the outside groups that may be interested in a company's financial data and what are their
particular interests?

 4. What are *generally accepted accounting principles* and what organization has primary responsibility for
their formulation in the United States?

 5. What are the main advantages and disadvantages of the corporate form of business?

 6. What role does financial accounting play in the allocation of society's financial resources?

 7. What is the accounting equation? Define *assets, liabilities,* and *stockholders' equity.*

 8. What are the three principal business activities and how do they differ?

 9. What is meant by corporate social responsibility?

10. What is the difference between generally accepted accounting principles (GAAP) and international financial reporting standards (IFRS)?

11. What are *revenues* and *expenses*?

12. What is the purpose of an income statement? The statement of stockholders' equity? The balance sheet? The statement of cash flows?

13. What is a *period-of-time statement*? Give three examples.

14. What is a *point-in-time statement*? Give one example.

15. On December 31, the Hill Company had $800,000 in total assets and owed $230,000 to creditors. If the corporation's common stock amounted to $400,000, what amount of retained earnings should appear on its December 31 balance sheet?

16. What are three aspects of the accounting environment that may create ethical pressure on an accountant?

17. What type of information might you find in the Management's Discussion and Analysis (MD&A) section of the annual report?

18. What is the purpose of having the financial statements audited by an independent auditor?

19. Determine whether the following statements are true or false and explain why:
    a. The accounting process is only interested in communicating economic activity.
    b. There are few potential users of financial accounting information.
    c. Financial accounting is primarily used to communicate to outside users.
    d. Auditors ensure the validity of a company's financial statements.

20. Why did the FASB develop a conceptual framework?

21. What are two primary qualities of accounting information that contribute to decision usefulness?

22. How would you describe, in one sentence, each of the following accounting principles, concepts and constraints?

Accounting entity	Consistency
Accounting period	Revenue recognition
Monetary unit	Expense recognition (matching)
Cost-benefit	Materiality
Going concern	Full disclosure

23. Which of the following is a primary qualitative characteristic of accounting information?
    a. Relevance
    b. Faithful representation
    c. Comparability
    d. All of the above are important characteristics.

SHORT EXERCISES

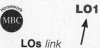

LO1   **SE1-1.   Forms of Business Organization** Match the following forms of business organization with the set of attributes that best describes that form of business: sole proprietorship, partnership, or corporation.
    a. Shared control, unlimited liability, tax advantages, increased skills and resources
    b. Best for raising large amounts of funds, double taxation, limited liability, easiest to transfer ownership interests
    c. Sole ownership, easiest to establish, tax advantages, unlimited liability

LOs link assignments to the Learning Objectives of each chapter.

LO4   **SE1-2.   Accounting Processes** Identify the following processes as either measuring or communicating.
    a. Prepare financial statements for the entity
    b. Identify relevant economic activities of the entity
    c. Record relevant economic activities of the entity
    d. Interpret financial results of the entity
    e. Quantify relevant economic activities of the entity

SE1-3. **Types of Statements** Match the following type of report with the most likely statement user: management, taxation authority, regulatory agency, or investor.   **LO3**

    a.   Financial statements   *c.*   Annual budget

    b.   Tax return   *d.*   Special report on a bank's financial health

SE1-4. **Accounting Organizations** Match the following organizations with the set of accounting guidelines: Financial Accounting Standards Board (FASB), International Accounting Standards Board (IASB).   **LO4**

    a.   Generally accepted accounting principles (GAAP)

    b.   International financial reporting standards (IFRS)

SE1-5. **Business Activities** Match the following activities with the type of activity: Operating, Investing, Financing.   **LO2**

    a.   Day-to-day business activities   *e.*   Payment of dividends

    b.   Purchase of land for a new warehouse   *f.*   Invest excess cash

    c.   Sale of merchandise inventory   *g.*   Purchase office supplies

    d.   Obtain a new bank loan   *h.*   Sell old equipment that is no longer needed

SE1-6. **Financial Statement Items** Identify the financial statement (or statements) in which each of the following items would appear: income statement (IS), statement of stockholders' equity (SSE), balance sheet (BS), or statement of cash flows (SCF).   **LO5**

    a.   Assets   *e.*   Expenses

    b.   Revenues   *f.*   Net change in cash

    c.   Cash flow from investing activities   *g.*   Net income

    d.   Stockholders' equity   *h.*   Liabilities

SE1-7. **Annual Report Components** Which of the following would not be part of the notes to the financial statements in a company's annual report?   **LO6**

    a.   Qualitative information about potential lawsuits

    b.   Additional information about the reported total of notes payable

    c.   Details about potential new products to be introduced during the next year

    d.   Details of estimates used to compute the expected amount of warranty expense

SE1-8. **Sarbanes-Oxley Act** The Sarbanes-Oxley Act was enacted to help restore confidence in financial reporting. Which of the following was **not** part of the legislation?   **LO3**

    a.   Severe penalties for fraudulent reporting

    b.   A requirement for certification of the financial statements by top management

    c.   A new statement of social responsibility

    d.   A report on internal controls to help prevent and detect errors in the reporting process

SE1-9. **Financial Accounting and Generally Accepted Accounting Principles** Answer the following multiple-choice questions: **LO4**

    1.   What is not a primary function of financial accounting in society?

       a.   Provide comedy material for late-night talk shows.

       b.   Aid in the proper allocation of financial resources in a free enterprise economic system.

       c.   Aid users to make better investing decisions.

    2.   IFRS refers to:

       a.   A random set of letters.

       b.   A set of standards and procedures that form guidelines for international financial accounting.

       c.   A set of standards and procedures that form guidelines for international managerial accounting.

    3.   GAAP:

       a.   Is the distance between two objects.

       b.   Is a set of guidelines for preparing managerial reports in the United States.

       c.   Is a set of guidelines for preparing financial reports in the United States.

LO2 **SE1-10. Cash Flow Activity Classification** Classify each activity as financing, investing, or operating:

1. Repay a loan from a bank.
2. Sell merchandise from a storefront operation.
3. Dispose of an old delivery truck.
4. Pay rent on a company warehouse.
5. Repurchase shares of stock from stockholders.
6. Pay utilities.

LO5 **SE1-11. Using the Basic Accounting Equation** Use the basic accounting equation to answer the following:

a. Hawkins Company has total assets of $150,000 and total liabilities of $110,000. How much is the company's total stockholders' equity?

b. Paul Company has total liabilities of $170,000 and total stockholders' equity of $105,000. How much total assets does the company have?

c. If Black Company's total assets increased by $35,000 during the year, and its total liabilities decreased during the same year by $20,000, what was the change in the company's total stockholders' equity?

LO5 **SE1-12. Using the Basic Accounting Equation** Floyd Company had beginning-of-the-year total assets of $320,000 and total liabilities of $180,000.

a. If during the year total assets increased by $15,000 and total liabilities increased by $40,000, what is the end-of-year total stockholders' equity?

b. If during the year total assets increased by $60,000 and total liabilities decreased by $5,000, what is the end-of-year total stockholders' equity?

c. If during the year total liabilities increased by $40,000 and total stockholders' equity increased by $35,000, what are the end-of-year total assets?

LO5 **SE1-13. Financial Statements** Indicate which statement (or statements) you would examine to locate the following items: balance sheet (BS), income statement (IS), statement of stockholders' equity (SSE), or statement of cash flows (SCF).

a. Expenses for the period
b. Cash at year-end
c. Cash used to purchase new equipment
d. Dividends for the period

LO5 **SE1-14. Financial Statements** Indicate which statement (or statements) you would examine to locate the following items: balance sheet (BS), income statement (IS), statement of stockholders' equity (SSE), or statement of cash flows (SCF).

a. Revenues for the period
b. Cash at beginning of the year
c. Cash used to pay back borrowings
d. Dividends for the period

LO4 **SE1-15. International Accounting Principles** The worldwide acceptance of a global set of international accounting principles will provide certain benefits.

a. Which group has taken the lead in developing a set of international accounting principles?

b. Identify and briefly discuss a benefit that would result from the adoption of a global set of international accounting principles.

LO8
(Appendix 1A) **SE1-16. Principles of Accounting** Which of the following accounting principles applies to the statement of cash flows?

a. Materiality
b. Conservatism
c. Accrual basis of accounting
d. Cash basis of accounting

LO8
(Appendix 1A) **SE1-17. Generally Accepted Accounting Principles** Select the best answer to each of the following questions:

1. Accounting rules are developed to provide:
   a. Simplicity
   b. Useful information
   c. Complexity
   d. Ability to change over time

2. The conceptual framework consists of each of the following except:
   a. Financial reporting objectives
   b. Financial statement elements
   c. Ratio analysis guidelines for analysts
   d. Recognition criteria for financial statement items

3. Which of the following is a financial statement element?
   a. Income statement
   b. Liabilities
   c. Balance sheet
   d. Statement of cash flows

SE1-18. Basic Accounting Principles Match the following list of accounting concepts, principles, and assumptions with the definitions below:

LO8
(Appendix 1A)

Accounting period concept	Consistency	Cost principle
Going concern concept	Materiality constraint	Full disclosure principle
	Comparability	

1. Ability to compare the financial performance of different companies.
2. Assumption that a company will continue to operate beyond the current period.
3. Only items large enough to make a difference to a user must be disclosed in the financial statements.
4. Prepare financial statements at set time intervals.
5. Record assets on the balance sheet at an amount equal to what was paid for them.
6. A company prepares its financial statements using the same methods used in prior periods.
7. All items of importance to the users of financial statements should be disclosed in the annual report.

SE1-19. FASB Codification Which of the following is not one of the reasons for the FASB's codification project:

LO4

a. provide a single source of authoritative U.S. GAAP
b. provide a concise history of the FASB
c. make it easier to research accounting standards
d. provide real-time updates as new standards are released

SE1-20. Basic Accounting Principles Which of the following is not considered a qualitative characteristic of accounting information?

LO8
(Appendix 1A)

a. Faithful representation
b. Comparability
c. Assets must equal liabilities and stockholders' equity
d. Relevance

SE1-21. Basic Accounting Principles Identify whether the following statements are true or false.

LO8
(Appendix 1A)

1. Together the revenue recognition principle and the expense recognition (matching) principle define the accrual basis of accounting.
2. The cash basis of accounting is only used in the preparation of the statement of cash flows.
3. The accrual basis of accounting is used in the preparation of the income statement and the balance sheet.

DATA ANALYTICS

DA1-1. Preparing Data Visualizations in Excel Using Doughnut Charts The Excel file associated with this exercise includes data obtained from the U.S. Bureau of Labor Statistics regarding the employers of the categories of (1) accountants and auditors and (2) financial analysts.[2] We would like to create a data visualization for each employer group in Excel using a doughnut chart, a form of a pie chart.

Data Analytics

Required

1. Download the Excel file DA1-1 found in myBusinessCourse.
2. Create a new row in each dataset for "Other employers."
3. Add the applicable percentage to the new category, "Other employers." *Hint:* When creating a doughnut chart, we are showing proportions of a total. Thus, the total percentage for each dataset must add up to 100%.
4. Create a doughnut chart for each dataset. *Hint:* Highlight the dataset, click on Insert, click on the Pie icon, and click on Doughnut.
5. Update the features of your doughnut charts by either choosing one of the chart design templates or updating manually. *Hint:* To update manually, resize the chart and legend by dragging the sizing handles, change the font size of the legend, change colors and/or shading of the plot area, and add a title.
6. Add percentages to each proportion of the doughnut charts. *Hint:* Right-click on your chart, and click on Add data labels. Click on your chart labels to allow editing of the color or font size.

---

[2] Bureau of Labor Statistics, U.S. Department of Labor, *Occupational Outlook Handbook*, Accountants and Auditors, at https://www.bls.gov/ooh/business-and-financial/accountants-and-auditors.htm (visited August 18, 2021).

7. Calculate the difference between the largest and smallest proportion in the doughnut chart for Dataset A.

8. Calculate the difference between the largest and smallest proportion in the doughnut chart for Dataset B.

9. List any employer categories that overlap between the two occupations.

10. List the formula associated with the chart. *Hint:* Double-click on the Doughnut chart in Dataset A, which will allow the formula to be visible in the formula bar.

LO1   DA1-2.   Explaining the Role of Artificial Intelligence in Accounting Artificial intelligence (AI) are machines that simulate human intelligence. Machines are programmed to sense, recognize speech, problem solve, learn, act or react. In a post by Nigel Duffy and Karsten Fuser called Six Ways the CFO Can Use Artificial Intelligence Today (found at https://www.ey.com/en_us/ai/six-ways-the-cfo-can-use-artificial-intelligence-today), the authors outline several uses of AI. Match a specific example that applies to each of the six uses of AI summarized by the authors.

Category of AI Usage

1. Customer data and predictive behavior
2. Beyond the book value
3. Management of bad debt
4. Fraud
5. Money laundering
6. Taking drudgery out of finance

Specific Example of AI Usage

a. ____ Using natural language processing software to review thousands of pages of contracts in order to identify possible lease agreements.

b. ____ Applying minute-by-minute pricing based upon correlations between customer demographics, type of product, and payment method with the goal of maximizing revenues.

c. ____ Using AI to predict which customers will pay and when they will pay, analyzing data such as the company's credit rating, industry type, purchase history, and company contact transactions.

d. ____ A lender assesses the fair value of collateral by assessing thousands of variables including market data and data specific to the collateral.

e. ____ Using AI to analyze trends in all recorded expenses, detecting patterns by certain employees.

f. ____ Classification of suspicious transactions according to the risk that they resulted in illegally obtained money.

DA1-3.   Preparing Executive Compensation Visualizations with Tableau: Part 1, Part II, Part III Refer to PF-17, PF-18, and PF-19 in Appendix F. This three-part problem uses Tableau to analyze compensation of chief executive officers and chief financial officers of S&P 500 companies.

DATA VISUALIZATION

Data Visualization Activities are available in myBusinessCourse. These assignments use Tableau Dashboards to expose students to visual depictions of data and introduce students to data analytics through data visualizations. These exercises are easily assignable and auto graded by MBC.

EXERCISES—SET A

LO1   E1-1A.   Forms of Business Organization Match the following organizational attributes in the left column with the organizational form in the right column. More than one organizational form may be associated with a given attribute.

1. Unlimited liability
2. Full control
3. Business income combined with owner(s) income for income tax purposes
4. Relatively more difficult to establish
5. Easier to raise funds

a. Sole proprietorship
b. Partnership
c. Corporation

E1-2A. Accounting Process Establish the correct sequence of steps in the accounting measurement process.   **LO4**

    a.   Record in a systematic fashion   *c.*   Quantify economic activity

    b.   Identify relevant economic activity

E1-3A. Types of Accounting Identify the type of accounting associated with each type of report: Managerial,   **LO3**
Financial, Tax, or some combination as needed.

    a.   Budget for internal use by management

    b.   Tax return for state income taxes

    c.   Audited financial statements

    d.   Special reports for regulators of a public utility

E1-4A. Environmental, Social, and Governance Which of the following is not part of the triple bottom line   **LO5**
reporting framework?

    a.   Economic bottom line   *c.*   Competitive bottom line

    b.   Social bottom line   *d.*   Environmental bottom line

E1-5A. Generally Accepted Accounting Principles Identify whether the following statements are true or   **LO4**
false:

    a.   U.S. GAAP is universally accepted in all countries in the world.

    b.   U.S. GAAP is established by the IASB.

    c.   Once established, U.S. GAAP is rarely, if ever, modified.

    d.   The international counterpart to the FASB is the IASB.

E1-6A. Business Activities Identify each of the following activities as operating (O), investing (I), or financ-   **LO2**
ing (F):

    a.   Payment of employee salaries

    b.   Repayment of a loan

    c.   Issuance of common stock

    d.   Purchase of equipment to manufacture a company's products

    e.   Sale of merchandise inventory

    f.   Investment of excess cash in the shares of another company

E1-7A. The Accounting Equation Determine the missing amount in each of the following cases: **LO5**

Assets	Liabilities	Stockholders' Equity
$190,000	$62,000	?
?	$55,000	$31,000
$115,000	?	$61,000

E1-8A. Determining Net Income The beginning and ending balances of retained earnings for the year were   **LO5**
$50,000 and $65,000, respectively. If dividend payments during the year were $0, determine the net
income or net loss for the year.

    a. $19,000 net loss   *c.* $15,000 net income

    b. $19,000 net income   *d.* $11,000 net income

E1-9A. Determining Retained Earnings and Net Income The following information appears in the records   **LO5**
of Becker Corporation at year-end:

Accounts receivable	$ 32,000	Retained earnings	$?
Accounts payable	12,000	Supplies	8,000
Cash	7,000	Equipment, net	145,000
Common stock	115,000		

    a.   Calculate the balance in retained earnings at year-end.

    b.   If the amount of the retained earnings at the beginning of the year was $38,000, and $13,000 in
dividends is paid during the year, calculate net income for the year.

LO5   **E1-10A. Determining Stockholders' Equity and Assets** Determine the following:

a.   The stockholders' equity of a corporation that has assets of $600,000 and liabilities of $306,000.
b.   The assets of a corporation that has liabilities of $250,000, common stock of $125,000, and retained earnings of $85,000.

LO5   **E1-11A. Financial Statements** Fred Flores operates a golf driving range. For each of the following financial items related to his business, indicate the financial statement (or statements) in which the item would be reported: balance sheet (BS), income statement (IS), statement of stockholders' equity (SSE) or statement of cash flows (SCF).

a.   Accounts receivable   e.   Notes payable
b.   Cash received from the sale of land   f.   Supplies expense
c.   Net income   g.   Land
d.   Cash invested in the business by Flores   h.   Supplies

LO5   **E1-12A. Omitted Financial Statement Data** For the following four unrelated situations, A through D, calculate the unknown amounts appearing in each column:

	A	B	C	D
Beginning				
Assets	$45,000	$32,000	$53,000	?
Liabilities	32,000	15,000	49,000	19,000
Ending				
Assets	50,000	30,000	41,000	52,000
Liabilities	22,000	?	20,000	24,000
During Year				
Sales revenue	?	30,000	31,000	27,000
Expenses	12,000	22,000	12,000	19,000
Dividends	2,000	3,000	?	8,000

LO6   **E1-13A. Other Components of the Annual Report** Identify where the following items will appear in a company's annual report: Management's Discussion and Analysis (MD&A), notes to the financial statements, or the auditor's report, or indicate that the item is not disclosed.

a.   A comment that the financial statements appear to be fairly presented
b.   A discussion about new competition likely to occur next year
c.   A quantitative summary of notes payable appearing on the balance sheet
d.   The "secret" ingredients in the company's special sauce

LO3   **E1-14A. Ethics** In each of the following cases, (a) identify the aspect of the accounting environment primarily responsible for the ethical pressure on the accountant as pressure to achieve a favorable outcome, to disclose confidential information, or to report good short-term results, and (b) indicate the appropriate behavioral response for the accountant.

Ethics
assignments are denoted by this icon.

1.   James Jehring, a tax accountant, is preparing an income tax return for a client. The client asks Jehring to take a sizable deduction on the tax return for business-related travel even though the client states that he has no documentation to support the deduction. "I don't think the IRS will audit my return," declares the client.
2.   Willa English, an accountant for Dome Construction Company, has just finished putting the numbers together for a construction project on which the firm is going to submit a bid next month. At a social gathering that evening, a friend casually asks English what Dome's bid is going to be. Ms. English knows that the friend's brother works for a competitor of Dome.
3.   The manager of Cross Department Store is ending his first year with the firm. December's business was slower than expected, and the firm's annual results are trailing last year's results. The manager instructs Kyle Tarpley, the store accountant, to include sales revenues from the first week of January in the December data. "This way, we'll show an increase over last year," declares the manager.

LO4   **E1-15A. International Accounting Principles** Identify whether the following statements are true or false.

1.   One argument for IFRS is that there is more globalization in the world.
2.   IFRS is accepted in every country of the world.
3.   The FASB is responsible for formulating both U.S. GAAP and IFRS.

E1-16A. The Conceptual Accounting Framework The Financial Accounting Standards Board worked many years to develop a conceptual framework for U.S. GAAP.   **LO8** (Appendix 1A)

    a.   What is the purpose of a conceptual framework?

    b.   Identify the financial reporting objectives that are specified in the conceptual framework.

E1-17A. Recognition and Measurement Criteria Indicate the accounting concepts, principles, or constraints that underlie each of the following independent situations: accounting entity concept, going concern concept, cost-benefit constraint, expense recognition (matching principle), materiality constraint, revenue recognition principle, full disclosure principle, cost principle.   **LO8** (Appendix 1A)

    a.   Dr. Lynn is a practicing pediatrician. Over the years, she has accumulated a personal investment portfolio of securities, virtually all of which have been purchased from her earnings as a pediatrician. The investment portfolio is not reflected in the accounting records of her medical practice.

    b.   A company purchases a desk tape dispenser for use by the office secretary. The tape dispenser cost $25 and has an estimated useful life of 15 years. The purchase is immediately expensed on the company's income statement.

    c.   A company sells a product that has a two-year warranty covering parts and labor. In the same period that revenues from product sales are recorded, an estimate of future warranty costs is recorded on the company's income statement.

    d.   A company is sued for $1.5 million by a customer claiming that a defective product caused an accident. The company believes that the lawsuit is without merit. Although the case will not be tried for a year, the company adds a note describing the lawsuit to its current financial statements.

E1-18A. Revenue Recognition Principle For each of the following situations, determine whether the criteria for revenue recognition have been met by December 31.   **LO8** (Appendix 1A)

    a.   A manufacturing company received $60,000 cash on December 31 as an advance payment on a special order for a piece of equipment. The equipment will be manufactured by March 31 of the next year.

    b.   A television dealer acquired six new high-definition television sets for $7,800 cash on December 31 and placed online advertisements selling them for $2,000 each.

    c.   A snow removal service signed a contract on November 15 with a shopping mall to clear its parking lot of all snowfalls over 1 inch during the months of December through March of the next year. The cost is $900 per month and payment is due in two $1,800 installments: January 2 and February 1. By December 31, no snowfall over 1 inch had occurred.

E1-19A. Accrual Basis of Accounting versus Cash Basis of Accounting On December 31, Greg Jones completed his first year as a financial planner. The following data are available from his accounting records: **LO5, 8** (Appendix 1A)

Fees billed to clients for		Rent expense for year just	
services rendered	$131,000	ended	$12,000
Cash received from clients	119,000	Utility expenses incurred	4,500
Supplies purchased for cash	7,100	Utility bills paid	3,300
Supplies used during the year	6,100	Salary earned by assistant	39,400
Cash paid for rent (rent is paid		Salary paid to assistant	35,100
through Mar. of next year)	15,000		

    a.   Compute Greg's net income for the year just ended using the accrual basis of accounting.

    b.   Compute Greg's net income for the year just ended using the cash basis of accounting.

    c.   Which net income amount is computed in accordance with generally accepted accounting principles?

E1-20A. Recognition and Measurement Criteria The following are unrelated accounting practices: **LO8** (Appendix 1A)

    1.   Pine Company purchased a new $30 snow shovel that is expected to last six years. The shovel is used to clear the firm's front steps during the winter months. The shovel's cost is recorded on the company's balance sheet as an asset.

    2.   Penny Corporation has been named as the defendant in a $50 million pollution lawsuit. Because the lawsuit will take several years to resolve and the outcome is uncertain, Penny's management decides not to mention the lawsuit in the current year financial statements.

Required
For each of the given practices, indicate which accounting concepts, principles, or constraints apply and whether they have been applied appropriately. For each inappropriate accounting practice, indicate the proper accounting procedure.

EXERCISES—SET B

 LO1   **E1-1B.   Forms of Business Organization** Match the following organizational attributes in the left column with the organizational form in the right column. More than one organizational form may be associated with a given attribute.

1.	Limited liability	*a.*	Sole proprietorship
2.	Shared control	*b.*	Partnership
3.	Double taxation	*c.*	Corporation
4.	Easiest to form		
5.	Easier to transfer ownership		

 LO4   **E1-2B.   The Accounting Process** Which of the following items is not part of the three-step accounting process?

a.   Quantify economic activity   *c.*   Record in a systematic fashion
b.   Identify relevant economic activity   *d.*   Audit the financial results

 LO3   **E1-3B.   Types of Accounting** Identify the type of accounting associated with each type of report: Managerial, Financial, Tax, or some combination as needed.

a.   Cost report for a new product
b.   Tax return for federal income taxes
c.   Unaudited financial statements requested for a bank loan
d.   Special report for banking regulators

 LO5   **E1-4B.   Environmental, Social, and Governance** Which of the following is not part of the triple bottom line reporting framework?

a.   Social bottom line   *c.*   Economic bottom line
b.   Environmental bottom line   *d.*   Efficiency bottom line

 LO4   **E1-5B.   Generally Accepted Accounting Principles** Identify whether the following statements are true or false.

a.   GAAP can differ from one country to another.
b.   U.S. GAAP is established by the FASB.
c.   U.S. GAAP is a guide to action that may change over time.
d.   At this time there is no international counterpart to the FASB.

 LO2   **E1-6B.   Business Activities** Identify each of the following activities as operating (O), investing (I), or financing (F).

a.   Payment of rent on the company headquarters   *c.*   Obtain a long-term bank loan
b.   Repurchase of the company's common stock   *d.*   Sale of an empty warehouse
                                                       e.   Delivery of consulting service
                                                       f.   Sale of short-term investments

 LO5   **E1-7B.   The Accounting Equation** Determine the missing amount in each of the following cases:

Assets	Liabilities	Stockholders' Equity
$350,000	?	$225,000
$155,000	$95,000	?
?	$40,000	$ 59,000

E1-8B. Determining Net Income The beginning and ending balances of retained earnings for the year were $63,000 and $82,000, respectively. If dividend payments during the year were $8,000, determine the net income or net loss for the year.   **LO5**

a. $14,000 net loss   c. $35,000 net income
b. $27,000 net income   d. $14,000 net income

E1-9B. Determining Retained Earnings and Net Income The following information appears in the records of Poco Corporation at year-end: **LO5**

Accounts receivable	$ 42,000	Retained earnings	$?
Accounts payable	21,000	Supplies	30,000
Cash	18,000	Equipment, net	105,000
Common stock	139,000		

a.   Calculate the amount of retained earnings at year-end.
b.   If the amount of the retained earnings at the beginning of the year was $25,000, and $10,000 in dividends is paid during the year, calculate net income for the year.

E1-10B. Determining Stockholders' Equity and Assets Determine the following: **LO5**

a.   The stockholders' equity of a corporation that has assets of $850,000 and liabilities of $190,000.
b.   The assets of a corporation that has liabilities of $195,000, common stock of $90,000, and retained earnings of $80,000.

E1-11B. Financial Statements Julie Jason operates a bakery. For each of the following financial statement items related to her business, indicate the financial statement (or statements) in which the item would be reported: balance sheet (BS), income statement (IS), statement of stockholders' equity (SSE) or statement of cash flows (SCF).   **LO5**

a.   Accounts payable   e.   Notes receivable
b.   Cash received from the sale of equipment   f.   Rent expense
c.   Net loss   g.   Building
d.   Cash invested in the business by Jason   h.   Inventory

E1-12B. Omitted Financial Statement Data For the following four unrelated situations, A through D, calculate the unknown amounts appearing in each column: **LO5**

	A	B	C	D
Beginning				
Assets	$38,000	$22,000	$38,000	?
Liabilities	22,000	15,000	29,000	19,000
Ending				
Assets	40,000	36,000	44,000	65,000
Liabilities	22,000	?	27,000	24,000
During Year				
Sales revenue	?	26,000	31,000	27,000
Expense	12,000	22,000	12,000	19,000
Dividends	2,000	5,500	?	4,000

E1-13B. Other Components of the Annual Report Identify where the following items will appear in a company's annual report: Management's Discussion and Analysis (MD&A), notes to the financial statements, or the auditor's report, or indicate that the item is not disclosed.   **LO6**

a.   A comment that the statements are presented in conformity with generally accepted accounting principles
b.   A discussion about new products to be introduced next year
c.   A quantitative summary of property, plant, and equipment appearing on the balance sheet
d.   The salaries of every employee

E1-14B. Ethics In each of the following cases, (a) identify the aspect of the accounting environment primarily responsible for the ethical pressure on the accountant as pressure to achieve a favorable outcome, to disclose confidential information, or to report good short-term results, and (b) indicate the appropriate behavioral response for the accountant.   **LO3**

1. Jenny Jones, a tax accountant, is preparing an income tax return for a client. The client asks Jones to omit some income she received for consulting services because the amount was paid in cash. "I don't think the IRS will audit my return," declares the client. "And even if they do, what are the chances they would catch this?"

2. Fred French, an accountant for Top Electronics Company, has just finished estimating the cost for a new iPod device that the company plans to introduce. Cost estimates help the company to determine the price it can charge for new products. At a social gathering that evening, a friend casually asks Fred what Top's cost for the iPod device came out to be. Fred knows that the friend's brother works for a competitor of Top Electronics.

3. The manager of Jazz Department Store is ending his first year with the firm. December's business was slower than expected, and the firm's annual results are below Wall Street's expectations. The manager instructs Chris Green, store accountant, to record some of December's expenses in the following year. "This way, we'll meet Wall Street's expectations," declares the manager.

LO4

E1-15B. International Accounting Principles Although there are obstacles to the worldwide acceptance of a global set of international accounting principles, the potential benefits appear significant.

Identify and briefly discuss three potential benefits to the worldwide acceptance of a global set of international accounting principles.

LO8
(Appendix 1A)

E1-16B. The Conceptual Framework The Financial Accounting Standards Board worked many years to develop a conceptual framework for U.S. GAAP.

a. Identify the financial statement elements that are specified in the conceptual framework.
b. Before a financial statement element may be recorded in the accounts, certain recognition criteria must be met. What are those recognition criteria?

LO8
(Appendix 1A)

E1-17B. Recognition and Measurement Criteria Indicate the accounting concepts, principles, or constraints that underlie each of the following independent situations: accounting entity concept, going concern concept, cost-benefit constraint, expense recognition (matching principle), materiality constraint, revenue recognition principle, full disclosure principle, cost principle.

a. General Motors reports in its annual report to stockholders that revenues from automotive sales "are recorded by the company when products are shipped to dealers."

b. The annual financial report of Fiat Chrysler Corporation and subsidiaries includes the financial data of its significant subsidiaries, including Chrysler Financial Corporation (which provides financing for dealers and customers), Chrysler Technologies Corporation (which manufactures high-technology electronic products), and Pentastar Transportation Group, Inc. (which includes Thrifty Rent-A-Car System, Inc., and Dollar Rent A Car Systems, Inc.).

c. A company purchased a parcel of land several years ago for $70,000. The land's estimated current market value is $80,000. The Land account balance is not increased but remains at $70,000.

d. A company has a calendar-year fiscal year-end. On January 8 prior year, a tornado destroyed its largest warehouse, causing a $2,000,000 loss. This information is reported in a footnote to the 2018 financial statements.

LO8
(Appendix 1A)

E1-18B. Revenue Recognition Principle For each of the following situations, determine whether the criteria for revenue recognition have been met by December 31.

a. A manufacturing company received $85,000 cash on December 31 as an advance payment on a special order for a piece of equipment. The equipment will be manufactured by March 31 of the next year.

b. An appliance dealer acquired ten new washer/dryer sets for $6,800 cash on December 31 and advertised their availability, at $1,000 for each set.

c. A yard maintenance service signed a contract on October 15 with an apartment complex to maintain its grounds during the months of November through June the next year. The cost is $750 per month and payment is due in two $3,000 installments: December 15 and March 15.

LO5, 8
(Appendix 1A)

E1-19B. Accrual Basis of Accounting versus Cash Basis of Accounting On December 31, John Bush completed his first year as a financial planner. The following data are available from his accounting records:

Fees billed to clients for services rendered	$137,000	Rent expense for year just ended.	$12,000
Cash received from clients	115,000	Utility expense incurred	3,100
Supplies purchased for cash	9,000	Utility bills paid	3,200
Supplies used during the year	6,800	Salary earned by assistant.	39,000
Cash paid for rent (rent is paid through		Salary paid to assistant	35,000
Feb. of next year)	14,000		

    a.   Compute John's net income for the year just ended using the accrual basis of accounting.

    b.   Compute John's net income for the year just ended using the cash basis of accounting.

    c.   Which net income amount is computed in accordance with generally accepted accounting principles?

E1-20B. Recognition and Measurement Criteria The following are unrelated accounting practices: **LO8**
(Appendix 1A)

    1. A recession has caused a slowing of business activity and lower profits for Penn Company. Consequently, the firm delays making its payments for December's rent and utilities until January and does not record either of these expenses in December.

    2. Joan Jeffrey, a consultant operating as a sole proprietorship, used her business car for a personal, month-long vacation. A full year's gas and oil expenditures on the car are charged to the firm's gas and oil expense account.

Required

For each of the given practices, indicate which accounting concepts, principles, or constraints apply and whether they have been applied appropriately. For each inappropriate accounting practice, indicate the proper accounting procedure.

PROBLEMS—SET A

P1-1A. **Forms of Business Organization** Presented below are four independent situations: **LO1**

    a.   Kent Jones, a senior in college looking for summer employment, decided to start a dog-walking business. Each morning and evening he picks up a group of dogs and walks them around the city park.

    b.   Brothers Jack and Jim Stevens each owned a separate electronics repair shop. They decided to combine their talents and resources in order to expand the amount of business they could undertake.

    c.   Three chemists at a large engineering company decided to start their own business based on an experimental chemical process they had developed outside the company. The process had the potential to be very successful; however, it was quite dangerous and could result in large legal problems.

    d.   Jason King ran a small, but successful holistic healing spa. The spa has gained a strong reputation beyond the community where it is located. Jason decided to open a chain of similar spas across the state to capitalize on his reputation. This will require a substantial investment in supplies and employee training. In addition, since Jason will not be able to closely supervise each location, he is worried about potential liability.

Required

Explain the form of organization that would be best in each situation—sole proprietorship, partnership, or corporation. Explain what factors you considered important in each situation.

P1-2A. **Financial Statements** While each of the financial statements is likely to aid in any business decision, **LO5**
it is often the case that a particular financial statement may be best suited to help in a particular decision. Consider each decision below independently:

    a.   You are trying to determine whether a particular firm is a good investment. You understand that share price increases are impacted heavily by a company's earnings potential.

    b.   You are employed in the lending department of a large bank. You are trying to determine if you should lend to a potential customer. If you do make the loan you are especially concerned that the company will have sufficient collateral in the event that it is unable to repay the loan.

c. You wish to invest in a firm that provides you with a steady source of income. You especially want a firm that pays out a large part of its net income as dividends.

d. You are trying to determine if a particular firm will have sufficient cash flow in order to keep expanding without relying too heavily on external sources of financing.

Required

Determine which of the financial statements contains the most useful information to help in your decision. Explain what information you used from each statement to help you make your decision.

LO5   P1-3A.   Balance Sheet The following balance sheet data are for Brintany Coastal Catering Service, a corporation, at May 31:

Accounts receivable	$27,300	Accounts payable	10,200
Notes payable	29,000	Cash	16,300
Equipment, net	61,000	Common stock	41,500
Supplies	15,400	Retained earnings	?

Required

Prepare a balance sheet for Brintany as of May 31.

LO5   P1-4A.   Statement of Stockholders' Equity and Balance Sheet The following is balance sheet information for Tuttle Janitorial Service, Inc., as of December 31 for Year 1 and Year 2:

	December 31, Year 2	December 31, Year 1
Accounts payable	$ 6,000	$ 9,000
Cash	25,000	22,000
Accounts receivable	39,000	31,000
Land	56,000	46,000
Building, net	250,000	260,000
Equipment, net	44,000	46,000
Mortgage payable	93,000	88,000
Supplies	18,000	16,000
Common stock	225,000	225,000
Dividends	12,000	0
Retained earnings	?	?

Required

a. Prepare a balance sheet as of December 31 of each year.

b. Prepare a statement of stockholders' equity for Year 2. (*Hint:* The increase in retained earnings is equal to the net income less the dividend.)

LO5   P1-5A.   Statement of Stockholders' Equity and Balance Sheet The following is balance sheet information for Flush Janitorial Service, Inc., as of December 31 for Year 1 and Year 2:

	December 31, Year 2	December 31, Year 1
Accounts payable	$ 17,000	$ 18,000
Cash	50,000	44,000
Accounts receivable	78,000	62,000
Land	92,000	92,000
Building, net	500,000	520,000
Equipment, net	75,000	77,000
Mortgage payable	175,000	205,000
Supplies	27,000	22,000
Common stock	420,000	420,000
Dividends	20,000	0
Retained earnings	?	?

Required

a. Prepare a balance sheet as of December 31 of each year.

b. Prepare a statement of stockholders' equity for Year 2. (*Hint:* The increase in retained earnings is equal to the net income less the dividend.)

P1-6A. **Income Statement and Balance Sheet** On March 1, Janet Dodge began Dodge Delivery Service, which provides delivery of bulk mailings to the post office, neighborhood delivery of weekly newspapers, data delivery to computer service centers, and various other delivery services using leased vans. On February 28, Dodge invested $20,000 of her own funds in the firm and borrowed $8,000 from her father on a six-month, non-interest-bearing note payable. The following information is available at March 31:

LO5

Excel icons denote assignments with Excel templates available.

Accounts receivable	$10,700	Delivery fees earned	$23,300
Rent expense	2,500	Cash	12,700
Advertising expense	1,100	Supplies inventory	14,800
Supplies expense	2,500	Notes payable	8,000
Accounts payable	1,400	Insurance expense	900
Salaries expense	6,200	Common stock	20,000
Miscellaneous expense	1,300	Retained earnings	?

Required

a. Prepare an income statement for the month of March.

b. Prepare a balance sheet as of March 31.

P1-7A. **Statement of Cash Flows** Shown below is selected information from the financial records of Merris Corporation as of December 31:

LO5

Inventory	$165,000	Cash purchase of equipment	$ 29,000
Cash collected from customers	350,000	Buildings, net	810,000
Equipment, net	355,000	Sales revenue	910,000
Retained earnings	480,000	Cash paid for operating activities	225,000
Cash dividends paid	38,000	Principal payments on existing note payable	41,000
Salary expense	215,000	Common stock	529,000

Required

a. Determine which of the above items will appear on the statement of cash flows and then prepare the statement for Merris Corporation for the year ended December 31.

b. Comment on the adequacy of Merris's operations to provide cash for its investing and financing activities.

P1-8A. **Ethics** In each of the following cases, (a) identify the aspect of the accounting environment primarily responsible for the ethical pressure on the accountant as pressure to achieve a favorable outcome, to disclose confidential information, or to report good short-term results, and (b) indicate the appropriate behavioral response that the accountant should take.

LO3

1. Patricia Kelly, an accountant for Wooden Company, is reviewing the costs charged to a government contract that Wooden worked on this year. Wooden is manufacturing special parts for the government and is allowed to charge the government for its actual manufacturing costs plus a fixed fee. Kelly notes that $75,000 worth of art objects purchased for the president's office is buried among the miscellaneous costs charged to the contract. Upon inquiry, the firm's vice president replies, "This sort of thing is done all the time."

2. Barry Marklin, accountant for Smith & Wesson partnership, is working on the year-end financial data for this year. The partnership agreement calls for Smith and Wesson to share this year's net income equally. Next year, the partners will share the net income 60 percent to Smith and 40 percent to Wesson. Wesson plans to cut back his involvement in the firm. Smith wants Marklin to delay recording sales revenue from work done at the end of this year until January of next year. "We haven't received the cash yet from those services," declares Smith.

3. The St. Louis Wheelers, a professional football franchise, just signed its first-round draft pick to a multiyear contract that is reported in the newspapers as a four-year, $20 million contract. Johanna Factor, the Wheelers' accountant, receives a call from an agent of another team's first-round pick. "Just calling to confirm the contract terms reported in the papers," states the agent. "My client should receive a similar contract, and I'm sure you don't want him to get shortchanged."

LO5, 6   **P1-9A.**   **Financial Statements and Other Components** Match each of the items in the left column with the appropriate annual report component from the right column:

1. The company's total liabilities	a. Income Statement
2. The sources of cash during the period	b. Balance Sheet
3. An opinion about whether the financial statements are fairly stated	c. Statement of Cash Flows
4. The amount of dividends that are distributed to the company's stockholders	d. Statement of Stockholders' Equity
5. A discussion of potential new products to be introduced the next year	e. Notes to the Financial Statements
6. Information regarding accounting methods used	f. Management's Discussion and Analysis (MD&A)
7. The company's total revenue for the period	g. Auditor's report

LO5   **P1-10A.** **Income Statement, Statement of Stockholders' Equity, and Balance Sheet** Petty Corporation started business on January 1. The following information was compiled by Petty's accountant on December 31:

Sales revenue.	$32,000	Equipment, net.	$25,000
Expenses	20,000	Building, net	59,000
Dividends	8,000	Accounts payable	7,000
Cash.	3,250	Notes payable.	50,500
Accounts receivable	2,750	Common stock	33,000
Inventory.	4,500	Retained earnings	?

Required

a. You have been asked to assist the accountant for the Petty Corporation in preparing year-end financial statements. Use the above information to prepare an income statement, statement of stockholders' equity, and a balance sheet as of December 31.

b. Comment on the decision to pay an $8,000 dividend.

LO8
(Appendix 1A)   **P1-11A.** **Recognition and Measurement Criteria** The following are unrelated accounting situations and the accounting treatment that was followed in each firm's records:

1. John Company mounts an $800,000 year-long advertising campaign on a national cable television network. The firm's annual accounting period is the calendar year. The television network required full payment in December at the beginning of the campaign. Accounting treatment is
   Increase Advertising Expense, $800,000
   Decrease Cash, $800,000

2. Because of a local bankruptcy, machinery worth $225,000 was acquired at a "bargain" purchase price of $170,000. Accounting treatment is
   Increase Machinery, $170,000
   Decrease Cash, $170,000

3. Tony Voes, a consultant operating a sole proprietorship, withdrew $30,000 from the business and purchased stocks as an investment gift to his wife. Accounting treatment is
   Increase Investments, $30,000
   Decrease Cash, $30,000

4. Channy Company received a firm offer of $96,000 for a parcel of land it owns that cost $50,000 two years ago. The offer was refused, but the indicated gain was recorded in the accounts. Accounting treatment is
   Increase Land, $46,000
   Increase Revenue from Change in Land Value, $46,000

Required

In each of the given situations, indicate which accounting concepts, principles or constraints apply and whether they have been applied appropriately. If you decide the accounting treatment is not generally accepted, discuss the effect of the departure on the balance sheet.

PROBLEMS—SET B

P1-1B. Forms of Business Organization   LO1

Presented below are four independent situations:

a. Larry Jordon, a photography major in college, decided to start a photography business specializing in weddings and similar occasions. Larry is still able to go to school full-time as all of his
jobs are on weekends or holidays.

b. Joe Friday and Jay Holmes each owned a separate detective agency. They decided to combine
their talents and resources in order to expand the amount of business they could undertake.

c. Three business school professors at a large university decided to start their own consulting business based on their combined talents. They feel that the insurance they can obtain will satisfy any
possible legal issues they may face. They plan to use one professor's home office to meet clients,
so start-up costs should be minimal.

d. Verna Zilver runs a small, but successful beauty salon. The salon has gained a strong reputation
beyond the community where it is located. Verna has decided to open a chain of similar salons
across the state to capitalize on her reputation. This will require a substantial investment in facilities and supplies. In addition, since Verna will not be able to closely supervise each location, she
is worried about potential liability.

Required

Explain the form of organization that would be best in each situation—sole proprietorship, partnership,
or corporation. Explain what factors you considered important in each situation.

P1-2B. Financial Statements While each of the financial statements is likely to aid in any business decision,   LO5
it is often the case that a particular financial statement may be best suited to help in a particular decision. Consider each decision below independently:

a. You are trying to determine whether a particular firm is a good investment. You want to invest in
a firm that has strong revenue growth.

b. You are employed as a financial analyst for a large investment firm. You are trying to assess the
riskiness of a particular investment opportunity. You understand that the more debt a firm has
relative to its stockholders' equity, the riskier the firm is.

c. You are trying to determine how much of a firm's net income it distributes to its stockholders.

d. You are trying to determine how a particular firm was able to finance its large expansion during
the year.

Required

Determine which of the financial statements contains the most useful information to help in your decision. Explain what information you used from each statement to help you make your decision.

P1-3B. Balance Sheet The following balance sheet data are for Better Plumbing Contractors, Inc., a corpora-   LO5
tion, at May 31:

Accounts payable	$ 9,900	Common stock	$101,000
Cash	15,700	Retained earnings	?
Equipment, net	100,000	Notes payable	31,000
Supplies	28,500	Accounts receivable	9,200
Land	31,000		

Required

Prepare a balance sheet for Better as of May 31.

LO5 **P1-4B.** **Statement of Stockholders' Equity and Balance Sheet** The following is balance sheet information for Bryant Packaging Service as of December 31 for Year 1 and Year 2:

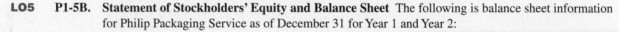

	December 31, Year 2	December 31, Year 1
Accounts payable	$ 2,800	$ 2,600
Cash	11,000	12,000
Accounts receivable	23,800	19,500
Equipment, net	33,000	31,000
Notes payable	21,000	21,000
Supplies	5,700	5,200
Common stock	6,000	6,000
Dividends	13,000	0
Retained earnings	?	?

Required

a. Prepare a balance sheet as of December 31 of each year.
b. Prepare a statement of stockholders' equity for Year 2. (*Hint:* The increase in retained earnings is equal to the net income less the dividend.)

LO5 **P1-5B.** **Statement of Stockholders' Equity and Balance Sheet** The following is balance sheet information for Philip Packaging Service as of December 31 for Year 1 and Year 2:

	December 31, Year 2	December 31, Year 1
Accounts payable	$ 16,000	$ 14,000
Cash	53,000	49,000
Accounts receivable	80,000	64,000
Equipment, net	76,000	78,000
Notes payable	175,000	175,000
Supplies	29,000	31,000
Common stock	30,000	30,000
Dividends	15,000	0
Retained earnings	?	?

Required

a. Prepare a balance sheet as of December 31 of each year.
b. Prepare a statement of stockholders' equity for Year 2. (*Hint:* The increase in retained earnings is equal to the net income less the dividend.)

LO5 **P1-6B.** **Income Statement and Balance Sheet** The first year records of R. Levitt, Interior Decorator, show the following information for the year-end December 31:

Notes payable	$ 6,000	Supplies	$ 6,500
Decorating fees earned	57,600	Cash	6,200
Insurance expense	1,600	Accounts receivable	8,600
Supplies expense	8,100	Advertising expense	700
Miscellaneous expense	1,200	Salaries expense	36,000
Common stock	7,000	Rent expense	4,500
Retained earnings	?	Accounts payable	2,800

Required

a. Prepare an income statement for the year.
b. Prepare a balance sheet as of December 31.

P1-7B. Statement of Cash Flows Shown below is selected information from the financial records of Willy Corporation as of December 31:

Inventory	$155,000	Cash purchase of equipment	$129,000
Cash collected from customers	670,000	Buildings, net	860,000
Equipment, net	255,000	Sales revenue	940,000
Retained earnings	580,000	Cash paid for operating activities	425,000
Cash dividends paid	90,000	Principal payments on existing note payable	128,000
Salary expense	226,000	Common stock	329,000

Required

a. Determine which of the above items will appear on the statement of cash flows and then prepare the statement for Willy Corporation for the year ended December 31.

b. Comment on the adequacy of Willy's operations to provide cash for its investing and financing activities.

P1-8B. Ethics In each of the following cases, (a) identify the aspect of the accounting environment primarily responsible for the ethical pressure on the accountant as pressure to achieve a favorable outcome, to disclose confidential information, or to report good short-term results, and (b) indicate the appropriate behavioral response that the accountant should take:

1. Jim Miller, an accountant for the Geary Company, is reviewing costs charged to a big government contract to supply logistical support. The contract specifies that Geary is entitled to its cost plus 10 percent extra for profit. Jim notices that gardening services at the home of the company president, Stuart Geary, are included under miscellaneous expenses. The company's vice president, Slick Herve, tells you not to worry about this since the government expects a little bit of fancy accounting to be included in all of its contracts.

2. Juan Salles, an accountant for the law partnership Dewy and Suem, is working on the year-end financial statements. Currently the two partners, Dewy and Suem, each receive one-half of the firm's net income. Next year the allocation will change to a two-thirds, one-third split since Suem will be taking considerable time off to do pro bono work, something Dewy never does. Dewy suggested to Salles that he delay booking a large partial settlement the partnership received in December until January of next year when they will receive the final cash payment. Dewy commented that it would be "cleaner" to keep it all together.

3. Pete Jackson is the accountant for a large professional services firm. Part of his responsibility is to complete payroll tax reports based on the salaries paid to all the employees. Pete received a call from a friend at a search firm that specializes in personnel such as those employed at Pete's place of employment. Pete's friend casually asked how much certain employees were making, explaining he wanted to be able to calibrate market wages for work he was doing.

P1-9B. Financial Statements and Other Components Match each of the items in the left column with the appropriate annual report component from the right column:

1. The company's total assets	a. Income Statement
2. An opinion regarding whether the financial statements followed GAAP	b. Statement of Stockholders' Equity
3. Information regarding the estimates used in the financial statements	c. Balance Sheet
4. The use of cash during the period	d. Statement of Cash Flows
5. The company's total expenses for the period	e. Management's Discussion and Analysis (MD&A)
6. A discussion of potential risks that a company may encounter in the future	f. Notes to the Financial Statements
7. The amount of a company's earnings that are distributed to the company's stockholders	g. Auditor's report

LO5   **P1-10B. Income Statement, Statement of Stockholders' Equity, and Balance Sheet** Pick Corporation started business on January 1. The following information was compiled by Pick's accountant on December 31:

Sales revenue	$52,000	Equipment, net	$31,000
Expenses	41,000	Building, net	49,000
Dividends	4,000	Accounts payable	8,000
Cash	5,250	Notes payable	49,500
Accounts receivable	6,750	Common stock	33,000
Inventory	5,500	Retained earnings	?

Required

a. You have been asked to assist the accountant for the Pick Corporation in preparing year-end financial statements. Use the above information to prepare an income statement, statement of stockholders' equity, and a balance sheet as of December 31.

b. Comment on the decision to pay a $4,000 dividend.

LO8   **P1-11B. Recognition and Measurement Criteria** The following are unrelated accounting situations and the
(Appendix 1A)   accounting treatment that was followed in each firm's records:

1. The Buchanan Company mounts a $900,000 year-long advertising campaign on a new national cable television network. The firm's annual accounting period is the calendar year. The television network required full payment in December at the beginning of the campaign. Accounting treatment is

    Increase Advertising Expense, $900,000
    Decrease Cash, $900,000

2. Because of a local bankruptcy, machinery worth $320,000 was acquired at a "bargain" purchase price of $150,000. Accounting treatment is

    Increase Machinery, $150,000
    Decrease Cash, $150,000

3. J.R. Brown, a consultant operating a sole proprietorship, withdrew $50,000 from the business and purchased stocks as an investment gift to his wife. Accounting treatment is

    Increase Investments, $50,000
    Decrease Cash, $50,000

4. Puite Company received a firm offer of $106,000 for a parcel of land it owns that cost $56,000 two years ago. The offer was refused, but the indicated gain was recorded in the accounts. Accounting treatment is

    Increase Land, $50,000
    Increase Revenue from Change in Land Value, $50,000

Required

In each of the given situations, indicate which accounting concepts, principles or constraints apply and whether they have been applied appropriately. If you decide the accounting treatment is not generally accepted, discuss the effect of the departure on the balance sheet.

SERIAL PROBLEM: KATE'S CARDS

SP1.   Kate Collins has always been good at putting together rhymes for any occasion. Kate is a recent college graduate with a double major in business and art. Kate has always had a bit of an entrepreneurial streak and has decided to open her own business designing and selling greeting cards.

Kate decided that she would rent a small studio where she would design the cards on a new Apple iMac that she is planning to purchase. Kate also decided to offer classes in greeting card design to other aspiring greeting card producers. After much thought, Kate decided to name her business "Kate's Cards."

Required

a. What form of business—sole proprietorship, partnership, or corporation—should Kate choose? Discuss why the organizational form that you selected is most appropriate for Kate.

Kate's Cards *is a continuous problem that requires students to apply the concepts from the current chapter. There is a Kate's Cards assignment in each chapter.*

Extending Your Knowledge
assignments require use of real world financial statements and critical thinking skills.

b.   What accounting information will Kate need to run her business?

c.   What balance sheet accounts—assets, liabilities, and stockholders' equity—and income statement accounts—revenues and expenses—will Kate likely need to use?

d.   Should Kate use her personal bank account or open a separate business bank account?

EXTENDING YOUR KNOWLEDGE

REPORTING AND ANALYSIS

EYK1-1.   Financial Reporting Problem: Columbia Sportswear Company Financial statements for the **Columbia Sportswear Company** are reported in **Appendix A** at the end of the textbook.

COLUMBIA
SPORTSWEAR
COMPANY

Financial Statements for Columbia Sportswear and Under Armour are located at the end of the book in Appendix A and Appendix B.

Required
Refer to Columbia Sportswear's financial statements to answer the following questions:

a.   How much did Columbia's total assets increase or decrease from December 31, 2019, to December 31, 2020?

b.   How much did Columbia's cash and cash equivalents increase or decrease from December 31, 2019, to December 31, 2020, and how much cash did Columbia report on its December 31, 2020, balance sheet?

c.   How much accounts receivable and accounts payable did Columbia report on December 31, 2020?

d.   Did Columbia experience sales growth in 2020?

e.   Was Columbia profitable in 2020? How does the company's 2020 net income compare to 2019?

EYK1-2.   Comparative Analysis Problem: Columbia Sportswear Company vs. Under Armour, Inc. Simplified financial statements for the **Columbia Sportswear Company** are reported in **Exhibit 1-10** and **Under Armour**'s financial statements are presented in **Appendix B** at the end of this book.

COLUMBIA
SPORTSWEAR
COMPANY

UNDER ARMOUR

Required
1.   Based on the information in these financial statements, compare the following for each company as of December 31, 2020:

a.   Total assets

c.   Net income

b.   Sales

d.   Cash flow from operations

2.   From this information, what can you conclude about the relative size and operating performance of each company?

EYK1-3.   Business Decision Problem Paul Seger, a friend of yours, is negotiating the purchase of an exterminating company called Complete Pest Control. Seger has been employed by a national pest control service and knows the technical side of the business. However, he knows little about accounting, so he asks for your assistance. The owner of Complete Pest Control, Greg Krum, provided Seger with income statements for the past three years, which showed an average net income of $75,000 per year. The latest balance sheet shows total assets of $360,000 and liabilities of $60,000. Seger brings the following matters to your attention:

1.   Krum is asking $375,000 for the firm. He told Seger that because the firm has been earning a 20 percent return on stockholders' equity, the price should be higher than the net assets reported on the balance sheet. (Note: The return on stockholders' equity is calculated as net income divided by total stockholders' equity.)

2.   Seger noticed that there was no salary expense reported for Krum on the income statements, even though he worked half-time in the business. Krum explained that, because he had other income, he withdrew only $15,000 each year from the firm for personal use. If he purchases the firm, Seger will hire a full-time manager to run the firm at an annual salary of $30,000.

3.   Krum's tax returns for the past three years report a lower net income for the firm than the amounts shown in the financial statements. Seger is skeptical about the accounting principles used in preparing the company's financial statements.

Required

a. If Seger accepts Krum's average annual income figure of $75,000, what would Seger's return on stockholders' equity be, assuming that the net income remained at the same level and that the firm was purchased for $375,000?

b. Should Krum's withdrawals of $15,000 per year affect the net income reported in the financial statements? What will Seger's percentage return be if he takes into consideration the $30,000 salary he plans to pay a full-time manager?

c. Could there be legitimate reasons for the difference between net income as shown in the financial statements and net income as reported on the tax returns, as mentioned in point 3? How might Seger obtain additional assurances about the propriety of the company's financial statements?

EYK1-4.   Financial Analysis Problem Todd Jansen is deciding among several job offers. One job offer he is considering is in the marketing department at Columbia Sportswear. Before he makes his decision, he decides to review the financial reports of the company.

Required

Use the Columbia Sportswear annual report located in Appendix A at the end of this book to answer the following questions:

a. Were the financial statements of Columbia audited? If so, what firm performed the audit?

b. What was the amount of Columbia's 2020 net income? How does this compare with 2019 net income?

c. How much cash was provided or used for investing activities? What were the major sources and uses of cash from investing activities?

d. How much were accrued liabilities in 2020? What makes up this balance?

e. What are some of the more significant estimates used in the preparation of the company's financial statements?

f. To what amount are the financial statements rounded?

CRITICAL THINKING

GENERAL MILLS, INC.

EYK1-5.   Accounting Research Problem Go to this book's Website and locate the annual report of **General Mills, Inc.** for the year ending May 31, 2020 (fiscal year 2020).

Required

a. Refer to the company's balance sheet.
  1. What form of business organization does General Mills use? What evidence supports your answer?
  2. What is the date of the most recent balance sheet?
  3. For the most recent balance sheet, what is the largest asset reported? The largest liability?

b. Refer to the company's income statement.
  1. What time period is covered by the fiscal year 2020 statement of earnings?
  2. What total amount of sales revenue did General Mills generate in the most recent period? What is the change in sales revenues from last year to the current report year?
  3. What is the net income (i.e., net earnings, including earnings attributable to noncontrolling interests) for the most recent period?

c. Refer to the company's statement of cash flows.
  1. For the most recent period, what is the amount and trend of the cash flow from operating activities?
  2. For the most recent period, what is the amount and trend of the cash flow from investing activities?
  3. For the most recent period, what is the amount and trend of the cash flow from financing activities?

Writing *assignments are denoted by this icon.*

↓

EYK1-6.   Accounting Communication Activity Bruce Smith is an intern for the Start Company. He knows the company's balance sheet is supposed to balance, but he is not having much luck getting it to balance. Bruce knows that you are taking a course in accounting so he asks for your help. Bruce provides you with the following balance sheet that is currently out of balance:

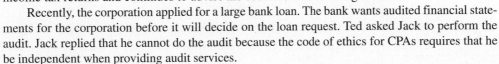

START COMPANY Balance Sheet December 31			
Assets		**Liabilities**	
Cash	15,000	Inventory	20,000
Accounts receivable	30,000	Notes payable	34,000
Equipment, net	28,000	**Stockholders' Equity**	
Accounts payable	(22,000)	Dividends	(11,000)
		Common stock	10,000
		Retained earnings, beginning of year	10,000
Total	51,000	Total	67,000

In addition, Bruce provides you with a correct income statement that reports a net income of $28,000.

Required

a. Prepare a corrected balance sheet for the Start Company.
b. Write a memo to Bruce explaining what he did wrong.
c. In the memo explain the purpose of the balance sheet.

EYK1-7. **Accounting Ethics Case** Jack Hardy, CPA, has a brother, Ted, in the retail clothing business. Ted ran the business as a sole proprietor for 10 years. During this 10-year period, Jack helped Ted with various accounting matters. For example, Jack designed the accounting system for the company, prepared Ted's personal income tax returns (which included financial data about the clothing business), and recommended various cost control procedures. Ted paid Jack for all of these services. A year ago, Ted expanded the business and incorporated. Ted is president of the corporation and also chairs the corporation's board of directors. The board of directors has overall responsibility for corporate affairs. When the corporation was formed, Ted asked Jack to serve on its board of directors. Jack accepted. In addition, Jack now prepares the corporation's income tax returns and continues to advise his brother on accounting matters.

Recently, the corporation applied for a large bank loan. The bank wants audited financial statements for the corporation before it will decide on the loan request. Ted asked Jack to perform the audit. Jack replied that he cannot do the audit because the code of ethics for CPAs requires that he be independent when providing audit services.

Required

Why is it important that a CPA be independent when providing audit services? Which of Jack's activities or relationships impair his independence?

EYK1-8. **Ethics** As the accountant for Minkow Corporation, you are responsible for reporting the company's profit. It appears that the company's actual results are much better than was expected by Wall Street analysts. Your supervisor has requested that you report some of next period's expenses now so that this period's profits will be in line with analyst expectations. He states that you are not really doing anything wrong since the reported results will be more conservative. In addition, this will make it easier to make next year's numbers. What should you do?

EYK1-9. **Environmental, Social, and Governance Problem** Go to the **Columbia Sportswear Company** Website and find the section on their commitment to corporate and environmental responsibility. These sections can be found near the bottom of their home page under the section "About Us."

COLUMBIA
SPORTSWEAR
COMPANY

Required

Answer the following questions.

a. How does Columbia describe the company's efforts at corporate responsibility?
b. How is the Higg Index used by Columbia's environmental responsibility efforts?
c. What featured initiative has Columbia embarked upon?
d. Why do you think Columbia produces a separate annual Corporate Responsibility Report to showcase these efforts?

Forensic Accounting
*assignments are denoted
by this icon.*

EYK1-10. **Forensic Accounting Problem** Go to the Association of Certified Fraud Examiners Website and find their description of a forensic accountant. This can be found under the Career tab, Career Paths, then click on Accounting followed by Forensic Accountant (www.acfe.com/career-path-forensic-accountant.aspx).

Required
Answer the following questions.

a.   What do forensic accountants do?
b.   What knowledge, skills, and abilities should a forensic accountant possess?
c.   How might the knowledge learned from this course help you to become a forensic accountant?

LVMH MOET
HENNESSEY-LOUIS
VUITTON S.A.

EYK1-11. **Analyzing IFRS Financial Statements** The 2020 financial statements of **LVMH Moet Hennessey-Louis Vuitton S.A.** are presented in **Appendix C** at the end of this book. LVMH is a Paris-based holding company and one of the world's largest and best-known luxury goods companies. As a member of the European Union, French companies are required to prepare their consolidated (group) financial statements using International Financial Reporting Standards (IFRS). After reviewing LVMH's consolidated financial statements, consider the following questions:

a.   What is LVMH's second largest asset account on its 2020 balance sheet? What percentage of total assets does this asset represent?
b.   Is LVMH principally debt financed or equity financed in 2020? What percentage of LVMH's assets is financed with debt?
c.   Is LVMH profitable in 2020? What percentage of the company's sales revenue in 2020 is represented by its "profit for the year," or its net income?
d.   How much is LVMH's cash flow from operating activities in 2020? How does LVMH's profit for the year (net income) compare with its cash flow from operating activities?

EYK1-12. **Working with the Takeaways** You have just learned that you inherited a large sum of money. You know that it is important to invest this money wisely, and you have decided to invest in the shares of several different companies. One of those companies is the Columbia Sportswear Company.

Required
Answer the following questions regarding your potential investment in Columbia Sportswear shares:

a.   Should you request financial statements from the company, and if so, which ones?
b.   Is it important that the financial statements be audited by an independent auditor? Explain.
c.   What does each of the four financial statements tell you about Columbia's financial health or operating performance?

ANSWERS TO SELF-STUDY QUESTIONS:

1. c   2. d   3. a   4. b   5. c   6. b   7. b   8. c   9. d

10.   1.   Sole proprietorship and partnership   4.   Corporation
      2.   Sole proprietorship and partnership   5.   Corporation
      3.   Partnership   6.   Sole proprietorship

11. c   12. c   13. b

YOUR TURN! SOLUTIONS

Solution 1.1

Sole proprietorship: Ease of formation, owner controlled, and tax advantages.

Partnership: Relatively easy to establish, larger skill set, and tax advantages.

Corporations: Easiest to raise capital, easiest to transfer ownership, and protection against personal liability.

Solution 1.2

1. Financing
2. Operating
3. Investing

4. Operating
5. Financing
6. Operating

Solution 1.3

1. The financial statements are the primary output of financial accounting. External users require information on a business's performance and financial position. This is the type of information provided by the financial statements. Managerial accounting involves the process of generating and analyzing financial data to use for internal decision making and management of the business.
2. Internal users include management, the marketing department, and the finance department, among others. Each of these groups require data to help them run their departments and make good business decisions.
3. External users include, among others, investors, lenders, and regulators. These external groups require accounting information to help them make decisions regarding a company's performance and financial position.

Solution 1.4

Your supervisor is asking you to participate in the preparation of fraudulent financial statements. This is not only unethical it is also illegal and could subject you to criminal prosecution. By reporting the sales revenue early, the financial statements will mislead users into thinking the company is doing better than it actually is. This in turn may lead them to make erroneous investment decisions. You should not follow your supervisor's request. Instead you should explain to your supervisor why reporting sales revenue prior to when it is earned is unethical. If your supervisor continues to pressure you, you should report your supervisor's request to a higher level of management in the company.

Solution 1.5

1. c
2. a

3. d
4. b

Solution 1.6

KANZU CORPORATION Income Statement For Year Ended December 31	
Sales revenue.	$20,000
Expenses	12,000
Net income	$ 8,000

KANZU CORPORATION Statement of Stockholders' Equity For Year Ended December 31	Common Stock	Retained Earnings	Total
Balance, January 1.	$ 0	$ 0	$ 0
Add: Common stock issued	20,000		20,000
Net income		8,000	8,000
Less: Dividends		(3,000)	(3,000)
Balance, December 31.	$20,000	$5,000	$25,000

KANZU CORPORATION Balance Sheet December 31			
Assets		**Liabilities**	
Cash	$ 1,500	Accounts payable	$ 4,000
Accounts receivable	2,500	Notes payable	33,000
Inventory	3,000	Total liabilities	$37,000
Building	40,000	**Stockholders' Equity**	
Equipment	15,000	Common stock	20,000
		Retained earnings	5,000
		Total stockholders' equity	25,000
Total assets	$62,000	Total liabilities and stockholders' equity	$62,000

KANZU CORPORATION Statement of Cash Flows For Year Ended December 31	
Cash flow from operating activities	$ 6,500
Cash flow from investing activities	(55,000)
Cash flow from financing activities	50,000
Net increase in cash	1,500
Cash at January 1, 2019	0
Cash at December 31, 2019	$ 1,500

Solution 1.7

1. c
2. b
3. a

Chapter 2
Processing Accounting Information

Road Map

LO	Learning Objective	Page	eLecture	Guided Example	Assignments
LO1	**Identify the five major steps in the accounting cycle.**	2-3	E2-1	YT2.1	SS15, SS17, SE10
LO2	**Analyze and record transactions using the accounting equation.**	2-4	E2-2	YT2.2	SS1, SS2, SS3, SS16, SE6, E1A, E2A, E3A, E4A, E11A, E15A, E1B, E2B, E3B, E4B, E11B, E15B, P1A, P2A, P3A, P4A, P5A, P6A, P7A, P8A, P9A, P10A, P11A, P1B, P2B, P3B, P4B, P5B, P6B, P7B, P8B, P9B, P10B, P11B
LO3	**Explain the nature, format, and purpose of an account.**	2-11	E2-3		SS4, SE11, E14A, E14B
LO4	**Describe the system of debits and credits and its use in recording transactions.**	2-11	E2-4	YT2.3, YT2.4	SS5, SS6, SS7, SS8, SS9, SS10, SE1, SE2, SE3, SE4, SE5, E5A, E8A, E9A, E10A, E11A, E5B, E8B, E9B, E10B, E11B, P12A, P13A, P14A, P15A, P16A, P12B, P13B, P14B, P15B, P16B
LO5	**Explain the process of journalizing and posting transactions.**	2-14	E2-5	YT2.5	SS11, SS13, SS14, SE7, E4A, E6A, E7A, E8A, E9A, E10A, E12A, E13A, E16A, E4B, E6B, E7B, E8B, E9B, E10B, E12B, E13B, E16B, P12A, P13A, P14A, P15A, P16A, P17A, P12B, P13B, P14B, P15B, P16B, P17B
LO6	**Describe the trial balance.**	2-22	E2-6	YT2.6	SS12, SE8, SE9, E12A, E13A, E12B, E13B, P12A, P13A, P14A, P15A, P16A, P17A, P12B, P13B, P14B, P15B, P16B, P17B

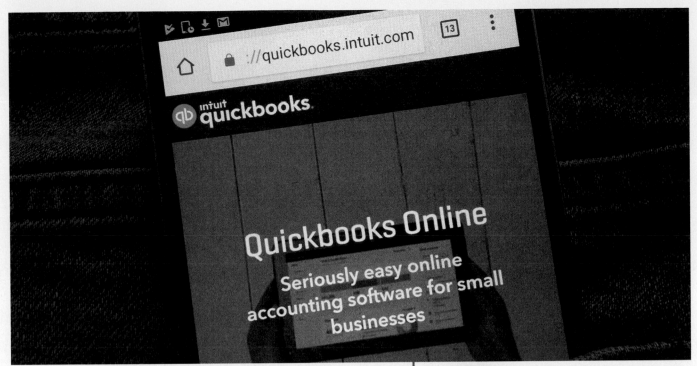

While not everyone is familiar with the company **Intuit Inc.**, nearly everyone who works in the business world is familiar with some of its products. Intuit is a software company based in Mountain View, California, that develops the popular financial and tax preparation software QuickBooks, Mint, and TurboTax.

This chapter describes the details of the accounting system of debits and credits that is applied throughout the world and is the foundation for all accounting software. This chapter also explains the process of journalizing and posting transactions so that financial statements can be prepared for both internal and external users of accounting.

PAST

Chapter 1 described the environment of financial accounting. It also introduced the financial statements and how they are related.

PRESENT

This chapter explains the accounting system, including transaction analysis, the system of debits and credits, and the journalizing of transactions.

FUTURE

Chapter 3 describes accounting adjustments, the construction of financial statements, and the period-end closing process.

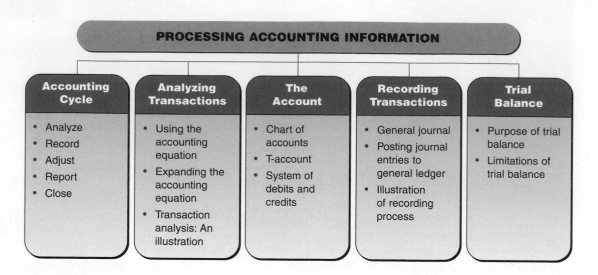

ACCOUNTING CYCLE

LO1 **Identify** the five major steps in the accounting cycle.

Businesses engage in economic activities. The role of accounting is to analyze these activities for their impact on a company's accounting equation, and then enter the results of that analysis in the company's accounting system. When a company's management team needs financial data for decision-making purposes and for reports to external parties, the company's financial statements are prepared and communicated. At the end of the accounting period, the "books are closed," a process that prepares the accounting records for the next accounting period. These accounting activities constitute the major steps in the **accounting cycle**—a sequence of activities undertaken by accountants to accumulate and report the financial information of a business. Stated succinctly, these steps are analyze, record, adjust, report, and close. **Exhibit 2-1** shows the sequence of the major steps in the accounting cycle.

EXHIBIT 2-1   Five Major Steps in the Accounting Cycle

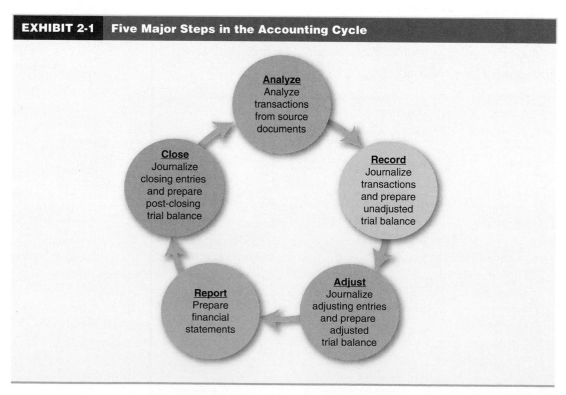

The five steps in the accounting cycle do not occur with equal frequency. A business analyzes and records financial transactions daily during the accounting period. It adjusts and reports accumulated financial data whenever management needs financial information, usually at weekly, monthly, or quarterly intervals, but at least annually. Closing the books occurs just once, at the end of the accounting period. This chapter focuses on the first two steps of the accounting cycle—analyze and record. In Chapter 3, we examine the final three steps of the cycle.

This chapter explains the accounting cycle using WebWork, a website development and consulting business launched on December 1, 2022.

ACCOUNTING IN PRACTICE   **Accounting Periods**

The annual accounting period is known as a **fiscal year**. Businesses with fiscal year-ends on December 31 are said to be on a **calendar year**. About 60 percent of U.S. businesses are on a calendar year. Many companies prefer to have their accounting year coincide with their "natural" year—that is, at a point in time when business activity is at a low point. For example, many retailers conclude their fiscal year when inventory quantities are low and easier to count, as year-end accounting procedures are more efficiently accomplished when there is less inventory. The "natural" year does not necessarily coincide with the calendar year. For example, **The Gap**, a retailer, ends its fiscal year on the Saturday nearest January 31. The company's busiest period is November through January, when its customers are holiday shopping. Similarly, the **Madison Square Garden Sports Corp.**, owner of the **New York Knicks** professional basketball team, concludes its fiscal year on June 30, following completion of the NBA finals.

YOUR TURN! 2.1

Place the following five major steps in the accounting cycle in the proper order:

a. Report   c. Close   e. Adjust

b. Record   d. Analyze

The solution is on page 2-59.

ANALYZING TRANSACTIONS

LO2   Analyze and record transactions using the accounting equation.

Many companies utilize a computer-based accounting system to record their financial transactions. You may have some personal experience using accounting software programs like QuickBooks by Intuit. While these computer-based accounting systems are not as sophisticated as the systems used by major corporations, they work in much the same way. Similarly, manual systems might lack the sophistication of large accounting systems utilized by companies like **Ford Motor Company**, but the basic process remains the same.

eLecture

MBC

As we saw in Chapter 1, the accounting equation is written as:

$$\text{Assets (A)} = \text{Liabilities (L)} + \text{Stockholders' equity (SE)}$$

The accounting equation provides a convenient way to analyze and summarize a company's financial transactions and data. The first step in the accounting cycle—analyze—is to determine what information (if any) must be recorded in a company's accounting records. Only items that can be expressed in monetary terms are recorded in financial statements. (The monetary unit concept was discussed in Appendix 1A.) For example, the payment of salary to Carol Tomé, the CEO of **United Parcel Service**, is recorded because it can be expressed in monetary terms.

An **accounting transaction** is an economic event that must be recorded in the company's accounting records. In general, an event that affects any of the elements of the accounting equation—assets, liabilities, or stockholders' equity—must be recorded in a company's accounting records. Some activities—for example, ordering supplies, bidding on a contract, or negotiating the purchase of an asset—may represent a business activity, but an accounting transaction does not occur until such activities result in a change in an asset, liability, or stockholders' equity account.

An accounting transaction affects at least two elements of the accounting equation, so that the equation always remains in balance. This is where the term **double-entry accounting** comes from. For example, if an asset account such as Cash is increased, one of the following financial events must also occur to keep the accounting equation in balance:

a.   Another asset, such as Accounts Receivable, must decrease; or

b.   A liability, such as Notes Payable, must increase; or

c.   Stockholders' equity, such as Common Stock, must increase.

Accounting Equation Expanded

Stockholders' equity has two primary components—the amount invested by stockholders (common stock) and the cumulative net income of the business that has not been distributed to stockholders as a dividend (retained earnings). Common stock increases when the company issues shares of stock. Retained earnings increases with revenues and decreases with expenses (revenues and expenses are the elements of a company's net income or net loss). Retained earnings also decreases when the company pays dividends. Incorporating these components into stockholders' equity, the *expanded accounting equation* is illustrated in **Exhibit 2-2**.

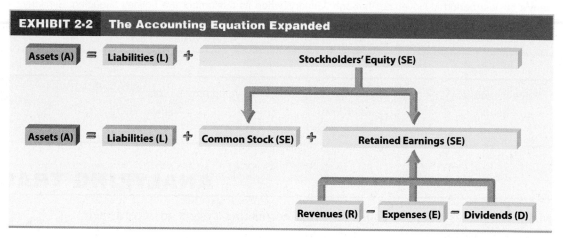

EXHIBIT 2-2   The Accounting Equation Expanded

Assets (A) = Liabilities (L) + Stockholders' Equity (SE)

Assets (A) = Liabilities (L) + Common Stock (SE) + Retained Earnings (SE)

Revenues (R) − Expenses (E) − Dividends (D)

Transactions and the Accounting Equation: An Illustration

We now consider the transactions of WebWork, Inc., a developer of web-based applications, to illustrate how various economic activities and events are analyzed and recorded.

Steve Gates first established WebWork on December 2, 2022. The company's transactions for December, the first month of operations, are analyzed on the following pages. The accounting equation for WebWork is shown after each transaction so that the financial effects of each transaction can be examined. The accounting equation remains in balance following each transaction. This is not a coincidence; it is the result of the fundamental structure of the accounting system.

The following pages illustrate eleven transactions that occurred at WebWork during December 2022. Avoid the temptation to skip any of these transactions because each transaction is included to illustrate a particular concept or approach to recording an economic event utilizing the accounting equation.

Transaction 1. Issued Stock

On December 2, 2022, Steve Gates invested $30,000 cash in exchange for all of the company's common stock. This transaction increased the company's assets, Cash, by $30,000 and increased its stockholders' equity, Common Stock, by $30,000, as illustrated below using the accounting equation. (For each transaction that impacts stockholders' equity, we add a brief description—in this case "Issued stock.")

	Assets	=	Liabilities	+	Stockholders' Equity	
	Cash	=		+	Common Stock	
(1)	+30,000	=			+30,000	Issued stock
	$30,000				$30,000	

It is important to verify the equality of the accounting equation following each transaction. After the above transaction is recorded, both sides of the equation total $30,000.

Transaction 2. Paid Rent in Advance

On December 2, WebWork prepaid its office rent for the next six months, December 2022 through May 2023. WebWork's rent is $1,800 per month, meaning it paid a total of $10,800 cash (6 × $1,800). This transaction decreased Cash by $10,800 and increased Prepaid Rent by $10,800.

	Assets			=	Liabilities	+	Stockholders' Equity
	Cash	+	Prepaid Rent	=		+	Common Stock
Beg. Bal.	30,000						30,000
(2)	−10,800		+10,800				
End Bal.	19,200	+	10,800				30,000
		$30,000		=			$30,000

The expenditure for prepaid rent is recorded as an asset because the advance payment is a future economic benefit to the company. This outlay of cash has value to the business beyond the current accounting period, but any rent that is used up in the current accounting period will be recorded as an expense for the month of December.

A.K.A. Prepaid assets are also called prepaid expenses.

Transaction 3. Purchased Office Supplies on Account

On December 2, WebWork purchased office supplies on account totaling $2,850. Businesses often extend credit to their customers. Credit allows businesses to pay for goods or services at a later date. When credit is used to purchase goods or services, the purchase is said to be made *on account*. This transaction increased Office Supplies by $2,850 and increased Accounts Payable by the same amount.

	Assets					=	Liabilities	+	Stockholders' Equity
	Cash	+	Office Supplies	+	Prepaid Rent	=	Accounts Payable	+	Common Stock
Beg. Bal.	19,200				10,800				30,000
(3)			+2,850				+2,850		
End Bal.	19,200	+	2,850		+10,800	=	2,850	+	30,000
		$32,850				=	$32,850		

Office supplies are recorded as an asset because they are expected to be used by the business in future periods beyond the current accounting period. Any supplies that are used up in the current accounting period will be recorded as an expense for the month of December. Following the purchase of office supplies, WebWork's assets total $32,850, which is equal to the sum of total liabilities of $2,850 plus stockholders' equity of $30,000.

Transaction 4. Signed Bank Note in Exchange for Cash

On December 2, WebWork obtained a two-year bank loan in the amount of $36,000, after signing a note payable. Annual interest of 10 percent is due each November 30. As a consequence of this loan, the company's Cash account increased by $36,000, and the Notes Payable account, a liability, increased by $36,000.

	Assets			=	Liabilities		+	Stockholders' Equity
	Cash	+	Office Supplies	+	Prepaid Rent	=	Accounts Payable	+	Notes Payable	+	Common Stock
Beg. Bal.	19,200		2,850		10,800		2,850				30,000
(4)	+36,000								+36,000		
End Bal.	55,200	+	2,850	+	10,800	=	2,850	+	36,000	+	30,000
			$68,850						$68,850		

Transaction 5. Purchased Equipment with Cash

On December 3, WebWork used cash to purchase office equipment costing $32,400. This transaction decreased Cash by $32,400 and increased Office Equipment by the same amount. The accounting equation remains in balance because an equal amount, $32,400, is added to one asset (Equipment) and subtracted from another asset (Cash).

	Assets				=	Liabilities		+	Stockholders' Equity
	Cash	+	Office Supplies	+	Prepaid Rent	+	Equip-ment	=	Accounts Payable	+	Notes Payable	+	Common Stock
Beg. Bal.	55,200		2,850		10,800				2,850		36,000		30,000
(5)	−32,400						+32,400						
End Bal.	22,800	+	2,850	+	10,800	+	32,400	=	2,850	+	36,000	+	30,000
				$68,850							$68,850		

Transaction 6. Received Customer Prepayment

On December 5, WebWork received a prepayment in the amount of $3,000 for services to be performed over the next few months. Because WebWork has not yet performed the services, it does not record the $3,000 payment as revenue. This practice follows the revenue recognition principle discussed in Appendix 1A. Instead, a liability account, **Unearned Revenue**, is increased by $3,000, and the Cash account is increased by $3,000. Unearned revenue is a liability because the company accepted payment for goods or services that have not yet been provided. Once WebWork performs the services, the unearned revenue liability will be reduced and revenue will be recognized.

	Assets				=	Liabilities			+	Stockholders' Equity
	Cash	+	Office Supplies	+	Prepaid Rent	+	Equip-ment	=	Accounts Payable	+	Unearned Revenue	+	Notes Payable	+	Common Stock
Beg. Bal.	22,800		2,850		10,800		32,400		2,850				36,000		30,000
(6)	+3,000										+3,000				
End Bal.	25,800	+	2,850	+	10,800	+	32,400	=	2,850	+	3,000	+	36,000	+	30,000
				$71,850								$71,850		

Non-Accounting Transaction. Hired an Employee

On December 6, WebWork hired an employee to provide administrative help in the office. The employee will be paid $1,620 every two weeks and begins work Monday, December 9. At the time the employee is hired there is no immediate financial effect on the assets, liabilities, or stockholders' equity of the company. There is only an employment agreement between the employee and the company. The employee has not yet performed any work, nor has the employee received any wages.

Transaction 7. Provided Services to Customers for Cash

On December 10, WebWork performed services for several customers and was paid $13,510 cash. This transaction increased Cash by $13,510 and increased Fee Revenue by the same amount.

	Assets				=	Liabilities			+	Stockholders' Equity			
											Retained Earnings		
	Cash	+ Office Supplies	+ Prepaid Rent	+ Equip- ment	=	Accounts Payable	+ Unearned Revenue	+ Notes Payable	+ Common Stock	+	Revenue	– Expense	– Dividend
Beg. Bal.	25,800	2,850	10,800	32,400		2,850	3,000	36,000	30,000				
(7)	+13,510										+13,510		Fee revenue
End Bal.	39,310 +	2,850 +	10,800 +	32,400 =		2,850 +	3,000 +	36,000 +	30,000 +		13,510		
		$85,360						$85,360					

This transaction is recorded as earned revenue because WebWork has performed the services for which it was paid. We use the expanded accounting equation to record revenues which, by definition, increase retained earnings.

Transaction 8. Provided Services for Cash and on Account

On December 18, WebWork performed $4,740 of services and received $1,000 in cash with the remaining $3,740 to be paid to WebWork by customers within 90 days. As previously noted in transaction 3 above, businesses often extend credit to customers, allowing them to pay for goods or services at a later date. Under accrual accounting, revenue must be recorded when goods or services are transferred from the seller to the buyer, regardless of when payment is received. Consequently, this transaction increased Cash by $1,000 and Accounts Receivable by $3,740, and it increased Fee Revenue by the total amount of $4,740. The accounting equation remains in balance because both sides of the equation are increased by $4,740.

A.K.A. Delivering goods or services in advance of payment is referred to as providing goods or services "on account" or "on credit."

	Assets					=	Liabilities			+	Stockholders' Equity			
											Retained Earnings		
	Cash	+ Accounts Receivable	+ Office Supplies	+ Prepaid Rent	+ Equip- ment	=	Accounts Payable	+ Unearned Revenue	+ Notes Payable	+ Common Stock	+	Revenue	– Expense	– Dividend
Beg. Bal.	39,310		2,850	+ 10,800	+ 32,400	=	2,850	+ 3,000	+ 36,000	+ 30,000	+	13,510		
(8)	+1,000	+3,740										+4,740		Fee revenue
End. Bal.	40,310+	3,740	+ 2,850	+ 10,800	+ 32,400	=	2,850	+ 3,000	+ 36,000	+ 30,000	+	18,250		
		$90,100							$90,100					

Transaction 9. Paid Employee Wages

On December 20, WebWork paid the employee after she completed her first two weeks on the job. This transaction decreased Cash by $1,620 and increased Wage Expense by $1,620. By definition, an increase in expenses decreases retained earnings.

	Assets				=	Liabilities			+	Stockholders' Equity		
Cash +	Accounts Receivable +	Office Supplies +	Prepaid Rent +	Equip-ment =		Accounts Payable +	Unearned Revenue +	Notes Payable +	Common Stock +	Retained Earnings Revenue –	Expense –	Dividend
Beg. Bal. 40,310	3,740	2,850	10,800	32,400		2,850	3,000	36,000	30,000	18,250		
(9) –1,620											–1,620	Wage expense
End Bal. 38,690 +	3,740 +	2,850 +	10,800 +	32,400 =		2,850 +	3,000 +	36,000 +	30,000 +	18,250 –	1,620	
$88,480									$88,480			

Transaction 10. Received Payment on Account from Customer

On December 27, WebWork received a payment of $2,400 cash from a customer who had previously received services performed on account (see Transaction 8). This transaction increased Cash by $2,400 and decreased Accounts Receivable by $2,400.

	Assets				=	Liabilities			+	Stockholders' Equity		
Cash +	Accounts Receivable +	Office Supplies +	Prepaid Rent +	Equip-ment =		Accounts Payable +	Unearned Revenue +	Notes Payable +	Common Stock +	Retained Earnings Revenue –	Expense –	Dividend
Beg. Bal. 38,690	3,740	2,850	10,800	32,400		2,850	3,000	36,000	30,000	18,250	1,620	
(10) +2,400	–2,400											
End Bal. 41,090 +	1,340 +	2,850 +	10,800 +	32,400 =		2,850 +	3,000 +	36,000 +	30,000 +	18,250 –	1,620	
$88,480									$88,480			

After recording this transaction, the balance in Accounts Receivable is $1,340. This represents the amount still owed to WebWork for services that were previously performed on account but remain unpaid.

Transaction 11. Paid Cash Dividend

On December 30, WebWork paid a cash dividend. Dividends are not a business expense and are not included in the calculation of net income. Rather, dividends are a distribution of the company's accumulated net income to its stockholders. Payment of the dividend decreased Cash by $500 and increased Dividends by $500. By definition, an increase in dividends causes a decrease in retained earnings.

	Assets				=	Liabilities			+	Stockholders' Equity		
Cash +	Accounts Receivable +	Office Supplies +	Prepaid Rent +	Equip-ment =		Accounts Payable +	Unearned Revenue +	Notes Payable +	Common Stock +	Retained Earnings Revenue –	Expense –	Dividend
Beg. Bal. 41,090	1,340	2,850	10,800	32,400		2,850	3,000	36,000	30,000	18,250	1,620	
(11) –500												–500 Dividends
End Bal. 40,590 +	1,340 +	2,850 +	10,800 +	32,400 =		2,850 +	3,000 +	36,000 +	30,000 +	18,250 –	1,620 –	500
$87,980									$87,980			

Transaction Summary

Exhibit 2-3 provides a summary of the eleven accounting transactions for WebWork, for the month of December. The exhibit illustrates the financial effect of each transaction using the expanded accounting equation. It is important that the accounting equation remains in balance at all times, and that the equality between total assets and the sum of total liabilities and stockholders' equity is maintained following each transaction.

EXHIBIT 2-3   Summary of December Transactions and Their Effect on the Expanded Accounting Equation

	Assets				=	Liabilities			+	Stockholders' Equity			
											Retained Earnings		
Cash	+ Accounts Receivable	+ Office Supplies	+ Prepaid Rent	+ Equip-ment	= Accounts Payable	+ Unearned Revenue	+ Notes Payable	+ Common Stock	+ Revenue	– Expense	– Dividend
(1) +30,000								+30,000			
(2) –10,800			+10,800								
(3)		+2,850			+2,850						
(4) +36,000							+36,000				
(5) –32,400				+32,400							
(6) +3,000						+3,000					
(7) +13,510									+13,510		
(8) +1,000	+3,740								+4,740		
(9) –1,620										–1,620	
(10) +2,400	–2,400										
(11) –500											–500
40,590 +	1,340 +	2,850 +	10,800 +	32,400 =	2,850 +	3,000 +	36,000 +	30,000 +	18,250 –	1,620 –	500

$87,980 $87,980

Concept ⟶	Method ⟶	Assessment	**TAKEAWAY 2.1**
When should an event be recorded in a company's accounting records?	Review the event details. Does the event affect the company's assets, liabilities, or stockholders' equity?	If the event affects any of the elements of the accounting equation, it must be recorded in a company's accounting records.	

YOUR TURN! 2.2

GuidedExample

MBC

The solution is on page 2-59.

Ford Fitness Studio, Inc., operates as a corporation. The firm rents studio space (including a sound system) and specializes in offering spin classes. On January 1, the assets, liabilities, and stockholders' equity of the business were as follows: Cash, $5,000; Accounts Receivable, $5,200; Accounts Payable, $1,000; Notes Payable, $2,500; Common Stock, $5,500; and Retained Earnings, $1,200. The January business activities for the studio were as follows.

1. Paid $600 cash on accounts payable.
2. Paid January rent of $3,600 cash.
3. Billed clients for January classes in the amount of $11,500.
4. Received a $500 invoice from a supplier for T-shirts given free to January's class members as an advertising promotion.
5. Collected $10,000 cash on account from clients for prior classes.
6. Paid employee wages of $2,400 cash.
7. Received a $680 invoice for January's utilities.
8. Paid $20 cash to the bank as January interest on an outstanding note payable.
9. Paid $900 cash in dividends to stockholders.
10. Paid $4,000 cash on January 31 to purchase a sound system to replace the rented system.

Required

a. Set up an accounting equation in columnar form with the following individual assets, liabilities, and stockholders' equity accounts: Cash, Accounts Receivable, Equipment, Accounts Payable, Notes Payable, Common Stock, and Retained Earnings. Enter the January 1 balances below each account. (The beginning balance in the Equipment account is $0.)

b. Record the financial impact (increase or decrease) of each transaction (1) through (10) on the beginning account balances. Then total the columns to demonstrate that total assets equal the sum of total liabilities plus stockholders' equity as of January 31.

THE ACCOUNT SYSTEM

LO3 **Explain** the nature, format, and purpose of an account.

The basic component of an accounting system is the **account**, which is an individual record of the increases and decreases in a specific asset, liability, or stockholders' equity item. An account is created for each individual asset, liability, and stockholders' equity item on a company's financial statements. Some common account titles are Cash, Accounts Receivable, Notes Payable, Fee Revenue, and Rent Expense.

Chart of Accounts

Businesses maintain a chart of accounts to facilitate the analysis of a company's business activities. A **chart of accounts** is a list of the titles of all accounts in a business's accounting system. Account titles are grouped by, and in the order of, the six major components of the expanded accounting equation: assets, liabilities, stockholders' equity, revenues, expenses, and dividends. **Exhibit 2-4** shows the chart of accounts for WebWork and indicates the account numbers that will be used throughout this illustration. (Each company maintains its own unique set of accounts and its own numbering system.)

EXHIBIT 2-4 Chart of Accounts for WebWork	
Assets	**Equity**
110 Cash	310 Common Stock
120 Accounts Receivable	320 Retained Earnings
130 Office Supplies	
150 Prepaid Rent	**Revenues**
170 Office Equipment	410 Fee Revenue
175 Accumulated Depreciation—	
Office Equipment	**Expenses**
	510 Supplies Expense
Liabilities	520 Wage Expense
210 Accounts Payable	530 Rent Expense
220 Interest Payable	540 Depreciation Expense—
230 Wages Payable	Office Equipment
250 Unearned Revenue	550 Interest Expense
260 Notes Payable	
	Dividends
	610 Dividends

System of Debits and Credits

LO4 **Describe** the system of debits and credits and its use in recording transactions.

One basic characteristic of all accounts is that data entries separately record the increases and decreases to an account. The method of recording data entries in the accounts is a matter of convention; that is, a simple set of rules is followed, which involves debits and credits.

A **T-account** is a simplified form of an account that is used to capture these effects. T-accounts are so named because they resemble the letter "T," as shown below:

Account Title (e.g., Cash)

Debit	**Credit**
Always the left side	Always the right side

The terms **debit** and **credit** refer to the left side and the right side, respectively, of an account. Regardless of what amount is recorded in an account, any entry made on the left side is a debit to the account while any entry recorded on the right side is a credit to the account.

The words *debit* and *credit* are abbreviated *dr.* (from the Latin *debere*) and *cr.* (from the Latin *credere*), respectively.

The system of debits and credits identifies which side of the account, debit or credit, is used to increase the account and which side of the account is used to decrease the account. **Exhibit 2-5** summarizes these rules for each of the six primary categories of accounts: assets, liabilities, stockholders' equity, revenues, expenses, and dividends.

Observe the following relations in **Exhibit 2-5**:

1. Debit always refers to the left side of an account; credit always refers to the right side.

2. The pattern of increases and decreases in accounts derives from the accounting equation. Assets are on the left side of the accounting equation and increase with debit (or left side) entries. Assets decrease with credit entries.

3. Liabilities and stockholders' equity are on the right side of the accounting equation and increase with credit (or right side) entries. Liabilities and stockholders' equity decrease with debit entries.

4. The **normal balance** of an account is the side on which increases to the account are recorded. This is because increases in an account are usually greater than, or equal to, decreases in an account. Asset accounts normally have debit balances while liability and stockholders' equity accounts normally have credit balances.

5. Revenue, expense, and dividends are temporary subdivisions of retained earnings. The pattern of increases and decreases in these accounts derives from their relation to retained earnings. Revenues increase earnings, and just like the retained earnings account, revenue accounts increase with credit entries and decrease with debit entries. On the other hand, expenses decrease earnings, and so have the opposite pattern as retained earnings; expense accounts increase with debit entries and decrease with credit entries.

6. Dividends are distributions of retained earnings to shareholders, and like expense accounts have the opposite pattern as retained earnings; dividends increase with debit entries and decrease with credit entries.

EXHIBIT 2-5   System of Increases and Decreases, Debits and Credits, and Normal Balances

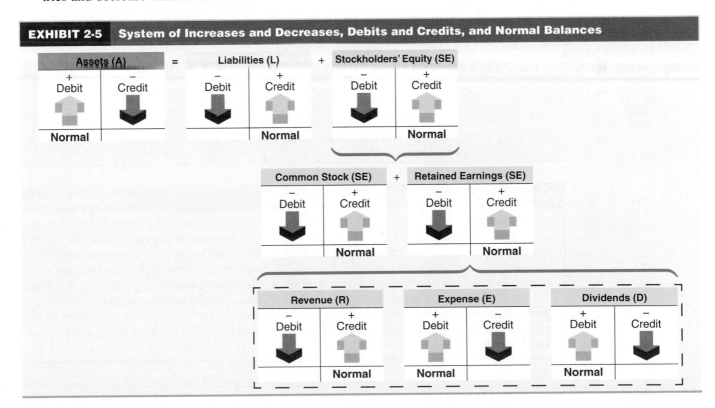

For each of the following accounts, identify whether the account's normal balance is a debit or a credit.

a. Cash	c. Wage expense	e. Dividends g. Inventory
b. Common stock	d. Notes payable	f. Sales revenue

As an example of the system of debits and credits, the Cash T-account with the December transactions for WebWork is presented in **Exhibit 2-6**.

EXHIBIT 2-6   Cash T-account

To compute the T-account balance, sum the numbers in each column and subtract the smaller total from the larger total. In this example, subtract 45,320 from 85,910 to compute the 40,590 balance.

+	Cash (A)		–
(1)	30,000	10,800	(2)
(4)	36,000	32,400	(5)
(6)	3,000	1,620	(9)
(7)	13,510	500	(11)
(8)	1,000		
(10)	2,400		
	85,910	45,320	
Bal.	40,590		

Note that amounts are not indicated with either a plus (+) or minus (–) sign in a T-account because, as shown in **Exhibit 2-5**, the type of the account and whether the data entry is a debit or credit to that account tell us if the amount is an increase or decrease. Because Cash is an asset, increases are always shown on the left as debits and decreases on the right as credits.

A T-account consists of (1) the account title (such as Cash), (2) amounts reflecting increases and decreases, and (3) cross-references to other accounting records. It is customary to reference (or link) the data entries in a T-account with a number or a letter to identify the related accounting transaction that originated the data. This permits a systematic review of the data entries in the event of a recording error. It also enables a company, and its independent auditor, to review the company's set of accounts and match the account information with the related accounting transactions. The numerical references in the Cash T-account above are the ones used to identify the December transactions for WebWork from **Exhibit 2-3**.

Using the information in **Exhibit 2-3**, construct the T-account for Accounts Receivable in proper form.

ENVIRONMENTAL, SOCIAL, AND GOVERNANCE   **What to Record?**

An important element of the conceptual framework discussed in Appendix 1A in Chapter 1 is the monetary unit concept, which states that only those items that can be expressed in monetary terms are reported in financial statements. This causes many items of interest to be excluded from financial statements. Reporting of a company's ESG activities, for example, would be compromised if it were constrained to the activities that can be expressed in monetary terms. Reporting guidelines established by the Global Reporting Initiative, the organization that pioneered the world's most widely used sustainability reporting framework, allow for a wider range of activities to be measured and reported. For example, **Bayer Group**, a global healthcare company, reports such items as greenhouse emissions, net water usage, and employee safety records in its annual Sustainability Report.

RECORDING TRANSACTIONS

Earlier in this chapter we analyzed the transactions of WebWork using the accounting equation. This approach enabled us to see how accounting transactions affect a company's financial position and operations. This approach is not feasible, however, for even a modest-sized business because of the large number of transactions and accounts involved. Consequently, we now explain the process of analyzing and recording accounting information in an actual accounting system.

LO5 Explain the process of journalizing and posting transactions.

eLecture
MBC

An initial step in the analysis and recording process is to identify evidence of a business transaction. This usually comes in the form of a source document. **Source documents** are printed forms or computer records that are generated when a firm engages in a business transaction. At a minimum, a source document usually specifies the dollar amount involved, the date of the transaction, and possibly the party dealing with the firm. Some examples of source documents include (1) a supplier's invoice showing evidence of a purchase of supplies on account, (2) a bank check indicating the payment of an obligation, (3) a deposit slip showing the amount of cash deposited in a bank, and (4) a cash receipt indicating the amount of cash received from a customer for services rendered. An example of an invoice follows. Regardless of its form, the source document serves as the basis for the analysis of the underlying business event.

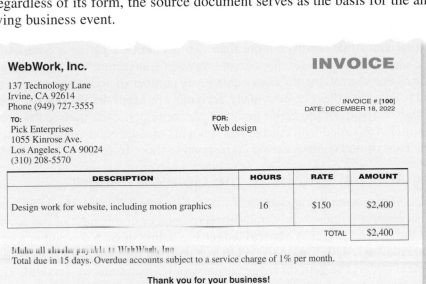

WebWork, Inc.

137 Technology Lane
Irvine, CA 92614
Phone (949) 727-3555

INVOICE

INVOICE # [100]
DATE: DECEMBER 18, 2022

TO:
Pick Enterprises
1055 Kinrose Ave.
Los Angeles, CA 90024
(310) 208-5570

FOR:
Web design

DESCRIPTION	HOURS	RATE	AMOUNT
Design work for website, including motion graphics	16	$150	$2,400
		TOTAL	$2,400

Make all checks payable to WebWork, Inc.
Total due in 15 days. Overdue accounts subject to a service charge of 1% per month.

Thank you for your business!

Once the source document has been analyzed to determine the accounts affected and the amounts involved, we then record the transaction. All accounting transactions are initially recorded in a journal. A **journal**, or *book of original entry,* is a tabular record in which a business's activities are reflected in terms of debits and credits and recorded in chronological order. A journal organizes information by date and thus serves as a chronological diary of a company's business activities. The word *journalize* means to record a transaction in a journal. An entry in a journal is called a **journal entry**.

A.K.A. A company's journals are also referred to as its "books."

A.K.A. Another term often used to describe the recording of a transaction is to "book" the transaction.

General Journal

The **general journal** is a record with enough flexibility that any type of business transaction can be recorded in it. Like all journals in an accounting system, the general journal is a book of original entry in which accounting data are entered into a company's accounting system. **Exhibit 2-7** shows the first transaction as it is recorded in WebWork's general journal. The procedure for recording entries in the general journal follows:

❶ Indicate the year, month, and date of entry. (Usually the year and month are rewritten only at the top of each page of the journal or at the point in the journal where the year and month change.)

❷ Enter the titles of accounts affected (from the chart of accounts) in the Description column. Accounts to receive debits are entered close to the left margin and are recorded first. Accounts to receive credits are recorded next and indented slightly to the right.

❸ Enter dollar amounts in the left (Debit) and right (Credit) columns.

❹ Provide an explanation of the transaction below the account titles; it should be brief, disclosing information necessary to understand the event recorded.

EXHIBIT 2-7	General Journal with First Entry of WebWork		
	GENERAL JOURNAL		
Date	**Description**	**Debit**	**Credit**
2022			
❶ Dec. 2	Cash ❷	30,000 ❸	
	Common stock		30,000
	Issued stock in exchange for cash. ❹		

A journal entry that involves more than two accounts is called a **compound journal entry**. (As shown on page 2-18, the journal entry for Transaction 8 is an example of a compound journal entry involving three accounts.) Any number of accounts can appear in a compound entry; but, regardless of how many accounts are used, the sum of the debit amounts always equals the sum of the credit amounts. Accordingly, each transaction entered in the general journal is recorded with equal dollar amounts of debits and credits. The account titles cited in the Description column should correspond to those from the chart of accounts.

Posting Journal Entries to the General Ledger

After an accounting transaction is journalized in the general journal, the debits and credits in each journal entry are immediately transferred to another component of the accounting system called the general ledger. A **general ledger** is a listing of each account of a company and the amounts making up each account. **While the general journal organizes transactions in chronological order, the general ledger organizes transactions by account.** This makes it easier to determine the balance of each account, which in turn facilitates the preparation of the company's financial statements. Although businesses can use various ledgers to accumulate detailed accounting information, all firms have a general ledger.

The process of transferring the debit and credit information from the general journal to the general ledger is called **posting**. It is important to be able to trace each data entry appearing in a general ledger account to the general journal location from which it was posted; consequently, both the general journal and general ledger accounts have a **posting reference** code. The posting reference of the general journal indicates the account to which the related debit or credit has been posted. The posting references in the general journal and ledger accounts are entered when the journal entries are posted to the ledger accounts (automatically when computerized, or by hand for a manual system). We will use the transaction number as the posting reference in the examples that follow.

Data Analytics

DATA ANALYTICS **Data Science Projects at Intuit**

Intuit has been focused on personal and small business finance for nearly 40 years with industry-leading products such as TurboTax and QuickBooks. Intuit realizes the importance of data science to its product portfolio and recently hired its first Chief Data Officer to lead Intuit's 60-plus data scientists.

Intuit's software helps companies manage their cashflow, taxes, payroll, and accounting. Intuit's data scientists use machine learning to eliminate much of the work involved in these processes, which creates a positive and efficient customer experience. Transaction categorization is an example of Intuit's application of data science. Categorizing each transaction is a common task in any accounting system. Manually labeling each transaction is very time consuming, so Intuit offers users the option of directly downloading transactions from their bank and having the Intuit software use algorithms to classify the transactions into the proper accounts. This use of data science frees up time for the customer to perform more value-added activities and analysis.

Illustration of the Recording Process

We now apply the recording process to the transactions of WebWork that were summarized in **Exhibit 2-3**. For each transaction, we **(1) analyze** the transaction using the accounting equation, **(2) journalize** the transaction, and **(3) post** journal entries to the general ledger (for simplicity, we use the T-account structure for each ledger account). To make this process easier to follow, we indicate debit amounts in **purple** and credit amounts in **blue**.

TRANSACTION 1 **Issued Stock**

On December 2, Steve Gates invested $30,000 in exchange for common stock of WebWork.

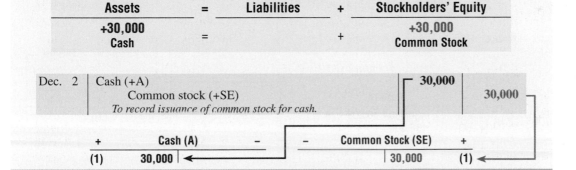

❶ **ANALYZE**

Assets	=	Liabilities	+	Stockholders' Equity
+30,000 Cash	=		+	+30,000 Common Stock

❷ **JOURNALIZE**

Dec. 2	Cash (+A)	30,000	
	Common stock (+SE)		30,000
	To record issuance of common stock for cash.		

❸ **POST**

| + Cash (A) − | | − Common Stock (SE) + |
| (1) 30,000 | | 30,000 (1) |

TRANSACTION 2 **Paid Rent in Advance**

On December 2, WebWork prepaid rent for the office covering the next six months, December 2022 through May 2023. Monthly rent is $1,800; the total amount prepaid was $10,800 cash.

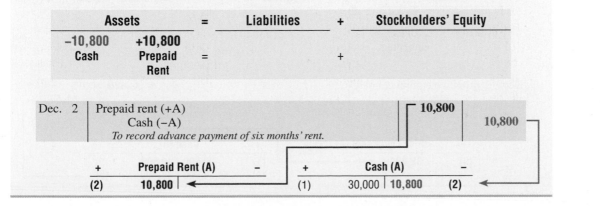

❶ **ANALYZE**

Assets		=	Liabilities	+	Stockholders' Equity
−10,800 Cash	+10,800 Prepaid Rent	=		+	

❷ **JOURNALIZE**

Dec. 2	Prepaid rent (+A)	10,800	
	Cash (−A)		10,800
	To record advance payment of six months' rent.		

❸ **POST**

| + Prepaid Rent (A) − | | + Cash (A) − |
| (2) 10,800 | | (1) 30,000 \| 10,800 (2) |

TRANSACTION 3   Purchased Office Supplies on Account

On December 2, WebWork purchased $2,850 of office supplies on account.

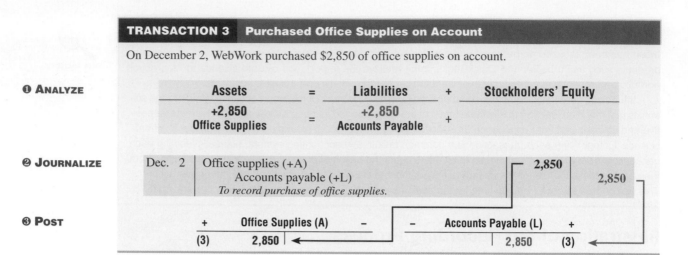

❶ ANALYZE

Assets	=	Liabilities	+	Stockholders' Equity
+2,850	=	+2,850	+	
Office Supplies		Accounts Payable		

❷ JOURNALIZE

Dec. 2 | Office supplies (+A)   2,850
       | Accounts payable (+L)   2,850
       | *To record purchase of office supplies.*

❸ POST

+ Office Supplies (A) –	– Accounts Payable (L) +
(3) 2,850	2,850 (3)

TRANSACTION 4   Signed Bank Note in Exchange for Cash

On December 2, WebWork obtained a two-year bank loan for $36,000, signing a note payable. Annual interest of 10 percent is due each November 30.

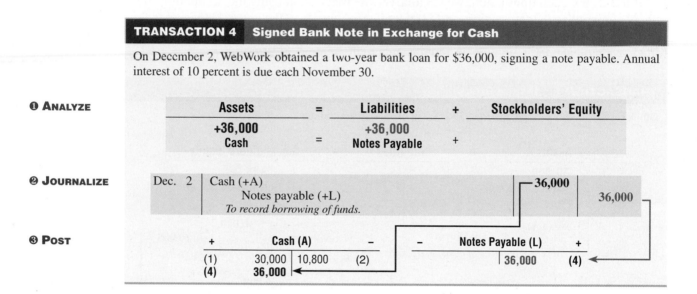

❶ ANALYZE

Assets	=	Liabilities	+	Stockholders' Equity
+36,000	=	+36,000	+	
Cash		Notes Payable		

❷ JOURNALIZE

Dec. 2 | Cash (+A)   36,000
       | Notes payable (+L)   36,000
       | *To record borrowing of funds.*

❸ POST

+ Cash (A) –		– Notes Payable (L) +
(1) 30,000	10,800 (2)	36,000 (4)
(4) 36,000		

TRANSACTION 5   Purchased Equipment with Cash

On December 3, WebWork used cash to purchase $32,400 of office equipment.

❶ ANALYZE

Assets		=	Liabilities	+	Stockholders' Equity
–32,400	+32,400	=		+	
Cash	Office Equipment				

❷ JOURNALIZE

Dec. 3 | Office equipment (+A)   32,400
       | Cash (–A)   32,400
       | *To record purchase of office equipment.*

❸ POST

+ Office Equipment (A) –		+ Cash (A) –
(5) 32,400	(1) 30,000	10,800 (2)
	(4) 36,000	32,400 (5)

TRANSACTION 6   Received Customer Prepayment

On December 5, WebWork received $3,000 cash for services to be performed in the future.

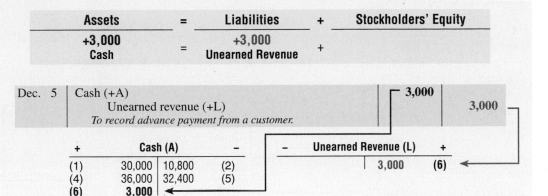

❶ **ANALYZE**

Assets	=	Liabilities	+	Stockholders' Equity
+3,000	=	+3,000	+	
Cash		Unearned Revenue		

❷ **JOURNALIZE**

Dec. 5	Cash (+A)		3,000	
	Unearned revenue (+L)			3,000
	To record advance payment from a customer.			

❸ **POST**

+	Cash (A)	–		–	Unearned Revenue (L)	+
(1)	30,000	10,800	(2)		3,000	(6)
(4)	36,000	32,400	(5)			
(6)	3,000					

TRANSACTION 7   Provided Services to Customers for Cash

On December 10, WebWork performed services for several customers and was paid $13,510 cash.

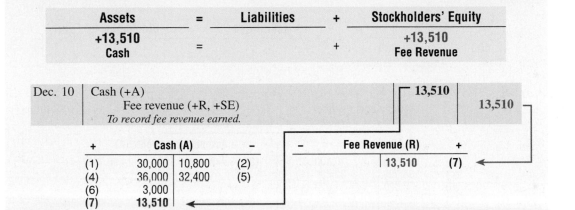

❶ **ANALYZE**

Assets	=	Liabilities	+	Stockholders' Equity
+13,510	=		+	+13,510
Cash				Fee Revenue

❷ **JOURNALIZE**

Dec. 10	Cash (+A)		13,510	
	Fee revenue (+R, +SE)			13,510
	To record fee revenue earned.			

❸ **POST**

+	Cash (A)	–		–	Fee Revenue (R)	+
(1)	30,000	10,800	(2)		13,510	(7)
(4)	36,000	32,400	(5)			
(6)	3,000					
(7)	13,510					

TRANSACTION 8   Provided Services for Cash and on Account

On December 18, WebWork performed $4,740 of services for which it received $1,000 cash with the remaining $3,740 to be paid in the future.

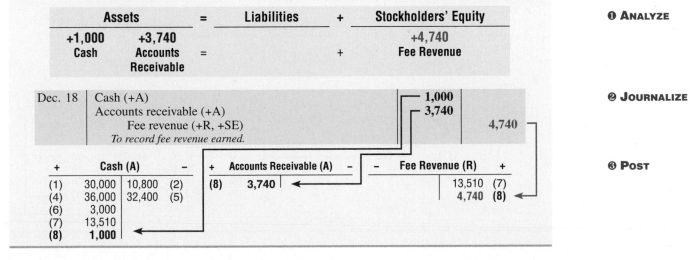

❶ **ANALYZE**

Assets		=	Liabilities	+	Stockholders' Equity
+1,000	+3,740	=		+	+4,740
Cash	Accounts Receivable				Fee Revenue

❷ **JOURNALIZE**

Dec. 18	Cash (+A)		1,000	
	Accounts receivable (+A)		3,740	
	Fee revenue (+R, +SE)			4,740
	To record fee revenue earned.			

❸ **POST**

+	Cash (A)	–		+	Accounts Receivable (A)	–		–	Fee Revenue (R)	+
(1)	30,000	10,800	(2)	(8)	3,740				13,510	(7)
(4)	36,000	32,400	(5)						4,740	(8)
(6)	3,000									
(7)	13,510									
(8)	1,000									

TRANSACTION 9   Paid Employee Wages

On December 20, WebWork paid its employee $1,620 cash upon completion of her first two weeks on the job.

❶ ANALYZE

Assets	=	Liabilities	+	Stockholders' Equity
−1,620 Cash	=		+	−1,620 Wage Expense

❷ JOURNALIZE

Dec. 20	Wage expense (+E, −SE)	1,620	
	Cash (−A)		1,620
	To record payment of employee wages.		

❸ POST

+	Wage Expense (E)	−		+	Cash (A)	−	
(9)	1,620			(1)	30,000	10,800	(2)
				(4)	36,000	32,400	(5)
				(6)	3,000	1,620	(9)
				(7)	13,510		
				(8)	1,000		

TRANSACTION 10   Received Payment on Account from Customer

On December 27, WebWork received $2,400 cash from a customer for services previously performed on account.

❶ ANALYZE

Assets		=	Liabilities	+	Stockholders' Equity
+2,400 Cash	−2,400 Accounts Receivable	=		+	

❷ JOURNALIZE

Dec. 27	Cash (+A)	2,400	
	Accounts receivable (−A)		2,400
	To record receipt of payment on account.		

❸ POST

+	Cash (A)	−		+	Accounts Receivable (A)	−	
(1)	30,000	10,800	(2)	(8)	3,740	2,400	(10)
(4)	36,000	32,400	(5)				
(6)	3,000	1,620	(9)				
(7)	13,510						
(8)	1,000						
(10)	2,400						

TRANSACTION 11   Paid Cash Dividend

On December 30, WebWork paid a $500 cash dividend.

❶ ANALYZE

Assets	=	Liabilities	+	Stockholders' Equity
−500 Cash	=		+	−500 Dividends

❷ JOURNALIZE

Dec. 30	Dividends (+D, −SE)	500	
	Cash (−A)		500
	To record payment of cash dividends.		

❸ POST

+	Dividends (D)	−		+	Cash (A)	−	
(11)	500			(1)	30,000	10,800	(2)
				(4)	36,000	32,400	(5)
				(6)	3,000	1,620	(9)
				(7)	13,510	500	(11)
				(8)	1,000		
				(10)	2,400		

Summary Illustration of Journalizing and Posting Transactions

Exhibit 2-8 presents the general journal for WebWork for the month of December 2022. All journal entries appearing in **Exhibit 2-8** have been posted to the general ledger accounts in **Exhibit 2-9**. The accounts in WebWork's general ledger are grouped by category as follows: (1) assets, (2) liabilities, (3) stockholders' equity, (4) dividends, (5) revenues, and (6) expenses. Each general ledger account in **Exhibit 2-9** has been totaled with the ending balance appearing in **red**. Note that total assets ($87,980) is equal to the sum of total liabilities ($41,850) and stockholders' equity ($46,130).

	EXHIBIT 2-8	**General Journal for WebWork**		
		General Journal		
	Date	**Account Titles and Explanation**	**Debit**	**Credit**
(1)	2022 Dec. 2	Cash (+A) Common stock (+SE) *To record issuance of common stock for cash.*	30,000	30,000
(2)	2	Prepaid rent (+A) Cash (−A) *To record advance payment of six months' rent.*	10,800	10,800
(3)	2	Office supplies (+A) Accounts payable (+L) *To record purchase of office supplies.*	2,850	2,850
(4)	2	Cash (+A) Notes payable (+L) *To record borrowing of funds.*	36,000	36,000
(5)	3	Office equipment (+A) Cash (−A) *To record purchase of office equipment.*	32,400	32,400
(6)	5	Cash (+A) Unearned revenue (+L) *To record advance payment from a customer.*	3,000	3,000
(7)	10	Cash (+A) Fee revenue (+R, +SE) *To record fee revenue earned.*	13,510	13,510
(8)	18	Cash (+A) Accounts receivable (+A) Fee revenue (+R, +SE) *To record fee revenue earned.*	1,000 3,740	4,740
(9)	20	Wage expense (+E, −SE) Cash (−A) *To record payment of employee wages.*	1,620	1,620
(10)	27	Cash (+A) Accounts receivable (−A) *To record receipt of payment on account.*	2,400	2,400
(11)	30	Dividends (+D, −SE) Cash (−A) *To record payment of cash dividends.*	500	500

EXHIBIT 2-9   General Ledger for WebWork

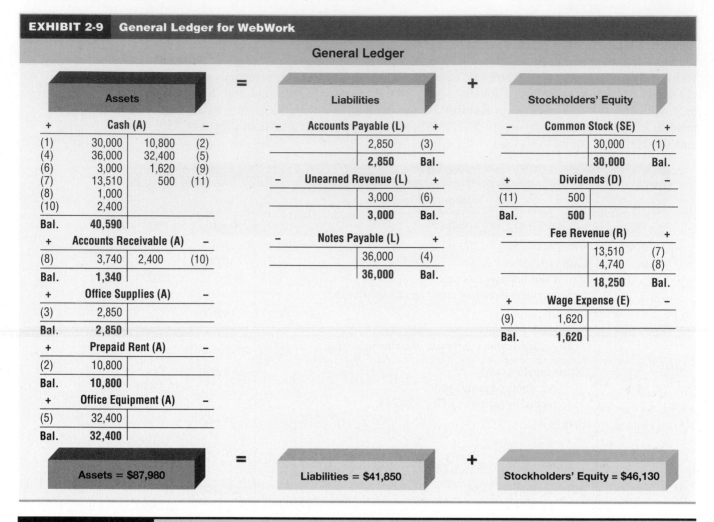

General Ledger

Assets   =   **Liabilities**   +   **Stockholders' Equity**

+	Cash (A)		–
(1)	30,000	10,800	(2)
(4)	36,000	32,400	(5)
(6)	3,000	1,620	(9)
(7)	13,510	500	(11)
(8)	1,000		
(10)	2,400		
Bal.	**40,590**		

+	Accounts Receivable (A)		–
(8)	3,740	2,400	(10)
Bal.	**1,340**		

+	Office Supplies (A)		–
(3)	2,850		
Bal.	**2,850**		

+	Prepaid Rent (A)		–
(2)	10,800		
Bal.	**10,800**		

+	Office Equipment (A)		–
(5)	32,400		
Bal.	**32,400**		

–	Accounts Payable (L)		+
		2,850	(3)
		2,850	Bal.

–	Unearned Revenue (L)		+
		3,000	(6)
		3,000	Bal.

–	Notes Payable (L)		+
		36,000	(4)
		36,000	Bal.

–	Common Stock (SE)		+
		30,000	(1)
		30,000	Bal.

+	Dividends (D)		–
(11)	500		
Bal.	**500**		

–	Fee Revenue (R)		+
		13,510	(7)
		4,740	(8)
		18,250	Bal.

+	Wage Expense (E)		–
(9)	1,620		
Bal.	**1,620**		

Assets = $87,980   =   **Liabilities = $41,850**   +   **Stockholders' Equity = $46,130**

YOUR TURN! 2.5

MBC

The solution is on page 2-59.

For each of the transactions below, complete the following requirements:

1. Record the effect of each transaction using the expanded accounting equation.
2. Prepare journal entries for each transaction.
3. Post the journal entries for each transaction to the appropriate T-accounts.

Transactions:

a. The company received $1,300 cash from clients for services rendered.

b. The company paid $2,400 cash for wages to employees.

c. The company collected $600 cash from clients on account.

d. The company paid a $400 cash dividend.

e. The company purchased $700 of office supplies on account.

f. The company billed clients $900 for services rendered, which will be paid in the future.

g. The company paid $500 cash to suppliers on account.

ACCOUNTING IN PRACTICE   **Careers at Intuit**

A company like Intuit obviously needs employees with a strong knowledge of accounting. However, understanding accounting and how accounting is used is important for many career paths. For example, sales and marketing uses accounting to track and forecast sales activity, human resources uses accounting in employee performance evaluation, and corporate strategy uses accounting to research investment opportunities and communicate with corporate stakeholders. Clearly, knowledge of accounting will help you go far whatever your chosen career.

TRIAL BALANCE

A **trial balance** is a listing of all accounts from the general ledger with their respective debit or credit balance. A trial balance is prepared at the end of an accounting period after all transactions have been recorded. **Exhibit 2-10** shows the trial balance for WebWork, Inc. The heading provides the name of the company and the date the trial balance was prepared, December 31, 2022. The sequence of the accounts and the dollar amounts are taken directly from the general ledger T-accounts in **Exhibit 2-9** (which follow the order of the account numbering system in WebWork's chart of accounts). The debit and credit columns from the trial balance are in balance; that is, the $90,100 sum of the debit account balances equals the $90,100 sum of the credit account balances.

LO6 Describe the trial balance.

eLecture

MBC

The two principal reasons for preparing a trial balance are:

1. To serve as a check on whether the sum of the debit balances and the sum of the credit balances from the general ledger accounts are equal. If the totals are not equal, it would indicate the presence of some type of recording error.

2. To show all general ledger account balances in one location, which facilitates the preparation of financial statements. The trial balance, however, is *not* a financial statement.

A trial balance must be dated. In **Exhibit 2-10**, the trial balance of WebWork, Inc., was prepared as of December 31, 2022.

While it is required that a trial balance be in balance—that is, that the total of the debit column equal the total of the credit column—this equality does not guarantee that the accounting data are error-free. Potential data errors could still exist as a consequence of (1) transactions not being journalized, (2) journal entries not being posted, (3) journal entries being posted in the wrong amount, or (4) journal entries being posted to the wrong accounts.

EXHIBIT 2-10	Unadjusted Trial Balance for WebWork

WEBWORK, INC. Unadjusted Trial Balance December 31, 2022	Debit	Credit
Cash.	$40,590	
Accounts receivable	1,340	
Office supplies	2,850	
Prepaid rent	10,800	
Office equipment	32,400	
Accounts payable		$ 2,850
Unearned revenue		3,000
Notes payable.		36,000
Common stock		30,000
Dividends	500	
Fee revenue		18,250
Wage expense	1,620	
Totals	$90,100	$90,100

It is required that the sum of all debits equal the sum of all credits in the trial balance.

Concept ⟶	Method ⟶	Assessment	TAKEAWAY 2.2
Is the trial balance in balance?	Ending balances for all of the general ledger accounts entered on the trial balance. Total the debit column and the credit column on the trial balance.	Verify that the sum of the debit account balances equals the sum of the credit account balances.	

YOUR TURN! 2.6

MBC

The solution is on page 2-60.

Each of the following accounts from the Devin Company has a normal balance. The account balances are as of December 31, the end of Devin's first year of operations:

Cash.	1,500	Common stock	7,500
Accounts receivable	4,500	Sales revenue.	12,000
Inventory.	3,750	Salary expense.	4,500
Property, plant, and equipment.	11,250	Administrative expenses.	750
Accounts payable	2,250	Dividends	1,500
Notes payable.	6,000		

Prepare a trial balance for the Devin Company as of December 31.

Data Analytics

DATA ANALYTICS   Big Data, Artificial Intelligence, and the Future of Accounting

While accountants are often known as paper pushers, the future of accounting is likely much different. According to an article in *Forbes*, the digital world for accountants will look much different. We already see accounting software such as QuickBooks replacing paper ledgers and services such as **PayPal** replacing paper checks. But what does the future hold with Big Data and Artificial Intelligence (AI) entering the mainstream?

The audits of tomorrow will benefit from the speed and rigorous checking provided by computers programed with AI. Computers with AI will also aid in regulatory compliance as transactions and reporting requirements become more complex. Machine readable receipts will make quick order of reconciliations. And computers and AI, already becoming very good at fraud detection, will excel at risk management in the future.

Does this spell the demise of the accounting profession? Quite the contrary. Accountants willing to accept this future will learn to work with, rather than compete with, these technologies. Just as the spreadsheet made accountants more efficient at their jobs, so will Big Data and AI.

Bernard Marr, "Big Data, AI and the Uncertain Future for Accountants," *Forbes*, October 7, 2016, https://www.forbes.com/sites /bernardmarr/2016/10/07/big-data-ai-and-the-uncertain-future-for-accountants/?sh=5b0a21f2749a.

FORENSIC ACCOUNTING   Fraudulent Reporting

Verifying that the sum of the debit account balances from the general ledger is equal to the sum of the credit account balances is not sufficient to guarantee the accuracy of financial records. The infamous accounting scandal at **WorldCom** provides a case in point. To inflate its net income, WorldCom improperly "capitalized expenses"—that is, it inappropriately debited property, plant, and equipment, an asset account, when it should have debited an expense account. While the sum of the debit account balances on WorldCom's books did equal the sum of the credit account balances, assets were overstated and expenses were understated by almost $7 billion. WorldCom's CEO, Bernard Ebbers, the mastermind of this fraudulent accounting scheme, was convicted of conspiracy to commit fraud, securities fraud, and making false filings with the SEC. Mr. Ebbers was sentenced to 25 years in prison.

COMPREHENSIVE PROBLEM

MBC

Juan Rios acted upon his entrepreneurial spirit and started a graphic design business called Juan's Designs. Based on an excellent business plan, Juan was able to raise sufficient capital to begin operations in October. During the month of October, the following events occurred related to the business.

1. Stockholders invested $40,000 cash in the business in exchange for common stock.
2. Paid $2,500 cash for rent on an office suite for the month of October.
3. Purchased two desktop computers, software, and a printer for $10,000 cash.
4. Purchased on account miscellaneous supplies for $500 that will be used during the month.

5. Purchased digital advertising for $300 cash, announcing the opening of his new business.
6. Performed $5,500 of design work on account.
7. Received $3,500 cash from customers for design work previously completed.
8. Paid $350 cash toward the company's accounts payable balance.
9. Paid $2,500 cash for employee wages.

Required

a. Use the following accounts to create a general ledger using T-accounts.

Cash	Common Stock	Wage Expense
Accounts Receivable	Service Revenue	Advertising Expense
Equipment	Supplies Expense	Rent Expense
Accounts Payable		

   Prepare journal entries and post the above accounting transactions to their general ledger T-accounts.

b. Prepare an unadjusted trial balance as of October 31.

Solution

Date	Description	Post Ref.	Debit	Credit
October	Cash (+A)	1	40,000	
	Common stock (+SE)	1		40,000
	Owner purchased shares for cash.			
	Rent expense (+E, −SE)	2	2,500	
	Cash (−A)	2		2,500
	Paid rent for office suite.			
	Equipment (+A)	3	10,000	
	Cash (−A)	3		10,000
	Purchased office equipment.			
	Supplies expense (+E, −SE)	4	500	
	Accounts payable (+L)	4		500
	Purchased supplies on account to be used in current month.			
	Advertising expense (+E, −SE)	5	300	
	Cash (−A)	5		300
	Purchased advertising.			
	Accounts receivable (+A)	6	5,500	
	Service revenue (+R, +SE)	6		5,500
	Performed design work on account.			
	Cash (+A)	7	3,500	
	Accounts receivable (−A)	7		3,500
	Received cash from previously billed work.			
	Accounts payable (−L)	8	350	
	Cash (−A)	8		350
	Paid cash toward accounts payable.			
	Wage expense (+E, −SE)	9	2,500	
	Cash (−A)	9		2,500
	Paid wages.			

+	Cash (A)		–
(1)	40,000	2,500	(2)
(7)	3,500	10,000	(3)
		300	(5)
		350	(8)
		2,500	(9)
Bal.	27,850		

+	Accounts Receivable (A)		–
(6)	5,500	3,500	(7)
Bal.	2,000		

+	Equipment (A)		–
(3)	10,000		

–	Accounts Payable (L)		+
(8)	350	500	(4)
		150	Bal.

–	Common Stock (SE)		+
		40,000	(1)

–	Service Revenue (R)		+
		5,500	(6)

+	Supplies Expense (E)		–
(4)	500		

+	Wage Expense (E)		–
(9)	2,500		

+	Advertising Expense (E)		–
(5)	300		

+	Rent Expense (E)		–
(2)	2,500		

JUAN'S DESIGNS
Unadjusted Trial Balance
October 31

	Debit	Credit
Cash.	$27,850	
Accounts receivable	2,000	
Equipment	10,000	
Accounts payable		$ 150
Common stock		40,000
Service revenue		5,500
Supplies expense	500	
Wage expense	2,500	
Advertising expense	300	
Rent expense	2,500	
Totals	$45,650	$45,650

SUMMARY OF LEARNING OBJECTIVES

LO1   **Identify the five major steps in the accounting cycle. (p. 2-3)**
- The five major steps in the accounting cycle are:
  1. Analyze.
  2. Record.
  3. Adjust.
  4. Report.
  5. Close.

LO2   **Analyze and record transactions using the accounting equation. (p. 2-4)**
- The accounting equation provides a convenient way to summarize the recording of financial information.
- The initial step in the accounting process—analyze—is to determine which transactions (if any) need to be recorded.
- An *accounting transaction* is an economic event that requires accounting recognition. An event that affects any of the elements of the basic accounting equation (assets, liabilities, or stockholders' equity) must be recorded.

LO3   **Explain the nature, format, and purpose of an account. (p. 2-11)**
- An account is an individual record of the increases and decreases in specific assets, liabilities, stockholders' equity, dividends, revenues, or expenses.
- Information provided by the account includes its title, amounts reflecting increases and decreases, cross-references to other accounting records, and dates and descriptive notations.

Describe the system of debits and credits and its use in recording transactions. (p. 2-11) **LO4**

- The left side of an account is always the debit side; the right side of an account is always the credit side.
- Increases in assets, dividends, and expenses are debit entries; increases in liabilities, stockholders' equity, and revenues are credit entries. Decreases are the opposite.
- The normal balance of any account appears on the account side used for recording account increases.
- For each accounting transaction, the sum of the debit amounts must always equal the sum of the credit amounts.
- All accounting transactions are analyzed using one or more of the basic account categories: (1) assets, (2) liabilities, (3) stockholders' equity, (4) dividends, (5) revenues, and (6) expenses.

Explain the process of journalizing and posting transactions. (p. 2-14) **LO5**

- Source documents provide the basis for analyzing business transactions.
- Accounting entries are initially recorded in a journal in chronological order; the journal is a book of original entry and acts like a diary of a business's activities.
- A general ledger is a grouping of all of the accounts that are used to prepare the basic financial statements.
- Posting is the transfer of information from a journal to the general ledger accounts.
- Posting references are used to cross-reference the information in journals and the general ledger accounts.

Describe the trial balance. (p. 2-22) **LO6**

- A trial balance is a list of the accounts in the general ledger with their respective debit or credit balance.
- A trial balance is prepared after all transactions have been recorded for an accounting period.
- A trial balance serves as a mechanical check to evaluate the equality of the sum of the debit account balances and the sum of the credit account balances.
- A trial balance facilitates the preparation of the financial statements by showing all account balances in one concise record.

Concept ⟶	Method ⟶	Assessment	SUMMARY
When should an event be recorded in a company's accounting records?	Review the event details. Does the event affect the company's assets, liabilities, or stockholders' equity?	If the event affects any of the elements of the accounting equation, it must be recorded in a company's accounting records.	TAKEAWAY 2.1
Is the trial balance in balance?	Ending balances for all of the general ledger accounts entered on the trial balance. Total the debit column and the credit column on the trial balance.	Verify that the sum of the debit account balances equals the sum of the credit account balances.	TAKEAWAY 2.2

KEY TERMS

Account (p. 2-11)	Debit (p. 2-11)	Journal entry (p. 2-14)
Accounting cycle (p. 2-3)	Deferred revenue (p. 2-7)	Normal balance (p. 2-12)
Accounting transaction (p. 2-4)	Double-entry accounting (p. 2-5)	Posting (p. 2-15)
Calendar year (p. 2-4)		Posting reference (p. 2-15)
Chart of accounts (p. 2-11)	Fiscal year (p. 2-4)	Source documents (p. 2-14)
Compound journal entry (p. 2-15)	General journal (p. 2-14)	T-account (p. 2-11)
	General ledger (p. 2-15)	Trial balance (p. 2-22)
Credit (p. 2-11)	Journal (p. 2-14)	Unearned revenue (p. 2-7)

Assignments with the ⬤ logo in the margin are available in **BusinessCourse**.
See the Preface of the book for details.

SELF-STUDY QUESTIONS

(Answers to Self-Study Questions are at the end of this chapter.)

LO2 1. **Which of the following transactions does not affect the balance sheet totals?**
   a. Purchased $500 supplies on account
   b. Paid off a $3,000 note payable
   c. Received $4,000 cash from a bank after signing a note payable
   d. Ordered a new machine that will be paid for upon its delivery in two months

LO2 2. **Tobias Company purchased inventory on account. This transaction will affect:**
   a. Only the balance sheet
   b. Only the income statement
   c. The income statement and the statement of retained earnings
   d. The income statement, balance sheet, and statement of retained earnings

LO2 3. **If assets increase by $50 and liabilities decrease by $30, stockholders' equity must:**
   a. Remain unchanged   c. Decrease by $70
   b. Increase by $80   d. Decrease by $130

LO3 4. **The chart of accounts is a listing of:**
   a. Customers and suppliers   c. General ledger account names and numbers
   b. Each inventory item   d. Shareholders

LO4 5. **Which of the following is true?**
   a. The debit is on the right side of an asset account
   b. The debit is on the left side of an asset account
   c. The credit is on the left side of a liability account
   d. The debit is on the right side of an expense account

LO4 6. **Which of the following accounts has a normal debit balance?**
   a. Accounts Payable   c. Common Stock
   b. Notes Payable   d. Advertising Expense

LO4 7. **Which of the following accounts is increased by a credit?**
   a. Accounts Receivable   c. Dividends
   b. Sales Revenue   d. Advertising Expense

LO4 8. **Which of the following is true?**
   a. A debit will increase a liability account   c. A credit will increase a revenue account
   b. A credit will increase an asset account   d. A debit will decrease an expense account

LO4 9. **In applying the rules of debits and credits, which of the following statements is correct?**
   a. The word *debit* means to increase and the word *credit* means to decrease
   b. Asset, expense, and common stock accounts are debited for increases
   c. Liability, revenue, and common stock accounts are debited for increases
   d. Asset, expense, and dividends are debited for increases

LO4 10. **Which of these accounts has a normal debit balance?**
   a. Assets, expenses, dividends   c. Liabilities, revenues, common stock
   b. Assets, revenues, common stock   d. Assets, liabilities, dividends

LO5 11. **The general ledger includes accounts for all but which of the following?**
   a. Assets   c. Dividends
   b. Expenses   d. All of the above are in the general ledger

LO6 12. **Which of the following will cause a trial balance to be out of balance?**
   a. Mistakenly debiting an asset account instead of an expense account
   b. Posting $123 as $213 to both a debit and a credit account
   c. Posting the same transaction twice by mistake
   d. Posting only the debit part of a transaction

LO5 13. **A journal entry that contains more than just two accounts is called:**
   a. A posted journal entry   c. An erroneous journal entry
   b. An adjusting journal entry   d. A compound journal entry

14. **Posting refers to the process of transferring information from:**   LO5
    a. A journal to the general ledger accounts   *c.* Source documents to a journal
    b. General ledger accounts to a journal   *d.* A journal to source documents

15. **Which of the following is not one of the five steps in the accounting cycle?**   LO1
    a. Analyze   *c.* Eliminate
    b. Adjust   *d.* Report

16. **The purchase of $500 of supplies on account will:**   LO2
    a. Increase both assets and stockholders' equity by $500
    b. Increase assets and decrease liabilities by $500
    c. Increase assets and decrease stockholders' equity by $500
    d. Increase both assets and liabilities by $500

17. **Match steps in the accounting cycle to their definitions.**   LO1

1. Analyze	a. Prepare financial statements
2. Record	b. Analyze transactions from source documents
3. Adjust	c. Journalize closing entries and prepare post-closing trial balance
4. Report	d. Journalize adjusting entries and prepare adjusted trial balance
5. Close	e. Journalize transactions and prepare unadjusted trial balance

QUESTIONS

1. List the five major steps in the accounting cycle in their proper order.

2. Define the term *fiscal year*.

3. Provide three examples of source documents that underlie business transactions.

4. Provide an example of a transaction that would:
    a. Increase one asset account but not change the amount of total assets
    b. Decrease an asset account and a liability account
    c. Decrease an asset account and increase an expense account
    d. Increase an asset account and a liability account

5. Explain the financial effect (increase, decrease, or no effect) of each of the following transactions on stockholders' equity:
    a. Purchased supplies for cash   *e.* Invested cash in business
    b. Paid an account payable   *f.* Rendered services to customers, on account
    c. Paid salaries   *g.* Rendered services to customers, for cash
    d. Purchased equipment for cash

6. The retained earnings on a balance sheet are $80,000. Without seeing the rest of the balance sheet, can you conclude that stockholders should be able to receive a dividend in the amount of $80,000 cash from the business? Justify your answer.

7. On December 31, the Milers Company had $800,000 in total assets and owed $300,000 to creditors. If the corporation's common stock amounted to $250,000, what amount of retained earnings should appear on the company's December 31 balance sheet?

8. Some accounting students believe that debits are good and credits are bad. Explain why this is not an accurate way to think about debits and credits.

9. What is an account?

10. What information is recorded in an account?

11. What does the term *debit* mean? What does the term *credit* mean?

12. What type of account—asset, liability, stockholders' equity, dividend, revenue, or expense—is each of the following accounts? Indicate whether a debit entry or a credit entry increases the balance of the account.

    Professional Fees Earned   Common Stock
    Accounts Receivable   Advertising Expense
    Accounts Payable   Supplies
    Cash   Dividends

13. How is the normal side of an account determined?

14. What is the normal balance (debit or credit) of each of the accounts in Discussion Question 12?

15. Describe the nature and purpose of a general journal.

16. What is the justification for the use of posting references?

17. Describe a compound journal entry.

18. What is a chart of accounts?

19. Explain the terms *general ledger* and *trial balance*. What are the primary reasons for preparing a trial balance?

20. Explain how it is possible for a trial balance to be in balance but still be in error.

21. What is a T-account and how is it used?

22. Is it possible for an accounting transaction to only affect the left side of the accounting equation and still leave the equation in balance? If so, provide an example.

23. Would a company record a transaction in its general ledger when an order is placed for the purchase of a machine that will be paid for at the time of its delivery in three months? Explain your answer.

SHORT EXERCISES

LO4 **SE2-1.** **Normal Balances** Indicate for each of the following accounts whether the normal balance is a debit or a credit:

a.	Accounts Receivable	e.	Inventory
b.	Accounts Payable	f.	Interest Income
c.	Dividends	g.	Retained Earnings
d.	Wage Expense		

LO4 **SE2-2.** **Debit and Credit Effects** Indicate the account that will be debited for each of the following transactions:

a.	Issued common stock for cash	d.	Purchased inventory on account
b.	Borrowed money from a bank	e.	Collected cash from customers that owed a
c.	Provided services on account		balance due

LO4 **SE2-3.** **Debit and Credit Effects** Indicate the account that will be credited for each of the following transactions:

a.	Issued common stock for cash	d.	Purchased inventory on account
b.	Borrowed money from a bank	e.	Collected cash from customers that owed a
c.	Provided services on account		balance due

LO4 **SE2-4.** **Determine a Transaction** The Pearce Company recorded a transaction by debiting Accounts Receivable and crediting Sales Revenue. What event was being recorded?

LO4 **SE2-5.** **Determine the Cash Balance** The beginning-of-the-period cash balance for the Taylor Company was a $12,000 debit. Cash sales for the month were $8,000, and sales on account were $8,000. The company paid $2,500 cash for current-period purchases and also paid $3,000 cash for amounts due from last month. What is the ending debit or credit balance in the Cash account?

LO2 **SE2-6.** **Recording Transactions with the Accounting Equation** During the year, the Flight Company experienced the following accounting transactions:

1. Issued common stock in the amount of $150,000
2. Paid a $30,000 cash dividend
3. Borrowed $25,000 from a bank
4. Made a principal payment of $3,500 on an outstanding bank loan
5. Made an interest payment of $1,200 on an outstanding bank loan

Using the accounting equation, record each of the transactions in columnar format using the following template:

Assets	=	Liabilities	+	Stockholders' Equity		
Cash	=	Notes Payable	+	Common Stock	+	Retained Earnings

SE2-7. **Posting Transactions to T-accounts** Using the data from short exercise SE2-6, prepare journal entries and post your transaction analysis to the appropriate T-accounts.

LO5

SE2-8. **Prepare a Trial Balance** The following balances were taken from the general ledger of Doogie Corporation as of December 31. All balances are normal. Prepare a trial balance.

LO6

Cash.	$ 6,000	Accounts receivable	$10,800
Accounts payable	6,000	Common stock	51,000
Equipment	45,000	Dividends	2,400
Utilities expense	2,000	Administrative expenses.	8,000
Sales revenue.	17,200		

SE2-9. **Prepare a Corrected Trial Balance** The following trial balance for Hill Company has errors that cause it to be out of balance. Prepare a corrected version of the trial balance for Hill Company.

LO6

HILL COMPANY Unadjusted Trial Balance December 31		
	Debit	Credit
Cash.	$ 20,000	
Inventory.		$ 85,000
Accounts receivable	42,000	
Accounts payable		12,000
Common stock		52,000
Retained earnings		58,000
Sales revenue.	100,000	
Utilities expense	60,000	
Selling expenses	15,000	
Totals	$237,000	$207,000

SE2-10. **The Accounting Cycle** The following is the correct order of the five steps in the accounting cycle:

LO1

a. Analyze; adjust; record; report; close
b. Analyze; record; adjust; report; close
c. Analyze; record; adjust; close; report
d. Analyze; report; adjust; record; close

SE2-11. **The Account** Which of the following is not part of the T-account?

LO3

a. Title
b. Amount
c. Cross-reference
d. Analysis

DATA ANALYTICS

DA2-1. **Preparing Basic Data Visualization in Excel Using a Doughnut Chart** The Excel file associated with this exercise includes total liabilities, common stock, and retained earnings balances as of December 31 for Monona Inc. We will prepare data visualizations focusing on how these amounts relate to one other and how the relations can be expressed through proportions.

Data Analytics

Required

1. Download Excel file DA2-1 found in myBusinessCourse.
2. Prepare a doughnut chart showing total liabilities, total common stock, and total retained earnings as components of total liabilities plus stockholders' equity.
3. Enter your first account label in cell A6 and its related dollar amount in cell B6.
4. Display a percentage label for each proportion on your chart. *Hint:* Right-click on the doughnut chart, select Format data labels, and select Percentage.
5. List the formula for the Y values from the Select data source window associated with your chart. *Hint:* Right-click on the chart, click Select data, and see the formula in the Y values box.
6. List the percentage amount (or combination of percentage amounts) on the doughnut chart that reflects the stockholders' equity proportion.
7. List the larger percentage: the total liabilities proportion or the total equity proportion of the pie chart.

8. List the percentage amount (or combination of percentage amounts) on the doughnut chart that reflects the total assets proportion.

9. List the dollar amount of total assets.

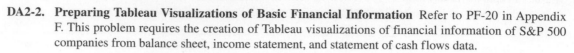

DA2-2. Preparing Tableau Visualizations of Basic Financial Information Refer to PF-20 in Appendix F. This problem requires the creation of Tableau visualizations of financial information of S&P 500 companies from balance sheet, income statement, and statement of cash flows data.

DATA VISUALIZATION

Data Visualization Activities are available in myBusinessCourse. These assignments use Tableau Dashboards to expose students to visual depictions of data and introduce students to data analytics through data visualizations. These exercises are easily assignable and auto graded by MBC.

EXERCISES—SET A

LO2 E2-1A. Accounting Equation Determine the missing amount in each of the following cases:

	Assets	Liabilities	Stockholders' Equity
a.	$420,000	$175,000	?
b.	?	$ 31,000	$42,000
c.	$121,000	?	$90,000

LO2 E2-2A. Transaction Analysis Following the example shown in (a) below, indicate the accounting effects of the listed transactions on the assets, liabilities, and stockholders' equity of Martin & Company, a corporation:

a. Purchased, for cash, a desktop computer for use in the office.
   ANSWER: Increase assets (Office Equipment)
         Decrease assets (Cash)
b. Rendered services and billed the client.
c. Paid rent for the month.
d. Rendered services to a client for cash.
e. Received amount due from a client in Transaction (b).
f. Purchased an office desk on account.
g. Paid employees' salaries for the month.
h. Paid for desk purchased in Transaction (f).
i. The company paid a dividend.

LO2 E2-3A. Analysis of Accounts Calculate the unknown amount in each of the following five independent situations. The answer to situation *(a)* is given as an example.

	Account	Beginning Balance	Ending Balance	Other Information
a.	Cash.................	$ 7,000	$ 5,250	Total cash disbursed, $5,400.
b.	Accounts receivable.....	11,000	9,300	Services on account, $16,500.
c.	Notes payable..........	17,500	23,000	Borrowed funds by issuing a note, $30,000.
d.	Accounts payable.......	2,500	1,720	Payments on account, $3,900.
e.	Stockholders' equity.....	29,000	46,000	Capital contribution, $7,000.

	Unknown Amounts Required	
a.	Total cash received.....................................	$3,650
b.	Total cash collected from credit customers................	_____
c.	Notes payable repaid during the period	_____
d.	Goods and services received from suppliers on account.....	_____
e.	Net income, assuming that no dividends were paid.........	_____

E2-4A. Transaction Analysis The accounts below are from the general ledger of The Bast Company. For each letter given in the T-accounts, describe the type of business transaction(s) or event(s) that would most likely be reflected by entries on that side of the account. For example, the answer to (a) is amounts for services performed for clients on account.   **LO2, 5**

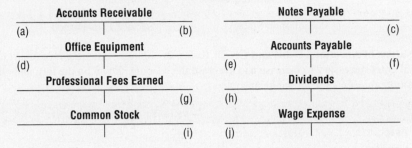

Accounts Receivable		Notes Payable	
(a)	(b)		(c)
Office Equipment		**Accounts Payable**	
(d)		(e)	(f)
Professional Fees Earned		**Dividends**	
	(g)	(h)	
Common Stock		**Wage Expense**	
	(i)	(j)	

E2-5A. Transaction Analysis Match each of the following transactions of Lesch & Company with the appropriate letters, indicating the debits and credits to be made. The key for the letters follows the list of transactions. The correct answer for Transaction (1) is given as an illustration: **LO4**

		Answer
1.	Purchased supplies on account.	*a, d*
2.	Paid interest on note payable.	_____
3.	Paid cash dividend to stockholders.	_____
4.	Returned some defective supplies and received a reduction in the amount owed.	_____
5.	Made payment to settle note payable.	_____
6.	Received an invoice for utilities used.	_____
7.	Received payment in advance from client for work to be done next month.	_____
8.	Received additional capital contribution from stockholders.	_____

Financial Effect of Transaction

a.	Debit an asset	*g.*	Debit dividends
b.	Credit an asset	*h.*	Credit dividends
c.	Debit a liability	*i.*	Debit a revenue
d.	Credit a liability	*j.*	Credit a revenue
e.	Debit common stock	*k.*	Debit an expense
f.	Credit common stock	*l.*	Credit an expense

E2-6A. Transaction Entries Unique Designs, a firm providing art services for advertisers, began business on June 1. The following accounts in its general ledger are needed to record the transactions for June: Cash; Accounts Receivable; Supplies; Office Equipment; Accounts Payable; Common Stock; Dividends; Service Fees Earned; Rent Expense; Utilities Expense; and Salaries Expense.   **LO5**

a. Using the accounting equation, record each of the transactions in columnar format.

b. Use journal entries to record the following transactions for June in the general journal.

June	1	Emily Holmes invested $8,000 cash to begin the business; she received common stock for her investment.
	2	Paid rent for June, $375.
	3	Purchased office equipment on account, $2,800.
	6	Purchased art materials and other supplies costing $2,500; paid $900 down with the remainder due within 30 days.
	11	Billed clients for services, $4,750.
	17	Collected $2,600 from clients on account.
	19	Paid $2,000 on account to office equipment company (see June 3 transaction).
	25	Emily Holmes received a $750 dividend.
	30	Paid utility bill for June, $525.
	30	Paid salaries for June, $2,750.

E2-7A. Source Documents For each transaction in E2-6A, indicate the related source document or documents that provide evidence supporting the transaction.   **LO5**

LO4, 5   E2-8A.   Nature of Accounts, Debit and Credit Rules For each of the accounts listed below, indicate whether the account is increased by a debit or a credit:

Accounts Payable	Dividends
Advertising Expense	Equipment
Cash	Land
Common Stock	Service Fees Earned

LO4, 5   E2-9A.   Nature of Accounts, Debit and Credit Rules In columns, enter *debit* or *credit* to describe the journal entry necessary to increase and decrease the account shown on the left, and which side of the account represents its normal balance.

	Increase	Decrease	Normal Balance
Asset...........................	_____	_____	_____
Liability	_____	_____	_____
Common stock	_____	_____	_____
Dividends	_____	_____	_____
Revenue	_____	_____	_____
Expense	_____	_____	_____

LO4, 5   E2-10A.   Nature of Accounts, Debit and Credit Rules For each of the accounts listed below, indicate whether the account is increased by a debit or a credit:

Accounts Receivable	Notes Payable
Advertising Revenue	Retained Earnings
Building	Supplies
Common Stock	Utilities Expense

LO2, 4   E2-11A.   Transaction Analysis Match each of the following transactions of L. Boyd & Company with the appropriate letters, indicating the debits and credits to be made. The key for the letters follows the list of transactions. The correct answer for Transaction 1 is given as an illustration:

		Answer
1.	Stockholders contributed cash to the business.	*a, f*
2.	Purchased equipment on account.	_____
3.	Received and immediately paid advertising bill.	_____
4.	Purchased supplies for cash.	_____
5.	Borrowed money from a bank, giving a note payable.	_____
6.	Billed customers for services rendered.	_____
7.	Made a partial payment on account for equipment.	_____
8.	Paid employee's salary.	_____
9.	Collected amounts due from customers billed in Transaction 6.	_____

Financial Effect of Transaction

a.	Debit an asset	*e.*	Debit common stock	*h.*	Credit a revenue
b.	Credit an asset	*f.*	Credit common stock	*i.*	Debit an expense
c.	Debit a liability	*g.*	Debit a revenue	*j.*	Credit an expense
d.	Credit a liability				

LO5, 6   E2-12A.   Transaction Analysis and Trial Balance Make T-accounts for the following accounts that appear in the general ledger of Dave Jennings, an attorney: Cash; Accounts Receivable; Office Equipment; Legal Database Subscription; Accounts Payable; Common Stock; Dividends; Legal Fees Earned; Salaries Expense; Rent Expense; and Utilities Expense. Using the accounting equation, record each of the transactions in columnar format. Prepare journal entries and record the following October transactions in the T-accounts and key all entries with the number identifying the transaction. Determine the balance in each account and prepare a trial balance sheet as of October 31.

1 Jennings started his law practice by contributing $21,500 cash to the business on October 1, receiving shares of common stock in the company.
2 Purchased office equipment on account, $11,400.
3 Paid office rent for October, $1,100.
4 Paid $9,750 to access online legal database for two years.

5 Billed clients for services rendered, $14,000.
6 Made $6,000 payment on account for the equipment purchased on October 2.
7 Paid legal assistant's salary, $2,800.
8 Collected $7,500 from clients previously billed for services.
9 Received invoice for October utilities, $190; it will be paid in November.
10 Paid stockholders $1,500 as a cash dividend.

E2-13A. Transaction Analysis and Trial Balance Make T-accounts for the following accounts that appear in the general ledger of Miller Cat Hospital, owned by R. Miller, a veterinarian: Cash; Accounts Receivable; Supplies; Office Equipment; Accounts Payable; Common Stock; Dividends; Professional Fees Earned; Salaries Expense; and Rent Expense. Using the accounting equation, record each of the transactions in columnar format. Prepare journal entries and record the following December transactions in the T-accounts and key all entries with the number identifying the transaction. Finally, determine the balance in each account and prepare a trial balance as of December 31.

LO5, 6

1 Miller opened a checking account on December 1 at United Bank in the name of Miller Cat Hospital and deposited $25,000 cash. Miller received common stock for his investment.
2 Paid rent for December, $1,500.
3 Purchased office equipment on account, $2,900.
4 Purchased supplies for cash, $1,900.
5 Billed clients for services rendered, $7,300.
6 Paid secretary's salary, $1,950.
7 Paid $1,500 on account for the equipment purchased on December 3.
8 Collected $5,800 from clients previously billed for services.
9 Paid stockholders $3,000 as a cash dividend.

E2-14A. The Account The following transactions occurred during December, the first month of operations for Farly Company. Prepare journal entries and create a T-account for accounts payable that includes the following five transactions.

LO3

1. Purchased $900 of inventory on account.   4. Purchased $500 of inventory on account.
2. Purchased $200 of inventory on account.   5. Paid suppliers $300.
3. Paid suppliers $550.

E2-15A. Recording Transactions with the Accounting Equation During the year, the Riley Company experienced the following accounting transactions:

LO2

1. Purchased equipment with cash in the amount of $165,000.
2. Purchased supplies on account in the amount of $15,000.
3. Collected $19,500 cash from customers.
4. Paid a cash dividend of $11,000.

Using the accounting equation, record each of the transactions in columnar format using the following template:

Assets				=	Liabilities	+	Stockholders' Equity
Cash +	Accounts Receivable	+ Supplies	+ Equipment =		Accounts Payable	+	Retained Earnings

E2-16A. Posting Transactions to T-accounts Using the data from short exercise E2-15A, prepare journal entries and post your transaction analysis to the appropriate T-accounts.

LO5

EXERCISES—SET B

E2-1B. Accounting Equation Determine the missing amount in each of the following cases:

LO2

	Assets	Liabilities	Stockholders' Equity
a.	$425,000	$115,000	?
b.	?	$ 79,000	$19,000
c.	$152,000	?	$93,000

LO2 **E2-2B.** **Transaction Analysis** Following the example shown in (a) below, indicate the effects of the listed transactions on the assets, liabilities, and stockholders' equity of John Dallmus, certified public accountant, a corporation:

a. Purchased, for cash, a desktop computer for use in the office.
   ANSWER: Increase assets (Office Equipment)
                Decrease assets (Cash)
b. Rendered accounting services and billed client.
c. Paid utilities for month.
d. Rendered tax services to client for cash.
e. Received amount due from client in Transaction (b).
f. Purchased a copying machine on account.
g. Paid employees' salaries for the month.
h. Paid for copying machine purchased in Transaction (f).
i. The company paid a dividend.

LO2 **E2-3B.** **Analysis of Accounts** Compute the unknown amount required in each of the following five independent situations. The answer to situation (a) is given as an illustration:

	Account	Beginning Balance	Ending Balance	Other Information
a.	Cash..............	$ 8,100	$ 5,250	Total cash disbursed, $6,100.
b.	Accounts receivable.....	8,500	7,500	Services on account, $17,000.
c.	Notes payable.........	17,000	14,000	Borrowed funds by issuing a note, $33,000.
d.	Accounts payable.......	5,280	1,750	Payments on account, $5,500.
e.	Stockholders' equity.....	29,500	41,000	Capital contribution, $6,100.

	Unknown Amounts Required	
a.	Total cash received.....................................	$3,250
b.	Total cash collected from credit customers..................	_____
c.	Notes payable repaid during the period	_____
d.	Goods and services received from suppliers on account.......	_____
e.	Net income, assuming that no dividends were paid...........	_____

LO2, 5 **E2-4B.** **Transaction Analysis** The accounts below are from the general ledger of Andrew Miller & Company, an architectural firm. For each letter given in the T-accounts, describe the type of business transaction(s) or event(s) that would most likely be reflected by entries on that side of the account. For example, the answer to (a) is amounts for services performed for clients on account.

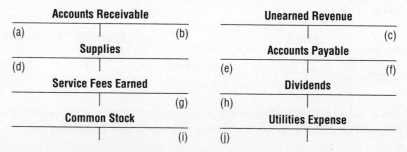

LO4 **E2-5B.** **Transaction Analysis** Match each of the following transactions of Ardon Peralta & Company, a landscape design firm, with the appropriate letters, indicating the debits and credits to be made. The key for the letters follows the list of transactions. The correct answer for Transaction 1 is given as an illustration:

Answer

1. Purchased supplies on account. _a, d_
2. Paid interest on a bank loan. _____
3. The business paid the stockholders a dividend. _____
4. Returned some defective supplies and received a reduction in the amount owed. _____
5. Made payment to repay bank loan. _____
6. Received an invoice for supplies used. _____
7. Received payment in advance from client for work to be done next month. _____
8. Paid employee's salary. _____
9. Peralta contributed additional capital to the business. _____

Financial Effect of Transaction

_a._ Debit an asset	_e._ Debit common stock	_i._ Debit a revenue
_b._ Credit an asset	_f._ Credit common stock	_j._ Credit a revenue
_c._ Debit a liability	_g._ Debit dividends	_k._ Debit an expense
_d._ Credit a liability	_h._ Credit dividends	_l._ Credit an expense

E2-6B. Transaction Entries Final Clean, a firm providing house-cleaning services, began business on April 1. **LO5**
The following accounts in its general ledger are needed to record the transactions for April: Cash; Accounts Receivable; Supplies; Prepaid Van Lease; Equipment; Accounts Payable; Notes Payable; Common Stock; Retained Earnings; Dividends; Cleaning Fees Earned; Wage Expense; Advertising Expense; and Fuel Expense.

    _a._ Using the accounting equation, record each of the transactions in columnar format.
    _b._ Use journal entries to record the following transactions for April in the general journal.

April	1	Randy Smith invested $14,000 cash to begin the business; he received common stock for his investment.
	2	Paid six months' lease on a van, $2,850.
	3	Borrowed $10,000 from a bank and signed a note payable agreeing to repay the $10,000 in one year plus 10 percent interest.
	3	Purchased $5,500 of cleaning equipment; paid $2,000 down with the remainder due within 30 days.
	4	Purchased cleaning supplies for $4,300 cash.
	7	Paid $350 for newspaper advertisements to run during April.
	21	Billed customers for services, $3,500
	23	Paid $1,500 on account to cleaning equipment firm (see April 3 transaction).
	28	Collected $2,300 from customers on account.
	29	Randy Smith received a $1,000 cash dividend.
	30	Paid wages for April, $1,750.
	30	Paid service station for gasoline used during April, $350.

E2-7B. Source Documents For each transaction in E2-6B, indicate the related source document or documents that provide evidence supporting the transaction. **LO5**

E2-8B. Nature of Accounts, Debit and Credit Rules For each of the accounts listed below, indicate whether **LO4, 5**
the account is increased by a debit or a credit:

Accounts Receivable	Common Stock
Supplies Expense	Dividends
Cash	Building
Equipment	Professional Fees Earned

E2-9B. Nature of Accounts, Debit and Credit Rules In the three columns, enter _debit_ or _credit_ to describe **LO4, 5**
the journal entry necessary to increase and decrease the account shown to the left, and indicate which
side of the account represents its normal balance.

	Increase	Decrease	Normal Balance
Cash	_____	_____	_____
Accounts payable	_____	_____	_____
Common stock	_____	_____	_____
Retained earnings	_____	_____	_____
Fee revenue	_____	_____	_____
Wage expense	_____	_____	_____

LO4, 5   **E2-10B. Nature of Accounts, Debit and Credit Rules** For each of the accounts listed below, indicate whether the account is increased by a debit or a credit:

Accounts Receivable	Notes Payable
Sales Revenue	Retained Earnings
Equipment	Inventory
Common Stock	Rent Expense

LO2, 4   **E2-11B. Transaction Analysis** Match each of the following transactions of R. Couche & Company, a printing company, with the appropriate letters, indicating the debits and credits to be made. The key for letters follows the list of transactions. The correct answer for Transaction (1) is given as an illustration:

		Answer
1.	Stockholders contributed cash to the business.	*a, f*
2.	Purchased inventory on account.	_____
3.	Received and immediately paid a utility bill.	_____
4.	Purchased supplies for cash.	_____
5.	Borrowed money from a bank, giving a note payable.	_____
6.	Billed customers for services rendered.	_____
7.	Made a partial payment on account.	_____
8.	Paid employee's salary.	_____
9.	Collected amounts due from customers billed in Transaction 6.	_____

Financial Effect of Transaction

a.	Debit an asset	*e.*	Debit common stock	*h.*	Credit a revenue
b.	Credit an asset	*f.*	Credit common stock	*i.*	Debit an expense
c.	Debit a liability	*g.*	Debit a revenue	*j.*	Credit an expense
d.	Credit a liability				

LO5, 6   **E2-12B. Transaction Analysis and the Trial Balance** Make T-accounts for the following accounts that appear in the general ledger of Matt Langley, an attorney: Cash; Accounts Receivable; Office Equipment; Legal Database Subscription; Accounts Payable; Common Stock; Dividends; Legal Fees Earned; Salaries Expense; Rent Expense; and Utilities Expense. Using the accounting equation, record each of the transactions in columnar format. Prepare journal entries and record the following October transactions in the T-accounts and key all entries with the number identifying the transaction. Determine the balance in each account and prepare a trial balance as of October 31.

1   Langley started his law practice by contributing $18,000 cash to the business on October 1; he received common stock for his investment.
2   Purchased office equipment on account, $14,000.
3   Paid office rent for October, $700.
4   Paid $12,500 to access online legal database for two years.
5   Billed clients for services rendered, $11,300.
6   Made $6,000 payment on account for the equipment purchased on October 2.
7   Paid legal assistant's salary, $3,100.
8   Collected $9,400 from clients previously billed for services.
9   Received invoice for October utilities, $250; it will be paid in November.
10   The firm paid stockholders $1,500 cash as a dividend.

LO5, 6   **E2-13B. Transaction Analysis and Trial Balance** Make T-accounts for the following accounts that appear in the general ledger of The Canine Hospital, owned by Kali Wells, a veterinarian: Cash; Accounts Receivable; Supplies; Office Equipment; Accounts Payable; Common Stock; Dividends; Professional Fees Earned; Salaries Expense; and Rent Expense. Using the accounting equation, record each of the transactions in columnar format. Prepare journal entries and record the following December transactions in the T-accounts and key all entries with the number identifying the transaction. Finally, determine the balance in each account and prepare a trial balance as of December 31.

1 Wells opened a checking account on December 1 at Biltmore Bank in the name of The Canine Hospital and deposited $31,000 cash; Wells received common stock for her investment.
2 Paid rent for December, $2,750.
3 Purchased office equipment on account, $2,900.
4 Purchased supplies for cash, $1,800.
5 Billed clients for services rendered, $8,300.
6 Paid secretary's salary, $1,950.
7 Paid $1,500 on account for the equipment purchased on December 3.
8 Collected $4,900 from clients previously billed for services.
9 The firm paid stockholders $1,500 cash as a dividend.

E2-14B. The Account The following transactions occurred during January, the first month of operations for Red Corporation. Prepare journal entries and create a T-account for inventory that includes the following five transactions. (*Hint:* When inventory is sold, it should be expensed to a Cost of Goods Sold expense account.) **LO3**

1. Purchased $1,100 of inventory on account.
2. Purchased $1,800 of inventory on account.
3. Sold inventory with an original cost of $450.
4. Purchased $1,100 of inventory on account.
5. Sold inventory with an original cost of $1,750.

E2-15B. Recording Transactions with the Accounting Equation During the year, the Fletcher Company experienced the following accounting transactions: **LO2**

1. Purchased equipment with cash in the amount of $130,000.
2. Purchased supplies on account in the amount of $16,500.
3. Collected $37,000 cash from customers.
4. Paid a cash dividend of $17,000.

Using the accounting equation, record each of the transactions in columnar format using the following template:

Assets				=	Liabilities	+	Stockholders' Equity
Cash +	Accounts Receivable	+ Supplies +	Equipment =		Accounts Payable	+	Retained Earnings

E2-16B. Posting Transactions to T-accounts Using the data from E2-15B, (a) prepare journal entries and (b) post your transactions to the appropriate T-accounts. **LO5**

PROBLEMS—SET A

P2-1A. Transaction Analysis The accounting equation of L. Lee & Company as of the beginning of the accounting period is given below, followed by seven transactions whose effects on the accounting equation are shown. Describe each transaction that occurred. Of the transactions affecting Retained Earnings, transaction (e) had no effect on net income for the period. **LO2**

	Cash	+	Accounts Receivable	+	Supplies	=	Accounts Payable	+	Notes Payable	+	Common Stock	+	Retained Earnings
Balance	$4,100	+	$9,000	+	$700	=	$800	+	$2,500	+	$2,000	+	$8,500
(a)	+8,000		−8,000										
(b)	−400				+400								
(c)			+7,000										+7,000
(d)	−750						−750						
(e)	−4,900												−4,900
(f)	−300				+300								
(g)	+2,200								+2,200				

LO2   P2-2A.   Transaction Analysis An analysis of the transactions of Pruitt Detective Agency for the month of May appears below. Line 1 summarizes the company's accounting equation data as of May 1; lines 2–10 represent the transactions for May:

	Cash	+	Accounts Receivable	+	Supplies	+	Equipment	=	Accounts Payable	+	Notes Payable	+	Common Stock	+	Retained Earnings
(1)	$2,400	+	$7,600	+	$1,500	+	$8,000	=	$300	+	$6,000	+	$10,000	+	$3,200
(2)	+2,000										+2,000				
(3)	+6,100		−6,100												
(4)					+980				+980						
(5)			+5,200												+5,200
(6)	−300								−300						
(7)	+1,500														+1,500
(8)	−800														−800
(9)	−900						+900								
(10)	−2,500										−2,500				

Required

a. Show that assets equal liabilities plus stockholders' equity as of May 1.

b. Describe the apparent transaction indicated by each line. (For example, line 2: Borrowed $2,000, giving a note payable.) If any line could reasonably represent more than one type of transaction, describe each type. Transaction (8) does not affect net income.

c. Show that assets equal liabilities plus stockholders' equity as of May 31.

LO2   P2-3A.   Transaction Analysis Grand Appraisal Service provides commercial and industrial appraisals and feasibility studies. On January 1, the assets and liabilities of the business were the following: Cash, $11,700; Accounts Receivable, $15,800; Accounts Payable, $600; and Notes Payable, $3,500. Common Stock had a balance of $18,400. Assume that Retained Earnings as of January 1 were $5,000. The following transactions occurred during the month of January:

1   Paid rent for January, $950.
2   Received $8,800 payment on customers' accounts.
3   Paid $750 on accounts payable.
4   Received $2,500 for services performed for cash customers.
5   Borrowed $5,000 from a bank and signed a note payable for that amount.
6   Billed the city $6,200 for a feasibility study performed; billed various other credit customers, $1,900.
7   Paid the salary of an assistant, $3,500.
8   Received invoice for January utilities, $410.
9   Paid $6,000 cash for employee salaries.
10 Purchased a van (on January 31) for business use, $7,200.
11 Paid $150 to bank as January interest on the outstanding notes payable.

Required

a. Set up an accounting equation in columnar form with the following individual assets, liabilities, and stockholders' equity accounts: Cash, Accounts Receivable, Van, Accounts Payable, Notes Payable, Common Stock, and Retained Earnings. Enter the January 1 balances below each item. (*Note:* The beginning Van account balance is $0.)

b. Show the impact (increase or decrease) of transactions 1–11 on the beginning balances, and total the columns to show that assets equal liabilities plus stockholders' equity as of January 31.

LO2   P2-4A.   Transaction Analysis On June 1, a group of bush pilots in Thunder Bay, Ontario, Canada, formed the Thunder Fly-In Service, Inc., by selling $80,000 of common stock for cash. The group then leased several amphibious aircraft and docking facilities, equipping them to transport campers and hunters to outpost camps owned by various resorts. The following transactions occurred during June:

1   Sold common stock for cash, $80,000.
2   Paid June rent for aircraft, dockage, and dockside office, $4,250.
3   Received invoice for the cost of a reception the firm gave to entertain resort owners, $1,600.
4   Paid for June advertising in various sports magazines, $800.

5   Paid insurance premium for June, $1,800.
6   Rendered fly-in services for various groups for cash, $26,500.
7   Billed the Canadian Ministry of Natural Resources for transporting mapping personnel, $1,900, and billed various firms for fly-in services, $14,000.
8   Paid $1,500 on accounts payable.
9   Received $13,200 on account from clients.
10   Paid June wages, $21,000.
11   Received invoice for the cost of fuel used during June, $3,500.
12   Paid a cash dividend, $4,000.

Required

a.   Set up an accounting equation in columnar form with the following column headings: Cash, Accounts Receivable, Accounts Payable, Common Stock, and Retained Earnings.
b.   Show how the June transactions affect the items in the accounting equation, and total all columns to show that assets equal liabilities plus stockholders' equity as of June 30. (*Note:* Revenues, expenses, and dividends affect Retained Earnings.)

P2-5A.   **Accounting Equation** Determine the following: **LO2**

a.   The stockholders' equity of a company that has assets of $625,000 and liabilities of $310,000.
b.   The retained earnings of a company that has assets of $725,000, liabilities of $325,000, and common stock of $225,000.
c.   The assets of a corporation that has liabilities of $375,000, common stock of $425,000, and retained earnings of $185,000.

P2-6A.   **Transaction Analysis** Following the example shown in (a) below, indicate the effects of the listed   **LO2** transactions on the assets, liabilities, and stockholders' equity of Martin Andrews & Company.

a.   Rendered legal services to clients for cash.
    ANSWER: Increase assets (Cash)
               Increase stockholders' equity (increase Revenue)
b.   Purchased office supplies on account.
c.   Andrews invested cash into the firm and received stock for his investment.
d.   Paid amount due on account for office supplies purchased in (b).
e.   Borrowed cash from a bank and signed a six-month note payable.
f.   Rendered services and billed clients.
g.   Purchased, for cash, a desk lamp for the office.
h.   Paid interest on a note payable to the bank.
i.   Received invoice for the current month's utilities.

P2-7A.   **Transaction Analysis** On October 1, Alice Rodstein started a consulting firm. The asset, liability,   **LO2** and stockholders' equity account balances <u>after</u> each of her first six transactions are shown below. Describe each of these six transactions:

	Amounts after Transaction											
	Cash	+	Accounts Receivable	+	Supplies	+	Equipment	=	Notes Payable	+	Common Stock	+	Retained Earnings
(a)	$7,000	+	$ 0	+	$ 0	+	$ 0	=	$ 0	+	$7,000	+	$ 0
(b)	5,000	+	0	+	2,000	+	0	=	0	+	7,000	+	0
(c)	8,500	+	0	+	2,000	+	0	=	3,500	+	7,000	+	0
(d)	3,000	+	0	+	2,000	+	5,500	=	3,500	+	7,000	+	0
(e)	3,000	+	1,000	+	2,000	+	5,500	=	3,500	+	7,000	+	1,000
(f)	3,400	+	600	+	2,000	+	5,500	=	3,500	+	7,000	+	1,000

P2-8A.   **Determination of Omitted Financial Statement Data** For the four unrelated situations, A–D, calcu-   **LO2** late the unknown amounts indicated by the letters appearing in each column:

	A	B	C	D
Beginning				
Assets.....................................	$28,000	$12,000	$28,000	$ (d)
Liabilities...............................	18,600	6,000	19,000	6,500
Ending				
Assets.....................................	31,000	26,000	36,000	40,000
Liabilities...............................	17,300	(b)	15,000	19,000
During the Year				
Common stock	2,000	4,500	(c)	2,500
Sales revenues...........................	(a)	28,000	18,000	24,000
Dividends	5,000	1,750	2,000	6,500
Expenses	9,000	21,000	11,000	17,000

LO2   P2-9A. Transaction Analysis Appearing below is an analysis of the June transactions for Island Consulting Services. Line 1 summarizes the company's accounting equation data as of June 1; lines 2–10 are the transactions for the month of June:

	Cash	+	Accounts Receivable	+	Supplies	+	Equipment	=	Accounts Payable	+	Notes Payable	+	Common Stock	+	Retained Earnings
(1)	$3,500	+	$6,000	+	$820	+	$9,000	=	$600	+	$3,000	+	$10,920	+	$4,800
(2)					+670				+670						
(3)							3,750				3,750				
(4)	+4,200		−4,200												
(5)			+7,800												+7,800
(6)	−600								−600						
(7)	−200				+200										
(8)	−5,500														−5,500
(9)	+2,000										+2,000				
(10)							+750						+750		

Required

a. Show that assets equal liabilities plus stockholders' equity as of June 1.

b. Describe the transaction indicated by each line. For example, line 2: Purchased supplies on account, $670. If any line could reasonably represent more than one type of transaction, describe each type.

c. Show that assets equal liabilities plus stockholders' equity as of June 30.

LO2   P2-10A. Transaction Analysis Grace Stewart began the Stewart Answering Service in December. The firm provides services for professional people and is currently operating with leased equipment. On January 1, the assets and liabilities of the business were Cash, $6,400; Accounts Receivable, $6,900; Accounts Payable, $1,600; and Notes Payable, $1,500. Assume that Retained Earnings as of January 1 were zero. The balance of Common Stock was $10,200. The following transactions occurred during the month of January:

1   Paid rent on office and equipment for January, $1,800.
2   Collected $6,000 on account from clients.
3   Borrowed $3,000 from a bank and signed a note payable for that amount.
4   Billed clients for work performed on account, $12,500.
5   Paid $1,400 on accounts payable.
6   Received invoice for January advertising, $800.
7   Paid January salaries, $3,200.
8   Paid January utilities, $430.
9   Paid stockholders a dividend of $3,600 cash.
10 Purchased a printer (on January 31) for business use, $1,400.
11 Paid $30 to the bank as January interest on the outstanding notes payable.

Required

a. Set up an accounting equation in columnar form with the following individual assets, liabilities, and stockholders' equity accounts: Cash, Accounts Receivable, Equipment, Accounts Payable, Notes Payable, Common Stock, and Retained Earnings. Enter the January 1 balances below each item. (*Note:* The beginning Equipment account balance is $0.)

b. Show the impact (increase or decrease) of the January transactions on the beginning balances, and total all columns to show that assets equal liabilities plus stockholders' equity as of January 31.

P2-11A. Transaction Analysis On December 1, Fred Allen started Job Services Inc., providing career and vocational counseling services. The following transactions took place during the month of December:

LO2

1   Allen invested $7,000 in the business, receiving common shares.
2   Paid rent for December on furnished office space, $1,750.
3   Received invoice for December advertising, $660.
4   Borrowed $16,000 from a bank and signed a note payable for that amount.
5   Received $1,200 for counseling services rendered for cash.
6   Billed certain governmental agencies and other clients for counseling services, $7,150.
7   Paid secretary's salary, $2,200.
8   Paid December utilities, $910.
9   Paid stockholders a dividend of $900 cash.
10 Purchased land for cash to use as a site for a new facility, $13,000.
11 Paid $950 to the bank as December interest on a note payable.

Required

a. Set up an accounting equation in columnar form with the following column headings: Cash, Accounts Receivable, Land, Accounts Payable, Notes Payable, Common Stock, and Retained Earnings.

b. Show how the December transactions affect the items in the accounting equation, and total all columns to show that assets equal liabilities plus stockholders' equity as of December 31.

P2-12A. Transaction Analysis and the Effect of Errors on the Trial Balance The following T-accounts contain numbered entries for the May transactions of Carol Miller, a market analyst, who opened her business on May 1:

LO4, 5, 6

	Cash		
(1)	13,000	4,800	(2)
(9)	3,150	810	(4)
		1,950	(6)
		600	(8)

	Common Stock	
	13,000	(1)

	Accounts Receivable		
(5)	6,400	3,150	(9)

	Dividends	
(8)	600	

	Office Supplies	
(3)	3,100	

	Professional Fees Earned	
	6,400	(5)

	Office Equipment	
(2)	4,800	

	Rent Expense	
(4)	810	

	Accounts Payable		
(6)	1,950	3,100	(3)
		355	(7)

	Utilities Expense	
(7)	355	

Required

a. Give a description of each of the nine numbered transactions entered in the above T-accounts. Example: (1) Carol Miller invested $13,000 of her personal funds in her business.

b. The following trial balance, prepared from Miller's data as of May 31, contains several errors. Itemize the errors and indicate the correct totals for the trial balance.

CAROL MILLER & COMPANY Unadjusted Trial Balance May 31		
	Debit	Credit
Cash.	$ 9,790	
Accounts receivable	4,250	
Office supplies	3,100	
Office equipment	4,800	
Accounts payable		$ 1,505
Common stock		13,000
Dividends		600
Professional fees earned		6,400
Rent expense	810	
Totals	$22,750	$21,505

LO4, 5, 6   **P2-13A. Transaction Analysis and Trial Balance** Pam Black owns Artsy Graphics, a firm providing designs for advertisers and market analysts. On July 1, the business's general ledger showed the following normal account balances:

Cash.	$ 6,800	Accounts payable	$ 2,100
Accounts receivable	10,700	Notes payable.	4,200
		Common stock	2,000
		Retained earnings	9,200
Total Assets	$17,500	Total Liabilities and Stockholders' Equity	$17,500

The following transactions occurred during the month of July:

1   Paid July rent, $510.
2   Collected $7,100 on account from customers.
3   Paid $1,800 installment due on the $3,300 noninterest-bearing note payable.
4   Billed customers for design services rendered on account, $18,100.
5   Rendered design services and collected cash from customers, $1,200.
6   Paid $1,400 to creditors on account.
7   Collected $12,750 on account from customers.
8   Paid a delivery service for delivery of graphics to commercial firms, $650.
9   Paid July salaries, $5,300.
10 Received invoice for July advertising expense, to be paid in August, $600.
11 Paid utilities for July, $250.
12 Paid stockholders a dividend of $2,000 cash.
13 Received invoice for supplies used in July, to be paid in August, $2,260.
14 Purchased computer for $7,000 cash to be used in the business starting next month.

Required

a.   Set up accounts for the general ledger accounts with July 1 balances and enter the beginning balances. Also provide the following accounts: Equipment; Service Fees Earned; Rent Expense; Salaries Expense; Delivery Expense; Advertising Expense; Utilities Expense; Supplies Expense; and Dividends. Prepare journal entries and record the listed transactions in the appropriate T-accounts.
b.   Prepare a trial balance as of July 31.

LO4, 5, 6   **P2-14A. Transaction Analysis and Trial Balance** Fly-In Service, Inc., operates leased amphibious aircraft and docking facilities, equipping the firm to transport campers and hunters from Vancouver, Canada, to outpost camps owned by various resorts. On August 1, the firm's trial balance was as follows:

FLY-IN SERVICE, INC. Unadjusted Trial Balance August 1		
	Debit	Credit
Cash.	$48,600	
Accounts receivable	24,000	
Accounts payable		$ 2,500
Notes payable.		3,000
Common stock		50,000
Retained earnings		17,100
Totals	$72,600	$72,600

During the month of August, the following transactions occurred:

1 Paid August rental cost for aircraft, dockage, and dockside office, $5,000.
2 Paid insurance premium for August, $1,200.
3 Paid for August advertising in various sports magazines, $1,000.
4 Rendered fly-in services for various groups for cash, $15,500.
5 Billed the Canadian Ministry of Natural Resources for services in transporting mapping personnel, $4,400.
6 Received $17,400 on account from clients.
7 Paid $2,100 on accounts payable.
8 Billed various clients for services, $16,400.
9 Paid interest on a note payable for August, $25.
10 Paid August wages, $12,800.
11 Received invoice for the cost of fuel used during August, $3,800.
12 Paid a cash dividend, $5,000.

Required

a. Set up accounts for each item in the August 1 trial balance and enter the beginning balances. Also provide accounts for the following items: Service Fees Earned, Wage Expense, Advertising Expense, Rent Expense, Fuel Expense, Insurance Expense, and Interest Expense. Prepare journal entries and record the transactions for August in the appropriate T-accounts, using the references given.

b. Prepare a trial balance as of August 31.

P2-15A. Transaction Analysis and Trial Balance Mary Baker opened a tax practice on June 1. The following accounts will be needed to record her transactions for June: Cash; Accounts Receivable; Office Supplies; Tax Library; Office Furniture and Fixtures; Accounts Payable; Notes Payable; Common Stock; Dividends; Professional Fees Earned; Rent Expense; Salaries Expense; Advertising Expense; Utilities Expense; and Interest Expense. The following transactions occurred during the month of June:

LO4, 5, 6

1 Baker opened a business checking account at a local bank, investing $13,500 in her practice in exchange for common stock.
2 Purchased office furniture and fixtures for $9,800; paid $2,800 cash and gave a note payable for the balance.
3 Purchased books and software for a tax library on account, $4,500.
4 Purchased office supplies for cash, $950.
5 Paid rent for June, $750.
6 Returned $300 of books with defective bindings. The return reduced the amount owed to the supplier.
7 Billed clients for professional services rendered, $9,200.
8 Paid $1,700 on account for the library items purchased on June 3.
9 Collected $5,900 on account from clients billed on June 7.
10 Paid June salaries, $4,900.
11 Received invoice for June advertising, to be paid in July, $300.
12 Paid stockholders $800 cash as a dividend.
13 Paid utilities for June, $160.
14 Paid interest for June on note payable, $310.

Required

a.   Prepare journal entries and record the above transactions in T-accounts, and key entries with the number of the transactions.

b.   Prepare a trial balance as of June 30.

LO4, 5, 6   **P2-16A. Transaction Analysis and the Effect of Errors on the Trial Balance**

The following T-accounts contain numbered entries for the May transactions of Gomez Corporation, an architectural firm, which opened its offices on May 1:

	Cash				Accounts Payable		
(1)	25,000	1,400	(4)	(5)	400	1,530	(3)
(10)	5,200	5,950	(7)	(8)	750	290	(9)
		750	(8)				

	Accounts Receivable				Common Stock		
(6)	8,750	5,200	(10)			25,000	(1)

	Supplies				Professional Fees Earned		
(3)	1,530	400	(5)			8,750	(6)

	Office Equipment			Rent Expense		
(2)	5,000		(4)	1,400	

	Notes Payable			Utilities Expense		
		5,000	(2)	(9)	290	

	Salaries Expense	
(7)	5,950	

Required

a.   Give a description of each of the 10 numbered transactions entered in the above accounts. Example: (1) Gomez Corporation issued common stock for cash, $25,000.

b.   The following trial balance, prepared for Gomez Corporation as of May 31, contains several errors. Itemize the errors and indicate the correct totals for the trial balance.

GOMEZ CORPORATION Unadjusted Trial Balance May 31		
	Debit	**Credit**
Cash..	$21,200	
Accounts receivable.......................................	3,550	
Supplies...	1,130	
Office equipment		$ 5,000
Accounts payable..		670
Notes payable..		50,000
Common stock		2,500
Professional fees earned		8,570
Rent expense	1,400	
Utilities expense	290	
Salaries expense	5,950	
Totals	$33,520	$66,740

LO5, 6   **P2-17A. Transaction Analysis and Trial Balance** James Green, electrical contractor, began business on May 1. The following transactions occurred during the month of May:

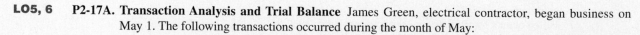

1   Green invested $15,500 of his personal funds in the business in exchange for common stock.

2   Purchased equipment on account, $4,200.

3   Returned $1,500 of equipment that was not satisfactory. The return reduced the amount owed to the supplier.

4   Purchased supplies on account, $860.

5   Purchased a truck for $9,500. Green paid $6,000 cash and gave a note payable for the balance.

6   Paid rent for May, $875.

7   Paid fuel cost for truck, $90.

8   Billed customers for services rendered, $13,700.

   9   Paid $2,500 on account for equipment purchased on May 2.
  10   Paid utilities for May, $210.
  11   Received invoice for May advertising, to be paid in June, $350.
  12   Paid employees' wages, $3,350.
  13   Collected $8,600 on accounts receivable.
  14   Paid stockholders $2,000 cash as a dividend.
  15   Paid interest for May on an outstanding note payable, $30.

Required

a.   Prepare journal entries and record the above transactions in T-accounts, and key entries with the numbers of the transactions. The following accounts will be needed to record the transactions for May: Cash; Accounts Receivable; Supplies; Equipment; Truck; Accounts Payable; Notes Payable; Common Stock; Dividends; Service Revenue; Rent Expense; Wages Expense; Utilities Expense; Truck Expense; Advertising Expense; and Interest Expense.

b.   Prepare a trial balance as of May 31.

PROBLEMS—SET B

P2-1B.   Transaction Analysis The accounting equation of Matthew Thomas, attorney, at the beginning of an accounting period is given below, followed by seven transactions whose effects on the accounting equation are shown. Describe each transaction that occurred. Of the transactions affecting retained earnings, transaction (e) had no effect on net income for the period.

LO2

	Cash	+	Accounts Receivable	+	Supplies	=	Accounts Payable	+	Notes Payable	+	Common Stock	+	Retained Earnings
Balance	$4,100	+	$9,000	+	$900	=	$1,000	+	$2,500	+	$7,500	+	$3,000
(a)	+7,500		−7,500										
(b)					+400		+400						
(c)			+8,000										+8,000
(d)	−800						−800						
(e)	−4,900												−4,900
(f)	−300				+300								
(g)	+3,200								+3,200				

P2-2B.   Transaction Analysis An analysis of the transactions of Pickett Shipping Services for the month of May appears below. Line 1 summarizes Pickett's accounting equation data as of May 1; lines 2–10 represent the transactions for the month of May:

LO2

	Cash	+	Accounts Receivable	+	Supplies	+	Equipment	=	Accounts Payable	+	Notes Payable	+	Common Stock	+	Retained Earnings
(1)	$3,500	+	$6,700	+	$2,100	+	$9,000	=	$ 700	+	$6,000	+	$4,400	+	$10,200
(2)	+3,500										+3,500				
(3)	+5,200		−5,200												
(4)					+1,500				+1,500						
(5)			+4,600												+4,600
(6)	−300								−300						
(7)	+1,900														+1,900
(8)	−800														−800
(9)	−750						+750								
(10)	−2,500										−2,500				

Required

a.   Show that assets equal liabilities plus stockholders' equity as of May 1.

b.   Describe the apparent transaction indicated by each line. (For example, line 2: Borrowed $3,500, giving a note payable.) If any line could reasonably represent more than one type of transaction, describe each type. Transaction (8) does not affect net income.

c.   Show that assets equal liabilities plus stockholders' equity as of May 31.

LO2   **P2-3B.**   **Transaction Analysis** Wesson Appraisal Service provides commercial and industrial appraisals and feasibility studies. On January 1, the assets and liabilities of the business were the following: Cash, $8,700; Accounts Receivable, $18,800; Accounts Payable, $5,200; and Notes Payable, $6,500. Assume that Retained Earnings as of January 1 were $1,000. The balance of Common Stock was $14,800. The following transactions occurred during the month of January:

1 Paid rent for January, $1,500.
2 Received $9,800 on customers' accounts.
3 Paid $900 on accounts payable.
4 Received $900 for services performed for cash customers.
5 Borrowed $8,000 from a bank and signed a note payable for that amount.
6 Billed the city $7,800 for a feasibility study performed; billed various other credit customers, $3,500.
7 Paid salary of assistant, $4,500.
8 Received invoice for January utilities, $610.
9 Paid $6,000 cash for employees salaries.
10 Purchased a van (on January 31) for business use, $9,800 cash.
11 Paid $400 to the bank as January interest on an outstanding note payable.

Required

a. Set up an accounting equation in columnar form with the following individual assets, liabilities, and stockholders' equity accounts: Cash, Accounts Receivable, Van, Accounts Payable, Notes Payable, Common Stock, and Retained Earnings. Enter January 1 balances below each item. (*Note:* The beginning Van amount is $0.)

b. Show the impact (increase or decrease) of transactions 1–11 on the beginning balances, and total the columns to show that assets equal liabilities plus stockholders' equity as of January 31.

LO2   **P2-4B.**   **Transaction Analysis** On June 1, a group of bush pilots in British Columbia, Canada, formed Adventure Airlines, Inc., by selling $51,000 of common stock for cash. The group then leased several aircraft and docking facilities, equipping them to transport campers and hunters to outpost camps owned by various resorts. The following transactions occurred during June:

1 Sold common stock for cash, $51,000.
2 Paid June rent for aircraft, dockage, and dockside office, $5,500.
3 Received invoice for the cost of a reception the firm gave to entertain resort owners, $3,100.
4 Paid for June advertising in various sports magazines, $1,900.
5 Paid insurance premium for June, $2,750.
6 Rendered services for various groups for cash, $25,000.
7 Billed the Canadian Ministry of Natural Resources for transporting mapping personnel, $4,900, and billed various firms for services, $16,750.
8 Paid $1,200 on accounts payable.
9 Received $14,200 on account from clients.
10 Paid June wages, $16,000.
11 Received an invoice for the cost of fuel used during June, $3,500.
12 Paid a cash dividend, $6,000.

Required

a. Set up an accounting equation in columnar form with the following column headings: Cash, Accounts Receivable, Accounts Payable, Common Stock, and Retained Earnings.

b. Show how the June transactions affect the items in the accounting equation, and total all columns to show that assets equal liabilities plus stockholders' equity as of June 30.

LO2   **P2-5B.**   **Accounting Equation** Determine the following:

a. The stockholders' equity of a company that has assets of $480,000 and liabilities of $360,000.

b. The retained earnings of a company that has assets of $625,000, liabilities of $225,000, and common stock of $165,000.

c. The assets of a corporation that has liabilities of $500,000, common stock of $350,000, and retained earnings of $255,000.

LO2   **P2-6B.**   **Transaction Analysis** Following the example shown in (a) below, indicate the effects of the listed transactions on the assets, liabilities, and stockholders' equity of McKay & Company:

a. Rendered services to clients for cash.
ANSWER: Increase assets (Cash)
          Increase stockholders' equity (increase Revenue)

   b.   Invested cash in the firm in exchange for common stock.
   c.   Purchased a document scanner on account.
   d.   Borrowed cash from a bank and signed a nine-month note.
   e.   Paid amount due on account for scanner purchased in (*c*).
   f.   Rendered services and billed clients.
   g.   Paid stockholders a cash dividend.
   h.   Paid interest on note payable to bank.
   i.   Received payment from clients billed in (*f*).

P2-7B. **Transaction Analysis** On October 1, Deloitte & Coopers Price started a consulting firm. The asset,   **LO2**
liability, and stockholders' equity account balances **after** each of the firm's first six transactions are
shown below. Describe each of these six transactions.

	Cash	+	Accounts Receivable	+	Supplies	+	Equipment	=	Notes Payable	+	Common Stock	+	Retained Earnings
(a)	$7,000	+	$ 0	+	$ 0	+	$ 0	=	$ 0	+	$7,000	+	$ 0
(b)	4,500	+	0	+	2,500	+	0	=	0	+	7,000	+	0
(c)	7,500	+	0	+	2,500	+	0	=	3,000	+	7,000	+	0
(d)	1,400	+	0	+	2,500	+	6,100	=	3,000	+	7,000	+	0
(e)	1,400	+	1,750	+	2,500	+	6,100	=	3,000	+	7,000	+	1,750
(f)	2,950	+	200	+	2,500	+	6,100	=	3,000	+	7,000	+	1,750

P2-8B. **Determination of Omitted Financial Statement Data** For the four unrelated situations, A–D, be-   **LO2**
low, calculate the unknown amounts indicated by the letters appearing in each column:

	A	B	C	D
Beginning				
Assets..	$40,000	$12,000	$28,000	$ (d)
Liabilities....................................	18,600	5,200	10,000	9,000
Ending				
Assets..	30,000	36,000	41,000	37,000
Liabilities....................................	17,300	(b)	13,000	15,000
During the Year				
Common stock............................	2,000	6,100	(c)	3,500
Revenues....................................	(a)	28,000	18,000	24,000
Dividends....................................	5,000	1,500	2,000	6,500
Expenses....................................	9,500	21,000	11,000	18,500

P2-9B. **Transaction Analysis** Appearing below is an analysis of the June transactions for Fisk Communica-   **LO2**
tions Company. Line 1 summarizes the company's accounting equation data as of June 1; lines 2–10
are the transactions for June:

	Cash	+	Accounts Receivable	+	Supplies	+	Equipment	=	Accounts Payable	+	Notes Payable	+	Common Stock	+	Retained Earnings
(1)	$3,500	+	$5,200	+	$1,100	+	$12,000	=	$600	+	$3,000	+	$11,200	+	$7,000
(2)					+670				+670					
(3)							+6,000				+6,000			
(4)	+6,000		−6,000											
(5)			+7,800											+7,800
(6)	−600								−600					
(7)	−200				+200									
(8)	−4,600													−4,600
(9)	+3,000										+3,000			
(10)	−500						+500							

   Required
   a.   Show that assets equal liabilities plus stockholders' equity as of June 1.
   b.   Describe the apparent transaction indicated by each line. For example, line 2: Purchased supplies
        on account, $670. If any line could reasonably represent more than one type of transaction, de-
        scribe each type.
   c.   Show that assets equal liabilities plus stockholders' equity as of June 30.

LO2 **P2-10B. Transaction Analysis** Torrey Peoples began the Peoples Word Processing Service in December. The firm provides word-processing services for businesses and is currently operating with leased equipment. On January 1, the assets and liabilities of the business were Cash, $6,400; Accounts Receivable, $7,500; Accounts Payable, $900; and Notes Payable, $3,500. Assume that Retained Earnings as of January 1 were zero. Common Stock balance was $9,500. The following transactions occurred during the month of January:

1   Paid rent on office and equipment for January, $1,100.
2   Collected $8,200 on account from clients.
3   Borrowed $5,000 from a bank and signed a note payable for that amount.
4   Billed clients for work performed on account, $9,150.
5   Paid $600 on accounts payable.
6   Received invoice for January advertising, $750.
7   Paid January salaries, $3,750.
8   Paid January utilities, $230.
9   Paid stockholders a dividend in the amount of $3,100.
10   Purchased a printer (on January 31) for business use, $1,750.
11   Paid $150 to bank as January interest on the outstanding notes payable.

Required

a.   Set up an accounting equation in columnar form with the following individual assets, liabilities, and stockholders' equity accounts: Cash, Accounts Receivable, Equipment, Accounts Payable, Notes Payable, Common Stock, and Retained Earnings. Enter the January 1 balances below each item. (*Note:* The beginning Equipment amount is $0.)

b.   Show the impact (increase or decrease) of the January transactions on the beginning balances, and total all columns to show that assets equal liabilities plus stockholders' equity as of January 31.

LO2 **P2-11B. Transaction Analysis** On December 1, Molly Frick started Advancement Career Services, which provides career and vocational counseling services to individuals. The following transactions took place during the month of December:

1   Frick invested $10,000 in the business in exchange for common stock.
2   Paid rent for December on furnished office space, $1,250.
3   Received invoice for December advertising, $600.
4   Borrowed $27,000 from a bank and signed a note payable for that amount.
5   Received $4,200 for counseling services rendered for cash.
6   Billed certain governmental agencies and other clients for counseling services, $9,800.
7   Paid secretary's salary, $2,700.
8   Paid December utilities, $370.
9   Paid stockholders a dividend in the amount of $900.
10   Purchased land for cash to use as a site for the company's future offices, $28,000.
11   Paid $100 to the bank as December interest on the outstanding notes payable.

Required

a.   Set up an accounting equation in columnar form with the following column headings: Cash, Accounts Receivable, Land, Accounts Payable, Notes Payable, Common Stock, and Retained Earnings.

b.   Show how the December transactions affect the items in the accounting equation, and total all columns to show that assets equal liabilities plus stockholders' equity as of December 31.

LO4, 5, 6 **P2-12B. Transaction Analysis and the Effect of Errors on the Trial Balance** The following T-accounts contain numbered entries for the May transactions of Valerie Vance, who opened a consulting services business on May 1:

	Cash				Common Stock	
(1)	20,000	4,800	(2)		20,000	(1)
(9)	3,700	810	(4)			
		1,950	(6)			
		600	(8)			

	Accounts Receivable				Dividends	
(5)	6,700	3,700	(9)	(8)	600	

	Office Supplies			Professional Fees Earned	
(3)	4,000				6,700	(5)

Office Equipment			Rent Expense	
(2)	4,800		(4)	810

Accounts Payable				Utilities Expense	
(6)	1,950	4,000	(3)	(7)	510
		510	(7)		

Required

a. Give a description of each of the nine numbered transactions entered in the above accounts. Example: (1) Valerie Vance invested $20,000 of her personal funds in the business in exchange for common stock.

b. The following trial balance, prepared for Rankine's firm as of May 31, contains several errors. Itemize the errors and indicate the correct totals for the trial balance.

VANCE CONSULTING SERVICES Unadjusted Trial Balance May 31		
	Debit	**Credit**
Cash.	$15,450	
Accounts receivable	4,000	
Office supplies	4,000	
Office equipment	4,800	
Accounts payable		$ 2,560
Common stock		20,000
Dividends		600
Professional fees earned		6,700
Rent expense	810	
Totals	$29,060	$29,860

P2-13B. **Transaction Analysis and Trial Balance** Ashley Conners owns La Jolla Art Company, a firm providing designs for advertisers, market analysts, and others. On July 1, the business's general ledger showed the following normal account balances:

LO4, 5, 6

Cash.	$14,500	Accounts payable	$ 2,100
Accounts receivable	9,800	Notes payable.	7,000
		Common stock	11,200
		Retained earnings	4,000
Total assets.	$24,300	Total liabilities and stockholders' equity	$24,300

The following transactions occurred during the month of July:

1   Paid July rent, $670.
2   Collected $8,100 on account from customers.
3   Paid $3,500 installment due on the $7,000 noninterest-bearing note payable to a relative.
4   Billed customers for design services rendered on account, $21,000.
5   Rendered design services and collected cash from customers, $1,400.
6   Paid $1,900 to creditors on account.
7   Collected $16,500 on account from customers.
8   Paid a delivery service for delivery of graphics to commercial firms, $400.
9   Paid July salaries, $4,600.
10 Received invoice for July advertising expense, to be paid in August, $620.
11 Paid utilities for July, $350.
12 The business paid a $2,000 cash dividend.
13 Received invoice for supplies used in July, to be paid in August, $1,575.
14 Purchased a computer for $4,300 cash to be used in the business starting next month.

Required

a. Set up accounts for the general ledger accounts with July 1 balances and enter the beginning balances. Also provide the following accounts: Equipment; Dividends; Service Fees Earned; Rent Expense; Salaries Expense; Delivery Expense; Advertising Expense; Utilities Expense; and

Supplies Expense. Prepare journal entries and record the listed transactions in the appropriate T-accounts.

b. Prepare a trial balance as of July 31.

LO4, 5, 6   **P2-14B. Transaction Analysis and Trial Balance** Great Outdoors Airlines, Inc., operates leased amphibious aircraft and docking facilities, equipping the firm to transport campers and hunters from British Columbia, Canada, to outpost camps owned by various resorts. On August 1, the firm's trial balance was as follows:

GREAT OUTDOORS AIRLINES, INC. Unadjusted Trial Balance August 1	Debit	Credit
Cash	$ 88,600	
Accounts receivable	23,200	
Accounts payable		$ 1,700
Notes payable		6,000
Common stock		83,000
Retained earnings		21,100
Totals	$111,800	$111,800

During August the following transactions occurred:

1   Paid August rental cost for aircraft, dockage, and dockside office, $8,100.
2   Paid the insurance premium for August, $2,800.
3   Paid for August advertising in various sports magazines, $1,500.
4   Rendered services for various groups for cash, $15,900.
5   Billed the Canadian Ministry of Natural Resources for services in transporting mapping personnel, $5,100.
6   Received $21,000 on account from clients.
7   Paid $1,700 on accounts payable.
8   Billed various clients for services, $19,400.
9   Paid interest on an outstanding note payable for August, $95.
10 Paid August wages, $14,800.
11 Received invoice for the cost of fuel used during August, $5,600.
12 Paid a cash dividend, $2,500.

Required

a. Set up accounts for each item in the August 1 trial balance and enter the beginning balances. Also provide similar accounts for the following items: Service Fees Earned, Dividends, Wages Expense, Advertising Expense, Rent Expense, Fuel Expense, Insurance Expense, and Interest Expense. Create journal entries and record the transactions for August in the appropriate T-accounts, using the references given.

b. Prepare a trial balance as of August 31.

LO4, 5, 6   **P2-15B. Transaction Analysis and Trial Balance** Bill Williams opened a tax practice (Bill Williams, Tax Accounting, Inc.) on June 1. The following accounts will be needed to record the business's transactions for June: Cash; Accounts Receivable; Office Supplies; Tax Library; Office Furniture and Fixtures; Accounts Payable; Notes Payable; Common Stock; Dividends; Professional Fees Earned; Rent Expense; Salaries Expense; Advertising Expense; Utilities Expense; and Interest Expense. The following transactions occurred in June:

1   Williams opened a business checking account at a local bank, investing $22,000 in his practice in exchange for common stock.
2   Purchased office furniture and fixtures for $9,800; paid $4,800 cash and gave a note payable for the balance.
3   Purchased books and software for a tax library on account, $6,700.
4   Purchased office supplies for cash, $390.
5   Paid rent for June, $850.

6   Returned $300 of books with defective bindings. The return reduced the amount owed to the supplier.
7   Billed clients for professional services rendered, $18,600.
8   Paid $1,700 on account for the library items purchased on June 3.
9   Collected $17,250 on account from clients billed on June 7.
10   Paid June salaries, $4,900.
11   Received an invoice for June advertising, to be paid in July, $400.
12   The business paid stockholders a cash dividend of $800.
13   Paid utilities for June, $210.
14   Paid interest for June on an outstanding note payable, $160.

Required

a. Prepare journal entries and record the above transactions in T-accounts, and key entries with the numbers of the transactions.

b. Prepare a trial balance from the general ledger as of June 30.

P2-16B. Transaction Analysis and the Effect of Errors on the Trial Balance   LO4, 5, 6

The following T-accounts contain numbered entries for the May transactions of the Upland Corporation, an architectural firm, which opened its offices on May 1:

Cash					Accounts Payable			
(1)	50,000	1,610	(4)	(5)	440	1,280	(3)
(10)	5,200	5,950	(7)	(8)	1,000	290	(9)
		1,000	(8)				

Accounts Receivable			
(6)	8,750	5,200	(10)

Common Stock		
	50,000	(1)

Supplies			
(3)	1,280	440	(5)

Professional Fees Earned		
	8,750	(6)

Office Equipment	
(2)	5,000

Rent Expense	
(4)	1,610

Notes Payable		
	5,000	(2)

Utilities Expense	
(9)	290

Salaries Expense	
(7)	5,950

Required

a. Give a description of each of the 10 numbered transactions entered in the above accounts. Example: (1) Upland Corporation issued common stock for cash, $50,000.

b. The following trial balance, prepared for Upland Corporation as of May 31, contains several errors. Itemize the errors and indicate the correct totals for the trial balance.

UPLAND CORPORATION
Unadjusted Trial Balance
May 31

	Debit	Credit
Cash	$46,460	
Accounts receivable	3,550	
Supplies	840	
Office equipment		$ 5,000
Accounts payable		130
Notes payable.		50,000
Common stock		50,000
Professional fees earned		8,570
Rent expense	1,610	
Utilities expense	290	
Salaries expense	5,950	
Totals	$58,700	$113,700

LO5, 6   **P2-17B.   Transaction Analysis and Trial Balance** Huff & Company, Electrical Contractors began operations on May 1. The following transactions occurred during the month of May:

1   Stockholders invested $65,000 in the business in exchange for common stock.
2   Purchased equipment on account, $4,200.
3   Returned $200 of equipment that was not satisfactory. The return reduced the amount owed to the supplier.
4   Purchased supplies on account, $940.
5   Purchased a truck for $12,500. The company paid $5,500 cash and gave a note payable for the balance.
6   Paid rent for May, $875.
7   Paid fuel cost for truck, $60.
8   Billed customers for services rendered, $15,700.
9   Paid $4,400 on account for equipment purchased on May 2.
10 Paid utilities for May, $210.
11 Received invoice for May advertising, to be paid in June, $280.
12 Paid employees' wages, $5,350.
13 Collected $8,600 on accounts receivable.
14 The company paid stockholders a dividend of $2,500 cash.
15 Paid interest for May on an outstanding note payable, $75.

Required

a.   Create journal entries and record the above transactions in T-accounts, and key entries with the numbers of the transactions. The following accounts will be needed to record the transactions for May: Cash; Accounts Receivable; Supplies; Equipment; Truck; Accounts Payable; Notes Payable; Common Stock; Dividends; Service Revenue; Rent Expense; Wages Expense; Utilities Expense; Truck Expense; Advertising Expense; and Interest Expense.

b.   Prepare a trial balance as of May 31.

SERIAL PROBLEM: KATE'S CARDS

(Note: This is a continuation of the Serial Problem: Kate's Cards from Chapter 1.)

SP2.   In September, Kate incorporated Kate's Cards after investigating different organizational forms, and began the process of getting her business up and running. The following events occurred during the month of September:

1.   Kate deposited $10,000 that she had saved into a newly opened business checking account. She received common stock in exchange.
2.   Kate designed a brochure that she will use to promote her greeting cards at local stationery stores.
3.   Kate paid Fred Simmons $50 to critique her brochure before undertaking her final design and printing.
4.   Kate purchased a new iMac computer tablet, specialized graphic arts software, and a commercial printer for the company, paying $4,800 in cash. She decided to record all of these items under the same equipment account.
5.   Kate purchased supplies such as paper and ink for $350 at the local stationery store. She opened a business account with the store and was granted 30 days credit on all purchases, including the one she just made.
6.   Kate designed her first five cards and prepared to show them to potential customers.
7.   The owner of the stationery store where Kate opened her account was impressed with Kate's work and ordered 1,000 of each of the five card designs at a cost of $1 per card, or $5,000 total. Kate tells the customer that she will have them printed and delivered within the week.
8.   Kate purchased additional supplies, on account, in the amount of $1,500.
9.   Kate delivered the 5,000 cards. Because the owner knows that Kate is just starting out, he paid her immediately in cash. He informed her that if the cards sell well that he will be ordering more, but would expect a 30-day credit period like the one he grants to his own business customers.
10. The cost to Kate for the order was $1,750 of the supplies she had purchased. (*Hint:* This cost should be recorded as a debit to an expense called Cost of Goods Sold.)
11. Kate paid her balance due for the supplies in full.

12. Kate purchased a one-year insurance policy for $1,200, paying the entire amount in cash. (*Hint:* Two accounts will need to be debited here, one for the current month expense and one for the prepaid amount.)

13. Kate determined that all of her equipment will have a useful life of 4 years (48 months), at which time it will not have any resale or scrap value. (*Hint:* Kate will expense 1/48th of the cost of the equipment each month to Depreciation Expense. The credit will be to Accumulated Depreciation.)

14. Kate paid herself a salary of $1,000 for the month.

15. Kate paid rent expense for the month in the amount of $1,200.

Required

a. Prepare a general ledger with the following accounts: Cash; Accounts Receivable; Supplies Inventory; Prepaid Insurance; Equipment; Accumulated Depreciation; Accounts Payable; Common Stock; Retained Earnings; Sales Revenue; Cost of Goods Sold; Consulting Expense; Insurance Expense; Depreciation Expense; Wages Expense; Rent Expense. Prepare journal entries for the above transactions using these accounts.

b. Post the accounting transactions for the month of September to the general ledger T-accounts.

c. Prepare a trial balance for Kate's Cards as of September 30.

EXTENDING YOUR KNOWLEDGE

REPORTING AND ANALYSIS

EYK2-1. **Financial Reporting Problem: Columbia Sportswear Company** The financial statements for the **Columbia Sportswear Company** can be found in Appendix A at the end of this book. The following selected accounts, in thousands, are from those statements:

COLUMBIA
SPORTSWEAR
COMPANY

Common stock	$ 20,165
Accounts payable	206,697
Accounts receivable	452,945
Inventories	556,530
Prepaid expenses and other current assets	54,197
Property, plant, and equipment	309,792
Net sales	2,501,554

Required

a. For each of these accounts, indicate whether a debit or a credit is required to increase its balance.

b. What other account is likely involved when:
   1. Accounts receivable is increased?   3. Net sales are increased?
   2. Accounts payable is decreased?

EYK2-2. **Comparative Analysis Problem: Columbia Sportswear Company vs. Under Armour, Inc.** The financial statements for the **Columbia Sportswear Company** can be found in Appendix A and **Under Armour, Inc.**'s financial statements can be found in Appendix B at the end of this book.

COLUMBIA
SPORTSWEAR
COMPANY

UNDER ARMOUR, INC.

Required

a. Each of the following accounts is listed in the company's financial statements:

	Columbia Sportswear		Under Armour, Inc.
1	Accounts receivable	1	Inventories
2	Property, plant, and equipment	2	Income tax expense
3	Accounts payable	3	Long-term debt
4	Common stock	4	Retained earnings
5	Interest income	5	Cost of goods sold

Determine the normal balance (debit or credit) for each of the accounts listed above.

b. Identify the probable other account involved when:

1. Cost of goods sold is increased.	3. Accounts receivable is decreased.
2. Interest income is increased.	4. Income taxes payable is increased.

EYK2-3.   Business Decision Problem

Mary Hernandez operates the Wildlife Image Gallery, selling original art and signed prints received on consignment (rather than purchased) from recognized wildlife artists throughout the country. The firm receives a 30 percent commission on all art sold and remits 70 percent of the sales price to the artist. All art is sold on a cash basis.

Mary began the business on March 1. She received a $20,000 loan from a relative to help her get started. Mary signed a note agreeing to repay the loan in one year. No interest is being charged on the loan, but the relative does expect to receive a set of financial statements each month. On April 1, Mary asks for your help in preparing the financial statements for the first month.

Mary has carefully kept the firm's checking account up to date and provides you with the following complete listing of the cash receipts and disbursements for March:

Cash Receipts	
Original investment by Mary Hernandez in exchange for common stock	$ 6,500
Loan from relative	20,000
Sales of art	95,000
Total cash receipts.	$121,500
Cash Disbursements	
Payments to artists for sales made.	$ 56,500
Payment of March rent for gallery space	900
Payment of March staff wages	4,900
Payment of airfare for personal vacation of Mary Hernandez (vacation will be taken in April) . . .	500
Total cash disbursements	62,800
Cash balance, March 31.	$ 58,700

Mary also gives you the following documents she has received:

1. A $350 invoice for March utilities; payment is due by April 15.
2. A $1,700 invoice from Careful Express for the shipping of the artwork sold during March; payment is due by April 10.
3. The one-year lease she signed for the gallery space; as an incentive to sign the lease, the landlord reduced the first month's rent by 25 percent; the monthly rent starting in April is $1,200.

In your discussions with Mary, she tells you that she has been so busy that she is behind in sending artists their share of the sales proceeds. She plans to catch up within the next week.

Required

From the above information, prepare the following financial statements for Wildlife Image Gallery: (a) income statement for the month of March; (b) statement of stockholders' equity for the month of March; and (c) balance sheet as of March 31. To obtain the data needed, you may wish to use T-accounts to construct the company's accounts.

EYK2-4.   Financial Analysis Problem   Tim Johnson runs a local photography studio, Action Images, Inc. Action Images is organized as a corporation. Tim's primary sources of revenue are the events he is contracted to photograph, mostly sporting events, and photography lessons given at a local community college. Most of Tim's photographic event customers pay him soon after they receive an invoice from Tim, approximately one week after the event, although in some cases Tim receives payment on the day of the event. The community college pays Tim at the end of each month that he teaches a class. Tim maintains the following accounts to account for these revenue transactions: Cash, Accounts Receivable, Photographic Revenue, and Teaching Revenue.

Tim leases the studio where he does most of his work. He owns all his equipment, which consists of cameras, lenses, lighting, a computer, printer, furniture, and miscellaneous office equipment. These assets are accounted for in the following accounts: Photographic Equipment, Office Equipment, and Furniture.

Tim does most of the work himself, but he does employ part-time help on days of his photo events, and he also employs a part-time bookkeeper. Most months Tim has expenses for the studio rent, utilities, advertising, supplies, and insurance. The following accounts are used to account for these expenses: Rent Expense, Utilities Expense, Salaries Expense, Advertising Expense, Supplies Expense, and Insurance Expense.

Tim pays himself a monthly salary. In addition, if his business does well, he will receive a dividend from Action Images. The following stockholders' equity accounts are maintained by Tim: Common Stock and Retained Earnings.

During the month of November, Tim hired a new bookkeeper while his regular bookkeeper was away on vacation. The new bookkeeper was inexperienced, and Tim is concerned that things may not have been recorded correctly. He has asked you to review the following transactions. For each transaction, Tim provides you with the account, the amount either debited or credited, and an explanation for the transaction. In each case, the explanation is correct.

	Account	Debit	Credit
1	Cash	5,000	
	Photographic revenue		5,000
	Issued common stock in exchange for cash.		
2	Cash	2,000	
	Teaching revenue		2,000
	Received $2,000 from the community college for course taught.		
3	Cash	4,500	
	Accounts receivable		5,400
	Received $4,500 from customers for work done last month.		
4	Supplies expense	1,600	
	Cash		1,600
	Purchase of a new camera for $1,600.		
5	Rent expense	3,000	
	Cash		3,000
	To pay the month's rent on the studio.		
6	Supplies expense	150	
	Accounts receivable		150
	Purchased printing supplies on account.		
7	Salaries expense	3,000	
	Cash		3,000
	Paid the salaries for the month.		

Required

a. For each entry, state if it is correct. If the entry is in error, make the necessary correction.

b. Will any of the errors cause the trial balance to be out of balance?

c. What effect did the errors have on Tim's net income for November?

CRITICAL THINKING

EYK2-5. **Accounting Research Problem** Go to this book's website and locate the annual report of General Mills, Inc. for the year ending May 31, 2020 (fiscal year 2020).

GENERAL MILLS, INC.

Required

1. For each of the income statement accounts, indicate the normal balance.

2. For each of the balance sheet accounts, indicate the normal balance.

EYK2-6. **Accounting Communication Activity** Jason Timmons is struggling with some accounting concepts and has come to you for help. In particular he does not understand what is meant by a debit and a credit. He was especially confused when he learned that sometimes debits result in account increases and sometimes debits result in account decreases.

Required

Write a short memorandum to Jason that explains what is meant by debits and credits as it applies to accounts used by a company.

EYK2-7.   **Accounting Ethics Case** Devon Myers and his supervisor are sent on an out-of-town assignment by their employer. At the supervisor's suggestion, they stay at the Spartan Inn, across the street from the Luxury Inn. After three days of work, they settle their lodging bills and leave. On the return trip, the supervisor gives Devon what appears to be a copy of a receipt from the Luxury Inn for three nights of lodging. Actually, the supervisor indicates that he prepared the Luxury Inn receipt on his office computer and plans to complete his expense reimbursement request using the higher lodging costs from the Luxury Inn.

Required

What are the ethical considerations that Devon faces when he prepares his expense reimbursement request?

EYK2-8.   **Environmental, Social, and Governance Problem** The Global Reporting Initiative (GRI) is a network-based organization that has pioneered the development of the world's most widely used sustainability reporting framework. The GRI website is located at http://www.globalreporting.org/. Go to the GRI website and find one of the member firms of the GRI Community (Reporting Support > GRI Community > Member directory). Select any listed member and go to their website to find their Corporate Responsibility Report. What are some of the areas the company reports on, and what measures do they use?

Required

Go to the GRI website and select Disclosure Database, https://database.globalreporting.org/search/. Use the Search feature to select a report of one of the listed firms. What are some of the areas that the company reports on, and what measures do they use?

EYK2-9.   **Forensic Accounting Problem** Accrual accounting is based on the idea that revenue should be recognized when earned and that any resources consumed in the revenue-generating process (expenses) should be matched with those revenues in the same period. Another basic principle on which GAAP is based is that of the accounting period. This principle sets the time period for which the revenues and expenses are to be measured and matched. For many firms, this date is December 31. Revenues earned after December 31 are to be reported in the following period, and expenses in the following period are then matched to those revenues. One way that companies have been found to misrepresent their reported performance is to violate these principles by "holding the books open" beyond December 31. In other words, the firm will improperly record revenue earned after year-end as if it were earned in the current year, and at the same time, fail to properly match the expenses associated with those revenues. How might a forensic accountant who has been hired to investigate improper financial reporting catch this type of activity?

EYK2-10.   **IFRS Financial Statements** Thomson Reuters is a global information company created by the 2008 merger of the Thomson Corporation, a Canadian company, with the Reuters Company, a United Kingdom–based company. The company operates in over 100 countries and has over 50,000 employees. The company provides financial, legal, scientific, and tax information services to the public on a fee basis. The shares of Thomson Reuters are listed on the New York Stock Exchange and the Toronto Stock Exchange. The company prepares its financial statements using IFRS but also reconciles this information to various non-IFRS measures. You can view the company's financial statements and the Canadian GAAP-IFRS reconciliation at www.thomsonreuters.com.

Required

1. What are the advantages of having a single, global set of accounting standards like IFRS?
2. A competitor of Thomson Reuters is U.S.-based Bloomberg L.P, a closely held financial software, news, and data company founded by Michael Bloomberg, former mayor of New York City. Bloomberg prepares its financial statements using U.S. GAAP. What constraints would you face in trying to compare the financial results of Thomson Reuters to Bloomberg?

EYK2-11. Working with the Takeaways

Part A

Each of the following accounts from the Canam Company has a normal balance as of December 31, the end of Canam's first year of operations.

Cash.	$ 100	Common stock	$1,500
Accounts receivable	300	Dividends	100
Inventory.	250	Sales revenue.	800
Property, plant, and equipment.	1,750	Selling expenses	300
Accounts payable	150	Administrative expenses.	50
Notes payable.	400		

Required

Prepare a trial balance for Canam Company as of December 31.

Part B

Landers Distributors was formed to serve as a distributor of fine furnishings imported from overseas manufacturers. Assume the following trial balance was prepared as of December 31, at the end of Landers' first year of operations:

LANDERS DISTRIBUTORS Unadjusted Trial Balance December 31		
	Debit	**Credit**
Cash.	$ 23,000	
Accounts receivable	4,500	
Buildings.	75,500	
Equipment	20,500	
Inventory.	38,000	
Accounts payable		$ 5,500
Notes payable.		47,750
Common stock		45,000
Dividends	6,000	
Sales revenue.		280,250
Wage expense	100,000	
Selling expenses	31,000	
Rent expense	23,000	
Administrative expenses.	15,750	
Tax expense	23,000	
Totals	$360,250	$378,500

It is apparent that there is an error somewhere in the company's accounts since the sum of the debit account balances ($360,250) does not equal the sum of the credit account balances ($378,500). After further research, we learn the following:

1. A cash purchase of $20,000 in inventory, occurring near year-end, was not recorded.
2. By mistake, $10,000 that should have been recorded as Accounts Payable was recorded as Notes Payable.
3. A credit of $16,000 was accidentally recorded in the Wage Expense account rather than in Sales Revenue.
4. A sale on account of $18,750 was correctly recorded as Sales Revenue, but the other side of the entry was mistakenly never recorded.

Required

a.   Which of the four errors, if any, is the reason that the trial balance is not in balance?
b.   Which of the errors, if any, must be corrected?
c.   Prepare a corrected trial balance.

ANSWERS TO SELF-STUDY QUESTIONS:

1. d　2. a　3. b　4. c　5. b　6. d　7. b　8. c　9. d　10. a　11. d　12. d　13. d　14. a　15. c　16. d
17. (1) b, (2) e, (3) d, (4) a, (5) c

YOUR TURN! SOLUTIONS

Solution 2.1

d, b, e, a, c

Solution 2.2

		Cash	+	Accounts Receivable	+	Equipment	=	Accounts Payable	+	Notes Payable	+	Common Stock	+	Retained Earnings
a.		$ 5,000	+	$ 5,200	+	$ 0	=	$1,000	+	$2,500	+	$5,500	+	$1,200
b.	(1)	−600						−600						
	(2)	−3,600												−3,600
	(3)			+11,500										+11,500
	(4)							+500						−500
	(5)	+10,000		−10,000										
	(6)	−2,400												−2,400
	(7)							+680						−680
	(8)	−20												−20
	(9)	−900												−900
	(10)	−4,000				+4,000								
		$ 3,480	+	$ 6,700	+	$4,000	=	$1,580	+	$2,500	+	$5,500	+	$4,600

$14,180

$14,180

Solution 2.3

a. Debit
b. Credit
c. Debit
d. Credit

e. Debit
f. Credit
g. Debit

Solution 2.4

+	Accounts Receivable (A)	−
(8)	3,740	2,400　(10)
Bal.	1,340	

Solution 2.5

1.

		Assets				Liabilities		Equity			
									Retained Earnings		
	Cash	+ Accounts Receivable	+ Office Supplies	=	Accounts Payable	+ Revenues	− Expenses	− Dividends	
a.	$ 1,300					$1,300			Service revenue
b.	−2,400						−2,400		Wages expense
c.	600	−600							
d.	−400							−400	Dividends
e.			700		700				
f.		900				900			Service revenue
g.	−500				−500				

2.   *a.*   Cash (+A)   1,300

                  Service revenue (+R, +SE)   1,300

                  Revenue payment for services rendered.

   b.   Wages expense (+E, −SE)   2,400

                  Cash (−A)   2,400

                  Paid employee wages.

   c.   Cash (+A)   600

                  Accounts receivable (−A)   600

                  Received payment from clients.

   d.   Dividends (+D, −SE)   400

                  Cash (−A)   400

                  Paid cash dividend.

   e.   Office supplies (+A)   700

                  Accounts payable (+L)   700

                  Purchased office supplies on account.

   f.   Accounts receivable (+A)   900

                  Service revenue (+R, +SE)   900

                  Billed clients for services rendered.

   g.   Accounts payable (−L)   500

                  Cash (−A)   500

                  Paid suppliers.

3.

+	Cash (A)	−			+	Accounts Receivable (A)	−
(a)	1,300	2,400	(b)		(f)	900 600	(c)
(c)	600	400	(d)				
		500	(g)				

+	Office Supplies (A)	−			−	Accounts Payable (L)	+
(e)	700				(g)	500 700	(e)

−	Service Revenue (R)	+			+	Wages Expense (E)	−
		1,300	(a)		(b)	2,400	
		900	(f)				

+	Dividends (D)	−
(d)	400	

Solution 2.6

Devin Company Unadjusted Trial Balance December 31	Debit	Credit
Cash...	$ 1,500	
Accounts receivable...................................	4,500	
Inventory..	3,750	
Property, plant, and equipment.......................	11,250	
Accounts payable......................................		$ 2,250
Notes payable...		6,000
Common stock..		7,500
Dividends...	1,500	
Sales revenue...		12,000
Salary expense..	4,500	
Administrative expenses...............................	750	
Totals..	$27,750	$27,750

Chapter 3
Accrual Basis of Accounting

Road Map

LO	Learning Objective	Page	eLecture	Guided Example	Assignments
LO1	Explain the accrual basis of accounting.	3-3	E3-1	YT 3.1	SS4, SS7, SE2, E6A, E7A, E6B, E7B
LO2	Describe the adjusting process.	3-7	E3-2	YT 3.2	SS6, SE3
LO3	Illustrate deferral adjustments.	3-8	E3-3	YT 3.3	SS1, SE4, SE5, SE6, SE7, E2A, E3A, E9A, E10A, E2B, E3B, E9B, E10B, P1A, P2A, P3A, P4A, P5A, P6A, P7A, P12A, P13A, P1B, P2B, P3B, P4B, P5B, P6B, P7B, P12B, P13B
LO4	Illustrate accrual adjustments.	3-11	E3-4	YT 3.4	SS2, SE6, SE7, E1A, E2A, E3A, E9A, E10A, E1B, E2B, E3B, E9B, E10B, P1A, P2A, P3A, P4A, P5A, P6A, P7A, P12A, P13A, P1B, P2B, P3B, P4B, P5B, P6B, P7B, P12B, P13B
LO5	Explain the adjusted trial balance and use it to prepare financial statements.	3-15	E3-5	YT 3.5	SE8, SE10, E4A, E4B, P8A, P10A, P11A, P12A, P13A, P14A, P15A, P16A, P17A, P18A, P8B, P10B, P11B, P12B, P13B, P14B, P15B, P16B, P17B, P18B
LO6	Describe the closing process and summarize the accounting cycle.	3-19	E3-6	YT 3.6, 3.7	SS3, SS1, SE9, E5A, E8A, E11A, E5B, E8B, E11B, P8A, P9A, P13A, P8B, P9B, P12A, P12B
LO7	Appendix 3A: Describe the process of closing to the Income Summary account and summarize the accounting cycle.	3-26	E3-7	YT 3A.1, 3A.2	SE11, E12A, E13A, E15A, E12B, E13B, E15B, P18A, P19A, P18B, P19B
LO8	Appendix 3B: Explain how to use a worksheet in the adjusting and closing process.	3-30	E3-8		SE12, E14A, E16A, E14B, E16B, P20A, P20B

Salesforce is a cloud-based software company that provides a customer relationship management (CRM) platform that helps a company's sales, marketing, service, IT, and commerce groups manage customers. In 2020, *Fortune* magazine ranked Salesforce sixth in its listing of the "100 Best Companies to Work For." This ranking is likely the result of its strong corporate culture based on the concept of "Ohana," a Hawaiian term meaning family.

While CRM is not generally associated with the accounting department, that does not mean the department cannot benefit greatly from Salesforce. Salesforce's technology helps a company's various departments, including accounting, better communicate with each other using its Chatter networking cloud and other communication tools. In addition, Salesforce helps the company create reports and presentations. These reports and presentations are enhanced by Saleforce's information tracking features. In this chapter, we begin to explore the primary reports that the accounting department creates—the financial statements.

PAST

Chapter 2 explained how we analyze and record transactions (the first two steps in the *accounting cycle*), including the system of debits and credits.

PRESENT

This chapter completes our examination of the final three steps in the five-step accounting cycle: adjust, report, and close.

FUTURE

Chapter 4 examines the balance sheet and income statement more closely and introduces techniques for analyzing and interpreting financial statements.

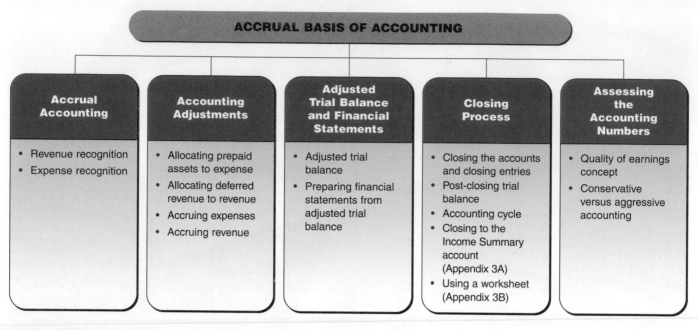

ACCRUAL BASIS OF ACCOUNTING

LO1 Explain the accrual basis of accounting.

Most individuals, and some small businesses, measure their financial performance by looking at their cash flow. For example, an individual is likely to evaluate her financial well-being in terms of her available cash. If she ends the period with a higher cash balance than she started with, she is likely to conclude that she generated a profit.

The cash basis of accounting is not considered generally accepted for most businesses. Generally accepted accounting principles require that companies use the accrual basis of accounting. The accrual basis of accounting requires a business to measure and report its operating performance regardless of whether all revenues have been collected in cash and all expenses have been paid with cash.

Revenue Recognition Principle

Under the cash basis of accounting, the receipt and payment of cash are the determining factors for when sales revenue is recognized and when expenses are deducted. Under the accrual basis of accounting, sales revenue is recognized as the amount the seller expects to be paid for the transfer of promised goods or services to customers. The selling company needs to apply the following five steps to determine the proper revenue to recognize:

1. Identify the contract with a customer.
2. Identify the performance obligations (or promises) in the contract.
3. Determine the transaction price.
4. Allocate the transaction price to the performance obligations in the contract.
5. Recognize revenue at the point the performance obligations have been satisfied.

For most businesses, this means that sales revenue is recognized at the time that goods and services are delivered to the customer. Revenue may be recognized before, after, or at the same time that cash is received.

Revenue Recognized *When* Cash Is Received

For most sales, **Krispy Kreme** will receive cash at the same time that the customer receives donuts. Under these circumstances, accrual accounting recognizes sales revenue at the same time that the company receives payment for its product. As a consequence, Krispy Kreme will debit Cash and credit Sales Revenue.

April 30	Cash (+A)	100		A = L + SE
	Sales revenue (+R, +SE)		100	+100 + 100 Rev.
	To record revenue at time of cash receipt.			

Revenue Recognized *Before* Cash Is Received

Safeway purchases large quantities of Krispy Kreme donuts for resale in its grocery stores. Assume that Safeway agrees to pay for the donuts thirty days after delivery. Even though Krispy Kreme has not received payment for the delivered donuts, the company has satisfied their performance obligation, and consequently, Krispy Kreme will recognize the sales revenue prior to cash collection. In this case, it will debit Accounts Receivable and credit Sales Revenue at the time of the sale. The subsequent collection of cash on the account does not result in sales revenue being recognized.

April 30	Accounts receivable (+A)	100		A = L + SE
	Sales revenue (+R, +SE)		100	+100 + 100 Rev.
	To recognize revenue earned.			
May 30	Cash (+A)	100		A = L + SE
	Accounts receivable (−A)		100	+100
	To recognize cash received.			−100

Revenue Recognized *After* Cash Is Received

Assume that Albertsons prepays for its donut purchases by giving Krispy Kreme a cash payment prior to receiving any donuts. Even though Krispy Kreme has received cash, it has not delivered the donuts, and thus, will defer the recognition of sales revenue until it does. Krispy Kreme will record a liability account, Unearned Revenue, for the cash received. When the donuts are delivered to Albertsons, it will recognize the revenue.

April 30	Cash (+A)	100		A = L + SE
	Unearned revenue (+L)		100	+100 +100
	To recognize the receipt of cash prior to revenue being earned.			
May 30	Unearned revenue (−L)	100		A = L + SE
	Sales revenue (+R, +SE)		100	−100 + 100 Rev.
	To recognize earned revenue.			

As these examples demonstrate, the timing of revenue recognition is determined by the revenue recognition principle, and not the timing of the cash collection.

Concept ➞	Method ➞	Assessment	TAKEAWAY 3.1
When should sales revenue be recognized?	Apply the five steps of the revenue recognition process.	Early recognition of revenue overstates current period revenue; recognizing revenue too late understates current period revenue.	

PRINCIPLE ALERT   Revenue Recognition

Applying the revenue recognition principle can be quite straightforward for simple situations such as the sale of a dozen donuts at a Krispy Kreme store. More complex situations, however, can lead to more difficulty in applying the five-step revenue recognition process. For example, when Xerox Corp. sells a laser printer along with a three-year maintenance agreement as part of a packaged deal, the five-step process would be applied as follows:

Step 1: Identify the contract with the customer. The revenue recognition standard treats every revenue transaction as a contract between the seller to provide goods or services and the buyer to provide payment to the seller. Contracts may be informal and implicit, such as the contract to purchase a dozen donuts from Krispy Kreme, or formal and explicit, such as a written contract to purchase a laser printer with a maintenance agreement from Xerox.

continued

continued from previous page

Step 2: Identify the separate performance obligations in the contract. Every contract requires the seller to perform at least one performance obligation, while some contracts may require multiple obligations. The purchase of a dozen donuts simply requires Krispy Kreme to deliver to the buyer the donuts in exchange for payment from the buyer. In contrast, the contract with Xerox contains two performance obligations: (1) the delivery of a laser printer and (2) the maintenance of the laser printer over a three-year period.

Step 3: Determine the transaction price. The transaction price is the amount the seller expects to receive for satisfying the performance obligations in the contract. The transaction price is easy to compute for the dozen donuts from Krispy Kreme. It is simply the price Krispy Kreme charges for the donuts. Determining the transaction price in the Xerox contract is more complex because it must be allocated between the two performance obligations in the contract, as discussed in the following step.

Step 4: Allocate the transaction price to the separate performance obligations in the contract. Step 4 is quite easy in the case of single performance obligation contracts such as the donut sale. Krispy Kreme simply allocates the entire transaction price to the sale of the donuts. A more complex allocation is necessary for the Xerox contract with two performance obligations. A widely used method in a contract like this is for Xerox to base the allocation on the price that would be charged for each performance obligation if they were sold separately.

For example, assume the contract with Xerox is for $15,000. Further assume that if sold separately the two performance obligations in the contract would be priced as follows:

Laser printer	$12,000
Maintenance agreement	4,000
Total	$16,000

The $15,000 transaction price would be allocated $11,250 to the sale of the laser printer and $3,750 to the sale of the maintenance agreement as follows:

$$\text{Laser printer} = \text{Transaction price} \times \frac{\text{Separate price of printer}}{\text{Total separate prices of printer and maintenance agreement}}$$

$$\text{Laser printer} = \$15,000 \times \frac{\$12,000}{\$16,000} = \$11,250$$

$$\text{Maintenance agreement} = \text{Transaction price} \times \frac{\text{Separate price of maintenance agreement}}{\text{Total separate prices of printer and maintenance agreement}}$$

$$\text{Maintenance agreement} = \$15,000 \times \frac{\$4,000}{\$16,000} = \$3,750$$

Step 5: Recognize revenue at the point the performance obligations have been satisfied. The seller should recognize revenue separately as each performance obligation is satisfied. In the simple Krispy Kreme example, revenue would be recognized by Krispy Kreme at the time the donuts are delivered to the buyer. In the more complex example, Xerox will recognize revenue for the sale of the laser printer at the time the buyer takes possession of the machine, and the revenue for the maintenance agreement over the three-year period of the agreement.

Continuing the example from above, the $11,250 revenue from the sale of the laser printer would be recognized by Xerox when it is delivered to the customer since the performance obligation is fulfilled at that point in time. The $3,750 revenue from the maintenance agreement would be recognized in the amount of $1,250 per year for each of the three years of the agreement.

Expense Recognition (Matching) Principle

Accounting requires that the expenses incurred to generate revenues be recognized in the same period. In other words, business expenses are recognized (matched) with sales revenues so that they are reported on the same income statement. Like the recognition of revenue, the recognition of expenses can occur prior to, simultaneously with, or subsequent to the payment of cash. It is the recognition of revenue, and not the payment of cash, that determines when expenses are recognized under the accrual basis of accounting.

Referring again to the Krispy Kreme example, assume the company pays $50 cash to acquire baking supplies for its donuts. A cash purchase is not considered to be a business expense until Krispy Kreme sells the donuts it produces. The cash purchase of materials prior to sale would be accounted for as a reduction of cash and an increase in supplies, both assets.

				A = L + SE
May 15	Baking supplies (+A)	50		+50
	Cash (−A)		50	−50
	To record cash payment for supplies.			

In this case, the cash payment precedes the recognition of revenue and the matching of expense. But what happens if the materials are purchased on account and used in donuts sold before Krispy Kreme pays for the baking materials? In this case, the accrual basis of accounting dictates the recognition of expense prior to the cash payment for the materials so that the expense is properly matched with the revenue recognized in the same accounting period.

				A = L + SE
May 15	Baking supplies (+A)	50		+50 +50
	Accounts payable (+L)		50	
	To record purchase of supplies on account.			

In both of the above cases, the expense for the cost of goods sold is recognized when the donuts are sold with the following journal entry:

				A = L + SE
May 15	Cost of goods sold (+E, −SE)	50		−50 −50
	Baking supplies (−A)		50	Exp.
	To record cost of product sold.			

The key point is that under accrual accounting, the recognition of expense is matched to the recognition of revenue in the same period. This may occur after the cash expenditure, before the cash expenditure, or at the same time as the cash expenditure. In addition, it should be stressed that the purpose of accrual accounting is to recognize revenues and expenses in the period the revenue is earned and the corresponding resources to earn the revenue are used rather than when cash is received or paid. Such matching would not necessarily occur under the cash basis of accounting. Ultimately, both cash-basis accounting and accrual-basis accounting will yield the same results; however, the results will likely differ period by period.

Concept ⟶	Method ⟶	Assessment	TAKEAWAY 3.2
When should expenses be recognized?	Recognize expenses with the related revenue in the same accounting period.	Early recognition of expenses overstates current period expenses; recognizing expenses too late understates current period expenses.	

YOUR TURN! 3.1

Prepare journal entries for Sawyer Enterprises for each of the following transactions on June 30.

1. Sawyer Enterprises sells $600 of merchandise to Apollo Inc. with terms of cash due in 30 days.
2. Apollo Inc. pays Sawyer Enterprises $700 for merchandise that will be delivered in 30 days.
3. Sawyer Enterprises purchases and receives inventory of $400 from its supplier Adamo Co. with terms of cash due in 45 days.

Guided Example

MBC

The solution is on page 3-65.

DATA ANALYTICS   **Salesforce Teams Up with Tableau**

Data Analytics

Salesforce is a worldwide leader in customer relationship management (CRM) software, and Tableau is a leader in data visualization software. Together they have teamed up to provide a way to discover what can be learned from a company's data. As Tableau tells it, "Tableau CRM empowers your Salesforce CRM users with actionable insights and AI-driven analytics right in their workflow." Tableau CRM is native to Salesforce, thus allowing a seamless experience for users to make decisions and to take actions based on what they have learned.

ADJUSTING ACCOUNTS

LO2 Describe the adjusting process.

eLecture

MBC

In Chapter 2, we analyzed a series of accounting transactions for WebWork, Inc., that occurred during the month of December. We prepared journal entries for those transactions and recorded them in the general journal. We then posted the company's journal entry data to the general ledger, which we set up in T-account form. Many of the general ledger account balances from Chapter 2, however, require an end-of-period adjustment to bring them to the correct balance for the preparation of WebWork's financial statements. For example, WebWork prepaid six months of rent for its office space on December 1. By December 31, one month's rent has expired. The prepaid rent account must be adjusted so that the account balance reflects the remaining amount of rent that is still prepaid and rent expense is recognized for the month of December. When it is time to prepare a company's financial statements, the company must review account balances and make any necessary end-of-period adjustments to bring those (unadjusted) accounts to their proper balance.

Unadjusted Trial Balance

The end-of-period adjustment process begins with the preparation of a trial balance of all general ledger accounts. Because this trial balance reports the account balances before any adjustments have been made, it is referred to as the **unadjusted trial balance**. An unadjusted trial balance is prepared to ensure that the general ledger is in balance before the end-of-period adjusting process begins. Accumulating all general ledger account balances in one location makes it easier to review the accounts and determine which account balances must be adjusted. The unadjusted trial balance of WebWork, Inc., as of December 31 is in **Exhibit 3-1**.

EXHIBIT 3-1	Unadjusted Trial Balance for WebWork, Inc.	

WEBWORK, INC.
Unadjusted Trial Balance
December 31, 2022

	Debit	Credit
Cash.	$40,590	
Accounts receivable	1,340	
Office supplies	2,850	
Prepaid rent	10,800	
Office equipment	32,400	
Accounts payable		$ 2,850
Unearned revenue		3,000
Notes payable.		36,000
Common stock		30,000
Dividends	500	
Fee revenue		18,250
Wage expense	1,620	
Totals	$90,100	$90,100

Types of Adjustments

There are four types of accounting adjustments made at the end of an accounting period:

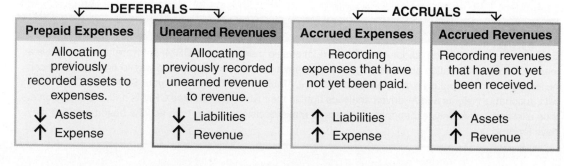

DEFERRALS		ACCRUALS	
Prepaid Expenses	**Unearned Revenues**	**Accrued Expenses**	**Accrued Revenues**
Allocating previously recorded assets to expenses.	Allocating previously recorded unearned revenue to revenue.	Recording expenses that have not yet been paid.	Recording revenues that have not yet been received.
↓ Assets	↓ Liabilities	↑ Liabilities	↑ Assets
↑ Expense	↑ Revenue	↑ Expense	↑ Revenue

Journal entries to record accounting adjustments are known as **adjusting entries**. Each adjusting entry affects one or more balance sheet accounts (an asset or liability account) and one or more income statement accounts (a revenue or expense account).

Adjustments in the first two categories—prepaid expenses and unearned revenues—are referred to as **deferrals**. The distinguishing characteristic of a deferral is that the adjustment deals with an amount that has previously been recorded, or deferred, in a balance sheet account. The adjusting entry, in effect, decreases the balance sheet account and increases an income statement account. Adjustments in the last two categories—accrued expenses and accrued revenues—are referred to as **accruals**. The unique characteristic of an accrual is that the adjustment deals with an amount that has not previously been recorded in an account. Consequently, the adjusting entry increases both a balance sheet account and an income statement account.

	YOUR TURN! 3.2
Match the transaction from the first column with the type of accounting adjustment from the second column.	The solution is on page 3-65.

1. Record depreciation for the month on buildings.
2. Record rental income for the month on equipment rented on a long-term rental agreement. Payment will be received next month.
3. Record rental income at month-end on amounts that had been received last month.
4. Record insurance expense at the end of the month for an annual policy that was previously purchased.

 a. Prepaid expenses
 b. Unearned revenue
 c. Accrued expenses
 d. Accrued revenues

ENVIRONMENTAL, SOCIAL, AND GOVERNANCE   Salesforce's Philanthropy Cloud

Salesforce has built what they call the Philanthropy Cloud as a foundation of their own corporate culture. With its success, they have now made the technology available to other companies that use the Salesforce platform. The goal of the Philanthropy Cloud is to increase the company's desired outcomes by helping them organize and track their philanthropic efforts. The Philanthropy Cloud teams with the United Way to "create a global network that connects companies and their employees to nonprofits at scale." The platform uses dashboards to display both individual and companywide efforts in achieving philanthropic goals.

DEFERRAL ADJUSTING ENTRIES

Allocating Previously Recorded Assets to Expenses

LO3

Illustrate deferral adjustments.

MBC

Prepaid Expenses

Many expenditures benefit multiple accounting periods. These expenditures must be allocated over the periods benefited. Common examples include purchases of buildings, equipment, and supplies; prepayments of rent and advertising; and prepayments of insurance premiums. Outlays for these expenditures are normally debited to an asset account at the time of payment. Then, at the end of each accounting period, the estimated portion of the expenditure that has expired, or that has been used, during the period is transferred from the asset account to an expense account to achieve a proper recognition of revenue and expenses.

These adjustments are commonly identified by inspecting the unadjusted trial balance for costs that benefit multiple accounting periods. For example, by looking at the December 31 trial balance of WebWork (**Exhibit 3-1**), we observe that adjustments are required to allocate costs of office supplies, prepaid rent, and office equipment to the current period (December) and subsequent accounting periods that benefit from these expenditures. The next three sections illustrate these adjustments.

Office Supplies
On December 1, WebWork purchased $2,850 of office supplies on account and recorded the expenditure in an asset account, Office Supplies:

A	=	L	+ SE
+2,850		+2,850	

Dec. 1	Office supplies (+A)	2,850	
	Accounts payable (+L)		2,850
	To record the purchase of office supplies.		

During December, office supplies were used as services were provided. The cost of office supplies used is an expense for December that reduces the amount of supplies available. It is unnecessary to record an expense as each individual supply item, such as a copier cartridge or LCD cleaner, is used. Instead, at the end of December, the company physically counts the supplies still available and then subtracts that amount from the total amount purchased to determine the amount used. For example, assume that a physical count of the office supplies reveals that $1,530 was available at the end of the month. This implies that $1,320 ($2,850 – $1,530) was used during December. An adjusting entry is needed to transfer this amount to an expense account, Supplies Expense, as follows:

A	= L +	SE	
–1,320		–1,320	
		Exp.	

Office Supplies

UNADJ	2,850		
		1,320	(a)
ADJ	1,530		

Supplies Expense

UNADJ	0	
(a)	1,320	
ADJ	1,530	

Dec. 31	Supplies expense (+E, –SE)	1,320	
	Office supplies (–A)		1,320
	To record expense of office supplies used in December.		

When this adjusting entry is posted, it properly shows the $1,320 December expense for office supplies and reduces the asset account, Office Supplies, to $1,530, the amount of the asset remaining as of December 31.

Prepaid Rent

On December 1, WebWork paid six months' rent in advance and debited the $10,800 payment to Prepaid Rent, an asset account. As each day passes and the rented space is occupied, rent expense is incurred, and the balance of the prepaid rent decreases. It is unnecessary to record rent expense on a daily basis because financial statements are not prepared daily; however, at the end of the accounting period, an adjusting entry is necessary to recognize the correct amount of rent expense for the period and to decrease the Prepaid Rent account. Specifically, on December 31, one month of WebWork's prepaid rent has been used; consequently, WebWork will transfer $1,800 ($10,800/6 months) from the Prepaid Rent account to the Rent Expense account, as follows:

A	= L +	SE	
–1,800		–1,800	
		Exp.	

Prepaid Rent

UNADJ	10,800		
		1,800	(b)
ADJ	9,000		

Rent Expense

UNADJ	0	
(b)	1,800	
ADJ	1,800	

Dec. 31	Rent expense (+E, –SE)	1,800	
	Prepaid rent (–A)		1,800
	To record rent expense for December.		

The posting of this adjusting entry shows the correct rent expense ($1,800) for December in the Rent Expense account and reduces the Prepaid Rent account balance to the correct balance ($9,000) that remains prepaid as of December 31. (Examples of other prepaid expenses for which similar adjustments are made include prepaid insurance and prepaid advertising.)

Depreciation

The process of allocating the cost of buildings and equipment to the periods benefiting from their use is called **depreciation**. Because these long-lived assets help generate revenue for a company over many years, each accounting period in which the assets are used must reflect a portion of their cost as an expense. The allocation of the cost of revenue-generating assets over the many periods that they help produce revenues is an application of the expense recognition principle. This periodic expense is known as *depreciation expense*.

There is no exact way to measure the amount of these assets used each period, which means that the periodic depreciation expense is an estimate. The procedure we illustrate in this chapter estimates the annual amount of depreciation expense by dividing the acquisition cost of the asset by its estimated useful life in years. This method is called **straight-line depreciation**. (We will explore other depreciation methods in a later chapter.)

When recording depreciation expense, the asset account is not reduced directly. Instead, the reduction is recorded in a contra account called **Accumulated Depreciation. Contra accounts**

Hint: A contra account is increased and decreased in the opposite way of its controlling account. Also, the normal balance of a contra account is opposite to the normal balance of its controlling account.

are so named because they are used to record reductions in, or offsets against, a controlling account. In this case, the Accumulated Depreciation contra account offsets the controlling account, Office Equipment, which has a normal debit balance. Accumulated depreciation therefore has a normal credit balance and appears in the balance sheet as a deduction against Office Equipment. Use of the contra account Accumulated Depreciation allows the original cost of the related asset to be reported in the company's balance sheet, followed by the accumulated amount of depreciation recorded to date. Users of financial statements want to see both of these amounts so that they can estimate how much of an asset has been used and how much remains to benefit the business in future periods.

To illustrate, assume that the office equipment purchased by WebWork for $32,400 is expected to last six years. Straight-line depreciation is $5,400 per year ($32,400/6 years), or $450 per month ($5,400/12 months). At the end of December, WebWork would make the following adjusting entry:

Dec. 31	Depreciation expense (+E, –SE)	450	
	Accumulated depreciation—Office equipment (+XA, –A)		450
	To record December depreciation expense.		

$$A = L + SE$$
$$-450 \qquad -450 \text{ Exp}$$

Accumulated Depreciation—Office Equipment

		0	UNADJ
		450	(c)
		450	ADJ

Depreciation Expense

| UNADJ (c) | 0 450 | | |
| ADJ | 450 | | |

When the preceding adjusting entry is posted, it shows the estimated cost of using the asset during December as an expense of $450 in the company's December income statement. On the balance sheet, the accumulated depreciation is subtracted from the related asset account (Office Equipment). The resulting balance (acquisition cost less accumulated depreciation) is called the asset's **book value** and represents the unexpired asset cost to be applied as an expense against future periods. For example, the December 31 balance sheet shows WebWork's office equipment with a book value of $31,950, presented as follows:

A.K.A. Book value is also called **carrying value.**

Office equipment	$32,400
Less: Accumulated depreciation	450
Office equipment, net	$31,950

Allocating Previously Recorded Unearned Revenue to Revenue

Unearned Revenues

Sometimes a business receives fees for services or products before the services or products are rendered. Such transactions are initially recorded by debiting the Cash account and crediting a liability account called **Unearned Revenue.** The Unearned Revenue account is also called **Deferred Revenue** and represents an obligation to perform a service or provide a product in the future. Once the service or product is provided, the revenue is recognized. The required adjusting entry is a debit to the Unearned Revenue account, which reduces the liability account, and a credit to the Revenue account for the amount of revenue earned in the current period.

Deferred Service Revenue

On December 5, WebWork signed a four-month contract to perform work for $750 per month, with the entire contract price of $3,000 received in advance. The journal entry on December 5 is:

Dec. 5	Cash (+A)	3,000	
	Unearned revenue (+L)		3,000
	Received $3,000 advance payment on a four-month contract.		

$$A = L + SE$$
$$+3,000 \quad +3,000$$

On December 31, the following adjusting entry transfers $750 ($3,000/4 months), the revenue earned in December, to Fee Revenue, and reduces the liability Unearned Revenue by the same amount:

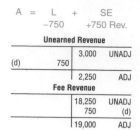

A	=	L	+	SE
		−750		+750 Rev.

Unearned Revenue

(d)	750	3,000	UNADJ
		2,250	ADJ

Fee Revenue

		18,250	UNADJ
		750	(d)
		19,000	ADJ

Dec. 31	Unearned revenue (−L)	750	
	Fee revenue (+R, +SE)		750
	To record portion of fee advance earned in December.		

After the journal entry is posted to the general ledger accounts, the liability account shows a balance of $2,250, the amount of future services still owed by WebWork, and the Fee Revenue account reflects the $750 earned in December.

Other examples of revenues received in advance include rental payments received in advance by real estate management companies, insurance premiums received in advance by insurance companies, subscription revenues received in advance by magazine and newspaper publishers, and membership fees received in advance by health and fitness clubs. In each case, a liability account is established when the prepayment is initially received. Later, an adjusting entry is made to reflect the revenues earned from the services provided or products delivered during the current accounting period.

YOUR TURN! 3.3

GuidedExample

MBC

The solution is on page 3-65.

Prepare journal entries for each of the following end-of-year accounting adjustments.

1. Record depreciation expense adjustment of $700 on the company's buildings.
2. Record $1,500 for rent expense. The company previously recorded a $2,000 advance rent payment to the landlord.

ACCRUAL ADJUSTING ENTRIES

LO4 Illustrate accrual adjustments.

eLecture

MBC

Accrued Expenses

Recording Previously Unrecorded Expenses

A company often incurs expenses before paying for them. Employee wages, utilities, and income taxes are all examples of expenses that are typically incurred by a business before payment is made. Usually the cash payments are made at regular time intervals, such as weekly, monthly, quarterly, or annually. If the accounting period ends on a date that does not coincide with a scheduled cash payment date, an adjusting entry must be recorded to reflect the expense incurred during the period. Such expenses are referred to as **accrued expenses**. WebWork has two such adjustments to make on December 31: one for its employee wages and the other for interest on its bank loan.

Accrued Wages

WebWork's employee is paid every two weeks at the rate of $810 per week. The employee was paid $1,620 on Friday, December 20. At the close of business on Friday, December 27, the employee has worked one week during December for which wages will not be paid until January. Because the employee's wages are $810 per week, an additional wage expense of $810 must be reflected in WebWork's income statement for December. The adjusting entry at the end of December to accrue one week of wage expense follows:

A	=	L	+	SE
		+ 810		−810 Exp

Wages Payable

		0	UNADJ
		810	(e)
		810	ADJ

Wage Expense

UNADJ	1,620		
(e)	810		
ADJ	2,430		

Dec. 31	Wage expense (+E, −SE)	810	
	Wages payable (+L)		810
	To record accrued wages for the final week of December.		

This adjustment enables WebWork's December income statement to show the cost of all wages *incurred* during the month rather than just the wages *paid*. Also, WebWork's balance sheet will correctly show a liability for unpaid wages at the end of December.

When the employee is paid on the next regular payday in January, WebWork must ensure that the one week of accrued wages for December is not again charged to expense. When the employee is paid $1,620 on Friday, January 3, the following entry is made:

Jan. 3	Wages payable (−L)	810	
	Wage expense (+E, −SE)	810	
	Cash (−A)		1,620
	To record two weeks wages paid.		

A	=	L	+	SE
−1,620		−810		−810
				Exp.

This entry eliminates the liability recorded in Wages Payable at the end of December and debits its January Wage Expense for only those wages earned by the employee in January.

Accrued Interest

On December 1, 2022, WebWork obtained a bank loan in the amount of $36,000 and signed a two-year note payable. The annual interest rate on the note is 10 percent, with interest payable each November 30. The amount of interest expense must be reflected in net income for the period. Interest expense (or interest revenue) is computed based on three factors: (1) the principal amount of the money borrowed (or loaned); (2) the rate of interest expressed as an annual rate; and (3) the amount of time that has passed. The first year's interest of $3,600 ($36,000 × 10 percent) is due on November 30, 2023. Because interest accumulates as time passes, an adjusting entry is needed on December 31, 2022, to reflect the interest expense for December. December's interest is $300 ($3,600/12 months), and the computation and adjusting entry at December 31 follow:

Principal Amount of Note	×	Annual Interest Rate	×	Time as a Fraction of a Year	=	Interest
$36,000	×	10%	×	1/12	=	$300

Dec. 31	Interest expense (+E, −SE)	300	
	Interest payable (+L)		300
	To record accrued interest expense for December.		

A	=	L	+	SE
		+300		−300 Exp

Interest Payable

		0	UNADJ
		300	(f)
		300	ADJ

Interest Expense

UNADJ	0		*
(f)	300		
ADJ	300		

When this adjusting entry is posted to the general ledger, the correct interest expense for December is shown as well as a liability for one month's interest that has accrued as of December 31.

When the first year's interest of $3,600 is paid on November 30, 2023, WebWork must remember that $300 of that amount relates to 2022. On November 30, 2023, the following entry records the interest payment:

Nov. 30	Interest payable (−L)	300	
	Interest expense (+E, −SE)	3,300	
	Cash (−A)		3,600
	To record payment of annual interest.		

A	=	L	+	SE
−3,600		−300		−3,300
				Exp.

This entry eliminates the interest payable that was accrued on December 31, 2022, and debits the Interest Expense account for $3,300 ($300 × 11 months), the correct interest expense for the first 11 months of 2023.

Recording Previously Unrecorded Revenues

Revenues from selling a product or providing a service must be recognized in the period in which the goods are sold or the services are performed. A company, however, may provide services during a period that are neither paid for by customers nor billed at the end of the period. The value of these services represents revenue that must be included in the current period income statement. To accomplish this, end-of-period adjusting entries are made to reflect any revenues for the period that have been earned but have not yet been paid or billed. Such accumulated revenue is often called **accrued revenue**.

Accrued Revenues

Accrued Fees

WebWork entered into a contract with a local company on December 2 that requires a December 31 adjusting entry to accrue revenue. Under the one-year contract, WebWork agreed to maintain that company's website in exchange for a monthly fee of $150, payable at the end of every three months. By December 31, WebWork has earned one month of fee revenue, and the following adjusting entry is made:

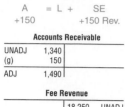

Dec. 31	Accounts receivable (+A)	150	
	Fee revenue (+R, +SE)		150
	To record accrued fee revenue earned in December.		

When WebWork receives the first $450 payment on February 28, 2023, the company must remember that $150 was previously earned and recorded in 2022. The following entry records the payment received on that date:

Feb. 28	Cash (+A)	450	
	Accounts receivable (−A)		150
	Fee revenue (+R, +SE)		300
	To record receipt of quarterly payment.		

This entry eliminates the accounts receivable established on December 31, 2022, and records $300 of fee revenue earned for the first two months of 2023.

Accrued Interest

Another example of accrued revenue involves a company that has loaned money to another entity on which interest has been earned but that has not yet been collected at the end of the accounting period. Assume WebWork loaned $2,000 to James Corporation on November 1, 2022, with annual interest at the rate of 6 percent. The loan balance, along with interest, is to be repaid one year later. On December 31, 2022, WebWork would make the following adjusting entry:

A = L + SE
+20   +20

Dec. 31	Interest receivable (+A)	20	
	Interest income (+R, +SE)		20
	To record interest earned on note.		

The $20 interest is computed as follows:

Principal Amount of Note	×	Annual Interest Rate	×	Time as a Fraction of a Year	=	Interest
$2,000	×	6%	×	2/12	=	$20

We show this entry only as an example of accrued interest. WebWork did not actually have a loan to James Corporation, so the adjustment calculated above will not be posted to the general ledger.

Summary of Accounting Adjustments

Exhibit 3-2 summarizes the adjusting entries for WebWork as recorded in its general journal. These adjustments would be posted to the company's general ledger.

EXHIBIT 3-2	Adjusting Entries for WebWork, Inc.		

GENERAL JOURNAL

Date	Description	Debit	Credit	
2022				
Dec. 31	Supplies expense (+E, −SE)	1,320		**(a)**
	Office supplies (−A)		1,320	
	To record expense of office supplies used in December.			
Dec. 31	Rent expense (+E, −SE)	1,800		**(b)**
	Prepaid rent (−A)		1,800	
	To record rent expense for December.			
Dec. 31	Depreciation expense (+E, −SE)	450		**(c)**
	Accumulated depreciation—Office equipment (+XA, −A)		450	
	To record December depreciation expense.			
Dec. 31	Unearned revenue (−L)	750		**(d)**
	Fee revenue (+R, +SE)		750	
	To record portion of fee advance earned in December.			
Dec. 31	Wage expense (+E, −SE)	810		**(e)**
	Wages payable (+L)		810	
	To record accrued wages for the final week of December.			
Dec. 31	Interest expense (+E, −SE)	300		**(f)**
	Interest payable (+L)		300	
	To record accrued interest expense for December.			
Dec. 31	Accounts receivable (+A)	150		**(g)**
	Fee revenue (+R, +SE)		150	
	To record accrued fee revenue earned in December.			

Exhibit 3-3 lists the four types of accounting adjustments and shows (1) examples of how each type of adjustment arises, (2) the generic adjusting entry for each type of adjustment, and (3) what accounts are overstated or understated *prior to* any adjustment. As we explained, each adjustment affects at least one balance sheet account (asset or liability), which we show in **blue** in Exhibit 3-3, and at least one income statement account (expense or revenue), which we show in **red**. Notice that if the adjusting entries are not properly recorded at the end of the accounting period, revenues and expenses for the period will be understated.

EXHIBIT 3-3	Four Types of Accounting Adjustments			

Accounting Adjustment	Examples	Adjusting Entry	Financial Effects If *Not* Adjusted	
			Balance Sheet	Income Statement
Deferrals ←				
Prepaid expenses	Expiration of prepaid rent, insurance, and advertising; depreciation of buildings and equipment	**Dr. Expense** **Cr. Asset** (or contra asset)	Asset overstated Equity overstated	Expense understated
Unearned revenues	Recognition of prepayments on customer orders, gift cards, and subscriptions	**Dr. Liability** **Cr. Revenue**	Liability overstated Equity understated	Revenue understated
Accruals ←				
Accrued expenses	Incurred but not yet paid amounts for wages, interest, and tax expenses	**Dr. Expense** **Cr. Liability**	Liability understated Equity overstated	Expense understated
Accrued revenues	Earned but not yet received amounts for service, sales, and interest revenues	**Dr. Asset** **Cr. Revenue**	Asset understated Equity understated	Revenue understated

Amounts that have previously been recorded in a balance sheet account.

Amounts that have not been previously recorded in an account.

TAKEAWAY 3.3	Concept ──────────▶	Method ──────────▶	Assessment
	When should an adjusting entry be made?	Inspect individual account balances and transaction details such as contracts and agreements. Determine the proper account balance. Adjustments involve (1) allocating assets to expense, (2) allocating unearned revenue to revenue, (3) accruing expenses, or (4) accruing revenues.	Record an adjusting entry so that accounts are correctly reported; otherwise, income and assets (and/or liabilities) are incorrectly reported.

YOUR TURN! 3.4

MBC

The solution is on page 3-65.

Prepare journal entries for each of the following end-of-year accounting adjustments.

1. Record $400 of revenue earned that was previously recorded as unearned revenue due to an advance payment from a customer.
2. Record $500 of accrued interest expense that applies to the company's bank loan. The $500 is part of the company's annual cash interest payment that is due next period.

ADJUSTED TRIAL BALANCE AND FINANCIAL STATEMENTS

LO5 Explain the adjusted trial balance and use it to prepare financial statements.

After the end-of-period adjustments are recorded in the general journal and posted to the general ledger, the company prepares an adjusted trial balance. The company then uses the adjusted trial balance to prepare the financial statements.

eLecture

MBC

Preparing the Adjusted Trial Balance

The **adjusted trial balance** lists all the general ledger account balances after the end-of-period adjustments have been posted. **Exhibit 3-4** presents WebWork's adjusted trial balance as of December 31 in the two right-hand columns of the exhibit. This exhibit begins with the unadjusted trial balance, shown in the two left-hand columns, and lists the seven adjustments in the middle columns. For example, Office Supplies has a $2,850 debit balance in the unadjusted trial balance. Adjusting entry (a), which is highlighted in the exhibit, credits Office Supplies for the $1,320 of supplies used in December. After the adjustment, Office Supplies has a debit balance of $1,530 in the adjusted trial balance.

This adjusting entry also affects supplies expense, as shown in the exhibit. Supplies expense has a zero balance in the unadjusted trial balance. The adjustment appears as a $1,320 debit in the adjustments column, leading to a $1,320 debit balance in the adjusted trial balance for supplies expense. Using this presentation, managers can readily see the adjustments made and their impact on the financial accounting numbers. Notice that the debit and credit columns are in balance in the unadjusted trial balance (equal to $90,100), in the adjustments (equal to $5,580), and in the adjusted trial balance (equal to $91,810). Another common format for the adjusted trial balance is to only show the two right-hand columns, as shown in **Exhibit 3-5**—either format is acceptable.

ACCOUNTING IN PRACTICE	Getting a Loan

Because of the size of many corporations like **McDonald's Corp.** and **Amazon.com Inc.**, it is easy to believe that corporations are the primary form of businesses in the United States. In reality, sole proprietorships, with a single owner, comprise about 70 percent of U.S. businesses according to the Small Business Administration (SBA). A common form of financing for these businesses is a 7(a) loan guaranteed by the SBA. While the procedures learned in this chapter needed to produce financial statements may seem like something only an accountant would need to know, this skill set is very useful for anybody applying for a loan. Listed near the top of the 7(a) loan application checklist is the preparation of personal and business financial statements.

EXHIBIT 3-4	Adjusted Trial Balance for WebWork, Inc.

WEBWORK, INC.
Adjusted Trial Balance
December 31, 2022

	Unadjusted Trial Balance		Adjustments		Adjusted Trial Balance	
	Debit	Credit	Debit	Credit	Debit	Credit
Cash..................	$40,590				$40,590	
Accounts receivable.......	1,340		(g) $ 150		1,490	
Office supplies	2,850			(a) $1,320	1,530	
Prepaid rent	10,800			(b) 1,800	9,000	
Office equipment	32,400				32,400	
Accumulated depreciation—						
Office equipment........				(c) 450		$ 450
Accounts payable.........		$ 2,850				2,850
Interest payable				(f) 300		300
Wages payable...........				(e) 810		810
Unearned revenue		3,000	(d) 750			2,250
Notes payable...........		36,000				36,000
Common stock...........		30,000				30,000
Dividends	500				500	
Fee revenue		18,250		(d) 750		19,150
				(g) 150		
Supplies expense.........			(a) 1,320		1,320	
Wage expense	1,620		(e) 810		2,430	
Rent expense			(b) 1,800		1,800	
Depreciation expense......			(c) 450		450	
Interest expense..........			(f) 300		300	
Totals	$90,100	$90,100	$5,580	$5,580	$91,810	$91,810

Preparing Financial Statements

The adjusted trial balance is used to prepare the income statement, the statement of stockholders' equity, and the balance sheet. (It is also helpful in preparing the statement of cash flows, although other information is also necessary to complete this financial statement.) We illustrate the preparation of financial statements for WebWork in **Exhibit 3-5.** Recall from Chapter 1 that financial statements are prepared in the following sequence: (1) the income statement, (2) the statement of stockholders' equity, (3) the balance sheet, and (4) the statement of cash flows.

STEP 1: Income Statement

The income statement presents a company's revenues and expenses and shows whether the company operated at a profit or a loss. WebWork's adjusted trial balance contains one revenue account and five expense accounts. The revenue and expense accounts are reported in Web-Work's income statement located in the lower right side of **Exhibit 3-5**. The income statement shows that net income for December is $12,850.

STEP 2: Statement of Stockholders' Equity

The statement of stockholders' equity reports the transactions and events causing a company's stockholders' equity to increase or decrease during an accounting period. The middle right side of **Exhibit 3-5** presents WebWork's statement of stockholders' equity for December. The stockholders' equity accounts in the general ledger provide some of the information for this statement, including the common stock and retained earnings balances at the beginning of the period, new common stock issuances, and dividends during the period. Since December was the first month of operations for WebWork, the beginning balances of the stockholders' equity accounts are equal to zero. The net income (or net loss) amount is obtained from the company's income statement.

EXHIBIT 3-5   Financial Statements Prepared from the Adjusted Trial Balance

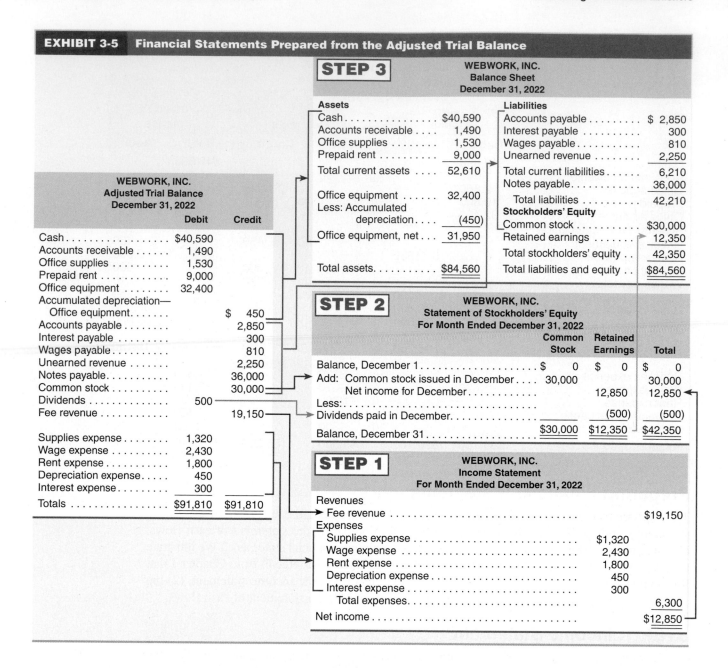

STEP 3: Balance Sheet

The balance sheet reports a company's assets, liabilities, and stockholders' equity. The assets and liabilities for WebWork as of December 31, 2022, shown in the upper right side of **Exhibit 3-5**, come from the adjusted trial balance. The $12,350 amount reported as retained earnings is taken from the statement of stockholders' equity as of December 31.

STEP 4: Statement of Cash Flows

The statement of cash flows reports information regarding a company's cash inflows and outflows. The statement of cash flows classifies cash flows into three activity categories: operating, investing, and financing. The procedures for preparing a statement of cash flows are discussed in Chapter 12.

Cassi Company has the following adjusted trial balance at December 31.

YOUR TURN! 3.5

GuidedExample

MBC

The solution is on page 3-65.

CASSI COMPANY Adjusted Trial Balance December 31		
	Debit	**Credit**
Cash.	$ 4,000	
Accounts receivable	15,000	
Inventory.	18,000	
Prepaid rent	5,000	
Equipment	50,000	
Accumulated depreciation		$ 10,000
Accounts payable		8,000
Salaries payable.		9,000
Dividends payable		2,000
Unearned revenue		5,000
Long-term debt.		35,000
Common stock		15,000
Retained earnings		5,000
Sales revenue.		52,000
Cost of goods sold	30,000	
Salaries expense	5,000	
Rent expense	6,000	
Depreciation expense.	6,000	
Dividends	2,000	
Totals	$141,000	$141,000

Required

Prepare an income statement, a statement of stockholders' equity, and a balance sheet for Cassi Company using its December 31 adjusted trial balance. There were no changes in stockholders' equity during the year other than for net income and dividends.

The following section illustrates closing temporary accounts directly to Retained Earnings. Appendix 3A presents an alternative process that closes temporary accounts using the Income Summary account. Your instructor can choose to cover either one or both processes. If the process using Retained Earnings is skipped, then read Appendix 3A and return to the section (four pages ahead) titled "Quality of Accounting Numbers."

CLOSING PROCESS

LO6 **Describe** the closing process and **summarize** the accounting cycle.

eLecture

MBC

A.K.A. The closing process is also known as **closing the books**.

All accounts can be identified as either permanent accounts or temporary accounts. **Permanent accounts** are the accounts presented on the balance sheet. They consist of the asset, liability, and stockholders' equity accounts. The distinguishing feature of a permanent account is that any balance in the account at the end of an accounting period is carried forward to the following accounting period. **Temporary accounts** are used to gather information for a particular accounting period. Revenue, expense, and dividend accounts are temporary subdivisions of stockholders' equity. At the end of the accounting period, temporary account balances are transferred to Retained Earnings, which is a permanent stockholders' equity account. The process of transferring the balances in temporary accounts to Retained Earnings is referred to as the **closing process** or **closing procedures**.

A temporary account is *closed* when an entry is made that changes its account balance to zero—that is, the entry is equal in amount to the account's ending balance but is opposite to the balance as a debit or credit. An account that is closed is said to be closed *to* the account that receives the offsetting debit or credit. Thus, a closing entry simply transfers the balance of one account to another account. Because closing entries bring temporary account balances to zero, the temporary accounts are then ready to start accumulating data for the next accounting period. In essence, closing the temporary accounts prevents information from the current accounting period from being carried forward to a subsequent period, which enables financial statement users to make meaningful comparisons of revenues and expenses from one period to the next. The following summarizes the classification of permanent and temporary accounts.

Permanent Accounts	Temporary Accounts
Assets	Revenues
Liabilities	Expenses
Common Stock	Dividends
Retained Earnings	

YOUR TURN! 3.6

The solution is on page 3-66.

Identify whether each of the following accounts is a permanent account or a temporary account:

a. Cash
b. Common Stock
c. Wage Expense
d. Notes Payable

e. Dividends
f. Sales Revenue
g. Inventory
h. Prepaid Expense

Journalizing and Posting the Closing Entries

The Retained Earnings account is used to close the temporary revenue, expense, and Dividends accounts. The closing entries occur only at the end of an accounting period and consist of three steps, which are illustrated in Exhibit 3-6.

1. **Close the revenue accounts.** Debit each revenue account for an amount equal to its current credit balance, and credit the Retained Earnings account for the total amount of revenues.

2. **Close the expense accounts.** Credit each expense account for an amount equal to its current debit balance, and debit the Retained Earnings account for the total amount of expenses.

3. **Close the Dividends account.** Debit the Retained Earnings account and credit the Dividends account for an amount equal to the balance in the Dividends account.

Closing Process for WebWork

Exhibit 3-6 illustrates the closing entries for WebWork as recorded in the company's general journal. The financial information in these entries is posted to the appropriate general ledger accounts, which is represented using T-accounts.

EXHIBIT 3-6	Closing Revenue, Expense, and Dividends Accounts—WebWork, Inc.		
GENERAL JOURNAL			
Date	**Description**	**Debit**	**Credit**
2022			
1 Dec. 31	Fee revenue (–R)	19,150	
	Retained earnings (+SE)		19,150
	To close the revenue account.		
2 Dec. 31	Retained earnings (–SE)	6,300	
	Supplies expense (–E)		1,320
	Wage expense (–E)		2,430
	Rent expense (–E)		1,800
	Depreciation expense (–E)		450
	Interest expense (–E)		300
	To close the expense accounts.		
3 Dec. 31	Retained earnings (–SE)	500	
	Dividends (–D)		500
	To close the dividends account.		

The financial effect of posting these entries on the general ledger is diagrammed below.

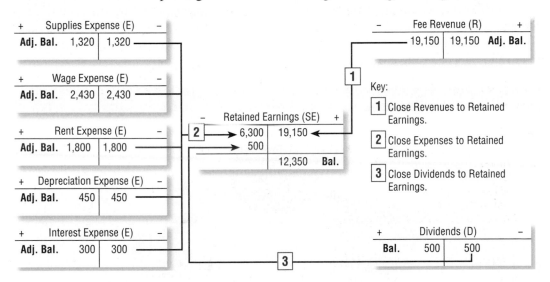

Preparing the Post-Closing Trial Balance

After closing entries are recorded in the general journal and posted to the general ledger, all of the temporary accounts have zero balances. At this point a **post-closing trial balance** is prepared. The post-closing trial balance provides evidence that the equality of debits and credits has been maintained in the general ledger throughout the adjusting and closing processes, and that the general ledger is in balance to start the next accounting period. Because the temporary accounts have been closed, only the balance sheet (or permanent) accounts appear in the post-closing trial balance. **Exhibit 3-7** presents the post-closing trial balance for WebWork.

EXHIBIT 3-7	Post-Closing Trial Balance for WebWork, Inc.

WEBWORK, INC.
Post-Closing Trial Balance
December 31, 2022

	Debit	Credit
Cash	$40,590	
Accounts receivable	1,490	
Office supplies	1,530	
Prepaid rent	9,000	
Office equipment	32,400	
Accumulated depreciation—Office equipment		$ 450
Accounts payable		2,850
Interest payable		300
Wages payable		810
Unearned revenue		2,250
Notes payable		36,000
Common stock		30,000
Retained earnings		12,350
Totals	$85,010	$85,010

Summary of the Accounting Cycle

The sequence of accounting procedures known as the *accounting cycle* occurs each fiscal period and represents a systematic process for accumulating and reporting the financial data of a business. **Exhibit 3-8** summarizes the five major steps in the accounting cycle as described in this and the preceding chapter.

EXHIBIT 3-8	The Accounting Cycle: A Summary

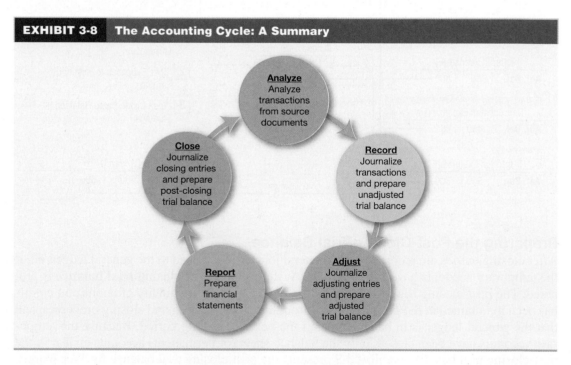

Prior to closing its books, the Morgan Company has the following balances in its temporary accounts as of December 31.

YOUR TURN! 3.7

GuidedExample

MBC

The solution is on page 3-66.

	Debit	Credit
Sales revenue.		$79,000
Cost of goods sold	$41,000	
Wage expense	22,000	
Rent expense	3,000	
Depreciation expense.	2,000	
Interest expense.	4,000	
Dividends	5,000	

Required

Prepare closing entries as of December 31 for the Morgan Company.

For readers skipping the closing process using Retained Earnings, please resume reading here.

QUALITY OF ACCOUNTING NUMBERS

Earnings quality is a phrase used to characterize the degree to which a company's financial statements reflect its true financial condition and performance. The better the statements represent the company's actual financial condition and performance, the higher a company's earnings quality is assumed to be.

While many end-of-period adjustments discussed in this chapter are based on direct calculations, such as the time remaining for a prepaid insurance policy or the interest rate on an outstanding loan, many other adjustments that we discuss in later chapters involve judgments on the part of the company's management. Examples of judgments leading to adjusting entries are the amount of future warranty work associated with a company's product, the amount of a company's accounts receivable that will not be collected, and the estimated depreciable lives of a company's plant and equipment. Each of these items involves estimates of future events that cannot be known with certainty. Consequently, each of these estimates can have a material affect on a company's reported financial results in any given period and can result in either higher or lower earnings quality for the company depending on how accurately management estimates these amounts.

Wall Street analysts often evaluate a company's quality of earnings by the degree to which these estimates are considered conservative or aggressive. Conservative estimates are those that lead to lower reported net income and net asset values, while aggressive estimates are those that result in higher reported net income and net asset values. The more conservative a company's estimates are judged to be, the higher a company's earnings quality is often assumed to be, although being overly conservative can also be viewed as a sign of low earnings quality. Investors may punish a company that is judged to have a low quality of earnings because they worry that a company using aggressive accounting estimates can surprise them with poor future performance that will cause the company's stock price to fall.

ENVIRONMENTAL, SOCIAL, AND GOVERNANCE   **Earnings Quality and ESG**

Does the stock market care about anything other than how much a company earns? Apparently so, at least according to a study by the **Center for Sustainable Business at New York University**. Based on an examination of more than 1,000 research papers, they find that a business strategy focused on ESG issues is synonymous with high-quality management and better financial performance. In addition, managers who embrace the ideals of ESG are more likely to act in a socially responsible manner to produce financial information that is transparent and reliable.

https://www.stern.nyu.edu/experience-stern/about/departments-centers-initiatives/centers-of-research/center-sustainable-business/research/research-initiatives/esg-and-financial-performance

"Is Earnings Quality Associated with Corporate Social Responsibility?" Kim, Park, and Wier, *The Accounting Review*, 2012

COMPREHENSIVE PROBLEM

Balke Laboratory began operations on July 1, 2021, and provides diagnostic services for physicians and medical clinics. The company's fiscal year ends on June 30, and the accounts are adjusted annually on this date. Balke's unadjusted trial balance as of June 30, 2023, is as follows:

BALKE LABORATORY Unadjusted Trial Balance June 30, 2023		
	Debit	**Credit**
Cash.	$ 1,000	
Accounts receivable	9,200	
Prepaid insurance.	6,000	
Supplies	31,300	
Laboratory equipment	270,000	
Accumulated depreciation—Laboratory equipment		$ 30,000
Accounts payable		3,100
Diagnostic fees received in advance		4,000
Common stock		90,000
Retained earnings		50,000
Diagnostic fees revenue		220,400
Wage expense	58,000	
Rent expense	22,000	
Totals	$397,500	$397,500

The following information is also available:

1. The Prepaid Insurance account balance represents a premium paid on January 1, 2023, for two years of fire and casualty insurance coverage. Before 2023, Balke Laboratory had no insurance protection.
2. The supplies were physically counted at June 30, 2023. The count totaled $6,300.
3. All laboratory equipment was purchased on July 1, 2021. It is expected to last nine years.
4. Balke Laboratory received a $4,000 cash payment on April 1, 2023, from Boll Clinic for diagnostic services to be provided uniformly over the four months beginning April 1, 2023. Balke credited the payment to Diagnostic Fees Received in Advance. The services for April, May, and June have been provided to Boll Clinic.
5. Unpaid wages at June 30, 2023, were $600.
6. Balke Laboratory rents facilities for $2,000 per month. Because of cash flow problems, Balke was unable to pay the rent for June 2023. The landlord gave Balke permission to delay the payment until July.

Required

a. Make the necessary adjusting entries as of June 30, 2023.
b. Prepare the adjusted trial balance as of June 30, 2023.
c. Prepare the Income Statement, Balance Sheet, and Statement of Stockholders' Equity for Balke Laboratory at June 30, 2023.
d. Make the necessary closing entries as of June 30, 2023.
e. Prepare the post-closing trial balance as of June 30, 2023.

Solution

a.

			Posting Ref.		
June 30	Insurance expense (+E, –SE)		1	1,500	
	Prepaid insurance (–A)		1		1,500
	To record 6 months' insurance expense.				
	($6,000 × 6/24 = $1,500).				
30	Supplies expense (+E, –SE)		2	25,000	
	Supplies (–A)		2		25,000
	To record supplies expense for the year.				
	($31,300 – $6,300 = $25,000).				
30	Depreciation expense—Laboratory equipment (+E, –SE)		3	30,000	
	Accumulated depreciation—Laboratory equipment (+XA, –A)		3		30,000
	To record depreciation for the year.				
	($270,000/9 years = $30,000).				
30	Diagnostic fees received in advance (–L)		4	3,000	
	Diagnostic fees revenue (+R, +SE)		4		3,000
	To record portion of advance payment that has been earned.				
	($4,000 × 3/4 = $3,000).				
30	Wage expense (+E, –SE)		5	600	
	Wages payable (+L)		5		600
	To record unpaid wages at June 30.				
30	Rent expense (+E, –SE)		6	2,000	
	Rent payable (+L)		6		2,000
	To record rent expense for June.				

b.

Balke Laboratory
Adjusted Trial Balance
June 30, 2023

	Unadjusted Trial Balance		Adjustments		Adjusted Trial Balance	
	Debit	Credit	Debit	Credit	Debit	Credit
Cash	$ 1,000				$ 1,000	
Accounts receivable	9,200				9,200	
Prepaid insurance	6,000			[1] $ 1,500	4,500	
Supplies	31,300			[2] 25,000	6,300	
Laboratory equipment	270,000				270,000	
Accumulated depreciation— Laboratory equipment		$ 30,000		[3] 30,000		$ 60,000
Accounts payable		3,100				3,100
Wages payable				[5] 600		600
Rent payable				[6] 2,000		2,000
Diagnostic fees received in advance		4,000	[4] $ 3,000			1,000
Common stock		90,000				90,000
Retained earnings		50,000				50,000
Diagnostic fees revenue		220,400		[4] 3,000		223,400
Wage expense	58,000		[5] 600		58,600	
Rent expense	22,000		[6] 2,000		24,000	
Insurance expense			[1] 1,500		1,500	
Supplies expense			[2] 25,000		25,000	
Depreciation expense— Laboratory equipment			[3] 30,000		30,000	
Totals	$397,500	$397,500	$62,100	$62,100	$430,100	$430,100

c.

Balke Laboratory
Income Statement
For the Year Ended June 30, 2023

Revenues		
Diagnostic fees revenue		$223,400
Expenses		
Wage expense	58,600	
Rent expense	24,000	
Insurance expense	1,500	
Supplies expense	25,000	
Depreciation expense	30,000	
Total expenses		139,100
Net income		$ 84,300

Balke Laboratory
Statement of Stockholders' Equity
For the Year Ended June 30, 2023

	Common Stock	Retained Earnings	Total
Balance, June 30, 2022	$90,000	$ 50,000	$140,000
Net income		84,300	84,300
Balance, June 30, 2023	$90,000	$134,300	$224,300

Balke Laboratory
Balance Sheet
June 30, 2023

Assets		Liabilities	
Cash	$ 1,000	Accounts payable	$ 3,100
Accounts receivable	9,200	Wages payable	600
Prepaid insurance	4,500	Rent payable	2,000
Supplies	6,300	Diagnostic fees received in advance	1,000
Total current assets	21,000	Total liabilities	6,700
		Stockholders' equity	
Laboratory equipment	270,000	Common stock	90,000
Less: Accumulated depreciation	(60,000)	Retained earnings	134,300
Laboratory equipment, net	210,000	Total stockholders' equity	224,300
Total assets	$231,000	Total liabilities and stockholders' equity	$231,000

d.	June 30	Diagnostic fees revenue (–R)	223,400	
		Retained earnings (+SE)		223,400
		To close the revenue account.		
		Retained earnings (–SE)	139,100	
		Wage expense (–E)		58,600
		Rent expense (–E)		24,000
		Insurance expense (–E)		1,500
		Supplies expense (–E)		25,000
		Depreciation expense—Laboratory equipment (–E)		30,000
		To close the expense accounts.		

e.

Balke Laboratory Post-Closing Trial Balance June 30, 2023	Debit	Credit
Cash.	$ 1,000	
Accounts receivable	9,200	
Prepaid insurance.	4,500	
Supplies	6,300	
Laboratory equipment	270,000	
Accumulated depreciation—Laboratory equipment		$ 60,000
Accounts payable		3,100
Wages payable.		600
Rent payable.		2,000
Diagnostic fees received in advance		1,000
Common stock		90,000
Retained earnings		134,300
Totals	$291,000	$291,000

APPENDIX 3A: Closing Process—Using Income Summary Account

All accounts can be identified as either permanent accounts or temporary accounts. **Permanent accounts** are the accounts presented on the balance sheet. They consist of the asset, liability, and stockholders' equity accounts. The distinguishing feature of a permanent account is that any balance in the account at the end of an accounting period is carried forward to the following accounting period. **Temporary accounts** are used to gather information for a particular accounting period. Revenue, expense, and dividend accounts are temporary subdivisions of stockholders' equity. At the end of the accounting period, temporary account balances are transferred to retained earnings, which is a permanent stockholders' equity account. The process of transferring the balances in temporary accounts to retained earnings is referred to as the **closing process** or **closing procedures**.

A temporary account is *closed* when an entry is made that changes its account balance to zero—that is, the entry is equal in amount to the account's ending balance but is opposite to the balance as a debit or credit. An account that is closed is said to be closed *to* the account that receives the offsetting debit or credit. Thus, a closing entry simply transfers the balance of one account to another account. Because closing entries bring temporary account balances to zero, the temporary accounts are then ready to start accumulating data for the next accounting period. In essence, closing the temporary accounts prevents information from the current accounting period from being carried forward to a subsequent period, which enables financial statement users to make meaningful comparisons of revenue and expenses from one period to the next.

A summary account can be used to close the temporary revenue and expense accounts. In this case, we use an account titled Income Summary. (Alternative titles for this account include Revenue and Expense Summary, Income and Expense Summary, and Profit and Loss Summary.) The Income Summary account is then closed to Retained Earnings. For this reason, it is also considered a temporary account. The following summarizes the classification of permanent and temporary accounts:

LO7 **Describe** the process of closing to the Income Summary account and **summarize** the accounting cycle.

eLecture
MBC

A.K.A. The closing process is also known as **closing the books**.

Permanent Accounts	Temporary Accounts
Assets	Revenues
Liabilities	Expenses
Common Stock	Dividends
Retained Earnings	Income Summary

YOUR TURN! 3A.1

The solution is on page 3-67.

For each of the following accounts, identify whether the account is either a permanent account or a temporary account:

a. Cash
b. Common Stock
c. Wage Expense
d. Notes Payable

e. Dividends
f. Sales Revenue
g. Inventory
h. Income Summary

Journalizing and Posting the Closing Entries

The closing entries occur only at the end of an accounting period and consist of four steps, which are illustrated in **Exhibit 3A-1**.

1. **Close the revenue accounts.** Debit each revenue account for an amount equal to its current credit balance, and credit the Income Summary account for the total amount of revenues.
2. **Close the expense accounts.** Credit each expense account for an amount equal to its current debit balance, and debit the Income Summary account for the total amount of expenses.

After steps 1 and 2, the balance of the Income Summary account equals the current period net income (if a credit balance) or net loss (if a debit balance).

3. **Close the Income Summary account.** In the case of net income, debit the Income Summary account and credit the Retained Earnings account for an amount equal to net income. In the case of a net loss, debit the Retained Earnings account and credit the Income Summary account for an amount equal to the net loss.
4. **Close the Dividends account.** Because dividends are not a business expense and are not included in the calculation of net income, the Dividends account is closed directly to Retained Earnings. Debit the Retained Earnings account and credit the Dividends account for an amount equal to the balance in the Dividends account.

Closing Process for WebWork

Exhibit 3A-1 illustrates the closing entries for the revenue and expense accounts for WebWork as recorded in the company's general journal. The financial information in these entries is posted to the appropriate general ledger accounts, which is represented using T-accounts.

EXHIBIT 3A-1	Closing Revenue and Expense Accounts—WebWork, Inc.		
GENERAL JOURNAL			
Date	**Description**	**Debit**	**Credit**
2022			
Dec. 31	Fee revenue (–R)	19,150	
	Income summary (+SE)		19,150
	To close the revenue account.		
Dec. 31	Income summary (–SE)	6,300	
	Supplies expense (–E)		1,320
	Wage expense (–E)		2,430
	Rent expense (–E)		1,800
	Depreciation expense (–E)		450
	Interest expense (–E)		300
	To close the expense accounts.		

After steps 1 and 2, the Income Summary account has a credit balance equal to WebWork's net income of $12,850. Steps 3 and 4 close the Income Summary account and the Dividends account to the Retained Earnings account. These two entries are recorded in WebWork's general journal in **Exhibit 3A-2**. The financial effect of posting these entries on the general ledger is diagrammed below.

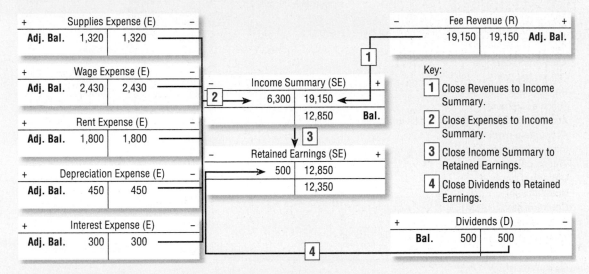

EXHIBIT 3A-2	Closing the Income Summary and Dividends Accounts—WebWork, Inc.

	GENERAL JOURNAL		
Date	**Description**	**Debit**	**Credit**
2022			
3 Dec. 31	Income summary (–SE)	12,850	
	Retained earnings (+SE)		12,850
	To close the Income Summary account.		
4 Dec. 31	Retained earnings (–SE)	500	
	Dividends (–D)		500
	To close the Dividends account.		

Preparing the Post-Closing Trial Balance

After closing entries are recorded in the general journal and posted to the general ledger, all of the temporary accounts have zero balances. At this point a **post-closing trial balance** is prepared. The post-closing trial balance provides evidence that the equality of debits and credits has been maintained in the general ledger throughout the adjusting and closing processes and that the general ledger is in balance to start the next accounting period. Because the temporary accounts have been closed, only the balance sheet (or permanent) accounts appear in the post-closing trial balance. **Exhibit 3A-3** presents the post-closing trial balance for WebWork.

EXHIBIT 3A-3   Post-Closing Trial Balance for WebWork, Inc.

WebWork, Inc.
Post-Closing Trial Balance
December 31, 2022

	Debit	Credit
Cash	$40,590	
Accounts receivable	1,490	
Office supplies	1,530	
Prepaid rent	9,000	
Office equipment	32,400	
Accumulated depreciation—Office equipment		$ 450
Accounts payable		2,850
Interest payable		300
Wages payable		810
Unearned revenue		2,250
Notes payable		36,000
Common stock		30,000
Retained earnings		12,350
Totals	$85,010	$85,010

Summary of the Accounting Cycle

The sequence of accounting procedures known as the *accounting cycle* occurs each fiscal period and represents a systematic process for accumulating and reporting the financial data of a business. **Exhibit 3A-4** summarizes the five major steps in the accounting cycle as described in this and the preceding chapter.

EXHIBIT 3A-4   The Accounting Cycle: A Summary

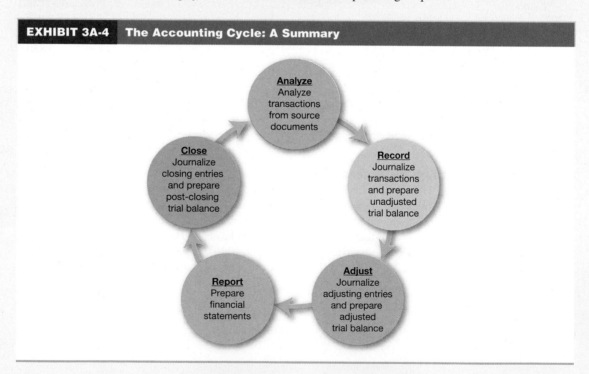

Prior to closing its books, the Morgan Company has the following balances in its temporary accounts as of December 31.

MBC

The solution is on page 3-67.

	Debit	Credit
Sales revenue.		$79,000
Cost of goods sold	$41,000	
Wage expense	22,000	
Rent expense	3,000	
Depreciation expense.	2,000	
Interest expense.	4,000	
Dividends	5,000	

Required
Prepare closing entries as of December 31 for the Morgan Company.

APPENDIX 3B: Using a Worksheet

A worksheet can be used to facilitate the adjusting and closing processes, and ultimately, the preparation of a company's financial statements. A **worksheet** is an informal document that helps accumulate the accounting information needed to prepare the financial statements. A worksheet is a tool; it is not part of a company's formal accounting records. In this section, we explain how a worksheet can be used to help compile information for a set of financial statements. Computer programs such as Microsoft Excel can simplify the preparation of a worksheet.

LO8 Explain how to use a worksheet in the adjusting and closing process.

eLecture

MBC

Preparing a Worksheet

A worksheet is prepared at that stage in the accounting cycle when it is time to adjust the accounts and prepare the financial statements. The basic structure of a worksheet is illustrated in **Exhibit 3B-1**, which includes an explanation of the format used. The worksheet is prepared in the order indicated by the numbered boxes in the exhibit.

EXHIBIT 3B-1

	1 (HEADING FOR WORKSHEET)									
	Unadjusted Trial Balance		**Adjustments**		**Adjusted Trial Balance**		**Income Statement**		**Balance Sheet**	
Description	**Debit**	**Credit**	**Debit**	**Credit**	**Debit**	**Credit**	**Debit**	**Credit**	**Debit**	**Credit**
	2 Unadjusted trial balance Accounts that arise for adjustments		**3** Adjustment amounts		**4** Adjusted account balances		**5** Classify adjusted balances into either the income statement or the balance sheet columns			
							6 Balancing of columns for each statement			

1 Heading The worksheet *heading* includes (1) the name of the entity, (2) the term *Worksheet* to indicate the type of analysis being performed, and (3) a date describing the period covered. The worksheet includes both income statement data (for the period described) and balance sheet data (for the end of the period described).

Exhibit 3B-2 illustrates the heading for WebWork's worksheet. The worksheet has a description column and 10 amount (monetary) columns. A set of Debit and Credit columns is provided for each of the five headings: Unadjusted Trial Balance, Adjustments, Adjusted Trial Balance, Income Statement, and Balance Sheet.

2 Unadjusted Trial Balance   The unadjusted trial balance is the starting point for the accounting analysis on the worksheet. It is entered in the worksheet's description column and the first pair of monetary columns. Once the trial balance is entered in the worksheet and double-ruled, it reflects the general ledger at the time the worksheet is prepared. **Exhibit 3B-2** shows the worksheet placement of WebWork's unadjusted trial balance as of December 31, 2022.

3 Adjustments   When a worksheet is used, all adjustments are first entered on the worksheet. This procedure permits the adjustments to be reviewed for completeness and accuracy. To adjust accounts already appearing in the unadjusted trial balance, we simply enter the amounts in the appropriate side (debit or credit) of the adjustments columns on the lines containing the accounts. When accounts not appearing in the unadjusted trial balance require adjustment, their titles are listed as needed in the Description column below the accounts already listed. Adjustments entered on the worksheet are not yet journalized; journalizing the adjustments occurs later. The adjustments recorded on WebWork's worksheet in **Exhibit 3B-2** are identical to those illustrated in the chapter (see **Exhibit 3-2**). After recording all the adjusting entries on the worksheet, we total the adjustments columns to verify that the sum of the debit entries equals the sum of the credit entries.

EXHIBIT 3B-2

WEBWORK, INC.
Worksheet
For Month Ended December 31, 2022

	Unadjusted Trial Balance Debit	Unadjusted Trial Balance Credit	Adjustments Debit	Adjustments Credit	Adjusted Trial Balance Debit	Adjusted Trial Balance Credit	Income Statement Debit	Income Statement Credit	Balance Sheet Debit	Balance Sheet Credit
Cash..............	$40,590				$40,590				$40,590	
Accounts receivable	1,340		(g) $ 150		1,490				1,490	
Office supplies	2,850			(a) $1,320	1,530				1,530	
Prepaid rent	10,800			(b) 1,800	9,000				9,000	
Office equipment	32,400				32,400				32,400	
Accumulated depreciation— Office equipment.....				(c) 450		$ 450				$ 450
Accounts payable......		$ 2,850				2,850				2,850
Interest payable				(f) 300		300				300
Wages payable........				(e) 810		810				810
Unearned revenue		3,000	(d) 750			2,250				2,250
Notes payable........		36,000				36,000				36,000
Common stock........		30,000				30,000				30,000
Dividends	500				500				500	
Fee revenue		18,250		(d) 750		19,150		$19,150		
				(g) 150						
Supplies expense......			(a) 1,320		1,320		1,320			
Wage expense	1,620		(e) 810		2,430		$ 2,430			
Rent expense.........			(b) 1,800		1,800		1,800			
Depreciation expense...			(c) 450		450		450			
Interest expense.......			(f) 300		300		300			
Totals.............	$90,100	$90,100	$5,580	$5,580	$91,810	$91,810	6,300	19,150	85,510	72,660
Net income							12,850			12,850
Totals..............							$19,150	$19,150	$85,510	$85,510

4 Adjusted Trial Balance   Once the adjustments have been entered on the worksheet, there is sufficient information available to complete an adjusted trial balance. The adjusted figures are determined by combining horizontally, line by line, the amounts in the first four columns—that is, the unadjusted trial balance and the adjustments. We review the calculations for two lines of **Exhibit 3B-2** to illustrate this process. The first line shows the Cash account with a debit amount of $40,590 in the unadjusted trial balance. Because Cash is not affected by any of the adjustments, the $40,590 appears in the debit column of the adjusted trial balance. On the third line, the Office Supplies account begins with a debit of $2,850 in the unadjusted trial balance and then shows a credit of $1,320 in the adjustments column. The $1,320 credit is subtracted from the $2,850 debit, and the remaining $1,530 is shown as a debit in the adjusted trial balance.

After calculating the adjusted trial balance amounts for all accounts on the worksheet, we total the debit and credit columns of the adjusted trial balance to verify that they are equal and that our worksheet is in balance.

5 **Extension of the Adjusted Trial Balance**   The amounts in the adjusted trial balance columns are extended into the two remaining pairs of columns as follows:

Expenses	→	Debit column of income statement
Revenues	→	Credit column of income statement
Assets and Dividends	→	Debit column of balance sheet
Liabilities, Common Stock, Retained Earnings, and Contra Assets	→	Credit column of balance sheet

Expense and revenue account balances are extended to the respective income statement columns because these accounts will be used to prepare the income statement. Similarly, asset, contra asset, liability, and stockholders' equity accounts are balance sheet accounts, so their balances are extended to the balance sheet columns. In addition, the Dividends debit balance is extended to the balance sheet debit column. **Exhibit 3B-2** shows the extension of WebWork's adjusted trial balance to the worksheet's income statement and balance sheet columns. Once the proper extensions are made, the worksheet is complete except for balancing the two pairs of debit and credit columns containing the adjusted balances.

6 **Balancing the Worksheet**   The first step in balancing is to add each of the income statement and balance sheet columns and record their respective totals on the same line as the totals of the adjusted trial balance columns. The difference between the total debits and total credits in the income statement columns is the difference between total revenues and total expenses—that is, the net income or net loss for the period. The net income or net loss must be the amount by which the debit and credit columns for the balance sheet differ. This is true because the Retained Earnings account balance, as extended, does not yet reflect the net income or net loss for the current period.

When revenues exceed expenses, we balance the two pairs of statement columns by adding the net income figure to both the debit column of the income statement and the credit column of the balance sheet. **Exhibit 3B-2** illustrates this balancing situation with WebWork's net income for December of $12,850. If expenses exceed revenues, we add the amount of net loss to the credit column of the income statement and to the debit column of the balance sheet. After we have added the net income (or loss) to the proper columns, we total and double-rule the four columns. The worksheet is now complete.

A completed worksheet aids in the last three steps of the accounting cycle—adjust, report, and close.

Adjust: The adjusting entries to be journalized and posted can be taken from the information in the adjustments columns. Because adjustments have first been entered on the worksheet, they can be reviewed for their financial effects before being journalized. Thus, the likelihood of incorrect adjustments appearing in the formal accounting records is reduced.

Report: The income statement can be prepared from the data in the income statement columns. Two pieces of information for the statement of stockholders' equity are available in the worksheet—the net income (or net loss) and dividends. The assets and liabilities needed for the balance sheet are available in the balance sheet columns. (The ending Retained Earnings balance for the balance sheet is obtained from the statement of stockholders' equity.)

Close: The closing entries to be journalized and posted can be prepared from data in the worksheet because it displays all of the temporary account balances. The revenue and expense account balances are shown in the income statement columns, and the cash dividends account balance is shown in the balance sheet debit column.

SUMMARY OF LEARNING OBJECTIVES

LO1   Explain the accrual basis of accounting. (p. 3-3)

- Revenue is recognized on an accrual basis by the transfer of promised goods or services to customers in an amount that reflects the consideration to which the seller expects to be paid in exchange for those goods or services. This may be prior to the receipt of cash, at the same time as the receipt of cash, or following the receipt of cash.
- Expenses are matched against revenues in the same accounting period that the associated revenue is recognized. This may be prior to cash payment, at the same time as cash payment, or following cash payment.
- Revenue recognition and the corresponding matching of expenses may differ in timing on an accrual basis versus on a cash basis.

LO2   Describe the adjusting process. (p. 3-7)

- Adjusting entries are made to achieve the appropriate recognition of revenues and matching of expenses with revenues, and consist of four general types of adjustments:
  1. Allocating previously recorded assets to expenses.
  2. Allocating previously recorded unearned revenue to revenue.
  3. Recording expenses that have not yet been paid.
  4. Recording revenues that have not yet been received.

LO3   Illustrate deferral adjustments. (p. 3-8)

- Deferral adjustments are amounts that have previously been recorded on the balance sheet and require adjustment to their correct amounts.
- The adjustment decreases the balance sheet amount and increases an income statement amount.
- Deferral adjustments include adjustments to prepaid expenses and adjustments to unearned revenues.

LO4   Illustrate accrual adjustments. (p. 3-11)

- Accrual adjustments are amounts that have not been previously recorded in an account.
- The adjustment increases both a balance sheet account and an income statement account.
- Accrual adjustments include adjustments to accrue expenses and adjustments to accrue revenues.

LO5   Explain the adjusted trial balance and use it to prepare financial statements. (p. 3-15)

- An income statement, statement of stockholders' equity, balance sheet, and statement of cash flows may be prepared from an adjusted trial balance and other information.
- The stockholders' equity accounts may need to be reviewed to obtain information regarding the beginning balances and additional capital contributions during the period for the statement of stockholders' equity.

LO6   Describe the closing process and summarize the accounting cycle. (p. 3-19)

- *Closing the books* means closing the revenue, expense, and dividend accounts by transferring the balances to the Retained Earnings account.

LO7   Appendix 3A: Describe the process of closing to the Income Summary account and summarize the accounting cycle. (p. 3-26)

- *Closing the books* means closing the revenue, expense, and other temporary accounts. Revenue and expense account balances are transferred to the Income Summary account. The balances of the Income Summary account and the Dividends account are then transferred to the Retained Earnings account.

LO8   Appendix 3B: Explain how to use a worksheet in the adjusting and closing process. (p. 3-30)

A worksheet is an informal document that helps in compiling the information needed for the preparation of the financial statements. A worksheet is a tool of the accountant; it is not part of a company's formal accounting records. The worksheet consists of a heading, along with the following columns:

a.	Unadjusted trial balance	*d.*	Income statement
b.	Adjustments	*e.*	Balance sheet
c.	Adjusted trial balance		

A completed worksheet aids in the last three steps of the accounting cycle: adjust, report, and close.

Concept →	Method →	Assessment	SUMMARY
When should sales revenue be recognized?	Apply the five steps of the revenue recognition process.	Early recognition of revenue overstates current period revenue; recognizing revenue too late understates current period revenue.	**TAKEAWAY 3.1**
When should expenses be recognized?	Recognized expenses with the related revenue in the same accounting period.	Early recognition of expenses overstates current period expenses; recognizing expenses too late understates current period expenses.	**TAKEAWAY 3.2**
When should an adjusting entry be made?	Inspect individual account balances and transaction details such as contracts and agreements. Determine the proper account balance. Adjustments involve (1) allocating assets to expense, (2) allocating unearned revenue to revenue, (3) accruing expenses, or (4) accruing revenues.	Record an adjusting entry so that accounts are correctly reported; otherwise, income and assets (and/or liabilities) are incorrectly reported.	**TAKEAWAY 3.3**

KEY TERMS

Accruals (p. 3-8)

Accrued expenses (p. 3-11)

Accrued revenue (p. 3-12)

Accumulated depreciation (p. 3-9)

Adjusted trial balance (p. 3-15)

Adjusting entries (p. 3-8)

Book value (p. 3-10)

Carrying value (p. 3-10)

Closing procedures (p. 3-19, 3-26)

Closing process (p. 3-19, 3-26)

Closing the books (p. 3-19, 3-26)

Contra accounts (p. 3-9)

Deferrals (p. 3-8)

Deferred revenue (p. 3-10)

Depreciation (p. 3-9)

Earnings quality (p. 3-22)

Permanent accounts (p. 3-19, 3-26)

Post-closing trial balance (p. 3-20, 3-28)

Straight-line depreciation (p. 3-9)

Temporary accounts (p. 3-19, 3-26)

Unadjusted trial balance (p. 3-7)

Unearned revenue (p. 3-10)

Worksheet (p. 3-30)

**Assignments with the logo in the margin are available in BusinessCourse.
See the Preface of the book for details.**

SELF-STUDY QUESTIONS

(Answers to the Self-Study Questions are available at the end of the chapter.)

1. **Which of the following is an example of an adjusting entry?**   LO3
   a. Recording the purchase of supplies on account
   b. Recording depreciation expense on a truck
   c. Recording the billing of customers for services rendered
   d. Recording the payment of wages to employees

2. **An adjusting entry to record utilities used during a month for which no bill has yet been received is an example of**   LO4
   a. Allocating assets to expense
   b. Allocating revenues received in advance to revenue
   c. Accruing expenses
   d. Accruing revenues

3. **Which of the following is not an example of a closing entry?**   LO6
   a. Close each revenue account to the Retained Earnings account
   b. Close each expense account to the Retained Earnings account
   c. Close the Dividends account to the Retained Earnings account
   d. Close Unearned Revenue to Retained Earnings

LO1   4. **Which of the following transactions does not affect total assets, total liabilities, or total stockholders' equity on the balance sheet?**

    a. Purchasing $500 supplies on account   *c.* Collecting $4,000 from customers on account

    b. Paying a $3,000 note payable   *d.* Payment of an $800 dividend

LO5   5. **The beginning and ending balances of retained earnings for the year were $30,000 and $41,000, respectively. If yearly dividends totaled $3,000, what was the net income or net loss for the year?**

    a. $8,000 net loss   *c.* $2,000 net income

    b. $14,000 net income   *d.* $8,000 net income

LO2   6. **The ending balance of the Accounts Receivable account was $7,800. Services billed to customers for the period were $21,500, and collections on account from customers were $23,600. What was the beginning balance of Accounts Receivable?**

    a. $33,500   *c.* $9,900

    b. $14,100   *d.* $33,100

LO1   7. **Kelly Corporation received an advanced payment of $30,000 in 2018 from Rufus Company for consulting services. Kelly performed half of the consulting in 2018 and the remainder in 2019. Kelly reports using the accrual basis of accounting. How much revenue from this consulting project will Kelly report in 2018?**

    a. $20,000   *c.* $0

    b. $10,000   *d.* $15,000

QUESTIONS

1. Why is the adjusting step of the accounting cycle necessary?

2. What four different types of adjustments are frequently necessary at the close of an accounting period? Provide an example of each type.

3. On January 1, Prepaid Insurance was debited with the cost of a two-year premium in the amount of $3,744. What adjusting entry should be made on January 31 before the January financial statements are prepared?

4. What is a contra account? What contra account is used in reporting the book value of a depreciable asset?

5. At the beginning of January, the first month of the accounting year, the Supplies account had a debit balance of $825. During January, purchases of $260 of supplies were debited to the account. Although only $530 of supplies was on hand at the end of January, the necessary adjusting entry was omitted. How will the omission affect (a) the income statement for January and (b) the balance sheet prepared as of January 31?

6. The publisher of *International View*, a monthly magazine, received two-year subscriptions totaling $12,240 on January 1. (a) What entry should be made to record the receipt of the $12,240? (b) What entry should be made at the end of January before financial statements are prepared for the month?

7. Globe Travel Agency pays an employee $600 in wages each Friday for a five-day work week ending on that day. The last Friday of January falls on January 27. What adjusting entry should be made on January 31, the fiscal year-end?

8. The Bayou Company earns interest amounting to $425 per month on its investments. The company receives the interest every six months, on December 31 and June 30. Monthly financial statements are prepared. What adjusting entry should be made on January 31?

9. Define *permanent account*. Provide an example.

10. Define *temporary account*. Provide an example.

11. Which group of accounts is closed at the end of the accounting year? Why?

12. What is the purpose of a post-closing trial balance? Which of the following accounts should not appear in the post-closing trial balance: Cash, Unearned Revenue, Dividends, Depreciation Expense, Utilities Payable, Supplies Expense, Retained Earnings?

SHORT EXERCISES

LO6   **SE3-1.   Steps in the Accounting Cycle** Listed below, out of order, are the steps in an accounting cycle.

    1. Prepare the unadjusted trial balance.   *6.* Record transactions in a journal.

    2. Post journal entries to general ledger accounts.   *7.* Prepare the post-closing trial balance.

    3. Analyze transactions from source documents.   *8.* Prepare the adjusted trial balance.

    4. Journalize and post adjusting entries.   *9.* Journalize and post closing entries.

    5. Prepare the financial statements.

(a) Place the numbers from the above list in the order in which the steps in the accounting cycle are performed, and (b) identify the steps in the accounting cycle that occur daily.

SE3-2. **Accrual Accounting** Evan Corporation provided consulting services for Kensington Company in 2022. Evan incurred costs of $60,000 associated with the consulting and billed Kensington $130,000. Evan paid $40,000 of its costs in 2022 and the remaining $20,000 in 2023. Evan received $45,000 of its billing in 2022. Kensington paid the remaining $85,000 in 2023. Evan reports on the accrual basis of accounting. How much is Evan's 2022 and 2023 profit related to the Kensington consulting?

LO1

SE3-3. **Adjusting Accounts** MacKenzie Enterprises includes the following accounts in its general ledger. Explain why each of these accounts may need to be adjusted.

LO2

a.   Rent Payable
b.   Unearned Revenue

c.   Prepaid Subscriptions
d.   Depreciation Expense

SE3-4. **Adjusting Entry for Depreciation** Cowley Company just completed its first year of operations. The December 31 equipment account has a balance of $20,000. There is no balance in the Accumulated Depreciation—Equipment account or in the Depreciation Expense account. The accountant estimates the yearly equipment depreciation to be $5,000. Prepare the required adjusting entry to record the yearly depreciation for equipment.

LO3

SE3-5. **Adjusting Entry for Prepaid Insurance** Cooper Inc. recorded the purchase of a three-year insurance policy on July 1 in the amount of $4,800 by debiting Prepaid Insurance and crediting Cash. Prepare the necessary December 31 year-end adjusting entry.

LO3

SE3-6. **Accrual Adjusting Entries** Prepare adjusting journal entries for Sparky Electronics for the following items:

LO3, 4

a.   Salaries for employees in the amount of $2,750 have not been paid.
b.   Interest expense of $1,400 for an outstanding note.
c.   Work performed but not yet billed for $3,800.

SE3-7. **Analyze an Adjusted Trial Balance** The trial balance of Fisher Supplies contains the following balance sheet accounts that require adjustment. Identify the likely income statement account that will be used to adjust these accounts.

LO3, 4

a.   Prepaid Insurance
b.   Accumulated Depreciation

c.   Supplies
d.   Unearned Revenue

e.   Interest Payable

SE3-8. **Prepare an Income Statement from an Adjusted Trial Balance** The Decade Company's adjusted trial balance contains the following balances as of December 31: Retained Earnings $8,500; Dividends $2,000; Sales $22,000; Cost of Goods Sold $8,000; Selling and Administrative Expenses $3,000; Interest Expense $1,500. Prepare an income statement for the year.

LO5

SE3-9. **Prepare Closing Entries to Retained Earnings** Use the data from SE3-8 to prepare the closing entries for The Decade Company. Close the temporary accounts straight to retained earnings. The balance of $8,500 in the retained earnings account is from the beginning of the year. What is the ending retained earnings balance after posting the closing entries?

LO6

SE3-10. **Identify Financial Statements from Adjusted Trial Balance Accounts** Trowel Corp reports the following accounts in its adjusted trial balance. Identify which financial statement each account would appear on:

LO5

a.   Cash
b.   Sales

c.   Accounts Payable
d.   Unearned Revenue

e.   Retained Earnings
f.   Interest Income

SE3-11. **Prepare Closing Entries Using the Income Summary Account** Use the data from SE3-8 to prepare the closing entries for The Decade Company. Close the temporary accounts to income summary. The balance of $8,500 in the retained earnings account is from the beginning of the year. What is the ending retained earnings balance after posting the closing entries?

LO7
(Appendix 3A)

SE3-12. **The Accounting Worksheet** The adjusted trial balance section of Menlo Company's worksheet shows a $1,500 debit balance in utility expense. At the end of the accounting period the accounting manager accrues an additional $300 of utility expense for the last week of the period. This will result in the following amounts appearing on Menlo's worksheet for utilities expense:

LO8
(Appendix 3B)

a. $300 debit adjustment; $1,800 debit adjusted trial balance; $1,800 debit balance sheet
b. $300 debit adjustment; $1,800 debit adjusted trial balance; $1,800 debit income statement
c. $300 credit adjustment; $1,200 debit adjusted trial balance; $1,800 debit income statement
d. $300 credit adjustment; $1,800 debit adjusted trial balance; $1,800 debit income statement

DATA ANALYTICS

Data Analytics

DA3-1. **Matching Chart Types and Aims to Data Measures** In the process of preparing a data visualization, determine which chart would be best suited for each data measure and determine what is the aim of that particular chart. Refer to LO5 from the Data Analytics Appendix F for a description of each chart type.

	Data Measure	Chart Type	Aim of Chart
a.	Relation of daily clicks on digital ads with daily online sales	__ Column chart	__ Compare different categories
b.	Sales by major city for a company's best-selling product.	__ Pie chart	__ Analyze changes over time
c.	Level of eight types of digital marketing expenses for the year	__ Line chart	__ Show parts that make up a whole
d.	Common stock and retained earnings portions of total equity	__ Scatter Plot	__ Show correlation between two variables
e.	Ten-year trend in digital marketing expense.	__ Map chart	__ Show differences across geographic locations

DA3-2. **Preparing Basic Visualization in Excel of Changes in Sales Data Over Time** The Excel file associated with this exercise includes daily sales for the month of December for Strickland Inc. In this exercise, we determine which sales amounts appear to be outliers, which means that they differ significantly from the other daily sales amounts.

Required

1. Download Excel file DA3-2 found in myBusinessCourse.
2. Prepare a line chart for the month of December. *Hint:* Highlight the data and open the Insert tab. Click the Line chart in the Charts group and select one of the 2-D lines. Do not include the column titles or the total row when highlighting the data.
3. Add a trendline to the chart. *Hint:* Right-click on the line in your chart to view the option to add a linear trendline.
4. Describe the position of the trendline on the chart on December 18.
5. List the point(s) (if any) on the chart that are positioned over +/−$1,200 beyond the trendline. *Hint:* Use the gridlines on the chart to help you visually detect outliers.

DATA VISUALIZATION

Data Visualization Activities are available in myBusinessCourse. These assignments use Tableau Dashboards to expose students to visual depictions of data and introduce students to data analytics through data visualizations. These exercises are easily assignable and auto graded by MBC.

Data Visualization

EXERCISES—SET A

LO4 **E3-1A.** **Transaction Entries and Adjusting Entries** Deluxe Building Services offers janitorial services on both a contract basis and an hourly basis. On January 1, Deluxe collected $42,000 in advance on a six-month contract for work to be performed evenly during the next six months.

a. Provide the general journal entry on January 1 to record the receipt of $42,000 for contract work.
b. Provide the adjusting entry to be made on January 31 for the contract work done during January.
c. At January 31, a total of 40 hours of hourly rate janitor work was unbilled. The billing rate is $25 per hour. Provide the adjusting entry needed on January 31. (*Note:* The firm uses the account Fees Receivable to reflect amounts due but not yet billed.)

LO3, 4 **E3-2A.** **Adjusting Entries** Selected accounts of Ideal Properties Inc., a real estate management firm, are shown below as of January 31, before any adjusting entries have been made:

	Debit	Credit
Prepaid insurance.	$7,200	
Supplies	2,100	
Office equipment	7,680	
Unearned rent revenue.		$ 5,400
Salaries expense	3,250	
Rent revenue		16,000

Monthly financial statements are prepared. Using the following information, record in a general journal the adjusting entries necessary on January 31:

a.   Prepaid Insurance represents a three-year premium paid on January 1.

b.   Supplies of $975 were on hand January 31.

c.   Office equipment is expected to last eight years. Depreciation is recorded monthly.

d.   On January 1, the firm collected six months' rent in advance from a tenant renting space for $925 per month.

e.   Accrued salaries not recorded as of January 31 are $625.

E3-3A.   Adjusting Entries For each of the following unrelated situations, prepare the necessary adjusting entry in general journal form: **LO3, 4**

a.   Unrecorded depreciation on equipment is $800.

b.   The Supplies account has a balance of $3,100. Supplies on hand at the end of the period totaled $1,200.

c.   On the date for preparing financial statements, an estimated utilities expense of $425 has been incurred, but no utility bill has been received.

d.   On the first day of the current month, rent for four months was paid and recorded as a $2,800 debit to Prepaid Rent and a $2,800 credit to Cash. Monthly statements are now being prepared.

e.   Nine months ago, Solid Insurance Company sold a one-year policy to a customer and recorded the receipt of the premium by debiting Cash for $800 and crediting Unearned Premium Revenue for $800. No adjusting entries have been prepared during the nine-month period. Annual financial statements are now being prepared.

f.   At the end of the accounting period, employee wages of $1,050 have been incurred but not paid.

g.   At the end of the accounting period, $411 of interest has been earned but not yet received on notes receivable that are held.

E3-4A.   Statement of Stockholders' Equity On January 1, the credit balance of the Retained Earnings account was $51,000. The company's Common Stock account had an opening balance of $65,000, and $8,000 in new capital contributions were made during the year. On December 31, at year-end, the Dividends account had a debit balance of $12,000 before closing. The income statement shows net income of $30,500. Prepare a statement of stockholders' equity for Stede & Company, architectural design firm.   **LO5**

E3-5A.   Closing Entries The adjusted trial balance prepared as of December 31, for Phyllis Howell & Company, Consultant, contains the following revenue and expense accounts: **LO6**

	Debit	Credit
Service fees earned		$91,000
Rent expense	$20,800	
Salaries expense	52,000	
Supplies expense	6,000	
Depreciation expense	11,300	
Retained earnings		72,000
Dividends	10,000	

Prepare journal entries to close the accounts directly to Retained Earnings. After these entries are posted, what is the balance in the Retained Earnings account?

E3-6A.   Revenue Recognition Identify the proper point to recognize revenue for each of the following transactions.   **LO1**

a.   Honey Industries sells a machine in January with terms of no payment due until six months later.

b.   Platt Company collects an advance deposit of $700 in July toward the purchase of a $3,000 piece of equipment that is delivered to the customer the following September.

c.   Naomi Corporation receives payment in October at the time of delivery of a rebuilt engine for a tractor.

E3-7A.   Expense Matching Identify the proper point to recognize expense for each of the following transactions.   **LO1**

a.   Kat Inc. purchases on credit six custom sofas for $800 each in June. Two of the sofas are sold for $1,200 each in June. One of the sofas is sold for $1,200 in July, and the remaining three sofas are sold for $1,500 each in August. All sales are for cash. Kat pays its supplier in July.

b. Kira Co. purchases $500 of supplies in January. Half the supplies are used in January, with the remaining half used in February.

c. Joseph Co. purchases $2,000 of inventory for cash in September. The entire inventory is sold in November.

LO6 **E3-8A. Closing Entries** In the midst of closing procedures, Echo Corporation's accountant became ill and was hospitalized. You have volunteered to complete the closing of the books. You find that all the revenue and expense accounts have zero balances. The Dividends account has a debit balance of $17,000. The Retained Earnings account has a beginning credit balance of $120,000. Expenses totaled $308,500, and revenues totaled $347,400. Prepare journal entries to complete the closing procedures as of year-end directly to Retained Earnings. After these entries are posted, what is the balance in the Retained Earnings account?

LO3, 4 **E3-9A. Analysis of Adjusted Data** Selected T-account balances for Coyle Company are shown below as of January 31; adjusting entries have already been posted. The firm uses a calendar-year accounting period and makes monthly adjustments.

Supplies			Supplies Expense		
Jan. 31	Bal. 800		Jan. 31	Bal. 960	
Prepaid Insurance			**Insurance Expense**		
Jan. 31	Bal. 492		Jan. 31	Bal. 82	
Wages Payable			**Wages Expense**		
		Bal. 650 Jan. 31	Jan. 31	Bal. 3,300	
Truck			**Accumulated Depreciation—Truck**		
Jan. 31	Bal. 8,700			Bal. 2,610	Jan. 31

a. If the amount in Supplies Expense represents the January 31 adjustment for the supplies used in January, and $825 worth of supplies were purchased during January, what was the January 1 balance of Supplies?

b. The amount in the Insurance Expense account represents the adjustment made at January 31 for January insurance expense. If the original insurance premium was for one year, what was the amount of the premium and on what date did the insurance policy start?

c. If we assume that no balance existed in Wages Payable or Wages Expense on January 1, how much cash was paid as wages during January?

d. If the truck has a useful life of five years, what is the monthly amount of depreciation expense, and how many months has Coyle owned the truck?

LO3, 4 **E3-10A. Analysis of the Impact of Adjustments on Financial Statements** At the end of the first month of operations, the Stephan Company's accountant prepared financial statements that showed the following amounts:

Assets.	$60,000
Liabilities.	20,000
Stockholders' equity	40,000
Net income	9,000

In preparing the statements, the accountant overlooked the following items:

a. Depreciation for the month, $925.

b. Service revenue earned but unbilled at month-end, $1,500.

c. Employee wages earned but unpaid at month-end, $410.

Determine the correct amounts of assets, liabilities, and stockholders' equity at month-end and net income for the month.

E3-11A. Closing Entries The adjusted trial balance of the Petal Corporation, prepared as of December 31, contains the following accounts:

LO6

	Debit	Credit
Service fees earned		$87,500
Interest income		2,600
Salaries expense	$41,800	
Advertising expense	6,300	
Depreciation expense	8,700	
Income tax expense	11,000	
Common stock		75,000
Retained earnings		60,000
Cash dividends	15,000	

Prepare journal entries to close the accounts directly to Retained Earnings. After these entries are posted, what is the ending balance in the Retained Earnings account?

E3-12A. Closing Entries Use the information provided in E3-5A to prepare journal entries to close the accounts using the Income Summary account. After these entries are posted, what is the balance in the Retained Earnings account?

LO7
(Appendix 3A)

E3-13A. Closing Entries In the midst of closing procedures, Park Corporation's accountant became ill and was hospitalized. You have volunteered to complete the closing of the books, and you find that all revenue and expense accounts have zero balances and that the Income Summary account has a single debit entry for $320,000 and a single credit entry for $352,000. The Dividends account has a debit balance of $17,500, and the Retained Earnings account has a credit balance of $120,000. Prepare journal entries to complete the closing procedures as of year-end.

LO7
(Appendix 3A)

E3-14A. Worksheet Identify each of the 10 amount columns of the worksheet and indicate to which column the adjusted balance of the following accounts would be extended:

LO8
(Appendix 3B)

a. Accounts Receivable
b. Accumulated Depreciation
c. Dividends
d. Wages Payable
e. Depreciation Expense
f. Rent Receivable
g. Prepaid Insurance
h. Service Fees Earned
i. Common Stock
j. Retained Earnings

E3-15A. Closing Entries Use the information provided in E3-11A to prepare journal entries to close the accounts using the Income Summary account. After these entries are posted, what is the balance in the Retained Earnings account?

LO7
(Appendix 3A)

E3-16A. Worksheet The adjusted trial balance columns of a worksheet for Bond Corporation are shown below. The worksheet is prepared for the year ended December 31.

LO8
(Appendix 3B)

	Adjusted Trial Balance	
	Debit	Credit
Cash	$ 6,000	
Accounts receivable	6,500	
Equipment	83,000	
Accumulated depreciation		$ 14,000
Notes payable		12,500
Common stock		48,000
Retained earnings		20,600
Cash dividends	8,000	
Service fees earned		71,900
Rent expense	18,000	
Salaries expense	38,500	
Depreciation expense	7,000	
Totals	$167,000	$167,000

Complete the worksheet by (a) entering the adjusted trial balance, (b) putting in the worksheet income statement and balance sheet columns, (c) extending the adjusted trial balance to the income statement and balance sheet columns, and (d) balancing the worksheet.

EXERCISES—SET B

LO4   E3-1B.   Transaction Entry and Adjusting Entries Burne Building Services offers janitorial services on both a contract basis and an hourly basis. On January 1, Burne collected $90,000 in advance on a six-month contract for work to be performed evenly during the next six months.

   a.   Provide the general journal entry on January 1 to record the receipt of $90,000 for contract work.
   b.   Provide the adjusting entry to be made on January 31 for the contract work done during January.
   c.   At January 31, a total of 35 hours of hourly rate janitor work was unbilled. The billing rate is $31 per hour. Provide the adjusting entry needed on January 31. (*Note:* The firm uses the account Fees Receivable to reflect amounts due but not yet billed.)

LO3, 4   E3-2B.   Adjusting Entries Judy Rock began Rock Refinishing Service on July 1. Selected accounts are shown below as of July 31, before any adjusting entries have been made:

	Debit	Credit
Prepaid rent	$6,000	
Prepaid advertising	930	
Supplies	3,000	
Unearned refinishing fees		$ 800
Refinishing fees revenue		2,500

Using the following information, record in a general journal the necessary adjusting entries on July 31:

   a.   On July 1, the firm paid one year's rent of $6,000.
   b.   On July 1, $930 was paid to a local newspaper for an advertisement to run daily for the months of July, August, and September.
   c.   Supplies on hand at July 31 total $1,100.
   d.   At July 31, refinishing services of $975 have been performed but not yet billed to customers. The firm uses the account Fees Receivable to reflect amounts due but not yet billed.
   e.   One customer paid $1,100 in advance for a refinishing project. At July 31, the project is one-half complete.

LO3, 4   E3-3B.   Adjusting Entries For each of the following unrelated situations, prepare the necessary adjusting entry in general journal form:

   a.   Unrecorded depreciation on equipment is $1,850.
   b.   The Supplies account has a balance of $5,000. Supplies on hand at the end of the period total $2,500.
   c.   On the date for preparing financial statements, an estimated utilities expense of $550 has been incurred, but no utility bill has been received.
   d.   On the first day of the current month, rent for four months was paid and recorded as a $2,800 debit to Prepaid Rent and a $2,800 credit to Cash. Monthly statements are now being prepared.
   e.   Nine months ago, Macke Insurance Company sold a one-year policy to a customer and recorded the receipt of the premium by debiting Cash for $624 and crediting Unearned Premium Revenue for $624. No adjusting entries have been prepared during the nine-month period. Annual financial statements are now being prepared.
   f.   At the end of the accounting period, employee wages of $700 have been incurred but not paid.
   g.   At the end of the accounting period, $800 of interest has been earned but not yet received on notes receivable that are held.

LO5   E3-4B.   Statement of Stockholders' Equity On January 1, the credit balance of the Retained Earnings account was $60,000. The company's common stock account had an opening balance of $85,000 and new contributions during the year totaled $9,000. On December 31, at year-end, the Dividends account had a debit balance of $6,500. The income statement shows net income of $40,000. Prepare a statement of stockholders' equity for Kim & Company, architectural design firm.

E3-5B. **Closing Entries** The adjusted trial balance prepared December 31 for Cheryl Lester & Company, **LO6**
shipping agent, contains the following accounts:

	Debit	Credit
Commissions earned		$94,900
Wages expense	$36,000	
Insurance expense	3,000	
Utilities expense	9,500	
Depreciation expense	9,800	
Dividends	12,000	
Common stock		90,000
Retained earnings		22,100

Prepare journal entries to close the accounts directly to Retained Earnings. After these entries are posted,
what is the ending balance in the Retained Earnings account?

E3-6B. **Revenue Recognition** Identify the proper point to recognize revenue for each of the following **LO1**
transactions.

   a.   Creed Industries sells a machine in January with terms of 50 percent due on delivery in January
and the remaining balance due three months later.

   b.   Pia Company collects an advance deposit of $950 in May toward the purchase of a $4,000 piece
of equipment that is delivered to the customer the following month.

   c.   Juan Corporation receives payment in March at the time of delivery of a rebuilt engine for a
forklift.

E3-7B. **Expense Matching** Identify the proper point to recognize expenses for each of the following **LO1**
transactions.

   a.   Julio Inc. purchases for cash five custom dining tables for $1,200 each in March. Three tables are
later sold for $1,750 each in April, and the remaining two tables are sold for $1,500 each in May.

   b.   Craig Company purchases $400 of office supplies that are both paid for and used in August.

   c.   Kerra Company purchases $500 of inventory on account in July. The inventory is sold for $650 in
August. Kerra pays its suppliers the $500 due in September.

E3-8B. **Closing Entries** In the midst of closing procedures, La Verne Corporation's accountant became ill **LO6**
and was hospitalized. You have volunteered to complete the closing of the books. You find that all
the revenue and expense accounts have zero balances. The Dividends account has a debit balance of
$35,000. The Retained Earnings account has a beginning credit balance of $191,000. Expenses totaled
$328,800, and revenues totaled $347,400. Prepare journal entries to complete the closing procedures
as of year-end directly to Retained Earnings. After these entries are posted, what is the balance in the
Retained Earnings account?

E3-9B. **Analysis of Adjusted Data** Selected T-account balances for the Rome Company are shown below as **LO3, 4**
of January 31; adjusting entries have already been posted. The firm uses a calendar-year accounting
period and makes monthly adjustments.

Supplies		Supplies Expense	
Jan. 31 Bal. 1,050		Jan. 31 Bal. 2,540	

Prepaid Insurance		Insurance Expense	
Jan. 31 Bal. 910		Jan. 31 Bal. 182	

Wages Payable		Wages Expense	
	Bal. 650 Jan. 31	Jan. 31 Bal. 2,700	

Truck		Accumulated Depreciation—Truck	
Jan. 31 Bal. 8,700			Bal. 2,610 Jan. 31

   a.   If the amount in Supplies Expense represents the January 31 adjustment for the supplies used in
January, and $700 worth of supplies were purchased during January, what was the January 1 bal-
ance of Supplies?

   b.   The amount in the Insurance Expense account represents the adjustment made at January 31 for
January insurance expense. If the original insurance premium was for one year, what was the
amount of the premium and on what date did the insurance policy start?

c. If we assume that no balance existed in Wages Payable or Wages Expense on January 1, how much cash was paid as wages during January?

d. If the truck has a useful life of five years, what is the monthly amount of depreciation expense, and how many months has Rome owned the truck?

LO3, 4   **E3-10B. Analysis of the Impact of Adjustments on Financial Statements** At the end of the first month of operations, the Lamar Company's accountant prepared financial statements that showed the following amounts:

Assets.	$90,000
Liabilities.	30,000
Stockholders' equity	60,000
Net income	11,000

In preparing the statements, the accountant overlooked the following items:

a. Depreciation for the month, $4,500.
b. Service revenue earned but unbilled at month-end, $1,850.
c. Employee wages earned but unpaid at month-end, $450.

Determine the correct amounts of assets, liabilities, and stockholders' equity at month-end and net income for the month.

LO6   **E3-11B. Closing Entries** The adjusted trial balance of the Murray Corporation, prepared December 31, contains the following accounts:

	Debit	Credit
Service fees earned		$102,500
Interest income.		7,000
Salaries expense	$49,800	
Advertising expense.	4,300	
Depreciation expense.	9,500	
Income tax expense	1,100	
Common stock		80,000
Retained earnings		57,700
Cash dividends.	17,000	

Prepare journal entries to close the accounts directly to Retained Earnings. After these entries are posted, what is the ending balance in the Retained Earnings account?

LO7
(Appendix 3A)   **E3-12B. Closing Entries** Use the information provided in E3-5B to prepare journal entries to close the accounts using the Income Summary account. After these entries are posted, what is the balance in the Retained Earnings account?

LO7
(Appendix 3A)   **E3-13B. Closing Entries** In the midst of closing procedures, La Verne Corporation's accountant became ill. You have volunteered to complete the closing of the books, and you find that all revenue and expense accounts have zero balances and that the Income Summary account has a single debit entry for $318,800 and a single credit entry for $370,000. The Cash Dividends account has a debit balance of $14,000, and the Retained Earnings account has a credit balance of $117,000. Prepare journal entries to complete the closing procedures as of year-end.

LO8
(Appendix 3B)   **E3-14B. Worksheet** Identify each of the 10 amount columns of the worksheet, and indicate to which column the adjusted balance of the following accounts would be extended:

a. Accounts Receivable
b. Accumulated Depreciation
c. Dividends
d. Salaries Payable
e. Wages Expense

f. Interest Receivable
g. Prepaid Rent
h. Service Fees Earned
i. Common Stock
j. Retained Earnings

LO7
(Appendix 3A)   **E3-15B. Closing Entries** Use the information provided in E3-11B to prepare journal entries to close the accounts using the Income Summary account. After these entries are posted, what is the balance in the Retained Earnings account?

E3-16B. Worksheet The adjusted trial balance columns of a worksheet for Levitt Corporation are shown below. The worksheet is prepared for the year ended December 31.

LO8
(Appendix 3B)

	Adjusted Trial Balance	
	Debit	Credit
Cash	$ 16,000	
Accounts receivable	18,500	
Equipment	76,000	
Accumulated depreciation		$ 24,000
Notes payable		16,000
Common stock		43,000
Retained earnings		20,600
Cash dividends	8,000	
Service fees earned		79,000
Rent expense	18,000	
Salaries expense	37,100	
Depreciation expense	9,000	
Totals	$182,600	$182,600

Complete the worksheet by (a) entering the adjusted trial balance, (b) putting in the worksheet income statement and balance sheet columns, (c) extending the adjusted trial balance to the income statement and balance sheet columns, and (d) balancing the worksheet.

PROBLEMS—SET A

P3-1A. Transaction Entries, Posting, Trial Balance, and Adjusting Entries Mark Gold opened Gold Roofing Service on April 1. Transactions for April are as follows:

LO3, 4

1 Gold contributed $15,000 of his personal funds in exchange for common stock to begin the business.
2 Purchased a used truck for $6,100 cash.
3 Purchased ladders and other equipment for a total of $3,100, paid $1,000 cash, with the balance due in 30 days.
4 Paid two-year premium on liability insurance, $6,000.
5 Purchased supplies on account, $1,200.
6 Received an advance payment of $1,800 from a customer for roof repair work to be done during April and May.
7 Billed customers for roofing services, $9,000.
8 Collected $6,500 on account from customers.
9 Paid bill for truck fuel used in April, $75.
10 Paid April newspaper advertising, $100.
11 Paid assistants' wages, $4,500.
12 Billed customers for roofing services, $5,000.

Required
a. Set up a general ledger with the following accounts: Cash; Accounts Receivable; Supplies; Prepaid Insurance; Trucks; Accumulated Depreciation—Trucks; Equipment; Accumulated Depreciation—Equipment; Accounts Payable; Unearned Roofing Fees; Common Stock; Roofing Fees Earned; Fuel Expense; Advertising Expense; Wages Expense; Insurance Expense; Supplies Expense; Depreciation Expense—Trucks; and Depreciation Expense—Equipment.
b. Record these transactions in the general journal and post to the ledger accounts.
c. Prepare an unadjusted trial balance as of April 30.
d. Prepare the journal entries to adjust the books for insurance expense, supplies expense, depreciation expense on the truck, depreciation expense on the equipment, and roofing fees earned. Supplies on hand on April 30 amounted to $950. Depreciation for April was $155 on the truck and $35 on the equipment. One-fourth of the roofing fee received in advance was earned by April 30. Post the adjusting entries.

LO3, 4   **P3-2A.**   **Transaction Entries, Posting, Trial Balance, and Adjusting Entries** The Healthy Catering Service
    had the following transactions in July, its first month of operations:

1 Kelly Foster contributed $18,000 of personal funds to the business in exchange for common stock.
2 Purchased the following items for cash from a catering firm that was going out of business (make
   a compound entry): delivery van, $3,780; equipment, $3,240; and supplies, $1,700.
3 Paid premium on a one-year liability insurance policy, $2,160.
4 Entered into a contract with a local service club to cater weekly luncheon meetings for one year
   at a fee of $1,000 per month. Received eight months' fees in advance.
5 Paid rent for July, August, and September, $2,340.
6 Paid employees' two weeks' wages (five-day week), $2,400.
7 Billed customers for services rendered, $5,000.
8 Purchased supplies on account, $3,000.
9 Paid employees' two weeks' wages, $1,800.
10 Paid July bill for gas, oil, and repairs on delivery van, $850.
11 Collected $3,700 from customers on account.
12 Billed customers for services rendered, $5,400.
13 Foster received a $2,000 dividend.

Required

a.   Set up a general ledger that includes the following accounts: Cash; Accounts Receivable; Sup-
     plies; Prepaid Rent; Prepaid Insurance; Delivery Van; Accumulated Depreciation—Delivery Van;
     Equipment; Accumulated Depreciation—Equipment; Accounts Payable; Wages Payable; Un-
     earned Catering Fees; Common Stock; Dividends; Catering Fees Revenue; Wages Expense; Rent
     Expense; Supplies Expense; Insurance Expense; Delivery Van Expense; Depreciation Expense—
     Delivery Van; and Depreciation Expense—Equipment.
b.   Record July transactions in the general journal and post to the ledger accounts.
c.   Prepare an unadjusted trial balance as of July 31.
d.   Record adjusting journal entries in the general journal and post to the ledger accounts. The fol-
     lowing information is available on July 31:

     Supplies on hand, $1,600
     Accrued wages, $550
     Estimated life of delivery van, three years (Assume van was purchased July 1)
     Estimated life of equipment, six years (Assume equipment was purchased July 1)

Also, make any necessary adjusting entries for insurance, rent, and catering fees indicated by the July
transactions. Assume original transactions occurred July 1.

LO3, 4   **P3-3A.**   **Trial Balance and Adjusting Entries** Image, Inc., a commercial photography studio, has just completed its first full year of operations on December 31. The general ledger account balances before
year-end adjustments follow. No adjusting entries have been made to the accounts at any time during
the year. Assume that all balances are normal.

Cash............................	$ 2,150	Accounts payable	$ 2,710
Accounts receivable	3,600	Unearned photography fees	2,600
Prepaid rent	12,600	Common stock	24,000
Prepaid insurance................	2,970	Photography fees earned	34,480
Supplies	5,250	Wages expense	11,000
Equipment	22,800	Utilities expense	3,420

An analysis of the firm's records discloses the following items:

1. Photography services of $1,250 have been rendered, but customers have not yet been billed. The
    firm uses the account Fees Receivable to reflect amounts due but not yet billed.
2. The equipment, purchased January 1, has an estimated life of 10 years.
3. Utilities expense for December is estimated to be $750, but the bill will not arrive until January of
    next year.
4. The balance in Prepaid Rent represents the amount paid on January 1 for a two-year lease on the
    studio.
5. In November, customers paid $2,600 in advance for pictures to be taken for the holiday season.
    When received, these fees were credited to Unearned Photography Fees. By December 31, all fees
    are earned.

6. A three-year insurance premium paid on January 1 was debited to Prepaid Insurance.
7. Supplies on hand at December 31 are $1,750.
8. At December 31, wages expense of $650 has been incurred but not paid.

Required

a. Prove that the sum of the debits equals the sum of the credits for Image's unadjusted account balances by preparing an unadjusted trial balance as of December 31.
b. Record adjusting entries in the general journal.

P3-4A. Adjusting Entries Foote Carpet Cleaners ended its first month of operations on June 30. Monthly financial statements will be prepared. The unadjusted account balances are as follows: **LO3, 4**

FOOTE CARPET CLEANERS Unadjusted Trial Balance June 30		
	Debit	**Credit**
Cash	$ 1,180	
Accounts receivable	450	
Prepaid rent	3,100	
Supplies	2,520	
Equipment	4,440	
Accounts payable		$ 760
Common stock		2,500
Retained earnings		5,200
Dividends	400	
Service fees earned		4,650
Wages expense	1,020	
	$13,110	$13,110

The following information is also available:

1. The balance in Prepaid Rent was the amount paid on June 1 for the first two months' rent.
2. Supplies on hand at June 30 were $1,250.
3. The equipment, purchased June 1, has an estimated life of five years.
4. Unpaid wages at June 30 were $450.
5. Utility services used during June were estimated at $650. A bill is expected early in July.
6. Fees earned for services performed but not yet billed on June 30 were $500. The firm uses the account Fees Receivable to reflect amounts due but not yet billed.

Required

Prepare the adjusting entries needed at June 30 for the general journal.

P3-5A. Adjusting Entries The following information relates to December 31 adjustments for Best Print, a printing company. The firm's fiscal year ends on December 31.   **LO3, 4**

1. Weekly salaries for a five-day week total $3,000, payable on Fridays. December 31 of the current year is a Tuesday.
2. Best Print has $25,000 of notes payable outstanding at December 31. Interest of $275 has accrued on these notes by December 31, but will not be paid until the notes mature next year.
3. During December, Best Print provided $1,000 of printing services to clients who will be billed on January 2. The firm uses the account Fees Receivable to reflect amounts due but not yet billed.
4. Starting December 1, all maintenance work on Best Print's equipment is handled by Prompt Repair Company under an agreement whereby Best Print pays a fixed monthly charge of $125. Best Print paid six months' service charge in advance on December 1, debiting Prepaid Maintenance for $750.
5. The firm paid $900 on December 15 for a series of radio commercials to run during December and January. One-third of the commercials have aired by December 31. The $900 payment was debited to Prepaid Advertising.
6. Starting December 16, Best Print rented 400 square feet of storage space from a neighboring business. The monthly rent of $0.90 per square foot is due in advance on the first of each month. Nothing was paid in December, however, because the neighbor agreed to add the rent for one-half of December to the January 1 payment.

7. Best Print invested $7,500 in securities on December 1 and earned interest of $62 on these securities by December 31. No interest will be received until January.
8. The annual depreciation on the firm's equipment is $2,600. No depreciation has been recorded during the year.

Required

Prepare the required December 31 adjusting entries in the general journal.

LO3, 4   P3-6A.   Adjusting Entries The following selected accounts appear in the Bullard Company's unadjusted trial balance as of December 31, the end of the fiscal year (all accounts have normal balances):

Prepaid advertising..........	$ 1,400	Unearned service fees........	$ 5,400
Wages expense............	43,800	Service fees earned..........	87,000
Prepaid insurance..........	3,420	Rental income.............	4,900

Required

Prepare the necessary adjusting entries in the general journal as of December 31, assuming the following:

1. Prepaid advertising at December 31 is $950.
2. Unpaid wages earned by employees in December are $1,800.
3. Prepaid insurance at December 31 is $2,750.
4. Unearned service fees at December 31 are $2,800.
5. Rent revenue of $1,250 owed by a tenant is not recorded at December 31.

LO3, 4   P3-7A.   Adjusting Entries The following selected accounts appear in the Birch Company's unadjusted trial balance as of December 31, the end of the fiscal year (all accounts have normal balances):

Prepaid maintenance..........	$2,700	Commission fees earned..........	$86,000
Supplies.................	9,400	Rent expense.............	10,800
Unearned commission fees......	9,000		

Required

Prepare the necessary adjusting entries in the general journal as of December 31, assuming the following:

1. On September 1, the company entered into a prepaid equipment maintenance contract. Birch Company paid $2,700 to cover maintenance service for six months, beginning September 1. The $2,700 payment was debited to Prepaid Maintenance.
2. Supplies on hand at December 31 are $2,900.
3. Unearned commission fees at December 31 are $4,000.
4. Commission fees earned but not yet billed at December 31 are $3,500. (*Note:* Debit Fees Receivable.)
5. Birch Company's lease calls for rent of $900 per month payable on the first of each month, plus an annual amount equal to 2 percent of annual commissions earned. This additional rent is payable on January 10 of the following year. (*Note:* Be sure to use the adjusted amount of commissions earned in computing the additional rent.)

LO5, 6   P3-8A.   Financial Statements and Closing Entries The adjusted trial balance shown below is for Sharpe Consulting Service as of December 31. Byran Sharpe made no capital contributions during the year.

	Adjusted Trial Balance	
	Debit	Credit
Cash.	$ 2,900	
Accounts receivable	3,270	
Supplies	5,060	
Prepaid insurance.	1,500	
Equipment	6,400	
Accumulated depreciation—Equipment		$ 1,080
Accounts payable		845
Long-term notes payable		7,200
Common stock		2,800
Retained earnings		5,205
Dividends	2,900	
Service fees earned		62,600
Rent expense	15,500	
Salaries expense	33,400	
Supplies expense	4,200	
Insurance expense	3,250	
Depreciation expense—Equipment	720	
Interest expense.	630	
Totals	$79,730	$79,730

Required

a. Prepare an income statement and a statement of stockholders' equity for the year, and a balance sheet as of December 31.

b. Prepare closing entries directly to Retained Earnings in general journal form.

P3-9A. **Closing Entries** The adjusted trial balance shown below is for Batton, Inc., at December 31:   **LO6**

	Adjusted Trial Balance	
	Debit	Credit
Cash.	$ 4,000	
Accounts receivable	8,000	
Prepaid insurance.	3,600	
Equipment	75,000	
Accumulated depreciation		$ 12,500
Accounts payable		600
Common stock		30,000
Retained earnings		14,100
Cash dividends.	7,000	
Service fees earned		101,200
Miscellaneous income		4,200
Salaries expense	42,800	
Rent expense	12,900	
Insurance expense	1,800	
Depreciation expense.	8,000	
Income tax expense	8,300	
Income tax payable.		8,800
Totals	$171,400	$171,400

Required

a. Prepare closing entries directly to Retained Earnings in general journal form.

b. After the closing entries are posted, what is the ending balance in the Retained Earnings account?

c. Prepare a post-closing trial balance.

P3-10A. **Balance Sheet and Net Income** At the beginning of the year, Azuza's Parking Lots had the following   **LO5**   balance sheet:

Assets		Liabilities	
Cash......................	$ 4,800	Accounts payable..................	$12,000
Accounts receivable............	14,700		
Land......................	67,000	**Stockholders' Equity**	
		Common stock................	27,000
		Retained earnings............	47,500
		Total Liabilities and	
Total Assets................	$86,500	Stockholders' Equity...........	$86,500

a. At the end of the year, Azuza had the following assets and liabilities: Cash, $7,800; Accounts Receivable, $17,400; Land, $67,000; Accounts Payable, $5,500; and Common Stock, $27,000. Prepare a year-end balance sheet for Azuza's Parking Lots.

b. Assume that stockholders did not invest any money in the business during the year but received $8,000 as a dividend; what was Azuza's net income or net loss the year?

LO5   **P3-11A. Determination of Retained Earnings and Net Income** The following information appears in the records of Stern Corporation at the end of the year:

Accounts receivable..............	$ 25,000	Retained earnings................	$?
Accounts payable.................	13,000	Supplies........................	9,000
Cash.........................	8,000	Equipment......................	138,000
Common stock..................	115,000		

a. Calculate the amount of retained earnings at the end of the year.

b. Using your answer from part *a*, if the amount of the retained earnings at the beginning of the year was $30,000, and $15,000 in dividends was paid during the year, what was the company's net income for the year?

LO3, 4, 5, 6   **P3-12A. Transaction Analysis, Trial Balance, and Financial Statements** Angela Mica operates the Mica Dance Studio. On June 1, the business's general ledger contained the following information:

Cash.........................	$ 5,930	Accounts payable..................	$ 480
Accounts receivable..............	8,400	Notes payable....................	3,980
		Common stock...................	7,870
		Retained earnings................	2,000
	$14,330		$14,330

The following transactions occurred during the month of June:

1 Paid June rent for practice studio, $875.
2 Paid June piano rental, $240 (Rent Expense).
3 Collected $5,320 from students on account.
4 Borrowed $1,500 and signed a promissory note payable due in six months.
5 Billed students for June instructional fees, $7,500.
6 Paid interest for June on notes payable, $30.
7 Paid $375 for advertising ballet performances.
8 Paid costume rental, $550 (Rent Expense).
9 Collected $2,100 admission fees from ballet performances given during the month.
10 Paid $480 owed on account.
11 Received invoice for June utilities, to be paid in July, $510.
12 Paid stockholders $900 cash as a dividend.
13 Purchased piano for $5,500 cash, to be used in business starting in July.

Required

a. Set up accounts for the general ledger with June 1 balances and enter the beginning balances. Also provide the following accounts: Piano; Dividends; Instructional Fees Earned; Performance Revenue; Rent Expense; Utilities Expense; Advertising Expense; and Interest Expense. Record the listed transactions in the accounts.

b. Prepare a trial balance as of June 30.

c. Prepare an income statement for the month of June.

d. Prepare a statement of stockholders' equity for the month of June.

e. Prepare a balance sheet as of June 30.

f. Prepare closing entries.

g. Prepare a post-closing trial balance.

P3-13A. Transaction Analysis, Trial Balance, and Financial Statements On December 1, a group of individuals formed a corporation to establish the *Local,* a neighborhood weekly newspaper featuring want ads of individuals and advertising of local firms. The free paper will be mailed to about 8,000 local residents; revenue will be generated from advertising and want ads. The December transactions are summarized as follows:

LO3, 4, 5

1 Sold common stock of Local, Inc., for cash, $40,000.

2 Paid December rent on furnished office, $1,200.

3 Purchased for $750, on account, T-shirts displaying company logo. The T-shirts were distributed at a grand opening.

4 Paid to creditor on account, $750.

5 Collected "Help wanted" ad revenue in cash, $5,000.

6 Paid post office for cost of bulk mailing, $910.

7 Billed various firms for advertising in the first two issues of the newspaper, $5,600.

8 Paid Acme Courier Service for transporting newspapers to post office, $50.

9 Paid for printing newspaper, $2,900.

10 Collected "Help wanted" ad revenue in cash, $2,570.

11 Received invoice for December utilities, to be paid in January, $890.

12 Paid for printing newspaper, $2,900.

13 Paid December salaries, $4,100.

14 Billed various firms for advertising in two issues of the newspaper, $8,850.

15 Paid post office for cost of bulk mailing, $775.

16 Paid Acme Courier Service for transporting newspapers to post office, $350.

17 Collected $5,100 on accounts receivable.

18 Purchased a printer for office in exchange for a six-month note payable, $1,400.

Required

a. Set up accounts for the following items: Cash, Accounts Receivable, Office Equipment, Accounts Payable, Notes Payable, Common Stock, Advertising Revenue, Want Ad Revenue, Printing Expense, Advertising Expense, Utilities Expense, Salaries Expense, Rent Expense, and Delivery Expense. Prepare journal entries in a general journal and record the foregoing transactions in the accounts.

b. Prepare a trial balance as of December 31.

c. Prepare an income statement for the month of December.

d. Prepare a balance sheet as of December 31. (*Note:* In this problem, the net income for December becomes the amount of retained earnings at December 31.)

P3-14A. Balance Sheets for a Corporation The following balance sheet data are given for Norman Catering Service, a corporation, as of May 31:

LO5

Accounts receivable	$20,300	Accounts payable	$ 5,200
Notes payable	23,000	Cash	12,200
Equipment	50,000	Common stock	42,500
Supplies	19,400	Retained earnings	?

Assume that on June 1, the following transactions occurred:

June 1 Purchased additional equipment costing $18,000, giving $3,000 cash and a $15,000 note payable.

1 Paid a cash dividend of $8,000.

Required

a. Prepare a balance sheet as of May 31.

b. Prepare a balance sheet as of June 2.

P3-15A. Determination of Net Income and Retained Earnings The following selected income statement and balance sheet information is available for Floyd Appraisers at the end of the current month:

LO5

Supplies	$ 6,500	Accounts payable	$ 4,000
Accounts receivable	17,800	Salaries expense	17,000
Utilities expense	700	Appraisal fees earned	31,000
Supplies expense	1,400	Common stock	10,000
Rent expense	3,000	Retained earnings (beginning)	5,000
Cash	3,600		

a. Calculate the net income or net loss for the month.

b. If Mr. Floyd made no additional investment in the business during the month but received $6,000 as a dividend, what is the balance in Retained Earnings at the end of the month?

LO5   P3-16A. Trial Balance and Financial Statements The following account balances were taken (out of order) from the general ledger of Howe & Company as of January 31. Howe trains dogs for competitive championship field trials. The firm's accounting year began on January 1. All accounts have normal balances.

Land	$22,810	Office rent expense	$ 800
Maintenance expense	950	Supplies expense	760
Supplies	1,200	Utilities expense	200
Advertising expense	380	Fees earned	18,400
Common stock	20,000	Accounts receivable	8,200
Retained earnings	9,000		
Cash	7,300	Salaries expense	4,480
Accounts payable	880	Dividends	1,200

Required

a. Prepare a trial balance from the given data.

b. Prepare an income statement for the month of January.

c. Prepare a statement of stockholders' equity for the month of January.

d. Prepare a balance sheet as of January 31.

LO5   P3-17A. Trial Balance and Financial Statements The following account balances, in alphabetical order, are from the general ledger of Milo's Waterproofing Service at January 31. The firm began business on January 1. All accounts have normal balances.

Accounts payable	$ 3,500	Notes payable	$ 5,000
Accounts receivable	19,000	Rent expense	1,500
Advertising expense	1,420	Salaries expense	8,000
Cash	12,600	Service fees earned	25,760
Common stock	29,740	Supplies	8,860
Dividends	2,000	Supplies expense	10,250
Interest expense	50	Utilities expense	320

Required

a. Prepare a trial balance from the given data.

b. Prepare an income statement for the month of January.

c. Prepare a statement of stockholders' equity for the month of January.

d. Prepare a balance sheet as of January 31.

LO5, 7   P3-18A. Financial Statements and Closing Entries Use the information provided in P3-8A.
(Appendix 3A)

Required

a. Prepare an income statement, a statement of stockholders' equity, and a balance sheet as of December 31.

b. Prepare closing entries using the Income Summary account.

LO7   P3-19A. Closing Entries Use the information provided in P3-9A.
(Appendix 3A)

Required

a. Prepare closing entries in general journal form using the Income Summary account.

b. After the closing entries are posted, what is the ending balance in the Retained Earnings account?

c. Prepare a post-closing trial balance.

P3-20A. Worksheet The following unadjusted trial balance was prepared as of March 31:

LO8
(Appendix 3B)

FOCUS TRAVEL AGENCY Unadjusted Trial Balance March 31	Debit	Credit
Cash	$ 2,400	
Commissions receivable	8,000	
Supplies	2,200	
Prepaid insurance	1,800	
Equipment	16,000	
Accumulated depreciation		$ 7,600
Accounts payable		550
Unearned commissions		700
Common stock		4,000
Retained earnings		9,300
Dividends	900	
Commissions earned		18,990
Salaries expense	6,500	
Rent expense	1,870	
Advertising expense	850	
Utilities expense	620	
Totals	$41,140	$41,140

Focus Travel Agency's fiscal year ends on March 31. The following additional information is available:

1. Depreciation for the year is $1,500.
2. Supplies on hand at March 31 amount to $820.
3. By March 31, the entire $700 of the unearned commissions was earned.
4. Insurance expense for the year is $1,200.
5. Accrued salaries payable total $1,100 at March 31.

Required

Enter the trial balance on a worksheet and complete the worksheet using the adjustment data given above.

PROBLEMS—SET B

P3-1B. Transaction Entries, Posting, Trial Balance, Adjusting Entries Zhou Karate School began business on June 1. Transactions for June were as follows:

LO3, 4

1. Po Zhou contributed $10,000 of his personal funds in exchange for common stock to begin the business.
2. Purchased equipment for $4,750, paying $950 cash, with the balance due in 30 days.
3. Paid six months' rent, $6,450.
4. Paid one-year premium on liability insurance, $876.
5. Paid June newspaper advertising, $715.
6. Billed participants for karate lessons to date, $2,200.
7. Received $885 from a local company to conduct a special three-session class on self-defense for its employees. The three sessions will be held on June 29, July 6, and July 13, at $295 per session.
8. Collected $3,000 on account from participants.
9. Paid $275 to repair damage to wall caused by an errant kick.
10. Billed participants for karate lessons to date, $2,000.
11. Paid assistant's wages, $950.

Required

a. Set up a general ledger with the following accounts: Cash; Accounts Receivable; Prepaid Rent; Prepaid Insurance; Equipment; Accumulated Depreciation—Equipment; Accounts Payable; Utilities Payable; Unearned Karate Fees; Common Stock; Karate Fees Earned; Advertising

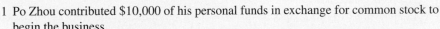

Expense; Repairs Expense; Wages Expense; Rent Expense; Insurance Expense; Depreciation Expense—Equipment; and Utilities Expense.

b. Record these transactions in general journal form and post to the ledger accounts.

c. Prepare an unadjusted trial balance as of June 30.

d. Prepare the adjusting entries for rent expense, insurance expense, depreciation expense, utilities expense, and karate fees earned. Depreciation expense for June is $175, and estimated utilities expense for June is $320. Post the adjusting entries.

LO3, 4   **P3-2B.**   **Transaction Entries, Posting, Trial Balance, and Adjusting Entries** Market-Tech, a market research firm, had the following transactions in June, its first month of operations.

1 J. Witson invested $28,000 of personal funds in the firm in exchange for common stock.

2 The firm purchased the following from an office supply company: office equipment, $11,040; office supplies, $2,840. Terms called for a cash payment of $3,500, with the remainder due in 60 days. (Make a compound entry.)

3 Paid June rent, $1,275.

4 Contracted for five months' advertising in a local newspaper at $325 per month and paid for the advertising in advance.

5 Signed a six-month contract with an electronics firm to provide research consulting services at a rate of $3,200 per month. Received two months' fees in advance. Work on the contract started immediately.

6 Billed various customers for services rendered, $8,000.

7 Paid two weeks' salaries (five-day week) to employees, $3,600.

8 Paid J. Witson's travel expenses to business conference, $1,440.

9 Paid $520 cash for postage to mail questionnaire.

10 Paid two weeks' salaries to employees, $3,600.

11 Billed various customers for services rendered, $7,200.

12 Collected $7,900 from customers on account.

13 J. Witson received a $2,500 cash dividend.

Required

a. Set up a general ledger that includes the following accounts: Cash; Accounts Receivable; Office Supplies; Prepaid Advertising; Office Equipment; Accumulated Depreciation—Office Equipment; Accounts Payable; Salaries Payable; Unearned Service Fees; Common Stock; Dividends; Service Fees Earned; Salaries Expense; Advertising Expense; Supplies Expense; Rent Expense; Travel Expense; Depreciation Expense—Office Equipment; and Postage Expense.

b. Record June transactions in general journal form and post to the ledger accounts.

c. Prepare an unadjusted trial balance as of June 30.

d. Record adjusting journal entries in general journal form, and post to the ledger accounts. The following information is available on June 30:

  Office supplies on hand, $1,830.

  Accrued salaries, $875.

  Estimated life of office equipment, eight years. (Assume equipment was purchased June 1.)

Also, make any necessary adjusting entries for advertising and for service fees indicated by the June transactions. Assume original transactions occurred June 1.

LO3, 4   **P3-3B.**   **Trial Balance and Adjusting Entries** Sendall, a mailing service, has just completed its first full year of operations on December 31, 2022. The firm's general ledger account balances before year-end adjustments are given below. No adjusting entries have been made to the accounts at any time during the year. Assume that all balances are normal.

Cash	$ 2,600	Accounts payable	$ 2,700
Accounts receivable	5,120	Common stock	7,530
Prepaid advertising	1,680	Mailing fees earned	86,000
Supplies	6,570	Wages expense	38,800
Equipment	42,240	Rent expense	4,700
Notes payable	8,500	Utilities expense	3,020

An analysis of the firm's records reveals the following:

1. The balance in Prepaid Advertising represents the amount paid for newspaper advertising for one year. The agreement, which calls for the same amount of space each month, covers the period from February 1, 2022, to January 31, 2023. Sendall did not advertise during its first month of operations.
2. The equipment, purchased January 1, has an estimated life of eight years.
3. Utilities expense does not include expense for December, estimated at $525. The bill will not arrive until January 2023.
4. At year-end, employees have earned $1,750 in wages that will not be paid until January.
5. Supplies on hand at year-end amounted to $1,720.
6. At year-end, unpaid interest of $500 has accrued on the notes payable.
7. The firm's lease calls for rent of $525 per month payable on the first of each month, plus an amount equal to 1 percent of annual mailing fees earned. The rental percentage is payable within 15 days after the end of the year.

Required
a. Demonstrate that the sum of the debits equals the sum of the credits for the unadjusted account balances shown above by preparing an unadjusted trial balance as of December 31, 2022.
b. Record adjusting entries in general journal form.

P3-4B. Adjusting Entries The Spoke Place, Inc., began operations on March 1 to provide automotive wheel alignment and balancing services. On March 31, the unadjusted balances of the firm's accounts are as follows: **LO3, 4**

THE SPOKE PLACE, INC. Unadjusted Trial Balance March 31		
	Debit	**Credit**
Cash	$ 1,900	
Accounts receivable	5,820	
Prepaid rent	4,770	
Supplies	4,100	
Equipment	36,180	
Accounts payable		$ 4,510
Unearned service revenue		1,500
Common stock		38,800
Service revenue		12,360
Wages expense	4,400	
Totals	$57,170	$57,170

The following information is also available.

1. The balance in Prepaid Rent was the amount paid on March 1 to cover the first six months' rent.
2. Supplies on hand on March 31 amounted to $2,100.
3. The equipment has an estimated life of nine years.
4. Unpaid wages at March 31 were $660.
5. Utility services used during March were estimated at $650. A bill is expected early in April.
6. The balance in Unearned Service Revenue was the amount received on March 1 from a new car dealer to cover alignment and balancing services on all new cars sold by the dealer in March and April. The Spoke Place agreed to provide the services at a fixed fee of $750 each month.

Required
Prepare the adjusting entries needed at March 31 in general journal form.

P3-5B. Adjusting Entries The following information relates to the December 31 adjustments for Liquid Barrier, a firm providing waterproofing services for commercial and residential customers. The firm's fiscal year ends December 31; no adjusting entries have been made during the year.   **LO3, 4**

1. The firm paid a $4,500 premium for a three-year insurance policy, coverage to begin October 1. The premium payment was debited to Prepaid Insurance.

2. Weekly wages for a five-day work week total $1,250, payable on Fridays. December 31 is a Thursday.

3. Liquid Barrier received $3,000 in November for services to be performed during December through February of the following year. When received, this amount was credited to Unearned Service Fees. By December 31, one-third of this amount was earned.

4. Liquid Barrier receives a 6 percent commission from the manufacturer on sales of a waterproofing agent to Liquid Barrier's customers. By December 31, Liquid Barrier had sales of $10,000 (during November and December) for which no commissions had been received or recorded.

5. During December, fuel oil costs of $650 were incurred to heat the firm's buildings. Because the monthly bill from the oil company has not yet arrived, no entry has been made for this amount. (Fuel oil costs are charged to Utilities Expense.)

6. The Supplies account has a balance of $17,500 on December 31. A count of supplies on December 31 indicates that $3,500 worth of supplies are still on hand.

7. On December 1, Liquid Barrier borrowed $10,000 from the bank, giving a note payable. Interest is not payable until the note is due near the end of the following January. However, the interest for December is $115.

8. Liquid Barrier rents parking spaces in its lot to firms in the office building next door. On December 1, Liquid Barrier received $7,500 as advance payments to cover parking privileges in the lot for December through March of the following year. When received, the $7,500 was credited to Unearned Parking Fees.

Required
Prepare the necessary December 31 adjusting entries in general journal form.

LO3, 4   P3-6B.   Adjusting Entries The following selected accounts appear in the Gloria Company's unadjusted trial balance as of December 31, the end of the fiscal year. (All accounts have normal balances.)

Prepaid advertising.	$ 3,600	Unearned service fees	$ 4,800
Wages expense	45,800	Service fees earned	88,000
Prepaid insurance.	6,420	Rental income.	4,900

Required
Make the necessary adjusting entries in general journal form as of December 31 assuming the following:

a. Prepaid advertising at December 31 is $900.
b. Unpaid wages earned by employees in December are $1,900.
c. Prepaid insurance at December 31 is $2,380.
d. Unearned service fees at December 31 are $2,500.
e. Rent revenue of $4,200 owed by a tenant is not recorded at December 31.

LO3, 4   P3-7B.   Adjusting Entries The following selected accounts appear in the Hawkes Company's unadjusted trial balance as of December 31, the end of the fiscal year. (All accounts have normal balances.)

Prepaid maintenance	$ 6,000	Commission fees earned	$97,000
Supplies	10,800	Rent expense	11,200
Unearned commission fees	10,700		

Required
Make the necessary adjusting entries in general journal form at December 31, assuming the following:

1. On September 1, the company entered into a prepaid equipment maintenance contract. The Hawkes Company paid $6,000 to cover maintenance service for six months, beginning September 1. The $6,000 payment was debited to Prepaid Maintenance.

2. Supplies on hand at December 31 are $3,500.

3. Unearned commission fees at December 31 are $5,500.

4. Commission fees earned but not yet billed at December 31 are $4,100. (*Note:* Debit Fees Receivable.)

5. The Hawkes Company's lease calls for rent of $900 per month payable on the first of each month, plus an annual amount equal to 4 percent of annual commissions earned. This additional rent is payable on January 10 of the following year. (*Note:* Be sure to use the adjusted amount of commissions earned in calculating the additional rent.)

P3-8B. Financial Statements and Closing Entries Outside, Inc., publishes magazines for skiers and hikers. **LO5, 6**
The firm has the following adjusted trial balance at December 31:

OUTSIDE, INC. Adjusted Trial Balance December 31		
	Debit	**Credit**
Cash.	$ 5,400	
Accounts receivable	19,000	
Supplies	4,200	
Prepaid insurance.	930	
Office equipment	70,000	
Accumulated depreciation		$ 13,000
Accounts payable		17,000
Unearned subscription revenue		10,000
Salaries payable.		3,500
Common stock		21,000
Retained earnings		17,620
Subscription revenue		188,300
Advertising revenue		55,400
Salaries expense	120,230	
Printing and mailing expense	85,600	
Rent expense	5,400	
Supplies expense	6,100	
Insurance expense	1,860	
Depreciation expense.	5,500	
Income tax expense	1,600	
Totals	$325,820	$325,820

Required

a. Prepare an income statement for the year and a balance sheet as of December 31.
b. Prepare closing entries directly to Retained Earnings in general journal form.

P3-9B. Closing Entries The adjusted trial balance for Barry Moving Service as of December 31 is as **LO6**
follows:

	Adjusted Trial Balance	
	Debit	**Credit**
Cash.	$ 5,400	
Accounts receivable	5,250	
Supplies	5,300	
Prepaid advertising.	3,000	
Trucks.	30,300	
Accumulated depreciation—Trucks		$ 10,000
Equipment	7,600	
Accumulated depreciation—Equipment		2,100
Accounts payable		1,200
Unearned service fees		6,700
Common stock		11,000
Retained earnings		16,750
Dividends	7,700	
Service fees earned		81,000
Wages expense	31,200	
Rent expense	10,200	
Insurance expense	4,900	
Supplies expense	5,100	
Advertising expense	8,000	
Depreciation expense—Trucks.	4,000	
Depreciation expense—Equipment	800	
Totals	$128,750	$128,750

Required

a. Prepare the closing entries at December 31 directly to Retained Earnings in general journal form.
b. After the closing entries are posted, calculate the ending balance in the Retained Earnings account.
c. Prepare a post-closing trial balance.

LO5   P3-10B. Balance Sheet and Net Income Determination At the beginning of the year, Acme Parking Services had the following balance sheet:

Assets		Liabilities	
Cash	$ 6,400	Accounts payable	$16,500
Accounts receivable	18,700		
Land	62,500	**Stockholders' Equity**	
		Common stock	63,000
		Retained earnings	8,100
		Total Liabilities and	
Total Assets	$87,600	Stockholders' Equity	$87,600

a. At the end of the year, Acme Parking Services had the following assets and liabilities: Cash, $9,200; Accounts Receivable, $18,400; Land, $62,500; and Accounts Payable, $11,750. Prepare a year-end balance sheet for Acme Parking Services assuming that no additional stock was issued.
b. Assuming that stockholders did not invest any money in the business during the year but received a $12,000 dividend, what was the company's net income or net loss for the year?

LO5   P3-11B. Determination of Retained Earnings and Net Income The following information appears in the records of the Aukland Corporation at year-end:

Accounts receivable	$ 40,000	Retained earnings	$?
Accounts payable	8,000	Supplies	9,000
Cash	7,000	Equipment	140,000
Common stock	130,000		

a. Calculate the amount of retained earnings at the end of the year.
b. Using your answer to part *a*, if the amount of the retained earnings at the beginning of the year was $30,000, and $6,000 in dividends was paid during the year, what was the net income for the year?

LO3, 4, 5, 6   P3-12B. Transaction Analysis, Trial Balance, and Financial Statements Kate Smith operates the Smith Dance Studio. On June 1, the studio's general ledger contained the following information:

Cash	$10,930	Accounts payable	$ 480
Accounts receivable	18,200	Notes payable	3,000
		Common stock	11,870
		Retained earnings	13,780
	$29,130		$29,130

The following transactions occurred during the month of June:

1 Paid June rent for practice studio, $3,000.
2 Paid June piano rental, $800 (Rent Expense).
3 Collected $14,320 from students on account.
4 Borrowed $6,500 and signed a promissory note payable due in six months.
5 Billed students for June instructional fees, $9,600.
6 Paid interest for June on the outstanding notes payable, $110.
7 Paid $550 for advertising ballet performances.
8 Paid costume rental, $800 (Rent Expense).
9 Collected $6,300 admission fees from ballet performances given during June.
10 Paid $780 owed on account.
11 Received invoice for June utilities, to be paid in July, $480.

12 The studio paid stockholders a cash dividend of $900.

13 Purchased piano for $6,000 cash, to be used in business starting in July.

Required

a. Set up accounts for the general ledger with June 1 balances and enter the beginning balances. Also provide the following accounts: Piano; Dividends; Instructional Fees Earned; Performance Revenue; Rent Expense; Utilities Expense; Advertising Expense; and Interest Expense. Record the listed transactions in the accounts.

b. Prepare a trial balance as of June 30.

c. Prepare an income statement for the month of June.

d. Prepare a statement of stockholders' equity for the month of June.

e. Prepare a balance sheet as of June 30.

f. Prepare closing entries.

g. Prepare a post-closing trial balance.

P3-13B. Transaction Analysis, Trial Balance, and Financial Statements On December 1, a group of individuals formed a corporation to establish the *Humbolt News,* a neighborhood newspaper featuring "Help wanted" ads by individuals and advertising by local firms. The free paper will be mailed to about 20,000 local residents; revenue will be generated from advertising and the want ads. The December transactions are summarized below:

LO3, 4

1 Sold common stock for cash, $65,000.

2 Paid December rent on furnished office, $5,000.

3 Purchased for $550, on account, T-shirts displaying company logo. The T-shirts were distributed at a grand opening.

4 Paid to creditor on account, $475.

5 Collected want ad revenue in cash, $2,800.

6 Paid post office for cost of bulk mailing, $810.

7 Billed various firms for advertising in the first two issues of the newspaper, $6,300.

8 Paid Tucson Courier Service for transporting newspapers to the post office, $70.

9 Paid for printing newspaper, $3,900.

10 Collected want ad revenue in cash, $4,570.

11 Received invoice for December utilities, to be paid in January, $510.

12 Paid for printing newspaper, $4,400.

13 Paid December salaries, $6,100.

14 Billed various firms for advertising in two issues of the newspaper, $8,950.

15 Paid post office for cost of bulk mailing, $630.

16 Paid Tucson Courier Service for transporting newspapers to the post office, $90.

17 Collected $5,100 on accounts receivable.

18 Purchased a printer for the office in exchange for a six-month note payable, $3,100.

Required

a. Set up accounts for the following: Cash, Accounts Receivable, Office Equipment, Accounts Payable, Notes Payable, Common Stock, Advertising Revenue, Want Ad Revenue, Printing Expense, Advertising Expense, Utilities Expense, Salaries Expense, Rent Expense, and Delivery Expense. Prepare journal entries in a general journal and record the foregoing transactions in the accounts.

b. Prepare a trial balance as of December 31.

c. Prepare an income statement for the month of December.

d. Prepare a balance sheet as of December 31. (*Note:* In this problem, the net income for December becomes the amount of retained earnings at December 31.)

P3-14B. Balance Sheets for a Corporation The following balance sheet data are given for Harvard Catering Service, a corporation, at May 31:

LO5

Accounts receivable	$30,300	Accounts payable	$ 5,200
Notes payable	20,000	Cash	12,200
Equipment	60,000	Common stock	62,500
Supplies	16,400	Retained earnings	?

Assume that on June 1, the following transactions occurred:

June 1 Purchased additional equipment costing $26,000, giving $2,000 cash and a $24,000 note payable.

2 Paid a cash dividend of $7,000.

Required

a.   Prepare a balance sheet as of May 31.
b.   Prepare a balance sheet as of June 2.

LO5   **P3-15B. Determination of Net Income and Stockholders' Equity** The following selected income statement and balance sheet information is available for Xin Land Appraisers at the end of the current month:

Supplies	$ 7,400	Accounts payable	$ 4,500
Accounts receivable	24,600	Salaries expense	15,000
Utilities expense	700	Appraisal fees earned.	31,000
Supplies expense	1,300	Common stock	15,000
Rent expense	2,900	Retained earnings (beginning)	5,000
Cash	3,600		

a.   Calculate the net income or net loss for the month.
b.   If stockholders made no additional investment during the month but received $6,000 as a dividend, what is the amount of retained earnings at the end of the month?

LO5   **P3-16B. Trial Balance and Financial Statements** The following account balances were prepared (out of order) from the general ledger of The Cat Whisperer, Inc., as of January 31. The company trains cats having behavioral problems. The firm's business began on January 1. All accounts have normal balances.

Facilities	$32,000	Office rent expense	$ 800
Maintenance expense	460	Supplies expense	1,760
Supplies	1,640	Utilities expense	200
Advertising expense	550	Fees earned	20,470
Common stock	37,600	Accounts receivable	8,200
Cash	7,300	Salaries expense	4,480
Accounts payable	1,420	Dividends	2,100

Required

a.   Prepare a trial balance from the given data.
b.   Prepare an income statement for the month of January.
c.   Prepare a statement of stockholders' equity for the month of January.
d.   Prepare a balance sheet as of January 31.

LO5   **P3-17B. Trial Balance and Financial Statements** The following account balances, in alphabetical order, are from the general ledger of The Nina Service Company at January 31. The firm's business began on January 1. All accounts have normal balances.

Accounts payable	$ 9,200	Notes payable.	$12,000
Accounts receivable	39,000	Rent expense	2,900
Advertising expense	840	Salaries expense	16,000
Cash	20,800	Service fees earned	53,020
Common stock	56,180	Supplies	17,920
Dividends	11,000	Supplies expense	20,500
Interest expense	800	Utilities expense	640

Required

a.   Prepare a trial balance from the given data.
b.   Prepare an income statement for the month of January.
c.   Prepare a statement of stockholders' equity for the month of January.
d.   Prepare a balance sheet as of January 31.

LO5, 7   **P3-18B. Financial Statements and Closing Entries** Use the information provided in P3-8B.
(Appendix 3A)

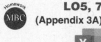

Required

a.   Prepare an income statement, a statement of stockholders' equity, and a balance sheet as of December 31.
b.   Prepare closing entries in general journal form using the Income Summary account.

P3-19B. Closing Entries Use the information provided in P3-9B.

LO7
(Appendix 3A)

Required

a.   Prepare closing entries at December 31 in general journal form using the Income Summary account.

b.   After the closing entries are posted, calculate the ending balance in the Retained Earnings account.

c.   Prepare a post-closing trial balance.

P3-20B. Worksheet The July 31 unadjusted trial balance of Lake Outfitters, a firm renting various types of equipment to canoeists and campers, follows.

LO8
(Appendix 3B)

LAKE OUTFITTERS Unadjusted Trial Balance July 31	Debit	Credit
Cash.	$ 3,750	
Supplies	8,600	
Prepaid insurance.	3,200	
Equipment	91,000	
Accumulated depreciation		$ 16,500
Accounts payable.		3,500
Unearned rental fees		8,850
Common stock		33,000
Retained earnings		3,000
Dividends	1,200	
Rental fees earned.		78,150
Wages expense	28,800	
Rent expense	3,300	
Advertising expense.	2,300	
Travel expense	850	
	$143,000	$143,000

Lake Outfitters' fiscal year ends on July 31. The following additional information is available:

1.   Supplies on hand at July 31 amount to $2,300.
2.   Insurance expense for the year is $1,600.
3.   Depreciation for the year is $8,750.
4.   The unearned rental fees consist of deposits received from customers in advance when reservations are made. During the year, $4,850 of the unearned rental fees were earned. The remaining deposits apply to rentals for August and September.
5.   At July 31, revenue from rental services earned during July but not yet billed or received amounts to $3,500. (*Note:* Debit Fees Receivable.)
6.   Accrued wages payable for equipment handlers and guides amounts to $700 at July 31.

Required
Enter the trial balance in a worksheet and complete the worksheet using the adjustment data given above.

SERIAL PROBLEM: KATE'S CARDS

(Note: This is a continuation of the Serial Problem: Kate's Cards from Chapters 1 and 2.)

SP3.   Getting ready for the upcoming holiday season is traditionally a busy time for greeting card companies, and it was no exception for Kate. The following transactions occurred during the month of October:

Kate's Cards

1. Hired an assistant at an hourly rate of $10 per hour to help with some of the computer layouts and administrative chores.
2. Supplements her business by teaching a class to aspiring card designers. She charges and receives a total of $450.
3. Delivers greeting cards to several new customers. She bills them a total of $3,500.
4. Pays a utility bill in the amount of $250 that she determines is the business portion of her utility bill.
5. Receives an advance deposit of $500 for a new set of cards she is designing for a new customer.
6. Pays her assistant $200 for the work done this month.
7. Determines that the assistant has worked 10 additional hours this month that have not yet been paid.
8. Ordered and receives additional supplies in the amount of $1,000. These were paid for during the month.
9. Counts her remaining inventory of supplies at the end of the month and determines the balance to be $300. Don't forget to consider the supplies inventory balance at September 30, from Chapter 2. (*Hint:* This expense will be a debit to Cost of Goods Sold.)
10. Records the adjusting entries for depreciation and insurance expense for the month.
11. Pays herself a salary of $1,000.
12. Paid monthly rent of $1,200 in cash.
13. Receives her next utility bill during December and determines $85 applies to October's operations.
14. Deciding she needs a little more cash, Kate pays herself a $100 dividend.

Required

Using the information that you gathered and the general ledger accounts that you prepared through Chapter 2, plus the new information above, complete the following:

a. Journalize the above transactions and adjusting entries.
b. Post the October transactions and adjusting entries. (Use the general ledger accounts prepared in Chapter 2 and add any new accounts that you may need.)
c. Prepare a trial balance as of October 31.
d. Prepare an income statement and a statement of stockholders' equity for the two-month period ending October 31, and a balance sheet as of October 31.
e. Prepare the closing entries as of October 31.
f. Prepare a post-closing trial balance.

EXTENDING YOUR KNOWLEDGE

REPORTING AND ANALYSIS

COLUMBIA
SPORTSWEAR
COMPANY

EYK3-1.   **Financial Reporting Problem: Columbia Sportswear Company** The financial statements for the **Columbia Sportswear Company** can be found in Appendix A at the end of this book.

Required
Answer the following questions using Columbia's Consolidated Financial Statements and the Notes to the consolidated financial statements:

a. Identify an item that likely requires adjusting entries for prepayments.
b. Identify an item that likely requires an adjusting accrual.
c. Examine the statement of cash flows and identify the amount of depreciation and amortization expense for 2020. Where on the balance sheet was this accrual likely also shown?
d. Identify the items that will require closing entries. What account will they be ultimately closed to?

COLUMBIA
SPORTSWEAR
COMPANY

UNDER ARMOUR, INC.

EYK3-2.   **Comparative Analysis Problem: Columbia Sportswear Company vs. Under Armour, Inc.** The financial statements for the **Columbia Sportswear Company** can be found in Appendix A, and **Under Armour, Inc.'s** financial statements can be found in Appendix B at the end of this book.

Required

a. Examine the balance sheet of Columbia Sportswear and identify three items that indicate that the company uses the accrual method of accounting. In each case, identify the likely income statement account that is affected by these accruals.

b. Examine the balance sheet of Under Armour, Inc., and identify three items that indicate the company uses the accrual method of accounting. In each case, identify the likely income statement account that is affected by these accruals.

EYK3-3. **Business Decision Problem** Gilbert Consulting Services, a firm started three years ago by Bruce Gilbert, offers consulting services for material handling and plant layout. The balance sheet prepared by the firm's accountant at the close of 2021 is shown here.

GILBERT CONSULTING SERVICES
Balance Sheet
As of December 31, 2021

Assets			Liabilities	
Cash.........................		$ 3,400	Notes payable.............	$30,000
Accounts receivable		22,875	Accounts payable	4,200
Supplies		13,200	Unearned consulting fees....	11,300
Prepaid insurance...............		4,500	Wages payable.............	400
Equipment	$68,500		Total Liabilities	45,900
Less: Accumulated depreciation....	(23,975)	44,525	**Stockholders' Equity**	
			Common stock	20,000
			Retained earnings	22,600
			Total Stockholders' Equity....	42,600
			Total Liabilities and	
Total Assets		$88,500	Stockholders' Equity	$88,500

Earlier in the year, Gilbert obtained a bank loan of $30,000 for the firm. One of the provisions of the loan is that the year-end debt-to-equity ratio (ratio of total liabilities to total stockholders' equity) shall not exceed 1.0. Based on the above balance sheet, the ratio at the end of 2021 is 1.08 ($45,900/$42,600).

Gilbert is concerned about being in violation of the loan agreement and asks your assistance in reviewing the situation. Gilbert believes that his rather inexperienced accountant may have overlooked some items at year-end.

In discussions with Gilbert and the accountant, you learn the following:

1. On January 1, 2021, the firm paid a $4,500 insurance premium for two years of coverage. The amount in Prepaid Insurance has not been adjusted.
2. Depreciation on the equipment should be 10 percent of cost per year. The accountant inadvertently recorded 15 percent for 2021.
3. Interest on the bank loan has been paid through the end of 2021.
4. The firm concluded a major consulting engagement in December, doing a plant layout analysis for a new factory. The $6,000 fee has not been billed or recorded in the accounts.
5. On December 1, 2021, the firm received an $11,300 advance payment from Croy Corporation for consulting services to be rendered over a two-month period. This payment was credited to the Unearned Consulting Fees account. One-half of this fee was earned by December 31, 2021.
6. Supplies costing $4,800 were on hand on December 31. The accountant filed the record of the count but made no entry in the accounts.

Required

a. What is the correct debt-to-equity ratio at December 31, 2021? Is the firm in violation of the loan agreement? Prepare a schedule to support your computation of the correct total liabilities and total stockholders' equity as of December 31, 2021.

b. Why might the loan agreement have contained the debt-to-equity provision?

EYK3-4. **Financial Analysis Problem** Purpose: To learn more about the Financial Accounting Standards Board (FASB)
Address: http://www.fasb.org

Required
Use the information on the FASB site to answer the following questions:
a.   When was the FASB established?
b.   What is the mission of the FASB?
c.   Who has oversight responsibility for the FASB?
d.   What are some of the current projects of the FASB?

CRITICAL THINKING

GENERAL MILLS, INC.

EYK3-5. **Accounting Research Problem** Refer to the annual report of **General Mills, Inc.,** for the year ending May 31, 2020 (fiscal year 2020), available on this book's website. Review the consolidated balance sheets.

Required
a.   Identify two assets listed in the consolidated balance sheets that indicate that General Mills uses the accrual basis of accounting. Which income statement accounts of General Mills are affected by adjustments to these assets accounts?
b.   Identify two liabilities listed in the consolidated balance sheets that indicate that General Mills uses the accrual basis of accounting. Which income statement accounts of General Mills are affected by these adjustments?

EYK3-6. **Accounting Communications Activity** Many people do not understand the concept of accrual accounting and how it differs from accounting on a cash basis. In particular, they are confused as to why a company's results in any one accounting period can differ so much between the two methods of accounting. Because the cash basis is understood to a far larger degree, many people argue that the cash basis should be the primary basis of accounting.

Required
Write a short memorandum that explains the difference between accrual accounting and the cash basis of accounting. In your memo give a simple example of how the accrual basis can give a clearer picture of a company's performance in a given period.

EYK3-7. **Accounting Ethics Case** It is the end of an accounting year for Juliet Kravetz, controller of a medium-sized, publicly held corporation specializing in toxic waste cleanup. Within the corporation, only Kravetz and the president know that the firm has been negotiating for several months to land a very large contract for waste cleanup in Western Europe. The president has hired another firm with excellent contacts in Western Europe to help with the negotiations. The outside firm charges an hourly fee plus expenses but has agreed not to submit a bill until the negotiations are in their final stages (expected to occur in another three to four months). Even if the contract falls through, the outside firm is entitled to receive payment for its services. Based upon her discussion with a member of the outside firm, Kravetz knows that its charge for services provided to date will be $150,000. This is a material amount for the company.

Kravetz knows that the president wants the negotiations to remain as secret as possible so that competitors will not learn of the European contract that the company is pursuing. Indeed, the president recently stated to her, "This is not the time to reveal our actions in Western Europe to other staff members, our auditors, or readers of our financial statements; securing this contract is crucial to our future growth." No entry has been made in the accounting records for the cost of the contract negotiations. Kravetz now faces an uncomfortable situation. The company's outside auditor has just asked her if she knows of any year-end adjustments that have not yet been recorded.

Required
What are the ethical considerations that Kravetz faces in answering the auditor's question? How should she respond to the question?

EYK3-8. **Environmental, Social, and Governance Problem** Unlike financial reporting that requires all reported amounts to be expressed in monetary terms, Environmental, Social, and Governance (ESG) reporting is often more qualitative than quantitative. This has caused some individuals to discount the ESG reports as too subjective.

Required
a. Can you identify any subjective areas within a financial statement prepared under GAAP?
b. Discuss the reasons both financial reporting, and to a larger extent ESG reporting, allow subjective estimates to be part of the report.

EYK3-9. **Forensic Accounting Problem** Most employees who choose to commit fraud against their employers feel justified in doing so. For example, a demotion with a corresponding pay cut can provide motivation to produce what is called "wages in kind," where the employee creates his or her own wages.

Required
What actions might an organization take to prevent "wages in kind"?

EYK3-10. **Analyzing IFRS Financial Statements** The 2020 financial statements of LVMH Moet Hennessey-Louis Vuitton S.A. are presented in Appendix C at the end of this book. LVMH is a Paris-based holding company and one of the world's largest and best-known luxury goods companies. As a member of the European Union, French companies are required to prepare their consolidated (group) financial statements using International Financial Reporting Standards (IFRS). After reviewing LVMH's consolidated financial statements, consider the following questions.

Required
a. Identify two assets listed in the group balance sheets that indicate that LVMH uses the accrual basis of accounting. Which income statement accounts of LVMH are affected by adjustments to these assets accounts?
b. Identify two liabilities listed in the group balance sheets that indicate that LVMH uses the accrual basis of accounting. Which income statement accounts of LVMH are affected by these adjustments?

EYK3-11. **Working with the Takeaways** The Vail Company has the following items that require adjustments as of December 31.
a. Service revenue of $600 had been received prior to work being performed. This amount was properly recorded as unearned revenue. At year-end, $500 of the services have now been performed.
b. Interest expense of $975 has not been recorded.
c. Services in the amount of $350 have been performed but not yet billed.
d. A physical count determined that supplies still available were $250. The Supplies asset account shows a balance of $800.

Required
Provide the adjusting entry needed to correct the balance in each of the affected accounts.

ANSWERS TO SELF-STUDY QUESTIONS:

1. b   2. c   3. d   4. c   5. b   6. c   7. d

YOUR TURN! SOLUTIONS

Solution 3.1

1.	June 30	Accounts receivable (+A)	600	
		Sales revenue (+R, +SE)		600
		To recognize revenue earned.		
2.	June 30	Cash (+A)	700	
		Unearned revenue (+L)		700
		To recognize cash prior to revenue being earned.		
3.	June 30	Inventory (+A)	400	
		Accounts payable (+L)		400
		To record the purchase of inventory on account.		

Solution 3.2

1. c,   2. d,   3. b,   4. a

Solution 3.3

1.	Dec. 31	Depreciation expense (+E, −SE)	700	
		Accumulated depreciation—Buildings (+XA, −A)		700
		To record depreciation on buildings.		
2.	Dec. 31	Rent expense (+E, −SE)	1,500	
		Prepaid rent (−A)		1,500
		To record rent expense.		

Solution 3.4

1.	Dec. 31	Unearned revenue (−L)	400	
		Revenue (+R, +SE)		400
		To recognize revenue earned on a previously recorded advance payment from a customer.		
2.	Dec. 31	Interest expense (+E, −SE)	500	
		Interest payable (+L)		500
		To accrue interest expense.		

Solution 3.5

CASSI COMPANY Income Statement For the Year Ended December 31		
Sales revenues		$52,000
Expenses		
Cost of goods sold	$30,000	
Salaries expense	5,000	
Rent expense	6,000	
Depreciation expense	6,000	
Total expenses		47,000
Net income		$ 5,000

CASSI COMPANY Statement of Stockholders' Equity For the Year Ended December 31	Common Stock	Retained Earnings	Total
Balance, December 1, 2019	$15,000	$5,000	$20,000
Add: Net income for December		5,000	5,000
Less: Dividends in December		(2,000)	(2,000)
Balance, December 31, 2019	$15,000	$8,000	$23,000

CASSI COMPANY
Balance Sheet
As of December 31

Assets			Liabilities		
Current assets			Current liabilities		
Cash	$ 4,000		Accounts payable	$ 8,000	
Accounts receivable	15,000		Salaries payable	9,000	
Inventory	18,000		Dividends payable	2,000	
Prepaid rent	5,000		Unearned service	5,000	
Total current assets		$42,000	Total current liabilities		$24,000
			Long-term debt		35,000
Equipment	50,000		Total liabilities		59,000
Less: Accumulated depreciation	(10,000)	40,000	**Stockholders' Equity**		
			Common stock	15,000	
			Retained earnings	8,000	
			Total stockholders' equity		23,000
Total Assets		$82,000	Total Liabilities and Stockholders' Equity		$82,000

Solution 3.6

a. Permanent
b. Permanent
c. Temporary
d. Permanent

e. Temporary
f. Temporary
g. Permanent
h. Permanent

Solution 3.7

Dec. 31	Sales revenue (–R)	79,000	
	Retained earnings (+SE)		79,000
	To close the revenue account.		
Dec. 31	Retained earnings (–SE)	72,000	
	Cost of goods sold (–E)		41,000
	Wage expense (–E)		22,000
	Rent expense (–E)		3,000
	Depreciation expense (–E)		2,000
	Interest expense (–E)		4,000
	To close the expense accounts.		
Dec. 31	Retained earnings (–SE)	5,000	
	Dividends (–D)		5,000
	To close the dividends account.		

Solution 3A.1

a. Permanent
b. Permanent
c. Temporary
d. Permanent

e. Temporary
f. Temporary
g. Permanent
h. Temporary

Solution 3A.2

Dec. 31	Sales revenue (–R)	79,000	
	Income summary (+SE)		79,000
	To close the revenue account.		
Dec. 31	Income summary (–SE)	72,000	
	Cost of goods sold (–E)		41,000
	Wage expense (–E)		22,000
	Rent expense (–E)		3,000
	Depreciation expense (–E)		2,000
	Interest expense (–E)		4,000
	To close the expense accounts.		
Dec. 31	Income summary (–SE)	7,000	
	Retained earnings (+SE)		7,000
	To close the Income Summary account.		
Dec. 31	Retained earnings (–SE)	5,000	
	Dividends (–D)		5,000
	To close the Dividends account.		

Chapter 4

Understanding Financial Statements

Road Map

LO	Learning Objective	Page	eLecture	Guided Example	Assignments
LO1	Describe a classified balance sheet.	4-3	E4-1	YT4.1	SS1, SS2, SS3, SS4, SS5, SE1, E1A, E4A, E1B, E4B, P1A, P2A, P4A, P1B, P2B, P4B
LO2	Describe a single-step and multi-step income statement.	4-7	E4-2	YT4.2	SS13, SE10, E2A, E2B, P3A, P6A, P10A, P3B, P6B, P10B
LO3	Discuss use of the balance sheet and ratios to assess liquidity and solvency.	4-11	E4-3	YT4.3	SS6, SS7, SS11, SE3, SE4, SE7, E3A, E5A, E6A, E3B, E5B, E6B, P5A, P8A, P9A, P5B, P8B, P9B
LO4	Discuss use of the income statement and ratios to assess profitability.	4-14	E4-4	YT4.4	SS8, SS9, SE2, SE9, E3A, E5A, E8A, E3B, E5B, E8B, P5A, P6A, P8A, P9A, P5B, P6B, P8B, P9B
LO5	Explain the components of the statement of stockholders' equity.	4-15	E4-5	YT4.5	SS10, SS12, E7A, E10A, E7B, E10B, P7A, P7B
LO6	Explain use of the statement of cash flows to help assess solvency.	4-16	E4-6	YT4.6	SE5, SE6, SE8, SE11, E3A, E5A, E9A, E3B, E5B, E9B, P4A, P4B

After a visit to one of **Apple**'s many retail stores, you will likely find it hard to believe that the company ever faced financial difficulties. The company has a cult-like following for its products, including its MacBook and iMac computers, the iPhone, iPad, and Apple Watch. Business has not always been so good for the company. In fact, Apple suffered crippling financial losses and record low stock prices in the mid-1990s. Steve Jobs, who left the company in 1985 to start another business, was brought back to Apple in 1997 as chief executive officer (CEO). Over the next few years, Jobs was able to return the company to profitability.

Being a profitable company has allowed Apple to benefit from what some refer to as a virtuous cycle in which the company is able to both do good financially and do good socially. The company's solid financial resources provide the ability to do good, whereas doing good helps the company do well financially.

But what if we decide to consider investing in a company like Apple? How should we go about determining whether Apple is a good investment? We first want to do some research to determine if the company is profitable and financially sound. In this and future chapters, we will begin to accumulate the financial skills needed to evaluate the financial health and operating performance of companies.

PAST

Chapters 1 through 3 explained the five-step accounting cycle: analyze, record, adjust, report, and close.

PRESENT

This chapter introduces classified financial statements and some key ratios computed from those statements.

FUTURE

Later chapters expand on ratios used in analyzing financial statements, starting in Chapter 5, which focuses on analyzing and recording merchandising transactions.

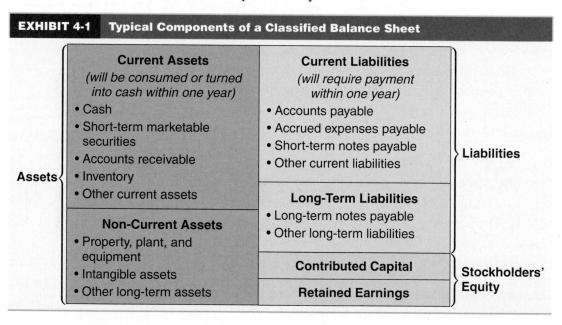

BALANCE SHEET CLASSIFICATION AND ANALYSIS

LO1   Describe a classified balance sheet.

MBC

A **classified balance sheet** presents the assets and liabilities of a business in separate subgroups. Such classification aids our financial analysis and business decision-making. **Exhibit 4-1** presents a list of the typical components of a classified balance sheet. A company need not use all of the components, and each company will use only those components necessary to report its financial position. **Exhibit 4-1** shows that a company's assets are commonly classified into two subgroups: current assets and long-term assets. Similarly, liabilities are classified into two subgroups: current liabilities and long-term liabilities. Classified balance sheets are presented by most businesses.

EXHIBIT 4-1   **Typical Components of a Classified Balance Sheet**

Assets		Liabilities / Stockholders' Equity	
Current Assets *(will be consumed or turned into cash within one year)* • Cash • Short-term marketable securities • Accounts receivable • Inventory • Other current assets		**Current Liabilities** *(will require payment within one year)* • Accounts payable • Accrued expenses payable • Short-term notes payable • Other current liabilities	**Liabilities**
Non-Current Assets • Property, plant, and equipment • Intangible assets • Other long-term assets		**Long-Term Liabilities** • Long-term notes payable • Other long-term liabilities	
		Contributed Capital	**Stockholders' Equity**
		Retained Earnings	

Current Assets

Current assets consist of cash and other assets that will be converted into cash or used within the normal operating cycle of a business or one year, whichever is longer. The **normal operating cycle** of a business is the average period of time between the payment of cash to deliver a service or to buy goods for resale and the subsequent collection of cash from customers who purchase those services or products. For most businesses, the normal operating cycle is less than one year. For example, the normal operating cycle for a grocery store chain like **Safeway** might be as short as a week or two, on average, and even only a day or two for perishable products like bread and fresh vegetables.

   Current assets are listed on a classified balance sheet in the order of their expected liquidity. **Liquidity** is the ability of an asset to be readily converted into cash. **Exhibit 4-1** lists five examples of current assets in the order of their expected liquidity: cash, short-term marketable securities, accounts receivable, inventory, and other current assets. Short-term marketable securities represent short-term investments in the securities of other firms that can be quickly sold for cash. Accounts receivable and inventory are converted into cash as part of the normal operations of a business; that is, inventory is sold for cash or on credit (accounts receivable) that is subsequently collected as cash from customers. Other current assets, such as supplies, are consumed during the normal operating cycle rather than converted into cash, and thus, represent the least liquid of the current assets. The following excerpt shows the current asset section of **Apple**'s balance sheet.

APPLE INC. Balance Sheet (Partial) September 26, 2020 (in millions)	
Cash.	$ 39,789
Short-term investments	52,927
Accounts receivable	16,120
Inventory.	4,061
Other current assets.	30,816
Total current assets.	$143,713

> Assets that will be converted into cash or used within the normal operating cycle of a business or one year, whichever is longer.

Long-Term Assets

Long-term assets are assets that the company does not expect to convert into cash within the next year or use during the course of the normal operating cycle, whichever is longer. As shown in **Exhibit 4-1**, long-term assets include property, plant, and equipment, intangible assets, and other long-term assets.

Property, Plant, and Equipment

Property, plant, and equipment consists of the land, buildings, equipment, vehicles, furniture, and fixtures that a company uses in its day-to-day operations. The following excerpt shows the PP&E section of **Apple**'s balance sheet.

APPLE INC. Balance Sheet (Partial) September 26, 2020 (in millions)		
Property, plant, and equipment		
Land and buildings	$17,952	
Equipment.	75,291	
Leasehold improvements	10,283	$103,526
Less: accumulated depreciation and amortization		66,760
Total property, plant, and equipment, net		$ 36,766

Companies can either report the components of PP&E in the balance sheet or report only the total and include the components in an accompanying note to the financial statements. Apple followed the second approach, reporting the total PP&E of $36,766 in the balance sheet and the components shown above in a note.

Intangible Assets

Intangible assets consist of brand names, copyrights, patents, and trademarks that a company acquires. These assets are referred to as "intangible" because, unlike buildings and equipment, they lack a physical presence. But, like buildings and equipment, intangible assets enable a company to generate revenue from its customers who recognize the quality associated with products bearing a brand name or trademark. Although Apple has several trademarks, patents, and copyrights, they are not reported on its September 26, 2020, balance sheet because they were developed by Apple rather than acquired from another company.

Other Long-Term Assets

Other long-term assets consist of resources that a company reports in a single miscellaneous category for purposes of presentation on the balance sheet. The following excerpt shows the other long-term assets included in **Apple**'s balance sheet.

APPLE INC. Balance Sheet (Partial) September 26, 2020 (in millions)	
Other long-term assets	
Long-term marketable securities	$100,887
Other assets	42,522
	$143,409

Current Liabilities

Current liabilities consist of liabilities that must be settled within the normal operating cycle or one year, whichever is longer. **Exhibit 4-1** lists four types of current liabilities: accounts payable, accrued expenses payable, short-term notes payable, and other current liabilities. Accounts payable reflects the amounts owed for inventory that was purchased from suppliers on credit. Accrued expenses payable include wages, utilities, interest, income tax, and property taxes that are legally owed by a company but have not yet been paid. Short-term notes payable represent amounts owed that are specified in a formal contract called a note. Other current liabilities consist of current obligations that the company aggregates into a single miscellaneous category. One example is the advance payments received from customers (deferred revenue), such as for goods under a layaway plan that will be recognized as revenue within the normal operating cycle or one year, whichever is longer. The following excerpt shows the current liabilities section of **Apple**'s balance sheet.

APPLE INC. Balance Sheet (Partial) September 26, 2020 (in millions)	
Current liabilities	
Accounts payable	$ 42,296
Accrued expenses	47,680
Deferred revenue	6,643
Short-term loans	8,773
Total current liabilities	$105,392

Liabilities that must be settled within the normal operating cycle or one year, whichever is longer.

Long-Term Liabilities

A.K.A. Long-term liabilities are also referred to as **noncurrent liabilities**.

Long-term liabilities consist of debt obligations not due to be settled within the normal operating cycle or one year, whichever is longer. Long-term notes payable and bonds payable are two examples of long-term liabilities. Other long-term liabilities include employee retirement plans that will be funded by the company in the future, or deferred revenue that will be recognized as revenue over longer periods. The following excerpt shows the long-term liabilities section of **Apple**'s balance sheet.

APPLE INC.
Balance Sheet (Partial)
September 26, 2020 (in millions)

Long-term liabilities	
Long-term debt	$ 98,667
Other long-term liabilities	54,490
Total long-term liabilities	$153,157

Stockholders' Equity

Stockholders' equity is the residual ownership interest in the assets of a business after its liabilities have been settled. The stockholders' equity of a corporation is divided into two main categories: amounts invested by stockholders (common stock) and the cumulative net income of a business that has not yet been distributed to its stockholders as a dividend (retained earnings). The following excerpt shows the stockholders' equity section of **Apple**'s balance sheet.

A.K.A. Stockholders' equity is also referred to as **shareholders' equity**.

APPLE INC.
Balance Sheet (Partial)
September 26, 2020 (in millions)

Stockholders' equity	
Common stock	$50,779
Retained earnings	14,966
Other equity	(406)
Total stockholders' equity	$65,339

Presentation Format

There are two generally accepted formats for presenting a classified balance sheet—the account form and the report form. In the **account form**, assets are displayed on the left side and liabilities and stockholders' equity are displayed on the right side. In the **report form**, assets are displayed at the top, followed by liabilities, and finally by stockholders' equity. Apple's 2020 and 2019 balance sheets in report form are presented in **Exhibit 4-2**. The report form is the more widely used format.

Hint: According to Accounting Trends and Techniques, a recent survey of 600 large U.S. companies shows that 88% use the report form for their balance sheet while 12% use the account form.

DATA ANALYTICS   **The Next Frontier: Data Analytics and the Audit**

Auditors use data analytics to gain a deeper understanding of the companies they audit and to perform the audit more efficiently and effectively. Some of the ways that data analytics could improve financial statement auditing include the testing of complete data sets rather than sampling and risk assessment through the identification of anomalies and trends. To achieve the full potential of data analytics in auditing, several things must happen, including broadening the education of accountants. The auditors of the future will need a better understanding of data science, information technology, statistics, modeling, and machine learning. With a staff knowledgeable in these areas, CPA firms will be able to expand their services to include areas such as data quality, cybersecurity, fraud prevention and detection, and internal controls.

Source: *Journal of Accountancy* online, Data analytics helps auditors gain deep insight, Murphy and Tysiac

Data Analytics

EXHIBIT 4-2	Report Form of a Classified Balance Sheet	

APPLE INC.
Balance Sheet
September 26, 2020, and September 28, 2019 (in millions)

(in millions)	2020	2019
Assets		
Current assets		
Cash	$ 39,789	$ 50,224
Short-term investments	52,927	51,713
Accounts receivable	16,120	22,926
Inventory	4,061	4,106
Other current assets	30,816	33,850
Total current assets	143,713	162,819
Long-term assets		
Property, plant, and equipment	36,766	37,378
Other noncurrent assets	143,409	138,319
Total long-term assets	180,175	175,697
Total assets	323,888	338,516
Liabilities		
Current liabilities		
Accounts payable	$ 42,296	$ 46,236
Other current liabilities	63,096	59,482
Total current liabilities	105,392	105,718
Long-term liabilities	153,157	142,310
Total liabilities	258,549	248,028
Stockholders' Equity		
Common stock	$ 50,779	$ 45,174
Retained earnings	14,966	45,898
Other equity	(406)	(584)
Total stockholders' equity	65,339	90,488
Total liabilities and stockholders' equity	$323,888	$338,516

YOUR TURN! 4.1

MBC

The solution is on
page 4-39.

The President of Musicland Company requests that you prepare a classified balance sheet in report form for the company. The following financial data are available from the company's accounting records as of December 31.

Other current liabilities	$ 2,000	Other current assets	$ 1,500
Long-term notes payable	20,000	Inventory	12,200
Stockholders' equity	17,500	Property, plant, & equipment, net	25,000
Accounts payable	2,500	Accounts receivable	3,000
Cash	300		

INCOME STATEMENT CLASSIFICATION AND ANALYSIS

Describe a single-step and multi-step income statement.

MBC

A **single-step income statement** is the simplest form of an income statement. The name originates from the way the statement is constructed. The sum of the expenses is subtracted from the sum of the revenues in a single step to arrive at net income. An example of a single-step income statement for **Apple** for the years ended September 26, 2020, and September 28, 2019, is in **Exhibit 4-3**.

EXHIBIT 4-3	Single-Step Income Statement for Apple Inc.	

APPLE INC.
Income Statement
For Years Ended September 26, 2020, and September 28, 2019

(in millions)	2020	2019
Revenues		
Net sales.	$274,515	$260,174
Other income	803	1,807
Total revenues.	275,318	261,981
Expenses		
Cost of goods sold	169,559	161,782
Research and development expenses	18,752	16,217
Selling, general, and administrative	19,916	18,245
Income tax expenses	9,680	10,481
Total expenses.	217,907	206,725
Net income.	$ 57,411	$ 55,256

Specifically, Apple's 2020 revenue totaled $275,318 million. From this amount, Apple subtracts total expenses of $217,907 million to yield 2020 net income of $57,411 million.

A **multi-step income statement** presents revenues and expenses in distinct categories to facilitate financial analysis and management decision-making. A multi-step income statement provides financial statement users with more information, and thus, enables them to make better and more informed decisions about a business. A multi-step income statement is divided into two main sections; the operating section and the non-operating section. The operating section contains revenues and expenses related to the principal business activities of the company. The non-operating section contains revenues and expenses that are incidental to the company's principal business activities, such as gains or losses on the sale of equipment and interest revenue or expense.

A.K.A A multi-step income statement is also known as a **classified income statement**.

The format of a multi-step income statement will differ somewhat depending on whether the company is a service firm or a merchandising firm. The difference in format between service firms and merchandising firms is because service firms do not sell a physical product and therefore do not have cost of goods sold. Examples of service companies include accounting firms, health care providers, and architects. In contrast, merchandising companies sell goods to customers. We discuss merchandisers in more detail in Chapter 5.

For a service company, total operating expenses are subtracted from service revenues to determine income from operations. Operating expenses are those expenses that relate to the primary operating activities of a business. Operating expenses are commonly called selling, general, and administrative expenses. Revenue and expense items that do not relate to the primary operating activities of the company appear in a separate category called *Other Income and Expense*. The net amount of other income and expense is either added to or subtracted from income from operations to determine pretax income.

For a merchandising company, the cost of goods sold is subtracted from the firm's net sales to determine its gross profit on sales. **Gross profit**, or gross profit on sales, is defined as the difference between net sales and cost of goods sold and reveals the amount of sales revenue remaining after subtracting the cost of products sold. **Net sales** are total sales less an estimate of **sales returns and allowances** and **sales discounts**. Sales returns and allowances represent the expected amount given to the customer for the return of merchandise or in lieu of a return. Sales discounts represent an expected amount allowed to the buyer for early payment. These items are discussed further in Chapter 5. Gross profit also reveals the amount of sales revenue available to cover a business's operating expenses. The remainder of the

A.K.A. Gross profit is often referred to as **gross margin**.

structure of a merchandising company's multi-step income statement (following gross profit) is the same as the structure of the service company's multi-step income statement.

A.K.A. Income before income tax is also known as **pretax income**.

Exhibit 4-4 presents a multi-step income statement for **Apple**. Apple's multi-step income statement provides more detail to the financial statement user with four measures of company performance: gross profit on sales, income from operations, income before income taxes, and net income. Gross profit on sales indicates how well the company performed in terms of purchasing goods, warehousing those goods, and pricing the goods for sale. Income from operations reports Apple's performance after considering the cost of running its stores, paying its employees, advertising to its customers, and administering the business. The income before income taxes reports the company's performance after considering various nonoperating items like interest expense and interest income but before subtracting the expected cost of income taxes. Income tax is then subtracted from income before income taxes to compute net income. Income tax is computed as a percentage of income before income taxes.

> A multi-step income statement for a service firm will not have cost of goods sold, nor will it have a subtotal for gross profit on sales.

EXHIBIT 4-4	Multi-Step Income Statement for a Merchandising Company	
APPLE INC.		
Income Statement		
For Years Ended September 26, 2020, and September 28, 2019		
(in millions)	**2020**	**2019**
Net sales.	$274,515	$260,174
Less cost of goods sold	169,559	161,782
Gross profit on sales	104,956	98,392
Operating expenses		
Research and development expenses	18,752	16,217
Selling, general, and administrative	19,916	18,245
Total operating expenses.	38,668	34,462
Income from operations.	66,288	63,930
Other income	803	1,807
Income before income taxes.	67,091	65,737
Income tax expense	9,680	10,481
Net income	$ 57,411	$ 55,256

Net sales for Apple consists primarily of sales of hardware, software, digital content, and support contracts, less amounts for estimated future product returns. Cost of goods sold represents the cost to Apple for the items sold. Cost of goods sold is typically the largest expense for a retail company such as Apple. Cost of goods sold is subtracted directly from net sales to highlight the gross profit on sales. The gross profit on sales is an important financial indicator for investment professionals who follow retail companies like Apple. Analysts compare the gross profit on sales between retailers as a way to assess the effectiveness of the retailer's pricing and purchasing policies.

The operating expenses section includes expenses that relate to the primary operating activities of a business. Operating expenses consist primarily of selling expenses and administrative expenses. Examples of Apple's selling, general, and administrative expenses include salaries expense, delivery expense, advertising expense, depreciation expense, rent expense, and supplies expense.

The other income and expense section of the income statement is sometimes labeled nonoperating activities. Examples of revenues and expenses that do not relate to the primary operating activities of a merchandising firm include:

Other Revenues and Gains	Other Expenses and Losses
• Interest revenue • Gains on asset sales • Dividend income	• Interest expense • Losses on asset sales

These items are reported in the other income and expense section that follows the financial information regarding a business's primary operating activities.

Net income measures Apple's bottom-line performance—that is after all costs of running the business are subtracted. Net income is the same whether the company uses a single-step or a multi-step income statement format.

Exhibit 4-5 presents the components of a multi-step income statement for Webwork (a service company) and for Apple (a merchandising company). We see the absence of the cost of goods sold section, including the gross profit subtotal, in the service company's income statement. Otherwise, the income statements follow the same format.

EXHIBIT 4-5	Classified Income Statements for Service and Merchandising Companies

WEBWORK, INC. Income Statement For Year Ended December 31		APPLE INC. Income Statement For Year Ended September 26	
Revenues	$19,150	Net sales.	$274,515
		Less cost of goods sold	169,559
		Gross profit on sales	104,956
Operating expenses		Operating expenses	
Wage, rent, and supplies expenses . . .	5,550	Research and development expenses . . .	18,752
Depreciation and interest expenses . . .	750	Selling, general, and administrative	19,916
Total operating expenses	6,300	Total operating expenses.	38,668
Income from operations	12,850	Income from operations	66,288
Other income and expenses.	—	Other income and expenses.	803
Income before income taxes.	12,850	Income before income taxes.	67,091
Income tax expense	2,570	Income tax expense	9,680
Net income	$10,280	Net income	$ 57,411

THINKING GLOBALLY

Appendix C at the end of this book presents the classified balance sheet and the multi-step income statement for LVMH Moet Hennessy, Louis Vuitton. LVMH is a Paris-based holding company and one of the world's largest and best-known luxury goods companies. As a member of the European Union, French companies are required to prepare their consolidated (group) financial statements using International Financial Reporting Standards (IFRS). After reviewing the LVMH statements, make a list of the similarities and differences between LVMH's IFRS balance sheet and income statement and Apple's U.S. GAAP balance sheet and income statement presented in Exhibits 4-2 and 4-4. Differences between LVMH's and Apple's balance sheets include: (1) LVMH presents noncurrent assets before its current assets—that is, it lists the company's assets in reverse order of liquidity; (2) LVMH presents shareholders' equity before liabilities; (3) LVMH presents noncurrent liabilities before current liabilities; and (4) LVMH uses slightly different labeling for some of its balance sheet accounts—for instance, common stock is referred to as "share capital." As for the income statements, like Apple, LVMH reports several measures of company performance: gross margin, profit from recurring operations, operating profit, net financial income (expense). Differences include (1) LVMH includes more subsections; (2) LVMH uses the word "profit" instead of "income"; (3) LVMH separates out minority interest (less than 100 percent owned subsidiaries that are consolidated with the parent LVMH); (4) LVMH refers to its interest expense as "cost of financial debt." Other than these labeling differences, LVMH's multi-step income statement under IFRS is strikingly similar to Apple's U.S. GAAP multi-step income statement.

YOUR TURN! 4.2

GuidedExample

MBC

The solution is on page 4-39.

Musicland provides the following information and requests that we prepare a multi-step income statement for the year ended December 31. Musicland pays income tax at the rate of 30 percent of income.

Selling, general, and administrative expenses ..	$25,000	Cost of goods sold.	$ 45,000
Research & development expense.	10,000	Net sales	100,000
Interest expense	5,000		

WORKING WITH FINANCIAL STATEMENTS

So far we have introduced the basic financial statements. We now demonstrate how financial statements are used to address questions about a company's operating performance and financial health.

Analysis Based on Ratios

If Apple's net income in 2020 totaled $57,411 million, would we conclude that the company had a good year or a bad year? While $57,411 million is a large number, some frame of reference is needed before we can conclude that this amount represents a good, bad, or mediocre level of operating performance. For example, $57,411 million is a phenomenal performance if the company had only $1 million in assets to operate with during the year. But it is not as exceptional if the company had $100,000 million in assets to operate with during the year.

Investment professionals use a variety of methods to develop a better understanding of how to interpret a net income number like $57,411 million. One such method involves ratio analysis. **Ratio analysis** expresses the relation of one relevant accounting number to another relevant accounting number through the process of division. The result of the division is expressed as a percentage, a rate, or a proportion.

To illustrate how a ratio can provide additional meaning to Apple's net income of $57,411 million, we can divide Apple's net income by its total assets of $323,888 million, which is known as its **return on assets (ROA)**.

$$\text{Return on assets (ROA)} = \frac{\text{Net income}}{\text{Total assets}}$$

The result tells us that Apple earned a rate of return of 17.7 percent on each dollar of assets invested in the business in 2020.

Although a single number like Apple's net income is difficult to interpret in isolation, a single ratio is also difficult to interpret without some point of reference or benchmark. Business professionals often use one of two techniques to further their understanding of ratios. **Trend analysis** compares a company's results, or the results of a ratio, over time. This technique helps the financial statement user identify any readily observable trends in a company's performance. **Benchmarking analysis** compares a company's performance, or a ratio, to that of its competitors, or to an industry average. Under benchmarking analysis, we compare, or benchmark, a company's performance against similar companies or against an industry standard. Trend analysis and benchmarking analysis are powerful tools to place a company's results into a meaningful context.

Working with the Balance Sheet

LO3   Discuss use of the balance sheet and ratios to assess liquidity and solvency.

The balance sheet helps users evaluate the financial health of a company. The balance sheet also provides information on how the company finances the acquisition of its assets, with debt or with equity.

Terms such as liquidity and solvency refer to the financial well-being of a company. For a company to remain in business, it must be able to pay its bills when they come due. Before a bank such as **Bank of America** will commit to extend a loan to a company like Apple, it needs to assess the likelihood that it will be repaid the amount borrowed and be

eLecture

MBC

paid the interest due on the amount borrowed, both in a timely manner. This assessment involves evaluating Apple's *liquidity*, the ability to pay obligations that come due in the current year, and *solvency*, the ability to pay obligations over the long term.

Liquidity

Liquidity refers to a company's ability to pay its short-term financial obligations. It depends on several factors, including the level of cash a company has and how quickly it can generate cash from operations or its assets.

Current Ratio   One widely used measure of a company's liquidity is the **current ratio**. The current ratio is defined as current assets divided by current liabilities. Current assets provide a measure of the cash available and expected to be generated in the current period. Current liabilities provide a measure of the cash that will be needed in the current period to pay existing or expected obligations.

$$\text{Current ratio} = \frac{\text{Current assets}}{\text{Current liabilities}}$$

A current ratio greater than one implies that a company has more cash and current assets than needed to pay off its current obligations, and a ratio less than one implies the opposite. While this interpretation is overly simplistic, it does provide an easily understood assessment of a company's liquidity. In general, the greater the current ratio, the more liquid a company is, and the less concern a lender has in extending a loan to the company.

    One of Apple's competitors is **Hewlett-Packard Inc.**, an online retailer of personal computers. The current ratios for both Apple and Hewlett-Packard are shown in **Exhibit 4-6**. Based on this ratio, we would conclude that Apple is more liquid than Hewlett-Packard in both years. Apple reports a higher current ratio than Hewlett-Packard in both years (1.36 compared to .88 in 2020 and 1.54 compared to .79 in 2019).

EXHIBIT 4-6	**Current Ratio**	
Current Ratio	**2020**	**2019**
Apple	$\frac{\$143{,}713}{\$105{,}392} = 1.36{:}1$	$\frac{\$162{,}819}{\$105{,}718} = 1.54{:}1$
Hewlett-Packard	$\frac{\$16{,}556}{\$18{,}738} = 0.88{:}1$	$\frac{\$15{,}143}{\$19{,}159} = 0.79{:}1$

Concept ⟶	Method ⟶	Assessment	**TAKEAWAY 4.1**
Can a company meet its short-term obligations?	Current assets and current liabilities from the balance sheet. $\text{Current ratio} = \frac{\text{Current assets}}{\text{Current liabilities}}$	A larger current ratio implies greater liquidity and a greater ability to pay short-term obligations.	

Solvency

Lenders often provide loans that have repayment terms that extend over several years. In such cases the lender is interested in evaluating a company's solvency. **Solvency** refers to a company's ability to pay its long-term financial obligations. It depends on several factors, including the amount of assets held by a company. Solvency, therefore, is a measure of a company's ability to survive over the long term. (Both liquidity and solvency are important indicators of financial health, but a company must first be liquid. If a company is unable to pay its bills in the short term, it is irrelevant whether it is solvent in the long term.)

Debt-to-Total-Assets Ratio   In general, the more debt a company uses to finance its assets and day-to-day operations, the riskier it is. This follows because the amount borrowed and the interest on that amount must be paid on a regular schedule. If a company is unable to meet the cash outflows required to satisfy its debt repayment schedule or meet its regular interest payments, a lender can legally demand immediate repayment of a loan, potentially forcing a company into bankruptcy if it is unable to repay that amount. The **debt-to-total-assets ratio**, calculated as total liabilities divided by total assets, provides a measure of this risk and is one ratio used to assess a company's solvency.

$$\text{Debt-to-total-assets ratio} = \frac{\text{Total liabilities}}{\text{Total assets}}$$

The greater the debt-to-total-assets ratio, the greater is a company's risk of not being able to pay its interest payments or principal repayments on a timely basis, and the lower is the company's solvency. Like the current ratio, the debt-to-total-assets ratio should not be used in isolation. There are many factors that must be considered when judging a company's solvency.

Exhibit 4-7 shows the debt-to-total-assets ratios for Apple and Hewlett-Packard. This exhibit reveals that in both 2020 and 2019 Apple used more debt to finance its assets than did Hewlett-Packard (79.8 percent versus 70.2 percent in 2020). While a higher debt-to-total-assets ratio could be an indication of a riskier, less solvent company, this is not likely the case in this example. Apple's debt-to-total-assets ratio is still within a range that is unlikely to concern a lender, such as **Citibank**.

EXHIBIT 4-7 Debt-to-Total-Assets Ratio		
(in millions)	**2020**	**2019**
Apple	$\frac{\$258,549}{\$323,888} = 79.8\%$	$\frac{\$248,028}{\$338,516} = 73.3\%$
Hewlett-Packard	$\frac{\$37,919}{\$54,015} = 70.2\%$	$\frac{\$34,654}{\$51,803} = 66.9\%$

TAKEAWAY 4.2	Concept ⟶	Method ⟶	Assessment
	Can a company meet its long-term obligations?	Total assets and total liabilities from the balance sheet. $\text{Debt-to-total-assets ratio} = \frac{\text{Total liabilities}}{\text{Total assets}}$	A larger ratio implies reduced solvency and a reduced ability to repay outstanding obligations over the long term.

YOUR TURN! 4.3

MBC

The solution is on page 4-40.

The following information is available from the financial statements of the Philips Company.

	Current Year	Prior Year
Net sales.	$120,000	$110,000
Net income	20,000	15,000
Cash provided by operating activities.	25,000	22,000
Expenditures on property, plant, and equipment . . .	7,000	6,000
Current assets	75,000	65,000
Current liabilities.	50,000	45,000
Total assets.	220,000	190,000
Total liabilities	$150,000	$145,000

Compute the current ratio and the debt-to-total-assets ratio and comment on any trends observed between the current year and the prior year.

Working with the Income Statement

Apple generates income by selling computers, iPads, iPhones, watches, peripherals, and downloads from its Apps store. The company's income statement provides a report detailing how much net income Apple was able to generate from these activities. A review of a company's income and its components is called profitability analysis. Apple's net income of $57,411 million for the year ended September 26, 2020, indicates that Apple was able to sell these products at a price that exceeded manufacturing and other costs of running the business.

LO4   **Discuss** use of the income statement and ratios to assess profitability.

eLecture

MBC

Apple's income statement, presented in **Exhibit 4-4**, also shows that the company's net income increased by $2,155 million, from $55,256 million in 2019 to $57,411 million in 2020. During a similar period, Hewlett-Packard's net income decreased by $1,371 million, from $1,049 million in 2019 to a loss of $322 million in 2020. This suggests that Apple outperformed one of its leading competitors during this period. How was that possible? Perhaps Apple's success reflects its superior product line or possibly its greater product focus. Alternatively, it might reflect the superior operating acumen of Apple's management team.

Measures for Profitability Analysis

There are many ways to measure a company's success. One such measure is profitability. Profitability indicates whether or not a company is able to bring its products or services to the market efficiently, and whether it produces products or services that are valued by the market. The more profitable a company is, the better are its long-term prospects. Consistently unprofitable companies are on a path to failure.

Return on Sales Ratio (Profit Margin)   It is somewhat unfair, and potentially misleading, to compare two companies of differing size on the basis of net income. A larger company is expected to generate a larger net income. But a large net income does not necessarily indicate that a company is performing more efficiently than a company with a smaller net income. One measure that facilitates a comparison of the profitability between companies of different size is the return on assets ratio, which we already explained. Another useful measure is the **return on sales (ROS) ratio (profit margin)**, calculated as net income divided by net sales.

$$\text{Return on sales ratio} = \frac{\text{Net income}}{\text{Net sales}}$$

Exhibit 4-8 shows the calculation of return on sales for both Apple and Hewlett-Packard. Apple is larger than Hewlett-Packard based on sales generated in 2020 ($274,515 million for Apple versus $26,982 million for Hewlett-Packard). Apple also generated more net income than Hewlett-Packard ($57,411 for Apple versus a loss of $322 million for Hewlett-Packard in 2020). Together this translates into a much more favorable return on sales for Apple (20.9 percent for Apple versus –1.2 percent for Hewlett-Packard in 2020). An ROS of 20.9 percent indicates Apple has 20.9 cents left over for each dollar of sales revenue after subtracting all of its expenses. This result suggests that Apple is a more profitable company than Hewlett-Packard, possibly because it is able to command a premium price for its products and/or because it runs a more efficient operation.

EXHIBIT 4-8	Return on Sales		
(in millions)		**2020**	**2019**
Apple		$\dfrac{\$57,411}{\$274,515} = 20.9\%$	$\dfrac{\$55,256}{\$260,174} = 21.2\%$
Hewlett-Packard		$\dfrac{\$(322)}{\$26,982} = -1.2\%$	$\dfrac{\$1,049}{\$29,135} = 3.6\%$

TAKEAWAY 4.3	Concept ⟶	Method ⟶	Assessment
	How much net income does a company generate from each dollar of sales revenue?	Net sales and net income from the income statement. $$\text{Return on sales ratio} = \frac{\text{Net income}}{\text{Net sales}}$$	A larger ratio indicates that a company is more profitable on each sales dollar because it commands a premium price for its products and/or is more operationally efficient.

YOUR TURN! 4.4

MBC

The solution is on page 4-40.

The following information is available from the financial statements of the Philips Company.

	Current Year	Prior Year
Net sales.	$120,000	$110,000
Net income	20,000	15,000
Cash provided by operating activities.	25,000	22,000
Expenditures on property, plant, and equipment . . .	7,000	6,000
Current assets	75,000	65,000
Current liabilities.	50,000	45,000
Total assets.	220,000	190,000
Total liabilities	150,000	145,000

Compute the return on sales ratio and comment on any trends observed between the current year and the prior year.

Working with the Statement of Stockholders' Equity

LO5

Explain the components of the statement of stockholders' equity.

eLecture

MBC

Chapter 1 introduced the statement of stockholder's equity, which summarizes the changes in a company's stockholders' equity during the period. The statement of stockholders' equity consists of two parts—contributed capital and earned capital. **Contributed capital** is a measure of the capital contributed by the stockholders of a company when they purchase ownership shares in the company. Ownership shares are called common shares or common stock. **Earned capital** is a measure of the capital that is earned by the company, reinvested in the business, and not distributed to its stockholders—that is, its retained earnings. Retained earnings at the end of a fiscal period is calculated as retained earnings at the start of the period, plus net income for the period, less any dividends during the period.

Retained earnings, beginning of period
+ Net income
– Dividends
_____
Retained earnings, end of period

ENVIRONMENTAL, SOCIAL, AND GOVERNANCE   Investing with a Social Conscience

Not all investors are singularly focused on the financial performance of businesses they invest in. For a segment of the investing community, corporate social responsibility goes hand in hand with financial performance in choosing an investment. **Socially responsible investing (SRI)**, also known as sustainable investing, considers a firm's environmental stewardship, consumer protection, human rights, and diversity, along with its financial performance. Investments in SRI funds are near $3 trillion and have grown in recent years at a pace almost six times greater than the growth of professionally managed investments.

Exhibit 4-9 presents the statement of stockholders' equity for Apple. The column labeled Common Stock represents the change in Apple's contributed capital during the period covered by the statement. The change to common stock resulted from the issuance of additional shares to Apple's existing stockholders, to new stockholders, or possibly to Apple's employees.

The column labeled Retained Earnings in **Exhibit 4-9** represents Apple's earned capital. The primary adjustments in this column are Apple's net income and the dividends Apple distributes to its shareholders.

EXHIBIT 4-9	Statement of Stockholders' Equity

APPLE INC.
Statement of Stockholders' Equity

(in millions)	Common Stock	Retained Earnings	Other Equity	Total Equity
Balance at September 29, 2018...........	$40,201	$70,400	$(3,454)	$107,147
Issuance of common stock...............	4,973			4,973
Net income............................		55,256		55,256
Dividends.............................		(14,129)		(14,129)
Other adjustments		(65,629)	2,870	(62,759)
Balance at September 28, 2019...........	45,174	45,898	(584)	90,488
Issuance of common stock...............	5,605			5,605
Net income............................		57,411		57,411
Dividends.............................		(14,087)		(14,087)
Other adjustments		(74,256)	178	(74,078)
Balance at September 29, 2020...........	$50,779	$14,966	$ (406)	$ 65,339

The following information is available for the Owner Company:

Beginning of the year common stock.....................	$120,000
Beginning of the year retained earnings	85,000
Additional common stock issued during the year	7,500
Net income..	16,000
Dividends...	4,000

Prepare a statement of stockholders' equity for the Owner Company. How much of the total equity is considered contributed capital, and how much is considered earned capital?

YOUR TURN! 4.5

GuidedExample

MBC

The solution is on page 4-40.

Working with the Statement of Cash Flows

A common refrain heard from business people is that "cash is king!" While net income is eventually converted into cash, it is the cash available that a company uses to run its business and pay its bills. The statement of cash flows provides information on a company's sources and uses of cash.

LO6 Explain use of the statement of cash flows to help assess solvency.

eLecture

MBC

The statement of cash flows aids in understanding the change in cash reported by a company over a period of time. It explains the change in the cash reported between two balance sheet dates, segmented into three activity categories: (1) cash flow from operating activities, (2) cash flow from investing activities, and (3) cash flow from financing activities. The separation into these three activities increases the statement's usefulness. For example, knowing that cash increased is not as useful as knowing that cash increased because of increased operating cash flow or because of a bank loan.

Exhibit 4-10 shows a simplified version of Apple's statement of cash flows. Apple reported a decrease of $10,435 million in cash in 2020, from $50,224 million in 2019 to $39,789 million in 2020. These cash balances are on Apple's balance sheet in **Exhibit 4-2**. Most of Apple's cash flow in 2020 was generated from operating activities ($80,674). Apple used some of its operating cash flow in its investing activities, mostly for the purchase of $8,833 of additional property, plant, and equipment. Apple also used a large amount of cash in its financing activities. The largest of these financing activities was the repurchase of $72,358 million of its common stock.

EXHIBIT 4-10	Statement of Cash Flows		
APPLE INC. **Statement of Cash Flows** **For Years Ended September 26, 2020, and September 28, 2019**			
(in millions)		2020	2019
Cash flow provided by operating activities			
Cash receipts less cash disbursements from operating activities . . .		$80,674	$69,391
Net cash provided by operations.		80,674	69,391
Cash flow provided by investing activities			
Net purchases of investments.		5,335	58,093
Net payments for property, plant, and equipment		(8,833)	(11,119)
Other cash payments		(791)	(1,078)
Net cash used by investing		(4,289)	45,896
Cash flow provided by financing activities			
Net cash from issuance of common stock		$ (2,754)	$ (2,036)
Net cash from issuance of debt		2,499	(7,819)
Payment of dividends		(14,081)	(14,119)
Repurchase of common stock		(72,358)	(66,897)
Other receipts		(126)	(105)
Net cash used by financing		(86,820)	(90,976)
Net increase (decrease) in cash.		(10,435)	24,311
Cash at beginning of year.		50,224	25,913
Cash at year-end		$39,789	$50,224

Free Cash Flow

Hint: When calculating a firm's free cash flow, "capital expenditures" is the cash spent for purchases of PP&E less the cash proceeds received from sale of PP&E. Both amounts are reported on a statement of cash flows.

The level of cash flow provided by operating activities is valuable information on a company's ability to generate cash from its day-to-day operations. Another measure of cash flow health is **free cash flow**. Free cash flow is often calculated by subtracting a company's capital expenditures for PP&E from its cash flow provided by operating activities. A company's free cash flow is an indicator of its ability to expand operations, repay lenders, or pay stockholders a dividend after replacing the value of any property, plant, and equipment used in operations.

Free cash flow = Cash flow from operations – Capital expenditures

We calculate Apple's free cash flow in 2020 and 2019 with information reported in Apple's statement of cash flows in **Exhibit 4-10**.

(in millions)	2020	2019
Cash flow provided by operating activities	$80,674	$69,391
Less: Expenditures on property, plant, and equipment.	(8,833)	(11,119)
Free cash flow	$71,841	$58,272

Apple's free cash flow of $71,841 in 2020 and $58,272 in 2019 indicates that it generates a healthy free cash flow. It also suggests that Apple should have no trouble financing future purchases of property, plant, and equipment, repaying its lenders, or paying dividends to its stockholders.

Concept	Method	Assessment	TAKEAWAY 4.4
How much free cash flow does a company generate?	Cash provided by operating activities less cash expended on purchases of property, plant, and equipment. Cash provided by operations – Capital expenditures = Free cash flow	Larger free cash flow indicates a greater ability to expand operations, repay debt, or pay dividends without external financing.	

YOUR TURN! 4.6

The solution is on page 4-40.

The following information is available from the financial statements of the Philips Company.

	Current Year	Prior Year
Net sales.	$120,000	$110,000
Net income	20,000	15,000
Cash provided by operating activities.	25,000	22,000
Expenditures on property, plant, and equipment	7,000	6,000
Current assets	75,000	65,000
Current liabilities.	50,000	45,000
Total assets.	220,000	190,000
Total liabilities	150,000	145,000

Compute the free cash flow and comment on any trends observed between the current year and the prior year.

FORENSIC ACCOUNTING   **Cash Fraud Schemes**

Frauds involving cash are the most common frauds, and are more common than corruption or fraudulent financial statements. The more common cash schemes include (1) skimming, where an employee accepts cash from a customer but does not record a sales transaction, (2) cash larceny, where an employee steals cash from the daily receipts before they are deposited in a bank, (3) check tampering, where an employee steals blank company checks and makes them out to him/herself or an accomplice, and (4) cash register disbursement, where an employee fraudulently voids a sale on his or her cash register and steals the cash.

COMPREHENSIVE PROBLEM

Following are items reported on the financial statements of MicroTech Corporation as of June 30, 2022. Amounts given are in millions of dollars.

Cash flow provided by operating activities ...	$ 39,507	Operating expenses	$33,363
Cash at June 30, 2021	6,510	Other income	823
Cash at June 30, 2022	7,663	Intangible assets.	45,228
Net revenue	89,950	Other long-term assets.	12,273
Cash flow used by investing activities	(46,781)	Income tax expense	1,945
Inventory.	2,181	Accounts payable.	7,390
Accounts receivable.	19,792	Other current liabilities	57,137
Cost of goods sold	34,261	Long-term liabilities	104,165
Cash flow provided by financing activities ...	8,427	Common stock	69,315
Other current assets.	130,215	Retained earnings	2,648
Property, plant, and equipment.	23,734	Other stockholders' equity	431

a. Prepare a multi-step income statement, a classified balance sheet, and a statement of cash flows using the accounts listed above.

b. Compute the following ratios:
   Current ratio
   Debt-to-total-assets ratio
   Return on sales ratio

Solution

a.

MICROTECH CORPORATION
Income Statement
For Year Ended June 30, 2022 (in millions)

Net revenue	$89,950
Less cost of goods sold	34,261
Gross profit on sales	55,689
Operating expenses	33,363
Income from operations	22,326
Other income	823
Income before income taxes	23,149
Income tax expense	1,945
Net income	$21,204

MICROTECH CORPORATION
Balance Sheet
June 30, 2022 (in millions)

Assets

Current assets

Cash	$ 7,663	
Accounts receivable	19,792	
Inventory	2,181	
Other current assets	130,215	
Total current assets		$159,851
Property, plant, and equipment		23,734
Intangible assets		45,228
Other long-term assets		12,273
Total assets		$241,086

Liabilities and Stockholders' Equity

Current liabilities

Accounts payable	$ 7,390	
Other current liabilities	57,137	
Total current liabilities		$ 64,527
Long-term liabilities		104,165
Total liabilities		168,692
Stockholders' equity		
Common stock	69,315	
Retained earnings	2,648	
Other stockholders' equity	431	
Total stockholders' equity		72,394
Total liabilities and stockholders' equity		$241,086

MICROTECH CORPORATION
Statement of Cash Flows
For Year Ended June 30, 2022 (in millions)

Cash flow provided by operating activities	$39,507
Cash flow used by investing activities	(46,781)
Cash flow used by financing activities	8,427
Net increase in cash	1,153
Cash at June 30, 2021	6,510
Cash at June 30, 2022	$ 7,663

b.

Current ratio	$\dfrac{\$159{,}851}{\$64{,}527}$	= 2.48:1
Debt-to-total-assets ratio	$\dfrac{\$168{,}692}{\$241{,}086}$	= 70.0%
Return on sales ratio	$\dfrac{\$21{,}204}{\$89{,}950}$	= 23.6%

SUMMARY OF LEARNING OBJECTIVES

Describe a classified balance sheet. (p. 4-3)   **LO1**

- A classified balance sheet contains two subgroups of assets (current assets and long-term assets) and two subgroups of liabilities (current liabilities and long-term liabilities).
- A classified balance sheet can be presented in account form or report form.

Describe a single-step and multi-step income statement. (p. 4-7)   **LO2**

- A multi-step income statement classifies items into subgroups to facilitate analysis and decision-making.
- A multi-step income statement for a merchandising firm often includes one line item for sales revenue; two line items for expenses (cost of goods sold and operating expenses) and a line item for other income and expenses.
- A multi-step income statement for a service firm is similar but does not have a line item for cost of goods sold.

Discuss use of the balance sheet and ratios to assess liquidity and solvency. (p. 4-11)   **LO3**

- Ratio analysis involves expressing the relation of one relevant accounting number with another relevant accounting number through the process of division. This process helps to provide a context to interpret a particular number.
- Two techniques that are often used in ratio analysis are (1) trend analysis where ratios are examined over time and (2) benchmarking analysis where a company's ratios are compared to those of another company or to an average of an industry as a whole.
- Liquidity refers to a company's ability to pay obligations that are expected to come due in the next year.
- The current ratio, or current assets divided by current liabilities, provides a measure of a company's liquidity.
- Solvency refers to a company's ability to repay its debts over the long term.
- The debt-to-total-assets ratio, calculated as total debt divided by total assets, provides one measure of a company's solvency.

Discuss use of the income statement and ratios to assess profitability. (p. 4-14)   **LO4**

- Return on sales, or net income divided by net sales, provides a measure of a company's profitability by indicating how much net income a company earns on each dollar of sales revenue.

Explain the components of the statement of stockholders' equity. (p. 4-15)   **LO5**

- Stockholders' equity comprises two parts: (1) contributed capital and (2) earned capital.
- Contributed capital is the capital contributed to a firm by stockholders when they purchase ownership shares in the company.
- Earned capital represents the net income that has been earned by a company and not distributed to stockholders as a dividend.

Explain use of the statement of cash flows to help assess solvency. (p. 4-16)   **LO6**

- The statement of cash flows provides information regarding a company's sources and uses of cash.
- Free cash flow, calculated as cash provided from operating activities less cash expended on property, plant, and equipment, provides information regarding management's ability to expand operations, repay debt, or make distributions to stockholders, using a firm's operating cash flow.

SUMMARY	Concept	→ Method →	Assessment
TAKEAWAY 4.1	Can a company meet its short-term obligations?	Current assets and current liabilities from the balance sheet. $$\text{Current ratio} = \frac{\text{Current assets}}{\text{Current liabilities}}$$	A larger current ratio implies greater liquidity and a greater ability to pay short-term obligations.
TAKEAWAY 4.2	Can a company meet its long-term obligations?	Total assets and total liabilities from the balance sheet. $$\text{Debt-to-total-assets ratio} = \frac{\text{Total liabilities}}{\text{Total assets}}$$	A larger ratio implies reduced solvency and a reduced ability to repay outstanding obligations over the long term.
TAKEAWAY 4.3	How much net income does a company generate from each dollar of sales revenue?	Net sales and net income from the income statement. $$\text{Return on sales ratio} = \frac{\text{Net income}}{\text{Net sales}}$$	A larger ratio indicates that a company is more profitable on each sales dollar because it commands a premium price for its products and/or is more operationally efficient.
TAKEAWAY 4.4	How much free cash flow does a company generate?	Cash provided by operating activities less cash expended on purchases of property, plant, and equipment. Cash provided by operations – Capital expenditures ——————————— Free cash flow	Larger free cash flow indicates a greater ability to expand operations, repay debt, or pay dividends without external financing.

KEY TERMS

Account form (p. 4-6)

Benchmarking
   analysis (p. 4-11)

Classified balance sheet (p. 4-3)

Classified income
   statement (p. 4-8)

Contributed capital (p. 4-15)

Current assets (p. 4-3)

Current liabilities (p. 4-5)

Current ratio (p. 4-12)

Debt-to-total-assets
   ratio (p. 4-13)

Earned capital (p. 4-15)

Free cash flow (p. 4-17)

Gross margin (p. 4-8)

Gross profit (p. 4-8)

Intangible assets (p. 4-4)

Liquidity (p. 4-4, 4-12)

Long-term liabilities (p. 4-5)

Multi-step income
   statement (p. 4-8)

Net sales (p. 4-8)

Noncurrent liabilities (p. 4-5)

Normal operating cycle (p. 4-3)

Pretax income (p. 4-9)

Property, plant, and
   equipment (p. 4-4)

Ratio analysis (p. 4-11)

Report form (p. 4-6)

Return on assets
   (ROA) (p. 4-11)

Return on sales (ROS) ratio
   (profit margin) (p. 4-14)

Sales discounts (p. 4-8)

Sales returns and
   allowances (p. 4-8)

Shareholders' equity (p. 4-6)

Single-step income
   statement (p. 4-7)

Socially Responsible Investing
   (SRI) (p. 4-15)

Solvency (p. 4-12)

Stockholders' equity (p. 4-6)

Trend analysis (p. 4-11)

Assignments with the 🔵 logo in the margin are available in ^{my}BusinessCourse.
See the Preface of the book for details.

SELF-STUDY QUESTIONS

(Answers to Self-Study Questions are at the end of this chapter.)

LO1   **1. Which of the following items will not be reported on a classified balance sheet?**
   a.   Current assets   *c.*   Total liabilities
   b.   Net income   *d.*   Common stock

LO1   **2. Which of the following would not be considered a current asset?**
   a.   Inventory   *c.*   Property, plant, and equipment
   b.   Accounts receivable   *d.*   Cash

3. **For the balance sheet to be in balance, the following must exist:**   **LO1**
   a. Total assets must be greater than total liabilities.
   b. Total assets must be less than total liabilities.
   c. Total assets must equal total liabilities plus stockholders' equity.
   d. Total liabilities must equal total stockholders' equity.

4. **Which of the following would be considered an intangible asset?**   **LO1**
   a. Cash   c. Accounts payable
   b. Land   d. Patents

5. **Which of the following would most likely be classified as a long-term liability?**   **LO1**
   a. Accounts payable   c. Accounts receivable
   b. Notes payable   d. Common stock

6. **Ratio analysis always involves which type of arithmetic operation?**   **LO3**
   a. Addition   c. Multiplication
   b. Subtraction   d. Division

7. **Which of the following is not a true statement?**   **LO3**
   a. Benchmarking analysis involves comparing a company to its industry's averages.
   b. Benchmarking analysis involves comparing a company to its competitors.
   c. Trend analysis involves comparing a company's ratios over time.
   d. Benchmarking analysis involves comparing a company's ratios over time.

8. **A company reported net income of $200 on net sales of $2,000. The company's return on sales is:**   **LO4**
   a. $1,800.   c. 0.1 percent.
   b. 10 percent.   d. None of the above.

9. **The return on sales ratio does *not* provide insight on which of the following?**   **LO4**
   a. A company's net income per dollar of sales
   b. A measure of a company's financial performance
   c. A measure of a company's cash flow flexibility
   d. A measure of a company's operating efficiency

10. **Which of the following is not shown on the statement of stockholders' equity?**   **LO5**
    a. Contributed capital   c. Common stock
    b. Retained earnings   d. Total liabilities

11. **The following data appear in the financial statements of a company. Calculate its current ratio.**   **LO3**

Current assets	$10,000
Current liabilities	$5,000

    a. 2:1   c. $5,000
    b. 1:2   d. ($5,000)

12. **The following data pertains to Smith Consulting, Inc., for 2018. Compute its ending retained earnings.**   **LO5**

Beginning-of-year retained earnings	$120,000
Net income	37,500
Dividends paid	5,000

    a. $157,500   c. $162,500
    b. $152,500   d. $115,000

13. **A merchandising company's multi-step income statement differs from that of a service company in what way?**   **LO2**
    a. There is no difference.
    b. A service company does not include a line for cost of goods sold.
    c. A service company has a line for selling expenses, whereas a merchandising company does not.
    d. A merchandising company will have a line for income from operations, whereas a service company will not.

QUESTIONS

1. List three subgroups of assets that may be found in the asset section of a classified balance sheet.
2. Define *current asset* and *normal operating cycle*.
3. Which of the following are current assets: land, cash, prepaid expense, building, accounts receivable, inventory, equipment?
4. What is meant by Environmental, Social, and Governance (ESG)?
5. Define the following ratios: current ratio, debt-to-total-assets ratio, and return on sales ratio.
6. What is meant by socially responsible investing?
7. Which of the following measures are best computed using a classified balance sheet?
   - *a.* Liquidity
   - *b.* Solvency
   - *c.* Free cash flow
   - *d.* Both a. and b.
8. Which of the following is a correct statement?
   - *a.* The current ratio is a measure of firm solvency.
   - *b.* The current ratio is a measure of firm liquidity.
   - *c.* The debt-to-total-assets ratio is a measure of firm liquidity.
   - *d.* None of the above is correct.
9. Free cash flow is measured using information from which financial statement?
   - *a.* Balance sheet
   - *b.* Income statement
   - *c.* Statement of cash flows
   - *d.* Statement of retained earnings
10. Socially Responsible Investing
   - *a.* Means making as much money on your investments as you can as your only goal.
   - *b.* Means investing in companies that adhere to environmental and social policies in their operations.
   - *c.* Is too small of a concept to matter much.

SHORT EXERCISES

LO1   **SE4-1.   Preparing a Classified Balance Sheet** Desi Company, a merchandising firm, reports the following data as of January 31:

Stockholders' equity	$ 5,700
Property, plant, and equipment	10,000
Inventory	3,500
Accounts receivable	1,200
Other current liabilities	600
Accounts payable	800
Long-term notes payable	8,000
Cash	400

Prepare a classified balance sheet for Desi Company as of January 31.

LO4   **SE4-2.   Evaluating Firm Profitability** The following financial information is taken from the annual reports of the Billy Company and the Ball Company:

	Billy	Ball
Net income	$10,000	$100,000
Net sales	40,000	500,000

Calculate the return on sales ratio for each company, and determine which firm is more profitable.

LO3   **SE4-3.   Evaluating Firm Liquidity** The following financial information is taken from the balance sheets of the Peter Company and the Paul Company:

	Peter	Paul
Current assets	$200,000	$50,000
Current liabilities	40,000	20,000

Calculate the current ratio for each company, and determine which firm has the higher level of liquidity.

SE4-4. **Evaluating Firm Solvency** The following financial information is taken from the balance sheets of the Benny Company and the Walter Company: **LO3**

	Benny	Walter
Total debt	$400,000	$ 900,000
Total assets.	500,000	1,000,000

Calculate the debt-to-total-assets ratio, and determine which firm has the higher level of solvency.

SE4-5. **Calculating Free Cash Flow** The following financial information is taken from the annual reports of the Ira Company and the Paul Company: **LO6**

	Ira	Paul
Cash flow from operating activities.	$300,000	$650,000
Cash investment in property & equipment	75,000	240,000

Calculate the free cash flow for each company, and determine which firm has better cash flow health.

SE4-6. **Statement of Cash Flows** Which of the following would not appear on a company's statement of cash flows? **LO6**
  a. Cash flow from operating activities
  b. Net change in cash
  c. Total assets
  d. Cash flow for investing activities

SE4-7. **Debt-to-Total-Assets Ratio** Red Company's balance sheet reports the following totals: Assets = $80,000; Liabilities = $50,000; Stockholders' Equity = $30,000. Determine the company's debt-to-total-assets ratio. **LO3**
  a. 37.5%
  b. 62.5%
  c. $15,000
  d. 166.7%

SE4-8. **Free Cash Flow** Debra Linens reports the following items on its statement of cash flows: **LO6**

Cash flow provided by operating activities = $100,000
Cash flow used by investing activities = $50,000
Cash flow used by financing activities = $25,000
Capital expenditures = $40,000

Determine Debra's free cash flow:
  a. $40,000
  b. $5,000
  c. 40%
  d. $60,000

SE4-9. **Return on Sales** The following data are from the financial statements of Pluto Wines, Inc. Compute Pluto's return on sales ratio. **LO4**

Total revenues: $3,500,000
Total expenses: $2,800,000
  a. 125%
  b. 80%
  c. 25%
  d. 20%

SE4-10. **The Multi-Step Income Statement** Robert Company, a merchandising firm, reports the following data for the month ended January 31: **LO2**

Operating expenses	$ 7,000	Income tax expense	$900
Cost of goods sold	4,000	Other income	500
Net sales.	15,000		

Prepare a multi-step income statement for Robert Company for the month of January.

SE4-11. **Statement of Cash Flows** Identify whether the following statements are true or false. **LO6**
  a. The statement of cash flows provides information about whether a firm is "rich" or not.
  b. The statement of cash flows provides information about a firm's financial health.
  c. The statement of cash flows provides information about a firm's liquidity.
  d. The statement of cash flows provides information about a firm's solvency.

DATA ANALYTICS

DA4-1. **Preparing a Basic Data Visualization in Excel to Highlight Changes in Expenses Over Time** The Excel file associated with this exercise includes three years of operating expenses of **Starbucks Corporation** reported in recent annual reports on Form 10-K. We will use data visualizations to analyze the trends of expenses over this three-year period.

Required
1. Download the Excel file DA4-1 found in myBusinessCourse.
2. Create a data visualization within the worksheet in Excel, through the Sparkline feature: Line option. *Hint:* Highlight the cells with data and click on Insert, click on Sparklines, click on Line. Next, select where to place Sparklines by highlighting the empty cells in the column to the right of your last column of data.
3. Format the Sparklines by adding color markers to the high and low points of your chart and adding thickness to the chart lines. *Hint:* Highlight your Sparkline, and under the Sparkline tab, click on High Point and Low Point and choose your desired color scheme from the options listed. To add thickness, click on Sparkline Color and Weight to make an adjustment.
4. Determine which Sparkline (and thus pattern of activity) is most similar to the Sparkline for Product and distribution.
5. Determine which Sparkline is most similar to the Sparkline for Store operating expenses.

DA4-2. **Analyzing the Liquidity of Companies by Industry Segments in Excel** The Excel file associated with this exercise includes Compustat data for S&P 500 companies for five years. In this exercise, we will prepare the data in the Excel file and convert the information in the data file to a PivotTable. Lastly, we will prepare a PivotChart to discern data trends in liquidity by industry segment, measured through the current ratio.

Required
Part 1 Preparing Data; Creating a PivotTable; Mining Data
1. Download Excel file DA4-2 found in myBusinessCourse.
2. Add a column to the worksheet in the Excel file that computes the current ratio per each row of data.
3. Sort data in the current ratio column in ascending order to group together rows where errors appear. *Hint:* Use the filter button in the column heading field to sort the data.
4. Identify the industry that had the most instances in which current assets and current liabilities were not provided which resulted in errors in the current ratio column. *Hint:* Use the filter button in the current ratio column heading field and select only those rows with errors (#DIV/0 rows). Then use the filter button in the column heading of the Segment field to sort the column in alphabetical order.
5. Delete all rows in the worksheet where errors appeared in the current ratio calculated cell. *Hint:* Start by clearing the filter in the Current Ratio column. If necessary, re-sort Current Ratio column in ascending order.
6. Create a PivotTable displaying the average current ratio for years 1 through 5 by industry segment. *Hint:* To create a PivotTable, click anywhere inside the table. Open Insert tab and select PivotTable in the Tables group. Add the PivotTable to a new worksheet. Drag Segment to Columns, drag Year to Rows, and drag Current ratio to Values. Select Value Field Settings in the dropdown menu next to Current Ratio in the Values box. Select Average in the Summarize Value Field box.
7. List for each year the industry that has the highest and lowest current ratio.
8. List the company with the highest and lowest current ratio for the Health Care segment in Year 4. *Hint:* Double-click on the average current ratio for Health Care in Year 4 to automatically open up a new sheet that holds the supporting details.

Part 2 Creating a PivotChart and Analyzing Trends
1. Create a visualization through a PivotChart in the form of a line chart of the current ratio by industry segment over the five-year period. *Hint:* Click anywhere inside the PivotTable created in Part 1. Open the PivotTable Analyze tab and click PivotChart in the Tools group. Click Line.
2. Based only on the visualization, answer the following questions.
   a. What two industries appear to have had the least fluctuation from year to year?
   b. What three industries appear to have had the most fluctuation from year to year?
3. Describe the trend in liquidity from Year 1 to Year 5 for the Consumer Staples segment.

Current Ratio

$$\frac{\text{Current assets}}{\text{Current liabilities}}$$

DA4-3. Preparing Tableau Visualizations to Analyze Liquidity through the Current Ratio Refer to PF-27 in Appendix F. This problem uses Tableau to analyze liquidity of S&P 500 companies through the current ratio. The visualization is exported to PowerPoint for communication purposes.

DATA VISUALIZATION

Data Visualization Activities are available in myBusinessCourse. These assignments use Tableau Dashboards to expose students to visual depictions of data and introduce students to data analytics through data visualizations. These exercises are easily assignable and auto graded by MBC.

Data Visualization

EXERCISES—SET A

E4-1A. Preparing a Classified Balance Sheet From the following accounts, listed in alphabetical order, prepare a classified balance sheet for Oakland Wholesalers as of December 31. All accounts have normal balances.

LO1

Accounts payable	$ 50,000	Inventory	$117,000
Accounts receivable	40,000	Land	39,000
Building	67,000	Mortgage payable (long term)	79,000
Cash	28,000	Office supplies	1,000
Common stock	120,000	Retained earnings	?
		Salaries payable	7,000

E4-2A. Multi-Step Income Statement From the following accounts, listed in alphabetical order, prepare a multi-step income statement for Carl Distributors for the year ended December 31. All accounts have normal balances.

LO2

Selling, general, and administrative expense	$225,000	Sales revenue	$580,000
Cost of goods sold	335,000	Income tax expense	10,000
Interest expense	5,000		

E4-3A. Evaluating the Liquidity and Solvency of a Company Identify whether the following statements are true or false.

LO3, 4, 6

a. The current ratio is a measure of a firm's liquidity.
b. Free cash flow is a measure of a firm's solvency.
c. The return on sales ratio is a measure of a firm's liquidity.
d. The debt-to-total-assets ratio is a measure of a firm's liquidity.

E4-4A. Classified Balance Sheet The George Company collected the following information for the preparation of its December 31 classified balance sheet:

LO1

Accounts receivable	$22,000	Property, plant, and equipment	$200,000
Cash	17,000	Inventory	57,000
Other current assets	25,000	Other long-term assets	40,000
Accounts payable	25,000	Common stock	92,000
Long-term liabilities	60,000	Retained earnings	?
Other current liabilities	19,000		

Prepare a classified balance sheet for the George Company.

E4-5A. Profitability, Liquidity, and Solvency Ratios Alex Corporation gathered the following information from its financial statements:

LO3, 4, 6

Net sales	$175,000
Net income	35,000
Cash provided by operating activities	40,000
Expenditures on property, plant, and equipment	15,000
Current assets	47,250
Current liabilities	27,000
Total assets	135,000
Total liabilities	94,500

Using the above data, calculate the following: (1) return on sales ratio, (2) current ratio, (3) debt-to-total-assets ratio, and (4) free cash flow.

LO3   **E4-6A.** **Return on Assets** The following information was taken from **Apple Inc.**'s 2020 financial statements. Numbers are in millions.

APPLE INC.
AAPL

	2020	2019
Net income	$ 57,411	$ 55,256
Total assets	323,888	338,516

Required

a.   What was Apple's return on assets for 2020 and 2019?

b.   Based on your answer from part *a*, how did the company's performance change from 2019 to 2020?

LO5   **E4-7A.** **Statement of Stockholders' Equity** You have been asked to assist with the preparation of a statement of stockholders' equity for Minimus Company for the year ended December 31, Year 2. You determine the following balances:

Common stock at December 31, Year 1	$10,000
Retained earnings at December 31, Year 1	7,500
Net income during Year 2	6,000
Dividends during Year 2	900
Issuance of common stock during Year 2	600

Required

Prepare a statement of stockholders' equity for Minimus Company for Year 2.

LO4   **E4-8A.** **Return on Sales** Peyton Co.'s sales rose 12 percent over prior year sales of $100,000; however, net income increased by only 5 percent over the prior year's net income. If Peyton's prior year return on sales ratio was 8 percent, what is the current year return on sales ratio?

LO6   **E4-9A.** **Free Cash Flow** Katty Co. reports the following financial data for the current year:

Cash flow from operating activities	$23,200
Cash flow from investing activities	(10,555)
Cash flow from financing activities	5,000
Cash disbursed for capital expenditures	(4,325)

Compute Katty's free cash flow.

LO5   **E4-10A.** **Statement of Stockholders' Equity** Jay Co. reported the following financial data for its most current year:

Beginning-of-year common stock	$105,000
Beginning-of-year retained earning	175,400
Net income	33,400
Dividends paid	10,500
Issuance of common stock	24,000

Compute Jay's end-of-year total stockholders' equity.

EXERCISES—SET B

LO1   **E4-1B.** **Preparing a Classified Balance Sheet** From the following accounts, listed in alphabetical order, prepare a classified balance sheet for Halford Wholesalers as of December 31. All accounts have normal balances.

Accounts payable	$ 55,000	Inventory	$142,000
Accounts receivable	61,000	Land	58,000
Building and equipment	87,000	Mortgage payable (long-term)	82,000
Cash	40,000	Office supplies	2,000
Common stock	125,000	Retained earnings	?
		Salaries payable	8,000

E4-2B. Multi-Step Income Statement From the following accounts, listed in alphabetical order, prepare a multi-step income statement for Moto Wholesale for the year ended December 31. All accounts have normal balances.

LO2

Selling, general, and administrative expenses	$260,000	Sales revenue..........	$580,000
Cost of goods sold	275,000	Income tax expense	6,000
Interest expense..........................	10,000		

E4-3B. Evaluating the Liquidity and Solvency of a Company Identify whether the following statements are true or false.

LO3, 4, 6

  a.   The current ratio is a measure of a firm's solvency.
  b.   Free cash flow is a measure of a firm's liquidity.
  c.   The return on sales ratio is a measure of a firm's solvency.
  d.   The debt-to-total-assets ratio is a measure of a firm's solvency.

E4-4B. Classified Balance Sheet The Oxford Company collected the following information for the preparation of its December 31 classified balance sheet:

LO1

Accounts receivable	$26,000	Property, plant, and equipment.......	$200,000
Cash..........................	20,000	Inventory........................	75,000
Other current assets...............	32,000	Other long-term assets.............	40,000
Accounts payable	30,000	Common stock	115,000
Long-term liabilities	60,000	Retained earnings	?
Other current liabilities	18,000		

Prepare a classified balance sheet for Oxford Company.

E4-5B. Profitability, Liquidity, and Solvency Ratios O'Reilly Corporation gathered the following information from its financial statements:

LO3, 4, 6

Net sales.....................................	$300,000	Current assets	$ 75,000
Net income	90,000	Current liabilities.........	25,000
Cash provided by operating activities............	100,000	Total assets.............	140,000
Expenditures on property, plant, and equipment ...	19,000	Total liabilities	112,000

Using the above data, calculate the following: (1) return on sales ratio, (2) current ratio, (3) debt-to-total-assets ratio, and (4) free cash flow.

E4-6B. Return on Assets Sue Company reports the following information in its financial statements. Numbers are in thousands.

LO3

	Current Year	Prior Year
Net sales..	$42,075	$44,100
Net income	12,780	15,732
Total assets...	63,900	87,400

There were 5,000 outstanding shares at December 31 of the current year.

Required
  a.   What was Sue's return on assets ratio for the current and previous years?
  b.   Based on your answer from part *a*, how did the company's performance change from the previous to the current year?

E4-7B. Statement of Stockholders' Equity You have been asked to assist with the preparation of a statement of stockholders' equity for Pal Company for the year ended December 31, Year 2. You determine the following balances:

LO5

Common stock at December 31, Year 1	$47,000
Retained earnings at December 31, Year 1	19,500
Net income during Year 2	23,400
Dividends during Year 2	7,800
Issuance of common stock during Year 2	5,000

Required

Prepare a statement of stockholders' equity for Pal Company for Year 2.

LO4 **E4-8B.** **Return on Sales** Trevor Co.'s sales rose 10 percent over prior year sales of $300,000; however, net income increased by 6 percent over the prior year's net income. If Trevor's prior year return on sales ratio was 25 percent, what is the current year return on sales ratio?

LO6 **E4-9B.** **Free Cash Flow** Madison Co. reports the following financial data for the current year:

Cash flow from operating activities. . .	$41,500	Cash flow from financing activities	$21,175
Cash flow from investing activities . . .	30,100	Cash disbursed for capital expenditures. . .	(12,500)

Compute Madison's free cash flow.

LO5 **E4-10B.** **Statement of Stockholders' Equity** Wally Co. reported the following financial data for its most current year:

Beginning-of-year common stock	$140,000
Beginning-of-year retained earnings	325,500
Net income	10,500
Dividends paid	10,000
Issuance of common stock	15,000

Compute Wally's end-of-year total stockholders' equity.

PROBLEMS—SET A

LO1 **P4-1A.** **Preparing a Classified Balance Sheet** The following financial data for Kravis Distributors was collected as of December 31. All accounts have normal balances.

Accounts payable	$ 80,000	Accounts receivable	$120,200
Delivery equipment.	90,000	Accumulated depreciation	55,000
Inventory.	114,000	Cash	15,200
Retained earnings	?	Common stock	130,000
Supplies	6,400	Prepaid insurance.	4,000

Required

Prepare a classified balance sheet as of December 31 for Kravis Distributors.

LO1 **P4-2A.** **Preparing a Classified Balance Sheet** The following financial data for the Revel Corporation was collected as of December 31. All accounts have normal balances.

Furniture and equipment . . .	$107,000	Accumulated depreciation—furniture and equipment. . .	$ 48,800
Cash	61,000	Accounts receivable	95,200
Common stock	190,000	Accounts payable	19,200
Prepaid insurance.	300	Inventory.	93,000
Retained earnings	?		

Required

Prepare a classified balance sheet as of December 31.

LO2 **P4-3A.** **Multi-Step Income Statements** The adjusted trial balance of Molly Distributors on December 31 is shown below.

MOLLY DISTRIBUTORS Adjusted Trial Balance December 31		
	Debit	Credit
Cash	$ 30,200	
Accounts receivable	110,200	
Inventory	94,000	
Prepaid insurance	2,400	
Supplies	6,400	
Delivery equipment	85,000	
Accumulated depreciation		$ 35,000
Accounts payable		100,000
Common stock		105,000
Retained earnings		22,800
Sales revenue		791,000
Cost of goods sold	513,400	
Salaries expense	123,000	
Rent expense	40,000	
Supplies expense	6,400	
Utilities expense	4,000	
Depreciation expense	16,000	
Insurance expense	6,800	
Income tax expense	16,000	
	$1,053,800	$1,053,800

Required

Prepare a multi-step income statement for the year ended December 31. Combine all the operating expenses into one line on the income statement for selling, general, and administrative expenses.

P4-4A. Preparing the Financial Statements Listed below are items reported on the financial statements of the Irvine Company as of June 30, Year 2:

LO1, 6

Cash flow provided by operating activities	$39,000	Other long-term assets	$17,500
Cash at June 30, Year 1	8,000	Cash flow from financing activities	1,300
Cash at June 30, Year 2	38,000	Current liabilities	24,000
Inventory	5,500	Long-term liabilities	16,250
Accounts receivable	15,200	Intangible assets	9,500
Cash flow from investing activities	(10,300)	Common stock	60,000
Other current assets	1,500	Retained earnings	?
Property, plant, and equipment	60,000		

Required

Prepare a classified balance sheet as of June 30, and statement of cash flows for the year.

P4-5A. Assessing a Firm's Profitability, Liquidity, and Solvency Presented below is financial data for the Outback Company as of the year-ends of the prior and current years.

LO3, 4

	Current Year	Prior Year
Current assets	$ 70,000	$ 68,750
Total assets	130,000	100,000
Current liabilities	40,000	27,500
Total liabilities	91,000	80,000
Net sales	190,000	140,000
Net income	26,600	22,400

Required

Calculate Outback's current ratio, debt-to-total-assets ratio, and return on sales ratio. Comment on the trend in the company's profitability, liquidity, and solvency from the prior and the current years.

LO2, 4   **P4-6A.**   **Profitability and the Income Statement** Presented below is income statement data for Short & Company as of year-end:

Income tax expense	$ 5,400	Net revenue	$62,950
Cost of goods sold	14,300	Operating expenses	27,000
Other expenses	500		

Required

Prepare a multi-step income statement and calculate the company's return on sales ratio. If Short's return on sales was 16 percent in the prior year, is the company's profitability improving or declining?

LO5   **P4-7A.**   **Preparing the Statement of Stockholders' Equity** Presented below is financial data for Jason & Co. as of year-end:

Cash	$ 8,500	Accumulated depreciation	$(14,000)
Retained earnings, Jan. 1	17,000	Net income	35,000
Intangible assets	25,000	Stockholders' equity, Jan. 1	67,000
Common stock	50,000	Retained earnings, Dec. 31	38,000
Accounts payable	4,000	Stockholders' equity, Dec. 31	88,000
Dividends paid	14,000	Building	72,500

Required

Prepare a statement of stockholders' equity for Jason & Co. as of December 31.

LO3, 4   **P4-8A.**   **Interpreting Liquidity, Solvency, and Profitability Ratios** Presented below are financial data for two retail companies:

	Company A	Company B
Return on sales ratio	15.5%	13.9%
Current ratio	0.4	2.0
Debt-to-total-assets	65%	35%

Required

Consider the financial ratio data for the two companies. Which company represents the better investment opportunity in your view and why?

LO3, 4   **P4-9A.**   **Ratio Analysis** The following balances were reported in the financial statements for Nadir Company.

	Current Year	Prior Year
Net sales	$1,000,000	$750,000
Net income	120,000	75,000
Current assets	220,000	270,000
Current liabilities	80,000	90,000
Total liabilities	250,000	240,000
Total assets	800,000	600,000

Required

1. Compute the following ratios for the current and the prior years for Nadir Company.
   a. Return on sales ratio
   b. Current ratio
   c. Debt-to-total-assets ratio
2. Comment on changes to Nadir Company's profitability, liquidity, and solvency.

P4-10A.　Multi-Step Income Statement and Adjusting Entries The New England Trading Company, whose accounting year ends on December 31, had the following normal balances in its general ledger at December 31:

Cash..........................	$17,000	Sales revenue....................	$620,000
Accounts receivable	56,600	Cost of goods sold	394,000
Inventory.......................	74,000	Utilities expense	4,800
Prepaid insurance.................	3,000	Sales salaries expense............	77,000
Office supplies	4,200	Delivery expense	10,800
Furniture and fixtures	21,000	Advertising expense..............	5,600
Accumulated depreciation—		Rent expense....................	9,400
furniture and fixtures.............	7,000	Office salaries expense	56,000
Delivery equipment................	86,000	Income tax expense	9,000
Accumulated depreciation—			
delivery equipment	12,000		
Accounts payable	37,000		
Long-term notes payable	28,000		
Common stock	70,000		
Retained earnings	56,400		

During the year, the accounting department prepared monthly statements, but no adjusting entries were made in the journals and ledgers. Data for the year-end procedures are as follows:

1. Prepaid insurance, December 31, was $1,800.
2. Depreciation expense on furniture and fixtures for the year was $2,200.
3. Depreciation expense on delivery equipment for the year was $11,000.
4. Salaries payable, December 31 ($1,900 sales and $1,200 office), was $3,100.
5. Unused office supplies on December 31 were $1,400.

Required
a. Record the necessary adjusting entries at December 31.
b. Prepare a multi-step income statement for the year. Combine all the operating expenses into one line on the income statement for selling, general, and administrative expenses.

PROBLEMS—SET B

P4-1B.　Preparing a Classified Balance Sheet The following financial data for Brandon & Company was collected as of December 31. All accounts have normal balances.

Accounts receivable	$223,000	Accumulated depreciation	$110,000
Inventory........................	268,000	Cash............................	40,000
Common stock	200,000	Accounts payable	155,000
Prepaid insurance.................	7,000	Supplies	12,800
Retained earnings	?	Delivery equipment................	160,000

Required
Prepare a classified balance sheet as of December 31 for Brandon & Company.

P4-2B.　Preparing a Classified Balance Sheet The following financial data for the St. Joseph Corporation was collected as of December 31. All accounts have normal balances.

Accounts receivable	$203,400	Furniture and equipment	$196,000
Accounts payable	36,800	Cash...........................	92,800
Prepaid insurance.................	900	Accumulated Depreciation—	
Common stock	410,000	furniture and equipment	77,600
Retained earnings	?	Inventory.......................	175,000

Required
Prepare a classified balance sheet as of December 31.

LO2   P4-3B. Multi-Step Income Statement The adjusted trial balance of Patton Corporation on December 31 is shown below.

PATTON CORPORATION Adjusted Trial Balance December 31		
	Debit	**Credit**
Cash.	$ 50,400	
Accounts receivable	95,200	
Inventory.	87,000	
Prepaid insurance.	1,300	
Furniture and fixtures	32,000	
Accumulated depreciation—furniture and fixtures		$ 6,800
Delivery equipment.	66,000	
Accumulated depreciation—delivery equipment		34,000
Accounts payable		17,400
Common stock		208,000
Retained earnings		50,000
Sales revenue.		381,000
Cost of goods sold	214,800	
Salaries expense	97,000	
Rent expense	20,800	
Utilities expense	6,800	
Insurance expense	1,500	
Depreciation expense—furniture and fixtures	3,200	
Depreciation expense—delivery equipment.	18,000	
Income tax expense	3,200	
	$697,200	$697,200

Required

Prepare a multi-step income statement for the year ended December 31. Combine all the operating expenses into one line on the income statement for selling, general, and administrative expenses.

LO1, 6   P4-4B. Preparing the Financial Statements Listed below are items reported on the financial statements of the La Playa Company as of June 30, Year 2:

Cash flow provided by operating activities . . .	$ 50,000	Other long-term assets.	$ 35,000
Cash at June 30, Year 1	21,000	Cash flow from financing activities . . .	2,600
Cash at June 30, Year 2	43,000	Current liabilities.	46,000
Inventory.	12,000	Long-term liabilities	36,500
Accounts receivable	24,400	Intangible assets.	19,000
Cash flow from investing activities	(30,600)	Common stock	102,000
Other current assets.	3,000	Retained earnings	?
Property, plant, and equipment.	85,000		

Required

Prepare a classified balance sheet as of June 30, and statement of cash flows for Year 2.

LO3, 4   P4-5B. Assessing a Firm's Profitability, Liquidity, and Solvency Presented below is financial data for the Lite Company as of the year-ends of the prior and the current years.

	Current Year	**Prior Year**
Current assets	$112,000	$ 90,000
Total assets.	350,000	250,000
Current liabilities.	140,000	60,000
Total liabilities	227,500	160,000
Net sales	375,000	265,000
Net income	50,250	35,775

Required
Calculate Lite's current ratio, debt-to-total-assets ratio, and return on sales ratio. Comment on the trend in the company's profitability, liquidity, and solvency from the prior to the current year.

P4-6B. Profitability and the Income Statement Presented below are income statement data for Poole & Company:

Income tax expense	$16,000	Sales revenue	$150,000
Cost of goods sold	30,000	Operating expenses	57,000
Other expenses	2,000		

Required
Prepare a multi-step income statement and calculate the company's return on sales ratio. If Poole's return on sales was 26 percent in the prior year, is the company's profitability improving or declining?

P4-7B. Preparing a Statement of Stockholders' Equity Presented below is financial data for Thomas & Co. as of December 31:

Cash	$ 25,000	Inventory	$ 14,000
Retained earnings, Jan. 1	31,000	Net income	60,000
Building	150,000	Stockholders' equity, Jan. 1	151,000
Common stock	120,000	Retained earnings, Dec. 31	?
Accrued expenses payable	8,000	Stockholders' equity, Dec. 31	181,000
Dividends paid	30,000		

Required
Prepare a statement of stockholders' equity as of December 31.

P4-8B. Interpreting Profitability, Liquidity, and Solvency Ratios Presented below is financial data for two furniture manufacturing companies:

	Company B	Company D
Return on sales ratio	9.0%	10.9%
Current ratio	2.1	1.0
Debt-to-total-assets ratio	41%	72%

Required
Consider the financial data of the two companies. Which company represents the better investment opportunity in your opinion and why?

P4-9B. Ratio Analysis The following balances were reported in the financial statements for Rudy Company.

	Current Year	Prior Year
Net sales	$1,700,000	$1,750,000
Net income	170,000	204,750
Current assets	408,000	525,000
Current liabilities	170,000	210,000
Total liabilities	496,000	661,500
Total assets	1,550,000	2,450,000

Required
1. Compute the following ratios for the current and the prior year for Rudy Company.
   a. Return on sales ratio
   b. Current ratio
   c. Debt-to-total-assets ratio
2. Comment on changes to Rudy Company's profitability, liquidity, and solvency.

LO2   **P4-10B. Multi-Step Income Statement and Adjusting Entries** Washington Distributors, whose accounting year ends on December 31, had the following normal balances in its ledger accounts at December 31:

Cash	$45,750	Common stock	$ 125,000
Accounts receivable	92,000	Retained earnings	?
Inventory	84,400	Sales revenue	1,170,000
Prepaid insurance	7,200	Cost of goods sold	822,200
Office supplies	4,800	Utilities expense	5,600
Furniture and fixtures	28,000	Sales salaries expense	108,000
Accumulated depreciation—		Delivery expense	37,000
furniture and fixtures	10,800	Advertising expense	28,200
Delivery equipment	70,000	Rent expense	30,000
Accumulated depreciation—		Office salaries expense	72,000
delivery equipment	24,400		
Accounts payable	69,400		
Long-term notes payable	30,000		
Income tax expense	11,000		

During the year, the accounting department prepared monthly statements, but no adjusting entries were made in the journals and ledgers. Data for the year-end procedures are as follows:

1. Prepaid insurance, December 31, was $2,800.
2. Depreciation expense on furniture and fixtures for the year was $3,000.
3. Depreciation expense on delivery equipment for the year was $10,000.
4. Salaries payable, December 31 ($2,300 sales and $800 office), was $3,100.
5. Office supplies on hand, December 31, were $1,900.

Required
a.   Record the necessary adjusting entries in general journal form at December 31.
b.   Prepare a multi-step income statement for the year. Combine all the operating expenses into one line on the income statement for selling, general, and administrative expenses.

SERIAL PROBLEM: KATE'S CARDS

(Note: This is a continuation of the Serial Problem: Kate's Cards from Chapter 3.)

SP4.   In order to learn more about the industry and to meet people who could give her advice, Kate attended several industry trade shows. At the most recent trade show, Kate was introduced to Fred Abbott, operations manager of "Sentiments," a national card distributor. After much discussion, Fred asked Kate to consider being one of Sentiments' card suppliers. He provided Kate with a copy of the company's recent financial statements. Fred indicated that he expects that Kate will need to supply Sentiments with approximately 50 card designs per month. Kate is to send Sentiments a monthly invoice, and she will be paid approximately 30 days from the date the invoice is received in Sentiments' corporate office. Naturally, Kate was thrilled with this offer, since this will certainly give her business a big boost.

Required
Kate has several questions. Answer the following questions for Kate.

a.   What type of information does each of Sentiments' financial statements provide to Kate?
b.   What financial statements would Kate need to evaluate whether Sentiments will have enough cash to meet its current liabilities? Explain what to look for.
c.   What financial statement would Kate need to evaluate whether Sentiments will be able to survive over a long period of time? Explain what to look for.
d.   What financial statement would Kate need to evaluate Sentiments' profitability? Explain what to look for.
e.   Where can Kate find out whether Sentiments has outstanding debt? How can Kate determine whether Sentiments will be able to meet its interest and principal payments on any debts that it has?
f.   How could Kate determine whether Sentiments pays a dividend?
g.   In deciding whether to go ahead with this opportunity, are there other areas of concern that Kate should be aware of?

EXTENDING YOUR KNOWLEDGE

REPORTING AND ANALYSIS

EYK4-1. **Financial Reporting Problem: Columbia Sportswear Company** The financial statements for **Columbia Sportswear** can be found in Appendix A at the end of this textbook.

COLUMBIA
SPORTSWEAR
COMPANY

Required

Answer the following questions using the Consolidated Balance Sheet and the Notes to the consolidated financial statements:

a. What were the combined totals of Columbia's liabilities and stockholders' equity for 2020 and 2019?

b. How do these amounts compare with Columbia's total assets for each year?

c. What was the largest, in dollar value, of Columbia's assets each year? What does this asset represent?

d. What is the balance of accrued liabilities made up of?

EYK4-2. **Comparative Analysis Problem: Columbia Sportswear Company vs. Under Armour, Inc.** The financial statements for **Columbia Sportswear** can be found in Appendix A, and **Under Armour**'s financial statements can be found in Appendix B at the end of this textbook.

COLUMBIA
SPORTSWEAR
COMPANY

UNDER ARMOUR, INC.

Required

a. Calculate for each company the following ratios for 2020:
1. Current ratio
2. Debt-to-total-assets ratio
3. Return on sales ratio

b. Comment on the companies' relative profitability, liquidity, and solvency.

EYK4-3. **Business Decision Problem** Memoryman, a maker of computer memory devices, reports the following information in its financial statements. Assume that you are a loan officer at a major bank and have been assigned the task of evaluating whether to extend a loan for a plant expansion to the company.

(in millions)	2022	2021	2020
Current assets	$ 4,356	$1,033	$2,915
Total assets	10,175	8,777	6,002
Current liabilities	1,093	960	871
Total liabilities	3,114	2,997	2,093
Retained earnings	1,797	813	(487)
Net sales	5,662	4,827	3,567
Cost of goods sold	3,223	2,565	2,282
Net income	987	1,300	415
Cash flow from operating activities	1,054	1,452	488
Cash flow from investing activities	(667)	(2,715)	(375)
Cash flow from financing activities	(48)	991	25
Expenditures for property, plant, and equipment	(193)	(108)	(60)

Required

a. Calculate the company's current ratio, debt-to-total-assets ratio, return on sales ratio, and free cash flow for each year.

b. Comment on Memoryman's liquidity, solvency, and profitability.

c. Based on what you have learned about Memoryman, would you recommend offering the company a loan?

EYK4-4. **Financial Analysis Problem** As part of your internship at Howe Inc. you have been assigned the job of developing a few important ratios from the company's financial statements. This information is intended to be used by the company to help Howe obtain a large bank loan. In particular, the data will need to convince the bank that Howe is a good loan risk based on its liquidity, solvency, and profitability. Below are the data you pulled together:

	Current Year	Prior Year
Current ratio	2.4:1	1.5:1
Debt-to-total-assets ratio	57 percent	66 percent
Return on sales ratio	9.3 percent	9.2 percent
Free cash flow	Up 18 percent	Up 19 percent
Net income	Up 16 percent	Down 12 percent

Required

Prepare brief comments that discuss how each of these items can be used to support the argument that Howe is showing improving financial health.

CRITICAL THINKING

GENERAL MILLS, INC.

EYK4-5. **Accounting Research Problem** Go to this book's website and locate the annual report of **General Mills, Inc.**, for the year ending May 31, 2020 (fiscal year 2020).

Required

1. Calculate the company's return on sales for 2018, 2019, and 2020. What is the trend?
2. Calculate the company's current ratio for 2019 and 2020. What is the trend?
3. Calculate the company's debt-to-total-assets ratio for 2019 and 2020. What is the trend?
4. Calculate the company's free cash flow for 2018, 2019, and 2020. What is the trend? (*Hint:* Proceeds from disposal of land, buildings, and equipment offset capital expenditures.)

EYK4-6. **Accounting Communication Activity** V. J. Simmons is the President of Forward Engineering Associates. He is a very good engineer, but his accounting knowledge is quite limited.

Required

V. J. has heard that ratio analysis can help him determine the financial condition of his company. In particular, he would like you to explain to him in a memo how to calculate and interpret the following three ratios: (1) return on sales ratio, (2) current ratio, and (3) debt-to-total-assets ratio. Prepare a memo for V. J.

EYK4-7. **Accounting Ethics Case** In the post-Enron environment, and with the enactment of the Sarbanes-Oxley legislation, many firms are proactively portraying themselves as being "ethical." Ethical behavior is, for example, part of the Environmental, Social, and Governance movement. This behavior includes many dimensions, from the ethical treatment of employees and the environment, to ethical financial reporting. Academic research has found a positive correlation between a firm's reputation and its financial performance. Do you feel that strong ethics makes good business sense? Why do you think that there is a positive correlation between ethical behavior and successful corporate financial performance?

EYK4-8. **Environmental, Social, and Governance Problem** Many investors consider past performance, fees, and investment objectives as the sole criteria for selecting a mutual fund for investment purposes. A growing number of investors are also asking about the actions and philosophies of the companies that form a fund's underlying investment portfolio. Socially responsible mutual funds have been developed to fill this need. These funds are designed for investors who want to align their investments with their religious, political, or social convictions.

Because there is no universally accepted definition as to what makes a company responsible or an investment a socially responsible investment, socially responsible funds are quite diverse. Not surprisingly, different funds may take opposite positions on certain controversial issues such as family planning, gay rights, and animal testing.

For the most part, socially responsible funds select their underlying investment firms through either a negative filter or a positive filter. A negative filter is used to screen out firms that are not considered acceptable to the positions advocated by the fund. Examples of firms that may be screened out include firms that are involved in gambling, alcohol, tobacco, or weapons. A positive filter is used to include firms that are seen to be leaders in areas advocated by the fund, such as environmental, diversity, or human rights records.

Required

a. Go to the websites of three socially responsible mutual funds:
    1. Calvert Signature Funds: https://www.calvert.com/calvert-responsible-indexes.php
    2. Domini Social Equity Fund: http://www.domini.com/investing-for-impact/impact-investment-standards
    3. Green Century Balanced Fund: https://www.greencentury.com/balanced-fund/
b. Compare the screening criteria used by each fund. How do they differ, and how are they alike?

EYK4-9.   **Forensic Accounting Problem** Debra Day, a business major at a local college, was recently hired for the summer at Sweet Delights, a popular ice cream parlor near the campus. Debra spent most of her time tending the cash register, where she noticed that most of the customers paid in cash and never seemed to care about getting a receipt. Debra soon figured out that she could ring up a much lesser amount on the register, charge the customer the full amount, then toss the receipt. For example, on a $7 order she would charge and collect the full $7 from the customer but only ring up $5. She would then deposit $5 in the register so that it would agree with the register tape and pocket the $2.

Required

a. What type of fraud is Debra committing?
b. The store manager recently hired you as a forensic accountant to critique the controls at Sweet Delights. He has noticed that while the store seems as busy as ever, and the cash in the register agrees with the tapes, the store is not as profitable as it previously was. What control would you recommend to help prevent the type of fraud being committed by Debra?

EYK4-10. **Working with the Takeaways** Throughout this chapter we have considered the financial statements of Apple Inc. and have undertaken select financial analysis using the Takeaways. Utilize these same tools to analyze the financial data of **Logitech International**, a manufacturer of computer peripherals. The following information was reported by Logitech in the company's financial statements as of year-end March 31, 2020 and 2019:

LOGITECH
INTERNATIONAL

March 31 (in thousands)	2020	2019
Current assets	$1,414,478	$1,350,436
Total assets	2,363,474	2,024,124
Current liabilities	714,144	717,819
Total liabilities	874,206	847,785
Net sales	2,975,851	2,708,322
Net income	449,726	257,573
Cash provided by operating activities	425,000	305,181
Expenditures on property, plant, and equipment	39,484	35,930

Required

1. Calculate the return on sales ratio for each year and comment on Logitech's profitability.
2. Calculate the current ratio for each year and comment on Logitech's liquidity.
3. Calculate the debt-to-total-assets ratio for each year and comment on Logitech's solvency.
4. Calculate the free cash flow for each year and comment on what this means for Logitech.
5. Apple's fiscal year-end occurs near the end of September, whereas Logitech uses a March year-end. How might this affect a comparison of the financial results of the two companies?

EYK4-11. **Evaluating Firm Liquidity, Solvency, Profitability, and Free Cash Flow: IFRS Financial Statements** The 2020 financial statements of **LVMH Moet Hennessey-Louis Vuitton S.A.** are presented in Appendix C at the end of this book. LVMH is a Paris-based holding company and one of the world's largest and best-known luxury goods companies. As a member of the European Union, French companies are required to prepare their consolidated (group) financial statements using International Financial Reporting Standards (IFRS). Using this financial data, calculate the company's (a) return on sales ratio using net profit, group share, (b) current ratio, (c) debt-to-total-assets ratio, and (d) free cash flow for 2019 and 2020. Comment on the trend in LVMH's liquidity, solvency, profitability, and free cash flow from 2019 to 2020.

LVMH MOET
HENNESSEY-LOUIS
VUITTON S.A.

ANSWERS TO SELF-STUDY QUESTIONS:

1. b 2. c 3. c 4. d 5. b 6. d 7. d 8. b 9. c 10. d 11. a 12. b 13. b

YOUR TURN! SOLUTIONS

Solution 4.1

MUSICLAND COMPANY Balance Sheet December 31	
Assets	
Current assets	
Cash	$ 300
Accounts receivable	3,000
Inventory	12,200
Other current assets	1,500
Total current assets	17,000
Property, plant, & equipment, net	25,000
Total assets	$42,000
Liabilities and Stockholders' Equity	
Current liabilities	
Accounts payable	$ 2,500
Other current liabilities	2,000
Total current liabilities	4,500
Long-term notes payable	20,000
Total liabilities	24,500
Stockholders' equity	17,500
Total liabilities and stockholders' equity	$42,000

Solution 4.2

MUSICLAND COMPANY Income Statement For Year Ended December 31	
Net sales	$100,000
Less cost of goods sold	45,000
Gross profit on sales	55,000
Operating expenses	
Selling, general, and administrative	25,000
Research and development expenses	10,000
Total operating expenses	35,000
Income from operations	20,000
Other income and expense	
Interest expense	5,000
Income before income taxes	15,000
Income tax expense	4,500
Net income	$ 10,500

Solution 4.3

	Current Year	Prior Year
Current ratio	$\dfrac{75,000}{50,000} = 1.50{:}1$	$\dfrac{65,000}{45,000} = 1.44{:}1$
Debt-to-total-assets ratio . . .	$\dfrac{150,000}{220,000} = 68.2\,\%$	$\dfrac{145,000}{190,000} = 76.3\%$

The Philips Company has improved its performance on both measures. Both its liquidity as reflected by the current ratio and its solvency as reflected by the debt-to-total-assets ratio are trending in a positive direction. (The current ratio is increasing, and the debt-to-total assets ratio is decreasing.)

Solution 4.4

	Current Year	Prior Year
Return on sales	$\dfrac{20,000}{120,000} = 16.7\,\%$	$\dfrac{15,000}{110,000} = 13.6\%$

The Philips Company has improved its performance from the prior year to the current year. The company is earning more net income on every dollar of sales revenue as indicated by its return on sales ratio.

Solution 4.5

Owner Company Statement of Stockholders' Equity	Common Stock	Retained Earnings	Total Equity
Balance at beginning of the year	$120,000	$85,000	$205,000
Issuance of common stock.	7,500		7,500
Net income		16,000	16,000
Dividends		(4,000)	(4,000)
Balance at the end of the year	$127,500	$97,000	$224,500

Contributed capital is $127,500, and earned capital is $97,000.

Solution 4.6

Current Year	Prior Year
$25,000 – $7,000 = $18,000	$22,000 – $6,000 = $16,000

The Philips Company has improved its free cash flow from the prior year to the current year. The company has more cash for a possible plant expansion, repayment of debt, or payment of dividends to shareholders.

Chapter **5**
Accounting for Merchandising Operations

Road Map

LO	Learning Objective	Page	eLecture	Guided Example	Assignments
LO1	**Explain the operations of a merchandising company and contrast that with the operations of a service company.**	5-3	E5-1	YT5.1	SS9, SE1
LO2	**Describe the accounting for purchases of merchandise.**	5-6	E5-2	YT5.2	SS1, SS2, SS3, SS5, SS6, SE2, SE3, SE4, SE5, E3A, E4A, E5A, E3B, E4B, E5B, P1A, P2A, P3A, P4A, P1B, P2B, P3B, P4B
LO3	**Describe the accounting for sales of merchandise.**	5-10	E5-3	YT5.3	SE6, E1A, E2A, E4A, E1B, E2B, E4B, P1A, P2A, P3A, P4A, P1B, P2B, P3B, P4B
LO4	**Define the gross profit percentage and the return on sales ratio, and explain their use in profitability analysis.**	5-13	E5-4	YT5.4	SS4, SS7, SS8, SE7, SE8, E6A, E6B, P5A, P5B
LO5	**Appendix 5A: Describe and illustrate a periodic inventory system.**	5-17	E5-5	YT5A.1, 5A.2, 5A.3	SS10, SS11, SE9, SE10, SE11, E7A, E8A, E9A, E7B, E8B, E9B, P6A, P7A, P6B, P7B
LO6	**Appendix 5B: Describe and illustrate the revenue recognition standard for sales returns and allowances and sales discounts.**	5-21	E5-6	YT5B.1	SE12, SE13, E10A, E11A, E10B, E11B

Target Corporation is one of the largest merchandising companies in the world, with nearly 1,900 stores and sales of over $93 billion. Target sells products, often referred to as *inventory*. However, Target does not manufacture the inventory it sells. Instead, it buys this inventory from manufacturers such as **Sony** and **Panasonic**, and then resells that inventory to consumers.

This chapter describes the most common inventory accounting system used by merchandising companies. This system *perpetually* tracks all purchases and sales of inventory. Such tracking is important for managers to effectively manage this key asset and to regularly compute measures that report on management's ability to generate profit from inventory.

PAST

Chapters 1 through 4 explained the five-step accounting cycle: analyze, record, adjust, report, and close.

PRESENT

This chapter focuses on analyzing and recording merchandising transactions.

FUTURE

Chapter 6 describes the accounting for inventory, including cost assumptions, the lower of cost or market approach, and inventory analysis.

ACCOUNTING FOR MERCHANDISING OPERATIONS

Merchandising	Accounting for Purchases of Merchandise	Accounting for Sales of Merchandise	Profitability Analysis	Periodic Inventory System (Appendix 5A)	Revenue Recognition Standard (Appendix 5B)
• Operating cycle • Cost flows • Inventory systems—perpetual and periodic	• Transportation costs • Purchase returns and allowances • Purchase discounts • Credit period	• Sales returns and allowances • Sales discounts • Net sales	• Gross profit percentage • Return on sales ratio	• Purchases of merchandise • Sales of merchandise • Comparing periodic and perpetual systems • Cost of goods sold using a periodic system	• Sales discounts • Sales returns and allowances

THE NATURE OF MERCHANDISING

LO1 **Explain** the operations of a merchandising company and **contrast** that with the operations of a service company.

eLecture

MBC

Manufacturers are companies that make goods for sale. They convert raw materials and component parts into a finished product through the application of skilled labor and machine operations. **Ford Motor Company**, for example, converts raw materials such as sheets of steel and components such as tires into automobiles and trucks. Similarly, **Del Monte** converts raw materials such as fresh peaches and components such as metal cans into canned peaches.

Merchandisers buy the finished products, warehouse or display them, and then resell the products to customers. Merchandising firms do not manufacture products, nor do they consume the products that they purchase. Merchandising firms often provide additional services to their customers, but their primary business is the resale of goods produced by other companies. **Exhibit 5-1** illustrates the typical relationship among these types of companies and the final consumer.

EXHIBIT 5-1	Distribution of Products to Individual Consumers

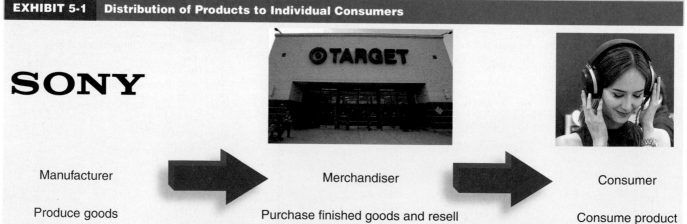

Manufacturer	Merchandiser	Consumer
Produce goods	Purchase finished goods and resell	Consume product

© Shutterstock.com

Wholesalers and retailers are types of merchandising firms. **Wholesalers** buy finished products from manufacturing firms in large quantities. Manufacturers typically only sell their products to wholesalers in what is referred to as a business-to-business or "B2B" transaction.

The wholesaler then sells and ships the products to various retailers in smaller quantities to satisfy the local demand for the product. Some wholesalers handle the products of only one manufacturer, while others handle the products of many manufacturers. **Retailers** typically buy products from wholesalers and resell the finished products to individual consumers in what is referred to as a business-to-consumer transaction (a "B2C" transaction). Retailers often have multiple store locations, and an online website, where they display the products they are offering for sale, enabling customers to view and buy the products. Radio, television, newspaper, and online advertisements inform potential customers of product availability and price. Retailers may range in size from small, with only one store location, to large, with thousands of store locations along with an online website, such as **Target.com**.

Operating Cycle of a Merchandising Firm

Exhibit 5-2 presents the **operating cycle** of a merchandising firm. There are three primary transactions involved in a merchandising firm's operating cycle: ❶ purchase merchandise and place in inventory; ❷ sell merchandise inventory to customers; and ❸ receive cash from customers. These transactions involve three current asset accounts—cash, accounts receivable, and inventory—and one current liability account—accounts payable. The merchandising firm purchases products with cash or on credit. Purchasing on credit creates an accounts payable. The purchased merchandise becomes part of the merchandiser's inventory until sold. An accounts receivable is created when the merchandise is sold to a customer on credit with cash received later when the customer pays the amount owed on account. In cases where the customer pays immediately with cash for the purchased merchandise, no accounts receivable is created. The merchandising firm uses the cash received from customers to pay the balances owed on accounts payable and to purchase more merchandise to resell, beginning a new operating cycle.

EXHIBIT 5-2	Comparison of Operating Cycle for a Merchandising Firm and a Service Firm

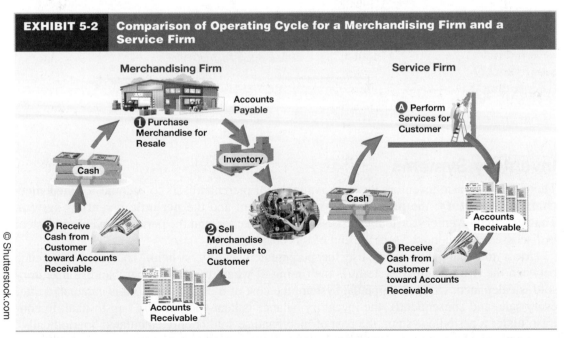

In contrast, there are only two primary transactions involved in the operating cycle of a service firm: ❹ perform service and ❺ receive cash from the customer. Service firms have no inventory to warehouse or display, and consequently, the length of their operating cycle is typically much shorter than that of a merchandising firm.

The three primary transactions for a merchandising firm repeat frequently, creating the cycle depicted in **Exhibit 5-2**. The timing of the cash collection depends upon the credit terms associated with the sale. When a wholesaler sells to a retailer, a B2B transaction, the sale is usually made on a credit basis. That is, the retailer is allowed some period of time following the sale, frequently 30 days or more, to pay the wholesaler for the purchased goods. Some retailers call a credit sale a **sale on account** (also referred to as **sale on credit**). "On account" means on a credit basis.

When retailers such as **Nordstrom** sell to individual consumers, the consumer can (1) pay cash at the time of the sale; (2) use a credit card such as **Discover**, **MasterCard**, or **Visa**; or (3) use an "open account" with the retailer. An **open account** is a charge account provided by a retailer for its customers. Many retailers such as Nordstrom have their own private label credit card to facilitate open account sales. If a customer pays cash, the retailer receives cash immediately. If the customer uses a major credit card issued by a financial institution like **Citibank**, the retailer transmits the credit card information to the card-issuing financial institution and collects the cash either on the same day or within a few days following the credit-sale transaction. If the customer uses an open account, the retailer may not collect the cash from the customer for 30 to 60 days or longer, depending upon the length of the credit terms allowed by the retailer.

Cost Flows

The costs of inventory for merchandisers flow through its accounting system as shown in the diagram below. Specifically, a company adds its *costs of goods purchased* during a period to its *beginning inventory* balance. These two components make up the company's *cost of goods available for sale*. The portion of the goods available for sale that the company sells during the period is recorded in *cost of goods sold*. The portion that is not sold is the *ending inventory* balance that is carried forward into the next period.

The mathematical representation of this cost flow relation is:

	Beginning inventory
+	Cost of goods purchased
=	Cost of goods available for sale
−	Ending inventory
=	Cost of goods sold

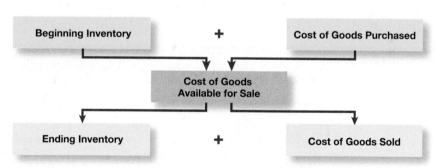

Inventory Systems

There are two basic inventory systems available for merchandisers to account for their **merchandise inventory**: the **perpetual inventory system** and the **periodic inventory system**. The perpetual inventory system is discussed in this chapter, and the periodic inventory system is discussed in Appendix 5A at the end of this chapter.

Most merchandising firms use the perpetual inventory system. The main difference between the two inventory systems is the timing of when the cost of merchandise inventory sold is calculated. Under a perpetual system, the cost of merchandise sold is calculated after every sale, and consequently, the inventory balance is kept "perpetually" up-to-date. In contrast, under a periodic system, the cost of merchandise sold is only calculated "periodically" when a physical count of the inventory is done. A physical inventory count is time consuming and usually occurs only at the end of a fiscal period. As a consequence, the actual inventory balance remains unknown until the end of a fiscal period.

A major advantage of the perpetual system is the increased control it provides over the inventory. Since the inventory is being continuously updated, management is able to determine whether current inventory levels are adequate to satisfy pending or expected sales. In addition, having a record of exactly how much inventory is available allows management to compare these amounts to a physical count of the inventory. Management can then investigate any difference between the amounts to identify the presence of theft or spoilage (in the case of perishable goods).

Jenny Company began the year with $110,000 of inventory and purchased an additional $245,000 of inventory during the year. At year end, a physical count of inventory revealed that Jenny Company still had $90,000 of inventory.
  a. How much was Jenny's cost of goods available for sale for the year?
  b. How much was Jenny's cost of goods sold for the year?

ACCOUNTING FOR PURCHASES OF MERCHANDISE

The first step of the merchandiser's operating cycle is the purchase of merchandise inventory. When a company using the perpetual inventory system purchases merchandise, it debits the Inventory account for the acquisition cost of the merchandise purchased to reflect an increase in the amount of inventory and credits the Accounts Payable account to reflect an increase in the amount owed to the supplier. For example, the Barton Wholesale Electronics' purchase invoice for inventory shown in **Exhibit 5-3** requires Barton to record the company's purchase of merchandise from Malibu Manufacturing on November 10 with the following journal entry:

LO2 **Describe** the accounting for purchases of merchandise.

Nov. 10	Inventory (+A)	21,000	
	Accounts payable (+L)		21,000
	To record the purchase of 100 disk drives from Malibu Manufacturing		
	with credit terms of 2/10, n/30.		

A   =   L   +   SE
+21,000   +21,000

Transportation Costs

Transportation Costs Incurred by Buyer

Transportation costs are sometimes incurred by a merchandising company when it acquires goods, and these costs are included as part of the acquisition cost of the inventory. When the buyer is responsible for shipping costs, it is referred to as **FOB shipping point**. An example of an invoice that specifies the shipping and payment terms is shown in **Exhibit 5-3**. (Shipping terms are explained further in Chapter 6.) Assume Barton (buyer) pays $126 to a freight company on November 11, for transportation costs on the 100 disk drives purchased from Malibu Manufacturing (seller). Barton makes the following journal entry to record the payment of $126:

Nov. 11	Inventory (+A)	126	
	Cash (−A)		126
	To record the payment of $126 of transportation costs for the purchase		
	of 100 disk drives.		

A   =   L   +   SE
+126
−126

PRINCIPLE ALERT   **Cost Principle**

The inclusion of transportation costs in the acquisition cost of inventory is consistent with the *cost principle*. The cost principle states that an asset is initially recorded at the amount paid to acquire the asset. There can be multiple expenditures associated with an asset acquisition, and all expenditures that are reasonable and necessary to acquire an asset are added to the asset's initial recorded cost.

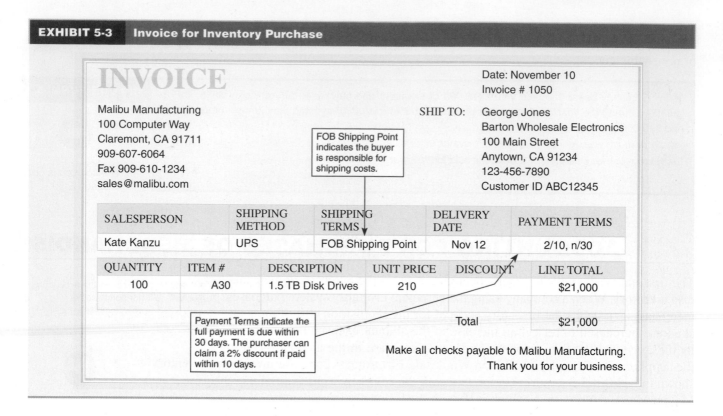

EXHIBIT 5-3   **Invoice for Inventory Purchase**

Transportation Costs Incurred by Seller

When the seller is responsible for shipping costs, it is referred to as **FOB destination**. Instead of the shipping terms stated in the invoice above, assume that the seller, Malibu Manufacturing, is responsible for and paid the $126 transportation costs. In this case the transportation costs would be considered an operating expense of the seller, and Malibu Manufacturing would debit an expense account titled Freight-out Expense as follows:

A	=	L	+	SE				
−126				−126	Nov. 11	Freight-out expense (+E, −SE)	126	
				Exp		Cash (−A)		126
						To record payment for the transportation costs for goods sold.		

Malibu paid the freight charges on the Barton purchase of disk drives, and it will attempt to pass on this cost to the buyer in the form of a higher sales price for the items purchased.

Purchase Returns and Allowances

Occasionally, a purchaser is dissatisfied with some or all of the merchandise purchased because, for example, the merchandise was manufactured poorly, the wrong merchandise was shipped, or the merchandise was damaged during shipping. When such circumstances are encountered, the purchaser and the seller can remedy the problem by agreeing to treat the value of the unwanted items either as a purchase return or as a purchase allowance.

With a **purchase return**, the purchaser ships the unsatisfactory merchandise back to the seller and receives a credit against the amount due equal to the **invoice price** of the returned merchandise. With a **purchase allowance**, the purchaser retains the merchandise, and the seller reduces the amount that the purchaser owes the seller for the shipment, in effect reducing the sales price.

As an example of a purchase return, assume that on November 15, Barton returns 10 of the 100 disk drives purchased on November 10. Barton has not yet paid Malibu Manufacturing for the goods purchased. Accordingly, Barton makes the following journal entry on November 15 to record the purchase return:

Nov. 15	Accounts payable (–L)	2,100		A	=	L	+ SE
	Inventory (–A)		2,100	–2,100		–2,100	
	To record a purchase return of 10 disk drives at an invoice price of						
	$210 each to Malibu Manufacturing.						

This entry reduces the Inventory account balance and reduces the amount owed. When the purchaser and seller reach agreement on how to handle a purchase return, they also must agree on which party pays the freight charges on the returned merchandise. (Usually the seller pays freight charges when goods are returned, in an attempt to maintain a positive customer relationship and to increase the likelihood of future repeat business.)

Data Analytics

DATA ANALYTICS **How Merchandising Analytics Help Retailers**

Merchandising analytics have the potential to reshape how merchandisers gain insights and make business decisions that improve their operations. The battle for shelf space illustrates how data analytics can lead to better purchasing decisions. It is the job of a company's brand representative to convince store managers to allocate desirable shelf space for the company's products. For example, imagine a brand representative for Coca-Cola trying to convince the local grocery store manager to allocate more shelf space for Coke Zero. With quality merchandising analytics, the brand representative is better able to argue for and obtain more shelf space for his or her product lines using actual sales data that can be filtered on a global, national, regional, and local level. In addition, real-time merchandising analytics help avoid inventory outages by providing the data necessary to reorder merchandise on a timely basis.

Purchase Discounts

Credit Period

When merchandise is sold on credit, the **credit period** is the maximum amount of time, often stated in days, that a purchaser can take to pay a seller for the purchased items. A typical credit period for a wholesale distributor is 30 days. The credit period is frequently described as the *net credit period*, or net terms. Merchandisers use the notation "**n/**" followed by the number of days in the credit period to designate the time period that a customer can take before paying cash for purchased goods. For example, **n/30** indicates a credit period of 30 days, and n/45 indicates a credit period of 45 days.

To encourage the early payment of unpaid bills, many firms offer their customers a cash discount if payment is made within a designated discount period. A **cash discount**, or **sales discount**, is the amount that the seller deducts from the invoice price if payment is made within the allowed discount period. Some refer to the cash discount offered to credit customers as a "quick-pay incentive." Sellers usually state cash discounts as a percent of the invoice price. The **discount period** is the maximum amount of time, stated in days, that a purchaser has to pay the seller if the purchaser wants to claim the cash discount. The discount period is always shorter than the credit period. Most merchandisers use the format "cash discount percent/discount period" to designate the cash discount and the discount period. For example, 1/10 indicates a cash discount of 1 percent of the invoice price and a discount period of 10 days following the invoice date. Finally, merchandisers usually combine the notation for the cash discount and the discount period with the notation for the credit period. For example, 1/10, n/30 represents a cash discount of 1 percent if paid within 10 days of the sale with a total credit period of 30 days following the date of the sale.

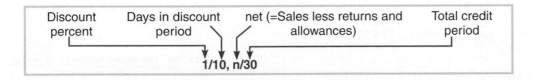

To illustrate, let's return to the Barton example in which Malibu Manufacturing and Barton agree on terms of 2/10, n/30, for the sale on November 10. Barton deducts 2 percent of the $21,000 invoice price ($420) if it pays Malibu by November 20. In that case, Barton pays $20,580 cash [computed as $21,000 × (1 − 0.02)]. If Barton pays Malibu after November 20 but no later than December 10, the amount that Barton must pay is $21,000. After December 10, the $21,000 amount would become overdue and often incurs additional interest cost depending on the invoice terms. **Exhibit 5-4** illustrates this example.

Discounts are normally attractive to merchandisers. For instance, if Barton did not take the discount offered by Malibu, this is like Barton paying an interest rate of 2 percent on the $21,000 for 20 days (30-day credit period less 10-day discount period). This is similar to paying an annual interest rate of 36.5 percent, computed as 2 percent × 365/20. Barton can borrow money at lower rates.

EXHIBIT 5-4   Purchase Discounts

Discount Period		No Discount	
Invoice Date	Discount Period Ends		Credit Period Ends
	Amount owed $20,580	Amount owed $21,000	
November 10	November 20		December 10

Accounting for Discounts

Let's extend the prior example where Barton owes $18,900 to Malibu Manufacturing; recall that Barton made a $21,000 purchase, then had a $2,100 purchase return, yielding a balance of $18,900 in the Accounts Payable T-account.

Accounts Payable	
	21,000 Nov. 10
Nov. 15 2,100	
	18,900 **Balance**

Pay within Discount Period   Assume that Barton makes a cash payment to Malibu on November 20, the last day of the discount period. (November 11, the first day following the date of sale, is the first day of the discount period, and November 20 is the tenth or last day of the discount period.) Barton records the cash payment, less the cash discount, with the following journal entry:

A	=	L	+ SE				
−378		−18,900		Nov. 20	Accounts payable (−L)	18,900	
−18,522					Inventory (−A)		378
					Cash (−A)		18,522
					To record the purchase discount and payment to Malibu Manufacturing within the discount period.		

This entry reduces to zero the amount that Barton owes Malibu Manufacturing. It also records the purchase discount of 2 percent ($18,900 × 2 percent = $378) as a reduction of the cost in the Inventory account. The entry reveals that $18,522 in cash was paid by Barton to Malibu Manufacturing ($18,900 − $378 = $18,522). Two aspects of this transaction should be noted. First, the cash discount applies only to the cost of the merchandise and not to the transportation cost. Second, the invoice price of the returned merchandise is subtracted from the total invoice price before the cash discount is calculated.

The net total cost reflected in Barton's Inventory account for the disk drives follows:

	+		Inventory (A)		−	
Purchase (+100 units)	Nov 10	21,000				
Freight-in	Nov 11	126				
			2,100	Nov 15	Purchase return (−10 units)	
			378	Nov 20	Purchase discount	
	Balance	18,648				

A total cost of $18,648 is assigned to the 90 disk drives in Barton's inventory (100 purchased less 10 returned). This results in an average cost per disk drive of $207.20 ($18,648/90).

Pay after Discount Period If Barton made a cash payment to Malibu sometime between November 21 and December 10, after the discount period expired, Barton is not eligible to receive the 2 percent purchase discount. Consequently, Barton would record a full cash payment on November 25 with the following journal entry:

Nov. 25	Accounts payable (–L)	18,900	
	Cash (–A)		18,900
	To record full payment to Malibu Manufacturing following expiration		
	of the discount period.		

A   =   L   + SE
–18,900 –18,900

When Barton makes the payment to Malibu outside of the allowed discount period, the net total cost in Barton's Inventory account for the 90 disk drives is:

	+	Inventory (A)	–	
Purchase (+100 units)	Nov 10	21,000		
Freight-in	Nov 11	126		
			2,100	Nov 15 Purchase return (–10 units)
	Balance	19,026		

A total cost of $19,026 is assigned to the 90 disk drives in Barton's inventory, resulting in an average cost per disk drive of $211.40 ($19,026/90). The cost per disk drive is higher in this situation because Barton did not make the payment for the inventory in a timely fashion to make it eligible for the cash discount.

On June 1, Musicland Inc. purchases 125 CDs at $4.08 each on account from its distributor for a total of $510. The credit terms of the purchase were 2/10, n/30. Also on June 1, Musicland paid freight charges of $22.18 cash for delivery of the CDs. On June 4, Musicland returned 15 defective CDs for an account credit of $61.20. On June 8, Musicland paid for the remaining 110 CDs.
    Record these transactions in journal entry form for Musicland.

YOUR TURN! 5.2

Guided Example

MBC

The solution is on page 5-40.

ACCOUNTING FOR SALES OF MERCHANDISE

The second step of the merchandiser's operating cycle is the sale of inventory to customers. Merchandising firms credit the Sales Revenue account when they sell products, regardless of whether the sales transaction is for cash or on credit. The Sales Revenue account has a normal credit balance.

LO3 Describe the accounting for sales of merchandise.

eLecture

MBC

Let's return to our example and assume that Barton sells 15 disk drives purchased from Malibu Manufacturing (the assumed cost per unit = $18,648/90 disk drives = $207.20 per disk drive) to The Computer Outlet Store at a sales price of $280 per unit. Barton makes the credit sale on December 12, with terms of 1/10, n/15, and The Computer Outlet Store pays shipping costs. Barton makes the following *two* journal entries to record the sale:

Dec. 12	Accounts receivable (+A)	4,200	
	Sales revenue (+R, +SE)		4,200
	To record sale of 15 disk drives at a sales price of $280 each to The		
	Computer Outlet Store with credit terms of 1/10, n/15.		

A = L + SE
+4,200   +4,200
Rev

Dec. 12	Cost of goods sold (+E, –SE)	3,108	
	Inventory (–A)		3,108
	To record sale of 15 disk drives with a unit cost of $207.20 to The		
	Computer Outlet Store.		

A = L + SE
–3,108   –3,108
Exp

A.K.A. Sales revenue is also referred to as revenue.

Revenue Side   The first journal entry records $4,200 of sales revenue ($280 × 15 disk drives) from the sale to The Computer Outlet Store. The debit to Accounts Receivable increases the amount due from customers, and the credit to Sales Revenue increases the total revenue from sales of merchandise during the accounting period.

A.K.A. Cost of goods sold is often abbreviated as COGS, and is also referred to as cost of sales.

Cost Side   The second journal entry transfers the $3,108 cost of merchandise sold ($207.20 × 15 disk drives) from the Inventory account, an asset account, to the Cost of Goods Sold account, an expense account. The debit to Cost of Goods Sold increases the total cost of merchandise sold during the accounting period, and the credit to Inventory removes the cost of the merchandise sold from the Inventory account. **Cost of goods sold** is the total cost of merchandise sold to customers during the accounting period.

After recording this sale, the net cost in Barton's Inventory account related to the disk drives is $15,540, as follows:

	+	Inventory (A)		–	
Purchase (+100 units)	Nov 10	21,000	2,100	Nov 15	Purchase return (–10 units)
Freight-in	Nov 11	126	378	Nov 20	Purchase discount
			3,108	Dec 12	Cost of goods sold (–15 units)
	Balance	**15,540**			

The $15,540 cost relates to the 75 disk drives (100 purchased – 10 returned – 15 sold) remaining in inventory. The average cost per disk drive remains $207.20 ($15,540/75 disk drives).

PRINCIPLE ALERT   **Revenue and Expense Recognition**

The entry to record sales revenue when 15 disk drives are sold to The Computer Outlet Store illustrates the *revenue recognition principle*. Under the revenue recognition principle, a merchandising firm will record revenue when goods are sold. Normally, this is the earliest point in time that the company has satisfied its performance obligation by delivering the goods to the customer. The entry to record the cost of goods sold illustrates the *expense recognition (matching) principle*. Under the expense recognition principle, expenses should be recorded in the same accounting period as the revenues they help generate.

Sales Returns and Allowances

When customers have returns and allowances, there are sellers that must record those same returns and allowances. With a sales return, the customer ships the merchandise back to the seller and the customer receives a reduction in the amount due to the seller. For example, textbook publishers often allow college bookstores to return any unsold textbooks to publishers at the conclusion of a term. With a sales allowance, the customer retains the merchandise, and the seller reduces the amount the customer owes, in effect reducing the sales price.

Accounting for **sales returns** requires two journal entries. The first entry offsets the sales revenue generated from the transaction and reduces the amount owed by the customer. The second entry transfers the cost of merchandise from Cost of Goods Sold back to the Inventory account. In the case of a **sales allowance**, the goods are not returned to the seller. As a result, only the first of these two entries is required.

Extending the previous example, assume that on December 15, The Computer Outlet Store returned five of the disk drives that it had purchased on December 12. Computer Outlet returned the units because it ordered five units too many; there is nothing wrong with the disk drives. Barton records the sales return by making the following two journal entries:

A = L + SE					
–1,400 –1,400	Dec. 15	Sales returns and allowances (+XR, –SE)		1,400	
Contra–Rev		Accounts receivable (–A)			1,400
		To record the return of 5 disk drives by The Computer Outlet Store,			
		with a sales price of $280 each.			

Dec. 15	Inventory (+A)	1,036	
	Cost of goods sold (−E, +SE)		1,036
	To record the return of 5 disk drives with a unit cost of $207.20 from The Computer Outlet Store.		

A = L + SE
+1,036   +1,036
           Exp

The first entry offsets the revenue generated from the sale by debiting Sales Returns and Allowances and reduces the amount the customer owes by crediting Accounts Receivable. The Sales Returns and Allowances account is a *contra-revenue account* and is subtracted from gross sales revenue on the income statement.

The second journal entry transfers the cost of the merchandise from Cost of Goods Sold back to the Inventory account by debiting Inventory (increasing it) and by crediting Cost of Goods Sold (decreasing it). After recording the transfer from Cost of Goods Sold to Inventory, the net total cost in Barton's Inventory account related to the disk drives is:

Hint: Contra accounts, such as the contra-revenue account, are useful because they provide more information than if the related account were used by itself. For example, by using both the revenue and the contra-revenue accounts, it is possible to track how much of the original sales have had returns or allowances.

+	Inventory (A)		−	
Purchase (+100 units)	**Nov 10**	21,000	2,100	**Nov 15** Purchase return (−10 units)
Freight-in	**Nov 11**	126	378	**Nov 20** Purchase discount
Sales return (+5 units)	**Dec 15**	1,036	3,108	**Dec 12** Cost of goods sold (−15 units)
	Balance	16,576		

The $16,576 total cost relates to 80 units (100 purchased − 10 purchase return − 15 sold + 5 sales return); the average cost of the inventory remains $207.20 ($16,576/80).

ACCOUNTING IN PRACTICE   **Monitoring Sales Returns and Allowances**

Companies accumulate sales revenue in one account and sales returns and allowances in another account so that they can separately monitor both types of activities. A high ratio of sales returns and allowances to sales revenue is undesirable, often indicating a problem in the quality of the merchandise or its packaging. A company can compare the ratio for the current year to prior-year ratios, or to a target ratio set for the current year, to determine how well the company is managing its product and packaging quality.

Sales Discounts

When making a cash payment for purchased goods, a customer is entitled to take a cash discount if the payment is made during the allowed discount period. If a cash discount is taken, the seller records it in a separate account called Sales Discounts.

Pay within Discount Period

Returning to the previous example, assume that The Computer Outlet Store agrees to terms of 1/10, n/15 and pays the amount due Barton after deducting the 1 percent cash discount on December 22, the last day of the cash discount period. (December 13 is the first day of the discount period, and December 22 is the tenth or last day of the discount period.) Barton makes the following journal entry to record the cash received from Computer Outlet:

Dec. 22	Cash (+A)	2,772	
	Sales discounts (+XR, −SE)	28	
	Accounts receivable (−A)		2,800
	To record the sales discount and cash payment from The Computer Outlet Store within the allowed discount period.		

A = L + SE
+2,772   −28
−2,800   Contra−Rev

This entry reduces the amount the customer, The Computer Outlet Store, owes the seller, Barton, to zero. The total undiscounted amount due was $2,800 ($4,200 sales − $1,400 sales return). With terms of 1/10, n/15, the sales discount is $28 ($2,800 × 1 percent) and the cash collected is $2,772 ($2,800 − $28).

Companies accumulate sales discounts in a separate account so that management can monitor the dollar amount of sales discounts being taken by customers. Sales Discounts is a *contra-revenue account* like Sales Returns and Allowances. Both accounts are contra to, or subtracted from, gross Sales Revenue on the income statement.

There are two important aspects of the sales discount calculation. First, the cash discount applies only to the sales price of the merchandise sold and not to any transportation costs. Second, the sales price of any merchandise returned must be subtracted from the total amount before calculating the cash discount.

Pay after Discount Period

If The Computer Outlet Store makes a cash payment after December 22 (after the discount period has expired), the cash discount does not apply. For example, if cash is received in full payment from The Computer Outlet Store on December 27, Barton would record the following journal entry:

A = L + SE				
+2,800	Dec. 27	Cash (+A)	2,800	
−2,800		Accounts receivable (−A)		2,800
		To record cash received from The Computer Outlet Store outside the allowed discount period.		

Net Sales

Gross sales revenue
− Sales returns and allowances
− Sales discounts
= Net sales

Net sales is the gross sales revenue generated through merchandise sales less any sales returns and allowances and any sales (cash) discounts. A company calculates its net sales for the period by subtracting the balances of the Sales Returns and Allowances account (normal debit balance) and the Sales Discounts account (normal debit balance) from the balance of the Sales Revenue account (normal credit balance).

YOUR TURN! 5.3

MBC

The solution is on page 5-40.

On June 15, a customer buys 75 CDs on account from Musicland for $10 each, for a total of $750. The **list price** of the CDs is $12 each, but Musicland gave the customer a $2 per CD discount because of the large order. On June 20, the customer returned, unopened, five of the CDs and was given a purchase credit of $50. The customer paid its full balance of $700 on June 25. Record these transactions in journal entry form for Musicland. The unit cost of the CDs in inventory is $4.20 each.*

*$4.20 is calculated from Your Turn! 5.2 as follows:

    Inventory cost = $510.00 + $22.18 − $61.20 − $8.98 = $462.00

    Inventory quantity = 125 − 15 = 110

    Cost per unit = $462.00/110 = $4.20

PROFITABILITY ANALYSIS

LO4 **Define** the gross profit percentage and the return on sales ratio, and **explain** their use in profitability analysis.

eLecture

MBC

A.K.A. Gross profit is often referred to as gross margin.

Gross Profit Percentage

Managers, investment professionals, and stockholders closely monitor a company's gross profit on sales. They know that if gross profit on sales declines from one year to the next, net income for the current and following year is also likely to decline. A declining gross profit can indicate problems in a company's purchasing activities or problems selling its goods at an acceptable price. **Gross profit (gross margin)**, or **gross profit on sales**, is defined as the difference between Net Sales and Cost of Goods Sold and reveals the amount of sales revenue remaining after subtracting the cost of products sold. (Recall that net sales equals gross sales revenue less any sales returns and allowances and sales discounts.)

© Shutterstock.com

Financial statement users who monitor a company's gross profit are also interested in its **gross profit percentage**—that is, the rate at which a company earns gross profit on its sales revenue. The gross profit percentage is computed as follows:

$$\text{Gross profit percentage} = \frac{\text{Gross profit on sales}}{\text{Net sales}}$$

Using the data in **Exhibit 5-5**, the 2020 gross profit percentage for **Target** is 29.8 percent.

Financial analysis of the gross profit percentage frequently involves comparing the company against its performance in prior years and against the performance of competitor companies. Gross profit percentages for a two-year period are presented in **Exhibit 5-5** for both **Target Corporation** and one of its chief competitors, **Walmart Corporation**.

EXHIBIT 5-5 Gross Profit Percentage for Target Corporation and Walmart Corporation

(in millions)	2020	2019
Target	$\frac{\$23,248}{\$78,112}$ = 29.8 percent	$\frac{\$22,057}{\$75,356}$ = 29.3 percent
Walmart	$\frac{\$129,359}{\$523,964}$ = 24.7 percent	$\frac{\$129,104}{\$514,405}$ = 25.1 percent

Target's gross profit percentage increased 0.5 percent, from 29.3 percent in 2019 to 29.8 percent in 2020; further, in both years Target has a higher gross profit percentage than Walmart. Walmart's gross profit percentage is only 25.1 percent in 2019 and 24.7 percent in 2020. One explanation for the large difference between the gross profit percentages of the two companies is their different business strategies. Target attempts to sell higher-quality products at a reasonable price, whereas Walmart focuses more on low prices and less on product quality.

Concept →	Method →	Assessment	TAKEAWAY 5.1
Is a company able to maintain prices on its goods consistent with changes in the cost of its inventory?	Gross profit and net sales Gross profit percentage = $\frac{\text{Gross profit on sales}}{\text{Net sales}}$	A higher ratio suggests the company has market power to command higher retail prices. A lower ratio suggests competitive pressures on price setting.	

Return on Sales Ratio (Profit Margin)

First introduced in Chapter 4, the **return on sales ratio (profit margin)** reveals the net income earned on each dollar of net sales and is computed by dividing net income by net sales:

A.K.A. Return on sales is often referred to as profit margin.

$$\text{Return on sales ratio} = \frac{\text{Net income}}{\text{Net sales}}$$

Return on sales ratios for **Target Corporation** and **Walmart Corporation** are presented in **Exhibit 5-6**. Target's return on sales ratio for 2020 is 4.2 percent.

EXHIBIT 5-6 Return on Sales Ratios for Target Corporation and Walmart Corporation

(in millions)	2020	2019
Target	$\frac{\$3,281}{\$78,112}$ = 4.2 percent	$\frac{\$2,937}{\$75,356}$ = 3.9 percent
Walmart	$\frac{\$14,881}{\$523,964}$ = 2.8 percent	$\frac{\$6,670}{\$514,405}$ = 1.3 percent

Walmart's return on sales ratio for 2020 indicates that it earned 2.8 cents for each dollar of sales. The return on sales ratio allows us to compare a company's ability to earn profits on its sales regardless of company size. Walmart generates nearly seven times the sales revenue as does Target ($78,112 million for Target versus $523,964 million for Walmart), yet Walmart has a return on sales ratio that is lower than Target's. A company has a number of ways to improve its return on sales ratio, for example, by raising its retail prices or by purchase discounts from buying in larger quantities. It could also reduce operating expenses by reducing salaries, administrative costs, or selling and marketing costs, or discontinuing poorly performing segments of the business. Analysts like to compare return on sales ratios for a company over time to detect any trends. They also like to compare the ratio with those of competitors.

TAKEAWAY 5.2	Concept ⟶	Method ⟶	Assessment
	Is a company able to maintain prices on its goods consistent with changes in its total expenses?	Net income and net sales Return on sales ratio = $\dfrac{\text{Net income}}{\text{Net sales}}$	A higher ratio suggests the company is providing a higher net income on each dollar of net sales.

YOUR TURN! 5.4

MBC

The solution is on page 5-40.

The President of Musicland has asked for help to evaluate the company's performance during the current year. In particular, calculate Musicland's gross profit percentage and its return on sales ratio and then explain what these measures indicate. The following information is from Musicland's financial statements:

Net sales.	$100,000
Cost of goods sold	45,000
Net income	10,500

ENVIRONMENTAL, SOCIAL, AND GOVERNANCE   Governance and Conflicts of Interest

Good corporate governance helps to cultivate a company culture of ethical business practices. **Target** publishes a Business Conduct Guide for its employees as part of its governance program. Included in this handbook are guidelines concerning conflicts of interest. The list below provides examples of potential conflicts of interest:

- Owning a substantial amount of stock in any competing business or in any organization that does business with us.
- Serving as a director, manager, consultant, employee, or independent contractor for any organization that does business with us, or is a competitor—except with our company's specific prior knowledge and consent.
- Accepting or receiving gifts of any value or favors, compensation, loans, excessive entertainment, or similar activities from any individual or organization that does business or wants to do business with us, or is a competitor.
- Representing the company in any transaction in which you or a related person has a substantial interest.
- Disclosing or using for your benefit confidential or non-public information about Target or other organizations with which we do business.
- Taking personal advantage of a business opportunity that is within the scope of Target's business—such as by purchasing property that Target is interested in acquiring.

Williams Distributing Company is a merchandising company. Williams uses the perpetual inventory system. Record each of the following transactions related to the company's purchasing and selling of merchandise:

March   1 Purchased merchandise on account for $6,000; terms were 2/10, n/30.
        3 Paid $200 cash for freight on the March 1 purchase.
        6 Returned merchandise costing $300 (part of the $6,000 purchase).
     10 Paid for merchandise purchased on March 1.
     12 Sold merchandise on account costing $8,000 for $10,000; terms were 2/10, n/30.
     15 Accepted returned and undamaged merchandise from a customer costing $400 that had been
           sold on account for $500 (part of the $10,000 sale).
     20 Received payment from customer for merchandise sold on March 12.

Solution

March	1	Inventory (+A)	6,000	
		Accounts payable (+L)		6,000
		Purchased merchandise with 2/10, n/30 terms.		
	3	Inventory (+A)	200	
		Cash (−A)		200
		Paid freight on March 1 purchase.		
	6	Accounts payable (−L)	300	
		Inventory (−A)		300
		Returned merchandise from March 1 purchase.		
	10	Accounts payable (−L)	5,700	
		Inventory (−A)		114
		Cash (−A)		5,586
		Paid for merchandise purchased on March 1 within the discount period		
		[($6,000 − $300) × 2% = $114].		
	12	Accounts receivable (+A)	10,000	
		Sales revenue (+R, +SE)		10,000
		To record revenue from sale of merchandise.		
	12	Cost of goods sold (+E, −SE)	8,000	
		Inventory (−A)		8,000
		To record cost of merchandise sold and to reduce inventory.		
	15	Sales returns and allowances (+XR, −SE)	500	
		Accounts receivable (−A)		500
		To record sales return by customer.		
	15	Inventory (+A)	400	
		Cost of goods sold (−E, +SE)		400
		To record cost of goods returned by customer.		
	20	Cash (+A)	9,310	
		Sales discounts (+XR, −SE)	190	
		Accounts receivable (−A)		9,500
		To record receipt of cash from customer within the discount period.		
		[($10,000 − $500) × 2% = $190].		

APPENDIX 5A: Periodic Inventory System

LO5
Describe and **illustrate** a periodic inventory system.

eLecture

MBC

An alternative to the perpetual inventory system illustrated in the chapter is the periodic inventory system. The **periodic inventory system** does not update the Inventory account or the Cost of Goods Sold account as merchandise transactions occur during the year. Instead, the Inventory account and the Cost of Goods Sold account are updated only at the end of the accounting period when a physical count of the inventory on hand is completed. Cost of goods sold is then calculated by subtracting the ending inventory balance from the cost of goods available for sale. The periodic inventory system is unacceptable for most companies because up-to-date inventory amounts are not available during the year for managerial decision making. The following section illustrates the journal entries that Barton Wholesale Electronics would make if it used the periodic inventory system. We utilize the same data from the chapter to illustrate the perpetual inventory system to facilitate an easy comparison of the two systems.

Accounting for Purchases of Merchandise

When a company uses the periodic inventory system, it records the purchase of merchandise by debiting the cost of the merchandise to the Purchases account, rather than the Inventory account, and crediting the cost to Accounts Payable. The Purchases account is a temporary account with a normal debit balance. On November 10, Barton records the purchase of 100 disk drives with a list price of $210 each and terms of 2/10, n/30 by making the following journal entry:

A	=	L	+	SE			
		+21,000		−21,000	Nov. 10	Purchases (+E, −SE)	21,000	
						Accounts payable (+L)		21,000
						To record the purchase of 100 disk drives from Malibu with 2/10, n/30 terms.		

Transportation Costs

When a purchaser using the periodic inventory system bears the cost of transporting the merchandise from the seller, the purchaser records the transportation costs in the Freight-in account, rather than in the Inventory account. Freight-in is a temporary account with a normal debit balance. Barton makes the following journal entry on November 11 to record payment of $126 of transportation costs on the purchase of 100 disk drives:

A	=	L	+	SE			
−126				−126 Exp	Nov. 11	Freight-in (+E, −SE)	126	
						Cash (−A)		126
						To record the payment of $126 of transportation costs on the purchase of 100 disk drives.		

Purchase Returns and Allowances

If a purchaser is dissatisfied with merchandise that was purchased and a purchase return or allowance is granted, the purchaser records the purchase return or allowance using the Purchase Returns and Allowances account, rather than the Inventory account. Purchase Returns and Allowances is a contra-Purchases account with a normal credit balance. On November 15, Barton records the return of 10 disk drives to Malibu Manufacturing by making the following journal entry:

A	=	L	+	SE			
		−2,100		+2,100	Nov. 15	Accounts payable (−L)	2,100	
						Purchase returns and allowances (−E, +SE)		2,100
						To record the return of 10 disk drives at a list price of $210.		

Purchase Discounts

If a purchaser makes a cash payment to the seller before the end of the allowed discount period, the purchaser deducts a cash discount. Otherwise, the purchaser pays the full invoice price. When a purchaser takes a cash discount, the purchaser credits the Purchase Discounts account, rather than the Inventory account. Purchase Discounts is a contra-Purchases account with a normal credit balance. Barton makes the following journal entry on November 20 to record its cash payment to Malibu Manufacturing after deducting the cash discount:

A	=	L	+	SE			
−18,522		−18,900		+378	Nov. 20	Accounts payable (−L)	18,900	
						Purchase discounts (−E, +SE)		378
						Cash (−A)		18,522
						To record the payment to Malibu Manufacturing within the allowed discount period.		

If Barton pays between November 21 and December 10, after the discount period has expired, the cash discount does not apply. In this case, Barton records a cash payment on November 25 with the following journal entry:

Nov. 25	Accounts payable (–L)	18,900	
	Cash (–A)		18,900
	To record the payment to Malibu Manufacturing outside the allowed		
	discount period.		

A = L + SE
−18,900 −18,900

YOUR TURN! 5A.1

Assume that Musicland uses the *periodic system*. On June 1, Musicland purchased 125 CDs at $4.08 each on account from its distributor for $510. The terms of the purchase were 2/10, n/30. Also on June 1, Musicland paid in cash a freight charge of $22.18 for delivery of the CDs. On June 4, Musicland returned 15 defective CDs for a credit of $61.20. On June 8, Musicland paid for the remaining 110 CDs. Record the transactions in journal entry form for Musicland.

GuidedExample

MBC

The solution is on page 5-40.

Accounting for Sales of Merchandise

Under the periodic inventory system, a seller makes only one journal entry to record a sale of merchandise. The entry records the amount received from the customer and the sales revenue from the sale by debiting Accounts Receivable and crediting Sales Revenue. Barton records the December 12 sale of 15 disk drives to The Computer Outlet Store at a sales price of $280 each with terms of 1/10, n/15 by making the following entry:

Dec. 12	Accounts receivable (+A)	4,200	
	Sales revenue (+R, +SE)		4,200
	To record the sale of 15 disk drives at a sales price of $280 each to		
	The Computer Outlet Store with credit terms of 1/10, n/15.		

A = L + SE
+4,200   +4,200
          Rev

The same journal entry is made under the perpetual inventory system. Under the periodic inventory system, however, there is no concurrent entry to transfer the cost of merchandise sold from the Inventory account to the Cost of Goods Sold account.

Sales Returns and Allowances

Under the periodic inventory system, only one journal entry is used to record a sales return or allowance. The entry records the reduction of the revenue from the sale and the reduction of the accounts receivable from the customer by debiting Sales Returns and Allowances and crediting Accounts Receivable. Barton records the December 15 return by The Computer Outlet Store of five disk drives by making the following journal entry:

Dec. 15	Sales returns and allowances (+XR, –SE)	1,400	
	Accounts receivable (–A)		1,400
	To record the return of 5 disk drives by The Computer Outlet Store;		
	sales price was $280 each.		

A = L + SE
−1,400   −1,400
      Contra-Rev

This entry is the same as the first journal entry under the perpetual inventory system; however, Barton does not make the second journal entry under the perpetual inventory system. Under the periodic inventory system, there is no immediate reinstatement of the returned merchandise to the Inventory account or corresponding reduction in the Cost of Goods Sold account.

Sales Discounts

The journal entry to record the receipt of a cash payment from a customer is exactly the same under either the perpetual inventory system or the periodic inventory system. If the payment is made within the allowed discount period, the entry includes a debit to Sales Discounts, a contra-Revenue account. Barton records the cash received from The Computer Outlet Store on December 22 (within the discount period) as follows:

A = L + SE +2,772   −28 −2,800 Contra-Rev

Dec. 22 | Cash (+A) | 2,772 | |
Sales discounts (+XR, −SE)	28	
Accounts receivable (−A)		2,800
To record the cash payment from The Computer Outlet Store within		
the discount period.		

If The Computer Outlet Store makes its cash payment any time between December 13 and December 27 (after the discount period), the cash discount does not apply. Barton records the cash received from The Computer Outlet Store on December 27 with the following journal entry:

A = L + SE +2,800 −2,800

Dec. 27 | Cash (+A) | 2,800 | |
Accounts receivable (−A)		2,800
To record the cash payment from The Computer Outlet Store outside		
the discount period.		

YOUR TURN! 5A.2

MBC

The solution is on page 5-41.

Assume Musicland uses the *periodic system*. On June 15, a customer buys on account 75 CDs from Musicland for $10 each, for a total of $750. The list price of the CDs is $12 each, but Musicland provided the customer with a $2 per CD discount because of the large order. On June 20, the customer returned, unopened, five of the CDs and was given a credit of $50. The customer paid its full balance of $700 on June 25. Record these transactions on Musicland's books. The unit cost of the CDs in inventory is $4.20 each.*

*$4.20 is calculated from Your Turn 5A.1 as follows:
Inventory cost = $510.00 + $22.18 − $61.20 − $8.98 = $462.00
Inventory quantity = 125 − 15 = 110
Cost per unit = $462.00/110 = $4.20

Comparison of Entries under the Perpetual and Periodic Systems

Exhibit 5A-1 summarizes all key journal entries under both the perpetual and periodic inventory systems for purchases and sales of merchandise. Differences in the periodic inventory system are highlighted.

EXHIBIT 5A-1 **Comparison of Journal Entries under the Perpetual and Periodic Systems**

Date	Transaction	Perpetual Inventory System			Periodic Inventory System		

Nov 10	Purchase of merchandise on credit	Inventory
		  Accounts payable
			21,000	21,000	Purchases
					  Accounts payable
						21,000	21,000

Nov 11	Freight cost	Inventory
		  Cash
			126	126	Freight-in
					  Cash
						126	126

Nov 15	Purchase returns	Accounts payable
		  Inventory
			2,100	2,100	Accounts payable
					  Purchase returns and allowances
						2,100	2,100

Nov 20	Purchase discount and payment	Accounts payable
		  Inventory
		  Cash
			18,900	378
				18,522
					Accounts payable
					  Purchase discounts
					  Cash
						18,900	378
							18,522

Dec 12	Sale of merchandise on credit	Accounts receivable
		  Sales revenue
			4,200	4,200	Accounts receivable
					  Sales revenue
						4,200	4,200

		Cost of goods sold Inventory	3,108	3,108	No entry		

Dec 15	Return of sales merchandise	Sales returns and allowances
		  Accounts receivable
			1,400	1,400	Sales returns and allowances
					  Accounts receivable
						1,400	1,400

		Inventory Cost of goods sold	1,036	1,036	No entry		

Dec 22	Sales discount and payment	Cash
		Sales discounts
		  Accounts receivable
			2,772
			28
				2,800	Cash
					Sales discounts
					  Accounts receivable
						2,772
						28
							2,800

Cost of Goods Sold Using a Periodic System

If a firm uses a periodic system rather than a perpetual system, it does not record cost of goods sold at the time sales revenue is recorded. Instead, cost of goods sold is calculated periodically at the end of the accounting period when the inventory is physically counted. Cost of goods sold is then calculated by subtracting the ending inventory from the **cost of goods available for sale**. The calculation of cost of goods sold using the periodic method is shown in **Exhibit 5A-2**.

EXHIBIT 5A-2	Cost of Goods Sold Computation Using the Periodic Method

	Beginning inventory
+	Cost of goods purchased during the period
=	Cost of goods available for sale
−	Ending inventory
=	Cost of goods sold

One additional difference between the periodic method and the perpetual method is how a company keeps track of items that affect the Inventory account. Under the perpetual system, items such as transportation charges, purchase returns, and purchase discounts are recorded directly to the Inventory account. Under the periodic system, separate accounts are used for each of these items, which are then added to beginning inventory to arrive at the cost of goods available for sale. An illustration of this is shown in **Exhibit 5A-3**, assuming that there was no beginning inventory.

EXHIBIT 5A-3	Cost of Goods Sold Illustration Using the Periodic Method

BARTON WHOLESALE ELECTRONICS
Cost of Goods Sold
For Year Ended December 31

Inventory, January 1			$ 0
Purchases.		$21,000	
Less: Purchase returns and allowances	$2,100		
Purchase discounts	378	2,478	
Net purchases		18,522	
Add: Freight-in		126	
Cost of goods purchased			18,648
Cost of goods available for sale			18,648
Less: Inventory, December 31			16,576
Cost of goods sold			$ 2,072

YOUR TURN! 5A.3

Assume that Musicland uses a periodic inventory system. Prepare a schedule of cost of goods sold as of December 31 using the following information:

Inventory, January 1	$10,000
Purchases.	50,000
Purchase returns and allowances	2,000
Freight-in.	200
Purchase discounts	1,000
Inventory, December 31	12,200

GuidedExample

MBC

The solution is on page 5-41.

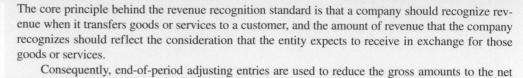

APPENDIX 5B: The Revenue Recognition Standard

LO6 Describe and illustrate the revenue recognition standard for sales returns and allowances and sales discounts.

eLecture

MBC

The core principle behind the revenue recognition standard is that a company should recognize revenue when it transfers goods or services to a customer, and the amount of revenue that the company recognizes should reflect the consideration that the entity expects to receive in exchange for those goods or services.

Consequently, end-of-period adjusting entries are used to reduce the gross amounts to the net amounts that the company expects to receive after sales discounts are taken and returns and allowances are made. A company must use its judgment to estimate the amount of sales discounts that will be taken and sales returns and allowances that will be made in future periods for sales that occur in the current period. It is reasonable to assume that nearly all customers will take the sales discounts because of the financial benefits of doing so. It is also likely that companies will use past experience to estimate sales returns and allowances.

The following example illustrates the accounting for sales of merchandise for Barton Wholesale Electronics using the approach required in the revenue recognition standard. Barton's fiscal year-end is December 31.

Assume that during the year Barton sells merchandise on account totaling $500,000. Further assume the cost to Barton of this merchandise was $400,000. The following two journal entries summarize Barton's credit sales during the year, along with the associated cost of goods sold.

Various dates	Accounts receivable (+A)	500,000	
	Sales revenue (+R, +SE)		500,000
	To record sale of merchandise on account.		
Various dates	Cost of goods sold (+E, −SE)	400,000	
	Inventory (−A)		400,000
	To record cost of goods sold.		

The revenue recognition standard requires Barton to estimate the amount of both sales discounts and sales returns and allowances. Below we illustrate three adjusting journal entries made at year-end to comply with the revenue recognition standard. The first adjusting journal entry applies to estimated sales discounts, and the other two adjusting journal entries apply to estimated sales returns and allowances.

Adjusting Journal Entry for Sales Discounts

Barton offers credit terms of 1/10, n/15 to encourage early payment. At year-end, Barton recognizes that there are $9,000 of sales on account still eligible for the 1 percent discount. Barton believes that all companies will pay within the discount period to receive the 1 percent discount. Barton makes the following adjusting journal entry at year-end to provide for these estimated sales discounts:

Dec. 31	Sales discounts (+XR, −SE)	90	
	Allowance for sales discounts (+XA, −A)		90
	To record the estimated sales discount of 1 percent on credit sales		
	still eligible for discount at year-end ($9,000 × 0.01).		

This adjusting journal entry debits Sales discounts for the amount of discounts Barton estimates will be taken. The Sales discounts account is a contra account to Sales revenue. The credit in this entry is to the Allowance for sales discounts, which is a contra account to Accounts receivable.

Adjusting Journal Entry for Sales Returns and Allowances

Barton allows a 60-day return privilege for the merchandise it sells. At year-end, Barton estimates there remain $100,000 of sales (with a cost to Barton of $80,000) that are still within the 60-day return period and that, from past experience, 10 percent of this merchandise will be returned. Barton makes the following adjusting journal entries at year-end to provide for these estimated returns.

Dec. 31	Sales returns and allowances (+XR, −SE)	10,000	
	Sales refunds payable (+L)		10,000
	To record the estimated return of 10 percent of the merchandise sold		
	that is still eligible for return at year-end ($100,000 × 0.10).		
Dec. 31	Estimated inventory return (+A)	8,000	
	Cost of goods sold (−E, +SE)		8,000
	To record the estimated return of 10 percent of the merchandise sold		
	that is still eligible for return at year-end ($80,000 × 0.10).		

The first adjusting journal entry debits Sales returns and allowances for the amount of merchandise that Barton estimates will be returned within the return period. Sales returns and allowance represents a contra account to Sales revenue. The credit in this entry is to Sales refunds payable, a liability account representing the refund that will be due upon the return of the merchandise.

The second adjusting journal entry debits Estimated inventory return for the amount of inventory Barton estimates will be returned. Estimated inventory return is an asset account.

In subsequent periods, management will assess these three important accounts: Allowance for Sales Discounts, Sales Refunds Payable, and Estimated Inventory Return. Management would adjust upward or downward as necessary during the year-end adjustment process to report balances for these accounts that reflect economic circumstances. All other entries during the period for returns, allowances, and discounts are identical to those described in the chapter.

YOUR TURN! 5B.1

WikiTech's fiscal year-end is December 31. Assume that during the year, WikiTech sells merchandise on account totaling $1,000,000. Further assume the cost to WikiTech of this merchandise was $300,000. WikiTech offers credit terms of 2/10, n/30 to encourage early payment. At year-end, WikiTech recognizes that there are $150,000 of sales on account still eligible for the 2 percent discount. WikiTech believes that all companies will pay within the discount period to receive the 2 percent discount. In addition, WikiTech allows a 90-day return privilege for the merchandise it sells. At year-end, WikiTech estimates there remain $200,000 of sales (with a cost to WikiTech of $60,000) that are still within the 90-day return period and that, from past experience, 7.5 percent of this merchandise is expected to be returned. Prepare the period-end adjusting journal entries needed for WikiTech to comply with the revenue recognition standard.

GuidedExample

MBC

The solution is on page 5-41.

SUMMARY OF LEARNING OBJECTIVES

Explain the operations of a merchandising company and contrast that with the operations of a service company. (p. 5-3)   **LO1**

- Merchandise inventory is a stock of products that a company buys from another company and makes available for sale to its customers.
- Merchandising firms sell merchandise. There are two types of merchandising firms: wholesale distributors and retailers.
- Manufacturing companies convert raw materials and components into finished products through the application of skilled labor and machine operations; wholesale distributors buy finished products from manufacturing firms in large quantities and sell smaller quantities to retailers; retailers sell the products to individual consumers.
- The operating cycle of a merchandising firm consists of three types of transactions: purchase merchandise for resale and warehouse the inventory, remove goods from inventory and ship to the customer at sale, and receive cash from the customer.
- The primary revenue source for a service firm is providing services to customers, rather than manufacturing or selling a physical product.

Describe the accounting for purchases of merchandise. (p. 5-6)   **LO2**

- The perpetual inventory system records the cost of merchandise in the Inventory account at the time of purchase and updates the Inventory account for subsequent transactions as they occur.
- When the perpetual inventory system is used, the Inventory account is affected by merchandise transactions as follows:
  - Debited for the invoice price of purchases.
  - Debited for transportation costs.
  - Credited for the cost of purchase returns and allowances.
  - Credited for cash discounts taken.
  - Credited for the cost of the merchandise sold.
  - Debited for the cost of any sales returns.

LO3   **Describe the accounting for sales of merchandise. (p. 5-10)**

- When a perpetual inventory system is used, the following procedure is followed to account for the sale of merchandise:
  - Credit Sales Revenue at the time of the sale, and debit Cash or Accounts Receivable.
  - Debit Cost of Goods Sold and credit Inventory at the time of sale to match expenses with revenue and to update the inventory balance.

LO4   **Define the gross profit percentage and the return on sales ratio, and explain their use in profitability analysis. (p. 5-13)**

- The gross profit percentage is the rate at which a company earns gross profit on net sales.
- The gross profit percentage is calculated as net sales less the cost of goods sold, all divided by net sales.
- The return on sales ratio reveals how much of each dollar of net sales is earned by the company after subtracting all expenses.
- The return on sales ratio is calculated by dividing net income by net sales.

LO5   **Appendix 5A: Describe and illustrate a periodic inventory system. (p. 5-17)**

- The periodic inventory system updates both the Inventory account and the Cost of Goods Sold account at the end of the accounting period when a physical count of the inventory is taken.
- Under the periodic inventory system separate accounts are used to record merchandise purchases, transportation costs, purchase returns and allowances, and purchase discounts, rather than recording these items to the Inventory account.
- The periodic inventory system does not update the Inventory account or the Cost of Goods Sold account as merchandise transactions occur during the year. Instead, the Inventory account and the Cost of Goods Sold account are updated only at the end of the accounting period when a physical count of the inventory is taken. Other accounts are used to record purchases, transportation costs, purchase returns and allowances, and purchase discounts.
- Cost of goods sold is calculated by subtracting the remaining inventory on hand from the cost of goods available for sale, which represents the aggregate inventory that was available to be sold.
- The basic formula for calculating the cost of goods sold under the periodic system is to calculate goods available for sale consisting of beginning inventory plus purchases during the period, net of purchase returns and allowances and purchase discounts, and then subtract ending inventory from this amount.

LO6   **Appendix 5B: Describe and illustrate the revenue recognition standard for sales returns and allowances and sales discounts. (p. 5-21)**

- The core principle underlying the revenue recognition standard is that a company should recognize revenue in the amount of consideration it expects to receive in exchange for the transfer of goods or services to a customer.

SUMMARY	Concept	Method	Assessment
TAKEAWAY 5.1	Is a company able to maintain prices on its goods consistent with changes in the cost of its inventory?	Gross profit and net sales $\text{Gross profit percentage} = \dfrac{\text{Gross profit on sales}}{\text{Net sales}}$	A higher ratio suggests the company has market power to command higher retail prices. A lower ratio suggests competitive pressures on price setting.
TAKEAWAY 5.2	Is a company able to maintain prices on its goods consistent with changes in its total expenses?	Net income and net sales $\text{Return on sales ratio} = \dfrac{\text{Net income}}{\text{Net sales}}$	A higher ratio suggests the company is providing a higher net income on each dollar of net sales.

KEY TERMS

Cash discount (p. 5-8)	Invoice price (p. 5-7)	Purchase allowance (p. 5-7)
Cost of goods available for sale (p. 5-20)	List price (p. 5-13)	Purchase return (p. 5-7)
	Manufacturers (p. 5-3)	Retailers (p. 5-4)
Cost of goods sold (p. 5-11)	Merchandise inventory (p. 5-5)	Return on sales ratio (profit margin) (p. 5-14)
Credit period (p. 5-8)	Merchandisers (p. 5-3)	
Discount period (p. 5-8)	Net sales (p. 5-13)	Sale on account (p. 5-5)
FOB destination (p. 5-7)	Open account (p. 5-5)	Sale on credit (p. 5-5)
FOB shipping point (p. 5-6)	Operating cycle (p. 5-4)	Sales allowance (p. 5-11)
Gross profit (gross margin) (p. 5-13)	Periodic inventory system (p. 5-5)	Sales discount (p. 5-8)
Gross profit on sales (p. 5-13)	Perpetual inventory system (p. 5-5)	Sales returns (p. 5-11)
Gross profit percentage (p. 5-14)		Wholesalers (p. 5-3)

Assignments with the (MBC) logo in the margin are available in BusinessCourse.
See the Preface of the book for details.

SELF-STUDY QUESTIONS

(Answers to Self-Study Questions are at the end of this chapter.)

1. On March 1, Kate Company purchased merchandise with an invoice price of $2,700 and 2/10, n/30 terms. On March 3, Kate pays $98 transportation costs on the purchased goods. On March 10, Kate pays for the merchandise. What is Kate's total cost of the purchased merchandise? **LO2**

   a. $2,700   *c.* $2,746
   b. $2,744   *d.* $2,800

2. Angle Company started business on January 1. During the year, the company purchased merchandise with an invoice price of $500,000. Angle also paid $20,000 freight on the merchandise. During the year, Angle returned $80,000 of the merchandise to its suppliers. All purchases were paid for in a timely manner, and a $10,000 cash discount was taken. Merchandise costing $418,000 was sold for $627,000. What is the December 31 balance in the Inventory account? **LO2**

   a. $82,000   *c.* $12,000
   b. $32,000   *d.* $2,000

3. Samuel Company uses the perpetual inventory system. Samuel purchased merchandise with an invoice price of $800, terms 2/10, n/30. If Samuel returns merchandise with an invoice price of $200 to the supplier, what should the journal entry to record the return include? **LO2**

   a. Debit to Inventory of $200   *c.* Credit to Inventory of $200
   b. Debit to Inventory of $196   *d.* Credit to Inventory of $100

4. Jackson Company reports net sales of $500, cost of sales of $300, and net income of $50. What is the gross profit percentage and return on sales ratio for Jackson? **LO4**

   a. Gross profit percentage is 10 percent and return on sales ratio is 40 percent.
   b. Gross profit percentage is 60 percent and return on sales ratio is 10 percent.
   c. Gross profit percentage is 40 percent and return on sales ratio is 10 percent.
   d. Gross profit percentage is 40 percent and return on sales ratio is 25 percent.

5. Jefferson & Sons purchased $5,000 of merchandise from the Claremont Company with terms of 3/10, n/30. How much discount is Jefferson & Sons entitled to take if it pays within the allowed discount period of 10 days? **LO2**

   a. $50   *c.* $150
   b. $100   *d.* $300

6. Adams Inc. purchased merchandise with a list price of $6,000 from the Sprague Company. Sprague offers its customers credit terms of 2/10, n/30. What amount should Adams pay if the cash discount is taken? **LO2**

   a. $5,940   *c.* $6,120
   b. $6,060   *d.* $5,880

LO4   7. The Eureka Company is a merchandiser and reports the following data at year-end:

Net sales.	$100,000
Cost of goods sold	60,000
Net income	15,000

What is the company's gross profit percentage?

   a. 40 percent   *c.* 15 percent
   b. 60 percent   *d.* None of the above

LO4   8. **Using the data in Question 7, what is The Eureka Company's return on sales ratio?**

   a. 40 percent   *c.* 15 percent
   b. 60 percent   *d.* None of the above

LO1   9. **Which of the following statements regarding cost flows is true?**

   a. Cost of goods available for sale is equal to beginning inventory minus cost of goods purchased.
   b. Cost of goods available for sale is equal to beginning inventory plus cost of goods purchased.
   c. Cost of goods available for sale = beginning inventory minus ending inventory.
   d. Cost of goods available for sale = cost of goods sold minus cost of goods purchased.

LO5
(Appendix 5A)   10. **Daniel Co. uses the periodic inventory system. When goods are purchased, Daniel will:**

   a. debit freight costs to Inventory.
   b. debit purchase returns and allowance for returned items.
   c. debit the Purchases account for purchases on account.
   d. debit the Inventory account for purchases on account.

LO5
(Appendix 5A)   11. **Bleu Company began the period with $20,000 in inventory. The company also purchased an additional $20,000 of inventory and returned $2,000 for a full credit. A physical count of the inventory at year-end revealed an inventory on hand of $16,000. What was Bleu's cost of goods sold for the period?**

   a. $16,000   *c.* $48,000
   b. $22,000   *d.* $50,000

QUESTIONS

1. Describe the differences between (a) a manufacturer, (b) a wholesale distributor, and (c) a retailer.

2. Describe the three primary transactions in the operating cycle of a merchandising firm.

3. What is the difference between a credit period and a discount period? What is a cash discount?

4. Spink Company purchased merchandise with a list price of $4,000 from the Thompson Company. Thompson offers a 2 percent cash discount if payment is received within 10 days. What is the payment amount if the cash discount is taken?

5. Carole Company purchased $6,000 of merchandise and paid $300 in transportation costs to deliver the merchandise. Carole then returned $1,000 of the merchandise before paying the supplier within the discount period. Carole was entitled to a 2 percent cash discount. How much did Carole pay the supplier?

6. What is the primary difference between a merchandise return and a merchandise allowance?

7. Define the *return on sales ratio*. What does this ratio measure?

8. Define *gross profit on sales*.

9. Define *gross profit percentage*. How is this percentage used by analysts and investors?

10. When merchandisers and manufacturers prepare income statements for their annual reports to shareholders, they usually begin the statement with net sales. For internal reporting purposes, however, the income statements will show gross sales and the related contra-revenue accounts of sales returns and allowances and sales discounts. What might explain this difference in the financial information disclosed to external parties and management? Do you consider the more limited disclosure in the annual reports to be inconsistent with the full disclosure principle? Briefly explain your point of view.

SHORT EXERCISES

SE5-1. Merchandising versus Service Firm For each of the following accounts, indicate whether it would be found in the records of a merchandising firm, a service firm, or both. **LO1**

a. Cost of goods sold.
b. Service revenue.
c. Purchase returns and allowances.
d. Inventory.
e. Accounts receivable.
f. Accounts payable.
g. Sales revenue.
h. Freight-out.

SE5-2. Accounting for Purchase Transactions Donna Company began operations on June 1. The following transactions took place in June: **LO2**

a. Purchases of merchandise on account were $750,000.
b. The cost of freight to receive the inventory was $20,000. This was paid in cash.
c. Donna returned $10,000 of the merchandise due to an ordering error. Donna received a full credit for the return.
d. Donna paid the remaining balance for the merchandise.

Calculate the dollar amount that Donna will have in inventory at the end of the month. Assume Donna uses the perpetual inventory system and there were no sales.

SE5-3. Accounting for Purchase Transactions Use the data from SE5-2 and prepare the journal entries to record the June transactions. **LO2**

SE5-4. Accounting for Purchase Discounts Kurt Company purchased $5,000 of merchandise from Marilyn Company with terms of 2/10, n/40. What percent discount will Kurt Company get if it pays within the allowed discount period? If Kurt Company fails to pay within the discount period, how many days does Kurt Company have from the date of purchase before the payment is considered to be late? **LO2**

SE5-5. Accounting for Purchase Discounts Using the information in SE5-4, what amount will Kurt Company pay to Marilyn Company if Kurt Company takes advantage of the purchase discount? **LO2**

SE5-6. Accounting for Sales Transactions Madison Company uses the perpetual inventory system. Record the journal entries for the following transactions: **LO3**

a. On July 16, Madison sold $500 of merchandise with terms of 3/10, n/30. The cost of the merchandise was $200.
b. On July 19, the customer returned $100 of the merchandise from (a). The cost of the merchandise was $40.
c. On July 22, the customer paid the entire balance due to Madison.

SE5-7. Gross Profit Percentage Using the data below, compute Ian's gross profit percentage for the month of January. **LO4**

Net sales.	$12,000
Cost of goods sold	3,000
Operating expenses	7,000
Other income	500
Income tax expense	1,000

SE5-8. Return on Sales Ratio Using the data in SE5-7, compute Ian's return on sales ratio for the month of January. **LO4**

SE5-9. Cost of Goods Sold and the Periodic System Kuyu Company uses the periodic inventory system. Kuyu started the period with $12,000 in inventory. The company purchased an additional $25,000 of merchandise, and returned $1,500 for a full credit. A physical count of inventory at the end of the period revealed that there was an ending inventory balance of $6,000. What was Kuyu's cost of goods sold during the period? **LO5** (Appendix 5A)

SE5-10. Cost of Goods Sold and the Periodic System Layla Company uses the periodic inventory system. Layla started the period with $22,000 in inventory. The company purchased an additional $25,000 of merchandise and returned $3,000 for a full credit. If Layla's cost of goods sold during the period was $31,000, what must have been the total of the physical inventory count? **LO5** (Appendix 5A)

LO5
(Appendix 5A)

SE5-11. Journalize Periodic Inventory Entries Prepare the journal entries to record the following transactions for the Kristen Company using a periodic inventory system.

    a.   On June 2, Kristen purchased $250,000 of merchandise from the Ferway Company, with terms 3/15, n/30.

    b.   On June 5, Kristen returned $50,000 of the merchandise purchased on June 2.

    c.   On June 13, Kristen paid the balance due to Ferway.

LO6
(Appendix 5B)

SE5-12. Revenue Recognition Standard—Adjusting Journal Entry—Sales Discounts Douglas Corporation reports it sold merchandise on account for a total of $800,000 for the current year. The cost to Douglas for the merchandise was $300,000. To encourage early payment, Douglas offers its customers credit terms of 1/10, n/30. At year-end, there are $150,000 of sales on account still eligible for the 1 percent discount. Douglas believes that all customers will pay within the discount period to receive the discount. Prepare the adjusting journal entry needed for Douglas Corporation to comply with the revenue recognition standard. Assume Douglas's fiscal year-end is December 31.

LO6
(Appendix 5B)

SE5-13. Revenue Recognition Standard—Adjusting Journal Entries—Sales Returns and Allowances During the year, Raul Company sells merchandise on account totaling $2,000,000 (the cost to Raul for this merchandise was $800,000). Raul allows a 60-day return privilege for the merchandise it sells. At year-end, Raul estimates there remain $400,000 of sales (with a cost to Raul of $160,000) that are still within the 60-day return period. Based on past experience, Raul expects 5 percent of this merchandise to be returned. Prepare the period-end adjusting journal entries needed for Raul Company to comply with the revenue recognition standard. Raul's fiscal year-end is December 31.

DATA ANALYTICS

Data Analytics

DA5-1. Preparing Excel Visualizations of Gross Profit Data Over Time Financial information for the following five retailers is included in the Excel file associated with this chapter: **The Home Depot, Inc.** (Home Depot), **Lowe's Companies, Inc.** (Lowe's), **Target Corporation** (Target), **The ODP Corporation** (ODP), and **Costco Wholesale Corporation** (Costco). In this problem we analyze the gross profit percentage of retail companies with different business models. The gross profit percentage measures a company's ability to cover its operating costs from revenues after allowing for costs of goods and services sold. A gross profit percentage will vary by industry (some industries require extensive manufacturing operations for example) and is also affected by a company's business strategy. For example, a company with a lower gross profit percentage (a grocery store) will make up for profits with higher sales volume. A company with a high gross profit percentage (high-end jewelry store) can afford to sell fewer products when each item has a higher gross profit percentage.

Gross Profit Percentage

$$\frac{\text{Sales revenue} - \text{Cost of goods sold}}{\text{Sales revenue}}$$

Required

1. Download Excel file DA5-1 found in myBusinessCourse.
2. Calculate the gross profit percentage for each of the three years (with Year 3 being the most recent year).
3. Create a line chart showing the trend of the gross profit percentage for each company over the three-year period.
4. List the companies in order from the highest to the lowest gross profit percentage for each of the three years.
5. Add a trendline to the line chart for each company and forecast one additional period. *Hint:* Right-click on each line in your chart and add trendline. In the format trendline area under Forecast, forward 1 period.
6. List the companies in order from the highest to the lowest gross profit percentage for the forecasted year.
7. Describe the trends in the line chart.
8. Describe the likely source of the difference between the company with the highest gross profit percentage and the lowest gross profit percentage.

DA5-2. Preparing and Interpreting Sales Data in Excel Wakeboards Inc. manufactures and sells three types of wakeboards to fifty customers located primarily in oceanside cities in the U.S. The Excel file

associated with this exercise contains daily sales data for its three different models over the past year. Using this file, we will drill down to and rank sales by model number, by customer name, and by time period.

Part 1 Creating PivotTable One

1. Download the Excel file DA5-2 found in myBusinessCourse.
2. Prepare a PivotTable showing sales by customer by month. *Hint:* With your cursor on a cell in the worksheet, click on Insert, PivotChart. Drag Date into Columns and Customer name into Rows, and desired Model (such as Model 1) into Values.
3. Answer the following questions based upon data in your PivotTable.
   a. How many units of Model 1 did Villager Store purchase for the year?
   b. How many units of Model 1 did Carmel Sports purchase in April?
   c. How many units of Model 2 did West Loop Inc. purchase during the year?
   d. How many units of Model 2 did Marina Inc. purchase in July?
   e. How many units of Model 3 did East Beach purchase in May? What dates were the purchases? (*Hint:* Double-click on Total Purchases, and a worksheet will automatically open with the detail for the May purchases.)
4. Apply conditional formatting to the PivotTable, highlighting all orders > 50 units of Model 1. (*Hint:* Highlight cells in the table. Then under the Home tab, click on Conditional Formatting, Highlight Cell Rules, and Greater Than; Specify Your Rule.)
5. List the companies with four or more orders that are greater than 50 units of Model 1.

Part 2 Creating PivotTable Two

1. Prepare a second PivotTable showing the total sales of Model 1 by month. *Hint:* Uncheck Customers but check Model One to show total sales of Model One.
2. List the amount of the highest monthly sales and the month in which it occurs.
3. Calculate the number of months where unit sales fall below 500 units.

DA5-3. Preparing Tableau Visualizations to Analyze Gross Profit Refer to PF-21 in Appendix F. This problem uses Tableau to create and analyze visualizations of gross profit percentages of S&P 500 companies.

DATA VISUALIZATION

Data Visualization Activities are available in myBusinessCourse. These assignments use Tableau Dashboards to expose students to visual depictions of data and introduce students to data analytics through data visualizations. These exercises are easily assignable and auto graded by MBC.

Data Visualization

EXERCISES—SET A

E5-1A. Cash Discount Calculations On June 1, Meadow Company sold merchandise with a list price of $40,000. For each of the sales terms below, determine the proper amount of cash received:

LO3

	Credit Terms	Date Paid
1.	2/10, n/30	June 8
2.	1/10, n/30	June 15
3.	1/15, n/30	June 14
4.	n/30	June 28

E5-2A. Journal Entries for Sale, Return, and Remittance—Perpetual System On September 13, Tomas Company sold merchandise with an invoice price of $1,200 ($600 cost), with terms of 2/10, n/30, to Dalton Company. On September 17, $250 of the merchandise ($80 cost) was returned because it was the wrong model. On September 23, Tomas Company received a check for the amount due from Dalton Company.

LO3

Required

Prepare the journal entries made by Tomas Company for these transactions. Tomas uses the perpetual inventory system.

LO2　E5-3A.　Journal Entries for Purchase, Return, and Remittance—Perpetual System　On April 13, the Albert Company purchased $26,000 of merchandise from the Krausman Company, with terms of 1/10, n/30. On April 15, Albert paid $400 to Ace Trucking Company for freight on the shipment. On April 18, Albert Company returned $900 of merchandise for credit. Final payment was made to Krausman on April 22. Albert Company records purchases using the perpetual inventory system.

Required

Prepare the journal entries that Albert Company should make on April 13, 15, 18, and 22.

LO2, 3　E5-4A.　Journal Entries for Merchandise Transactions on Seller's and Buyer's Books—Perpetual System　The following are selected transactions for Kim, Inc., during the month of June:

June 21　Sold and shipped on account to Lowery Company, $4,000 ($2,000 cost) of merchandise, with terms of 2/10, n/30.

　　28　Lowery Company returned defective merchandise billed at $400 on June 21 ($200 cost).

　　30　Received from Lowery Company a check for full settlement of the June 21 transaction.

Required

Prepare the necessary journal entries for (a) Kim, Inc., and (b) Lowery Company. Both companies use the perpetual inventory system.

LO2　E5-5A.　Recording Purchases—Perpetual System　On July 1, Hernandez, Inc., purchased merchandise for $2,500, with terms of 1/10, n/30. On July 5, the firm returned $1,000 of the merchandise to the seller. Payment of the account occurred on July 8. Hernandez uses the perpetual inventory system.

Required

a.　Prepare the journal entries for July 1, July 5, and July 8.

b.　Assuming that the account was paid on July 14, prepare the journal entry for payment on that date.

LO4　E5-6A.　Profitability Analysis　Erin Enterprises reports the following information on its year-end income statement:

Net sales.	$200,000	Operating expenses	$40,000
Cost of goods sold	110,000	Other income	25,000

Required

Calculate Erin's gross profit percentage and return on sales ratio.

LO5　E5-7A.　Journal Entries for Sale, Return, and Remittance—Periodic System　On June 8, James Company
(Appendix 5A)　sold merchandise listing for $1,850 to Dalton Company, terms 3/10, n/30. On June 12, $550 worth of the merchandise was returned because it was the wrong color. On June 18, James Company received a check for the amount due.

Required

Record the journal entries made by James Company for these transactions. James uses the periodic inventory system.

LO5　E5-8A.　Journal Entries for Purchase, Return, and Remittance—Periodic System　On March 10, Horne
(Appendix 5A)　Company purchased $21,000 worth of merchandise from James Company, terms 1/10, n/30. On March 12, Horne paid $300 freight on the shipment. On March 15, Horne returned $300 of merchandise for credit. Final payment was made to James on March 19. Horne Company uses the periodic inventory system.

Required

Prepare the journal entries that Horne should make on March 10, March 12, March 15, and March 19.

E5-9A. **Journal Entries for Merchandise Transactions for Seller and Buyer—Periodic System** The following are selected transactions for Jefferson, Inc., during the month of April:

LO5
(Appendix 5A)

April   20   Sold and shipped on account to Lind Stores merchandise for $3,000, with terms of 1/10,
n/30.
27   Lind Stores returned defective merchandise billed at $300 on April 20.
29   Received from Lind Stores a check for full settlement of the April 20 transaction.

Required
Prepare the necessary journal entries for (a) Jefferson, Inc., and (b) Lind Stores. Both companies use
the periodic inventory system.

E5-10A. **Revenue Recognition Standard—Adjusting Journal Entries** TheOne sold $5,000,000 of merchan-
dise on account during the current year. The cost for this merchandise to TheOne was $1,400,000. To
encourage early payment from its customers, TheOne offers credit terms of 2/10, n/30. At year-end,
TheOne recognizes that there are $500,000 of sales on account still eligible for the 2 percent discount.
TheOne believes that all customers will pay within the discount period to receive this discount. In
addition, TheOne allows a 60-day return privilege for the merchandise it sells. At year-end, TheOne
estimates there remain $600,000 of sales (with a cost to TheOne of $168,000) that are still within the
60-day return period and that, based on past experience, 4 percent of this merchandise is expected to
be returned. Prepare the period-end adjusting journal entries needed for TheOne to comply with the
new revenue recognition standard. Assume TheOne's fiscal year-end is December 31.

LO6
(Appendix 5B)

E5-11A. **Revenue Recognition Standard—Adjusting Journal Entries** During the year, Price Company sells
merchandise on account totaling $10,000,000 with a cost of merchandise to Price of $5,000,000. Price
offers its customers credit terms of 1/15, n/30. Price recognizes that there are $900,000 of sales on
account still eligible for the 1 percent discount at year-end and believes that all customers will pay
within the discount period. Additionally, Price allows a 90-day return privilege for the merchandise
it sells. At year-end, Price estimates sales of $2,500,000 (with a cost to Price of $1,250,000) remain
that are still within the 90-day return period. From past experience, 8 percent of this merchandise is
expected to be returned. Prepare the period-end adjusting journal entries needed for Price Company to
comply with the revenue recognition standard. Price's fiscal year-end is December 31.

LO6
(Appendix 5B)

EXERCISES—SET B

E5-1B. **Cash Discount Calculations** On April 1, the Gerald Company sold merchandise with a list price of
$75,000. For each of the sales terms below, determine the proper amount of cash received:

LO3

	Credit Terms	Date Paid
1.	1/15, n/30 . . .	April 14
2.	n/30.	April 28
3.	2/10, n/30 . . .	April 8
4.	1/10, n/30 . . .	April 15

E5-2B. **Journal Entries for Sale, Return, and Remittance—Perpetual System** On October 14, the Henry
Company sold merchandise with an invoice price of $1,300 ($750 cost), with terms of 1/10, n/30, to
the Baxter Company. On October 18, $300 of merchandise ($175 cost) was returned because it was
the wrong size. On October 24, the Henry Company received a check for the amount due from the
Baxter Company.

LO3

Required
Prepare the journal entries for the Henry Company using the perpetual inventory system.

E5-3B. **Journal Entries for Purchase, Return, and Remittance—Perpetual System** On May 15, Walter
Company purchased $30,000 of merchandise from the Terrell Company, with terms of 1/10, n/30. On
May 17, Walter paid $400 to Swift Trucking Company for freight on the shipment. On May 20, Walter
Company returned $1,200 of merchandise for credit. Final payment was made to Terrell on May 24.
Walter Company records purchases using the perpetual inventory system.

LO2

Required
Prepare the journal entries that Walter Company should make on May 15, 17, 20, and 24.

LO2, 3   E5-4B.   Journal Entries for Merchandise Transactions on Seller's and Buyer's Books—Perpetual System The following are selected transactions of Candy, Inc., during the month of June:

June 18 Sold and shipped on account to Dante Company $5,000 ($3,000 cost) of merchandise, with terms of 2/10, n/30.
      25 Dante Company returned merchandise billed at $700 on June 18 ($300 cost).
      27 Received from Dante Company a check for full settlement of the June 18 transaction.

Required
Prepare the necessary journal entries for (a) Candy, Inc., and (b) Dante Company. Both companies use the perpetual inventory system.

LO2   E5-5B.   Recording Purchases—Perpetual System On September 12, Burt, Inc., purchased merchandise for $4,800, with terms of 2/10, n/30. On September 16, the firm returned $500 of the merchandise to the seller. Payment of the account occurred on September 19. Burt uses the perpetual inventory system.

Required
a. Prepare the journal entries for September 12, September 16, and September 19.
b. Assuming that the account was paid on September 25, prepare the journal entry for payment on that date.

LO4   E5-6B.   Profitability Analysis Shannon Enterprises reports the following information on its year-end income statement:

Net sales..................	$200,000	Operating expenses............	$20,000
Cost of goods sold............	130,000	Other income................	10,000

Required
Calculate Shannon's gross profit percentage and return on sales ratio.

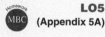

LO5   E5-7B.   Journal Entries for Sale, Return, and Remittance—Periodic System On March 10, the Stone
(Appendix 5A)   Company sold merchandise listing for $3,000 to the Dillard Company with terms of 1/10, n/30. On March 14, $200 of merchandise was returned because it was the wrong size. On March 20, Stone Company received a check for the amount due.

Required
Prepare the journal entries made by Stone Company for these transactions. Stone uses the periodic inventory system.

LO5   E5-8B.   Journal Entries for Purchase, Return, and Remittance—Periodic System On August 15, the Ford
(Appendix 5A)   Company purchased $17,500 of merchandise from Jason Company with terms of 2/10, n/30. On August 17, Ford paid $350 freight on the shipment. On August 20, Ford returned $500 worth of the merchandise for credit. Final payment was made to Jason on August 24. Ford Company records purchases using the periodic inventory system.

Required
Prepare the journal entries that Ford should make on August 15, August 17, August 20, and August 24.

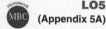

LO5   E5-9B.   Journal Entries for Merchandise Transactions on Seller's and Buyer's Books—Periodic System
(Appendix 5A)   The following are selected transactions of Fedor, Inc., during the month of January:

Jan. 20 Sold and shipped on account to Lawrence Stores merchandise listing for $4,500 with terms of 2/10, n/30.
      27 Lawrence Stores was granted a $500 allowance on goods shipped January 20.
      29 Received from Lawrence Stores a check for full settlement of the January 20 transaction.

Required
Prepare journal entries for (a) Fedor, Inc., and (b) Lawrence Stores. Both companies use the periodic inventory system.

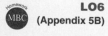

LO6   E5-10B.   Revenue Recognition Standard—Adjusting Journal Entries Prime sold $2,000,000 of merchan-
(Appendix 5B)   dise on account during the current year. The cost for this merchandise to Prime was $800,000. To encourage early payment from its customers, Prime offers credit terms of 2/10, n/30. At year-end, Prime recognizes that there are $350,000 of sales on account still eligible for the 2 percent discount. Prime believes that all customers will pay within the discount period to receive this discount. In addition, Prime allows a 60-day return privilege for the merchandise it sells. At year-end, Prime estimates there

remain $450,000 of sales (with a cost to Prime of $180,000) that are still within the 60-day return period and that, based on past experience, 7 percent of this merchandise is expected to be returned. Prepare the period-end adjusting journal entries needed for Prime to comply with the revenue recognition standard. Assume Prime's fiscal year-end is December 31.

E5-11B. Revenue Recognition Standard—Adjusting Journal Entries During the year, Carrie Corporation sells merchandise on account totaling $4,000,000 with a cost of merchandise to Carrie of $2,000,000. Carrie offers its customers credit terms of 1/15, n/30. Carrie recognizes that there are $410,000 of sales on account still eligible for the 1 percent discount at year-end and believes that all companies will pay within the discount period. Additionally, Carrie allows a 90-day return privilege for the merchandise it sells. At year-end, Carrie estimates sales of $1,200,000 (with a cost to Carrie of $600,000) remain that are still within the 90-day return period. From past experience, 6 percent of this merchandise is expected to be returned. Prepare the period-end adjusting journal entries needed for Carrie Corporation to comply with the revenue recognition standard. Carrie Corporation's fiscal year-end is December 31.

LO6
(Appendix 5B)

PROBLEMS—SET A

P5-1A. **Journal Entries for Merchandise Transactions on Seller's and Buyer's Books—Perpetual System** The following transactions occurred between the Decker Company and Mann Stores, Inc., during March:

LO2, 3

Mar. 8 Decker sold $14,000 worth of merchandise ($9,600 cost) to Mann Stores with terms of 2/10, n/30.
10 Mann Stores paid freight charges on the shipment from Decker Company, $500.
12 Mann Stores returned $2,000 of the merchandise ($1,600 cost) shipped on March 8.
17 Decker received full payment for the net amount due from the March 8 sale.
20 Mann Stores returned goods that had been billed originally at $800 ($600 cost). Decker issued a check for $784.

Required
Prepare the necessary journal entries for (a) the books of Decker Company and (b) the books of Mann Stores, Inc. Assume that both companies use the perpetual inventory system.

P5-2A. **Journal Entries for Merchandise Transactions—Perpetual System** Rockford Corporation, which began business on August 1, sells on terms of 2/10, n/30. Credit terms for its purchases vary with the supplier. Selected transactions for August are given below. Unless noted, all transactions are on account and involve merchandise held for resale. The perpetual inventory system is used.

LO2, 3

Aug. 1 Purchased merchandise from Norris, Inc., $4,000, terms 2/10, n/30.
5 Paid freight on shipment from Norris, Inc., $220.
7 Sold merchandise to Denton Corporation, $5,500 ($4,100 cost).
7 Paid $300 freight on August 7 shipment and billed Denton for the charges.
9 Returned $800 worth of the merchandise purchased August 1 from Norris, Inc., because it was defective. Norris approved the return.
9 Received $750 of returned merchandise ($500 cost) from Denton Corporation. Rockford approved the return.
10 Paid Norris, Inc., the amount due.
14 Purchased from Chambers, Inc., goods with a price of $9,000. Terms 1/10, n/30.
15 Paid freight on shipment from Chambers, Inc., $320.
17 Received the amount due from Denton Corporation.
18 Sold merchandise to Weber, Inc., $9,600 ($6,600 cost).
20 Paid $350 freight on August 18 shipment and billed Weber for the charges.
24 Paid Chambers, Inc., the amount due.
28 Received the amount due from Weber, Inc.

Required
Prepare journal entries for these transactions for Rockford Corporation.

P5-3A. **Effects of Transactions on the Inventory Account—Perpetual System** Watt Wholesale Company purchases merchandise from a variety of manufacturers and sells the merchandise to a variety of retailers. All sales are subject to a cash discount (2/10, n/30). Watt uses a perpetual inventory system. The May 1 balance in Watt's Inventory account was a $70,000 debit. The following transactions occurred during May:

LO2, 3

May   2 Purchased $5,500 of merchandise from Ajax Manufacturing; terms are 1/10, n/30.
       4 Paid $200 freight on the May 2 purchase.
      12 Paid Ajax for the May 2 purchase.
      14 Purchased $4,000 of merchandise from Baker Manufacturing; terms are 2/10, n/45.
      16 Received a $300 allowance on the May 14 purchase since some of the merchandise was
          the wrong color. All of the merchandise is salable at regular prices.
      18 Purchased $2,500 of merchandise from Charles Industries; terms are 2/10, n/30.
      19 Sold merchandise with a list price of $2,000 ($1,200 cost) to Daytime Industries.
      22 Daytime Industries returned 40 percent of the merchandise from the May 19 sale.
      26 Paid Baker Manufacturing for the May 14 purchase.
      29 Paid Charles Industries for the May 18 purchase.

Required

Prepare a schedule that shows the impact of these transactions on Watt's Inventory account. Use the following headings:

Date	Transaction	Debit Amount	Credit Amount	Account Balance

LO2, 3   P5-4A.   Journal Entries for Merchandise Transactions—Perpetual System Cushing Distributing Company uses the perpetual inventory system. Cushing had the following transactions related to merchandise during the month of June:

June   1 Purchased on account merchandise for resale for $10,000; terms were 2/10, n/30.
        3 Paid $550 cash for freight on the June 1 purchase.
        7 Returned merchandise costing $600 (part of the $10,000 purchase).
       10 Paid for merchandise purchased on June 1.
       13 Sold merchandise on account costing $8,000 for $10,000; terms were 2/10, n/30.
       16 Customer returned merchandise costing $750 that had been sold on account for $1,000
           (part of the $10,000 sale).
       22 Received payment from customer for merchandise sold on June 13.

Required

Prepare journal entries for each of the transactions for the Cushing Distributing Company.

LO4   P5-5A.   Profitability Analysis Kolby Enterprises reports the following information on its income statement:

Net sales..................	$250,000	Administrative expenses........	$10,000
Cost of goods sold............	150,000	Other income	15,000
Selling expenses	50,000	Other expense	10,000

Required

Calculate Kolby's gross profit percentage and return on sales ratio. Explain what each ratio tells us about Kolby's performance. Kolby is planning to add a new product and expects net sales to be $45,000 and cost of goods to be $38,000. No other income or expenses are expected to change. How will this affect Kolby's gross profit percentage and return on sales ratio? What do you advise regarding the new product offering?

LO5   P5-6A.   Journal Entries for Merchandise Transactions on Seller's and Buyer's Books—Periodic System
(Appendix 5A) The following transactions occurred between Southwick Company and Mann Stores, Inc., during March:

Mar.   8 Southwick sold $7,100 worth of merchandise to Mann Stores, terms 2/10, n/30.
       10 Mann Stores paid freight charges on the shipment from Southwick Company, $200.
       12 Mann Stores returned $700 of the merchandise shipped on March 8.
       17 Southwick received full payment for the net amount due from the March 8 sale.
       20 Mann Stores returned goods that had been billed originally at $400. Southwick issued a
           check for $392.

Required

Prepare the necessary journal entries for (a) the books of Southwick Company and (b) the books of Mann Stores, Inc. Assume that both companies use the periodic inventory system.

LO5   P5-7A.   Journal Entries for Merchandise Transactions—Periodic System The Malvado Corporation sells
(Appendix 5A) goods on terms of 2/10, n/30. Credit terms for its purchases vary with the supplier. Selected transactions for August are given below. Unless noted, all transactions are on account and involve merchandise held for resale. The periodic inventory system is used.

Aug.	1	Purchased merchandise from Norris, Inc., $2,500; terms 2/10, n/30.
	5	Paid freight on shipment from Norris, Inc., $120.
	7	Sold merchandise to Denton Corporation, $3,100.
	7	Paid freight on shipment to Denton Corporation, $150, and billed Denton for the charges.
	9	Returned $400 worth of the merchandise purchased August 1 from Norris, Inc., because it was defective. Norris approved the return.
	9	Received $500 of returned merchandise from Denton Corporation.
	10	Paid Norris, Inc., the amount due.
	14	Purchased from Chambers, Inc., goods with a price of $4,500. Terms 1/10, n/30.
	15	Paid freight on shipment from Chambers, Inc., $160.
	17	Received the amount due from Denton Corporation.
	18	Sold merchandise to Weber, Inc., $4,800.
	20	Paid freight on August 18 shipment to Weber, Inc., $160, and billed Weber.
	24	Paid Chambers, Inc., the amount due.
	28	Received the amount due from Weber, Inc.

Required
Prepare the necessary journal entries for the Malvado Corporation.

PROBLEMS—SET B

P5-1B. Journal Entries for Merchandise Transactions on Seller's and Buyer's Books—Perpetual System   **LO2, 3**
Ryan Distributing Company had the following transactions with Arlington, Inc., during the month of November:

Nov.	10	Ryan sold and shipped $8,000 worth of merchandise ($4,500 cost) to Arlington, terms 1/10, n/30.
	12	Arlington, Inc., paid freight charges on the shipment from Ryan Company, $450.
	14	Ryan received $600 of merchandise returned by Arlington ($340 cost) from the November 10 sale.
	19	Ryan received payment in full for the net amount due on the November 10 sale.
	24	Arlington returned goods that had originally been billed at $400 ($280 cost). Ryan issued a check for $396.

Required
Prepare the necessary journal entries (a) on the books of Ryan Distributing Company and (b) on the books of Arlington, Inc. Assume that both companies use the perpetual inventory system.

P5-2B. Journal Entries for Merchandise Transactions—Perpetual System   Webb Company was established   **LO2, 3**
on July 1. Its sales terms are 3/10, n/30. Credit terms for its purchases vary with the supplier. Selected transactions for the first month of operations are given below. Unless noted, all transactions are on account and involve merchandise held for resale. Webb Company uses the perpetual inventory system.

July	1	Purchased goods from Dawson, Inc., $2,500; terms 1/10, n/30.
	2	Purchased goods from Penn Company, $5,500; terms 2/10, n/30.
	3	Paid freight on shipment from Dawson, $300.
	5	Sold merchandise to Ward, Inc., $1,400 ($1,100 cost).
	5	Paid freight on shipment to Ward, Inc., $90. (*Hint:* debit Delivery Expense)
	8	Returned $700 worth of the goods purchased July 1 from Dawson, Inc., because some goods were damaged. Dawson approved the return.
	9	Received returned goods from Ward, Inc., worth $200 ($150 cost).
	10	Paid Dawson, Inc., the amount due.
	10	Purchased goods from Dorn Company with a list price of $3,000. Terms 2/10, n/30.
	11	Paid freight on shipment from Dorn Company, $150.
	15	Received the amount due from Ward, Inc.
	15	Sold merchandise to Colby Corporation, $3,200 ($2,400 cost).
	16	Mailed a check to Penn Company for the amount due on its July 2 invoice.
	18	Received an allowance of $250 from Dorn Company for defective merchandise purchased on July 10.
	19	Paid Dorn Company the amount due.
	25	Received the amount due from Colby Corporation.

Required
Prepare the necessary journal entries for the Webb Company.

LO2, 3   P5-3B.   Effects of Transactions on the Inventory Account—Perpetual System Rand Wholesale Company purchases merchandise from a variety of manufacturers and sells the merchandise to a variety of retailers. All sales are subject to a cash discount (2/10, n/30). Rand has a perpetual inventory system. The February 1 balance in Rand's Inventory account was a $50,000 debit. The following transactions occurred during February:

Feb. 2 Purchased $8,600 of merchandise from Sweet Manufacturing; terms are 1/10, n/30.
      5 Paid $270 freight on the February 2 purchase.
     11 Paid Sweet for the February 2 purchase.
     13 Purchased $5,000 of merchandise from Tayler Manufacturing; terms are 2/10, n/45.
     16 Received a $300 allowance on the February 13 purchase since some of the merchandise was the wrong size. All of the merchandise is salable at regular prices.
     17 Purchased $5,200 of merchandise from Zorn Industries; terms are 2/10, n/30.
     20 Sold merchandise with a list price of $3,000 ($1,200 cost) to Valley Mart.
     22 Valley Mart returned 30 percent of the merchandise from the February 20 sale.
     23 Paid Tayler Manufacturing for the February 13 purchase.
     28 Paid Zorn Industries for the February 17 purchase.

Required

Prepare a schedule that shows the impact of these transactions on Rand's Inventory account. Use the following headings:

Date	Transaction	Debit Amount	Credit Amount	Account Balance

LO2, 3   P5-4B.   Journal Entries for Merchandise Transactions Jane Distributing Company uses the perpetual inventory system. Jane had the following transactions related to merchandise during the month of August:

Aug. 10 Purchased on account merchandise for resale for $9,000; terms were 2/10, n/30.
     12 Paid $450 cash for freight on the August 10 purchase.
     16 Returned merchandise costing $800 (part of the $9,000 purchase).
     19 Paid for merchandise purchased on August 10.
     22 Sold merchandise on account costing $8,500 for $11,000; terms were 2/10, n/30.
     25 Customer returned merchandise costing $750 that had been sold on account for $900 (part of the $11,000 sale).
     31 Received payment from customer for merchandise sold on August 22.

Required

Record each of the transactions related to purchasing and selling merchandise for the Jane Distributing Company.

LO4   P5-5B.   Profitability Analysis Emily Enterprises reports the following information on its income statement:

Net sales.	$400,000	Administrative expenses.	$20,000
Cost of goods sold	170,000	Other income	15,000
Selling expenses	50,000	Other expense	10,000

Required

Compute Emily's gross profit percentage and return on sales ratio. Explain what each ratio tells us about Emily's performance. Emily is planning to add a new product and expects net sales to be $40,000 and cost of goods to be $28,000. No other income or expenses are expected to change. How will this affect Emily's gross profit percentage and return on sales ratio? What do you advise regarding the new product offering?

LO5   P5-6B.   Journal Entries for Merchandise Transactions on Seller's and Buyer's Books—Periodic System
(Appendix 5A) Fame Distributing Company had the following transactions with Arlington, Inc., during November:

Nov. 10 Fame sold and shipped $8,000 worth of merchandise to Arlington, terms 2/10, n/30.
     12 Arlington, Inc., paid freight charges on the shipment from Fame Company, $450.
     14 Fame received $850 of merchandise returned by Arlington from the November 10 sale.
     19 Fame received payment in full for the net amount due on the November 10 sale.
     24 Arlington returned goods that had originally been billed at $700. Fame issued a check for $686.

Required

Prepare the necessary journal entries (a) on the books of Fame Distributing Company and (b) on the books of Arlington, Inc. Assume that both companies use the periodic inventory system.

P5-7B. **Journal Entries for Merchandise Transactions—Periodic System** Drake Company was established on July 1. Its sales terms are 2/10, n/30. Credit terms for its purchases vary with the supplier. Selected transactions for the first month of operations are given below. Unless noted, all transactions are on account and involve merchandise held for resale. All purchases are recorded using the periodic inventory system.

LO5
(Appendix 5A)

July 1 Purchased goods from Dawson, Inc., $3,500; terms 1/10, n/30.
      2 Purchased goods from Penn Company, $5,100; terms 2/10, n/30.
      3 Paid freight on shipment from Dawson, $200.
      5 Sold merchandise to Ward, Inc., $1,700.
      5 Paid freight on shipment to Ward, Inc., $80. (*Hint:* debit Delivery Expense)
July 8 Returned $300 worth of the goods purchased July 1 from Dawson, Inc., because some goods were damaged. Dawson approved the return.
      9 Received returned merchandise from Ward, Inc., $200.
    10 Paid Dawson, Inc., the amount due.
    10 Purchased goods from Dorn Company with a price of $2,200. Terms 2/10, n/30.
    11 Paid freight on shipment from Dorn Company, $130.
    15 Received the amount due from Ward, Inc.
    15 Sold merchandise to Colby Corporation, $4,200.
    16 Mailed a check to Penn Company for the amount due on its July 2 invoice.
    18 Received an allowance of $100 from Dorn Company for defective merchandise purchased on July 10.
    19 Paid Dorn Company the amount due.
    25 Received the amount due from Colby Corporation.

Required

Prepare the necessary journal entries for Drake Company.

SERIAL PROBLEM: KATE'S CARDS

Kate's Cards

(Note: This is a continuation of the Serial Problem: Kate's Cards from Chapters 1 through 4.)

SP5. Kate was a little worried about some of the practices of Fred Abbott, the CEO of Sentiments, and decided that an association with Sentiments could damage the reputation of her own company. Kate is very concerned that her business be viewed as socially responsible, and any damage to her reputation at this early stage could prove very difficult to overcome. She therefore decided to concentrate her efforts on producing a quality product that consumers would be proud to purchase and send to their loved ones.

As expected, November saw a boom in Kate's greeting card business. She invested in additional computer graphics equipment, which she partially funded with a bank loan of $15,000 and an additional investment of her own funds into the business. The loan carries an interest rate of six percent with interest payments required semiannually. The entire principal balance is due in one balloon payment in two years. Kate uses a perpetual inventory system. As of December 2, Kate's Cards had the following account balances:

Cash	$11,900	Accumulated depreciation	$ 1,600
Accounts receivable	16,800	Accounts payable	13,800
Inventory	16,000	Other current liabilities	900
Other current assets	3,600	Long-term note payable	15,000
Computer equipment	38,900	Common stock	25,000
		Retained earnings	30,900

The company had the following transactions during December:

Dec. 1 Paid $1,200 rent for the month.
      7 Paid $1,800 to employees. Of this amount, $900 was for an amount owed from November. Wages due to employees at the end of each month are recorded as Other Current Liabilities.
      9 Received $5,400 from customers as payment on account.

Dec. 12 Sold, for cash, $11,000 of greeting cards. This merchandise had cost $6,000 to produce.
   14 Purchased additional inventory totaling $7,000 on account with terms of 2/10, n/45.
   15 Paid cash for supplies (listed as Other Current Assets) in the amount of $600.
   19 Sold, on account with terms of 2/10, n/30, greeting cards totaling $6,000. The merchandise had cost $4,000 to produce.
   21 Paid additional wages of $1,400.
   25 Paid the total owed for the merchandise that was purchased on December 14.
   28 Received payment in full from the customer that purchased the merchandise on December 19.
   31 Depreciation for the month totaled $900.
   31 A physical count of inventory and supplies revealed that $13,000 and $2,000, respectively, were on hand at year-end. Assume that Other Current Assets consists only of the cost of supplies.

Required

a. Prepare journal entries for the December transactions.
b. Prepare a classified income statement for the month of December.
c. Calculate Kate's gross profit percentage and return on sales ratio for December.

EXTENDING YOUR KNOWLEDGE

REPORTING AND ANALYSIS

COLUMBIA
SPORTSWEAR
COMPANY

EYK5-1. **Financial Reporting Problem: The Columbia Sportswear Company** The financial statements for the **Columbia Sportswear Company** are in Appendix A at the end of this book.

Required

Using the company's Consolidated Statement of Operations (which is another name for Income Statement), answer the following questions.

a. What was the change in net sales and in net income from 2019 to 2020?
b. What was the gross profit percentage in each of the three years, 2018 through 2020? Comment on the trend in this ratio.
c. What was the return on sales ratio in each of the three years, 2018 through 2020? Comment on the trend in this ratio.

COLUMBIA
SPORTSWEAR
COMPANY

UNDER ARMOUR, INC.

EYK5-2. **Comparative Analysis Problem: The Columbia Sportswear Company vs. Under Armour, Inc.** The financial statements for the **Columbia Sportswear Company** and **Under Armour, Inc.**, are in Appendix A and B, respectively, at the end of this book.

Required

a. Based on the information you find in these financial statements, determine the following values for each company:
   1. Gross profit for 2020
   2. Gross profit percentage for 2020
   3. Net income for 2020
   4. Return on sales ratio for 2020
b. Based on this information, what can you say about the relative performance of these two companies?

EYK5-3. **Business Decision Problem** Northern Corporation started a retail clothing business on July 1. During the year, Northern Corporation had the following summary transactions related to merchandise inventory:

	Purchases	Sales
July	$240,000	$ 360,000
August	384,000	696,000
September	312,000	576,000
October	360,000	660,000
November	900,000	1,020,000
December	264,000	1,344,000

On average, Northern's cost of goods sold is 50 percent of sales. Assume that there were no sales returns and allowances or purchase returns and allowances during this six-month time period.

Required

a. Calculate the ending merchandise inventory for each of the six months.

b. Northern's purchases peaked during November; its sales peaked during December. Did Northern plan its purchases wisely? Should Northern expect a similar pattern in future years?

EYK5-4.   **Financial Analysis Problem** Johnson & Johnson is a worldwide manufacturer of healthcare   JOHNSON & JOHNSON
products, including Band-Aid bandages and Mylanta antacid. It reported the following results for three recent years:

(in millions)	2020	2019	2018
Net sales.	$82,584	$82,059	$81,581
Cost of goods sold	28,427	27,556	27,091

Assume that similar-sized companies in the same basic industries have experienced an average gross profit percentage of 65 percent each year.

Required

a. Calculate the gross profit percentage for Johnson & Johnson for the three years.

b. Compare the three-year trend in gross profit percentage for Johnson & Johnson to the assumed industry average. Analyze the trend and evaluate the performance of Johnson & Johnson compared to the assumed industry average.

CRITICAL THINKING

EYK5-5.   **Accounting Research Problem** Refer to the fiscal year 2020 annual report of **General Mills,**   GENERAL MILLS, INC.
Inc., available on this book's website.

Required

a. How much sales revenue did General Mills report in 2019 and 2020?

b. What was the company's gross profit percentage in 2019 and 2020?

c. How much net income did the company earn in 2019 and 2020?

d. What was the company's return on sales for 2019 and 2020? What can we conclude about the company's performance over the two-year period?

EYK5-6.   **Accounting Communication Activity** Geary Company produces custom machinery that has few competitors. As such, Geary is able to charge a large markup that is reflected in its large gross profit percentage. Recently the marketing director proposed offering a new set of products that are more generic in nature, and therefore will not allow large markups. The accounting department has, however, determined the products will add to Geary's overall net income. The following table provides estimates of Geary's profitability both with and without the new products:

	Without New Products	With New Products
Net sales.	$250,000	$350,000
Cost of goods sold	125,000	210,000
Net income	25,000	31,500

Required

The President of Geary, Jack Brown, has asked you to write a memo answering the following questions.

a. How will the new product line affect the company's profitability as measured by its gross profit percentage and the return on sales ratio?

b. How is it possible for net income to improve, while at the same time these profitability ratios may deteriorate?

c. Should the company expand by offering this new product line?

EYK5-7.   **Accounting Ethics Case** During the last week of 2017, George Green, controller of We 'R' Appliances, received a memorandum from the firm's president, Jane Anderson. The memorandum stated that Anderson had negotiated a very large sale with a new customer and directed Green to see that the order was processed and the goods shipped before the end of the year. Anderson noted that she had to depart from the usual credit terms of n/30 and allow terms of n/60 to clinch the sale.

Although the credit terms were unusual for the company, Green was particularly pleased with the news because business had been somewhat slow. The goods were shipped on December 29 and the sale was incorporated into the 2017 financial data.

It is now mid-February 2018, and two events have occurred recently that, together, cause concern for Green. First, he was inadvertently copied on a letter from the firm's bank to Anderson. The letter stated that the bank had reconsidered its decision to deny a loan to the company and is now granting the loan based on the new, and favorable, sales data supplied by the president. The bank was "particularly impressed with the sales improvement shown in December." Although Green had been involved in the initial loan application that was denied, he had been unaware that the president had reapplied for the loan.

The second event was that all of the goods shipped on December 29, 2017, to the new customer had just been returned.

Required

What are the ethical considerations George Green faces as a result of the recent events?

TARGET

EYK5-8. **Environmental, Social, and Governance Problem** Target is one of a large growing number of companies that publish an annual Environmental, Social, and Governance (ESG) report. Go to the Target website and navigate to the section on corporate responsibility to download Target's latest corporate responsibility report. This can be found under the More tab at the bottom right of the Target website. Discuss some of the ways that Target documents its good citizenship.

EYK5-9. **Analyzing IFRS Financial Statements** The 2020 financial statements of LVMH Moët Hennessy-Louis Vuitton S.A. are presented in Appendix C at the end of this book. LVMH is a Paris-based holding company and one of the world's largest and best-known luxury goods companies. As members of the European Union, French companies are required to prepare their consolidated (group) financial statements using International Financial Reporting Standards (IFRS). Using the company's financial statements, calculate the company's (a) gross profit percentage and (b) return on sales ratio for 2019 and 2020. Comment on the trend in the company's profitability over the two-year period.

COSTCO

EYK5-10. **Working with the Takeaways** Costco Wholesale Corporation is the largest membership warehouse club chain in the world based on sales volume. It is the fifth-largest general retailer in the United States. Costco is also one of the fastest-growing retailers, having grown to over 600 locations since its start in 1983. A look at Costco's income statement reveals the following data:

COSTCO WHOLESALE CORPORATION		
(in millions)	2020	2019
Net sales.	$163,220	$149,351
Cost of goods sold	144,939	132,886
Net income	4,002	3,659

Required

Evaluate Costco's performance in terms of gross profit percentage and return on sales ratio. How does Costco compare to Target and Walmart? (See **Exhibits 5-5** and **5-6** on page 5-14.)

ANSWERS TO SELF-STUDY QUESTIONS:

1. b   2. c   3. c   4. c   5. c   6. d   7. a   8. c   9. b   10. c   11. b

YOUR TURN! SOLUTIONS

Solution 5.1
a. Cost of goods available for sale = $110,000 + $245,000 = $355,000.
b. Cost of goods sold = $355,000 − $90,000 = $265,000.

Solution 5.2

June 1	Inventory (+A)	510.00	
	Accounts payable (+L)		510.00
	To record merchandise purchased on account (125 CDs @ $4.08 each)		

June 1	Inventory (+A)	22.18	
	Cash (−A)		22.18
	To record payment of freight charges on merchandise purchased.		

June 4	Accounts payable (−L)	61.20	
	Inventory (−A)		61.20
	To record the return of defective merchandise		
	(15 CDs @ $4.08 per unit).		

June 8	Accounts payable (−L)	448.80	
	Cash (−A)		439.82
	Inventory (−A)		8.98
	To record full payment within discount period. Cash discount		
	earned = ($510.00 − $61.20) × 2% = $8.98.		

Solution 5.3

June 15	Accounts receivable (+A)	750.00	
	Sales revenue (+R, +SE)		750.00
	To record the sale of 75 CDs on account.		

June 15	Cost of goods sold (+E, −SE)	315.00	
	Inventory (−A)		315.00
	To record cost of goods sold for 75 CDs.		

June 20	Sales returns and allowances (+XR, −SE)	50.00	
	Accounts receivable (−A)		50.00
	To record the return of 5 CDs for credit.		

June 20	Inventory (+A)	21.00	
	Cost of goods sold (−E, +SE)		21.00
	To record the return of 5 CDs for credit.		

June 25	Cash (+A)	700.00	
	Accounts receivable (−A)		700.00
	To record cash payment from customer.		

Solution 5.4

Gross profit percentage = ($100,000 − $45,000)/$100,000 = 55 percent
Return on sales ratio = $10,500/$100,000 = 10.5 percent

    A gross profit percentage of 55 percent indicates that Musicland was able to earn 55 cents for each dollar of net sales after considering just its cost of goods sold. In other words, Musicland still has 55 cents available from each dollar of net sales to cover its remaining expenses and to earn a net profit.

    A return on sales ratio of 10.5 percent indicates that Musicland was able to earn 10.5 cents in net income from each dollar of net sales after subtracting all of the business's expenses.

Solution 5A.1

June 1	Purchases (+E, −SE)	510.00	
	Accounts payable (+L)		510.00
	To record merchandise purchased on account (125 @ $4.08 each) with		
	2/10, n/30 terms.		

June 1	Freight-in (+E, −SE)	22.18	
	Cash (−A)		22.18
	To record payment of freight charge on merchandise purchase.		

June 4	Accounts payable (–L)	61.20	
	Purchase returns and allowances (–E, +SE)		61.20
	To record the return of defective merchandise (15 units).		
June 8	Accounts payable (–L)	448.80	
	Cash (–A)		439.82
	Purchase discounts (–E, +SE)		8.98
	To record payment for merchandise purchased.		

Solution 5A.2

June 15	Accounts receivable (+A)	750.00	
	Sales revenue (+R, +SE)		750.00
	To record the sale of 75 CDs on account.		
June 20	Sales returns and allowances (+XR, –SE)	50.00	
	Accounts receivable (–A)		50.00
	To record the return of 5 CDs for credit.		
June 25	Cash (+A)	700.00	
	Accounts receivable (–A)		700.00
	To record cash payment from customer.		

Solution 5A.3

MUSICLAND COMPANY **Cost of Goods Sold** **For Year Ended December 31**			
Inventory, January 1			$10,000
Purchases.		$50,000	
Less: Purchase returns and allowances.	$2,000		
Purchase discounts	1,000	3,000	
Net purchases.		47,000	
Add: Freight-in.		200	
Cost of goods purchased			47,200
Cost of goods available for sale			57,200
Less: Inventory, December 31.			12,200
Cost of goods sold.			$45,000

Solution 5B.1

Adjusting Journal Entry for Sales Discount

Dec. 31	Sales discounts (+XR, –SE)	3,000	
	Allowance for sales discounts (+XA, –A)		3,000
	To record the estimated sales discount of 2 percent on credit sales		
	still eligible for discount at year-end ($150,000 × 0.02).		

Adjusting Journal Entry for Sales Returns

Dec. 31	Sales returns and allowances (+XR, –SE)	15,000	
	Sales refunds payable (+L)		15,000
	To record the estimated return of 7.5 percent of the merchandise sold		
	that is still eligible for return at year-end ($200,000 × 0.075).		
Dec. 31	Estimated inventory return (+A)	4,500	
	Cost of goods sold (–E, +SE)		4,500
	To record the estimated return of 7.5 percent of the merchandise sold		
	that is still eligible for return at year-end ($60,000 × 0.075).		

Chapter **6**
Accounting for Inventory

Road Map

LO	Learning Objective	Page	eLecture	Guided Example	Assignments
LO1	**Explain inventory concepts and management practices.**	6-3	E6-1	YT6.1	SS1, SS4, SE3, E1A, E3A, E1B, E3B, P1A, P6A, P9A, P1B, P6B, P9B
LO2	**Describe inventory costing using specific identification, FIFO, LIFO, and weighted-average cost.**	6-7	E6-2	YT6.2	SS2, SE2, SE8, SE9, SE11, E2A, E4A, E7A, E8A, E2B, E4B, E7B, E8B, P2A, P4A, P8A, P2B, P4B, P8B
LO3	**Analyze the effects of different inventory costing methods on company profit.**	6-12	E6-3	YT6.3	SS3, SS6, SS7, SS8, SS9, SE10, E5A, E5B, P4A, P4B
LO4	**Apply the lower-of-cost-or-net realizable value method.**	6-17	E6-4	YT6.4	SS5, SS10, SE1, SE4, SE5, E6A, E9A, E10A, E12A,E6B, E9B, E10B, E12B, P3A, P7A, P3B, P7B
LO5	**Define inventory turnover and days' sales in inventory and explain the use of these ratios.**	6-19	E6-5	YT6.5	SS11, SE6, SE7, E9A, E11A, E9B, E11B, P5A, P5B
LO6	**Appendix 6A: Describe inventory costing under a perpetual inventory system using specific identification, FIFO, LIFO, and weighted-average cost.**	6-21	E6-6	YT6A.1	SS13, SE12, SE13, E14A, E15A, E16A, E14B, E15B, E16B, P10A, P11A, P13A, P10B, P11B, P13B
LO7	**Appendix 6B: Define the LIFO reserve and explain how it is used to compare the performance of companies using LIFO and FIFO inventory costing methods.**	6-26	E6-7	YT6B.1	SS12, SE14, E13A, E13B, P12A, P12B, EYK11

Inventory represents a very important asset for many companies. For example, in **Nike Inc.**'s third quarter balance sheet dated February 28, 2021, inventory made up 18% of total assets, down from nearly 25% at the end of their previous fiscal year on May 31, 2020. For companies like Nike, the management of inventory has a significant impact on a firm's profitability. The challenge of inventory management for Nike was highlighted during the Covid-19 pandemic, which disrupted global supply chains. Supply chain bottlenecks caused by global container shortages and U.S. port congestion contributed to the relatively low balance of inventory in the third quarter of 2021 and to an 11% revenue decline in Nike's North American segment.

Many retail brands, like Nike, have embraced a just-in-time inventory model in an effort to increase their inventory turnover and keep their inventory holding costs at lower levels. This strategy has worked well in the past; however, the pandemic has caused these same firms to rethink their inventory supply chains. Changes being considered include supplier diversification across different geographical locations, increasing domestic production, and increasing the use of automation.

How is Nike's inventory valued and recorded on its balance sheet? What measures exist for management and financial statement users to evaluate how effectively those inventories are being managed? We discuss the answers to these and other important questions in this chapter.

Source: Nike Misses Revenue Mark As Covid-19 Bottelnecks Continue To Plague Retail Brands." by Rose Celestin, Forbes.com, March 19, 2021.

PAST

Chapter 5 focused on accounting for merchandising transactions.

PRESENT

This chapter explains the accounting for inventory and the cost flow assumptions we make to simplify computations.

FUTURE

Chapter 7 focuses on fraud risks faced by businesses and internal controls used to combat fraud and errors.

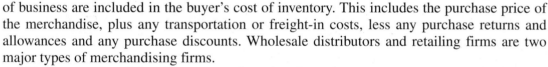

ACCOUNTING FOR INVENTORY

Inventory Concepts	Inventoriable Items	Inventory Costing Methods (Under Periodic Inventory System)	Inventory Analysis
• Inventory categories • Inventory management methods and objectives	• Goods in transit • Consignment goods • Physical inventory count • Inventory shrinkage and overage	• Specific identification • First-In, first-out (FIFO) • Last-In, first-out (LIFO) • Weighted-average cost • Gross profit effects • Income tax effects • Inventory errors • Lower-of-cost-or-net realizable value	• Inventory turnover • Days' sales in inventory • Perpetual Inventory System (Appendix 6A) • LIFO inventory reserve (Appendix 6B)

INVENTORY CATEGORIES AND CONCEPTS

LO1 Explain inventory concepts and management practices.

eLecture

MBC

Categories of Inventory

Merchandise inventory consists of the goods that a merchandising company buys from a manufacturing company and makes available for sale to its customers. All necessary costs incurred to acquire the merchandise inventory and deliver it to the buyer's place of business are included in the buyer's cost of inventory. This includes the purchase price of the merchandise, plus any transportation or freight-in costs, less any purchase returns and allowances and any purchase discounts. Wholesale distributors and retailing firms are two major types of merchandising firms.

Unlike merchandising firms, manufacturing firms do not purchase merchandise that is ready for sale. Instead, they purchase various raw materials and components and convert them into salable merchandise. At any point in time, manufacturing firms have units of merchandise at various stages of completion. Consequently, a manufacturing firm usually maintains three separate categories of inventory: raw materials inventory, work-in-process inventory, and finished goods inventory.

Raw materials inventory includes raw materials and components that have been purchased for use in the production of a product but that have not yet been placed into the production process. Sheets of steel are an example of raw material, and computer chips are an example of a component. A *component* is an item in the raw materials inventory account that was a finished product for the manufacturer that produced it. For example, **Intel Corporation** manufactures computer chips that other manufacturers incorporate into their final products. **Dell Inc.**, a computer manufacturer, is an example of a company that incorporates the finished goods of Intel into the computers that it manufactures.

Work-in-process inventory consists of units of product that have been placed into production but that are not fully assembled. All of the costs related to raw materials and components, human labor in the factory, factory utilities, and other factory-related costs are included in the work-in-process inventory. Items in this inventory category are not ready for sale since they are not yet a finished product.

Finished goods inventory includes all units that have been fully manufactured and are ready to be sold to customers. The cost of each item in the finished goods inventory is accumulated in the work-in-process inventory account and is then transferred to the finished goods inventory when the inventory is ready for sale.

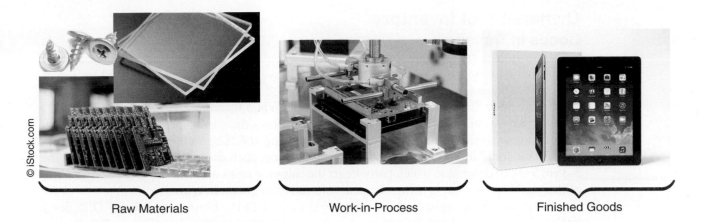

Raw Materials   Work-in-Process   Finished Goods

Concepts of Inventory Management

Merchandising and manufacturing companies often find it desirable to maintain a large and varied inventory of merchandise to satisfy the diverse needs and preferences of their customers. Not having enough inventory to meet customer demand can result in missed sales opportunities, called **stock-out costs**. At the same time, carrying more inventory than is needed to meet demand also leads to additional costs. Companies will use inventory management techniques to control these costs.

Just-in-Case Inventory

Manufacturing companies have traditionally maintained inventories as a buffer against unforeseen shipping delays and unforeseen demand by customers. This extra quantity is known as **just-in-case inventory**. Just-in-case inventories create **inventory carrying costs**, which include insurance, building usage costs, and the cost of the capital invested in the inventory.

Just-in-Time Manufacturing

Just-in-time (JIT) manufacturing seeks to eliminate or minimize inventory quantities and their related costs. The key to just-in-time manufacturing involves careful raw material purchase planning and careful management of the manufacturing and sales processes to avoid stock-out costs.

DATA ANALYTICS Data Analytics Can Make Order Fulfillment Faster and More Efficient

Many large retailers, such as **Amazon**, use data analytics to make order fulfillment faster and more efficient. Using automated shipping rules, an order is assigned to the fulfillment center nearest to the order destination, thereby reducing transportation time and cost. Inventory management software also optimizes warehousing by dictating inventory locations within a facility to ensure efficient product picking routes. Through the use of data analytics, retailers can optimize good flows within the warehouse, which leads to faster order fulfillment and lower operating costs.

Data Analytics

INVENTORY OWNERSHIP AND PHYSICAL COUNT

To determine the quantity of inventory, it is necessary to take a physical count of the inventory, usually at the end of a fiscal period. This involves not only physically counting the inventory, but also determining ownership of the inventory.

Ownership of Inventory

Goods in Transit

Goods in transit can present some uncertainty when trying to determine the end-of-period inventory quantities. It is important to include all inventory items that are owned by a company and exclude any items that are no longer owned, regardless of whether a company has the merchandise in its physical possession or not. When merchandise is shipped by a common carrier—a railroad, trucking company, or airline—the carrier prepares a *freight bill* in accordance with the instructions of the party making the transportation arrangements. The accountant could look at the freight bill or the invoice, such as the one illustrated in **Exhibit 5-3** (p. 5-7), to determine which party bears the shipping costs and which party has ownership of the merchandise that is being shipped, referred to as **goods in transit**.

These documents usually show shipping terms of **F.O.B. shipping point** or **F.O.B. destination**. *F.O.B.* is an abbreviation for "free on board." When the freight terms are F.O.B. shipping point, the buyer assumes ownership of the merchandise at the time the common carrier accepts the items from the seller. When the terms are F.O.B. destination, the seller maintains ownership of the merchandise until the buyer takes possession at delivery. In sum, ownership of goods in transit is determined by the freight terms when goods are shipped from a seller to a buyer, as illustrated in **Exhibit 6-1**.

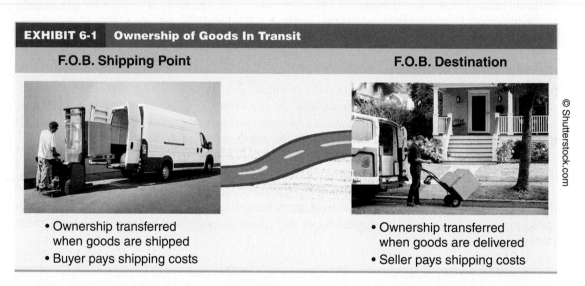

EXHIBIT 6-1   Ownership of Goods In Transit

F.O.B. Shipping Point

- Ownership transferred when goods are shipped
- Buyer pays shipping costs

F.O.B. Destination

- Ownership transferred when goods are delivered
- Seller pays shipping costs

© Shutterstock.com

ACCOUNTING IN PRACTICE   **Goods in Transit**

As a practical matter most companies ignore inventory in transit for inventory purchases because it has no profit effect. In a perpetual inventory system, the accounts affected are accounts payable and inventory. In a periodic inventory system, purchases and ending inventory are both increased, so there is no change in cost of goods sold.

Consignment Goods

Another uncertainty when assessing inventory ownership involves consignment goods. **Consignment goods** are items held for sale by parties other than the owner. An example of a consignment good is used cars held for sale at a used car lot specializing in selling cars for private parties. The car lot does not assume ownership of the cars, but simply attempts to sell the cars, collecting a commission on any completed sales. Since consignment goods do not involve a transfer of title, they are included in the determination of the end-of-period inventory quantity by the owner until sold.

Physical Count of Inventory

A company takes a **physical count of inventory** to verify the balance of inventory. It is possible that changes in the quantity of particular items could have taken place without a transaction being recognized. For example, quantities of various items may have been stolen, damaged, or destroyed. Also, the seller might have shipped an incorrect quantity to a customer even though the seller reflected the correct quantity in a journal entry. The physical count of inventory is usually taken at year-end and consists of the following steps:

1. Count the number of individual items of inventory available at the end of the period.
2. Determine the unit cost of each individual item and multiply the unit cost times the quantity to obtain the total cost for each individual inventory item.
3. Add the total cost of all the individual inventory items to obtain the total cost of the aggregate inventory available.

In a perpetual inventory system, if the physical count of inventory results in a total that does not agree with the balance in the Inventory account, the company makes a year-end adjusting entry. If the physical inventory total is less than the Inventory account balance, the company makes an adjusting entry debiting Cost of Goods Sold and crediting Inventory for the difference between the physical inventory total and the balance in the Inventory account. This entry decreases the balance in the Inventory account and adds the cost of the inventory shortage to Cost of Goods Sold. The cost associated with an inventory shortage is known as **inventory shrinkage**.

Adjusting entry for inventory shrinkage:

Cost of goods sold (+E, –SE)
   Inventory (–A)

FORENSIC ACCOUNTING   **Employee Theft of Inventory**

 Inventory shrinkage arises from employee and/or customer theft, physical damage or deterioration, and obsolescence. Shrinkage is typically discovered following a physical count of inventory. According to the 2020 National Retail Security Survey, shrinkage for U.S. retailers reached an all-time high of $61.7 billion in 2019, up from $50.6 billion the prior year. Employee theft represents a substantial part of this overall loss. Preventing inventory theft is difficult. However, there are several ways that companies can help prevent it, such as:

- Give different passwords to each cashier. Using separate passwords and log-ins reveals which employee was manning the cash register at the times when theft occurs.
- Verify any transaction that is voided or canceled. This is a common way for inventory to be removed from a store.
- Review inventory reports daily to be sure sales match current inventory quantities.
- Install an alarm system on a store's back door that is activated each time the door is opened without authorization.
- Inspect the garbage nightly. Use clear, plastic bags so that the contents are easily inspected to ensure that no inventory is hidden inside.
- Install security cameras in the store and in the back storage to allow the store manager to keep an eye on items on the store racks as well as in stock.

If the physical inventory total is greater than the Inventory account balance, the company makes an adjusting entry debiting Inventory and crediting Cost of Goods Sold for the difference between the physical inventory and the Inventory account balance. This entry increases the balance in the Inventory account and subtracts the cost of this **inventory overage** from Cost of Goods Sold.

To illustrate shrinkage (the usual situation), assume that the December 31 balance of the Inventory account (including all items) is $120,600. Also assume that a physical count of the inventory produced a total cost at December 31 of $120,000. The following period-end adjusting entry is required at December 31 to adjust the balance in the Inventory account from $120,600 to $120,000:

Adjusting entry for inventory overage:

Inventory (+A)
   Cost of goods sold (–E, +SE)

A = L + SE	Dec. 31	Cost of Goods Sold (+E, −SE)	600	
−600 −600		Inventory (−A)		600
Exp		*To adjust the inventory account balance to the total cost determined by*		
		a physical inventory count in a perpetual inventory system.		

YOUR TURN! 6.1

GuidedExample

MBC

The solution is on
page 6-50.

The Counter Company just completed the year-end physical count of its inventory. The total value of inventory was determined to be $300,000. The following additional information came to light following the conclusion of the physical count:

1. The company included $20,000 of inventory that was shipped F.O.B. destination.
2. The company included $15,000 of inventory that was shipped F.O.B. shipping point.
3. The company did not include $25,000 of inventory that was being sold on consignment by Johnson Sales, a consignment dealer. The inventory is located at Johnson Sales, but it was still owned by The Counter Company at the time of its physical count of inventory.

Discuss how this additional information affects the $300,000 value that The Counter Company initially determined to be the value of its ending inventory.

INVENTORY COSTING METHODS

LO2 Describe inventory costing using specific identification, FIFO, LIFO, and weighted-average cost.

eLecture

MBC

In general, the value of a company's inventory is entered into the accounting records at its acquisition cost. Inventory costing is simple when the acquisition cost remains constant. For example, assume that the Fletcher Motor Company purchased electric motors four times during the year, as shown in **Exhibit 6-2**.

EXHIBIT 6-2	Illustration of Cost Flows When Prices Do Not Change
February 10 purchase	100 motors at $180 each
April 25 purchase	150 motors at $180 each
July 16 purchase	150 motors at $180 each
October 8 purchase	200 motors at $180 each
December 31 ending inventory.	40 motors at $? each

The December 31 ending inventory of 40 electric motors includes some from the July 16 purchase and some from the October 8 purchase. In this case, it is easy to determine the cost to be assigned to the 40 motors (40 × $180 = $7,200) because all of the inventory purchases were made at the exact same purchase price of $180. In real business situations, however, the purchase price of an item of inventory often changes. The trend is usually toward increasing prices, although in some cases purchase prices may decline. When purchase prices change during the year, a company must either keep track of the acquisition cost of each specific unit or make an assumption about which units have been sold and which units remain in inventory. Most companies choose the latter option because the cost of keeping track of exactly which units are sold can be prohibitively expensive.

Goods Flow vs. Cost Flow

Two concepts that are helpful in understanding the problem of assigning a cost to inventory when purchase prices are changing are goods flow and cost flow. **Goods flow** describes the actual physical movement of inventory through a business. **Cost flow** is the assumed assignment of costs to goods sold and to ending inventory. The cost flow need not, and often does not, reflect the actual goods flow through a business.

Generally accepted accounting principles permit businesses to use a cost flow that does not reflect the company's actual goods flow. For example, the goods flow in a grocery store chain like **Safeway** will almost always be such that the goods brought in first will be the first goods to be sold. This physical goods flow results in the least amount of loss due to spoilage. However, just because Safeway operates with this physical goods flow through its stores does not mean that the company is required to adopt a similar cost flow to calculate the value of its inventory. The *cost flow assumption* adopted could be one in which the most recent goods added to inventory are assumed to be the first goods sold.

> The following sections use a periodic inventory system to illustrate the different cost flow assumptions. Using the same data from this illustration, Appendix 6A explains the different cost flow assumptions using a perpetual inventory system. Your instructor can choose to cover either one or both systems. If the following periodic system is skipped, then read Appendix 6A and return to the section (on page 6-14) titled "Income Tax Effects."

Data for Illustration of Cost Flow Assumptions

In this section, we introduce and illustrate four generally accepted methods of costing inventories: (1) specific identification, (2) first-in, first-out (FIFO), (3) last-in, first-out (LIFO), and (4) weighted-average cost. Following an illustration of the four methods, a comparative analysis of the financial results of the methods is presented. To facilitate this comparison, we use a common set of data. Assume that Claremont Company's purchases and sales of inventory during the year are as shown in **Exhibit 6-3**.

EXHIBIT 6-3	Purchases and Sales for Application of Inventory Methods			
Date	**Event**	**No. of Units**	**Unit Cost**	**Total Cost**
Jan. 1	Beginning inventory	60	@ $10 =	$ 600
Mar. 27	Purchase inventory	90	@ $11 =	$ 990
May 2	**Sell inventory**	(130)		
Aug. 15	Purchase inventory	100	@ $13 =	$1,300
Nov. 6	Purchase inventory	50	@ $16 =	$ 800
Dec. 10	**Sell inventory**	(90)		
Dec. 31	Ending inventory	80		

The four inventory costing methods differ in the way they assign costs to the 80 units in ending inventory and the 220 units in cost of goods sold. Under the periodic inventory system, the Inventory account and the Cost of Goods Sold account are updated only at the end of the period, following a physical count of the ending inventory. Once the total cost of ending inventory is determined using one of the four inventory costing methods, the ending inventory amount is subtracted from cost of goods available for sale to derive the period's cost of goods sold.

Specific Identification Method

The **specific identification method** involves (1) keeping track of the purchase cost of each specific unit available for sale and (2) costing the ending inventory at the actual costs of the specific units in ending inventory. Assume that the 80 units in ending inventory consist of 10 units from beginning inventory, 20 units from the August 15 purchase, and all 50 of the units purchased on November 6. The cost assigned to the ending inventory and to the cost of goods sold is shown in **Exhibit 6-4**. Observe that the entire $3,690 of cost of the goods available for sale is assigned as either ending inventory ($1,160) or as cost of goods sold ($2,530).

This information is used to compute ending inventory.

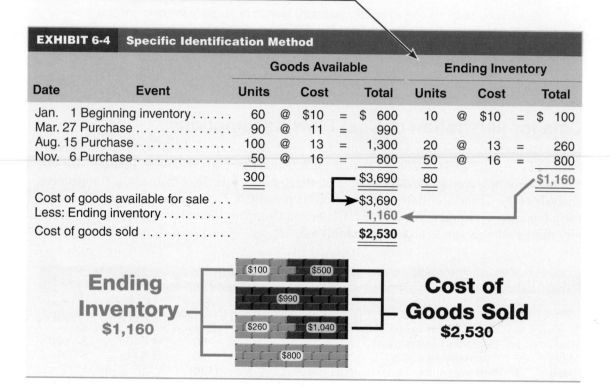

EXHIBIT 6-4	Specific Identification Method									
		Goods Available				**Ending Inventory**				
Date	**Event**	**Units**		**Cost**		**Total**	**Units**		**Cost**		**Total**
Jan. 1 Beginning inventory......		60	@	$10	=	$ 600	10	@	$10	=	$ 100
Mar. 27 Purchase..............		90	@	11	=	990					
Aug. 15 Purchase.............		100	@	13	=	1,300	20	@	13	=	260
Nov. 6 Purchase.............		50	@	16	=	800	50	@	16	=	800
		300				$3,690	80				$1,160
Cost of goods available for sale ...						$3,690					
Less: Ending inventory..........						1,160					
Cost of goods sold						$2,530					

Ending Inventory $1,160 $100 $500 $990 $260 $1,040 $800   **Cost of Goods Sold $2,530**

First-In, First-Out (FIFO) Method

The **first-in, first-out (FIFO) method** assumes that the oldest goods (or earliest purchased) are sold first. This means that the costs assigned to ending inventory are from the most recent purchases. FIFO results in the cost allocations as shown in **Exhibit 6-5**. This method assumes the first 220 units acquired are sold first, and the last 80 units purchased remain in ending inventory.

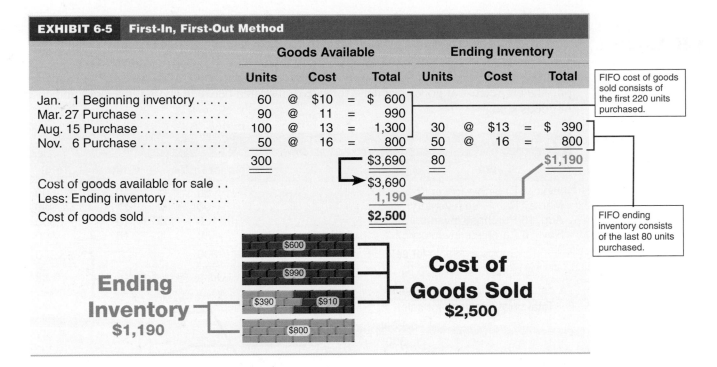

EXHIBIT 6-5   **First-In, First-Out Method**

	Goods Available			Ending Inventory			
	Units	Cost	Total	Units	Cost	Total	
Jan. 1 Beginning inventory	60	@ $10	= $ 600				FIFO cost of goods sold consists of the first 220 units purchased.
Mar. 27 Purchase	90	@ 11	= 990				
Aug. 15 Purchase	100	@ 13	= 1,300	30	@ $13	= $ 390	
Nov. 6 Purchase	50	@ 16	= 800	50	@ 16	= 800	
	300		$3,690	80		$1,190	
Cost of goods available for sale . .			$3,690				
Less: Ending inventory			1,190				FIFO ending inventory consists of the last 80 units purchased.
Cost of goods sold			$2,500				

Ending Inventory $1,190

$600
$990
$390 $910
$800

Cost of Goods Sold $2,500

Last-In, First-Out (LIFO) Method

The **last-in, first-out (LIFO) method** assumes that the most recent purchases are sold first. **Exhibit 6-6** illustrates the calculation of LIFO cost of goods sold. LIFO assumes that the 220 units last (most recently) purchased are sold first, and the 80 oldest units available for sale remain in inventory at the end of the period.

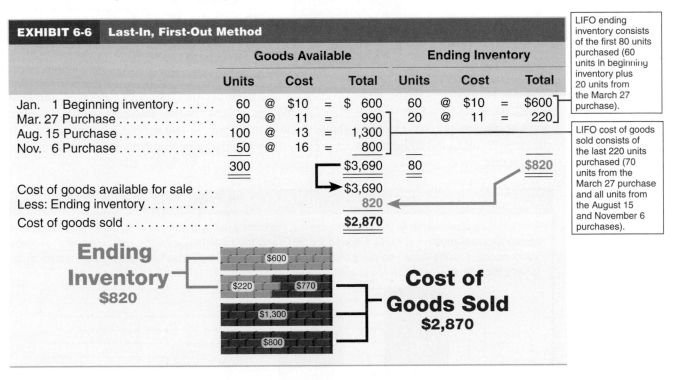

EXHIBIT 6-6   **Last-In, First-Out Method**

	Goods Available			Ending Inventory			
	Units	Cost	Total	Units	Cost	Total	
Jan. 1 Beginning inventory	60	@ $10	= $ 600	60	@ $10	= $600	LIFO ending inventory consists of the first 80 units purchased (60 units in beginning inventory plus 20 units from the March 27 purchase).
Mar. 27 Purchase	90	@ 11	= 990	20	@ 11	= 220	
Aug. 15 Purchase	100	@ 13	= 1,300				
Nov. 6 Purchase	50	@ 16	= 800				
	300		$3,690	80		$820	LIFO cost of goods sold consists of the last 220 units purchased (70 units from the March 27 purchase and all units from the August 15 and November 6 purchases).
Cost of goods available for sale . . .			$3,690				
Less: Ending inventory			820				
Cost of goods sold			$2,870				

Ending Inventory $820

$600
$220 $770
$1,300
$800

Cost of Goods Sold $2,870

Weighted-Average Cost Method

A.K.A. The weighted-average cost method is often referred to as the average cost method.

The **weighted-average cost method** spreads the total dollar cost of the goods available for sale equally among all units. In our illustration, the weighted-average cost per unit is $12.30, computed as $3,690/300 units. **Exhibit 6-7** diagrams the assignment of costs under this method. The entire cost of goods available for sale is allocated between ending inventory and cost of goods sold.

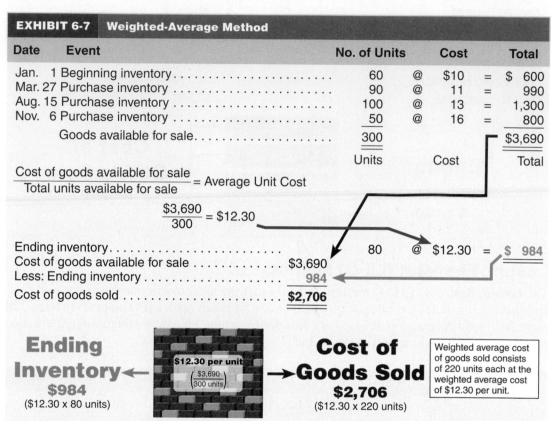

EXHIBIT 6-7	**Weighted-Average Method**				
Date	**Event**	**No. of Units**		**Cost**	**Total**
Jan. 1	Beginning inventory..................	60	@	$10 =	$ 600
Mar. 27	Purchase inventory.................	90	@	11 =	990
Aug. 15	Purchase inventory.................	100	@	13 =	1,300
Nov. 6	Purchase inventory.................	50	@	16 =	800
	Goods available for sale...........	300			$3,690
		Units		Cost	Total

$$\frac{\text{Cost of goods available for sale}}{\text{Total units available for sale}} = \text{Average Unit Cost}$$

$$\frac{\$3,690}{300} = \$12.30$$

Ending inventory....................	80	@ $12.30 =	$ 984
Cost of goods available for sale.............	$3,690		
Less: Ending inventory.................	984		
Cost of goods sold......................	$2,706		

Weighted average ending inventory consists of 80 units, each at the weighted average cost of $12.30 per unit.

Ending Inventory $984 ($12.30 x 80 units) ← **$12.30 per unit** $3,690 / 300 units → **Cost of Goods Sold** $2,706 ($12.30 x 220 units)

Weighted average cost of goods sold consists of 220 units each at the weighted average cost of $12.30 per unit.

It would be incorrect to use a *simple* average of the unit costs. The simple average unit cost is $12.50, or [($10 + $11 + $13 + $16)/4]. This figure does not take into account the different number of units purchased and available at the various prices. The simple average cost yields the same result as the weighted-average cost only when the same number of units is purchased at each unit price.

ACCOUNTING IN PRACTICE   **Inventory Costing Methods**

The following chart identifies the inventory costing methods used by a sample of 600 U.S. firms. The most frequently used method is FIFO, followed by LIFO and then weighted-average cost. (The total exceeds 100% because some firms use more than one method to value their inventory, which is permitted under GAAP.) [Source: Accounting Trends and Techniques]

	FIFO	LIFO	Weighted-average	Other
70%				
60%				
50%				
40%				
30%				
20%				
10%				
0%				

The following inventory information is gathered from the accounting records of Tucker Enterprises:

Beginning inventory	4,000 units at $ 5 each
Purchases.	6,000 units at $ 7 each
Sales.	9,000 units at $10 each

Calculate (a) ending inventory, (b) cost of goods sold, and (c) the gross profit using each of the following methods (i) FIFO, (ii) LIFO, and (iii) weighted-average cost.

MBC

The solution is on page 6-50.

Comparative Analysis of Inventory Costing Methods and Gross Profit

The purchase price data used in the Claremont Company illustration has an important characteristic: the purchase price of the inventory increased each time that a purchase was made, from $11 per unit to $13 per unit to $16 per unit. Increasing inventory prices are frequently encountered in the real world where price inflation is common and price deflation is uncommon. **Exhibit 6-8** summarizes the results of applying the four inventory costing methods to the Claremont Company data and reveals that the FIFO method produces the lowest cost of goods sold ($2,500), while the LIFO method produces the highest cost of goods sold ($2,870). The exhibit also reveals that FIFO produces the highest year-end value of ending inventory ($1,190), while LIFO produces the lowest year-end value of ending inventory ($820). Weighted-average cost produces ending inventory values and cost of goods sold values that fall in between the results obtained using FIFO and LIFO.

LO3 Analyze the effects of different inventory costing methods on company profit.

These results, however, are highly dependent on the purchase prices for the inventory. If the inventory's purchase price had been decreasing rather than increasing, the financial effects would have been just the opposite, with LIFO producing the lowest cost of goods sold and FIFO the highest. If the purchase prices had been perfectly stable, there would be no difference between the cost of goods sold or the ending inventory for any of the four methods.

EXHIBIT 6-8	Results of Different Inventory Costing Methods			
	Specific Identification	FIFO	LIFO	Weighted-Average
Cost of goods sold	$2,530	$2,500	$2,870	$2,706
Ending inventory.	1,160	1,190	820	984

To illustrate the financial effects of the different inventory costing methods, assume that the 220 units sold by the Claremont Company were sold for $20 each, producing sales of $4,400 ($20 × 220). **Exhibit 6-9** shows the difference in gross profit under each of the four inventory costing methods. Remember that the difference in reported gross profit results from the assumptions made about cost flow, not from any difference in the physical flow of goods. In each case, 220 units were sold and 80 units remained. Each of the inventory costing methods is in accord with generally accepted accounting principles, yet the methods have different financial effects on gross profit and net income.

EXHIBIT 6-9	Gross Profit Using Alternative Inventory Costing Methods			
	Specific Identification	FIFO	LIFO	Weighted-Average
Sales (220 units @ $20).....................	$4,400	$4,400	$4,400	$4,400
Cost of goods sold	2,530	2,500	2,870	2,706
Gross profit................................	$1,870	$1,900	$1,530	$1,694
Increased gross profit compared with LIFO	$ 340	$ 370		$ 164

Income Statement and Balance Sheet Effects

As **Exhibit 6-9** reveals, LIFO results in the smallest gross profit ($1,530), with FIFO producing the highest ($1,900) gross profit. This result occurs because the purchase price of inventory was increasing throughout the year, from $11 per unit to $13 per unit to $16 per unit. When costs are rising, FIFO tends to overstate gross profit (and income) because older, lower unit costs are included in the cost of goods sold and matched with current sales prices. In other words, the units sold are charged to costs of goods sold under FIFO at unit costs of $10, $11, and $13. If the latest purchase price reflects the inventory's current acquisition cost, the units sold must be replaced by units costing $16 (or more if costs continue to rise).

It is frequently argued that LIFO provides a better matching of current costs with current revenues since the cost of the most recent purchases constitutes the LIFO cost of goods sold. While LIFO associates the current, higher unit costs with cost of goods sold, it assigns costs to ending inventory using the older, lower unit costs. As a consequence, the value of the LIFO ending inventory on the balance sheet is often undervalued in terms of the inventory's current value. When inventory quantities are maintained or increased, the LIFO method prevents older costs from appearing in the cost of goods sold. No doubt, some firms still carry LIFO inventories at unit costs that existed more than 10 years ago. Under FIFO, the ending inventory is measured at relatively recent costs.

Selecting Inventory Methods

Under generally accepted accounting principles, a company is permitted to select one or more of the four methods for purposes of assigning costs to ending inventory and cost of goods sold. Which method (or methods, since a company may elect to value some of its inventory using FIFO, some using LIFO, and some using weighted-average cost) is selected by a company depends upon a number of factors, including the type of product, the cost of the product, whether the product is perishable, whether the company desires to report a high or a low net income, and income tax considerations.

Specific Identification Method

Companies might choose to use specific identification for unique items with small volume and high unit cost, such as fine art or jewelry, that would justify the cost of tracking the specific unit cost of each inventory item. Specific identification is usually not cost-justified for inventories that have a low unit cost or involve high volumes of similar products.

FIFO Method

Many companies, especially those with perishable, time-dated, or style-affected merchandise, attempt to sell their oldest merchandise first. This is especially true for companies that sell food products, chemicals, and drugs. For these types of companies, the cost flow produced by the FIFO method most closely matches the physical goods flow. However, a company is not required to use the cost flow assumption that most closely matches its physical goods flow. When costs are rising, FIFO will result in the lowest cost of goods sold, and therefore, the highest net income. The desire to show a higher net income by some companies partly explains the popularity of the FIFO method.

LIFO Method

Although LIFO does not reflect the physical goods flow for most businesses, its popularity is likely linked to the potential income tax savings associated with its use. We illustrate the income tax advantages of the LIFO method in the next section. For some industries, however, LIFO does depict the physical goods flow. For example, in industries that extract natural resources, such as mining, the product is frequently dumped onto a storage pile from an overhead trestle, and sold inventory is taken from the top of the pile. One disadvantage of using LIFO when the quantity of beginning inventories has been maintained or increased is that a firm's ending inventory can be substantially undervalued since old purchase prices tend to be retained on a company's books under the LIFO method. This, in turn, will cause a firm's current assets and total assets to likewise be undervalued.

Weighted-Average Cost Method

Weighted-average cost is best suited for businesses that warehouse a large volume of identical goods in a common area. Liquid fuels, grains, and other commodities are examples. Weighted-average cost typically generates a cost of goods sold amount that is neither high nor low as compared to the other methods, as is revealed in **Exhibit 6-8**.

Summary

We can broadly summarize the choice among the cost flow assumptions as follows:

1. Specific identification identifies the actual cost of goods sold and ending inventory but can be costly to implement.
2. FIFO approximates the actual physical flow of goods for most firms.
3. LIFO is popular because of the income tax savings associated with its use.
4. Weighted-average cost is most often associated with businesses in which identical goods are commingled in a common area like a warehouse.

PRINCIPLE ALERT   **Consistency and Full Disclosure**

Inventory costing requires the application of *consistency* and *full disclosure*. Because of the possible variation in gross profit and ending inventory values that result from the use of different inventory costing methods, it is important that a firm use the same inventory costing method from one fiscal period to the next. This application of consistency enhances the comparability of a firm's cost of goods sold, gross profit, net income, inventory, current assets, and total assets over time. In addition, a firm should disclose which inventory costing method it is using, either in its financial statements or in the notes to the statements. This information is required by the full disclosure principle and is important to users who compare financial data across firms.

For readers skipping the periodic system, please resume reading here.

Income Tax Effects

Management is usually free to select different accounting treatments for financial reporting to shareholders and for income tax reporting to the Internal Revenue Service (IRS). For example, it is acceptable for a business to use different methods of computing depreciation when reporting under GAAP on the income statement and for reporting under income tax regulations on a company's income tax return. An exception to this flexibility occurs when a company chooses to use LIFO for income tax reporting. A U.S. federal tax regulation known as the **LIFO conformity rule** requires any company that selects LIFO for income tax reporting to also use LIFO for financial reporting to shareholders.

During periods of rising purchase prices, LIFO results in a lower gross profit than any of the alternative inventory costing methods. A lower gross profit, and net income, means that lower amounts of income taxes need to be paid. Hence, the desire to reduce current income tax payments is a major reason for widespread use of LIFO.

To illustrate LIFO's income tax advantage, assume that the Huntington Corporation has beginning inventory of 10 units costing $500 each, and that only two transactions occur. In the first transaction, it purchases 10 more units costing $630 each, for a total cash purchase price of $6,300. In the second transaction, it sells 10 units for $700 each, for a total cash sale of $7,000. Both transactions are for cash and, for simplicity, we assume that the company's operating expenses are zero and the applicable income tax rate is 20 percent. **Exhibit 6-10** presents the income statements and cash flows for Huntington under both FIFO and LIFO.

EXHIBIT 6-10	**FIFO vs. LIFO Comparison: Phantom Profit Effect and Tax Benefit**			
	FIFO		**LIFO**	
	Income Statement	Cash In (Out)	Income Statement	Cash In (Out)
Sales (10 @ $700)	$ 7,000	$7,000	$ 7,000	$7,000
Cost of goods sold				
Beginning inventory (10 @ $500)	5,000		5,000	
Purchases (10 @ $630)	6,300	(6,300)	6,300	(6,300)
Goods available (20 units)	11,300		11,300	
Ending inventory				
10 @ FIFO	6,300			
10 @ LIFO.			5,000	
Cost of goods sold	5,000		6,300	
Pretax income.	2,000		700	
Income tax (at 20%)	400	(400)	140	(140)
Net income	$ 1,600		$ 560	
Net cash proceeds		$ 300		$ 560

Under FIFO, Huntington reports $1,600 of net income on cash sales of $7,000; however, after replacing the 10 units of inventory sold at the current cost of $6,300 and paying income tax of $400 on the $2,000 in FIFO pretax net income, the company only has net cash proceeds of $300. The net income of $1,600 is not fully realized in cash, and consequently, is unavailable to pay dividends or be reinvested in the business. As a consequence, FIFO net income is sometimes referred to as *phantom profit*.

Under LIFO, Huntington reports net income of $560 as a consequence of its higher cost of goods sold ($6,300). With a lower net income, it incurs a smaller cash outflow for income taxes ($140). The attractiveness of LIFO during periods of rising inventory purchase prices is evidenced by LIFO's more favorable net cash flow ($560) compared with FIFO ($300). Using LIFO during times of falling inventory purchase prices, however, has the opposite income tax effect.

Errors in the Inventory Count

A physical count of inventory is necessary to determine the value of a company's ending inventory regardless of what inventory method is used. Unfortunately, errors in the inventory count, for example failing to count some items or counting some items twice, can occur. These errors affect not only the value of ending inventory reported on the balance sheet in the period of the error, but also cost of goods sold and gross profit. Further, the error is not limited to only the current period—cost of goods sold and gross profit in the following period are also affected. To illustrate, assume that the Arrow Company began operations in 2014. **Exhibit 6-11** summarizes Arrow's 2020 and 2021 transactions.

EXHIBIT 6-11	Inventory Transactions for Arrow Company	Inventory Units	Inventory Balance
2020	Beginning inventory	0	0
	Purchased 1,000 units of merchandise inventory for $3 per unit . . .	1000	$3,000
	Sold 400 units of merchandise inventory	(400)	(1,200)*
	Ending inventory.	600	$1,800
2021	Beginning inventory	600	$1,800
	Purchased 2,000 units of merchandise inventory for $3 per unit . . .	2,000	6,000
	Sold 1,500 units of merchandise inventory.	(1,500)	(4,500)*
	Ending inventory.	1,100	$3,300

* Cost of goods sold.

Assume that Arrow Company made an error in its physical count of inventory at the end of 2020, mistakenly double-counting 40 units of inventory, and consequently, overstating ending inventory by $120 (40 units × $3). An error in the ending inventory account in the current year affects the value of ending inventory in the current year, as well as current year gross profit through cost of goods sold. The error also affects, in an opposite direction, gross profit in the following year (through its effect on cost of goods sold).

EXHIBIT 6-12	Inventory Error Effects				
Cost of Goods Sold	**=**	**Beginning Inventory**	**+ Purchases**	**–**	**Ending Inventory**
2020: $1,080 (instead of $1,200)	=	$ 0	+ $3,000	–	$1,920**
2021: $4,620 (instead of $4,500)	=	$1,920	+ $6,000	–	$3,300
Gross Profit		**No Error**	**With Error**		
2020					
Cost of goods sold		$1,200	$1,080		
Gross profit (under)/over stated			$ 120		
2021					
Cost of goods sold		$4,500	$4,620		
Gross profit (under)/over stated			$ (120)		

** ($1,800 + $120)

To show the effect of inventory errors using the Arrow Company example in **Exhibit 6-12**, notice that the combined cost of goods sold for both years is $5,700, without the error ($1,200 + $4,500) or with the error ($1,080 + $4,620). Further, we see that ending inventory was overstated in 2020 by $120, which resulted in 2020 cost of goods sold being understated by $120, and 2020 gross profit being overstated by $120. The same $120 error is carried through to 2021, where it causes cost of goods sold to be overstated by $120 (because of the overstatement of beginning inventory), and gross profit to be understated by $120.

YOUR TURN! 6.3

MBC

The solution is on page 6-50.

Assume Pointer Company began operations two years ago. The table below summarizes Pointer's inventory transactions for those two years.

		Inventory Units	Inventory Balance	Sales
Year 1	Beginning inventory	0	0	
	Purchased 2,000 units of merchandise for $5 per unit. . . .	2,000	$10,000	
	Sold 1,500 units of merchandise for $10 per unit.	(1,500)	(7,500)	$15,000
	Ending inventory.	500	$ 2,500	
Year 2	Beginning inventory	500	$ 2,500	
	Purchased 3,000 units of merchandise for $5 per unit. . . .	3,000	15,000	
	Sold 2,500 units of merchandise for $10 per unit.	(2,500)	(12,500)	$25,000
	Ending inventory.	1,000	$ 5,000	

Assume that Pointer made an error in its physical count of inventory at the end of Year 1, mistakenly omitting 100 units of inventory, and consequently, understating ending inventory by $500 (100 units × $5). Determine Pointer's Year 1 and Year 2 ending inventory with the error. Also compute Pointer's sales, cost of goods sold, and gross profit for Year 1 and Year 2 both with and without the error.

LOWER-OF-COST-OR-NET REALIZABLE VALUE METHOD

LO4 **Apply** the lower-of-cost-or-net realizable value method.

eLecture

MBC

In general, inventory is valued at its acquisition cost using one of the generally accepted inventory costing methods explained earlier in this chapter. However, it can be necessary to report inventory at a lower value if there is evidence that the inventory's utility to a business—that is, the inventory's revenue-generating ability—has fallen below its acquisition cost. Such *inventory write-downs* can occur when (1) merchandise must be sold at reduced prices because it is damaged or otherwise not in normal salable condition or when (2) the cost of replacing the ending inventory has declined below the inventory's recorded acquisition cost.

Net Realizable Value

Damaged, physically deteriorated, or obsolete merchandise should be measured and reported at its net realizable value on the balance sheet when this value is less than the inventory's acquisition cost. **Net realizable value (NRV)** is an item's estimated selling price less the expected cost of the eventual sale or disposal of the item. For example, assume that an inventory item cost $300 but can be sold for only $200 because it is damaged. If the related selling costs are estimated to be $20, the inventory should be written down to its net realizable value of $180 ($200 estimated selling price less $20 estimated disposal cost), and a $120 inventory write-down loss ($300 − $180) should be reported on the income statement for the current period.

Lower-of-Cost-or-Net Realizable Value

The **lower-of-cost-or-net realizable value** method provides for the recognition of an inventory write-down loss when the inventory's net realizable value declines below its recorded acquisition cost. Under this method, a loss is reported in the period when the inventory's net realizable value declines, rather than during a subsequent period when the actual sale of the inventory takes place. This procedure assumes that decreases in the net realizable value of inventory are accompanied by proportionate decreases in the selling price of the inventory.

To illustrate, assume that an inventory item that cost $80 has been selling at a retail price of $100, yielding a gross profit percentage of 20 percent. Assume also that by year-end, the item's net realizable value has declined to $60 (calculated as a sales price of $64 with an estimated cost of $4 to sell the item). In this case, the inventory is written down to its $60 net realizable value, and the current period's net income is reduced by a $20 write-down loss ($80 – $60). If the inventory is sold in a subsequent period for $75 (assuming the normal gross profit percentage of 20 percent on sales), a gross profit of $15 will be reported ($75 – $60).

The lower-of-cost-or-net realizable value method can be applied to each individual item in inventory or to the total of all inventory. In **Exhibit 6-13**, if the lower-of-cost-or-net realizable value method is applied on an individual item basis, the value of ending inventory is $6,820. If the lower-of-cost-or-net realizable value method was instead applied to all inventory, the value of ending inventory is $7,120.

EXHIBIT 6-13	Application of the Lower-of-Cost-or-Net Realizable Value					
		Per Unit		**Total**		**Lower-of-Cost-or-Net Realizable Value**
Inventory Item	Quantity	Cost	NRV	Cost	NRV	Individual Item
Cameras						
Model V70......	40	$80	$75	$3,200	$3,000	$3,000
Model V85......	30	60	64	1,800	1,920	1,800
Subtotal......				$5,000	$4,920	—
Calculators						
Model C20......	90	13	15	$1,170	$1,350	1,170
Model C40......	50	20	17	1,000	850	850
Subtotal......				$2,170	$2,200	—
Total				$7,170	$7,120	$6,820

PRINCIPLE ALERT   **Conservatism**

The lower-of-cost-or-net realizable value method for inventory is a good illustration of *conservatism*. When the net realizable value for an inventory item falls below its acquisition cost, there is increased uncertainty about the future profitability of the item. Conservatism is the reaction to significant uncertainties in the measurement of net assets and net income. In choosing between alternative financial measures, conservatism causes the least optimistic measure to be selected. When an item's net realizable value falls below its historical acquisition cost, the least optimistic measure is its lower NRV. The lower-of-cost-or-net realizable value method applies to all inventory methods except LIFO. For LIFO inventory, companies report inventory at the lower of cost or market, where market is typically the replacement cost of the inventory. The replacement cost is never greater than net realizable value.

THINKING GLOBALLY

Under IFRS, LIFO is not generally accepted. Further, under U.S. GAAP, inventory may not be revalued upward, even if it has been revalued downward. IFRS permits reversal of inventory write-downs, with the reversal limited to the amount of the original write-down.

YOUR TURN! 6.4

The Images Company sells three types of video equipment—DSLR cameras, Point and Shoot cameras, and Camcorders. The cost and net realizable value of its inventory of video equipment follow:

	Cost	NRV
DSLR	$110,000	$125,000
Point and Shoot	73,000	92,000
Camcorders	57,000	48,000

Compute the value of the Images Company's ending inventory under the lower-of-cost-or-net realizable value method applied on an item-by-item basis.

GuidedExample

MBC

The solution is on page 6-50.

INVENTORY ANALYSIS

LO5 Define *inventory turnover* and *days' sales in inventory* and **explain** the use of these ratios.

© Shutterstock.com

Inventory Turnover and Days' Sales in Inventory

The **inventory turnover ratio** indicates how many times a year, on average, a firm sells its inventory, and it is calculated as:

$$\text{Inventory turnover} = \frac{\text{Cost of goods sold}}{\text{Average inventory}}$$

This ratio relates data from two financial statements: the income statement and the balance sheet. Cost of goods sold is taken from the income statement, while the average inventory is calculated from balance sheet data—that is, the beginning and ending inventories are summed, and the total is divided by two.

In general, the faster a company can turn over its inventory, the more profitable the company will be. Further, the higher the inventory turnover ratio, the less time a firm has its funds tied up in inventory and the less risk the firm faces from trying to sell out-of-date merchandise. What is considered to be a satisfactory inventory turnover varies from industry to industry. A grocery store chain like **Safeway**, for example, should have a much higher inventory turnover than a jewelry store like **Zales**.

To illustrate the inventory turnover ratio, **Best Buy** reported the following financial data:

($ millions)	2020	2019
Cost of goods sold	$36,689	$33,590
Beginning inventory	5,174	5,409
Ending inventory	5,612	5,174

Best Buy's inventory turnover in 2020 is 6.80, computed as $36,689/[($5,174 + $5,612)/2]. A similar calculation reveals that Best Buy's inventory turnover was 6.35 in 2019, indicating an improvement from 2019 to 2020.

The inventory turnover ratio can be influenced by a firm's choice of inventory costing method. Inventory amounts calculated using LIFO, for example, will typically be smaller than the same inventory calculated using FIFO. An investor comparing inventory turnover ratios between different firms will need to verify that the firms are using the same inventory costing method; otherwise, any ratio comparisons will not be meaningful.

An extension of the inventory turnover ratio is the **days' sales in inventory**, calculated as:

$$\text{Days' sales in inventory} = \frac{365}{\text{Inventory turnover}}$$

A.K.A. The days' sales in inventory ratio is also referred to as the days' inventory-on-hand ratio and the inventory-on-hand period.

This ratio indicates how many days it takes, on average, for a firm to sell its inventory. During 2020, for example, Best Buy's days' sales in inventory was 53.7 days, or 365/6.80; that is, Best Buy took about 54 days to sell its inventory. Similar calculations reveal it took an average of 57.5 days for Best Buy to sell its inventory in 2019. Do these ratio results indicate that Best Buy is doing a good job of managing its investment in inventory? Without comparable ratio data from a competitor like Target Corporation, it is difficult to conclude whether a days' sales in inventory ratio of 53.7 days indicates that Best Buy is doing a good or bad job of managing its inventory.

Concept	➝	Method	➝	Assessment	TAKEAWAY 6.1
How long, on average, does it take to sell the inventory?		Cost of goods sold, beginning inventory, and ending inventory $\text{Inventory turnover} = \dfrac{\text{Cost of goods sold}}{\text{Average inventory}}$ $\text{Days' sales in inventory} = \dfrac{365}{\text{Inventory turnover}}$		A higher inventory turnover or a lower days' sales in inventory indicates that the company is able to sell its inventory more quickly.	

YOUR TURN! 6.5

MBC

The solution is on page 6-50.

Flip Company installed a new inventory management system. Shown below are financial data from the company's accounting records:

	Year 1	Year 2
Sales revenue.	$4,000,000	$4,400,000
Cost of goods sold	2,000,000	2,300,000
Beginning inventory	450,000	430,000
Ending inventory.	430,000	320,000

Calculate the inventory turnover and days' sales in inventory for both years. Discuss your findings.

ENVIRONMENTAL, SOCIAL, AND GOVERNANCE   **Best Buy and an Ethical Supply Chain**

Many businesses strive to not only do well financially, but also do good environmentally and socially. **Best Buy** serves as the ultimate seller of many products manufactured by other companies, such as TVs by **Sony**, cameras by **Nikon**, and computers by **Dell**. Best Buy also sells its exclusive brands. As the manufacturer of these products, Best Buy faces decisions on how and where these products are produced. Best Buy's 2020 Environmental, Social, and Governance Report discloses that "Best Buy partners with approximately 190 factories, to produce our private label (or Exclusive Brands) products. We work with these suppliers on the design, production and testing of these products, and we also partner with them to ensure they meet our expectations for safe workplaces where workers are treated fairly." In their fourth annual ranking of the 100 Most Sustainable Companies, Barron's ranked Best Buy at the top of the list.

COMPREHENSIVE PROBLEM

The Montclair Corporation had the following inventory transactions for its only product during the curent year:

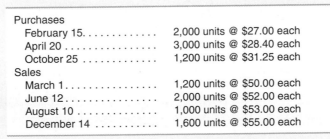

Purchases	
February 15.	2,000 units @ $27.00 each
April 20	3,000 units @ $28.40 each
October 25	1,200 units @ $31.25 each
Sales	
March 1.	1,200 units @ $50.00 each
June 12.	2,000 units @ $52.00 each
August 10	1,000 units @ $53.00 each
December 14	1,600 units @ $55.00 each

The Montclair Corporation had 1,000 units in its January 1 beginning inventory with a unit cost of $24 each. Montclair uses the periodic inventory system.

Required

a. Determine the cost assigned to Montclair's December 31 ending inventory and Montclair's cost of goods sold for the current year under each of the following inventory costing methods:

   1. Weighted-average cost   2. FIFO   3. LIFO

b. Determine Montclair's gross profit for the current year under each of the following inventory costing methods:

   1. Weighted-average cost   2. FIFO   3. LIFO

c. Determine Montclair's inventory turnover and days' sales in inventory for the current year under each of the following inventory costing methods:

   1. Weighted-average cost   2. FIFO   3. LIFO

Solution

a. Units available:

1,000 units @ $24.00 =	$ 24,000
2,000 units @ $27.00 =	54,000
3,000 units @ $28.40 =	85,200
1,200 units @ $31.25 =	37,500
7,200	$200,700

1. **Weighted-average cost:**

Weighted-average unit cost: $200,700/7,200 units = $ 27.875

Ending inventory: 1,400 units × $27.875 = $ 39,025

Cost of goods sold: $200,700 − $39,025 = $161,675

2. **FIFO:**

Ending inventory:	1,200 units @ $31.25 =	$ 37,500
	200 units @ $28.40 =	5,680
	1,400	$ 43,180

Cost of goods sold: $200,700 − $43,180 = $157,520

3. **LIFO:**

Ending inventory:	1,000 units @ $24.00 =	$ 24,000
	400 units @ $27.00 =	10,800
	1,400	$ 34,800

Cost of goods sold: $200,700 − $34,800 = $165,900

b. Sales revenue:

1,200 units @ $50.00 =	$ 60,000
2,000 units @ $52.00 =	104,000
1,000 units @ $53.00 =	53,000
1,600 units @ $55.00 =	88,000
5,800	$305,000

1. Weighted-average gross profit = $305,000 − $161,675 = $143,325
2. FIFO gross profit = $305,000 − $157,520 = $147,480
3. LIFO gross profit = $305,000 − $165,900 = $139,100

c.

	Inventory Turnover	Days' Sales in Inventory
Weighted-average cost...	5.13 = $161,675 / [($24,000 + $39,025) / 2]	71.2 days = 365 / 5.13
FIFO..............	4.69 = $157,5220 / [($24,000 + $43,180) / 2]	77.8 days = 365 / 4.69
LIFO..............	5.64 = $165,900 / [($24,000 + $34,800) / 2]	64.7 days = 365 / 5.64

APPENDIX 6A: Inventory Costing Methods and the Perpetual Inventory System

LO6 **Describe** inventory costing under a perpetual inventory system using specific identification, FIFO, LIFO, and weighted-average cost.

This appendix illustrates the accounting for inventories using the perpetual inventory system under the four generally accepted costing methods: (1) specific identification; (2) first-in, first-out (FIFO); (3) last-in, first-out (LIFO); and (4) weighted-average cost. All four methods are illustrated using the following data for Claremont Company.

MBC

Date	Event	No. of Units	Unit Cost		Total Cost
Jan. 1	Beginning inventory	60	@	$10 =	$ 600
Mar. 27	Purchase inventory.	90	@	11 =	990
	Goods available for sale	150			$1,590
May 2	**Sell inventory**	**(130)**			
Aug. 15	Purchase inventory.	100	@	13 =	1,300
Nov. 6	Purchase inventory.	50	@	16 =	800
	Goods available for sale	170			$3,690
Dec. 10	**Sell inventory**	**(90)**			
Dec. 31	Ending inventory.	80			

Under all four inventory costing methods, the Inventory account is increased each time a purchase occurs for the amount of the purchase and is decreased each time a sale occurs by an amount equal to the cost of goods sold. The methods differ only in the computation of cost of goods sold, consisting of 220 units (130 + 90 = 220), and the year-end Inventory account balance, consisting of 80 units remaining.

Specific Identification Method

Under the **specific identification method**, the actual cost of the specific units sold is identified and used to compute the cost of goods sold. To illustrate, assume that 50 of the 130 units sold on May 2 came from the beginning inventory of 60 units, and the remaining 80 units sold (50 + 80 = 130) came from the purchase of 90 units on March 27. Also, assume that 10 of the 90 units sold on December 10 came from the purchase of 90 units on March 27, and the remaining 80 units sold (10 + 80 = 90) came from the purchase of 100 units on August 15. **Exhibit 6A-1** illustrates the calculation of cost of goods sold and ending inventory using specific identification. The cost of goods sold is $2,530 (sum of the Sold Total column), and the ending inventory of 80 units, consisting of 10 units from the beginning inventory, 20 units from the August 15 purchase, and 50 units from the November 6 purchase, is valued at $1,160 (final amount in the Inventory Balance Total column).

EXHIBIT 6A-1	**Specific Identification Method (Perpetual Inventory System)**								
	Purchased			**Sold**			**Inventory Balance**		
Date	Units	Unit Cost	Total	Units	Unit Cost	Total	Units	Unit Cost	Total
Jan. 1							60	$10	$ 600
Mar. 27	90	$11	$ 990				60	10	⎤ 1,590
							90	11	⎦
May 2				50	$10	$ 500	10	10	⎤ 210
				80	11	880	10	11	⎦
Aug. 15	100	13	1,300				10	10	⎤
							10	11	1,510
							100	13	⎦
Nov. 6	50	16	800				10	10	⎤
							10	11	2,310
							100	13	
							50	16	⎦
Dec. 10				10	11	110	10	10	⎤
				80	13	1,040	20	13	1,160
							50	16	⎦
Total						$2,530			

First-In, First-Out (FIFO) Method

Under the **first-in, first-out (FIFO) method**, each time that a sale is made, the cost of the oldest goods available at that time are charged to cost of goods sold.

Results of the FIFO method are in **Exhibit 6A-2**. FIFO handles the May 2 sale of 130 units as follows: The oldest units are the units in the January 1 beginning inventory. These are the first 60 units assumed to be sold. The next oldest units are the units purchased on March 27; 70 units are needed from this purchase (130 sold – 60 from January 1) to provide all of the units sold on May 2. After the May 2 sale, only 20 units remain, all from the March 27 purchase.

The December 10 sale of 90 units is handled in a similar manner. The oldest units at December 10 are the 20 units remaining from the March 27 purchase. These are the first units assumed to be sold. The next oldest units are the 100 units purchased on August 15; 70 additional units are needed for the sale (90 sold − 20 from the March 27 purchase). Therefore, 70 of the 100 units purchased on August 15 are assumed to be included in the units sold on December 10. After the December 10 sale, 30 units remain from the August 15 purchase, and 50 units remain from the November 6 purchase.

Cost of goods sold using the FIFO method is $2,500 (sum of the Sold Total column), and the ending inventory is $1,190 (final amount in the Inventory Balance Total column).

EXHIBIT 6A-2	First-In, First-Out Method (Perpetual Inventory System)								
	Purchased			**Sold**			**Inventory Balance**		
Date	**Units**	**Unit Cost**	**Total**	**Units**	**Unit Cost**	**Total**	**Units**	**Unit Cost**	**Total**
Jan. 1							60	$10	$ 600
Mar. 27	90	$11	$ 990				60	10	}1,590
							90	11	
May 2				60	$10	$ 600			
				70	11	770	20	11	220
Aug. 15	100	13	1,300				20	11	}1,520
							100	13	
Nov. 6	50	16	800				20	11	}
							100	13	}2,320
							50	16	
Dec. 10				20	11	220	30	13	}1,190
				70	13	910	50	16	
Total						$2,500			

Last-In, First-Out (LIFO) Method

When the **last-in, first-out (LIFO) method** is used, the cost of the most recent inventory purchased is charged to cost of goods sold when a sale occurs.

Exhibit 6A-3 illustrates the results using LIFO. The LIFO method handles the May 2 sale of 130 units as follows: The most recently purchased units (newest units) are the units from the March 27 purchase. These are the first 90 units assumed to be sold. The next newest units are the units in the January 1 beginning inventory; 40 units from the January 1 units are needed (130 sold − 90 from the March 27 purchase) to provide all of the units sold on May 2. After the May 2 sale, only 20 units remain, all from the January 1 beginning inventory.

The December 10 sale of 90 units is handled in a similar manner. The newest units at December 10 are the 50 units purchased on November 6. These are the first units assumed to be sold. The next newest units are the 100 units purchased on August 15; 40 additional units are needed for the sale (90 sold − 50 from the November 6 purchase). Therefore, 40 of the 100 units purchased on August 15 are assumed to be included in the units sold on December 10. After the sale, 20 units remain from the January 1 inventory, and 60 units remain from the August 15 purchase.

Cost of goods sold using LIFO is $2,710 (sum of the Sold Total column), and the ending inventory is $980 (final amount in the Inventory Balance Total column).

EXHIBIT 6A-3	Last-In, First-Out Method (Perpetual Inventory System)									
	Purchased			**Sold**			**Inventory Balance**			
Date	Units	Unit Cost	Total	Units	Unit Cost	Total	Units	Unit Cost	Total	
Jan. 1							60	$10	$ 600	
Mar. 27	90	$11	$ 990				60	10	⎱ 1,590	
							90	11	⎰	
May 2				90	$11	$ 990				
				40	10	400	20	10	200	
Aug. 15	100	13	1,300				20	10	⎱ 1,500	
							100	13	⎰	
Nov. 6	50	16	800				20	10	⎱	
							100	13	⎰ 2,300	
							50	16		
Dec. 10				50	16	800	20	10	⎱ 980	
				40	13	520	60	13	⎰	
Total						$2,710				

Weighted-Average Cost Method

When the **weighted-average cost method** is used, a new weighted-average unit cost is calculated (**equal to the total cost divided by total units**) each time that goods are purchased and added to inventory. The cost of goods sold for each sale is calculated by multiplying the weighted-average unit cost at the time of sale by the number of units sold. **Exhibit 6A-4** illustrates the calculation of cost of goods sold and ending inventory under the weighted-average cost method. The weighted-average unit cost is calculated three times in **Exhibit 6A-4**. On March 27, 90 units were purchased at a unit cost of $11, and the updated weighted-average unit cost on this date is:

$$[\$600 + \$990]/[60 \text{ units} + 90 \text{ units}] = \$10.60$$

The weighted-average unit cost of $10.60 is used to calculate the cost of the 130 units sold on May 2, or $130 \times \$10.60 = \$1,378$.

On August 15, 100 units were purchased at a unit cost of $13. The updated weighted-average unit cost on this date is:

$$[\$212 + \$1,300]/[20 \text{ units} + 100 \text{ units}] = \$12.60$$

On November 6, 50 units were purchased at a unit cost of $16. The updated weighted-average unit cost on this date is:

$$[\$1,512 + \$800]/[120 \text{ units} + 50 \text{ units}] = \$13.60$$

The weighted-average unit cost of $13.60 is used to calculate the cost of the 130 units sold on December 10, or $90 \times \$13.60 = \$1,224$.

The total cost of goods sold is $2,602 (sum of the Sold Total column), and the ending inventory is $1,088 (final amount in the Inventory Balance Total column).

EXHIBIT 6A-4	Weighted-Average Cost Method (Perpetual Inventory System)								
	Purchased			**Sold**			**Inventory Balance**		
Date	Units	Unit Cost	Total	Units	Unit Cost	Total	Units	Weighted-Average Unit Cost	Total
Jan. 1							60	$10.00	$ 600
Mar. 27	90	$11	$ 990				150	10.60	1,590
May 2				130	$10.60	$1,378	20	10.60	212
Aug. 15	100	13	1,300				120	12.60	1,512
Nov. 6	50	16	800				170	13.60	2,312
Dec. 10				90	13.60	1,224	80	13.60	1,088
Total						$2,602			

Comparative Analysis of Inventory Costing Methods

The purchase price data used in the Claremont Company illustration has an important characteristic: the purchase price of the inventory increased each time that a purchase was made, from $11 per unit to $13 per unit to $16 per unit. Increasing inventory prices are frequently encountered in the real world where price inflation is common and price deflation is uncommon. **Exhibit 6A-5** summarizes the results of applying the four inventory costing methods to the Claremont Company data and reveals that the FIFO method produces the lowest cost of goods sold ($2,500), while the LIFO method produces the highest cost of goods sold ($2,710). The exhibit also reveals that FIFO produces the highest year-end value of ending inventory ($1,190), while LIFO produces the lowest year-end value of ending inventory ($980). Weighted-average cost produces ending inventory values and cost of goods sold values that fall in between the results obtained using FIFO and LIFO.

These results, however, are highly dependent on the purchase prices for the inventory. If the inventory's purchase price had been decreasing rather than increasing, the financial effects would have been just the opposite, with LIFO producing the lowest cost of goods sold and FIFO the highest. If the purchase prices had been perfectly stable, there would be no difference between the cost of goods sold or the ending inventory for any of the four methods.

EXHIBIT 6A-5	Results of Different Inventory Costing Methods			
	Specific Identification	FIFO	LIFO	Weighted-Average
Cost of goods sold	$2,530	$2,500	$2,710	$2,602
Ending inventory.	1,160	1,190	980	1,088

To illustrate the financial effects of the different inventory costing methods, assume that the 220 units sold by the Claremont Company were sold for $20 each, producing sales of $4,400 ($20 × 220). **Exhibit 6A-6** shows the difference in gross profit under each of the four inventory costing methods. Remember that the difference in reported gross profit results from the assumptions made about cost flow, not from any difference in the physical flow of goods. In each case, 220 units were sold and 80 units remained. Each of the inventory costing methods is in accord with generally accepted accounting principles, yet the methods have different financial effects on gross profit and net income.

EXHIBIT 6A-6	Gross Profit Using Alternative Inventory Costing Methods			
	Specific Identification	FIFO	LIFO	Weighted-Average
Sales (220 units @ $20).	$4,400	$4,400	$4,400	$4,400
Cost of goods sold	2,530	2,500	2,710	2,602
Gross profit.	$1,870	$1,900	$1,690	$1,798
Increased gross profit compared with LIFO	$ 180	$ 210		$ 108

Income Statement and Balance Sheet Effects

As **Exhibit 6A-6** reveals, LIFO results in the smallest gross profit ($1,690), with FIFO producing the highest ($1,900) gross profit. This result occurs because the purchase price of inventory was increasing throughout the year, from $11 per unit to $13 per unit to $16 per unit. When costs are rising, FIFO tends to overstate gross profit (and income) because older, lower unit costs are included in the cost of goods sold and matched with current sales prices. In other words, the units sold are charged to costs of goods sold under FIFO at unit costs of $10, $11, and $13. If the latest purchase price reflects the inventory's current acquisition cost, the units sold must be replaced by units costing $16 (or more if costs continue to rise).

It is frequently argued that LIFO provides a better matching of current costs with current revenues since the cost of the most recent purchases constitutes the LIFO cost of goods sold. While LIFO associates the current, higher unit costs with cost of goods sold, it assigns costs to ending inventory using the older, lower unit costs. As a consequence, the value of the LIFO ending inventory on the balance sheet is often undervalued in terms of the inventory's current value. When inventory quantities are maintained or increased, the LIFO method prevents older costs from appearing in the cost of goods sold. No doubt, some firms still carry LIFO inventories at unit costs that existed more than 10 years ago. Under FIFO, the ending inventory is measured at relatively recent costs.

Comparison of Inventory Costing Methods for Periodic and Perpetual Inventory Systems

Exhibit 6A-7 summarizes the results of applying the periodic and perpetual inventory systems under the four costing methods using the same Claremont data. The specific identification method and the FIFO method yield the same results for ending inventory and cost of goods sold regardless of whether the periodic or the perpetual method is being used. Only the LIFO and weighted-average methods produce different results under the periodic and perpetual systems.

EXHIBIT 6A-7	Summary Results of Different Inventory Costing Methods		
Costing Method		**Ending Inventory**	**Cost of Goods Sold**
Specific identification			
Periodic		$1,160	$2,530
Perpetual		1,160	2,530
FIFO			
Periodic		1,190	2,500
Perpetual		1,190	2,500
LIFO			
Periodic		820	2,870
Perpetual		980	2,710
Average			
Periodic		984	2,706
Perpetual		1,088	2,602

Choice of a periodic versus perpetual system does *not* affect specific identification or FIFO.

Choice of a periodic versus perpetual system does affect LIFO and weighted-average results.

The following information applies to the Kensington Company.

Jan. 1 Beginning inventory 1,000 units at $5 each

Jan. 5 Purchased 600 units at $6 each

Jan. 15 Sold 200 units

Jan. 17 Purchased 300 units at $7 each

Jan. 25 Sold 400 units

Kensington Company utilizes a perpetual inventory system. Calculate the cost of goods sold and ending inventory using the following methods.

a. FIFO   *b.* LIFO   *c.* Weighted-average

Guided Example

MBC

The solution is on page 6-51.

APPENDIX 6B: LIFO Reserve

As shown in this chapter, the LIFO inventory costing method can produce significantly different results relative to other inventory costing methods for both ending inventory and cost of goods sold, and therefore gross profit and net income. The difference is greatest when compared to results obtained using FIFO. When costs are rising, FIFO will result in higher reported ending inventory, lower cost of goods sold, and higher net income relative to LIFO.

L07 **Define** the LIFO reserve and **explain** how it is used to compare the performance of companies using LIFO and FIFO inventory costing methods.

To make comparisons between companies using LIFO and companies using FIFO, we need to use the **LIFO inventory reserve**, or simply *LIFO reserve*. Companies that use LIFO are required under generally accepted accounting principles to report the difference between ending inventory using LIFO and the inventory that would have been reported under FIFO. This difference is called the LIFO inventory reserve and is disclosed in notes to financial statements.

eLecture

MBC

Referring to **Exhibit 6-8** in the chapter, FIFO ending inventory is valued at $1,190 and LIFO ending inventory at $820. The LIFO reserve is $370 ($1,190 – $820). Use of LIFO can have a material impact on many ratios, and one way to compensate for these effects is to use the LIFO reserve to restate the reported inventory and cost of goods sold to a FIFO basis. To illustrate, assume that Claremont Company, whose inventory costing method results are compared in **Exhibit 6-8**, has current assets of $2,100 and current liabilities of $1,400 under the LIFO method. **Exhibit 6B-1** calculates the current ratio (current assets divided by current liabilities) under both LIFO and FIFO. (The current ratio is discussed in Chapter 2.)

Hint: The LIFO
reserve is also
used to restate
the LIFO cost
of goods sold
to that under
FIFO. The LIFO
cost of goods
sold minus
the change
in the LIFO
reserve from the
beginning to the
end of the period
equals FIFO cost
of goods sold.

EXHIBIT 6B-1   Impact of the LIFO Inventory Reserve on the Current Ratio

	LIFO	FIFO
Current ratio	$\dfrac{\$2,100}{\$1,400} = 1.50$	$\dfrac{(\$2,100 + \$370)}{\$1,400} = 1.76$

As shown in **Exhibit 6B-1**, the current ratio is higher under FIFO (1.76) than under LIFO (1.50). Differences occur between LIFO and FIFO companies for many ratios, with FIFO resulting in more favorable ratios in most cases since FIFO generally results in higher inventory values and higher net earnings. For some ratios, however, LIFO produces more favorable results. Two examples are the inventory turnover ratio and the days' sales in inventory ratio. Because LIFO results in lower inventory values, the inventory turnover (and consequently, the days' sales in inventory) under LIFO appears higher (lower) than it does under FIFO. (The LIFO reserve also affects cost of goods sold and therefore the numerator of the inventory turnover ratio; in most cases the adjustment to cost of goods sold is much smaller than the adjustment to average inventory, leading to a higher inventory turnover under LIFO than under FIFO.)

TAKEAWAY 6.2

Concept ➡	Method ➡	Assessment ➡
What effect does the use of LIFO have on ending inventory relative to the use of FIFO?	Ending inventory and the LIFO inventory reserve The value of LIFO ending inventory + the LIFO inventory reserve = The value of FIFO ending inventory	If the LIFO reserve is material, it can have a significant impact on many ratios when compared to FIFO. The calculation of these ratios can be adjusted using the LIFO inventory reserve to provide a more comparable set of results.

YOUR TURN! 6B.1

The solution is on page 6-51.

Adams Inc. reports ending inventory under the LIFO method at $165,000. Adams also discloses a LIFO reserve of $20,000. What would Adams have reported for ending inventory if it had used FIFO rather than LIFO?.

SUMMARY OF LEARNING OBJECTIVES

LO1   **Explain inventory concepts and management practices. (p. 6-3)**

- Merchandise inventory is a stock of goods that a merchandising company buys from a manufacturer and makes available for sale to its customers.
- A manufacturing firm maintains three different inventory categories: raw materials inventory, work-in-process inventory, and finished goods inventory.
- Traditionally, manufacturers have maintained just-in-case inventories of raw materials and components to provide for unplanned production or delayed raw material shipments, resulting in high levels of inventory carrying costs.
- Many manufacturers have adopted a just-in-time (JIT) manufacturing philosophy, which is designed to eliminate or minimize raw materials, work-in-process, and finished goods inventories. The key to JIT manufacturing is careful inventory order planning and sophisticated production management.
- Ownership of goods in transit depends on the shipping terms. The buyer assumes ownership of goods in transit shipped F.O.B. shipping point, whereas the seller maintains ownership of goods shipped F.O.B. destination until the buyer assumes possession at delivery.
- Consignment goods are goods held for sale by parties other than the owner. The owner maintains legal ownership of these inventory items while they are held for sale by the consignment seller.
- The year-end physical count of inventory is taken to verify the inventory balance. It consists of three steps:
  1. Count the number of individual items of merchandise on hand at the end of the year.
  2. Determine the unit cost of each item and multiply the unit cost times the quantity on hand to obtain the total cost for each item of merchandise.
  3. Add together the total cost of all the items to obtain the total cost of the inventory on hand.

Describe inventory costing under specific identification, FIFO, LIFO, and weighted-average cost. (p. 6-7)   **LO2**

- To assign cost to units sold (cost of goods sold) and units available (inventory), a company must either keep track of the cost of each specific unit (specific identification method) or make an assumption about which units have been sold (weighted-average cost, FIFO, and LIFO methods).
- The weighted-average cost method assumes that a mix of the goods available is sold; the FIFO method assumes that the oldest goods are sold first; and the LIFO method assumes that the newest goods are sold first.

Analyze the effects of different inventory costing methods on company profit. (p. 6-12)   **LO3**

- Each of the alternative inventory costing methods produces a different cost of goods sold and gross profit unless purchase prices have been perfectly stable.
- When costs are rising, the LIFO method does the best job of matching current costs with revenues; LIFO also produces a lower gross profit and lower income taxes than either weighted-average cost or FIFO.

Apply the lower-of-cost-or-net realizable value method. (p. 6-17)   **LO4**

- Damaged, physically deteriorated, or obsolete merchandise should be valued and reported at its net realizable value—that is, its estimated selling price less the expected cost of disposal.
- The lower-of-cost-or-net realizable value method provides for inventory write-downs to be recorded in the period that the net realizable value of inventory declines below the inventory's acquisition cost.

Define *inventory turnover* and *day's sales in inventory* and explain the use of these ratios. (p. 6-19)   **LO5**

- Inventory turnover and days' sales in inventory indicate, respectively, how many times on average during the year a firm sells its inventory and how many days on average it takes a firm to sell its inventory.
- Inventory turnover and days' sales in inventory provide evidence regarding a firm's ability to sell its inventory and its ability to effectively manage its investment in inventory.

Appendix 6A: Describe inventory costing under a perpetual inventory system using specific identification, FIFO, LIFO, and weighted-average cost. (p. 6-21)   **LO6**

- To assign cost to units sold (cost of goods sold) and units available (inventory), a company must either keep track of the cost of each specific unit (specific identification method) or make an assumption about which units have been sold (weighted-average cost, FIFO, and LIFO methods).
- The weighted-average cost method assumes that a mix of the goods available is sold; the FIFO method assumes that the oldest goods are sold; and the LIFO method assumes that the newest goods are sold.
- The specific identification method and the FIFO method yield the same results for ending inventory and for cost of goods sold regardless of whether the periodic or the perpetual method is being used. Only LIFO and weighted-average methods produce different results.

Appendix 6B: Define the LIFO reserve and explain how it is used to compare the performance of companies using LIFO and FIFO inventory costing methods. (p. 6-26)   **LO7**

- The LIFO inventory reserve represents the difference between the value of LIFO ending inventory and what the value of ending inventory would have been under FIFO.
- The LIFO inventory reserve can cause a material effect on many ratios. These ratios should be adjusted for the LIFO inventory reserve when comparing a company using LIFO with a FIFO company.

Concept ⟶	Method ⟶	Assessment	SUMMARY
How long, on average, does it take to sell the inventory?	Cost of goods sold, beginning inventory, and ending inventory $\text{Inventory turnover} = \dfrac{\text{Cost of goods sold}}{\text{Average inventory}}$ $\text{Days' sales in inventory} = \dfrac{365}{\text{Inventory turnover}}$	A higher inventory turnover or a lower days' sales in inventory indicates that the company is able to sell its inventory more quickly.	**TAKEAWAY 6.1**
What effect does the use of LIFO have on ending inventory relative to the use of FIFO?	Ending inventory and the LIFO inventory reserve The value of LIFO ending inventory + the LIFO inventory reserve = The value of FIFO ending inventory	If the LIFO reserve is material, it can have a significant impact on many ratios when compared to FIFO. The calculation of these ratios can be adjusted using the LIFO inventory reserve to provide a more comparable set of results.	**TAKEAWAY 6.2**

KEY TERMS

Consignment goods (p. 6-5)

Cost flow (p. 6-7)

Days' sales in inventory (p. 6-19)

Finished goods inventory (p. 6-3)

First-in, first-out (FIFO) method (p. 6-9, 6-22)

F.O.B. destination (p. 6-5)

F.O.B. shipping point (p. 6-5)

Goods flow (p. 6-7)

Goods in transit (p. 6-5)

Inventory carrying costs (p. 6-4)

Inventory overage (p. 6-6)

Inventory shrinkage (p. 6-6)

Inventory turnover ratio (p. 6-19)

Just-in-case inventory (p. 6-4)

Just-in-time (JIT) manufacturing (p. 6-4)

Last-in, first-out (LIFO) method (p. 6-10, 6-23)

LIFO conformity rule (p. 6-14)

LIFO inventory reserve (p. 6-26)

Lower-of-cost-or-net realizable value (p. 6-17)

Net realizable value (NRV) (p. 6-17)

Physical count of inventory (p. 6-6)

Raw materials inventory (p. 6-3)

Specific identification method (p. 6-8, 6-22)

Stock-out costs (p. 6-4)

Weighted-average cost method (p. 6-11, 6-24)

Work-in-process inventory (p. 6-3)

Assignments with the (MBC) logo in the margin are available in BusinessCourse.
See the Preface of the book for details.

SELF-STUDY QUESTIONS

(Answers to Self-Study Questions are at the end of this chapter.)

LO1 1. **Which of the following concepts relates to the elimination or minimization of inventories by a manufacturing firm?**

    a. Quick response   *c.* Just-in-case

    b. Just-in-time   *d.* Specific identification

LO2 2. **Which inventory costing method assumes that the most recently purchased merchandise is sold first?**

    a. Specific identification   *c.* FIFO

    b. Weighted-average cost   *d.* LIFO

LO3 3. **Which inventory costing method results in the highest-valued ending inventory during a period of rising unit costs?**

    a. Specific identification   *c.* FIFO

    b. Weighted-average cost   *d.* LIFO

LO1 4. **Under which of the following freight terms does the seller retain ownership of the shipped goods?**

    a. F.O.B. shipping point   *b.* F.O.B. destination

LO4 5. **When should ending inventory be written down below its acquisition cost on the balance sheet?**

    a. When units are damaged, physically deteriorated, or obsolete.

    b. When the inventory's net realizable value exceeds its acquisition cost.

    c. When the inventory's net realizable value is below its acquisition cost.

    d. Both a and c.

LO3 6. **Which inventory costing method results in the highest net income during a period of rising unit prices?**

    a. Specific identification   *c.* FIFO

    b. Weighted-average cost   *d.* LIFO

LO3 7. **Which inventory costing method is expensive to implement?**

    a. Specific identification   *c.* FIFO

    b. Weighted-average cost   *d.* LIFO

LO3 8. **Which inventory costing method is frequently used when identical units are stored in a common area?**

    a. Specific identification   *c.* FIFO

    b. Weighted-average cost   *d.* LIFO

LO3 9. **Which inventory costing method results in the lowest net income during a period of rising unit prices?**

    a. Specific identification   *c.* FIFO

    b. Weighted-average cost   *d.* LIFO

10. Which inventory costing method does not require the use of the lower-of-cost-or-net realizable value method? **LO4**

    a. Specific Identification   *c.* FIFO

    b. Weighted-average cost   *d.* LIFO

11. Mack Corp. reported annual cost of goods sold of $30,000 and average inventory on hand during the year of $3,750. What was Mack's inventory turnover? **LO5**

    a. 0.125 times   *c.* $26,250

    b. 8.0 times   *d.* 8.0%

12. The Molly Company reports ending inventory under the LIFO method of $15,000. Had Molly used FIFO, the ending inventory would have been reported as $16,500. Molly's LIFO inventory reserve is: **LO7** (Appendix 6B)

    a. $31,500   *c.* $1,500

    b. $15,000   *d.* 91%

13. The periodic inventory system differs from the perpetual inventory system: **LO6** (Appendix 6A)

    a. because the periodic system is not compatible with modern technology.

    b. because the perpetual system continually updates inventory, while the periodic inventory system only updates inventory at the end of the period.

    c. because the periodic system continually updates inventory, while the perpetual inventory system only updates inventory at the end of the period.

    d. because the periodic system is more complex and costly.

QUESTIONS

1. What are the three inventory accounts maintained by a manufacturing firm? Define each.

2. ShopMart Stores use point-of-sale equipment at their checkout counters to read universal bar codes. They also use a quick response system. What is a quick response system?

3. What are *just-in-case inventory* and *inventory carrying costs?*

4. What is the *just-in-time manufacturing philosophy?* Describe it.

5. What is meant by *goods flow* and *cost flow?*

6. Describe how each of the following inventory costing methods is used with the perpetual inventory system: (a) Specific identification; (b) Weighted-average cost; (c) First-in, first-out; and (d) Last-in, first-out.

7. Describe the type of inventory for which the goods flow would most naturally correspond to the cost flow for each of the inventory costing methods: (a) Specific identification, (b) Weighted-average cost, (c) FIFO, and (d) LIFO.

8. Why do relatively stable purchase prices reduce the significance of the choice of an inventory costing method?

9. What is the nature of FIFO *phantom profits* during periods of rising inventory purchase prices?

10. If costs have been rising, which inventory costing method—weighted-average cost; first-in, first-out; or last-in, first-out—yields (a) the lowest ending inventory value? (b) the lowest net income? (c) the largest ending inventory value? (d) the largest net income?

11. Even though it does not represent their goods flow, why might firms adopt last-in, first-out inventory costing during periods when inventory costs are rising?

12. Describe a situation in which merchandise must be valued on the balance sheet at an amount less than its acquisition cost.

13. Which of the following is not an inventory costing method?

    a. Specific identification   *c.* Just-in-time manufacturing

    b. Weighted-average cost   *d.* FIFO

14. What is the effect on reported net income of applying the lower-of-cost-or-net realizable value method to ending inventory?

15. How do the accounting principles of consistency and full disclosure apply to inventory costing?

16. Which party, the seller or the buyer, bears the freight cost when the terms are F.O.B. shipping point? When the terms are F.O.B. destination?

17. What is a LIFO inventory reserve, and how can it be useful to an analyst?

18. Moyer Company has an inventory turnover of 4.51. What is Moyer's days' sales in inventory?

CRAFTMADE
INTERNATIONAL, INC.

19. In an annual report, **Craftmade International, Inc.**, describes its inventory accounting policies as follows:

> Inventories are stated at the lower-of-cost-or-net realizable value, with inventory cost determined using the first-in, first-out (FIFO) method. The cost of inventory includes freight-in and duties on imported goods.

KAISER ALUMINUM
CORPORATION

Also in an annual report, **Kaiser Aluminum Corporation** made the following statement in discussing its inventories:

> The Company recorded pretax charges of approximately $19.4 million because of a reduction in the carrying values of its inventories caused principally by prevailing lower prices for alumina, primary aluminum, and fabricated products.

What accounting principle did Craftmade International follow when it included the costs of freight-in and duties on imported goods in its Inventory account? Briefly describe how a firm determines which costs to include in its inventory account. What accounting principle did Kaiser Aluminum follow when it recorded the $19.4 million pretax charge? Briefly describe the rationale for this principle.

20. What are the three steps that make up the year-end physical count of inventory?

SHORT EXERCISES

LO4

MBC

SE6-1. Departures from Acquisition Cost At year-end, The Kitchen Shop has a refrigerator that has been used as a demonstration model. The refrigerator cost $585 and sells for $750 when new. In its present condition, the refrigerator will be sold for $530. Related selling costs are an estimated $15. At what amount should the refrigerator be carried in inventory?

a. $550   c. $525
b. $535   d. $515

LO2

MBC

SE6-2. Inventory Costing Methods Which inventory costing method requires that a company keep track of the cost of each specific unit of inventory?

a.   Specific identification   c.   LIFO
b.   Lower of cost or market method   d.   All of the above

LO1

MBC

SE6-3. Identify Goods to Be Included in Inventory Lisa Company has the following items at year-end. Identify which items should be included in Lisa's year-end inventory count.

1. Goods held on consignment by Sell For You Company.
2. Goods held by Lisa on consignment that will be sold for another company.
3. Goods in transit sent to a client F.O.B. shipping point.
4. Goods in transit sent to a client F.O.B. destination.

LO4

MBC

SE6-4. Lower-of-Cost-or-Net Realizable Value Method The Claremont Company's ending inventory is composed of 50 units that had cost $20 each and 100 units that had cost $15 each. If all 150 units have an NRV of $16 each, what value should be assigned to the company's ending inventory assuming that it applies lower-of-cost-or-net realizable value on a group-wise basis?

LO4

MBC

SE6-5. Lower-of-Cost-or-Net Realizable Value Method The McQuenny Company's ending inventory is composed of 100 units that had an acquisition cost of $25 per unit and 50 units that had an acquisition cost of $30 per unit. If 150 units have an NRV of $27 per unit, what value should be assigned to the company's ending inventory assuming that it applies the lower-of-cost-or-net realizable value method on an individual item basis?

LO5

MBC

SE6-6. Inventory Turnover and Days' Sales in Inventory Bass & Company reported the following information in its recent annual report:

	Year 1	Year 2
Cost of goods sold	$4,000,000	$4,600,000
Beginning inventory	880,000	860,000
Ending inventory	860,000	760,000

Calculate the company's inventory turnover and days' sales in inventory for both years.

SE6-7. **Inventory Turnover and Days' Sales in Inventory** Hamm & Company disclosed the following information in its recent annual report: **LO5**

	Year 1	Year 2
Cost of goods sold	$16,000,000	$22,000,000
Beginning inventory	2,000,000	4,000,000
Ending inventory.	3,000,000	5,000,000

Calculate the company's inventory turnover and days' sales in inventory for both years.

SE6-8. **Inventory Costing Methods and the Periodic Method** Lamb Company experienced the following events in January: **LO2**

Date	Event	Units		Unit Cost	Total Cost
Jan. 10	Purchased inventory.	100	@	$14	$1,400
Jan. 20	Purchased inventory.	200	@	16	3,200
Jan. 30	Sold inventory.	150			

If the Lamb Company uses the FIFO inventory costing method, calculate the company's cost of goods sold and its ending inventory as of January 31 assuming the periodic method.

SE6-9. **Inventory Costing Methods and the Periodic Method** Deer Company experienced the following events in February: **LO2**

Date	Event	Units		Unit Cost	Total Cost
Feb. 1	Purchased inventory.	100	@	$18	$1,800
Feb. 4	Sold inventory.	50			
Feb. 9	Purchased inventory.	100	@	$21	$2,100
Feb. 27	Sold inventory.	100			

If the Deer Company uses the LIFO inventory costing method, calculate the company's cost of goods sold and ending inventory as of February 28 assuming the periodic method.

SE6-10. **Errors in Inventory Count** Pow Corp. accidentally overstated its previous year ending inventory by $750. Assume that ending current year inventory is accurately counted. The previous year error will have what effect on Pow Corp.? **LO3**

a. Previous year net income is understated by $750.

b. Previous year net income is overstated by $750.

c. Current year net income is understated by $750.

d. Both *b* and *c* are correct.

SE6-11. **Inventory Costing Methods and the Periodic Method** Kay & Company experienced the following events in March: **LO2**

Date	Event	Units		Unit Cost	Total Cost
Mar. 1	Purchased inventory.	100	@	$16	$1,600
Mar. 3	Sold inventory.	60			
Mar. 15	Purchased inventory.	100	@	$18	$1,800
Mar. 20	Sold inventory.	40			

If Kay & Company uses the weighted-average cost method, calculate the company's cost of goods sold and ending inventory as of March 31 assuming the periodic method.

SE6-12. **Inventory Costing Methods and the Perpetual Method** Refer to the information in SE6-11 and assume the perpetual inventory system is used. Use the weighted-average inventory costing method to calculate the company's cost of goods sold and ending inventory as of March 31. Round your final answers to the nearest dollar. **LO6** (Appendix 6A)

SE6-13. **Inventory Costing Methods and the Perpetual Method** Refer to the information in SE6-9 and assume the perpetual inventory system is used. Use the LIFO inventory costing method to calculate the company's cost of goods sold and ending inventory as of February 28. **LO6** (Appendix 6A)

LO7
(Appendix 6B)

SE6-14. LIFO Inventory Reserve Lamar Company reports ending inventory of $150,000 on a LIFO basis and also reports a LIFO inventory reserve of $32,000. If Lamar had used FIFO rather than LIFO, ending inventory would have been:

a. $123,000.   c. $177,000.
b. $150,000.   d. $182,000.

DATA ANALYTICS

DA6-1. Preparing an Excel Worksheet to Record Inventory at the Lower of Cost or Net Realizable Value The Excel file associated with this exercise includes a sheet (Inventory Data Sheet) with information regarding Lain Company's inventory including unit cost, cost of disposal, unit selling price, and quantity on hand. A second sheet (Inventory Obsolescence Sheet) includes information about inventory markdowns on the selling price due to obsolescence concerns. In this exercise, we calculate the value of inventory at the lower of cost or net realizable value. In doing so, we first update sales data with the latest inventory obsolescence information using a useful Excel function: VLOOKUP.

Required

1. Download Excel file DA6-1 found in myBusinessCourse.
2. In the Data-Inventory Obsolescence worksheet, use VLOOKUP to pull in the original selling price from the Data-Inventory worksheet. *Hint:* Use the Item number in the first column as the lookup value, the table in the Inventory Data Sheet for the source to pull from, the column titled Selling price per unit for the source data. This must be an exact match.
3. List the formula that is currently in cell D4 of your Inventory Obsolescence sheet.
4. Calculate the updated selling price, considering the mark-down percentage in the Updated Selling Price per Unit column. Round to two decimal places. What is the updated selling price for Item No.1823555?
5. Using the VLOOKUP function, add the updated selling price from the Data-Inventory Obsolescence worksheet to the Updated Selling Price per Unit column in the Data-Inventory worksheet.
6. Eliminate the errors in the cells in the Updated Selling Price per Unit column on the Data-Inventory worksheet by replacing the error with the original selling price per unit using the IFERROR function. *Hint:* Enclose the formula used in part 5 within the IFERRROR function: replace the error sign with the original selling price per unit.
7. List the formula that is currently in cell G5 of your Inventory Data sheet.
8. For each item, enter the net realizable value in the Net Realizable Value per Unit column.
9. Using an IF statement, calculate the lower of cost per unit or net realizable value per unit in the Lower of Cost or NRV per Unit column. *Hint:* If the cost per unit is less than the net realizable value per unit, show the cost per unit value in the cell; otherwise, show the net realizable value per unit in the cell.
10. Calculate the total inventory value at the lower of cost or net realizable value for each item in the Total Inventory Value column. What is the lower of cost or net realizable value for Item no. 1124503 (in total)? Item no. 1122812 (in total)?
11. List the total inventory value at the lower of cost or net realizable value.

DA6-2. Preparing Tableau Visualizations to Analyze Inventory Management Refer to PF-22 in Appendix F. This problem uses Tableau to create and analyze visualizations of inventory ratios of certain market segments of S&P 500 companies.

DATA VISUALIZATION

Data Visualization Activities are available in myBusinessCourse. These assignments use Tableau Dashboards to expose students to visual depictions of data and introduce students to data analytics through data visualizations. These exercises are easily assignable and auto graded by MBC.

EXERCISES—SET A

LO1

E6-1A. Just-in-Time Inventories Mitch Manufacturing Company uses the perpetual inventory system and plans to use raw materials costing $1,200,000 in manufacturing its products. Mitch will operate its factory 300 days during the year. Currently, Mitch follows the just-in-case philosophy with its raw materials inventory, keeping raw materials costing $12,000 in its raw materials inventory. Mitch plans to switch to the just-in-time manufacturing philosophy by keeping only the raw materials needed for the next two days of production. Calculate the new raw materials inventory level after Mitch implements the just-in-time manufacturing philosophy in its factory.

E6-2A. **Inventory Costing Methods—Periodic Method** The Luann Company uses the periodic inventory system. The following July data are for an item in Luann's inventory: **LO2**

July 1 Beginning inventory, 30 units @ $9 per unit.
  10 Purchased 50 units @ $11 per unit.
  15 Sold 60 units.
  26 Purchased 25 units @ $13 per unit.

Calculate the cost of goods sold for July and ending inventory at July 31 using (a) first-in, first-out, (b) last-in, first-out, and (c) the weighted-average cost methods. Round the cost per unit to three decimal places and your final answers to the nearest dollar.

E6-3A. **Year-End Physical Inventory** The December 31 inventory for the Jeremy Company included five products. The year-end physical count revealed the following: **LO1**

Product	Quantity Available
A	26
B	50
C	71
D	75
E	55

The related unit costs were: A, $10; B, $6; C, $9; D, $8; and E, $11.

Required
Calculate the total cost of the December 31 physical inventory.

E6-4A. **Inventory Costing Methods—Periodic Method** Arrow Company is a retailer that uses the periodic inventory system. On August 1, it had 80 units of product A at a total cost of $1,600. On August 5, Arrow purchased 100 units of A for $2,116. On August 8, it purchased 200 units of A for $4,416. On August 11, it sold 170 units of A for $4,800. Calculate the August cost of goods sold and the ending inventory at August 31 using (a) first-in, first-out, (b) last-in, first-out, and (c) the weighted-average cost methods. Round your final answers to the nearest dollar. **LO2**

E6-5A. **Errors in Inventory Counts** The following information was taken from the records of Tinker Enterprises: **LO3**

	Year 1	Year 2
Beginning inventory	$ 50,000	$ 60,000
Cost of goods purchased	400,000	420,000
Cost of goods available for sale	450,000	480,000
Ending inventory	60,000	55,000
Cost of goods sold	$390,000	$425,000

The following two errors were made in the physical inventory counts:
1. Year 1 ending inventory was understated by $8,000.
2. Year 2 ending inventory was overstated by $4,000.

Compute the correct cost of goods sold for both years.

E6-6A. **Departures from Acquisition Cost** Determine the proper total inventory value for each of the following items in Viking Company's ending inventory: **LO4**

a. Viking has 500 video games in stock. The games cost $36 each, but their year-end net realizable value is $28.

b. Viking has 400 rolls of photographic film that are past the expiration date marked on the film's box. The films cost $1.65 each and are normally sold for $3.30. To clear out these old films, Viking will drop their selling price to $1.30. There are no related selling costs.

c.   Viking has seven cameras in stock that have been used as demonstration models. The cameras cost $380 and normally sell for $480. Because these cameras are in used condition, Viking has set the selling price at $360 each. Expected selling costs are $15 per camera.

LO2   E6-7A. Inventory Costing Methods—Periodic Method The following information is for the Bud Company; the company sells just one product:

		Units	Unit Cost
Beginning inventory		200	$10
Purchases:	Feb. 11	500	14
	May 18	400	16
	October 23	100	22

At year-end, there was an ending inventory of 340 units. Assume the use of the periodic inventory method. Calculate the value of ending inventory and the cost of goods sold for the year using (a) first-in, first-out, (b) last-in, first-out, and (c) the weighted-average cost method.

LO2   E6-8A. Inventory Costing Methods—Periodic Method The following data are for the Vista Company, which sells just one product:

		Units	Unit Cost
Beginning inventory, January 1.		200	$10
Purchases:	February 11	500	14
	May 18	400	17
	October 23	100	18
Sales	March 1.	400	
	July 1	380	

Calculate the value of ending inventory and cost of goods sold using the periodic method and (a) first-in, first-out, (b) last-in, first-out, and (c) weighted-average cost method. Round your final answers to the nearest dollar.

LO4, 5   E6-9A. Applying IFRS LVMH is a Paris-based manufacturer of luxury goods that prepares its financial statements using IFRS. During the year, the management of the company undertook a review of the fair value of its inventory and found that the inventory had appreciated above its book value of 12 million euros. According to the company's management, the inventory was undervalued by 3 million euros. (*Hint:* Credit Asset, revaluation reserve. Prepare the journal entry to revalue the company's inventory. How would the revaluation immediately affect the company's (a) current ratio, (b) inventory turnover, and (c) days' sales in inventory?

LO4   E6-10A. Lower-of-Cost-or-Net Realizable Value Method The following data are taken from the Browning Corporation's inventory accounts:

Item Code	Quantity	Unit Cost	Net Realizable Value
ACE	100	$27	$25
BDF	300	29	31
GHJ	400	22	18
MBS	200	23	27

Calculate the value of the company's ending inventory using the lower-of-cost-or-net realizable value method applied to each item of inventory.

LO5   E6-11A. Inventory Turnover and Days' Sales in Inventory Shown below are data from the Northern Company's accounting records:

	Year 1	Year 2
Sales revenue.	$8,000,000	$11,000,000
Cost of goods sold	4,000,000	4,800,000
Beginning inventory	510,000	540,000
Ending inventory.	550,000	600,000

Calculate the company's (a) inventory turnover and (b) days' sales in inventory for both years. Comment on your results.

E6-12A. Lower-of-Cost-or-Net Realizable Value Method The following data refer to the Ian Company's ending inventory: **LO4**

Item Code	Quantity	Unit Cost	Net Realizable Value
ABX	80	$50	$55
TYG	200	38	42
JIL	175	28	24
GGH	90	44	38

Calculate the value of the company's ending inventory by using the lower-of-cost-or-net realizable value applied to each item of inventory.

E6-13A. The LIFO Inventory Reserve Southeast Steel Company uses the LIFO inventory costing method to value its ending inventory. The following data were obtained from the company's accounting records: **LO7** **(Appendix 6B)**

Current assets (under FIFO)	$9,000,000
Current liabilities	6,000,000
Inventory under LIFO	2,200,000
Inventory under FIFO	2,800,000

Calculate the company's (a) LIFO inventory reserve and (b) the current ratio assuming (i) FIFO and (ii) LIFO.

E6-14A. Inventory Costing Methods—Perpetual Method Refer to the information in E6-2A and assume the perpetual inventory system is used. Calculate the cost of goods sold for the July 15 sale using (a) first-in, first-out, (b) last-in, first-out, and (c) the weighted-average cost methods. Round your final answers to the nearest dollar. **LO6** **(Appendix 6A)**

E6-15A. Inventory Costing Methods—Perpetual Method Refer to the information in E6-4A and assume the perpetual inventory system is used. Calculate the inventory cost of product A on August 11 (after the sale) using (a) first-in, first-out, (b) last-in, first-out, and (c) the weighted-average cost methods. Round your final answers to the nearest dollar. **LO6** **(Appendix 6A)**

E6-16A. Inventory Costing Methods—Perpetual Method Refer to the information in E6-8A and assume the perpetual inventory system is used. Calculate the value of ending inventory and cost of goods sold using the perpetual method and (a) first-in, first-out, (b) last-in, first-out, and (c) weighted-average cost method. Round the cost per unit to three decimal places and round your final answers to the nearest dollar. **LO6** **(Appendix 6A)**

EXERCISES—SET B

E6-1B. Just-in-Time Inventories Nevada Manufacturing Company uses the perpetual inventory system and plans to use raw material costing $2,100,000 in making its products. Nevada will operate its factory 300 days during the year. Currently, Nevada follows the just-in-case philosophy with its raw materials inventory, keeping raw materials costing $20,000 in its raw materials inventory. Nevada plans to switch to the just-in-time manufacturing philosophy by keeping only the raw materials needed for the next two days of production. Calculate the new raw materials inventory level after Nevada implements the just-in-time manufacturing philosophy. **LO1**

E6-2B. Inventory Costing Methods—Periodic Method Mary Company uses the periodic inventory system. The following May data are for an item in Mary's inventory: **LO2**

May   1 Beginning inventory, 150 units @ $30 per unit.
      12 Purchased 100 units @ $35 per unit.
      16 Sold 180 units.
      24 Purchased 170 units @ $40 per unit.

Calculate the cost of goods sold for May and ending inventory at May 31 using (a) first-in, first-out, (b) last-in, first-out, and (c) the weighted-average cost method. Round the cost per unit to three decimal places and your final answers to the nearest dollar.

LO1   E6-3B.   Year-End Physical Inventory The December 31 inventory for the Simpson Company included five products. The year-end physical count revealed the following quantities on hand:

Product	Quantity Available
K	40
L	42
M	60
N	52
P	55

The related unit costs were: K, $7; L, $10; M, $9; N, $5; and P, $7.

Required
Calculate the total cost of the December 31 physical inventory.

LO2   E6-4B.   Inventory Costing Methods—Periodic Method Spanner Company is a retailer that uses the periodic inventory system. On March 1, it had 100 units of product M at a total cost of $1,590. On March 6, Spanner purchased 200 units of M for $3,600. On March 10, it purchased 125 units of M for $3,000. On March 15, it sold 200 units of M for $6,000. Calculate the March cost of goods sold and the ending inventory at March 31 using (a) first-in, first-out, (b) last-in, first-out, and (c) the weighted-average cost method. Round your final answers to the nearest dollar.

LO3   E6-5B.   Errors in Inventory Counts The following information was taken from the records of Hawk Enterprises:

	Year 1	Year 2
Beginning inventory	$ 75,000	$ 55,000
Cost of goods purchased	500,000	540,000
Cost of goods available for sale	575,000	595,000
Ending inventory	55,000	85,000
Cost of goods sold	$520,000	$510,000

The following two errors were made in the physical inventory counts:

1. Year 1 ending inventory was overstated by $28,000.
2. Year 2 ending inventory was understated by $17,000.

Compute the correct cost of goods sold for both years.

LO4   E6-6B.   Departures from Acquisition Cost Determine the proper total inventory value for each of the following items in Parker Company's ending inventory:

a.   Parker has 70 model X3 cameras in stock. The cameras cost $360 each, but their year-end net realizable value is only $340.
b.   Parker has 600 rolls of film that are past the expiration date since film is now a slow moving item. The film cost $2.00 each and normally sells for $4.00. Parker has put the expired film on clearance and is selling it for $1.50 per roll. There are no related selling costs.
c.   Parker has five computers in stock that have been used as demonstration models. These computers cost $600 and normally sell for $750. Because they are used, Parker is selling them for $550 each. Expected selling costs are $10 per computer. New models of the computer (on order Z) will cost Parker $620 and will be priced to sell at $790.

LO2   E6-7B.   Inventory Costing Methods—Periodic Method The Caitlin Company, which uses the periodic inventory system, has the following records:

		Units	Unit Cost
Beginning inventory		100	$49
Purchases:	Jan. 6	650	42
	July 15	550	38
	Dec. 28	200	36

Ending inventory was 400 units. Compute the ending inventory and the cost of goods sold for the year using (a) first-in, first out, (b) weighted-average cost, and (c) last-in, first-out.

E6-8B. Inventory Costing Methods—Periodic Method The following data are for the Lite Corporation, which sells just one product: **LO2**

		Units	Unit Cost
Beginning inventory, January 1.		200	$12
Purchases	February 11	500	13
	May 18	400	15
	October 23	100	17
Sales	March 1.	350	
	July 1	440	

Calculate the value of ending inventory and cost of goods sold using the periodic method and (a) first-in, first-out, (b) last-in, first-out, and (c) weighted-average cost method. Round your final answers to the nearest dollar.

E6-9B. Applying IFRS The French Petroleum Company is a Paris-based oil and gas company that prepares   **LO4, 5**
its financial statements using IFRS. During the year, the management of the company undertook a review of the fair value of its oil and gas inventory and found that the inventory had appreciated above its book value of 55 million euros. According to the company's management, the oil and gas inventory was undervalued by 8 million euros. Prepare the journal entry to revalue the company's inventory. (*Hint:* Credit Asset, revaluation reserve.) How would the revaluation immediately affect the company's (a) current ratio, (b) inventory turnover, and (c) days' sales in inventory?

E6-10B. Lower-of-Cost-or-Net Realizable Value Method The following data are taken from the Smith &   **LO4**
Barney Corporation's inventory accounts:

Item Code	Quantity	Unit Cost	Net Realizable Value
ZKE.	100	$22	$16
XYF.	300	33	37
MNJ	400	23	18
UBS	220	33	39

Calculate the value of the company's ending inventory using the lower-of-cost-or-net realizable value method applied to each item of inventory.

E6-11B. Inventory Turnover and Days' Sales in Inventory Shown below are data from the Western Com-   **LO5**
pany's accounting records:

	Year 1	Year 2
Sales revenue.	$11,000,000	$14,000,000
Cost of goods sold	5,000,000	6,000,000
Beginning inventory	620,000	630,000
Ending inventory.	630,000	750,000

Calculate the company's (a) inventory turnover and (b) days' sales in inventory for both years. Comment on your results.

E6-12B. Lower-of-Cost-or-Net Realizable Value Method The following data refer to the Fanning Compa-   **LO4**
ny's ending inventory:

Item Code	Quantity	Unit Cost	Net Realizable Value
LXC.	60	$40	$48
KWT	260	38	34
MOR.	400	25	20
NES	100	26	32

Calculate the value of the company's ending inventory by using the lower-of-cost-or-net realizable value method applied to each item of inventory.

LO7
(Appendix 6B)

E6-13B. The LIFO Inventory Reserve Eastern Steel Company uses the LIFO inventory costing method to value its ending inventory. The following data were obtained from the company's accounting records:

Current assets (under FIFO)	$9,500,000
Current liabilities..	7,500,000
Inventory under LIFO	4,000,000
Inventory under FIFO	5,700,000

Calculate the company's (a) LIFO inventory reserve and (b) current ratio assuming (i) FIFO and (ii) LIFO.

LO6
(Appendix 6A)

E6-14B. Inventory Costing Methods—Perpetual Method Refer to the information in E6-2B and assume the perpetual inventory system is used. Calculate the cost of goods sold for the May 16 sale using (a) first-in, first-out, (b) last-in, first-out, and (c) the weighted-average cost method. Round your final answers to the nearest dollar.

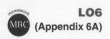

LO6
(Appendix 6A)

E6-15B. Inventory Costing Methods—Perpetual Method Refer to the information in E6-4B and assume the perpetual inventory system is used. Calculate the ending inventory cost of product M on March 15 (after the sale) using (a) first-in, first-out, (b) last-in, first-out, and (c) the weighted-average cost method. Round your final answers to the nearest dollar.

LO6
(Appendix 6A)

E6-16B. Inventory Costing Methods—Perpetual Method Refer to the information in E6-8B and assume the perpetual inventory system is used. Calculate the value of ending inventory and cost of goods sold using the perpetual method and (a) first-in, first-out, (b) last-in, first-out, and (c) weighted-average cost method. Round the cost per unit to three decimal places and your final answers to the nearest dollar.

PROBLEMS—SET A

LO1

P6-1A. Just-in-Time Inventory The Mason Manufacturing Company uses the perpetual inventory system with its raw material inventory. Mason plans to include raw material costing $2,700,000 in the products that it manufactures. John Mason, president of the company, wants to adopt the just-in-time manufacturing philosophy for the raw materials inventory. He wants to have only the raw material needed for the next day's production at the end of each day. The factory operates 300 days each year. Historically, the raw materials inventory balance at the end of the day has averaged $40,000 cost. Mason has an annual inventory carrying cost equal to 20 percent of total inventory cost.

Required
a. What is the anticipated inventory carrying cost (in dollars) if Mason does not adopt the just-in-time manufacturing philosophy?
b. Calculate the average level (in dollars) for the raw materials inventory if Mason adopts the just-in-time manufacturing philosophy.
c. Calculate the reductions in the raw materials inventory level and the raw materials inventory annual carrying cost if Mason adopts the just-in-time manufacturing philosophy.
d. What other factors or situations should Mason consider before deciding to have only one day's supply of raw material? (*Hint:* Consider factors and situations related to environment, supplier problems, labor problems, etc.)

LO2

P6-2A. Inventory Costing Methods—Periodic Method Tally Stores uses the periodic inventory system for its merchandise inventory. The April 1 inventory for one of the items in the merchandise inventory consisted of 120 units with a unit cost of $330. Transactions for this item during April were as follows:

April	9	Purchased 40 units @ $345 per unit.
	14	Sold 80 units @ $550 per unit.
	23	Purchased 20 units @ $360 per unit.
	29	Sold 40 units @ $550 per unit.

Required
a. Calculate the cost of goods sold and the ending inventory cost for the month of April using the weighted-average cost method. Round the cost per unit to three decimal places and your final answers to the nearest dollar.

b. Calculate the cost of goods sold and the ending inventory cost for the month of April using the first-in, first-out method.

c. Calculate the cost of goods sold and the ending inventory cost for the month of April using the last-in, first-out method.

P6-3A. Lower-of-Cost-or-Net Realizable Value Method The following data are taken from the Daley Corporation's inventory accounts:

LO4

Item Code	Quantity	Unit Cost	Net Realizable Value
Product 1			
ZKE.	100	$22	$18
ZKF.	300	31	36
Product 2			
MNJ.	400	22	19
MNS	250	31	37

Calculate the value of the company's ending inventory using the lower-of-cost-or-net realizable value method applied to each item of inventory.

P6-4A. Inventory Costing Methods—Periodic Method Chou Sales Corporation uses the periodic inventory system. On January 1, Chou had 1,000 units of product A with a unit cost of $20 per unit. A summary of purchases and sales during the year follows:

LO2, 3

	Unit Cost	Units Purchased	Units Sold
Feb. 2			400
Apr. 6	$22	1,800	
July 10			1,600
Aug. 9	25	800	
Oct. 23			800
Dec. 30	28	1,400	

Required

a. Assume that Chou uses the first-in, first-out method. Compute the cost of goods sold for the year and the ending inventory balance at December 31 for product A.

b. Assume that Chou uses the last-in, first-out method. Compute the cost of goods sold for the year and the ending inventory balance at December 31 for product A.

c. Assume that Chou uses the weighted-average cost method. Compute the cost of goods sold for the year and the ending inventory balance at December 31 for product A.

d. Assuming that Chou's products are perishable items, which of the three inventory costing methods would you choose to:

1. Reflect the likely goods flow through the business?
2. Minimize income taxes for the period?
3. Report the largest amount of net income for the period?

Explain your answers.

P6-5A. Inventory Turnover and Days' Sales in Inventory Shown below are data from the Southern Corporation's accounting records:

LO5

	Year 1	Year 2
Sales revenue.	$19,000,000	$20,000,000
Cost of goods sold	8,600,000	9,200,000
Beginning inventory	2,500,000	2,530,000
Ending inventory.	2,530,000	2,600,000

Calculate the company's (a) inventory turnover (round to three decimal places) and (b) days' sales in inventory for both years. Comment on your results.

LO1   P6-6A.   Goods in Transit The Yankee Wholesale Company sells merchandise to a variety of retailers. Yankee uses different freight terms with its various customers and suppliers. All sales are made on account.

Required

For each of the following transactions, indicate which company has ownership of the goods in transit:

a. Yankee sold merchandise to X-Mart Stores, with shipping terms of F.O.B. shipping point.

b. Yankee purchased merchandise from Zendo Manufacturing Company, with shipping terms of F.O.B. destination.

c. Yankee sold merchandise to Mary's Boutique, with shipping terms of F.O.B. destination.

d. Sunshine Manufacturing Company sold merchandise to Yankee, with shipping terms of F.O.B. shipping point.

e. Yankee purchased merchandise from Warfield Manufacturing Company, with freight terms of F.O.B. shipping point.

f. Stevenson Stores purchased merchandise from Yankee, with shipping terms of F.O.B. shipping point.

LO4   P6-7A.   Lower-of-Cost-or-Net Realizable Value Method The Vandy Company had the following inventory at year-end:

	Quantity	Unit Price Cost	Unit Price Net Realizable Value
Fans			
Model X1.	300	$18	$19
Model X2.	250	23	24
Model X3.	450	29	25
Heaters			
Model B7.	500	24	30
Model B8.	290	35	32
Model B9.	100	41	37

Required

a. Determine the value of ending inventory after applying the lower-of-cost-or-net realizable value method to each item of inventory.

b. Would the net income be lower under the cost method or the lower-of-cost-or-net realizable value method?

LO2   P6-8A.   Inventory Costing Methods—Periodic Method The following data are for the Porter Corporation, which sells just one product:

		Units	Unit Cost
Beginning inventory, January 1.		1,200	$ 8
Purchases	February 11	1,500	9
	May 18	1,400	12
	October 23	1,100	14
Sales	March 1.	1,400	
	July 1	1,400	
	October 29	1,200	

Calculate the value of ending inventory and cost of goods sold at year-end using the periodic method and (a) first-in, first-out, (b) last-in, first-out, and (c) weighted-average cost method. Round the cost per unit to three decimal places and round your final answers to the nearest dollar. If the net realizable value of the inventory at year-end is $15, how will the cost of goods sold under each method be affected?

LO1   P6-9A.   Physical Inventory Calculation Comanche Stores conducted a physical inventory at December 31. The items counted during the physical inventory are listed below. Comanche's accountant provided the unit costs.

Item Description	December 31	
	Count	Unit Cost
Colorado wool sweaters.................................	48	$32
Magnum wool sweaters	27	34
Johnson jackets	50	30
Magnum caps..	45	12
Evans caps..	30	10
Colorado shirts..	72	20
Johnson shirts	68	25
Magnum boots	45	60

Required

Prepare a schedule to determine the total cost of each item in the inventory and the total cost of the complete inventory at December 31.

P6-10A. Inventory Costing Methods—Perpetual Method Refer to the information in P6-2A and assume the perpetual inventory system is used.

LO6
(Appendix 6A)

Required

a. Calculate the cost of goods sold and the ending inventory cost for the month of April using the weighted-average cost method.

b. Calculate the cost of goods sold and the ending inventory cost for the month of April using the first-in, first-out method.

c. Calculate the cost of goods sold and the ending inventory cost for the month of April using the last-in, first-out method.

P6-11A. Inventory Costing Methods—Perpetual Method Refer to the information in P6-4A and assume the perpetual inventory system is used.

LO6
(Appendix 6A)

Required

a. Assume that Chou uses the first-in, first-out method. Compute the cost of goods sold for the year and the ending inventory balance at December 31 for product A.

b. Assume that Chou uses the last-in, first-out method. Compute the cost of goods sold for the year and the ending inventory balance at December 31 for product A.

c. Assume that Chou uses the weighted-average cost method. Compute the cost of goods sold for the year and the ending inventory balance at December 31 for product A.

d. Assuming that Chou's products are perishable items, which of the three inventory costing methods would you choose to:

1. Reflect the likely goods flow through the business?
2. Minimize income taxes for the period?
3. Report the largest amount of net income for the period?

Explain your answers.

P6-12A. The LIFO Inventory Reserve Alaska Manufacturing Company uses the LIFO inventory costing method to value its ending inventory. The following data were obtained from the company's accounting records:

LO7
(Appendix 6B)

Current assets (under FIFO)	$20,000,000
Current liabilities...	15,000,000
Inventory under LIFO	7,000,000
Inventory under FIFO	7,700,000

Calculate the company's (a) LIFO inventory reserve and (b) current ratio assuming (i) FIFO and (ii) LIFO. If the company's LIFO gross profit was $10,000,000 and the change in the LIFO inventory reserve was $1,400,000, calculate the company's gross profit under FIFO.

P6-13A. Inventory Costing Methods—Perpetual Method Using the data in P6-8A, assume that Porter Corporation uses the perpetual inventory system. Calculate the value of ending inventory and cost of goods sold at year-end using the perpetual method and (a) first-in, first-out, (b) last-in, first-out, and (c) weighted-average cost method. Round the cost per unit to three decimal places and round your final answers to the nearest dollar. If the net realizable value of the inventory at year-end is $15, how will the cost of goods sold under each method be affected?

LO6
(Appendix 6A)

PROBLEMS—SET B

LO1   P6-1B.   Just-in-Time Inventory The Track Manufacturing Company uses the perpetual inventory system for its raw materials inventory. Track plans to include raw material costing $2,500,000 in the products that it manufactures. Henry Track, president of the company, wants to adopt the just-in-time manufacturing philosophy for the raw materials inventory. He wants to have only the raw material needed for the next day's production at the end of each day. The factory operates 250 days each year. Historically, the raw materials inventory balance at the end of the day has averaged $55,000 cost. Track has an annual inventory carrying cost equal to 22 percent of total inventory cost.

Required

a.   What is the anticipated annual inventory carrying cost (in dollars) if Track does not adopt the just-in-time manufacturing philosophy?

b.   Calculate the average level (in dollars) for the raw materials inventory if Track adopts the just-in-time manufacturing philosophy.

c.   Calculate the reduction in the raw materials inventory level and the raw materials inventory annual carrying cost if Track adopts the just-in-time manufacturing philosophy.

d.   What other factors or situations should Track consider before deciding to have only one day's supply of material? (*Hint:* Consider factors and situations related to environment, supplier problems, labor problems, etc.)

LO2   P6-2B.   Inventory Costing Methods—Periodic Method The Kali Company uses the periodic inventory system for its merchandise inventory. The June 1 inventory for one of the items in the merchandise inventory consisted of 60 units with a unit cost of $45. Transactions for this item during June were as follows:

June   5   Purchased 40 units @ $50 per unit.
        13 Sold 50 units @ $95 per unit.
        25 Purchased 40 units @ $53 per unit.
        29 Sold 20 units @ $110 per unit.

Required

a.   Compute the cost of goods sold and the ending inventory cost for the month of June using the weighted-average cost method. Round the cost per unit to three decimal places and round your final answers to the nearest dollar.

b.   Compute the cost of goods sold and the ending inventory cost for the month of June using the first-in, first-out method.

c.   Compute the cost of goods sold and the ending inventory cost for the month of June using the last-in, first-out method.

LO4   P6-3B.   Lower-of-Cost-or-Net Realizable Value Method The following data are taken from the Hilton Corporation's inventory accounts:

Item Code	Quantity	Unit Cost	Net Realizable Value
Product 1			
XKE....................................	100	$32	$28
XKF....................................	400	43	44
Product 2			
ZNJ....................................	400	32	29
ZNS....................................	300	43	48

Calculate the value of the company's ending inventory using the lower-of-cost-or-net realizable value method applied to each item of inventory.

LO2, 3   P6-4B.   Inventory Costing Methods—Periodic Method The Glenn Sales Corporation uses the periodic inventory system. On January 1 Glenn had 2,600 units of product B with a unit cost of $40 per unit. A summary of purchases and sales during the year follows:

	Unit Cost	Units Purchased	Units Sold
Jan. 3			1,600
Mar. 8	$44	3,000	
June 13...			2,000
Sept. 19	46	800	
Nov. 23	50	1,200	
Dec. 28...			1,800

Required

a.   Assume that Glenn uses the first-in, first-out method. Compute the cost of goods sold for the year and the ending inventory balance at December 31 for product B.

b.   Assume that Glenn uses the last-in, first-out method. Compute the cost of goods sold for the year and the ending inventory balance at December 31 for product B.

c.   Assume that Glenn uses the weighted-average cost method. Compute the cost of goods sold for the year and the ending inventory balance at December 31 for product B.

d.   Assuming that Glenn sells items that quickly become obsolete, which of these three inventory costing methods would you choose to:
1.   Reflect the likely goods flow through the business?
2.   Minimize income tax for the period?
3.   Report the largest amount of net income for the period?
Explain your answers.

P6-5B.   Inventory Turnover and Days' Sales in Inventory Shown below are data from the Southwestern States Corporation's accounting records:

LO5

	Year 1	Year 2
Sales revenue.	$49,000,000	$42,000,000
Cost of goods sold	30,000,000	29,500,000
Beginning inventory	16,250,000	16,500,000
Ending inventory.	17,000,000	20,500,000

Calculate the company's (a) inventory turnover (round to three decimal places) and (b) days' sales in inventory for both years. Comment on your results.

P6-6B.   Goods in Transit Field Distributors sells merchandise to a variety of retailers. Field uses different freight terms with its various customers and suppliers. All sales are made on account.

LO1

Required

For each of the following transactions, indicate which company has ownership of the goods in transit:

a.   Field sold merchandise to Clay Boutique, with shipping terms of F.O.B. destination.

b.   Field purchased merchandise from Campbell Manufacturing Company, with freight terms of F.O.B. shipping point.

c.   Field sold merchandise to Save-A-Lot Stores, with shipping terms of F.O.B. shipping point.

d.   Field purchased merchandise from Central Manufacturing Company, with shipping terms of F.O.B. destination.

e.   Levinson Stores purchased merchandise from Field, with shipping terms of F.O.B. shipping point.

f.   Connor Manufacturing Company sold merchandise to Field, with shipping terms of F.O.B. shipping point.

P6-7B.   Lower-of-Cost-or-Net Realizable Value Method The Crow Company had the following inventory at year-end:

LO4

		Unit Price	
	Quantity	Cost	Net Realizable Value
Desks			
Model 9001.	70	$190	$215
Model 9002.	45	310	268
Model 9003.	20	345	360
Cabinets			
Model 7001.	120	60	68
Model 7002.	80	95	85
Model 7003.	60	135	126

Required

a.   Determine the value of the ending inventory after applying the lower-of-cost-or-net realizable value method to each item of inventory.

b.   Would the net income be lower under the cost method or the lower-of-cost-or-net realizable value method?

LO2   P6-8B.   Inventory Costing Methods—Periodic Method The following data are for the Cracker Corporation, which sells just one product:

		Units	Unit Cost
Beginning inventory, January 1.		1,200	$18
Purchases	February 11	1,500	19
	May 18	1,400	20
	October 23	1,100	23
Sales	March 1.	1,400	
	July 1	1,400	
	October 29	1,000	

Calculate the value of ending inventory and cost of goods sold for the year using the periodic method and (a) first-in, first-out, (b) last-in, first-out, and (c) weighted-average cost method. Round the cost per unit to three decimal places and round your final answers to the nearest dollar. If the replacement cost of the inventory at year-end is $25, how will the cost of goods sold under each method be affected?

LO1   P6-9B.   Physical Inventory Calculation Household City conducted a physical inventory at December 31. The items counted during the physical inventory are listed below. Household City's accountant provided the unit costs.

Item Description	December 31 Count	Unit Cost
Taylor sofas.	10	$250
Georgia sofas	8	300
Taylor chairs	22	175
Taylor recliners	16	200
Georgia recliners	4	220
Carolina lamps	16	30
Chicago lamps	20	28
Georgia tables	10	155

Required
Prepare a schedule to determine the total cost of each item in the inventory and the total cost of the complete inventory at December 31.

LO6   P6-10B.   Inventory Costing Methods—Perpetual Method Refer to the information in P6-2B and assume the
(Appendix 6A)   perpetual inventory system is used.

Required
a.   Compute the cost of goods sold and the ending inventory cost for the month of June using the weighted-average cost method.
b.   Compute the cost of goods sold and the ending inventory cost for the month of June using the first-in, first-out method.
c.   Compute the cost of goods sold and the ending inventory cost for the month of June using the last-in, first-out method.

LO6   P6-11B.   Inventory Costing Methods—Perpetual Method Refer to the information in P6-4B and assume the
(Appendix 6A)   perpetual inventory system is used.

Required
a.   Assume that Glenn uses the first-in, first-out method. Compute the cost of goods sold for the year and the ending inventory balance at December 31 for product B.
b.   Assume that Glenn uses the last-in, first-out method. Compute the cost of goods sold for the year and the ending inventory balance at December 31 for product B.
c.   Assume that Glenn uses the weighted-average cost method. Compute the cost of goods sold for the year and the ending inventory balance at December 31 for product B.
d.   Assuming that Glenn sells items that quickly become obsolete, which of these three inventory costing methods would you choose to:
1.   Reflect the likely goods flow through the business?
2.   Minimize income tax for the period?
3.   Report the largest amount of net income for the period?
Explain your answers.

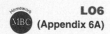

P6-12B. The LIFO Inventory Reserve The Midwestern Manufacturing Company uses the LIFO inventory costing method to value its ending inventory. The following data were obtained from the company's accounting records:

LO7
(Appendix 6B) MBC

Current assets (under FIFO)	$50,000,000
Current liabilities	38,000,000
Inventory under LIFO	16,000,000
Inventory under FIFO	18,700,000

Calculate the company's (a) LIFO inventory reserve and (b) current ratio assuming (i) FIFO and (ii) LIFO. If the company's LIFO gross profit was $18,000,000 and the change in the LIFO inventory reserve was $3,000,000, calculate the company's gross profit under FIFO.

P6-13B. Inventory Costing Methods—Perpetual Method Using the data in P6-8B, assume that Cracker Corporation uses the perpetual inventory system. Calculate the value of ending inventory and cost of goods sold for the year using the perpetual method and (a) first-in, first-out, (b) last-in, first-out, and (c) weighted-average cost method. Round the cost per unit to three decimal places and round your final answers to the nearest dollar. If the net realizable value of the inventory at year-end is $25, how will the cost of goods sold under each method be affected?

LO6
(Appendix 6A) MBC

SERIAL PROBLEM: KATE'S CARDS

(Note: This is a continuation of the Serial Problem: Kate's Cards from Chapters 1 through 5.)

SP6. As expected, the holiday season was very busy for Kate and her greeting card company. In fact, most of her supplies were fully depleted by year-end, necessitating a restocking of inventory. Assume that Kate uses the periodic method of accounting for inventory and that her January beginning inventory was $0. The following transactions occurred for Kate's Cards during January of the New Year:

Kate's
Cards

MBC

Purchases	Units		Unit Cost	Total Cost
Jan. 10	400	@	$3.00 per unit	$1,200
Jan. 17	500	@	$3.50 per unit	1,750
Jan. 23	300	@	$4.00 per unit	1,200
Total	1,200			$4,150

Sales	Units			
Jan. 15	360			
Jan. 21	420			
Jan. 27	380			
Total	1,160			

Required

a. Calculate the company's cost of goods sold and value of ending inventory for the month of January using (1) FIFO, (2) LIFO, and (3) the weighted-average cost method. Round the cost per unit to three decimal places and round your final answers to the nearest dollar.

b. If the net realizable value of Kate's inventory is $4.00 per unit on January 31, what value should be reported for her ending inventory on the January 31 balance sheet under each of the three inventory costing methods?

EXTENDING YOUR KNOWLEDGE

REPORTING AND ANALYSIS

COLUMBIA
SPORTSWEAR
COMPANY

EYK6-1. **Financial Reporting Problem: The Columbia Sportswear Company** The financial statements for the **Columbia Sportswear Company** can be found in Appendix A at the end of this textbook.

Required

Answer the following questions using Columbia's Consolidated Financial Statements:
a. How much inventory does Columbia carry on its balance sheet? What percentage of Columbia's total assets does inventory represent in 2020 and 2019?
b. Compute the inventory turnover and days' sales in inventory for 2020 and 2019. Calculate inventory turnover using end of year inventory.
c. Is Columbia's inventory management improving?

COLUMBIA
SPORTSWEAR
COMPANY

UNDER ARMOUR, INC.

EYK6-2. **Comparative Analysis Problem: Columbia Sportswear Company vs Under Armour, Inc.** The financial statements for **Columbia Sportswear Company** can be found in Appendix A at the end of this textbook, and the financial statements of **Under Armour, Inc.**, can be found in Appendix B.

Required

a. Compare the dollar value of inventory carried on the balance sheet by each company in 2020 and 2019. Which company carries the greatest dollar amount of inventory? Compare the ratio of inventory divided by total assets for each company for 2020 and 2019. Which company carries the largest relative investment in inventory?
b. Calculate the inventory turnover and days' sales in inventory for 2020 and 2019 for each company. Inventory at December 31, 2018, for Columbia and Under Armour, Inc., was $521.8 million and $1,019.5 million, respectively.
c. Which company appears to be doing the better job of managing its investment in inventory?

EYK6-3. **Business Decision Problem** Margaret Company is a wholesaler that uses the perpetual inventory system. On January 1, 2021, Margaret had 3,000 units of its product at a cost of $5 per unit. Transactions related to inventory during 2021 were as follows:

Purchases				Sales			
Feb. 5	9,000 units	@	$6	March 8	8,000 units	@	$ 9
May 19	20,000 units	@	7	June 21	19,000 units	@	10
Dec. 15	3,000 units	@	9	Dec. 28	4,000 units	@	12

Margaret is trying to decide whether to use the first-in, first-out (FIFO) inventory costing method or the last-in, first-out (LIFO) inventory costing method.

Required

a. Assume that Margaret decides to use the FIFO inventory costing method.
   1. What would gross profit be for 2021?
   2. How would Margaret's gross profit and ending inventory for 2021 change if the December 15, 2021, purchase had been made on January 3, 2022, instead?
   3. How would Margaret's gross profit and ending inventory for 2021 change if the December 15, 2021, purchase had been for 6,000 units instead of 3,000 units?
b. Assume that Margaret decides to use the LIFO inventory costing method.
   1. What would gross profit be for 2021?
   2. How would Margaret's gross profit and ending inventory for 2021 change if the December 15, 2021, purchase had been made on January 3, 2022, instead?
   3. How would Margaret's gross profit and ending inventory for 2021 change if the December 15, 2021, purchase had been for 6,000 units instead of 3,000 units?
c. Which inventory costing method should Margaret choose and why?

EYK6-4.   **Financial Analysis Problem** Purpose: To use annual financial report filings to learn about how a company accounts for its inventory.

Select any publicly traded company not discussed in this chapter and go to its website. Find the section on investor information and download its latest annual report. (You may download its 10K report rather than the annual report.)

Required

Using this report, answer the following questions.

a.   What is the name of the company you chose, and what is the primary industry that it operates in?

b.   Does the company list inventory on its balance sheet? If so, where on the balance sheet does it appear?

c.   Does the company have a separate note in the notes to the financial statements that provides a more detailed breakdown of the amount of inventory listed? If so, what is that breakdown?

d.   What inventory method does the company use?

e.   Calculate the inventory turnover ratio and days' sales in inventory for the most current year shown.

CRITICAL THINKING

EYK6-5.   **Accounting Research Problem** The fiscal year 2020 annual report of **General Mills, Inc.,** is available on this book's website.

GENERAL MILLS, INC.

Required

a.   What percentage of total assets is represented by General Mills' investment in inventory in 2020 and 2019?

b.   Compute the inventory turnover and days' sales in inventory for General Mills for 2020 and 2019. Calculate inventory turnover using end-of-year inventory.

c.   Is the company doing a better job of managing its investment in inventory in 2019?

d.   What inventory costing method does General Mills use?

e.   What is the value of the company's LIFO reserve at year-end 2020? General Mills labels its LIFO reserve as the "Excess of FIFO over LIFO cost" in Note 18.

EYK6-6.   **Accounting Communications Activity** **Pactiv Corporation** is a leader in the consumer and foodservice packaging market. In December 2009 the company announced a change in the accounting for inventories. https://www.streetinsider.com/Corporate+News/Pactiv+(PTV)+Annou nces+Inventory+Accounting+Changes+from+LIFO+to+FIFO%3B+Guides+FY09+EPS/5199200. html

PACTIV CORPORATION

Required

Sarah Jenkins, CEO of a competing firm, read this announcement but was confused about what exactly Pactiv was doing. She asked that you write a memo explaining the following items.

a.   What about its accounting for inventory was Pactiv changing?

b.   Why does Pactiv believe the new method is preferable?

c.   What benefit does Pactiv believe will be realized from the change?

EYK6-7.   **Accounting Ethics Case** Reed Kohler is in his final year of employment as controller for Quality Sales Corporation; he hopes to retire next year. As a member of top management, Kohler participates in an attractive company bonus plan. The overall size of the bonus is a function of the firm's net income before bonus and income taxes—the larger the net income, the larger the bonus.

Due to a slowdown in the economy, Quality Sales Corporation has encountered difficulties in managing its cash flow. To improve its cash flow by reducing cash payments for income taxes, the firm's auditors have recommended that the company change its inventory costing method from FIFO to LIFO. This change would cause a significant increase in the cost of goods sold for the year. Kohler believes the firm should not switch to LIFO this year because its inventory quantities are too large. He believes that the firm should work to reduce its inventory quantities and then switch to LIFO. (The switch could be made in a year or two.) After expressing this opinion to the firm's treasurer, Kohler is stunned when the treasurer replies: "Reed, I can't believe that after all these years with the firm, you put your personal interests ahead of the firm's interests."

Explain why Kohler may be viewed as holding a position that favors his personal interests. What can Kohler do to increase his credibility when the possible change to LIFO is discussed at a meeting of the firm's top management next week?

BEST BUY

EYK6-8.   Environmental, Social, and Governance Problem The Environmental, Social, and Governance (ESG) highlight in this chapter discussed how **Best Buy** is working to make sure its supply chain complies with the company's high ethical standards. One of the ways this is done is for Best Buy's Global Sourcing team to work with their Social and Environmental Responsibility team.

Go to the Best Buy website and its page on Environmental Sustainability (https://corporate.bestbuy.com/sustainability/) and locate Best Buy's Fiscal Year 2020 ESG Report. Open the report and find the section on Responsible supply chain. The responsible supply chain seeks to control risk, enhance the partnership with suppliers (by building their capacity for responsible business practices), and create value for all stakeholders. The supplier code of conduct and the audit methodology are intended to create business value by improving working and environmental conditions in the supply chain. Explain the six parts of the code of conduct and the factory audit program utilized in the SCS program.

CRAZY EDDIE

COMPTRONIX
CORPORATION

LESLIE FAY COMPANY

LARIBEE
MANUFACTURING
COMPANY

PHAR-MOR

EYK6-9.   Forensic Accounting Problem The chapter highlights an inventory fraud case at **Crazy Eddie**. Unfortunately, there have been many other serious inventory frauds where the auditors were fooled by illegal acts. A few of these cases include (1) **Comptronix Corporation**, (2) **Leslie Fay Company**, (3) **Laribee Manufacturing Company**, and (4) **Phar-Mor** drug stores.

Do a computer search of one of these cases and explain how inventory was used to commit the fraud. List some ways the auditors can lessen the chance such frauds could go undetected.

LO5

EYK6-10.   Inventory Turnover and Days' Sales in Inventory: IFRS Financial Statements The 2020 financial statements of LVMH Moet Hennessey-Louis Vuitton S.A. are presented in Appendix C at the end of this book. LVMH is a Paris-based holding company and one of the world's largest and best-known luxury goods companies. As a member of the European Union, French companies are required to prepare their consolidated (group) financial statements using International Financial Reporting Standards (IFRS). LVMH's IFRS financial statements are presented in Appendix C at the end of this textbook. Using these financial statements, calculate the company's (a) inventory turnover and (b) days' sales in inventory for 2019 and 2020. Comment on the company's trend in inventory management effectiveness.

LO7
(Appendix 6B)

EYK6-11.   Working with the Takeaways Unger Company uses the LIFO inventory costing method to value inventory. The following financial data were obtained from its accounting records for the current year:

Current assets (including inventory)	$4,000
Current liabilities	2,000
Inventory under LIFO	575
Inventory under FIFO	775

Compute (a) the current ratio assuming (i) LIFO and (ii) FIFO and (b) the LIFO inventory reserve.

ANSWERS TO SELF-STUDY QUESTIONS:

1. b   2. d   3. c   4. b   5. d   6. c   7. a   8. b   9. d   10. d   11. b   12. c   13. b

YOUR TURN! SOLUTIONS

Solution 6.1

The $15,000 of goods shipped F.O.B. shipping point should be deducted from the inventory valuation, and the $25,000 of consignment goods should be included in the inventory valuation. The corrected ending inventory total should be $310,000 ($300,000 − $15,000 + $25,000).

Solution 6.2

a. Ending inventory using:

   i. FIFO: 1,000 × $7 = $7,000
   ii. LIFO: 1,000 × $5 = $5,000
   iii. Weighted-average cost: 1,000 × [(4,000 × $5) + (6,000 × $7)]/10,000 = 1,000 × $6.20 = $6,200

b. Cost of goods sold using:

   i. FIFO: (4,000 × $5) + (5,000 × $7) = $55,000
   ii. LIFO: (6,000 × $7) + (3,000 × $5) = $57,000
   iii. Weighted-average cost: 9,000 × [(4,000 × $5) + (6,000 × $7)]/10,000 = 9,000 × $6.20 = $55,800

c. Gross profit using:

   i. FIFO: $90,000 − $55,000 = $35,000
   ii. LIFO: $90,000 − $57,000 = $33,000
   iii. Weighted-average cost: $90,000 − $55,800 = $34,200

Solution 6.3

	Cost of Goods Sold	Beginning Inventory		Purchases		Ending Inventory
Year 1	$7,000 (instead of $7,500)	$ —	+	$10,000	–	$3,000
Year 2	$13,000 (instead of $12,500)	$ 3,000	+	$15,000	–	$5,000

		With Error	Without Error
Year 1			
	Sales.	$15,000	$15,000
	Cost of goods sold	7,500	7,000
	Gross profit.	$ 7,500	$ 8,000
Year 2			
	Sales.	$25,000	$25,000
	Cost of goods sold	12,500	13,000
	Gross profit.	$12,500	$12,000

Solution 6.4

The lowest value for each inventory item is: DSLR $110,000, Point and Shoot $73,000, and Camcorders $48,000. The total of the inventory is therefore valued under the lower of cost or NRV method at $231,000 ($110,000 + $73,000 + $48,000).

Solution 6.5

	Year 1	Year 2
Inventory turnover.	$\dfrac{\$2,000,000}{(\$450,000 + \$430,000)/2} = 4.55$	$\dfrac{\$2,300,000}{(\$430,000 + \$320,000)/2} = 6.13$
Days' sales in inventory	365/4.5 = 80.2 days	365/6.13 = 59.5 days

The company increased its sales by $400,000 from Year 1 to Year 2, and at the same time, decreased its average inventory by $65,000 ($440,000 − $375,000) as a consequence of improved inventory management. This resulted in a significantly improved inventory turnover (6.13 versus 4.55) and 20.7 (80.2 − 59.5) less days' sales in inventory. It appears that the new inventory management system is a financial success

Solution 6A.1

FIFO

Date	Units	Purchased Unit Cost	Total	Units	Sold Unit Cost	Total	Units	Unit Cost	Total
Jan. 1							1,000	$5.00	$5,000
Jan. 5	600	$6.00	$3,600				1,000	5.00	
							600	6.00	8,600
Jan. 15 ...				200	$5.00	$1,000	800	5.00	
							600	6.00	7,600
Jan. 17 ...	300	7.00	2,100				800	5.00	
							600	6.00	9,700
							300	7.00	
Jan. 25 ...				400	5.00	2,000	400	5.00	
							600	6.00	7,700
							300	7.00	
						$3,000			

LIFO

Date	Units	Purchased Unit Cost	Total	Units	Sold Unit Cost	Total	Units	Unit Cost	Total
Jan. 1							1,000	$5.00	$5,000
Jan. 5	600	$6.00	$3,600				1,000	5.00	
							600	6.00	8,600
Jan. 15 ...				200	$6.00	$1,200	1,000	5.00	
							400	6.00	7,400
Jan. 17 ...	300	7.00	2,100				1,000	5.00	
							400	6.00	9,500
							300	7.00	
Jan. 25 ...				300	7.00		1,000	5.00	
				100	6.00	2,700	300	6.00	6,800
						$3,900			

Weighted Average

Date	Units	Purchased Unit Cost	Total	Units	Sold Unit Cost	Total	Units	Weighted-Average Unit Cost	Total
Jan. 1							1,000	$5.000	$5,000
Jan. 5	600	$6.00	$3,600				1,600	5.375	8,600
Jan. 15 ...				200	$5.375	$1,075	1,400	5.375	7,525
Jan. 17 ...	300	7.00	2,100				1,700	5.662	9,625
Jan. 25 ...				400	5.662	2,265	1,300	5.662	7,360
						$3,340			

Solution 6B.1
$165,000 + $20,000 = $185,000

Chapter 7
Internal Control and Cash

Road Map

LO	Learning Objective	Page	eLecture	Guided Example	Assignments
LO1	**Define the three elements of fraud.**	7-3	E7-1	YT7.1	SS1, SE1
LO2	**Discuss how the COSO framework helps prevent fraud, identify potential internal control failures, and discuss SOX regulations.**	7-4	E7-2	YT7.2	SS2, SS3, SS4, SE2, SE3, SE4, SE5, E1A, E5A, E1B, E5B, P1A, P2A, P7A, P8A, P1B, P2B, P7B, P8B
LO3	**Define cash and discuss the accounting for cash.**	7-9	E7-3	YT7.3	SS6, SE6, SE7, E7A, E7B, P6A, P6B
LO4	**Describe the internal controls for cash.**	7-11	E7-4	YT7.4	SS7, SS10, SE8, SE9, E2A, E2B, P1A, P2A, P3A, P8A, P1B, P2B, P3B, P8B
LO5	**Illustrate the bank reconciliation process.**	7-17	E7-5	YT7.5	SS8, SS9, E3A, E4A, E3B, E4B, P4A, P5A, P9A, P4B, P5B, P9B
LO6	**Describe the four primary activities of effective cash management.**	7-22	E7-6	YT7.6, YT7.7	SE10, E6A, E6B, P10A
LO7	**Appendix 7A: Describe financial statement audits and operational audits.**	7-25	E7-7	YT7A.1	SS5, SE4, E8A, E9A, E8B, E9B

If someone asked you which company has the most coffee stores in China and you answered **Starbucks**, you would be wrong. The correct answer is **Luckin Coffee**, a Chinese coffee company that was founded in 2017.

Luckin Coffee opened its first store in January 2018, and by October 2018 it had become the second-largest coffee brand in China with 1,300 stores. In January 2019, Luckin Coffee announced plans to open an additional 2,500 stores to surpass Starbucks as the number one coffee brand in China. Around the same time, Luckin began trading on the NASDAQ stock exchange at $17 per share. On January 8, 2020, Luckin announced that it had opened 4,507 stores and had become the largest coffee brand in China. Unfortunately, though, things were not as rosy as they appeared; on February 5, 2021, Luckin Coffee filed for bankruptcy in New York.

What happened? Simply put, much of Luckin Coffee's accounting earnings were fraudulent. As far back as January 2020, the short selling firm, Muddy Waters Research, published a report claiming that it had evidence that sales in the second half of 2019 were inflated by nearly 80 percent. Although Luckin aggressively denied any wrongdoing at the time, within a year the stock plummeted from nearly $50 per share to under $2 per share and was delisted from the NASDAQ. China's market regulators fined Luckin Coffee for falsification of its financial reports, the U.S. SEC settled an accounting fraud case with Luckin Coffee for $180 million and in late 2021 the company reached a $175 million settlement of a shareholder class-action lawsuit.

Although detecting fraud is important, it is far better to keep fraud from occurring in the first place. Developing a knowledge of the elements of fraud and understanding how internal controls can prevent fraud are critical to all organizations. In this chapter, we study internal controls. Perhaps this discussion will inspire you to embark on a career in forensic accounting.

PAST

Chapter 6 explained the accounting for inventory. We described and applied the costing methods of specific identification, FIFO, LIFO, and weighted average.

PRESENT

In this chapter, we focus our attention on another current asset, cash. In addition, we study how internal control can be used to prevent errors and fraud associated with assets such as cash and inventory.

FUTURE

Chapter 8 explains the accounting for accounts and notes receivable. We will explain the reporting of uncollectible accounts and how managers monitor such accounts.

7-2

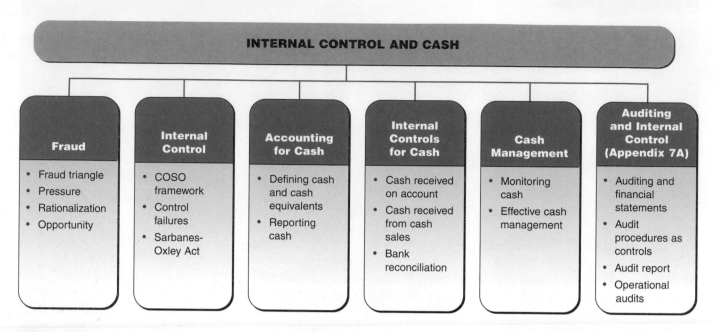

FRAUD

LO1   Define the three elements of fraud..

eLecture

MBC

Infamous stories of fraud involving **Enron Corporation** and **Madoff Investment Securities LLC**, or more recent frauds such as **Luckin Coffee** or **Wirecard AG**, illustrate the potential cost that fraud can have on so many people. Unfortunately, it is nearly impossible to completely prevent fraud; however, we do know much about why fraud is committed and what can be done to lower the risk of it occurring. Research shows that any individual, under the right circumstances, can commit fraud. This does not mean, however, that everyone will commit fraud. What it does mean is that it is very difficult to determine prior to the commission of a fraud exactly which employee will be the one to commit fraud.

Fraud refers to any act by the management or employees of a business involving an intentional deception for personal gain. Fraud may include, among other acts, embezzlement of a business's cash, theft of assets, filing false insurance claims, filing false health claims, and financial statement fraud. Fraud is a punishable crime and is also a violation of civil law.

Fraud Triangle

Research shows that three elements are almost always present when a fraud occurs. These elements are often referred to as the **fraud triangle** and include (1) a perceived pressure, (2) some way to rationalize the fraudulent act, and (3) a perceived opportunity. Reducing any of the three elements of the fraud triangle reduces the likelihood of fraud occurring in a business.

Unfortunately, the fraud triangle is not well understood. Because of this, nearly all fraud prevention efforts by businesses are devoted to the third element—reducing the opportunity to commit fraud. Too often, little effort is expended on the other elements of fraud even though efforts in any one area can reduce the effort needed in the other two areas.

Pressure

Pressure can be divided into several categories, but research shows that nearly all frauds are committed by individuals who feel perceived pressure from some sort of financial need. Financial pressure could come from living beyond one's means and being unable to pay one's bills, experiencing large medical bills, or the financial pressure from vices like gambling, drugs, or alcohol. The latter pressure is sometimes referred to as vice pressure.

Financial statement fraud, such as the overstatement of revenues or the understatement of expenses, usually occurs because of pressure on management to "make the numbers," either to satisfy Wall Street analyst expectations or to attain a bonus based on meeting an earnings target. Although it is not possible to completely eliminate this element of fraud, numerous methods have proven successful at lowering the risk of financial statement fraud. An obvious action is to perform careful personnel screening before hiring any employee to reduce the likelihood of employing individuals with known histories of fraud.

Rationalization

Very few individuals want to commit fraud since they recognize that it is wrong. In order to overcome this tremendous feeling of guilt, most employees need to come up with some form of rationalization so that they can live with their actions. Common rationalizations include such attitudes as (1) I am underpaid and the company owes it to me; (2) Everyone else is doing it; or (3) I am only borrowing the money and I will pay it back later.

The best way to reduce this element of fraud is to create an environment in which it is difficult to rationalize unethical behavior. A company that promotes a culture of honesty and integrity, within which unethical behavior is considered unacceptable, is much less likely to encounter fraudulent behavior by management or its employees. The key to building organization-wide attitudes regarding ethical behavior starts with the "tone at the top"—that is, the behaviors and attitudes displayed by a company's CEO or president.

Opportunity

The third element of the fraud triangle is perceived opportunity. An individual will only attempt to commit a fraud if he or she perceives that there is an opportunity to succeed. Of course this element is related to the other two elements. For example, if an employee is under tremendous pressure either at work or outside the workplace, he may attempt to commit a fraud even if he perceives only a small chance of success, while an individual under much less pressure will likely only attempt the fraud if it is perceived to be easy to commit.

YOUR TURN! 7.1

Identify the element of the fraud triangle associated with each of the following statements:
1. "I take full responsibility for what happened. But saying that, I know in my mind that I did nothing criminal."
2. "We were constantly told we would end up working for McDonald's. If we did not make the sales quotas, we had to stay for what felt like after-school detention, or report to a call session on Saturdays."
3. "The attitude was sort of, 'If you're doing something wrong, we don't want to know.'"

The solution is on page 7-47.

INTERNAL CONTROL

Reducing the opportunity to commit fraud often involves implementing a system of internal control, including such measures as physical control over cash and proper authorization over cash disbursements.

LO2 Discuss how the COSO framework helps prevent fraud, **identify** potential internal control failures, and **discuss** SOX regulations.

COSO Framework

eLecture

MBC

In 1992, the Committee of Sponsoring Organizations of the Treadway Commission (COSO) released a framework to help companies structure and evaluate their internal controls. Twenty years later, in 2013, COSO updated its framework to reflect changes in business environments brought about by developments including technological advancements and increasing globalization.

The COSO framework identifies five internal control components: (1) the control environment, (2) risk assessment, (3) control activities, (4) information and communication, and (5) monitoring activities.

1. Control Environment

The **control environment** sets the tone of the organization. An environment of ethical values and integrity is crucial to keeping employees from feeling that it is acceptable to commit fraud. The control environment provides the foundation for all other components of internal control. Included in the control environment are management's philosophy and management style; the organizational structure and assignment of authority and responsibility; the process for attracting and developing competent employees; and the rewards to drive accountability for performance.

ENVIRONMENTAL, SOCIAL, AND GOVERNANCE   Governance and Conflicts of Interest
Much of what was done at Enron was perfectly legal. Enron's management became very skilled at staying within the letter of the law, even if it meant violating the spirit of the law. For example, Enron used specialized accounting rules that allowed the company to mask the true level of its debt so that financial statement users would be unable to obtain a transparent view of the company's financial position. Top executives at Enron created a culture of deceit within the company that provided employees with an easy rationalization for their own misdeeds. Corporate social responsibility, by way of contrast, espouses the notion that not only is it important to make money, but it is important to do so in a responsible way. Cutting corners and playing fast and loose with the rules may work in the short term, but it is not sustainable in the long run, as the Enron saga reveals. Creating a culture of ethical behavior within a business is perhaps the most important internal control that exists to not only prevent fraud, but to provide a foundation for a sustainable enterprise.

2. Risk Assessment

Every organization faces a variety of different risks from both internal and external sources. Risk is defined as the possibility that an event will occur that has a negative impact on the organization's objectives. **Risk assessment** involves identifying and analyzing relevant risks to an organization's objectives. Because factors external to the organization such as the economic conditions, industry competitors, and regulations, along with internal factors such as operating conditions, are constantly changing, risk assessment must be an ongoing dynamic and iterative process.

3. Control Activities

The accounting system represents a cornerstone of the control environment that is necessary to reduce the opportunity for, and success of, fraudulent behavior. A critical aspect of the accounting system is a strong system of internal controls. **Internal controls** are the measures undertaken by a business to ensure the reliability of its accounting data, protect its assets from theft or unauthorized use, ensure that employees are following the company's policies and procedures, and evaluate the performance of employees, departments, divisions, and the company as a whole. Management is responsible for designing, installing, and monitoring internal controls throughout the business with the intent of attaining "reasonable assurance," rather than "absolute assurance," that the controls will meet their objectives.

   Control activities are the specific policies and procedures designed to reduce risk. A control activity can be either a prevention control or a detection control. A **prevention control** is intended to deter a problem or fraud before it can arise. A **detection control**, on the other hand, is designed to discover a problem or fraud shortly after it arises. Prevention controls are generally more desirable and preferred than detection controls, reflecting the old saying that "an ounce of prevention is worth a pound of detection."

   A company should incorporate the following elements when it designs its prevention and detection controls:

- Establish clear lines of authority and responsibility.
- Implement segregation of duties.
- Hire competent personnel.
- Use control numbers on all business documents.
- Develop plans and budgets.

■   Maintain adequate accounting records.

■   Provide physical and electronic controls.

We consider each of these elements in the following paragraphs and provide examples of their use as a prevention control or a detection control.

Establish Clear Lines of Authority and Responsibility

Establish Clear Lines of Authority and Responsibility   The organizational structure of a company defines the lines of authority and responsibility within the company. It informs employees about who is in charge of which functions and to whom each person reports.

The existence of an identified supervisor is a prevention control. Employees know that the supervisor is evaluating their performance; consequently, they are more likely to perform according to a company's established policies and rules. Supervision is also a detection control. A supervisor is likely to discover errors or irregularities when he or she reviews the work performance of employees.

Implement Segregation of Duties

Implement Segregation of Duties   **Segregation of duties** requires that when allocating various duties within the accounting system, management should make sure that no employee is assigned too many different responsibilities. As a general rule, no individual employee should be able to perpetrate and conceal irregularities in the transaction processing system. To accomplish this, management must separate three functions: the authorization function, the recording function, and the custody function.

When an employee prepares a purchase order to buy merchandise, that employee is effectively "authorizing" the transaction. When the merchandise is received, a second employee should prepare the receiving report when he or she gains "custody" of the merchandise. And, neither of these two employees should be allowed to "record" the purchase order, the receipt of the merchandise, or the payment of cash for the goods in the accounting records. Separating the work functions in this manner will reduce the likelihood of fraud occurring because committing a fraud when work duties are separated requires collusion among multiple employees. Proper segregation of duties is a prevention control.

Hire Competent Personnel

Hire Competent Personnel   Because people are the most important element of an accounting system, it is vital that a company hire competent personnel. Management must screen each job applicant to determine that he or she has sufficient education, training, and experience to qualify for the job. After hiring an employee, the company should provide specific formal training so that the employee is able to complete all of the tasks that the job requires. The training should refer to written policy statements, procedure manuals, and job descriptions so that the employee can become familiar with all aspects and expectations of his or her job. Hiring and training employees is a prevention control.

Some companies routinely rotate personnel among various jobs. For example, a company might switch jobs between an employee working exclusively with accounts receivable and an employee working exclusively with accounts payable. This rotation may disclose errors or irregularities resulting from over-familiarity with a job or just carelessness. Requiring employees to take vacations of at least one week in duration may also disclose errors or irregularities when another employee performs the vacationing employee's duties. These personnel policies act as a detection control.

ACCOUNTING IN PRACTICE   Job Rotation and Mandatory Vacations as Internal Controls

Job rotation and mandatory vacations are some of the best internal controls for uncovering fraud. For many frauds, it is necessary for the perpetrator to actively cover up his or her misdeeds through the falsification of accounting records. Requiring job rotation and vacations allows another employee to perform these job responsibilities, often leading to the discovery of fraud. And you thought your employer was only giving you that vacation to be nice!

Source: Association of Certified Fraud Examiners 2008 Report.

Use Control Numbers on All Business Documents

All business documents such as purchase orders, sales invoices, credit memos, and checks should have **control numbers** preprinted on them. Each control number should be unique for that type of document. For example, the bank checks that you use to pay your personal expenses have control numbers on them, usually in the upper right-hand corner of the check, referred to as a *check number*. These numbers act as a detection control enabling you to track each check written, and to ensure that no one has written an improper check against your account.

Develop Plans and Budgets

Top management should initiate the planning and budgeting process to establish forward thinking about the business and to provide a basis for evaluating department and employee performance. Every company should prepare an annual operating plan and budget. These items provide guidance for all levels of management regarding how to respond to various situations. The **budget** also provides a basis for comparing actual operating results to planned results when management evaluates operating unit performance. An example of evaluating performance involves comparing the actual advertising expense to the budgeted advertising expense. When variances between actual and budgeted amounts are observed, those variances should be investigated by management. This type of control activity is both a prevention control and a detection control.

Maintain Adequate Accounting Records

In previous chapters, we discussed a number of detection controls that help ensure that a business has adequate accounting records. These controls include using the double-entry accounting system to record transactions (debits must equal credits), preparing trial balances (total debits must equal total credits), and taking a physical count of the inventory on hand (physical inventory total should equal perpetual inventory total).

Many control activities related to maintaining accurate accounting records involve comparisons of various amounts. For instance, each business should periodically make a physical inspection of its plant assets to compare the data in the plant assets' ledger account to the plant assets actually in use. This inspection identifies any missing assets and any

Data Analytics

DATA ANALYTICS	Benford's Law and Data Analytics Aid Accounting Sleuths

How often should the number 9 appear as the first digit of an amount reported on a financial statement? If you say one out of ten times you, like most people, you would be wrong. It turns out that the number 9 should appear less than 5 percent of the time, whereas the number 1 should appear as the first digit of a reported amount over 30 percent of the time! This numerical phenomenon, known as Benford's Law, was discovered by Frank Benford while he was working as a physicist at the GE Research Laboratories.

An intuitive explanation of Benford's Law appeared in the *Journal of Accountancy* in the article "I've Got Your Number" written by Mark Nigrini. Nigrini offered an explanation that considered "the total assets of a mutual fund that is growing at 10 percent per year. When the total assets are $100 million, the first digit of total assets is 1. The first digit will continue to be 1 until total assets reach $200 million. This will require a 100 percent increase (from 100 to 200), which, at a growth rate of 10 percent per year, will take about 7.3 years (with compounding). At $500 million the first digit will be 5. Growing at 10 percent per year, the total assets will rise from $500 million to $600 million in about 1.9 years, significantly less time than assets took to grow from $100 million to $200 million. At $900 million, the first digit will be 9 until total assets reach $1 billion, or about 1.1 years at 10 percent. Once total assets are $1 billion the first digit will again be 1, until total assets again grow by another 100 percent. The persistence of a 1 as a first digit will occur with any phenomenon that has a constant (or even an erratic) growth rate."

The expected frequency of the first digits in a dataset of numbers is as follows:

1	2	3	4	5	6	7	8	9
30.1%	17.6%	12.5%	9.7%	7.9%	6.7%	5.8%	5.1%	4.6%

An excellent example of accountants at KPMG leveraging data analytics occurred when Benford's Law was used in the audit of a call center. The call center allowed hundreds of operators to issue refunds up to $50 without manager approval. What the audit found was that there were way too many refunds that began with a 4. The accountants soon found that several operators were issuing refunds just under the $50 limit to friends, family members, and, even more boldly, to themselves. The total fraud, uncovered with the aid of data analytics and Benford's Law, amounted to hundreds of thousands of dollars of fraudulent refunds.

assets not recorded in the asset account. Similarly, a business should periodically confirm the amounts owed to suppliers (Accounts Payable) and the amounts due from customers (Accounts Receivable) by contacting the suppliers and customers to verify any amounts owed or to be received. This internal control process is known as accounts receivable confirmation and accounts payable confirmation.

Provide Physical and Electronic Controls   Physical and electronic controls are prevention controls that take many forms. Locked doors are an important physical control. Locked doors help prevent the theft of assets and protect the integrity of the accounting system. Many companies install safes and vaults to store cash prior to depositing it in a bank and to hold important business documents such as mortgages and securities. Any installed safes and vaults should be of sufficient quality that they can withstand fire and such natural disasters as flooding and tornados. Fencing off company property and assigning security guards at the gates are other commonly used physical controls.

Electronic controls are also widely used by businesses. Merchandising firms use electronic cash registers to ensure that each salesperson records each transaction as it occurs and that the salesperson stores cash in a locked drawer. Retailers, convenience stores, and banks use observation cameras to monitor their operations. Retailers also attach special plastic tags to merchandise, which activate electronic sensors and set off alarms if an individual attempts to leave a store without having the plastic tag removed by a salesperson.

4. Information and Communication

The fourth control component of the COSO framework involves communication. It is important that individuals receive a clear message from senior management that control responsibilities must be taken seriously. To do this, management must obtain or generate relevant and quality information from both internal and external sources. This information must then be communicated in a continual and iterative process of providing, sharing, and then obtaining new information.

5. Monitoring Activities

It is necessary for the internal control system to be monitored in order to assess the quality of the system's performance over time. **Monitoring activities** involve ongoing evaluations, special evaluations, or some combination of each. Ongoing evaluations are built into the business processes at various levels of the organization and provide timely information. Special evaluations are conducted periodically and vary in scope and frequency based on risk assessments, results from ongoing evaluations, and other management considerations.

Internal Audits   Internal audits are one type of monitoring activity. In a small company, internal auditing is a function typically assigned to an employee who has other duties as well. In a large company, internal auditing is an activity assigned to an independent department that reports to top management or the board of directors of the corporation. **Internal auditing** is a company function that provides independent appraisals of the company's financial statements, its internal control, and its operations.

The evaluation of a company's internal control involves two phases. First, the internal auditor determines whether sufficient internal controls are in place. Second, the internal auditor determines whether the internal controls in place are functioning as planned. After completing the appraisal, the internal auditor makes recommendations to management regarding additional controls that are needed or improvements that are required for existing controls.

Control Failures

Occasionally, internal controls fail. For example, an employee may forget to lock an exterior door and a thief will steal some merchandise. Or, an employee with custody responsibilities steals cash received from customers. A company cannot completely prevent these types of incidents from occurring. Consequently, many businesses purchase insurance to compensate the company if any of these types of incidents do occur. Casualty insurance provides financial compensation to a business for losses from fire, natural disasters, and theft. A **fidelity bond** is an insurance policy that provides financial compensation for theft by employees specifically covered by the insurance.

Another reason that internal controls fail is **employee collusion**. When two or more employees work together to circumvent or avoid prescribed internal controls, this act is known as *employee collusion*. For example, an employee with custody of an asset (like cash) can work with an employee with recording responsibilities to steal the asset and cover up the theft in the accounting records. Employee collusion is difficult to prevent or detect. Hiring high-quality employees and paying them market wages is the best approach to avoid collusion. Close employee supervision is also important.

THINKING GLOBALLY

Unfortunately, financial fraud is a world wide problem. For example, in 2008, India's leading software services firm, **Satyam Computer Services**, was found to have defrauded stockholders for more than a decade by overstating the company's revenues and its cash by more than $1 billion. The company's independent auditors, from **PricewaterhouseCoopers**, were arrested shortly thereafter on charges of being an accomplice to the financial fraud.

As with employee collusion, senior management can often circumvent internal controls. Additionally, in small companies where proper segregation of duties is not possible, the owner must serve as the mitigating control. This requires the owner to be present most of the time and also provides opportunity for the owner to circumvent internal controls.

Sarbanes-Oxley Act

For public companies, strong internal controls like those described above are no longer simply a matter of good business practice; they are required by law. Following the **Enron** and **WorldCom** accounting scandals, the U.S. Congress passed landmark legislation called the Sarbanes-Oxley Act (SOX). This act mandates that all publicly traded U.S. corporations maintain an adequate system of internal controls. Further, top management must ensure the reliability of these controls and outside independent auditors must attest to the adequacy of the controls. Failing to do so can result in prison sentences of up to 20 years and/or monetary fines of up to $5 million.

TAKEAWAY 7.1	Concept ⟶	Method ⟶	Assessment
	Are the internal controls adequate?	The COSO framework identifies five internal control components: (1) the control environment, (2) risk assessment, (3) control activities, (4) information and communication, and (5) monitoring activities.	Monitoring activities include appraisals of the company's internal control system. If weaknesses are reported, be cautious in relying on the reported financial statements.

YOUR TURN! 7.2

The solution is on page 7-47.

Identify which internal control concept is being violated and explain how this may cause an opportunity for fraud to occur within a business:

1. The supervisor for the purchasing department has not taken a vacation in three years.
2. Inventory is left in a receiving area at the back of the store by an open door.
3. The purchasing supervisor has the authority to order a purchase and also to receive the merchandise, record its receipt, and authorize the accounting department to issue a check.

ACCOUNTING FOR CASH

Cash includes coins, currency (paper money), checks, money orders, traveler's checks, and funds on deposit at a financial institution in a company's checking and savings accounts. An item is considered to be an element of cash if (1) it is accepted by a bank or other financial institution (brokerage firm or credit union) for deposit, and (2) it is free from restrictions that would prevent its use for paying debts.

LO3 Define cash and **discuss** the accounting for cash.

eLecture
MBC

Many near-cash items such as certificates of deposit, postdated checks, not-sufficient-funds checks, and IOUs are not considered to be cash. **Certificates of deposit** (CDs) are securities issued by a bank when cash is invested for a short period of time, typically three months to one year. CDs pay a fixed rate of interest on any deposited funds. A **postdated check** is a check from another person or company with a date that is later than the current date. A postdated check does not become equivalent to cash until the actual calendar date on the check. A **not-sufficient-funds check** (**NSF** check) is a check from an individual or company that had an insufficient cash balance in the bank when the holder of the check presented it to the bank for payment. IOU is a slang term for a note receivable—that is, a written document that states that one party promises to pay another party a certain amount of cash on a certain date. CDs are accounted for as investments, whereas postdated checks, NSF checks, and IOUs are accounted for as Other Receivables.

Reporting Cash

A company may have only one Cash account in the general ledger, or it may have multiple cash accounts, such as Cash in Bank, Cash on Hand, and Petty Cash. Cash in Bank includes any cash held in a company's checking and savings accounts, while Cash on Hand includes cash items not yet deposited in the bank. Petty Cash is an example of cash on hand that is used for small disbursements and is maintained at the company's business location.

When a company has several bank accounts, it may maintain a separate general ledger account for each account or use a single Cash in Bank account. Although a company may prepare for internal use only a balance sheet that shows each individual bank account separately, the balance sheet that the company prepares for external users typically shows the combined balances of all bank accounts and other cash accounts under a single heading of Cash. Management is likely to want to see the detail involving the multiple cash accounts that the company maintains so that it can monitor and control the various accounts and on hand amounts. Most external users, however, are only interested in the total amount of cash and its relationship to other items on the balance sheet.

Cash is a current asset and is shown first in the balance sheet listing of assets. Some of a company's cash may be **restricted cash**, meaning that the cash is restricted for a special purpose. For example, a company may have a restriction on its cash to cover a litigation settlement. Restricted cash should be reported separately on the balance sheet as either a current or a noncurrent asset depending on the length of the restriction. Sometimes a company's total cash includes one or more compensating balances. A **compensating balance** is a minimum cash balance that a bank requires a firm to maintain in its bank account as part of a borrowing arrangement. Compensating balances related to short-term borrowings are current assets, which, if significant, are reported separately from the cash amount among the current assets. Compensating balances related to long-term borrowings are reported as long-term assets.

Cash and Cash Equivalents

A company may combine certain short-term, highly liquid investments with cash and present a single amount called **cash and cash equivalents** on the balance sheet. Cash equivalents are highly liquid, short-term investments of 90 days maturity or less in such risk-free securities as U.S. Treasury bills and money market funds. A company presents this combined amount on the balance sheet so that it reconciles with the change in cash and cash equivalents appearing on the company's statement of cash flows. The statement of cash flows explains the changes in a firm's total cash and cash equivalents during an accounting period.

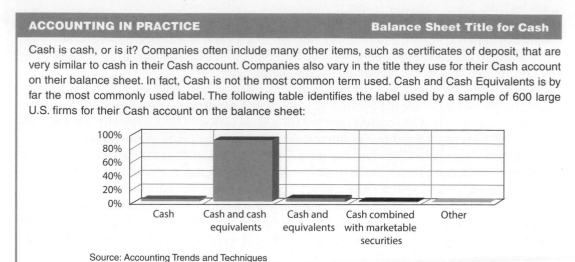

ACCOUNTING IN PRACTICE   **Balance Sheet Title for Cash**

Cash is cash, or is it? Companies often include many other items, such as certificates of deposit, that are very similar to cash in their Cash account. Companies also vary in the title they use for their Cash account on their balance sheet. In fact, Cash is not the most common term used. Cash and Cash Equivalents is by far the most commonly used label. The following table identifies the label used by a sample of 600 large U.S. firms for their Cash account on the balance sheet:

Source: Accounting Trends and Techniques

TAKEAWAY 7.2	Concept	→	Method	→	Assessment
	Are there any restrictions on a company's use of its cash and cash equivalents?		Balance sheet and the notes to the financial statements. Identify any restrictions to cash or compensating cash balances.		Consider any existing cash restrictions when assessing liquidity.

YOUR TURN! 7.3

The solution is on page 7-47.

All of the following are typically included in the cash and cash equivalents account except:

a. Cash
b. Marketable securities
c. Money market funds
d. 30-day U.S. Treasury bills

INTERNAL CONTROL OF CASH RECEIPTS TRANSACTIONS

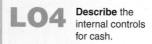

LO4 Describe the internal controls for cash.

eLecture

MBC

Most companies develop elaborate internal controls to protect their cash because it is their most liquid asset, and in all likelihood, an important operating asset. Cash is highly desirable, easily taken and concealed, and quickly converted into other assets. In addition, a high percentage of a company's transactions involve cash. Cash is received from customers following a sale and cash is paid to suppliers and employees for goods and services. A company receives cash from customers, for example, as payment on account and as payment for cash sales. The following sections describe cash handling procedures and the related internal controls for these two types of cash receipts.

Cash Received on Account

A company receives cash through the mail from customers who are making payments on their accounts receivable balance. Four departments play major roles in processing cash receipts that arrive via the mail: the mailroom, the treasurer's department, the controller's department, and the internal audit department. **Exhibit 7-1** and the following paragraphs describe the role that each department plays in processing mailed cash receipts.

EXHIBIT 7-1 **Processing Cash Received on Account through the Mail**

Mailroom

1. Opens mail from separate post office box.
2. Compares checks to remittance advices.
3. Endorses checks.
4. Prepares remittance list and compares it to total of checks.
5. Sends checks to treasurer.
6. Sends remittance list and remittance advices to controller.

Treasurer (Custody)

1. Prepares deposit slip.
2. Sends deposit slips and checks to bank.
3. Sends copy of deposit slip to controller.
4. Files a copy of the deposit slip.

Controller (Recording)

1. Compares deposit slip from treasurer to remittance list total.
2. Uses the total on the remittance list to prepare the journal entry to record the cash receipt.
3. Uses the remittance advices to post to the accounts receivable subsidiary ledger.
4. Files the remittance list, remittance advices, and deposit slip copy.

Internal Audit

1. Receives monthly bank statement directly from the bank.
2. Prepares bank reconciliation.
3. Prepares adjusting entries.

Mailroom

A company often sets up a separate post office box and requests that its customers mail any cash payments on account to that post office box. All other mail and company correspondence are directed to another company address or a different post office box. This approach automatically sorts a company's mail into two groups: (1) cash receipts from customers and (2) all other mail.

Mailroom employees open the envelopes containing cash receipts from customers. Each envelope should contain two items: a check and a remittance advice. A **remittance advice** is a form that accompanies a check to inform the company receiving the check about the purpose of the check. The remittance advice includes the customer's name, the amount paid, and such reference numbers as the invoice number and the customer account number.

Mailroom employees ensure that the dollar amount on each check and the related remittance advice are the same and then place the two documents in separate piles. An employee then endorses each check "For Deposit Only" so that no one can cash the check. The mailroom employees also prepare a remittance list. A **remittance list** is a list of all of the checks received on a given day. For each check, the remittance list includes the customer name and/or account number, the check number, and the amount received.

A separate mailroom employee compares the remittance list total to a list totaling the checks and another list totaling the remittance advices to ensure that the check amounts are listed correctly and that they agree with the remittance advices. The mailroom then sends the checks to the treasurer's department and the remittance list and the remittance advices to the controller's department.

Treasurer

The treasurer's department is a *custodial* department. It maintains custody of the received customer checks. It has no responsibilities for any recording or posting activities. The duties of this department include preparing a bank deposit slip (original plus two copies) for each batch of checks received and sending the original deposit slip and the customer checks to the bank. One copy of the deposit slip is forwarded to the controller's department, and the treasurer's department files the second copy for future reference.

Controller

The controller's department is a *recording* department. It records the cash receipts in a journal and posts the cash receipts to the company's general ledger and the Accounts Receivable account. The controller's department never has access to, or custody of, the received customer checks.

Before recording and posting the cash receipts, the controller's department compares the total on the deposit slip copy from the treasurer's department to the remittance list obtained from the mailroom to ensure that the treasurer's department deposited all of the checks sent from the mailroom. The controller's department then prepares a journal entry (debit Cash and credit Accounts Receivable) to record the cash receipts. The dollar amount of the debit and credit is the total from the deposit slip.

The controller's department uses the individual remittance advices to post the cash payments to the Accounts Receivable account of each individual customer. After processing, the remittance list, the remittance advices, and the deposit slip copy are filed in the controller's department for future reference.

Internal Audit

Internal audit is an independent department; it has no recurring custody, recording, or authorization duties related to accounting transactions. Once each month, the internal audit department performs its independent review and **reconciliation** duties related to the cash received. The internal auditor receives the monthly bank statement directly from the bank. This ensures that no one can alter the information returned with the bank statement. The internal audit department uses the bank statement to prepare the monthly bank reconciliation and create any needed journal entries. These internally prepared bank reconciliations can be part of a good internal control environment and serve as schedules that the independent auditors can more easily verify and test as a part of their audit process. The preparation of the bank reconciliation and related journal entries are discussed later in this chapter.

Data Analytics

DATA ANALYTICS	**How Data Analytics Is Changing the Internal Audit Function**

Data analytics at its most basic level is the process of collecting and manipulating data to draw insights from the data. One area in which data analytics has proven extremely valuable is the field of internal auditing. Internal auditors have automated many processes that had been manual. Using data analytics, they have been able to develop a more comprehensive view of the business, identify risks earlier in the audit process, improve communication with visualizations, and shorten the audit, which reduces costs.

Cash Received from Retail Cash Sales

A retailer receives cash from customers when the retailer sells merchandise. The retailer must design internal controls to protect any cash received. Five groups play major roles in collecting, protecting, processing, and recording cash received from retail customers: the retail sales area, the retail sales supervisor, the treasurer's department, the controller's department, and the internal audit department. **Exhibit 7-2** and the following paragraphs describe the role that each group plays.

Retail Sales Area

Sales associates use cash registers to record cash sales and to control and protect the cash collected from customers. Each sales associate uses a unique **password** or key to identify him- or herself to the cash register. Each associate should have a separate cash drawer for collecting cash from customers and making change. Each sales associate begins their shift with a fixed amount of change in his or her cash drawer. The sales associates enter details of each sale into the cash register and place any cash received from customers into the assigned cash drawer. The cash register prints a paper tape listing the description and price of the items sold and the total amount due. The cash register also records this information either in the memory of the cash register or in a computer memory that the cash register accesses.

Retail Sales Supervisor

The retail sales supervisor oversees the retail sales operations of a business. Throughout the day, the supervisor approves any unusual transactions such as merchandise returns. At the end of the sales associate's shift, the supervisor counts the contents of each cash drawer. He or she compares the amount of cash in each drawer in excess of the beginning amount to the sales total accumulated by the cash register for each sales associate. The supervisor then prepares a written report (three copies) to document the total sales and the total cash received.

The supervisor delivers the cash in excess of the initial change amount and a copy of the written report to the treasurer's department. The cash register tape and another copy of the written report are taken to the controller's department. The supervisor files the third copy of the written report for future use if needed.

Treasurer

The treasurer's department takes custody of any cash from the retail sales supervisor after signing a receipt that the supervisor retains as proof of the cash delivery. Employees of the treasurer's department count the cash and prepare a deposit slip (original plus two copies). The employees then send the original deposit slip and cash to the bank for deposit. One copy of the deposit slip is sent to the controller's department, and the treasurer's department files the final copy for future reference.

Controller

The controller's department is responsible for recording cash sales. The controller's department never has access to or custody of the cash. Before recording and posting the cash receipts, the controller's department compares the total on the deposit slip copy from the treasurer's department to the written report from the retail sales supervisor to ensure that the treasurer's department deposited all of the cash received. The controller's department then prepares a journal entry to record the cash sales. This entry also reflects any shortage or overage of cash, should this occur. The written report and the deposit receipt are filed for future reference.

Internal Audit

The duties of the internal audit department with respect to cash received from retail sales are identical to its duties with respect to cash received on account. Note again that the bank sends the monthly bank statement directly to a company's internal auditor. If a company does not have an internal auditor, the bank sends the monthly bank statement to an appropriate person designated by the company, usually someone who does not have custody or recording responsibilities for cash. The internal audit department prepares a bank reconciliation statement and makes any needed journal entries.

EXHIBIT 7-2   Processing Cash Received from Retail Cash Sales

Retail Sales Area

1. Begin each shift with a fixed amount of change in drawer of each cash register.
2. Sales associate enters details of each sale into a cash register and places cash received from the customer into the cash register drawer assigned to that sales associate.

Retail Sales Supervisor

1. Observes the sales operation during the day.
2. Approves any unusual transactions during the day.
3. At the end of the shift, counts the contents of each drawer with the sales associate responsible for the drawer.
4. Compares the amount in the drawer in excess of the beginning amount to the sales total accumulated by the cash register for that sales associate.
5. Prepares written report of sales and cash received.
6. Sends cash and a copy of the written report to the treasurer.
7. Sends cash register tape and a copy of the report to the controller.

Treasurer (Custody)

1. Prepares deposit slip.
2. Sends deposit slip and cash to bank.
3. Sends copy of deposit slip to controller.
4. Files a copy of the deposit slip.

Controller (Recording)

1. Compares deposit slip from treasurer to written report and cash register tape.
2. Uses the written report to prepare the journal entry to record cash sales.
3. Files written report and deposit slip.

Internal Auditor

1. Receives monthly bank statement directly from the bank.
2. Prepares bank reconciliation.
3. Prepares adjusting entries.

Checks

When a company opens a checking account at a bank, the bank requires each company employee who will sign checks to sign a signature card. Occasionally, a bank employee compares the signatures on the checks presented for payment by various parties to the authorized signatures on the signature cards. This comparison provides an internal control for the bank that it is not cashing a check written by an unauthorized employee. The bank is responsible for any amounts erroneously paid out of a company's checking account.

A **check** is a written order signed by a checking account owner (also known as the *maker*) directing the bank (called the *payer*) to pay a specified amount of money to the person or company named on the check (called the *payee*). A check is a negotiable instrument; it can be transferred to another person or company by writing "pay to the order of" and the name of the other person or company on the back of the check and then signing the back of the check.

Exhibit 7-3 presents a sample check. As noted previously, proper internal control requires that business documents such as checks be prenumbered in numerical sequence. The printed check number appears in two locations in **Exhibit 7-3**: in standard type in the upper right corner ❶ and in MICR (magnetic ink character recognition) form on the bottom of the check ❷. Also printed twice on the check are alternative formats of the routing number for the check, a fraction format ❸ and an MICR format ❹. The check printer also places the customer's account number on the check in MICR form ❺. When the check is processed by the banking system, the MICR check amount ❻ is added at the bottom right of the check. Banks use special equipment that reads MICR codes directly into computer files.

EXHIBIT 7-3   Sample Check

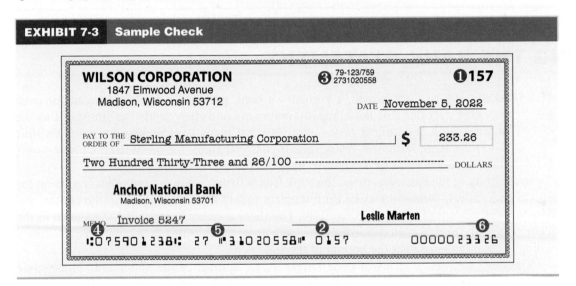

Using Electronic Funds Transfer

Many companies receive payments from customers or make payments to suppliers using electronic funds transfer rather than writing and mailing checks. **Electronic funds transfer**, commonly known as EFT, involves sending an electronic message from one computer to another to cause a transfer of money from one financial institution to another, or directly to a company. Actually, two electronic messages are sent. To illustrate, assume that a company wants to use EFT to transfer money to a second company to pay an invoice. The paying company has its computer send a message to its bank's computer to request the funds transfer. This is known as *retail EFT*. Then, the paying company's bank uses EFT to transfer funds to the receiving company's bank. This is known as *wholesale EFT* or *bank-to-bank EFT*. Wholesale EFT usually involves a central bank (such as a Federal Reserve Bank) that acts as an automated clearinghouse by increasing the balance of one bank and decreasing the balance of the other bank.

Petty Cash Fund

Most businesses find it inconvenient and expensive to write checks for small expenditures. Instead, these businesses establish a petty cash fund. A **petty cash fund** is a small amount of cash, for example, $300, that is placed in a secure location on a business's premises to be used to pay for small expenditures such as postage, delivery service charges, and minor purchases of supplies. The size of the petty cash fund depends on how often it is used and the amount of the disbursements. Firms often select an amount that will last for three or four weeks.

Although the use of a petty cash fund violates the rule that all cash payments should be made by check or EFT, control can be maintained by handling the fund on an imprest basis with documented procedures. An imprest fund contains a fixed amount of cash. A business establishes a petty cash fund by writing a check against the firm's checking account and cashing the check at the bank. All replenishments of the petty cash fund are also made by check. As a result, all expenditures are ultimately controlled by check, providing a paper trail of all cash transfers to the petty cash fund.

YOUR TURN! 7.4 GuidedExample **MBC** The solution is on page 7-47.	Match the internal control function from the left-hand column with the area of responsibility in the right-hand column: 1. Prepares deposit receipt. 2. Approves unusual transactions. 3. Prepares remittance list. 4. Prepares bank reconciliation. 5. Compares deposit receipt to remittance list. *a.* Retail sales supervisor *b.* Mailroom *c.* Treasurer's department *d.* Controller's department *e.* Internal audit department

RECONCILING THE BANK STATEMENT

Illustrate the bank reconciliation process.

eLecture

MBC

At the end of each month, a company's bank prepares a bank statement for each checking account that the company maintains and then sends the statement to the internal audit department of the company that owns the checking account. **Exhibit 7-4** is the bank statement from Anchor National Bank for the Wilson Corporation's checking account as of November 30.

In the body of the bank statement, the bank lists Wilson's deposits and other credits on the left (in date order), Wilson's checks (in numerical order) and other debits in the center, and Wilson's daily account balance on the right. The daily account balance is the balance in the account as of the end of each day listed. The bank presents a summary calculation of Wilson's ending account balance near the bottom of the statement.

The bank defines a series of code letters at the bottom of the statement. These code letters identify debits and credits not related to paying checks or making deposits. These code letters are not standard from bank to bank. In **Exhibit 7-4**, EC identifies corrections of errors made by the bank; DM (debit memo) identifies automatic loan payments and bank charges for items such as collecting notes; CM (credit memo) identifies amounts collected by the bank for the depositor; SC (service charge) identifies fees charged by the bank for the checking account; OD (overdraft) indicates a negative balance in the account; RT (returned item) identifies items such as posted checks and NSF checks for which the bank could not collect cash; and IN (interest earned) identifies interest added to the account.

ACCOUNTING IN PRACTICE   **Debits or Credits?**
Debit and credit terminology may seem backward on a bank statement. Debits decrease a bank account balance and credits increase a bank account balance. To understand this, realize that bank statements are prepared from the perspective of the bank, not the customer of the bank. In other words, when a company deposits cash in its checking account, the bank debits Cash and credits a liability account called a Customer Deposit. The bank statement sent to a company each month is a statement of its Customer Deposit account held by the bank. As with any liability, debits decrease its balance and credits increase its balance.

EXHIBIT 7-4	Bank Statement of Wilson Corporation

ANCHOR NATIONAL BANK
123 Center Street
Madison, Wisconsin 53701

Wilson Corporation
1847 Elmwood Avenue
Madison, Wisconsin 53712

Account Number   27-31020558
Statement Date   November 30

Deposits and Credits		Checks and Debits			Daily Balance	
Date	Amount	Number	Date	Amount	Date	Amount
Nov. 01	420.00	149	Nov. 02	125.00	Nov. 01	6,060.30
Nov. 02	630.00	154	Nov. 03	56.25	Nov. 02	6,565.30
Nov. 07	560.80	155	Nov. 10	135.00	Nov. 03	6,509.05
Nov. 10	480.25	156	Nov. 08	315.10	Nov. 07	6,801.19
Nov. 14	525.00	157	Nov. 07	233.26	Nov. 08	6,486.09
Nov. 17	270.25	158	Nov. 11	27.14	Nov. 10	6,831.34
Nov. 21	640.20	159	Nov. 18	275.00	Nov. 11	6,804.20
Nov. 26	300.00CM	160	Nov. 15	315.37	Nov. 14	7,329.20
Nov. 26	475.00	161	Nov. 17	76.40	Nov. 15	7,013.83
Nov. 30	471.40	162	Nov. 21	325.60	Nov. 17	7,207.68
		163	Nov. 21	450.00	Nov. 18	6,932.68
		164	Nov. 23	239.00	Nov. 21	6,731.58
		165	Nov. 21	65.70	Nov. 23	6,492.58
		166	Nov. 28	482.43	Nov. 26	7,262.58
		169	Nov. 28	260.00	Nov. 28	6,520.15
		170	Nov. 30	122.50	Nov. 30	6,488.95
		171	Nov. 30	370.10		
			Nov. 07	35.40RT		
			Nov. 26	5.00DM		
			Nov. 30	10.00SC		

Beginning Balance	+	Deposits and Credits	–	Checks and Debits	=	Ending Balance
$5,640.30	+	$4,772.90	–	$3,924.25	=	$6,488.95

Item Codes: EC: Error Correction   DM: Debit Memo   CM: Credit Memo
SC: Service Charge   OD: Overdraft   RT: Returned Item
IN: Interest Earned

The Bank Reconciliation Process

The internal audit department prepares a bank reconciliation as of the end of each month. A **bank reconciliation** is a schedule that (1) accounts for all differences between the ending cash balance on the bank statement and the ending cash balance in the Cash account in the company's general ledger and (2) determines the reconciled cash balance as of the end of the month. The internal audit department employee preparing the bank reconciliation needs access to the bank statement, the general ledger, cash receipts records, and cash disbursements records to prepare the reconciliation.

Exhibit 7-5 outlines the structure of a company's bank reconciliation. The bank reconciliation is really two schedules prepared side by side. The schedule on the left includes bank items, and the schedule on the right includes items related to the company's general ledger.

The schedule on the left begins with the ending cash balance from the bank statement (the month-end balance according to the bank's records). The internal audit department employee preparing the reconciliation adds (1) deposits not yet recorded by the bank, called **deposits in transit**, and (2) any corrections not yet made by the bank that will increase the bank balance. The preparer then subtracts (1) checks not yet recorded by the bank, called

EXHIBIT 7-5   **Structure of a Company's Bank Reconciliation**

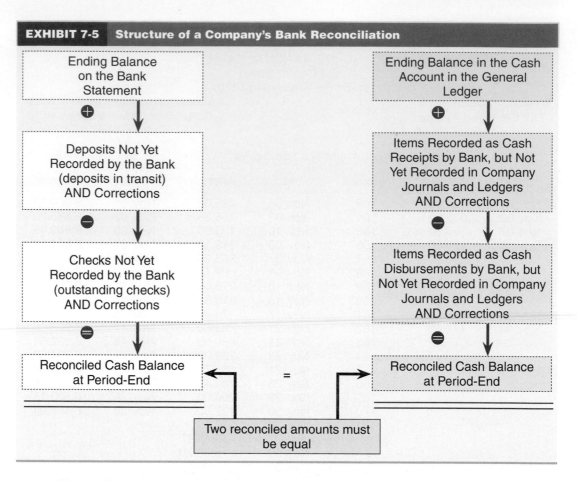

outstanding checks, and (2) any corrections not yet made by the bank that will decrease the bank balance. The resulting total is the reconciled cash balance at the end of the month.

The schedule on the right begins with the ending balance in the Cash account in the company's general ledger. The internal audit department employee adds (1) items recorded as cash receipts by the bank but not yet recorded in the company's journals and ledgers and (2) any corrections not yet made by the company that will increase the general ledger cash balance. The preparer subtracts (1) items recorded as cash disbursements by the bank but not yet recorded in the company's journals and ledgers and (2) any corrections not yet made by the company that will decrease the general ledger cash balance. The resulting total is the reconciled cash balance at the end of the month. The totals of the two schedules will be the same if the bank reconciliation is completed properly.

Bank Reconciliation Illustrated   Assume that the internal auditor of the Wilson Corporation is preparing the November 30 bank reconciliation. She uses the following procedures to reconcile the November 30 bank statement balance of $6,488.95 to the November 30 general ledger Cash account balance of $5,322.69:

1. **Trace outstanding items on the bank reconciliation for the previous month to the current bank statement.** Any items on the previous bank reconciliation that have still not been processed by the bank must appear on the current bank reconciliation. The October 31 reconciliation included the following:

Deposit in transit		$420.00
Outstanding checks:	Number 149	$125.00
	Number 154	56.25
	Number 155	135.00

The November 30 bank statement includes the $420 deposit and all three checks listed above. Therefore, none of these items will appear on the November 30 bank reconciliation.

2. **Compare the deposits made during the month to the deposits on the bank statement.**
   The Wilson Corporation made the following deposits during November:

November 2	$630.00	November 21	$640.20
November 7	560.80	November 26	475.00
November 10	480.25	November 29	471.40
November 14	525.00	November 30	225.00
November 17	270.25		

   All of these deposits appear on the bank statement except for the November 30 deposit of $225. The $225 deposit will appear on the left side of the November 30 bank reconciliation as a deposit in transit.

3. **Compare the checks issued during the month to the checks on the bank statement.**
   The Wilson Corporation issued the following checks during November:

Number 156	$315.10	Number 165	$ 65.70
Number 157	233.26	Number 166	482.43
Number 158	27.14	Number 167	301.66
Number 159	275.00	Number 168	149.50
Number 160	315.37	Number 169	260.00
Number 161	76.40	Number 170	122.50
Number 162	325.60	Number 171	370.10
Number 163	450.00	Number 172	450.00
Number 164	239.00	Number 173	240.50

   Four of the checks—numbers 167, 168, 172, and 173—do not appear on the bank statement. These four checks will appear on the left side of the November 30 bank reconciliation as outstanding checks.

4. **Scan the bank statement for charges and credits not yet reflected in the general ledger.** The Wilson Corporation's bank statement contains a charge of $35.40 for a returned item, a debit memo of $5.00, and a service charge of $10.00 in the Checks and Debits column. The Deposits and Credits column contains a credit memo for $300.00. Supplemental information sent by the bank with the bank statement reveals that the bank charged a $35.40 NSF check against Wilson's account, collected a $300.00 note for Wilson and charged a $5.00 collection fee, and that the service charge for the month of November was $10.00. These four items have not yet been recorded by Wilson Corporation. Therefore, they must be listed on the right side of the bank reconciliation.

5. **Check for errors.** A review of Wilson Corporation's journals and ledgers reveals that they recorded check number 159 as $725.00. The correct amount of $275.00 appears on the bank statement. The check was written to pay for office supplies. The correction of the transposition in the amount of $450 must be listed on the right side of the bank reconciliation.

After the five steps have been completed, the November 30 bank reconciliation for the Wilson Corporation appears as shown in **Exhibit 7-6**. Note that both the left side and the right side of the reconciliation end with a reconciled cash balance and that the two amounts are the same. This reconciled cash balance of $5,572.29 is the amount that will appear on the November 30 balance sheet for the company.

EXHIBIT 7-6	November 30, 2019, Bank Reconciliation for Wilson Corporation

WILSON CORPORATION
Bank Reconciliation
November 30

Ending balance from bank statement....	$6,488.95	Balance from general ledger			$4,872.69
Add: Deposits in transit................	225.00	Add: Check 159 for $275			
		recorded as $725			450.00
		Collection of note	$300.00		
	6,713.95	Less: Collection fee	5.00		295.00
					5,617.69
Less: Outstanding checks:					
No. 167	$301.66	Less: NSF check		35.40	
No. 168	149.50	Service charge		10.00	45.40
No. 172	450.00				
No. 173	240.50	1,141.66			
Reconciled cash balance		$5,572.29	Reconciled cash balance		$5,572.29

Before the Wilson Corporation prepares its financial statements for November, they must make journal entries to bring the balance in the Cash account into agreement with the reconciled cash balance on the bank reconciliation. These entries incorporate the items on the company's side of the bank reconciliation as follows:

A = L + SE	Nov. 30	Cash (+A)			450.00	
+450.00 +450.00 Exp		Office supplies expense (−E, +SE)				450.00
		To correct recording error on check number 159.				
A = L + SE	Nov. 30	Cash (+A)			295.00	
+295.00 −5.00 Exp		Miscellaneous expense (+E, −SE)			5.00	
−300.00		Notes receivable (−A)				300.00
		To record a note collected by the bank, less a collection fee.				
A = L + SE	Nov. 30	Accounts receivable (+A)			35.40	
+35.40		Cash (−A)				35.40
−35.40		*To reclassify an NSF check as an account receivable.*				
A = L + SE	Nov. 30	Miscellaneous expense (+E, −SE)			10.00	
−10.00 −10.00 Exp		Cash (−A)				10.00
		To record bank service charge for November.				

ACCOUNTING IN PRACTICE	Accounting Trick to Catch Transpositions

Transposing numbers is one of the most frequent causes of errors in bank reconciliations. Transposing numbers occurs when they are written in the wrong sequence. Recording 87 instead of 78 or 149 instead of 194 are examples of transposition errors. Anybody who has recorded lists of numbers has probably made these kinds of errors at some point. Fortunately, there is an easy way to detect transposition errors. If, when doing a bank reconciliation, you find that the number you arrive at differs from the bank's number by a multiple of 9, chances are it is a transposition error. Assume you think you have $120 in your account, but the bank claims your balance is only $66. The difference between $120 and $66 is $54, a number evenly divisible by 9. There is a good chance that this difference is the result of a transposition error because all transpositions, no matter what numbers are transposed, will cause an error evenly divisible by 9. Recall our two examples above, 78 and 194 transposed as 87 and 149. The differences are 9 and 45, and both are evenly divisible by 9. Go ahead and try it with any number. Of course this trick can be used anytime you are recording numbers, not just with bank reconciliations.

Match the reconciling items from the left-hand column with the proper reconciling action from the right-hand column:

1. Deposits in transit
2. Outstanding checks
3. Bank service charge
4. Cash collected by bank on note

a. Add to bank statement balance
b. Subtract from bank statement balance
c. Add to cash general ledger account
d. Subtract from cash general ledger account

The solution is on page 7-47.

EFFECTIVE CASH MANAGEMENT

Cash is typically one of a company's most important assets. Without cash, a company would be unable to pay its employees or its suppliers. In short, a company would be unable to continue operating. As a consequence, managers spend considerable time and effort managing and monitoring this key asset. Similarly, investors and lenders spend considerable time understanding where a company's cash came from and how the company spent it.

LO6 Describe the four primary activities of effective cash management.

Monitoring Cash

The most effective tool for external parties to monitor a company's cash is the statement of cash flows.[1] As discussed in Chapter 1, the statement of cash flows identifies a company's cash inflows and cash outflows, segmenting them into the three business activities of operating, investing, and financing. **Exhibit 7-7** presents the statement of cash flows for WebWork, Inc., for the month ended December 31.

EXHIBIT 7-7	Statement of Cash Flows for WebWork, Inc.

WEBWORK, INC.
Statement of Cash Flows
For Month Ended December 31

Cash flow from operating activities		
Cash received from clients	$19,910	
Cash paid to employees and suppliers	(1,620)	
Cash paid for rent	(10,800)	
Cash provided by operating activities		$ 7,490
Cash flow from investing activities		
Purchase of office equipment	(32,400)	
Cash used by investing activities		(32,400)
Cash flow from financing activities		
Stock issued	30,000	
Borrowing from bank	36,000	
Cash dividends	(500)	
Cash provided by financing activities		65,500
Net increase in cash		40,590
Cash at December 1		0
Cash at December 31		$40,590

---

[1] The statement of cash flows provides an after-the-fact monitoring of cash sources and uses. Many companies use a cash budget to plan anticipated cash inflows and outflows so that they are able to manage the amount of cash on hand at an appropriate level. Cash budgets are covered in most managerial accounting textbooks.

The positive numbers on the statement of cash flows represent a company's cash inflows and the negative numbers represent a company's cash outflows. WebWork's primary cash inflows involved the sale of stock ($30,000) and bank borrowings ($36,000). The company's primary uses of cash involved the purchase of office equipment ($32,400) and the payment of rent ($10,800). Not only does the statement of cash flows identify the sources and uses of cash, but it also identifies whether a company's cash balance increased or decreased for the period. **Exhibit 7-7** reveals that WebWork's cash account increased by $40,590 for the month of December.

While having some cash on hand is important to enable a company to pay its employees and its suppliers on a timely basis, having too much cash on hand may indicate that a company is not maximizing the return on its assets. Thus, it is important for managers to not only monitor a company's cash but also to manage it effectively to ensure that the company is earning an adequate return on this key asset.

Primary Activities of Effective Cash Management

Effective cash management generally involves four primary activities:

1. **Manage accounts receivable.** Since accounts receivable rarely include interest charges for late payment, the sooner that cash from sales can be collected, the sooner the cash can be used to pay suppliers, pay debt, or be invested in operations. Thus, managers should try to increase the rate at which accounts receivable are collected.

2. **Manage inventory levels.** Inventory should be maintained at levels that allow a company to satisfy customer needs while at the same time avoid having too much of the company's resources tied up in inventory for extended periods of time. Thus, managers should try to keep inventory levels as low as possible without losing any sales.

3. **Manage accounts payable.** Since accounts payable rarely include an interest charge for late payment, the longer a manager takes to pay off these accounts, the longer a company can use its cash to fund operations. Thus, managers should delay the payment of accounts payable. However, they should not be delayed beyond the point at which suppliers are no longer willing to do business with the company on reasonable terms. When accounts payable have credit terms that provide a discount for prompt payment, managers must evaluate the trade-off involved by delaying payment versus the reduced purchase price that results from timely payment.

4. **Invest excess cash.** Since cash on hand or in a bank account yields a very low rate of return, it is important to invest any excess cash. Thus, an important management activity is forecasting a company's cash needs by constructing a cash budget each period. Only a sufficient amount of cash necessary to cover a company's day-to-day needs should be kept on hand; any excess amounts should be invested in an effort to earn an adequate rate of return on this asset.

YOUR TURN! 7.6	Match the activities from column 1 with the activities described in column 2.	
The solution is on page 7-47.	**1**	**2**
	a. Manage accounts receivable	1. Acquire additional production machinery using additional cash beyond what the company normally needs to fund day-to-day operations.
	b. Manage inventory levels	2. Develop a forecast of demand for the company's products, taking into account factors such as seasonal fluctuations.
	c. Manage accounts payable	3. Contact customers with a reminder the first day a payment is late rather than waiting until the next month.
	d. Invest excess cash	4. Set up a schedule to pay invoices based on the credit terms offered by each vendor.

COMPREHENSIVE PROBLEM

At December 31 the Cash account in the Tyler Company's general ledger had a debit balance of $18,434.27. The December 31 bank statement showed a balance of $19,726.40. In reconciling the two amounts, you discover the following:

1. Bank deposits made by Tyler on December 31 amounting to $2,145.40 do not appear on the bank statement.
2. A noninterest-bearing note receivable from the Smith Company for $2,000 was collected by the bank at the end of December. The bank credited the proceeds, less a $5 collection fee, on the bank statement. Tyler Company has not recorded the collection.
3. Accompanying the bank statement is a debit memorandum indicating that John Miller's check for $450 was charged against Tyler's bank account on December 30 because of insufficient funds.
4. Check No. 586, written for advertising expense of $869.10, was recorded as $896.10 by Tyler Company.
5. A comparison of the paid checks returned by the bank with the recorded disbursements revealed that the following checks are still outstanding as of December 31:

No. 561	$306.63	No. 591	$190.00
No. 585	440.00	No. 592	282.50
No. 588	476.40	No. 593	243.00

6. The bank mistakenly charged Tyler Company's account for check printing costs of $30.50, which should have been charged to Taylor Company.
7. The bank charged Tyler Company's account $42.50 for the rental of a safe deposit box. No entry has been made in Tyler's records for this expense.

Required

a. Prepare a bank reconciliation as of December 31.
b. Prepare any necessary journal entries at December 31.

Solution

a.

TYLER COMPANY
Bank Reconciliation
December 31

Ending balance from bank statement.....		$19,726.40	Balance from general ledger		$18,434.27
Add: Deposits in transit................		2,145.40	Add: Collection of note $2,000.00		
Error by bank (Check printing			Less: Collection charge 5.00		1,995.00
charge of Taylor Co.)................		30.50	Error in recording check No. 586		27.00
		21,902.30			20,456.27
Less: Outstanding checks:			Less:		
No. 561	$306.63		NSF check 450.00		
No. 585	440.00		Charge for safe deposit box 42.50		492.50
No. 588	476.40				
No. 591	190.00				
No. 592	282.50				
No. 593	243.00	1,938.53			
Reconciled cash balance		$19,963.77	Reconciled cash balance		$19,963.77

A = L + SE				
+1,995.00 −5.00 −2,000.00	*b.* Dec. 31	Cash (+A)	1,995.00	
		Miscellaneous expense (+E, −SE)	5.00	
		Notes receivable—Smith Company (−A)		2,000.00
		To record collection of Smith Company's note by bank, less		
		collection charge.		
A = L + SE +27.00 +27.00	31	Cash (+A)	27.00	
		Advertising expense (−E, +SE)		27.00
		To correct error in recording advertising expense.		
A = L + SE +450.00 −450.00	31	Accounts receivable—John Miller (+A)	450.00	
		Cash (−A)		450.00
		To reclassify NSF check as an account receivable.		
A = L + SE −42.50 −42.50	31	Miscellaneous expense (+E, −SE)	42.50	
		Cash (−A)		42.50
		To record rental expense of safety deposit box.		

APPENDIX 7A: Auditing and Internal Control

L07   Describe financial statement audits and operational audits.

MBC

One of the internal control concepts previously discussed is conducting internal company audits. Internal audits provide appraisals of a company's financial statements, its internal control, and its operations. Internal auditors, who are employees of the company that they audit, conduct internal audits under the direction of top management or a company's board of directors.

    Parties outside the company, such as bankers and stockholders, prefer independent appraisals of a company's performance. These parties are usually unwilling to accept an audit report prepared by company-employed internal auditors because of possible bias and conflicts of interest. Consequently, creditors and stockholders usually require that an independent, professional auditing firm conduct an audit of the annual financial statements. Moreover, U.S. securities law requires that all corporations whose common stock is publicly traded have an independent firm of certified public accountants (CPAs) audit the company's annual financial statements.

FORENSIC ACCOUNTING   **Not Your Ordinary Audit**

The financial statement audit is performed to enable the independent auditor to express an opinion regarding whether the financial statements present fairly, in all material respects, the financial position and results of operations of a company. In so doing, the independent auditor is looking for material errors, whether the errors are a result of unintentional misstatement or fraud. To perform the audit, the auditor will perform statistical sampling of the reported transactions to make judgments regarding the fairness of the reported statements. The auditor is not specifically looking for fraud, and likely will not find it even if present, because the financial statement audit is not designed to uncover fraud. The forensic accountant, by way of contrast, is specifically looking for fraud. Forensic accountants concentrate their efforts where fraud is likely to occur or is suspected, rather than on the financial statements as a whole. The forensic accountant will also utilize additional investigative techniques and follow leads suggested by what appear to be immaterial items. The forensic accountant will often have additional skills not common to financial statement auditors, such as surveillance tactics and interviewing and interrogation skills.

Financial Statement Audits

A **financial statement audit** is an examination of a company's annual financial statements by a firm of independent certified public accountants. (The quarterly financial reports of U.S. publicly traded companies are "reviewed" by an independent audit firm but they are not subject to a full audit like the annual financial statements.) The independent audit firm conducts this examination so it can prepare a report that expresses an opinion regarding whether (or not) the financial statements fairly present the results of operations, cash flows, and financial position of a company.

Audit Procedures

The independent audit firm conducts the annual financial statement audit according to standards established by the **Public Company Accounting Oversight Board (PCAOB)**, a quasi-governmental agency established by the Sarbanes-Oxley Act. The PCAOB is responsible for establishing auditing standards, inspecting the auditing practices of independent audit firms, and disciplining those firms that fail to maintain acceptable audit standards and practices.

The annual financial statement audit includes many different stages of work. During the early stage of an audit, the independent auditor reviews and evaluates the internal controls embedded in a company's accounting system and other systems. This review and evaluation help the auditor determine what additional investigative steps, if any, should be included in the audit. The auditor then collects and analyzes data that substantiate the amounts in the financial statements. The auditor obtains most of these data from accounting records (such as journals and ledgers), business documents (such as purchase orders, sales invoices, and payment approval forms), and outside sources (such as banks, insurance companies, and suppliers).

The Audit Report

The **audit report** that the independent auditor issues following the annual audit specifies the financial statements that were audited, summarizes the audit process, and states the auditor's opinion regarding the financial statement data. The opinion usually states that the financial statements "fairly present" the results of operations, cash flow, and financial position of the company. The independent auditor does not conduct the audit to determine whether the financial statements are absolutely correct. Instead, the audit is conducted to determine whether the financial statements are a fair representation of operating results, cash flow, and financial position.

The primary purpose of the annual financial statement audit is *not* the discovery of fraudulent acts by management or employees of the company. Many audit procedures use statistical samples of transactions and data rather than examining the complete population of transactions. The auditors use samples to minimize the time required to conduct the audit, and consequently, to minimize its cost. As a result, there is the possibility that some errors or irregularities will exist in the transactions and data that the auditor does not review or evaluate. However, the independent auditor carefully designs the sampling procedures to detect errors and irregularities that are material in relation to the financial statements.

Report of Independent Registered Public Accounting Firm
In our opinion, such consolidated financial statements present fairly, in all material respects, the financial position of the Company as of December 31, 2022 and 2021, and the results of its operations and its cash flows for each of the three years in the period ended December 31, 2022, in conformity with accounting principles generally accepted in the United States of America. Also, in our opinion, such a financial statement schedule, when considered in relation to the basic consolidated financial statements taken as a whole, presents fairly, in all material respects, the information set forth therein.

DELOITTE & TOUCHE LLP

Operational Audits

Both internal audit departments and independent audit firms perform operational audits. An **operational audit** is an evaluation of activities, systems, and internal controls within a company to determine their efficiency, effectiveness, and economy. Operational auditing goes beyond accounting records and financial statements to obtain a full understanding of the operations of a company. Companies dedicated to continuous quality improvement often use operational audits to identify specific areas where they need to improve the quality of their operations or products.

Auditors design operational audits to assess the quality and efficiency of operational performance, identify opportunities for improvement, and develop specific recommendations for improvement. The scope of an operational audit can be very narrow, such as a review and evaluation of the procedures for processing cash receipts, or quite broad, such as a review and evaluation of all of the internal controls in a computerized accounting system.

YOUR TURN! 7A.1

Match the description in the left-hand column with the type of audit in the right-hand column:

1. Conducted by company employees
2. Conducted by independent auditors
3. Conducted by both independent auditors and internal auditors
4. Primary purpose is to report on the fairness of a company's financial statements
5. Evaluation of the efficiency and effectiveness of company activities

a. Internal audit
b. Financial statement audit
c. Operational audit

MBC

The solution is on page 7-47.

SUMMARY OF LEARNING OBJECTIVES

LO1   Define the three elements of fraud. (p. 7-3)
- The fraud triangle consists of three parts: (1) pressure, (2) rationalization, and (3) opportunity.

LO2   Discuss how the COSO framework helps prevent fraud, identify potential internal control failures, and discuss SOX regulations. (p. 7-4)
- The COSO framework identifies five internal control components: (1) the control environment; (2) risk assessment; (3) control activities; (4) information and communication; and (5) monitoring activities.
- Internal controls are the measures undertaken by a company to ensure the reliability of its accounting data, protect its assets from theft or unauthorized use, ensure that employees follow the company's policies and procedures, and evaluate the performance of employees, departments, divisions, and the company as a whole.
- A prevention control is designed to deter problems before they arise. A detection control is designed to discover problems soon after they arise. Prevention controls are generally more desirable than detection controls.
- A company should incorporate the following concepts when it designs its internal control:
  - Establish clear lines of authority and responsibility.
  - Implement segregation of duties.
  - Hire competent personnel.
  - Use control numbers on all business documents.
  - Develop plans and budgets.
  - Maintain adequate accounting records.
  - Provide physical and electronic controls.
- The internal control system must be monitored to assess the quality of the system's performance over time. One type of monitoring activity is an internal audit.
- Occasionally, internal controls fail. To compensate, many businesses purchase a fidelity bond, an insurance policy that provides financial compensation for theft by employees specifically covered by the insurance.
- For public companies, strong internal controls are required by law. The Sarbanes-Oxley Act (SOX) mandates that all publicly traded U.S. corporations maintain an adequate system of internal controls, that top management ensures the reliability of these controls, and that outside independent auditors attest to the adequacy of the controls. Failing to do so can result in prison sentences of up to 20 years and/or monetary fines of up to $5 million.

LO3   Define cash and discuss the accounting for cash. (p. 7-9)
- Cash includes coins, currency (paper money), checks, money orders, traveler's checks, and funds on deposit at a financial institution in a company's checking accounts and savings accounts.
- A company can have one or more cash accounts in its general ledger. Cash is a current asset.
- A company may combine certain short-term, highly liquid investments with cash and present a single amount called *cash and cash equivalents.*
- Not all of the company's cash may be available for general use. Restricted cash represents cash that has been restricted for specific uses. A compensating balance is an amount that a company must maintain in a bank account as part of a loan agreement.

LO4   Describe the internal controls for cash. (p. 7-11)
- Companies develop elaborate internal controls to protect cash, their most liquid asset.
- Four departments play major roles in processing cash received on account: the mailroom (open mail, endorse checks, list checks), the treasurer's department (deposit checks), the controller's department (update general ledger accounts), and the internal audit department (reconcile bank statement).
- Five departments play major roles in processing cash received from retail sales: the retail sales area (enter sales in cash register and place cash in drawer), the retail sales supervisor (count cash and prepare reports), the treasurer's department (deposit cash), the controller's department (update general ledger), and the internal audit department (reconcile bank statement).
- Many companies receive payments from customers or make payments to suppliers using electronic funds transfer (EFT) rather than writing and mailing checks. EFT involves sending an electronic message from one computer to another to cause a transfer of money from one financial institution to another, or directly to a company.

- A petty cash fund is a small amount of cash placed in a secure location on a company's premises to be used to pay for small expenditures such as postage and delivery service.

Illustrate the bank reconciliation process. (p. 7-17)   **LO5**

- A bank reconciliation is a schedule that (1) accounts for all differences between the ending cash balance of the bank statement and the ending cash balance of the Cash account in a company's general ledger and (2) determines the reconciled cash balance as of the end of the month.
- The procedure used to prepare the bank reconciliation involves five steps:

  (1) Trace outstanding items on the bank reconciliation from the previous month to the current bank statement.
  (2) Compare the deposits made during the month to the deposits on the bank statement.
  (3) Compare the checks issued during the month to the checks on the bank statement.
  (4) Scan the bank statement for charges and credits not yet reflected in the general ledger.
  (5) Check for errors.

Describe the four primary activities of effective cash management. (p. 7-22)   **LO6**

- Effective cash management includes monitoring and managing accounts receivable, inventory, and accounts payable, and investing any excess cash.
- Cash should be monitored using the statement of cash flows.

Appendix 7A: Describe financial statement audits and operational audits. (p. 7-25)   **LO7**

- A financial statement audit is an examination of a company's financial statements by a firm of independent certified public accountants. The firm issues an audit report upon completion of the audit.
- An operational audit is an evaluation of activities, systems, and internal controls within a company to determine their efficiency, effectiveness, and economy.

Concept	Method	Assessment	SUMMARY
Are the internal controls adequate?	The COSO framework identifies five internal control components: (1) the control environment, (2) risk assessment, (3) control activities, (4) information and communication, and (5) monitoring activities.	Monitoring activities include appraisals of the company's internal control system. If weaknesses are reported, be cautious in relying on the reported financial statements.	TAKEAWAY 7.1
Are there any restrictions on a company's use of its cash and cash equivalents?	Balance sheet and the notes to the financial statements. Identify restrictions to cash or compensating cash balances.	Consider any existing cash restrictions when assessing liquidity.	TAKEAWAY 7.2

KEY TERMS

Audit report (p. 7-26)
Bank reconciliation (p. 7-18)
Budget (p. 7-7)
Cash (p. 7-10)
Cash and cash
  equivalents (p. 7-10)
Certificates of deposit (p. 7-10)
Check (p. 7-16)
Compensating balance (p. 7-10)
Control activities (p. 7-5)
Control environment (p. 7-5)
Control numbers (p. 7-7)
Deposits in transit (p. 7-18)
Detection control (p. 7-5)

Electronic funds
  transfer (p. 7-16)
Employee collusion (p. 7-9)
Fidelity bond (p. 7-9)
Financial statement
  audit (p. 7-25)
Fraud (p. 7-3)
Fraud triangle (p. 7-3)
Internal auditing (p. 7-8)
Internal controls (p. 7-5)
Monitoring activities (p. 7-8)
Not-sufficient-funds
  check (p. 7-10)
Operational audit (p. 7-26)
Outstanding checks (p. 7-19)

Password (p. 7-14)
Petty cash fund (p. 7-16)
Postdated check (p. 7-10)
Prevention control (p. 7-5)
Public Company Accounting
  Oversight Board
  (PCAOB) (p. 7-25)
Reconciliation (p. 7-13)
Remittance advice (p. 7-12)
Remittance list (p. 7-12)
Restricted cash (p. 7-10)
Risk assessment (p. 7-5)
Segregation of duties (p. 7-6)

Assignments with the (MBC) logo in the margin are available in myBusinessCourse.
See the Preface of the book for details.

SELF-STUDY QUESTIONS

(Answers to the Self-Study Questions are at the end of the chapter.)

LO1   1. **Which of the following is not one of the three elements of the fraud triangle?**

    a. Pressure   *c.* Embezzlement

    b. Rationalization   *d.* Opportunity

LO2   2. **Which of the following is not a common internal control concept?**

    a. Establish clear lines of responsibility   *c.* Collusion among employees

    b. Provide physical and electronic controls   *d.* Separate work functions

LO2   3. **Which of the following are considered good internal control practice?**

    a. Job rotation   *c.* Only promoting from within

    b. Required vacations   *d.* Both *a* and *b*

LO2   4. **Burton Company should utilize all except one of the following concepts related to placing control numbers on business documents. Which concept should Burton not use?**

    a. Write the control number on the document when it is used.

    b. Place control numbers on all business documents.

    c. Use the documents in strict numerical sequence.

    d. Periodically account for all numbers used.

LO7   5. **An operational audit is:**

    a. Just another word for a financial statement audit.

    b. Only performed by independent auditors.

    c. Used to assess the quality and efficiency of operational performance.

    d. Usually reported to the public along with the financial statements.

LO3   6. **Which of the following statements is correct regarding the reporting of cash?**

    a. Restricted cash is always shown as a noncurrent asset.

    b. Cash is shown as the first asset on the balance sheet.

    c. Restricted cash is usually combined with unrestricted cash on the balance sheet.

    d. If a company maintains more than one bank account, each must be shown separately on the balance sheet.

LO4   7. **The treasurer is responsible for each of the following except:**

    a. Prepare the deposit slip.   *c.* Prepare the bank reconciliation.

    b. Send deposit slips and checks to the bank.   *d.* File a copy of the deposit receipt.

LO5   8. **What is a bank reconciliation?**

    a. A formal financial statement that lists all of a firm's bank account balances.

    b. A merger of two banks that previously were competitors.

    c. A statement sent monthly by a bank to a depositor that lists all deposits, checks paid, and other credits and charges to the depositor's account for the month.

    d. A schedule that accounts for differences between a firm's cash balance as shown on its bank statement and the balance shown in its general ledger Cash account.

LO5   9. **In a bank reconciliation, outstanding checks are:**

    a. Deducted from the bank balance.   *c.* Deducted from the general ledger balance.

    b. Added to the bank balance.   *d.* Added to the general ledger balance.

LO4   10. **Which of the following statements about a petty cash fund is not true?**

    a. The fund is managed on an imprest basis.

    b. The fund is used to pay for minor items such as postage and delivery charges.

    c. The fund should have a balance large enough to support one replenishment per year.

    d. All replenishments are made by check.

QUESTIONS

1. Describe the three elements of the fraud triangle and how they relate to each other.

2. Explain why supervision is an important internal control.

3. Define and contrast prevention controls and detection controls. Which are more desirable?

4. Yates Company is reviewing its internal procedures to try to improve the company's internal control. It specifically wants to separate work functions. What three types of work functions must be separated to improve internal control?

5. Janet Jones is considered one of the rising stars at Finch Company. Janet is very hard working and has not taken a vacation in three years. Explain why this is a violation of good internal control.

6. Why does the control environment provide the foundation for the entire internal control system?

7. In what way did the Sarbanes-Oxley Act impact the need for internal control?

8. How are a financial statement audit and an operational audit similar and different?

9. What types of items are included in cash? What are the two important characteristics of an item of cash?

10. Which of the following are considered to be cash: paper money, certificates of deposit, postdated checks, traveler's checks, funds in a checking account, and money orders?

11. What is a remittance advice? What types of data are included on a remittance advice?

12. What is electronic funds transfer (EFT)? What are retail EFT and wholesale EFT?

13. What is the purpose of a bank reconciliation?

14. In preparing a bank reconciliation, how should you determine (a) deposits not recorded in the bank statement and (b) outstanding checks?

15. Indicate whether the following bank reconciliation items should be (1) added to the bank statement balance, (2) deducted from the bank statement balance, (3) added to the ledger account balance, or (4) deducted from the ledger account balance:
    a. Bank service charge
    b. NSF check
    c. Deposit in transit
    d. Outstanding check
    e. Bank error charging company's account with another company's check
    f. Difference of $270 in amount of check written for $410 but recorded by the company as $140

16. Which of the items listed in Discussion Question 15 require a journal entry on the company's books?

17. What is an imprest petty cash fund? How is such a fund established and replenished?

18. Carter Manufacturing Company makes a variety of consumer products. For the year just ended (and the two prior years), sales of private-label product to Mega-Mart (1,200 stores nationwide) have made up 60 to 65 percent of total sales. On December 31 of the year just ended, Mega-Mart informed Carter that it would be buying all private-label products from another manufacturer under a five-year contract. Losing this business will result in a 50 to 55 percent reduction in total gross profit for Carter.
    a. What is the going concern concept and how does it apply to this situation?
    b. How should the full disclosure principle be applied when preparing the annual report for the year just ended?
    c. What is the independent auditor's responsibility in this situation?

SHORT EXERCISES

SE7-1. The Fraud Triangle Each of the following is part of the fraud triangle except: **LO1**
    a. pressure.   c. concealment.
    b. opportunity.   d. rationalization.

SE7-2. Segregation of Duties Having one person responsible for the related activities of ordering merchandise, receiving the merchandise, and paying for the merchandise: **LO2**
    a. provides increased security over the firm's assets.
    b. is an example of good internal control.
    c. is a good example of segregation of duties.
    d. increases the potential of fraud.

SE7-3. Internal Control Internal controls do each of the following except: **LO2**
    a. protect assets from theft.
    b. evaluate the performance of employees.
    c. guarantee the accuracy of the accounting records.
    d. increase the likelihood that any errors will be caught.

LO2, 7   **SE7-4.   Auditors** Which of the following is true?
  a.   Internal auditors are independent of the company they audit.
  b.   Internal audits provide appraisals of a company's internal control.
  c.   The company being audited cannot pay the external auditing firm since this would violate its independence.
  d.   Outside parties prefer appraisals by internal auditors over those of external auditors since they know more about the company being audited.

LO2   **SE7-5.   The COSO framework identifies five internal control components.** Which of the following is not one of the five components?
  a.   segregation of duties   c.   monitoring activities
  b.   risk assessment   d.   control activities

LO3   **SE7-6.   Cash** Cash includes each of the following except:
  a.   a postdated check.   c.   money orders.
  b.   currency.   d.   funds in a checking account.

LO3   **SE7-7.   Restricted Cash** Restricted cash:
  a.   must be shown as a current asset.   c.   is shown as a liability.
  b.   must be shown as a noncurrent asset.   d.   is reported separate from unrestricted cash.

LO4   **SE7-8.   Electronic Funds Transfer** Electronic funds transfer (EFT) involves transferring cash from one location to another using:
  a.   armored trucks.   c.   bicycle messengers.
  b.   computers.   d.   the mail service.

LO4   **SE7-9.   Cash Internal Control** Good internal control over cash received on account involves the mailroom doing each of the following activities except:
  a.   Opening the mail.   c.   Preparing the remittance list.
  b.   Preparing the deposit receipt.   d.   Sending checks to the treasurer.

LO6   **SE7-10. Cash Management** Effective cash management involves all the following except:
  a.   Managing accounts receivable.   c.   Investing excess cash.
  b.   Managing inventory.   d.   Conducting internal audits.

DATA ANALYTICS

DA7-1.   Differentiating Between Different Types of Data Analytics For CPAs, we commonly consider four types of data analytics: descriptive analytics, diagnostic analytics, predictive analytics, and prescriptive analytics. To understand the differences between these four types, review Appendix B to this text and refer to *The Next Frontier in Data Analytics* by N. Tschakert, J. Kokina, S. Kozlowski, and M. Vasarhelyi in the *Journal of Accountancy* found at https://www.journalofaccountancy.com/issues/2016/aug/data-analytics-skills.html.

Required
For each of the following ten examples, indicate which type of data analytics best applies (descriptive, diagnostic, predictive, or prescriptive).

1. Analyzing the trends of collections over the past three years for a customer and using that information to estimate the customer's collection schedule over the upcoming year.
2. Preparing a horizontal analysis, showing changes in expenses over the prior year.
3. Analyzing a significant change in operating expenses over the prior year by drilling down to specific categories that were over budget, down to specific departments, down to specific time periods.
4. An analysis of inventory turns by product in conjunction with an analysis of web clicks for the related product resulted in a list of products to phase out over the next year.
5. Preparing a forecast of sales by major segment using a regression analysis.
6. The relation of a digital marketing campaign and resulting sales is used to budget sales in the following year given the plan for upcoming digital marketing campaigns.
7. An analysis of the relations between the costs of five recent digital marketing campaigns and resulting sales was used to recommend digital marking campaigns to pursue in the future.
8. Preparing monthly unaudited financial statements by department.

9. Examining trends in gross margin at a product level to understand the cause of a drop in overall gross margin.

10. Preparing a data visualization showing how many of the company's current customers are self-employed.

DA7-2. Displaying Key Performance Indicators in Excel A key performance indicator (KPI) is a quantifiable measure used to track a company's overall performance. Managers can create a KPI dashboard, which is a data visualization that displays all indicators in one central location. This allows a manager to conveniently track and monitor key operational data. Information in KPI dashboards may even be updated in real time. For this exercise, we use the data included in the Excel file associated with this exercise for Wakeboards Inc. to create a data visualization (dashboard). Wakeboards Inc. manufactures and sells three types of wakeboards to 50 customers located primarily in oceanside cities in the U.S.

Required

1. Download Excel file DA7-2 found in myBusinessCourse.

2. Create the following six PivotCharts arranged as one KPI dashboard using the data included in file DA7-2.

   a. Top five customers for Model 1 in a bar chart. *Hint:* Click anywhere inside the data table and open the Insert tab. Click PivotTable in the Tables group. Add the PivotTable to a new worksheet. Drag Customer Name to Rows; Model 1 Sales Units to Values. In the PivotTable, open the dropdown menu next to RowLabels and select Top 10 in the Values Filter menu. Change to Top 5. Click anywhere inside the PivotTable and open the PivotTable Analyze tab. Click PivotChart in the Tools group. Select Bar. Click inside the bars and click Format Data Labels.

   b. Top five customers for Model 2 in a bar chart. *Hint:* Highlight all cells in the PivotTable created in part *a*. Right-click and select Copy. Move to another location on the same worksheet. Right-click and select Paste. Make the appropriate changes to the second PivotTable.

   c. Top five customers for Model 3 in a bar chart.

   d. Sales in units by model by month in a line chart. *Hint:* Months in Rows; Model 1, 2, and 3 Sales Units fields to Values.

   e. Most recent monthly sales (December) in a pie chart showing the proportion by Model number. *Hint:* Months in Columns; Model 1, 2, and 3 Sales Units fields to Values.

   f. Sales in units by customer by month with a slicer for Customer name and Months. *Hint:* Customer Name and Months fields to Rows; Model 1, 2, and 3 Sales Units fields to Values. Click inside the chart and open the PivotTable Analyze tab. Click Insert Slicer and select Customer Name and Months. Slicers are used to filter the data included in PivotTables.

3. Use the visualizations to answer the following questions.

   a. List the third largest customer for Model 1.

   b. List the first largest customer for Model 2.

   c. List the fifth largest customer for Model 3.

   d. List the peak month for sales of Model 1.

   e. List the quantity of sales in December for Model 2.

   f. List the quantity of sales of Model 1, Model 2, and Model 3 for Marina Inc. in June.

DA7-3. Using Tableau for Fraud Detection Refer to PF-25 in Appendix F. This problem uses Tableau to apply Benford's Law in order to detect fraud in reimbursement request data from an actual court case.

DATA VISUALIZATION

Data Visualization Activities are available in myBusinessCourse. These assignments use Tableau Dashboards to expose students to visual depictions of data and introduce students to data analytics through data visualizations. These exercises are easily assignable and auto graded by MBC.

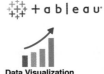

EXERCISES—SET A

E7-1A. Internal Control Explain how each of the following procedures strengthens a company's internal control:

   a. After preparing a check for a cash disbursement, the accountant for Timber Lumber Company cancels the supporting business documents (purchase order, receiving report, and invoice) by stamping them PAID.

LO2

b. The salespeople for Phinney Department Store give each customer a cash register receipt along with the proper change. A sign on each cash register states that no refunds or exchanges are allowed without the related cash register receipt.

c. The ticket-taker at the Sunrise Theater tears each admission ticket in half and gives one half back to the ticket purchaser. The seat number is printed on each half of the ticket.

d. John Verde's restaurant provides servers with prenumbered customers' checks. The servers are to void checks with mistakes on them and issue new ones rather than make corrections on them. Voided checks must be given to the manager every day.

LO4   E7-2A. Internal Controls for Cash Received on Account Oregon Company sells supplies to restaurants. Most sales are made on open account (credit sales). Oregon has requested your help in designing procedures for processing checks received from its customers. Briefly describe the procedures that should be used in each of the following departments:

a. Mailroom   b. Treasurer's department   c. Controller's department

LO5   E7-3A. Bank Reconciliation Use the following information to prepare a bank reconciliation for Fast Company at June 30:

1. Balance per Cash account, June 30, $7,015.40.
2. Balance per bank statement, June 30, $7,235.85.
3. Deposits not reflected on bank statement, $975.
4. Outstanding checks, June 30, $1,260.45.
5. Service charge on bank statement not recorded in books, $50.
6. Error by bank—Yertel Company check charged on Fast Company's bank statement, $375.
7. Check for advertising expense, $260, incorrectly recorded in books as $620.

LO5   E7-4A. Bank Reconciliation Components Identify the requested amount in each of the following situations:

a. Munster Company's May 31 bank reconciliation shows deposits in transit of $1,400. The general ledger Cash in Bank account shows total cash receipts during June of $55,600. The June bank statement shows total cash deposits of $54,300 (and no credit memos). What amount of deposits in transit should appear in the June 30 bank reconciliation?

b. Sanders Company's August 31 bank reconciliation shows outstanding checks of $1,850. The general ledger Cash in Bank account shows total cash disbursements (all by check) during September of $49,800. The September bank statement shows $49,200 of checks clearing the bank. What amount of outstanding checks should appear in the September 30 bank reconciliation?

c. Burkle Corporation's March 31 bank reconciliation shows deposits in transit of $700. The general ledger Cash in Bank account shows total cash receipts during April of $41,000. The April bank statement shows total cash deposits of $37,100 (including $1,000 from the collection of a note; the note collection has not yet been recorded by Burkle). What amount of deposits in transit should appear in the April 30 bank reconciliation?

LO2   E7-5A. Internal Control Explain how each of the following actions strengthens a company's system of internal control:

a. Separate work functions.
b. Hire competent personnel.
c. Develop plans and budgets.

d. Use control numbers on all business documents.

LO6   E7-6A. Effective Cash Management Explain how each of the following activities can improve a company's cash management:

a. Manage accounts receivable.
b. Manage inventory.

c. Manage accounts payable.
d. Invest excess cash.

LO3   E7-7A. Cash and Cash Equivalents Identify each of the following items as either cash (C), cash equivalents (CE), or neither (N):

a. Coin
b. U.S. treasury bills
c. Checks

d. Six-month certificate of deposit
e. Currency

E7-8A. **External versus Internal Audit** Explain why parties outside the company, such as bankers and stockholders, prefer an independent appraisal of the company's financial results rather than relying on the work of internal auditors.
LO7
(Appendix 7A)

E7-9A. **Operational Audits** Explain the nature of an operational audit.
LO7
(Appendix 7A)

EXERCISES—SET B

E7-1B. **Internal Control** Explain how each of the following procedures strengthens a company's internal control:
LO2

   a. Susan Corporation's photocopy machines are activated by keying a code number. Each employee is assigned a different, confidential code number. Each copy machine keeps track of the number of copies run under each employee number.

   b. Pike Company's bank requires a signature card on file for each Pike Company employee who is authorized to sign checks.

   c. Speedy Stop Convenience Stores have programmed their cash registers to imprint a blue star on every 300th receipt printed. A sign by each cash register states that the customer will receive $2 if his or her receipt has a blue star on it.

   d. Wurst Corporation has a policy that every employee must take two weeks of vacation each year.

E7-2B. **Internal Controls for Cash Received from Retail Sales** Dunn Company operates a retail department store. Most customers pay cash for their purchases. Edwards has asked you to help it design procedures for processing cash received from customers for cash sales. Briefly describe the procedures that should be used in each of the following departments:
LO4

   a. Retail sales departments   *c.* Treasurer's department

   b. Retail sales supervisor   *d.* Controller's department

E7-3B. **Bank Reconciliation** Use the following information to prepare a bank reconciliation for Dylan Company at April 30:
LO5

   1. Balance per Cash account, April 30, $6,042.10.

   2. Balance per bank statement, April 30, $6,428.28.

   3. Deposits not reflected on bank statement, $575.

   4. Outstanding checks, April 30, $1,340.18.

   5. Service charge on bank statement not recorded in books, $19.

   6. Error by bank—Dillard Company check charged on Dylan Company's bank statement, $450.

   7. Check for advertising expense, $230, incorrectly recorded in books as $320.

E7-4B. **Bank Reconciliation Components** Identify the requested amount in each of the following situations:
LO5

   a. MaryAnn Company's August 31 bank reconciliation shows deposits in transit of $2,250. The general ledger Cash in Bank account shows total cash receipts during September of $86,050. The September bank statement shows total cash deposits of $87,000 (and no credit memos). What amount of deposits in transit should appear in the September 30 bank reconciliation?

   b. Ginger Corporation's March 31 bank reconciliation shows deposits in transit of $1,400. The general ledger Cash in Bank account shows total cash receipts during April of $64,600. The April bank statement shows total cash deposits of $63,100 (including $700 from the collection of a note; the note collection has not yet been recorded by Ginger). What amount of deposits in transit should appear in the April 30 bank reconciliation?

   c. Skipper Company's October 31 bank reconciliation shows outstanding checks of $2,400. The general ledger Cash in Bank account shows total cash disbursements (all by check) during November of $69,300. The November bank statement shows $67,200 of checks clearing the bank. What amount of outstanding checks should appear in the November 30 bank reconciliation?

E7-5B. **Internal Control** Explain how each of the following items strengthens a company's system of internal control:
LO2

   a. Conduct internal audits.

   b. Establish clear lines of authority and responsibility.

   c. Maintain adequate accounting records.

   d. Provide physical and electronic controls.

LO6   **E7-6B.   Effective Cash Management** Presented below is the statement of cash flows for Professor & Sons for the month ended December 31. Identify (a) the major sources of cash, (b) the major uses of cash, and (c) the change in the cash balance during the month.

PROFESSOR & SONS Statement of Cash Flows For the Month Ended December 31	
Cash flows from operating activities	
Cash receipts from customers	$13,275
Cash payments for operating activities	(11,131)
Cash provided by operating activities	2,144
Cash flows from investing activities	
Net purchases of investments	(140)
Net capital expenditures	(30,000)
Cash used by investing activities	(30,140)
Cash flows for financing activities	
Repurchase of common stock	(7,300)
Cash dividends paid	(7,000)
Cash used in financing activities	(14,300)
Net decrease in cash	(42,296)
Cash at beginning of month	95,000
Cash at end of month	$52,704

LO3   **E7-7B.   Cash and Cash Equivalents** Identify each of the following items as either cash (C), cash equivalents (CE), or neither (N):

a.   Money market funds   d.   A savings account
b.   Euros   e.   Traveler's checks
c.   A postdated check

LO7
(Appendix 7A)   **E7-8B.   External versus Internal Audit** Compare the purpose of an external audit to that of an internal audit.

LO7
(Appendix 7A)   **E7-9B.   The External Audit and Fraud** Explain why the external audit is not considered a fraud audit.

PROBLEMS—SET A

LO2, 4   **P7-1A.   Internal Control** Xiley Company encountered the following situations:

a.   The person who opens the mail for Xiley, Bill Stevens, stole a check from a customer and cashed it. To cover up the theft, he debited Sales Returns and Allowances and credited Accounts Receivable in the general ledger. He also posted the amount to the customer's account in the accounts receivable subsidiary ledger.

b.   The purchasing agent, Susan Martin, used a company purchase order to order building materials from Lumber Mart. Later, she telephoned Lumber Mart and changed the delivery address to her home address. She told Lumber Mart to charge the material to the company. At month-end, she approved the invoice from Lumber Mart for payment.

c.   Nash Supply Company sent two invoices for the same order: the first on June 10 and the second on July 20. The accountant authorized payment of both invoices and both were paid.

d.   On January 1, Jack Monty, a junior accountant for Xiley, was given the responsibility of recording all general journal entries. At the end of the year, the auditors discovered that Monty had made 150 serious errors in recording transactions. The chief accountant was unaware that Monty had been making mistakes.

Required
For each situation, describe any violations of good internal control procedures and identify the steps that you would take to prevent each situation.

LO2, 4   **P7-2A.   Internal Control** Each of the following lettered paragraphs briefly describes an independent situation involving some aspect of internal control.

Required

Answer the questions at the end of each paragraph or numbered section.

a. Robert Flynn is the office manager of Oakwood Company, a small wholesaling company. Flynn opens all incoming mail, makes bank deposits, and maintains both the general ledger and the accounts receivable subsidiary ledger. An assistant records transactions in the credit sales journal and the cash receipts journal. The assistant also prepares a monthly statement for each customer and mails the statements to the customers. These statements list the beginning balance, credit sales, cash receipts, adjustments, and ending balance for the month.

1. If Flynn stole Customer A's $200 check (payment in full) and made no effort to conceal his embezzlement in the ledgers, how would the misappropriation be discovered?
2. What routine accounting procedure would disclose Flynn's $200 embezzlement in part (1), even if Flynn destroyed Customer A's subsidiary ledger account?
3. What circumstances might disclose Flynn's theft if he posted a payment to Customer A's account in the accounts receivable subsidiary ledger and set up a $200 account for a fictitious customer?
4. In part (3), why might Flynn be anxious to open the mail himself each morning?
5. In part (3), why might Flynn want to have the authority to write off accounts considered uncollectible?

b. A bagel shop uses a cash register that produces a printed receipt for each sale. The register also prints each transaction on a paper tape that is locked inside the cash register. Only the supervisor has access to the cash-register tape. A prominently displayed sign promises a free bagel to any customer who is not given a cash-register receipt with his or her purchase. How is this procedure an internal control device for the bagel shop?

c. Jason Philber, a swindler, sent several businesses invoices requesting payment for office supplies that had never been ordered or delivered to the businesses. A 5 percent discount was offered for prompt payment. What internal control procedures should prevent this swindle from being successful?

d. The cashier for Downtown Cafeteria is located at the end of the food line. After customers have selected their food items, the cashier rings up the prices of the food and the customer pays the bill. The customer line frequently stalls while the person paying searches for the correct amount of cash. To speed things up, the cashier often collects money from the next customer or two who have the correct change without ringing up their food on the register. After the first customer finally pays, the cashier rings up the amounts for the customers who have already paid. What is the internal control weakness in this procedure? How might the internal control over the collection of cash from the cafeteria customers be strengthened?

P7-3A. Internal Controls for Cash Received on Account Blue Company sells plumbing supplies to plumbing contractors on account. The procedures that Blue uses to handle checks received from customers via the mail are described below: **LO4**

a. Blue instructs its customers to send payment checks to its street address, 619 Main Street, Scottsdale, Arizona.
b. Blue does not provide a remittance advice to its customers for return with payment checks.
c. Checks are endorsed by the treasurer's office just prior to sending the checks to the bank for deposit.
d. The mailroom prepares a remittance list of all the checks received and files the only copy of the remittance list in a mailroom file cabinet.
e. The checks are sent to the controller's office. The controller's office uses the checks to post the accounts receivable subsidiary ledger and prepare the journal entry to record cash receipts. The checks are then sent to the treasurer's office.
f. The treasurer's office prepares the deposit slip (two copies) and sends one copy and the checks to the bank. The other copy of the deposit slip is filed in the treasurer's file cabinet.
g. The bank statement is sent to the controller, who prepares the bank reconciliation.

Required

Indicate how Blue Company could improve each of these procedures. (Refer to **Exhibit 7-1** in the chapter to help you generate ideas.)

P7-4A. Bank Reconciliation On July 31, Arthur Company's Cash in Bank account had a balance of $8,112.62. On that date, the bank statement indicated a balance of $10,170.62. A comparison of returned checks and bank advices revealed the following: **LO5**

1. Deposits in transit July 31 amounted to $3,316.12.
2. Outstanding checks July 31 totaled $1,251.12.
3. The bank erroneously charged a $215 check of Solomon Company against the Arthur bank account.
4. A $15 bank service charge has not yet been recorded by Arthur Company.
5. Arthur neglected to record $4,000 borrowed from the bank on a 10 percent six-month note. The bank statement shows the $4,000 as a deposit.
6. Included with the returned checks is a memo indicating that J. Martin's check for $610 had been returned NSF. Martin, a customer, had sent the check to pay an account of $660 less a $50 discount.
7. Arthur Company recorded a $107 payment for repairs as $1,070.

Required
a. Prepare a bank reconciliation for Arthur Company at July 31.
b. Prepare the journal entry (or entries) necessary to bring the Cash in Bank account into agreement with the reconciled cash balance on the bank reconciliation.

LO5   **P7-5A.** **Bank Reconciliation** The bank reconciliation made by Thurman, Inc., on August 31 showed a deposit in transit of $1,170 and two outstanding checks, No. 597 for $650 and No. 603 for $710. The
reconciled cash balance on August 31 was $14,110.

The following bank statement is available for September:

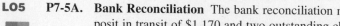

				Bank Statement					
TO	Thurman, Inc. St. Louis, MO								**September 30 STATE BANK**
	Date	**Deposits**	**No.**		**Date**	**Charges**		**Date**	**Balance**
								Aug. 31	$14,300
Sept. 1	$1,170		597	Sept. 1		$ 650		Sept. 1	14,820
2	1,120		607	5		1,850		2	15,940
5	850		608	5		1,100		5	13,840
9	744		609	8		640		8	13,200
15	585		610	9		552		9	13,392
17	1,540		611	15		817		15	13,160
25	1,028		612	17		488		17	14,212
30	680		614	25		920		25	14,320
			NSF	29		991		29	13,329
			SC	30		36		30	13,973
Item Codes:	EC: Error Correction SC: Service Charge IN: Interest Earned			DM: Debit Memo OD: Overdraft NSF: Non-sufficient Funds				CM: Credit Memo RT: Returned Item	

A list of deposits made and checks written during September is shown below:

	Deposits Made		**Checks Written**	
Sept. 1	$1,120	No. 607	$1,850
4	850	608	1,100
8	744	609	552
12	585	610	640
16	1,540	611	871
24	1,028	612	488
29	680	613	310
30	1,266	614	920
	$7,813	615	386
		616	420
			$7,537

The Cash in Bank account balance on September 30 was $14,386. In reviewing checks returned by the bank, the accountant discovered that check No. 611, written for $817 for advertising expense, was recorded in the cash disbursements journal as $871. The NSF check for $991, which Thurman deposited on September 24, was a payment on account from customer D. Walker.

Required

a. Prepare a bank reconciliation for Thurman, Inc., at September 30.

b. Prepare the necessary journal entries to bring the Cash in Bank account into agreement with the reconciled cash balance on the bank reconciliation.

P7-6A.   Reporting Cash   Tina Company has the following items at year-end.   **LO3**

Currency and coin in safe...	$ 4,100
Funds in savings account (requires $2,500 compensating balance)	26,540
Funds in checking account...	6,750
Traveler's checks	625
Postdated check...	1,250
Not-sufficient-funds check	1,880
Money market fund...	35,100

Required

Identify the amount of the above items that should be reported as cash and cash equivalents on Tina Company's balance sheet.

P7-7A.   Internal Control   Bart Simons has worked for Dr. Homer Spring for many years. Bart has been a   **LO2**
model employee. He has not taken a vacation in over four years, always stating that work was too important. One of Bart's primary jobs at the clinic is to open mail and list the checks received. He also collects cash from patients at the cashier's window as patients leave. There are times that things are so hectic that Bart does not bother to give the patient a receipt; however, he assures them that he will make sure their account is properly credited. When things slow down at the clinic, Bart often offers to help Lisa post payments to the patients' accounts receivable ledger. Lisa is always happy to receive help since she is also quite busy and because Bart is such a careful worker.

Required

Identify any internal control principles that may be violated in Dr. Spring's clinic.

P7-8A.   Internal Control   Listed below are (a) four potential errors or problems that could occur in the process-   **LO2, 4**
ing of cash transactions and (b) internal control principles. Review each error or problem and identify an internal control principle that could reduce the chance of the error or problem occurring. You may also cite more than one principle if more than one applies, or write none if none of the principles will correct the error or problem.

1. An employee steals cash collected from a customer's accounts receivable and hides the theft by issuing a credit memorandum indicating the customer returned the merchandise.

2. An official with authority to sign checks is able to steal blank checks and issue them without detection.

3. Due to a labor shortage many employees are hired without sufficient skills with the thought they can "learn on the job."

4. A salesperson often rings up a sale for less than the actual amount and then pockets the additional cash collected from the customer.

Internal control principles:

a. Establish clear lines of authority and responsibility.

b. Implement segregation of duties.

c. Hire competent personnel.

d. Use control numbers on all business documents.

e. Develop plans and budgets.

f. Maintain adequate accounting records.

g. Provide physical and electronic controls.

h. Conduct internal audits.

P7-9A.   Bank Reconciliation   The Seattle First Company's bank statement for the month of September in-   **LO5**
dicated a balance of $13,375. The company's cash account in the general ledger showed a balance of $10,030 on September 30. Other relevant information includes the following:

1. Deposits in transit on September 30 total $9,850.
2. The bank statement shows a debit memorandum for a $95 check printing charge.
3. Check No. 238 payable to Simon Company was recorded in the accounting records for $496 and cleared the bank for this same amount. A review of the records indicated that the Simon account now has a $72 credit balance and the check to them should have been $568.
4. Outstanding checks as of September 30 totaled $11,600.
5. Check No. 276 was correctly written and paid by the bank for $574. The check was recorded in the accounting records as a debit to accounts payable and a credit to cash for $754.
6. The bank returned an NSF check in the amount of $1,110.
7. The bank included a credit memorandum for $2,620 representing a collection of a customer's note. The principal portion was $2,400 and the interest portion was $220. The interest had not been accrued.

Required
a. Prepare the September bank reconciliation for Seattle First Company.
b. Prepare any necessary adjusting entries.

LO6   P7-10A. Effective Cash Management Shorte LLP is a new law firm struggling to manage its cash flow. Like many new businesses, the firm has not yet developed a sufficient client base to cover its operating costs. Additionally, the firm faced a number of large initial, but nonrecurring, start-up costs at the beginning of the year. Ongoing monthly costs include office rent and salary for a paralegal staff member. Another problem that the firm faces is that several of its major clients have failed to pay their current, but overdue, bills. Mick Shorte, one of the two founding partners, has not taken any salary since the firm began operations over eight months ago, and has decided to maintain a part-time job bartending on weekends at a local resort to ensure that he has some cash to cover day-to-day expenses like travel.

Required
What suggestions would you make to Mick Shorte to improve his firm's cash management practices?

PROBLEMS—SET B

LO2, 4   P7-1B.   Internal Control Walt Company encountered the following situations:
a. Jenny Farrell, head of the receiving department, created a fictitious company named Speedy Forms and used it to send invoices to Walt Company for business documents that Walt never ordered or received. Farrell prepared receiving reports that stated that the business documents had been received. Walt's controller compared the receiving reports to the invoices and paid each one.
b. Walt Company lost one day's cash receipts. An employee took the receipts to the bank after the bank's closing hours to deposit them in the night depository slot. A creative thief had placed a sign on the slot saying it was out of order and all deposits should be placed in a metal canister placed next to the building. Walt's employee placed the deposit in the canister and left. Employees from two other companies did the same thing. Later that night, the thief returned and stole the deposits from the canister. (This is an actual case.)
c. Walt Company does not prenumber the sales invoices used for over-the-counter sales. A cashier pocketed cash receipts and destroyed all copies of the related sales invoices.

Required
For each situation, describe any violations of good internal control procedures and identify the steps that you would take to prevent each situation.

LO2, 4   P7-2B.   Internal Control The Mountain amusement ride has the following system of internal control over cash receipts. All persons pay the same price for a ride. A person taking the ride pays cash to the cashier and receives a prenumbered ticket. The tickets are issued in strict number sequence. The individual then walks to the ride site, hands the ticket to a ticket-taker (who controls the number of people getting on each ride), and passes through a turnstile. At the end of each day, the beginning ticket number is subtracted from the ending ticket number to determine the number of tickets sold. The cash is counted and compared with the number of tickets sold. The turnstile records how many people pass through it.

At the end of each day, the beginning turnstile count is subtracted from the ending count to determine the number of riders that day. The number of riders is compared with the number of tickets sold.

Required

Which internal control feature would reveal each of the following irregularities?

a. The ticket-taker lets her friends on the ride without tickets.

b. The cashier gives his friends tickets without receiving cash from them.

c. The cashier gives too much change.

d. The ticket-taker returns the tickets she has collected to the cashier. The cashier then resells these tickets and splits the proceeds with the ticket-taker.

e. A person sneaks into the ride line without paying the cashier.

P7-3B. **Internal Controls for Cash Received from Retail Sales** Ocean Stores is a retailer of men's clothing. Most customers pay cash for their purchases. The procedures that Ocean uses for handling cash are described below: **LO4**

a. Each department begins the day with whatever amount of cash remains in the cash register from the prior day. This is not a predetermined amount.

b. All sales associates share one cash drawer.

c. Each sales associate can handle all transactions, including returns and unusual transactions, without approval from a supervisor.

d. At the end of each day, one of the sales associates takes the cash drawer and the cash register totals to a private area where no one can observe what is being done, counts the cash in the drawer, and prepares a written report of sales and cash received. The cash, the register tape, and a copy of the report are sent to the controller's department.

e. The controller prepares the deposit slip and sends the deposit to the bank. The controller then prepares the journal entry to record the cash sales.

f. The controller does not keep any copies of the written report or the deposit slip.

g. The bank statement is sent to the controller, who prepares the bank reconciliation.

Required

Indicate how Ocean could improve each of these procedures. (Refer to **Exhibit 7-2** in the chapter to help you generate ideas.)

P7-4B. **Bank Reconciliation** On May 31, the Cash in Bank account of James Company, a sole proprietorship, had a balance of $5,950.30. On that date, the bank statement indicated a balance of $7,868.50. A comparison of returned checks and bank advices revealed the following: **LO5**

1. Deposits in transit May 31 totaled $2,603.05.

2. Outstanding checks May 31 totaled $3,152.45.

3. The bank added to the account $19.80 of interest income earned by James during May.

4. The bank collected a $2,400 note receivable for James and charged a $30 collection fee. Both items appear on the bank statement.

5. Bank service charges in addition to the collection fee, not yet recorded, were $65.

6. Included with the returned checks is a memo indicating that L. Ryder's check for $686 had been returned NSF. Ryder, a customer, had sent the check to pay an account of $700 less a 2% discount.

7. James Company incorrectly recorded the payment of an account payable as $360; the check was for $630.

Required

a. Prepare a bank reconciliation for James Company at May 31.

b. Prepare the journal entry (or entries) necessary to bring the Cash in Bank account into agreement with the reconciled cash balance on the bank reconciliation.

P7-5B. **Bank Reconciliation** The bank reconciliation made by Adam Company, a sole proprietorship, on March 31 showed a deposit in transit of $1,300 and two outstanding checks, No. 797 for $550 and No. 804 for $690. The reconciled cash balance on March 31 was $12,020. **LO5**

The following bank statement is available for April 30:

Bank Statement							
TO	Adam Company Fairbanks, AK					April 30 FAIRBANKS NATIONAL BANK	
Date	Deposits	No.	Date	Charges		Date	Balance
						Mar. 31	$11,960
Apr. 1	$1,300	804	Apr. 2	$ 690		Apr. 1	13,260
3	1,680	807	3	730		2	12,570
7	1,250	808	7	1,240		3	13,520
13	1,020	809	7	838		7	12,692
18	840	810	13	541		13	13,171
23	990	811	16	1,040		16	12,131
27	1,340	813	18	500		18	12,471
30	1,160	814	23	600		23	12,861
30	95IN	NSF	27	640		27	13,561
		SC	30	40		30	14,776

Item Codes:	EC: Error Correction	DM: Debit Memo	CM: Credit Memo
	SC: Service Charge	OD: Overdraft	RT: Returned Item
	IN: Interest Earned	NSF: Non-sufficient Funds	

A list of deposits made and checks written during April is shown below:

Deposits Made		Checks Written	
Apr. 2	$1,680	No. 807	$ 730
6	1,250	808	1,240
10	1,020	809	838
17	840	810	1,040
22	990	811	451
24	1,340	812	948
29	1,160	813	640
30	1,425	814	600
	$9,705	815	372
		816	875
			$7,734

The Cash in Bank account balance on April 30 was $13,991. In reviewing checks returned by the bank, the accountant discovered that check No. 811, written for $541 for delivery expense, was recorded in the cash disbursements journal as $451. The NSF check for $500 was that of customer R. Koppa, deposited in April. Interest for April added to the account by the bank was $95.

Required

a.   Prepare a bank reconciliation for Adam Company at April 30.

b.   Prepare the necessary journal entries to bring the Cash in Bank account into agreement with the reconciled cash balance on the bank reconciliation.

LO3   P7-6B.   Reporting Cash Janzen Company has the following items at year-end:

Currency and coin in safe..	$ 5,300
Funds in savings account (requires $2,500 compensating balance)	17,300
Funds in checking account...	1,750
Traveler's checks	1,900
Postdated check..	2,250
Not-sufficient-funds check	575
Money market fund...	12,600

Required

Identify the amount of the above items that should be reported as cash and cash equivalents on Janzen Company's balance sheet.

LO2   P7-7B.   Internal Control Jerry Finch has worked for Jane Hardware for many years. Jerry has been a model employee. He has not taken a vacation in over three years, always stating that work was too important. One of Jerry's primary jobs at the store is to open mail and list the checks received. He also collects cash from customers at the store's outdoor nursery area. There are times that things are so hectic that Jerry does not bother to use the register, simply making change from cash he carries with him. When things slow down at the store Jerry often offers to help Cindy post payments to the customer's accounts receivable ledger. Cindy is always happy to receive help since she is also quite busy and because Jerry is such a careful worker.

Required

Identify any internal control principles that may be violated in the Jane Hardware store.

P7-8B. **Internal Control** Listed below are (a) four potential errors or problems that could occur in the processing of cash transactions and (b) internal control principles. For each error or problem, identify an internal control principle that could reduce the chance of the error or problem occurring. You may also cite more than one principle if more than one applies, or write none if none of the principles will correct the error or problem.

1. Three cashiers use one cash register and the cash in the drawer is often short of the recorded balance.
2. The same employee is responsible for opening the mail, listing any checks received, preparing the deposit receipt, and recording to the accounts receivable journal. Several customers have complained that their balances are incorrect.
3. In an effort to save printing costs, generic receipts without numbers are used for customer sales.
4. Because things have been hectic, no budgets were prepared this year. One department seems to be doing less volume in revenue, but cost of goods sold appear to be high relative to sales.

Internal control principles:

a.   Establish clear lines of authority and responsibility.
b.   Implement segregation of duties.
c.   Hire competent personnel.
d.   Use control numbers on all business documents.
e.   Develop plans and budgets.
f.   Maintain adequate accounting records.
g.   Provide physical and electronic controls.
h.   Conduct internal audits.

P7-9B. **Bank Reconciliation** The Chicago Skate Company's bank statement for the month of June indicated a balance of $4,320. The company's cash account in the general ledger showed a balance of $3,377 on June 30. Other relevant information includes the following:

1. Deposits in transit on June 30 total $2,550.
2. The bank statement shows a debit memorandum for a $10 check printing charge.
3. Check No. 160 payable to Simon Company was recorded in the accounting records for $124 and cleared the bank for this same amount. A review of the records indicated that the Simon account now has a $28 credit balance and the check to them should have been $142.
4. Outstanding checks as of June 30 totaled $3,175.
5. Check No. 176 was correctly written and paid by the bank for $345. The check was recorded in the accounting records as a debit to accounts payable and a credit to cash for $354.
6. The bank returned an NSF check in the amount of $311.
7. The bank included a credit memorandum for $630 representing a collection of a customer's note. The principal portion was $610 and the interest portion was $20. The interest had not been accrued.

Required

a.   Prepare the June bank reconciliation for the Chicago Skate Company.
b.   Prepare any necessary adjusting entries.

SERIAL PROBLEM: KATE'S CARDS

(Note: This is a continuation of the Serial Problem: Kate's Cards from Chapters 1 through 6.)

SP7.   On February 15, 2022, Kate Collins, owner of Kate's Cards, asks you to investigate the cash handling activities in her business. She believes that a new employee might be stealing funds. "I have no proof," she says, "but I'm fairly certain that the January 31, 2022, undeposited receipts amounted to more than $12,000, although the January 31 bank reconciliation prepared by the cashier (who works in the treasurer's department) shows only $7,238.40. Also, the January bank reconciliation doesn't

Kate's
Cards

show several checks that have been outstanding for a long time. The cashier told me that these checks needn't appear on the reconciliation because he had notified the bank to stop payment on them and he had made the necessary adjustment on the books. Does that sound reasonable to you?"

At your request, Kate shows you the following (unaudited) January 31, 2022, bank reconciliation prepared by the cashier:

KATE'S CARDS Bank Reconciliation January 31, 2022					
Ending balance from bank statement...		$ 4,843.69	Balance from general ledger ...		$10,893.89
Add: Deposits in transit.............		7,238.40			
		$12,082.09			
Less:			Less:		
Outstanding checks:			Bank service charge........ $ 60.00		
No. 2351	$1,100.20		Unrecorded credit.......... 1,200.00		(1,260.00)
No. 2353	578.32				
No. 2354	969.68	(2,448.20)			
Reconciled cash balance		$ 9,633.89	Reconciled cash balance		$ 9,633.89

You discover that the $1,200 unrecorded bank credit represents a note collected by the bank on Kate's behalf; it appears in the deposits column of the January bank statement. Your investigation also reveals that the December 31, 2021, bank reconciliation showed three checks that had been outstanding longer than 10 months: No. 1432 for $600, No. 1458 for $466.90, and No. 1512 for $253.10. You also discover that these items were never added back into the Cash account in Kate's books. In confirming that the checks shown on the cashier's January 31 bank reconciliation were outstanding on that date, you discover that check No. 2353 was actually a payment of $1,658.32 and had been recorded on the books for that amount.

To confirm the amount of undeposited receipts at January 31, you request a bank statement for February 1–12 (called a cutoff bank statement). This indeed shows a January 1 deposit of $7,238.40.

Required
a. Calculate the amount of funds stolen by the employee.
b. Describe how the employee concealed the theft.
c. What suggestions would you make to Kate about cash control procedures?

EXTENDING YOUR KNOWLEDGE

REPORTING AND ANALYSIS

EYK7-1. **Financial Reporting Problem: Columbia Sportswear Company** The financial statements for the **Columbia Sportswear Company** can be found in Appendix A at the end of this book.

COLUMBIA
SPORTSWEAR
COMPANY

Required
Use the financial statements and the accompanying notes to the financial statements to answer the following questions about Columbia Sportswear:
a. What title is used on Columbia's consolidated balance sheet for cash?
b. According to the information given in Note 2, what is the makeup of the cash and cash equivalents account?
c. According to information in Item 9A. Controls and Procedures, who is responsible for establishing and maintaining adequate internal control over financial reporting?
d. Deloitte and Touche, the independent auditor of Columbia Sportswear, issued a report on its audit of Columbia's internal control. What did Deloitte and Touche conclude?

EYK7-2. **Comparative Analysis Problem: Columbia Sportswear Company versus Under Armour, Inc.** The financial statements for **Columbia Sportswear Company** can be found in Appendix A and **Under Armour, Inc.**'s financial statements can be found in Appendix B at the end of this book.

COLUMBIA
SPORTSWEAR
COMPANY

UNDER ARMOUR, INC.

Required
Use the information in the companies' financial statements to answer the following questions:

    a. What is the balance in cash and cash equivalents as of December 31, 2020?

    b. What percentage of each company's total assets is made up of cash and cash equivalents as of December 31, 2020?

    c. How much did cash and cash equivalents change during 2020 for each firm?

    d. For each company, how did the change in cash for 2020 compare to its cash provided by operating activities?

EYK7-3. **Business Decision Problem** Quality Electronics Company is a distributor of microcomputers and related electronic equipment. The company has grown very rapidly. It is located in a large building near Chicago, Illinois. Jack Flanigan, the president of Quality, has hired you to perform an internal control review of the company. You conduct interviews of key employees, tour the operations, and observe various company functions. You discover the following:

    1. Quality has not changed its ordering procedures since it was formed eight years ago. Anyone in the company can prepare a purchase order and send it to the vendor without getting any managerial approval. When the invoice arrives from the vendor, it is compared only to the purchase order before authorizing payment.

    2. Quality does not have an organization chart. In fact, employees are encouraged to work on their own, without supervision. Flanigan believes that this approach increases creativity.

    3. Business documents have been carefully designed by the controller. When the printer prints the documents, no control numbers are printed on them. Instead, employees using a form write the next sequential number on the form. The controller believes that this approach ensures that a proper sequencing of numbers will be maintained.

    4. No budgets are prepared for the company.

    5. All doors to the building remain unlocked from 7:00 a.m. to 11:00 p.m. Employees normally work from 7:30 a.m. to 5:00 p.m. A private security firm drives to the building to unlock it each morning and lock it each night. The security firm's employee leaves immediately after unlocking or locking. The company does not use time clocks or employee badges.

    6. Flanigan believes that audits (either external or internal) are a waste of time. He has resisted the bank president's urging to hire a CPA firm to conduct an audit.

Required

Analyze the findings listed above. Then list all the internal control weaknesses that you can identify. For each weakness, describe one or more internal controls that Quality should install to overcome the weakness.

EYK7-4. **Financial Analysis Problem** The **Public Company Accounting Oversight Board (PCAOB)** was created as part of the Sarbanes-Oxley legislation to provide oversight to U.S. accounting firms. The PCAOB's web address is http://www.pcaobus.org.

Required

Answer the following questions:

    a. What is the mission of the PCAOB?

    b. What is the title of the first auditing standard AS1001 issued by the PCAOB?

    c. According to the rules section of the site, what is required for a PCAOB rule to take effect?

CRITICAL THINKING

EYK7-5. **Accounting Research Problem** Refer to the consolidated balance sheets in the fiscal year 2020 annual report of **General Mills, Inc.,** available on this book's website.

GENERAL MILLS, INC.

Required

    a. What was the amount of cash and cash equivalents as of May 31, 2020?

    b. By what amount did cash and cash equivalents increase or decrease during the year?

    c. What statement elsewhere in the annual report contains an explanation of the increase or decrease in the cash and cash equivalents amount? In that statement, what amount of cash was provided or used by (1) operating activities, (2) investment activities, and (3) financing activities?

    d. What members of the company signed off as to the assessment of the company's internal control (see Reports of management and Independent Registered Public Accounting Firm)?

    e. What firm conducted the audit of General Mills?

    f. What opinion did the accounting firm express about General Mills's financial statements?

    g. In addition to its audit of the financial statements, what else did the auditing firm audit?

EYK7-6. **Accounting Communication Activity** You were recently hired as the head of a company's ethics division. As one of your first acts, you decide to prepare a letter to the company's Chairman of the Board explaining the importance of ethics within the company. What are some of the items that should be included in your letter?

EYK7-7. **Accounting Ethics Case** Gina Pullen is the petty cash cashier for a large family-owned restaurant. She has been presented on numerous occasions with properly approved receipts for reimbursement from petty cash that she believes are personal expenses of one of the five owners of the restaurant. She reports to the controller of the company. The controller is also a family member and is the person who approves the receipts for payment out of petty cash.

Required

What are the accounting implications if Pullen is correct? What alternatives should she consider?

EYK7-8. **Environmental, Social, and Governance Problem** Corporate social responsibility and fraud prevention are often related. One way that the two are connected is in the creation of a culture of honesty and the ethical treatment of employees. This is often the result of the tone from the top, where the company leaders not only talk about these concepts, but also practice them.

Required

Discuss how a culture of honesty and the ethical treatment of employees can reduce the risk of fraud.

EYK7-9. **Forensic Accounting Problem** Internal control follows the concept of reasonable assurance. Pete Simmons, the chief compliance officer of Salem Company, stated that he does not want simply reasonable assurance. He wants absolute assurance in all aspects that apply to the financial statements of the company. Specifically, Pete stated, "As long as I am working here, we will run a perfectly tight system that ensures absolutely no fraud in our financial statements." Betty Flint, the controller, disagreed with Pete and argued that anything more than reasonable assurance is both financially and practically impossible.

Required

Do you agree with Pete or Betty, and why?

EYK7-10. **Forensic Accounting Problem** Wayne James Nelson, a manager in the office of the Arizona State Treasurer, was found guilty of trying to defraud the state of nearly $2 million. Nelson's scheme involved issuing checks to bogus vendors. The amounts of the 23 checks issued are shown below:

The table lists the checks that a manager in the office of the Arizona State Treasurer wrote to divert funds for his own use. The vendors to whom the checks were issued were fictitious.

Date of Check	Amount
October 9	$ 1,927.48
	27,902.31
October 14	86,241.90
	72,117.46
	81,321.75
	97,473.96
October 19	93,249.11
	89,658.17
	87,776.89
	92,105.83
	79,949.16
	87,602.93
	96,879.27
	91,806.47
	84,991.67
	90,831.83
	93,766.67
	88,338.72
	94,639.49
	83,709.28
	96,412.21
	88,432.86
	71,552.16
TOTAL	**$1,878,687.58**

Required

Refer to the chart shown below that reports the occurrences of various digits in a number. Compare the first digit of the fraudulent checks to the table of Benford's Law. How do the two compare? Are there any other unusual patterns you detect in the check amounts?

Position of digit in number				
Digit	**First**	**Second**	**Third**	**Fourth**
0	.	.11968	.10178	.10018
1	.30103	.11389	.10138	.10014
2	.17609	.10882	.10097	.10010
3	.12494	.10433	.10057	.10006
4	.09691	.10031	.10018	.10002
5	.07918	.09668	.09979	.09998
6	.06695	.09337	.09940	.09994
7	.05799	.09035	.09902	.09990
8	.05115	.08757	.09864	.09986
9	.04576	.08500	.09827	.09982

Example: The number 147 has three digits, with 1 as the first digit, 4 as the second digit, and 7 as the third digit. The table shows that under Benford's Law the expected proportion of numbers with a first digit 1 is 30.103% and the expected proportion of numbers with a third digit 7 is 9.902%.

Source: M. J. Nigrini, "A Taxpayer Compliance Application of Benford's Law," *Journal of the American Taxation Association* 18 (1996).

EYK7-11. Analyzing IFRS Financial Statements The 2020 financial statements of LVMH Moët Hennessy-Louis Vuitton S.A. are presented in Appendix C at the end of this book. LVMH is a Paris-based holding company and one of the world's largest and best-known luxury goods companies. As members of the European Union, French companies are required to prepare their consolidated (group) financial statements using International Financial Reporting Standards (IFRS). After reviewing LVMH's consolidated financial statements, consider the following questions:

Required

a.   What was the amount of cash and cash equivalents as of December 31, 2020?

b.   By what amount did cash and cash equivalents increase or decrease during the year?

c.   What statement elsewhere in the annual report contains an explanation of the increase or decrease in the cash and cash equivalents amount? In that statement, what amount of cash was provided or used by (1) operating activities and (2) financing activities?

EYK7-12. Working with the Takeaways The following conditions of material weaknesses were reported in a prior year independent auditors' report on internal control of the U.S. Department of Transportation Highway Trust Fund (HTF):

1. Weaknesses with respect to journal entry preparation:
   a.   Lack of indication of preparer
   b.   Lack of supporting documentation
   c.   Lack of proper review and approval
2. Weaknesses with respect to the consolidated financial statement preparation and analysis process:
   a.   Inadequate analysis of abnormal balances
   b.   Inadequate analysis of account relationships
   c.   Inadequate controls over journal entry processing
   d.   Lack of oversight related to allocation transfers

Required

a.   What is the possible negative effect of these material weaknesses?

b.   If you were the reporting auditor, what would you recommend be done?

ANSWERS TO SELF-STUDY QUESTIONS:

1. c   2. c   3. d   4. a   5. c   6. b   7. c   8. d   9. a   10. c

YOUR TURN! SOLUTIONS

Solution 7.1

1. **Rationalization.** This quote is from CEO Kenneth Lay rationalizing his role in the accounting fraud at Enron.
2. **Pressure.** This quote is from an employee at Wells Fargo who was one of at least 5,000 employees pressured to open fake bank and credit card accounts.[2]
3. **Opportunity.** This quote is from Bernie Madoff describing how the "willful blindness" of regulators and investors provided the opportunity to keep his Ponzi scheme afloat.[3]

Solution 7.2

1. This is a personnel policy control violation. The supervisor may be committing a fraud and covering up his acts. If the supervisor were forced to take a vacation, the employee filling in might observe some suspicious activity and uncover the fraud.
2. This is a physical control violation. The unattended inventory could be stolen through the open door.
3. This is a segregation of duties violation. The supervisor is in a position to order an improper purchase, receive the goods for his own purposes, record the goods as received by the company, and then have the company pay for the purchase.

Solution 7.3

b. Marketable securities are often held for longer than 90 days and are reported separately from cash and cash equivalents.

Solution 7.4

1. (c) Treasurer's department
2. (a) Retail sales supervisor
3. (b) Mailroom
4. (e) Internal audit department
5. (d) Controller's department

Solution 7.5

1. (a) Add to bank statement balance
2. (b) Subtract from bank statement balance
3. (d) Subtract from cash general ledger account
4. (c) Add to cash general ledger account

Solution 7.6

a. 3   b. 2   c. 4   d. 1

Solution 7A.1

1. (a) Internal audit
2. (b) Financial statement audit
3. (c) Operational audit
4. (b) Financial statement audit
5. (c) Operational audit

---

[2] Elizabeth C. Tippett, "This Is How Wells Fargo Encouraged Employees to Commit Fraud, *New Republic*, October 7, 2016, https://newrepublic.com/article/137571/wells-fargo-encouraged-employees-commit-fraud.
[3] Diana B. Henriques, "From Prison, Madoff Says Banks 'Had to Know' of Fraud," *New York Times*, February 15, 2011 https://www.nytimes.com/2011/02/16/business/madoff-prison-interview.html.

Chapter **8**

Accounting for Receivables

Road Map

LO	Learning Objective	Page	eLecture	Guided Example	Assignments
LO1	Define accounts receivable, explain losses from uncollectible accounts, and describe the allowance method of accounting for doubtful accounts.	8-3	E8-1	YT8.1	SS1, SS7, SS9, SE1, E2A, E3A, E9A, E2B, E3B, E9B, P2A, P7A, P2B, P7B
LO2	Describe and illustrate the percentage of net sales method and the accounts receivable aging method for estimating a business's bad debts expense.	8-7	E8-2	YT8.2 YT8.3	SS1, SS2, SS7, SS9, SE1, SE2, SE3, E1A, E2A, E8A, E9A, E1B, E2B, E8B, E9B, P1A, P2A, P3A, P5A, P6A, P7A, P8A, P10A, P1B, P2B, P3B, P5B, P6B, P7B, P8B, P10B
LO3	Discuss the accounting treatment of credit card sales.	8-11	E8-3	YT8.4	SS8, SE6, E4A, E11A, E4B, E11B, P4A, P9A, P4B, P9B
LO4	Illustrate a promissory note receivable, discuss the calculation of interest on notes receivable, and present journal entries to record notes receivable and interest.	8-12	E8-4	YT8.5	SS3, SS6, SS10, SE5, SE7, SE8, E5A, E6A, E12A, E13A, E5B, E6B, E12B, E13B, P5A, P10A, P5B, P10B
LO5	Define accounts receivable turnover and average collection period and explain their use in the analysis and management of accounts and notes receivable.	8-15	E8-5	YT8.6	SS4, SS5, SE4, SE9, E7A, E10A, E7B, E10B
LO6	Appendix 8A: Illustrate the direct write-off method and contrast it with the allowance method for accounting for doubtful accounts.	8-19	E8-6	YT8.7	SS9, SE10, E14A, E15A, E14B, E15B

Tesla is an American company that promotes clean energy. It is best known for its electric vehicles (EVs). However, Tesla and its subsidiary, Solar City, also develop and install solar photovoltaic systems and battery storage. Tesla's 2020 EV sales accounted for nearly a quarter of the entire EV market and its 3-gigawatt hour of battery storage makes it one of the world's largest suppliers of battery energy storage.

Although Tesla is a pioneer in these markets and is arguably the best known company selling EVs, the company nearly went bankrupt before becoming profitable. In fact, Tesla reported an accounting loss every year since its founding in 2003 until finally reporting a profit in 2020. Tesla has certainly had its share of accounting controversies during its path to profitability. The U.S. Securities and Exchange Commission has questioned the company's warranty reserves and lease accounting. Fortune magazine has claimed that Tesla uses creative accounting to improve quarterly profits. Bloomberg has written that Tesla's financial reporting may violate Generally Accepted Accounting Principles. One area of Tesla's accounting that has drawn attention for possible accounting abuses is the subject of this chapter, accounts receivable. In 2020, hedge fund manager, David Einhorn, accused Tesla's CEO, Elon Musk, of committing fraud and claiming that he was, ". . . beginning to wonder whether your accounts receivable exist."[1] In this chapter, we examine the reporting and analysis of accounts receivable.

PAST

In Chapter 7 we studied how companies can prevent errors and fraud with the use of internal controls.

PRESENT

In this chapter we turn our attention to the accounting for two important assets— accounts and notes receivable.

FUTURE

In Chapter 9 we will continue our study of a company's assets by looking at long-lived assets.

---

[1] Querolo, Nic; Trudell, Craig (April 30, 2020). "Tesla Declines After Einhorn Questions Musk's Accounting." *Bloomberg.com.*

ACCOUNTING FOR RECEIVABLES

Accounts Receivable	Credit Card Sales	Notes Receivable	Analyzing and Managing Receivables
• Recording accounts receivable • Accounting for bad debts • Allowance methods: percentage of net sales and aging of receivables • Direct write-off method (Appendix 8A)	• Recording receivables from credit card sales	• Promissory note • Interest on note • Maturity date • Recording entries • Disclosure of notes	• Accounts receivable turnover • Average collection period • Factoring and discounting

ACCOUNTS RECEIVABLE

LO1 **Define** accounts receivable, explain losses from uncollectible accounts, and **describe** the allowance method of accounting for doubtful accounts.

eLecture

MBC

A.K.A. Accounts receivable are also sometimes referred to as trade receivables.

Receivables are assets representing a company's right to receive cash or other assets at some point in the future. Accounts receivable includes only those amounts relating to credit sales of goods or services. Other amounts due, such as from advances to employees or loans to affiliated companies, should be included with the Other Receivables account on the balance sheet. Other Receivables may be either a current asset or a noncurrent asset.

Many businesses sell goods and services to their customers on a credit basis, allowing customers to pay for their purchases over a period of time called the credit period. **Accounts receivable** is the asset, usually classified as current, that is created when a sale or service transaction is executed on a credit basis.

When a company makes a credit sale, or a "sale on account," it debits the Accounts Receivable account and credits the Sales Revenue account. To illustrate, assume that on December 1 the Claremont Company sells $20,000 of merchandise on account. The company will make the following journal entry on its books for the credit sale transaction:

A = L + SE
+20,000   +20,000
          Rev

Dec. 1	Accounts receivable (+A)	20,000	
	Sales revenue (+R, +SE)		20,000
	To record credit sales to customers.		

When the credit sale is collected on December 20, the following entry is made:

A = L + SE
+20,000
−20,000

Dec. 20	Cash (+A)	20,000	
	Accounts receivable (−A)		20,000
	To record cash collection.		

Accounting for Bad Debts

Businesses that extend credit to their customers anticipate some amount of credit losses—that is, losses from customers who fail to pay for their credit purchases. The magnitude of these losses is usually closely related to a firm's credit-granting policy. A **credit-granting policy** is a policy that a company follows to decide which customers should be allowed to buy goods and services on credit and how much credit those customers should be granted. Companies often base their credit-granting policy on a computerized credit score. (See Accounting in Practice: "Credit Scoring Systems" on the next page.) A company may deliberately relax its credit-granting policy to increase its sales, but should recognize that this will likely cause a corresponding increase in its credit losses.

Businesses must also establish a **credit-collection policy**; that is, a policy establishing the amount of time that its customers may take before they are required to pay their outstanding accounts receivable. In Chapter 5, we discussed the *credit period*, or the allowed time period that customers may take to pay for their credit purchases, and *sales discounts*, or the dollar amount that customers may deduct from the purchase price of goods if they pay within an allowed discount period. Together, sales discounts, the discount period, and the credit period constitute a company's credit-collection policy. Maintaining an effective credit-collection policy is important for those businesses that allow their customers to buy goods and services on credit, since companies can have millions of dollars tied up in uncollected accounts receivable.

Most large companies have credit departments that administer the company's credit-granting and credit-collection policies. Credit personnel conduct credit investigations, establish credit limits, and follow up on any unpaid accounts. They also decide, following written collection procedures, when an account receivable becomes uncollectible, and consequently, when it should be written off a company's balance sheet.

Credit losses are considered to be an operating expense of a business, and consequently, they are debited to an account called **Bad Debts Expense**. Normally, the Bad Debts Expense account is classified as a selling expense on the income statement, although some companies include it as part of their administrative expenses.

A.K.A. The Bad Debts Expense is also sometimes referred to as the Provision for Bad Debts.

ACCOUNTING IN PRACTICE   **Credit Scoring Systems**

Most companies use a computerized credit scoring system to decide whether to extend credit to customers. The credit scoring system is based on a set of formulas with multiple variables. Data from a customer's credit application and from credit reporting agencies are used by the system to calculate a credit score. The system then compares the score to predetermined limits and recommends whether or not credit be extended.

If credit is extended, the scoring system often recommends an upper limit on the amount of credit to be extended. Scoring systems focus on a customer's ability to generate income and cash flow, the customer's current level of debt and required repayment schedule, and current assets. Many of the financial statement ratios discussed throughout this text are incorporated into credit scoring systems.

Allowance Method

Credit losses are an unfortunate but predictable consequence of a business extending credit to its customers. At the time that a credit sale is made, the seller does not know whether the account receivable will be collected in full, in part, or not at all. Further, any loss from an uncollectible account may not be known for several months, or even a year or more, following the credit sale. To achieve a proper matching of sales revenues and expenses, however, a company's accountants must estimate the amount of the bad debts expense to report on the income statement. This estimate is recorded in an end-of-period adjusting entry. The process of estimating and recording the bad debts expense for a business is most often done using the **allowance method**.

PRINCIPLE ALERT   **Matching Concept**

The *matching concept* states that expenses should be linked with, or matched with, the revenues that they help to generate. A company sells its goods and services on credit because this business practice attracts more customers and, therefore, more sales revenue than if the company only permitted cash transactions. One of the costs associated with extending credit to customers is the bad debts expense. The matching concept requires that this expense be reported in the same accounting period as the related sales revenue. To accomplish the appropriate matching of sales revenue and expenses, accountants must estimate the bad debts expense because the specific accounts that will be uncollectible may not be known until a later accounting period.

Recording Estimated Bad Debts Expense Under the Allowance Method

The allowance method gets its name from the end-of-period adjusting entry, which credits a contra-asset account called the **Allowance for Doubtful Accounts**. The credit is to the Allowance for Doubtful accounts, rather than a specific customer account, because at the time

A.K.A. The Allowance for Doubtful Accounts is also often referred to as the Allowance for Uncollectible Accounts.

the firm records its estimate of uncollectible accounts, it does not know precisely which of its customer accounts in the Accounts Receivable ledger will be uncollectible. The allowance method not only matches credit losses with the related credit sales in the same time period in which the sale occurs, but it also reports accounts receivable at their estimated realizable value in the end-of-period balance sheet. To illustrate, assume that the Claremont Corporation estimates its bad debts expense for 2022 to be $1,600 and makes the following adjusting entry in its general journal:

A   = L +   SE
−1,600   −1,600 Exp

2022			
Dec. 31	Bad debts expense (+E, −SE)	1,600	
	Allowance for doubtful accounts (+XA, −A)		1,600
	To record the bad debts expense for the year.		

The Allowance for Doubtful Accounts is a contra-asset account with a normal credit balance. To report the amount of accounts receivable that the business expects to collect on the balance sheet, the Allowance for Doubtful Accounts is subtracted from the Accounts Receivable account. Assuming that the Claremont Corporation had $100,000 of accounts receivable (and a zero balance in the Allowance for Doubtful Accounts prior to the December 31, adjusting entry), the year-end balance sheet presentation would appear as follows:

Current Assets		
Cash		$ 52,000
Accounts receivable	$100,000	
Less: Allowance for doubtful accounts	1,600	
Accounts receivable, net.		98,400
Inventory		125,000
Other current assets		31,000
Total Current Assets		$306,400

The Allowance for Doubtful Accounts of $1,600 is subtracted from the $100,000 of Accounts Receivable to obtain the net realizable value of $98,400. In other words, customers owe Claremont Corporation $100,000 but Claremont does not expect to collect $1,600 of this amount. Instead, Claremont only expects to collect $98,400, referred to as the net balance of Accounts Receivable.

PRINCIPLE ALERT   **Going Concern Concept**

Accounts receivable are reported on the balance sheet at the amount that a company expects to collect in the future from its credit customers. This presentation assumes that the company will be in existence long enough to collect its accounts receivable, and therefore, it is an example of the *going concern concept*. As a principle of accounting, the going concern concept assumes that a business entity will continue to operate indefinitely in the future.

Writing Off Specific Accounts Receivable under the Allowance Method

A company's credit department manager is usually the employee with the authority to determine when a specific account receivable is uncollectible, and hence, when it should be written off and removed from a company's balance sheet. This might occur, for example, if the customer has not made any payments on its account for a specified period of time, say four months, or if the customer has declared bankruptcy. Assume, for example, that the credit manager of the Claremont Corporation authorizes a $300 write-off of the Monroe Company's account receivable during the following January. When the accounting department is notified of the credit department manager's decision, it will make the following journal entry:

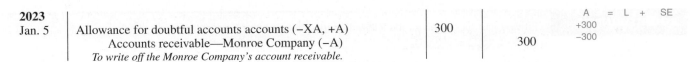

2023					A = L + SE
Jan. 5	Allowance for doubtful accounts accounts (−XA, +A)		300		+300
	Accounts receivable—Monroe Company (−A)			300	−300
	To write off the Monroe Company's account receivable.				

Notice that the journal entry to write off an account receivable does not affect a company's net income or total assets. Net income is reduced when the company records the year-end adjusting entry for bad debts expense. And because the Allowance for Doubtful Accounts is deducted from the Accounts Receivable account, the *net* realizable value of accounts receivable in the assets section of the balance sheet is unchanged by the account write-off. After the Monroe Company's account receivable has been written off, the Accounts Receivable and the Allowance for Doubtful Accounts T-accounts of Claremont Corporation appear as follows:

+	Accounts Receivable (A)		−		−	Allowance for Doubtful Accounts (XA)		+
Beg.	100,000	300	Jan. 5		Jan. 5	300	1,600	Beg.
Bal.	99,700						1,300	Bal.

As can be seen in the above T-accounts, the net realizable value of Claremont's accounts receivable as of January 1, 2023, is $98,400 ($100,000 less $1,600 allowance for doubtful accounts). Following the January 5, 2023, account write-off, the net realizable value of the Claremont Corporation's accounts receivable remains $98,400 ($99,700 less $1,300 allowance for doubtful accounts) since Accounts Receivable and the Allowance for Doubtful Accounts are reduced by the same amount ($300). The following table summarizes the allowance method.

Action	Journal Entry	Balance Sheet Effect (Increase/Decrease)	Income Statement Effect (Increase/Decrease)
Recording Estimated Bad Debts Expense (In period when sale occurred)	**DEBIT** Bad debts expense **CREDIT** Allowance for doubtful accounts	▲ Allowance for doubtful accounts ▼ Accounts receivable, net	▲ Bad debts expense ▼ Net income
Writing-Off Bad Debt (In period when receivable is determined uncollectible)	**DEBIT** Allowance for doubtful accounts **CREDIT** Accounts receivable	▼ Accounts receivable ▼ Allowance for doubtful accounts No Change Accounts receivable, net	**No Change**

ACCOUNTING IN PRACTICE   Balance Sheet Title for Uncollectible Accounts

No doubt about it, not all receivables will be collected! So how should a company title the amount that it likely will be unable to collect? Allowance for Doubtful Accounts is the most common account title, although several other titles are also used, as can be seen from a survey of 600 large U.S. companies:

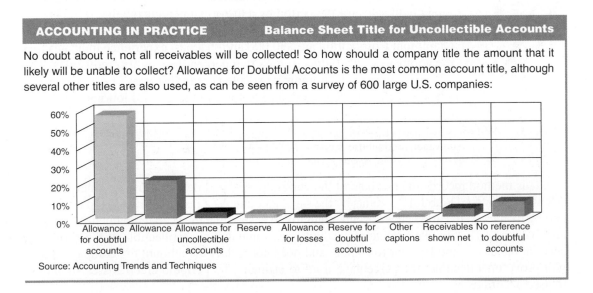

Source: Accounting Trends and Techniques

YOUR TURN! 8.1

GuidedExample

MBC

The solution is on page 8-42.

Provide journal entries for the following transactions for the Turner Company:

May   2   Sold $40,000 of merchandise on account
May 17   Collected $35,000 of the May 2nd sale
May 31   Estimated $500 of the remaining accounts receivable may not be collected
June 15   Wrote off $200 of the existing accounts receivable

ESTIMATING CREDIT LOSSES

LO2 **Describe** and **illustrate** the percentage of net sales method and the accounts receivable aging method for estimating a business's bad debts expense.

eLecture

MBC

When the allowance method is used, estimates of a company's expected credit losses are generally based on past business experience, with additional consideration given to forecasts of future sales activity, economic conditions, and any planned changes to a company's credit-granting policy. The most commonly used methods to estimate expected credit losses are as a percentage of a company's credit sales for the period, or as a percentage of accounts receivable outstanding at the end of a fiscal period. Companies may use one or both methods, and a variety of different assumptions with each method, before deciding on the best estimate that will be recorded in the financial statements.

Method	① Estimate	② Calculate
Percentage of Net Sales	Bad Debt Expense →	Ending Balance in Allowance for Doubtful Accounts
Accounts Receivable Aging	Ending Balance in Allowance for Doubtful Accounts →	Bad Debt Expense

Percentage of Net Sales Method

The percentage of net sales method first estimates the amount of the end-of-period adjusting entry for bad debts expense, and then calculates the ending balance of the Allowance for Doubtful accounts given this bad debts expense. The bad debts expense is estimated by multiplying the company's total credit sales for the period by a historical percentage that reflects past credit losses. For example, suppose that the current year credit sales for the Claremont Corporation are $80,000 and that past experience indicates that the company is likely to sustain a two percent loss on its credit sales. The adjusting entry for Claremont's expected credit losses of $1,600 (2 percent × $80,000) would be recorded as follows in the general journal:

A = L + SE				
−1,600 −1,600	Dec. 31	Bad debts expense (+E, −SE)	1,600	
Exp		Allowance for doubtful accounts (+XA, −A)		1,600
		To record the bad debts expense for the year.		

This method records the estimate of the current period bad debt expense and increases the Allowance for for Doubtful Accounts by the same amount. As a result, a firm should review the ending balance in the allowance account regularly to ensure that the account maintains a reasonable balance reflecting the amount of accounts receivable that is uncollectible. If the allowance account balance is too large or too small, and does not reflect the amount the company thinks will prove uncollectible, the percentage used to estimate the periodic credit losses should be revised accordingly.

A company that uses the **percentage of net sales method** usually applies the estimated uncollectible percentage only to its credit sales, excluding cash sales, since only credit sales are subject to credit losses. Further, any sales discounts and sales returns and allowances should be deducted from total credit sales before applying the historical uncollectible percentage.

YOUR TURN! 8.2

Taylor Company estimates three percent of its $600,000 credit sales will prove uncollectible. What is the journal entry to record this estimate?

GuidedExample

MBC

The solution is on page 8-42.

Accounts Receivable Aging Method

The accounts receivable aging method first estimates the appropriate balance for the Allowance for Doubtful Accounts account at year-end and then calculates the bad debts expense necessary to achieve this balance. The difference between the estimated Allowance and the balance in the Allowance account just prior to making the year-end adjusting journal entry is equal to the current period estimate of the company's bad debts expense. This approach is called the **accounts receivable aging method**.

When using the accounts receivable aging method, a company estimates the amount needed in the allowance account by analyzing its outstanding accounts receivable balances using an aging schedule similar to the one in **Exhibit 8-1**. An **aging schedule** is simply an analysis that reveals how much time has elapsed since a credit sale originally occurred, and consequently, how long a customer's account receivable has remained unpaid. Assume, for example, that the firm whose aging schedule appears in **Exhibit 8-1** sells its goods on credit with a credit period of 30 days. The exhibit reveals that the Alton account is current, which means that the $320 billing was made within the last 30 days; however, the Bailey account is 0–30 days *past due*, which means that the account receivable is from 31 to 60 days old. The aging schedule also reveals that the Wall balance consists of a $50 billing that is 61 to 120 days past due and a $100 billing that is 121 days to 6 months past due, and so on. In total, $42,000 of the $50,000 in Accounts Receivable is current, while the remaining $8,000 is past due from one month to over six months.

EXHIBIT 8-1	Aging Schedule of Customer Balances, December 31						
					Past Due		
Customer	Account Balance	Current	0–30 Days	31–60 Days	61–120 Days	121 Days to 6 Mos.	Over 6 Mos.
Alton, J............	$ 320	$ 320					
Bailey, C.	400		$ 400				
many more accts ...	...	...	...	$ ...	$ ...	$ ...	$ ...
Wall, M...........	150				50	100	
Zorn, W.	210			210			
	$50,000	$42,000	$4,000	$2,000	$1,000	$800	$200

Companies that analyze their uncollectible accounts experience using aged account balances develop probability-of-noncollection percentages corresponding to each age category. At the end of each period, the probability-of-noncollection percentages are applied to the totals of each age category to determine the appropriate allowance account balance for a given category. For our example, these percentages are shown in the table below. As one might expect, the estimated probability-of-noncollection increases as the number of days past due increases. Applying the percentages to the totals in our aging schedule, we can calculate the required balance for the Allowance for Doubtful Accounts—that is, $1,560:

	Amount	Probability of Noncollection	Allowance Required
Current	$42,000	2%	$ 840
0–30 days past due	4,000	3%	120
31–60 days past due	2,000	5%	100
61–120 days past due	1,000	20%	200
121–180 days past due	800	25%	200
Over 180 days past due	200	50%	100
Total allowance required			$1,560

If the Allowance for Doubtful Accounts has an existing $400 credit balance, the company calculates the required bad debt expense as $1,560 – $400, or $1,160. The year-end adjusting entry is:

A = L + SE
–1,160   –1,160 Exp

Dec. 31	Bad debts expense (+E, –SE)	1,160	
	Allowance for doubtful accounts (+XA, –A)		1,160
	To record the bad debts expense for the period.		

This entry brings the credit balance in the Allowance for Doubtful Accounts account to the estimated amount of $1,560, as shown below:

Hint: *In contrast to the percentage of net sales method, the accounts receivable aging method takes into account the beginning balance of the Allowance for Doubtful Accounts.*

–	Allowance for Doubtful Accounts (XA)	+
	400	Beg.
	1,160	Dec. 31
	1,560	Bal.

It is also possible to have a debit balance in the allowance account before the year-end adjustment. This would occur whenever the write-off of specific accounts receivable during the year exceeded the credit balance in the account as of the beginning of the year. Assume, for example, that the Allowance for Doubtful Accounts had a $350 debit balance prior to recording the December 31 adjusting entry, and that the aging schedule showed that the allowance account should have a $1,560 credit balance. The year-end adjusting entry would then be as follows:

A = L + SE
–1,910   –1,910 Exp

Dec. 31	Bad debts expense (+E, –SE)	1,910	
	Allowance for doubtful accounts (+XA, –A)		1,910
	To record the bad debts expense for the period.		

The following Allowance for Doubtful Accounts T-account shows that this entry creates the desired year-end credit balance in the allowance account of $1,560:

–	Allowance for Doubtful Accounts (XA)		+
Beg.	350	1,910	Dec. 31
		1,560	Bal.

Just when an account receivable is judged to be uncollectible is very much a cultural issue. In some Central and South American countries, buying goods and services on credit is almost unheard of. In these countries, it is considered in bad taste to owe someone money, and consequently, to preserve a company's good reputation and standing in the business community, companies pay cash for their purchases and avoid buying goods and services on credit. Therefore, in these countries it is extremely rare to see accounts receivable on the financial statements of businesses. In the United States, on the other hand, buying goods and services on credit is considered to be a normal business activity. In fact, a business manager would be chastised for failing to take advantage of any offered trade credit by paying cash for purchased goods or services. In the United States, most large businesses consider an account receivable to be uncollectible when it becomes 120 days old. Buying goods and services on credit in China is, likewise, quite common; however, buyers often take several years to pay for purchased goods, and consequently, accounts receivable are not considered to be uncollectible until 2 to 3 years have elapsed since the original credit sales transaction.

Concept ➝	Method ➝	Assessment	TAKEAWAY 8.1
Are the accounts receivable being collected in a timely manner?	List of accounts receivable along with how long they have been outstanding. Prepare an aging schedule.	Accounts in the older categories require additional collection attention.	

Recoveries of Accounts Written Off under the Allowance Method

Occasionally, an account written off against the allowance for doubtful accounts as uncollectible will later prove to be wholly or partially collectible. In such situations, a firm must first reinstate the customer's account receivable for the amount recovered before recording the collection of cash. Then the cash payment can be recorded in the customer's account. In other words, the journal entry made for the original account write-off is reversed to the extent of the recovery amount and the receipt of cash is recorded in the usual manner. For example, assume that the Claremont Corporation is using the allowance method and wrote off the Monroe Company's $300 account on January 5, 2023, but subsequently received a $200 payment on April 20, 2023. The following journal entries illustrate the write-off and subsequent recovery procedure:

	To write off the account			A = L + SE
Jan. 5	Allowance for doubtful accounts (−XA, +A)	300		+300
	Accounts receivable—Monroe Company (−A)		300	−300
	To write off the Monroe Company's account.			

	To reinstate the account			A = L + SE
Apr. 20	Accounts receivable—Monroe Company (+A)	200		+200
	Allowance for doubtful accounts (−A)		200	−200
	To reinstate the Monroe Company's account to the extent of the recovery.			

	To record receipt of cash			A = L + SE
Apr. 20	Cash (+A)	200		+200
	Accounts receivable—Monroe Company (−A)		200	−200
	To record collection of cash on account.			

YOUR TURN! 8.3

GuidedExample

MBC

The solution is on page 8-42.

Phisher, Inc., analyzed its accounts receivable at the end of the current year, and arrived at the aged balances listed below, along with the percentage that is estimated to be uncollectible:

Age Group	Balance	Estimated Loss Percentage
0–30 days past due	$100,000	1
31–60 days past due	15,000	3
61–120 days past due	10,000	5
Over 120 days past due	20,000	10
	$145,000	

The company handles credit losses with the allowance method. The company has an existing credit balance in the Allowance account of $750.

a. Prepare the adjusting entry for estimated credit losses on December 31.

b. Prepare the journal entry to write off the account of one of their customers, Phorest Company, on May 12 of the following year in the amount of $480.

CREDIT CARD SALES

LO3 Discuss the accounting treatment of credit card sales.

eLecture

MBC

Many businesses, especially retailers, allow their customers to use credit cards for their purchase transactions. Popular credit cards include VISA, MasterCard, Discover, and American Express. When a customer uses a credit card to make a purchase, the seller collects cash from the credit card company, and the customer pays cash to the credit card company when billed at a later date.

The issuer of a credit card, frequently a financial institution like **Chase Bank** or **Citibank**, will charge the seller a fee each time a card is used. The **credit card fee** usually ranges from one percent to five percent of the amount of the credit card purchase. Businesses are willing to incur this fee because credit cards provide considerable benefits to a seller. For example, the seller does not have to evaluate the creditworthiness of the customer using a credit card, and the business avoids any risk of noncollection of the account since this risk remains with the credit card issuer. Finally, the seller typically receives the cash from the credit card issuer faster than if the customer were granted trade credit by the seller.

To illustrate, the journal entry to record a $1,000 credit card sale on March 15, with a three percent credit card fee, is as follows:

Mar. 15	Cash (+A)	970		A = L + SE
	Credit card fee expense (+E, −SE)	30		+970 −30 Exp
	Sales revenue (+R, +SE)		1,000	+1,000 Rev
	To record credit card sales and collection, less a three percent fee.			

YOUR TURN! 8.4

Nafooz Company pays a two percent credit card fee on all credit sales, and receives a cash deposit immediately following each credit card transaction. If credit sales for the company total $50,000, what journal entry should be recorded to recognize the receipt of cash and the credit card fee expense?

MBC

The solution is on page 8-42.

NOTES RECEIVABLE

Promissory notes receivable are often used in sale transactions when the credit period is longer than the 30- to 60-day credit period that is typical for accounts receivable. Promissory notes are also used frequently in sales involving equipment and property because the dollar amount of these transactions can be quite large. Occasionally, a note will be substituted for an account receivable when an extension of the usual credit period is granted. Also, promissory notes are normally prepared when financial institutions make a loan to a business or an individual.

LO4 Illustrate a promissory note receivable, **discuss** the calculation of interest on notes receivable, and **present** journal entries to record notes receivable and interest.

A **promissory note** is a written promise to pay a certain sum of money on demand or at a fixed (or determinable) future date. The note is signed by the **maker** and made payable to the order of either a specific **payee** or to the **bearer**. The interest rate specified on the note is typically an annual rate. **Exhibit 8-2** illustrates a promissory note.

eLecture

MBC

A note from a debtor is called a **note receivable** by the noteholder. A note is usually regarded as a stronger claim against a debtor than an account receivable because the terms of payment are specified in writing.

EXHIBIT 8-2 A Promissory Note

> **PROMISSORY NOTE**
>
> $ __2,000. 00__ __May 3__ 20 __22__
>
> __60 days__ after the above date the undersigned promises to pay
>
> to the order of __Susan Robinson__ , the
>
> sum of __Two thousand no/100..............__ dollars, with __9__ %
>
> interest. Payable at __First Bank of Los Angeles, CA__ .
>
> __James Stone__
>
> NAME OF BORROWER

Interest on Notes Receivable

Interest is a charge for the use of money over time. Interest incurred on a promissory note receivable is interest income to the noteholder or payee of the note and interest expense to the maker of the note. Interest on a short-term promissory note is paid at the maturity date of the note. The formula for determining the amount of interest expense to the maker and interest income to the noteholder is as follows:

$$\text{Interest} = \text{Principal} \times \text{Interest rate} \times \text{Interest time}$$

The principal is the face amount of a note and the interest rate is the annual rate of interest specified in the note agreement. Interest time is the fraction of a year that a note receivable is outstanding.

When a note is written for a certain number of months, interest time is expressed in twelfths of a year. For example, interest on a six-month note for $2,000 with a nine percent annual interest rate is calculated as:

$$\text{Interest} = \$2,000 \times 0.09 \times 6/12 = \$90$$

When a note's duration, or time to maturity, is given in days, interest time is expressed as a fraction of a year; the numerator is the number of days that the note receivable will be outstanding and the denominator is 360 days. (Some lenders use 360 days, while others use 365 days; we use 360 days in our examples, exercises, and problems.) For example, interest on a 60 day note for $2,000 with a nine percent annual interest rate is:

$$\text{Interest} = \$2,000 \times 0.09 \times 60/360 = \$30$$

Businesses are required to distinguish between operating and non-operating items in their income statements; consequently, they place any interest expense or interest income on outstanding notes under the other income and expense heading in the income statement so that financial statement users will readily identify interest income or expense as being nonoperating in nature.

Determining Maturity Date

When a note's duration is expressed in days, it is customary to count the exact number of days in each calendar month to determine the note's **maturity date**. For example, a 90 day note dated July 21 has an October 19 maturity date, which is determined as follows:

10	days in July (remainder of month—31 days minus 21 days)
31	days in August
30	days in September
19	days in October (number of days required to total 90)
90	

If the duration of a note is expressed in months, the maturity date is calculated simply by counting the number of months from the date of issue. For example, a two-month note dated January 31 would mature on March 31, a three-month note of the same date would mature on April 30 (the last day of the month), and a four-month note would mature on May 31.

Recording Notes Receivable and Interest

When a note is exchanged to settle an account receivable, a journal entry is made to reflect the note receivable and to reduce the balance of the related account receivable. For example, suppose that Jordon Company sold $12,000 of merchandise on account to Bowman Company. On October 1, after the regular credit period had elapsed, the Bowman Company gave the Jordon Company a 60 day, nine percent note receivable for $12,000. Jordon Company makes the following journal entry to record receiving the note:

Oct. 1	Notes receivable—Bowman Company (+A)	12,000		A = L + SE
	Accounts receivable—Bowman Company (–A)		12,000	+12,000
	Received 60 day, nine percent note in payment of account.			–12,000

If the Bowman Company pays the note on the November 30 maturity date, the Jordon Company makes the following journal entry:

Nov. 30	Cash (+A)	12,180		A = L + SE
	Interest income (+R, +SE)		180	+12,180 +180 Rev
	Notes receivable—Bowman Company (–A)		12,000	–12,000
	Collected Bowman Company note. ($12,000 × 0.09 × 60/360 = $180).			

Recording Dishonored Notes

In the prior example, interest for 60 days at nine percent is recorded on the maturity date of the note even if the maker of the note (Bowman Company) defaults on or dishonors the note. When a note is dishonored at maturity, the amount of the combined principal plus interest is converted to an account receivable. This procedure leaves only the current, unmatured notes in the note-holder's Notes Receivable account. If the Bowman Company, for example, failed to pay its note on November 30 as expected, the Jordon Company would make the following journal entry:

Nov. 30	Accounts receivable—Bowman Company (+A)	12,180		A = L + SE
	Interest income (+R, +SE)		180	+12,180 +180 Rev
	Notes receivable—Bowman Company (–A)		12,000	–12,000
	To record the dishonoring of a note by Bowman Company.			

Adjusting Entry for Interest

When the term of a promissory note extends beyond the end of an accounting period, a year-end adjusting entry is necessary to reflect the interest earned. To illustrate, assume that Jordon Company has a note receivable outstanding at December 31, 2022. The note receivable from the Garcia Company is dated December 21, 2022, has a principal amount of $6,000, an interest rate of 12 percent, and a maturity date of February 19, 2023. The adjusting entry that Jordon Company makes at December 31, 2022, to record the earned, but uncollected, interest income is as follows:

Dec. 31	Interest receivable (+A)	20		A = L + SE
Ⓐ	Interest income (+R, +SE)		20	+20 +20 Rev
	To accrue interest income on the note from Garcia Company			
	($6,000 × 0.12 × 10/360 = $20).			

When the note is subsequently paid on February 19, Jordon Company makes the following journal entry:

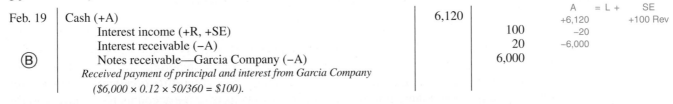

Feb. 19	Cash (+A)	6,120		A = L + SE
	Interest income (+R, +SE)		100	+6,120 +100 Rev
	Interest receivable (–A)		20	–20
Ⓑ	Notes receivable—Garcia Company (–A)		6,000	–6,000
	Received payment of principal and interest from Garcia Company			
	($6,000 × 0.12 × 50/360 = $100).			

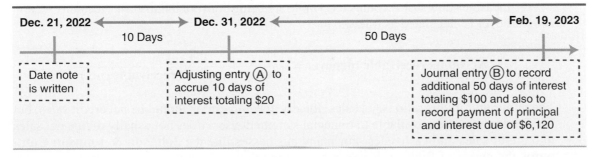

Reporting Notes Receivable on the Balance Sheet

Short-Term Notes Receivable are a current asset on the balance sheet and are often reported below Accounts Receivable in the current asset section. As with accounts receivable, notes receivable are reported separately from other notes receivable from officers and employees and notes representing advances to affiliated companies. If the notes are not short term, they should be classified as noncurrent assets. Interest Receivable on a note receivable is also a current asset.

Sometimes companies with a large volume of notes receivable must provide for possible losses on the outstanding notes. Frequently, the Allowance for Doubtful Accounts also covers potential credit losses on notes as well. In such cases, the Allowance for Doubtful Accounts account is deducted from the aggregate total of Accounts Receivable and Notes Receivable on the balance sheet. Estimating the potential credit losses on outstanding notes receivable follows the same procedures as for accounts receivable.

ENVIRONMENTAL, SOCIAL, AND GOVERNANCE   Good Business Practice at Tesla

Tesla is well known for its efforts to produce clean energy and its fight against climate change. Tesla's efforts have led to increased sales of its products, but that is not the whole reason for Tesla's profitability. Many U.S. states mandate that automakers sell a certain number of electric vehicles (EVs) relative to their total sales. Automobile manufacturers must maintain state mandated EV sales levels or risk paying hefty fines. In contrast, Tesla amasses regulatory credits due to its all-electric product line. If a manufacturer such as Fiat Chrysler is unable to meet a state's EV sales requirement, it has the option to buy credits from an EV manufacturer such as Tesla that has surplus credits. In 2020, the year Tesla was able to report its fourth consecutive quarter of GAAP profitability, a significant portion of that profit came from selling regulatory credits to other automobile manufacturers. Without the sale of those credits, Tesla would not have been able to report four consecutive quarters of GAAP profitability; a requirement that Tesla needed to fulfill to join the S&P 500. Tesla is a good example of how ESG and shrewd business practices can work together.

YOUR TURN! 8.5

GuidedExample

MBC

The solution is on page 8-42.

Ruby Company received a four month, five percent note receivable for $40,000 on October 1. How much interest income should be accrued on December 31?

ANALYZING AND MANAGING RECEIVABLES

LO5 **Define** accounts receivable turnover and average collection period and **explain** their use in the analysis and management of accounts and notes receivable.

eLecture

MBC

Most companies transact the majority of their sales on credit, which creates accounts receivable. Management and financial analysts closely monitor a company's accounts receivable using a variety of financial measures, including the accounts receivable turnover ratio and the average collection period. **Accounts receivable turnover** indicates how many times a year a firm collects its average accounts receivable, and thus, measures how fast accounts receivable are being converted into cash. Accounts receivable turnover is calculated as follows:

$$\text{Accounts receivable turnover} = \frac{\text{Net sales}}{\text{Average accounts receivable (net)}}$$

The numerator in this ratio is net sales. Ideally, the numerator should be net credit sales, but financial information available to financial statement users does not usually divide net sales into credit sales and cash sales. For many businesses like the **Johnson & Johnson Company**, the maker of Band-Aids and baby shampoo, over 99 percent of the company's sales are credit sales. Unless there is other information available on the amount of credit sales, it is common to assume that a company's net sales is a good proxy for its credit sales. Average accounts receivable (net of the allowance for doubtful accounts) is calculated by summing the beginning and ending accounts receivable (net) balances and dividing the sum by two.

To illustrate the calculation of this ratio, consider the financial results for the Claremont Corporation.

	Current Year	Prior Year
Net sales.	$40,831	$33,548
Beginning accounts receivable (net).	1,848	1,948
Ending accounts receivable (net)	1,799	1,848

Claremont's accounts receivable turnover for the current year is 22.39, or $40,831/[$1,848 + $1,799)/2], and for the prior year is 17.68, or $33,548/[($1,948 + $1,848)/2]. In general, the higher the accounts receivable turnover ratio, the faster a company is converting its receivables into cash. The increase in accounts receivable turnover in the current year is a positive sign regarding how well the Claremont Corporation is managing its accounts receivable.

An extension of the accounts receivable turnover ratio is the **average collection period**, calculated as follows:

$$\text{Average collection period} = \frac{365}{\text{Accounts receivable turnover}}$$

This ratio indicates how many days it takes on average to collect an account receivable. During the current year, Claremont's average collection period was 16.3 days, or 365/22.39. During the prior year, Claremont's average collection period was 20.6 days, or 365/17.68. The ratio reveals that Claremont is taking four fewer days to collect its accounts receivable in the current year, another sign of improved accounts receivable management.

The average collection period may also be used to evaluate the effectiveness of a company's credit policies. One rule of thumb states that the average collection period should not exceed a business's allowed credit period by more than 15 days. Thus, if a firm grants credit terms of 30 days to its customers, its average collection period should not exceed 45 days.

YOUR TURN! 8.6

MBC

The solution is on page 8-42.

The Forrester Corporation disclosed the following financial information (in millions) in its recent annual report:

Net sales.	$30,000
Beginning accounts receivable (net).	2,800
Ending accounts receivable (net)	3,200

a. Calculate the accounts receivable turnover ratio.

b. Calculate the average collection period.

Factoring and Discounting

A company can accelerate the collection of cash on an account receivable or a note receivable by selling the receivable to a finance company or a financial institution. Selling an account receivable is called **factoring** and selling a note receivable is called **discounting**. Finance companies and financial institutions that buy receivables are called **factors**.

When receivables are sold, the factor pays the selling company the amount of the account receivable or note receivable less a fee, often ranging from two percent to five percent of the value of the sold receivable. The factor then collects the cash payments directly from the customer who originally purchased the goods or services on credit. This approach speeds the collection of cash to the selling company and releases it from the work of billing and collecting the account.

Accounts and notes receivable may be sold under two conditions—with recourse and without recourse. "With recourse" indicates that in the event that a factor is unable to collect a specific customer's account or note receivable, the factor has the right to request that the selling company return the amount of the uncollected receivable. "Without recourse" indicates that a factor is unable to request reimbursement from the selling company if the factor is unable to collect a specific account or note receivable. Selling receivables without recourse is more expensive than selling receivables with recourse because the factor is forced to assume additional collection risk.

TAKEAWAY 8.2	Concept ⟶	Method ⟶	Assessment
	Are any of the existing accounts receivable in need of further attention?	Net sales and average accounts receivable $\text{Accounts receivable turnover} = \dfrac{\text{Net sales}}{\text{Average accounts receivable (net)}}$ $\text{Average collection period} = \dfrac{365}{\text{Accounts receivable turnover}}$	Compare the average collection period to the company credit policy. Longer collection periods suggest the need for management attention.

Data Analytics

DATA ANALYTICS   Tesla Uses Customer Data to Refine the Cars It Builds

Many consider **Tesla** a pioneer in the manufacturing of electric vehicles (EVs); however, Tesla was not the first to build EVs. It is more accurate to think of Tesla as a pioneer in the use of big data and data analytics to build and improve its cars. One of Tesla's goals is to collect as much user data as possible from the owners of its cars. Tesla collects data from various sources. One such source is its optional technology package, which, for example, includes cameras and sensors to help warn drivers of potential road hazards. Although this option provides a valuable service to Tesla owners, it also provides Tesla access to a trove of data, it compiles and analyzes to improve its cars.

COMPREHENSIVE PROBLEM

GuidedExample

MBC

At December 31, 2022, the following selected accounts appeared in Delta Company's unadjusted trial balance:

Accounts receivable	$81,000
Allowance for doubtful accounts.	1,200 (credit)
Notes receivable (Jason, Inc.)	12,000

Net credit sales for 2022 were $250,000. The $12,000 note receivable was a 90 day, eight percent note dated December 13, 2022. The following adjusting entries and transactions occurred at the end of 2022 and during 2023:

2022

Dec. 31 Recorded the adjusting entry for the bad debts expense, at 1.5 percent of net credit sales.
     31 Recorded the adjusting entry for interest on the $12,000 note receivable.

2023

Mar. 13 Received payment on the $12,000 note receivable from Jason, Inc., plus interest.
Apr. 5 Wrote off the account of Abilene Company, $2,850.

July   9   Wrote off the account of Acme Suppliers, $1,450.

Sept.   5   Received payment from Acme Suppliers, which is in bankruptcy proceedings, for $450 in final settlement of the account written off on July 9.

Dec.   6   Wrote off the account of Walton, Inc., $1,300.

       31   Changed from the percentage-of-net-sales method of providing for uncollectible accounts to an estimate based on the accounts receivable aging method. The account analysis indicated a desired credit balance of $4,500 in the Allowance for Doubtful Accounts.

Required

Prepare the journal entries for these adjustments and transactions.

Solution

2022

Dec. 31	Bad debts expense (+E, −SE)	3,750	
	Allowance for doubtful accounts (+XA, −A)		3,750
	To provide for bad debts expense at 1.5 percent of net credit sales, $250,000.		
31	Interest receivable (+A)	48	
	Interest income (+R, +SE)		48
	To accrue interest on Jason, Inc., note receivable ($12,000 × 0.08 × 18/360 = $48).		

2023

Mar. 13	Cash (+A)	12,240	
	Interest income (+R, +SE)		192
	Interest receivable (−A)		48
	Notes receivable—Jason, Inc. (−A)		12,000
	To record receipt of payment of Jason, Inc., note receivable ($12,000 × 0.08 × 72/360 = $192). (31 + 28 + 13 = 72 days)		
Apr. 5	Allowance for doubtful accounts (−XA, +A)	2,850	
	Accounts receivable—Abilene Company (−A)		2,850
	To write off the account of Abilene Company as uncollectible.		
July 9	Allowance for doubtful accounts (−XA, +A)	1,450	
	Accounts receivable—Acme Suppliers (−A)		1,450
	To write off the account of Acme Suppliers as uncollectible.		
Sept. 5	Accounts receivable—Acme Suppliers (+A)	450	
	Allowance for doubtful accounts (+XA, −A)		450
	To reinstate $450 of the account of Acme Suppliers that proved collectible.		
5	Cash (+A)	450	
	Accounts receivable—Acme Suppliers (−A)		450
	To record payment of Acme Suppliers' account.		

2023

Dec. 6	Allowance for doubtful accounts (−XA, +A)	1,300	
	Accounts receivable—Walton, Inc. (−A)		1,300
	To write off the account of Walton, Inc., as uncollectible.		
Dec. 31	Bad debts expense (+E, −SE)	4,700	
	Allowance for doubtful accounts (+XA, −A)		4,700
	To provide for bad debts expense ($4,500 desired balance + $200 existing debit balance = $4,700).		

Allowance for Doubtful Accounts	
Beginning balance	($1,200)
Bad Debts Expense, 12/31/2022	(3,750)
Write-offs ($2,850 + $1,450 + $1,300)	5,600
Recovery	(450)
Balance.	200
Bad Debts Expense, 12/31/2023	(4,700)
Ending Balance	($4,500)

APPENDIX 8A: Direct Write-Off Method

LO6 **Illustrate** the direct write-off method and **contrast** it with the allowance method for accounting for doubtful accounts.

The direct write-off method of accounting for credit losses is an alternative to the allowance method. Under the **direct write-off method**, doubtful accounts are charged to the bad debts expense on the income statement in the period in which the accounts are determined to be uncollectible. Under this approach, there is no attempt to estimate the bad debts expense, nor is there any attempt to match this expense with sales revenues in the period in which the credit sales transaction originally occurred. As a consequence, U.S. GAAP does not permit the use of the direct write-off method unless the amount of the credit losses is immaterial. The reason for this is because the direct write-off method does not properly match credit losses with credit sales in the appropriate time period, violating the matching concept.

For example, an account receivable may not be determined to be uncollectible, and therefore not written off, until several periods after the actual credit sales revenue is recorded. By way of contrast, the allowance method, through the use of an estimate of the bad debts expense, properly matches this expense with the associated sales revenue in the same period. The use of the direct write-off method also causes a consistent overstatement of accounts receivable on the balance sheet. Although not generally accepted for accounting purposes for most businesses, the direct write-off method is used by all companies for U.S. federal income tax purposes.

The journal entries made when the direct write-off method is used are illustrated below using data from the Claremont Corporation illustration appearing on pages 8-5 to 8-6:

To write off the account

A = L + SE
−300   −300 Exp
	Jan. 5	Bad debts expense (+E, −SE)
		    Accounts receivable—Monroe Company (−A)
		    To write off the Monroe Company's account.
			300	300

To reinstate the account

A = L + SE
+200   +200 Exp
	Apr. 20	Accounts receivable—Monroe Company (+A)
		    Bad debts expense (−E, +SE)
		    To reinstate the Monroe Company's account to the extent of the recovery.
			200	200

To record receipt of cash

A = L + SE
+200
−200
	Apr. 20	Cash (+A)
		    Accounts receivable—Monroe Company (−A)
		    To record collection of cash on account.
			200	200

If an account receivable written off in a prior year is reinstated during the current year and the Bad Debts Expense account has no existing balance from other write-offs (and no more write-offs are expected), then the account credited in the reinstatement entry is the Doubtful Accounts Recovery, a revenue account.

YOUR TURN! 8A.1

The solution is on page 8-42.

Harley Company has determined an account receivable in the amount of $750 from Rhea Inc. is uncollectible and has decided to write the account off. Harley Company uses the direct write-off method because write-offs are considered immaterial. Provide the journal entry to write off the Rhea account.

SUMMARY OF LEARNING OBJECTIVES

LO1 **Define accounts receivable, explain losses from uncollectible accounts, and describe the allowance method of accounting for doubtful accounts. (p. 8-3)**

- Accounts receivable is a current asset created when a sales transaction is executed on a credit basis.
- Accounts receivable does not include such receivables as loans to affiliate companies or advances to employees.
- The credit department of a company is responsible for conducting credit investigations of customers, establishing credit limits, and following up on overdue accounts.
- The allowance method is designed to record the bad debts expense in the same accounting period as the related credit sale.
- When the allowance method is used, specific accounts are written off by debiting the Allowance for Doubtful Accounts and crediting the Accounts Receivable account.

Describe and illustrate the percentage of net sales method and the accounts receivable aging method for estimating a business's bad debts expense. (p. 8-7)   **LO2**

- The percentage of net sales method is used to determine estimated credit losses directly. Estimated credit losses are determined by multiplying credit sales (net of any sales discounts and sales returns and allowances) times the estimated percentage of uncollectible credit sales.
- The accounts receivable aging method determines the estimated credit loss indirectly. The balance in the Accounts Receivable account is segmented into age categories. Then the balance of each category is multiplied by the estimated uncollectible percentage for that age category. The results are added to obtain the desired balance in the Allowance for Doubtful Accounts. The desired balance is then compared to the existing balance in the Allowance for Doubtful Accounts to determine the estimated credit losses and bad debts expense for the period.
- Occasionally, accounts written off against the Allowance for Doubtful Accounts later prove to be wholly or partially collectible. When this happens, the Accounts Receivable account is first reinstated to the extent of the recovery, and then the cash collection is recorded.

Discuss the accounting treatment of credit card sales. (p. 8-11)   **LO3**

- Credit card fee expense is recognized when the credit card sales transaction is recorded.
- Credit card fee expense reduces the amount of cash received by the company from the credit card issuer.

Illustrate a promissory note receivable, discuss the calculation of interest on notes receivable, and present journal entries to record notes receivable and interest. (p. 8-12)   **LO4**

- Interest on a short-term promissory note is determined using the following formula:

$$\text{Interest} = \text{Principal} \times \text{Interest rate} \times \text{Interest time}$$

- When a note is received in payment of an account receivable balance, the Notes Receivable account is debited and the Accounts Receivable account is credited.
- The noteholder recognizes interest income at the maturity date or in an end-of-period adjusting entry if the financial statements are prepared before the note matures.

Define accounts receivable turnover and average collection period and explain their use in the analysis and management of accounts and notes receivable. (p. 8-15)   **LO5**

- Accounts receivable turnover = Net sales/Average accounts receivable
- Average collection period = 365/Accounts receivable turnover
- *Accounts receivable turnover* indicates how many times a year, on average, that a firm collects its accounts receivable. *Average collection period* indicates how many days it takes, on average, to collect an account receivable.

Appendix 8A: Illustrate the direct write-off method and contrast it with the allowance method for accounting for doubtful accounts. (p. 8-19)   **LO6**

- Under the direct write-off method, uncollectible accounts are charged to the bad debts expense in the period in which they are determined to be uncollectible.
- For most companies, the direct write-off method is not a generally accepted method of accounting for credit losses; however, most companies use the direct write-off method for income tax purposes.
- U.S. GAAP does not permit the use of the direct write-off method unless the amount of the credit losses is immaterial.

Concept ➡	Method ➡	Assessment	**SUMMARY**
Are the accounts receivable being collected in a timely manner?	List of accounts receivable along with how long they have been outstanding. Prepare an aging schedule.	Accounts in the older categories require additional collection attention.	**TAKEAWAY 8.1**
Are any of the existing accounts receivable in need of further attention?	Net sales and average accounts receivable $\text{Accounts receivable turnover} = \dfrac{\text{Net sales}}{\text{Average accounts receivable (net)}}$ $\text{Average collection period} = \dfrac{365}{\text{Accounts receivable turnover}}$	Compare the average collection period to the company credit policy. Longer collection periods suggest the need for management attention.	**TAKEAWAY 8.2**

KEY TERMS

Accounts receivable (p. 366)	Allowance method (p. 368)	Discounting (p. 380)
Accounts receivable aging method (p. 371)	Average collection period (p. 379)	Factoring (p. 380)
Accounts receivable turnover (p. 379)	Bad Debts Expense (Provision for Bad Debts) (p. 367)	Factors (p. 380)
Aging schedule (p. 372)	Bearer (p. 375)	Maker (p. 375)
Allowance for Doubtful Accounts (Allowance for Uncollectible Accounts) (p. 368)	Credit card fee (p. 375)	Maturity date (p. 376)
	Credit-collection policy (p. 367)	Note receivable (p. 375)
	Credit-granting policy (p. 367)	Payee (p. 375)
	Direct write-off method (p. 382)	Percentage of net sales method (p. 371)
		Promissory note (p. 375)

Assignments with the (MBC) logo in the margin are available in **BusinessCourse**.
See the Preface of the book for details.

SELF-STUDY QUESTIONS

(Answers to the Self-Study Questions are available at the end of this chapter.)

LO1, 2

1. A firm, using the allowance method of recording credit losses, wrote off a customer's account in the amount of $500. Later, the customer paid the account. The firm reinstated the account by means of a journal entry and then recorded the collection. What is the result of these procedures?

   a. Increases total assets by $500
   b. Decreases total assets by $500
   c. Decreases total assets by $1,000
   d. Has no effect on total assets

LO2

2. A firm has accounts receivable of $90,000 and a debit balance of $900 in the Allowance for Doubtful Accounts. Two-thirds of the accounts receivable are current and one-third is past due. The firm estimates that two percent of the current accounts and five percent of the past due accounts will prove to be uncollectible. The adjusting entry to provide for the bad debts expense under the aging method should be for what amount?

   a. $2,700
   b. $3,600
   c. $1,800
   d. $4,500

LO4

3. A firm receives a six-month note from a customer. The note has a face amount of $4,000 and an interest rate of nine percent. What is the total amount of interest to be received?

   a. $1,080
   b. $30
   c. $360
   d. $180

LO5

4. A business has net sales of $60,000, a beginning balance in Accounts Receivable of $5,000, and an ending balance in Accounts Receivable of $7,000. What is the company's accounts receivable turnover?

   a. 10.0
   b. 12.0
   c. 8.6
   d. 9.2

LO5

5. A business has an accounts receivable turnover of ten. What is the company's average collection period?

   a. 36.0
   b. 30.8
   c. 34.6
   d. 36.5

LO4

6. Lite Company received a 90 day, six percent note receivable for $10,000 on December 1. How much interest should be accrued on December 31?

   a. $150
   b. $90
   c. $50
   d. $25

LO1, 2

7. Wesson Company uses the allowance method to record its expected credit losses. It estimates its losses at one percent of credit sales, which were $750,000 during the year. The Accounts Receivable balance was $220,000 and the Allowance for Doubtful Accounts had a credit balance of $1,000 at year-end. What amount is the debit to the Bad Debts Expense?

   a. $7,500
   b. $8,500
   c. $6,500
   d. $3,200

8. **Rufus & Company pays a three percent credit card fee on all credit sales, and receives a cash deposit immediately following each credit card transaction. If credit sales for the company total $15,000 on December 13, what journal entry should be recorded to recognize the receipt of cash and the credit card fee expense?**   **LO3**
   - *a.*   Debit Cash $14,550; debit Credit Card Fee Expense $450; credit Sales Revenue $15,000.
   - *b.*   Debit Cash $15,000; credit Credit Card Fee Expense $450; credit Sales Revenue $14,550.
   - *c.*   Debit Cash $15,450; debit Credit Card Fee Expense $450; credit Sales Revenue $15,900.
   - *d.*   Debit Cash $15,450; credit Credit Card Fee Expense $450; credit Sales Revenue $15,000.

9. **Which of the following statements is true?**   **LO1, 2, 6**
   - *a.*   The direct write-off method is generally accepted.
   - *b.*   The percentage of net sales method estimates the bad debts expense indirectly.
   - *c.*   The accounts receivable aging method estimates the bad debts expense indirectly.
   - *d.*   None of the above is true.

10. **On September 1, the Pavey Company accepted a $24,000, 60 day, nine percent, promissory note in exchange for overdue accounts receivable balance for the same amount from the Wagner Company. On November 30, the Wagner Company dishonored the note. What journal entry should be recorded on November 30?**   **LO4**
   - *a.*   Debit Dishonored Note Receivable Expense; credit Notes Receivable.
   - *b.*   Debit Allowance for Doubtful Accounts; credit Notes Receivable.
   - *c.*   Debit Accounts Receivable; credit Interest Income; credit Notes Receivable.
   - *d.*   None of the above entries is correct.

QUESTIONS

1. In dealing with receivables, what do the terms *factoring* and *discounting* mean?
2. How does a credit scoring system work?
3. How do the allowance method and the direct write-off method of handling credit losses differ with respect to the timing of bad debts expense recognition?
4. When a firm provides for credit losses under the allowance method, why is the Allowance for Doubtful Accounts credited rather than Accounts Receivable?
5. What are the two most commonly used methods of estimating the bad debts expense when the allowance method is employed? Describe them.
6. Haley Company estimates its bad debts expense by aging its accounts receivable and applying percentages to various age groups of the accounts. Haley calculated a total of $2,100 in possible credit losses as of December 31. Accounts Receivable has a balance of $98,000, and the Allowance for Doubtful Accounts has a credit balance of $500 before adjustment at December 31. What is the December 31 adjusting entry to provide for credit losses? What is the net amount of accounts receivable that should be included in current assets?
7. On June 15, Vance, Inc., sold $750 worth of merchandise to Dell Company. On November 20, Vance, Inc., wrote off Dell's account. On March 10 of the following year, Dell Company paid the account in full. What are the journal entries that Vance, Inc., should make for the write-off and the recovery assuming that Vance, Inc., uses (a) the allowance method of handling credit losses and (b) the direct write-off method?
8. Fiber Company sold a $675 refrigerator to a customer who charged the sale using a VISA credit card. Fiber Company deposits credit card sales slips daily; cash is deposited in Fiber Company's checking account at the same time. Fiber Company's bank charges a credit card fee of four percent of sales revenue. What journal entry should Fiber Company make to record the sale?
9. Volt Inc. received a 60 day, nine percent note for $15,000 on March 5 from a customer. What is the maturity date of the note?
10. Stafford Company received a 150 day, eight percent note for $15,000 on December 1. What adjusting entry is needed to accrue the interest due on December 31?
11. Define *accounts receivable turnover* and explain its use. How is the *average collection period* determined?
12. At a recent board of directors meeting of Ascot, Inc., one of the directors expressed concern over the Allowance for Doubtful Accounts appearing on the company's balance sheet. "I don't understand this account," he said. "Why don't we just show accounts receivable at the amount we would receive if we sold them to a financial institution and get rid of that allowance account?"

Prepare a written response to the director. Include in your response (1) an explanation of why the company has an allowance account, (2) what the balance sheet presentation of accounts receivable is supposed to show, and (3) how the basic principles of accounting relate to the analysis and presentation of accounts receivable.

13. What generally accepted accounting principle is being implemented when a company estimates its potential credit losses from its outstanding accounts receivable?

14. Why is the direct write-off method of accounting for credit losses not generally accepted?

15. When a previously written-off account receivable is collected, it must first be reinstated by debiting the Accounts Receivable account and crediting the Allowance for Doubtful Accounts. Explain the credit portion of the reinstatement journal entry.

SHORT EXERCISES

LO1, 2   **SE8-1.**   **Accounting for Doubtful Accounts** Randall Company estimates its bad debts expense by aging its accounts receivable and applying percentages to various age groups of the accounts. Randall calculated a total of $3,000 in possible credit losses as of December 31. Accounts Receivable has a balance of $128,000, and the Allowance for Doubtful Accounts has a credit balance of $500 before adjustment at December 31. What is the December 31 adjusting entry to provide for credit losses? What is the net amount of accounts receivable that should be included in current assets?

LO2   **SE8-2.**   **Reinstating Written-Off Accounts** The Stonegate Company uses the allowance method of recording credit losses and wrote off a customer's account in the amount of $800. Later, the customer paid the account. The company reinstated the account by means of a journal entry and then recorded the collection. What is the result of these procedures?

  a.   Increases total assets by $800   c.   Decreases total assets by $1,600
  b.   Decreases total assets by $800   d.   Has no effect on total assets

LO2   **SE8-3.**   **Estimating the Bad Debts Expense** Winter & Company has accounts receivable of $120,000 and a debit balance of $1,000 in the Allowance for Doubtful Accounts. Two-thirds of the accounts receivable are current and one-third is past due. The firm estimates that two percent of the current accounts and five percent of the past due accounts will prove to be uncollectible. The adjusting entry to provide for the bad debts expense under the aging method should be for what amount?

  a. $3,600   c. $2,600
  b. $4,600   d. $1,600

LO5   **SE8-4.**   **Average Collection Period** Smyth & Sons has an accounts receivable turnover of 20. What is the company's average collection period?

  a.   18.25 days   c.   22.25 days
  b.   20.0 days   d.   24.25 days

LO4   **SE8-5.**   **Recording Dishonored Promissory Notes Receivable** On October 1, the Humpback Company accepted a $50,000, 60 day, nine percent, promissory note in exchange for an overdue accounts receivable balance for the same amount from the Schwartz Company. On November 30, the Schwartz Company dishonored the note. What journal entry should be recorded on November 30?

  a.   Debit Dishonored Note Receivable Expense; credit Notes Receivable.
  b.   Debit Allowance for Doubtful Accounts; credit Notes Receivable.
  c.   Debit Accounts Receivable; credit Interest Income; credit Notes Receivable.
  d.   None of the above entries is correct.

LO3   **SE8-6.**   **Accounting for Credit Card Sales** Carter & Company pays a three percent credit card fee on all credit sales, and receives a cash deposit immediately following each credit card transaction. If credit sales for the company total $30,000 on January 15, what journal entry should be recorded to recognize the receipt of cash and the credit card fee expense?

  a.   Debit Cash $29,100; debit Credit Card Fee Expense $900.
  b.   Debit Cash $29,100; credit Credit Card Fee Expense $900.
  c.   Debit Cash $30,900; debit Credit Card Fee Expense $900.
  d.   Debit Cash $30,900; credit Credit Card Fee Expense $900.

SE8-7. Calculating Accrued Interest Income on Promissory Notes Receivable Pickett Company received a 90 day, six percent note receivable for $20,000 on November 1. How much interest income should be accrued on December 31?   **LO4**

a. $100
b. $200
c. $300
d. $400

SE8-8. Calculating Interest on Promissory Notes Receivable Houston Company receives a six-month note from a customer. The note has a face amount of $8,000 and an interest rate of nine percent. What is the total amount of interest income to be received?   **LO4**

a. $720
b. $540
c. $360
d. $180

SE8-9. Accounts Receivable Turnover Taver Company has net sales of $120,000, a beginning balance in Accounts Receivable of $10,000, and an ending balance in Accounts Receivable of $14,000. What is the company's accounts receivable turnover?   **LO5**

a. 10.0
b. 12.0
c. 8.6
d. 9.2

SE8-10. Direct Write-Off Method The direct write-off method is not generally accepted because: **LO6** (Appendix 8A)

a. The method overstates the bad debts expense.
b. It is too complex.
c. The method fails to match sales revenue with expenses in the appropriate time period.
d. The method causes liabilities to be overstated.

DATA ANALYTICS

DA8-1. Preparing Accounts Receivable Aging Using Excel A review of open invoices of Sketchers Inc. results in a schedule shown in the Excel file associated with this exercise. For this exercise, we will convert the list of open invoices into an accounts receivable aging schedule.

Data Analytics

Part 1 Cleaning the Data

1. Download Excel file DA8-1 found in myBusinessCourse.
2. Separate the items listed in one column in the worksheet into three columns using Text to Columns feature under the Data tab.
3. Determine which method to use to divide the data into columns, delimited or fixed width.
4. List the invoice that required a manual adjustment after applying the Text to columns feature.
5. Create a new column in your worksheet that calculates the number of days the invoices are outstanding. *Hint:* Enter: Dec 31 (the date of reference) in a new cell; next, in a new column, for each invoice, subtract the cell holding each invoice date from the cell holding Dec 31 (using an absolute reference). Add $ before the column and row cell reference in a formula to make it absolute. Absolute references don't change when formulas are copied. Change the format in your new column to Number, if necessary. Add headings to your columns.
6. Determine how many days invoice #204 is outstanding based upon data included in your worksheet.

Part 2 Creating a PivotTable

1. Create a PivotTable which results in an aging schedule that lists invoices in categories of (1) less than 30 days due, (2) 31–60 days due, (3) 60–90 days due, and (4) greater than 90 days due. *Hint:* After selecting your data and creating a PivotTable, drag Days outstanding to Rows, and drag Amount to Values. PivotTables are created by highlighting the data, including column titles, and clicking PivotTable on the Insert tab. To group your PivotTable into 30-day increments, right-click on the first column, select Group, and enter 1 for "starting," enter 90 for "ending," and enter 30 for "by." Lastly, drag Invoice to Rows to show invoices within each aging category.
2. Determine the total amount in each category, 1–30, 31–60, 61–90, and >91 based on data in the PivotTable.
3. Determine how many invoices are in the 61–90 day category based on data in the PivotTable. *Hint:* Copy the PivotTable from 1. Remove Invoice number from Rows. Open the dropdown menu next to

Sum of Amount in the Values box and select Value Field Settings. Select Count in the Summarize value field by box.

4. Create a new PivotTable, updating the aging categories to show aging categories by 30 days through 180 days past due.

5. Determine the total amount in each category, 1–30, 31–60, 61–90, 91–120, 121–150, 151–180 and >181.

6. Determine how many invoices are in the 151–180 category.

DA8-2. Preparing Excel Visualizations to Analyze Industry Trends Over Time The file associated with this exercise includes data extracted from the Estimates of Monthly Retail and Food Services Sales by Kind of Business obtained at the United States Census Bureau at https://www.census.gov/retail/index. html. In this exercise, we will analyze the trends in sales of *automobile and other motor vehicles* over a five-year period.

Required

1. Download Excel file DA8-2 found in myBusinessCourse.

2. Transpose the data so that it is shown in a column instead of a long row. *Hint:* Copy, Paste Special, Transpose.

3. Prepare a line chart showing trends in the sales of automobile and other motor vehicle dealers from 2017 to 2021. *Hint:* Highlight data and open Insert tab. Click Line graph in Charts group and select one of the 2-D graphs.

4. Answer the following questions using the visualization for reference.
   a. What was the lowest month of sales during the period of January 2017 to June of 2021?
   b. What was the peak month of sales during the period of January 2017 to June of 2021?
   c. How would you describe the trends in 2020 through the first half of 2021?
   d. What is a likely cause of the low point described in part *a*?

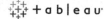

DA8-3. Preparing Tableau Visualizations of Accounting Receivable Aging Refer to PF-23 in Appendix F. This problem uses Tableau to create accounts receivable aging visualizations based on invoice data provided for Hugo Enterprises.

DA8-4. Preparing Tableau Visualizations of Accounting Receivable Aging Refer to PF-24 in Appendix F. This problem uses Tableau to create accounts receivable aging visualizations based on invoice data provided for Javier Enterprises.

DATA VISUALIZATION

Data Visualization Activities are available in myBusinessCourse. These assignments use Tableau Dashboards to expose students to visual depictions of data and introduce students to data analytics through data visualizations. These exercises are easily assignable and auto graded by MBC.

Data Visualization

EXERCISES—SET A

LO2   E8-1A. Credit Losses Based on Credit Sales Gregg Company uses the allowance method for recording its expected credit losses. It estimates credit losses at three percent of credit sales, which were $900,000 during the year. On December 31, the Accounts Receivable balance was $150,000, and the Allowance for Doubtful Accounts had a credit balance of $12,200 before adjustment.

a. Prepare the adjusting entry to record the credit losses for the year.

b. Show how Accounts Receivable and the Allowance for Doubtful Accounts would appear in the December 31 balance sheet.

LO1, 2   E8-2A. Credit Losses Based on Accounts Receivable Hunter, Inc., analyzed its accounts receivable balances at December 31, and arrived at the aged balances listed below, along with the percentage that is estimated to be uncollectible:

Age Group	Balance	Probability of Noncollection
0–30 days past due	$ 90,000	1
31–60 days past due	20,000	2
61–120 days past due	11,000	5
121–180 days past due	6,000	10
Over 180 days past due	6,000	25
	$133,000	

The company handles credit losses using the allowance method. The credit balance of the Allowance for Doubtful Accounts is $820 on December 31, before any adjustments.

a. Prepare the adjusting entry for estimated credit losses on December 31.
b. Prepare the journal entry to write off the Rose Company's account on April 10 of the following year in the amount of $650.

E8-3A. Recognizing Accounts Receivable On June 7, Pixer Co. sells $1,500 of merchandise to Jasmine Co. on account. Jasmine Co. pays for this merchandise on June 21.   **LO1**

a. Prepare the entry on Pixer's books to record the sale.
b. Prepare the entry on Pixer's books to record the receipt of payment.

E8-4A. Credit Card Sales Jamie's Fabrics accepts cash, personal checks, and two credit cards when customers buy merchandise. With the Great American Bank Card, Jamie's Fabrics receives an immediate deposit in its checking account when credit card sales slips are deposited at the bank. The bank charges a three percent fee. With the United Merchants Card, Jamie's Fabrics mails the credit card sales slips to United Merchants' regional processing center each day. United Merchants accumulates these slips for two days and then mails a check to Jamie's Fabrics, after deducting a three percent fee. Prepare journal entries to record the following: **LO3**

a. Sales for March 15 were as follows:

Cash and checks	$ 950
Great American Bank Card (Deposited at the end of the day)	1,200
United Merchants Card (Mailed at the end of the day)	700
	$2,850

b. Received a check for $1,900 from United Merchants on March 20.

E8-5A. Maturity Dates of Notes Receivable Determine the maturity date and compute the interest for each of the following notes: **LO4**

	Date of Note	Principal	Interest Rate (%)	Term
a.	August 5	$ 6,000	8	120 days
b.	May 10	16,800	7	30 days
c.	October 20	25,000	9	45 days
d.	July 6	4,500	11	60 days
e.	September 15	9,000	9	75 days

E8-6A. Computing Accrued Interest Compute the interest accrued on each of the following notes receivable held by Southland, Inc., on December 31: (Round your answer to the nearest dollar.)   **LO4**

Maker	Date of Note	Principal	Interest Rate (%)	Term
Maple	11/21	$20,000	10	120 days
Wyman	12/13	14,000	9	90 days
Nahn	12/24	21,000	6	60 days

E8-7A. Accounts Receivable Turnover and Average Collection Period The Outback Corporation disclosed the following financial information (in millions) in its recent annual report: **LO5**

	Previous Year	Current Year
Net sales.	$72,500	$83,750
Beginning accounts receivable (net).	3,896	4,100
Ending accounts receivable (net)	4,100	3,596

a.   Calculate the accounts receivable turnover ratio for both years.
b.   Calculate the average collection period for both years.
c.   Is the company's accounts receivable management improving or deteriorating?

LO2   **E8-8A.   Credit Losses Based on Credit Sales** Fritters & Sons uses the allowance method of handling its credit losses. It estimates credit losses at three percent of credit sales, which were $1,900,000 during the year. On December 31, the Accounts Receivable balance was $300,000, and the Allowance for Doubtful Accounts had a credit balance of $23,200 before adjustment.

a.   Prepare the adjusting entry to record the credit losses for the year.
b.   Show how Accounts Receivable and the Allowance for Doubtful Accounts would appear in the December 31 balance sheet.

LO1, 2   **E8-9A.   Credit Losses Based on Accounts Receivable** Miller, Inc., analyzed its accounts receivable balances at December 31 and arrived at the aged balances listed below, along with the percentage that is estimated to be uncollectible:

Age Group	Balance	Probability of Noncollection
0–30 days past due	$180,000	1
31–60 days past due	40,000	4
61–120 days past due	22,000	5
121–180 days past due	14,000	12
Over 180 days past due	8,000	25
	$264,000	

The company handles credit losses using the allowance method. The credit balance of the Allowance for Doubtful Accounts is $1,150 on December 31, before any adjustments.

a.   Prepare the adjusting entry for estimated credit losses on December 31.
b.   Prepare the journal entry to write off the Lyons Company's account on April 10 of the following year in the amount of $575.

LO5   **E8-10A.   Accounts Receivable Turnover and Average Collection Period** Verne Corporation disclosed the following financial information (in millions) in its recent annual report:

	Previous Year	Current Year
Net sales.	$167,096	$181,662
Beginning accounts receivable (net).	13,896	15,100
Ending accounts receivable (net)	15,100	13,598

a.   Calculate the accounts receivable turnover ratio for both years.
b.   Calculate the average collection period for both years.
c.   Is the company's accounts receivable management improving or deteriorating?

LO3   **E8-11A.   Credit Card Sales** The Green Roof accepts cash, personal checks, and two credit cards when customers buy merchandise. With the Great American Bank Card, The Green Roof receives an immediate deposit in its checking account when credit card sales slips are deposited at the bank. The bank charges a two percent fee. With the United Merchants Card, The Green Roof mails the credit card sales slips to United Merchants' regional processing center each day. United Merchants accumulates these slips for three days and then mails a check to The Green Roof, after deducting a two percent fee. Prepare journal entries to record the following:

a.   Sales for March 15 were as follows:

Cash and checks	$1,800
Great American Bank Card (Deposited at the end of the day)	2,500
United Merchants Card (Mailed at the end of the day)	1,400
	$5,700

    b.   Received a check for $4,050 from United Merchants on March 20.

E8-12A. Maturity Dates of Notes Receivable Determine the maturity date and compute the interest for each of the following notes: **LO4**

	Date of Note	Principal	Interest Rate (%)	Term
a.	August 5	$12,000	9	120 days
b.	May 10	33,600	7	90 days
c.	October 20	48,000	12	45 days
d.	July 16	9,000	10	60 days
e.	September 15	19,000	7	75 days

E8-13A. Computing Accrued Interest Compute the interest accrued on each of the following notes receivable held by Kirkland, Inc., on December 31: **LO4**

Maker	Date of Note	Principal	Interest Rate (%)	Term
Abel	11/21	$42,000	12	120 days
Baker	12/13	32,000	9	90 days
Charlie	12/19	25,000	6	60 days

E8-14A. Allowance Method versus Direct Write-Off Method On March 10, May, Inc., declared a $2,500 account receivable from Anders Company as uncollectible and wrote off the account. On November 18, May received an $800 payment on the account from Anders. **LO6 (Appendix 8A)**

    a.   Assume that May uses the allowance method of handling credit losses. Prepare the journal entries to record the write-off and the subsequent recovery of Anders's account.

    b.   Assume that May uses the direct write-off method of handling credit losses. Prepare the journal entries to record the write-off and the subsequent recovery of Anders's account.

    c.   Assume that the payment from Anders arrives on the following February 5, rather than on November 18 of the current year. (1) Prepare the journal entries to record the write-off and subsequent recovery of Anders's account under the allowance method. (2) Prepare the journal entries to record the write-off and subsequent recovery of Anders's account under the direct write-off method.

E8-15A. Allowance Method versus Direct Write-Off Method On March 10, Chancey, Inc., declared a $700 account receivable from the Gates Company as uncollectible and wrote off the account. On November 18, Chancey received a $200 payment on the account from Gates. **LO6 (Appendix 8A)**

    a.   Assume that Chancey uses the allowance method of handling credit losses. Prepare the journal entries to record the write-off and the subsequent recovery of Gates's account.

    b.   Assume that Chancey uses the direct write-off method of handling credit losses. Prepare the journal entries to record the write-off and the subsequent recovery of Gates's account.

    c.   Assume that the payment from Gates arrives on February 5 of the following year rather than on November 18 of the current year. (1) Prepare the journal entries to record the write-off and subsequent recovery of Gates's account under the allowance method. (2) Prepare the journal entries to record the write-off and subsequent recovery of Gates's account under the direct write-off method.

EXERCISES—SET B

E8-1B. Credit Losses Based on Credit Sales Lowland Company uses the allowance method of handling credit losses. It estimates losses at two percent of credit sales, which were $1,400,000 during the year. On December 31, the Accounts Receivable balance was $280,000, and the Allowance for Doubtful Accounts had a credit balance of $2,100 before adjustment. **LO2**

    a. Prepare the adjusting entry to record credit losses for the year.

    b. Show how the Accounts Receivable account and the Allowance for Doubtful Accounts would appear on the December 31 balance sheet.

LO1, 2   E8-2B. Credit Losses Based on Accounts Receivable Marvel, Inc., analyzed its accounts receivable balances at December 31 and arrived at the aged balances listed below, along with the percentage that is estimated to be uncollectible:

Age Group	Balance	Probability of Noncollection
0–30 days past due	$100,000	1
31–60 days past due	20,000	2
61–120 days past due	20,000	6
121–180 days past due	9,000	11
Over 180 days past due	2,000	20
	$151,000	

The company handles credit losses with the allowance method. The credit balance of the Allowance for Doubtful Accounts is $840 on December 31, before any adjustments.

    a. Prepare the adjusting entry for estimated credit losses on December 31.

    b. Prepare the journal entry to write off Porter Company's account on the following May 12, in the amount of $680.

LO1   E8-3B. Recognizing Accounts Receivable On August 9, Gait Co. sells $980 of merchandise to Taylor Co. on account. Taylor Co. pays for this merchandise on September 1.

    a. Prepare the entry on Gait's books to record the sale.

    b. Prepare the entry on Gait's books to record the receipt of payment.

LO3   E8-4B. Credit Card Sales Historically, 60 percent of the customer bills at the Andrews' Supper Club have been paid with cash or check, and 40 percent have been paid using either the Great American Bank Card or the United Merchants Card. Andrews pays a four percent fee with both cards. Great American Bank deposits cash in Andrews' checking account when the credit card sales slips are deposited. United Merchants makes an electronic funds transfer three days after the sales slips are mailed. Prepare journal entries to record the following:

    a. Sales for September 10 were as follows:

Cash and checks	$1,340
Great American Bank Card (Deposited at the end of the day)	500
United Merchants Card (Mailed at the end of the day)	300
	$2,140

    b. On September 13, Andrews received an electronic funds transfer from United Merchants for the September 10 sales.

LO4   E8-5B. Maturity Dates of Notes Receivable Determine the maturity date and compute the interest for each of the following notes:

	Date of Note	Principal	Interest Rate (%)	Term
a.	July 10	$ 7,200	9	90 days
b.	April 25	12,000	5	120 days
c.	May 19	11,200	7	120 days
d.	June 10	5,400	11	45 days
e.	October 29	30,000	6	75 days

LO4   E8-6B. Computing Accrued Interest Compute the interest accrued on each of the following notes receivable held by Gallow, Inc., on December 31: (Round your answer to the nearest dollar.)

Maker	Date of Note	Principal	Interest Rate (%)	Term
Barton....................	12/14	$ 8,000	8	120 days
Lawson...................	12/13	26,000	9	90 days
Riley	12/19	12,000	11	60 days

E8-7B. Accounts Receivable Turnover and Average Collection Period The Bud Miller Corporation disclosed the following financial information (in millions) in its recent annual report:

LO5

	Previous Year	Current Year
Net sales...	$97,096	$111,662
Beginning accounts receivable (net)..........................	6,450	6,355
Ending accounts receivable (net).............................	6,355	6,598

    a.   Calculate the accounts receivable turnover ratio for both years.
    b.   Calculate the average collection period for both years.
    c.   Is the company's accounts receivable management improving or deteriorating?

E8-8B. Credit Losses Based on Credit Sales Ranch Company uses the allowance method of handling its credit losses. It estimates credit losses at 2.5 percent of credit sales, which were $2,700,000 during the year. On December 31, the Accounts Receivable balance was $475,000, and the Allowance for Doubtful Accounts had a credit balance of $30,600 before adjustment.

LO2

    a.   Prepare the adjusting entry to record the credit losses for the year.
    b.   Show how Accounts Receivable and the Allowance for Doubtful Accounts would appear in the December 31 balance sheet.

E8-9B. Credit Losses Based on Accounts Receivable Billy, Inc., analyzed its accounts receivable balances at December 31 and arrived at the aged balances listed below, along with the percentage that is estimated to be uncollectible:

LO1, 2

Age Group	Balance	Probability of Noncollection
0–30 days past due	$320,000	1
31–60 days past due	60,000	3
61–120 days past due	33,000	6
121–180 days past due	18,000	10
Over 180 days past due	14,000	25
	$445,000	

The company handles credit losses using the allowance method. The credit balance of the Allowance for Doubtful Accounts is $1,560 on December 31, before any adjustments.

    a.   Prepare the adjusting entry for estimated credit losses on December 31.
    b.   Prepare the journal entry to write off the Matthews Company's account on the following April 10, in the amount of $460.

E8-10B. Accounts Receivable Turnover and Average Collection Period The Yale Corporation disclosed the following financial information (in millions) in its recent annual report:

LO5

	Previous Year	Current Year
Net sales...	$127,096	$112,550
Beginning accounts receivable (net)..........................	8,896	8,120
Ending accounts receivable (net).............................	8,120	6,598

    a.   Calculate the accounts receivable turnover ratio for both years.
    b.   Calculate the average collection period for both years.
    c.   Is the company's accounts receivable management improving or deteriorating?

LO3 **E8-11B. Credit Card Sales** The Kitchen Store accepts cash, personal checks, and two credit cards when customers buy merchandise. With the Great American Bank Card, The Kitchen Store receives an immediate deposit in its checking account when credit card sales slips are deposited at the bank. The bank charges a three percent fee. With the United Merchants Card, The Kitchen Store mails the credit card sales slips to United Merchants' regional processing center each day. United Merchants accumulates these slips for three days and then mails a check to The Kitchen Store, after deducting a two percent fee. Prepare journal entries to record the following:

a.   Sales for March 15 were as follows:

Cash and checks	$2,550
Great American Bank Card (Deposited at the end of the day)	3,300
United Merchants Card (Mailed at the end of the day)	2,100
	$7,950

b.   Received a check for $9,250 from United Merchants on March 20.

LO4 **E8-12B. Maturity Dates of Notes Receivable** Determine the maturity date and compute the interest for each of the following notes:

	Date of Note	Principal	Interest Rate (%)	Term
a.	August 5	$20,000	8	120 days
b.	May 10	50,400	7	90 days
c.	October 30	72,000	9	45 days
d.	July 6	13,750	11	60 days
e.	September 15	27,000	8	60 days

LO4 **E8-13B. Computing Accrued Interest** Compute the interest accrued on each of the following notes receivable held by Northland, Inc., on December 31:

	Maker	Date of Note	Principal	Interest Rate (%)	Term
a.	Delta	11/21	$54,000	7	120 days
b.	Echo	12/13	42,000	9	90 days
c.	Foxtrot	12/17	63,000	8	60 days

LO6
(Appendix 8A) **E8-14B. Allowance Method versus Direct Write-Off Method** On March 10, Barnes, Inc., declared a $3,700 account receivable from Lamas Company as uncollectible and wrote off the account. On November 18, Barnes received a $1,600 payment on the account from Lamas.

a.   Assume that Barnes uses the allowance method of handling credit losses. Prepare the journal entries to record the write-off and the subsequent recovery of Lamas's account.

b.   Assume that Barnes uses the direct write-off method of handling credit losses. Prepare the journal entries to record the write-off and the subsequent recovery of Lamas's account.

c.   Assume that the payment from Lamas arrives on the following February 5, rather than on November 18 of the current year. (1) Prepare the journal entries to record the write-off and subsequent recovery of Lamas's account under the allowance method. (2) Prepare the journal entries to record the write-off and subsequent recovery of Lamas's account under the direct write-off method.

LO6
(Appendix 8A) **E8-15B. Allowance Method versus Direct Write-Off Method** On April 12, Mitch Company declared a $2,000 account receivable from the Ward Company as uncollectible and wrote off the account. On December 5, Mitch received a $600 payment on the account from Ward.

a.   Assume that Mitch uses the allowance method of handling credit losses. Prepare the journal entries to record the write-off and the subsequent recovery of Ward's account.

b.   Assume that Mitch uses the direct write-off method of handling credit losses. Prepare the journal entries to record the write-off and the subsequent recovery of Ward's account.

c.   Assume that the payment from Ward arrives on the following January 18, rather than on December 5 of the current year. (1) Prepare the journal entries to record the write-off and subsequent recovery of Ward's account under the allowance method. (2) Prepare the journal entries to record the write-off and subsequent recovery of Ward's account under the direct write-off method.

PROBLEMS—SET A

P8-1A. Allowance Method David Company, which has been in business for three years, makes all of its sales on account and does not offer cash discounts. The firm's credit sales, collections from customers, and write-offs of uncollectible accounts for the three-year period are summarized below: **LO2**

Year	Sales	Collections	Accounts Written Off
Year 1	$300,000	$287,000	$2,200
Year 2	385,000	390,000	3,350
Year 3	430,000	407,000	3,650

Required

a. If David Company had used the allowance method of recognizing credit losses and had provided for such losses at the rate of 1.6 percent of credit sales, what amounts in accounts receivable and the allowance for doubtful accounts would appear on the firm's balance sheet at the end of the third year? What total amount of bad debts expense would have appeared on the firm's income statement during the three-year period?

b. Comment on the use of the 1.6 percent rate to provide for credit losses in part *a*.

P8-2A. Journal Entries for Credit Losses At the beginning of the year, Portal Company had the following accounts on its books: **LO1, 2**

Accounts receivable	$140,000 (debit)
Allowance for doubtful accounts.	8,000 (credit)

During the year, credit sales were $1,173,000 and collections on account were $1,175,000. The following transactions, among others, occurred during the year:

Feb.   17   Wrote off R. Lowell's account, $4,000.
May   28   Wrote off G. Boyd's account, $3,400.
Oct.   13   Received $600 from G. Boyd, who is in bankruptcy proceedings, in final settlement of the account written off on May 28. This amount is not included in the $1,175,000 collections.
Dec.   15   Wrote off K. Marshall's account, $1,600.
       31   In an adjusting entry, recorded the allowance for doubtful accounts at 0.9 percent of credit sales for the year.

Required

a. Prepare journal entries to record the credit sales, the collections on account, and the preceding transactions and adjustment.

b. Show how Accounts Receivable and the Allowance for Doubtful Accounts would appear on the December 31 balance sheet.

P8-3A. Credit Losses Based on Accounts Receivable At December 31, Mueller Company had a balance of $409,000 in its Accounts Receivable account and a credit balance of $4,200 in the Allowance for Doubtful Accounts account. The accounts receivable T-account consisted of $414,000 in debit balances and $5,000 in credit balances. The company aged its accounts as follows: **LO2**

Current	$344,000
0–60 days past due	44,000
61–180 days past due	18,000
Over 180 days past due	8,000
	$414,000

In the past, the company has experienced credit losses as follows: one percent of current balances, five percent of balances 0–60 days past due, 18 percent of balances 61–180 days past due, and 30 percent of balances over six months past due. The company bases its allowance for doubtful accounts on an aging analysis of accounts receivable.

Required

a. Prepare the adjusting entry to record the allowance for doubtful accounts for the year.

b. Show how Accounts Receivable (including the credit balances) and the Allowance for Doubtful Accounts would appear on the December 31 balance sheet.

LO3   **P8-4A.** **Credit Card Sales** Katy's Gallery sells quality art work, with prices for individual pieces ranging from $300 to $25,000. Sales are infrequent, typically only three to five pieces per week. The following transactions occurred during the first week of June. Perpetual inventory is used.

June   1   Sold a $900 framed print ($450 cost) to Kerwin Antiques on account, with 3/10, n/30 credit terms.

2   Sold three framed etchings totaling $2,400 ($1,500 cost) to Maria Alvado, who used the United Merchants Card to charge the cost of the etchings. Katy mailed the credit card sales slip to United Merchants the same day. United Merchants will send a check within seven days after deducting a one percent fee.

4   Sold a $1,900 oil painting ($1,000 cost) to Shaun Chandler, who paid with a personal check.

5   Sold a $2,100 watercolor ($1,500 cost) to Julie and John Malbie, who used their Great American Bank Card to charge the purchase of the painting. Katy deposited the credit card sales slip the same day and received immediate credit in the company's checking account. The bank charged a one percent fee.

6   Received payment from Kerwin Antiques for its June 1 purchase.

7   Received a check from United Merchants for the June 2 sale.

Required
Prepare journal entries to record Katy's Gallery transactions.

LO2, 4   **P8-5A.** **Journal Entries for Accounts and Notes Receivable** Pomona Inc. began business on January 1. Certain transactions for the year follow:

June   8   Received a $30,000, 60 day, six percent note on account from R. Elliot.
Aug.   7   Received payment from R. Elliot on her note (principal plus interest).
Sept.   1   Received an $18,000, 120 day, seven percent note from B. Shore Company on account.
Dec.   16   Received a $14,400, 45 day, eight percent note from C. Judd on account.
30   B. Shore Company failed to pay its note.
31   Wrote off B. Shore's account as uncollectible. Pomona, Inc., uses the allowance method of providing for credit losses.
31   Recorded expected credit losses for the year by an adjusting entry. Accounts written off during this first year have created a debit balance in the Allowance for Doubtful Accounts of $24,500. An analysis of aged receivables indicates that the desired balance of the allowance account should be $21,300.
31   Made the appropriate adjusting entries for interest.

Required
Record the foregoing transactions and adjustments in general journal form.

LO2   **P8-6A.** **Allowance Method** The Irvine Company, which has been in business for three years, makes all of its sales on account and does not offer cash discounts. The firm's credit sales, collections from customers, and write-offs of uncollectible accounts for the three-year period are summarized below:

Year	Sales	Collections	Accounts Written Off
Year 1	$600,000	$574,000	$4,200
Year 2	770,000	740,000	6,900
Year 3	860,000	814,000	7,300

Required
a.   If the Irvine Company had used the allowance method of recognizing credit losses and had provided for such losses at the rate of 1.3 percent of credit sales, what amounts in Accounts Receivable and the Allowance for Doubtful Accounts would appear on the firm's balance sheet at the end of the third year? What total amount of bad debts expense would have appeared on the firm's income statement during the three-year period?
b.   Comment on the use of the 1.3 percent rate to provide for credit losses in part *a*.

LO1, 2   **P8-7A.** **Journal Entries for Credit Losses** At the beginning of the year, the Dallas Company had the following accounts on its books:

Accounts receivable...	$264,000 (debit)
Allowance for doubtful accounts...	16,500 (credit)

During the year, credit sales were $2,346,000 and collections on account were $2,350,000. The following transactions, among others, occurred during the year:

Feb. 17 Wrote off R. St. John's account, $7,500.

May 28 Wrote off G. Herberger's account, $4,800.

Oct. 13 Received $1,200 from G. Herberger, who is in bankruptcy proceedings, in final settlement of the account written off on May 28. This amount is not included in the $2,350,000 collections.

Dec. 15 Wrote off R. Clancy's account, $5,000.

31 In an adjusting entry, recorded the allowance for doubtful accounts at 0.8 percent of credit sales for the year.

Required

a. Prepare journal entries to record the credit sales, the collections on account, and the preceding transactions and adjustment.

b. Show how Accounts Receivable and the Allowance for Doubtful Accounts would appear on the December 31 balance sheet.

P8-8A. Credit Losses Based on Accounts Receivable At December 31, the Azuza Company had a balance of $754,000 in its Accounts Receivable account and a credit balance of $9,000 in the Allowance for Doubtful Accounts account. The company aged its accounts as follows:

Current...	$608,000
0–60 days past due...	88,000
61–180 days past due......................................	40,000
Over 180 days past due....................................	18,000
	$754,000

In the past, the company has experienced credit losses as follows: one percent of current balances, five percent of balances 0–60 days past due, 20 percent of balances 61–180 days past due, and 40 percent of balances over six months past due. The company bases its allowance for doubtful accounts on an aging analysis of accounts receivable.

Required

a. Prepare the adjusting entry to record the allowance for doubtful accounts for the year.

b. Show how Accounts Receivable and the Allowance for Doubtful Accounts would appear on the December 31 balance sheet.

P8-9A. Credit Card Sales Le Kai Arts sells quality art work, with prices for individual pieces ranging from $1,000 to $50,000. Sales are infrequent, typically only six to ten pieces per week. The following transactions occurred during the first week of June. Perpetual inventory is used.

June 1 Sold an $1,800 framed print ($1,200 cost) to Likert Antiques on account, with 2/10, n/30 credit terms.

2 Sold three framed etchings totaling $5,200 ($2,800 cost) to Annabelle Herrera, who used the United Merchants Card to charge the cost of the etchings. Le Kai mailed the credit card sales slip to United Merchants the same day. United Merchants will send a check within seven days after deducting a two percent fee.

4 Sold a $3,600 oil painting ($2,000 cost) to Ryan LaLander, who paid with a personal check.

5 Sold a $6,000 watercolor ($2,200 cost) to Julie and Bobby Herman, who used their Great American Bank Card to charge the purchase of the painting. Le Kai deposited the credit card sales slip the same day and received immediate credit in the company's checking account. The bank charged a one percent fee.

6 Received payment from Likert Antiques for its June 1 purchase.

7 Received a check from United Merchants for the June 2 sale.

Required

Prepare journal entries to record the Le Kai Gallery transactions.

LO2

LO3

LO2, 4   **P8-10A.   Journal Entries for Accounts and Notes Receivable**   Philly, Inc., began business on January 1. Certain transactions for the year follow:

June   8   Received a $15,000, 60 day, nine percent note on account from J. Albert.
Aug.   7   Received payment from J. Albert on his note (principal plus interest).
Sept.   1   Received a $40,000, 120 day, six percent note from R.T. Matthews Company on account.
Dec.   16   Received a $28,800, 45 day, ten percent note from D. LeRoy on account.
        30   R.T. Matthews Company failed to pay its note.
        31   Wrote off R.T. Matthews' account as uncollectible. Philly, Inc., uses the allowance method of providing for credit losses.
        31   Recorded expected credit losses for the year by an adjusting entry. Accounts written off during this first year have created a debit balance in the allowance for doubtful accounts of $45,200. An analysis of aged receivables indicates that the desired balance of the allowance account should be $42,000.
        31   Made the appropriate adjusting entries for interest.

Required
Record the foregoing transactions and adjustments in general journal form.

PROBLEMS—SET B

LO2   **P8-1B.   Allowance Method**   Brooke Company, which has been in business for three years, makes all of its sales on account and does not offer cash discounts. The firm's credit sales, collections from customers, and write-offs of uncollectible accounts for the three-year period are summarized as follows:

Year	Sales	Collections	Accounts Written Off
Year 1	$751,000	$733,000	$5,300
Year 2	876,000	864,000	6,400
Year 3	980,000	938,000	6,500

Required
a.   If Brooke Company used an allowance method of recognizing credit losses and provided for such losses at the rate of one percent of credit sales, what amounts of accounts receivable and the allowance for doubtful accounts should appear on the firm's balance sheet at the end of the third year? What total amount of bad debts expense should appear on the firm's income statement during the three-year period?
b.   Comment on the use of the one percent rate to provide for credit losses in part *a*.

LO1, 2   **P8-2B.   Journal Entries for Credit Losses**   At January 1, the Blake Company had the following accounts on its books:

Accounts receivable	$130,000 (debit)
Allowance for doubtful accounts	7,000 (credit)

During the year, credit sales were $850,000 and collections on account were $794,000. The following transactions, among others, occurred during the year:

Jan.   11   Wrote off J. Wolf's account, $3,000.
Apr.   29   Wrote off B. Avery's account, $2,000.
Nov.   15   Received $1,000 from B. Avery to pay a debt that had been written off April 29. This amount is not included in the $794,000 collections.
Dec.   5   Wrote off D. Wright's account, $2,250.
        31   In an adjusting entry, recorded the allowance for doubtful accounts at one percent of credit sales for the year.

Required
a.   Prepare journal entries to record the credit sales, the collections on account, the transactions, and the adjustment.
b.   Show how Accounts Receivable and the Allowance for Doubtful Accounts appear on the December 31 balance sheet.

P8-3B. Credit Losses Based on Accounts Receivable At December 31, Rhine Company had a balance of $307,000 in its Accounts Receivable account and a credit balance of $2,800 in the Allowance for Doubtful Accounts account. The accounts receivable T-account consisted of $310,600 in debit balances and $3,600 in credit balances. The company has aged its accounts as follows:

LO2

Current	$262,000
0–60 days past due	28,000
61–180 days past due	11,200
Over 180 days past due	9,400
	$310,600

In the past, the company has experienced credit losses as follows: two percent of current balances, six percent of balances 0–60 days past due, 15 percent of balances 61–180 days past due, and 30 percent of balances more than six months past due. The company bases its allowance for doubtful accounts on an aging analysis of accounts receivable.

Required

a. Prepare the adjusting journal entry to record the provision for credit losses for the year.
b. Show how Accounts Receivable (including the credit balances) and the Allowance for Doubtful Accounts appear on the December 31 balance sheet.

P8-4B. Credit Card Sales Captain Peter's Marina sells boats and other water recreational vehicles (approximately three vehicles are sold each week). The following transactions occurred during the third week of May:

LO3

May 15 Sold an $800 boat trailer ($500 cost) to Sam and Myrna Marston, who paid using a personal check.
      16 Sold a $10,000 boat ($6,500 cost) to the Calumet Lake Patrol on account, with 2/10, n/30 terms.
      18 Sold a $1,200 water scooter ($700 cost) to Kyle Bronson, who used the United Merchants Card to charge the cost of the water scooter. Captain Peter's mailed the credit card sales slip to United Merchants the same day. United Merchants will send a check within seven days, net of a two percent fee.
      19 Sold a $6,000 fishing boat ($3,500 cost) to Michael Ferguson, who used the Great American Bank Card to pay for the boat. Captain Peter's deposited the credit card sales slip the same day and received an immediate credit in the company's checking account, net of a three percent fee.
      20 Received payment from Calumet Lake Patrol for the boat purchased on May 16.
      21 Received payment from United Merchants for the May 18 transaction.

Required
Prepare journal entries to record these transactions. Captain Peter's Marina uses the perpetual inventory system.

P8-5B. Journal Entries for Accounts and Notes Receivable Lance, Inc., began business on January 1. Several transactions for the year follow:

LO2, 4

May   2 Received an $18,000, 60 day, ten percent note on account from the Holt Company.
July   1 Received payment from Holt for its note plus interest.
      1 Received a $30,000, 120 day, ten percent note from B. Rich Company on account.
Oct. 29 B. Rich failed to pay its note.
Dec.   9 Wrote off B. Rich's account as uncollectible. Lance, Inc., uses the allowance method of providing for credit losses.
      11 Received a $35,000, 90 day, nine percent note from W. Maling on account.
      31 Recorded expected credit losses for the year by an adjusting entry. The allowance for doubtful accounts has a debit balance of $28,300 as a result of accounts written off during this first year. An analysis of aged accounts receivables indicates that the desired balance of the allowance account is $5,800.
      31 Made the appropriate adjusting entries for interest.

Required
Record the foregoing transactions and adjustments in general journal form.

LO2 P8-6B. Allowance Method The Fallbrook Company, which has been in business for three years, makes all of its sales on account and does not offer cash discounts. The firm's credit sales, collections from customers, and write-offs of uncollectible accounts for the three-year period are summarized below:

Year	Sales	Collections	Accounts Written Off
Year 1	$1,602,000	$1,466,000	$10,600
Year 2	1,752,000	1,728,000	12,500
Year 3	2,050,000	1,876,000	14,000

Required

a. If the Fallbrook Company used an allowance method of recognizing credit losses and provided for such losses at the rate of one percent of credit sales, what amounts of accounts receivable and the allowance for doubtful accounts should appear on the firm's balance sheet at the end of the third year? What total amount of bad debts expense should appear on the firm's income statement during the three-year period?

b. Comment on the use of the one percent rate to provide for credit losses in part a.

LO1, 2 P8-7B. Journal Entries for Credit Losses At January 1, the Sherry Company had the following accounts on its books:

Accounts receivable	$255,000 (debit)
Allowance for doubtful accounts	13,600 (credit)

During the year, credit sales were $1,750,000 and collections on account were $1,588,000. The following transactions, among others, occurred during the year:

Jan. 11 Wrote off J. Smith's account, $5,800.
Apr. 29 Wrote off B. Bird's account, $2,500.
Nov. 15 Received $1,500 from B. Bird to pay a debt that had been written off April 29. This amount is not included in the $1,588,000 collections.
Dec. 5 Wrote off D. Finger's account, $4,300.
      31 In an adjusting entry, recorded the allowance for doubtful accounts at three percent of credit sales for the year.

Required

a. Prepare journal entries to record the credit sales, the collections on account, the transactions, and the adjustment.

b. Show how Accounts Receivable and the Allowance for Doubtful Accounts appear on the December 31 balance sheet.

LO2 P8-8B. Credit Losses Based on Accounts Receivable At December 31, the Lange Company had a balance of $622,000 in its accounts receivable account and a credit balance of $7,500 in the allowance for doubtful accounts account. The company has aged its accounts as follows:

Current	$524,000
0–60 days past due	56,000
61–180 days past due	25,200
Over 180 days past due	16,800
	$622,000

In the past, the company has experienced credit losses as follows: two percent of current balances, six percent of balances 0–60 days past due, 20 percent of balances 61–180 days past due, and 30 percent of balances more than six months past due. The company bases its allowance for doubtful accounts on an aging analysis of accounts receivable.

Required

a. Prepare the adjusting journal entry to record the provision for credit losses for the year.

b. Show how Accounts Receivable and the Allowance for Doubtful Accounts appear on the December 31 balance sheet.

P8-9B. Credit Card Sales Lake Heart Marina sells boats and other water recreational vehicles (approximately three vehicles are sold each week). The following transactions occurred during the third week of May:

LO3

May 15 Sold a $1,500 boat trailer ($760 cost) to Ed and Jane Peeler, who paid using a personal check.
16 Sold a $20,000 boat ($13,000 cost) to the Lake Heart Lake Patrol on account, with 2/10, n/30 terms.
18 Sold a $2,800 water scooter ($1,500 cost) to Bryan Wagner, who used the United Merchants Card to charge the cost of the water scooter. Lake Heart Marina mailed the credit card sales slip to United Merchants the same day. United Merchants will send a check within seven days, net of a three percent fee.
19 Sold a $9,000 fishing boat ($5,000 cost) to Michael Moffett, who used the Great American Bank Card to pay for the boat. Lake Heart Marina deposited the credit card sales slip the same day and received an immediate credit in the company's checking account, net of a two percent fee.
20 Received payment from the Lake Heart Lake Patrol for the boat purchased on May 16.
21 Received payment from United Merchants for the May 18 transaction.

Required
Prepare journal entries to record these transactions. The Lake Heart Marina uses a perpetual inventory system.

P8-10B. Journal Entries for Accounts and Notes Receivable Austin, Inc., began business on January 1. Several transactions for the year follow:

LO2, 4

May 2 Received a $30,000, 60 day, ten percent note on account from the Haskins Company.
July 1 Received payment from Haskins for its note plus interest.
1 Received a $61,000, 120 day, nine percent note from R. Longo Company on account.
Oct. 29 R. Longo failed to pay its note.
Dec. 9 Wrote off R. Longo's account as uncollectible. Austin, Inc., uses the allowance method of providing for credit losses.
11 Received a $42,000, 90 day, 12 percent note from R. Canal on account.
31 Recorded expected credit losses for the year by an adjusting entry. Accounts written off during this first year have created a debit balance in the Allowance for Doubtful Accounts of $61,000. An analysis of aged accounts receivables indicates that the desired balance of the allowance account should be $13,200.
31 Made the appropriate adjusting entries for interest.

Required
Record the foregoing transactions and adjustments in general journal form.

SERIAL PROBLEM: KATE'S CARDS

(Note: This is a continuation of the Serial Problem: Kate's Cards from Chapters 1 through 7.)

SP8. Kate has put a lot of time and effort into streamlining the process to design and produce a greeting card. She has documented the entire process in a QuickTime video she produced on her iMac. The video takes the viewer through the step-by-step process of selecting hardware and software, and shows how to design and produce the card. Kate has met many people who would like to get into the production of greeting cards, but are overwhelmed by the process. Kate has decided to sell the entire package (hardware, software, and video tutorial) to aspiring card producers. The cost of the entire package to Kate is $4,500 and she plans to mark it up by $500 and sell it for $5,000.

John Stevens, an individual Kate met recently at a greeting card conference, would like to buy the package from Kate. Unfortunately, John does not have this much cash and would like for Kate to extend credit.

Kate believes that many of her customers will not be able to pay cash and, therefore, she will need to find some way to provide financing. One option she is exploring is to accept credit cards. She learned that the credit card provider charges a 2.5 percent fee and provides immediate cash upon receiving the sales receipts.

Kate would like you to answer the following questions:

1. What are the advantages and disadvantages of offering credit?
2. What precautions should she take before offering credit to people like John?

3. If Kate grants credit to John, the terms will be 2/10, n/30. Assuming the payment is made during the 10-day discount period, what would be the journal entry to record the sale and then the subsequent payment?

4. If instead of paying early, John pays in 25 days, what would be the journal entry to record the payment?

5. Rather than providing the financing directly, assume that Kate decides to allow the use of credit cards. Further, assume that during the month there is $15,000 worth of credit card sales. Provide the journal entry to record the sales, along with the associated credit card fee. The cost of the goods sold total $13,500.

EXTENDING YOUR KNOWLEDGE

REPORTING AND ANALYSIS

COLUMBIA SPORTSWEAR COMPANY

EYK8-1.   Financial Reporting Problem: Columbia Sportswear Company The annual report of the **Columbia Sportswear Company** is presented in Appendix A at the end of this book.

a. What was the gross amount of Accounts Receivables and the Allowance for Doubtful Accounts at the end of 2019 and 2020?

b. What percent of net accounts receivables was the allowance for doubtful accounts at the end of 2019 and 2020?

COLUMBIA SPORTSWEAR COMPANY

UNDER ARMOUR, INC.

EYK8-2.   Comparative Analysis Problem: Columbia Sportswear Company vs. Under Armour, Inc. The annual report of the **Columbia Sportswear Company** is presented in Appendix A at the end of this book and the complete annual report of **Under Armour, Inc.**, is on this book's website.

Required

a. Calculate the accounts receivable turnover and the average collection period for Columbia Sportswear and Under Armour, Inc., for 2020 and 2019. (To calculate the accounts receivable turnover, use the ending net accounts receivable balance as the denominator rather than average net accounts receivable.)

b. Compare the average collection periods for the two companies and comment on possible reasons for the difference in the average collection periods for the two companies.

EYK8-3.   Business Decision Problem Sally Smith owned a dance studio in San Francisco, California. Students could buy access to the dance classes by paying a monthly fee. Unfortunately, many of Sally's students were struggling actors and actresses who lacked the ability to pay their bills in a timely manner. Although the students were expected to pay for classes in advance, Sally had begun offering credit to many of her students in order to grow her business. This, however, created a serious liquidity problem for Sally.

Age Classification	Trade Receivables Outstanding Balance	Historical Estimate of Noncollection
0–30 days	$44,000	4%
31–60 days	31,000	8%
61–90 days	22,000	12%
91–120 days	13,000	14%
121–150 days	9,000	20%
> 150 days	5,000	50%

Sally's accountant, Matt Thomas, had tried to help her get a handle on the problem, but to little avail. One trick he had successfully used in the past to make Sally realize the seriousness of the problem was to overestimate the extent of Sally's debts; consequently, there currently existed a balance in the Allowance for Uncollectible Accounts totaling $2,700.

Required

1. The first step to help get Sally's business back on track is to write off all receivables having a very low probability of collection (i.e., those accounts over 150 days). Which accounts are affected and by what amount?

2. Prepare an aging of Sally's remaining accounts receivable. What should be the balance in the Allowance for Uncollectible Accounts?

3. Sally is in need of an immediate cash infusion and Matt has advised her to sell some of her receivables. A local bank has offered her two alternatives:

    a. Factor $40,000 of "current" receivables (i.e., 0–30 days old) on a nonrecourse basis at a flat fee of 11 percent of the receivables sold.

    b. Factor $40,000 of "current" receivables on a recourse basis at a flat fee of six percent of the receivables sold.

    Which option should Sally choose? Why?

EYK8-4. **Financial Analysis Problem** **Abbott Laboratories** is a diversified health care company devoted to the discovery, development, manufacture, and marketing of innovative products that improve diagnostic, therapeutic, and nutritional practices. Abbott markets products in more than 130 countries and employs 50,000 people. **Pfizer Inc.** is a research-based, global health care company. Its mission is to discover and develop innovative, value-added products that improve the quality of life of people around the world. Pfizer manufactures products in 31 countries and markets these products worldwide. These two companies reported the following information in their financial reports:

ABBOTT
LABORATORIES

PFIZER INC.

(in millions)	2020
Abbott Laboratories	
Net sales.	$34,608
Beginning accounts receivable (net).	5,425
Ending accounts receivable (net)	6,414
Pfizer Inc.	
Net sales.	$41,908
Beginning accounts receivable (net).	12,068
Ending accounts receivable (net)	11,194

Required

a. Calculate the accounts receivable turnover and the average collection period for Abbott Laboratories and Pfizer Inc. for 2020.

b. Compare the average collection periods for the two companies and comment on possible reasons for the difference in average collection periods for the two companies.

CRITICAL THINKING

EYK8-5. **Accounting Research Problem** Access the fiscal year 2020 annual report of **General Mills, Inc.,** available on this book's website.

GENERAL MILLS, INC.

Required

a. What was the amount of total Accounts Receivables and the Allowance for Doubtful Accounts at the end of fiscal-year 2020 and 2019? (Note: This information can be found in Note 18.)

b. What percent of total accounts receivables was the allowance for doubtful accounts at the end of 2020 and 2019?

c. Calculate the accounts receivable turnover and the average collection period for General Mills for 2020 and 2019. (For purposes of calculating the accounts receivable turnover, use the ending total accounts receivable balance [net] as the denominator rather than the average total accounts receivable [net].)

d. Comment on whether General Mills' management of accounts receivable improved (or not) over the two-year period.

EYK8-6. **Accounting Communications Activity** You have been hired as the accounting manager of Taylor, Inc., a provider of custom furniture. The company recently switched its method of paying its salespeople from a straight salary to a commission basis in order to encourage them to increase sales. The salespeople receive ten percent of the sales price at the time of the sale. You have noticed that the company's accounts receivable balance is growing because the salespeople are granting more credit to their customers.

Required

Draft a memorandum explaining why it is important to closely monitor the company's accounts receivable balance and why a large balance could lead to cash flow problems.

EYK8-7. **Accounting Ethics Case** Tractor Motors' best salesperson is Marie Glazer. Glazer's largest sales have been to Farmers Cooperative, a customer she brought to the company. Another salesperson, Bryan Blanchard, has been told in confidence by his cousin (an employee of Farmers Cooperative) that Farmers Cooperative is experiencing financial difficulties and may not be able to pay Tractor Motors what is owed.

Both Glazer and Blanchard are being considered for promotion to a new sales manager position.

Required
What are the ethical considerations that face Bryan Blanchard? What alternatives does he have?

MGM RESORTS
INTERNATIONAL

EYK8-8. **Environmental, Social, and Governance Problem** Tesla's mission is to accelerate the world's transition to sustainable energy. In order to highlight its efforts in this regard, the company publishes an annual impact report. To find this report go to Tesla's website at www.Tesla.com and navigate to the investor's section by clicking on Tesla in the bottom left, then Investors in the top right. Choose Other Documents & Events and then the 2019 Impact Report. Next click on View Impact Report. Tesla explains its environmental impact over several pages. Explain some of Tesla's efforts in this regard.

EYK8-9. **Forensic Accounting Problem** The chapter highlight on forensic accounting discussed the technique of covering up receivables theft by lapping (see Forensic Accounting: Lapping on page 8-11), where one account is credited with the receipt from another account. The highlight stated that lapping may be detected by an auditor through the confirmation of accounts receivables. While detection is important, it is far better to prevent lapping from occurring in the first place. Can you think of any controls that can be put in place to help prevent lapping?

LVMH MOET
HENNESSEY-LOUIS
VUITTON S.A.

EYK8-10. **Analyzing IFRS Financial Statements** The 2020 financial statements of **LVMH Moet Hennessey-Louis Vuitton S.A.** are presented in Appendix C at the end of this book. LVMH is a Paris-based holding company and one of the world's largest and best-known luxury goods companies. As a member of the European Union, French companies are required to prepare their consolidated (group) financial statements using International Financial Reporting Standards (IFRS). At year-end 2020 (2019), LVMH's allowance account was 124 (89) million euros. After reviewing LVMH's consolidated financial statements, consider the following questions. (Additional information can be found in LVMH's complete annual report provided on this book's website.)

Required
a. What was the gross amount of Trade and Other Receivables at fiscal year-end 2019 and 2020?
b. What percent of net trade and other receivables were the provision for impairment as of the end of 2019 and 2020?
c. Calculate the accounts receivable turnover and the average collection period for the company for 2019 and 2020.
d. Comment on whether LVMH's management of its trade receivables improved (or not) over the two-year period.

MGM RESORTS
INTERNATIONAL

EYK8-11. **Working with the Takeaways** Below are selected data from a recent **MGM Resorts International** financial statement. Amounts are in thousands.

Net sales:	$9,455,123
Beginning of year accounts receivable:	480,559
End of year accounts receivable:	542,924

Required
Calculate the MGM Resorts International (a) accounts receivable turnover, and (b) average collection period.

ANSWERS TO SELF-STUDY QUESTIONS:

1. d 2. b 3. d 4. a 5. d 6. c 7. a 8. a 9. c 10. c

YOUR TURN! SOLUTIONS

Solution 8.1

May 2	Accounts receivable (+A)	40,000	
	Sales revenue (+R, +SE)		40,000
	To record credit sales.		

May 17	Cash (+A)	35,000	
	Accounts receivable (−A)		35,000
	To record cash collections.		

May 31	Bad debts expense (+E, −SE)	500	
	Allowance for doubtful accounts (+XA, −A)		500
	To record bad debts expense.		

June 15	Allowance for doubtful accounts (−XA, +A)	200	
	Accounts receivable (−A)		200
	To write off accounts receivable.		

Solution 8.2

Bad debts expense (+E, −SE)	18,000	
Allowance for doubtful accounts (+XA, −A)		18,000
To record the bad debts expense for the period.		

Solution 8.3

a.

Bad debts expense (+E, −SE)	3,200	
Allowance for doubtful accounts (+XA, −A)		3,200
To record the bad debts expense for the period.		

$$\text{Bad debt expense} = \frac{(\$100{,}000 \times 1\%) + (\$15{,}000 \times 3\%) +}{(\$10{,}000 \times 5\%) + (\$20{,}000 \times 10\%) - \$750}$$
$$= \$3{,}200$$

b.

Allowance for doubtful accounts (−XA, +A)	480	
Accounts receivable—Phorest Company (−A)		480
To write off the Phorest Company uncollectible account.		

Solution 8.4

Cash (+A)	49,000	
Credit card fee expense (+E, −SE)	1,000	
Sales revenue (+R, +SE)		50,000
To record credit sales and collection, less a two percent fee.		

Solution 8.5

$40,000 × .05 × 3/12 = $500

Solution 8.6

a. Accounts receivable turnover = $30,000/[($2,800 + $3,200)/2] = 10

b. Average collection period = 365/10 = 36.5 days

Solution 8A.1

Bad debts expense (+E, −SE)	750	
Accounts receivable (−A)		750
To write off the Rhea Inc. uncollectible account.		

Chapter 9

Accounting for Long-Lived and Intangible Assets

Road Map

LO	Learning Objective	Page	eLecture	Guided Example	Assignments
LO1	Discuss the nature of plant assets and identify the accounting guidelines relating to their initial measurement.	9-4	E9-1	YT9.1	SS1, SE1, E1A, E2A, E1B, E2B, P1A, P2A, P4A, P6A, P8A, P1B, P2B, P4B, P6B, P8B
LO2	Discuss the nature of depreciation, illustrate three depreciation methods, and explain impairment losses.	9-7	E9-2	YT9.2	SS2, SE2, SE3, SE4, E3A, E4A, E5A, E3B, E4B, E5B, P2A, P3A, P4A, P6A, P8A, P9A, P2B, P3B, P4B, P6B, P8B, P9B
LO3	Discuss the distinction between revenue expenditures and capital expenditures.	9-15	E9-3	YT9.3	SS7, E6A, E6B, P4A, P8A, P9A, P4B, P8B, P9B
LO4	Explain and illustrate the accounting for disposals of plant assets.	9-17	E9-4	YT9.4	SS3, SS11, SE5, SE11, E7A, E7B, P5A, P5B
LO5	Discuss the nature of, and the accounting for, intangible assets and natural resources.	9-18	E9-5	YT9.5, YT9.6	SS4, SS5, SS6, SS12, SE6, SE7, SE13, E8A, E8B, P6A, P6B
LO6	Illustrate the balance sheet presentation of long-lived assets.	9-22	E9-6		SS8, SE12, E10A, E11A, E10B, E11B, P7A, P7B
LO7	Define the return on assets ratio and the asset turnover ratio and explain their use.	9-23	E9-7	YT9.7	SS9, SS10, SE8, SE9, SE10, E9A, E9B

Activewear and athleisure brands have grown steadily in recent years, fueled by consumer interest in health and wellness and changing workplace dress codes. These trends were amplified by the Covid-19 pandemic. One of the top ten players in this market is **lululemon athletica inc.**, a designer, distributor, and retailer of healthy lifestyle inspired athletic apparel and accessories.

To meet the demand for their products, lululemon operates over 500 stores in 17 countries, and distribution facilities in the United States, Canada, and Australia. This large footprint is reflected in lululemon's fixed assets, including land, buildings, leasehold improvements, furniture and fixtures, equipment, and vehicles. The acquisition cost of these fixed assets is $1.4 billion, and the book value after deducting accumulated depreciation is $750 million, which is almost 20 percent of its total assets.

In addition to their physical presence, lululemon has trademark rights on many of their brands, slogans, fabrics, and products, which they consider to be one of the company's most valuable assets. They also own several patents on their product innovations, distinctive apparel, and accessory designs. All told, the book value of lululemon's intangible assets, including goodwill, is close to half a billion dollars.

In this chapter, we will study how companies like lululemon account for their plant assets and intangible assets, along with some measures that can be used to analyze how well a company utilizes those assets.

PAST

In Chapter 8 we studied how to account for accounts and notes receivable.

PRESENT

This chapter focuses on another important set of assets—long-lived and intangible assets.

FUTURE

Chapter 10 begins our study of the accounting for liabilities.

ACCOUNTING FOR LONG-LIVED AND INTANGIBLE ASSETS

Plant Assets	Intangible Assets and Natural Resources	Analyzing Long-Lived Assets
• Measuring acquisition cost • Recording plant assets • Computing depreciation • Revenue and capital expenditures • Disposing of plant assets	• Measuring intangible asset costs • Recording intangible assets • Computing amortization • Examples of intangibles • Accounting for natural resources • Balance sheet presentation	• Return on assets • Asset turnover

OVERVIEW OF LONG-LIVED ASSETS

A.K.A. Plant assets are often referred to as fixed assets.

A.K.A. Natural resources are also known as wasting assets because they are consumed (exhausted) through extraction or removal from their natural setting.

Long-lived assets are expected to provide benefits to a business for more than one year. There are three major categories of long-lived assets. **Plant assets** refer to a firm's *long-lived property, plant, and equipment*, often referred to simply as PP&E. **Intangible assets** are those economic resources that benefit a company's operations but which lack the physical substance that characterizes plant assets. Examples of intangible assets include copyrights, franchises, and patents. Resources supplied by nature, such as timber stands, mineral deposits, and oil and gas deposits are **natural resources**.

The carrying value of long-lived assets is initially based on the asset's historical cost—that is, the cost incurred to acquire and place the asset into a revenue-producing state. The costs related to the use of long-lived assets must be matched with the revenues that they help to generate to ensure that a business's net income is correctly determined. The portion of an asset's cost that is consumed or used up in any given period is called depreciation expense when referring to plant assets, amortization expense when referring to intangible assets, and depletion expense when referring to natural resources. Depreciation, amortization, and depletion all refer to the process of allocating a portion of a long-term asset's acquisition cost to expense on the income statement to reflect the consumption of the asset as it produces revenue for a business.

Exhibit 9-1 provides several examples for each category of long-lived assets. The exhibit also identifies the appropriate term for the periodic consumption of the asset and its write-off to expense. Because the land a company owns has an indefinite useful life, it does not require a periodic write-off to expense.

EXHIBIT 9-1	Long-Lived Assets That Require Periodic Write-Off	
Asset Category	**Examples**	**Term for the Periodic Write-Off to Expense**
Plant Assets	*Buildings, equipment, tools, furniture, fixtures, vehicles*	Depreciation
Intangible Assets	*Patents, copyrights, leaseholds, franchises, trademarks, brand names*	Amortization
Natural Resources	*Timber, coal, oil and gas reserves, mineral deposits*	Depletion

MEASURING ACQUISITION COST OF PLANT ASSETS

Exhibit 9-2 illustrates the accounting issues associated with plant assets during their useful life: ❶ Identifying the type, and amount, of expenditures to include in the acquisition cost of the asset. ❷ Determining the appropriate amount of an asset's cost to periodically charge against revenue to reflect the asset's consumption. This involves estimating the asset's useful life and its probable salvage value at disposal. ❸ Differentiating expenditures related to the maintenance of an asset from expenditures that increase an asset's productive capacity or extend its useful life. ❹ Determining any gain or loss to be recognized when a plant asset is disposed.

LO1 **Discuss** the nature of plant assets and **identify** the accounting guidelines relating to their initial measurement.

eLecture
MBC

EXHIBIT 9-2   Issues Associated with the Accounting for Plant Assets

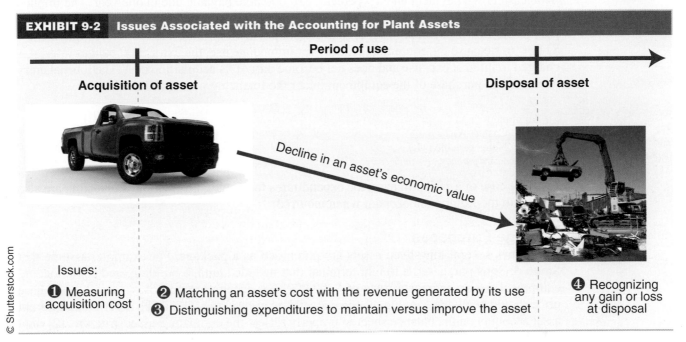

Period of use

Acquisition of asset

Disposal of asset

Decline in an asset's economic value

© Shutterstock.com

Issues:
❶ Measuring acquisition cost
❷ Matching an asset's cost with the revenue generated by its use
❸ Distinguishing expenditures to maintain versus improve the asset
❹ Recognizing any gain or loss at disposal

Acquisition Cost

Plant assets are initially recorded on the balance sheet at their acquisition cost. This measure is also called the asset's *historical cost* because it represents the amount expended when the asset was originally acquired. In general, the acquisition cost equals the cash and/or cash equivalent given up to acquire the asset *and* to prepare it for its intended use.

Cash Purchases

An asset's acquisition cost is often simply the amount of cash paid when the asset is acquired and readied for use by a business. Consider, for example, the following expenditures made by Smith & Sons to acquire a piece of equipment:

Purchase price components:		
Gross invoice price	$10,000	
Less: Cash discount (1/10, n/30)	(100)	
Sales tax	500	$10,400
Related expenditures:		
Freight charges	200	
Installation costs	500	
Testing of installed machine	300	1,000
Acquisition cost of equipment		**$11,400**

The total acquisition cost of the Smith & Sons equipment is $11,400, consisting of a cash purchase price of $10,400 and related preparation costs of $1,000. The sales tax is a necessary component of the purchase price and should also be included in the asset's acquisition cost. Similarly, the costs of freight, installation, and testing are expenditures necessary to get the asset to the desired business location and ready for its intended use.

Deferred Payment Purchases

If an asset's purchase price is not immediately paid in cash, the cash-equivalent purchase price at the date of acquisition is determined and recorded in the asset account. Suppose, for example, that Smith & Sons purchased its equipment under a financing plan requiring a $400 cash down payment and a 9 percent, $10,000 note payable due in one year. The implied cash price is $10,400 even though more than $10,400 is eventually paid under the financing plan ($400 down payment + $10,000 principal payment on note + $900 interest payment = $11,300). Because the equipment is ready for immediate use, the extra $900 paid as interest is charged to interest expense and does not become part of its acquisition cost. The journal entry to record the purchase of the equipment under the financing plan is as follows:

A = L + SE		
+10,400 +10,000	Equipment (+A)	10,400
−400	Cash (−A)	400
	Notes payable (+L)	10,000
	To record purchase of equipment.	

As in the case of a cash purchase, the expenditures for freight, installation, and testing are also debited to the Equipment account when incurred.

Package Purchases

Sometimes several long-lived assets are purchased as a package. For example, assume that Smith & Sons purchased a freight terminal that included land, a building, and some loading equipment for an aggregate price of $190,000. For accounting purposes, the total purchase price should be divided among the three assets because (1) they should be reported in different asset accounts on the balance sheet to properly reflect the company's asset structure, (2) only the building and equipment are subject to depreciation, and (3) the equipment is likely to have an estimated useful life different from that of the building.

The total package price is allocated among the acquired assets on the basis of their relative market or appraisal values. For example, if the estimated market value of the land, building, and equipment is $60,000, $120,000, and $20,000, respectively, the allocation of the $190,000 acquisition price would be as follows:

Asset	Estimated Market Value	Percent of Total	Allocation of Purchase Price	Estimated Useful Life
Land	$ 60,000	30	$ 57,000 (30% × $190,000)	Indefinite
Building.	120,000	60	114,000 (60% × $190,000)	30 years
Equipment	20,000	10	19,000 (10% × $190,000)	8 years
Totals.	$200,000	100	$190,000	

Acquisition Costs Related to Land

The purchase of land often raises a number of accounting issues. Suppose, for example, that Smith & Sons retains a local real estate broker at a fee of $2,000 to locate an appropriate site for the company's new office building. Assume, also, that the property selected for purchase has an existing building on it that will need to be razed. The terms of the sale include a down payment of $40,000 to the seller, with the buyer paying off an existing mortgage of $10,000 and $300 of accrued interest. In addition, Smith & Sons agrees to pay accrued real estate taxes of $800 owed by the seller. Other related expenditures include legal fees of $400 and a title insurance premium of $500. A local salvage company will be hired to raze the old building, paying Smith & Sons $200 for reclaimed materials. Applying the cost principle, the acquisition cost of the land is calculated as follows:

Payment to the seller	$40,000
Commission to real estate agent	2,000
Payment of mortgage and accrued interest due at time of sale	10,300
Payment of property taxes owed by seller	800
Legal fees.	400
Title insurance premium	500
	$54,000
Less: Net recovery from material reclamation.	**200**
Cost of land.	$53,800

Again, any expenditure for the property taxes, insurance, and legal fees should be capitalized, or added to, the acquisition cost of the land because they are necessary to complete the purchase transaction. Similarly, removing the old building also prepares the land for its intended use. The $200 net recovery from razing the existing structure, therefore, *reduces* the land's cost. A net payment to remove the old building would *increase* the land's cost.

When a land site is acquired in an undeveloped area, a firm may pay a special assessment to the local government for such property improvements as streets, sidewalks, and sewers. These improvements are considered to be permanent improvements; and consequently, the special assessment is capitalized to (added to) the acquisition cost of the land.

A firm may also make property improvements that have limited lives. Classified as **land improvements**, they include such improvements as paved parking lots, driveways, private sidewalks, and fences. Expenditures for these assets are charged to a separate Land Improvement account on the balance sheet and depreciated over the estimated useful life of the improvements.

Leasehold Improvements

Expenditures made by a business to alter or improve leased property are called **leasehold improvements**. For example, a merchandising firm may make improvements, with the permission of the owner, to a leased building. **The Home Depot, Inc.**, a home improvement retail chain, leases a significant portion of its more than 2,000 U.S. stores and reports nearly $2 billion of leasehold improvements on its balance sheet. The improvements, or alterations, become part of the leased property and revert to the owner of the property at the end of the lease. The cost of the leasehold improvements is capitalized to the Leasehold Improvements account on the balance sheet and is depreciated over the life of the lease or the life of the improvements, whichever is shorter.

YOUR TURN! 9.1

Kelly Company purchased manufacturing equipment for $20,000 cash. In addition to the $20,000 purchase price, Kelly paid sales tax of $1,600, freight costs of $400, installation costs of $600, testing costs of $100, and $300 for unrelated supplies from the same company. Explain the accounting treatment for each of the expenditures.

MBC

The solution is on page 9-43.

NATURE OF DEPRECIATION

LO2 **Discuss** the nature of depreciation, **illustrate** three depreciation methods, and **explain** impairment losses.

MBC

With the exception of land, the use of plant assets to generate revenue consumes the economic benefit provided by the assets. At some point—usually before they are totally worthless—these assets are disposed of, and often replaced. A diagram of a typical pattern of plant asset utilization is illustrated below:

| Acquisition cost $1,000 | —— Useful life ——→ | Salvage value $100 |

Decline in recorded value, $900

In this example, a plant asset is acquired for $1,000, used for several accounting periods, and then sold for $100. The $900 decline in recorded value is called **depreciation** and is a cost of generating the revenues recognized during the periods that the asset was in use. Thus, if a company's net income is to be a meaningful representation of the business's operating performance, $900 of expense must be allocated to the periods of asset use and matched with sales revenue. Failure to do so would overstate the company's net income for these periods.

As part of this allocation process, it is necessary to estimate the asset's useful life and its expected future salvage value. **Useful life** is the expected period of economic usefulness to the business—that is, the period from the date of acquisition to the expected date of disposal. **Salvage value** (or *residual value*) is the expected net recovery (sales proceeds less disposal costs) when the asset is sold or removed from service. When the salvage value is insignificant, it may be ignored in the depreciation process under the materiality concept.

A.K.A. The salvage value of a plant asset is also often referred to as its residual value or scrap value.

Depreciation Accounting: Allocation versus Valuation

Although the idea is theoretically appealing, accountants do not base an asset's periodic depreciation expense on changes in the asset's market value or on the measured wear of the asset, primarily because a reliable, objective, and practical source for such data rarely exists. Rather, the purpose of **depreciation accounting** is to allocate, in a *systematic* and *rational* manner, the difference between an asset's acquisition cost and its estimated salvage value over the *estimated* useful life of the asset. Consequently, depreciation accounting techniques are convenient expedients for estimating asset utilization and should not be considered precise. Although imperfect, depreciation estimates facilitate a better assessment of a business's net income than would result from expensing the asset in full at either its date of acquisition or its date of disposal.

PRINCIPLE ALERT   **Expense Recognition (Matching) Concept**

Depreciation accounting represents an application of the *expense recognition* (*matching*) *concept.* Depreciable plant assets are used in a business's operating activities to help generate revenues. Each period that benefits from the use of a plant asset is assigned part of the asset's cost as depreciation expense. In so doing, the depreciation expense is matched with the sales revenue that the asset helps to generate. The matching that occurs through this allocation process extends throughout the asset's useful life.

Several factors are related to the periodic allocation of depreciation, including wear from use, from natural deterioration, and from technical obsolescence. Each factor reduces the economic value of an asset. To some extent, maintenance (lubrication, adjustments, parts replacements, and cleaning) may partially arrest or offset wear and deterioration. Thus, when an asset's useful life and salvage value are estimated, a given level of maintenance is assumed.

Calculating Depreciation Expense

Estimating the periodic depreciation of a plant asset can be achieved in many ways. In this section, three widely used methods for calculating depreciation are illustrated.

1. Straight-line
2. Declining-balance
3. Units-of-production

For each method, we assume that equipment is purchased for $1,000. The equipment is assumed to have an estimated useful life of five years and has an estimated salvage value of $100.

Straight-Line Method

The **straight-line method** is the easiest depreciation method to understand and calculate, and it is the most widely used depreciation method by U.S. businesses. Under the straight-line method, an equal amount of depreciation expense is allocated to each period of an asset's useful life. Straight-line depreciation is calculated as follows:

$$\text{Annual depreciation} = \frac{\textbf{(Acquisition cost – Salvage value)}}{\textbf{Estimated useful life (in years)}}$$

For the purchased equipment in our example, the annual straight-line depreciation expense is:

$$\frac{(\$1,000 - \$100)}{5 \text{ years}} = \$180 \text{ per year}$$

The journal entry to record the annual depreciation expense is:

Depreciation expense—Equipment (+E, –SE)	180	
Accumulated depreciation—Equipment (+XA, –A)		180
To record depreciation expense for the year.		

A	=	L	+	SE
–180				–180
				Exp

Like other expense accounts, Depreciation Expense is deducted from sales revenue on the income statement and is closed at year-end to Retained Earnings. The offsetting credit entry is posted to a contra-asset account, Accumulated Depreciation, which is deducted from the Equipment account on the balance sheet to calculate the asset's book value. This means that as long as the asset is in service, the original acquisition cost of the asset is maintained in the asset account, and the cumulative balance of depreciation taken to date is carried in the contra-asset account. When an asset is disposed of, the asset's acquisition cost and accumulated depreciation are removed from the respective accounts.

A.K.A. The book value of an asset (acquisition cost less accumulated depreciation) is also referred to as the **net book value**.

The following table shows the depreciation schedule for the equipment's five-year life under the straight-line method:

			End-of-Period Balance	
Year of Useful Life	Balance of Equipment Account	Annual Depreciation Expense	Accumulated Depreciation Account	Asset's Book Value
1	$1,000	$180	$180	$820
2	1,000	180	360	640
3	1,000	180	540	460
4	1,000	180	720	280
5	1,000	180	900	100
Total		$900		

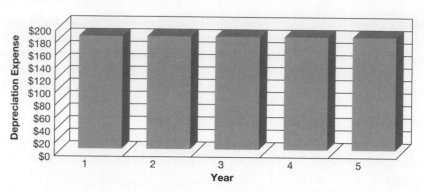

Notice that (1) the Equipment account always shows the original acquisition cost ($1,000) of the asset; (2) each period reflects $180 of depreciation expense; (3) the Accumulated Depreciation account balance is cumulative and shows the portion of the acquisition cost taken as depreciation to date; (4) the asset's book value is the original acquisition cost of the asset less the accumulated depreciation taken to date; and (5) the asset's book value at the end of the five-year period is equal to the asset's estimated salvage value. Thus, an asset's book value declines to its estimated salvage value as the asset is depreciated over its useful life.

For periods of less than one year, straight-line depreciation amounts are simply proportions of the annual depreciation charge. For example, if an asset is acquired on April 1, depreciation for the period ended December 31 would be $135, or 9/12 × $180. Assets acquired or disposed of during the first half of any month are usually treated as if the acquisition or disposal occurred on the first day of the month. When either event occurs during the last half of any month, it is assumed that the event occurred on the first day of the following month.

Data Analytics

DATA ANALYTICS	Using Manufacturing Analytics to Optimize Performance

Optimizing the performance of plant assets is a key concern for manufacturers. **Intel Corp.** uses a sophisticated sensor network to collect data on fan filter units in their clean rooms. That data goes directly to the cloud where Intel uses analytics to predict the circumstances and timing of unit failures and schedule maintenance. By using data analytics techniques, they were able to reduce unscheduled downtime by two-thirds. In addition to reducing costs, manufacturing analytics can help companies reduce energy consumption and implement safer worker and environmental protocols. Some predict that the next wave of efficiency will come from "digital twins"—virtual models of an entire manufacturing plant, including the physical assets and their behavior. Used in concert with machine learning models, digital twins will help manufacturers automatically detect issues and make recommendations.

Declining-Balance Method

The **declining-balance method** is an **accelerated depreciation method**. It calculates a company's depreciation expense as a constant percentage of an asset's book value as of the beginning of each period. The method takes its name from the fact that, over time, an asset's book value (acquisition cost − accumulated depreciation) declines as the asset is used up, yielding a decreasing depreciation expense. An asset's salvage value is *not* considered in the calculation of declining-balance depreciation, except that the depreciation of an asset stops when the asset's book value equals its estimated salvage value.

The declining-balance method is an "accelerated" method because the constant depreciation percentage it uses is a multiple of the straight-line depreciation rate (The straight-line depreciation rate = 100 percent/expected useful life in years.) There are many versions of the declining-balance method because different multiples of the straight-line rate may be used. *Double-declining balance depreciation* uses a depreciation rate that is twice the straight-line rate; similarly, *150 percent-declining balance depreciation* uses a depreciation rate that is one and one-half times the straight-line rate.

For example, the straight-line depreciation rate for an asset with a five-year useful life is 20 percent per year (100 percent/5 years). Thus, to depreciate a five-year asset on an accelerated basis, the double-declining balance method uses a 40 percent depreciation rate (2 × 20 percent), while the 150 percent declining-balance method uses a 30 percent depreciation rate (1.5 × 20 percent).

Under the double-declining balance method, the annual depreciation expense is calculated as follows:

Annual depreciation = Book value at beginning of year × Double-declining balance rate

Referring to our example of the equipment purchased for $1,000, with a useful life of five years and an expected salvage value of $100, the periodic double-declining balance depreciation is calculated as follows (amounts rounded to the nearest dollar):

Year of Useful Life	Acquisition Cost	Beginning Accumulated Depreciation	Beginning Book Value		Twice Straight-Line Percentage		Annual Depreciation Expense
1	$1,000	$ 0	$1,000	×	40 percent	=	$400
2	1,000	400	600	×	40 percent	=	240
3	1,000	640	360	×	40 percent	=	144
4	1,000	784	216	×	40 percent	=	86
5	1,000	870	130		[exceeds limit]		30
Total							$900

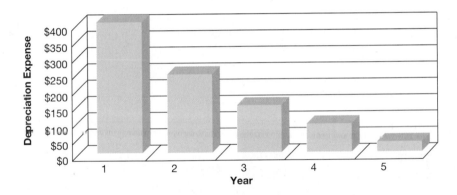

Notice in the fifth year that the depreciation expense is only $30, the amount needed to reduce the asset's book value to its estimated salvage value of $100. Assets are not depreciated below their estimated salvage value.

If an asset is purchased during a fiscal period, a pro-rata allocation of the first year's depreciation is calculated. If, for example, an asset is acquired on April 1, depreciation for the period ended December 31 would be $300, or [9/12 × (40 percent × $1,000)]. In subsequent periods, the usual procedure is followed; that is, the asset's book value at the beginning of the period is multiplied by the constant depreciation rate. For example, in the second year, depreciation on the asset would be $280, or [40 percent × ($1,000 – $300)].

Units-of-Production Method

The **units-of-production method** allocates depreciation in proportion to an asset's use in operations. Under this method, the depreciation per unit of production is first calculated by dividing the total depreciable cost of the asset (in our example, $1000 – $100 = $900) by the asset's total projected units-of-production capacity:

Hint: An asset's salvage value must be considered when calculating the depreciation expense for an asset using the straight-line method or the units-of-production method. Salvage value is not considered when calculating double-declining balance depreciation until the final year.

$$\text{Depreciation per unit} = \frac{\text{(Acquisition cost – Salvage value)}}{\text{Total estimated units of production}}$$

The total estimated units of production may represent the total expected miles that an asset will be driven, the total tons expected to be hauled, the total hours expected to be used, or the total number of expected cuttings, drillings, or stampings of parts by a piece of equipment. To illustrate, assume that a drilling tool will drill an estimated 45,000 parts during its expected useful life. The tool is purchased for $1,000 and has an expected salvage value of $100. Consequently, the depreciation per unit of production is:

$$\frac{(\$1,000 - \$100)}{45,000 \text{ parts}} = \$0.02 \text{ per part}$$

To find the asset's annual depreciation expense, the depreciation per unit of production is multiplied by the number of units actually produced during a given year:

Annual depreciation = Depreciation per unit × Units of production for the period

Assuming that the number of parts drilled over the five years was 8,000, 14,000, 10,000, 4,000, and 9,000, respectively, in Year 1 through Year 5, the units-of-production depreciation expense is calculated as follows:

Year of Useful Life	Depreciation per Unit		Annual Units of Production		Annual Depreciation Expense
1	$0.02	×	8,000	=	$160
2	0.02	×	14,000	=	280
3	0.02	×	10,000	=	200
4	0.02	×	4,000	=	80
5	0.02	×	9,000	=	180
Total					$900

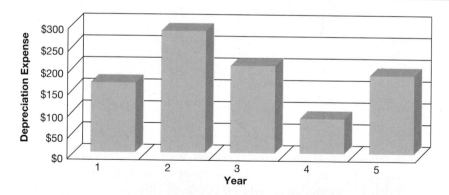

A Comparison of Alternative Depreciation Methods

The following charts compare the periodic depreciation expense and accumulated depreciation from our equipment illustration. The charts show the accelerated nature of the double-declining balance method relative to the straight-line method. Notice, for example, that the depreciation expense in Year 1 under the double-declining balance method is $400 but is only $180 under the straight-line method. In Year 2, the double-declining balance depreciation is $240 but again is only $180 for the straight-line method. It is not until Year 3 that the straight-line method produces a depreciation charge that exceeds the double-declining balance charge. Depreciation expense for the units-of-production method reflects the assumptions presented previously in the chapter. There is no general pattern for the annual depreciation expense under this method. The annual depreciation for the units-of-production method depends on the yearly productive activity of an asset, and this activity will vary from asset to asset. Finally, note that the total accumulated depreciation over the life of the asset is the same under all three methods and is equal to the acquisition cost less salvage value, or $900.

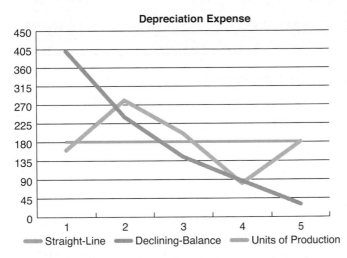

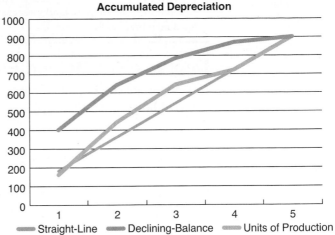

Annual Depreciation Expense			
Year	Straight-Line	Declining-Balance	Units-of-Production
1	$180	$400	$160
2	180	240	280
3	180	144	200
4	180	86	80
5	180	30	180
Total	$900	$900	$900

ACCOUNTING IN PRACTICE   **Depreciation Methods**

So many assets, so little time. Some accountants may feel that way when it comes to calculating the periodic depreciation expense for a business. They may also feel that variety is the spice of life. At least it appears that way given the various methods that companies choose to calculate the depreciation expense that appears in their income statements. Below are the depreciation methods used by 600 large U.S. companies. As can be seen, the straight-line method is by far the most popular depreciation method used:

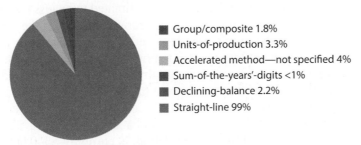

Group/composite 1.8%
Units-of-production 3.3%
Accelerated method—not specified 4%
Sum-of-the-years'-digits <1%
Declining-balance 2.2%
Straight-line 99%

*The totals exceed 100 percent because some firms use more than one method.
Source: *Accounting Trends and Techniques*

The Salsbury Company purchased equipment costing $10,000 at the start of the year. The equipment has an estimated useful life of five years and a salvage value of $2,000. The CEO is unsure if the company should use the straight-line method or the double-declining balance method to depreciate the new equipment.

Required:
Prepare the journal entry for depreciation for the second year under each of the alternative depreciation accounting methods.

Depreciation Method Estimate Changes

It is important to remember that a business's periodic depreciation expense is based on estimates of both an asset's useful life and its salvage value. Circumstances change, however, and the estimates originally made when the asset was acquired may subsequently be found to be too high or too low. Once it is determined that the original estimates of either an asset's useful life or salvage value were incorrect, the calculation of the periodic depreciation expense for an asset's remaining useful life may be revised. When a revision in one or both of the depreciation estimates is found to be warranted, the revision is executed by allocating the remaining undepreciated balance of the asset's book value over the revised remaining useful life and using the revised estimated salvage value. To illustrate this process, refer again to our example of equipment costing $1,000, with a five-year life, and an estimated salvage value of $100.

If, based on original estimates, straight-line depreciation of $180 has been recorded for each of the first three years of the asset's useful life, the accumulated depreciation to date would total $540, or 3 × $180. Now, suppose that just before recording the depreciation expense for the fourth year, circumstances indicate that the equipment's useful life will total six years instead of five, and that its salvage value at the end of the sixth year will be $40 instead of $100. The revised depreciation expense to be taken during the revised remaining useful life (Year Four through Year Six) of the equipment is calculated as follows:

Original acquisition cost	$1,000
Depreciation previously recorded (3 years @ $180)	(540)
Book value at start of fourth year	$ 460
Revised salvage value	**(40)**
Revised remaining depreciable cost	$ 420
Revised remaining useful life	3 years
Revised depreciation for fourth, fifth, and sixth years	$420/3 = $140 per year

Impairment Losses

Sometimes a change in the circumstances relating to a depreciable asset is so severe that the future cash flows from the asset's use and disposal are estimated to be *less* than its current book value. If an asset's remaining book value cannot be recovered through the future cash flows expected to be generated from the asset's use, the asset's value is said to be *impaired*. Under these circumstances, an impairment loss is recorded on the income statement, and the asset's book value on the balance sheet is reduced. The **impairment loss** is calculated as the difference between the asset's current book value and its current fair value.

To illustrate, assume that two years ago Salesforce purchased computer servers costing $500,000, with an estimated useful life of six years and a salvage value of $20,000. The book value of the servers, assuming straight-line depreciation, is currently $340,000 ($500,000 cost less $160,000 accumulated depreciation). Unanticipated technological advances in server technology used by competitors, however, now severely limit the use of Salesforce's equipment. An analysis by the company's CFO indicates that they now expect that the net future cash flows to be generated from the use and disposal of the equipment over the next four years will be $300,000. The limited uses for the equipment cause its current fair value to be only $200,000.

   Salesforce's equipment is impaired because its book value is not recoverable through its expected future cash flows—the $300,000 of expected future cash flows is less than the equipment's $340,000 current book value. Thus, an impairment loss is computed by comparing the equipment's book value with its current fair value, as follows:

Equipment book value	$340,000
Equipment current fair value	**(200,000)**
Impairment loss	$140,000

The journal entry to record the impairment loss is as follows:

Impairment loss on equipment (+Loss, −SE)	140,000	
Accumulated depreciation—Equipment (+XA, −A)		140,000
To record impairment loss on equipment.		

A = L + SE
−140,000   −140,000
Loss

Principle Alert   Conservatism Concept

The accounting for impaired plant assets illustrates the *conservatism concept*. In selecting between alternative accounting measures, the conservatism concept states that the least optimistic measure should be used. When a plant asset is impaired, it is reported on the balance sheet at its current fair value, an amount lower than its book value before any impairment loss is recorded. Unimpaired plant assets remain on the balance sheet at their book value, however, even though current fair values may be higher. U.S. GAAP mandates that asset values be written down when impaired, but prohibits the write-up of assets when their value appreciates.

THINKING GLOBALLY

While U.S. GAAP requires that long-lived assets be written down in value when they are judged to be impaired, they may not be written up in value if there is a subsequent recovery in their fair market value. Under International Financial Reporting Standards (IFRS), however, the accounting treatment of long-lived asset value recoveries is substantially different. Under IFRS, the company may choose to revalue long-lived assets to full value. If an asset's value increases above its current book value, the asset's balance sheet value may be written up to the higher value by debiting the asset account for the amount of the increase. The balancing credit entry is to a stockholders' equity account called the asset revaluation reserve.

   To illustrate, assume that Peabody International PLC, based in the United Kingdom, owns land in London that was originally purchased for 20 million British pounds. Current real estate appraisals, however, indicate that the fair market value of the land is now 50 million pounds. To recognize the increase in the land's fair market value, Peabody International would record the following journal entry:

Land (+A)	30 million pounds	
Asset revaluation reserve—Land (+SE)		30 million pounds
To record the revaluation of land.		

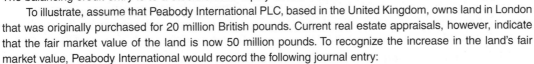

Depreciation for Income Tax Purposes

Depreciation expense may be deducted by a business on its federal income tax return as a normal business expense. As a consequence, some refer to the tax deductibility of depreciation as a "tax shield" since depreciation expense lowers a business's taxable income, and hence, lowers the actual income taxes that must be paid. The depreciation expense deducted on a business's income tax return, however, may differ substantially from the depreciation expense reported on a company's income statement because the calculation of tax depreciation follows income tax regulations referred to as the **modified accelerated cost recovery system (MACRS)**.

   MACRS establishes several asset classes with prescribed useful lives ranging from three years to 31.5 years. Most machinery and equipment, for example, are in the seven-year asset class. When acquired, an asset is placed in the appropriate asset class (per MACRS guidelines) and depreciated over the prescribed useful life specified for that class.[1]

MACRS was introduced into U.S. tax law to encourage companies to invest in plant assets. Because the useful life specified under MACRS is usually shorter than an asset's accounting useful life, this method provides larger depreciation deductions during an asset's early years, much like the declining-balance method used for financial statement reporting. In a sense, the accelerated deductions under MACRS provide an interest-free loan to a business because they allow the firm to pay less income tax in the early years of an asset's life and more in the later years. During the intervening time period, the firm can use the postponed income tax payments to support the business's operations, without incurring interest charges.

Change and modification characterize U.S. tax law. Tax depreciation guidelines will likely be modified again in the future. Keep in mind, however, that depreciation changes in the tax law do not affect the depreciation methods and estimates that a firm may use in preparing its financial statements using U.S. GAAP for its shareholders and lenders.

REVENUE VERSUS CAPITAL EXPENDITURES

LO3 Discuss the distinction between revenue expenditures and capital expenditures.

eLecture

MBC

Revenue Expenditures

Revenue expenditures are expenditures relating to plant assets that are expensed when incurred. The following list identifies two common types of revenue expenditures:

1. Expenditures for ordinary maintenance and repairs of existing plant assets.
2. Expenditures to acquire low-cost items that benefit the firm for several periods.

Maintenance and Repairs

Some level of maintenance and repairs must be assumed when estimating the useful lives and salvage values of property, plant, and equipment. For example, a plant asset that is not maintained or repaired will have a shorter useful life than a similar asset that is properly maintained. Periodic upkeep—such as lubrication, cleaning, and replacement of minor parts—is necessary to maintain an asset's expected level and length of usefulness. These periodic upkeep costs—referred to as maintenance costs—are charged to expense as they are incurred.

Low-Cost Items

Most businesses purchase items that provide years of service at a relatively small cost, such as paperweights, staplers, and wastebaskets. Because of the small dollar amounts involved, establishing these items as assets on the balance sheet and depreciating them over their expected useful lives serves no useful purpose. The effect on the financial statements is insignificant and consequently, expensing these expenditures at the time of purchase is more efficient. The accounting for such low-cost items is thus completed in the period in which they are acquired.

PRINCIPLE ALERT   **Materiality Concept**

The practice of accounting for small dollar transactions in the most expedient fashion follows the *materiality concept*. Under this accounting concept, generally accepted accounting principles apply only to items of significance to the users of financial statements. Because the judgment of users will be unaffected by the accounting for immaterial dollar amounts, their immediate expensing does not diminish the usefulness of financial statements.

---

[1] Depreciation in most asset classes must follow a half-year convention whereby one-half of the first year's depreciation expense is taken in the first year, regardless of when the asset was acquired, and one-half of the asset's last year's depreciation is taken in the year of disposal, regardless of when during the year the asset is disposed. The half-year convention means that assets in the three-year asset class are effectively depreciated over four accounting periods, assets in the five-year property class are depreciated over six accounting periods, and so on.

Capital Expenditures

Capital expenditures increase the book value of long-lived assets. To *capitalize* an amount means to increase an asset's book value by that amount. The following list identifies two typical capital expenditures related to property, plant, and equipment:

1. Initial acquisitions and additions.
2. Betterments.

Initial Acquisitions and Additions

At the beginning of this chapter, the accounting guidelines governing the initial measurement of long-lived assets were discussed. We noted that expenditures equal to an asset's implied cash purchase price, plus any costs necessary to prepare the asset for use, were debited to the asset account. These amounts are commonly referred to as capital expenditures.

These same accounting guidelines apply for additions to existing plant assets. Adding a new wing to a building and expanding the size of an asphalt parking lot are examples of additions. These capital expenditures should also be debited to an asset account. A separate account (and depreciation schedule) should be used for an addition when its estimated useful life differs from the remaining useful life of the existing plant asset.

Betterments

Betterments are expenditures that (1) extend the useful life of an asset, (2) improve the quality and/or quantity of the asset's output, or (3) reduce the asset's operating expenses. Examples include overhauling the engine or adding a power winch to a highway service truck, improving the precision of a machining device to reduce defects, and converting a building to solar power. Expenditures for betterments are generally debited to the appropriate asset account, and the subsequent periodic depreciation expense is increased to allocate the additional cost over the asset's remaining useful life.

YOUR TURN! 9.3

MBC

The solution is on page 9-44.

Hastings Company recorded the following expenditures during the year with regard to its delivery van:

1. Changed the engine oil
2. Repainted the van
3. Overhauled the engine that is expected to increase the useful life of the van
4. Repaired a dent in a fender
5. Converted the van to run on a biofuel with an estimated annual fuel cost savings of 30 percent

Required:
Determine whether each of the above expenditures is a revenue expenditure or a capital expenditure.

FORENSIC ACCOUNTING   **WorldCom's Bad Accounting**

 On the surface, the decision to capitalize or expense an expenditure related to a plant asset does not seem like the subject matter for one of the most infamous accounting scandals of all time. Unfortunately, to the many investors in **WorldCom** who saw the value of their investment disappear, this accounting decision had profound consequences.

Beginning in 2001, and continuing through mid-2002, WorldCom, under the direction of its CEO, CFO, Controller, and Director of General Accounting, used fraudulent accounting methods to portray a false picture of the company's financial health. The principal accounting gimmickry used by the company was to misclassify "line costs," a cost that should have been expensed each year, as a capital expenditure, thus adding to WorldCom's assets rather than adding to its expenses.

The fraud was discovered and brought to the attention of WorldCom's Board of Directors by a small team of internal auditors who had been conducting their investigation in secret, mostly at night. The Securities and Exchange Commission followed with its own investigation. The final conclusion—WorldCom's assets and pre-tax net income had been inflated by nearly $11 billion! Following a conviction for filing false financial reports with the SEC, WorldCom's CEO Bernard Ebbers was sentenced to 25 years in prison.

DISPOSALS OF PLANT ASSETS

LO4 **Explain** and **illustrate** the accounting for disposals of plant assets.

eLecture

MBC

A business may dispose of its plant assets in a variety of ways. An asset may be sold, retired, or exchanged as partial payment for a new asset. The asset's usefulness to a firm may also be ended by an unfavorable or unanticipated event, such as the asset being stolen or destroyed by a natural disaster.

Depreciation must extend through an asset's total useful life to a business. Consequently, depreciation must be recorded up to the disposal date, regardless of the manner of the asset's disposal. Should the disposal date not coincide with the end of an accounting period, a journal entry must record depreciation for the partial period—that is, the period from the date that depreciation was last recorded to the asset's disposal date.

The following data is used to illustrate the disposal of plant assets:

Equipment's acquisition cost	$1,000
Estimated salvage value after five years	100
Annual straight-line depreciation	180
(Assume that depreciation to the date of disposal has been recorded.)	

Sale of Plant Assets

Most sales of plant assets involve the following factors:

1. The sale transaction involves an exchange of a used plant asset for cash. Because the plant asset is no longer on hand, a journal entry must remove the asset account and the accumulated depreciation account from the books. These amounts together reflect the asset's book value.

2. Because plant assets are often sold for an amount higher or lower than their book value, a gain or loss will result. Sale proceeds in excess of book value create a gain, whereas book values in excess of sales proceeds create a loss.

Asset Sales for More Than Book Value

Assume that the equipment is sold for $230 midway through its fifth year of use. Depreciation was last recorded at the end of the fourth year. The journal entries to record the sale are:

A = L + SE
−90   −90 Exp

Depreciation expense—Equipment (+E, −SE)	90	
Accumulated depreciation—Equipment (+XA, −A)		90
To record depreciation expense for six months ($180/2).		

A = L + SE
+230   +40 Gain
+810
−1,000

Cash (+A)	230	
Accumulated depreciation—Equipment (−XA, +A)	810	
Equipment (−A)		1,000
Gain on sale of plant assets (+Gain, +SE)		40
To record the sale of equipment for $230.		

Cash		Equip.
230		1,000

Gain on Sale		Accum. Dep.
40		810

Note that recording depreciation to the date of sale adds $90 to the Accumulated Depreciation account, which totals $810, calculated as [(4 × $180) + $90]. To reflect the sale properly, it is necessary to remove the entire amount of accumulated depreciation ($810) from the books. The gain of $40 is calculated as the sale proceeds of $230 minus the asset's book value of $190 ($1,000 − $810).

Asset Sales for Less Than Book Value

Assume that the equipment is sold for $30 at the end of the fifth year. The journal entry to record this sale is:

		30	
Cash (+A)		30	
Loss on sale of plant assets (+Loss, –SE)		70	
Accumulated depreciation—Equipment (–XA, +A)		900	
Equipment (–A)			1,000
To record the sale of equipment for $30.			

```
A    =  L  +   SE
+30            –70 Loss
+900
–1,000
```

Cash	Equip.
30	1,000

Loss on Sale	Accum. Dep.
70	900

The loss on the asset sale equals the book value of $100 minus the sales proceeds of $30. The cash received is recorded, and the balances from both the Equipment account and the Accumulated Depreciation account are removed from the books.

If the equipment is sold for an amount exactly equal to its book value, no gain or loss results. Should the equipment be abandoned, stolen, or destroyed (with no insurance coverage) before the end of its expected useful life, a loss equal to its book value is recorded.

Exchange of Plant Assets

A plant asset may be exchanged for another plant asset. The accounting for long-lived asset exchanges can be complex depending upon the relationship between the new asset and the asset being traded in. Consequently, the accounting for asset exchanges is covered in intermediate accounting textbooks.

YOUR TURN! 9.4

MBC

The solution is on page 9-44.

The Jones Company is self-insured, and consequently the company does not receive any insurance payments if one of its vehicles it is involved in an accident. One of the Jones Company trucks was involved in a major accident, and the company decided to sell the truck for scrap. At the time of the accident, the truck had a cost basis of $22,500 and accumulated depreciation of $15,000. The proceeds from the sale totaled $750.

Required:
Record the journal entry for the disposal of the truck.

INTANGIBLE ASSETS AND NATURAL RESOURCES

Intangible assets are the various resources that benefit a business's operations, but which lack physical characteristics or substance. Intangible assets include, for example, the exclusive rights or privileges obtained from a governmental unit or by legal contract, such as patents, copyrights, franchises, trademarks, and leaseholds. Another intangible asset is goodwill, which reflects the beneficial attributes acquired in the acquisition of another company that cannot be attributed to any other recorded asset.

LO5 Discuss the nature of, and the accounting for, intangible assets and natural resources.

eLecture

MBC

Some resources that lack physical substance are considered monetary assets, such as prepaid insurance, accounts receivable, and investments, rather than intangible assets. Because intangible assets lack physical characteristics, the related accounting procedures are more subjective than for such tangible assets as property, plant, and equipment.

Measurement of Intangible Assets (Cost Determination)

A firm should record intangible assets acquired from outside entities at their acquisition cost. Similarly, some costs associated with intangible assets created internally by a firm are capitalized to the balance sheet. For example, the costs to secure a trademark or patent—such as attorney's fees and registration fees—are charged to an Intangibles Asset account, if they are material.

The accounting for other expenditures related to intangible assets varies depending upon the type of expenditure and the nature of the intangible asset. Notably, **research and development costs** are not capitalized to the balance sheet as an intangible asset because GAAP requires that these expenditures be expensed when incurred. As a result, some companies may have important intangible assets that are carried at a nominal amount or may even fail to appear at all on the firm's balance sheet. It is noteworthy that one U.S. industry is exempted from the conservative accounting treatment of research and development costs. Under U.S. GAAP, software development companies may capitalize some costs associated with the development of software.

> **THINKING GLOBALLY**
>
> The accounting for some intangible assets under IFRS differs significantly from the accounting under U.S. GAAP. For instance, under U.S. GAAP, research and development costs are usually expensed when incurred; however, under IFRS, development costs may be capitalized if a commercially viable product results from the original research effort. A significant consequence of this alternative accounting treatment is that IFRS companies enjoy a more fairly presented balance sheet, since most intangible assets are fully disclosed. On the balance sheets of many U.S. GAAP companies, there are many unreported intangible assets.

Amortization of Intangibles

The **amortization** of an intangible asset carried on the balance sheet involves the periodic expensing of the asset's cost over the term of its expected useful life. Because salvage values are ordinarily not involved, the amortization of intangible assets typically entails (1) determining the asset's cost, (2) estimating the period over which it will benefit a company, and (3) allocating the cost to each accounting period involved. Straight-line amortization is typically used for intangible assets unless another method is shown to be more appropriate.

The amortization entry debits the Amortization Expense account and credits the Intangible Asset account. An Accumulated Amortization account could be used for the credit entry, but generally there is no particular benefit to financial statement users from accumulating amortization in a separate contra-asset account.

Not all intangible assets are amortized. Some intangible assets have a limited life because of legal or regulatory restrictions. Intangible assets classified as having a limited life are amortized over their expected useful life. Other intangible assets are considered to have an indefinite life because they are expected to generate cash flows for the company for the foreseeable future. Goodwill is an example of an intangible asset with an indefinite life. Intangible assets with an indefinite life are not amortized.

EXAMPLES OF INTANGIBLE ASSETS

Patents

A **patent** is an exclusive privilege granted to an inventor by the U.S. Patent Office for a period of 20 years from the date the patent application is filed. A patent gives the patent holder the right to exclude others from making, using, or selling the invention. Patent laws originated to encourage inventors by protecting them from imitators who might usurp the invention for commercial gain. Just what qualifies as a patentable idea, however, has become quite complex in the modern realm of technical knowledge. Consequently, long periods of patent "searching," and frequently, successful defense of infringement suits may precede the validation of a patent. Even though patents have a legal life of 20 years from application date, changes in technology or consumer tastes may shorten their economic life. Because of their uncertain value, patents are accounted for conservatively by most businesses. For example, most businesses amortize patents over a shorter period than 20 years. When patents are purchased, the buyer enjoys patent protection for the patent's remaining legal life.

Copyright

A **copyright** protects its owner against the unauthorized reproduction of a specific written work, recorded work, or artwork. A copyright lasts for the life of the author plus 70 years. The purchase price of valuable copyrights can be substantial, and proper measurement and amortization are necessary for valid business income determination.

Franchises

Franchises most often involve exclusive rights to operate or sell a specific brand of products in a given geographic area. Franchises may be for definite or indefinite periods. Although many franchises are agreements between two private firms, various governmental units award franchises for public utility operations within their legal jurisdictions. The right to operate a **Kentucky Fried Chicken (KFC)** restaurant or to sell **Midas Mufflers** in a specific area illustrates franchise agreements in the private sector.

ACCOUNTING IN PRACTICE   **Types of Intangible Assets**

Intangible assets are perhaps the most difficult asset category to fully comprehend. Intangible assets appearing on a company's balance sheet represent a varied collection of assets, as can be seen from a sample of 600 large U.S. firms:

Type of Intangible Asset	Number	%
Goodwill	542	90%
Trademarks, brand names, copyrights	330	55%
Customer lists/relationships	320	53%
Technology	162	27%
Patents	161	27%
Licenses, franchises, memberships	114	19%
Non-compete covenants	112	18.7%
Contracts, agreements	104	17.3%
Other—described	65	10.8%

Source: *Accounting Trends and Techniques.*

Trademarks

Trademarks and **trade names** represent the exclusive and continuing right to use certain terms, names, or symbols, usually to identify a brand or family of products. An original trademark or trade name can be registered with the U.S. federal government for a nominal cost. A company may spend considerable time and money to determine an appropriate name or symbol for a product. Also, the purchase of well-known, and thus valuable, trademarks or trade names may involve substantial amounts of money. When the cost of a trademark or trade name is material, the amount is debited to an appropriate intangible asset account—Trademarks—and amortized over the period of expected benefit to a business.

Goodwill

Goodwill is an often misunderstood concept. In common usage, goodwill may represent the favorable reputation a firm has earned based on its prior operations, quality of service, or positive product characteristics. The term "goodwill," however, has a much different meaning when used in accounting. Goodwill represents the amount paid by one company in the acquisition of another company above the amount that can be attributed to the identifiable net assets of the acquired company, including the other intangibles like those discussed above. The measurement of goodwill is complex because it can stem from many factors. Examples of such factors include exceptional customer relations, advantageous business location, operating efficiency, superior personnel, favorable financial sources, and perceived synergies between the acquiring company and the acquired company. Unlike most intangible assets, goodwill is not subject to periodic amortization because it is considered to have an indefinite life. Instead, goodwill is evaluated annually for any impairment in value. If a company's goodwill is found to be impaired, the Goodwill account is written down to its fair value and an Impairment Loss is recorded on the income statement.

Match the descriptive explanation below with the correct term:

| Amortization | Patent | Copyright |
| Franchise | Trademark | |

1. An exclusive right that protects an owner against the unauthorized reproduction of a specific written work.
2. The periodic write-off of an intangible asset to expense on the income statement.
3. An exclusive and continuing right to use a certain symbol to identify a brand or family of products.
4. An exclusive right to operate or sell a specific brand of products in a given geographic area.
5. An exclusive privilege granted to an inventor that gives the asset holder the right to exclude others from making, using, or selling the invention.

NATURAL RESOURCES

Natural resources include assets such as standing timber, iron ore, coal, gold, silver, and other metal ores. Natural resource assets are recorded on the balance sheet at their acquisition cost plus exploration and development costs.[2] Similar to the units-of-production depreciation method for plant assets, GAAP requires natural resources to be *depleted* over the asset's expected useful life.

Depletion represents the removal of the natural resource from the resource's natural setting and subsequent sale or placement into inventory for sale. Because it is not known with certainty the amount of natural resources in their natural state, the depletion recorded in an accounting period represents an estimate of the actual amount of natural resources extracted in the period.

To illustrate, assume that on January 1, Silverton Mining acquires for $1,000,000 a mineral deposit with an estimated 400,000 tons of ore. Silverton spends an additional $200,000 on exploration and development. Silverton expects zero salvage value once the ore is fully mined. The acquisition would be recorded with the following journal entry:

A	=	L	+	SE
+1,200,000				
−1,200,000				

Jan. 1	Mineral deposits (+A)	1,200,000	
	Cash (−A)		1,200,000
	To record the purchase of mineral deposits and associated exploration and development costs.		

Assume Silverton mined a total of 60,000 tons of ore in the initial year. The depletion charge is computed as follows:

$$\text{Depletion rate} = \frac{\text{Cost of natural resource} - \text{Salvage}}{\text{Estimated total units of natural resource}} = \frac{\$1,200,000}{400,000} = \$3.00 \text{ per ton}$$

The current year depletion expense is $180,000 (60,000 tons × $3.00 per ton). The depletion expense would be recorded with the following journal entry.

A	=	L	+	SE
−180,000				−180,000
				Exp

Dec. 31	Depletion expense (+E, −SE)	180,000	
	Accumulated depletion (+XA, −A)		180,000
	To record the depletion of mineral deposits.		

In the above example it is assumed that Silverton sold all the $180,000 of ore that was mined during the year. If instead one-half of the mined ore was still unsold at year-end, the proper journal entry to record depletion would be:

---

[2] The accounting for another type of natural resource—oil and gas reserves—is more complicated and depends on which of two available methods the company selects: the full cost method or the successful efforts method. These methods are described in advanced accounting textbooks.

Dec. 31	Inventory—mineral deposits (+A)	90,000			A	= L +	SE
	Depletion expense (+E, −SE)	90,000			+90,000		−90,000
	Accumulated depletion (+XA, −A)		180,000		−180,000		Exp
	To record the depletion of mineral deposits.						

Hardwoods, Inc., purchased a tract of timber for a total cost of $500,000. The tract is estimated to contain 200,000 board feet of lumber once the timber is harvested. Hardwoods expects the land will be worth $100,000 once the timber is fully harvested. Hardwoods harvests 40,000 board feet of timber in the initial year and sells all but 5,000 board feet.

    Record separate journal entries for the purchase of the tract of timber and for the recording of depletion in the first year.

YOUR TURN! 9.6

The solution is on page 9-44.

BALANCE SHEET PRESENTATION

Long-lived assets are presented on the balance sheet below the Current Assets category. (Recall that assets are listed on a classified balance sheet in descending order of liquidity.) Although goodwill is an intangible asset, GAAP rules require companies to report it separately from any other intangible assets. Natural resources are usually shown on the balance sheet as either a part of plant assets or as a separate category among noncurrent assets with a title such as "oil reserves" or "timber stands." For example, **Boise Cascade** reports a separate line item titled "Timber deposits," while **ExxonMobil** includes natural resources with other property, plant, and equipment. In either case, natural resources are reported at their total cost less accumulated depletion. For example, **Exhibit 9-3** reveals how these assets appear on the balance sheet of **Weyerhaeuser Company**.

LO6 **Illustrate** the balance sheet presentation of long-lived assets.

EXHIBIT 9-3   **Weyerhaeuser Company**

WEYERHAEUSER COMPANY
Balance Sheet (asset section only)
Dollar Amounts in Millions

	December 31	
	2020	**2019**
Current assets:		
Cash and cash equivalents..............................	$ 495	$ 139
Accounts receivable	450	309
Inventories	443	416
Prepaid expenses and other current assets	221	747
Total current assets	1,609	1,611
Property and equipment, less depreciation	2,013	1,969
Construction in progress......................................	73	130
Timber and timberlands at cost, less depletion	11,827	11,929
Minerals and mineral rights, less depletion	268	281
Other assets...	521	486
Total assets...	**$16,311**	**$16,406**

RETURN ON ASSETS AND ASSET TURNOVER

LO7 Define the return on assets ratio and the asset turnover ratio, and **explain** their use.

eLecture

MBC

© Shutterstock.com

The ability of a firm to use its assets effectively and efficiently is a sign of a healthy, well-managed company. The rate of return generated on a company's assets, referred to as the *return on assets ratio,* is a widely used indicator that focuses on this dimension of a firm's financial performance. In practice, there is some variation in the calculation of this ratio, but one commonly used definition of **return on assets** is:

$$\text{Return on assets} = \frac{\text{Net income}}{\text{Average total assets}}$$

This ratio relates data from two financial statements—the income statement and the balance sheet. The numerator consists of the net income for the year from the income statement.[3] The denominator in the ratio is the average balance of total assets for the year (computed by adding the total assets at the beginning of the year to the total assets at the end of the year and dividing the sum by two) obtained from the balance sheet.

To illustrate the calculation of the return on assets ratio, we use data from General Motors Company, a manufacturing firm with a large investment in long-lived assets. The company reported 2020 net income of $6,247 million, total assets at the beginning of the year of $228,037 million, and year-end total assets of $235,194 million. GM's return on assets for the year is 2.7 percent, calculated as $6,247/[($228,037 + $235,194)/2]. To evaluate a firm's return on assets, it is useful to consider the trend in the ratio, the return for other firms in the same industry, the industry's average return on assets, and the company's economic environment.

TAKEAWAY 9.1	Concept ⟶	Method ⟶	Assessment
	How effective is a company in using its assets to produce net income?	Net income and average total assets $$\text{Return on assets ratio} = \frac{\text{Net income}}{\text{Average total assets}}$$	A higher ratio value implies a higher, more effective level of asset utilization.

The **asset turnover** ratio is another ratio that evaluates a company's use of its assets. This ratio measures how effectively a firm uses its assets to generate sales revenue. The asset turnover ratio is calculated as follows:

$$\text{Asset turnover} = \frac{\text{Net sales}}{\text{Average total assets}}$$

Referring again to the 2020 GM data, the company reported net sales of $122,485 million. Consequently, GM's asset turnover for the year is 0.53, or $156,776/[($228,037 + $235,194)/2], indicating that the company was able to generate $0.53 of sales revenue for every dollar invested in assets. For the preceding year, GM's asset turnover was 0.60. Thus, GM generated $0.60 in net sales in 2019 for each dollar invested in total assets. The decrease in GM's asset turnover from 0.60 to 0.53 indicates that the firm used its assets less effectively in 2020 than in 2019 to generate sales revenue, likely due to the Covid-19 pandemic.

YOUR TURN! 9.7

GuidedExample

MBC

The solution is on page 9-44.

Rollins Co. reported the following information in its latest financial statements:	
Net sales.	$150,000
Net income	25,000
Beginning of year total assets	130,000
End of year total assets	120,000

Compute the return on assets and asset turnover for Rollins Co.

---

[3] An alternative calculation of the return on assets ratio adds interest expense to net income in the ratio's numerator. This calculation keeps the method of financing a company's assets from influencing the calculation of the ratio.

Concept →	Method →	Assessment	TAKEAWAY 9.2
How effective is a company in generating sales revenue using its assets?	Average total assets and net sales Asset turnover ratio = $\dfrac{\text{Net sales}}{\text{Average total assets}}$	A higher ratio value implies a higher level of sales revenue generated for each dollar invested in assets.	

COMPREHENSIVE PROBLEM

Segman Company purchased a machine on January 2 for $24,300. The machine has an expected useful life of three years and an expected salvage value of $900. The company expects to use the machine for 1,400 hours in the first year, 2,000 hours in the second year, and 1,600 hours in the third year.

Required

a. Calculate the depreciation expense for each year using each of the following depreciation methods: (1) straight-line, (2) units-of-production (assume that actual usage equals expected usage), (3) double-declining balance.

b. Assume that the machine was purchased June 1. Calculate the depreciation expense for each year using the following depreciation methods: (1) straight-line, (2) double-declining balance.

Solution

a. 1. Straight-line:
        Year 1: ($24,300 – $900)/3 = $7,800
        Year 2: ($24,300 – $900)/3 = $7,800
        Year 3: ($24,300 – $900)/3 = $7,800

    2. Units-of-production:
        Depreciation per hour = ($24,300 – $900)/5,000 hours = $4.68 per hour
        Year 1: 1,400 hours × $4.68 = $6,552
        Year 2: 2,000 hours × $4.68 = $9,360
        Year 3: 1,600 hours × $4.68 = $7,488

    3. Double-declining balance:
        Depreciation rate = (100/3) × 2 = 66 2/3 percent
        Year 1: $24,300 × 66 2/3 percent = $16,200
        Year 2: ($24,300 – $16,200) × 66 2/3 percent = $5,400
        Year 3: ($24,300 – $21,600) × 66 2/3 percent = $1,800

b. 1. Straight-line: Refer to calculations in (a)1.
        Year 1: $7,800 × 7/12 = $4,550
        Year 2: $7,800 (full year's depreciation)
        Year 3: $7,800 (full year's depreciation)
        Year 4: $7,800 × 5/12 = $3,250

    2. Double-declining balance: Refer to calculations in (a)3.
        Year 1: $16,200 × 7/12 = $9,450
        Year 2: ($24,300 – $9,450) × 66 2/3 percent = $9,900
        Year 3: ($24,300 – $19,350) × 66 2/3 percent= $3,300
        Year 4: $750 [This amount reduces the machine's book value to its salvage value of $900 and is the maximum depreciation expense for the year. ($24,300 – $22,650) × 66 2/3 percent = $1,100 gives an amount in excess of the maximum $750 depreciation.]

SUMMARY OF LEARNING OBJECTIVES

Discuss the nature of long-lived assets and identify the accounting guidelines relating to their initial measurement. (p. 9-4)   **LO1**

■ The accounting for long-lived assets involves the determination of an asset's acquisition cost, periodic depreciation expense, subsequent capital expenditures, and disposal.

■ The initial cost of a plant asset is its implied cash price plus any expenditure necessary to prepare the asset for its intended use.

LO2 **Discuss the nature of depreciation, illustrate three depreciation methods, and explain impairment losses. (p. 9-7)**

- Depreciation is a cost allocation process; it allocates a plant asset's depreciable cost (acquisition cost less salvage value) in a systematic manner over the asset's estimated useful life.
- The most commonly used depreciation methods are straight-line, units-of-production, and declining-balance.
- Revisions of depreciation estimates are accomplished by recalculating depreciation charges for current and subsequent periods.
- When a plant asset is impaired, a loss is recognized equal to the difference between the asset's book value and its current fair value.

LO3 **Discuss the distinction between revenue expenditures and capital expenditures. (p. 9-15)**

- Revenue expenditures are expensed as incurred and include the cost of ordinary repairs and maintenance and the purchase of low-cost items.
- Capital expenditures, which increase a plant asset's book value, include initial acquisitions, additions, and betterments.

LO4 **Explain and illustrate the accounting for disposals of plant assets. (p. 9-17)**

- When a firm disposes of a plant asset, depreciation must be recorded on the asset up to the disposal date.
- Gains and losses on plant asset dispositions are determined by comparing an asset's book value to the proceeds received.

LO5 **Discuss the nature of, and the accounting for, intangible assets and natural resources. (p. 9-18)**

- Intangible assets acquired from other entities are initially valued at their acquisition cost. Some internally created intangible assets are also measured at their cost, but most expenditures related to internally developed intangible assets are expensed rather than capitalized.
- Research and development costs related to a firm's products and its production processes are expensed as incurred.
- Amortization is the periodic write-off to expense of an intangible asset's cost over the asset's useful life.
- Goodwill may be shown in the accounts only when it has been purchased as part of the acquisition of another business.
- Natural resources include assets such as standing timber, oil and gas reserves, and mineral ores.
- Depletion represents the removal of the natural resources from their natural setting.

LO6 **Illustrate the balance sheet presentation of long-lived assets. (p. 9-22)**

- Long-lived assets are shown on the balance sheet after long-term investments. Although technically an intangible asset, goodwill is reported separately on the balance sheet since it is not subject to amortization.

LO7 **Define the return on assets ratio and the asset turnover ratio, and explain their use. (p. 9-23)**

- The return on assets ratio is calculated by dividing net income by average total assets; it represents an overall measure of a firm's profitability and how efficiently a company is using its assets to generate net income.
- The asset turnover ratio is calculated by dividing net sales by average total assets; it provides an indication of the effective utilization of business assets to generate sales revenues.

SUMMARY	Concept ⟶	Method ⟶	Assessment
TAKEAWAY 9.1	How effective is a company in using its assets to produce net income?	Net income and average total assets $\text{Return on assets ratio} = \dfrac{\text{Net income}}{\text{Average total assets}}$	A higher ratio value implies a higher, more effective level of asset utilization.
TAKEAWAY 9.2	How effective is a company at generating sales using its assets?	Average total assets and net sales $\text{Asset turnover ratio} = \dfrac{\text{Net sales}}{\text{Average total assets}}$	A higher ratio value implies a higher level of sales revenue generated for each dollar invested in assets.

KEY TERMS

Accelerated depreciation
   method (p. 9-9)
Amortization (p. 9-19)
Asset turnover (p. 9-23)
Betterments (p. 9-16)
Capital expenditures (p. 9-16)
Copyright (p. 9-19)
Declining-balance
   method (p. 9-9)
Depletion (p. 9-21)
Depreciation (p. 9-7)
Depreciation accounting (p. 9-7)

Franchises (p. 9-20)
Goodwill (p. 9-20)
Impairment loss (p. 9-13)
Intangible assets (p. 9-3, 9-18)
Land improvements (p. 9-6)
Leasehold
   improvements (p. 9-6)
Modified accelerated
   cost recovery system
   (MACRS) (p. 9-14)
Natural resources (p. 9-3, 9-21)
Net book value (p. 9-8)
Patent (p. 9-19)

Plant assets (p. 9-3)
Research and development
   costs (p. 9-18)
Return on assets (p. 9-23)
Revenue expenditures (p. 9-15)
Salvage value (p. 9-7)
Straight-line method (p. 9-8)
Trademarks (p. 9-20)
Trade names (p. 9-20)
Units-of-production
   method (p. 9-10)
Useful life (p. 9-7)

Assignments with the 🅜🅑🅒 logo in the margin are available in BusinessCourse.
See the Preface of the book for details.

SELF-STUDY QUESTIONS

(Answers for the Self-Study Questions are available at the end of this chapter.)

1. **The acquisition cost of a plant asset is equal to the asset's implied cash price and:**   **LO1**
   a. The interest paid on any debt incurred to finance the asset's purchase.
   b. The market value of any noncash assets given up to acquire the plant asset.
   c. The reasonable and necessary costs incurred to prepare the asset for its intended use.
   d. The asset's estimated salvage value.

2. **On January 1, Bush Company purchased a delivery truck for $10,000. The company estimates**   **LO2**
   the truck will be driven 80,000 miles over its eight-year useful life. The estimated salvage value
   is $2,000. The truck was driven 12,000 miles in its first year. Which method results in the largest
   depreciation expense for the first year?
   a. Units-of-production   c. Double-declining balance
   b. Straight-line

3. **On the first day of the current year, Griffin Company sold equipment for less than its book value.**   **LO4**
   Which of the following is part of the journal entry to record the sale?
   a. A debit to Equipment
   b. A credit to Accumulated Depreciation—Equipment
   c. A credit to Gain on Sale of Plant Assets
   d. A debit to Loss on Sale of Plant Assets

4. **Accounting for the periodic amortization of intangible assets is similar to which depreciation**   **LO5**
   method?
   a. Straight-line   c. Double-declining balance
   b. Units-of-production

5. **An exclusive right to operate or sell a specific brand of products in a given geographic area is called:**   **LO5**
   a. A franchise.   c. A patent.
   b. Goodwill.   d. A copyright.

6. **Which of the following statements is true?**   **LO5**
   a. Goodwill is subject to amortization.
   b. Research and development costs may be capitalized to the balance sheet.
   c. Intangible assets are amortized to expense on the income statement.
   d. Goodwill arises because of a company's positive corporate image among its customers.

7. **Which of the following statements is false?**   **LO3**
   a. Expenditures for ordinary repairs are a capital expenditure.
   b. Betterment expenditures are a capital expenditure.
   c. Expenditures to acquire low-cost assets are revenue expenditures.
   d. Material additions to a plant asset are capital expenditures.

LO6   **8. Which of the following statements is true?**
   a.   Intangible assets are shown on the balance sheet net of the Accumulated Amortization account.
   b.   Goodwill is shown on the balance sheet net of the Accumulated Amortization account.
   c.   The Accumulated Depreciation account need not be used for plant assets.
   d.   Plant assets are shown on the balance sheet net of the Accumulated Depreciation account.

LO7   **9. A company reports net income of $12,000, net sales of $30,000, and average total assets of $48,000. What is the company's return on assets?**

   a.   62.5 percent   c.   40.0 percent
   b.   25.0 percent   d.   None of the above

LO7   **10. A company reports net income of $12,000, net sales of $30,000, and average total assets of $48,000. What is the company's asset turnover?**
   a.   0.625   c.   0.400
   b.   0.250   d.   None of the above

LO4   **11. Davidson Company sold one of its worn-out delivery trucks on December 31, 2022. The truck was purchased on January 1, 2019, for $50,000 and was depreciated on a straight-line basis over a five-year life. There was no salvage value associated with the truck. If the truck was sold for $14,000, what was the amount of gain or loss recorded at the time of the sale?**
   a. $4,000 loss   c. $4,000 gain
   b. $14,000 gain   d. $6,000 loss

LO5   **12. Which of the following is not an example of a natural resource?**
   a.   Oil reserves   c.   Oil rig
   b.   Standing timber   d.   Mineral deposits

QUESTIONS

1. What are the three major types of long-term assets that require a periodic write-off? Present examples of each, and indicate for each type of asset the term that denotes the periodic write-off to expense.

2. In what way is land different from other plant assets?

3. In general, what amounts constitute the acquisition cost of plant assets?

4. Foss Company bought land with a vacant building for $400,000. Foss will use the building in its operations. Must Foss allocate the purchase price between the land and building? Why or why not? Would your answer be different if Foss intends to raze the building and build a new one? Why or why not?

5. Why is the recognition of depreciation expense necessary to match revenue and expense properly?

6. What is the pattern of plant asset utilization (or benefit) that corresponds to each of the following depreciation methods: (a) straight-line, (b) units-of-production, (c) double-declining balance?

7. How should a revision of depreciation charges due to a change in an asset's estimated useful life or salvage value be handled? Which periods—past, present, or future—are affected by the revision?

8. When is a plant asset considered to be impaired? How is an impairment loss calculated?

9. What is the benefit of accelerating depreciation for income tax purposes when the total depreciation taken is no more than if straight-line depreciation were used?

10. Identify two types of revenue expenditures. What is the proper accounting for revenue expenditures?

11. Identify two types of capital expenditures. What is the proper accounting for capital expenditures?

12. What factors determine the gain or loss on the sale of a plant asset?

13. Folger Company installed a conveyor system that cost $192,000. The system can be used only in the excavation of gravel at a particular site. Folger expects to excavate gravel at the site for 10 years. Over how many years should the conveyor be depreciated if its physical life is estimated at (a) 8 years and (b) 12 years?

14. What are five different types of intangible assets? Briefly explain the nature of each type.

15. How should a firm account for research and development costs?

16. Under what circumstances is goodwill recorded?

17. How is the *return on assets* ratio calculated? What does this ratio reveal about a business?

18. How is the *asset turnover ratio* calculated? What does this ratio reveal about a business?

SHORT EXERCISES

SE9-1. Calculate Amount to Capitalize The Bud Company paid $12,000 to acquire a 100 ton press. Freight charges to deliver the equipment amounted to $1,500 and were paid by Bud. Installation costs amounted to $570, and machine testing charges amounted to $400. Calculate the amount that should be capitalized to the Equipment account.   **LO1**

SE9-2. Depreciation Expense Using the Straight-Line Method The Peete Company purchased an office building for $4,500,000. The building had an estimated useful life of 25 years and an expected salvage value of $500,000. Calculate the depreciation expense for the second year using the straight-line method.   **LO2**

SE9-3. Depreciation Expense Using the Double-Declining Balance Method The Peete Company purchased an office building for $4,500,000. The building had an estimated useful life of 25 years and an expected salvage value of $500,000. Calculate the depreciation expense for the second year using the double-declining balance method.   **LO2**

SE9-4. Depreciation Expense Using the Units-of-Production Method The Sonya Company is a coal company based in West Virginia. The company recently purchased a new coal truck for $50,000. The truck had an expected useful life of 200,000 miles and an expected salvage value of $2,000. Calculate the depreciation expense using the units-of-production method assuming the truck travelled 40,000 miles on company business during the year.   **LO2**

SE9-5. Sale of a Building The Mite Company sold a building for $350,000 that had a book value of $450,000. The building had originally cost the company $12,000,000 and had accumulated depreciation to date of $11,550,000. Prepare a journal entry to record the sale of the building.   **LO4**

SE9-6. Goodwill Impairment Bruce Farms Equipment Company had goodwill valued at $80 million on its balance sheet at year-end. A review of the goodwill by the company's CFO indicated that the goodwill was impaired and was now only worth $45 million. Prepare a journal entry to record the goodwill impairment on the books of the company.   **LO5**

SE9-7. Amortization Expense Smith & Daughters obtained a patent for a new optical scanning device. The fees incurred to file for the patent and to defend the patent in court against several companies that challenged the patent amounted to $90,000. Smith & Daughters concluded that the expected economic life of the patent was 12 years. Calculate the amortization expense that should be recorded in the second year, and record the journal entry for the amortization expense on the books of Smith & Daughters.   **LO5**

SE9-8. Return on Assets The Queen Company reported net income of $80,000 and average total assets of $450,000. Calculate the company's return on assets.   **LO7**

SE9-9. Asset Turnover The Kingwood Company reported sales revenue of $520,000 and average total assets of $500,000. Calculate the company's asset turnover.   **LO7**

SE9-10. Return on Assets and Asset Turnover Last year, the Miller Company reported a return on assets of 15 percent and an asset turnover of 1.6. In the current year, the company reported a return on assets of 19 percent but an asset turnover of only 1.2. If sales revenue remained unchanged from last year to the current year, what would explain the two ratio results?   **LO7**

SE9-11. Sale of Equipment Prepare the journal entry for the following transactions: (1) Geysler Company sold some old equipment that initially cost $30,000 and had $25,000 of accumulated depreciation and received cash in the amount of $2,000. (2) Assume the same facts except Geysler received $8,000.   **LO4**

SE9-12. Financial Statement Placement Name the financial statement where each of the following will appear: (IS) Income Statement; (BS) Balance Sheet; (SCF) Statement of Cash Flows; (N) None.   **LO6**
  a. Book value of equipment purchased five years ago   d. Gain on the sale of buildings
  b. Market value of equipment purchased five years ago   e. Accumulated depreciation on equipment
  c. Cash proceeds from the sale of land   f. Impairment loss on land

SE9-13. Depletion expense Digger, Inc., paid $100,000 for the rights to mineral deposits containing an estimated 20,000 tons of ore. Digger paid an additional $20,000 for exploration and development and estimated there would be no salvage value once the ore was fully extracted. Calculate depletion expense if Digger extracted and sold 8,000 tons of ore.   **LO5**

DATA ANALYTICS

DA9-1. **Preparing an Excel Visualization of Property and Equipment Components Over Time** The Excel file associated with this exercise includes information regarding **Fastenal Company**'s disclosures on its property and equipment in its Form 10-Ks over a six-year period. For this exercise, we analyze the changes in the composition of property and equipment over time.

Required

1. Download Excel file DA9-1 found in myBusinessCourse.
2. Create a Stacked Area chart showing the gross balances (before accumulated depreciation) of its property and equipment accounts. *Hint:* Highlight your data and open the Insert tab. Click Recommended Charts in the Charts group. Open the All Charts tab and click Area. Select the Stacked Area chart.
3. Answer the following questions based on the visualization.
    a. In which two years did total property and equipment rise at a slightly faster pace than the other years shown?
    b. From Year 1 to Year 6, which category of property and equipment showed the most growth?
    c. Which category of property and equipment appeared to drop (in proportion to the other categories) from Year 1 to Year 6?
    d. What is the largest category of property and equipment in Year 6?
4. Create two Pie charts, one for Year 1, and one for Year 6, showing gross balances (before accumulated depreciation) of property and equipment accounts.
5. If necessary, add chart titles to state the year. *Hint:* Click inside the chart and open the Chart Design tab. Click Add Chart Element in the Charts Layout group and select Chart Title.
6. Add data labels to the pie charts and edit data labels to only show percentages and not values. *Hint:* Right-click inside the pie and select Format Data Labels. Select Percentages under Label Options in the sidebar. Deselect Value, if necessary.
7. Answer the following questions based on the visualization.
    a. Which component has the highest proportion in Year 1? What is the percentage?
    b. Which component has the highest proportion in Year 6? What is the percentage?
    c. Which component had the greatest increase in proportion of the total from Year 1 to Year 6? What was the percentage difference?
    d. Which component had the greatest decrease in proportion from Year 1 to Year 6? What was the percentage difference?
    e. Which components showed a 2% or less difference in proportion of the total between Year 1 and Year 6?

DA9-2. **Using Excel Visualizations to Analyze Property and Equipment** The Excel file associated with this exercise includes data for **Delta Air Lines, Inc.**, as reported in its Form 10-K reports over a 10-year period. The percent depreciated of depreciable fixed assets measures the age of the assets compared to useful life. A company that has made substantial investments in new fixed assets will have a lower ratio compared to a company with fixed assets nearing the end of their useful life. In this exercise, we review the trend of percent depreciated of gross property and equipment for Delta Airlines over a 10-year period.

Required

1. Download Excel file DA9-2 found in myBusinessCourse.
2. Compute the ratio of accumulated depreciation to gross property and equipment for each year. Assume all assets are depreciable.

Percent Depreciated

Accumulated depreciation
Cost of depreciable asset

3. Prepare the following three charts in Excel.
    *   Chart 1: A bar chart showing accumulated depreciation and gross property and equipment per year over the 10-year period.
    *   Chart 2: A line chart showing property and equipment additions over the 10-year period, with the earliest year on the left hand side. *Hint:* To reverse the order of the years, right-click inside the horizontal axis. A Format Axis sidebar will appear. Open the bar chart icon tab. Click Categories in reverse order under Axis options.
    *   Chart 3: A line chart showing the ratio of accumulated depreciation to gross property and equipment over the 10-year period.

4. Answer the following questions based on your visualizations.
   a. In Chart 1, in what year(s) was the trend of increasing values not evident in the chart?
   b. In Chart 2, what year(s) showed a drop in property and equipment additions?
   c. In Chart 2, what year showed the most significant change?
   d. Describe the trend shown in Chart 3.
   e. What is the likely cause of the increase shown in Year 10 in Chart 3.

DA9-3. Determining the Method Used to Produce a Depreciation Visualization The Excel file associated with this exercise includes four charts depicting depreciation under four different methods over the life of a fixed asset with a useful life of five years. In this exercise, we match each depreciation method provided to the appropriate depreciation chart based upon the trend in depreciation over the five-year period.

Required
1. Download Excel file DA9-3 found in myBusinessCourse.
2. Calculate the fixed asset's original cost if the residual value of the asset is $5,000.
3. Match each of the charts with the depreciation method used: straight-line, sum-of-the-years'-digits, declining-balance, or units-of-production methods.
4. Indicate which chart(s) can be prepared upon purchase of the fixed asset and which chart(s) can only be prepared over time.

DA9-4. Using Excel Visualizations to Analyze Research & Development Expense Trends The Excel file associated with this exercise includes six years of financial information including research and development (R&D) expense and sales for seven companies in the Health sector. In this exercise, we analyze trends of the ratio of R&D to total sales. An increase in the ratio means that a higher portion of sales was devoted to R&D activities for the period.

Required
1. Download Excel file DA9-4 found in myBusinessCourse.
2. Calculate in Excel, R&D expense as a percentage of sales for six years for each of the following companies: **Abbott Laboratories, Baxter International, Inc., Bristol-Myers Squibb Co., Boston Scientific Corp., Johnson & Johnson, Merck & Co.,** and **Pfizer Inc.**
3. Prepare a line chart in Excel showing the trend of R&D expense as a percentage of sales over the six-year period. *Hint:* The vertical axis should be percentages; the horizontal axis should be Year. The series (lines) should be the seven companies. To edit the chart, open the Chart Design Tab and click Select Data. You may need to switch rows/columns.
4. Describe the trend in the chart for each company. *Hint:* Review the trend but also notice the beginning and ending point of your line chart.
5. Indicate which two companies showed the most growth in research as a percentage of sales over the six-year period.

R&D Expense to Sales
R&D Expense
Total Sales

DATA VISUALIZATION

Data Visualization Activities are available in myBusinessCourse. These assignments use Tableau Dashboards to expose students to visual depictions of data and introduce students to data analytics through data visualizations. These exercises are easily assignable and auto graded by MBC.

Data Visualization

EXERCISES—SET A

E9-1A. Acquisition Cost of Long-Lived Asset The following data relate to a firm's purchase of a machine used in the manufacture of its product:

LO1

Invoice price	$34,000
Applicable sales tax	2,000
Cash discount taken for prompt payment	400
Freight paid	260
Cost of insurance coverage on machine while in transit	125
Installation costs	2,000
Testing and adjusting costs	475
Repair of damages to machine caused by the firm's employees	750
Prepaid maintenance contract for first year of machine's use	400

Determine the acquisition cost of the machine.

LO1 **E9-2A. Allocation of Package Purchase Price** Tamarack Company purchased a plant from one of its suppliers. The $1,000,000 purchase price included the land, a building, and factory machinery. Tamarack also paid $6,000 in legal fees to negotiate the purchase of the plant. An appraisal showed the following values for the items purchased:

Property	Assessed Value
Land.	$126,000
Building.	456,000
Machinery.	318,000
Total.	$900,000

Using the assessed value as a guide, allocate the total purchase price of the plant to the land, building, and machinery accounts in Tamarack Company's records.

LO2 **E9-3A. Depreciation Methods** A delivery truck costing $22,000 is expected to have a $2,000 salvage value at the end of its useful life of four years or 100,000 miles. Assume that the truck was purchased on January 2. Calculate the depreciation expense for the second year using each of the following depreciation methods: (a) straight-line, (b) double-declining balance, and (c) units-of-production. (Assume that the truck was driven 30,000 miles in the second year.)

LO2 **E9-4A. Revision of Depreciation** On January 2, 2018, Moser, Inc., purchased equipment for $100,000. The equipment was expected to have a $10,000 salvage value at the end of its estimated six-year useful life. Straight-line depreciation has been recorded. Before adjusting the accounts for 2022, Moser decided that the useful life of the equipment should be extended by three years and the salvage value decreased to $8,000.

    a.   Prepare a journal entry to record depreciation expense on the equipment for 2022.

    b.   What is the book value of the equipment at the end of 2022 (after recording the depreciation expense for 2022)?

LO2 **E9-5A. Impairment Loss** On July 1, 2018, Karen Company purchased equipment for $325,000; the estimated useful life was 10 years and the expected salvage value was $40,000. Straight-line depreciation is used. On July 1, 2022, economic factors cause the market value of the equipment to decrease to $90,000. On this date, Karen evaluates if the equipment is impaired and estimates future cash flows relating to the use and disposal of the equipment to be $195,000.

    a.   Is the equipment impaired at July 1, 2022? Explain.

    b.   If the equipment is impaired at July 1, 2022, calculate the amount of the impairment loss.

    c.   If the equipment is impaired at July 1, 2022, prepare the journal entry to record the impairment loss.

LO3 **E9-6A. Revenue and Capital Expenditures** Shriver Company built an addition to its chemical plant. Indicate whether each of the following expenditures related to the addition is a revenue expenditure or a capital expenditure:

    a.   Shriver's initial application for a building permit was denied by the city as not conforming to environmental standards. Shriver disagreed with the decision and spent $8,000 in attorney's fees to convince the city to reverse its position and issue the permit.

    b.   Due to unanticipated sandy soil conditions, and on the advice of construction engineers, Shriver spent $58,000 to extend the footings for the addition to a greater depth than originally planned.

    c.   Shriver spent $3,000 to send each of the addition's subcontractors a side of beef as a thank-you gift for completing the project on schedule.

    d.   Shriver invited the mayor to a ribbon-cutting ceremony to open the plant addition. It spent $40 to purchase the ribbon and scissors.

    e.   Shriver spent $4,100 to have the company logo sandblasted into the concrete above the entrance to the addition.

LO4 **E9-7A. Sale of Plant Asset** Lone Pine Company has a machine that originally cost $60,000. Depreciation has been recorded for four years using the straight-line method, with a $5,000 estimated salvage value at the end of an expected ten-year life. After recording depreciation at the end of four years, Lone Pine sells the machine. Prepare the journal entry to record the machine's sale for:

    a. $39,000 cash.   *c.* $28,000 cash.

    b. $38,000 cash.

E9-8A. **Amortization Expense** For each of the following unrelated situations, calculate the annual amortization expense and prepare a journal entry to record the expense: **LO5**

    a.   A patent with a 10-year remaining legal life was purchased for $350,000. The patent will be commercially exploitable for another eight years.

    b.   A patent was acquired on a device designed by a production worker. Although the cost of the patent to date consisted of $52,300 in legal fees for handling the patent application, the patent should be commercially valuable during its entire remaining legal life of 10 years and is currently worth $400,000.

    c.   A franchise granting exclusive distribution rights for a new solar water heater within a three-state area for five years was obtained at a cost of $70,000. Satisfactory sales performance over the five years permits renewal of the franchise for another three years (at an additional cost determined at renewal).

E9-9A. **Return on Assets Ratio and Asset Turnover Ratio** Northern Systems reported the following financial data (in millions) in its annual report: **LO7**

	Previous Year	Current Year
Net income	$ 9,050	$ 7,500
Net sales	52,350	37,200
Total assets	58,734	68,128

If the company's total assets are $55,676 at the beginning of the previous year, calculate the company's (a) return on assets and (b) asset turnover for both years.

E9-10A. **Financial Statement Presentation** Alexa Corp. reported the following amounts for the year just ended: **LO6**

Land	$150,000
Patents	25,000
Equipment	40,000
Buildings	150,000
Goodwill	37,000
Accumulated amortization	13,000
Accumulated depreciation	90,000

Prepare a partial balance sheet for these amounts.

E9-11A. **Natural Resources** The Hollister Company acquires a silver mine at the cost of $1,300,000 on January 1. Along with the purchase price Hollister pays additional costs associated with development of $50,000. Hollister expects the mine will have a salvage value of $100,000 once all the silver has been mined. Best estimates are that the mine contains 250,000 tons of ore.   **LO6**

Required

    a.   Prepare the entry to record the purchase of the silver mine.

    b.   Prepare the December 31 year-end adjusting entry to record depletion if 60,000 tons of ore are mined and all the ore is sold.

    c.   Prepare the December 31 year-end adjusting entry to record depletion if 60,000 tons of ore are mined but only 15,000 tons of the ore are sold.

EXERCISES—SET B

E9-1B. **Acquisition Cost of Long-Lived Asset** Derrick Construction purchased a used front-end loader for $32,000, terms 2/10, n/30, F.O.B. shipping point, freight collect. Derrick paid the freight charges of $330 and sent the seller a check for $31,360 one week after the machine was delivered. The loader required a new battery, which cost Fischer $180. Derrick also spent $240 to have the company name printed on the loader and $375 for one year's insurance coverage on it. Derrick hired a new employee to operate it at a wage of $20 per hour; the employee spent one morning (eight hours) practicing with the machine and went to work at a construction site that afternoon. Calculate the amount at which the front-end loader should be reported on the company's balance sheet.   **LO1**

LO1   E9-2B.   Allocation of Package Purchase Price Joe Comey went into business by purchasing a car lubrication station, consisting of land, a building, and equipment. The seller's original asking price was $240,000. Comey hired an appraiser for $3,000 to appraise the assets. The appraised valuations were land, $43,000; building, $95,000; and equipment, $62,000. After receiving the appraisal, Comey offered $183,000 for the business. The seller refused this offer. Comey then offered $190,000 for the business, which the seller accepted. Using the appraisal values as a guide, allocate the total purchase price of the car lubrication station to the Land, Building, and Equipment accounts.

LO2   E9-3B.   Depreciation Methods A machine costing $180,000 was purchased May 1. The machine should be obsolete after four years and, therefore, no longer useful to the company. The estimated salvage value is $15,000. Calculate the depreciation expense for each year of its expected useful life using each of the following depreciation methods: (a) straight-line, (b) double-declining balance.

LO2   E9-4B.   Revision of Depreciation People's Clinic purchased a special machine for use in its laboratory on January 2, 2019. The machine cost $100,000 and was expected to last 10 years. Its salvage value was estimated to be $6,000. By early 2021, it was evident that the machine will be useful for a total of only seven years. The salvage value after seven years was estimated to be $7,500. People's Clinic uses straight-line depreciation. Compute the proper depreciation expense on the machine for 2021.

LO2   E9-5B.   Impairment Loss On May 1, 2019, Smooth, Inc., purchased machinery for $360,000; the estimated useful life was eight years, and the expected salvage value was $15,000. Straight-line depreciation is used. On May 1, 2021, economic factors cause the market value of the machinery to decrease to $190,000. On this date, Smooth evaluates whether the machinery is impaired.

   a.   Assume that on May 1, 2021, Smooth estimates future cash flows relating to the use and disposal of the machinery to be $270,000. Is the machinery impaired at May 1, 2021? Explain. If it is impaired, what is the amount of the impairment loss?

   b.   Assume that on May 1, 2021, Smooth estimates future cash flows relating to the use and disposal of the machinery to be $230,000. Is the machinery impaired at May 1, 2021? Explain. If it is impaired, what is the amount of the impairment loss?

LO3   E9-6B.   Revenue and Capital Expenditures Indicate whether each of the following expenditures is a revenue expenditure or a capital expenditure for Linda Company:

   a.   Paid $300 to replace a truck windshield that was cracked by a stone thrown up by another vehicle while the truck was being used to make a delivery.

   b.   Paid $10 for a "No Smoking" sign for the conference room.

   c.   Paid $900 to add a hard disk to an employee's computer.

   d.   Paid $25 for a dust cover for a computer printer.

   e.   Paid $280 to replace a cracked windshield on a used truck that was just purchased for company use. The company bought the truck knowing the windshield was cracked.

   f.   Paid $750 for a building permit from the city for a storage shed the company is going to have built.

LO4   E9-7B.   Sale of Plant Asset Shannon Company has equipment that originally cost $68,000. Depreciation has been recorded for six years using the straight-line method, with a $9,000 estimated salvage value at the end of an expected eight-year life. After recording depreciation at the end of six years, Shannon sells the equipment. Prepare the journal entry to record the equipment's sale for:

   a. $30,000 cash.   c. $21,000 cash.

   b. $23,750 cash.

LO5   E9-8B.   Amortization Expense For each of the following unrelated situations, calculate the annual amortization expense and prepare a journal entry to record the expense:

   a.   A patent with a 15-year remaining legal life was purchased for $756,000. The patent will be commercially exploitable for another six years.

   b.   A patent was acquired on a device designed by a production worker. Although the cost of the patent to date consisted of $88,200 in legal fees for handling the patent application, the patent should be commercially valuable during its entire remaining legal life of 15 years and is currently worth $720,000.

   c.   A franchise granting exclusive distribution rights for a new wind turbine within a three-state area for four years was obtained at a cost of $72,000. Satisfactory sales performance over the four years permits renewal of the franchise for another four years (at an additional cost determined at renewal).

E9-9B. Return on Assets Ratio and Asset Turnover Ratio United Systems reported the following financial   **LO7**
data (in millions) in its annual report:

	Previous Year	Current Year
Net income	$21,500	$16,134
Net sales	49,540	52,250
Total assets	68,734	78,128

If the company's total assets are $65,676 at the beginning of the previous year, calculate the company's
(a) return on assets and (b) asset turnover for both years.

E9-10B. Financial Statement Presentation Olin Corp. reported the following amounts for the year just ended: **LO6**

Land	$ 90
Trademarks	16
Equipment	83
Buildings	110
Goodwill	32
Accumulated amortization	10
Accumulated depreciation	55

Prepare a partial balance sheet for these amounts.

E9-11B. Natural Resources The Stein Company acquires a silver mine at the cost of $950,000 on January 1.   **LO6**
Along with the purchase price Stein pays additional costs associated with development of $75,000.
Stein expects the mine will have a salvage value of $125,000 once all the silver has been mined. Best
estimates are that the mine contains 300,000 tons of ore.

Required
a. Prepare the entry to record the purchase of the silver mine.
b. Prepare the December 31 year-end adjusting entry to record depletion if 40,000 tons of ore are
mined and all the ore is sold.
c. Prepare the December 31 year-end adjusting entry to record depletion if 40,000 tons of ore are
mined but only 10,000 tons of the ore are sold.

PROBLEMS—SET A

P9-1A. Acquisition Cost of Long-Lived Assets The following items represent expenditures (or receipts)   **LO1**
related to the construction of a new home office for Norma Company.

Cost of land site, which included an old apartment building appraised at $75,000	$ 180,000
Legal fees, including fee for title search	2,100
Payment of apartment building mortgage and related interest due at time of sale	9,300
Payment for delinquent property taxes assumed by the purchaser	6,000
Cost of razing the apartment building	19,000
Proceeds from sale of salvaged materials	(3,800)
Grading to establish proper drainage flow on land site	2,100
Architect's fees on new building	310,000
Proceeds from sales of excess dirt (from basement excavation) to owner of adjoining property (dirt was used to fill in a low area on property)	(2,000)
Payment to building contractor	5,000,000
Payment of medical bills of employee accidentally injured while inspecting building construction	1,600
Special assessment for paving city sidewalks (paid to city)	20,000
Cost of paving driveway and parking lot	30,000
Cost of installing lights in parking lot	9,500
Premium for insurance on building during construction	7,800
Cost of open house party to celebrate opening of new building	10,000

Required
From the given data, calculate the proper balances for the Land, Building, and Land Improvements
accounts of Norma Company.

LO1, 2

P9-2A. **Allocation of Package Purchase Price and Depreciation Methods** To expand its business, Renee Company paid $760,000 for most of the property, plant, and equipment of a small trucking company that was going out of business. Before agreeing to the price, Small hired a consultant for $10,000 to appraise the assets. The appraised values were as follows:

Land	$120,000
Building.	440,000
Trucks	144,000
Equipment	96,000
Total.	$800,000

Small issued two checks totaling $770,000 to acquire the assets and pay the consultant on July 1. Renee depreciated the assets using the straight-line method on the building and on the equipment, and the double-declining balance method on the trucks. Estimated useful lives and salvage values were as follows:

	Useful Life	Salvage Value
Building.	20 years	$42,000
Trucks	4 years	15,000
Equipment	8 years	10,000

Required

a. Calculate the amounts allocated to the various types of plant assets acquired on July 1.
b. Prepare the July 1 journal entries to record the purchase of the assets and the payment to the consultant.
c. Prepare the December 31 journal entries to record depreciation expense for the year on the building, trucks, and equipment.

LO2

P9-3A. **Depreciation Methods** On January 2 Skyler, Inc., purchased a laser cutting machine to be used in the fabrication of a part for one of its key products. The machine cost $120,000, and its estimated useful life was four years or 920,000 cuttings, after which it could be sold for $5,000.

Required

a. Calculate each year's depreciation expense for the period under each of the following depreciation methods:
    1. Straight-line.
    2. Double-declining balance.
    3. Units-of-production. Assume annual production in cuttings of 200,000; 350,000; 260,000; and 110,000.
b. Assume that the machine was purchased on July 1. Calculate each year's depreciation expense for the period under each of the following depreciation methods:
    1. Straight-line.
    2. Double-declining balance.

LO1, 2, 3

P9-4A. **Accounting for Plant Assets** Ethan Corporation had the following transactions related to its delivery truck:

Year 1
Jan.	5	Purchased for $28,000 cash a new truck with an estimated useful life of four years and a salvage value of $4,000.
Feb.	20	Installed a new set of side-view mirrors at a cost of $80 cash.
June	9	Paid $325 for an engine tune-up, wheel balancing, and a periodic chassis lubrication.
Aug.	2	Paid a $410 repair bill for the uninsured portion of damages to the truck caused by Ethan's own driver.
Dec.	31	Recorded depreciation on the truck for the year.

Year 2
May	1	Installed a set of parts bins in the truck at a cost of $950 cash. This expenditure was not expected to increase the salvage value of the truck.
Dec.	31	Recorded depreciation on the truck for the year.

Year 3
Dec.	31	Recorded depreciation on the truck for the year.

Ethan's depreciation policies include (1) using straight-line depreciation, (2) recording depreciation to the nearest whole month, and (3) expensing all truck expenditures of $100 or less.

Required
Prepare journal entries to record these transactions and adjustments.

P9-5A. **Disposal of Plant Asset** Ben Company has a used executive charter plane that originally cost **LO4** $1,000,000. Straight-line depreciation on the plane has been recorded for six years, with a $100,000 expected salvage value at the end of its estimated eight-year useful life. The last depreciation entry was made at the end of the sixth year. Eight months into the seventh year, Ben disposes of the plane.

Required
Prepare journal entries to record:

a. Depreciation expense to the date of disposal.
b. Sale of the plane for cash at its book value.
c. Sale of the plane for $300,000 cash.
d. Sale of the plane for $220,000 cash.
e. Destruction of the plane in a fire. Ben expects a $210,000 insurance settlement.

P9-6A. **Accounting for Intangible Assets and Leasehold Improvements** Jeffrey Company owns several **LO1, 2, 5** retail outlets. During the year, it expanded operations and entered into the following transactions:

Jan. 2 Signed an eight-year lease for additional retail space for an annual rent of $32,000. Paid the first year's rent on this date. (*Hint:* Debit the first year's rent to Prepaid Rent.)
   3 Paid $23,600 to a contractor for installation of a new oak floor in the leased facility. The oak floor's life is an estimated 50 years with no salvage value.
Mar. 1 Paid $60,000 to obtain an exclusive area franchise for five years to distribute a new line of gourmet chocolates.
July 1 Paid $46,000 to LogoLab, Inc., for designing a trademark for a new line of gourmet chocolates that Jeffrey will distribute nationally. Jeffrey will use the trademark for as long as the firm remains in business. Jeffrey expects to be in business for at least another 50 years.
   1 Paid $40,000 for advertisement in a national magazine (June issue) introducing the new line of gourmet chocolates and the trademark.

Required
a. Prepare journal entries to record these transactions.
b. Prepare the necessary adjusting entries on December 31 for these transactions. Jeffrey makes adjusting entries once a year. Jeffrey uses straight-line depreciation and amortization.

P9-7A. **Preparation of Balance Sheet** Ari Company's December 31 post-closing trial balance contains the **LO6** following normal balances:

Cash	$ 19,000
Accounts payable	20,000
Building	439,500
Long-term notes payable	785,000
Common stock	950,000
Retained earnings	75,000
Accumulated depreciation—Equipment	180,000
Land	877,000
Accounts receivable	22,500
Accumulated depreciation—Building	135,000
Wages payable	6,000
Patent (net of amortization)	120,000
Notes payable (short term)	131,000
Inventory	206,000
Equipment	600,000
Allowance for doubtful accounts	2,000

Required
Prepare a December 31 classified balance sheet for Ari Company.

LO1, 2, 3   P9-8A.   Journal Entries for Plant Assets During the first few days of the year, Jules Company entered into the following transactions:

1. Purchased a parcel of land with a building on it for $900,000 cash. The building, which will be used in operations, has an estimated useful life of 20 years and a salvage value of $60,000. The assessed valuations for property tax purposes show the land at $80,000 and the building at $720,000.
2. Paid $31,200 for the construction of an asphalt parking lot for customers. The parking lot is expected to last 12 years and has no salvage value.
3. Paid $50,000 for the construction of a new entrance to the building.
4. Purchased store equipment, paying the invoice price (including seven percent sales tax) of $78,760 in cash. The estimated useful life of the equipment is eight years, and the salvage value is $6,000.
5. Paid $240 freight on the new equipment.
6. Paid $1,650 to repair damages to floor caused when the store equipment was accidentally dropped as it was moved into place.
7. Paid $75 for an umbrella holder to place inside front door. (Customers may place wet umbrellas in the holder.) The holder is expected to last 20 years.

Required

a. Prepare journal entries to record these transactions.
b. Prepare the December 31 journal entries to record depreciation expense for the year. Double-declining balance depreciation is used for the equipment, and straight-line depreciation is used for the building and parking lot.

LO2, 3   P9-9A.   Revision of Depreciation and Capital Expenditure Eric Company uses straight-line depreciation for its equipment. On January 1, 2016, Eric purchased a new piece of equipment for $168,000 cash. The equipment's estimated useful life was eight years with $15,000 salvage value. In 2021, the company decided its original useful life estimate should be increased by six years. Beginning in 2021, depreciation was based on a 14-year total useful life, and no change was made in the salvage value estimate. On January 3, 2022, Eric added a modification to the equipment that increased its productivity at a cost of $21,100 cash. These modifications did not change the equipment's useful life but did increase the estimated salvage value by $3,980.

Required

a. Prepare journal entries to record (1) the purchase of the equipment, (2) 2016 depreciation expense, (3) 2021 depreciation expense, (4) the 2022 modification, and (5) 2022 depreciation expense.
b. Calculate the book value of the equipment at the end of 2022 (that is, after recording the depreciation expense for 2022).

PROBLEMS—SET B

LO1   P9-1B.   Acquisition Cost of Long-Lived Assets The following items represent expenditures (or receipts) related to the construction of a new home office for Ryan Investment Company.

Cost of land site, which included an abandoned railroad spur	$ 185,000
Legal fees, including title search, relating to land purchase	4,300
Cost of surveying land to confirm boundaries	3,000
Cost of removing railroad tracks	7,000
Payment of delinquent property taxes assumed by the purchaser	6,000
Proceeds from sale of timber from walnut trees cut down to prepare site for construction	(20,000)
Proceeds from sale of salvaged railroad track	(4,700)
Grading to prepare land site for construction	4,000
Cost of basement excavation (contracted separately)	3,700
Architect's fees on new building	142,000
Payment to building contractor—original contract price	3,200,000
Cost of changes during construction to make building more energy efficient	91,000
Cost of replacing windows broken by vandals	3,400
Cost of paving driveway and parking lot	17,000
Out-of-court settlement for mud slide onto adjacent property	12,500
Special assessment for paving city sidewalks (paid to city)	22,000
Cost of brick and wrought iron fence installed across front of property	17,500

Required

From the given data, compute the proper balances for the Land, Building, and Land Improvements accounts of Ryan Investment Company.

P9-2B. Allocation of Package Purchase Price and Depreciation Methods In an expansion move, James Company paid $2,190,000 for most of the property, plant, and equipment of a small manufacturing firm that was going out of business. Before agreeing to the price, James hired a consultant for $25,000 to appraise the assets. The appraised values were as follows:

Land	$ 384,000
Building.	912,000
Equipment	960,000
Trucks	144,000
Total.	$2,400,000

James issued two checks totaling $2,215,000 to acquire the assets and pay the consultant on April 1. James depreciated the assets using the straight-line method for the building and equipment, and the double-declining balance method for the trucks. Estimated useful lives and salvage values were as follows:

	Useful Life	Salvage Value
Building.	30 years	$86,000
Equipment	10 years	70,000
Trucks	4 years	13,000

Required
a. Calculate the amounts allocated to the various types of plant assets acquired on April 1.
b. Prepare the April 1 journal entries to record the purchase of the assets and the payment of the consultant.
c. Prepare the December 31 journal entries to record the depreciation expense on the building, equipment, and trucks for the year.

P9-3B. Depreciation Methods On January 2 Javier Company purchased an electroplating machine to help manufacture a part for one of its key products. The machine cost $437,400 and was estimated to have a useful life of six years or 781,200 platings, after which it could be sold for $46,800.

Required
a. Calculate each year's depreciation expense for the period under each of the following depreciation methods:
  1. Straight-line.
  2. Double-declining balance.
  3. Units-of-production. (Assume annual production in platings of 140,000; 180,000; 150,000; 125,000; 95,000; and 91,200.)
b. Assume that the machine was purchased on September 1. Calculate each year's depreciation expense for the period under each of the following depreciation methods:
  1. Straight-line.
  2. Double-declining balance.

P9-4B. Journal Entries for Plant Assets Ediza Delivery Service had the following transactions related to its delivery truck:

Year 1
Mar.   1 Purchased for $32,500 cash a new delivery truck with an estimated useful life of five years and a $6,850 salvage value.
       2 Paid $750 for painting the company name and logo on the truck.
Dec.   31 Recorded depreciation on the truck for the year.
Year 2
July   1 Installed air conditioning in the truck at a cost of $1,808 cash. Although the truck's estimated useful life was unaffected, its estimated salvage value was increased by $400.
Sept.   7 Paid $600 for truck tune-up and safety inspection.
Dec.   31 Recorded depreciation on the truck for the year.
Year 3
Sept.   3 Installed a set of front and rear bumper guards at a cost of $125 cash.
Dec.   31 Recorded depreciation on the truck for the year.
Year 4
Dec.   31 Recorded depreciation on the truck for the year.

Ediza's depreciation policies include (1) using straight-line depreciation, (2) recording depreciation to the nearest whole month, and (3) expensing all truck expenditures of $150 or less.

Required

Prepare journal entries to record these transactions and adjustments.

LO4   P9-5B.   Disposal of Plant Asset Crystal Company has a used delivery truck that originally cost $24,200. Straight-line depreciation on the truck has been recorded for three years, with a $3,500 expected salvage value at the end of its estimated six-year useful life. The last depreciation entry was made at the end of the third year. Four months into the fourth year, Crystal disposes of the truck.

Required

Prepare journal entries to record:

a.   Depreciation expense to the date of disposal.
b.   Sale of the truck for cash at its book value.
c.   Sale of the truck for $17,000 cash.
d.   Sale of the truck for $10,000 cash.
e.   Theft of the truck. Crystal carries no insurance for theft.

LO1, 2, 5   P9-6B.   Accounting for Plant and Intangible Assets Selected transactions of Global Publishers, Inc., for the current year are given below:

Jan.   2   Paid $170,000 to purchase copyrights to a series of romantic novels. The copyrights expire in 40 years, although sales of the novels are expected to stop after 10 years.

Mar.   1   Discovered a satellite dish antenna has been destroyed by lightning. The loss is covered by insurance and a claim is filed today. The antenna cost $18,360 when installed on July 1, 2018, and was being depreciated over 12 years with a $1,800 salvage value. Straight-line depreciation was last recorded on December 31, 2018. Global expects to receive an insurance settlement of $17,000.

April   1   Paid $140,000 to remodel space to create an employee exercise area on the lower level in a leased building. The building's remaining useful life is 40 years; the lease on the building expires in 12 years.

July   1   Paid $540,000 to acquire a patent on a new publishing process. The patent has a remaining legal life of 15 years. Global estimates the new process will be utilized for 6 years before it becomes obsolete.

Nov.   1   Paid $180,000 to obtain a four-year franchise to sell a new series of computerized do-it-yourself manuals.

Required

a.   Prepare journal entries to record these transactions.
b.   Prepare the December 31 journal entries to record depreciation and amortization expense for assets acquired during the year. Global uses straight-line depreciation and amortization.

LO6   P9-7B.   Preparation of Balance Sheet Conner Corporation's December 31 post-closing trial balance contains the following normal account balances:

Cash	$ 10,000
Accounts payable	13,000
Building	260,000
Long-term notes payable	940,000
Common stock	420,000
Retained earnings	342,000
Accumulated depreciation—Equipment	130,000
Land	1,129,000
Accounts receivable	21,000
Accumulated depreciation—Building	70,000
Interest payable	24,000
Patent (net of amortization)	60,000
Notes payable (short term)	80,000
Inventory	137,000
Equipment	266,000
Allowance for doubtful accounts	1,000
Accumulated depreciation - Leasehold improvements	22,000
Leasehold improvements	140,000
Trademark (net of amortization)	19,000

Required

Prepare a December 31 classified balance sheet for Conner Corporation.

P9-8B. **Journal Entries for Plant Assets** During the first few days of the year, Coastal Company entered   **LO1, 2, 3**
into the following transactions:

1. Purchased a parcel of land with a building on it for $3,500,000 cash. The building, which will be used in operations, has an estimated useful life of 30 years and a salvage value of $200,000. The assessed valuations for property tax purposes show the land at $280,000 and the building at $2,520,000.
2. Paid $180,000 for the construction of an asphalt parking lot for customers. The parking lot is expected to last 15 years and has no salvage value.
3. Paid $500,000 for the construction of a new entrance to the building.
4. Purchased store equipment, paying the invoice price (including seven percent sales tax) of $89,660 in cash. The estimated useful life of the equipment is five years, and the salvage value is $4,000.
5. Paid $640 freight on the new equipment.
6. Paid $1,200 to repair damages to floor caused when the store equipment was accidentally dropped as it was moved into place.
7. Paid $50 for an umbrella holder to place inside front door. (Customers may place wet umbrellas in the holder.) The holder is expected to last 30 years.

Required
a. Prepare journal entries to record these transactions.
b. Prepare the December 31 journal entries to record depreciation expense for the year. Double declining balance depreciation is used for the equipment, and straight-line depreciation is used for the building and parking lot.

P9-9B. **Revision of Depreciation and Capital Expenditure** Pinecrest Company uses straight-line depreciation in accounting for its machines. On January 2, 2016, Pinecrest purchased a new machine for   **LO2, 3**
$258,000 cash. The machine's estimated useful life was seven years with a $20,000 salvage value. In 2021, the company decided its original useful life estimate should be increased by three years. Beginning in 2021, depreciation was based on a 10-year total useful life, and no change was made in the salvage value estimate. On January 3, 2022, Pinecrest added an automatic cut-off switch and a self-sharpening blade mechanism to the machine at a cost of $9,200 cash. These improvements did not change the machine's useful life but did increase the estimated salvage value to $11,200.

Required
a. Prepare journal entries to record (1) the purchase of the machine, (2) 2016 depreciation expense, (3) 2021 depreciation expense, (4) the 2022 improvements, and (5) 2019 depreciation expense.
b. Calculate the book value of the machine at the end of 2022 (that is, after recording the depreciation expense for 2022).

SERIAL PROBLEM: KATE'S CARDS

(Note: This is a continuation of the Serial Problem: Kate's Cards from Chapters 1 through 8.)

SP9. Kate's business is growing faster than she had predicted. In order to keep up, she will need to purchase improved computer hardware. Kate has learned that the software that she uses runs much faster if her computer has a lot of memory. In addition, her files are very large and she is running out of free space on her existing hard drive. Finally, Kate has heard horror stories about hard disk drive crashes and the possibility that all of her work will be destroyed. In order to protect against this possibility, she has decided to invest in a large commercial grade backup system.

The cost of the memory and hard disk drive upgrade to Kate's computer will total $420. The cost of the backup system is $3,000. The memory and hard disk upgrade will increase the productivity of Kate's current computer; however, it will not extend its useful life. The backup system is expected to have a five-year useful life.

Kate would like to know the following items:

1. How should the expenditure for the memory and hard disk drive upgrade be recorded? Provide the journal entry.
2. Kate's current computer has 42 months remaining for depreciation purposes (under the straight-line method). The original cost of the computer was $4,800 and had a four-year useful life. The current monthly depreciation is $100. How will this current expenditure affect the monthly depreciation?
3. Kate would like to know how depreciation on the backup system under both the straight-line method and the double-declining method differ. She is assigning a $500 salvage value to the equipment. Construct a table showing yearly depreciation under both methods.

EXTENDING YOUR KNOWLEDGE

REPORTING AND ANALYSIS

COLUMBIA
SPORTSWEAR
COMPANY

EYK9-1. **Financial Reporting Problem: Columbia Sportswear Company** The financial statements for the **Columbia Sportswear Company** can be found in Appendix A at the end of this book.

Required

Answer the following questions.

a. What was the total cost of Columbia's property, plant, and equipment at December 31, 2020?
b. What was the total accumulated depreciation at December 31, 2020?
c. What percentage of the total cost of property, plant, and equipment at December 31, 2020, was from building and improvements?
d. How much depreciation and amortization expense was taken in 2020?
e. What amount of property, plant, and equipment purchases (capital expenditures) occurred in 2020?

COLUMBIA
SPORTSWEAR
COMPANY

UNDER ARMOUR, INC.

EYK9-2. **Comparative Analysis Problem: Columbia Sportswear Company vs. Under Armour, Inc.** The financial statements for the **Columbia Sportswear Company** can be found in Appendix A at the end of this book, and the financial statements of **Under Armour, Inc.**, can be found in Appendix B. (The complete annual report is available on this book's website.)

Required

a. Calculate the following ratios for Columbia Sportswear and for Under Armour, Inc., for 2020:
   1. Return on assets
   2. Asset turnover
b. Comment on your findings.

EYK9-3. **Business Decision Problem** Lyle Fleming, president of Fleming, Inc., wants you to resolve his dispute with Mia Gooden over the amount of a finder's fee due Gooden. Fleming hired Gooden to locate a new plant site to expand the business. By agreement, Gooden's fee was to be 15 percent of the "cost of the property (excluding the finder's fee), measured according to generally accepted accounting principles."

Gooden located Site 1 and Site 2 for Fleming to consider. Each site had a selling price of $150,000, and the geographic locations of both sites were equally acceptable to Fleming. Fleming employed an engineering firm to conduct the geological tests necessary to determine the relative quality of the two sites for construction. The tests, which cost $10,000 for each site, showed that Site 1 was superior to Site 2.

The owner of Site 1 initially gave Fleming 30 days—a reasonable period—to decide whether or not to buy the property. However, Fleming procrastinated in contracting the geological tests, and the results were not available by the end of the 30-day period. Fleming requested a two-week extension. The Site 1 owner granted Fleming the additional two weeks but charged him $6,000 for the extension (which Fleming paid). Fleming eventually bought Site 1.

Fleming sent Gooden a fee of $24,000, which was 15 percent of a cost computed as follows:

Sales price, Site 1.	$150,000
Geological tests, Site 1.	10,000
Total.	$160,000

Gooden believes that she is entitled to $26,400, based on a cost computed as follows:

Sales price, Site 1.	$150,000
Geological tests, Site 1.	10,000
Geological tests, Site 2.	10,000
Fee for time extension	6,000
Total.	$176,000

Required

What fee is Gooden entitled to under the agreement? Explain.

EYK9-4.   **Financial Analysis Problem** **Target Corporation** is headquartered in Minneapolis, Minnesota.   TARGET CORPORATION
The company sells food, apparel, household goods, and many other items. Selected financial data
for Target Corporation follow (amounts in millions):

	2020	2019	2018
Total assets, beginning of year	$42,779	$41,290	$39,999
Total assets, end of year	51,248	42,779	41,290
Revenues for the year	93,561	78,112	75,356
Net income for the year	4,368	3,281	2,937

Required

a.   Calculate the return on assets for 2018–2020.

b.   In 2020, Target Corporation's revenues grew by 19.8 percent, and in 2019 they grew by 3.7
percent. How did this revenue growth correspond to Target Corporation's ROA for 2020 and
2019?

CRITICAL THINKING

EYK9-5.   **Accounting Research Problem** The 2020 annual report of **General Mills, Inc.,** for fiscal year   GENERAL MILLS, INC.
2020 is available on this book's website. Review the consolidated statements of earnings, the con-
solidated balance sheets, and Notes 2 and 18.

Required

a.   What is General Mills' gross cost of land, buildings, and equipment at May 31, 2020?

b.   What depreciation method is used in the financial statements?

c.   How much depreciation and amortization were expensed in fiscal 2020?

d.   How much depreciation has accumulated by May 31, 2020?

e.   How much research and development cost was expensed in fiscal 2020?

f.   What is General Mills' return on assets for fiscal 2020?

EYK9-6.   **Accounting Communication Activity** Peggy Zimmer, a friend of yours taking her first accounting class, is confused as to why there is a separate accumulated depreciation account. She argues
that it would be much simpler to just credit the asset that is being depreciated directly instead of
crediting accumulated depreciation.

Required

Explain to your friend in an informal memo a possible advantage that keeping the cost and accumulated depreciation separate can have for an analyst.

EYK9-7.   **Accounting Ethics Case** Linda Tristan, assistant controller for Ag-Growth, Inc., a biotechnology
firm, has concerns about the accounting analysis for the firm's purchase of a land site and building
from Hylite Corporation. The price for this package purchase was $1,800,000 cash. A memoran-
dum from the controller, Greg Fister, stated that the journal entry for this purchase should debit
Land for $1,350,000, debit Building for $450,000, and credit Cash for $1,800,000. The building, a
used laboratory facility, is to be depreciated over 10 years with a zero salvage value.

The source documents supporting the transaction include two appraisals of the property, one
done for Ag-Growth and one done for Hylite Corporation. The appraisal for Ag-Growth valued the
land at $1,000,000 and the building at $500,000. The appraisal for Hylite Corporation (done by a
different appraiser) valued the land at $1,500,000 and the building at $750,000. Negotiations between
the two firms finally settled on an overall price of $1,800,000 for the land and the building.

Tristan asked Fister how he arrived at the amounts to be recorded for the land and building since
each appraisal valued the land at only twice the building's value. "Well," replied Fister, "I used the
$1,500,000 land value from Hylite's appraiser and the $500,000 building value from our appraiser.
That relationship shows the land to be worth three times the building's value. Using that relationship, I assigned 75 percent of our actual purchase price of $1,800,000 to the land and 25 percent of
the purchase price to the building."

"But why do it that way?" asked Tristan.

"Because it will improve our profits, before income taxes, by $150,000 over the next decade,"
replied Fister.

"But it just doesn't seem right," commented Tristan.

Required

a.   How does the accounting analysis by Fister improve profits before income taxes by $150,000
over the next decade?

    b. Is the goal of improving profits a sufficient rationale to defend the accounting analysis by Fister?

    c. Do you agree with Fister's analysis? Briefly explain.

    d. What actions are available to Tristan to resolve her concerns with Fister's analysis?

CUMMINS INC.

EYK9-8. **Environmental, Social, and Governance Problem** Unlike Tesla Motors' emphasis on electric engines, Cummins, Inc., is best known for its design and manufacturing of diesel engines. Go to the **Cummins**' website at http://cummins.com and navigate to the section on sustainability.

    Required

    1. Articulate Cummins' approach to corporate responsibility.

    2. Cummins states that "corporate responsibility contributes directly to the long-term health, growth, and profitability of our company." Explain how being a good corporate citizen may lead to increased growth and profitability.

WASTE MANAGEMENT, INC.

EYK9-9. **Forensic Accounting Problem Waste Management** is a leading provider of comprehensive trash and waste removal, recycling, and waste management services. In 2002, the Securities and Exchange Commission sued several members and former members of Waste Management's management team for fraud. Go to the S.E.C. press release at https://www.sec.gov/litigation/litreleases/lr17435.htm to answer the following questions:

    1. What does the complaint claim about Dean L. Buntrock, the company's founder, chairman of the board, and chief executive officer?

    2. What accounting methods does the complaint claim were used by Waste Management in order to perpetuate the fraud?

LVMH MOËT HENNESSY-LOUIS VUITTON S.A.

EYK9-10. **Analyzing IFRS Financial Statements** The 2020 financial statements of **LVMH Moët Hennessy-Louis Vuitton S.A.** are presented in Appendix C at the end of this book. LVMH is a Paris-based holding company and one of the world's largest and best-known luxury goods companies. As a member of the European Union, French companies are required to prepare their consolidated (group) financial statements using International Financial Reporting Standards (IFRS). After reviewing LVMH's consolidated financial statements, consider the following questions. (Additional information can be found in LVMH's complete annual report provided on this book's website.)

    Required

    a. What is LVMH's net cost of property, plant, and equipment at December 31, 2020?

    b. What depreciation method is used in the company?

    c. What is LVMH's net cost of goodwill and other intangible assets at December 31, 2020?

    d. How does LVMH account for its research costs? Development costs?

    e. What is LVMH's return on assets for the year ended December 31, 2020?

ALPHABET INC.

EYK9-11. **Working with the Takeaways** The following data (in millions) are taken from **Alphabet's (Google)** 2020 financial statements:

(in millions)	2020	2019
Net sales	$182,527	$161,857
Net income	40,269	34,343
Total assets	319,616	275,909

Calculate Alphabet's 2020 asset turnover and return on assets.

ANSWERS TO SELF-STUDY QUESTIONS:

1. c   2. c   3. d   4. a   5. a   6. c   7. a   8. d   9. b   10. a   11. c   12. c

YOUR TURN! SOLUTIONS

Solution 9.1

All of the costs, with the exception of the unrelated supplies, are considered to be part of the equipment's acquisition cost, and therefore should be capitalized to the equipment account. This includes the $20,000 purchase price, along with the $1,600 sales tax, $400 freight cost, $600 installation cost, and $100 testing cost, for a total acquisition cost of $22,700. The cost of the $300 of supplies should be accounted for as a supplies inventory (an asset) and allocated to expense on the income statement as it is used.

Solution 9.2

(a) Under the straight-line method, the annual depreciation expense is calculated as ($10,000 – $2,000)/5 years = $1,600 for each year. Thus, depreciation for the second year will require the following journal entry:

Depreciation expense (+E, –SE)	1,600	
Accumulated depreciation (+XA, –A)		1,600
To record depreciation expense.		

(b) The depreciation rate for a five-year asset under the double-declining balance method is 40 percent, or [(100 percent/5 years) × 2]. Depreciation expense is calculated as 40 percent times the book value of the asset as of the beginning of the year. Thus, the first year depreciation is $4,000 (40 percent × $10,000), and the second year depreciation is $2,400 [40 percent × ($10,000 – $4,000)]. Thus, the required journal entry is:

Depreciation expense (+E, –SE)	2,400	
Accumulated depreciation (+XA, –A)		2,400
To record depreciation expense.		

Solution 9.3

Items (1), (2), and (4) are revenue expenditures. Item (3) increases the van's useful life, and item (5) reduces the van's operating costs; thus, these items are capital expenditures.

Solution 9.4

Cash (+A)	750	
Accumulated depreciation (–XA, +A)	15,000	
Loss on sale of truck (+E, –SE)	6,750	
Truck (–A)		22,500
To record the sale of truck.		

Solution 9.5

1. Copyright
2. Amortization
3. Trademark

4. Franchise
5. Patent

Solution 9.6

Standing timber (+A)	500,000	
Cash (–A)		500,000
To record the purchase of a tract of timber.		

Inventory—timber (+A)	10,000	
Depletion expense (+E, –SE)	70,000	
Accumulated depletion (+XA, –A)		80,000
To record the depletion of timber.		

$$\text{Depletion rate} = \frac{\$500,000 - \$100,000}{200,000} = \$2.00 \text{ board foot}$$

Inventory = 5,000 × $2.00; Depletion expense = 35,000 × $2.00

Solution 9.7

Return on assets = $25,000 / [($130,000 + $120,000)/2] = 20 percent
Asset turnover = $150,000 / [($130,000 + $120,000)/2] = 1.20

Chapter 10
Accounting for Liabilities

Road Map

LO	Learning Objective	Page	eLecture	Guided Example	Assignments
LO1	Describe the nature of liabilities and discuss various current liabilities.	10-3	E10-1	YT10.1	SS1, SS2, SS4, E1A, E2A, E3A, E4A, E5A, E6A, E7A, E1B, E2B, E3B, E4B, E5B, E6B, E7B, P1A, P2A, P3A, P4A, P5A, P6A, P1B, P2B, P3B, P4B, P5B, P6B
LO2	Illustrate the accounting for long-term liabilities.	10-9	E10-2	YT10.2	SS8, SE2, SE8, SE9, SE10, E8A, E9A, E10A, E11A, E14A, E15A, E16A, E17A, E18A, E19A, E21A, E8B, E9B, E10B, E11B, E14B, E15B, E16B, E17B, E18B, E19B, E21B, P7A, P7B
LO3	Define contingent liabilities and explain the rules for their accounting and disclosure in the financial statements.	10-19	E10-3	YT10.3	SS3, SS5, SE1, SE3, E1A, E7A, E7B, E12A, E12B, P6A, P6B
LO4	Define the current ratio, quick ratio, and times-interest-earned ratio and explain their use.	10-22	E10-4	YT10.4	SS10, SS11, SE5, SE6, SE7, E13A, E13B, P8A, P8B
LO5	Appendix 10A: Explain bond pricing and illustrate the straight-line and effective interest methods of amortizing bond discounts/ premiums.	10-25	E10-5	YT10A.1	SS6, SS7, E14A, E15A, E16A, E17A, E18A, E19A, E14B, E15B, E16B, E17B, E18B, E19B, P9A, P10A, P11A, P12A, P9B, P10B, P11B, P12B
LO6	Appendix 10B: Describe the accounting for leases.	10-32	E10-6	YT10B.1	SS9, SE4, E20A, E20B

© Cambridge Business Publishers

Microsoft Corporation is one of the world's most well-recognized technology companies.

Until 2009, Microsoft remained largely debt free. The company's business model was so successful that it was unnecessary for the company to borrow money. The high profit margins on the company's products enabled Microsoft to finance its growth using internally generated operating cash flow. In 2009, however, the company issued its first bonds to the capital market. Wall Street analysts speculated that Microsoft really didn't need the cash but rather sold the bonds to take advantage of the extremely low interest rates available at that time and possibly to "bulk up" the company's cash position in anticipation of a major corporate acquisition. Microsoft issued bonds almost every year from 2009 through 2021, eventually accumulating borrowings of $58 billion, or 41 percent of total stockholders' equity.

In this chapter, we examine how companies, like Microsoft, value and disclose liabilities on their balance sheets. We consider current liabilities such as accounts payable and accrued expenses payable, noncurrent liabilities such as bonds payable and term loans payable, and contingent liabilities such as pending lawsuits and environmental cleanup obligations.

PAST

Chapter 9 concluded our investigation of the accounting for assets.

PRESENT

In this chapter we turn our attention to the accounting for liabilities.

FUTURE

Chapter 11 examines the accounting for stockholders' equity.

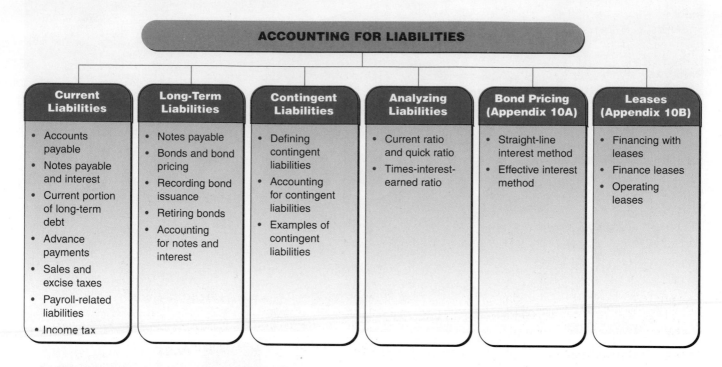

CURRENT LIABILITIES

LO1   **Describe** the nature of liabilities and **discuss** various current liabilities.

eLecture

MBC

Liabilities are obligations resulting from past transactions or events that require a business to pay money, provide goods, or perform services in the future. **Current liabilities** are obligations that will require (1) the use of existing current assets or (2) the creation of other current liabilities. Most current liabilities are settled by using current assets, but sometimes a current liability is settled by the issuance of another current liability. A past due account payable, for example, may be settled by issuing a short-term note payable. Liabilities are classified as current using the same time frame used to classify current assets—the longer of one year or a firm's normal operating cycle. We discuss some typical current liabilities in this section.

Accounts Payable

In a balance sheet listing of current liabilities, amounts due to short-term creditors on accounts payable and notes payable are commonly shown first. Short-term creditors send invoices specifying the amount owed for goods or services that they have provided. As a result, the amount of any account or note payable is easily determined because it is based on the invoices received from a creditor.

At the end of an accounting period, accountants need to know whether any goods are in transit and what the shipping terms are for such goods. If the goods are shipped FOB shipping point, ownership of the goods has transferred to the buyer and an account payable should be recorded at year-end (as well as an increase in inventory) even though the goods and an invoice have not yet arrived.

Notes Payable and Interest

Promissory notes are often issued in transactions when the credit period is longer than the 30 or 60 days typical for accounts payable. Although promissory notes are commonly used in credit sales transactions involving equipment and real property, a note may sometimes be exchanged for merchandise. A note payable may also be substituted for an account payable when an extension of the usual credit period is granted. And, a promissory note is prepared when a loan is obtained from a bank.

Interest is a charge for the use of money. Consequently, interest incurred on a promissory note is an expense to the maker of a note. Since businesses are required under GAAP to distinguish between operating and nonoperating expenses in their income statements, interest expense is reported under the Other Income and Expense category to highlight the fact that this expense is not considered to be an operating expense and, instead, is a financing expense of the business.

Interest on promissory notes can be structured in either of two ways: (1) as an amount paid in addition to the face amount of the note, called the *add-on interest method*, or (2) as an amount included in the face amount of the note, called the *discount method*. The add-on interest method is most commonly used, and consequently, we focus on that approach.

Add-On Interest Method

Interest on a short-term note payable using the *add-on interest method* is paid at the maturity date of the note. The formula for determining the amount of interest to be paid is as follows:

$$\textbf{Interest = Principal} \times \textbf{Interest Rate} \times \textbf{Time}$$

The principal, or face amount, of a note is the amount borrowed. The interest rate is the annual rate of interest. Time is the fraction of a year that a note is outstanding.

When a note is written for a certain number of months, time is expressed in twelfths of a year. For example, interest on a three-month note for $4,000, with a 9 percent annual interest rate is:

$$\textbf{Interest = \$4,000} \times \textbf{0.09} \times \textbf{3/12 = \$90}$$

When a note's duration—that is, the length of the borrowing period—is given in days, time is expressed as a fraction of a year; the numerator is the number of days that the note will be outstanding and the denominator is 360 days. (Some lenders use 360 days, while others use 365 days; we will use 360 days in our examples.) For example, interest on a 60-day note for $3,000, with a 9 percent annual interest rate is:

$$\textbf{Interest = \$3,000} \times \textbf{0.09} \times \textbf{60/360 = \$45}$$

Determining the Maturity Date of a Note

When the duration of a note is expressed in months, the **maturity date** is determined by counting the number of months from the date of issue. For example, a two-month note dated January 31 matures on March 31, a three-month note of the same date matures on April 30 (the last day of the month), and a four-month note matures on May 31.

When a note's duration is expressed in days, the exact number of days in each calendar month is counted to determine the note's maturity date. For example, a 90-day note dated July 21 has an October 19 maturity date, determined as follows:

July (**remainder of month, 31 days minus 21 days**)	10 days
August	31 days
September	30 days
October (**number of days required to total 90**)	19 days
	90

Recording Notes Payable and Interest Expense

When a note payable is exchanged to settle an account payable, a journal entry is made to reflect the note payable and to reduce the balance of the related account payable. For example, suppose that the Jordon Company sold $12,000 of merchandise on account to Bowman Company. On October 1, after the regular credit period had expired, Bowman Company gave the

Jordon Company a 60-day, 9 percent note for $12,000. As a consequence, the Bowman Company makes the following journal entry on October 1:

A = L + SE
−12,000
+12,000

Oct. 1	Accounts payable—Jordon Company (−L)	12,000	
	Notes payable—Jordon Company (+L)		12,000
	Gave 60-day, 9 percent note in payment of account.		

If the Bowman Company pays the note on the November 30 maturity date, the company makes the following journal entry:

A = L + SE
−12,180 −12,000 −180
             Exp

Nov. 30	Notes payable—Jordon Company (−L)	12,000	
	Interest expense (+E, −SE)	180	
	Cash (−A)		12,180
	Paid note to Jordon Company ($12,000 × 0.09 × 60/360 = $180).		

Interest Payable

At the end of the fiscal year, adjusting entries must be made to reflect any accrued but unpaid interest expense. For example, assume that the Bowman Company has one note payable outstanding at December 31 to Garcia Company. The note dated December 21 has a principal amount of $6,000, an interest rate of 12 percent, and a maturity date of February 19 of the following year. The adjusting entry that Bowman Company makes at December 31 is as follows:

A = L + SE
   +20 −20
        Exp

Dec. 31	Interest expense (+E, −SE)	20	
	Interest payable (+L)		20
	To accrue interest expense on the note to Garcia Company		
	($6,000 × 0.12 × 10/360 = $20).		

When the note payable to Garcia Company is subsequently paid on February 19, the Bowman Company makes the following entry:

A = L + SE
−6,120 −6,000 −100
    −20 Exp

Feb. 19	Notes payable—Garcia Company (−L)	6,000	
	Interest payable (−L)	20	
	Interest expense (+E, −SE)	100	
	Cash (−A)		6,120
	Paid principal and interest to Garcia Company		
	($6,000 × 0.12 × 50/360 = $100).		

Current Portion of Long-Term Debt

The repayment of long-term obligations often involves a series of principal payment installments over several years. To report liabilities involving installments properly, any principal due within one year (or the operating cycle, if longer) is reported as a current liability on the balance sheet. For example, of Microsoft's total long-term debt of $58 billion, they report $8 billion as the current portion. Failure to reclassify the currently maturing portion of any long-term debt as a current liability can mislead readers regarding the total current obligations of a business.

Advance Payments—Unearned Revenue

Airline tickets, gift cards, cruise-line tickets, season football tickets, and cellular phone connection charges are examples of advance payments for services. A customer pays cash in advance for these services and the service provider agrees to provide future services. As an example, assume that **Southwest Airlines Co.** sells a ticket for $400 on March 20 for travel on May 25. Southwest makes the following entry when the ticket is sold:

A = L + SE
+400 +400

Mar. 20	Cash (+A)	400	
	Unearned ticket revenue (+L)		400
	To record the sale of an airline ticket.		

When the passenger takes the scheduled flight, the airline makes the following entry:

May 25	Unearned ticket revenue (–L)	400	
	Ticket revenue (+R, +SE)		400
	To record ticket revenue earned.		

$$A = L + SE$$
$$-400 \quad +400$$
$$Rev$$

Sales and Excise Taxes Payable

Many products and services are subject to sales and excise taxes. The laws governing these taxes usually require the selling firm to collect the tax at the time of sale and to send the collections periodically to the appropriate tax collection agency. For example, assume that a particular product selling for $1,000 is subject to a 6 percent state sales tax and a 10 percent federal excise tax. Each tax should be figured on the basic sale price only. The sale is recorded as follows:

Accounts receivable (*or* Cash) (+A)	1,160	
Sales revenue (+R, +SE)		1,000
Sales tax payable (+L)		60
Excise tax payable (+L)		100
To record sales and related taxes.		

$$A = L + SE$$
$$+1,160 \quad +60 \quad +1,000$$
$$+100 \quad Rev$$

The selling firm will periodically complete a tax reporting form and send the period's tax collections to the appropriate collection agency. The tax liability accounts are then debited and the Cash account is credited.

Payroll-Related Liabilities

Salaries and wages represent a major outlay in the cost structure of many businesses. For service firms, the largest expense category is usually the compensation paid to employees and the related payroll taxes and fringe benefits paid by the employer. Three types of current liabilities arise from a company's payroll: (1) accrued salaries and wages payable (discussed in Chapter 4), (2) amounts withheld from employees' paychecks by the employer, and (3) payroll taxes and fringe benefits paid by the employer.

Amounts Withheld from Employee Paychecks

When a business hires an employee, the firm establishes the employee's rate of pay. At the end of each pay period, the employer uses the employee's salary to determine the employee's **gross pay**, the amount earned before any withholdings. The employer then subtracts any withheld amounts to determine the employee's **net pay**, the amount of the paycheck. **Exhibit 10-1** demonstrates these relations.

Amounts Withheld by Legal Mandate Some amounts withheld from an employee's gross pay are mandated by law. These amounts include federal income tax, state income tax, Social Security taxes, and Medicare taxes.

The amount of federal income tax withheld from an employee's paycheck is determined by referencing a table that uses the amount of the employee's gross pay, the employee's marital status, and the number of withholding allowances claimed by the employee. Most states require employers to use similar information in calculating state income tax withholding, although not all states have an income tax.

The Federal Insurance Contributions Act (FICA) dictates the percentages to be used in calculating the withholding amounts for Social Security and Medicare. The rates for employee withholding for 2021 were 6.2 percent of the first $142,800 of gross pay for Social Security and 1.45 percent of all gross pay for Medicare.

Amounts Withheld by Employee Request Other amounts are withheld from an employee's gross pay by employee request. These amounts include premiums for life or health insurance, union dues, and payments into a self-funded retirement plan.

Recording Gross Pay and Net Pay

To illustrate the recording of employee gross and net pay, assume that the payroll for the week ended August 15 for Centerline Company totaled $6,000. Amounts withheld were $1,200 for federal income tax, $405 for state income tax, $372 for Social Security, and $87 for Medicare. In addition, Centerline withheld $100 for union dues and $320 for health insurance premiums. Centerline makes the following entry to record the payroll:

A	=	L	+	SE			
		+1,200		−6,000	Aug. 15	Salaries and wage expense (+E, −SE)	6,000	
		+405		Exp		Federal income tax withholding payable (+L)		1,200
		+459				State income tax withholding payable (+L)		405
		+100				FICA taxes payable (+L)		459
		+320				Union dues payable (+L)		100
		+3,516				Health insurance premiums payable (+L)		320
						Payroll payable (+L)		3,516
						To record the payroll for the week ended August 15.		

At the appropriate time, the employer will remit the amounts withheld from employees to the proper recipients. To the extent that any of the payable amounts are not paid at the end of an accounting period, they are reported as current liabilities.

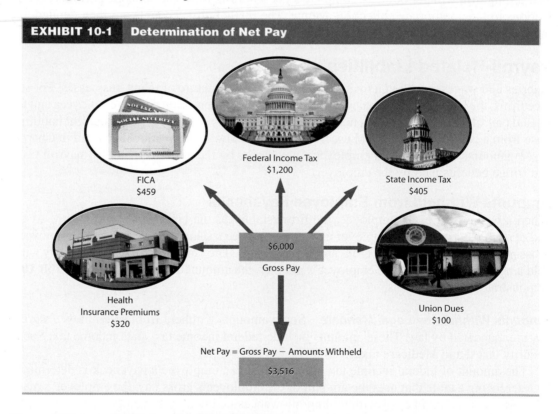

EXHIBIT 10-1   Determination of Net Pay

FICA $459

Federal Income Tax $1,200

State Income Tax $405

$6,000 Gross Pay

Health Insurance Premiums $320

Union Dues $100

Net Pay = Gross Pay − Amounts Withheld

$3,516

Payroll Taxes Paid by the Employer

An employer pays three types of taxes on the gross payroll amount: FICA taxes (Social Security and Medicare), federal unemployment tax, and state unemployment tax.

Each employer is required to pay an amount equal to the FICA taxes withheld from the employees' gross pay (2021 rates were 6.2 percent of the first $142,800 of gross pay for Social Security and 1.45 percent of gross pay for Medicare). As a result, the total Social Security collected in 2021 for each employee was 12.4 percent of the first $142,800 of gross pay, and the total Medicare collected was 2.9 percent of all gross pay.

Federal and state unemployment taxes are levied only on employers as a percentage of the gross payroll, subject to various limits. The current federal unemployment tax rate is 6.0 percent of the first $7,000 of an employee's gross pay. However, an employer is entitled to a credit against this tax for unemployment taxes paid to the state. The maximum credit allowed is 5.4 percent of the first $7,000 of gross pay. Many states set their basic unemployment tax rate at this maximum credit. In these states, the effective federal unemployment tax rate is 0.6 percent (6.0 percent − 5.4 percent), and the effective state unemployment tax rate is 5.4 percent.

Recording Payroll Taxes Paid by the Employer   Assume that the payroll for the week ended August 15 for Centerline Company totaled $6,000. Amounts withheld included $372 for Social Security and $87 for Medicare. Federal unemployment tax payable for the week was $36 (0.6 percent) and state unemployment tax payable was $324 (5.4 percent). Centerline makes the following entry to record its payroll taxes:

Aug. 15	Payroll tax expense (+E, −SE)	819	
	FICA taxes payable (+L)		459
	Federal unemployment tax payable (+L)		36
	State unemployment tax payable (+L)		324
	To record the payroll taxes for the week ended August 15.		

$$A = L + SE$$
$$+459 \quad -819$$
$$+36 \quad \text{Exp}$$
$$+324$$

If payroll taxes have not been remitted to the proper government agency by the end of the accounting period, they are classified as current liabilities in the balance sheet.

YOUR TURN! 10.1

MBC

The solution is on page 10-56.

Archer Corporation had the following payroll data for April:

Office salaries.	$ 40,000
Sales salaries.	86,000
Federal income taxes withheld.	25,600
Health insurance premiums withheld.	1,850
Union dues withheld.	950
Salaries (included above):	
Subject to both FICA taxes.	126,000
Subject to federal unemployment taxes.	76,000
Subject to state unemployment taxes.	88,000

Assume the combined FICA tax rate (for both employee withholding and employer) is 7.65 percent (6.2 percent plus 1.45 percent), the federal unemployment compensation tax rate is 0.6 percent, and the state unemployment compensation tax rate is 5.4 percent. The amounts subject to these taxes are given above.

Required

Prepare journal entries to record the following on April 30:

a. Accrual of the payroll.

b. Payment of the net payroll.

c. Accrual of the employer's payroll taxes.

d. Payment of all liabilities related to the payroll. (Assume that all liabilities are paid at the same time.)

Income Taxes Payable

The U.S. federal government, most states, and some municipalities levy income taxes against corporations, individuals, estates, and trusts. Sole proprietorships and partnerships are not taxable entities—their owners include any business income on the owner's personal income tax return.

The tax due is determined in accordance with tax law, rulings by taxing agencies, and court decisions. Because the administration of tax law is quite complex and many honest differences exist in their interpretation, the tax obligation reported on a tax return is only an estimate until the government reviews and accepts a firm's (or individual's) calculations.

Because corporations are separate taxable entities, they incur a legal obligation for income taxes whenever income is earned. Therefore, corporate financial statements routinely include income tax liabilities. For example, business income taxes of $8,000 are recorded as follows:

A = L + SE
   +8,000 −8,000
         Exp

Income tax expense (+E, −SE)	8,000	
Income tax payable (+L)		8,000
To record estimated income tax.		

Corporations usually pay their estimated income taxes quarterly, with an annual tax return and final payment due within a few months following the end of a calendar year. Thus, any liability for income taxes in the financial statements is classified as a current liability since payment is expected in the short term.

Data Analytics

DATA ANALYTICS   **Power of Data Analytics for Managing Procurement**

In most large businesses, the accounts payable function represents a very large volume of transactions and a significant percentage of the business's costs. Although most business have a variety of controls in place to manage this process, payment errors still do occur. While these errors as a percentage of total invoices may be very small, the total dollar amounts can still be meaningful to the business's overall profitability. The accounting firm, **Deloitte**, believes using data analytics can help uncover invalid payments and at the same time protect the business from future erroneous invoices. They have developed a sophisticated software package that tests, scores, and then presents the findings to allow interactive views of all suspect vendors, invoices, or payments, thus helping manage this very important function.

LONG-TERM LIABILITIES

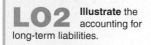

LO2 **Illustrate** the accounting for long-term liabilities.

eLecture

MBC

Most businesses will need to secure long-term funds to finance operations or acquire operating assets. When a business elects to finance with long-term debt, it may do so by borrowing money with long-term notes or issuing bonds. An obligation in the form of a written note due after the current period is referred to as a **term loan** or long-term note payable. The borrower typically signs a note payable and the debt is referred to as a term loan. While long-term notes are usually arranged with a single lender, bonds are usually issued to a large number of buyers. A **bond** is a long-term debt instrument that promises to pay interest periodically as well as a principal amount at maturity, to the bond investor. In the United States, bond interest is usually paid semiannually. The principal amount is referred to as the bond's face value because it is printed on the face of the bond certificate.

Long-Term Notes (Term Loans)

Term loans are often repaid in equal periodic installments. The agreement may require installment payments to be made monthly, quarterly, or semiannually. Each payment contains an interest amount and a partial repayment of principal. Because the installment payments are equal, the amounts that are allocated to interest and principal repayments change over time because the interest is computed on the unpaid principal, and the unpaid principal is reduced with each payment.

To illustrate, assume that on December 31, 2021, Reid, Inc., borrows $100,000 from a bank on a 12 percent, 10-year mortgage note payable. The note is to be repaid with equal quarterly installments of $4,326 (please see Appendix E for explanation on how to do this calculation). Thus, there will be 40 quarterly payments, and the quarterly interest rate is 3 percent (12 percent/4 quarters). **Exhibit 10-2** presents the first eight quarterly payments (of the complete 40 quarterly payment schedule) and their division between interest expense and principal repayment. As the book value of the note declines over time (column D), the amount of interest expense also declines (column B). As a result, the amount of the fixed quarterly cash payment (column A) that is applied to repayment of the principal increases over time (column C). The entries to record the mortgage note payable and the first quarterly payment follow:

2021			
Dec. 31	Cash (+A)	100,000	
	Mortgage note payable (+L)		100,000
	To record mortgage loan.		

A = L + SE
100,000 100,000

2022			
Mar. 31	Interest expense (+E, −SE)	3,000	
	Mortgage note payable (−L)	1,326	
	Cash (−A)		4,326
	To record quarterly mortgage loan payment.		

A = L + SE
−4,326 −1,326 −3,000
Exp

EXHIBIT 10-2   Partial Mortgage Note Payment Schedule

**$100,000 mortgage note payable with quarterly payments
of $4,326 and quarterly interest rate of 3 percent**

Payment Date	A Cash Payment	B Interest Expense (3% × D)*	C Principal Repaid (A − B)	D Book Value of Note (Unpaid Principal)
2021				
December 31 (issue date). . . .				$100,000
2022				
March 31.	$4,326	$3,000	$1,326	98,674
June 30.	4,326	2,960	1,366	97,308
September 30	4,326	2,919	1,407	95,901
December 31	4,326	2,877	1,449	94,452
2023				
March 31.	4,326	2,834	1,492	92,960
June 30	4,326	2,789	1,537	91,423
September 30	4,326	2,743	1,583	89,840
December 31	4,326	2,695	1,631	88,209

* Three percent × unpaid principal after previous payment (rounded to nearest dollar).

Types of Bonds

Companies issue different types of bonds to capitalize on certain lending situations, appeal to special investor groups, or provide special repayment patterns.

Secured bonds, for example, pledge specific property as security for meeting the terms of the bond agreement. The specific title of the bonds may indicate the type of property pledged—for example, real estate mortgage bonds (land or buildings), chattel mortgage bonds (machinery or equipment), and collateral trust bonds (negotiable securities).

Bonds that have no specific property pledged as security for their repayment are called **debenture bonds.** Buyers of debenture bonds rely on a borrower's general credit reputation. Because a lender's risk is usually greater than with secured bonds, the sale of unsecured bonds may require offering a higher rate of interest to attract bond buyers.

The maturity dates of **serial bonds** are staggered over a series of years. For example, a serial bond issue of $15 million may provide for $1 million of the bonds to mature each year for 15 years. An advantage of serial bonds is that bond investors can choose bonds with maturity dates that correspond with their desired length of investment.

Sinking fund bonds require that a borrower make payments each year to a trustee who is responsible for managing the funds needed to retire the bonds at maturity. The orderly retirement of bonds, or the accumulation of funds needed at maturity, as required by a sinking fund provision is generally viewed as making any bond safer (less risky) for the bondholders.

Convertible bonds grant the bondholder the right to convert the bonds into a company's common stock at some specific exchange (or conversion) ratio. This provision gives an investor the security of being a creditor during a certain stage of a firm's life, with the option of becoming a stockholder if the firm becomes sufficiently profitable. Because the conversion feature is attractive to potential investors, a company may issue convertible bonds at a lower interest rate than it would pay without the conversion feature.

Callable bonds allow the bond issuer to call in the bonds for redemption. Usually, an extra amount or premium must be paid to the holders of a called bond. A call provision offers borrowers additional financing flexibility that may be significant if funds become available at interest rates substantially lower than those currently being paid on the bonds. Borrowers can, in effect, also "call" any of their bonds by buying them on the open market.

ACCOUNTING IN PRACTICE   **Bond Risk Ratings**

The relative riskiness of different bonds may vary considerably. Bond investors who want to know the relative quality of a particular bond issue can consult a bond-rating service. Two major firms that rate the riskiness of bonds are **Standard & Poor's Corporation** (S&P) and **Moody's Investors Service** (Moody's). The rating categories used by these firms are similar. The schedule below shows the relation between the ratings and the degree of risk using Standard & Poor's rating system:

Low Risk							High Risk
AAA	AA	A	BBB	BB	B	CCC	D

|- - - - - - - - - Investment Grade Bonds - - - - - - - - -|- - - - - - - - - Junk Bonds - - - - - - - - -|

Investment grade bonds are highly rated bonds with little risk that the issuing company will fail to pay interest as scheduled or fail to repay the principal at a bond's maturity. Junk bonds, on the other hand, are low-quality, high-yield bonds. In the S&P rating system, junk bonds are any bonds rated BB and lower. Generally, bonds with poor credit ratings must offer higher interest rates than highly rated bonds to attract potential buyers.

A.K.A. Junk bonds are often referred to as **high-yield bonds** because of the higher yield rates that typically accompany this type of debt investment.

Bond Prices

A.K.A. A bond's face value is also referred to as its **maturity value**, stated value, par value, or settlement value.

Bonds are typically sold in units (denominations) of $1,000 face (maturity) value, and the market price is expressed as a percentage of **face value**. Thus, a $1,000 face value bond that is quoted at 98 will sell for $980. For example, in the bond certificate illustrated in **Exhibit 10-3**, shows that Walmart issued a total of $2 billion of unsecured bonds in minimum denominations of $2,000. The bonds were priced (issued) at 99.645. Generally, bond prices fluctuate in response to changes in market interest rates, which are determined by government monetary policies (managing the demand and supply of money) and economic expectations. Bond prices are also affected by the financial outlook for the issuing firm and the specific features of the bond being issued, as discussed previously.

A.K.A. A bond's coupon rate of interest is also referred to as its nominal rate or stated rate of interest.

A bond specifies a pattern of future cash flows, usually a series of interest payments and a single payment at maturity equal to the bond's face value. The amount of the periodic interest payment is determined by the **coupon rate** stated on the bond certificate. The Walmart bonds have a coupon rate of 1.8 percent. Interest rates are usually quoted as annual rates, so the coupon rate will need to be converted to a per period interest rate when interest is paid more than once a year. For example, in the U.S., bond interest is usually paid semiannually, with the payments six months apart. The Walmart bonds pay interest semiannually on March 22 and September 22 of each year. Thus, the amount of interest paid semiannually is calculated by multiplying one-half the coupon rate of interest times the bond's face value.

A.K.A. A bond's market rate of interest is also referred to as its real rate of interest or its effective yield rate.

A bond's market price is determined by discounting the bond's future cash flows (both its principal and its interest payments) to the present using the current **market rate of interest** for the bond as the discount rate, a process known as *computing the bond's present value*. The market rate is the rate of return investors expect on their investment.

EXHIBIT 10-3	Bond Certificate

Walmart Inc. ◄——— Bond Issuer

$2,000,000,000 ◄——— Face value

1.8% Notes due 2031 ◄——— Coupon rate

Issue price: 99.645%

We will pay interest on the notes semiannually on March 22 and September 22 of each year, beginning March 22, 2022. The notes will mature on September 22, 2031. The notes will be redeemable, as a whole or in part, at our option. ◄——— Maturity date

The notes will be senior unsecured obligations and rank equally with our other senior unsecured debt securities. The notes will be issued in minimum denominations of $2,000 and multiples of $1,000 in excess thereof.

Neither the Securities and Exchange Commission nor any state securities commission has approved or disapproved of the notes or determined if this prospectus supplement or the accompanying prospectus is truthful or complete. Any representation to the contrary is a criminal offense.

	Per Note	Total
Public Offering Price (1)	99.645%	$1,992,900,000
Underwriting Discounts	.450%	$ 9,000,000
Proceeds to Walmart	99.195%	$1,983,900,000

(1) Plus accrued interest if any, from September 22, 2021.

The underwriters expect to deliver the notes in book-entry form only through the facilities of The Depository Trust Company, for the credit of the accounts of its direct and indirect participants, including Clearstream Banking, S.A. and Euroclear Bank SA/NV on or about September 22, 2021.

Joint Book-Running Managers

AmeriVet Securities	**BofA Securities**	**Citigroup**	**C.L. King & Associates**
	Green Structuring Agent		

Morgan Stanley	**Ramirez & Co., Inc.**	**Siebert Williams Shank**

Senior Co-Managers

BBVA	**Goldman Sachs & Co., LLC**	**Santander**
Scotiabank	**Standard Chartered Bank**	**US Bancorp**

Co-Managers

Barclays	BNP PARIBA	Credit Suisse	NatWest Markets	SMBC Nikko	TD Securities
Academy Securities	CastleOak Securities, L.P.	Guzman & Company	ICBC Standard Bank	Lloyds Securities	Loop Capital Markets

---

THINKING GLOBALLY

U.S. GAAP and IFRS are substantially aligned when it comes to the reporting of liabilities. Under both accounting systems, for example, current liabilities, like Accounts Payable, are reported at their settlement or future value, or the amount of money required to satisfy the obligation when it becomes due. Similarly, both systems require that long-term liabilities, like Bonds Payable, be reported at their present value. Where the two systems diverge is in regard to the reporting of some contingent liabilities (to be discussed shortly).

The **effective interest rate** is the market rate of interest used to price the bonds when they are originally issued. A bond's price may be equal to, less than, or greater than its face value. Bonds sell at *face value* when the market rate of interest equals the bond's coupon rate. Bonds sell at a *discount* (less than face value) when the market interest rate exceeds the bond's coupon rate, and bonds sell at a *premium* (more than face value) when the market interest rate is less than the bond's coupon rate.

Since bonds are usually printed on one date and sold at a later date, the market rate and coupon rate will often differ due to a change in market interest rates after the bonds are printed. Market rates and coupon rates are frequently stated in percentage terms, although increasingly, these rates are stated as "basis points." One percentage point is equal to 100 basis points. Thus, a bond with a coupon rate of 3 percent is said to have a coupon rate of 300 basis points.

Exhibit 10-4 shows the calculation of a bond's selling price using different market rates of interest. (See Appendix 10A for a discussion of the calculation of a bond's present value.) The bond is a $1,000, 8 percent annual coupon rate, four-year bond with interest payable semiannually. The periodic interest payment is $40 ($1,000 × 0.08 × 1/2).

EXHIBIT 10-4	Calculation of Bond Selling Price at Different Market Rates		
Four-year $1,000 bond, 8 percent annual coupon rate, interest payable semiannually. Eight semiannual interest payments of $40 ($1,000 × 0.08 × 1/2)			
	Yield Rate, Compounded Semiannually		
	10%	8%	6%
Present value of $1,000 at maturity			
$1,000 × 0.67684 present value factor* ..... =	$677		
$1,000 × 0.73069 present value factor ...... =		$ 731	
$1,000 × 0.78941 present value factor ...... =			$ 789
Present value of eight $40 interest payments (rounded to nearest dollar)			
$40 × 6.46321 present value factor* .... =	259		
$40 × 6.73274 present value factor .... =		269	
$40 × 7.01969 present value factor .... =			281
Bond selling price......................	$936	$1,000	$1,070
Bond priced at	Discount	Face value	Premium

*See Appendix 10A for a discussion of present value factors.

As shown in the exhibit, the bond will:

1. Sell at a *discount* ($936 bond price) when the market rate (10 percent) exceeds the coupon rate (8 percent).

2. Sell at *face value* ($1,000 bond price) when the market rate (8 percent) equals the coupon rate (8 percent).

3. Sell at a *premium* ($1,070 bond price) when the market rate (6 percent) is less than the coupon rate (8 percent).

Bond coupon rate	Market rate of interest is	Bond will sell at
Bond coupon rate is 8 percent Sold when	10 percent	Discount
	8 percent	Face Value
	6 percent	Premium

Recording Bonds

Bonds Issued at Face Value

To provide a simple illustration, we use a bond with a short period to maturity. Assume that on December 31, 2021, Reid, Inc., issues at face value $100,000 of 8 percent bonds that mature in four years with interest paid on June 30 and December 31. The following entry records the bond, which is sold at its face value:

2021				
Dec. 31	Cash (+A)	100,000		
	Bonds payable (+L)		100,000	
	To record the issuance of bonds.			

A	=	L	+ SE
+100,000		+100,000	

Interest of $4,000 ($100,000 × 0.08 × 6/12) will be paid on each of the eight payment dates (four years, semiannual payments). For example, the entry on June 30, 2022, the first interest payment date, is:

2022				
June 30	Bond interest expense (+E, −SE)	4,000		
	Cash (−A)		4,000	
	To record the payment of semiannual interest on bonds.			

A	=	L	+	SE
−4,000				−4,000
				Exp

When the bonds mature, Reid, Inc., records their retirement as follows (this assumes the December 31 interest payment has already been recorded):

2022				
Dec. 31	Bonds payable (−L)	100,000		
	Cash (−A)		100,000	
	To record the retirement of bonds.			

A	=	L	+ SE
−100,000		−100,000	

Issuance between Interest Dates

Not all bonds are sold on the exact day on which their interest payment period begins. Investors who buy bonds after the interest period begins are expected to "buy" any interest that has accrued on the bonds. Such bonds are said to be sold at a given price "plus accrued interest." The accrued interest is returned to the investor at the next interest payment date. This procedure simplifies the bond issuer's administrative work. Regardless of when bonds are issued, a full six months' interest is paid to all bondholders on each interest payment date.

To illustrate, assume that Reid, Inc., sold its $100,000, 8 percent, four-year bonds at 100 plus accrued interest on February 28, 2022, instead of on December 31, 2021. The following journal entry is made:

2022				
Feb. 28	Cash (+A)	101,333		
	Bonds payable (+L)		100,000	
	Bond interest payable (+L)		1,333	
	To record bond issuance at 100 plus two months' accrued interest.			

A	=	L	+ SE
+101,333		+100,000	
		+1,333	

The interest accrued on the bonds on February 28 is $1,333 ($100,000 × 0.08 × 2/12, rounded). On the first interest payment date, June 30, 2022, Reid, Inc., makes the following entry:

2022				
June 30	Bond interest payable (−L)	1,333		
	Bond interest expense (+E, −SE)	2,667		
	Cash (−A)		4,000	
	To record the payment of semiannual interest on bonds payable.			

A	=	L	+	SE
−4,000		−1,333		−2,667
				Exp

Bond interest expense recorded by Reid relates only to the four months since the bonds were issued.

Bonds Issued at a Discount

If the coupon rate of interest on the bonds issued is less than the current market rate, the bonds will be sold at a price less than their face value. In such cases, investors "discount" the price of the bonds to enable the buyer to earn the current market rate of interest. For example, assume that Reid, Inc.'s $100,000 issue of 8 percent, four-year bonds is sold on December 31, 2021, for $93,537. This price permits investors to earn an effective interest rate of 10 percent even though the bonds are only paying a cash coupon rate of 8 percent.

(For calculations, please see Appendix 10A.) The following entry records the issuance of the bonds at a discount:

A	=	L	+ SE
+93,537		−6,463	
		+100,000	

Cash		Bonds Payable	
93,537			100,000

Disc. on Bonds	
6,463	

2021				
Dec. 31	Cash (+A)		93,537	
	Discount on bonds payable (+XL, −L)		**6,463**	
	Bonds payable (+L)			100,000
	To record the issuance of bonds.			

Discount on Bonds Payable is a contra account that reduces the value of Bonds Payable on the balance sheet. The $6,463 discount is not a loss or an expense to Reid, Inc. Instead, it represents an adjustment to interest expense that will be made over the life of the bonds. This can be illustrated by comparing the funds that Reid, Inc., receives with the funds it must pay to the bondholders. Regardless of their selling price, the bonds represent an agreement to pay $132,000 to the bondholders ($100,000 principal at maturity plus eight semiannual interest payments of $4,000 each).

Total funds paid to bondholders	$132,000
Total funds received from bond sale.	(93,537)
Difference equals total interest expense.	38,463
Total semiannual interest payments ([$100,000 × 8% = $8,000] × 4 years). . . .	(32,000)
Increase in interest expense beyond semiannual interest payments	
(***bond discount***).	$ 6,463

The total interest expense for this four-year bond issue is $38,463, the difference between the total cash paid to the bondholders and the proceeds from the sale of the bonds. The semiannual interest payments to bondholders total $32,000, so an additional $6,463 must be recognized as interest expense over the life of the bonds. The $6,463 is the amount of the bond discount. To reflect the larger periodic interest expense, the bond discount is *amortized over the eight interest payment periods*. Amortization of a bond discount means that, periodically, an amount is transferred from the Discount on Bonds Payable account to the Bond Interest Expense account.

There are two methods of bond amortization: the straight-line method and the effective interest method. Under the **straight-line interest method**, equal amounts are transferred from bond discount to interest expense for each interest payment period. The **effective interest method**, on the other hand, reflects a constant rate of interest over the life of the bonds. Appendix 10A illustrates both methods, but the effective interest method is the more commonly used accounting method for bond amortization.

Zero-coupon bonds are a special type of discount bond. As the name implies, these bonds pay no periodic interest payments, which causes them to be issued at a substantial discount from their face value. The face value is paid to the bondholder at maturity. The total interest implicit in the bond contract is the difference between the bond's original issue price and its face value at maturity. For example, a five-year, $1,000 zero-coupon bond issued for $713 will pay the lender $1,000 at the end of the five years. The total interest associated with this bond is $287 ($1,000 − $713). Zero-coupon bonds are particularly helpful to a borrower when the project being financed with the bond proceeds provides no cash inflows until the bond maturity date.

Bonds Issued at a Premium

If the coupon rate of interest is higher than the current market rate, the bonds will be sold at a price that exceeds their face value. For example, suppose that the effective interest rate was 6 percent. Reid Inc.'s $100,000, 8 percent, four-year bonds would sell for $107,020 (for calculations, please see Appendix 10A). The issuance of the bonds on December 31, 2021, is recorded as follows:

2021				
Dec. 31	Cash (+A)	107,020		
	Bonds payable (+L)		100,000	
	Premium on bonds payable (+XL, +L)		**7,020**	
	To record issuance of bonds.			

A	=	L	+ SE
+107,020		+100,000	
		+7,020	

Cash	Bonds Payable
107,020	100,000

	Prem. on Bonds
	7,020

When bonds are issued at a premium, the book value of the bond liability is determined by adding the Premium on Bonds Payable account balance to the Bonds Payable account balance.

Premium on Bonds Payable is a contra account that increases the value of Bonds Payable on the balance sheet. Like a bond discount, a bond premium is considered an adjustment of interest expense over the life of the bonds. We saw that a bond discount represents the excess of total interest expense over the total semiannual interest payments. A similar analysis shows that a bond premium represents the amount by which the total semiannual interest payments exceed the total interest expense. The analysis begins by comparing the total funds that will be paid to the bondholders over the four years (again, it is $132,000) with the proceeds received when the bonds are issued:

Total funds paid to bondholders	$132,000
Total funds received from bond sale.	(107,020)
Difference equals total interest expense.	24,980
Total semiannual interest payments ([$100,000 × 8% = $8,000] × 4 years).	(32,000)
Decrease in interest expense below semiannual interest payments **(*bond premium*)**.	**$ 7,020**

The total interest expense for this four-year bond issue is $24,980, an amount that is $7,020 less than the total semiannual interest payments to be made to bondholders. The $7,020 is the amount of the bond premium. The bond premium is amortized to cause the periodic interest expense to be less than the semiannual interest payment.

Year-End Adjustments

When a periodic interest payment does not correspond with the fiscal year-end, an adjusting entry should be recorded reflecting the amount of interest expense incurred but not yet recorded. The adjusting entry includes a pro rata amortization of bond discount or bond premium for the portion of the year involved.

ENVIRONMENTAL, SOCIAL, AND GOVERNANCE   **Financing Green Investment**

Being a "green" company takes a lot of green—money that is. **Walmart** created their Green Financing Framework to finance investments that will enable the company to meet its environmental objectives. Their Framework is designed to meet the best practice guidelines of the International Capital Markets Association (ICMA) Green Bond Principles. In September 2021, Walmart launched its inaugural $2 billion green bond offering to fund current and future projects to advance the company's sustainability goals (see **Exhibit 10-3**). The bonds fund investment in renewable energy, high performance buildings, sustainable transport, zero waste projects, water stewardship, and habitat restoration and conservation.

Bonds Payable Disclosed on the Balance Sheet

Bonds payable that mature more than one year in the future are classified as long-term liabilities on the balance sheet. Bonds payable maturing within the next year are classified as current liabilities. Discount on Bonds Payable and Premium on Bonds Payable are contra accounts that adjust the value of Bonds Payable on the balance sheet. Discount on Bonds Payable is a deduction from face value and Premium on Bonds Payable is an addition to face value. Many companies do not separately disclose the Discount on Bonds Payable account or the Premium on Bonds Payable account on their balance sheet, but rather net these amounts against the Bonds Payable account.

At December 31, 2022, the Reid, Inc., bonds issued at a discount (see **Exhibit 10A-4**) appear on Reid's balance sheet as follows:

Bonds payable	$100,000
Less: Discount on bonds payable	6,463
Bonds payable, net	$ 93,537

On the same date, the Reid, Inc., bonds issued at a premium (see **Exhibit 10A-5**) appear as follows:

Bonds payable	$100,000
Add: Premium on bonds payable	7,020
Bonds payable, net	$107,020

Retirement of Bonds before Maturity

Bonds are usually retired at their maturity dates with a journal entry debiting the Bonds Payable account and crediting the Cash account for the face value of the bonds. However, bonds can be retired before maturity—for example, to take advantage of more attractive financing terms. In accounting for the retirement of bonds before maturity, the following steps are used:

1. Remove the book value of the bonds being retired from the accounts (that is, remove the Bonds Payable amount and any related bond premium or discount).

2. Record the cash paid to retire the bonds.

3. Recognize any difference between the bonds' book value and the cash paid as a gain or loss on bond retirement.

To illustrate, assume that the Reid, Inc., bonds issued at a premium for $107,020 in our previous example were called for retirement at 105 at the end of 2024, after paying the semiannual interest on December 31, 2024. According to **Exhibit 10A-5**, the bonds' book value at the end of 2024 is $101,915. The following entry records the bond retirement:

A	=	L	+	SE
−105,000		−100,000		−3,085
		−1,915		Loss

Cash		Bonds Payable
105,000		100,000

Loss on Retire.		Prem. on Bonds
3,085		1,915

2024			
Dec. 31	Bonds payable (−L)	100,000	
	Premium on bonds payable (−XL, −L)	1,915	
	Loss on bond retirement (+LOSS, −SE)	3,085	
	Cash (−A)		105,000
	To retire bonds at 105 and record loss on retirement.		

YOUR TURN! 10.2

GuidedExample

MBC

The solution is on page 10-57.

Koby Company issued $300,000 of bonds for $325,000. (a) Prepare the journal entry to record the issuance of the bonds, and (b) illustrate how the bonds will be shown on the Koby Company's balance sheet at the issuance date.

Advantages and Disadvantages of Long-Term Bonds and Notes

Issuing bonds and notes versus issuing common stock is an alternative way for a corporation to obtain needed long-term funds. The advantages of obtaining long-term funds by issuing bonds and notes instead of common stock include:

1. **No dilution of ownership interest.** Bondholders and noteholders are creditors, not shareholders, of a corporation. Issuing bonds and notes rather than common stock maintains the number of outstanding shares of stock at their current level.

2. **Tax deductibility of interest expense.** Interest expense is deductible as an expense on a corporation's income tax return. Dividend payments to shareholders are not tax deductible.

3. **Income available to common shareholders can increase.** **Leverage** refers to the use of borrowed funds, particularly long-term debt, to finance a business's growth. When a firm is able to earn a return on its borrowed funds that exceeds the cost of borrowing the funds, then leverage is said to build shareholder value.

For example, assume that a firm can earn 15 percent on a $5,000,000 project financed by issuing bonds and notes that have a 10 percent interest rate. If the firm pays income taxes at a 20 percent rate, its net income will increase $200,000 each year, as follows:

Earnings on funds borrowed: 15 percent × $5,000,000	$750,000
Interest cost on funds borrowed: 10 percent × $5,000,000	**(500,000)**
Increase in income before income tax expense	$250,000
Income tax expense on increase: 20 percent × $250,000	**(50,000)**
Increase in net income	$200,000

The $200,000 increase in net income accrues exclusively to the company's common shareholders.

Not all aspects of issuing bonds and notes, however, are necessarily desirable for the borrowing company. Among the disadvantages of issuing bonds and notes are the following:

1. **Interest expense is a contractual obligation.** In contrast to dividends on common stock, interest represents a fixed periodic expenditure that the firm is contractually obligated to pay. In the previous example, if the project earns less than 10 percent, say 8 percent, the company is still obligated to pay interest on the borrowed funds at 10 percent. This shortfall will reduce income available to common shareholders.

2. **Funds borrowed have a specific repayment date.** Because bonds and notes normally have a defined maturity date, the borrower has a specific obligation to repay the borrowings at maturity. There is no obligation to return funds to shareholders by a specific date.

3. **The borrowing agreement can restrict company actions.** The legal document setting forth the terms of a debt issue is called an *indenture*. Some of the provisions in an indenture may involve restrictions on dividend payments, restrictions on additional financing, and specification of minimum financial ratios that must be maintained. These provisions, called *debt covenants*, are intended to provide protection for debtholders by limiting a company's flexibility to act.

ACCOUNTING IN PRACTICE　　　　　　　**Why Issue Bonds? Or Is Debt Really Bad?**

The opening vignette of this chapter mentions that **Microsoft**, a company with seemingly no need to borrow money, issued bonds to obtain additional cash. Microsoft is not alone in this behavior. **Apple**, on its 2020 balance sheet, reported just over $90 billion in cash and marketable securities. Still, Apple has continued to issue debt, reporting almost $100 billion on its 2020 balance sheet. Nearly all of this debt was raised in the past few years. Why would companies like Microsoft and Apple take on more debt when they clearly have sufficient cash on hand? As finance theory teaches us, as long as a company can earn a higher rate of return on borrowed funds than the cost of those funds, the excess returns flow to the shareholders in the way of a higher return on equity.

CONTINGENT LIABILITIES

LO3 **Define** contingent liabilities and **explain** the rules for their accounting and disclosure in the financial statements.

eLecture

MBC

Previously, we defined a liability as an obligation resulting from past transactions or events that require a firm to pay money, provide goods, or perform services in the future. Even though a past transaction or event has taken place, the existence of some liabilities still depends on the occurrence of a future event. These types of liabilities are called **contingent liabilities.** Whether or not a contingent liability is recorded depends on the likelihood of the future event occurring and the measurability of the obligation.

If the future event will *probably occur* and the amount of the liability is known or can be *reasonably estimated,* an estimated liability should be recorded. The estimated liability for product warranties is a good example of this situation. Many firms guarantee their products for a period of time following their sale. Customers are likely to make claims under a warranty for goods that they had purchased, and a reasonable estimate of the amount of the warranty obligation can usually be made.

Some contingent liabilities are not recorded but must be disclosed in a note to the financial statements. Contingent liabilities disclosed in this manner are (1) those for which the likelihood of the future event occurring is probable but no reasonable estimate of the future obligation can be made or (2) those for which the likelihood of the future event occurring is only *reasonably possible* (but not probable), regardless of the ability to measure the future amount. When the future amount is not determinable, the note should state that the amount cannot be estimated.

PRINCIPLE ALERT   **Measuring Unit Concept and Full Disclosure Principle**

The accounting guidelines for contingent liabilities illustrate the application of two principles of accounting: the *measuring unit concept* and the *full disclosure principle.* The measuring unit concept requires that information reported in the body of the financial statements be expressed in money terms. If a reasonable estimate of a contingent liability's dollar amount cannot be made, the measuring unit concept prevents the item from appearing in the balance sheet, even if its future occurrence is probable. However, the full disclosure principle requires that firms disclose all significant financial facts and circumstances to financial statement users. This principle leads to the reporting of likely but unmeasurable contingent liabilities in the notes to the financial statements.

If the likelihood of the future event occurring is *remote,* the contingent liability is neither recorded in the accounts nor disclosed in the notes to the financial statements, regardless of the ability to measure the future amount. One exception to this guideline, however, is when a company guarantees the credit of others (discussed in the following section). Even remote contingent liabilities associated with credit guarantees must be disclosed in the notes to the financial statements. **Exhibit 10-5** summarizes when contingent liabilities should be recorded or disclosed.

EXHIBIT 10-5   When contingent liabilities should be recorded or disclosed

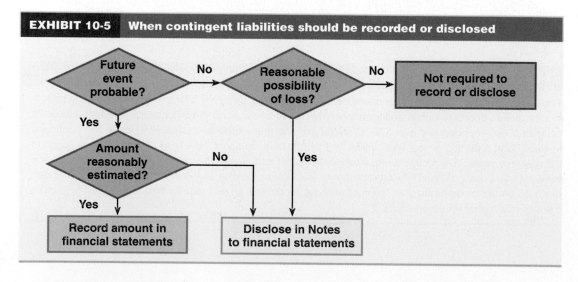

Examples of Contingent Liabilities

Situations that may create contingent liabilities are discussed in the following sections. In each of these situations, accountants must assess the likelihood of the future event occurring and the measurability of the future amount because these factors determine the proper accounting treatment of the contingent liability.

Product Warranties

A proper matching of sales revenue and expenses requires that the estimated cost of **product warranties** be recognized as an expense in the period of sale rather than in a later period when the warranty costs are actually incurred and paid.

To illustrate, assume that a firm sells a product for $300 per unit, which includes a 30-day warranty against defects. Past experience indicates that 3 percent of the units will prove defective and that the average repair cost will be $40 per defective unit. Furthermore, during a particular month, product sales were $240,000, and 13 of the units sold during the month were defective and were repaired. Using this information, the accrued liability for product warranties at the end of the month is calculated as follows:

Number of units sold ($240,000/$300)	800
Rate of projected defective units	× 0.03
Total units expected to fail	24
Less: Units that failed in the month of sale	13
Units expected to fail in the remainder of the warranty period	11
Average repair cost per unit	× $40
Estimated liability for product warranty at end of month	$440

This accrued liability is recorded at the end of the month of sale as follows:

Product warranty expense (+E, −SE)	440	
Estimated liability for product warranty (+L)		440
To record estimated warranty expense		

A	=	L	+	SE
		+440		−440
				Exp

When a unit fails in a future period, the repair costs will be recorded by debiting the Estimated Liability for Product Warranty account and crediting Cash, Supplies, and so forth.

PRINCIPLE ALERT   **Matching Concept**

The accounting for product warranties follows the *expense recognition (matching) concept.* This accounting concept states that expenses must be recorded in the same accounting period as the revenues they help generate. Product warranties make a company's products more attractive to buyers; consequently, product warranties help generate incremental sales revenues. Hence, one of the expenses that must be matched with sales revenues is the cost of honoring and servicing a product warranty. Because most warranty costs are incurred in periods following the period of sale, it is necessary to estimate these costs and record them in the same period when the sale of the product occurs to achieve a proper matching of revenues and expenses.

Lawsuits

In the course of its operations, a firm may be a defendant in one or more lawsuits involving potentially material financial settlements. Examples of litigation issues include product liability, patent infringement, unfair labor practices and environmental matters. The resolution of a lawsuit may take many years. During the time a lawsuit is pending, the defendant has a contingent liability for any future financial settlement although it is impossible in most cases to arrive at a reasonable estimate of a company's possible losses. For this reason, lawsuit liabilities are most commonly disclosed in the notes to the financial statements.

Environmental Cleanup Costs

Past actions by many companies in disposing of various types of industrial waste have caused subsequent environmental damage. Some estimates of the total cleanup costs for the United States run as high as $100 billion. Firms owning sites that require environmental remediation or that may require cleanup face a contingent liability for the remediation costs. Cleanup costs for a particular site may be very difficult to estimate. The party responsible for bearing the cost—the company or its insurance company—may also be at issue.

Credit Guarantees

To accommodate important but less financially secure suppliers or customers, a firm may create a **credit guarantee** by cosigning a note payable. Until the original debtor satisfies the obligation, the cosigning firm is contingently liable for the debt. Even when the likelihood of default by a debtor is considered remote, the contingent liability associated with credit guarantees must be disclosed in the notes to the financial statements.

THINKING GLOBALLY

The accounting for some contingent liabilities under U.S. GAAP and IFRS differs significantly. For example, under U.S. GAAP, purchase commitments—that is, an agreement by one company to buy merchandise from another company at a future date—are not reported on the balance sheet but, if material in amount, are disclosed in the notes to the financial statements. Under IFRS, however, purchase commitments are reported on the balance sheet when a company has a clear and demonstrable commitment to a second company to buy its goods. In essence, IFRS adopts a broader definition of what constitutes an accounting liability than does U.S. GAAP. Under U.S. GAAP, while purchase commitments are acknowledged to be economic liabilities of a business, they do not constitute an accounting liability until an exchange of assets occurs between the two companies.

Summary of Accounting Treatment for Liabilities

Exhibit 10-6 summarizes the accounting for different types of liabilities according to their unique characteristics.

EXHIBIT 10-6	Liabilities: Criteria and Financial Statement Treatment				
Characteristics That Determine the Type of Liability and How It Is Recorded or Disclosed	**Recorded in Accounts and Reported on Balance Sheet**		**Disclosed in Footnote to Financial Statements**		**No Disclosure Required**
	Noncontingent	**Contingent**	**Contingent**	**Contingent**	**Contingent**
Dependent on future event...	No	No	Yes	Yes	Yes	Yes
Likelihood of future event..............	Already occurred	Already occurred	**Probable**	**Probable**	**Reasonably possible**	**Remote**
Amount of future obligation...........	Known	Reasonably estimable	Known, or Reasonably estimable	Not reasonably estimable	Known, or Reasonably estimable, or Not reasonably estimable	Known, or Reasonably estimable, or Not reasonably estimable
Common examples........	Notes payable, Accounts payable, Dividends payable	Income tax payable	Estimated liability for product warranty	Lawsuits, Environmental cleanup, Guarantee of others' credit	Lawsuits, Environmental cleanup, Guarantee of others' credit	Lawsuits, Environmental cleanup

YOUR TURN! 10.3

MBC

The solution is on page 10-57.

For each of the following scenarios, determine if the firm should (a) record as a liability, (b) disclose as a contingent liability, or (c) neither:

1. The Seco Co. has been sued by a group of individuals claiming the products they purchased from the company were defective and caused injuries. Seco's lawyers have determined that the product in question could not possibly have caused the types of damages claimed and, further, that the same group of individuals has unsuccessfully sued several other companies claiming their products caused the same injuries. The likelihood of losing this lawsuit is deemed remote.
2. The Everett Co. has guaranteed the loan of a subsidiary that is suffering minor financial distress. The chance that the loan will not be repaid is deemed remote.
3. Hiller Inc. has acquired a defunct mining company and assumed all its liabilities. Toxic waste from the defunct company was recently discovered to have leaked into some nearby wells. The evidence that the waste came from the mining company is very strong and the cost of cleanup is estimated to be $4 million.

Concept →	Method →	Assessment	TAKEAWAY 10.1
Does the company have any contingent liabilities?	Notes to the financial statements Read the notes to the financial statements to identify contingent liabilities.	Consider the likely outcome and size of contingent liabilities. If significant, consider these items in the analysis of the firm's liabilities.	

FORENSIC ACCOUNTING   **Accounting Software**

One definition of forensic accounting is "the use of accounting records and documents to determine the legality of past activities." Possible uses of forensic accounting include financial statements, government investigations, contract disputes, or even culling through a shoebox of receipts in preparation for an IRS audit. As a business owner, would you rather defend yourself in an investigation with a shoebox full of documents or with a detailed set of accounting records? While some small business owners feel that entry-level accounting systems such as **Intuit**'s QuickBooks are fine for their needs, they may want to consider the benefits of a more robust accounting package, such as **Microsoft** Dynamics GP accounting system. In today's technology-driven society, a security breach is only a few keystrokes away. A hacker will have a much easier time penetrating the single layer of security in most entry-level packages than the eight levels of security in Microsoft Dynamics GP. In addition, the more robust accounting systems provide a richer data repository from which a forensic accountant can mine data in an effort to identify inconsistencies, a major weapon in the detection of fraud.

ANALYZING LIABILITIES

Current Ratio and Quick Ratio

The **working capital** of a firm is the difference between the amount of its current assets and the amount of its current liabilities. In general, having a higher working capital position is preferred to having a lower working capital position. In analyzing the adequacy of a firm's working capital, the current ratio is a widely used financial metric. The **current ratio** is calculated as follows:

LO4   **Define** the current ratio, quick ratio, and times-interest-earned ratio and **explain** their use.

MBC

$$\text{Current ratio} = \frac{\text{Current assets}}{\text{Current liabilities}}$$

Historically, a current ratio of 2.00 has been considered an acceptable current ratio; however, this is a general guide only. Many businesses operate successfully with a current ratio below 2.00, particularly service firms, because they do not need to maintain large amounts of inventory among their current assets. Similarly, many

fast-food franchises operate successfully with a negative working capital position. These businesses produce large amounts of operating cash flow, have no accounts receivable, and extensively utilize the trade credit (accounts payable) provided by their suppliers.

The **quick ratio** is another ratio used to evaluate a company's working capital position. The quick ratio is calculated as follows:

$$\text{Quick ratio} = \frac{[\text{Cash and cash equivalents} + \text{Short-term investments} + \text{Accounts receivable}]}{\text{Current liabilities}}$$

Cash and cash equivalents, short-term investments, and accounts receivable are also known as quick assets. Quick assets are converted to cash more quickly than other current assets such as inventory or prepaid assets that are omitted from the numerator of the ratio. Consequently, the quick ratio is often preferred by investment professionals because it gives a more accurate picture of a company's ability to pay current liabilities.

The following are examples of the current and quick ratios for companies in different industries:

	Current Ratio	Quick Ratio
Verizon Communications (telecommunications)	1.16	1.38
Johnson & Johnson (healthcare products)	0.91	1.21
Duke Energy (utility)	0.21	0.53
Alphabet (technology)	3.21	3.37

As can be seen from the above data, the current and quick ratios vary dramatically between industries.

FORENSIC ACCOUNTING   **Cooking the Books**

One of the key measures indicating the amount of liabilities, or leverage, used by a company is its net debt. Net debt is calculated as a firm's total liabilities minus its liquid (or quick) assets. The higher a firm's net debt, the higher the firm's leverage, or use of debt financing. Because of the widespread use of net debt as an indicator of a firm's use of leverage by investment professionals, some firms have attempted to manage the level of their reported net debt. To illustrate, consider the case of **Parmalat SpA**, an Italian dairy company. In late 2003, the company filed for bankruptcy after revealing that it had massively underreported its outstanding net debt. According to the company's forensic investigative auditor, **PricewaterhouseCoopers LLP**, Parmalat underreported its net debt position by overstating the amount of cash on hand and retaining worthless accounts receivable on the company's balance sheet.

TAKEAWAY 10.2	Concept	Method	Assessment
	Can a firm pay its current liabilities?	Current assets, Quick assets, Current liabilities $\text{Current ratio} = \dfrac{\text{Current assets}}{\text{Current liabilities}}$ $\text{Quick ratio} = \dfrac{\text{Quick assets}}{\text{Current liabilities}}$	A higher current ratio and quick ratio indicate that a firm can readily pay its current liabilities.

Times-Interest-Earned Ratio

A financial ratio of particular interest to current and potential long-term creditors is the times-interest-earned ratio. The **times-interest-earned ratio** is computed as follows:

$$\text{Times-interest-earned ratio} = \frac{\text{Income before interest expense and income taxes}}{\text{Interest expense}}$$

The principal on long-term debt, such as bonds payable, is not due until maturity, which may be many years into the future. Interest payments, however, are due every six months, and possibly monthly on term loans. Thus, creditors examine the times-interest-earned ratio to help assess the ability of a company to meet its periodic interest commitments. The ratio indicates the number of times that the fixed interest charges were earned during the year. Many investment professionals believe that the times-interest-earned ratio should be at least in the range of 3.0–4.0 for the extension of long-term credit to be considered a safe investment. The trend of the ratio in recent years and the nature of the industry (volatile or stable, for example) also influence the interpretation of this ratio.

A.K.A. The times-interest-earned ratio is also referred to as the interest coverage ratio.

Both the numerator and the denominator in the times-interest-earned ratio are obtained from the income statement. The numerator uses income before interest expense and income taxes because that is the amount available to cover a business's current interest charges. The denominator is the business's total interest expense for the period. To illustrate, Reid, Inc., issued $100,000 of 8 percent bonds at face value. The annual interest expense was $8,000. If this was Reid's only interest expense and Reid's income before interest expense and income taxes was $28,000, Reid's times-interest-earned ratio for the year would be 3.5, or $28,000/$8,000.

The times-interest-earned ratio may differ substantially among industries and firms, depending upon a company's decision to use leverage to finance its assets and operations. The following are examples of times-interest-earned ratios for several companies in different industries:

Kellogg Company (grocery products)	6.65
Kimberly-Clark Corporation (consumer goods)	13.19
Amazon.com Inc. (online retailing)	8.95
Cisco Systems, Inc. (computer communications equip.)	24.88

Concept	Method	Assessment	TAKEAWAY 10.3
Can a firm pay its current periodic interest payments?	Income before income taxes and interest expense, Interest expense Times-interest-earned ratio $= \dfrac{\text{Income before income taxes and interest expense}}{\text{Interest expense}}$	A higher times-interest-earned ratio indicates that a firm will have less difficulty paying its current interest expense.	

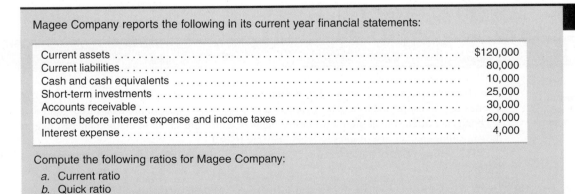

Magee Company reports the following in its current year financial statements:

Current assets	$120,000
Current liabilities	80,000
Cash and cash equivalents	10,000
Short-term investments	25,000
Accounts receivable	30,000
Income before interest expense and income taxes	20,000
Interest expense	4,000

Compute the following ratios for Magee Company:

a. Current ratio
b. Quick ratio
c. Times-interest-earned ratio

YOUR TURN! 10.4

GuidedExample

MBC

The solution is on page 10-57.

COMPREHENSIVE PROBLEM

MBC

The following are selected transactions for Tyler, Inc., for the prior and current year. The firm closes its books on December 31.

Prior year

Dec. 31   Issued $500,000 of 12 percent, 10-year bonds for $562,360, yielding an effective rate of 10 percent. Interest is payable June 30 and December 31.

Current year

June 30   Paid semiannual interest and recorded semiannual premium amortization on bonds.

Dec. 31   Paid semiannual interest and recorded semiannual premium amortization on bonds.

    31   Called one-half of the bonds in for retirement at 104.

Required

Record the transactions using (a) straight-line amortization and (b) effective interest amortization. Round amounts to the nearest dollar. You should read Appendix 10A prior to attempting this comprehensive problem.

Solution:

Prior year

		(a) Straight-line Amortization		(b) Effective Interest Amortization	
Dec. 31	Cash (+A)	562,360		562,360	
	Bonds payable (+L)		500,000		500,000
	Premium on bonds payable (+XL, +L)		62,360		62,360
	Issued $500,000 of 12 percent, 10-year bonds for $562,360.				

Current year

June 30	Bond interest expense (+E, −SE)	26,882		28,118	
	Premium on bonds payable (−XL, −L)	3,118		1,882	
	Cash (−A)		30,000		30,000
	To record semiannual interest payment and premium amortization.	*[$62,360 ÷ 20 = $3,118].*		*[$562,360 × 0.05 = $28,118].*	
Dec. 31	Bond interest expense (+E, −SE)	26,882		28,024	
	Premium on bonds payable (−XL, −L)	3,118		1,976	
	Cash (−A)		30,000		30,000
	To record semiannual interest payment and premium amortization.	*[$62,360 ÷ 20 = $3,118].*		*[($562,360 − $1,882) × 0.05 = $28,024, rounded].*	
31	Bonds payable (−L)	250,000		250,000	
	Premium on bonds payable (−XL, −L)	28,062		29,251	
	Cash (−A)		260,000		260,000
	Gain on bond retirement (+Gain, +SE)		18,062		19,251
	To record retirement of $250,000 of bonds; Retirement payment: $250,000 × 1.04 = $260,000.	*[$56,124 × 50% = $28,062].*		*[$58,502 × 50% = $29,251].*	

APPENDIX 10A: Bond Pricing

L05 Explain bond pricing and **illustrate** the straight-line and effective interest methods of amortizing bond discounts/premiums.

This chapter explains that (1) a bond agreement specifies a pattern of future cash flows—usually a series of interest payments and a single payment at maturity equal to the face value—and that (2) bonds are often sold at premiums or discounts to adjust the stated or coupon interest rate to the prevailing market rate of interest when they are issued.

    The selling price of a bond that is necessary to yield a specific rate can be determined as follows:

❶ Use Appendix E's Table III to calculate the present value of the future principal repayment at the bond's effective rate of interest.

❷ Use Appendix E's Table IV to calculate the present value of the future series of interest payments at the bond's effective rate of interest.

❸ Add the two present value calculations obtained in steps one and two.

Exhibit 10A-1 illustrates the pricing of a $100,000 issue of 10 percent, four-year bonds paying interest semiannually and sold on the date of issue to yield (1) 8 percent, (2) 10 percent, or (3) 6 percent. The price of the 8 percent bonds sold to yield 8 percent equals the face (or par) value of the bonds. However, the bonds must sell for $93,537 to provide a yield of 10 percent, whereas the bonds must sell for $107,020 to provide a yield of 6 percent.

EXHIBIT 10A-1	Calculating Bond Issue Price Using Present Value Tables

(1) $100,000 of 8 percent, four-year bonds with interest payable semiannually sold to yield 8 percent:

Future Cash Flows	Multiplier (Table III)	Multiplier (Table IV)	Present Values at 4% Semiannually
Principal repayment, $100,000 (a single amount received eight semiannual periods hence)	0.73069		$ 73,069
Interest payments, $4,000 at end of each of eight semiannual interest periods		6.73274	26,931
Total present value (or issue price) of bonds			$100,000

(2) $100,000 of 8 percent, four-year bonds with interest payable semiannually sold to yield 10 percent:

Future Cash Flows	Multiplier (Table III)	Multiplier (Table IV)	Present Values at 5% Semiannually
Principal repayment, $100,000 (a single amount received eight semiannual periods hence)	0.67684		$ 67,684
Interest payments, $4,000 at end of each of eight semiannual interest periods		6.46321	25,853
Total present value (or issue price) of bonds			$ 93,537

(3) $100,000 of 8 percent, four-year bonds with interest payable semiannually sold to yield 6 percent:

Future Cash Flows	Multiplier (Table III)	Multiplier (Table IV)	Present Values at 3% Semiannually
Principal repayment, $100,000 (a single amount received eight semiannual periods hence)	0.78941		$ 78,941
Interest payments, $4,000 at end of each of eight semiannual interest periods		7.01969	28,079
Total present value (or issue price) of bonds			$107,020

Straight-line Interest Method of Discount Amortization

When bonds are sold at either a discount or a premium, the amount of interest that the company pays to bond-holders will differ from the amount of interest expense that is reported on the income statement. To see why this is the case, we will first consider the bond in **Exhibit 10A-1** that sells for $93,537; a discount of $6,463 from the face value of $100,000. This $6,463 discount represents an additional interest cost that the issuing company, Reid, Inc., must pay because it borrowed $93,537 but will have to pay back $100,000 in addition to the semiannual $4,000 interest payments. To properly apply the matching principle, Reid, Inc., will recognize a portion of the $6,463 discount as additional interest expense each time it makes an interest payment, thus spreading the additional interest of $6,463 over the life of the bond.

Under the **straight-line interest method** an equal amount of the discount is amortized to expense at each payment date. **Exhibit 10A-2** presents an amortization table illustrating the straight-line method. Column A lists the constant amount of interest paid every six months—that is, the coupon interest rate times the face value (4 percent × $100,000). The amount of the discount amortized in each period in column B is obtained by dividing the $6,463 discount by the eight interest payments, or $808 per semiannual period (rounded). The total interest expense in column C is the interest payment in column A *plus* the discount amortization in column B. The original $6,463 discount is reduced by $808 each period as shown in column D. As a result, the reported value of the bonds, shown in column E, changes each period. For discounted bonds, the reported value increases each period until it reaches the face value on the maturity date because the discount is being reduced each period until it becomes zero.

EXHIBIT 10A-2	Bonds Sold at a Discount: Straight-line Interest Method

$100,000 of 8% four-year bonds with interest payable semiannually issued on December 31, 2021, at $93,537 to yield 10%

		A	B	C	D	E
Date	Interest Period	Interest Paid (4% of face value)	Discount Amortization*	Total Interest Expense (A + B)	Balance of Unamortized Discount (D − B)	Book Value of Bonds, End of Period ($100,000 − D)
Dec. 31, 2021 . . . At issue					$6,463	$ 93,537
June 30, 2022 . . . 1		$4,000	$808	$4,808	5,655	94,345
Dec. 31, 2022 . . . 2		4,000	808	4,808	4,847	95,153
June 30, 2023 . . . 3		4,000	808	4,808	4,039	95,961
Dec. 31, 2023 . . . 4		4,000	808	4,808	3,231	96,769
June 30, 2024 . . . 5		4,000	808	4,808	2,423	97,577
Dec. 31, 2024 . . . 6		4,000	808	4,808	1,615	98,385
June 30, 2025 . . . 7		4,000	808	4,808	808	99,192
Dec. 31, 2025 . . . 8		4,000	808	4,808	0	100,000

* $6,463 / 8 interest periods = $808 (rounded)

The following journal entry records the interest expense and discount amortization each period:

A = L + SE		2022			
−4,000 +808 −4,808		June 30	Bond interest expense (+E, −SE)	4,808	
			Discount on bonds payable (−XL, +L)		808
			Cash (−A)		4,000
			To record semiannual interest payments and amortization.		

Amortizing the bond discount over the four-year life of the bonds leaves a zero balance in the Discount on Bonds Payable account on the maturity date of the bonds. The retirement of the bonds at maturity is then recorded by debiting Bonds Payable and crediting Cash for $100,000, equal to the face value of the bonds.

Straight-line Interest Method of Premium Amortization

When bonds are issued at a premium, the interest expense each period will be less than the amount of cash paid. We can see this by again considering the Reid, Inc., bond from **Exhibit 10A-1**, this time considering the bond issued for $107,020, a premium of $7,020 over the face value of $100,000. The $7,020 premium represents a reduction of interest cost to Reid, Inc., because Reid borrowed $107,020 but will have to pay back only $100,000 in addition to the semiannual $4,000 interest payments. As with the discount discussed above, to properly apply the matching principle, Reid, Inc., will recognize a portion of the $7,020 premium as a reduction of interest expense each time it makes an interest payment, thus spreading the $7,020 premium over the life of the bond.

Exhibit 10A-3 presents an amortization table illustrating the straight-line method. Column A lists the constant amount of interest paid every six months—that is, the coupon interest rate times the face value (4 percent ×

EXHIBIT 10A-3	Bonds Sold at a Premium: Straight-line Interest Method

$100,000 of 8% four-year bonds with interest payable semiannually issued on December 31, 2021, at $107,020 to yield 6%

		A	B	C	D	E
Date	Interest Period	Interest Paid (4% of face value)	Premium Amortization*	Total Interest Expense (A − B)	Balance of Unamortized Premium (D − B)	Book Value of Bonds, End of Period ($100,000 + D)
Dec. 31, 2021 . . . At issue					$7,020.00	$107,020.00
June 30, 2022 . . . 1		$4,000	$877.50	$3,122.50	6,142.50	106,142.50
Dec. 31, 2022 . . . 2		4,000	877.50	3,122.50	5,265.00	105,265.00
June 30, 2023 . . . 3		4,000	877.50	3,122.50	4,387.50	104,387.50
Dec. 31, 2023 . . . 4		4,000	877.50	3,122.50	3,510.00	103,510.00
June 30, 2024 . . . 5		4,000	877.50	3,122.50	2,632.50	102,632.50
Dec. 31, 2024 . . . 6		4,000	877.50	3,122.50	1,755.00	101,755.00
June 30, 2025 . . . 7		4,000	877.50	3,122.50	877.50	100,877.50
Dec. 31, 2025 . . . 8		4,000	877.50	3,122.50	0.00	100,000.00

* $7,020 / 8 interest periods = $877.50

$100,000). The amount of the premium amortized in each period in column B is obtained by dividing the $7,020 premium by the eight interest payments, or $877.50 per semiannual period. The total interest expense in column C is the interest payment in column A *minus* the premium amortization in column B. The original $7,020 premium is reduced by $877.50 each period as shown in column D. As a result, the reported value of the bonds, shown in column E, changes each period. For bonds issued at a premium, the value decreases each period until it reaches the face value on the maturity date because the premium is being reduced each period until it becomes zero.

The following journal entry records the interest expense and premium amortization each period:

2022				
June 30	Bond interest expense (+E, −SE)	3,122.50		
	Premium on bonds payable (−XL, −L)	877.50		
	Cash (−A)		4,000	
	To record semiannual interest payments and amortization.			

A = L + SE
−4,000.00 −877.50 −3,122.50

Amortizing the bond premium over the four-year life of the bonds leaves a zero balance in the Premium on Bonds Payable account on the maturity date of the bonds. The retirement of the bonds at maturity is then recorded by debiting Bonds Payable and crediting Cash for $100,000, equal to the face value of the bonds.

Effective Interest Method of Discount Amortization

A bond premium or discount can be amortized to interest expense using the straight-line method or the effective interest method. GAAP requires the effective interest method, except in cases where the differences between the two methods are not material. The **effective interest method** of amortization recognizes a constant *percentage* of the book value of a bond as interest expense for each interest payment period. For bonds issued at a discount, the book value of a bond is the balance in the Bonds Payable account less the balance in the Discount on Bonds Payable account. To obtain interest expense under the effective interest method, we multiply the bond's book value at the beginning of each period by the effective interest rate. The **effective interest rate** is the market rate of interest used to price the bonds when they are originally issued. The difference between this amount and the amount of interest paid (coupon interest rate × face value of bonds) is the amount of discount amortized.

When using the effective interest method of amortization, accountants often prepare an amortization schedule similar to the one in **Exhibit 10A-4**. This schedule covers the four-year life of the Reid, Inc., bonds issued at a discount. The interest rates shown in columns A and B are one-half the annual rates. Column A lists the constant amount of interest paid every six months—that is, the coupon interest rate times the face value (4 percent × $100,000). The amounts in Column B are obtained by multiplying the book value as of the beginning of each period (column E) by the 5 percent effective interest rate. For example, the $4,677 interest expense for the first period is 5 percent times $93,537; for the second period, it is 5 percent times $94,214, or $4,711, and so on. The amount of discount amortization for each period, given in column C, is the difference between the interest expense in Column B and the interest paid in Column A. This periodic amortization is subtracted from the beginning balance of the unamortized discount to give the balance at the end of each period in Column D. Because the unamortized discount decreases each period, the book value of the discount bond in Column E increases each period until it reaches the face value on the maturity date.

EXHIBIT 10A-4	**Bonds Sold at a Discount: Effective Interest Method**

**$100,000 of 8%, four-year bonds with interest payable semiannually
issued on December 31, 2021, at $93,537 to yield 10%**

Date	Interest Period	A Interest Paid (4% of face value)	B Interest Expense (5% of bond book value)	C Discount Amortization (B − A)	D Balance of Unamortized Discount (D − C)	E Book Value of Bonds, End of Period ($100,000 − D)
Dec. 31, 2021 . . .	At issue				$6,463	$ 93,537
June 30, 2022 . . .	1	$4,000	$4,677	$677	5,786	94,214
Dec. 31, 2022 . . .	2	4,000	4,711	711	5,075	94,925
June 30, 2023 . . .	3	4,000	4,746	746	4,329	95,671
Dec. 31, 2023 . . .	4	4,000	4,784	784	3,545	96,455
June 30, 2024 . . .	5	4,000	4,823	823	2,722	97,278
Dec. 31, 2024 . . .	6	4,000	4,864	864	1,858	98,142
June 30, 2025 . . .	7	4,000	4,907	907	951	99,049
Dec. 31, 2025 . . .	8	4,000	4,952	951	0	100,000

The amounts recorded for each interest payment can be read directly from the amortization schedule. The following journal entries record the interest expense and discount amortization for the first two interest payments:

A	=	L	+	SE					
−4,000		+677		−4,677 Exp	**2022** June 30	Bond interest expense (+E, −SE)		4,677	
						Discount on bonds payable (−XL, +L)			677
						Cash (−A)			4,000
						To record semiannual interest payment and amortization.			

A	=	L	+	SE					
−4,000		+711		−4,711 Exp	Dec. 31	Bond interest expense (+E, −SE)		4,711	
						Discount on bonds payable (−XL, +L)			711
						Cash (−A)			4,000
						To record semiannual interest payment and amortization.			

Amortizing the bond discount over the four-year life of the bonds leaves a zero balance in the Discount on Bonds Payable account on the maturity date of the bonds. The retirement of the bonds at maturity is then recorded by debiting Bonds Payable and crediting Cash for $100,000, equal to the face value of the bonds.

PRINCIPLE ALERT   **Materiality Concept**

Under U.S. GAAP, the effective interest method is the preferred method of bond amortization. It is generally accepted because it uses the actual market rate of interest when the bonds were originally issued to determine the amount of interest expense each period. The effective interest method, however, is somewhat more complex than the straight-line method. Accounting standards permit the straight-line method of amortization to be used when the results are not materially different from those achieved under the effective interest method. This exception represents an application of the *materiality concept*. As previously discussed, the materiality concept permits insignificant accounting transactions to be recorded most expediently. Here, the materiality concept permits a simpler (and, thus, more expedient) straight-line method to be used when it results in insignificant differences from the theoretically superior effective interest method.

Effective Interest Method of Premium Amortization

The effective interest method of amortizing a bond premium is handled the same way as a bond discount amortization. Each interest period, a constant percentage of the bonds' book value as of the beginning of the period is recognized as interest expense; the difference between the interest expense and the semiannual interest payment is the amount of the premium amortization.

Exhibit 10A-5 shows the amortization schedule for the four-year life of the Reid, Inc., bonds that were issued at a premium. The coupon rate of 4 percent in column A and the effective interest rate of 3 percent in column B are one-half the annual rates because the calculations are for six-month periods.

EXHIBIT 10A-5	**Bonds Sold at a Premium: Effective Interest Method**

$100,000 of 8%, four-year bonds with interest payable semiannually issued on December 31, 2021, at $107,020 to yield 6%

Date	Interest Period	A Interest Paid (4% of face value)	B Interest Expense (3% of bond book value)	C Premium Amortization (A − B)	D Balance of Unamortized Premium (D − C)	E Book Value of Bonds, End of Period ($100,000 + D)
Dec. 31, 2021 . . .	At issue				$7,020	$107,020
June 30, 2022 . . .	1	$4,000	$3,211	$789	6,231	106,231
Dec. 31, 2022 . . .	2	4,000	3,187	813	5,418	105,418
June 30, 2023 . . .	3	4,000	3,163	837	4,581	104,581
Dec. 31, 2023 . . .	4	4,000	3,137	863	3,718	103,718
June 30, 2024 . . .	5	4,000	3,112	888	2,830	102,830
Dec. 31, 2024 . . .	6	4,000	3,085	915	1,915	101,915
June 30, 2025 . . .	7	4,000	3,057	943	972	100,972
Dec. 31, 2025 . . .	8	4,000	3,030	972	0	100,000

The journal entries for each interest payment are taken directly from the amortization schedule. The entries for the first two interest payments follow. Note that the periodic interest expense is less than the semiannual interest payment.

2022				
June 30	Bond interest expense (+E, −SE)	3,211		A = L + SE
	Premium on bonds payable (−XL, −L)	789		−4,000 −789 −3,211
	Cash (−A)		4,000	Exp
	To record semiannual interest payment and amortization.			

Dec. 31	Bond interest expense (+E, −SE)	3,187		A = L + SE
	Premium on bonds payable (−XL, −L)	813		−4,000 −813 −3,187
	Cash (−A)		4,000	Exp
	To record semiannual interest payment and amortization.			

After amortizing the bond premium over the four-year life of the bonds, the balance in the Premium on Bonds Payable account is zero. When the bonds are retired at the end of four years, the journal entry to record the retirement debits Bonds Payable and credits Cash for the $100,000 face value of the bonds.

Exhibit 10A-6 illustrates the book value of the Reid, Inc., bonds from issuance to maturity. The bond issued at face value has a reported book value of $100,000 over its entire life. The book value of the bond sold at a premium is greater than the face value at issuance. As the premium is amortized over the life of the bond, the book value declines until it is equal to the face value. The book value of the bond sold at a discount behaves in the opposite fashion; it is less than the face value at issuance, and increases over time as the discount is amortized. At maturity, the book value of all three bonds is equal to the $100,000 face value.

EXHIBIT 10A-6 **Book Value of Bonds, End of Period**

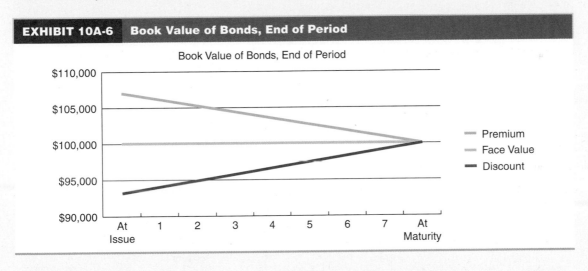

Using a Financial Calculator

While present value tables can provide a handy method to solve some time value of money problems, they are not suitable for many real-world situations. For example, many real-world interest rates are not "even integers" like those appearing in Table I through Table IV of Appendix E, nor are many problems limited to the number of time periods appearing in the tables. While it is still possible to solve these problems with the provided formulas, a financial calculator provides a quicker solution. Financial calculators can be distinguished from other calculators by the presence of dedicated keys for present and future values, along with keys for the number of periods, interest rates, and annuity payments. There are many brands of financial calculators; however, all of them work in much the same way. We will illustrate the calculation of bond issuance prices from **Exhibit 10A-1** using a Hewlett-Packard 10BII financial calculator, as illustrated in **Exhibit 10A-7**. (It is usually necessary to do some preliminary setup on a financial calculator before performing time value of money calculations. For example, the HP 10BII calculator has a default setting of monthly compounding; this may need to be changed if the problem calls for a different number of compounding periods, such as annual. In addition, the calculator assumes interest payments occur at the end of each period; this will need to be changed if the problem requires beginning of period payments. See your calculator manual to determine how to make these setting changes.)

EXHIBIT 10A-7	Hewlett-Packard 10BII Financial Calculator

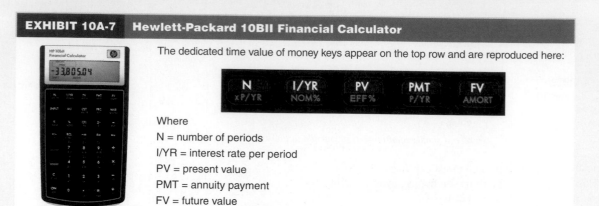

The dedicated time value of money keys appear on the top row and are reproduced here:

Where

N = number of periods

I/YR = interest rate per period

PV = present value

PMT = annuity payment

FV = future value

To solve a time value of money problem using a financial calculator, input the known values and then press the key of the unknown value. **Exhibit 10A-8** illustrates the bond value calculations from **Exhibit 10A-1**. The interest payment (PMT = $4,000) and principal at maturity (FV = $100,000) are shown as negative numbers, indicating cash outflows. Solving for the present value (PV) of these cash flows yields the price of the bond, which is equal to the amount of cash received at issuance. Financial calculators require cash outflows and inflows to be of opposite signs. If we were to enter PMT and FV as positive numbers, PV would be displayed as a negative number. Calculator solutions can be slightly different from the solutions using either the tables or the formulas due to rounding of the future value and present value multipliers.

EXHIBIT 10A-8	Calculating Bond Issue Prices Using a Financial Calculator

(1) $100,000 of 8 percent, four-year bonds with interest payable semiannually sold to yield 8 percent:

Enter		Display		
8	N	N	=	8
4	I/YR	I/YR	=	4
−4,000	PMT	PMT	=	−4,000
−100,000	FV	FV	=	−100,000
Press	PV	PV	=	100,000

(2) $100,000 of 8 percent, four-year bonds with interest payable semiannually sold to yield 10 percent:

Enter		Display		
8	N	N	=	8
5	I/YR	I/YR	=	5
−4,000	PMT	PMT	=	−4,000
−100,000	FV	FV	=	−100,000
Press	PV	PV	=	93,537

(3) $100,000 of 8 percent, four-year bonds with interest payable semiannually sold to yield 6 percent:

Enter		Display		
8	N	N	=	8
3	I/YR	I/YR	=	3
−4,000	PMT	PMT	=	−4,000
−100,000	FV	FV	=	−100,000
Press	PV	PV	=	107,020

ACCOUNTING IN PRACTICE	Getting a Car Loan

The expression "knowledge is power" certainly applies to the situation many of us face when shopping for a new car that we plan to finance. Sitting in the room with the car dealership's finance manager can be much more pleasant if one is armed with a financial calculator and the knowledge of how to calculate car payments. You no longer need to trust that the interest rate you are being quoted is the "real" interest rate you are being charged; you can simply do the calculation yourself and verify the number.

Using an Electronic Spreadsheet

In addition to present value tables and financial calculators, another way to solve time value of money problems is with an electronic spreadsheet such as Excel, which has several built-in functions that allow calculation of time value of money problems. Depending on the version of Excel, these functions are accessed differently. Within Excel, go to the Insert function f_x in the Formulas ribbon. The required functions are located under the FINANCIAL option. Below are examples of how to use the PV (present value) function in Excel to solve the same problems we previously solved using a financial calculator.

Example 1

Issue price of $100,000 of 8 percent, four-year bonds with interest payable semiannually sold to yield 8 percent.

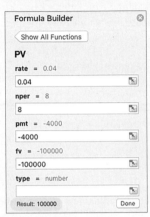

Example 2

Issue price of $100,000 of 8 percent, four-year bonds with interest payable semiannually sold to yield 10 percent.

Example 3

Issue price of $100,000 of 8 percent, four-year bonds with interest payable semiannually sold to yield 6 percent.

GuidedExample
MBC

YOUR TURN! 10A.1

Use an Excel spreadsheet to find the selling price (present value) of a three-year $100,000 face value bond with coupon semiannual payments at 4 percent that is issued when bonds of similar risk are yielding 6 percent.

The solution is on page 10-57.

APPENDIX 10B: Leases

A firm may rent property for a specified period of time under a contract called a **lease**. The company acquiring the right to use the property is the **lessee**, while the owner of the property is the **lessor**. The rights transferred to the lessee are called a **leasehold**. Examples of leased assets include land, buildings, factory machinery, and office equipment.

L06 Describe the accounting for leases.

The FASB updated its leasing standard effective for fiscal years beginning after December 15, 2019. The FASB believes the updated accounting standard for leases provides a more faithful representation of a lessee's rights and obligations arising from a lease. Before the update, companies were often able to structure a lease such that the leased asset and its corresponding liability failed to be reported on the balance sheet, a practice known as **off-balance sheet financing**.

eLecture
MBC

Under the revised standard, a lessee's accounting treatment of a leased asset and lease liability depends on whether a lease is categorized as a **finance lease** or an **operating lease**. If *any* of the following five criteria are met, the lease is categorized as a finance lease. Otherwise, the lease is categorized as an operating lease.

- Ownership of the leased asset is transferred to the lessee at the end of the lease.
- The lessee has the option to purchase the leased asset at a bargain price.
- The lease term is for a major part of the remaining economic life of the leased asset.
- The present value of the lease payments and any residual value guarantee is equal to, or more than, substantially all of the fair value of the leased asset.

- The leased asset has no alternative use to the lessor at the end of the term because of its specialized nature.

Whether classified as a finance or operating lease, the lessee records the leased asset and a corresponding lease liability on the balance sheet at an amount equal to the present value of the future lease payments. For example, assume Knight Inc. leases a building for 10 years with annual lease payments of $129,505 when Knight's borrowing rate is 5 percent. The present value of these lease payments is $1,000,000.[1] Knight would therefore make the following journal entry to record the lease:

Right-of-Use Asset (Building) (+A)	1,000,000	
Lease liability (Building) (−A)		1,000,000

There are some differences in the income statement treatment between an operating and a finance lease. These differences are covered in an intermediate accounting textbook.

YOUR TURN! 10B.1

MBC

The solution is on page 10-57.

Huff Company leased a new forklift for four years. Huff Co. will return the forklift at the end of the four years. The estimated economic life of the forklift is five years. At the time of the lease, the fair value of the forklift is $45,000. The monthly lease payments are $1,000 and the lease has an annual implied interest rate of 6 percent, for a present value of $42,580.

Determine whether the lease will be categorized as a finance or operating lease and provide the journal entry to record the lease.

SUMMARY OF LEARNING OBJECTIVES

LO1   Describe the nature of liabilities and discuss various current liabilities. (p. 10-3)

- Liabilities are obligations resulting from past transactions or events that require a business to pay money, provide goods, or perform services in the future.
- Current liabilities are obligations that will require, within the coming year or the normal operating cycle, whichever is longer, (1) the use of existing current assets or (2) the creation of other current liabilities.

LO2   Illustrate the accounting for long-term liabilities. (p. 10-9)

- A bond is a long-term debt instrument used by many businesses to provide financing for operations or asset purchases.
- Discounts and premiums may be recorded when the bonds are issued.
- Bonds payable are shown in the long-term liabilities section of the balance sheet, with any unamortized premium added or unamortized discount deducted.
- The entry for the retirement of bonds removes both the bonds payable and any related bond premium or bond discount from the accounts at the date of retirement and recognizes any gain or loss on retirement.

LO3   Define contingent liabilities and explain the rules for their accounting and disclosure in the financial statements. (p. 10-19)

- Even though a past transaction or event has taken place, the existence of some liabilities, called contingent liabilities, depends on the occurrence of a future event. Whether or not a contingent liability is recorded in the accounts depends on the likelihood of the future event occurring and the measurability of the obligation:
  1. If the future event will probably occur and the amount of the liability is known or can be reasonably estimated, the contingent liability should be recorded.
  2. If the likelihood of the future event occurring is probable, but no reasonable estimate of the future obligation is determinable, or the likelihood of the future event occurring is reasonably possible (but not probable), regardless of the ability to measure the future amount, the contingent liability should be disclosed in a note to the financial statements, but not recorded.
  3. If the likelihood of the future event occurring is remote, the contingent liability is not recorded or disclosed in a note to the financial statements. The only exception is a credit guarantee, which must be disclosed in a note to the financial statements.

---

[1] Annual lease payment of $129,505 times the present value of an ordinary annuity factor of 7.72173 (5 percent and 10 periods) equals 1,000,000 (rounded). (See Appendix E, Table IV.)

Define the current ratio, quick ratio, and times-interest-earned ratio and explain their use. (p. 10-22)   **LO4**

- The current ratio is calculated as follows:

$$\text{Current ratio} = \frac{\text{Current assets}}{\text{Current liabilities}}$$

- The quick ratio is calculated as follows:

$$\text{Quick ratio} = \frac{[\text{Cash and cash equivalents} + \text{Short-term investments} + \text{Accounts receivable}]}{\text{Current liabilities}}$$

- Both the current and quick ratios measure a firm's ability to pay its current liabilities, as well as the strength of its working capital position.
- The times-interest-earned ratio measures the ability of a firm to meet its periodic interest commitments, and is calculated as:

$$\text{Times-interest-earned ratio} = \frac{\text{Income before income taxes and interest expense}}{\text{Interest expense}}$$

Appendix 10A: Explain bond pricing and illustrate the straight-line and effective interest methods of amortizing bond discounts/premiums. (p. 10-25)   **LO5**

- Because of the role played by interest, the selling price of the bond often differs from the face amount of the bond.
- We account for this difference by utilizing bond premium (when the market rate of interest is less than the coupon rate) and bond discount (when the market rate of interest is more than the coupon rate) accounts, which affect the book value of the liability.
- The straight-line method amortizes an equal amount of the discount/premium to interest expense each period. The effective interest method amortizes the discount/premium such that interest expense is a constant percentage of the beginning book value of the bond.
- While the straight-line method may be simpler, the preferred method according to GAAP for amortizing bond premiums and discounts is the effective interest method.

Appendix 10B: Describe the accounting for leases. (p. 10-32)   **LO6**

- Leases are categorized as either finance leases or operating leases based on five criteria.
- All leases require the lessee to record the leased asset (Right-of-Use Asset) and a corresponding lease liability on the balance sheet.

Concept	→ Method →	Assessment	SUMMARY
Does the company have any contingent liabilities?	Notes to the financial statements Read the notes to the financial statements to identify contingent liabilities.	Consider the likely outcome and size of contingent liabilities. If significant, consider these items in the analysis of the firm's liabilities.	TAKEAWAY 10.1
Can a firm pay its current liabilities?	Current assets, Quick assets, Current liabilities Current ratio = $\dfrac{\text{Current assets}}{\text{Current liabilities}}$ Quick ratio = $\dfrac{\text{Quick assets}}{\text{Current liabilities}}$	A higher current ratio and quick ratio indicate that a firm can readily pay its current liabilities.	TAKEAWAY 10.2
Can a firm pay its current periodic interest payments?	Income before income taxes and interest expense, Interest expense Times-interest-earned ratio = $\dfrac{\text{Income before income taxes and interest expense}}{\text{Interest expense}}$	A higher times-interest-earned ratio indicates that a firm will have less difficulty paying its current interest expense.	TAKEAWAY 10.3

KEY TERMS

Bond (p. 10-9)	Gross pay (p. 10-6)	Off-balance sheet financing (p. 10-32)
Callable bonds (p. 10-11)	High-yield bonds (p. 10-11)	Operating lease (p. 10-32)
Contingent liabilities (p. 10-19)	Lease (p. 10-32)	Product warranties (p. 10-20)
Convertible bonds (p. 10-11)	Leasehold (p. 10-32)	Quick ratio (p. 10-23)
Coupon rate (p. 10-11)	Lessee (p. 10-32)	Secured bonds (p. 10-10)
Credit guarantee (p. 10-21)	Lessor (p. 10-32)	Serial bonds (p. 10-10)
Current liabilities (p. 10-3)	Leverage (p. 10-18)	Sinking fund bonds (p. 10-10)
Current ratio (p. 10-22)	Liabilities (p. 10-3)	Straight-line interest method (p. 10-15, 10-26)
Debenture bonds (p. 10-10)	Market rate of interest (Real rate of interest; effective yield rate) (p. 10-11)	Term loan (p. 10-9)
Effective interest method (p. 10-15, 10-28)	Maturity date (p. 10-4)	Times-interest-earned ratio (p. 10-23)
Effective interest rate (p. 10-12, 10-28)	Maturity value (p. 10-11)	Working capital (p. 10-22)
Face value (p. 10-11)	Net pay (p. 10-6)	Zero-coupon bonds (p. 10-15)
Finance lease (p. 10-32)		

Assignments with the (MBC) logo in the margin are available in ᵐʸBusinessCourse.
See the Preface of the book for details.

SELF-STUDY QUESTIONS

(Answers to the Self-Study Questions are available at the end of this chapter.)

LO1 **1. Goldsteen Corporation obtained a $5,000 loan from a bank on April 1. If the bank charges 8 percent interest annually, how much interest will be accrued at December 31?**

    a. $400   *c.* $275
    b. $300   *d.* $250

LO1 **2. Wong, Inc., sold merchandise on account for $1,840, which is subject to a 10 percent excise tax and a 5 percent sales tax. What would the entry to record this sale include?**

    a.   A debit of $1,600 to Accounts Receivable   *c.*   A credit of $1,600 to Sales
    b.   A debit of $2,116 to Accounts Receivable   *d.*   A debit of $1,840 to Sales

LO3 **3. Jansen Company sells a product for $400 per unit, which includes a 30-day warranty against product defects. Experience indicates that 4 percent of the units sold will prove defective, requiring an average repair cost of $50 per unit. During the first month of business, product sales were $320,000, and 20 of the units sold were found to be defective and repaired during the month. What is the accrued liability for product warranties at month-end?**

    a. $1,000   *c.* $1,600
    b. $600   *d.* $2,000

LO1 **4. Which of the following payroll-related taxes are not withheld from an employee's earnings?**

    a.   Medicare taxes   *c.*   Federal unemployment taxes
    b.   Income taxes   *d.*   Social Security taxes

LO3 **5. Which of the following is *not* considered to be a contingent liability?**

    a.   Environmental cleanup costs   *c.*   Credit guarantees
    b.   Notes payable   *d.*   Lawsuit

LO5
(Appendix 10A) **6. On May 1 a firm issued $400,000 of 12-year, 9 percent bonds payable at 96 1/2 plus accrued interest. The bonds are dated January 1, and interest is payable on January 1 and July 1 of each year. The amount the firm receives on May 1 from the sale of the bonds (see Appendix 10A) is:**

    a. $386,000.   *c.* $392,000.
    b. $422,000.   *d.* $398,000.

LO5
(Appendix 10A) **7. A firm issued $250,000 of 10-year, 12 percent bonds payable on January 1 for $281,180, yielding an effective rate of 10 percent. Interest is payable on January 1 and July 1 each year. The firm records**

amortization on each interest date. Bond interest expense for the first six months using effective interest amortization (see Appendix 10A) is:

a. $15,000.

c. $14,059.

b. $16,871.

d. $14,331.

8. In financial statement presentations, the Discount on Bonds Payable account is:

a. Added to Bond Interest Expense.

c. Added to Bonds Payable.

b. Deducted from Bonds Payable.

d. Deducted from Bond Interest Expense.

LO2

9. Which of the following is *not* one of the criteria for classifying a lease as finance or operating?

a. The lessee frequently leases the same type of asset.

b. The lessee has the option to purchase the leased asset at a bargain price.

c. Ownership of the leased asset transfers to the lessee at the end of the lease.

d. The lease term is for a major part of the remaining economic life of the leased asset.

LO6
(Appendix 10B)

10. Appolo Company reported year-end current assets of $75,000 and current liabilities of $25,000. The company's current ratio is:

a. 1/3

c. 4

b. 3

d. $50,000

LO4

11. Cristo Company reported net income of $50,000 after subtracting $10,000 for interest expense and $20,000 for taxes. Compute the company's times-interest-earned ratio:

a. 2.5

c. 8

b. 5

d. 3

LO4

QUESTIONS

1. For accounting purposes, how are liabilities defined?

2. At what amount are current liabilities presented on the balance sheet?

3. What does the term *current liabilities* mean?

4. What formula should Hardy Company use to calculate the total amount of interest on a note payable that uses add-on interest?

5. Gordon Company signed a note payable on November 20. Gordon has a December 31 year-end. It paid the note, including interest, on the maturity date, February 20. What accounts did Gordon debit and what account did it credit on February 20?

6. Jack Swanson gave a creditor a 90-day 8 percent note payable for $7,200 on December 16. What adjusting entry should Swanson make on December 31?

7. What are two examples of voluntary deductions from an employee's gross pay?

8. On whom is the FICA tax levied? What does the FICA tax finance?

9. What is the difference between accounting for product warranties on (a) failed units repaired in the month of sale and (b) failed units repaired in a subsequent month but that are still covered by warranty?

10. **American Paging, Inc.**, is the seventh-largest paging company in the United States. In a recent balance sheet, it reported a current liability of $8,452,379 that was labeled Unearned Revenues and Deposits. A note to the financial statements explained:

AMERICAN PAGING, INC.

> Unearned revenues and deposits primarily represent monthly charges to customers for radio paging rental and dispatch billed in advance. Such revenues and deposits are recognized in the following month when service is provided or are applied against the customer's final bill or last month's rent.

What basic principle of accounting guides American Paging's handling of its unearned revenues and deposits?

11. What do the following terms mean? (a) term loan, (b) bonds payable, (c) trustee, (d) secured bonds, (e) serial bonds, (f) call provision, (g) convertible bonds, (h) face value, (i) coupon rate, (j) bond discount, (k) bond premium, and (l) amortization of bond premium or discount.

12. What are the advantages and disadvantages of issuing bonds rather than common stock?

13. A $3,000,000 issue of 10-year, 9 percent bonds was sold at 98 plus accrued interest three months after the bonds were dated. What net amount of cash is received when the bonds are sold?

14. If the effective interest amortization method is used for bonds payable, how does the periodic interest expense change over the life of the bonds when they are issued (a) at a discount and (b) at a premium?

15. On April 30, one year before maturity, Eastern Company retired $200,000 of 9 percent bonds payable at 101. The book value of the bonds on April 30 was $197,600. Bond interest was last paid on April 30. What is the gain or loss on the retirement of the bonds?

16. What are *contingent liabilities*? List three examples of contingent liabilities. When should contingent liabilities be recorded in the accounts?

17. What is the difference between an operating lease and a finance lease?

18. Define the terms *current ratio* and *quick ratio*. What does each ratio tell us?

19. Define the times-interest-earned ratio and explain how it is used.

SHORT EXERCISES

LO3   **SE10-1.**   **Contingent Liabilities** The CEO of Evans & Sons, Inc., negotiated with its principal supplier of raw materials to purchase 10,000 units for a total price of $100,000. The units are to be delivered in 90 days. The CEO is uncertain whether she should record the purchase commitment on the company's balance sheet as a liability or not. She asks for your advice. What would you advise her?

LO2   **SE10-2.**   **Determining Bond Premium or Discount** Evans & Sons, Inc., decides to sell $1,000,000 in bonds to finance the construction of a new warehouse. The bonds will carry an annual coupon rate of interest of 3 percent, to be paid semiannually, and will mature in five years. (a) If the market rate of interest at the time of issuance is 5 percent, will the bonds sell at their face value, a discount, or a premium? (b) If the market rate of interest at the time of issuance is 3 percent, will the bonds sell at their face value, a discount, or a premium? (c) If the market rate of interest at the time of issuance is 2 percent, will the bonds sell at their face value, a discount, or a premium?

LO3   **SE10-3.**   **Contingent Liabilities** Evans & Sons, Inc., received notification from a local attorney that the company was being sued for $5,000,000 for patent infringement. A review of the situation by the company's CEO led to the conclusion that Evans & Sons had indeed infringed upon the other company's patented product. Nonetheless, the CEO thought the amount of $5,000,000 was excessive and intended to litigate the issue. How should the lawsuit be reported in Evans & Sons' annual report?

LO6
(Appendix 10B)   **SE10-4.**   **Operating and Capital Leases** The CEO of Evans & Sons, Inc., was considering a lease for a new administrative headquarters building. The building was old, but was very well located near the company's principal customers. The leasing agent estimated that the building's remaining useful life was 10 years, and at the end of its useful life, the building would probably be worth $100,000. The proposed lease term was eight years, and as an inducement to Smith & Sons' CEO to sign the lease, the leasing agent indicated a willingness to include a statement in the lease agreement that would allow Smith & Sons to buy the building at the end of the lease for only $75,000. As the CEO considered whether or not to sign the lease, she wondered whether the lease could be accounted for as a finance lease or an operating lease. What would you advise her?

The following information relates to SE10-5 through SE10-7:

EVANS & SONS, INC. Income Statement For Years Ended December 31		
(in millions)	Current Year	Previous Year
Net sales.	$ 9,800	$ 9,300
Cost of goods sold	(5,500)	(5,200)
Gross profit.	4,300	4,100
Selling and administrative expenses	(2,800)	(2,700)
Income from operations	1,500	1,400
Interest expense.	(300)	(250)
Income before income taxes.	1,200	1,150
Income tax expense	(220)	(200)
Net income	$ 980	$ 950

EVANS & SONS, INC. Balance Sheet December 31		
(in millions)	Current Year	Previous Year
Assets		
Current assets		
Cash and cash equivalents	$ 100	$ 300
Accounts receivable	900	800
Inventory	500	650
Other current assets	400	250
Total current assets	1,900	2,000
Property, plant, & equipment (net)	2,600	2,500
Other assets	5,700	5,900
Total Assets	$10,200	$10,400
Liabilities and Stockholders' Equity		
Current liabilities	$ 3,000	$ 2,900
Long-term liabilities	5,000	5,400
Total liabilities	8,000	8,300
Stockholders' equity—common	2,200	2,100
Total Liabilities and Stockholders' Equity	$10,200	$10,400

SE10-5. **Current Ratio** Calculate the current ratio for Evans & Sons, Inc., for each year, and comment on the company's working capital position. Did the company's ability to pay its current liabilities improve over the two years?   **LO4**

SE10-6. **Quick Ratio** Calculate the quick ratio for Evans & Sons, Inc., for each year, and comment on the company's working capital position. Did the company's ability to pay its current liabilities improve over the two years?   **LO4**

SE10-7. **Times-Interest-Earned Ratio** Calculate the times-interest-earned ratio for Evans & Sons, Inc., for each year, and comment on the company's ability to pay its current interest payments. Did the company's ability to pay its current interest charges improve?   **LO4**

SE10-8. **Premium and Discount of a Bond or Debenture** Evans & Sons, Inc., reported the following borrowings in a prior annual report: **LO2**

	Borrowing ($ in millions)	Amount	Effective Interest Rate (%)
a.	4.00 percent, zero-coupon bond, due 2020	$202	4.00
b.	4.80 percent debentures, due 2033	500	5.00
c.	3.80 percent debentures, due 2017	500	3.95
d.	6.95 percent bonds, due 2025	293	6.85

For each borrowing, indicate whether the bond or debenture was originally sold at its face value, a discount, or a premium.

SE10-9. **Bond Interest Expense** Evans & Sons, Inc., sold $100,000 face value, 6 percent coupon rate, four-year bonds, for an aggregate issue price of $95,000. Calculate the total interest expense to be recorded by the company over the four-year life of the bonds.   **LO2**

SE10-10. **Bond Interest Expense** During the current year, Evans & Sons, Inc., issued $400 million of zero-coupon bonds, due in seven years. The proceeds from the bond issuance were $184.2 million. Calculate the total interest expense that the company will incur over the life of the bonds.   **LO2**

DATA ANALYTICS

DA10-1. **Preparing an Excel Map Visualization of Sales Tax Across States** For this exercise, download the Excel file "Table 3: State Tax Collections by State and Type of Tax 2021" obtained at the United States Census Bureau at https://www.census.gov/data/tables/2021/econ/qtax/historical.html. For this exercise, we extract data for *sales and gross receipts taxes by state* for the first quarter of 2021. We then convert the data to a U.S. map chart and analyze the results.

Required

1. Download Excel file DA10-1 found in myBusinessCourse.
2. Prepare a table by extracting from the U.S. Census Bureau file: General Sales and Gross Receipts Taxes by state for 2021 Q1. You will only be using the General Sales and Gross Receipts data in your analysis. Do not include Washington, D.C. in your table. *Hint:* Eliminate unnecessary data. Then use the Transpose function. (You may want to unmerge cells before transposing the data. After the transposition, you can line up the amounts with the states.) Convert the data to a table as the final step.
3. List the total of the amounts in your table. (Leave the amounts in thousands.)
4. Using the table as a reference, list the states with no tax.
5. Prepare a map chart of the tax by state. *Hint:* Highlight your data; then click on Insert, Maps, and Filled Map. If you're having trouble with the map, try converting the Xs in the Receipts column for states with no taxes to 0s.
6. What is the top and bottom end of the legend automatically prepared for the chart?
7. Answer the following questions using the map visualization:
   a. What three states have the largest tax?
   b. Where is there a visible cluster of mid-range taxes on the map if we consider the map in four quadrants?
   c. Where is there the least amount of tax on the map if we consider the map in four quadrants?
8. Is the amount of sales tax dependent only on the volume of sales activity in the state?
9. Does the map visualization provide information on the sales tax rate by state?

DA10-2. Preparing Excel Schedules to Determine Compliance with Debt Agreements Monroe Inc. (the Company) obtained financing from Pro Bank in Year 8. Associated with the debt agreement are debt covenants, which place restrictions on the Company's activities. The intention of the covenants is to protect the lender (Pro Bank) from a situation where the Company is unable to pay the debt when it is due. A debt agreement will include any debt covenants along with details on any calculations involved. From the debt agreement between Monroe Inc. and Pro Bank, the financial covenants are included below. Key definitions of certain terms are also included.

Financial Covenants

1. Total Leverage Ratio. The Company will not, as of the last day of any fiscal quarter, permit the Total Leverage Ratio to be greater than 2.00 to 1.00.
2. Minimum EBITDA. The Company will not, as of the last day of any fiscal quarter, permit EBITDA, for the period of the quarter ending on or immediately prior to such date to be less than $300 million.
3. Funded Debt. The Company will not, at any time, permit the aggregate outstanding principal amount of all Funded Debt to exceed an amount equal to 10% of the Company's total assets (as determined as of the last day of the most recently ended fiscal quarter for which financial statements have been provided).

Definitions

- *Total Leverage Ratio:* As of any date of determination, the ratio of (a) Funded Debt on such date to (b) EBITDA for the quarter ending on or immediately prior to such date.
- *EBITDA:* For any period, the sum of the following, for the Company in accordance with GAAP: Net income for such period plus (b) the sum of the following, to the extent deducted in determining net income for such period: (1) income tax expense during such period, (2) interest expense, net of interest income for such period, and (3) amortization and depreciation expense.
- *Funded Debt:* As of the date of determination with respect to the Company, the sum of all liabilities of the Company due to borrowing money.

The Excel file associated with this exercise includes quarterly financial information for Monroe Inc. from Quarter 1 of Year 10 to Quarter 2 of Year 12.

Required

1. Download Excel file DA10-2 found in myBusinessCourse.
2. Determine the key financial categories needed to determine whether the company is in compliance with the three financial covenants for each quarter presented.
3. Calculate the key financial amounts within the Excel worksheet.

4. Create an IF statement for each financial covenant per quarter that returns a "YES" if the company is in compliance at quarter end, or a "NO" if the company is not in compliance at quarter end.

5. List the formula for the IF statement for Q1 Year 10 for the first financial statement covenant.

6. Add a rule to your IF statement to shade the cell where YES is contained in green and a rule to shade the cell where NO is contained in red. *Hint:* Under the Home tab, click on Conditional formatting, Highlight cell rules, Text that contains, and then set up two rules.

7. Indicate the quarter ends (if any) where the company is not in compliance with the financial covenants.

8. Create *What-if Scenario 1* by duplicating the original schedule created. Assume that Funded Debt was higher by 10% at each quarter-end. Increase interest expense by 10% as well as Funded Debt. Assume no other changes in the financial data provided.

9. Indicate the quarter ends (if any) where the company is not in compliance with the financial covenants based on the schedule created in part 8.

10. Create *What-if Scenario 2* by duplicating the original schedule created. Assume that total assets were lower by 10% each quarter-end. Assume no other changes in the financial data provided.

11. Indicate the quarter ends (if any) where the company is not in compliance with the financial covenants based on the schedule created in part 10.

12. Determine the minimum required net income for each quarter in order to be in compliance with the second financial covenant, using the original data. Use 30% of earnings before tax as an estimate for tax expense. Round tax expense to one decimal place.

13. Determine the quarter where there is the smallest difference between net income reported and the minimum net income required to meet the second financial covenant.

DATA VISUALIZATION

Data Visualization Activities are available in myBusinessCourse. These assignments use Tableau Dashboards to expose students to visual depictions of data and introduce students to data analytics through data visualizations. These exercises are easily assignable and auto graded by MBC.

Data Visualization

EXERCISES—SET A

E10-1A. Liabilities on the Balance Sheet For each of the following situations, indicate the amount shown as a liability on the balance sheet of Cooper, Inc., at December 31: **LO1, 3**

   a. Cooper has accounts payable of $120,000 for merchandise included in the year-end inventory.

   b. Cooper agreed to purchase a $30,000 drill press the following January.

   c. During November and December of the current year, Cooper sold products to a firm and guaranteed them against product failure for 90 days. Estimated costs of honoring this provision next year are $2,200.

   d. On December 15, Cooper declared a $60,000 cash dividend payable on January 15 of the following year to shareholders of record on December 31.

   e. Cooper provides a profit-sharing bonus for its executives equal to 5 percent of the reported before-tax income for the current year. The estimated before-tax income for the current year is $800,000.

E10-2A. Maturity Dates of Notes Payable Determine the maturity date and compute the interest for each of the following notes payable with add-on interest: **LO1**

	Date of Note	Principal	Interest Rate (%)	Term
a.	August 5	$20,000	9	120 days
b.	May 10	8,400	7	90 days
c.	October 5	12,000	6	45 days
d.	July 6	6,000	10	60 days
e.	September 15	12,000	8	75 days

E10-3A. Accrued Interest Payable Compute the interest accrued on each of the following notes payable owed by Northland, Inc., on December 31: **LO1**

Lender	Date of Note	Principal	Interest Rate (%)	Term
Maple	11/21	$18,000	10	120 days
Wyman	12/13	5,000	8	90 days
Nahn	12/10	16,000	12	60 days

LO1   **E10-4A.**   **Adjusting Entries for Interest**   The following note transactions occurred during the year for Towne Company:

Nov.   25   Towne issued a 90-day, 9 percent note payable for $8,000 to Hyatt Company for merchandise.

Dec.   7   Towne signed a 120-day, $30,000 note at the bank at 10 percent.
       22   Towne gave Barr, Inc., a $12,000, 4 percent, 60-day note in payment of account.

Prepare the general journal entries necessary to adjust the interest accounts at December 31.

LO1   **E10-5A.**   **Excise and Sales Tax Calculations**   Clifford Company has just billed a customer for $1,100, an amount that includes an 8 percent excise tax and a 2 percent state sales tax.

a.   What amount of revenue is recorded?
b.   Prepare a general journal entry to record the transaction on the books of Clifford Company.

LO1   **E10-6A.**   **Advance Payments for Goods**   The Petaluma Daily Times Corporation (CDT) publishes a daily newspaper. A 52-week subscription sells for $260. Assume that CDT sells 100 subscriptions on January 1. None of the subscriptions are cancelled as of March 31.

a.   Prepare a journal entry to record the receipt of the subscriptions on January 1.
b.   Prepare a journal entry to record one week of earned revenue on March 25.

LO3   **E10-7A.**   **Warranty Costs**   Zealand Company sells a motor that carries a 3-month unconditional warranty against product failure. Based on a reliable statistical analysis, Milford knows that between the sale and the end of the product warranty period, 4 percent of the units sold will require repair at an average cost of $60 per unit. The following data reflect Milford's recent experience:

	October	November	December	Dec. 31 Total
Units sold	23,000	22,000	25,000	70,000
Known product failures from sales in:				
October	120	180	160	460
November		130	220	350
December			210	210

Calculate and prepare a journal entry to record the estimated liability for product warranties at December 31. Assume that warranty costs of known failures have already been reflected in the records.

LO2   **E10-8A.**   **Financial Statement Presentation of Bond Accounts**   Indicate the proper financial statement classification for each of the following accounts:

       Gain on Bond Retirement (material amount)
       Discount on Long-Term Bonds Payable
       Mortgage Notes Payable
       Long-Term Bonds Payable
       Bond Interest Expense
       Bond Interest Payable
       Premium on Long-Term Bonds Payable

LO2   **E10-9A.**   **Early Retirement of Bonds**   Eaton Company issued $600,000 of 8 percent, 20-year bonds at 106 on January 1, 2016. Interest is payable semiannually on July 1 and January 1. Through January 1, 2022, Eaton amortized $5,000 of the bond premium. On January 1, 2022, Eaton retired the bonds at 103 (after making the interest payment on that date). Prepare the journal entry to record the bond retirement on January 1, 2022.

LO2   **E10-10A.**   **Installment Term Loan**   On December 31 Eppel, Inc., borrowed $900,000 on an 8 percent, 15-year mortgage note payable. The note is to be repaid in equal semiannual installments of $52,047 (payable on June 30 and December 31). Prepare journal entries to reflect (a) the issuance of the mortgage note payable, (b) the payment of the first installment on June 30, and (c) the payment of the second installment on December 31. Round amounts to the nearest dollar.

E10-11A. Installment Term Loan On December 31 Clarke, Inc., borrowed $900,000 on a 7 percent, 10-year mortgage note payable. The note is to be repaid in equal annual installments of $128,140 (payable on December 31). Prepare journal entries to reflect (a) the issuance of the mortgage note payable, (b) the payment of the first installment on December 31 of the following year, and (c) the payment of the second installment on December 31 two years later. Round amounts to the nearest dollar.

LO2

E10-12A. Contingent Liabilities Determine which of the following transactions represent contingent liabilities for Sawyer Rental and indicate the proper accounting treatment at the company's fiscal year-end by placing the letter of the correct accounting treatment in the space provided.

LO3

a. Accrue a liability and disclose in the financial statement notes
b. Disclose in the financial statement footnotes only
c. No disclosure

1. Sawyer Rental cosigned a loan for $75,000 due in one year for Wyler Company. Wyler is a very profitable company and is very liquid, making it a remote chance Sawyer will have to pay the loan.	
2. One of Sawyer's rental tents collapsed at a wedding and injured the bride and groom. Sawyer's legal counsel believes it is probable that Sawyer will have to pay damages of $400,000.	
3. Sawyer Rental is being audited by the Internal Revenue Service. Its tax returns for the past two years are being examined. At the company's year-end, the audit is still in process. Sawyer's CPA believes that payment of significant taxes is possible.	

E10-13A. Ratio Analysis Presented below are summary financial data from Porter's annual report:

LO4

Amounts in millions	
Balance sheet	
Cash and cash equivalents	$ 1,850
Marketable securities	19,100
Accounts receivable (net)	9,367
Total current assets	39,088
Total assets	123,078
Current liabilities	38,450
Long-term debt	7,279
Shareholders' equity	68,278
Income statement	
Interest expense	400
Net income before taxes	14,007

Calculate the following ratios:
a. Times-interest-earned ratio   *c.* Current ratio
b. Quick ratio

E10-14A. Issue Price of a Bond Matt Enterprises issued $200,000 of 10 percent, five-year bonds with interest payable semiannually. Determine the issue price if the bonds are priced to yield (a) 10 percent, (b) 6 percent, and (c) 12 percent.

LO2, 5
(Appendix 10A)

E10-15A. Issue Price of a Bond Abbott, Inc., plans to issue $500,000 of 10 percent bonds that will pay interest semiannually and mature in five years. Assume that the effective interest rate is 12 percent per year compounded semiannually. Calculate the selling price of the bonds.

LO2, 5
(Appendix 10A)

E10-16A. Bonds Payable Journal Entries; Straight-Line Interest Amortization On December 31 Brown Company issued $750,000 of 20-year, 8 percent bonds payable for $621,307, yielding an effective interest rate of 10 percent. Interest is payable semiannually on June 30 and December 31. Prepare journal entries to reflect (a) the issuance of the bonds, (b) the semiannual interest payment and discount amortization (straight-line interest method) on June 30, and (c) the semiannual interest payment and discount amortization on December 31. Round amounts to the nearest dollar.

LO2, 5
(Appendix 10A)

LO2, 5
(Appendix 10A)

E10-17A. **Bonds Payable Journal Entries; Straight-Line Interest Amortization** On December 31 Shade Company issued $250,000 of 20-year, 8 percent bonds payable for $276,694, yielding an effective interest rate of 7 percent. Interest is payable semiannually on June 30 and December 31. Prepare journal entries to reflect (a) the issuance of the bonds, (b) the semiannual interest payment and premium amortization (straight-line interest method) on June 30, and (c) the semiannual interest payment and premium amortization on December 31. Round amounts to the nearest dollar.

LO2, 5
(Appendix 10A)

E10-18A. **Bonds Payable Journal Entries; Effective Interest Amortization** On December 31 Phillip Company issued $600,000 of 10-year, 9 percent bonds payable for $496,771, yielding an effective interest rate of 12 percent. Interest is payable semiannually on June 30 and December 31. Prepare journal entries to reflect (a) the issuance of the bonds, (b) the semiannual interest payment and discount amortization (effective interest method) on June 30, and (c) the semiannual interest payment and discount amortization on December 31. Round amounts to the nearest dollar.

LO2, 5
(Appendix 10A)

E10-19A. **Bonds Payable Journal Entries; Effective Interest Amortization** On December 31 Karen Company issued $400,000 of 10-year, 10 percent bonds payable for $454,361, yielding an effective interest rate of 8 percent. Interest is payable semiannually on June 30 and December 31. Prepare journal entries to reflect (a) the issuance of the bonds, (b) the semiannual interest payment and premium amortization (effective interest method) on June 30, and (c) the semiannual interest payment and premium amortization on December 31. Round amounts to the nearest dollar.

LO6
(Appendix 10B)

E10-20A. **Leases** On January 1, Lorraine, Inc., entered into a lease contract. The lease contract was a 10-year lease for a computer with $15,000 annual lease payments due at the end of each year. Lorraine took possession of the computer on January 1. The present value of the lease payments under the lease contract is $108,703.

The lease contract is a finance lease. Prepare the journal entry for this lease on January 1.

LO2

E10-21A. **Coupon Rates, Yield Rates, and Bond Issuance Prices** The relation between a bond's coupon rate and yield rate is known to influence a bond's issuance price. Presented below are coupon rates and yield rates for a selection of corporate bonds. Identify whether each bond was sold at a discount, at its par value, or at a premium, and explain why.

Bond	Coupon Rate	Yield Rate
A....................	7.5%	7.55%
B....................	8.1	8.00
C....................	6.0	6.00
D....................	4.5	4.40
E....................	9.0	9.15

EXERCISES—SET B

LO1

E10-1B. **Liabilities on the Balance Sheet** For each of the following situations, indicate the amount shown as a liability on the balance sheet of Javier, Inc., at December 31:

a. Javier's general ledger shows a credit balance of $130,000 in Long-Term Notes Payable. Of this amount, a $30,000 installment becomes due on June 30 of the following year.

b. Javier estimates its unpaid income tax liability for the current year is $34,000; it plans to pay this amount in March of the following year.

c. On December 31, Javier received a $30,000 invoice for merchandise shipped on December 28. The merchandise has not yet been received. The merchandise was shipped FOB shipping point.

d. During the year, Javier collected $10,500 of state sales tax. At year-end, it has not yet remitted $1,400 of these taxes to the state department of revenue.

e. On December 31, Javier's bank approved a $10,000, 90-day loan. Javier plans to sign the note and receive the money on January 2 of the following year.

LO1

E10-2B. **Maturity Dates of Notes Payable** Determine the maturity date and compute the interest for each of the following notes payable:

	Date of Note	Principal	Interest Rate (%)	Term
a.	July 10	$ 8,400	9	90 days
b.	April 4	6,000	8	120 days
c.	May 19	5,600	7.5	180 days
d.	June 10.	6,500	8	45 days
e.	October 29	10,000	3	60 days

E10-3B. **Accrued Interest Payable** Compute the interest accrued on each of the following notes payable owed by Galloway, Inc., on December 31:   LO1

Lender	Date of Note	Principal	Interest Rate (%)	Term
Barton.	12/4	$12,000	12	150 days
Lawson.	12/13	14,000	10	90 days
Riley	12/19	15,000	11	90 days

E10-4B. **Adjusting Entries for Interest** The following note transactions occurred during the year for Zale Company: LO1

Nov. 25 Zale issued a 120-day, 12 percent note payable for $9,000 to Porter Company for merchandise.
Dec. 10 Zale signed a 180-day, $7,200 note at the bank at 10 percent.
     23 Zale gave Dale, Inc., a $9,000, 6 percent, 60-day note in payment of account.

Prepare the journal entries necessary to adjust the interest accounts at December 31.

E10-5B. **Excise and Sales Tax Calculations** Beck Company has just billed a customer for $1,400, an amount that includes an 8 percent excise tax and a 4 percent state sales tax.   LO1

  a. What amount of revenue is recorded?
  b. Prepare a journal entry to record the transaction on the books of Beck Company.

E10-6B. **Advance Payment for Services** The Whitney Bluebirds football team sells a 15-game season ticket for $180. Assume that the team sells 2,000 season tickets on August 10. The tickets are all used for admission.   LO1

  a. Prepare a journal entry to record the sale of the season tickets on August 10.
  b. Prepare a journal entry to record one game of earned revenue on September 12.

E10-7B. **Warranty Costs** Young Company sells an electric timer that carries a 3-month unconditional warranty against product failure. Based on a reliable statistical analysis, Young knows that between the sale and the end of the product warranty period, 4 percent of the units sold will require repair at an average cost of $50 per unit. The following data reflect Young's recent experience: LO3

	October	November	December	Dec. 31 Total
Units sold	36,000	34,000	45,000	115,000
Known product failures from sales in:				
October.........................	320	550	210	1,080
November		230	360	590
December.......................			410	410

Calculate and prepare a journal entry to record the estimated liability for product warranties at December 31. Assume that warranty costs of known failures have already been reflected in the records.

E10-8B. **Bonds Payable on the Balance Sheet** The adjusted trial balance for the Mammoth Corporation at the end of 2018 contains the following accounts: LO2

Bond interest payable.	$ 40,000
9% Bonds payable due 2020	600,000
10% Bonds payable due 2019	500,000
Discount on 9% bonds payable	19,000
Premium on 10% bonds payable	15,000
Zero-coupon bonds payable due 2021.	170,500
8% Bonds payable due 2023	200,000

Prepare the long-term liabilities section of the balance sheet. Indicate the balance sheet classification for any accounts listed above that do not belong in the long-term liabilities section.

LO2   E10-9B.   Early Retirement of Bonds Navarro, Inc., issued $250,000 of 8 percent, 20-year bonds at 98 on June 30, 2016. Interest is payable semiannually on December 31 and June 30. Through June 30, 2022, Navarro amortized $3,000 of the bond discount. On June 30, 2022, Navarro retired the bonds at 102 (after making the interest payment on that date). Prepare the journal entry to record the bond retirement on June 30, 2022.

LO2   E10-10B. Installment Term Loan On December 31 James, Inc., borrowed $500,000 on an 8 percent, 10-year mortgage note payable. The note is to be repaid in equal quarterly installments of $18,278 (beginning March 31). Prepare journal entries to reflect (a) the issuance of the mortgage note payable, (b) the payment of the first installment on March 31 and (c) the payment of the second installment on June 30. Round amounts to the nearest dollar.

LO2   E10-11B. Installment Term Loan On December 31 James, Inc., borrowed $300,000 on a 6 percent, 20-year mortgage note payable. The note is to be repaid in equal semiannual installments of $12,979 (beginning July 1). Prepare journal entries to reflect (a) the issuance of the mortgage note payable, (b) the payment of the first installment on July 1, and (c) the payment of the second installment on December 31. Round amounts to the nearest dollar.

LO3   E10-12B. Contingent Liabilities Determine which of the following transactions represent contingent liabilities for June Leasing and indicate the proper accounting treatment at the company's fiscal year-end by placing the letter of the correct accounting treatment in the space provided.

a. Accrue a liability and disclose in the financial statement notes
b. Disclose in the financial statement footnotes only
c. No disclosure

1. June Leasing was sued by a customer who claimed the equipment they leased was not up to the standards described by June. June stands by its claims and can support all the item's specifications. June plans to vigorously defend itself and believes the chances of losing the lawsuit are remote.	
2. A government audit of June found that the company is in violation of several work safety regulations. June has been notified that it will be assessed a fine of $25,000. June has agreed to make the safety changes so that it will be in compliance with the regulations.	
3. June Leasing has been served a lawsuit by a customer that claims he was injured from one of the products leased from June. June plans to defend itself in court, but its lawyers believe there is a 50/50 chance that June will lose and be forced to pay $50,000.	

LO4   E10-13B. Ratio Analysis Presented below are summary financial data from the Smith Co. annual report:

Amounts in millions	
Balance sheet	
Cash and cash equivalents	$ 2,200
Marketable securities	16,200
Accounts receivable (net)	10,000
Total current assets	42,000
Total assets	155,000
Current liabilities	25,000
Long-term debt	52,500
Shareholders' equity	79,500
Income statement	
Interest expense	6,400
Net income before taxes	37,800

Calculate the following ratios:

a. Times-interest-earned ratio
b. Quick ratio
c. Current ratio

E10-14B. Issue Price of a Bond May Enterprises issued $200,000 of 6 percent, 5-year bonds with interest payable semiannually. Determine the issue price if the bonds are priced to yield (a) 6 percent, (b) 10 percent, and (c) 2 percent.

LO2, 5
(Appendix 10A)

E10-15B. Issue Price of a Bond Atlantic, Inc., plans to issue $700,000 of 9 percent bonds that will pay interest semiannually and mature in 10 years. Assume that the effective interest is 8 percent per year compounded semiannually. Calculate the selling price of the bonds.

LO2, 5
(Appendix 10A)

E10-16B. Bonds Payable Journal Entries; Straight-Line Interest Amortization On December 31 Green Company issued $600,000 of 15-year, 10 percent bonds payable for $517,411, yielding an effective interest rate of 12 percent. Interest is payable semiannually on June 30 and December 31. Prepare journal entries to reflect (a) the issuance of the bonds, (b) the semiannual interest payment and discount amortization (straight-line interest method) on June 30, and (c) the semiannual interest payment and discount amortization on December 31. Round amounts to the nearest dollar.

LO2, 5
(Appendix 10A)

E10-17B. Bonds Payable Journal Entries; Straight-Line Interest Amortization On December 31 Tan Company issued $400,000 of 10-year, 12 percent bonds payable for $449,849, yielding an effective interest rate of 10 percent. Interest is payable semiannually on June 30 and December 31. Prepare journal entries to reflect (a) the issuance of the bonds, (b) the semiannual interest payment and premium amortization (straight-line interest method) on June 30, and (c) the semiannual interest payment and premium amortization on December 31. Round amounts to the nearest dollar.

LO2, 5
(Appendix 10A)

E10-18B. Bonds Payable Journal Entries; Effective Interest Amortization On December 31 Blair Company issued $600,000 of 20-year, 11 percent bonds payable for $554,861, yielding an effective interest rate of 12 percent. Interest is payable semiannually on June 30 and December 31. Prepare journal entries to reflect (a) the issuance of the bonds, (b) the semiannual interest payment and discount amortization (effective interest method) on June 30, and (c) the semiannual interest payment and discount amortization on December 31. Round amounts to the nearest dollar.

LO2, 5
(Appendix 10A)

E10-19B. Bonds Payable Journal Entries; Effective Interest Amortization On December 31 Kim Company issued $500,000 of five-year, 12 percent bonds payable for $538,609, yielding an effective interest rate of 10 percent. Interest is payable semiannually on June 30 and December 31. Prepare journal entries to reflect (a) the issuance of the bonds, (b) the semiannual interest payment and premium amortization (effective interest method) on June 30, and (c) the semiannual interest payment and premium amortization on December 31. Round amounts to the nearest dollar.

LO2, 5
(Appendix 10A)

E10-20B. Leases On January 1, Cheryl, Inc., entered into a lease contract. The lease contract was an eight-year lease for a sound system with $28,000 annual lease payments due at the end of each year. Cheryl took possession of the sound system on January 1. The present value of the lease payments under the lease contract is $173,778.

The lease contract is a finance lease. Prepare the journal entry for this lease on January 1.

LO6
(Appendix 10B)

E10-21B. Coupon Rates, Yield Rates, and Bond Issuance Prices The relation between a bond's coupon rate and yield rate is known to influence a bond's issuance price. Presented below are coupon rates and yield rates for a selection of corporate bonds. Identify whether each bond was sold at a discount, at its par value, or at a premium, and explain why.

LO2

Bond	Coupon Rate	Yield Rate
A	7.5%	7.45%
B	8.1	8.40
C	6.0	5.80
D	4.4	4.40
E	8.9	9.10

PROBLEMS—SET A

P10-1A. Journal Entries for Accounts and Notes Payable Lyon Company had the following transactions:

LO1

Apr.	8	Issued a 6,000, 60-day, 6 percent note payable in payment of an account with Bennett Company.
May	15	Borrowed $40,000 from Lincoln Bank, signing a 60-day note at 9 percent.
June	7	Paid Bennett Company the principal and interest due on the April 8 note payable.

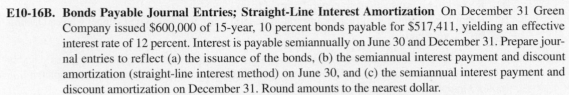

July	6	Purchased $14,000 of merchandise from Bolton Company; signed a 90-day note with 10 percent interest.
July	14	Paid the May 15 note due Lincoln Bank.
Oct.	2	Borrowed $30,000 from Lincoln Bank, signing a 120-day note at 9 percent.
	4	Defaulted on the note payable to Bolton Company.

Required

a. Record these transactions in general journal form.

b. Record any adjusting entries for interest in general journal form. Lyon Company has a December 31 year-end.

LO1 P10-2A. Adjusting Entries for Interest At December 31, 2021, Eric Corporation had two notes payable outstanding (notes 1 and 2). At December 31, 2022, Eric also had two notes payable outstanding (notes 3 and 4). These notes are described below:

	Date of Note	Principal Amount	Interest Rate	Number of Days
December 31, 2021				
Note 1	11/16/2021	$30,000	8%	120
Note 2	12/4/2021	16,000	9	60
December 31, 2022				
Note 3	12/7/2022	9,000	10	60
Note 4	12/21/2022	18,000	12	30

Required

a. Prepare the adjusting entries for interest at December 31, 2021.

b. Assume that the adjusting entries were made at December 31, 2021. Prepare the 2022 journal entries to record payment of the notes that were outstanding at December 31, 2021.

c. Prepare the adjusting entries for interest at December 31, 2022.

LO1 P10-3A. Recording Payroll and Payroll Taxes Ruth Corporation had the following payroll for April:

Officers' salaries	$36,000
Sales salaries	67,000
Federal income taxes withheld	19,000
FICA taxes withheld	7,500
Health insurance premiums withheld	1,800
Union dues withheld	1,400
Salaries (included above) subject to federal unemployment taxes	55,000
Salaries (included above) subject to state unemployment taxes	58,000

Required

Prepare journal entries on April 30 to record:

a. Accrual of the monthly payroll.

b. Payment of the net payroll.

c. Accrual of employer's payroll taxes. (Assume that the FICA tax matches the amount withheld, the federal unemployment tax is 0.6 percent, and the state unemployment tax is 5.4 percent.)

d. Payment of all liabilities related to this payroll. (Assume that all are settled at the same time.)

LO1 P10-4A. Recording Payroll and Payroll Taxes The following data are taken from Stockton Wholesale Company's May payroll:

Administrative salaries	$50,000
Sales salaries	51,000
Custodial salaries	7,000
Total payroll	$108,000
Salaries subject to 1.45 percent Medicare tax	$108,000
Salaries subject to 6.2 percent Social Security tax	85,000
Salaries subject to federal unemployment taxes	14,000
Salaries subject to state unemployment taxes	21,000
Federal income taxes withheld from all salaries	17,800

Assume that the company is subject to a 2 percent state unemployment tax (due to a favorable experience rating) and a 0.6 percent federal unemployment tax.

Required

Record the following in general journal form on May 31:

a. Accrual of the monthly payroll.

b. Payment of the net payroll.

c. Accrual of the employer's payroll taxes. (Assume that the FICA tax matches the amount withheld).

d. Payment of these payroll-related liabilities. (Assume that all are settled at the same time.)

P10-5A. Excise and Sales Tax Calculations Fullerton Corporation initially records its sales at amounts that exclude any related excise and sales taxes. During June, Fullerton recorded total sales of $700,000. An analysis of June sales indicated the following: **LO1**

1. Thirty percent of sales were subject to both a 10 percent excise tax and a 6 percent sales tax.

2. Fifty percent of sales were subject only to the sales tax.

3. The balance of sales was for labor charges not subject to either excise or sales tax.

Required

a. Calculate the related liabilities for excise and sales taxes for June.

b. Prepare the necessary journal entry at June 30 to record the monthly payment of excise tax and sales tax to the government.

P10-6A. Noncontingent and Contingent Liabilities The following independent situations represent various types of liabilities: **LO1, 3**

1. One of the employees of Martin Company was severely injured when hit by one of Martin's trucks in the parking lot. The 35-year-old employee will never be able to work again. Insurance coverage is minimal. The employee has sued Martin Company and a jury trial is scheduled.

2. A shareholder has filed a lawsuit against Sweitzer Corporation. Sweitzer's attorneys have reviewed the facts of the case. Their review revealed that similar lawsuits have never resulted in a cash award and it is highly unlikely that this lawsuit will either.

3. Armstrong Company signed a 60-day, 10 percent note when it purchased merchandise from Fischer Company.

4. Richmond Company has been notified by the Department of Environmental Protection (DEP) that a state where it has a plant is filing a lawsuit for groundwater pollution against Richmond and another company that has a plant adjacent to Richmond's plant. Test results have not identified the exact source of the pollution. Richmond's manufacturing process can produce by-products that pollute ground water.

5. Fredonia Company has cosigned a note payable to a bank for one of its customers. The customer received all of the proceeds of the note. Fredonia will have to repay the loan if the customer fails to do so. Fredonia Company believes that it is unlikely that it will have to pay the note.

6. Holt Company manufactured and sold products to Z-Mart, a retailer that sold the products to consumers. The manufacturer's warranty offers replacement of the product if it is found to be defective within 90 days of the sale to the consumer. Historically, 1.2 percent of the products are returned for replacement.

Required

Prepare a multicolumn analysis that presents the following information for each of these situations:

a. Number of the situation.

b. Type of liability: (1) noncontingent or (2) contingent.

c. Accounting treatment: (1) record in accounts, (2) disclose in a note to the financial statements, or (3) neither record nor disclose.

P10-7A. Bonds Payable Journal Entries; Issued at Par Plus Accrued Interest Ashton, Inc., which closes its books on December 31, is authorized to issue $800,000 of 9 percent, 20-year bonds dated May 1, with interest payments on November 1 and May 1.   **LO2**

Required

Prepare journal entries to record the following events, assuming that the bonds were sold at 100 plus accrued interest on October 1:

a. The bond issuance.

b. Payment of the first semiannual period's interest on November 1.

    c.   Accrual of bond interest expense at December 31.

    d.   Payment of the semiannual interest on May 1 of the following year.

    e.   Retirement of $400,000 of the bonds at 101 on May 1, Year 2 (immediately after the interest payment on that date).

LO4   **P10-8A.**   **Current Ratio, Quick Ratio, and Times-Interest-Earned Ratio** The following data are from the current accounting records of Rome Company:

Cash	$120
Accounts receivable (net of allowance of 40)	200
Inventory	150
Other current assets	80
Accounts payable	110
Other current liabilities	170

The president of the company is concerned that the company is in violation of a debt covenant that requires the company to maintain a minimum current ratio of 2.0. He believes the best way to rectify this is to reverse a bad debt write-off in the amount of $10 that the company just recorded. He argues that the write-off was done too early, and that the collections department should be given more time to collect the outstanding receivables. The CFO argues that this will have no effect on the current ratio, so a better idea is to use $10 of cash to pay accounts payable early.

Required

    a.   Which idea, the president's or the CFO's, is better for attaining a minimum 2.0 current ratio?

    b.   Will either the quick ratio or the times-interest-earned ratio be affected by either of these ideas?

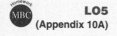

LO5   **P10-9A.**   **Effective Interest Amortization** On December 31, Casper, Inc., issued $300,000 of 8 percent,
(Appendix 10A)   10-year bonds for $262,613, yielding an effective interest rate of 10 percent. Semiannual interest is payable on June 30 and December 31 each year. The firm uses the effective interest method to amortize the discount.

Required

    a.   Prepare an amortization schedule showing the necessary information for the first two interest periods. Round amounts to the nearest dollar.

    b.   Prepare the journal entry for the bond issuance on December 31.

    c.   Prepare the journal entry to record the bond interest payment and discount amortization at June 30 of the following year.

    d.   Prepare the journal entry to record the bond interest payment and discount amortization at December 31 of the following year.

LO5   **P10-10A.**   **Effective Interest Amortization** On January 1, Lowe, Inc., issued $500,000 of 10 percent, 20-year
(Appendix 10A)   bonds for $598,964, yielding an effective interest rate of 8 percent. Semiannual interest is payable on June 30 and December 31 each year. The firm uses the effective interest method to amortize the premium.

Required

    a.   Prepare an amortization schedule showing the necessary information for the first two interest periods. Round amounts to the nearest dollar.

    b.   Prepare the journal entry for the bond issuance on January 1.

    c.   Prepare the journal entry to record the bond interest payment and premium amortization at June 30.

    d.   Prepare the journal entry to record the bond interest payment and premium amortization at December 31.

LO5   **P10-11A.**   **Accounting for Bonds Sold at a Discount** The Biltmore National Bank raised capital through the
(Appendix 10A)   sale of $150 million face value of 8 percent coupon rate, 10-year bonds. The bonds paid interest semiannually and were sold at a time when equivalent risk-rated bonds carried a yield rate of 10 percent.

    a.   Calculate the proceeds that The Biltmore National Bank received from the sale of the 8 percent bonds.

    b.   Calculate the interest expense on the bonds for the first year that the bonds are outstanding.

    c.   Calculate the book value of the bonds at the end of the first year.

P10-12A. Accounting for Bonds Issues at a Premium The Longo Corporation issued $50 million maturity value of 6 percent coupon rate bonds, with interest paid semiannually. At the time of the bond issuance, equivalent risk-rated debt instruments carried a yield rate of 4 percent. The bonds matured in five years.

LO5
(Appendix 10A)

   a. Calculate the proceeds that the Longo Corporation would receive from the sale of the bonds.
   b. Calculate the interest expense on the bonds for the first year.
   c. Calculate the book value of the bonds at the end of the first year.

PROBLEMS—SET B

P10-1B. Journal Entries for Accounts Payable and Notes Payable Geary Company had the following transactions:

LO1

Apr.	15	Issued a $6,000, 60-day, 8 percent note payable in payment of an account with Marion Company.
May	22	Borrowed $50,000 from Sinclair Bank, signing a 60-day note at 9 percent.
June	14	Paid Marion Company the principal and interest due on the April 15 note payable.
July	13	Purchased $15,000 of merchandise from Sharp Company; signed a 90-day note with 8 percent interest.
	21	Paid the May 22 note due Sinclair Bank.
Oct.	2	Borrowed $38,000 from Sinclair Bank, signing a 120-day note at 12 percent.
	11	Defaulted on the note payable to Sharp Company.

Required
   a. Record these transactions in general journal form.
   b. Record any adjusting entries for interest in general journal form. Geary Company has a December 31 year-end.

P10-2B. Adjusting Entries for Interest At December 31, 2021, Seattle Corporation had two notes payable outstanding (notes 1 and 2). At December 31, 2022, Seattle also had two notes payable outstanding (notes 3 and 4). These notes are described below.

LO1

	Date of Note	Principal Amount	Interest Rate	Number of Days
December 31, 2021				
Note 1................	11/25/2021	$35,000	8%	90
Note 2................	12/10/2021	16,900	10	60
December 31, 2022				
Note 3................	12/11/2022	15,400	9	120
Note 4................	12/7/2022	20,000	12	90

Required
   a. Prepare the adjusting entries for interest at December 31, 2021.
   b. Assume that the adjusting entries were made at December 31, 2021, and that no adjusting entries were made during 2022. Prepare the 2022 journal entries to record payment of the notes that were outstanding at December 31, 2021.
   c. Prepare the adjusting entries for interest at December 31, 2022.

P10-3B. Recording Payroll and Payroll Taxes England, Inc., had the following payroll for March:

LO1

Officers' salaries...	$39,000
Sales salaries..	60,000
Federal income taxes withheld...	21,000
FICA taxes withheld..	7,900
Health insurance premiums withheld.......................................	2,500
Salaries (included above) subject to federal unemployment taxes...........	55,000
Salaries (included above) subject to state unemployment taxes.............	65,000

Required
Prepare journal entries on March 31 to record:

   a. Accrual of the monthly payroll.

b. Payment of the net payroll.

c. Accrual of employer's payroll taxes. (Assume that the FICA tax matches the amount withheld, the federal unemployment tax is 0.6 percent, and the state unemployment tax is 5.4 percent.)

d. Payment of all liabilities related to this payroll. (Assume that all are settled at the same time.)

 LO1   P10-4B.   Recording Payroll and Payroll Taxes The following data are taken from Madison Distribution Company's March payroll:

Administrative salaries	$34,000
Sales salaries	58,000
Custodial salaries	8,000
Total payroll	$100,000
Salaries subject to 1.45 percent Medicare tax	$100,000
Salaries subject to 6.2 percent Social Security tax	100,000
Salaries subject to federal unemployment taxes	66,000
Salaries subject to state unemployment taxes	76,000
Federal income taxes withheld from all salaries	18,600

Assume that the company is subject to a 5.2 percent state unemployment tax and 0.6 percent federal unemployment tax.

Required

Record the following in general journal form on March 31:

a. Accrual of the monthly payroll.

b. Payment of the net payroll.

c. Accrual of the employer's payroll taxes. (Assume that the FICA tax matches the amount withheld.)

d. Payment of these payroll-related liabilities. (Assume that all are settled at the same time.)

 LO1   P10-5B.   Excise and Sales Tax Calculations Adams Corporation initially records its sales at amounts that exclude any related excise and sales taxes. During May, Adams recorded total sales of $750,000. An analysis of May sales indicated the following:

1. Thirty percent of sales were subject to both a 10 percent excise tax and a 5 percent sales tax.
2. Sixty-five percent of sales were subject only to the sales tax.
3. The balance of sales was for labor charges not subject to either excise or sales tax.

Required

a. Calculate the related liabilities for excise and sales taxes for May.

b. Prepare the necessary journal entry at May 31 to record the monthly payment of excise tax and sales tax to the government.

LO1, 3   P10-6B.   Noncontingent and Contingent Liabilities The following independent situations represent various types of liabilities:

1. Marshall Company has a manufacturing plant located in a small, rural community. The only other major employer in the area is Baker Company, which is experiencing financial problems. Marshall agrees to guarantee a loan for Baker, so Baker will remain in the community. Baker will receive all the proceeds of the loan. However, Marshall will have to repay the loan if Baker fails to do so. Marshall believes that Baker will repay the loan.

2. The village of High Creek and the town of Middlebury have been jointly using a rural dump site for 25 years. The state Department of Natural Resources has notified the two municipalities that wells on the nearby farms are polluted and that the dump site will be closed while further testing is done. Cleanup could cost as much as $25 million.

3. Two people walking on the sidewalk in front of the building owned by First United Bank were injured when part of the building collapsed on them. They are 25 years old and both are totally disabled. The building had been in poor condition for a long time. Insurance coverage is minimal. Both are suing First United Bank, and a jury trial is scheduled.

4. Winters Company sells garden tractors through 120 dealers located throughout the United States. Winters provides a two-year warranty for all parts and labor on these tractors. Each year, the average warranty cost per tractor sold is approximately $40.

5. Cronnin Company signed a 90-day note when it bought a new delivery truck for $25,000.

6. The CPA firm of Boyd and Lampe is being sued by one of the owners of an audit client that went bankrupt three years after Boyd and Lampe conducted an audit. The CPA firm has no insurance for this type of lawsuit. The attorneys for the CPA firm have stated that similar cases have never been successful, and they expect the same result here.

Required

Prepare a multicolumn analysis that presents the following information for each of these situations:

a. Number of the situation.
b. Type of liability: (1) noncontingent or (2) contingent.
c. Accounting treatment: (1) record in accounts, (2) disclose in a note to the financial statements, or (3) neither record nor disclose.

P10-7B. **Bonds Payable Journal Entries; Issued at Par Plus Accrued Interest** Richard, Inc., which closes its books on December 31, is authorized to issue $600,000 of 6 percent, 20-year bonds dated March 1, with interest payments on September 1 and March 1.

LO2

Required

Prepare journal entries to record the following events, assuming that the bonds were sold at 100 plus accrued interest on July 1.

a. The bond issuance.
b. Payment of the semiannual interest on September 1.
c. Accrual of bond interest expense at December 31.
d. Payment of the semiannual interest on March 1 of the following year.
e. Retirement of $200,000 of the bonds at 104 on March 1, Year 3 (immediately after the interest payment on that date).

P10-8B. **Current Ratio, Quick Ratio, and Times-Interest-Earned Ratio** The following data are from the current accounting records of Crest Company:

LO4

Cash.	$240
Accounts receivable (net of allowance of 80)	400
Inventory.	300
Other current assets.	160
Accounts payable	220
Other current liabilities	340

The president of the company is concerned that the company may be in violation of a debt covenant that requires the company to maintain a minimum current ratio of 2.0. He believes the best way to rectify the problem is to reverse a bad debt write-off in the amount of $20 that the company just recorded. He argues that the write-off was done too early and that the collections department should be given more time to collect the outstanding amounts. The CFO argues that this will have no effect on the current ratio, so a better idea is to use $20 of cash to pay accounts payable early.

Required

a. Which idea, the president's or the CFO's, is better for attaining a minimum 2.0 current ratio?
b. Will either the quick ratio or the times-interest-earned ratio be affected by either of these ideas?

P10-9B. **Effective Interest Amortization** On December 31 Edmand, Inc., issued $750,000 of 11 percent, five-year bonds for $722,400, yielding an effective interest rate of 12 percent. Semiannual interest is payable on June 30 and December 31 each year. The firm uses the effective interest method to amortize the discount.

LO5
(Appendix 10A)

Required

a. Prepare an amortization schedule showing the necessary information for the first two interest periods. Round amounts to the nearest dollar.
b. Prepare the journal entry for the bond issuance on December 31.
c. Prepare the journal entry to record bond interest expense and discount amortization at June 30 of the following year.
d. Prepare the journal entry to record bond interest expense and discount amortization at December 31 of the following year.

LO5
(Appendix 10A)

P10-10B. **Effective Interest Amortization** On January 1 Ranier, Inc., issued $300,000 of 10 percent, 15-year bonds for $351,876, yielding an effective interest rate of 8 percent. Semiannual interest is payable on June 30 and December 31 each year. The firm uses the effective interest method to amortize the premium.

Required
a.   Prepare an amortization schedule showing the necessary information for the first two interest periods. Round amounts to the nearest dollar.
b.   Prepare the journal entry for the bond issuance on January 1.
c.   Prepare the journal entry to record the bond interest payment and premium amortization at June 30.
d.   Prepare the journal entry to record the bond interest payment and premium amortization at December 31.

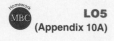

LO5
(Appendix 10A)

P10-11B. **Accounting for Bonds Sold at a Discount** The Peoples National Bank raised capital through the sale of $100 million face value of 4 percent coupon rate, 10-year bonds. The bonds paid interest semiannually and were sold at a time when equivalent risk-rated bonds carried a yield rate of 6 percent.

a.   Calculate the proceeds that The Peoples National Bank received from the sale of the 6 percent bonds.
b.   Calculate the interest expense on the bonds for the first year that the bonds are outstanding.
c.   Calculate the book value of the bonds at the end of the first year.

LO5
(Appendix 10A)

P10-12B. **Accounting for Bonds Issues at a Premium** The Miller Corporation issued $100 million maturity value of 6 percent coupon rate bonds, with interest paid semiannually. At the time of the bond issuance, equivalent risk-rated debt instruments carried a yield rate of 4 percent. The bonds matured in 10 years.

a.   Calculate the proceeds that the Miller Corporation would receive from the sale of the bonds.
b.   Calculate the interest expense on the bonds for the first year.
c.   Calculate the book value of the bonds at the end of the first year.

Kate's
Cards

SERIAL PROBLEM: KATE'S CARDS

(Note: This is a continuation of the Serial Problem: Kate's Cards from Chapters 1 through 9.)

SP10.   Recall that Kate previously obtained a $15,000 bank loan, signing a note payable, on November 30. The note required semiannual interest payments at the rate of 6 percent. The entire principal balance was due two years from the origination date of the note. Kate has been accruing interest on a monthly basis in the amount of $75. Kate would like to know how she should record the interest in May, the month she makes the first interest payment. She is unsure how much expense will need to be recorded in May.

The upcoming interest payment is really not Kate's main concern right now. She was just notified by a lawyer that she is being sued for copyright infringement. Mega Cards Incorporated, one of the largest greeting card companies, believes that one of Kate's designs is too similar to one of Mega's designs for it to be coincidence, and has, therefore, decided to sue Kate's Cards. Mega has a prior reputation for suing small companies and settling out of court for lesser damages. Kate, however, knows that her design is original and that she had never previously seen the Mega design that is the subject of the lawsuit. She has determined to fight the lawsuit, regardless of the cost. She doesn't know, however, how this will affect her financial statements.

1.   Record the May journal entry for Kate's first interest payment. How much interest expense is reported in May?
2.   How should Kate report the copyright infringement lawsuit in her financial statements?

EXTENDING YOUR KNOWLEDGE

REPORTING AND ANALYSIS

COLUMBIA
SPORTSWEAR
COMPANY

EYK10-1.   **Financial Reporting Problem: Columbia Sportswear Company** The financial statements for the **Columbia Sportswear Company** can be found in Appendix A at the end of this book.

Required
Answer the following questions:

a. How much were Columbia's current liabilities as of December 31, 2020?
b. What two items made up the largest percentage of Columbia's December 31, 2020, current liabilities?
c. What was the largest component of Columbia's December 31, 2020, accrued liabilities?

EYK10-2. Comparative Analysis Problem: Columbia Sportswear Company vs. Under Armour, Inc. The financial statements for the **Columbia Sportswear Company** can be found in Appendix A at the end of this book, and the financial statements of **Under Armour, Inc.**, can be found in Appendix B (the complete annual report is available on this book's website).

COLUMBIA SPORTSWEAR COMPANY

UNDER ARMOUR, INC.

Required
Answer the following questions:

a. Compute the current ratio for Columbia Sportswear and Under Armour, Inc., as of December 31, 2020, and comment on what this ratio implies about each company's liquidity and working capital position.
b. Compute the debt-to-total assets ratio for Columbia Sportswear and Under Armour, Inc., as of December 31, 2020, and comment on what this ratio implies about each company's solvency.

EYK10-3. Business Decision Problem Kingston Corporation has total assets of $5,200,000 and has been earning an average of $800,000 before income taxes the past several years. The firm is planning to expand plant facilities to manufacture a new product and needs an additional $2,000,000 in funds, on which it expects to earn 18 percent before income tax. The income tax rate is expected to be 20 percent for the next several years. The firm has no long-term debt outstanding and presently has 75,000 shares of common stock outstanding. The firm is considering three alternatives:

1. Obtain the $2,000,000 by issuing 25,000 shares of common stock at $80 per share.
2. Obtain the $2,000,000 by issuing $1,000,000 of 10 percent, 20-year bonds at face value and 12,500 shares of common stock at $80 per share.
3. Obtain the $2,000,000 by issuing $2,000,000 of 10 percent, 20-year bonds at face value.

Required
As a shareholder of Kingston Corporation, which of the three alternatives would you prefer if your main concern is enhancing the firm's earnings per share? (*Hint:* Divide net income by the number of outstanding common shares to determine the company's earnings per share.)

EYK10-4. Financial Analysis Problem **Abbott Laboratories** is a diversified healthcare company devoted to the discovery, development, manufacture, and marketing of innovative products that improve diagnostic, therapeutic, and nutritional practices. The company's balance sheet for three recent years contains the following data:

ABBOTT LABORATORIES

	2020	2019	2018
Cash and cash equivalents	$ 6,838,000	$3,860,000	$ 3,844,000
Short-term investments	310,000	280,000	242,000
Trade receivables (net of allowance)	6,414,000	5,425,000	5,182,000
Inventories	5,012,000	4,316,000	3,796,000
Other current assets.	1,867,000	1,786,000	1,568,000
Total current assets	$20,441,000	$15,667,000	$14,632,000
Total current liabilities.	$11,907,000	$10,863,000	$ 9,012,000

Required
a. Compute the current ratio for 2018–2020.
b. Compute the quick ratio for 2018–2020.
c. Comment on the three-year trend in these ratios.

CRITICAL THINKING

EYK10-5. Financial Analysis on the Web: General Mills, Inc. The fiscal year 2020 annual report of **General Mills, Inc.**, is available on this book's website. Refer to the consolidated balance sheet and Note 8.

GENERAL MILLS, INC.

Required
a. What was the total dollar amount of current liabilities as of May 31, 2020?
b. What percent of long-term debt was considered current as of May 31, 2020?

c.   What were the current ratio and quick ratio as of May 28, 2020?

d.   What is the total amount of long-term liabilities reported by General Mills as of May 31, 2020?

e.   How much in principal payments on the long-term debt is General Mills anticipating paying in fiscal year 2021?

EYK10-6.   Accounting Communication Activity Cedric Salos is considering different ways to raise money for the expansion of his company's operations. Cedric is not sure about the advantages of issuing bonds versus issuing common stock. In addition, he is not sure which features he should consider including with the bonds if he selects that form of financing. He asks you to explain, in simple terms, the answers to his questions.

Required

Write a short memorandum to Cedric explaining the advantages of issuing bonds over issuing common stock and the features that should be considered for inclusion with the bonds.

EYK10-7.   Accounting Ethics Case Sunrise Pools, Inc., is being sued by the Crescent Club for negligence when installing a new pool on Crescent Club's property. Crescent Club alleges that the employees of Sunrise Pools damaged the foundation of the clubhouse and part of the golf course while operating heavy machinery to install the pool.

The lawsuit is for $1.5 million. At the time of the alleged incident, Sunrise Pools carried only $600,000 of liability insurance.

While reviewing the draft of Sunrise Pools' annual report, its president deletes all references to this lawsuit. She is concerned that disclosure of this lawsuit in the annual report will be viewed by Crescent Club as admission of Sunrise's wrongdoing, even though she privately admits that Sunrise employees were careless and believes that Sunrise Pools will be found liable for an amount in excess of $1 million. The president sends the amended draft of the annual report to the vice president of finance with a note stating that the lawsuit will not be disclosed in the annual report and that the lawsuit will not be disclosed to the board of directors.

Required

Is the president's concern valid? What ethical problems will the vice president of finance face if he follows the president's instructions?

EYK10-8.   Environmental, Social, and Governance Problem The chapter highlights **Walmart**'s Green Investment initiative (see page 10-16). Go to Walmart's website and navigate to the section "Our Company"; then select "Global Responsibility," then navigate to the section on Environmental, Social and Governance. Download the ESG Summary. What are some of the ways that Walmart demonstrates its commitment to being a good corporate citizen?

EYK10-9.   Forensic Accounting Problem Billing schemes are frauds in which an employee causes the victim organization to issue fraudulent payments by submitting invoices for nonexistent goods or services, inflated invoices, or invoices for personal items. One type of billing scheme uses a shell company that is set up for the purpose of committing the fraud. The shell company is often nothing more than a fake corporate name and a post office mailbox.

What are some of the ways that shell company invoices can be detected?

EYK10-10. Working with the Takeaways Below are selected data from **Microsoft**'s recent financial statements:

	2020	2019
Net income	$ 44,281	$ 39,240
Tax expense	8,755	4,448
Cash and cash equivalents ..	13,576	11,356
Short-term investments	122,951	122,463
Accounts receivable	32,011	29,524
Inventory	1,895	2,063
Other current assets	11,482	10,146
Current liabilities	72,310	69,420

Required

Calculate the following ratios for 2020 and 2019 and comment on the trend:

a.   Current ratio   *b.*   Quick ratio

EYK10-11. Analyzing IFRS Financial Statements The 2020 financial statements of **LVMH Moët Hennessy-Louis Vuitton S.A.** are presented in Appendix C at the end of this book. LVMH is a Paris-based holding company and one of the world's largest and best-known luxury goods companies. As members of the European Union, French companies are required to prepare their consolidated (group) financial statements using International Financial Reporting Standards (IFRS). Using LVMH's financial data for 2019 and 2020, calculate the company's (a) current ratio, (b) quick ratio, and (c) times-interest-earned ratio. Is LVMH's working capital position improving or declining over the two-year period? Can LVMH readily service its interest payments from its income before interest expense and income taxes? (*Hint:* LVMH's interest expense is labeled "cost of net financial debt" on its consolidated income statement.)

LVMH MOËT
HENNESSY-LOUIS
VUITTON S.A.

ANSWERS TO SELF-STUDY QUESTIONS:

1. b   2. b   3. b   4. c   5. b   6. d   7. c   8. b   9. a   10. b   11. c

YOUR TURN! SOLUTIONS

Solution 10.1

a.	Apr. 30	Office salaries expense (+E, −SE)	40,000	
		Sales salaries expense (+E, −SE)	86,000	
		Federal income tax withholding payable (+L)		25,600
		FICA tax payable (+L)		9,639
		Health insurance premiums payable (+L)		1,850
		Union dues payable (+L)		950
		Payroll payable (+L)		87,961
		To accrue payroll for April		
		(FICA taxes = 0.0765 × $126,000 = $9,639).		
b.	30	Payroll payable (−L)	87,961	
		Cash (−A)		87,961
		To pay April payroll.		
c.	30	Payroll tax expense (+E, −SE)	14,847	
		FICA tax payable (+L)		9,639
		Federal unemployment tax payable (+L)		456
		State unemployment tax payable (+L)		4,752
		To record employer's payroll taxes (FICA Tax = 0.0765 ×		
		$126,000 = $9,639; Federal Unemployment Tax = 0.006 ×		
		$76,000 = $456; State Unemployment Tax = 0.054 × $88,000 =		
		$4,752).		
d.	30	Federal income tax withholding payable (−L)	25,600	
		FICA tax payable (−L)	19,278	
		Health insurance premiums payable (−L)	1,850	
		Union dues payable (−L)	950	
		Federal unemployment tax payable (−L)	456	
		State unemployment tax payable (−L)	4,752	
		Cash (−A)		52,886
		To record the payment of payroll-related liabilities.		

Solution 10.2

a.

Cash (+A)	325,000	
Bonds payable (+L)		300,000
Premium on bonds payable (+XL, +L)		25,000
To record the issuance of bonds payable.		

b.

Long-term liabilities	
Bonds payable	$300,000
Add: Premium on bonds payable	25,000
Bonds payable, net.	$325,000

Solution 10.3

1. Because the likelihood of losing the lawsuit is deemed remote, it does not need to be recognized or disclosed by Seco Co.
2. Even though the contingency is deemed remote, credit guarantees must be disclosed in the notes to the financial statements.
3. The liability should be recorded on the balance sheet because the likelihood of payment is both high and can be estimated.

Solution 10.4

a. Current ratio = $120,000 / $80,000 = 1.50
b. Quick ratio = ($10,000 + $25,000 + $30,000) / $80,000 = 0.81
c. Times-interest-earned ratio = $20,000 / $4,000 = 5.0

Solution 10A.1

The selling price will be $94,582.81.

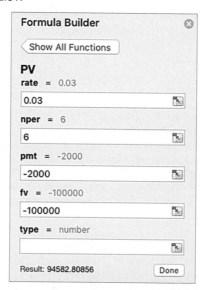

Solution 10B.1

The present value of the lease payments is $42,580, which is "substantially all" of the asset's fair value of $45,000. In addition, the four-year lease is for the "major part" of the asset's five-year economic life. Therefore the lease is a finance lease. The entry to record the lease is:

Right-of-Use Asset (Equipment)	42,580	
Lease liability (Equipment)		42,580

Chapter 11
Stockholders' Equity

Road Map

LO	Learning Objective	Page	eLecture	Guided Example	Assignments
LO1	Define the corporate form of organization and discuss its principal characteristics.	11-3	E11-1	YT11.1	SS1, SE1, E11A, E11B
LO2	Explain the difference between par value stock and no-par value stock.	11-6	E11-2	YT11.2	SE2
LO3	Identify and discuss the two types of capital stock and their respective stockholder rights.	11-7	E11-3	YT11.3	SS2, SS8, SE3, E8A, E8B
LO4	Describe the accounting for issuances of capital stock.	11-10	E11-4	YT11.4	SS3, SE4, E2A, E4A, E12A, E13A, E2B, E4B, E12B, E13B, P2A, P3A, P4A, P5A, P8A, P9A, P10A, P11A, P2B, P3B, P4B, P5B, P8B, P9B, P10B, P11B
LO5	Define and discuss the accounting for stock splits.	11-12	E11-5	YT11.5	SS6, SE5, E3A, E9A, E15A, E3B, E9B, E15B, P4A, P8A, P9A, P4B, P8B, P9B
LO6	Explain the accounting for treasury stock.	11-13	E11-6	YT11.6	SS4, SE6, E4A, E13A, E4B, E13B, P3A, P4A, P5A, P8A, P9A, P10A, P11A, P3B, P4B, P5B, P8B, P9B, P10B, P11B
LO7	Identify and distinguish between cash dividends and stock dividends.	11-15	E11-7	YT11.7	SS5, SS9, SE7, E1A, E5A, E6A, E14A, E15A, E1B, E5B, E6B, E14B, E15B, P1A, P6A, P7A, P10A, P1B, P6B, P7B, P10B
LO8	Illustrate the statement of retained earnings and the statement of stockholders' equity.	11-18	E11-8	YT11.8	SS10, SE11, E7A, E7B, P2A, P3A, P4A, P6A, P7A, P9A, P10A, P2B, P3B, P4B, P6B, P7B, P10B
LO9	Define return on equity, dividend yield, and dividend payout ratio and explain their use.	11-20	E11-9	YT11.9	SS7, SE8, SE9, SE10, E10A, E10B

The first **Starbucks** coffeehouse was opened in Seattle, Washington, in 1971 to sell high-quality coffee beans and equipment. Since that time, Starbucks has grown at an explosive rate. Starbucks is the largest coffeehouse company in the world with over 30,000 stores.

Where do firms get the necessary capital for expansion? While not every large firm is a corporation, many are, and one of the most important characteristics of the corporate form of organization is the ability to raise new capital by selling ownership shares in the company. Starbucks had its initial public offering of its common shares in 1992.

Without a doubt, the modern corporation dominates the national and international economic landscape. In the United States, corporations generate well over three-fourths of the combined sales revenue of all forms of business organization, even though less than one of every five businesses is organized as a corporation. The corporate form of organization is used in a variety of business settings—from large multinational corporations with more than a million stockholders operating in countries all over the world, to small, family-owned businesses operating only in their local community.

Why do fast-growing firms like Starbucks choose the corporate form of organization? There are several reasons, but certainly one of the primary reasons is the relative ease of attracting large amounts of capital as compared to other organizational forms of business.

PAST

Chapter 10 examined the accounting for liabilities.

PRESENT

In this chapter, we turn our attention to the accounting for stockholders' equity.

FUTURE

In Chapter 12, we shift our focus to the statement of cash flows.

11-2

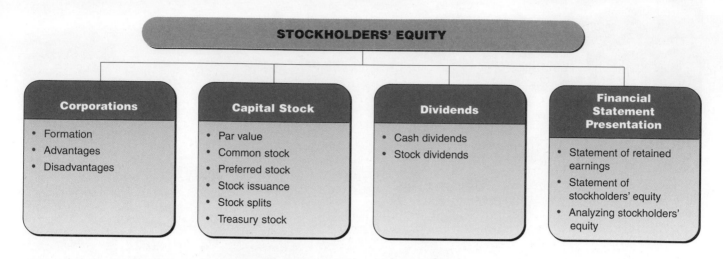

NATURE AND FORMATION OF A CORPORATION

LO1 **Define** the corporate form of organization and **discuss** its principal characteristics.

eLecture

MBC

A **corporation** is a legal entity created with the approval of a governmental authority. The right to conduct business as a corporation is granted by the state in which a corporation is formed (or chartered). All states have laws specifying the requirements for creating a corporation.

To form a corporation, the incorporators (founders) must apply for a charter. The incorporators prepare and file the **articles of incorporation**, which define the basic structure of the corporation, including the purpose for which it is formed and the amount of capital stock to be authorized. If the incorporators meet the requirements of the law, the government issues a charter or certificate of incorporation. After a charter has been granted, the founders hold an organizational meeting to elect the first board of directors and adopt the corporation's bylaws.

Because assets are essential to starting any business, a corporation issues (or sells) *certificates of capital stock* to obtain the necessary funds to acquire operating assets. As owners of a corporation, *stockholders* are entitled to a voice in the control and management of the company. Stockholders with voting stock may vote on specific issues at the annual meeting and participate in the election of the board of directors. The board of directors establishes the overall policies of a corporation and declares dividends. Normally, the board also hires a group of corporate officers, including a chief executive officer, a chief financial officer, one or more vice presidents, a controller, a treasurer, and a secretary, to execute the day-to-day operations of the company. The officers implement the policies of the board of directors and actively manage the affairs of the corporation. **Exhibit 11-1** depicts the responsibilities of these stakeholders in a corporation.

Advantages of the Corporate Form of Organization

A corporation has several advantages when compared with a sole proprietorship or partnership.

Separate Legal Entity

The corporation, as a separate legal entity, may acquire assets, incur debt, enter into contracts, sue, and be sued—all in its own name. The stockholders of a corporation are separate and distinct from the corporation. This characteristic contrasts with proprietorships and partnerships, which are accounting entities but not legal entities apart from their owners.

EXHIBIT 11-1 **Responsibilities of Selected Corporate Stakeholders**

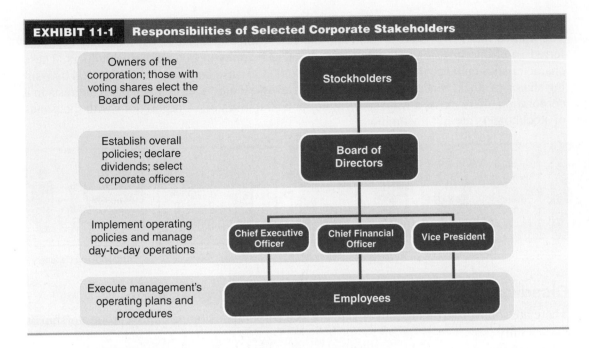

Limited Liability

The liability of stockholders with respect to a company's business affairs is usually limited to the value of their investment in the corporation. By way of contrast, the owners of proprietorships and partnerships can be held financially responsible, separately and collectively, for any unsatisfied obligations of the business. To protect a corporation's creditors, state laws limit the distribution of contributed capital to stockholders. Distributions of retained earnings (undistributed profits) are not legal unless the board of directors formally votes to declare a dividend. Because of the legal constraints regarding the amount of stockholder capital available for distribution, corporations must maintain clear distinctions in the accounts to identify the various elements of stockholders' equity.

Transferability of Ownership

Shares in a corporation may be routinely transferred without affecting a company's operations. The corporation merely notes such transfers of ownership in the stockholder records. Although a corporation must have stockholder records to notify stockholders of meetings and to pay dividends, the price at which shares transfer between investors is not recognized in the corporation's accounts.

Continuity of Existence

Because routine transfers of ownership do not affect a corporation's affairs, the corporation is said to have continuity of existence. In a partnership, any change in ownership technically results in a discontinuation of the old partnership and the formation of a new one.

PRINCIPLE ALERT   **Entity Concept and Going Concern Concept**

Two characteristics of the corporate form of organization mesh well with the basic principles of accounting. The separate legal status conferred upon a corporation conforms, for example, with the *entity concept*. When the corporation is the unit of focus for accounting purposes, the entity concept requires that the economic activity of the corporation be accounted for separately from the activities of its owners. Legally, the corporate entity is also distinct from its owners. Consequently, the corporation's continuity of existence also aligns well with the *going concern concept*, which assumes that the accounting entity will continue indefinitely into the future.

Capital Raising Capability

The limited liability of stockholders and the ease with which shares of stock may be transferred from one investor to another are attractive features to potential stockholders. These characteristics enhance the ability of the corporation to raise large amounts of capital by issuing shares of stock. Since both large and small investors may acquire ownership interests in a corporation, there exists a wide spectrum of potential investors. Corporations with thousands of stockholders are not uncommon.

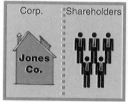
Separate Legal Entity

Limited Liability

Transferability of Ownership

Continuous Existence

Capital Raising Capability

Disadvantages of the Corporate Form of Organization

There are some disadvantages to organizing as a corporation compared to a proprietorship or partnership.

Organization Costs

Creating a corporation is more costly than organizing a proprietorship or partnership. The expenditures incurred to organize a corporation are charged to Organization Costs and expensed on the income statement when incurred. These costs include attorney's fees, fees paid to the state, and the costs of promoting the enterprise.

Taxation

As separate legal entities, corporations are subject to federal income taxes on any earned income. Stockholders are likewise subject to income taxation on any income received from a corporation as dividends, leading to a situation of double taxation of a corporation's distributed earnings.

In addition, corporations are usually subject to state income taxes in the states in which they are incorporated or are doing business. They may also be subject to real estate, personal property, and franchise taxes.

THINKING GLOBALLY

The equity ownership structure of most U.S. and United Kingdom companies is characterized by small diffuse investors, each of whom owns only a small fraction of the firm. But the ownership structure of public companies in most of the rest of the world is strikingly different, and is more commonly characterized by the presence of a large investor who holds a controlling interest in the company's shares. These large owners usually consist of families and are typically directly involved in managing the company's operations. To illustrate, consider the following seven East Asian countries and the percentage of their public companies that is controlled by families. South Korea has the highest percentage of family-controlled public companies at 78 percent:

Country	Percentage of Family-Controlled Companies
Hong Kong	65%
Indonesia	75
Malaysia	71
Singapore	50
South Korea	78
Taiwan	55
Thailand	68

Regulation and Supervision

Corporations are subject to greater degrees of regulation and supervision than are proprietorships and partnerships. Each state maintains the right to regulate the corporations it charters. State laws also limit the powers a corporation may exercise, identify reports that must be filed by a corporation, and define the rights and liabilities of stockholders. If shares of stock are issued to the public, the corporation must comply with any laws governing the sale of corporate securities. Furthermore, corporations whose shares are listed and traded on organized security exchanges, such as the New York Stock Exchange, are subject to the various reporting and disclosure requirements of these exchanges.

Accounting for Stockholders' Equity in Alternative Organizational Forms

Differences exist between the accounting for the stockholders' equity of a corporation and for that of a sole proprietorship or partnership. In a sole proprietorship, only a single owner's capital account is needed to reflect increases from capital contributions and net income as well as decreases from owner withdrawals and net losses. A similar situation exists in most partnerships, which customarily maintain capital and drawing accounts for each partner.

A corporation, on the other hand, is subject to certain legal restrictions imposed by the government approving its creation. These restrictions focus on the distinction between contributed capital and retained earnings and make accounting for stockholders' equity somewhat more complex for corporations than for other types of business organizations.

GuidedExample

MBC

YOUR TURN! 11.1

The following attributes are associated with the corporate form of organization. Identify each one as either an advantage or a disadvantage of the corporate form over other forms of organization:

1. Taxation
2. Limited liability
3. Capital raising capability
4. Regulation
5. Cost to organize
6. Transferability of ownership

The solution is on page 11-45.

PAR VALUE STOCK AND NO-PAR VALUE STOCK

A corporate charter may specify a face value, or **par value**, for each share of capital stock. In the early days of corporate stock issuances, par value represented the market value of the stock when it was issued. In more recent times, however, par values have typically been set at amounts well below a stock's fair market value on the date of issue. For example, the par value of Starbucks' common stock is $0.001 per share. As a consequence, a stock's par value has no economic significance today.

Par value, however, may have legal implications. In some states, par value may represent the minimum amount that must be contributed per share of stock. If stock is issued at a *discount* (that is, at less than its par value), the stockholder may have a liability for the amount of the discount should any creditor claims remain unsatisfied following a company's liquidation. Issuing stock at a discount rarely occurs, however, because boards of directors have generally established par values below fair market values at the time of issue.

Par value may also be used in some states to define a corporation's legal capital. *Legal capital* is the minimum amount of contributed capital that must remain in a corporation as a margin of protection for creditors. However, given the low par values typically assigned to common stock today, this protection has limited usefulness for creditors. Still, given the role that par value may play in defining legal capital, accountants carefully segregate and record the par value of stock transactions in a separate capital stock account.

Most states permit the issuance of capital stock without a par value, called **no-par value stock**. The company's board of directors, however, usually sets a **stated value** for the no-par stock. In such cases, the stated value will determine the corporation's legal capital. For

LO2 Explain the difference between par value stock and no-par value stock.

eLecture

MBC

accounting purposes, stated value amounts are treated similarly to par value amounts. In the absence of a stated value, the entire proceeds from the issuance of no-par value stock will likely establish a corporation's legal capital.

ENVIRONMENTAL, SOCIAL, AND GOVERNANCE   Purpose Beyond Profit at Starbucks
To some, corporate social responsibility means doing things for non-stockholder stakeholders, even if it means a lower rate of return for stockholders. This sort of thinking pits environmental and social impact against stockholder gains, as if the two were competitors for the corporate dollar. Companies that truly understand ESG have come to see it in a more strategic light, where doing good can lead to doing well. Further, these companies realize that they would not have the resources to do good if they were not making money. **Starbucks** is known to be not only a highly profitable company with 2020 profits of nearly $1 billion U.S. dollars, but also a company on the leading edge of social responsibility. Starbucks believes businesses should have a positive impact on the communities they serve. The company has set goals in such areas as ethical sourcing, recycling, diversity, and philanthropy.

YOUR TURN! 11.2

MBC

The solution is on page 11-45.

Which of the following sentences is false?

a. In the early days of corporations, the par value represented the market value of the stock.

b. Par value represents the average value of the stock.

c. In recent times, par value is typically set well below a stock's market value.

d. Par value may be related to a corporation's legal capital.

TYPES OF CAPITAL STOCK

LO3 Identify and discuss the two types of capital stock and their respective stockholder rights.

MBC

The amounts and kinds of capital stock that a corporation can issue are specified in a company's charter of incorporation. Providing for the sale of several classes of capital stock permits a company to raise capital from different types of investors with diverse risk preferences. The charter also specifies a corporation's **authorized shares**—the maximum number of shares of each class of capital stock that can be issued. Shares that have been sold and issued to stockholders constitute the **issued shares** of a corporation. Some of these shares may be repurchased by the corporation. When shares are repurchased, they may be retired and cancelled or held for reissuance. Shares actually held by stockholders are called **outstanding shares**, whereas those reacquired by a corporation (and not cancelled) are called **treasury stock**. We will discuss treasury stock later in the chapter.

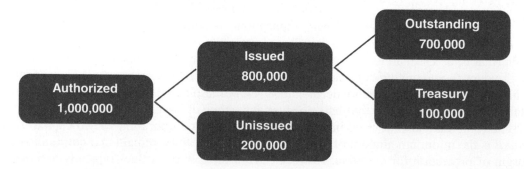

Common Stock

When only one class of stock is issued, it is called **common stock**. Common stockholders have the right to vote on corporate matters, to share in the corporation's net income, to participate in additional issuances of stock, and in the case of a corporate liquidation, to share in any asset distributions after any prior claims against the corporation by its creditors have been settled.

As the owners of a corporation, the common stockholders elect the board of directors and vote on all matters requiring the approval of the owners. Stockholders who do not attend the annual stockholders' meetings may vote by proxy.

A common stockholder has the right to a proportionate share of the corporation's earnings that are distributed as dividends. All earnings belong to the corporation, however, until the board of directors formally votes to declare a dividend.

Each stockholder of a corporation has a **preemptive right** to maintain his or her proportionate ownership interest in the corporation. If a company issues additional shares of stock, the current owners of that type of capital stock receive the first opportunity to acquire, on a pro rata basis, the new shares. In certain situations, management may request stockholders to waive their preemptive right. For example, a corporation may wish to issue additional shares of capital stock for use to acquire another company.

ACCOUNTING IN PRACTICE   Preemptive Right Prevents Wealth Transfer

A major reason for the preemptive right is to protect stockholders against a transfer of their wealth to new stockholders. To illustrate, assume that a firm has 10,000 shares of common stock outstanding with a market price of $20 per share. Thus, the firm's total market value is $200,000 (10,000 shares × $20). If the firm sells another 10,000 common shares at $10 per share (a price below its current market value), the additional $100,000 cash received would raise the firm's total market value to $300,000. With a new market value of $15 per share ($300,000/20,000 shares), the new share issuance causes the old stockholders to lose $5 per share and the new stockholders to gain $5 per share—that is, the sale of the new shares at a lower price transfers wealth from the old stockholders to the new stockholders. The preemptive right protects the existing stockholders from such wealth transfers by enabling them to purchase any newly issued shares.

When a corporation liquidates, it converts its assets to a form suitable for distribution, usually cash, which it then distributes to all parties having claims on the corporate assets. Any assets remaining after all claims have been satisfied belong to the residual owners of the corporation—that is, the common stockholders. Common stockholders are entitled to the final distribution of the balance of any remaining assets in a corporate liquidation.

A company may occasionally issue *classified* common stock; that is, it may issue more than one class of common stock. For example, when two classes of common stock are issued, they are often identified as Class A and Class B. The two classes usually differ in either their respective dividend rights or their respective voting powers. Usually, classified common stock is issued when the founders of a corporation wish to acquire funds from the public while retaining voting control of the corporation. For example, Google originally issued two classes of common stock: Class A shares that were sold to the public and Class B shares that were retained by the Company's founders. The Class A shares have one vote per share while the Class B shares have 10 votes per share.

Preferred Stock

Preferred stock is a class of stock with characteristics that differentiate it from common stock. Preferred stock, for example, has one or more preferences over common stock, usually with reference to (1) the payment of dividends and (2) the distribution of assets when a corporation liquidates. To determine the features of a particular preferred stock issue, it is necessary to examine the preferred stock contract. The majority of preferred shares, however, have certain typical features, which are discussed below.

Dividend Preference

When the board of directors declares a distribution of the company's net income, preferred stockholders are entitled to an annual dividend before common stockholders may receive any dividend distribution. The amount is usually specified in the preferred stock contract as a percentage of the par value of the stock or in dollars per share if the stock lacks a par value.

Thus, if the preferred stock has a $100 par value and a six percent dividend rate, the preferred stockholders receive $6 per share in dividends. However, the dividend is owed to the stockholders only if, and when, declared by the board of directors.

Preferred dividends are usually **cumulative**—that is, regular dividends to preferred stockholders omitted in the past must be paid in addition to the current year's dividend before any dividend distribution can be made to the common stockholders. If a preferred stock is **noncumulative**, omitted dividends do not carry forward.

To illustrate the difference between cumulative and noncumulative preferred stock, assume that a company ending its second year of operations has 1,000 shares of $100 par value, six percent preferred stock and 100,000 shares of $1 par value common stock outstanding. The company declared no dividends last year. This year a dividend of $27,000 is declared. The distribution of the $27,000 between the two stockholder classes depends on whether the preferred stock is cumulative or noncumulative. If the preferred stock is cumulative, preferred stockholders receive $12 per share before common stockholders receive anything, as illustrated below:

	Preferred	Common	Total
Total par value of outstanding shares..................	$100,000	$100,000	$200,000
Preferred stock is cumulative			
Preferred dividends in arrears (6 percent).........	$ 6,000		$ 6,000
Regular preferred dividend (6 percent).............	6,000		6,000
Remainder to common..........................		$ 15,000	15,000
Total distribution	$ 12,000	$ 15,000	$ 27,000
Preferred stock is noncumulative			
Regular preferred dividend (6 percent).............	$ 6,000		$ 6,000
Remainder to common..........................		$ 21,000	21,000
Total distribution	$ 6,000	$ 21,000	$ 27,000

Dividends in arrears (that is, dividends omitted in past years) on cumulative preferred stock are not an accounting liability and do not appear in the liability section of the balance sheet. They do not become an obligation of the corporation until the board of directors formally declares such dividends. Any dividends in arrears are disclosed to investors in the notes to the financial statements.

Asset Distribution Preference

Preferred stockholders normally have a preference over common stockholders with respect to the receipt of assets in the event of a corporate liquidation. When a corporation liquidates, any creditor claims are settled first. Preferred stockholders then have the right to receive assets equal to the par value of their shares, or a larger stated liquidation value per share, before any assets are distributed to common stockholders. The preferred stockholders' preference to assets in liquidation also includes any dividends in arrears.

Other Preferred Stock Features

Although preferred stockholders do not ordinarily have the right to vote in the election of the board of directors, this right can be accorded by contract. Some state laws require that all capital stock issued by a corporation be given voting rights. Further, preferred stock may contain features that cause the shares to resemble common stock. Preferred stock may, for example, be **convertible** into common stock at a specified conversion rate. When this feature is present, the market price of the preferred shares often moves in a fashion consistent with the related common shares. When the price of the common stock rises, the value of the conversion feature is enhanced, and consequently, the value of the preferred shares should also rise.

Preferred stock may be **participating** meaning that it shares any special dividend distributions with common stock beyond the regular preferred stock dividend rate. (Special dividends are discussed on p. 11-15.) After receiving its regular dividend preference, preferred stock normally does not participate in any special dividend distribution until the common stock is allowed a dividend amount corresponding to the regular preferred stock dividend rate. At this point, the two classes of stock begin to share the special dividend distribution at the same rate. The preferred stock participation feature may be partial (which limits the participation to a certain amount) or full (which places no limit on the rate of participation).

Preferred stock may be **callable**, which means that a corporation can redeem the shares after a length of time and at a price specified in the stock contract. The call feature makes the preferred stock similar to a bond, since many bonds are callable or have a limited life. Most preferred stocks are callable, with the call or redemption price set slightly above the original preferred stock issuance price.

ACCOUNTING IN PRACTICE   **Preferred Shares and the Capital Market**

Although legally, and from an accounting standpoint, preferred shares are considered to be part of a company's stockholders' equity, the capital market takes a different point of view. Most investment professionals consider a company's preferred stock to be part of the company's debt structure. Thus, from a capital market perspective, the only true stockholders of a business are its common stockholders.

Match the description in the right column with the appropriate term in the left column:

1. Authorized
2. Outstanding
3. Common stock
4. Preemptive right
5. Preferred stock
6. Cumulative preference

a. The right to receive dividends omitted in prior years.
b. The most basic class of stock ownership.
c. Stock with one or more preferences over common stock.
d. The maximum number of shares of each class of stock that may be issued.
e. Shares actually held by stockholders.
f. The right to maintain a proportionate ownership interest in a corporation.

YOUR TURN! 11.3

GuidedExample
MBC

The solution is on page 11-45.

STOCK ISSUANCES FOR CASH

When issuing capital stock to investors, a corporation may use the services of an investment bank, a specialist in marketing securities to the capital market. The investment bank may *underwrite* a stock issue by agreeing to sell the shares on a firm commitment basis—that is, buying the shares from the corporation and then reselling them to investors. Under a firm commitment agreement, a corporation does not risk being unable to sell its stock. The underwriter bears this risk in return for the fees and profits generated by selling the shares to investors at a price higher than it paid to the corporation. An investment bank that is unwilling to underwrite a stock issue may handle the issuance of the shares on a *best efforts* basis. In this case, the investment bank agrees to sell as many shares as possible at a set price, but the corporation bears the risk of any unsold shares.

LO4 Describe the accounting for issuances of capital stock.

eLecture
MBC

When capital stock is issued to investors, the appropriate capital stock account is credited for the par value of the stock issued, or if the stock is no-par value stock, with its stated value, if any. The asset received in exchange for the stock (usually cash) is debited, and any difference is credited to the Paid-in Capital in Excess of Par Value account.

To illustrate the journal entries to record various stock issuances in exchange for cash, assume that Smithson Corp. issued two different types of capital stock during its first year of operations:

Issuing Stock at a Premium

1. Issued 1,000 shares of $100 par value, nine percent preferred stock at $107 cash per share:

A	= L +	SE
+107,000		+100,000
		PS
		+7,000
		PS

Cash (+A)	107,000	
Preferred stock (+SE)		100,000
Paid-in capital in excess of par value—Preferred stock (+SE)		7,000

In this transaction, the preferred stock is issued at a price greater than its par value—that is, the shares were sold at a premium. The par value of the preferred stock issued is credited to the Preferred Stock account and the $7,000 premium is credited to the Paid-in Capital in Excess of Par Value account. If there is more than one class of par value stock, the account title may indicate the class of stock to which the premium relates, in this case Paid-in Capital in Excess of Par Value—Preferred Stock.

Issuing No-Par Stock

2. Issued 30,000 shares of no-par value common stock, stated value $5, at $8 cash per share:

A	= L +	SE
+240,000		+150,000
		CS
		+90,000
		CS

Cash (+A)	240,000	
Common stock (+SE)		150,000
Paid-in capital in excess of stated value—Common stock (+SE)		90,000

When no-par value stock has a stated value, as in Entry 2, the stated value of the total shares issued is credited to the proper capital stock account, and any additional amount received is credited to the account Paid-in Capital in Excess of Stated Value. If there is no stated value for the no-par value stock, the entire proceeds are credited to the appropriate capital stock account. In the second journal entry, if the common stock had no stated value, the entire $240,000 amount would have been credited to the Common Stock account.

These two stock issuances are reflected in **Exhibit 11-2**, which presents the stockholders' equity section from Smithson's year-end balance sheet. (Retained earnings are assumed to be $25,000.) The stockholders' equity section is divided into two major categories: ❶ Paid-in Capital and ❷ Retained Earnings. **Paid-in capital** is the amount of capital contributed to the corporation from various capital stock transactions such as the issuance of preferred stock and common stock. The capital contributed by stockholders through the issuance of stock is divided between the legal capital (the par value or stated value of the stock) and the amounts received in excess of the legal capital. Later in this chapter we discuss treasury stock transactions that may affect a corporation's paid-in capital. **Retained earnings** represent the cumulative net income and losses of the company that have not been distributed to stockholders as a dividend.

EXHIBIT 11-2	Stockholders' Equity Section of the Balance Sheet		
❶	**Paid-in Capital**		
	9% Preferred stock, $100 par value, 1,000 shares authorized, issued, and outstanding	$100,000	
	No-par common stock, stated value $5, 40,000 shares authorized; 30,000 shares issued and outstanding	150,000	$250,000
	Additional paid-in capital		
	In excess of par value—Preferred stock	7,000	
	In excess of stated value—Common stock	90,000	97,000
	Total Paid-in Capital		347,000
❷	Retained earnings		25,000
	Total Stockholders' Equity		$372,000

Noncash Stock Issuances

Sometimes a corporation will exchange its common stock for services, operating assets, or for its own convertible debt or convertible preferred stock. For example, some start-up companies lacking cash will exchange their common stock for professional services provided by attorneys and accountants. When this occurs, a journal entry is made to debit the Professional Services Expense account and a credit is made to Common Stock—Par Value and to the Paid-in Capital in Excess of Par Value—Common Stock account for the fair value of the services received.

When common stock is exchanged for operating assets, a similar journal entry is made, although the debit in this case is to the Land or Equipment account. When common stock is exchanged for convertible bonds (discussed in Chapter 10), the value of the newly issued stock is assumed to be equal to the book value of the bonds. An exchange of convertible bonds for common stock is executed by debiting the Bonds Payable account and the Premium on Bonds Payable account (or crediting the Discount on Bonds Payable account) and crediting the Common Stock account and the Paid-in Capital in Excess of Par Value—Common Stock for any excess of the bonds' book value over the stock's par value.

When preferred stock is converted into a company's common stock, the newly issued common stock assumes the book value of the preferred stock. That is, Preferred Stock—Par Value and Paid-in Capital in Excess of Par Value—Preferred Stock are debited while Common Stock—Par Value and Paid-in Capital in Excess of Par Value—Common Stock are credited.

Wyatt Industries began operations on June 1 by issuing 10,000 shares of $1 par value common stock for cash at $9 per share. How much Additional Paid-in Capital will be reported by Wyatt Industries?

YOUR TURN! 11.4

The solution is on page 11-45.

STOCK SPLITS

Occasionally, a corporation may issue additional shares of common stock to its stockholders through a **forward stock split**. The principal reason that companies execute a forward stock split is to reduce the market price of their shares. A forward stock split increases the number of shares outstanding and is accounted for by reducing the par value or stated value of the stock affected. A forward stock split does not change the balances of any of the stockholders' equity accounts; however, a memorandum entry is made in the general journal to show the altered par value or stated value of the stock and to note the increase in the number of shares issued and outstanding. For example, if Waylon Company has 10,000 shares of $10 par value common stock outstanding and announces a 2-for-1 forward stock split, it would simply reduce the par value of its common stock to $5 per share and issue to its stockholders 10,000 new common shares. Thus, after the forward stock split, each stockholder would have twice the number of shares held prior to the split, and the value of the Common Stock account would remain unchanged at $100,000 (10,000 shares × 2 = 20,000 shares × $5 = $100,000). If you owned one share of Waylon's $10 par value stock before the 2-for-1 forward stock split, you would own two shares of their $5 par value stock after the stock split.

 **LO5** Define and discuss the accounting for stock splits.

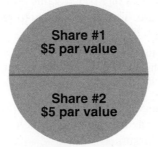

Before 2-for-1 forward stock split   **After 2-for-1 forward stock split**

Occasionally, a company may execute a **reverse stock split**, for example a 1-for-2 reverse stock split, which increases the par value of the stock and reduces the number of shares outstanding. Reverse stock splits are designed to increase a company's stock price. Most major stock exchanges have a minimum trading price that a company must meet or exceed to be traded on the exchange. When a company's stock price falls below the minimum trading price, the shares may be delisted, making it difficult for stockholders to find buyers for their shares. Meeting an exchange's minimum listing price is one of the principal reasons for reverse stock splits.

YOUR TURN! 11.5

The solution is on page 11-45.

Aston Enterprises currently has 500,000 common shares outstanding with a par value of $3.00. Mariam Hernandez owns 500 of those shares. If Aston were to execute a 3-for-1 split, what would be the resulting share information for both Aston and Hernandez?

TREASURY STOCK

LO6 Explain the accounting for treasury stock.

When a corporation acquires its own outstanding shares and does not retire (cancel) them, the acquired shares are called **treasury stock**. Treasury stock may be purchased for a variety of reasons, including reissuing them to officers and employees in profit sharing programs or employee stock option plans. Whatever the purpose, treasury stock purchases reduce a company's stockholders' equity. Treasury shares do not carry voting privileges or preemptive rights, are not paid dividends, and do not receive assets in the event of a corporation's liquidation.

THINKING GLOBALLY

Under IFRS and U.S. GAAP, treasury stock is reported on the balance sheet as a contra-stockholders' equity account. That is, the repurchase cost of any treasury stock is subtracted from total stockholders' equity. In addition, both IFRS and U.S. GAAP preclude the recognition of any gain or loss by a company from stock transactions involving its own shares—that is, any "gain" or "loss" from trading in a company's own shares is recorded as part of Paid-in Capital in Excess of Par Value. By way of contrast, some countries permit treasury stock to be reported on the asset side of the balance sheet as an investment in marketable securities. Under IFRS and U.S. GAAP, treasury stock does not satisfy the definition of an asset, and therefore, cannot be reported on the balance sheet as marketable securities. It is also noteworthy that in some countries, treasury stock purchases are illegal because they are viewed as a form of stock price manipulation.

Accounting for Treasury Stock

Accountants record treasury stock at its acquisition cost, debiting the Treasury Stock account and crediting the Cash account. The Treasury Stock account is a contra-stockholders' equity account, and its balance is deducted when deriving total stockholders' equity on the balance sheet. To illustrate the accounting for the purchase of treasury stock, assume that Chen Corporation had 20,000 shares of $10 par value common stock outstanding and then purchased 1,000 shares at $12 per share. The journal entry to record the purchase is:

A = L + SE		
−12,000 −12,000		
TS		

Treasury stock (+XSE, −SE)	12,000	
Cash (−A)		12,000
To record purchase of 1,000 shares of treasury stock at $12 per share.		

If a balance sheet is prepared following this transaction, the stockholders' equity section would appear as follows (the values for Paid-in Capital in Excess of Par Value and Retained Earnings are assumed):

CHEN CORPORATION Stockholders' Equity	
Paid-in Capital	
Common stock, $10 par value, authorized and issued 20,000 shares; 1,000 shares in treasury, 19,000 shares outstanding	$200,000
Paid-in capital in excess of par value	20,000
Total Paid-in Capital	220,000
Retained earnings	40,000
	260,000
Less: Treasury stock (1,000 shares) at cost	**12,000**
Total Stockholders' Equity	$248,000

Note that the $200,000 par value of all *issued* stock is disclosed, although the 1,000 treasury shares are no longer outstanding. The total cost of the 1,000 shares, however, is later deducted as the last component in the presentation of total stockholders' equity.

If Chen subsequently resells 500 shares of its treasury stock at $14 per share, the following journal entry is made:

Cash (+A)	7,000	
Treasury stock (−XSE, +SE)		6,000
Paid-in capital—Treasury stock (+SE)		1,000

A = L + SE
+7,000   +6,000 TS
                    +1,000 TS

Note that the $1,000 "gain" on the resale of the treasury stock is accounted for as an increase in shareholders' equity and not as an increase in net income.

ACCOUNTING IN PRACTICE   **Why Do Companies Buy Back Their Stock?**

There are many potential reasons why firms buy back their own shares. The company may feel that its shares are currently undervalued by the market and repurchasing its own outstanding shares takes advantages of this possible mispricing. This not only allows the company to benefit if and when the share price ultimately rises, but perhaps more importantly it also sends a strong positive signal to the financial markets about the company's value. While it is one thing for the CEO to simply claim the company's stock is undervalued, it is a far more powerful signal to "put their money where their mouth is" by repurchasing the shares.

Some companies repurchase their own shares as a means to build shareholder value. Distributing this excess cash to the shareholders prevents management from using the cash in ways that destroy value, such as investing in a pet project with little chance of succeeding or wasting it on lavish management benefits such as a new corporate jet. Further, repurchasing stock benefits the shareholders because what the shareholder earns on shares sold back to the company is often taxed at lower capital gains rates than the ordinary income tax rate used to tax dividends.

Other possible reasons for share repurchases include the need to have a sufficient number of shares available to execute an acquisition through a share exchange, or to meet the demand for new shares when employees exercise their stock options. Alternatively, some companies repurchase as a takeover defense, for example, when the company's share price is below its intrinsic value per share and outsiders have been accumulating the shares.

Finally, share repurchases have the potential to improve the company's earnings per share calculation. Recall earnings per share is computed by dividing the company's earnings by the number of outstanding shares of common stock. Treasury stock is not counted as outstanding, and therefore reduces the denominator in the earnings per share calculation.

GuidedExample

MBC

The Fullerton Corporation purchased 5,000 shares of its outstanding $2 par value common stock for $75,000 cash on November 1. Management anticipates holding the shares in treasury stock until it is resold. By how much would the Fullerton Corporation debit Treasury Stock for this purchase?	**YOUR TURN! 11.6** The solution is on page 11-45.

CASH DIVIDENDS AND STOCK DIVIDENDS

LO7 **Identify** and **distinguish** between cash dividends and stock dividends.

eLecture

MBC

Dividends are a distribution of assets or shares of stock from a corporation to its stockholders. A corporation can distribute dividends to stockholders only after its board of directors has formally voted to declare a distribution. Dividends are usually paid in cash but may also be paid as property or additional shares of stock in the firm. Legally, declared dividends are an obligation of the firm, and an entry to record the dividend obligation is made on the *dividend declaration date*. Cash and property dividends payable are carried as liabilities, and stock dividends to be issued are shown in the stockholders' equity section of the balance sheet. At the date of declaration, a *record date* and *payment date* are also established. For example, assume that on April 25 (the declaration date), the board of directors of Branson Inc. declares a cash dividend payable on June 1 (the payment date) to those investors who own shares of stock on May 15 (the record date). Stockholders owning stock on the record date receive the dividend even if they dispose of their shares before the payment date. Therefore, shares sold between the record date and the payment date are sold *ex dividend*—that is, they are sold without the right to receive the dividend.

Most dividend declarations are accounted for by reducing retained earnings. Dividends are distributions of earnings and are not shown as an expense on the income statement. Also, dividends cannot be deducted for income tax purposes. Under certain conditions, however, state laws may permit distributions from additional paid-in capital. Stockholders should be informed of the source of such dividends, because, in a sense, any dividend paid from a company's paid-in capital is a nontaxable return of capital rather than a taxable distribution of earnings.

Declaration Date	Record Date	Payment Date
April 25	May 15	June 1
Balance sheet effects	No effect	**Balance sheet effects**
Increase dividends payable		Decrease cash
Decrease retained earnings		Decrease dividends payable

THINKING GLOBALLY

While U.S. corporations principally distribute cash and/or stock dividends, property dividend distributions are common among Japanese corporations. For example, **McDonald's Holding Company of Japan** annually distributes to its stockholders coupons for a free Big Mac as a property dividend. **DyDo Drinco, Inc.**, distributes to its stockholders samples of its beverage products as a property dividend. Companies that distribute their products or coupons for their products to stockholders as a property dividend believe that by making stockholders more familiar with the company's products, they will retain the investment commitment of their stockholders on a longer term basis than would otherwise be the case.

Cash Dividends

The majority of dividends distributed by corporations are paid in cash. Although companies may pay such dividends annually, many firms pay quarterly dividends. Dividends that are paid routinely are called regular dividends. The **Johnson & Johnson Company** and **PepsiCo, Inc.**, for example, pay regular quarterly dividends. Some companies occasionally pay a special dividend. Special dividends occur infrequently and represent the distribution of excess cash that has been accumulated by a business for which the business has no immediate operational need.

When a company declares a **cash dividend**, the company must have both an appropriate amount of retained earnings and the necessary amount of cash on hand. However, a large retained earnings balance does not guarantee generous dividend distributions. A company may successfully accumulate earnings and at the same time not be sufficiently liquid to pay large cash dividends. Many companies, especially new firms in growth industries, finance their expansion from assets generated through earnings and pay out small cash dividends or none at all.

Cash dividends are based on the number of shares outstanding. When a company's directors declare a cash dividend, an entry is made debiting the Cash Dividends account and crediting the Dividends Payable account. The Cash Dividends account is a temporary account that is closed to the Retained Earnings account at year-end.[1] To illustrate, assume that Boseman Group has 1,000 shares of $100 par value, six percent preferred stock and 6,000 shares of $10 par value common stock outstanding. If the company declares the regular $6 dividend on the preferred stock and a $2 dividend on the common stock, the dividend payment totals $18,000. The following journal entry is made on the declaration date:

Cash dividends (−SE)	18,000	
Dividends payable—Preferred stock (+L)		6,000
Dividends payable—Common stock (+L)		12,000
To record the declaration of $6 dividend on preferred stock and		
$2 dividend on common stock.		

A	=	L	+	SE
		+6,000		−18,000
		+12,000		Div

Dividends Payable—Preferred Stock and Dividends Payable—Common Stock are reported as current liabilities on the balance sheet until paid. On the dividend payment date, the following journal entry is made:

Dividends payable—Preferred stock (−L)	6,000	
Dividends payable—Common stock (−L)	12,000	
Cash (−A)		18,000
To record the payment of dividends on preferred and common shares.		

A	=	L	+	SE
−18,000		−6,000		
		−12,000		

Stock Dividends

Companies may also distribute shares of their own stock as dividends to stockholders in lieu of, or in addition to, cash dividends. A company may issue **stock dividends** when it does not wish to deplete its working capital by paying a cash dividend. Young and growing companies often issue stock dividends because cash is usually needed to acquire new facilities and to expand.

The accounting for a stock dividend results in a transfer of a portion of retained earnings to the paid-in capital accounts. Thus, the distribution of a stock dividend signals to investors management's desire to "plow back" earnings into the company. Although stock dividends may take a number of forms, usually common shares are distributed to common stockholders. We limit our discussion to this type of stock dividend distribution.

Small Stock Dividends

Small stock dividends are share distributions that involve less than 25 percent of the total number of shares previously outstanding. Small stock dividends are *recorded at the market value* of the shares issued, causing retained earnings to decrease and paid-in capital to increase by this amount. To illustrate the journal entries for a declaration of a small stock dividend, assume that the stockholders' equity of Hopkins Inc. is as follows prior to the declaration of a ten percent stock dividend:

Common stock, $5 par value, 20,000 shares issued and outstanding	$100,000
Paid-in capital in excess of par value	20,000
Total Paid-in Capital	120,000
Retained earnings	65,000
Total Stockholders' Equity	$185,000

---

[1] Some companies, especially those paying regular dividends, debit the Retained Earnings account directly on the dividend declaration date.

With 20,000 shares outstanding, the declaration of a ten percent stock dividend requires the issuance of an additional 2,000 shares (10 percent × 20,000 shares). If the current market price per share is $11, the total market value of the shares to be distributed is $22,000 (2,000 shares × $11), resulting in the following journal entry:

A = L + SE
−22,000
Div
+10,000
CS
+12,000
CS
	Stock dividends (−SE)
	    Stock dividend distributable (+SE)
	    Paid-in capital in excess of par value (+SE)
	    To record declaration of 10 percent stock dividend on common shares.
		22,000
		    10,000
		    12,000

The amount of the credit to the Stock Dividend Distributable account is the par value of the shares to be distributed (2,000 shares × $5). If a balance sheet is prepared between the declaration date and the distribution date of a stock dividend, the Stock Dividend Distributable account is shown in stockholders' equity immediately after the Common Stock account. When the shares are distributed, the following journal entry is made:

A = L + SE
−10,000
CS
+10,000
CS
	Stock dividend distributable (−SE)
	    Common stock (+SE)
	    To record issuance of stock dividend on common shares.
		10,000
		    10,000

The Stock Dividends account is a temporary account that is closed to the Retained Earnings account at year-end, as shown by the following journal entry:

A = L + SE
−22,000
RE
+22,000
Div
	Retained earnings (−SE)
	    Stock dividends (+SE)
	    To close the Stock Dividends account.
		22,000
		    22,000

A comparison of the stockholders' equity and outstanding shares, before and after the stock dividend, appears below. Note that retained earnings decreased by $22,000 and paid-in capital increased by $22,000, but total stockholders' equity remains unchanged:

	Before Stock Dividend	After Stock Dividend
Common stock, $5 par value	$100,000	$110,000
Paid-in capital in excess of par value	20,000	32,000
Total Paid-in Capital	120,000	142,000
Retained earnings	65,000	43,000
Total Stockholders' Equity	$185,000	$185,000
Common shares issued and outstanding	20,000	22,000

Total stockholders' equity remains unchanged.

The relative ownership interest of a common stockholder is unaltered by the receipt of a common stock dividend. If a ten percent stock dividend is distributed, all stockholders increase their proportionate holdings by ten percent, and the total shares outstanding are increased in the same proportion. Small stock dividends rarely affect the market value of the underlying stock.

Large Stock Dividends

When the number of shares issued as a stock dividend is large enough to impact the stock's market value per share, stockholders may not perceive the same benefits as they do for a small stock dividend. This is because issuing a large number of shares is likely to reduce the market price of the shares, much the same way that a stock split, discussed earlier in the chapter, reduces the market price per share. To see this, note that a 100 percent large stock dividend is the same as a 2-for-1 forward stock split. Accordingly, the accounting for large stock dividends (those over 25 percent) differs from the accounting for small stock dividends. Large stock dividends are recorded *at the par value* of the shares issued. The journal entry to record the declaration of a large stock dividend debits the Stock Dividends account and credits the Stock Dividend Distributable account for the par or stated value of the shares issued. Once the stock is issued, the increase in paid-in capital is reflected in the Common Stock account.[2]

ACCOUNTING IN PRACTICE	How Big Will That Bonus Be?

Investors and creditors are not the only people with a keen interest in a company's reported accounting results. Employees often have a big reason to care as well. The reason is that their own well-being could be directly tied to how much profit the company reports in a couple of ways. First, some companies believe in sharing some of the wealth with their employees through profit sharing plans. In addition, it is not uncommon to have the size of an employee's bonus based on some accounting measure, such as net income or return on assets. All the more reason to understand the accounting numbers.

YOUR TURN! 11.7

Guided Example
MBC

The solution is on page 11-45.

Fango Company's president would like to know the financial impact that a cash dividend and a stock dividend will have on the company's retained earnings account. The current balance in retained earnings is $500,000. The company has 10,000 shares of $1 par value common stock outstanding with a current market value of $20 per share. The potential cash dividend will be $3 per share and the potential stock dividend will be ten percent.

Required
Compute the Fango Company retained earnings balance after

a. A $3 per share cash dividend

b. A ten percent stock dividend

RETAINED EARNINGS AND THE STATEMENT OF STOCKHOLDERS' EQUITY

A **statement of retained earnings** presents an analysis of the Retained Earnings account for a given accounting period. An example of a statement of retained earnings is presented in **Exhibit 11-3**. The statement begins with the retained earnings balance as of the beginning of the period ❶, then reports the items that caused retained earnings to change during the period ❷, and ends with the end-of-period balance in retained earnings ❸.

LO8 Illustrate the statement of retained earnings and the statement of stockholders' equity.

eLecture
MBC

EXHIBIT 11-3	Statement of Retained Earnings

GEYSER CORPORATION Statement of Retained Earnings For Year Ended December 31	
❶ { Retained earnings, January 1....................................	$48,000
❷ { Add: Net income...	32,000
	80,000
Less: Cash dividends declared................................	19,000
❸ { Retained earnings, December 31................................	$61,000

---

[2] A stock's par value or stated value per share is not changed by a stock dividend. However, a stock split reduces the par value or stated value in proportion to the increase in the number of shares issued. This difference leads to a difference in accounting treatment—only a memorandum entry is made for a stock split, whereas a large stock dividend requires a journal entry to transfer the legal capital of the shares to be issued from retained earnings to common stock.

Statement of Stockholders' Equity

Rather than reporting a statement of retained earnings, most corporations integrate the information regarding retained earnings into a more comprehensive statement called a **statement of stockholders' equity**. This statement shows an analysis of all of the stockholders' equity accounts for the period. **Exhibit 11-4** presents an example of a statement of stockholders' equity. The statement begins with the beginning balances of the various stockholders' equity accounts ❶, reports the items causing changes in these accounts ❷, and ends with the end-of-period balances ❸.

The statement of stockholders' equity in **Exhibit 11-4** reveals all of the events affecting the Geyser Corporation's stockholders' equity during the year. These events are the earning of net income, the issuance of common stock, the issuance of treasury stock, the declaration of a cash dividend, and the acquisition of treasury stock. Note that the information in the retained earnings column (highlighted using a dotted red box) contains the same information as a statement of retained earnings.

EXHIBIT 11-4	Statement of Stockholders' Equity

GEYSER CORPORATION
Statement of Stockholders' Equity
For Year Ended December 31

	Common Stock	Paid-in Capital in Excess of Par Value	Paid-in Capital from Treasury Stock	Retained Earnings	Treasury Stock	Total
❶ Balance, January 1............	$200,000	$120,000	$18,000	$48,000	$(14,000)	$372,000
Net income..................				32,000		32,000
6,000 Common shares issued ...	30,000	24,000				54,000
❷ 500 Treasury shares issued.....			2,000		3,500	5,500
Cash dividends declared				(19,000)		(19,000)
200 Treasury shares acquired ...					(2,000)	(2,000)
❸ Balance, December 31.........	$230,000	$144,000	$20,000	$61,000	$(12,500)	$442,500

THINKING GLOBALLY

There are a number of significant terminology differences between U.S. GAAP and IFRS with respect to the reporting of stockholders' equity:

U.S. GAAP	IFRS
Common stock	Share capital
Paid-in capital in excess of par value	Share premium
Retained earnings	Retained profits
Accumulated other comprehensive income	Other reserve accounts

---

YOUR TURN! 11.8

GuidedExample

MBC

The solution is on page 11-46.

Dior Company had beginning balances at January 1 of $100,000 Common Stock, $900,000 Paid-in Capital in Excess of Par Value, $50,000 Retained Earnings, and $10,000 Treasury Stock. Net income for the year was $30,000. Dior paid a cash dividend of $8,000. Dior also issued 1,000 new $1 par value common shares for $15 each.

Required
Prepare a statement of stockholders' equity for the Dior Company for the year.

ANALYZING STOCKHOLDERS' EQUITY

Return on Equity

A financial ratio of particular interest to stockholders is the **return on equity**. This ratio measures the overall profitability of the stockholders' investment in a company and is calculated as follows:[3]

LO9 Define the return on equity, dividend yield, and dividend payout ratio and **explain** their use.

$$\text{Return on equity} = \frac{\text{Net income}}{\text{Average stockholders' equity}}$$

The denominator averages the stockholders' equity for the year (sum the beginning and ending stockholders' equity and then divide by 2).

To illustrate the calculation of the return on equity, financial data from **Johnson Controls, Inc.**, is used. Johnson Controls manufactures automotive heating systems, environmental control systems, automotive batteries, and plastic packaging. The company's 2020 financial data are as follows (in millions of dollars):

Net income	$ 795
Stockholders' equity, beginning of year.	20,829
Stockholders' equity, end of year	18,533

Johnson Controls' return on equity for the year is 4.0 percent, calculated as $795/[($20,829 + $18,533)/2].

Concept ———————▶	Method ———————▶	Assessment	**TAKEAWAY 11.1**
How profitable is the stockholders' investment in a company?	Statement of stockholders' equity and the income statement. Calculate the return on equity.	The higher the return on equity, the higher the overall return on the stockholders' investment in a business.	

Dividend Yield and Dividend Payout Ratio

Investors differ in their expectations regarding their investments—some investors are primarily interested in appreciation in the market value of their shares, while other investors focus on receiving current income in the form of dividends. The dividend yield and dividend payout ratio are helpful to this latter group of investors.

Dividend Yield

Dividend yield measures the current rate of return in cash dividends from an investment in a company's shares. The ratio may be calculated for either common or preferred shares by dividing the latest annual dividend per share by the current market price per share of the stock:

$$\text{Dividend yield} = \frac{\text{Annual dividend per share}}{\text{Market price per share}}$$

To illustrate, **Worthington Industries**, a manufacturer of steel and plastic products, declared cash dividends per common share of $0.96. At fiscal year-end, Worthington's common stock had a market price of $29.92 per share. Consequently, the company's dividend yield was 3.2 percent, or $0.96/$29.92.

---

[3] A related ratio used by many investment professionals is the return on common stockholders' equity, calculated as: (Net income − Preferred stock dividends) / Average common stockholders' equity.

Dividend yields are included in the stock tables published in *The Wall Street Journal* and *Barrons,* as well as online resources such as Yahoo! Finance, so it is easy for investors to compare current dividend yields for different stocks. The following are 5-year average dividend yields for several well-known companies:

The Coca-Cola Company.	3.2 percent
AT&T	5.8 percent
IBM Corporation	4.3 percent
Microsoft Corp.	1.7 percent
Chevron Corp.	4.3 percent
Alphabet (Google)	0.0 percent

TAKEAWAY 11.2	Concept ➡	Method ➡	Assessment
	What is a company's current rate of return to stockholders in the form of dividends?	Statement of stockholders' equity and a company's current market price per share. Calculate the company's dividend yield by dividing the annual dividend per share by the company's market price per share.	The higher a company's dividend yield, the greater the rate of return to stockholders in the form of dividends.

Data Analytics

DATA ANALYTICS   **Using analytics for Starbucks' site selections**

Perhaps the only thing **Starbucks** has more of than beans is data. With over 17 million active users for its mobile app and over 13 million for its reward program, Starbucks knows what you buy, and where and when you make the purchase. This allows Starbucks to personalize your experience by knowing what you like and suggesting new products based on those preferences. In addition, Starbucks does not simply need to go with gut hunches on where to locate new stores. Instead, they use the data they collect and a mapping and business intelligence tool called Atlas to determine optimal store locations.

Dividend Payout Ratio

The **dividend payout ratio** measures the percentage of net income available to common stockholders that is paid out as dividends. The ratio is calculated as follows:

$$\text{Dividend payout ratio} = \frac{\text{Annual dividend per share}}{\text{Earnings per share}}$$

Dividend payout ratios vary considerably among corporations. Companies that are considered "growth" companies often have low payout ratios because they use the net income they generate to help finance their growth. In contrast, "mature" companies that lack significant growth opportunities often distribute a high percentage of their net income as dividends. A good example of a mature company is the local utility company whose growth is limited by the net increase of new homes and businesses in the community and the approved rate increases by the local public utility commission.

Some corporations try to maintain a reasonably stable dividend payout ratio, so their payout ratios do not vary much from one year to the next. Other corporations try to keep their dividend per share either constant or increasing each year at a constant rate. If net income fluctuates quite a bit from year to year, these latter corporations will show dividend payout ratios that are quite variable over time. However, no company likes to cut its dividend per share because of the negative signal it sends to stockholders.

The following are the recent dividend payout ratios for some well-known corporations:

Best Buy Co. Inc. (retail)	34 percent
Apple Inc. (technology)	22 percent
Procter & Gamble Co. (consumer goods)	62 percent

YOUR TURN! 11.9

Century Co. reports the following information for the current year:

Net income	$150,000
Beginning of year stockholders' equity	650,000
End of year stockholders' equity	700,000
Annual common dividend per share	0.75
Market price of common shares	33.00
Earnings per common share	3.00

Calculate Century's (a) return on equity; (b) dividend yield; and (c) dividend payout ratio.

The solution is on page 11-46.

Concept ⟶	Method ⟶	Assessment	**TAKEAWAY 11.3**
What percentage of a company's net income is paid out to stockholders as a dividend?	Statement of stockholders' equity and the income statement. Calculate the dividend payout ratio by dividing the annual dividend per share by a company's earnings per share.	The higher the dividend payout ratio, the higher the percentage of net income paid to stockholders as a dividend.	

COMPREHENSIVE PROBLEM

Following is the stockholders' equity section of Bayside Corporation's December 31 balance sheet:

MBC

Paid-in Capital		
7% preferred stock, $50 par value, 5,000 shares authorized,		
issued, and outstanding	$ 250,000	
Common stock, $6 par value, 700,000 shares authorized; 200,000 issued,		
of which 10,000 shares are in the treasury	1,200,000	$1,450,000
Additional Paid-in Capital		
In excess of par value—Preferred stock	80,000	
In excess of par value—Common stock	1,000,000	
From treasury stock.	22,000	1,102,000
Total Paid-in Capital.		2,552,000
Retained earnings.		2,223,000
		4,775,000
Less: Treasury stock (10,000 common shares) at cost.		140,000
Total Stockholders' Equity		$4,635,000

Required

a.   What is Bayside's legal capital at December 31?

b.   What is the number of common shares outstanding at December 31?

c.   What is the average amount per share received from the original issuance of common stock?

d.   Assuming that the preferred stock is cumulative with no dividends in arrears, what total dollar amount of preferred dividends needs to be declared at December 31, before the common stockholders may receive a dividend?

e.   Has Bayside ever sold treasury stock for more than the treasury stock cost when it was acquired? Briefly explain.

f. Assume that Bayside splits its common stock 3-for-1 on the following January 1. What is the total amount of paid-in capital immediately after the split?

Solution
a. $1,450,000 (the par value of the issued preferred stock and common stock).
b. 190,000 shares (200,000 issued common shares less 10,000 shares in the treasury).
c. $11 [($1,200,000 par value of issued shares + $1,000,000 paid-in capital in excess of par value)/200,000 issued shares].
d. $17,500 (7 percent × $250,000).
e. Yes, the stockholders' equity section shows additional paid-in capital of $22,000 from treasury stock. This type of paid-in capital represents the excess of proceeds from the sale of treasury stock over that treasury stock's cost.
f. $2,552,000 (splitting the common stock does not change any of the account balances composing paid-in capital; the common stock's par value will decrease to $2 per share, and the common shares issued will increase to 600,000).

SUMMARY OF LEARNING OBJECTIVES

LO1   Define the corporate form of organization and discuss its principal characteristics. (p. 11-3)
- A corporation is a separate legal entity chartered by the state in which it is formed.
- The liability of corporate stockholders for the debts of a business is limited to the value of their ownership interest in a corporation, whereas claims against partners and sole proprietors may extend to their personal resources.
- Unlike sole proprietorships and partnerships, corporations must report paid-in capital separately from the accumulated balance of retained earnings. Distributions to stockholders are limited by the amount of retained earnings and other capital as specified by state law.

LO2   Explain the difference between par value stock and no-par value stock. (p. 11-6)
- Par value is the face value printed on a stock certificate. It has no economic significance but may have legal significance.
- No-par value stock has no face value printed on the stock certificate, although generally the board of directors sets a stated value for a corporation's capital stock.

LO3   Identify and discuss the two types of capital stock and their respective stockholder rights. (p. 11-7)
- Common stock represents a corporation's basic ownership class of stock; common shares carry the right to vote and may or may not pay a dividend.
- Preferred stock may differ from common stock in several ways. Typically, preferred stock has, at a minimum, some type of dividend preference and a prior claim to assets in the event of a corporate liquidation, relative to common stock.

LO4   Describe the accounting for issuances of capital stock. (p. 11-10)
- When capital stock is issued, the appropriate capital stock account is credited with the par value or stated value of the shares issued. The asset exchanged for the stock (usually cash) is debited for its fair value. Any difference is placed in the Paid-in Capital in Excess of Par Value account.

LO5   Define and discuss the accounting for stock splits. (p. 11-12)
- Stock splits change the par or stated value of capital stock and affect the number of shares outstanding. Only a memorandum notation records stock splits in the general journal. Forward stock splits increase the number of shares outstanding and lower its par or stated value, while reverse stock splits do the opposite.

LO6   Explain the accounting for treasury stock. (p. 11-13)
- Treasury stock represents reacquired shares of a firm's capital stock. It is commonly recorded at its acquisition cost and is deducted from total stockholders' equity on the balance sheet.

LO7   Identify and distinguish between cash dividends and stock dividends. (p. 11-15)
- Cash dividends reduce retained earnings and are a current liability when declared.
- Stock dividends are accounted for by a transfer of retained earnings to the appropriate capital stock and paid-in capital accounts at the fair market value of the shares distributed for small stock dividends and at par value for large stock dividends.

LO8   Illustrate the statement of retained earnings and the statement of stockholders' equity. (p. 11-18)
- A statement of retained earnings presents the financial effect of events causing retained earnings to change during an accounting period.

- A statement of stockholders' equity presents the financial effect of events causing each component of stockholders' equity (including retained earnings) to change during an accounting period.

Define the return on equity, dividend yield, and dividend payout ratio and explain their use. (p. 11-20)   **LO9**

- The return on equity is computed as net income /average stockholders' equity. It indicates the profitability of the stockholders' investment in a company.
- Dividend yield is computed by dividing a stock's annual dividend per share by its current market price per share. This ratio identifies the annual rate of return in dividends from an investment in a company's shares.
- The dividend payout ratio is computed by dividing the annual dividend per share by a company's earnings per share.

Concept ➞	Method ➞	Assessment	SUMMARY
How profitable is the stockholders' investment in a company?	Statement of stockholders' equity and the income statement. Calculate the return on equity.	The higher the return on equity, the higher the overall return on the stockholders' investment in a business.	**TAKEAWAY 11.1**
What is a company's current rate of return to stockholders in the form of dividends?	Statement of stockholders' equity and a company's current market price per share. Calculate the company's dividend yield by dividing the annual dividend per share by the company's market price per share.	The higher a company's dividend yield, the greater the rate of return to stockholders in the form of dividends.	**TAKEAWAY 11.2**
What percentage of a company's net income is paid out to stockholders as a dividend?	Statement of stockholders' equity and the income statement. Calculate the dividend payout ratio by dividing the annual dividend per share by a company's earnings per share.	The higher the dividend payout ratio, the higher the percentage of net income paid to stockholders as a dividend.	**TAKEAWAY 11.3**

KEY TERMS

Articles of incorporation (p. 11-3)	Dividend yield (p. 11-20)	Retained earnings (p. 11-11)
Authorized shares (p. 11-7)	Forward stock split (p. 11-12)	Return on equity (p. 11-20)
Callable (p. 11-10)	Issued shares (p. 11-7)	Reverse stock split (p. 11-13)
Cash dividend (p. 11-15)	Noncumulative (p. 11-9)	Stated value (p. 11-6)
Common stock (p. 11-7)	No-par value stock (p. 11-6)	Statement of retained earnings (p. 11-18)
Convertible (p. 11-9)	Outstanding shares (p. 11-7)	
Corporation (p. 11-3)	Paid-in capital (p. 11-11)	Statement of stockholders' equity (p. 11-19)
Cumulative (p. 11-9)	Participating (p. 11-9)	
Dividend payout ratio (p. 11-21)	Par value (p. 11-6)	Stock dividends (p. 11-16)
Dividends (p. 11-15)	Preemptive right (p. 11-8)	Treasury stock (p. 11-7, 11-13)
Dividends in arrears (p. 11-9)	Preferred stock (p. 11-8)	

Assignments with the 🔵 logo in the margin are available in *BusinessCourse*.
See the Preface of the book for details.

SELF-STUDY QUESTIONS

(Answers to the Self-Study Questions are available at the end of this chapter.)

1. **What is the usual liability of stockholders for corporation actions?**   **LO1**
    a. Unlimited
    b. Limited to the par value or stated value of the shares of stock they hold
    c. Limited to the amount of their investment in the corporation
    d. Limited to the amount of a corporation's retained earnings

LO3   2. **Which type of stock may have dividends in arrears?**

  a.   Cumulative preferred stock   *c.*   Noncumulative preferred stock
  b.   Common stock   *d.*   Treasury stock

LO4   3. **Wyler Company issued 20,000 shares of $10 par value common stock in exchange for a building with a current fair value of $1,000,000. In recording this transaction, what amount should be credited to the Paid-in Capital in Excess of Par Value account?**

  a. $1,000,000   *c.* $800,000
  b. $200,000   *d.* $980,000

LO6   4. **Which of the following accounts has a normal debit balance?**

  a.   Common Stock   *c.*   Preferred Stock
  b.   Paid-in Capital in Excess of Stated Value   *d.*   Treasury Stock

LO7   5. **Which of the following events decreases a corporation's stockholders' equity?**

  a.   A payment of a previously declared cash dividend
  b.   A declaration of a six percent stock dividend
  c.   A 2-for-1 forward stock split
  d.   A declaration of a $1 cash dividend per share on preferred stock

LO5   6. **When a company wants to reduce the market price per share of its stock, what action should it take?**

  a.   Issue a cash dividend   *c.*   Do a reverse stock split
  b.   Issue a stock dividend   *d.*   Do a forward stock split

LO9   7. **What type of company is typically characterized by a high dividend payout ratio?**

  a.   Technology company   *c.*   Mature, low-growth company
  b.   High-growth company   *d.*   All of the above

LO3   8. **Preferred stock that may be converted into common stock has which of the following characteristics?**

  a.   Call feature   *c.*   Participation feature
  b.   Cumulative feature   *d.*   Convertible feature

LO7   9. **A dividend that is paid every quarter or every year is called?**

  a.   Regular dividend   *c.*   Property dividend
  b.   Special dividend   *d.*   Stock dividend

LO8   10. **The statement of stockholders' equity includes each of the following except:**

  a.   Retained Earnings   *c.*   Paid-in Capital in Excess of Par Value
  b.   Treasury Stock   *d.*   Accounts Receivable

QUESTIONS

1. What is the meaning of each of the following terms: *corporation, articles of incorporation, corporate charter, board of directors, corporate officers,* and *organization costs*?

2. What is meant by the limited liability of a stockholder? Does this characteristic enhance or reduce a corporation's ability to raise capital?

3. Contrast the federal income taxation of a corporation with that of a sole proprietorship and a partnership. Which of the three types of organizations must file a federal income tax return?

4. Define *par value stock*. What is the significance of a stock's par value?

5. What is the preemptive right of a stockholder?

6. What are the basic differences between preferred stock and common stock? What are the typical features of preferred stock?

7. What features make preferred stock similar to debt? What features make it similar to common stock?

8. What is meant by dividends in arrears? If dividends are two years in arrears on $500,000 of six percent preferred stock and dividends are declared this year, what amount of total dividends must preferred stockholders receive before any distributions can be made to common stockholders?

9. Distinguish between authorized shares and issued shares. Why might the number of shares issued be more than the number of shares outstanding?

10. What are the different sources of paid-in capital?

11. Define a *forward stock split*. What is the major reason for a forward stock split?

12. Define *treasury stock*. Why might a corporation acquire treasury stock? How is treasury stock shown on the balance sheet?

13. If a corporation purchases 600 shares of its own common stock at $10 per share and resells the shares at $14 per share, where would the $2,400 [($14 − $10) × 600 shares] increase in capital appear in the financial statements? Why is no gain reported?

14. Why is the average stockholders' equity used in the denominator when calculating return on equity?

15. What is a stock dividend? How does a common stock dividend paid to common stockholders affect their respective ownership interests?

16. What is the difference between the accounting for a small stock dividend and the accounting for a large stock dividend?

17. What information is presented in a statement of retained earnings? What information is presented in a statement of stockholders' equity?

18. Where do the following accounts (and their balances) appear in the balance sheet?
    a. Dividends Payable—Common Stock
    b. Stock Dividend Distributable

19. How is a corporation's dividend yield calculated?

20. Bleaker Company declares and pays its annual dividend near the end of its fiscal year. For the current year, Bleaker's dividend payout ratio was 40 percent, its earnings per common share were $5.80, and it had 50,000 shares of common stock outstanding all year. What total amount of dividends did Bleaker declare and pay in the current year?

SHORT EXERCISES

SE11-1. Issuance of Common Stock Evans & Sons, Inc., is authorized to issue one million shares of $1 par value common stock. In the company's initial public offering, 500,000 shares are sold to the investing public at a price of $5 per share. One month following Evan & Sons' initial public offering, 1,000 of its common shares were sold by one investor to another at a price of $15 per share. How should this transaction be recorded in the accounts of Evans & Sons? Why?   **LO1**

SE11-2. Issuance of No-Par Common Stock Browne & Company issued 200,000 shares of $1 par value common stock at a price of $5 per share and issued 10,000 shares of no-par value common stock at a price of $10 per share. Prepare the journal entry to record the issuance of the no-par value common stock. How does this entry differ from the entry to record the $1 par value common stock?   **LO2**

SE11-3. Allocating Liquidation Between Common Stockholders and Preferred Stockholders The Azuza Company is liquidating. After paying off all of its creditors, the company has $1.5 million to distribute between its preferred stockholders and its common stockholders. The aggregate par value of the preferred stock is $900,000 and the aggregate par value of its common stock is $2 million. How much of the remaining $1.5 million in assets should be distributed to the preferred stockholders and how much should be distributed to the common stockholders?   **LO3**

SE11-4. Issuance of Common Stock Evans & Sons, Inc., is authorized to issue one million shares of $1 par value common stock. The company actually sells 700,000 shares at $10 per share. Prepare the journal entry to record the issuance of the 700,000 shares.   **LO4**

SE11-5. Outstanding Shares Willis & Company has 20 million shares of $1 par value common stock outstanding. The company believes that its current market price of $100 per share is too high and decides to execute a 4-for-1 forward stock split to lower the price. How many shares will be outstanding following the stock split, and what will be the new par value per share?   **LO5**

SE11-6. Treasury Stock Purchase Browne & Company has no-par value common stock outstanding that is selling at $40 per share. The company's CEO believes that the stock price is undervalued and decides to buy back 10,000 shares. Prepare the journal entry to record the purchase of the treasury stock.   **LO6**

SE11-7. Dividends Paid and Dividends in Arrears The Glendora Company has 200,000 shares of cumulative, five percent, $100 par value preferred stock outstanding. Last year the company failed to pay its regular dividend, but the board of directors would like to resume paying its regular dividend this year. Calculate the dividends in arrears and the total dividend that must be paid this year.   **LO7**

The following information relates to SE11-8 through SE11-10:

Evans & Sons, Inc., disclosed the following information in a recent annual report:

	Previous Year	Current Year
Net income	$ 35,000	$ 48,000
Average stockholders' equity	1,000,000	1,500,000
Dividend per common share.	1.90	2.00
Earnings per share.	2.85	3.20
Market price per common share, year-end.	19.00	21.00

LO9   **SE11-8.**   **Return on Equity** Calculate the return on equity for Evans & Sons for each year. Did the return improve?

LO9   **SE11-9.**   **Dividend Yield** Calculate the dividend yield for Evans & Sons for each year. Did the dividend yield improve?

LO9   **SE11-10.**   **Dividend Payout Ratio** Calculate the dividend payout for Evans & Sons for each year. Did the dividend payout increase?

LO8   **SE11-11.**   **Change in Stockholders' Equity** Nikron Corporation issued 20,000 shares of $0.50 par value common stock during the year for $20 each. Nikron also repurchased treasury stock for $15,000. Net income for the year was $140,000. The company also paid cash dividends of $25,000. What was the total change in Nikron's stockholders' equity for the year?

DATA ANALYTICS

Data Analytics

DA11-1.   **Constructing and Analyzing a Dataset on Share-Based Compensation in Excel** For this exercise, we create and analyze a dataset in Excel of the changes in the composition of share-based compensation plans (restricted stock unit, performance share, and stock option plans) for **Target Corporation** over a 10-year period.

REQUIRED

1.   Download Excel file DA11-1 found in myBusinessCourse.
2.   Create a dataset that will provide information on the composition of Target's share-based compensation plans over a 10-year period from fiscal year 2011 to fiscal year 2020.
   - In your dataset, for each of the share-based awards (restricted stock unit, performance share, and stock options) include the following: number of units granted during the year and the unrecognized compensation expense at year-end.
   - Also include in your dataset the total share-based compensation expense included on the income statement for each year and the fair value per unit at grant date of the restricted stock units for each year.
   - *Hints*:
     - This information can be found in the note disclosures in the annual 10-K reports.
     - When collecting your data, note that some amounts are in thousands, and some in millions.
     - Fiscal years end in January or February of the following year; for example, Fiscal Year 2020 ends January 30, 2021.
3.   Prepare a line chart in Excel over the 10-year period showing the trends in units granted of the three different types of share-based awards. *Hint:* Highlight data; click Insert, Line. Chart should show the earliest year on the left and the latest year on the right. To change the order, right-click inside the horizontal axis. In the Format Axis sidebar, check Categories in reverse order.
4.   Describe the 10-year trend in the data visualization for each of the three awards.
5.   Prepare a line chart in Excel showing the trend of share-based compensation expense over the 10-year period.
6.   Indicate which year(s) in the data visualization prepared in part 5 showed a highly visible decline in share-based compensation expense.
7.   Indicate which year seems to be the start of an increasing trend in the visualization created in part 5.
8.   Prepare a line chart in Excel showing the trend of unrecognized share-based compensation expense over the 10-year period for all three share-based plan types.

9. Indicate which share-based plan type in the data visualization prepared in part 8 showed the highest value and lowest value in Fiscal Year 2011, 2015, and 2020.

10. Prepare a schedule for the total fair value of the restricted stock share awards at the date of grant for each of the 10 years. *Hint:* Multiply the number of restricted stock units by the unit price at the date of grant.

11. Indicate which year(s) showed a decrease in total value based on the data visualization prepared in part 10.

12. Describe the trend shown in fair value of restricted stock share awards from fiscal year 2016 to fiscal year 2020.

13. Summarize the result of your analysis.

DA11-2. **Preparing Tableau Visualizations to Analyze Dividend Payout Policies Through Ratios** Refer to PF-28 in Appendix F. This problem uses Tableau to analyze dividend payout policies of S&P 500 companies through the dividend yield and dividend payout ratio.

DATA VISUALIZATION

Data Visualization Activities are available in myBusinessCourse. These assignments use Tableau Dashboards to expose students to visual depictions of data and introduce students to data analytics through data visualizations. These exercises are easily assignable and auto graded by MBC.

Data Visualization

EXERCISES—SET A

E11-1A. **Dividend Distribution** Lake Company has the following shares outstanding: 20,000 shares of $50 par value, five percent cumulative preferred stock and 80,000 shares of $10 par value common stock. The company declared cash dividends amounting to $200,000.   **LO7**

  a. If no dividends in arrears on the preferred stock exist, how much in total dividends, and in dividends per share, is paid to each class of stock?

  b. If one year of dividends in arrears exist on the preferred stock, how much in total dividends, and in dividends per share, is paid to each class of stock?

E11-2A. **Share Issuances for Cash** Minaret, Inc., issued 10,000 shares of $50 par value preferred stock at $68 per share and 12,000 shares of no-par value common stock at $15 per share. The common stock has no stated value. All issuances were for cash.   **LO4**

  a. Prepare the journal entries to record the share issuances.

  b. Prepare the journal entry for the issuance of the common stock assuming that it had a stated value of $4 per share.

  c. Prepare the journal entry for the issuance of the common stock assuming that it had a par value of $2 per share.

E11-3A. **Forward Stock Split** On March 1 of the current year, Center Corporation has 500,000 shares of $10 par value common stock that are issued and outstanding. The general ledger shows the following account balances relating to the common stock: **LO5**

Common stock	$5,000,000
Paid-in capital in excess of par value	3,500,000

On March 2, Center Corporation splits its stock 2-for-1 and reduces the par value to $5 per share.

  a. How many shares of common stock are issued and outstanding immediately following the stock split?

  b. What is the balance in the Common Stock account immediately following the stock split?

  c. What is the balance in the Paid-in Capital in Excess of Par Value account immediately following the stock split?

  d. Is a journal entry required to record the forward stock split? If yes, prepare the entry.

LO4, 6   E11-4A.   Treasury Stock Inland Corporation issued 30,000 shares of $5 par value common stock at $15 per share and 8,000 shares of $50 par value, eight percent preferred stock at $85 per share. Later, the company purchased 3,000 shares of its own common stock at $20 per share.

　a.　Prepare the journal entries to record the share issuances and the purchase of the common shares.
　b.　Assume that Inland sold 2,000 shares of the treasury stock at $30 per share. Prepare the general journal entry to record the sale of this treasury stock.
　c.　Assume that Inland sold the remaining 1,000 shares of treasury stock at $18 per share. Prepare the journal entry to record the sale of this treasury stock.

LO7   E11-5A.   Cash Dividends Bernard Corporation has the following shares outstanding: 8,000 shares of $50 par value, six percent preferred stock and 50,000 shares of $1 par value common stock. The company has $328,000 of retained earnings. At year-end, the company declares its regular $3 per share cash dividend on the preferred stock and a $2.20 per share cash dividend on the common stock. Three weeks later, the company pays the dividends.

　a.　Prepare the journal entry for the declaration of the cash dividends.
　b.　Prepare the journal entry for the payment of the cash dividends.

LO7   E11-6A.   Stock Dividends White Corporation has 80,000 shares of $5 par value common stock outstanding. At year-end, the company declares a five percent stock dividend. The market price of the stock on the declaration date is $20 per share. Four weeks later, the company issues the shares of stock to stockholders.

　a.　Prepare the journal entry for the declaration of the stock dividend.
　b.　Prepare the journal entry for the issuance of the stock dividend.
　c.　Assume that the company declared a 30 percent stock dividend rather than a five percent stock dividend. Prepare the journal entries for (1) the declaration of the stock dividend and (2) the issuance of the stock dividend.

LO8   E11-7A.   Statement of Retained Earnings Use the following data to prepare a statement of retained earnings for Barney Corporation.

Total retained earnings originally reported at January 1.	$400,000
Cash dividends declared during the year	80,000
Net income for the year	193,000
Stock dividend declared during the year	40,000

LO3   E11-8A.   Conversion of Preferred Stock into Common Stock Evans & Sons, Inc., has 20,000 shares of $100 par value, six percent preferred stock and 100,000 shares of $1.00 par value common stock outstanding. The preferred stock is convertible into the company's common stock at a conversion rate of 1-to-20; that is, each share of preferred stock is convertible into 20 shares of common stock. The preferred stock had been sold for its par value when issued. Prepare the journal entry to record the conversion of all of the company's preferred stock into common stock.

LO5   E11-9A.   Reverse Stock Split Upland Metals Company had 20,000,000 shares of $0.01 par value common stock outstanding which had been sold for an aggregate amount of $300,000,000. The company's shares are traded on the New York Stock Exchange, which has a minimum listing price of $1 per share. Recently, the company's common stock has been trading on the exchange below $1 per share, and the exchange has notified the company that its common stock would be delisted in 30 days if the stock price did not rebound above its minimum listing price. In response to this notification, Upland Metals authorized a 1-for-40 reverse stock split. Following the reverse stock split:

　a.　How many common shares will be outstanding?
　b.　What will be the new par value per share?
　c.　How will the reverse stock split be recorded in the company's accounts?

LO9   E11-10A.   Return on Equity, Dividend Yield, and Dividend Payout The following information relates to Ontario Components, Inc.:

	Previous Year	Current Year
Net income	$ 65,000	$ 100,000
Average stockholders' equity	2,000,000	2,100,000
Dividend per common share	1.50	1.50
Earnings per share	2.90	3.00
Market price per common share, year-end	27.50	30.00

a. Calculate the company's return on equity for each year.
b. Calculate the company's dividend yield for each year.
c. Calculate the company's dividend payout for each year.

E11-11A. Characteristics of a Corporation Label each of the following characteristics of a corporation as either an (A) advantage or a (D) disadvantage: **LO1**

a. Limited liability
b. Taxation

c. Regulations
d. Transferability of ownership

E11-12A. Cash and Noncash Share Issuances Skelton Corporation was organized on June 1. The company's charter authorizes 500,000 shares of $5 par value common stock. On July 1, the attorney who helped organize the corporation accepted 600 shares of Skelton common stock in settlement for the services provided (the services were valued at $8,000). On July 15, Skelton issued 6,000 common shares for $65,000 cash. On September 15, Skelton issued 2,000 common shares to acquire a vacant land site appraised at $28,000. Prepare the journal entries to record the stock issuances on July 1, July 15, and September 15. **LO4**

E11-13A. Stock Issuance and Treasury Stock Decade, Inc., recorded certain capital stock transactions shown in the following journal entries: (1) issued common stock for $25 cash per share, (2) purchased treasury shares at $40 per share, and (3) sold some of the treasury shares: **LO4, 6**

1.	Cash	500,000	
	Common stock		75,000
	Paid-in capital in excess of par value		425,000
2.	Treasury stock	100,000	
	Cash		100,000
3.	Cash	81,000	
	Treasury stock		75,000
	Paid-in capital from treasury stock		6,000

a. How many shares were originally issued?
b. What was the par value of the shares issued?
c. How many shares of treasury stock were acquired?
d. How many shares of treasury stock were sold?
e. At what price per share was the treasury stock sold?

E11-14A. Cash and Stock Dividends Lester Corporation has 30,000 shares of $1 par value common stock outstanding. The company has $250,000 of retained earnings. At year-end, the company declares a cash dividend of $3.00 per share and a five percent stock dividend. The market price of the stock at the declaration date is $40 per share. Three weeks later, the company pays the dividends. **LO7**

a. Prepare the journal entry for the declaration of the cash dividend.
b. Prepare the journal entry for the declaration of the stock dividend.
c. Prepare the journal entry for the payment of the cash dividend.
d. Prepare the journal entry for the payment of the stock dividend.

E11-15A. Large Stock Dividend and Forward Stock Split High Corporation has 60,000 shares of $20 par value common stock outstanding and retained earnings of $800,000. The company declares a 100 percent stock dividend. The market price at the declaration date is $20 per share. **LO5, 7**

a. Prepare the journal entries for (1) the declaration of the dividend and (2) the issuance of the dividend.
b. Assume that the company splits its stock 2-for-1 and reduces the par value from $20 to $10 rather than declaring a 100 percent stock dividend. How does the accounting for the forward stock split differ from the accounting for the 100 percent stock dividend?

EXERCISES—SET B

LO7   **E11-1B.**   **Dividend Distribution** Bowen Corporation has the following shares outstanding: 15,000 shares of $50 par value, six percent preferred stock and 50,000 shares of $5 par value common stock. During its first three years in business, the firm declared no dividends in the first year, $140,000 of dividends in the second year, and $60,000 of dividends in the third year.

    a.   If the preferred stock is cumulative, determine the total amount of dividends paid to each class of stock in each of the three years.

    b.   If the preferred stock is noncumulative, determine the total amount of dividends paid to each class of stock in each of the three years.

LO4   **E11-2B.**   **Share Issuances for Cash** Chase, Inc., issued 10,000 shares of $20 par value preferred stock at $50 per share and 8,000 shares of no-par value common stock at $20 per share. The common stock has no stated value. All issuances were for cash.

    a.   Prepare the journal entries to record the share issuances.

    b.   Prepare the journal entry for the issuance of the common stock assuming that it had a stated value of $10 per share.

    c.   Prepare the journal entry for the issuance of the common stock assuming that it had a par value of $2 per share.

LO5   **E11-3B.**   **Forward Stock Split** On September 1, Cambridge Company has 500,000 shares of $15 par value common stock that are issued and outstanding. The general ledger shows the following account balances relating to the common stock:

Common stock	$7,500,000
Paid-in capital in excess of par value	$2,250,000

On September 2, Cambridge splits its stock 3-for-2 and reduces the par value to $10 per share.

    a.   How many shares of common stock are issued and outstanding immediately following the stock split?

    b.   What is the balance in the Common Stock account immediately following the stock split?

    c.   What is the likely reason that Cambridge Company split its stock?

LO4, 6   **E11-4B.**   **Treasury Stock** Pomona Corporation issued 60,000 shares of $3 par value common stock at $21 per share and 9,000 shares of $30 par value, ten percent preferred stock at $85 per share. Later, the company purchased 2,000 shares of its own common stock at $23 per share.

    a.   Prepare the journal entries to record the share issuances and the purchase of the common shares.

    b.   Assume that Pomona sold 1,500 shares of the treasury stock at $30 per share. Prepare the general journal entry to record the sale of this treasury stock.

    c.   Assume that Pomona sold the remaining 500 shares of treasury stock at $20 per share. Prepare the journal entry to record the sale of this treasury stock.

LO7   **E11-5B.**   **Cash Dividends** Sand Corporation has the following shares outstanding: 10,000 shares of $40 par value, ten percent preferred stock and 50,000 shares of $2 par value common stock. The company has $428,000 of retained earnings. At year-end, the company declares its regular $4 per share cash dividend on the preferred stock and a $3.20 per share cash dividend on the common stock. Two weeks later, the company pays the dividends.

    a.   Prepare the journal entry for the declaration of the cash dividends.

    b.   Prepare the journal entry for the payment of the cash dividends.

LO7   **E11-6B.**   **Stock Dividends** Mammoth Corporation has 100,000 shares of $10 par value common stock outstanding. At year-end, the company declares a five percent stock dividend. The market price of the stock on the declaration date is $30 per share. Three weeks later, the company issues the shares of stock to stockholders.

    a.   Prepare the journal entry for the declaration of the stock dividend.

    b.   Prepare the journal entry for the issuance of the stock dividend.

    c.   Assume that the company declared a 50 percent stock dividend rather than a five percent stock dividend. Prepare the journal entries for (1) the declaration of the stock dividend and (2) the issuance of the stock dividend.

E11-7B.   **Statement of Retained Earnings** Use the following data to prepare a statement of retained earnings for June Corporation.   **LO8**

Total retained earnings originally reported as of January 1	$347,000
Stock dividends declared during the year	25,000
Cash dividends declared during the year	40,000
Net income for the year	70,000

E11-8B.   **Conversion of Preferred Stock into Common Stock** Givens & Sons, Inc., has 20,000 shares of $50 par value, nine percent preferred stock and 100,000 shares of $0.50 par value common stock outstanding. The preferred stock is convertible into the company's common stock at a conversion rate of 1-to-40; that is, each share of preferred stock is convertible into 40 shares of common stock. The preferred stock had been sold for its par value when issued. Prepare the journal entry to record the conversion of all of the company's preferred stock into common stock.   **LO3**

E11-9B.   **Reverse Stock Split** The Crystal Company had 100,000,000 shares of $0.10 par value common stock outstanding which had been sold for an aggregate amount of $500,000,000. The company's shares are traded on the New York Stock Exchange, which has a minimum listing price of $1 per share. Recently, the company's common stock has been trading on the exchange below $1 per share, and the exchange has notified the company that its common stock would be delisted in 30 days if the stock price did not rebound above its minimum listing price. In response to this notification, Crystal authorized a 1-for-40 reverse stock split. Following the reverse stock split: **LO5**

a.   How many common shares will be outstanding?
b.   What will be the new par value per share?
c.   How will the reverse stock split be recorded in the company's accounts?

E11-10B.   **Return on Equity, Dividend Yield, and Dividend Payout** The following information relates to Menlo, Inc.:   **LO9**

	Previous Year	Current Year
Net income	$ 125,000	$ 200,000
Average stockholders' equity	5,000,000	4,200,000
Dividend per common share	2.80	3.00
Earnings per share	5.80	6.00
Market price per common share, year-end	60.00	59.50

a.   Calculate the company's return on equity for each year.
b.   Calculate the company's dividend yield for each year.
c.   Calculate the company's dividend payout for each year.

E11-11B.   **Characteristics of a Corporation** Label each of the following characteristics of a corporation as either an (A) advantage or a (D) disadvantage: **LO1**

a.   Organizational costs   *c.*   Capital raising capability
b.   Continuity of existence   *d.*   Separate legal entity

E11-12B.   **Cash and Noncash Share Issuances** Channey Corporation was organized on July 1. The company's charter authorizes 100,000 shares of $2 par value common stock. On August 1, the attorney who helped organize the corporation accepted 950 shares of Channey common stock in settlement for the services provided (the services were valued at $9,800). On August 15, Channey issued 6,000 common shares for $75,000 cash. On October 15, Channey issued 3,000 common shares to acquire a vacant land site appraised at $50,000. Prepare the journal entries to record the stock issuances on August 1, August 15, and October 15.   **LO4**

E11-13B.   **Stock Issuance and Treasury Stock** Omaha, Inc., recorded certain capital stock transactions shown in the following journal entries: (1) issued common stock for $40 cash per share, (2) purchased treasury shares at $50 per share, and (3) sold some of the treasury shares: **LO4, 6**

1.	Cash	437,000	
	Common stock		43,700
	Paid-in capital in excess of par value		393,300

2.	Treasury stock	77,000	
	Cash		77,000
3.	Cash	63,360	
	Treasury stock		52,800
	Paid-in capital from treasury stock		10,560

    a.   How many shares were originally issued?
    b.   What was the par value of the shares issued?
    c.   How many shares of treasury stock were acquired?
    d.   How many shares of treasury stock were sold?
    e.   At what price per share was the treasury stock sold?

LO7   **E11-14B. Cash and Stock Dividends** Murphy Corporation has 50,000 shares of $10 par value common stock outstanding. The company has $450,000 of retained earnings. At year-end, the company declares a cash dividend of $2.10 per share and a five percent stock dividend. The market price of the stock at the declaration date is $35 per share. Four weeks later, the company pays the dividends.

    a.   Prepare the journal entry for the declaration of the cash dividend.
    b.   Prepare the journal entry for the declaration of the stock dividend.
    c.   Prepare the journal entry for the payment of the cash dividend.
    d.   Prepare the journal entry for the payment of the stock dividend.

LO5, 7   **E11-15B. Large Stock Dividend and Forward Stock Split** Kitch Corporation has 50,000 shares of $5 par value common stock outstanding and retained earnings of $820,000. The company declares a 100 percent stock dividend. The market price at the declaration date is $17 per share.

    a.   Prepare the journal entries for (1) the declaration of the dividend and (2) the issuance of the dividend.
    b.   Assume that the company splits its stock 5-for-1 and reduces the par value from $5 to $1 rather than declaring a 100 percent stock dividend. How does the accounting for the forward stock split differ from the accounting for the 100 percent stock dividend?

PROBLEMS—SET A

LO7   **P11-1A. Dividend Distribution** Ryan Corporation began business on March 1, 2019. At that time, it issued 20,000 shares of $60 par value, seven percent cumulative preferred stock and 100,000 shares of $5 par value common stock. Through the end of 2021, there had been no change in the number of preferred and common shares outstanding.

Required
    a.   Assume that Ryan declared dividends of $0 in 2019, $195,000 in 2020, and $200,000 in 2021. Calculate the total dividends and the dividends per share paid to each class of stock in 2019, 2020, and 2021.
    b.   Assume that Ryan declared dividends of $0 in 2019, $90,000 in 2020, and $190,000 in 2021. Calculate the total dividends and the dividends per share paid to each class of stock in 2019, 2020, and 2021.

LO4, 8   **P11-2A. Stockholders' Equity: Transactions and Balance Sheet Presentation** Torey Corporation was organized on April 1, with an authorization of 25,000 shares of six percent, $50 par value preferred stock and 200,000 shares of $5 par value common stock. During April, the following transactions affecting stockholders' equity occurred:

Apr.   1   Issued 80,000 shares of common stock at $40 cash per share.
       3   Issued 2,000 shares of common stock to attorneys and promoters in exchange for their services in organizing the corporation. The services were valued at $31,000.
       8   Issued 3,000 shares of common stock in exchange for equipment with a fair market value of $55,000.
    20   Issued 6,000 shares of preferred stock for cash at $80 per share.

Required

a.   Prepare journal entries to record the above transactions.

b.   Prepare the stockholders' equity section of the balance sheet at April 30. Assume that the net income for April is $60,000.

P11-3A.   Stockholders' Equity: Transactions and Balance Sheet Presentation   The stockholders' equity accounts of Willis Corporation at January 1 appear below:

LO4, 6, 8

8% preferred stock, $10 par value, 50,000 shares authorized; 6,800 shares issued and outstanding...	$ 68,000
Common stock, $10 par value, 200,000 shares authorized; 50,000 shares issued and outstanding....	500,000
Paid-in capital in excess of par value—Preferred stock	68,000
Paid-in capital in excess of par value—Common stock	200,000
Retained earnings	270,000

During the year, the following transactions occurred:

Jan.   10   Issued 35,000 shares of common stock for $18 cash per share.

23   Purchased 10,000 shares of common stock as treasury stock at $19 per share.

Mar.   14   Sold one-half of the treasury shares acquired January 23 for $21 per share.

July   15   Issued 3,500 shares of preferred stock in exchange for equipment with a fair market value of $128,000.

Nov.   15   Sold 1,000 of the treasury shares acquired January 23 for $24 per share.

Dec.   31   Closed the net income of $59,000 to the Retained Earnings account.

Required

a.   Set up T-accounts for the stockholders' equity accounts as of the beginning of the year and enter the January 1 balances.

b.   Prepare journal entries to record the foregoing transactions and post to T-accounts (set up any additional T-accounts needed). Do not prepare the journal entry for the Dec. 31 transaction, but post the appropriate amount to the Retained Earnings T-account. Determine the ending balances for the stockholders' equity accounts.

c.   Prepare the December 31 stockholders' equity section of the balance sheet.

P11-4A.   Stockholders' Equity: Transactions and Balance Sheet Presentation   The stockholders' equity of Peak Corporation at January 1 follows:

LO4, 5, 6, 8

7% preferred stock, $100 par value, 20,000 shares authorized;	
5,000 shares issued and outstanding......................................	$ 500,000
Common stock, $15 par value, 100,000 shares authorized;	
40,000 shares issued and outstanding.....................................	600,000
Paid-in capital in excess of par value—Preferred stock	24,000
Paid-in capital in excess of par value—Common stock	360,000
Retained earnings	325,000
Total Stockholders' Equity	$1,809,000

The following transactions, among others, occurred during the year:

Jan.   12   Announced a 4-for-1 common stock split, reducing the par value of the common stock to $3.75 per share. The authorization was increased to 400,000 shares.

Mar.   31   Converted $40,000 face value of convertible bonds payable (the book value of the bonds was $43,000) to common stock. Each $1,000 bond converted to 125 shares of common stock.

June   1   Acquired equipment with a fair market value of $90,000 in exchange for 500 shares of preferred stock.

Sept.   1   Acquired 10,000 shares of common stock for cash at $10 per share.

Oct.   12   Sold 1,500 treasury shares at $12 per share.

Nov.   21   Issued 5,000 shares of common stock at $11 cash per share.

Dec.   28   Sold 1,200 treasury shares at $9 per share.

31   Closed net income of $105,000 to the Retained Earnings account.

Required

a. Set up T-accounts for the stockholders' equity accounts as of the beginning of the year and enter the January 1 balances.

b. Prepare journal entries for the given transactions and post them to the T-accounts (set up any additional T-accounts needed). Do not prepare the journal entry for the Dec. 31 transaction, but post the appropriate amount to the Retained Earnings T-account. Determine the ending balances for the stockholders' equity accounts.

c. Prepare the stockholders' equity section of the balance sheet at December 31.

LO4, 6   P11-5A.   Stockholders' Equity: Information and Entries from Comparative Data Comparative stockholders' equity sections from two successive years of balance sheets from Farrow, Inc., are as follows:

	Dec. 31, Current Year	Dec. 31, Previous Year
Paid-in Capital		
8% preferred stock, $40 par value, authorized 20,000 shares; issued and outstanding, current year: 12,000 shares; previous year: 10,000 shares	$ 480,000	$ 400,000
Common stock, no-par value, $5 stated value, authorized 80,000 shares; issued, current year: 40,000 shares; previous year: 32,000 shares	200,000	160,000
Additional Paid-in Capital		
In excess of par value—Preferred stock	224,000	144,000
In excess of stated value—Common stock	232,000	160,000
From treasury stock.	21,000	
Retained earnings.	350,000	229,000
		$1,093,000
Less: Treasury stock (8,000 shares common) at cost.	0	179,000
Total Stockholders' Equity	$1,507,000	$ 914,000

No dividends were declared or paid during the current year.

Required

Prepare the journal entries for the transactions affecting stockholders' equity that occurred during the current year. Do not prepare the journal entry for closing net income to retained earnings. Assume that any share transactions were for cash.

LO7, 8   P11-6A.   Retained Earnings: Transactions and Statement The stockholders' equity accounts of Raymund Corporation as of January 1 appear below:

Common stock, $1 par value, 400,000 shares authorized; 160,000 shares issued and outstanding	$160,000
Paid-in capital in excess of par value	920,000
Retained earnings	513,000

During the year, the following transactions occurred:

June   7   Declared a 20 percent stock dividend; market value of the common stock was $15 per share.
        28   Issued the stock dividend declared on June 7.
Dec.   5   Declared a cash dividend of $2.00 per share.
        26   Paid the cash dividend declared on December 5.

Required

a. Prepare journal entries to record the foregoing transactions.

b. Prepare a statement of retained earnings. The net income for the year is $435,000.

P11-7A. Retained Earnings: Transactions and Statement The stockholders' equity of Carly Corporation at January 1 follows:

6% preferred stock, $10 par value, 40,000 shares authorized; 25,000 shares issued and outstanding	$ 250,000
Common stock, $1 par value, 300,000 shares authorized; 80,000 shares issued and outstanding.	80,000
Paid-in capital in excess of par value—Common stock	560,000
Retained earnings	830,000
Total Stockholders' Equity	$1,720,000

The following transactions, among others, occurred during the year:

June   18   Declared a 70 percent stock dividend on all outstanding shares of common stock. The market value of the stock was $14 per share.

July   1   Issued the stock dividend declared on June 18.

Dec.   20   Declared the annual cash dividend on the preferred stock and a cash dividend of $1.80 per share on the common stock, payable on January 20 to stockholders of record on December 28.

Required

a.   Prepare journal entries to record the foregoing transactions.

b.   Prepare a statement of retained earnings. The net income for the year is $500,000.

P11-8A. Stockholders' Equity Transactions, Journal Entries, and T-Accounts The stockholders' equity of Black Corporation at January 1 follows:

8% preferred stock, $100 par value, 20,000 shares authorized; 5,000 shares issued and outstanding.	$ 500,000
Common stock, $1 par value, 100,000 shares authorized; 40,000 shares issued and outstanding.	40,000
Paid-in capital in excess of par value—Preferred stock	200,000
Paid-in capital in excess of par value—Common stock	800,000
Retained earnings	625,000
Total Stockholders' Equity	$2,165,000

The following transactions, among others, occurred during the year:

Jan.   1   Announced a 4-for-1 common stock split, reducing the par value of the common stock to $0.25 per share.

Mar.   31   Converted $75,000 face value of convertible bonds payable (the book value of the bonds was $83,000) to common stock. Each $1,000 bond converted to 110 shares of common stock. (Record common stock entry in whole dollars. Round up.)

June   1   Acquired equipment with a fair market value of $90,000 in exchange for 300 shares of preferred stock.

Sept.   1   Acquired 15,000 shares of common stock for cash at $20 per share.

Nov.   21   Issued 5,000 shares of common stock at $22 cash per share.

Dec.   28   Sold 1,000 treasury shares at $23 per share.

         31   Closed net income of $145,000, to the Retained Earnings account.

Required

a.   Set up T-accounts for the stockholders' equity accounts as of the beginning of the year and enter the January 1 balances.

b.   Prepare journal entries for the given transactions and post them to the T-accounts (set up any additional T-accounts needed). Do not prepare the journal entry for the Dec. 31 transaction, but post the appropriate amount to the Retained Earnings T-account. Determine the ending balances for the stockholders' equity accounts.

P11-9A. Stockholders' Equity Section of the Balance Sheet Using your analysis from P11-8A, prepare the stockholders' equity section of the Black Corporation's balance sheet.

LO4, 6, 7, 8   **P11-10A. Stockholders' Equity: Transactions and Statement** The stockholders' equity section of Day Corporation's balance sheet at January 1 follows:

Common stock, $5 par value, 300,000 shares authorized, 60,000 shares Issued, 6,000 shares in treasury.		$ 300,000
Additional paid-in capital.		
In excess of par value.	$480,000	
From treasury stock	30,000	510,000
Retained earnings		348,000
		1,158,000
Less: Treasury stock (6,000 shares) at cost.		138,000
		$1,020,000

The following transactions affecting stockholders' equity occurred during the year:

Jan.	8	Issued 15,000 shares of previously unissued common stock for $42 cash per share.
Mar.	12	Sold all of the treasury shares for $56 cash per share.
June	30	Declared a five percent stock dividend on all outstanding shares of common stock. The market value of the stock was $50 per share.
July	10	Issued the stock dividend declared on June 30.
Oct.	7	Acquired 2,500 shares of common stock as treasury stock at $52 cash per share.
Dec.	18	Declared a cash dividend of $1.00 per outstanding common share, payable on January 9 to stockholders of record on December 31.

Required

a.   Prepare journal entries to record the foregoing transactions.

b.   Prepare a statement of stockholders' equity. Net income for the year is $351,000.

 LO4, 6   **P11-11A. Stockholders' Equity: Transaction Descriptions from Account Data** The following T-accounts contain keyed entries representing five transactions involving the stockholders' equity of Riverside, Inc.:

Cash

(1)	90,000	15,600	(4)
(2)	120,000		
(5)	8,400		

Land

(3)	105,000	

Preferred Stock, $10 Par

	30,000	(1)

Paid-in Capital in Excess of Par Value—Preferred Stock

	60,000	(1)

Common Stock, $20 Par

	120,000	(2)
	90,000	(3)

Paid-in Capital in Excess of Par Value—Common Stock

	15,000	(3)

Paid-in Capital from Treasury Stock

	600	(5)

Treasury Stock

(4)	(600 shares of common)	7,800 15,600		(5)

Required

Using this information, give detailed descriptions, including number of shares and price per share when applicable, for each of the five transactions.

PROBLEMS—SET B

 LO7   **P11-1B.   Dividend Distribution** Chauncey Corporation began business on June 30, 2019. At that time, it issued 20,000 shares of $50 par value, six percent, cumulative preferred stock and 90,000 shares of $10 par value common stock. Through the end of 2021, there had been no change in the number of preferred and common shares outstanding.

Required

a. Assume that Chauncey declared dividends of $69,000 in 2019, $0 in 2020, and $354,000 in 2021. Calculate the total dividends and the dividends per share paid to each class of stock in 2019, 2020, and 2021.

b. Assume that Chauncey declared dividends of $0 in 2019, $120,000 in 2020, and $186,000 in 2021. Calculate the total dividends and the dividends per share paid to each class of stock in 2019, 2020, and 2021.

P11-2B. **Stockholders' Equity: Transactions and Balance Sheet Presentation** Baker Corporation was organized on July 1, with an authorization of 50,000 shares of $5 no-par value preferred stock ($5 is the annual dividend) and 100,000 shares of $10 par value common stock. During July, the following transactions affecting stockholders' equity occurred:

LO4, 8

July   1   Issued 62,000 shares of common stock at $21 cash per share.
       12   Issued 7,000 shares of common stock in exchange for equipment with a fair market value of $71,000.
       15   Issued 10,000 shares of preferred stock for cash at $40 per share.

Required

a. Prepare journal entries to record the foregoing transactions.
b. Prepare the stockholders' equity section of the balance sheet at July 31. The net income for July is $52,000.

P11-3B. **Stockholders' Equity: Transactions and Balance Sheet Presentation** The stockholders' equity accounts of Cooper Corporation at January 1 follow:

LO4, 6, 8

Common stock, $1 par value, 350,000 shares authorized;	
150,000 shares issued and outstanding	$150,000
Paid-in capital in excess of par value	600,000
Retained earnings	366,000

During the year, the following transactions occurred:

Jan.   5   Issued 20,000 shares of common stock for $15 cash per share.
      18   Purchased 4,000 shares of common stock as treasury stock at $14 cash per share.
Mar.   12   Sold one-fourth of the treasury shares acquired January 18 for $17 per share.
July   17   Sold 600 shares of the remaining treasury stock for $12 per share.
Oct.   1   Issued 5,000 shares of eight percent, $25 par value preferred stock for $35 cash per share. These are the first preferred shares issued out of 50,000 authorized shares.
Dec.   31   Closed the net income of $170,000 to the Retained Earnings account.

Required

a. Set up T-accounts for the stockholders' equity accounts as of the beginning of the year and enter the January 1 balances.
b. Prepare journal entries to record the foregoing transactions and post to T-accounts (set up any additional T-accounts needed). Do not prepare the journal entry for the Dec. 31 transaction, but post the appropriate amount to the Retained Earnings T-account. Determine the ending balances for the stockholders' equity accounts.
c. Prepare the December 31 stockholders' equity section of the balance sheet.

P11-4B. **Stockholders' Equity: Transactions and Balance Sheet Presentation** The following is the stockholders' equity of Laker Corporation at January 1:

LO4, 5, 6, 8

8% preferred stock, $40 par value, 10,000 shares authorized;	
7,000 shares issued and outstanding	$ 280,000
Common stock, $20 par value, 50,000 shares authorized;	
25,000 shares issued and outstanding	500,000
Paid-in capital in excess of par value—Preferred stock	70,000
Paid-in capital in excess of par value—Common stock	385,000
Retained earnings	238,000
Total Stockholders' Equity	$1,473,000

The following transactions, among others, occurred during the year:

Jan. 15 Issued 2,000 shares of preferred stock for $65 cash per share.
      20 Issued 4,000 shares of common stock at $40 cash per share.
      31 Converted $20,000 face value of convertible bonds payable (the book value of the bonds is $18,500) to common stock. Each $1,000 bond converted to 25 shares of common stock.

May   18 Announced a 2-for-1 common stock split, reducing the par value of the common stock to $10 per share. The authorization was increased to 100,000 shares.

June   1 Acquired equipment with a fair market value of $50,000 in exchange for 2,000 shares of common stock.

Sept. 1 Purchased 3,500 shares of common stock as treasury stock at $19 cash per share.
Oct. 12 Sold 900 treasury shares at $21 per share.
Dec. 22 Issued 600 shares of preferred stock for $59 cash per share.
      28 Sold 1,100 of the remaining treasury shares at $18 per share.
      31 Closed net income of $150,000 to the Retained Earnings account.

Required

a. Set up T-accounts for the stockholders' equity accounts as of the beginning of the year and enter the January 1 balances.
b. Prepare journal entries for the given transactions and post them to the T-accounts (set up any additional T-accounts needed). Do not prepare the journal entry for the Dec. 31 transaction, but post the appropriate amount to the Retained Earnings T-account. Determine the ending balances for the stockholders' equity accounts.
c. Prepare the stockholders' equity section of the balance sheet at December 31.

LO4, 6   P11-5B.   Stockholders' Equity: Information and Entries from Comparative Data Comparative stockholders' equity sections from two successive years of balance sheets from Kirkwood, Inc., are as follows:

	Dec. 31, Current Year	Dec. 31, Previous Year
Paid-in Capital		
10% preferred stock, $20 par value, authorized 50,000 shares; issued and outstanding, current year: 25,000 shares; previous year: 15,000 shares	$ 500,000	$ 400,000
Common stock, no-par value, $10 stated value, authorized 120,000 shares; issued, current year: 65,000 shares; previous year: 48,000 shares	600,000	480,000
Additional Paid-in Capital		
In excess of par value—Preferred stock	225,000	160,000
In excess of stated value—Common stock	540,000	336,000
From treasury stock	25,000	
Retained earnings	390,000	335,000
	2,275,000	1,711,000
Less: Treasury stock (10,000 shares common) at cost	0	136,000
Total stockholders' equity	$2,275,000	$1,575,000

No dividends were declared or paid during the current year.

Required

Prepare the journal entries for the transactions affecting stockholders' equity that occurred during the current year. Do not prepare the journal entry for closing net income to retained earnings. Assume that any share transactions were for cash.

LO7, 8   P11-6B.   Retained Earnings: Transactions and Statement The stockholders' equity of Ranger Corporation at January 1 appears below:

Common stock, $10 par value, 200,000 shares authorized; 80,000 shares issued and outstanding	$800,000
Paid-in capital in excess of par value	480,000
Retained earnings	305,000

During the year, the following transactions occurred:

May   12 Declared a 15 percent stock dividend; market value of the common stock was $22 per share.
June   6 Issued the stock dividend declared on May 12.
Dec.   5 Declared a cash dividend of $1.50 per share.
          30 Paid the cash dividend declared on December 5.

Required
a.   Prepare journal entries to record the foregoing transactions.
b.   Prepare a statement of retained earnings. Net income for the year is $275,000.

P11-7B.   Retained Earnings: Transactions and Statement The stockholders' equity of Elsworth Corpora- **LO7, 8**
tion at January 1 is shown below:

5% preferred stock, $100 par value, 10,000 shares authorized;	
4,000 shares issued and outstanding	$ 400,000
Common stock, $5 par value, 200,000 shares	
authorized; 50,000 shares issued and outstanding.	250,000
Paid-in capital in excess of par value—Preferred stock	40,000
Paid-in capital in excess of par value—Common stock	300,000
Retained earnings	656,000
Total Stockholders' Equity	$1,646,000

The following transactions, among others, occurred during the year:

Apr.   1 Declared a 100 percent stock dividend on all outstanding shares of common stock. The
          market value of the stock was $16 per share.
        15 Issued the stock dividend declared on April 1.
Dec.   7 Declared a two percent stock dividend on all outstanding shares of common stock. The
          market value of the stock was $18 per share.
        17 Issued the stock dividend declared on December 7.
        20 Declared the annual cash dividend on the preferred stock and a cash dividend of $1.20
          per common share, payable on January 15 to common stockholders of record on
          December 31.

Required
a.   Prepare journal entries to record the foregoing transactions.
b.   Prepare a statement of retained earnings. Net income for the year is $300,000.

P11-8B.   Stockholders' Equity Transactions, Journal Entries, and T-Accounts The stockholders' equity **LO4, 5, 6**
of Zhou Corporation at January 1 follows:

10% preferred stock, $100 par value, 20,000 shares authorized; 4,000 shares	
issued and outstanding.	$ 400,000
Common stock, $4 par value, 100,000 shares authorized;	
40,000 shares issued and outstanding	160,000
Paid-in capital in excess of par value—Preferred stock	400,000
Paid-in capital in excess of par value—Common stock	800,000
Retained earnings	850,000
Total Stockholders' Equity	$2,610,000

The following transactions, among others, occurred during the year:

Jan.   1 Announced a 4-for-1 common stock split, reducing the par value of the common stock
          to $1.00 per share.
Mar.   31 Converted $100,000 face value of convertible bonds payable (the book value of the
          bonds was $103,000) to common stock. Each $1,000 bond converted to 110 shares of
          common stock.
June   1 Acquired equipment with a fair market value of $40,000 in exchange for 200 shares of
          preferred stock.
Sept.   1 Acquired 10,000 shares of common stock for cash at $21 per share.
Nov.   21 Issued 5,000 shares of common stock at $22 cash per share.

Dec. 28 Sold 500 treasury shares at $23 per share.
      31 Closed net income of $150,000 to the Retained Earnings account.

Required

a. Set up T-accounts for the stockholders' equity accounts as of the beginning of the year and enter the January 1 balances.

b. Prepare journal entries for the given transactions and post them to the T-accounts (set up any additional T-accounts needed). Do not prepare the journal entry for the Dec. 31 transaction, but post the appropriate amount to the Retained Earnings T-account. Determine the ending balances for the stockholders' equity accounts.

 LO4, 5, 6, 8   P11-9B.   The Stockholders' Equity Section of the Balance Sheet Using your analysis from P11-8B, prepare the Stockholders' Equity section of the Zhou Corporation's balance sheet.

LO4, 6, 7, 8   P11-10B.   Stockholders' Equity: Transactions and Statement The stockholders' equity section of Light Corporation's balance sheet at January 1 follows:

Common stock, $10 par value, 200,000 shares authorized, 35,000 shares issued, 4,000 shares are in the treasury.		$350,000
Additional paid-in capital		
In excess of par value.	$315,000	
From treasury stock	18,000	333,000
Retained earnings		298,000
		981,000
Less: Treasury stock (4,000 shares) at cost		84,000
Total Stockholders' Equity.		$897,000

The following transactions affecting stockholders' equity occurred during the year:

Jan.   8 Issued 30,000 shares of previously unissued common stock for $23 cash per share.
Mar. 12 Sold all of the treasury shares for $29 cash per share.
June 30 Declared a six percent stock dividend on all outstanding shares of common stock. The market value of the stock was $35 per share.
July 10 Issued the stock dividend declared on June 30.
Oct.   7 Acquired 2,000 shares of common stock as treasury stock at $28 cash per share.
Dec. 18 Declared a cash dividend of $1.20 per outstanding common share, payable on January 9 to stockholders of record on December 31.

Required

a. Prepare journal entries to record the foregoing transactions.

b. Prepare a statement of stockholders' equity. Net income for the year is $200,000.

 LO4, 6   P11-11B.   Stockholders' Equity: Transaction Descriptions from Account Data The following T-accounts contain keyed entries representing five transactions involving the stockholders' equity of Meadow, Inc.:

Cash

(1)	96,000	13,500	(4)
(2)	50,000		
(5)	6,480		

Land

(3)	95,000	

Preferred Stock, $50 Par

	80,000	(1)

Paid-in Capital in Excess of Par Value—Preferred Stock

	16,000	(1)

Common Stock, $10 Par

	50,000	(2)
	60,000	(3)

Paid-in Capital in Excess of Par Value—Common Stock

	35,000	(3)

Paid-in Capital from Treasury Stock

	1,080	(5)

Treasury Stock

(4)	(900 shares of common)	13,500	5,400	(5)

Required

Using this information, give detailed descriptions, including number of shares and price per share when applicable, for each of the five transactions.

SERIAL PROBLEM: KATE'S CARDS

(Note: This is a continuation of the Serial Problem: Kate's Cards from Chapters 1 through 10.)

SP11.   Kate's business continues to flourish. It hardly seems that just eleven months ago, in September of last year, Kate started the business. She is especially pleased that she was able to successfully defend herself against what turned out to be a mistaken attempt to sue her for copyright infringement. She was able to clearly demonstrate that her card designs were unique and significantly different from the designs sold by Mega Cards.

Kate has decided to take on an investor. Taylor Kasey believes that Kate's Cards represents a good investment and wishes to invest money to help Kate expand the business. Kate, however, is somewhat unsure how to structure Taylor's investment. Taylor wishes to be an equity investor rather than simply providing a loan to Kate. Kate wants to know whether she should issue Taylor common stock or preferred stock for her investment.

1. Discuss the difference between the two classes of stock and suggest which type is more appropriate for Kate to issue.

2. Kate has decided that she does not want to give up voting control of Kate's Cards. Since Taylor prefers to be a passive investor, but does wish to have a steady income from dividends, the decision is made to issue 50 shares of $100 par value, six percent cumulative preferred stock.

   Provide the journal entry to record the issuance of the preferred stock for cash.

3. Kate also wishes to pay dividends on both her common shares and the preferred stock. She is a little confused between cash and stock dividends.

   Explain the difference between a cash dividend and a stock dividend. Since Kate is the only stockholder of the common stock, what would be the effect of issuing a 10 percent stock dividend?

4. Kate decides to issue cash dividends on both the common stock and the preferred stock. Currently there are 50 outstanding preferred shares and 500 common shares outstanding. The dividends that Kate paid were $6 per share on the preferred shares and $2 per share on the common shares.

   Provide the journal entry for the payment of the cash dividends.

5. Kate's Cards has a net income of $1,500 for the current month of August. Kate had decided that the business will have a fiscal year-end of August 31, so this is the completion of the company's first year. Kate will be preparing her annual financial statements; however, she would also like to see a monthly statement of retained earnings for August. In addition, she would like to see how the stockholders' equity section of the balance sheet will look after the addition of the preferred stock. The stockholders' equity section from July is shown below:

Stockholders' Equity
Common stock (5,000 shares authorized, 500 shares issued and outstanding)	$ 500
Paid-in capital in excess of par value—common stock	9,500
Retained earnings	15,000
Total stockholders' equity	$25,000

Prepare a statement of retained earnings for the month of August and the stockholders' equity section of the balance sheet as of August 31.

EXTENDING YOUR KNOWLEDGE

REPORTING AND ANALYSIS

EYK11-1.   Financial Reporting Problem: Columbia Sportswear Company The financial statements for the **Columbia Sportswear Company** can be found in Appendix A at the end of this book.

COLUMBIA
SPORTSWEAR
COMPANY

Required

Answer the following questions:

a. How many shares of common stock are authorized at the end of 2020?
b. What percentage of the common shares authorized are outstanding at the end of 2020?
c. Does Columbia Sportswear have any preferred shares outstanding at the end of 2020?
d. How many shares of common stock did Columbia Sportswear repurchase in 2020? What was the dollar amount of this repurchase?
e. What amount of dividends per share did Columbia Sportswear report for 2020? 2019?

COLUMBIA
SPORTSWEAR
COMPANY

UNDER ARMOUR, INC.

EYK11-2. Comparative Analysis Problem: Columbia Sportswear Company vs Under Armour, Inc. The financial statements for the **Columbia Sportswear Company** can be found in Appendix A at the end of this book, and the financial statements of **Under Armour, Inc.** can be found in Appendix B (the complete annual report is available on this book's website).

Required

Answer the following questions:

a. Calculate the return on equity for each company for 2020.
b. Calculate the dividend payout ratio for each company for 2020.
c. Based on these ratios, which company performed better for its shareholders during 2020?

EYK11-3. Business Decision Problem Egghead, Inc., was a software chain that had over 100 stores across the U.S. Initially its founders and employees owned the company privately. The company eventually went public with an initial public offering (IPO) of 3.6 million shares (the company had 12 million shares prior to the IPO). The new shares were priced at $15 each. The company did not hold any treasury shares.

Required

a. Assume that the common shares had a $1 par value. Provide the journal entry to record the issuance of new shares.
b. Discuss whether you think Egghead's board of directors and existing shareholders had to approve the public issuance before it occurred.
c. Provide some reasons why Egghead wished to raise $54 million with equity rather than debt.

GILLETTE COMPANY

PROCTER & GAMBLE

COLGATE-
PALMOLIVE COMPANY

EYK11-4. Financial Analysis Problem The following data were obtained prior to the acquisition of **Gillette Company** by **Procter & Gamble**. Gillette Company, the Procter & Gamble Company, and **Colgate-Palmolive Company** are three firms in the personal care consumer products industry. During the prior year, the average return on equity for the personal care consumer products industry was 28.1 percent. In the same year, the relevant financial data for Gillette, Procter & Gamble, and Colgate-Palmolive were as follows (in millions):

	Gillette	Procter & Gamble	Colgate-Palmolive
Stockholders' equity, beginning	1,397.2	5,472.0	2,201.5
Stockholders' equity, ending	1,380.0	6,890.0	1,460.7
Net income	426.9	2,211.0	548.1

Required

a. Calculate Gillette Company's return on equity.
b. Evaluate Gillette Company's return on equity by comparing it with the following:
    1. The average for the personal care consumer products industry.
    2. The return earned by the Procter & Gamble Company.
    3. The return earned by Colgate-Palmolive Company.

CRITICAL THINKING

GENERAL MILLS, INC.

EYK11-5. Financial Analysis on the Web: General Mills, Inc. The fiscal year 2020 annual report of **General Mills, Inc.** is available on this book's website.

Required

a. How many shares of common stock is General Mills authorized to issue? How many common shares are issued as of May 31, 2020?
b. What is the par value of General Mills' common stock?

    c.   Does General Mills have any preferred shares? If so, how many shares of preferred stock are outstanding on May 31, 2020?

    d.   How many treasury shares did General Mills purchase on the open market during the 2020 fiscal year? What did General Mills pay to purchase these shares? How many common shares are in the treasury as of May 31, 2020?

    e.   What is General Mills' return on equity for the 2020 fiscal year?

    f.   What is the cash dividend per share declared by General Mills in fiscal year 2020? 2019?

    g.   What are General Mills' basic earnings per share in fiscal year 2020? 2019?

    h.   What is General Mills' dividend payout ratio for fiscal year 2020? 2019?

EYK11-6. **Accounting Communication Activity** Your neighbor, Norman Vetter, has always been tinkering in his garage with his inventions. He believes he has finally come up with one that could really sell well. He is a little concerned about some potential safety issues, but he believes those issues will be worked out. He wants to form a business to manufacture and sell his invention and has come to you for advice. In particular, he would like to know the advantages and disadvantages of forming a corporation, rather than simply organizing as a sole proprietor.

Required
Write a brief memorandum to your neighbor explaining the advantages and disadvantages of the corporate form of organization.

EYK11-7. **Accounting Ethics Case** Colin Agee, chairperson of the board of directors and chief executive officer of Image, Inc., is pondering a recommendation to make to the firm's board of directors in response to actions taken by Sam Mecon. Mecon recently informed Agee and other board members that he (Mecon) had purchased 15 percent of the voting stock of Image at $12 per share and is considering an attempt to take control of the company. His effort to take control would include offering $16 per share to stockholders to induce them to sell shares to him. Mecon also indicated that he would abandon his takeover plans if the company would buy back his stock at a price 50 percent over its current market price of $13 per share.

    Agee views the proposed takeover by Mecon as a hostile maneuver. Mecon has a reputation of identifying companies that are undervalued (that is, their underlying net assets are worth more than the price of the outstanding shares), buying enough shares to take control of the company, replacing top management, and, on occasion, breaking up the company (that is, selling off the various divisions to the highest bidder). The process has proven profitable to Mecon and his financial backers. Stockholders of the companies taken over have also benefited because Mecon paid them attractive prices to buy their shares.

    Agee recognizes that Image is currently undervalued by the stock market but believes that eventually the company will significantly improve its financial performance to the long-run benefit of its stockholders.

Required
What are the ethical issues that Agee should consider in arriving at a recommendation to make to the board of directors regarding Mecon's offer to be "bought out" of his takeover plans?

EYK11-8. **Environmental, Social, and Governance Problem** In the ESG highlight regarding Starbucks on page 11-7 in this chapter, it was stated that Starbucks believes in measuring and monitoring the company's ESG progress. The forward to Starbucks' Global Social Impact 2019 Performance Report stated:

> At Starbucks we stand for being people positive, planet positive and profit positive, living our Mission and Values while working together as partners to build a different kind of company.
>
>   Our annual global social impact reporting focuses on three areas: leading in sustainability, creating meaningful opportunities, and strengthening our communities. These are areas critical to our business, and where we know we can have notable impact.

Go to: https://stories.starbucks.com/uploads/2020/06/2019-Starbucks-Global-Social-Impact-Report.pdf and select one of the three areas of focus and identify how the company is doing with respect to its goals.

GENERAL ELECTRIC
COMPANY

EYK11-9. **Working With The Takeaways** The following data are from a recent **General Electric Company** annual report. All amounts, except per share data, are in $ millions.

Net income	$ 8,176
Average stockholders' equity	87,051
Dividends per share	0.93
Earnings per share	0.90
Per share market price of common stock at year-end	29.70

Required

Compute the following ratios for the General Electric Company:

a.   Return on equity   *b.*   Dividend yield   *c.*   Dividend payout

LVMH MOET
HENNESSEY-LOUIS
VUITTON S.A.

EYK11-10. IFRS Financial Statements The 2020 financial statements of **LVMH Moet Hennessey-Louis Vuitton S.A.** are presented in Appendix C at the end of this book. LVMH is a Paris-based holding company and one of the world's largest and best-known luxury goods companies. As a member of the European Union, French companies are required to prepare their consolidated (group) financial statements using International Financial Reporting Standards (IFRS). Calculate LVMH's (a) return on equity, (b) dividend yield, and (c) dividend payout for 2020 and 2019. Additional information that you will need is below:

	2020	2019
Earnings per share (in euros)	9.33	14.25
Dividend per share (in euros)	6.00	4.80
Market price per share (in euros)	124.73	93.31

ANSWERS TO SELF-STUDY QUESTIONS:

1. c   2. a   3. c   4. d   5. d   6. d   7. c   8. d   9. a   10. d

YOUR TURN! SOLUTIONS

Solution 11.1
1. Disadvantage   3. Advantage   5. Disadvantage
2. Advantage   4. Disadvantage   6. Advantage

Solution 11.2
b.

Solution 11.3
1. d **2.** e **3.** b **4.** f **5.** c **6.** a

Solution 11.4
Paid-in capital in excess of par value = ($9 − $1) × 10,000 shares = $80,000

Solution 11.5
After the split Aston Enterprises would report 1,500,000 shares outstanding with a par value of $1.00. Mariam Hernandez would own 1,500 shares of Aston.

Solution 11.6
$75,000

Solution 11.7
a. A cash dividend will lower retained earnings by $30,000 ($3 × 10,000 shares) to $470,000.
b. A ten percent stock dividend will lower retained earnings by $20,000 (.10 × 10,000 × $20) to $480,000.

Solution 11.8

	Common Stock	Paid-in Capital in Excess of Par Value	Retained Earnings	Treasury Stock	Total
DIOR COMPANY Statement of Stockholders' Equity For Year Ended December 31					
Balance, January 1............	$100,000	$900,000	$50,000	$(10,000)	$1,040,000
Net income..................			30,000		30,000
1,000 common shares issued....	1,000	14,000			15,000
Cash dividend...............			(8,000)		(8,000)
Balance, December 31.........	$101,000	$914,000	$72,000	$(10,000)	$1,077,000

Solution 11.9

a. Return on equity = $150,000 / [($650,000 + $700,000)/2] = 22.2 percent
b. Dividend yield = $0.75/$33.00 = 2.3 percent
c. Dividend payout ratio = $0.75/$3.00 = 25 percent

Chapter **12**
Statement of Cash Flows

Road Map

LO	Learning Objective	Page	eLecture	Guided Example	Assignments
LO1	**Discuss the content and format of the statement of cash flows.**	12-3	E12-1	YT12.1	SS1, SS2, SS3, SS6, SS8, SE1, SE2, SE3, E1A, E2A, E1B, E2B
LO2	**Explain the preparation of a statement of cash flows using the indirect method.**	12-9	E12-2	YT12.2	SS4, SS9, SE1, SE2, SE3, E3A, E4A, E5A, E6A, E11A, E3B, E4B, E5B, E6B, E11B, P1A, P2A, P3A, P4A, P1B, P2B, P3B, P4B
LO3	**Define ratios used to analyze the statement of cash flows and explain their use.**	12-18	E12-3	YT12.3	SS5, SS7, SE4, SE5, SE6, E4A, E7A, E3B, E7B, P1A, P5A, P6A, P1B, P5B, P6B
LO4	**Appendix 12A: Explain the preparation of a statement of cash flows using the direct method.**	12-22	E12-4	YT12.4	SS10, SS11, SS12, SE7, SE8, SE9, SE10, E8A, E9A, E10A, E11A, E8B, E9B, E10B, E11B, P6A, P7A, P8A, P9A, P6B, P7B, P8B, P9B

Home Depot is the largest home improvement retailer in the United States. Founded in 1978 in Atlanta, Georgia, the company now operates nearly 2,000 stores in the United States, Canada, and Mexico.

It takes a lot of cash to build and operate a business as big as Home Depot, especially when the average size of each store is over 105,000 square feet. In fiscal year 2019 alone Home Depot spent over $2.6 billion on capital expenditures.

How can a financial statement user determine where a company obtained the cash to fund its growth? This chapter introduces the statement of cash flows and explores how a company discloses both the sources and uses of its cash. Understanding the content, format, and construction of the statement of cash flows enables a financial statement user to assess how a company like Home Depot was able to finance its capital expenditures for new store growth.

PAST

Chapter 11 examined the accounting for stockholders' equity.

PRESENT

In this chapter we turn our attention to the statement of cash flows.

FUTURE

Chapter 13 completes our study of financial accounting by looking at the analysis and interpretation of financial statements.

```
                    ┌──────────────────────────────────────────┐
                    │         STATEMENT OF CASH FLOWS          │
                    └──────────────────────────────────────────┘
```

Classification of Cash Flows	Preparing the Statement of Cash Flows	Analyzing Cash Flows
• Cash and cash equivalents • Operating activities • Investing activities • Financing activities	• Indirect method • Direct method (Appendix 12A)	• Free cash flow • Operating-cash-flow-to-current-liabilities • Operating-cash-flow-to-capital-expenditures ratio

CASH AND CASH EQUIVALENTS

LO1 **Discuss** the content and format of the statement of cash flows.

eLecture

MBC

In the eyes of most creditors, investors, and managers, cash is a business's most important asset. Without cash, a business would be unable to pay employees, lenders, suppliers, service providers, or shareholders. In short, cash is the only asset that a business can't operate without.

The dilemma for most managers, however, is knowing exactly how much cash to keep on hand. Although managers know that they need to keep some cash on hand in a checking account and/or petty cash fund to pay their immediate bills, they also know that cash is the lowest return generating asset that a business has. Keeping too much cash on hand means that a business is not maximizing the value of its assets. For this reason, most managers spend considerable time assessing their cash needs—an activity called **cash management**. Because the science of cash management is inexact, managers have derived ways to help them minimize the amount of cash that they need to keep on hand while also maximizing the return on a business's assets. One method is to invest any excess cash in alternative investments that are readily convertible back into cash and earn a higher rate of return than cash, but which do not place the invested cash at risk of loss. These alternative investments are known as cash equivalents.

Cash equivalents are short-term, highly liquid investments that are (1) easily convertible into cash and (2) close enough to maturity so that their market value is relatively insensitive to interest rate changes (generally, investments with maturities of three months or less). U.S. Treasury bills, certificates of deposit (CDs), commercial paper (short-term notes issued by corporations), and money market funds are examples of cash equivalents. Because firms may differ with respect to which investments they consider to be cash equivalents, GAAP requires that each firm disclose in the notes to the financial statements the company's policy regarding which investments are treated as cash equivalents.

When preparing a statement of cash flows, the cash and cash equivalents are added together and treated as a single amount because the purchase and sale of investments in cash equivalents are considered to be part of a firm's overall cash management strategy rather than a source or use of cash. As financial statement users evaluate a firm's cash flows, it should not matter whether the cash is on hand, deposited in a bank account, or invested in cash equivalents. Transfers back and forth between a firm's Cash account and its investments in cash equivalents, consequently, are not treated as cash inflows or outflows in the statement of cash flows.

When discussing the statement of cash flows, accountants often just use the word *cash* rather than the term *cash and cash equivalents*. We follow that practice in this chapter.

ACCOUNTING IN PRACTICE   **Definition of Cash Equivalents**

There are some differences between firms regarding which investments of cash are considered to be cash equivalents. For example, **PepsiCo, Inc.**, the beverage and snack food company, states in the notes to its financial statements that "Cash equivalents are investments with original maturities of three months or less." **International Game Technology**, a manufacturer of gaming machines and proprietary gaming software systems, on the other hand, notes that "In addition to cash deposits at major banks, cash and equivalents include other marketable securities with original maturities of 90 days or less, primarily in U.S. Treasury-backed money market funds." The commonality among all firms, however, is that cash equivalents represent a temporary investment of excess cash in risk-free investments until such time as the cash is needed to support a business's operations.

ACTIVITY CLASSIFICATIONS IN THE STATEMENT OF CASH FLOWS

A statement of cash flows classifies a company's cash receipts and cash payments into three major business activity categories: operating activities, investing activities, and financing activities. Grouping cash flows into these categories identifies the effect on cash of each of the major business activities of a firm (see Chapter 1). The combined effects on cash from all three categories explain the net change in cash for the period. The net change in cash is then reconciled with the beginning and ending balances of cash from the balance sheet. **Exhibit 12-1** illustrates the basic format for a statement of cash flows.

EXHIBIT 12-1 **Format for the Statement of Cash Flows**		
SAMPLE COMPANY Statement of Cash Flows For Year Ended December 31, Year 2		
Cash Flow from Operating Activities		
(Details of cash flow from operating activities)............................	$###	
Cash provided (used) by operating activities		$###
Cash Flow from Investing Activities		
(Details of investing cash inflows and outflows).........................	###	
Cash provided (used) by investing activities............................		###
Cash Flow from Financing Activities		
(Details of financing cash inflows and outflows)........................	###	
Cash provided (used) by financing activities...........................		###
Net increase (decrease) in cash......................................		###
Cash at beginning of year..		###
Cash at end of year		$###

Exhibit 12-2 illustrates the purpose of the statement of cash flows. In this illustration, the water level in the bucket represents the cash balance. The water level changes from the beginning of the period to the end of the period. Why does the water level change? Water is flowing into the bucket through three spigots, representing the three sources of cash inflows (operating, investing, and financing activities). However, the bucket also has three holes near the bottom, representing the three categories of cash outflows (operating, investing, and financing activities). Thus, water flows in and out of the bucket through all three types of activities and the cash flow statement explains the change in the water level (the cash balance) from the beginning to the end of the period.

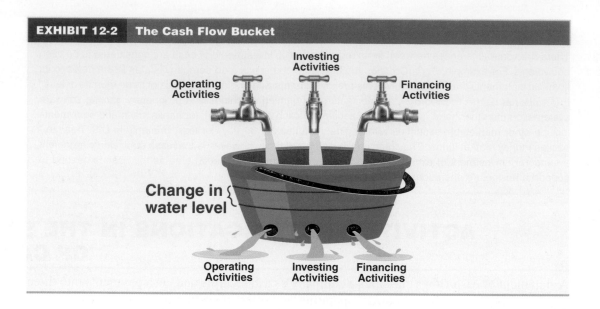

EXHIBIT 12-2   The Cash Flow Bucket

Operating Activities

A company's income statement reflects the transactions and events that constitute its operating activities. The focus of a firm's operating activities involves selling goods or rendering services. The cash flow from **operating activities** is defined broadly enough, however, to include any cash receipts or payments that are not classified as investing activities or financing activities. For example, cash received from a lawsuit settlement and cash payments to charity are treated as cash flow from operating activities. The following are examples of cash inflows and outflows relating to a firm's operating activities:

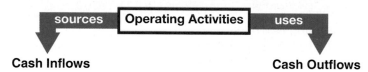

Cash Inflows	**Cash Outflows**
1. Receipts from customers for sales of goods or services.	1. Payments to suppliers.
2. Receipts of interest and dividends.	2. Payments to employees.
3. Other receipts that are not related to investing or financing activities, such as lawsuit settlements and refunds received from suppliers.	3. Payments of interest to creditors.
	4. Payments of taxes to governmental agencies.
	5. Other payments that are not related to investing or financing activities, such as contributions to charity.

Investing Activities

A firm's **investing activities** include transactions involving (1) the acquisition or disposal of plant assets and intangible assets, (2) the purchase or sale of stocks, bonds, and other securities (that are not cash equivalents), and (3) the lending and subsequent collection of money.[1] The related cash receipts and cash payments appear in the investing activities section of the statement of cash flows. Examples of these cash flows include:

---

[1] There are exceptions to the classification of these events as investing activities. For example, the purchase or sale of mortgage loans by a mortgage banker, like Bank of America, and the purchase or sale of securities in the trading account of a broker/dealer in financial securities, like Merrill Lynch, represent operating activities for these businesses.

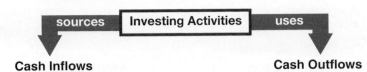

Cash Inflows	Cash Outflows
1. Receipts from the sale of plant assets and intangible assets.	1. Payments to purchase plant assets and intangible assets.
2. Receipts from sales of investments in stocks, bonds, and other securities (other than cash equivalents).	2. Payments to purchase stocks, bonds, and other securities (other than cash equivalents).
3. Receipts from repayments of loans by borrowers.	3. Payments made to lend money to borrowers.

Financing Activities

A firm engages in **financing activities** when it obtains cash from shareholders, returns cash to shareholders, borrows from creditors, and repays amounts borrowed from creditors. Cash flows related to these events are reported in the financing activities section of the statement of cash flows. Examples of these cash flows include:

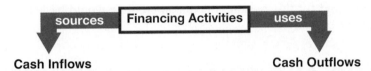

Cash Inflows	Cash Outflows
1. Receipts from the issuance of common stock and preferred stock and from sales of treasury stock.	1. Payments to acquire treasury stock.
2. Receipts from the issuance of bonds payable, mortgage notes payable, and other notes payable.	2. Payments of dividends.
	3. Payments to settle outstanding bonds payable, mortgage notes payable, and other notes payable.

Note that paying cash to settle obligations such as accounts payable, wages payable, interest payable, and income tax payable is an operating activity, not a financing activity. Also observe that cash received as interest and dividends and cash paid as interest are classified as cash flows from operating activities, although cash paid as dividends to a company's stockholders is classified as a financing activity.

THINKING GLOBALLY

Although the statement of cash flows under U.S. GAAP has three activity categories—operating, investing, and financing—this is not the case under International Financial Reporting Standards (IFRS). Under IFRS, the statement of cash flows may have either four or five activity categories: Operations, Investing, Debt Financing, Equity Financing, and sometimes a category called the Effect of Foreign Currency Translation. In essence, IFRS segments the financing activities category into two separate categories relating to financing with debt and financing with equity. The sum of these two categories is equivalent to the single category of financing activities under U.S. GAAP.

Usefulness of Activity Classification

The classification of cash flows into the three business activity categories helps financial statement users analyze and interpret a company's cash flow data. To illustrate, assume that companies D, E, and F operate in the same industry and that each company reported a $100,000 increase in cash during the period. Information from each company's statement of cash flows is summarized below:

	Company		
	D	**E**	**F**
Cash flow from operating activities...............	$100,000	$ 0	$ 0
Cash flow from investing activities:			
Sale of plant assets...........................	0	100,000	0
Cash flow from financing activities:			
Issuance of notes payable	0	0	100,000
Net increase in cash.........................	$100,000	$100,000	$100,000

Although each company's increase in cash is exactly $100,000, the source of the cash increase varied by company. This variation affects the analysis of the cash flow data, particularly for potential creditors who must evaluate the likelihood of the repayment of funds loaned to a company. Based only on this cash flow data, a potential creditor would feel more comfortable lending money to Company D than to either Company E or F. D's cash increase comes from its operating activities, whereas E's cash increase comes from the sale of plant assets, a source that is unlikely to recur, and F's cash increase comes from borrowed funds. Company F faces additional future uncertainty when the interest and principal payments on the existing notes become due, and for this reason, a potential creditor would be less inclined to extend additional loans to Company F.

NONCASH INVESTING AND FINANCING ACTIVITIES

Although many investing and financing activities affect cash and therefore are included in the investing and financing sections of the statement of cash flows, some significant investing and financing events do not affect current cash flow. An example of **noncash investing and financing activities** is the issuance of stock or bonds (a financing activity) in exchange for plant assets or intangible assets (an investing activity). Other examples include the exchange of long-term assets for other long-term assets, and the conversion of long-term debt into common stock. The key feature of each of these transactions is that no cash is exchanged between the parties involved in the transaction.

Noncash investing and financing transactions generally do, however, affect future cash flows. Issuing bonds in exchange for equipment, for example, requires future cash payments for interest and principal on the bonds. On the other hand, converting bonds into common stock eliminates the future cash payments related to the bonds' interest and principal, but may result in future cash dividend payments. Knowledge of these types of events, therefore, is helpful to financial statement users who wish to evaluate a firm's future cash flows.

Companies are required to disclose information regarding material noncash investing and financing transactions in a separate accounting schedule. The separate schedule may be placed immediately below the statement of cash flows, or it may be placed among the notes to the financial statements.

PRINCIPLE ALERT   **Objectivity Principle**

The *objectivity principle* asserts that the usefulness of financial statements is enhanced when the underlying data are objective and verifiable. Measuring cash and the changes in cash are among the most objective measurements that accountants make. The statement of cash flows, therefore, is the most objective financial statement required under generally accepted accounting principles. This characteristic of the statement of cash flows is welcomed by investors and creditors interested in evaluating the quality of a firm's net income and assets. Financial statement users often feel more confident about the quality of a company's net income and assets when there is a high correlation between, or relationship with, a company's cash flow from operating activities and its net income.

USING THE STATEMENT OF CASH FLOWS

The Financial Accounting Standards Board believes that one of the principal objectives of financial reporting is to help financial statement users assess the amount, timing, and uncertainty of a business's future cash flows. These assessments, in turn, help users evaluate prospective future cash receipts from their investments in, or loans to, a business. Although the statement of cash flows describes a company's past cash flows, the statement is also useful for assessing future cash flows since the recent past is often a very good predictor of the future.

The statement of cash flows shows the cash effects of a firm's operating, investing, and financing activities. Distinguishing among these different categories of cash flow helps financial statement users compare, evaluate, and predict a business's future cash flows. With cash flow information, creditors and investors are better able to assess a company's ability to repay its liabilities and pay dividends. A firm's need for outside financing can also be evaluated using the statement of cash flows. Further, the statement enables users to observe and analyze management's investing and financing policies, plans, and strategies.

The statement of cash flows also provides information useful in evaluating a firm's financial flexibility. **Financial flexibility** is a company's ability to generate sufficient amounts of cash to respond to unanticipated needs and opportunities. Information about past cash flows, particularly cash flow from operations, helps in assessing financial flexibility. An evaluation of a firm's ability to survive an unexpected drop in demand for its goods and services, for example, may include a review of its past cash flow from operations. The larger these past cash flows, the greater a firm's ability to withstand adverse changes in future economic conditions.

Some investors and creditors find the statement of cash flows useful in evaluating the "quality" of a firm's net income. As we saw in Chapter 4, determining net income under the accrual basis of accounting requires many accruals, deferrals, allocations, and valuations. These adjustment and measurement procedures introduce greater subjectivity into a company's income determination than some financial statement users are comfortable with. Consequently, these users can relate a more objective performance measure—a firm's cash flow from operations—to net income. To these users, the closer the relation between a company's net income and their cash flow from operations, the higher the quality of the firm's net income.

CASH FLOW FROM OPERATING ACTIVITIES

The first section of the statement of cash flows presents a firm's cash flow from operating activities. Two alternative formats are available to present cash flow from operating activities: the indirect method and the direct method. Both methods report the same amount of cash flow from operating activities and differ only in how the cash flow from operating activities is derived. The indirect method and direct method refer only to how the cash flow from operating activities section is prepared. The cash flow from investing activities and cash flow from financing activities sections do not change.

The **indirect method** starts with net income using the accrual basis of accounting and applies a series of adjustments to convert it to net income under the cash basis of accounting, which is equivalent to the cash flow from operating activities. The adjustments to net income do not represent specific cash flows; consequently, the indirect method does not report any detail concerning individual operating cash inflows and outflows.

The **direct method** shows individual amounts of cash inflows and cash outflows for the major operating activities. The net difference between these inflows and outflows is the cash flow from operating activities.

While the presentation of the operating section is different under the two methods, the adjustments in the indirect method to convert net income to operating cash flows are the same adjustments that are made to individual income statement line items to convert revenues and expenses under the accrual basis of accounting to cash inflows and outflows under the cash basis of accounting presented in the direct method. Thus, the two methods for presenting the operating section are really just "two sides of the same coin." We present the indirect method in this chapter, but we explain the direct method (and how the two methods integrate with one another) in Appendix 12A.

The Financial Accounting Standards Board encourages companies to use the direct method but permits the use of the indirect method. Despite the FASB's preference for the direct method, almost all companies use the indirect method. The indirect method is popular because (1) it is easier and less expensive to prepare than the direct method and (2) the direct method requires a supplemental disclosure showing cash flow from operating activities prepared under the indirect method.

ACCOUNTING IN PRACTICE   **Popularity of Direct and Indirect Method**

Do you think a direct approach in communicating with financial statement users is best, or should your approach be more indirect? When it comes to reporting the cash flow from operations, companies appear to favor the indirect approach by a wide margin, as evidenced by the responses to a survey of 600 large U.S. companies.

Source: Accounting Trends and Techniques

■ Direct
■ Indirect

YOUR TURN! 12.1

GuidedExample

MBC

The solution is on page 12-50.

Classify each of the cash flow events listed below as either an (1) operating activity, (2) investing activity, or (3) financing activity:

1. Cash received from customers
2. Cash sale of land
3. Cash paid to suppliers
4. Cash purchase of equipment
5. Payment on note payable

6. Cash dividend payment
7. Cash wages paid
8. Purchase of treasury stock
9. Cash sale of investments

The following section on preparing the statement of cash flows uses the indirect method. Appendix 12A uses the direct method. Your instructor can choose to cover either one or both methods. If the indirect method is skipped, then read Appendix 12A and return to the section (9 pages ahead) titled "Analyzing Cash Flows."

PREPARING THE STATEMENT OF CASH FLOWS USING THE INDIRECT METHOD

LO2 Explain the preparation of a statement of cash flows using the indirect method.

eLecture

MBC

To prepare the operating section of the statement of cash flows, the following information is needed: a company's income statement, balance sheets for the current and prior year, and possibly additional data taken from the company's financial statements. **Exhibit 12-3** presents this information for the Bennett Company. We will use these data to prepare Bennett's Year 2 statement of cash flows using the indirect method. As will be seen shortly, Bennett's statement of cash flows will explain the $25,000 increase in the company's cash account that occurred during Year 2 (from $10,000 at the beginning of the year to $35,000 at the end of the year) by classifying the firm's cash inflows and outflows into the three business activity categories of operating, investing, and financing.

EXHIBIT 12-3	Financial Data of Bennett Company

BENNETT COMPANY Income Statement For Year Ended December 31, Year 2		
Sales revenue.		$250,000
Cost of goods sold	$148,000	
Wages expense	52,000	
Insurance expense	5,000	
Depreciation expense.	10,000	
Income tax expense	11,000	
Gain on sale of plant assets.	(8,000)	218,000
Net income		$ 32,000

BENNETT COMPANY Balance Sheets		
As of December 31	Year 2	Year 1
Assets		
Cash	$ 35,000	$ 10,000
Accounts receivable	39,000	34,000
Inventory.	54,000	60,000
Prepaid insurance.	17,000	4,000
Long-term investments	15,000	—
Plant assets	180,000	200,000
Accumulated depreciation	(50,000)	(40,000)
Patent	60,000	—
Total assets.	$350,000	$268,000

Additional Data Year 2
1. Sold a plant asset (land) costing $20,000 for $28,000 cash.
2. Declared and paid cash dividends of $13,000.

Liabilities and Equity		
Accounts payable	$ 10,000	$ 19,000
Income tax payable.	5,000	3,000
Common stock	260,000	190,000
Retained earnings	75,000	56,000
Total liabilities and equity	$350,000	$268,000

To see that the statement of cash flows can be prepared using a company's income statement and the changes in its balance sheet accounts, consider again the balance sheet equation that was first introduced in Chapter 1:

$$\text{Assets (A) = Liabilities (L) + Stockholders' equity (SE)} \tag{1}$$

Separating a firm's assets into its cash and noncash assets (NCA) gives:

$$\text{Cash + NCA = L + SE} \tag{2}$$

And, rewriting the balance sheet equation in changes form yields:

$$\Delta\text{Cash} + \Delta\text{NCA} = \Delta\text{L} + \Delta\text{SE} \tag{3}$$

Finally, rearranging the components of the equation shows that the change in cash (which is the end result of the statement of cash flows) can be computed from the change in all of the other balance sheet accounts:

$$\Delta\text{Cash} = \Delta\text{L} - \Delta\text{NCA} + \Delta\text{SE} \tag{4}$$

Breaking non-current assets and liabilities into short- and long-term components allows us to better explain cash flows in terms of the three types of business activities (operating, investing, and financing).

Finally, separating assets and liabilities into short-and long-term categories allows us to specify a general set of rules for identifying changes in balance sheet accounts associated with operating, investing, and financing activities:

$$\Delta\text{Cash} = \underbrace{[\Delta\text{STL} - \Delta\text{STA}]}_{\substack{\textbf{Operating} \\ \textbf{Activities}}} - \underbrace{\Delta\text{LTA}}_{\substack{\textbf{Investing} \\ \textbf{Activities}}} + \underbrace{[\Delta\text{LTL} + \Delta\text{SE}]}_{\substack{\textbf{Financing} \\ \textbf{Activities}}} \tag{5}$$

As shown in equation (5), operating activities are generally associated with changes in short-term assets and liabilities, investing activities are generally associated with changes in long-term assets, and financing activities are usually associated with changes in long-term liabilities and equity accounts. We explain these concepts in more detail subsequently.

Five Steps to Preparing a Statement of Cash Flows

The process to prepare a statement of cash flows using the indirect method involves five steps. The approach begins by focusing initially only on the balance sheet and then proceeds to integrate a business's income statement through a series of systematic adjustments to a preliminary statement of cash flows derived solely from balance sheet data.

Step One: Calculate the change in all balance sheet accounts.   Using the beginning and ending balance sheets (see Columns 1 and 2 in **Exhibit 12-4**), calculate the change in each balance sheet account by subtracting the beginning balance sheet amount from the ending amount. Column 3 of **Exhibit 12-4** presents the results of this step for the Bennett Company. To simplify this step, we combine the change in the Plant Assets account with the Accumulated Depreciation account—that is, the change in the Plant Assets account is calculated net of accumulated depreciation.

EXHIBIT 12-4	Preparing a Statement of Cash Flows: The Indirect Method			
	BENNETT COMPANY Balance Sheet December 31, Year 2			
	(1) Beginning of Year	(2) End of Year	(3) Change for Year	(4) Cash Flow Classification
Assets				
Cash.	$ 10,000	$ 35,000	**$25,000**	**Cash flow increase**
Accounts receivable	34,000	39,000	5,000	Operating
Inventory.	60,000	54,000	(6,000)	Operating
Prepaid insurance.	4,000	17,000	13,000	Operating
Long-term investments.	0	15,000	15,000	Investing
Plant assets (net)	160,000	130,000	(30,000)	Investing
Patent.	0	60,000	60,000	Investing
Total assets.	$268,000	$350,000	$82,000	
Liabilities and Equity				
Accounts payable	$ 19,000	$ 10,000	$ (9,000)	Operating
Income tax payable.	3,000	5,000	2,000	Operating
Common stock	190,000	260,000	70,000	Financing
Retained earnings	56,000	75,000	19,000	Operating/Financing
Total liabilities and equity	$268,000	$350,000	$82,000	

To verify the accuracy of the Step One calculations, simply compare the sum of the changes in the asset accounts ($82,000) with the sum of the changes in the liability and stockholders' equity accounts ($82,000). These totals must be equal. If the totals are not equal, it indicates the presence of a calculation error that must be identified and corrected before proceeding to Step Two.

An important figure identified during Step One is the "bottom line" of the statement of cash flows—namely, the change in the cash account. **Exhibit 12-4** reveals that the cash account of the Bennett Company increased by $25,000 from the beginning of the year to the end of the year. Hence, the sum of the operating, investing, and financing cash flows for the company must aggregate to this figure.

Step Two: Classify each of the changes in balance sheet accounts as operating, investing, or financing.

As a general rule, the following cash flow activity classifications apply, although exceptions exist:

Balance Sheet Account	Cash Flow Activity Category
Current assets	Operating
Noncurrent assets	Investing
Current liabilities.	Operating
Noncurrent liabilities.	Financing
Capital stock.	Financing
Retained earnings	Operating/Financing

Examples of exceptions to these cash flow activity classifications include the following:

- Short-term investments, a current asset, are an investing activity item.
- Short-term (current) notes payable, a current liability, are a financing activity item.
- Current maturities of long-term debt, a current liability, are a financing activity item.
- Employee pension obligations, a noncurrent liability, are an operating activity item.

Column 4 of **Exhibit 12-4** presents the cash flow activity classifications. Although measuring the change in the balance sheet accounts in Step One is a straight-forward arithmetic activity, there can be some confusion over the correct activity classification for some of the balance sheet accounts in Step Two. The changes in accounts receivable, inventory, prepaid insurance, accounts payable, and income tax payable are all easily identified as operating activities because they are associated with the day-to-day operations of a business. The change in common stock, on the other hand, is clearly a financing activity because it is associated with raising capital to finance a business.

The change in net plant assets, however, is more complex. Purchases and sales of plant assets are associated with the capital investment needed to run a business, and thus are easily identified as investing activities. However, the depreciation expense associated with plant assets is deducted as an operating expense in the calculation of a company's net income. Similarly, the change in intangible assets such as patents, results from the acquisition or sale of intangibles and is easily identified as an investing activity. However, the amortization of intangibles is an operating expense deducted in the calculation of net income. Finally, the change in retained earnings can be associated with both operating and financing activities because retained earnings is increased by net income, an operating activity, but decreased by the payment of dividends, a financing activity.

Step Three: Prepare a preliminary statement of cash flows.
Having completed Steps One and Two, you are now ready to build a preliminary statement of cash flows using the calculated increases or decreases in the various balance sheet accounts from Step One and the identified activity classifications from Step Two. The preliminary statement of cash flows for the Bennett Company is presented in **Exhibit 12-5**.

The statement of cash flows measures the inflows and outflows of cash for a business. Recall from equation (4) that the change in cash is equal to the change in liabilities *minus* the change in non-cash assets plus the change in stockholder's equity accounts. Thus, we *add* changes in liability and equity accounts but *subtract* changes in asset accounts to explain the change in cash.

For instance, **Exhibit 12-5** shows that the change in accounts receivable is an increase of $5,000, whereas the change in inventory is a decrease of $6,000. When preparing the indirect method statement of cash flows, a $5,000 increase in accounts receivable is subtracted from net income, whereas a $6,000 decrease in inventory of $6,000 is added to net income, to arrive at the cash flow from operations. In other words, by subtracting the decrease in inventory, we end up adding it in our preliminary statement of cash flows.

To illustrate why an increase in accounts receivable must be subtracted from net income to arrive at operating cash flow, consider how sales revenue is initially recorded. Assume that a $2,000 sale of goods is paid for with $1,200 in cash and the remaining amount recorded as an increase in accounts receivable. In this example, net income increases by $2,000, but cash increases by only $1,200. Therefore, net income must be reduced by the $800 increase in accounts receivable to yield the correct cash flow from operations.

Cash	AR	Sales
1,200	800	2,000

Hence, when preparing the preliminary statement of cash flows in Step Three, it is important to remember to *subtract* the change in asset accounts and *add* changes in the liability and stockholders' equity accounts.

EXHIBIT 12-5	An Illustration of a Preliminary Statement of Cash Flows: The Indirect Method

BENNETT COMPANY
Preliminary Statement of Cash Flows
For Year Ended December 31, Year 2

Operating Activities	
Retained earnings	$19,000
Accounts receivable	(5,000)
Inventory	6,000
Prepaid insurance	(13,000)
Accounts payable	(9,000)
Income tax payable	2,000
Cash flow provided by operating activities	0
Investing Activities	
Long-term investments	(15,000)
Plant assets (net)	30,000
Patent	(60,000)
Cash flow used by investing activities	(45,000)
Financing Activities	
Common stock	70,000
Cash flow provided financing activities	70,000
Change in cash (from the balance sheet)	$25,000

Exhibit 12-5 presents the preliminary statement of cash flows for the Bennett Company. This preliminary statement indicates that the firm's cash flow provided by operating activities was $0, the cash flow used by investing activities was $45,000, and the cash flow provided financing activities was $70,000. As required, the cash inflows and outflows aggregate to the change in cash from the balance sheet, an increase of $25,000.

Step Four: Integrate income statement data.   To this point we have used the balance sheet exclusively to provide the needed inputs to our statement of cash flows. In Step Four, we integrate information from the income statement (see **Exhibit 12-3**) into the preliminary statement of cash flows in **Exhibit 12-5**.

First, we replace the change in retained earnings from the balance sheet with net income from the income statement. For the Bennett Company, the change in retained earnings of $19,000 does not equal net income of $32,000. The difference of $13,000 ($32,000 – $19,000) represents a cash dividend paid to Bennett's shareholders (see the Additional Data in **Exhibit**

12-3). Thus, when we replace retained earnings of $19,000 with net income of $32,000, it is also necessary to report the $13,000 cash dividend payment as a cash outflow under the financing activities section in **Exhibit 12-6**. Increasing the cash flow from operations and decreasing the cash flow from financing activities by an equivalent amount ($13,000) keeps the statement of cash flows in balance with the net change in cash of $25,000.

Retained Earnings

		56,000	Beginning Balance
		32,000	Net Income
Dividends Paid	13,000		
		75,000	Ending Balance

Second, we adjust the Bennett Company's net income for any **noncash expenses** such as the depreciation of plant assets and the amortization of intangibles that were deducted in the process of calculating the firm's accrual basis net income. Depreciation expense and amortization expense are called noncash expenses because these expenses do not involve a current cash outflow. Depreciation expense, for example, represents the allocation of the purchase price of plant assets over the many periods that these assets produce sales revenue for a business. The matching principle requires that the cost of plant assets be matched with the sales revenue produced by these assets, and this is accomplished on the income statement by the deduction of the periodic depreciation charge. The cash flows associated with the purchase and sale of plant assets and intangible assets are appropriately classified as cash flow from investing activities (see **Exhibit 12-5**). These noncash expenses must be *added back* to net income in the operating activities section to correctly measure the firm's operating cash flow.

The Income Statement in **Exhibit 12-3** indicates that $10,000 of depreciation expense was deducted in calculating net income. Thus, we will add this amount back to net income. (Note that there was no amortization expense on the patent because it was not purchased until Year 2.) To keep the statement of cash flows in balance with an increase in cash of $25,000, it is also necessary to subtract equivalent amounts in the investing activities section. We discuss this adjustment in Step Five.

To summarize, the adjustments to the Bennett Company's preliminary statement of cash flows in **Exhibit 12-5** are:

1. Net income of $32,000 replaces the change in retained earnings of $19,000 in the operating activities section. This action adds $13,000 to the cash flow from operating activities. To keep the statement of cash flows in balance with the change in cash of $25,000, it is necessary to subtract $13,000 elsewhere on the statement. Since retained earnings is calculated as follows:

	Retained earnings (beginning)
+	Net income for the period
−	Dividends declared
=	Retained earnings (ending)

the outflow of $13,000 is shown as a cash dividend to shareholders under the financing activities section.

2. Depreciation expense of $10,000, a noncash deduction from net income, is added back to net income to avoid understating the cash flow from operations. However, to keep the statement of cash flows in balance with the change in cash of $25,000, a similar amount is subtracted from plant assets under the investing activities section.

Step Five: Remove the financial effects of any nonrecurring or nonoperating transactions from net income. A firm's operating cash flow should include only the cash flows from operating activities. Consequently, to calculate the cash flow from operating activities, it is necessary to review a company's income statement to identify and remove the financial effects of any nonoperating transactions included in net income.[2]

To illustrate this point, note that Bennett Company sold a plant asset (land) during the year at a gain of $8,000 ($28,000 sales price less $20,000 cost). (See the Income Statement andAdditional Data in **Exhibit 12-3**.) The sale of a plant asset is an investing activity and therefore the cash received properly belongs in the investing activities section. However, the gain of $8,000 is included in net income in the operating activities section. Thus, to correctly assess Bennett's cash flows, it is necessary to subtract the gain from the operating activities section and add it to the change in plant assets in the investing activities section. (Note that if there had been a loss on the sale of plant assets, Bennett would have added it back to net income in the operating activities section because a loss reduces net income but does not represent an operating cash outflow). When combined with the adjustment for depreciation expense from Step Four, the cash flow from plant assets is $28,000 ($30,000 change in plant assets − $10,000 adjustment for depreciation expense + $8,000 adjustment for gain). The adjusted amount of $28,000 is equal to the cash received on the sale of plant assets.

FYI: The sale of a non-depreciable plant asset (like land) only affects the Plant Asset account, but if the plant asset sold had been a depreciable asset, the cost of the asset would be removed from the Plant Assets Account and the associated Accumulated Depreciation would also have to be removed.

Plant Assets				Accumulated Depreciation		
Beginning Balance	200,000				40,000	Beginning Balance
		20,000	Sale	Sale	0	10,000	Depreciation Expense
Ending Balance	180,000				50,000	Ending Balance

Cash proceeds	28,000	Investing cash flow
− Book value	(20,000)	
Gain on sale	8,000	

Exhibit 12-6 presents the final statement of cash flows for Bennett Company and includes not only the adjustments from Step Four, but also the adjustment to remove any nonoperating gains and losses from the cash flow from operating activities (Step Five). Note that the company's statement of cash flows remains in balance with the change in cash of $25,000 after the adjustments in both of these steps. This result is possible because whatever amount was added to (or subtracted from) net income under the cash flow from operating activities, an equivalent amount was subtracted from (or added to) the investing activities or the financing activities.

Bennett's statement of cash flows reveals that the cash flow provided by operating activities is $15,000, the cash flow used by investing activities is $47,000, and the cash flow provided by financing activities is $57,000. The resulting total cash flow of $25,000 exactly equals the increase in cash on the balance sheet of $25,000, as required.

---

[2] An exception is interest expense, which most investment professionals view as a financing activity. Regardless, interest payments are required to be included in the cash flow from operating activities.

EXHIBIT 12-6	Statement of Cash Flows—The Indirect Method

BENNETT COMPANY
Statement of Cash Flows
For Year Ended December 31, Year 2

Cash Flow from Operating Activities		
Net income	$32,000	
Add (deduct) items to convert net income to cash basis		
Depreciation	10,000	
Gain on sale of plant assets	(8,000)	
Accounts receivable increase	(5,000)	
Inventory decrease	6,000	
Prepaid insurance increase	(13,000)	
Accounts payable decrease	(9,000)	
Income tax payable increase	2,000	
Cash provided by operating activities		$15,000
Cash Flow from Investing Activities		
Purchase of long-term investments	(15,000)	
Sale of plant assets	28,000	
Purchase of patent	(60,000)	
Cash used by investing activities		(47,000)
Cash Flow from Financing Activities		
Issuance of common stock	70,000	
Payment of dividends	(13,000)	
Cash provided by financing activities		57,000
Net increase in cash		25,000
Cash at beginning of year		10,000
Cash at end of year		$35,000

The following illustration summarizes the five-step process to prepare an indirect method statement of cash flows:

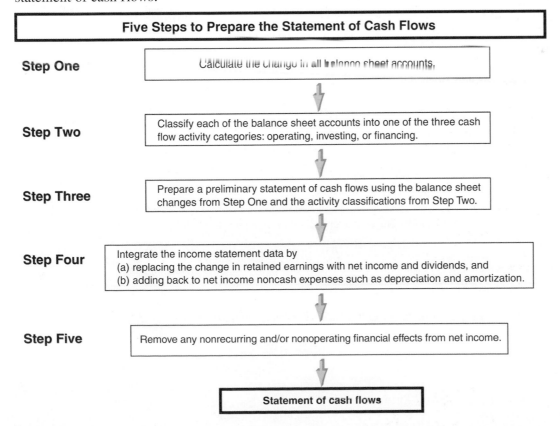

Five Steps to Prepare the Statement of Cash Flows

Step One — Calculate the change in all balance sheet accounts.

Step Two — Classify each of the balance sheet accounts into one of the three cash flow activity categories: operating, investing, or financing.

Step Three — Prepare a preliminary statement of cash flows using the balance sheet changes from Step One and the activity classifications from Step Two.

Step Four — Integrate the income statement data by
(a) replacing the change in retained earnings with net income and dividends, and
(b) adding back to net income noncash expenses such as depreciation and amortization.

Step Five — Remove any nonrecurring and/or nonoperating financial effects from net income.

Statement of cash flows

ENVIRONMENTAL, SOCIAL, AND GOVERNANCE   Serving Communities in Need

Home Depot doesn't just serve its customers, it serves its community. The Home Depot Foundation works to improve the homes and lives of U.S. veterans, train skilled tradespeople and help them find careers in the home improvement industry through their Path to Pro program, and support communities impacted by natural disasters. Assisting them on the ground are more than 55,000 store associates who, as Team Depot volunteers, donate their time and sweat to these causes.

YOUR TURN! 12.2

MBC

The solution is on page 12-50.

Husky Company's current year income statement and comparative balance sheets as of December 31 of the current and previous years are shown below:

HUSKY COMPANY Income Statement For Year Ended December 31, Current Year		
Sales revenue.		$1,270,000
Cost of goods sold	$860,000	
Wages expense	172,000	
Insurance expense	16,000	
Depreciation expense.	34,000	
Interest expense	18,000	
Income tax expense	58,000	1,158,000
Net income		$ 112,000

HUSKY COMPANY Balance Sheets	Dec. 31, Current Year	Dec. 31, Previous Year
Assets		
Cash.	$ 22,000	$ 10,000
Accounts receivable	82,000	64,000
Inventory.	180,000	120,000
Prepaid insurance.	10,000	14,000
Plant assets	500,000	390,000
Accumulated depreciation	(136,000)	(102,000)
Total assets.	$658,000	$496,000
Liabilities and Stockholders' Equity		
Accounts payable	$ 14,000	$ 20,000
Wages payable.	18,000	12,000
Income tax payable.	14,000	16,000
Bonds payable	260,000	150,000
Common stock	180,000	180,000
Retained earnings	172,000	118,000
Total liabilities and stockholders' equity	$658,000	$496,000

Cash dividends of $58,000 were declared and paid during the current year. Plant assets were purchased for cash, and bonds payable were issued for cash. Accounts payable relate to merchandise purchases.

Required
Prepare a statement of cash flows for the Husky Company using the indirect method.

For readers skipping the indirect method, please resume reading here.

ANALYZING CASH FLOWS

Data from the statement of cash flows are often used to calculate financial measures to evaluate a company's cash flow health. Three such measures include the company's free cash flow, the operating-cash-flow-to-current-liabilities ratio, and the operating-cash-flow-to-capital-expenditures ratio.

LO3 Define ratios used to analyze the statement of cash flows and **explain** their use.

eLecture
MBC

Free Cash Flow

Free cash flow (FCF) is often used by investment professionals and investors to evaluate a company's cash-flow strength. FCF is an important performance reference point for investment professionals because it indicates the amount of cash generated during the year beyond what is needed to operate the business at its current capacity. Free cash flow is calculated as follows:

FCF = Cash flow from operating activities – Capital expenditures

As discussed in Chapter 9, capital expenditures refer to investment in a business's plant and intangible assets necessary to enable a firm to remain a going concern. Subtracting capital expenditures from the firm's cash flow from operating activities measures the amount of excess or "free" cash flow that can be used for expansion, paying dividends, reducing debt, or other purposes. A firm with strong free cash flow will generally carry a higher stock value than one with weak (or no) free cash flow.

Concept	→ Method →	Assessment	**TAKEAWAY 12.1**
Does a company generate cash flows in excess of its capital expenditure needs?	Statement of cash flows. Free Cash Flow = Cash flow from operating activities – Capital expenditures	The higher the free cash flow, the greater is a company's ability to generate cash for needs other than capital expenditures.	

Operating-Cash-Flow-to-Current-Liabilities Ratio

Two measures previously introduced—the current ratio and the quick ratio—emphasize the relation between a company's current or quick assets and its current liabilities to measure the ability of a firm to pay its current liabilities. The **operating-cash-flow-to-current-liabilities ratio** is another measure of a company's ability to pay its current liabilities. While the current and quick ratios focus on a firm's ability to pay liabilities using existing current or quick assets, the operating cash flow to current liabilities ratio highlights a firm's ability to pay its current liabilities using its operating cash flow. The ratio is calculated as follows:

$$\text{Operating-cash-flow-to-current-liabilities ratio} = \frac{\text{Cash flow from operating activities}}{\text{Average current liabilities}}$$

The cash flow from operating activities is obtained from the statement of cash flows. The denominator is the average of the beginning and ending current liabilities for the year.

The following amounts (in thousands of dollars) were taken from the financial statements of the **Gannett Co., Inc.**, a diversified news and information company that publishes *USA Today*:

Cash flow from operating activities.	$ 57,770
Current liabilities at beginning of the year	$718,453
Current liabilities at end of the year	$741,300

The operating cash flow to current liabilities ratio for the Gannett Co. is calculated as follows (in millions):

$$\frac{\$57,770}{\left[\dfrac{(\$718,453 + \$741,300)}{2}\right]} = 0.08$$

The higher this ratio, the greater is a firm's ability to pay current liabilities using its operating cash flow. A ratio of 0.5 is considered a strong ratio; consequently, Gannett's ratio of 0.08 would be interpreted as a little weak. A ratio of 0.08 indicates that Gannett generates $0.08 of operating cash flow for every dollar of current liabilities.

TAKEAWAY 12.2	Concept ➝	Method ➝	Assessment
	Will a company have sufficient cash to pay its current liabilities as they become due?	Statement of cash flows and balance sheet. Operating-cash-flow-to-current-liabilities ratio $=$ $\dfrac{\text{Cash flow from operating activities}}{\text{Average current liabilities}}$	The higher the ratio, the higher the probability that a company will have sufficient operating cash flow to pay its current liabilities as they become due.

Operating-Cash-Flow-to-Capital-Expenditures Ratio

To remain competitive, a business must be able to replace, and expand when appropriate, its property, plant, and equipment. A ratio that evaluates a firm's ability to finance its capital investments from operating cash flow is the **operating-cash-flow-to-capital-expenditures ratio**. This ratio is calculated as follows:

$$\text{Operating-cash-flow-to-capital expenditures ratio} = \frac{\textbf{Cash flow from operating activities}}{\textbf{Annual net capital expenditures}}$$

The numerator in this ratio comes from the statement of cash flows. Information for the denominator may be found in one or more places in the financial statements. Data regarding a company's capital expenditures are presented in the investing activities section of the statement of cash flows. (When capital expenditures are reported in the statement of cash flows, the amount is often broken into two figures—(1) Proceeds from the sale of property, plant, and equipment and (2) Purchases of property, plant, and equipment. The appropriate "capital expenditures" figure for the purpose of calculating this ratio is the net of the two amounts.) Data on capital expenditures are also part of the required industry segment disclosures in the notes to the financial statements. Finally, management's discussion and analysis of the financial statements may identify the company's annual capital expenditures.

A ratio in excess of 1.0 indicates that a firm's current operating activities are providing sufficient cash to fund its desired investment in plant assets and would normally be considered a sign of financial strength. The interpretation of this ratio is influenced by the trend in recent years, the ratio being achieved by other firms in the same industry, and the stage of a firm's life cycle. A firm in the early stages of its life cycle—when periods of rapid expansion may occur—may be expected to experience a lower ratio than a firm in the later stage of its life cycle—when maintenance of plant capacity may be more likely than an expansion of plant capacity.

To illustrate the ratio's calculation, **Abbott Laboratories**, a manufacturer of pharmaceutical and health care products, reported capital expenditures (in millions of dollars) of $2,177. Abbott's cash flow from operating activities was $7,901. Thus, Abbott's operating-cash-flow-to-capital-expenditure ratio for the year was 3.63, or ($7,901/$2,177). The following are operating-cash-flow-to-capital-expenditures ratios for other well-known companies:

PepsiCo Inc. (Consumer foods and beverages)	2.50
Lockheed Martin Corporation (Aerospace).	4.63
Norfolk Southern Corporation (Freight transportation services).	2.43

DATA ANALYTICS — Using Analytics to Improve Cash Flow Management

Data Analytics

A firm's financial transactions can be complex, and with complexity comes risk. There is the risk of missing data, the risk of data duplication, and the risk that the information used for decisions is dated and doesn't reflect the current state of the firm's financial health. Business intelligence software such as Tableau can be of tremendous benefit by providing a clear understanding of a company's cash flow.

A shortcoming of using the traditional approach of reviewing month-end bank statements in a general ledger and then analyzing operating, investing, and financing activities is that this perspective is static and often not available in a timely fashion. In contrast, business intelligence software allows for real-time analysis from multiple sources. Further, the ability to display the data in easier to understand visualizations, and the ability to drill down into the data as needed provides business managers with a far better way to understand and manage cash flows.

Concept	→ Method →	Assessment	TAKEAWAY 12.3
Does a company generate sufficient operating cash flows to finance its capital expenditure needs?	Statement of cash flows. $$\text{Operating-cash-flow-to-capital-expenditures ratio} = \frac{\text{Cash flow from operating activities}}{\text{Annual net capital expenditures}}$$	The higher the ratio, the higher the probability that a company will generate sufficient operating cash flow to finance its capital expenditure needs.	

YOUR TURN! 12.3

GuidedExample

MBC

The solution is on page 12-51.

The following selected data were obtained from the financial statements of Blake Enterprises:

Cash flow from operating activities.	$40,000
Annual net capital expenditures	12,500
Average current liabilities	30,000

Calculate the following financial measures for Blake Enterprises:

1. Free cash flow
2. Operating-cash-flow-to-current-liabilities ratio
3. Operating-cash-flow-to-capital-expenditures ratio

COMPREHENSIVE PROBLEM

GuidedExample

MBC

Terry Company's income statement and comparative balance sheets at December 31 of the current and previous year are as follows:

TERRY COMPANY
Income Statement
For Year Ended December 31, Current Year

Sales revenue.		$385,000
Dividend income.		5,000
		390,000
Cost of goods sold	$233,000	
Wages expense	82,000	
Advertising expense.	10,000	
Depreciation expense.	11,000	
Income tax expense.	17,000	
Loss on sale of investments.	1,000	354,000
Net income.		$ 36,000

TERRY COMPANY Balance Sheets		
	Dec. 31, Current Year	Dec. 31, Previous Year
Assets		
Cash....	$ 8,000	$ 12,000
Accounts receivable .	22,000	28,000
Inventory.	94,000	66,000
Prepaid advertising.	12,000	9,000
Long-term investments.	30,000	40,000
Plant assets .	178,000	130,000
Accumulated depreciation .	(72,000)	(61,000)
Total assets....	$272,000	$224,000
Liabilities and Stockholders' Equity		
Accounts payable .	$ 27,000	$ 14,000
Wages payable.	6,000	2,500
Income tax payable.	3,000	4,500
Common stock .	139,000	125,000
Retained earnings .	97,000	78,000
Unrealized loss on investments .	—	—
Total liabilities and stockholders' equity .	$272,000	$224,000

Cash dividends of $17,000 were declared and paid during the year. Plant assets were purchased for cash, and, later in the year, additional common stock was issued for cash. Investments costing $10,000 were sold for cash at a $1,000 loss.

Required

a. Calculate the change in cash that occurred during the year.

b. Prepare a statement of cash flows using the indirect method.

Solution

a. $8,000 ending balance – $12,000 beginning balance = $4,000 decrease in cash

b. 1. Use the indirect method to determine the cash flow from operating activities.

  • The adjustments to convert Terry Company's net income of $36,000 to the cash provided by operating activities of $38,000 are shown in the following statement of cash flows.

2. Analyze changes in remaining noncash asset (and contra asset) accounts to determine cash flows from investing activities.

  • Long-term investments: $10,000 decrease resulted from sale of investments for cash at a $1,000 loss. Cash received from sale of investments = $9,000 ($10,000 cost – $1,000 loss).

  • Plant assets: $48,000 increase resulted from purchase of plant assets for cash. Cash paid to purchase plant assets = $48,000.

  • Accumulated depreciation: $11,000 increase resulted from the recording of 2019 depreciation. No cash flow effect.

3. Analyze changes in remaining liability and stockholders' equity accounts to determine cash flows from financing activities.

  • Common stock: $14,000 increase resulted from the issuance of stock for cash. Cash received from issuance of common stock = $14,000.

  • Retained earnings: $19,000 increase resulted from net income of $36,000 and dividend declaration of $17,000. Cash paid as dividends = $17,000.

The statement of cash flows (indirect method) is as follows:

TERRY COMPANY Statement of Cash Flows For the Year Ended December 31, Current Year		
Cash Flow from Operating Activities		
Net income	$36,000	
Add (deduct) items to convert net income to cash basis		
Depreciation	11,000	
Loss on sale of investments	1,000	
Accounts receivable decrease	6,000	
Inventory increase	(28,000)	
Prepaid advertising increase	(3,000)	
Accounts payable increase	13,000	
Wages payable increase	3,500	
Income tax payable decrease	(1,500)	
Cash provided by operating activities		$38,000
Cash Flow from Investing Activities		
Sale of investments	9,000	
Purchase of plant assets	(48,000)	
Cash used by investing activities		(39,000)
Cash Flow from Financing Activities		
Issuance of common stock	14,000	
Payment of dividends	(17,000)	
Cash used by financing activities		(3,000)
Net decrease in cash		(4,000)
Cash at beginning of year		12,000
Cash at end of year		$ 8,000

APPENDIX 12A: Preparing the Statement of Cash Flows Under the Direct Method

Although it is quite straightforward to create a direct method statement of cash flows given access to a company's internal accounting records, this type of access is rarely available to anyone except a company's management team. All that is necessary is to pull the numbers directly off the Cash general ledger account and place them in the appropriate section of the statement of cash flows. This is why the direct method is referred to as "direct." The cash flow from operations is taken directly from the company's general ledger, rather than being indirectly computed from net income. Unfortunately, investment professionals, lenders, and stockholders rarely have access to such proprietary internal data. Thus, it is necessary to be able to create direct method cash flow information using only publicly available data included in the indirect method statement of cash flows.

LO4 Explain the preparation of a statement of cash flows using the direct method.

eLecture
MBC

The adjustments in the indirect method to convert net income to operating cash flows are the same adjustments that are made to individual income statement line items to convert revenues and expenses under the accrual basis of accounting to cash inflows and outflows under the cash basis of accounting in the direct method. Thus, after learning the indirect method for preparing the operating section, it is quite simple to use the same adjustments to present the operating section using the direct method.

The process to convert an indirect method statement of cash flows to the direct method requires two steps. First, replace net income (the first line item under the operating activities section of the indirect method statement format) with the line items appearing on a firm's income statement. For instance, Bennett Company's income statement in **Exhibit 12-3** contains the following line items:

Sales revenue	$250,000
Cost of goods sold	(148,000)
Wages expense	(52,000)
Insurance expense	(5,000)
Depreciation expense	(10,000)
Income tax expense	(11,000)
Gain on sale of plant assets	8,000
Net income	$ 32,000

For the Bennett Company, we begin by replacing the net income of $32,000 under the operating activities section in **Exhibit 12-6** with the seven income statement line items, which aggregate to $32,000.

The second step involves adjusting the income statement line items by the relevant amounts from the operating activities section of the indirect method statement of cash flows. **Exhibit 12A-1** summarizes the procedures for converting individual income statement items to the corresponding cash flows from operating activities.

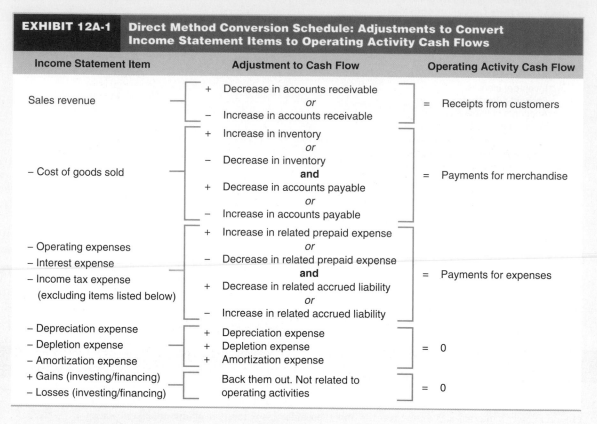

EXHIBIT 12A-1   **Direct Method Conversion Schedule: Adjustments to Convert Income Statement Items to Operating Activity Cash Flows**

In other words, rather than simply listing each adjustment to net income as in the indirect method, we align each adjustment with the associated income statement line item. For example, accounts receivable is used to record sales on credit, so we subtract the change in accounts receivable from sales revenue to calculate cash received from customers. Similarly, changes in inventory and accounts payable are used to convert cost of goods sold expense to cash payments for merchandise.

Using the Bennet Company data in **Exhibits 12-3** and **12-4**, we prepare the following schedule:

Income Statement Line Items		Operating Activities Line Items	Direct Method Operating Cash Flow	
Sales revenue	$250,000	− $5,000 ↑ accounts receivable	Cash received from customers	$245,000
Cost of goods sold	(148,000)	+ $6,000 ↓ inventory	Cash paid for merchandise	(151,000)
		− $9,000 ↓ accounts payable		
Wage expense	(52,000)	No adjustment	Cash paid to employees	(52,000)
Insurance expense	(5,000)	− $13,000 ↑ prepaid insurance	Cash paid for insurance	(18,000)
Depreciation expense	(10,000)	+ $10,000 depreciation		0
Income tax expense	(11,000)	+ $2,000 ↑ income tax payable	Cash paid for income taxes	(9,000)
Gain on sale of plant assets	8,000	− $8,000 gain on sale of plant assets		0
Net income	$ 32,000		Cash flow from operations	$ 15,000

↑ denotes increases and ↓ denotes decreases

The first column of this schedule lists each of the income statement line items, while the middle column lists the associated adjustments. Summing across, the final column provides the amount of operating cash receipts or payments. The highlighted cells in the far right column represent the direct method operating section.

Exhibit 12A-2 presents the Bennett Company's direct method statement of cash flows. As expected, the direct method cash flow from operating activities of $15,000 is exactly equivalent to the indirect method result of $15,000 as reported in **Exhibit 12-6**. Note that the cash flow from investing activities and the cash flow from financing activities sections are exactly the same in both **Exhibit 12-6** and **Exhibit 12A-2**. The only difference between the two exhibits is the manner in which the cash flow from operating activities is presented. In **Exhibit 12-6**, the cash flow from operating activities is calculated beginning with net income and then adjusting for various noncash expenses (depreciation expense) and nonoperating transactions (gain on sale of plant assets), as well as adjusting for the changes in the various working capital accounts (accounts receivable, inventory, prepaid insurance, accounts payable, and taxes payable). In **Exhibit 12A-2**, the direct method cash flow from operating activities lists each category of cash receipts and cash payments from the highlighted column in the schedule above. But in each case, the operating cash flow is $15,000. A company using the direct method must also separately disclose the reconciliation of net income to cash flow from operating activities prepared using the indirect method.

EXHIBIT 12A-2	Statement of Cash Flows Under the Direct Method

BENNETT COMPANY
Statement of Cash Flows
For Year Ended December 31, Year 2

Cash Flow from Operating Activities		
Cash received from customers.		$245,000
Cash paid for merchandise purchased.	$(151,000)	
Cash paid to employees.	(52,000)	
Cash paid for insurance	(18,000)	
Cash paid for income taxes	(9,000)	(230,000)
Cash provided by operating activities		15,000
Cash Flow from Investing Activities		
Purchase of long-term investments	(15,000)	
Sale of plant assets	28,000	
Purchase of patent.	(60,000)	
Cash used by investing activities		(47,000)
Cash Flow from Financing Activities		
Issuance of common stock.	70,000	
Payment of dividends	(13,000)	
Cash provided by financing activities		57,000
Net increase in cash.		25,000
Cash at beginning of year.		10,000
Cash at end of year		$ 35,000

Finally, note that this schedule can also be used to illustrate the connection between the direct and indirect methods. Specifically, the indirect method starts with net income and makes various adjustments to this summary number to arrive at operating cash flows, as highlighted in the schedule below. In other words, the direct and indirect methods are derived from the same data, proving that they are just "two sides of the same coin."

Income Statement Line Items		Operating Activities Line Items	Direct Method Operating Cash Flow	
Sales revenue	$250,000	− $5,000 ↑ accounts receivable	Cash received from customers	$245,000
Cost of goods sold	(148,000)	+ $6,000 ↓ inventory	Cash paid for merchandise	(151,000)
		− $9,000 ↓ accounts payable		
Wage expense	(52,000)	No adjustment	Cash paid to employees	(52,000)
Insurance expense	(5,000)	− $13,000 ↑ prepaid insurance	Cash paid for insurance	(18,000)
Depreciation expense	(10,000)	+ $10,000 depreciation		0
Income tax expense	(11,000)	+ $2,000 ↑ income tax payable	Cash paid for income taxes	(9,000)
Gain on sale of plant assets	8,000	− $8,000 gain on sale of plant assets		0
Net income	$ 32,000		Cash flow from operations	$ 15,000

↑ denotes increases and ↓ denotes decreases

YOUR TURN! 12A.1

GuidedExample

MBC

The solution is on page 12-51.

Husky Company's income statement and comparative balance sheets as of December 31 of the current and previous year are shown below:

HUSKY COMPANY		
Income Statement		
For the Year Ended December 31		
Sales revenue		$1,270,000
Cost of goods sold	$860,000	
Wages expense	172,000	
Insurance expense	16,000	
Depreciation expense	34,000	
Interest expense	18,000	
Income tax expense	58,000	1,158,000
Net income		$ 112,000

HUSKY COMPANY		
Balance Sheets		
	Dec. 31, Current Year	Dec. 31, Previous Year
Assets		
Cash	$ 22,000	$ 10,000
Accounts receivable	82,000	64,000
Inventory	180,000	120,000
Prepaid insurance	10,000	14,000
Plant assets	500,000	390,000
Accumulated depreciation	(136,000)	(102,000)
Total assets	$658,000	$496,000
Liabilities and Stockholders' Equity		
Accounts payable	$ 14,000	$ 20,000
Wages payable	18,000	12,000
Income tax payable	14,000	16,000
Bonds payable	260,000	150,000
Common stock	180,000	180,000
Retained earnings	172,000	118,000
Total liabilities and stockholders' equity	$658,000	$496,000

Cash dividends of $58,000 were declared and paid during the year. Plant assets were purchased for cash, and bonds payable were issued for cash. Bond interest is paid semiannually on June 30 and December 31. Accounts payable relate to merchandise purchases.

Required

Prepare a statement of cash flows using the direct method.

SUMMARY OF LEARNING OBJECTIVES

LO1   **Discuss the content and format of the statement of cash flows. (p. 12-3)**

■   The statement of cash flows explains the net increase or decrease in cash and cash equivalents during the period.

■   The statement of cash flows separates cash flows into operating, investing, and financing activity categories.

■   The statement of cash flows also provides a required supplemental disclosure reporting noncash investing and financing activities.

■   The statement of cash flows helps users compare, evaluate, and predict a firm's cash flows and also helps evaluate its financial flexibility.

Explain the preparation of a statement of cash flows using the indirect method. (p. 12-9)   **LO2**

■ The indirect method of preparing the cash flow from operating activities section reconciles net income to cash flow from operating activities.

Define ratios used to analyze the statement of cash flows and explain their use. (p. 12-18)   **LO3**

■ Free cash flow is defined as a company's cash flow from operations less its capital expenditures; the metric provides a measure of a firm's cash flow that can be used to fund business activities beyond the replacement of property, plant, and equipment.

■ The operating-cash-flow-to-current-liabilities ratio is calculated by dividing a company's cash flow from operating activities by its average current liabilities for the year; the ratio reveals a firm's ability to repay current liabilities from operating cash flow.

■ The operating-cash-flow-to-capital-expenditures ratio is calculated by dividing a firm's cash flow from operating activities by its annual net capital expenditures; the ratio evaluates a firm's ability to fund its capital investment using operating cash flow.

Appendix 12A: Explain the preparation of a statement of cash flows using the direct method. (p. 12-22)   **LO4**

■ The direct method of preparing the cash flow from operating activities section shows the major categories of operating cash receipts and payments.

■ The FASB encourages use of the direct method but permits use of either the direct or the indirect method.

■ A firm using the direct method must separately disclose the reconciliation of net income to cash flow from operating activities.

Concept	Method	Assessment	SUMMARY
Does a company generate cash flows in excess of its capital expenditure needs?	Statement of cash flows. Free Cash Flow = Cash flow from operating activities – Capital expenditures	The higher the free cash flow, the greater is a company's ability to generate cash for needs other than capital expenditures.	TAKEAWAY 12.1
Will a company have sufficient cash to pay its current liabilities as they become due?	Statement of cash flows and balance sheet. $\text{Operating-cash-flow-to-current-liabilities ratio} = \dfrac{\text{Cash flow from operating activities}}{\text{Average current liabilities}}$	The higher the ratio, the higher the probability that a company will have sufficient operating cash flow to pay its current liabilities as they become due.	TAKEAWAY 12.2
Does a company generate sufficient operating cash flows to finance its capital expenditure needs?	Statement of cash flows. $\text{Operating-cash-flow-to-capital-expenditures ratio} = \dfrac{\text{Cash flow from operating activities}}{\text{Annual net capital expenditures}}$	The higher the ratio, the higher the probability that a company will generate sufficient operating cash flow to finance its capital expenditure needs.	TAKEAWAY 12.3

KEY TERMS

Cash equivalents (p. 12-3)
Cash management (p. 12-3)
Direct method (p. 12-8)
Financial flexibility (p. 12-8)
Financing activities (p. 12-6)

Free cash flow (FCF) (p. 12-18)
Indirect method (p. 12-8)
Investing activities (p. 12-5)
Noncash expenses (p. 12-14)
Noncash investing and financing activities (p. 12-7)

Operating activities (p. 12-5)
Operating-cash-flow-to-capital-expenditures ratio (p. 12-19)
Operating-cash-flow-to-current-liabilities ratio (p. 12-18)

Assignments with the ⓂⒷⒸ logo in the margin are available in myBusinessCourse.
See the Preface of the book for details.

SELF-STUDY QUESTIONS

(Answers to the Self-Study Questions are at the end of the chapter.)

LO1 1. **Which of the following is not disclosed in a statement of cash flows?**
  a. A transfer of cash to a cash equivalent investment
  b. The amount of cash at year-end
  c. Cash outflows from investing activities during the period
  d. Cash inflows from financing activities during the period

LO1 2. **Which of the following events will appear in the cash flows from investing activities section of the statement of cash flows?**
  a. Cash received as interest   *c.* Cash purchase of truck
  b. Cash received from issuance of common stock *d.* Cash payment of dividends

LO1 3. **Which of the following events will appear in the cash flows from financing activities section of the statement of cash flows?**
  a. Cash purchase of equipment
  b. Cash purchase of bonds issued by another company
  c. Cash received as repayment for funds loaned
  d. Cash purchase of treasury stock

LO2 4. **Tyler Company has net income of $49,000 and the following related items:**

Depreciation expense	$ 5,000
Accounts receivable increase	2,000
Inventory increase	10,000
Accounts payable decrease	4,000

  Using the indirect method, what is Tyler's cash flow from operations?
  a. $42,000   *c.* $58,000
  b. $46,000   *d.* $38,000

LO3 5. **Free cash flow is a measure of a firm's**
  a. interest-free debt.
  b. ability to generate net income.
  c. ability to generate cash and invest in new capital expenditures.
  d. ability to collect accounts receivable in a timely manner.

LO1 6. **Which of the following events will not appear in the cash flows from financing activities section of the statement of cash flow?**
  a. Borrowing cash from a bank   *c.* Sales of common stock
  b. Issuance of stock in exchange for plant assets   *d.* Payment of dividends on preferred stock

LO3 7. **Taylor Company reports free cash flow of $15,000, total cash of $18,000, net income of $50,000, current assets of $90,000, average current liabilities of $38,400, and cash flow from operating activities of $48,000. Compute the operating-cash-flow-to-current-liabilities ratio for Taylor Company.**
  a. 0.83   *c.* 0.30
  b. 0.80   *d.* 1.25

LO1 8. **Which of the following is not a cash equivalent?**
  a. Short-term U.S. Treasury bill   *c.* Money-market account
  b. Short-term certificate of deposit   *d.* IBM common stock

LO2 9. **Which of the following expenses are not added back to net income when using the indirect method to prepare a statement of cash flows?**
  a. Amortization expense   *c.* Interest expense
  b. Depletion expense   *d.* Depreciation expense

LO4
(Appendix 12A) 10. **Smith & Sons reports interest expense of $90,000 on its income statement. The beginning and ending balances for interest payable reported on its balance sheet are $15,000 and $10,000, respectively. How much cash did Smith & Sons pay for interest expense this period?**
  a. $85,000   *c.* $100,000
  b. $95,000   *d.* $105,000

11. Which of the following methods will disclose the cash received from customers in the statement of cash flows?

LO4
(Appendix 12A)

a. Indirect method
b. Reconciliation method
c. Direct method
d. Both direct and indirect methods

12. Smith & Sons reports sales revenue of $1,000,000 on its income statement. Its balance sheet reveals beginning and ending accounts receivable of $92,000 and $60,000, respectively. What is the amount of cash collected from customers of the company?

LO4
(Appendix 12A)

a. $1,032,000
b. $968,000
c. $1,060,000
d. $1,092,000

QUESTIONS

1. What is the definition of *cash equivalents?* Give three examples of cash equivalents.

2. Why are cash equivalents included with cash in a statement of cash flows?

3. What are the three major types of activities classified on a statement of cash flows? Give an example of a cash inflow and a cash outflow in each classification.

4. In which of the three activity categories of a statement of cash flows would each of the following items appear? Indicate for each item whether it represents a cash inflow or a cash outflow:

a. Cash purchase of equipment
b. Cash collection on loans
c. Cash dividends paid
d. Cash dividends received
e. Cash proceeds from issuing stock
f. Cash receipts from customers
g. Cash interest paid
h. Cash interest received

5. Why is a statement of cash flows a useful financial statement?

6. What is the difference between the direct method and the indirect method of presenting the cash flow from operating activities?

7. In determining the cash flow from operating activities using the indirect method, why is it necessary to add depreciation back to net income? Give an example of another item that is added back to net income under the indirect method.

8. Vista Company sold land for $98,000 cash that had originally cost $70,000. The company recorded a gain on the sale of $28,000. How is this event reported in a statement of cash flows using the indirect method?

9. A firm uses the indirect method. Using the following information, what is its cash flow from operating activities?

Net income	$88,000
Accounts receivable decrease	13,000
Inventory increase	9,000
Accounts payable decrease	3,500
Income tax payable increase	1,500
Depreciation expense	6,000

10. If a business had a net loss for the year, under what circumstances would the statement of cash flows show a positive cash flow from operating activities?

11. A firm is converting its accrual revenues to corresponding cash amounts using the direct method. Sales revenue on the income statement are $925,000. Beginning and ending accounts receivable on the balance sheet are $58,000 and $44,000, respectively. What is the amount of cash received from customers?

12. A firm reports $86,000 wages expense in its income statement. If beginning and ending wages payable are $3,900 and $2,800, respectively, what is the amount of cash paid to employees?

13. A firm reports $43,000 advertising expense in its income statement. If beginning and ending prepaid advertising are $6,000 and $7,600, respectively, what is the amount of cash paid for advertising?

14. Rusk Company sold equipment for $5,100 cash that had cost $35,000 and had $29,000 of accumulated depreciation. How is this event reported in a statement of cash flows using the direct method?

15. What separate disclosures are required for a company that reports a statement of cash flows using the direct method?

16. How is the *operating-cash-flow-to-current-liabilities ratio* calculated? Explain its use.

17. How is the *operating-cash-flow-to capital-expenditures ratio* calculated? Explain its use.

18. The statement of cash flows provides information that may be useful in predicting future cash flows, evaluating financial flexibility, assessing liquidity, and identifying a company's financing needs. It is not,

however, the best financial statement for learning about a firm's financial performance during a period. Information about a company's financial performance is provided by the income statement. Two basic principles—the revenue recognition principle and the matching concept—work to distinguish the income statement from the statement of cash flows. (a) Define the revenue recognition principle and the matching concept. (b) Briefly explain how these two principles work to make the income statement a better report regarding a firm's periodic financial performance than the statement of cash flows.

SHORT EXERCISES

Use the following information regarding the Melville Corporation to answer Short Exercises 12-1 through 12-3:

Accounts payable increase	$12,000
Accounts receivable increase	4,000
Accrued liabilities decrease	5,000
Amortization expense	7,000
Cash balance, January 1	22,000
Cash balance, December 31	23,000
Cash paid as dividends	31,000
Cash paid to purchase land	90,000
Cash paid to retire bonds payable at par	60,000
Cash received from issuance of common stock	37,000
Cash received from sale of equipment	19,000
Depreciation expense	29,000
Gain on sale of equipment	4,000
Inventory decrease	13,000
Net income	80,000
Prepaid expenses increase	2,000

LO1, 2   **SE12-1.** **Cash Flow from Operating Activities** Using the information for the Melville Corporation above, calculate the cash flow from operating activities.

LO1, 2   **SE12-2.** **Cash Flow from Investing Activities** Using the information for the Melville Corporation above, calculate the cash flow from investing activities.

LO1, 2   **SE12-3.** **Cash Flow from Financing Activities** Using the information for the Melville Corporation above, calculate the cash flow from financing activities.

The following information for Evans & Sons relates to Short Exercises 12-4 through 12-6:

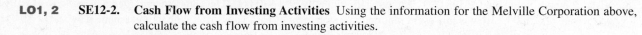

Cash flow from operating activities	$1,600,000
Capital expenditures	850,000
Current liabilities, beginning of year	300,000
Current liabilities, end of year	380,000

LO3   **SE12-4.** **Free Cash Flow** Using the above data, calculate the free cash flow for Evans & Sons.

LO3   **SE12-5.** **Operating-Cash-Flow-to-Current-Liabilities Ratio** Using the above data, calculate the operating-cash-flow-to-current-liabilities ratio for Evans & Sons.

LO3   **SE12-6.** **Operating-Cash-Flow-to-Capital-Expenditures Ratio** Using the above data, calculate the operating-cash-flow-to-capital-expenditures ratio for Evans & Sons.

LO4
(Appendix 12A)   **SE12-7.** **Converting Sales Revenue to Cash** Evans & Sons is converting its sales revenues to corresponding cash amounts using the direct method. Sales revenue on the income statement are $1,025,000. Beginning and ending accounts receivable on the balance sheet are $58,000 and $38,000, respectively. Calculate the amount of cash received from customers.

LO4
(Appendix 12A)   **SE12-8.** **Direct Method** Using the following data for Evans & Sons, calculate the cash paid for rent:

Rent expense	$80,000
Prepaid rent, January 1	10,000
Prepaid rent, December 31	8,000

SE12-9. **Direct Method** Using the following data for Evans & Sons, calculate the cash received as interest:

LO4
(Appendix 12A)

Interest income.	$30,000
Interest receivable, January 1.	3,000
Interest receivable, December 31.	3,700

SE12-10. **Direct Method** Using the following data for Evans & Sons, calculate the cash paid for merchandise purchased:

LO4
(Appendix 12A)

Cost of goods sold	$128,000
Inventory, January 1	19,000
Inventory, December 31	22,000
Accounts payable, January 1	11,000
Accounts payable, December 31	7,000

DATA ANALYTICS

DA12-1. **Preparing and Interpreting Excel Visualizations Created from Income and Cash Flow Data** The Excel file associated with this exercise includes data extracted from Form 10-K reports for **CVS Health Corporation** (CVS) and **Walgreens Boots Alliance** (Walgreens Boots) for six years. In this exercise, we analyze changes to and the relations between net income and operating cash flows over a six-year period.

Data Analytics

Required

1. Download Excel file DA12-1 found in myBusinessCourse.
2. Prepare a line chart for the six-year period for each company showing net income and operating cash flows. *Hint:* Highlight your data; click on Insert, Select line chart. There should be a separate line for net income and a separate line for operating cash flows. If necessary, edit the chart by opening the Chart Design tab and clicking Select Data. There should be two series.
3. Use the visualizations to answer the following questions.
   a. In what year(s) does net income exceed operating cash flows for CVS?
   b. In what year(s) do operating cash flows exceed net income for Walgreens Boots?
   c. Over the six-year period, which year showed the largest difference between net income and operating cash flows for CVS?
   d. What is a likely cause of the difference shown between net income and operating cash flows for the year identified in part *c*?
   e. For Walgreens Boots, in what year were net income and operating cash flows most similar?
   f. For CVS, in what year were net income and operating cash flows most similar?
   g. How would you compare the trend of operating cash flows for CVS vs. Walgreens Boots?

DA12-2. **Analyzing Cash Flow Ratio Trends by Industry Segment** The Excel file associated with this exercise includes Compustat data for S&P 500 companies for Year 1 through Year 5. For this exercise, we analyze trends in cash flow ratios by industry segment. The current cash debt coverage ratio is a liquidity ratio that measures whether a company can pay its *current* debts with cash provided from operating activities. The cash debt coverage ratio is a solvency ratio that measures a company's ability to pay *all* debts with cash provided from operating activities. In both cases, an increase in the ratio is generally viewed as favorable because it indicates that the company has a stronger ability to pay off obligations.

Part 1 Preparing the Data

1. Download Excel file DA12-2 found in myBusinessCourse.
2. Format the worksheet as a table. *Hint:* Highlight data in worksheet by clicking on keys Alt and A simultaneously. Select Insert, Table.
3. Sort data in table by Segment and delete all rows in the Financials and Real Estate Segments. Companies in these industries rarely report current assets or liabilities. *Hint:* Because this worksheet is formatted as a table, you can sort by any row using the dropdown at the column head.
4. Add a column to calculate average current liabilities for Years 2 through 5. *Hint:* Use the IF function to calculate the amount (the average current liabilities for that year). If the company name

agrees to the company name in the previous cell (Company Name column), then calculate the average; otherwise, put "n/a" in the cell. Year 1 will always be n/a.

5. Copy and Paste Special—Values back into the same cells. This will allow you to sort by other columns in the table without causing a recalculation error. *Hint:* To quickly highlight a long column, double-click on the bottom right corner of the first cell in the column.

6. Add a column to calculate average liabilities for Years 2 through 5. *Hint:* Use similar steps as in part 4.

Current Cash Debt Coverage

$$\frac{\text{Cash provided by operating activities}}{\text{Average current liabilities}}$$

Cash Debt Coverage

$$\frac{\text{Cash provided by operating activities}}{\text{Average total liabilities}}$$

7. Create a ratio column to calculate the current cash debt coverage ratio and a ratio column to calculate the cash debt coverage ratio. Sort your worksheet in ascending order by each ratio column and eliminate any rows with errors due to incomplete information (such as a Year 1 calculation) or where the answer is zero and it indicates an error or missing information.

8. Eliminate extreme outliers by deleting any company's information where it shows a ratio over +/−60. Be sure to eliminate all years of data of any company considered an outlier.

9. Check your output by answering the following questions:
   a. What is the Current cash debt coverage ratio for XRX for Year 3?
   b. What is the Cash debt coverage ratio for GD for Year 2?
   c. What is Cash flow from operations for HD for Year 5?
   d. How many rows are included for the Materials segment? *Hint:* Sort your worksheet by segment and then by the Materials column and view the "Count" at the bottom right of your screen.

Part 2   Creating a PivotTable

1. Create a PivotTable showing the average current cash debt coverage ratio and cash debt coverage ratio by segment by year. *Hint:* Drag Year then Segment to Rows and Current cash debt coverage and Cash debt coverage to Values. *Hint:* Right-click on a numeric field, select Value Field Settings, and change to Average.

2. Format your table to show two decimal places. *Hint:* Right-click on any item in the column to format and click on Number Format to update.

3. Eliminate totals from your chart. *Hint:* Click on the Design tab (it will be highlighted when you click anywhere in your PivotTable), Grand totals, Off for rows & columns.

4. Answer the following questions:
   a. Which industry segment has the highest average current cash debt coverage ratio in Year 2?
   b. Which industry segment has the lowest average current cash debt coverage ratio in Year 3?
   c. Which industry segment has the highest average cash debt coverage ratio in Year 5?
   d. Which industry segment has the lowest average cash debt coverage ratio in Year 5?
   e. What company had the largest current cash debt coverage ratio listed in the Telecommunications segment in Year 5? *Hint:* Double-click on the ratio amount in the PivotTable for Telecommunications, Year 5 to open up a new sheet with the supporting detail.

Part 3   Preparing and Analyzing a PivotChart

1. Create a PivotChart of the Cash Debt Coverage Ratio using a line chart.
2. Add a Slicer for Segment. *Hint:* Click inside the chart, click PivotChart Analyze, and click Add Slicer.
3. Describe the trend in each segment from Year 2 through Year 5.

DATA VISUALIZATION

Data Visualization Activities are available in myBusinessCourse. These assignments use Tableau Dashboards to expose students to visual depictions of data and introduce students to data analytics through data visualizations. These exercises are easily assignable and auto graded by MBC.

Data Visualization

EXERCISES—SET A

LO1   **E12-1A.   Classification of Cash Flows**   For each of the items below, indicate whether the cash flow item relates to an operating activity, an investing activity, or a financing activity:

   a.   Cash receipts from customers for services rendered

   b. Sale of long-term investments for cash
   c. Acquisition of plant assets for cash
   d. Payment of income taxes
   e. Bonds payable issued for cash
   f. Payment of cash dividends declared in previous year
   g. Purchase of short-term investments (not cash equivalents) for cash

E12-2A. Classification of Cash Flows For each of the items below, indicate whether it is (1) a cash flow   **LO1**
from an operating activity, (2) a cash flow from an investing activity, (3) a cash flow from a financing activity, (4) a noncash investing and financing activity, or (5) none of the above:

   a. Paid cash to retire bonds payable at a loss
   b. Received cash as settlement of a lawsuit
   c. Acquired a patent in exchange for common stock
   d. Received advance payments from customers on orders for custom-made goods
   e. Gave large cash contribution to local university
   f. Invested cash in 60-day commercial paper (a cash equivalent)

E12-3A. Cash Flow from Operating Activities (Indirect Method) The Washington Company owns no   **LO2**
plant assets and had the following income statement for the year:

Sales revenue.		$900,000
Cost of goods sold	$470,000	
Wages expense	120,000	
Rent expense	50,000	
Insurance expense	15,000	655,000
Net income		$245,000

Additional information about the company includes:

	End of Year	Beginning of Year
Accounts receivable	$54,000	$51,000
Inventory.	60,000	76,000
Prepaid insurance.	8,000	7,000
Accounts payable	24,000	18,000
Wages payable.	7,000	11,000

Use the preceding information to calculate the cash flow from operating activities using the indirect
method.

E12-4A. Statement of Cash Flows (Indirect Method) Use the following information regarding the Surpa   **LO2, 3**
Corporation to (a) prepare a statement of cash flows using the indirect method and (b) compute
Surpa's operating-cash-flow-to-current-liabilities ratio.

Accounts payable increase.	$ 13,000
Accounts receivable increase.	4,000
Accrued liabilities decrease	6,000
Amortization expense.	7,000
Cash balance, January 1	21,000
Cash balance, December 31	17,000
Cash paid as dividends	31,000
Cash paid to purchase land	90,000
Cash paid to retire bonds payable at par	60,000
Cash received from issuance of common stock	40,000
Cash received from sale of equipment.	17,000
Depreciation expense.	29,000
Gain on sale of equipment	7,000
Inventory decrease.	13,000
Net income	78,000
Prepaid expenses increase	3,000
Average current liabilities	140,000

LO2   **E12-5A.**   **Cash Flow from Operating Activities (Indirect Method)** The Azuza Company owns no plant assets and had the following income statement for the year:

Sales revenue.		$930,000
Cost of goods sold	$650,000	
Wages expense	210,000	
Rent expense	42,000	
Utilities expense	12,000	914,000
Net income		$ 16,000

Additional information about the company includes:

	End of Year	Beginning of Year
Accounts receivable	$67,000	$59,000
Inventory.	62,000	86,000
Prepaid rent	9,000	7,000
Accounts payable	22,000	30,000
Wages payable	9,000	7,000

Use the preceding information to calculate the cash flow from operating activities using the indirect method.

LO2   **E12-6A.**   **Statement of Cash Flows (Indirect Method)** Use the following information regarding the Hamilton Corporation to prepare a statement of cash flows using the indirect method:

Accounts payable decrease	$ 3,000
Accounts receivable increase.	10,000
Wages payable decrease	9,000
Amortization expense.	19,000
Cash balance, January 1	31,000
Cash balance, December 31	2,000
Cash paid as dividends	6,000
Cash paid to purchase land	110,000
Cash paid to retire bonds payable at par	65,000
Cash received from issuance of common stock.	45,000
Cash received from sale of equipment.	13,000
Depreciation expense.	39,000
Gain on sale of equipment	16,000
Inventory increase	11,000
Net income	94,000
Prepaid expenses increase	9,000

LO3   **E12-7A.**   **Cash Flow Ratios** Tracy Company reports the following amounts in its annual financial statements:

Cash flow from operating activities.	$90,000		Capital expenditures.	$ 31,000*
Cash flow from investing activities	(70,000)		Average current assets.	80,000
Cash flow from financing activities	(10,000)		Average current liabilities	60,000
Net income	44,000		Total assets.	180,000

* This amount is a cash outflow.

a.   Compute Tracy's free cash flow.
b.   Compute Tracy's operating-cash-flow-to-current-liabilities ratio.
c.   Compute Tracy's operating-cash-flow-to-capital-expenditures ratio.

E12-8A. **Operating Cash Flows (Direct Method)** Calculate the cash flow in each of the following cases:

    a. Cash paid for advertising:

Advertising expense	$62,000
Prepaid advertising, January 1	13,000
Prepaid advertising, December 31	15,000

    b. Cash paid for income taxes:

Income tax expense	$31,000
Income tax payable, January 1	7,100
Income tax payable, December 31	5,900

    c. Cash paid for merchandise purchased:

Cost of goods sold	$180,000
Inventory, January 1	30,000
Inventory, December 31	24,000
Accounts payable, January 1	10,000
Accounts payable, December 31	11,000

LO4
(Appendix 12A)

E12-9A. **Statement of Cash Flows (Direct Method)** Use the following information regarding the cash flows of Dixon Corporation to prepare a statement of cash flows using the direct method:

Cash balance, December 31	$ 9,000
Cash paid to employees and suppliers	158,000
Cash received from sale of land	42,000
Cash paid to acquire treasury stock	10,000
Cash balance, January 1	18,000
Cash received as interest	8,000
Cash paid as income taxes	9,000
Cash paid to purchase equipment	89,000
Cash received from customers	199,000
Cash received from issuing bonds payable	30,000
Cash paid as dividends	22,000

LO4
(Appendix 12A)

E12-10A. **Operating Cash Flows (Direct Method)** Refer to the information in Exercise E12-3A. Calculate the cash flow from operating activities using the direct method. Show a related cash flow for each revenue and expense.

LO4
(Appendix 12A)

E12-11A. **Investing and Financing Cash Flows** During the year, Paton Corporation's Long-Term Investments account (at cost) increased $20,000, the net result of purchasing stocks costing $85,000 and selling stocks costing $65,000 at a $7,000 loss. Also, the Bonds Payable account decreased by $35,000, the net result of issuing $100,000 of bonds at 102 and retiring bonds with a face value (and book value) of $135,000 at an $8,000 gain. What items and amounts will appear in the (a) cash flows from investing activities and the (b) cash flows from financing activities sections of Paton's statement of cash flows?

LO2, 4
(Appendix 12A)

EXERCISES—SET B

E12-1B. **Classification of Cash Flows** For each of the items below, indicate whether the cash flow item relates to an operating activity, an investing activity, or a financing activity:

    a. Cash loaned to borrowers
    b. Cash paid as interest on bonds payable
    c. Cash received from issuance of preferred stock
    d. Cash paid as state income taxes
    e. Cash received as dividends on stock investments
    f. Cash paid to acquire treasury stock
    g. Cash paid to acquire a franchise to distribute a product line

LO1

LO1   E12-2B.   Classification of Cash Flows For each of the items below, indicate whether it is (1) a cash flow from an operating activity, (2) a cash flow from an investing activity, (3) a cash flow from a financing activity, (4) a noncash investing and financing activity, or (5) none of the above:

a.   Received cash as interest earned on bond investment
b.   Received cash as refund from supplier
c.   Borrowed cash from bank on six-month note payable
d.   Exchanged, at a gain, stock held as an investment for a parcel of land
e.   Invested cash in a money market fund (cash may be easily withdrawn from the fund)
f.   Loaned cash to help finance the start of a new biotechnology firm

LO2, 3   E12-3B.   Cash Flow from Operating Activities (Indirect Method) The following information was obtained from Melville Company's comparative balance sheets:

	End of Year	Beginning of Year
Cash	$ 19,000	$ 9,000
Accounts receivable	50,000	35,000
Inventory	55,000	49,000
Prepaid rent	6,000	8,000
Long-term investments	21,000	32,000
Plant assets	140,000	106,000
Accumulated depreciation	(42,000)	(32,000)
Accounts payable	24,000	22,000
Income tax payable	4,000	6,000
Common stock	127,000	92,000
Retained earnings	106,000	91,000
Capital expenditures	15,200	

Assume that Melville Company's income statement showed depreciation expense of $10,000, a gain on sale of investments of $7,000, and a net income of $60,000. (a) Calculate the cash flow from operating activities using the indirect method and (b) compute Melville's operating-cash-flow-to-capital-expenditures ratio.

LO2   E12-4B.   Cash Flow from Operating Activities (Indirect Method) Zaire Company had a $26,000 net loss from operations. Depreciation expense for the year was $9,600, and a dividend of $2,000 was declared and paid. The balances of the current asset and current liability accounts at the beginning and end of the year are as follows:

	End	Beginning
Cash	$ 3,500	$ 7,000
Accounts receivable	16,000	27,000
Inventory	51,000	53,000
Prepaid expenses	5,000	9,000
Accounts payable	12,000	8,000
Accrued liabilities	6,000	7,600

Did Zaire Company's operating activities provide or use cash? Use the indirect method to determine your answer.

LO2   E12-5B.   Cash Flow from Operating Activities (Indirect Method) The Smith Company owns no plant assets and had the following income statement for the year:

Sales revenue		$1,140,000
Cost of goods sold	$770,000	
Wages expense	230,000	
Rent expense	65,000	
Insurance expense	47,000	1,112,000
Net income		$ 28,000

Additional information about the company includes:

	End of Year	Beginning of Year
Accounts receivable	$74,000	$49,000
Inventory.	70,000	74,000
Prepaid insurance.	5,000	8,000
Accounts payable	26,000	28,000
Wages payable	6,000	13,000

Use the preceding information to calculate the cash flow from operating activities using the indirect method.

E12-6B.   **Statement of Cash Flows (Indirect Method)** Use the following information regarding the Fremont Corporation to prepare a statement of cash flows using the indirect method:

LO2

Accounts payable increase.	$ 14,000
Accounts receivable increase.	7,000
Accrued liabilities decrease	5,000
Amortization expense.	31,000
Cash balance, January 1	21,000
Cash balance, December 31	141,000
Cash paid as dividends	41,000
Cash paid to purchase land	81,000
Cash paid to retire bonds payable at par	70,000
Cash received from issuance of common stock.	75,000
Cash received from sale of equipment.	17,000
Depreciation expense.	65,000
Gain on sale of equipment	12,000
Inventory decrease.	11,000
Net income	126,000
Prepaid expenses increase	3,000

E12-7B.   **Cash Flow Ratios** Morris Company reports the following amounts in its annual financial statements:

LO3

Cash flow from operating activities.	$75,000	Capital expenditures.	$ 47,500*
Cash flow from investing activities	(60,000)	Average current assets.	150,000
Cash flow from financing activities	(8,500)	Average current liabilities	90,000
Net income	37,500	Total assets.	225,000

* This amount is a cash outflow.

a.   Compute Morris' free cash flow.
b.   Compute Morris' operating-cash-flow-to-current-liabilities ratio.
c.   Compute Morris' operating-cash-flow-to-capital-expenditures ratio.

E12-8B.   **Operating Cash Flows (Direct Method)** Calculate the cash flow in each of the following cases:

LO4
(Appendix 12A)

a.   Cash paid for rent:

Rent expense	$62,000
Prepaid rent, January 1	10,000
Prepaid rent, December 31	6,000

b.   Cash received as interest:

Interest income.	$16,000
Interest receivable, January 1.	6,000
Interest receivable, December 31.	3,700

c.   Cash paid for merchandise purchased:

Cost of goods sold	$98,000
Inventory, January 1	19,000
Inventory, December 31	22,000
Accounts payable, January 1	11,000
Accounts payable, December 31	6,000

LO4
(Appendix 12A)

MBC

E12-9B. **Statement of Cash Flows (Direct Method)** Use the following information regarding the cash flows of Jack Corporation to prepare a statement of cash flows using the direct method:

Cash balance, December 31	$ 26,000
Cash paid to employees and suppliers	151,000
Cash received from sale of equipment	91,000
Cash paid to retire bonds payable	70,000
Cash balance, January 1	20,000
Cash paid as interest	4,000
Cash paid as income taxes	24,000
Cash paid to purchase patent	76,000
Cash received from customers	221,000
Cash received from issuing common stock	35,000
Cash paid as dividends	16,000

LO4
(Appendix 12A)

MBC

E12-10B. **Operating Cash Flows (Direct Method)** The Thurston Company's current year income statement contains the following data:

Sales revenue	$790,000
Cost of goods sold	550,000
Gross profit	$240,000

Thurston's comparative balance sheets show the following data (accounts payable relate to merchandise purchases):

	End of Year	Beginning of Year
Accounts receivable	$ 71,000	$61,000
Inventory	120,000	96,000
Prepaid expenses	3,000	10,000
Accounts payable	31,000	35,000

Compute Thurston's current-year cash received from customers and cash paid for merchandise purchased.

LO2, 4
(Appendix 12A)

MBC

E12-11B. **Investing and Financing Cash Flows** Refer to the information in Exercise 12-3B. During the year, Melville Company purchased plant assets for cash, sold investments for cash (the entire $7,000 gain developed during the year), and issued common stock for cash. The firm also declared and paid cash dividends. What items and amounts will appear in (a) the cash flow from investing activities and (b) the cash flow from financing activities sections of a statement of cash flows?

PROBLEMS—SET A

MBC

LO2, 3

P12-1A. **Statement of Cash Flows (Indirect Method)** The Artic Company's income statement and comparative balance sheets at December 31 of the current and the previous year are shown next:

ARTIC COMPANY Income Statement For the Year Ended December 31		
Sales revenue		$645,000
Cost of goods sold	$430,000	
Wages expense	91,000	
Insurance expense	12,000	
Depreciation expense	13,000	
Interest expense	15,000	
Income tax expense	29,000	590,000
Net income		$ 55,000

ARTIC COMPANY Balance Sheets		
	Dec. 31, Current Year	Dec. 31, Previous Year
Assets		
Cash.	$ 41,000	$ 8,000
Accounts receivable	41,000	32,000
Inventory.	90,000	65,000
Prepaid insurance.	5,000	7,000
Plant assets	219,000	202,000
Accumulated depreciation	(68,000)	(55,000)
Total assets.	$328,000	$259,000
Liabilities and Stockholders' Equity		
Accounts payable	$ 7,000	$ 10,000
Wages payable.	10,000	6,000
Income tax payable.	6,000	7,000
Bonds payable	141,000	87,000
Common stock	90,000	90,000
Retained earnings	74,000	59,000
Total liabilities and stockholders' equity	$328,000	$259,000

Cash dividends of $40,000 were declared and paid during the current year. Plant assets were purchased for cash, and bonds payable were issued for cash. Bond interest is paid semi-annually on June 30 and December 31. Accounts payable relate to merchandise purchases.

Required

a. Calculate the change in cash that occurred during the current year.
b. Prepare a statement of cash flows using the indirect method.
c. Compute the free cash flow.
d. Compute the operating-cash-flow-to-current-liabilities ratio.
e. Compute the operating-cash-flow-to-capital-expenditures ratio.

P12-2A. **Statement of Cash Flows (Indirect Method)** North Company's income statement and comparative balance sheets as of December 31 of the current and the previous year follow:

LO2

NORTH COMPANY Income Statement For the Year Ended December 31		
Sales revenue.		$770,000
Cost of goods sold	$550,000	
Wages expense	195,000	
Advertising expense.	31,000	
Depreciation expense.	24,000	
Interest expense.	20,000	
Gain on sale of land	(25,000)	795,000
Net loss.		$ (25,000)

NORTH COMPANY Balance Sheets	Dec. 31, Current Year	Dec. 31, Previous Year
Assets		
Cash	$ 80,000	$ 32,000
Accounts receivable	42,000	49,000
Inventory	107,000	115,000
Prepaid advertising	10,000	14,000
Plant assets	360,000	210,000
Accumulated depreciation	(80,000)	(56,000)
Total assets	$519,000	$364,000
Liabilities and Stockholders' Equity		
Accounts payable	$ 19,000	$ 25,000
Interest payable	6,000	—
Bonds payable	210,000	—
Common stock	245,000	245,000
Retained earnings	69,000	94,000
Treasury stock	(30,000)	—
Total liabilities and stockholders' equity	$519,000	$364,000

During the current year, North sold land for $70,000 cash that had originally cost $45,000. North also purchased equipment for cash, acquired treasury stock for cash, and issued bonds payable for cash. Accounts payable relate to merchandise purchases.

Required
a. Calculate the change in cash that occurred during the current year.
b. Prepare a statement of cash flows using the indirect method.

LO2   P12-3A.   Statement of Cash Flows (Indirect Method) The Pruitt Company's income statement and comparative balance sheets as of December 31 of the current and the previous year follow:

PRUITT COMPANY Income Statement For the Year Ended December 31		
Sales revenue		$770,000
Cost of goods sold	$450,000	
Wages and other operating expenses	195,000	
Depreciation expense	22,000	
Goodwill amortization expense	7,000	
Interest expense	5,000	
Income tax expense	36,000	
Loss on bond retirement	5,000	720,000
Net income		$ 50,000

PRUITT COMPANY Balance Sheets	Dec. 31, Current Year	Dec. 31, Previous Year
Assets		
Cash	$ 8,000	$ 19,000
Accounts receivable	43,000	28,000
Inventory	101,000	131,000
Prepaid expenses	12,000	11,000
Plant assets	360,000	334,000
Accumulated depreciation	(87,000)	(84,000)
Goodwill	43,000	50,000
Total assets	$480,000	$489,000

continued

continued from previous page

PRUITT COMPANY Balance Sheets	Dec. 31, Current Year	Dec. 31, Previous Year
Liabilities and Stockholders' Equity		
Accounts payable	$ 32,000	$ 28,000
Interest payable	3,000	7,000
Income tax payable.	6,000	8,000
Bonds payable	60,000	100,000
Common stock	252,000	248,000
Retained earnings	127,000	98,000
Total liabilities and stockholders' equity	$480,000	$489,000

During the year, the company sold for $15,000 cash old equipment that had cost $34,000 and had $19,000 accumulated depreciation. New equipment worth $60,000 was acquired in exchange for $60,000 of bonds payable. Bonds payable of $100,000 were retired for cash at a loss. A $21,000 cash dividend was declared and paid. All stock issuances were for cash.

Required
a.   Compute the change in cash that occurred in the current year.
b.   Prepare a statement of cash flows using the indirect method.

P12-4A.   Statement of Cash Flows (Indirect Method) The Sky Company's income statement and comparative balance sheets as of December 31 of the current and the previous year follow:

LO2

SKY COMPANY Income Statement For Year Ended December 31		
Sales revenue.		$800,000
Dividend income.		19,000
		819,000
Cost of goods sold	$440,000	
Wages and other operating expenses	130,000	
Depreciation expense.	39,000	
Patent amortization expense	7,000	
Interest expense	13,000	
Income tax expense	30,000	
Loss on sale of equipment	5,000	
Gain on sale of investments	(10,000)	654,000
Net income.		$165,000

SKY COMPANY Balance Sheets	Dec. 31, Current Year	Dec. 31, Previous Year
Assets		
Cash and cash equivalents	$ 63,000	$ 29,000
Accounts receivable	45,000	35,000
Inventory.	100,000	77,000
Prepaid expenses.	10,000	6,000
Long-term investments—available for sale.	—	50,000
Fair value adjustment to investments	—	7,000
Land	190,000	100,000
Buildings.	445,000	350,000
Accumulated depreciation—Buildings	(91,000)	(75,000)
Equipment	179,000	225,000
Accumulated depreciation—Equipment	(42,000)	(46,000)
Patents	50,000	32,000
Total assets.	$949,000	$790,000

continued

continued from previous page

SKY COMPANY Balance Sheets	Dec. 31, Current Year	Dec. 31, Previous Year
Liabilities and Stockholders' Equity		
Accounts payable	$ 21,000	$ 18,000
Interest payable	6,000	5,000
Income tax payable	8,000	12,000
Bonds payable	135,000	130,000
Preferred stock ($100 par value)	100,000	75,000
Common stock ($5 par value)	379,000	364,000
Paid-in-capital in excess of par value—Common	133,000	124,000
Retained earnings	167,000	55,000
Unrealized gain on investments	—	7,000
Total liabilities and stockholders' equity	$949,000	$790,000

During the year, the following transactions occurred:

1. Sold long-term investments costing $50,000 for $60,000 cash. Unrealized gains totaling $7,000 related to these investments had been recorded in earlier years. At year-end, the fair value adjustment and unrealized gain account balances were eliminated.
2. Purchased land for cash.
3. Capitalized an expenditure made to improve the building.
4. Sold equipment for $14,000 cash that originally cost $46,000 and had $27,000 accumulated depreciation.
5. Issued bonds payable at face value for cash.
6. Acquired a patent with a fair value of $25,000 by issuing 250 shares of preferred stock at par value.
7. Declared and paid a $53,000 cash dividend.
8. Issued 3,000 shares of common stock for cash at $8 per share.
9. Recorded depreciation of $16,000 on buildings and $23,000 on equipment.

Required

a. Calculate the change in cash and cash equivalents that occurred during the current year.
b. Prepare a statement of cash flows using the indirect method.

LO3   P12-5A.   Analyzing Cash Flow Ratios Pearce Enterprises reported the following information for the past year of operations:

Transaction	Free Cash Flow $250,000	Operating-Cash-Flow-to-Current-Liabilities Ratio 1.0 Times	Operating-Cash-Flow-to-Capital-Expenditures Ratio 3.0 Times
a. Recorded credit sales of $9,000			
b. Collected $4,000 owed from customers			
c. Purchased $28,000 of equipment on long-term credit			
d. Purchased $16,000 of equipment for cash			
e. Paid $10,000 of wages with cash			
f. Recorded utility bill of $1,750 that has not been paid			

For each transaction, indicate whether the ratio will (I) increase, (D) decrease, or (N) have no effect.

LO3, 4   P12-6A.   Statement of Cash Flows (Direct Method) Refer to the data given for the Artic Company in Problem P12-1A.
(Appendix 12A)

Required

a. Calculate the change in cash that occurred during the current year.
b. Prepare a statement of cash flows using the direct method.
c. Compute free cash flow.
d. Compute the operating-cash-flow-to-current-liabilities ratio.
e. Compute the operating-cash-flow-to-capital-expenditures ratio.

P12-7A. **Statement of Cash Flows (Direct Method)** Refer to the data given for the North Company in Problem P12-2A.

Required
a. Calculate the change in cash that occurred during the current year.
b. Prepare a statement of cash flows using the direct method.

P12-8A. **Statement of Cash Flows (Direct Method)** Refer to the data given for the Pruitt Company in Problem P12-3A.

Required
a. Compute the change in cash that occurred in the current year.
b. Prepare a statement of cash flows using the direct method. Use one cash outflow for "cash paid for wages and other operating expenses." Accounts payable relate to inventory purchases only.

P12-9A. **Statement of Cash Flows (Direct Method)** Refer to the data given for the Sky Company in Problem P12-4A.

Required
a. Calculate the change in cash that occurred in the current year.
b. Prepare a statement of cash flows using the direct method. Use one cash outflow for "cash paid for wages and other operating expenses." Accounts payable relate to inventory purchases only.

PROBLEMS—SET B

P12-1B. **Statement of Cash Flows (Indirect Method)** The Forrester Company's income statement and comparative balance sheets as of December 31 of the current and the previous year are shown below:

FORRESTER COMPANY Income Statement For the Year Ended December 31		
Sales revenue.		$660,000
Cost of goods sold	$376,000	
Wages expense	107,000	
Depreciation expense.	22,000	
Rent expense	28,000	
Income tax expense	24,000	557,000
Net income		$103,000

FORRESTER COMPANY Balance Sheets	Dec. 31, Current Year	Dec. 31, Previous Year
Assets		
Cash.	$ 58,000	$ 30,000
Accounts receivable	52,000	60,000
Inventory.	142,000	120,000
Prepaid rent	16,000	10,000
Plant assets	420,000	301,000
Accumulated depreciation	(127,000)	(105,000)
Total assets.	$561,000	$416,000
Liabilities and Stockholders' Equity		
Accounts payable	$ 29,000	$ 17,000
Wages payable.	14,000	9,000
Income tax payable.	7,000	8,000
Common stock	295,000	252,000
Paid-in-capital in excess of par value	72,000	58,000
Retained earnings	144,000	72,000
Total liabilities and stockholders' equity	$561,000	$416,000

Cash dividends of $31,000 were declared and paid during the current year. Plant assets were purchased for cash, and additional common stock was issued for cash. Accounts payable relate to merchandise purchases.

Required

a. Calculate the change in cash that occurred during the current year.
b. Prepare a statement of cash flows using the indirect method.
c. Compute free cash flow.
d. Compute the operating-cash-flow-to-current-liabilities ratio.
e. Compute the operating-cash-flows-to-capital-expenditures ratio.

LO2   P12-2B.   Statement of Cash Flows (Indirect Method) The Lowe Company's income statement and comparative balance sheets as of December 31 of the current and the previous year are presented below:

LOWE COMPANY Income Statement For the Year Ended December 31		
Sales revenue.		$925,000
Cost of goods sold	$490,000	
Wages expense	207,000	
Depreciation expense.	62,000	
Insurance expense.	17,000	
Interest expense.	12,000	
Income tax expense	57,000	
Gain on sale of equipment	(16,000)	829,000
Net income		$ 96,000

LOWE COMPANY Balance Sheets	Dec. 31, Current Year	Dec. 31, Previous Year
Assets		
Cash.	$ 25,000	$ 33,000
Accounts receivable	68,000	51,000
Inventory.	177,000	126,000
Prepaid insurance.	8,000	11,000
Plant assets	887,000	763,000
Accumulated depreciation	(191,000)	(175,000)
Total assets.	$974,000	$809,000
Liabilities and Stockholders' Equity		
Accounts payable	$ 37,000	$ 27,000
Interest payable	7,000	—
Income tax payable.	11,000	19,000
Bonds payable	145,000	80,000
Common stock	660,000	585,000
Retained earnings	166,000	98,000
Treasury stock	(52,000)	—
Total liabilities and stockholders' equity	$974,000	$809,000

During the year, Lowe Company sold equipment for $27,000 cash that originally cost $57,000 and had $46,000 accumulated depreciation. New equipment was purchased for cash. Bonds payable and common stock were issued for cash. Cash dividends of $28,000 were declared and paid. At the end of the year, shares of treasury stock were purchased for cash. Accounts payable relate to merchandise purchases.

Required

a. Compute the change in cash that occurred during the current year.
b. Prepare a statement of cash flows using the indirect method.

P12-3B. Statement of Cash Flows (Indirect Method) The Madison Company's income statement and comparative balance sheets as of December 31 of the current and the previous year follow:

LO2

MADISON COMPANY Income Statement For the Year Ended December 31		
Sales revenue.		$825,000
Cost of goods sold	$530,000	
Wages and other operating expenses	179,000	
Depreciation expense.	29,000	
Patent amortization expense	6,000	
Interest expense.	18,000	
Income tax expense	25,000	
Gain on exchange of land for patent.	(37,000)	750,000
Net income		$ 75,000

MADISON COMPANY Balance Sheets	Dec. 31, Current Year	Dec. 31, Previous Year
Assets		
Cash.	$ 67,000	$ 25,000
Accounts receivable	64,000	49,000
Inventory.	85,000	66,000
Land.	117,000	160,000
Building and equipment	441,000	353,000
Accumulated depreciation	(122,000)	(100,000)
Patent.	74,000	—
Total assets.	$726,000	$553,000
Liabilities and Stockholders' Equity		
Accounts payable	$ 36,000	$ 26,000
Interest payable	13,000	8,000
Income tax payable.	7,000	12,000
Bonds payable	190,000	75,000
Common stock	350,000	350,000
Retained earnings	130,000	82,000
Total liabilities and stockholders' equity	$726,000	$553,000

During the current year, $27,000 of cash dividends were declared and paid. A patent valued at $80,000 was obtained in exchange for land. Equipment that originally cost $20,000 and had $7,000 accumulated depreciation was sold for $13,000 cash. Bonds payable were sold for cash, and cash was used to pay for structural improvements to the building.

Required
a. Compute the change in cash that occurred during the current year.
b. Prepare a statement of cash flows using the indirect method.

P12-4B. Statement of Cash Flows (Indirect Method) The Geary Company's income statement and comparative balance sheets as of December 31 of the current and the previous year follow:

LO2

GEARY COMPANY Income Statement For the Year Ended December 31		
Service fees earned		$320,000
Dividend and interest income.		16,000
		$336,000
Wages and other operating expenses	$288,000	
Depreciation expense.	55,000	
Franchise amortization expense.	10,000	
Loss on sale of equipment	7,000	
Gain on sale of investments.	(17,000)	343,000
Net loss.		$ (7,000)

GEARY COMPANY Balance Sheets	Dec. 31, Current Year	Dec. 31, Previous Year
Assets		
Cash.	$ 21,000	$ 33,000
Accounts receivable	14,000	18,000
Interest receivable	—	4,000
Prepaid expenses.	16,000	10,000
Long-term investments—available for sale.	—	70,000
Fair value adjustment to investments	—	10,000
Plant assets	656,000	655,000
Accumulated depreciation	(237,000)	(185,000)
Franchise	91,000	29,000
Total assets.	$561,000	$644,000
Liabilities and Stockholders' Equity		
Accrued liabilities	$ 12,000	$ 14,000
Notes payable.	—	26,000
Common stock ($10 par value).	535,000	535,000
Retained earnings	34,000	59,000
Unrealized gain on investments	—	10,000
Treasury stock	(20,000)	—
Total liabilities and stockholders' equity	$561,000	$644,000

During the year, the following transactions occurred:

1. Sold equipment for $9,000 cash that originally cost $19,000 and had $3,000 accumulated depreciation.
2. Sold long-term investments that had cost $70,000 for $87,000 cash. Unrealized gains totaling $10,000 related to these investments had been recorded in earlier years. At year-end, the fair value adjustment and unrealized gain account balances were eliminated.
3. Paid cash to extend the company's exclusive franchise for another three years.
4. Paid off a note payable at the bank on January 1.
5. Declared and paid an $18,000 dividend.
6. Purchased treasury stock for cash.
7. Purchased land valued at $20,000.

Required

a. Compute the change in cash that occurred in the current year.
b. Prepare a statement of cash flows using the indirect method.

LO3   P12-5B.   Analyzing Cash Flow Ratios Meagan Enterprises reported the following information for the past year of operations:

Transaction	Free Cash Flow $400,000	Operating-Cash-Flow-to-Current-Liabilities Ratio 1.1 Times	Operating-Cash-Flow-to-Capital-Expenditures Ratio 5.0 Times
a. Recorded credit sales of $17,000			
b. Collected $6,000 owed from customers			
c. Purchased $50,000 of equipment on long-term credit			
d. Purchased $70,000 of equipment for cash			
e. Paid $17,000 of wages with cash			
f. Recorded utility bill of $14,750 that has not been paid			

For each transaction, indicate whether the ratio will (I) increase, (D) decrease, or (N) have no effect.

P12-6B. **Statement of Cash Flows (Direct Method)** Refer to the data given for the Forrester Company in Problem P12-1B.

LO3, 4
(Appendix 12A)

Required
- a. Compute the change in cash that occurred during the current year.
- b. Prepare a statement of cash flows using the direct method.
- c. Compute the free cash flow.
- d. Compute the operating-cash-flow-to-current-liabilities ratio.
- e. Compute the operating-cash-flow-to-capital-expenditures ratio.

P12-7B. **Statement of Cash Flows (Direct Method)** Refer to the data given for the Lowe Company in Problem P12-2B.

LO4
(Appendix 12A)

Required
- a. Compute the change in cash that occurred during the current year.
- b. Prepare a statement of cash flows using the direct method.

P12-8B. **Statement of Cash Flows (Direct Method)** Refer to the data given for the Madison Company in Problem P12-3B.

LO4
(Appendix 12A)

Required
- a. Compute the change in cash that occurred during the current year.
- b. Prepare a statement of cash flows using the direct method. Use one cash outflow for "cash paid for wages and other operating expenses." Accounts payable relate to inventory purchases only.

P12-9B. **Statement of Cash Flows (Direct Method)** Refer to the data given for the Geary Company in Problem P12-4B.

LO4
(Appendix 12A)

Required
- a. Compute the change in cash that occurred during the current year.
- b. Prepare a statement of cash flows using the direct method. Use one cash outflow for "cash paid for wages and other operating expenses."

SERIAL PROBLEM: KATE'S CARDS

(Note: This is a continuation of the Serial Problem: Kate's Cards from Chapter 1 through Chapter 11.)

SP12. Kate has just completed her first year running Kate's Cards. She has been preparing monthly income statements and balance sheets, so she knows that her company has been profitable and that there is cash in the bank. She has not, however, prepared a statement of cash flows. Kate provides you with the year-end income statement and balance sheet and asks that you prepare a statement of cash flows for Kate's Cards.

Additional information:

1. There were no disposals of equipment during the year.
2. Dividends in the amount of $1,300 were paid in cash during the year.
3. Prepaid expenses relate to operating expenses.

Required
- a. Prepare a statement of cash flows for Kate's Cards for the year ended August 31 using the indirect method. Hint: Since this was Kate's first year of operations, the beginning balance sheet account balances were zero.
- b. Prepare a statement of cash flows for Kate's Cards for the year ended August 31 using the direct method. (Appendix 12A)

KATE'S CARDS Income Statement Year Ended August 31	
Sales revenue	$185,000
Cost of goods sold	106,000
Gross profit	79,000
Operating expenses	
Wages	18,000
Consulting	11,850
Insurance	1,200
Utilities	2,400
Rent	14,400
Depreciation	3,250
Total operating expenses	51,100
Income from operations	27,900
Interest expense	900
Income before income tax	27,000
Income tax expense	5,400
Net income	$ 21,600

KATE'S CARDS Balance Sheet As of August 31	
Assets	
Current assets	
Cash	$17,400
Accounts receivable	11,000
Inventory	16,000
Prepaid insurance	1,000
Total current assets	45,400
Equipment	17,500
Accumulated depreciation	(3,250)
Total assets	$59,650
Liabilities	
Current liabilities	
Accounts payable	$ 6,200
Unearned revenue	1,250
Other current liabilities	1,900
Total current liabilities	9,350
Note payable	15,000
Total liabilities	24,350
Stockholders' equity	
Common stock	500
Additional paid-in-capital	9,500
Preferred stock	5,000
Retained earnings	20,300
Total stockholders' equity	35,300
Total liabilities and stockholders' equity	$59,650

EXTENDING YOUR KNOWLEDGE

REPORTING AND ANALYSIS

COLUMBIA
SPORTSWEAR
COMPANY

EYK12-1. Financial Reporting Problem: Columbia Sportswear Company The financial statements for the **Columbia Sportswear Company** can be found in Appendix A at the end of this book.

Required

Answer the following questions:

a. How much did Columbia Sportswear's cash and cash equivalents increase in 2020?

b. What was the largest source of cash and cash equivalents in 2020?

c. What was the single largest use of cash and cash equivalents in 2020?

d. How much dividends were paid in 2020?

e. Why do depreciation and amortization, both noncash items, appear on Columbia's statement of cash flows?

EYK12-2. **Comparative Analysis Problem: Columbia Sportswear Company vs Under Armour, Inc.** The financial statements for the Columbia Sportswear Company can be found in Appendix A at the end of this book, and the financial statements of Under Armour, Inc., can be found in Appendix B. (The complete annual report is available on this book's website.)

COLUMBIA
SPORTSWEAR
COMPANY

UNDER ARMOUR, INC.

Required

Answer the following questions:

a. Compute the free cash flow in 2020 for both Columbia Sportswear and Under Armour, Inc.

b. Compute the operating cash flows to capital expenditures for both Columbia Sportswear and Under Armour, Inc.

c. Comment on the ability of each company to finance its capital expenditures.

EYK12-3. **Business Decision Problem** Recently hired as assistant controller for Finite, Inc., you are sitting next to the controller as she responds to questions at the annual stockholders' meeting. The firm's financial statements contain a statement of cash flows prepared using the indirect method. A stockholder raises his hand.

Stockholder: "I notice that depreciation expense is shown as an addition in the calculation of the cash flow from operating activities."

Controller: "That's correct."

Stockholder: "What depreciation method do you use?"

Controller: "We use the straight-line method for all plant assets."

Stockholder: "Well, why don't you switch to an accelerated depreciation method, such as double-declining balance, increase the annual depreciation amount, and thus increase the cash flow from operating activities?"

The controller pauses, turns to you, and replies, "My assistant will answer your question."

Required

Prepare an answer to the stockholder's question

EYK12-4. **Financial Analysis Problem** **Parker Hannifin Corporation**, headquartered in Cleveland, Ohio, manufactures motion control and fluid system components for a variety of industrial users. The firm's financial statements contain the following data. (Year 3 is the most recent year; dollar amounts are in thousands.)

PARKER HANNIFIN
CORPORATION

	Year 3	Year 2	Year 1
Current assets at year-end.	$1,018,354	$1,056,443	$1,055,776
Current liabilities at year-end	504,444	468,254	358,729
Current liabilities at beginning of year	468,254	358,729	345,594
Cash provided by operating activities.	259,204	229,382	235,186
Capital expenditures.	99,914	91,484	84,955

a. Calculate Parker Hannifin's current ratio (current assets/current liabilities) for Years 1, 2, and 3.

b. Calculate Parker Hannifin's operating-cash-flow-to-current-liabilities ratio for Years 1, 2, and 3.

c. Comment on the three-year trend in Parker Hannifin's current ratio and operating-cash-flow-to-current-liabilities ratio. Do the trends in these two ratios reinforce each other or contradict each other as indicators of Parker Hannifin's ability to pay its current liabilities?

d. Calculate Parker Hannifin's operating-cash-flow-to-capital-expenditures ratio for Years 1, 2, and 3. Comment on the strength of this ratio over the three-year period.

CRITICAL THINKING

GENERAL MILLS, INC.

EYK12-5. **Accounting Research Problem: General Mills, Inc.** The fiscal year 2020 annual report of General Mills, Inc., is available on this book's website.

Required

a. Refer to Note 2. How does General Mills define its cash equivalents?
b. What method does General Mills use to report its cash provided by operating activities?
c. What is the change in cash and cash equivalents experienced by General Mills during fiscal 2020? What is the amount of cash and cash equivalents as of May 31, 2020?
d. What is General Mills' operating-cash-flow-to-capital-expenditures ratio for fiscal year 2020?
e. Calculate General Mills' 2020 operating-cash-flow-to-current-liabilities ratio.

EYK12-6. **Accounting Communication Activity** Susan Henderson, the vice president of marketing, was told by the CEO that she needs to understand the numbers because the company's existence depends on making money. It has been a long time since Susan took a class in accounting. She recalls that companies report net income and cash flows in two separate statements. She feels pretty comfortable with the income statement but is somewhat lost looking at the statement of cash flows. She asks you to help explain this statement.

Required

Write a brief memo to Susan explaining the form and content of the statement of cash flows, along with a short discussion of how to analyze the statement.

EYK12-7. **Accounting Ethics Case** Due to an economic recession, Anton Corporation faces severe cash flow problems. Management forecasts that payments to some suppliers will have to be delayed for several months. Jay Newton, controller, has asked his staff for suggestions on selecting the suppliers for which payments will be delayed.

"That's a fairly easy decision," observes Tim Haslem. "Some suppliers charge interest if our payment is late, but others do not. We should pay those suppliers that charge interest and delay payments to the ones that do not charge interest. If we do this, the savings in interest charges will be quite substantial."

"I disagree," states Tara Wirth. "That position is too 'bottom line' oriented. It's not fair to delay payments only to suppliers who don't charge interest for late payments. Most suppliers in that category are ones we have dealt with for years; selecting these suppliers would be taking dvantage of the excellent relationships we have developed over the years. The fair thing to do is to make pro-rata payments to each supplier."

"Well, making pro-rata payments to each supplier means that *all* our suppliers will be upset because no one receives full payment," comments Sue Myling. "I believe it is most important to maintain good relations with our long-term suppliers; we should pay them currently and delay payments to our newer suppliers. The interest costs we end up paying these newer suppliers are the price we must pay to keep our long-term relationships solid."

Required

Which suppliers should Jay Newton select for delayed payments? Discuss.

THE HOME DEPOT, INC.

EYK12-8. **Environmental, Social, and Governance Problem** The ESG highlighted in this chapter (see page 12-17) mentions that **Home Depot** believes in giving back. One of the ways the company has done this is through its Team Depot program of employee volunteerism. Under this program, Home Depot employees volunteer their own time to work together on projects that benefit communities in which the company does business. Each year the program provides millions of hours of employee volunteerism.

Do a computer search and report on Team Depot's activities.

EYK12-9. **Forensic Accounting Problem** Cash larceny involves the fraudulent stealing of an employer's cash. These schemes often target the company's bank deposits. The fraudster steals the money after the deposit has been prepared, but before the deposit is taken to the bank. Most often these schemes involve a deficiency in the internal control system where segregation of duties is not present. The perpetrator is often in charge of recording receipts, preparing the deposit, delivering the deposit to the bank, and verifying the receipted deposit slip. Without proper segregation of duties, the fraudster is able to cover up the theft.

In addition to segregation of duties, what internal control procedures might help deter and detect cash larceny?

EYK12-10. Working with the Takeaways For the fiscal year ended January 31, 2021, Home Depot reports (in millions) cash provided by operating activities of $18,839. For the same period, average current liabilities were reported to be $17,545, and annual capital expenditures were $2,463. Calculate the free cash flow, the operating-cash-flow-to-current-liabities ratio, and the operating-cash-flow-to-capital-expenditures ratio for Home Depot and comment on the results.

EYK12-11. Analyzing IFRS Financial Statements The 2020 financial statements of LVMH Moet Hennessey-Louis Vuitton S.A. are presented in Appendix C at the end of this book. LVMH is a Paris-based holding company and one of the world's largest and best-known luxury goods companies. As a member of the European Union, French companies are required to prepare their consolidated (group) financial statements using International Financial Reporting Standards (IFRS). After reviewing LVMH's consolidated financial statements, calculate LVMH's (a) free cash flow, (b) operating-cash-flow-to-current-liabilities ratio (use the year-end current liabilities instead of the average current liabilities), and (c) operating-cash-flow-to-capital-expenditures ratio for 2019 and 2020. What do the ratio results reveal about LVMH? *Hint:* Capital expenditures are classified as "Operating investments" on LVMH Consolidated cash flow statement.

ANSWERS TO SELF-STUDY QUESTIONS:

1. a   2. c   3. d   4. d   5. c   6. b   7. d   8. d   9. c   10. b   11. c   12. a

YOUR TURN! SOLUTIONS

Solution 12.1

1. Operating
2. Investing
3. Operating
4. Investing
5. Financing
6. Financing
7. Operating
8. Financing
9. Investing

Solution 12.2

HUSKY COMPANY Statement of Cash Flows For the Year Ended December 31		
Cash Flow from Operating Activities		
Net income	$112,000	
Add (deduct) items to convert net income to cash basis		
Depreciation	34,000	
Accounts receivable increase.	(18,000)	
Inventory increase	(60,000)	
Prepaid insurance decrease.	4,000	
Accounts payable decrease	(6,000)	
Wages payable increase.	6,000	
Income tax payable decrease.	(2,000)	
Cash provided by operating activities.		$ 70,000
Cash Flow from Investing Activities		
Purchase of plant assets		(110,000)
Cash Flow from Financing Activities		
Issuance of bonds payable.	110,000	
Payment of dividends	(58,000)	
Cash provided by financing activities		52,000
Net increase in cash.		12,000
Cash at beginning of year.		10,000
Cash at end of year		$ 22,000

Solution 12.3

Free cash flow: $40,000 – $12,500 = $27,500

Operating-cash-flow-to-current-liabilities-ratio: $40,000/$30,000 = 1.33

Operating-cash-flow-to-capital-expenditures-ratio: $40,000/$12,500 = 3.20

Solution 12A.1

Supporting Calculations:

Cash received from customers:

$1,270,000 Sales revenue – $18,000 Accounts receivable increase = $1,252,000

Cash paid for merchandise purchased:

$860,000 Cost of goods sold + $60,000 Inventory increase + $6,000 Accounts payable decrease = $926,000

Cash paid to employees:

$172,000 Wages expense – $6,000 Wages payable increase = $166,000

Cash paid for insurance:

$16,000 Insurance expense – $4,000 Prepaid insurance decrease = $12,000

Cash paid for interest:

Equal to the $18,000 balance in interest expense

Cash paid for income taxes:

$58,000 Income tax expense + $2,000 Income tax payable decrease = $60,000

Purchase of plant assets:

$500,000 Ending plant assets – $390,000 Beginning plant assets = $110,000

Issuance of bonds payable:

$260,000 Ending bonds payable – $150,000 Beginning bonds payable = $110,000

Payment of dividends

$58,000 given in problem data

Other Analysis

Accumulated depreciation increased by $34,000, which is the amount of depreciation expense.

Common stock account balance did not change.

Retained earnings increased by $54,000, which is the difference between the net income of $112,000 and the dividends declared of $58,000.

HUSKY COMPANY Statement of Cash Flows (Direct Method) For the Year Ended December 31		
Cash Flow from Operating Activities		
Cash received from customers		$1,252,000
Cash paid for merchandise purchased	$(926,000)	
Cash paid to employees	(166,000)	
Cash paid for insurance	(12,000)	
Cash paid for interest	(18,000)	
Cash paid for income taxes.	(60,000)	(1,182,000)
Cash provided by operating activities		70,000
Cash Flow from Investing Activities		
Purchase of plant assets.		(110,000)
Cash Flow from Financing Activities		
Issuance of bonds payable	110,000	
Payment of dividends	(58,000)	
Cash provided by financing activities		52,000
Net increase in cash.		12,000
Cash at beginning of year.		10,000
Cash at end of year		$ 22,000

Chapter 13
Analysis and Interpretation of Financial Statements

Road Map

LO	Learning Objective	Page	eLecture	Guided Example	Assignments
LO1	**Identify persistent earnings and discuss the content and format of the income statement.**	13-3	E13-1	YT13.1	SS1, SE11, E1A, E1B, P1A, P3A, P1B, P3B
LO2	**Identify the sources of financial information used by investment professionals and explain horizontal financial statement analysis.**	13-6	E13-2	YT13.2	SS10, SE12, E3A, E3B, P4A, P6A, P10A, P4B, P6B, P10B
LO3	**Explain vertical financial statement analysis.**	13-12	E13-3	YT13.3	SS2, SE13, E4A, E4B, P6A, P6B
LO4	**Define and discuss financial ratios for analyzing a firm.**	13-13	E13-4	YT13.4	SS3, SS4, SS5, SS6, SS7, SS8, SS9, SE1, SE2, SE3, SE4, SE5, SE6, SE7, SE8, SE9, SE10, E2A, E5A, E6A, E7A, E8A, E9A, E2B, E5B, E6B, E7B, E8B, P2A, P3A, P5A, P6A, P7A, P8A, P9A, P2B, P3B, P5B, P6B, P7B, P8B, P9B
LO5	**Discuss the limitations of financial statement analysis.**	13-27	E13-5	YT13.5	SS11, SE14, E10A, E10B
LO6	**Appendix 13A: Describe financial statement disclosures.**	13-29	E13-6	YT13.6	SS12, SE15, E11A, E11B

The **Procter & Gamble Company (P&G)** is one of America's oldest companies, dating back to 1837 when candle maker William Procter and soap maker James Gamble combined their small businesses. Over the next few decades the company introduced such well-known products as Ivory soap and Crisco shortening that are still sold today.

P&G has continued to grow, with annual sales of over $70 billion. Not all of the company's growth, however, is the result of internally developed products like Crest toothpaste, Head & Shoulders shampoo, and Pampers diapers. A significant part of P&G's growth has come from mergers and acquisitions. P&G's largest acquisition occurred in 2005 when it acquired Gillette for $57 billion.

Acquisitions, such as the one involving Gillette, are complex transactions. Perhaps the hardest part of any merger or acquisition is determining the appropriate price to pay. Many factors go into such an analysis, but it often comes down to how much a company like Gillette will be able to add to P&G's future persistent earnings.

In this chapter we explore some of the ways that investment professionals determine how much a company is worth. The process involves analyzing a company's persistent earnings potential as well as the various risks associated with a company's day-to-day operations.

PAST

In Chapter 12, we examined the statement of cash flows.

PRESENT

In this chapter we complete our study of financial accounting by looking at the analysis and interpretation of financial statements.

> ## ANALYSIS AND INTERPRETATION OF FINANCIAL STATEMENTS
>
> ### Income Statement and Persistent Earnings
>
> - Persistent earnings
> - Discontinued operations
> - Changes in accounting principles
> - Comprehensive income
>
> ### Analytical Techniques
>
> - Sources of information
> - Horizontal analysis
> - Trend analysis
> - Vertical analysis
> - Ratio analysis
> - Limitations of financial analysis
> - Financial statement disclosures (Appendix 13A)

PERSISTENT EARNINGS AND THE INCOME STATEMENT

LO1 **Identify** persistent earnings and **discuss** the content and format of the income statement.

eLecture

MBC

Net income is the "bottom line" measure of firm performance. It is a measure that depends on such accrual accounting procedures as the revenue recognition and expense matching policies selected by a firm's management. Generally accepted accounting principles have historically emphasized the importance of accounting earnings because past accounting earnings have been found to be a good predictor of a firm's future operating cash flow. Modern valuation theory tells us that the economic value of a company is the present value of the company's future operating cash flows. Thus, an important role for accounting numbers is their use by investment professionals when assessing the economic value of a company.

One of the determinants of the ability of historical accounting earnings to predict future cash flow is the extent to which earnings recur over time, or what is known as *earnings persistence*. Since the value of a share of common stock today is a function of a firm's ability to consistently generate earnings year in and year out, the persistence (or sustainability) of a company's operating earnings is closely linked to its economic value. **Persistent earnings** are also sometimes referred to as *sustainable earnings* or *permanent earnings*, whereas non-persistent earnings are often referred to as **transitory earnings**. In general, transitory earnings include such single-period events as special items, restructuring charges, changes in accounting principle, and discontinued operations.

Companies are required under GAAP to classify income statement accounts in a manner that aids a financial statement user in assessing persistent earnings, and hence in assessing a firm's economic value. In Chapter 4, we introduced the multiple-step or multi-step income statement. **Exhibit 13-1** illustrates the basic format of the multi-step income statement. While a **single-step income statement** derives the net income of a business in one step by subtracting total expenses from total revenues, a **multiple-step income statement** derives one or more intermediate performance measures before net income is reported. Examples of such intermediate performance measures are gross profit, net operating income, and net income from continuing operations before taxes.

The income statement is organized in such a way that items with greater persistence are reported higher up in the income statement, whereas items considered more transitory are reported further down in the statement. Thus, accounts representing financial events that are both usual and frequent are reported first. Usual refers to an item that is central to a firm's core operations, whereas **unusual items** are unrelated, or only incidentally related, to core operations. Frequent refers to how often an item is expected to occur, with infrequent items not reasonably expected to recur in the foreseeable future.

EXHIBIT 13-1	The Multi-Step Income Statement

KALI COMPANY
Income Statement
For Year Ended December 31

Sales revenue		$ 500	Usual and frequent
Cost of goods sold		200	Usual and frequent
Gross profit		300	
Operating expenses		250	Usual and frequent
Net operating income		50	
Other income and expense			
Interest income	25		**Unusual**
Interest expense	(35)		**Unusual**
Gain on sale of equipment	15	5	**Unusual**
Net income from continuing operations before tax		55	
Income tax expense		20	Usual and frequent
Net income from continuing operations		35	
Gain from operations of discontinued division (net of tax)	15		**Infrequent**
Loss on disposal of discontinued division (net of tax)	(5)	10	**Infrequent**
Net income		$ 45	
Earning per share (100 shares outstanding)		$0.45	

Usual and frequent items typically consist of such income statement accounts as sales revenue, cost of goods sold, and other operating expenses. Just below these usual and frequent items are items that are either unusual or infrequent, but not both. Income statement accounts such as interest expense, interest income, and gains on sales of equipment are often frequently recurring items; however, they are not considered part of a firm's central operations and therefore are considered unusual. Examples of infrequent items include such financial events as asset write-downs and restructuring charges. These items are not expected to occur regularly, but are not considered unusual in nature.

Each of the above items is reported as part of a company's continuing operations and is shown before any income tax expense. GAAP, however, requires certain single-period items, or one-time events, to be reported on an after-tax basis. For example, income from discontinued operations, or the part of a business that is being shuttered or sold, are shown net of the financial effect of any applicable income taxes. Reporting discontinued operations on a net-of-tax basis allows the income tax expense reported on the income statement to reflect only the income taxes associated with a firm's continuing operations. Segregating discontinued operations from the results of continuing operations also makes it easier for financial statement users to identify a company's persistent earnings.

Most believe that the income statement is more useful when certain types of transactions and events are reported in separate sections. The creation of sections within the income statement, however, complicates the reporting of a company's income tax expense. Items affecting the overall amount of income tax expense may appear in more than one section. If this is the case, accountants allocate a company's total income tax expense among those sections of the income statement in which the items affecting the tax expense appear.

Regardless of the format used for the income statement, companies are required to report net income on a per common share basis, called **earnings per share (EPS)**, on the income statement immediately following net income.

Discontinued Operations

© Shutterstock.com

Discontinued Operations

When a company sells, abandons, or otherwise disposes of a segment of its operations, a **discontinued operations** section of the income statement reports information about the discontinued business segment. The discontinued operations section presents two categories of information:

1. The income or loss from the segment's operations for the portion of the year before its discontinuance.

2. Any gain or loss from the disposal of the segment.

This section is reported on the income statement immediately after information regarding a firm's continuing operations.

To illustrate the reporting of discontinued operations, assume that on July 1, Kali Company, a diversified manufacturing company, sold its pet food division. **Exhibit 13-1** illustrates the income statement for Kali Company, including information regarding its pet food division in the discontinued operations section. From January 1 through June 30, Kali's pet food division operated at a profit, net of income taxes, of $15. The loss, net of income taxes, from the sale of the division's assets and liabilities was $5. Note that when there is a discontinued operations section, the difference between a firm's continuing sales revenues and expenses is labeled "net income from continuing operations."

Changes in Accounting Principles

Occasionally a company may implement a **change in accounting principle**—that is, a switch from one generally accepted method to another. For example, a company may change its inventory costing method, such as from FIFO to weighted-average cost. These changes are permitted when a business can demonstrate that the reported financial results under the new accounting method are preferable to the results reported under the replaced method.

Changing accounting principles can present a problem for financial statement users analyzing a company's performance over time because different accounting principles are likely to produce different financial statement results. Consequently, financial statements of prior years, issued in comparative form with current year financial statements, must also be presented using the new accounting principles as if the new method had been used all along.

Comprehensive Income

Most items that generate wealth changes in a business are required to be shown on the income statement. There are, however, a few items that do not appear as part of the regular content of the income statement and instead are classified under a category labeled **comprehensive income**. A business's comprehensive income includes, among other items, its net income, any changes in the market value of certain marketable securities (see Appendix D at the end of this book), and any unrealized gains and losses from translating foreign currency denominated financial statements into U.S. dollars. This latter topic is covered in more advanced accounting textbooks.

Companies are given some flexibility as to how they report their comprehensive income. They are allowed to utilize two alternative formats under GAAP: (1) appending comprehensive income to the bottom of the income statement; or (2) creating a separate statement of comprehensive income. In addition to comprehensive income for the current period, GAAP requires a company to report accumulated other comprehensive income as part of stockholders' equity on the balance sheet. Accumulated other comprehensive income serves the same role for comprehensive income as retained earnings serves for regular net income—it reports the cumulative amount of comprehensive income as of the balance sheet date.

ENVIRONMENTAL, SOCIAL, AND GOVERNANCE	Pampers and UNICEF

Maternal and neonatal tetanus is a disease that kills 59,000 people annually. **P&G**, through its Pampers product, has teamed up with UNICEF to fight this completely preventable disease. For every purchase of a pack of Pampers, P&G donates one dose of the tetanus vaccine. Pampers' funding has helped protect 100 million women and their babies against maternal and neonatal tetanus (MNT) and has helped eliminate this disease in Myanmar and Uganda. P&G and UNICEF are committed to the elimination of MNT from the face of the earth.

P&G and UNICEF have gone even further in their teamwork. P&G offers its employees in Europe, the Middle East, and Africa a three-month paid sabbatical to work with UNICEF. The program is aimed at employees who have always wanted to perform humanitarian work but have lacked the financial resources to do so.

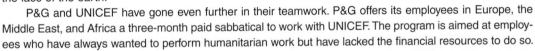

Conner Company, a retail company, entered into the following transactions during the year:

1. Sold merchandise to customers
2. Settled a major lawsuit
3. Wrote down the book value of a closed warehouse
4. Paid employee wages
5. Disposed of a line of discount stores
6. Paid income taxes

Required

Classify each of the above items as either persistent earnings or transitory earnings.

YOUR TURN! 13.1

GuidedExample

MBC

The solution is on page 13-63.

SOURCES OF INFORMATION

Except for closely held companies, businesses publish their financial statements at least annually. Most large companies also issue quarterly financial data. Normally, annual financial statements are attested to by a certified public accountant, and investment professionals carefully review the independent accountant's opinion to assess the reliability of the published financial data. Companies listed on stock exchanges must also submit financial statements, called a 10-K for the annual report and 10-Q for the quarterly report, to the U.S. Securities and Exchange Commission (SEC). These statements are available to any interested party and generally contain greater detail than the company's annual or quarterly reports.

Investment professionals may also want to compare the performance of a particular firm with that of the other firms in the same industry. Data on industry norms, median financial ratios by industry, and other relationships are available from such data collection services as Dun & Bradstreet, Moody's, and Standard and Poor's. In addition, some brokerage firms compile industry norms and financial ratios from their own computer databases.

LO2 Identify the sources of financial information used by investment professionals and **explain** horizontal financial statement analysis.

eLecture

MBC

ACCOUNTING IN PRACTICE   **SEC EDGAR Database**

An example of a financial database is **EDGAR**, the Electronic Data Gathering, Analysis, and Retrieval system, maintained by the U.S. SEC (www.sec.gov/edgar.shtml). This computer database aids financial statement analysis by performing automated data collection, validation, indexing, acceptance, and forwarding of submissions by companies and others who are required by law to file forms with the U.S. Securities and Exchange Commission. The primary intent of the SEC in creating EDGAR was to increase the efficiency of the securities market for the benefit of investors, corporations, and the economy by accelerating the receipt, acceptance, and dissemination of corporate information filed with the agency.

Analytical Techniques

The dollar amounts of net income, sales revenue, total assets, and other key data are usually not meaningful when analyzed in isolation. For example, knowing that a company's annual net income is $1 million is of little informational value unless the amount of the income can be related to other factors. A $1 million profit might represent excellent performance for a company with less than $10 million in invested capital. On the other hand, $1 million in net income would be considered meager for a firm that had several hundred million dollars in invested capital. Thus, significant information can be derived by examining the relation between two or more accounting variables, such as net income and total assets, net income and sales revenue, or net income and stockholders' equity. To describe these relations clearly and to make comparisons easy, they are often expressed in terms of ratios or percentages.

For example, we might express the relation between $15,000 in net income and $150,000 in sales revenue as a ten percent ($15,000/$150,000) rate of return on sales. To describe the relation between sales revenue of $150,000 and inventory of $20,000, we might use a ratio or a percentage; ($150,000/$20,000) may be expressed as 7.5, 7.5:1, or 750 percent.

Changes in selected financial statement items compared in successive financial statements are often expressed as percentages. For example, if a firm's net income increased from $40,000 last year to $48,000 this year, the $8,000 increase relative to last year (the base year) is expressed as a 20 percent increase ($8,000/$40,000) in net income. To express a dollar increase or decrease as a percentage, however, the base year amount must be a positive figure. If, for example, a firm had a net loss of $4,000 in one year and net income of $20,000 in the next, the $24,000 increase cannot be meaningfully expressed as a percentage. Similarly, if a firm reported no debt securities in last year's balance sheet but showed $15,000 of such securities in this year's statement, the $15,000 increase cannot be expressed as a meaningful percentage.

When evaluating a firm's financial statements for two or more years, analysts often use **horizontal analysis**. Horizontal analysis is a technique that can be useful for detecting an improvement or deterioration in a firm's performance and for spotting trends regarding a firm's financial well-being. The term **vertical analysis** is used to describe the analysis of a single year of financial data.

HORIZONTAL ANALYSIS

The type of horizontal analysis most often used by investment professionals is **comparative financial statement analysis** for two or more years, showing dollar or percentage changes for important financial statement items and totals. Dollar increases and decreases are divided by data from the base year to obtain percentage changes. To illustrate, the 2020 and 2019 financial statements of Procter & Gamble (P&G) are presented in **Exhibits 13-2**, **13-3**, and **13-4**. We will use the data in these statements throughout this chapter to illustrate various analytical techniques.

| EXHIBIT 13-2 | Procter & Gamble Income Statement |

THE PROCTER & GAMBLE COMPANY
Consolidated Income Statements

(in millions)	Year Ended 2020	Common-Size	Year Ended 2019	Common-Size	$ Change	% Change
Net sales.	$70,950	100.0%	$67,684	100.0%	$ 3,266	4.8 %
Cost of goods sold	35,250	49.7%	34,768	51.4%	482	1.4 %
Gross profit.	35,700	50.3%	32,916	48.6%	2,784	8.5 %
Selling, general, and administrative expense.	19,994	28.2%	27,429	40.5%	(7,435)	(27.1)%
Operating income	15,706	22.1%	5,487	8.1%	10,219	186.2 %
Interest expense.	465	0.7%	509	0.8%	(44)	(8.6)%
Other non-operating income (expense)	593	0.8%	1,091	1.6%	(498)	(45.6)%
Earnings from continuing operations before taxes	15,834	22.3%	6,069	9.0%	9,765	160.9 %
Income taxes on continuing operations.	2,731	3.8%	2,103	3.1%	628	29.9 %
Net earnings from continuing operations.	13,103	18.5%	3,966	5.9%	9,137	230.4 %
Net earnings attributable to noncontrolling interests.	76	0.1%	69	0.1%	7	10.1 %
Net earnings.	13,027	18.4%	3,897	5.8%	9,130	234.3 %
Earnings per share	5.13		1.45			
Dividends per share	3.03		2.90			

When analyzing financial statements, the investment professional is likely to focus his or her immediate attention on those financial statement items or percentages that are significant in amount. Although percentage changes are helpful in identifying significant items, they can sometimes be misleading. An unusually large percentage change may occur simply because the dollar amount of the base year is small. For example, P&G had a decrease in other non-operating income of $498, from $1,091 in 2019 to $593 in 2020 (**Exhibit 13-2**). This represents a decrease of 45.6 percent, yet the dollar amount of this line item is quite small and insignificant relative to the other reported dollar amounts on P&G's income statement. The financial statement user's attention should be directed first to changes in key financial statement totals: sales revenue, operating income, net income, total assets, total liabilities, and so on. Next, the changes in significant individual items, such as accounts receivable, inventory, and property, plant, and equipment should be examined.

P&G's total assets increased by 4.9 percent from 2019 to 2020 (**Exhibit 13-3**), consistent with an increase in net sales of 4.8 percent over the same time period (**Exhibit 13-2**). (Recall from Chapter 5 that net sales equals gross sales revenue less any sales returns and allowances and sales discounts.) P&G did report a very favorable 234.3 percent increase in net earnings from 2019 to 2020. This change appears to be mostly the result of cost control reflected in a large decrease of $7,435 million in selling, general, and administrative expense.

EXHIBIT 13-3	Procter & Gamble Balance Sheet					

THE PROCTER & GAMBLE COMPANY
Consolidated Balance Sheets

(in millions)	2020	Common-Size	2019	Common-Size	$ Change	% Change
Assets						
Current assets						
Cash and cash equivalents................	$ 16,181	13.4 %	$ 4,239	3.7 %	$11,942	281.7 %
Short-term investments...................			6,048	5.3 %	(6,048)	(100.0)%
Accounts receivable	4,178	3.5 %	4,951	4.3 %	(773)	(15.6)%
Inventories	5,498	4.6 %	5,017	4.4 %	481	9.6 %
Other current assets....................	2,130	1.8 %	2,218	1.9 %	(88)	(4.0)%
Total current assets...................	27,987	23.2 %	22,473	19.5 %	5,514	24.5 %
Property, plant, and equipment, net	20,692	17.1 %	21,271	18.5 %	(579)	(2.7)%
Intangible assets........................	63,693	52.8 %	64,488	56.0 %	(795)	(1.2)%
Other noncurrent assets..................	8,328	6.9 %	6,863	6.0 %	1,465	21.3 %
Total assets	$120,700	100.0 %	$115,095	100.0 %	$ 5,605	4.9 %
Liabilities and Stockholders' Equity						
Current liabilities						
Accounts payable	$ 12,071	10.0 %	$ 11,260	9.8 %	$ 811	7.2 %
Other current liabilities	20,905	17.3 %	18,751	16.3 %	2,154	11.5 %
Total current liabilities	32,976	27.3 %	30,011	26.1 %	2,965	9.9 %
Long-term debt........................	23,537	19.5 %	20,395	17.7 %	3,142	15.4 %
Other noncurrent liabilities	17,309	14.3 %	17,110	14.9 %	199	1.2 %
Total liabilities	73,822	61.2 %	67,516	58.7 %	6,306	9.3 %
Preferred stock.......................	897	0.7 %	928	0.8 %	(31)	(3.3)%
Common stock	4,009	3.3 %	4,009	3.5 %	—	0.0 %
Additional paid-in capital.................	64,194	53.2 %	63,827	55.5 %	367	0.6 %
Treasury stock	(105,573)	(87.5)%	(100,406)	(87.2)%	(5,167)	5.1 %
Retained earnings	100,239	83.0 %	94,918	82.5 %	5,321	5.6 %
Other stockholders' equity	(16,888)	(14.0)%	(15,697)	(13.6)%	(1,191)	7.6 %
Total stockholders' equity..............	46,878	38.8 %	47,579	41.3 %	(701)	(1.5)%
Total liabilities and stockholders' equity....	$120,700	100.0 %	$115,095	100.0 %	$ 5,605	4.9 %

We can see from P&G's statement of cash flows (**Exhibit 13-4**) that an increase in cash flow from operating activities from 2019 to 2020 and an increase in cash flow from investing activities during the same period resulted in a large increase in ending cash in 2020. Also, **Exhibit 13-4** reveals that P&G repurchased more of its common stock (treasury stock) and paid more cash dividends in 2020 than in 2019, both of which increased the amount of the cash it returned to shareholders during this period. Offsetting these financing cash outflows in 2020 was a large increase in funds borrowed.

From this limited analysis of comparative financial statements, an investment professional might conclude that P&G's operating performance for 2020 was an improvement when compared with that of 2019, mostly the result of cost controls in 2020. Further analysis using some of the techniques summarized later in the chapter, however, may cause that opinion to be either affirmed or modified.

EXHIBIT 13-4	Procter & Gamble Statement of Cash Flows

THE PROCTER & GAMBLE COMPANY
Consolidated Statements of Cash Flows

(in millions)	Year Ended 2020	Year Ended 2019	$ Change	% Change
Operating activities				
Net earnings.	$13,103	$ 3,966		
Depreciation and amortization	3,013	2,824		
Other adjustments to net income	(31)	7,771		
Changes in accounts receivable.	634	(276)		
Changes in inventories.	(637)	(239)		
Changes in liabilities.	1,923	1,856		
Changes in other operating activities	(602)	(660)		
Net cash flow provided by operating activities	17,403	15,242	$2,161	14.18%
Investing activities				
Capital expenditures.	(3,073)	(3,347)		
Investments	6,146	3,408		
Other cash flows from investing activities.	(28)	(3,551)		
Net cash flow used by investing activities.	3,045	(3,490)	6,535	(187.25)%
Financing activities				
Dividends	(7,789)	(7,498)		
Net stock purchases.	(7,405)	(5,003)		
Net borrowings	4,849	817		
Other cash flow from financing activities	1,978	3,324		
Net cash flow used by financing activities	(8,367)	(9,994)	$1,627	(16.28)%
Effect of exchange rate changes	(139)	(88)		
Change in cash and cash equivalents	11,942	1,670		
Beginning cash and cash equivalents	4,239	2,569		
Ending cash and cash equivalents.	$16,181	$ 4,239		

PRINCIPLE ALERT	Consistency Principle

Horizontal analysis is a technique for analyzing a firm's financial data across two or more years by examining dollar changes, percentage changes, or trend percentages. The utility of horizontal analysis, however, is dependent upon the effective implementation of the *consistency principle*. This accounting principle requires that a firm use the same accounting methods from one period to the next or, if a firm finds it necessary (or required) to change an accounting method, that the financial effects of any change be fully disclosed in the financial statements. The consistency principle assures financial analysts that, unless otherwise noted, changes in the accounts over time represent underlying economic changes in a business, and not the result of an accounting method change.

TREND ANALYSIS

To observe percentage changes over time in selected financial data, investment professionals often calculate **trend percentages**. Most companies provide summaries of their key financial data for the past five or ten years in their annual reports. With such information, the financial statement user can examine changes over periods longer than just the past two years. For example, suppose an analyst is interested in the trend in sales and net income for P&G for the past five years. The following are P&G's sales revenue and net income figures for 2016 through 2020:

	PROCTER & GAMBLE COMPANY Annual Performance									
	2016		**2017**		**2018**		**2019**		**2020**	
	Millions of Dollars	Percentage of Base Year	Millions of Dollars	Percentage of Base Year	Millions of Dollars	Percentage of Base Year	Millions of Dollars	Percentage of Base Year	Millions of Dollars	Percentage of Base Year
Net sales...............	$65,299	100%	$65,058	100%	$66,832	102%	$67,684	104%	$70,950	109%
Net earnings from continuing operations...............	10,027	100%	10,194	102%	9,861	98%	3,966	40%	13,103	131%

The pattern of changes from year to year can be determined more precisely by calculating trend percentages. To do this, we select a base year and then divide the data for each of the remaining years by the base-year data. The result is an index of the changes occurring throughout the period. If, for example, 2016 is selected as the base year, all data for 2017 through 2020 will be related to 2016, which is represented as 100 percent.

To create the table of data displayed above, we divide each year's net sales—from 2016 through 2020, by $65,299, P&G's 2016 net sales (in millions of dollars). Similarly, P&G's net earnings from continuing operations for 2016 through 2020 is divided by $10,027, the company's 2016 net earnings from continuing operations (in millions of dollars).

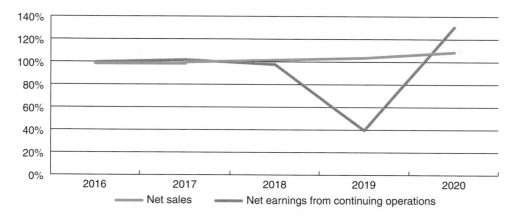

P&G's trend percentages above reveal that the company's growth in net earnings from continuing operations decreased in 2019 before recovering in 2020. In contrast, the company's net sales showed an increasing trend throughout the five-year period.

It is important to exercise care when interpreting trend percentages. Since all index percentages are related to a base year, it is important to select a good representative base year. For example, if 2016 was an unusual year for the firm, perhaps because of some large transitory items, its use in the trend analysis would be of limited value.

Other data items that an investment professional may relate to sales revenue and net income over multiple years include total assets, a company's investment in plant assets and its cash flow from operations, among others.

YOUR TURN! 13.2

MBC

The solution is on page 13-63.

The following data pertain to the Farrow Company:

	Current Year	Previous Year
Sales revenue...	$800,000	$750,000
Net income...	120,000	100,000
Total assets...	300,000	290,000

Calculate both the amount in dollars and the percentage change in the current year using horizontal analysis and the previous year as the base year.

Concept	➡	Method	➡	Assessment	TAKEAWAY 13.1
How does a company's current performance compare with the prior year?		Income statement, balance sheet, and statement of cash flows for current and prior year. The financial statements should be compared using the prior year as the base. Percentage changes in financial statement amounts can be computed as the change between years divided by the base year amount.		Significant changes should be analyzed to determine the reason for any change.	

VERTICAL ANALYSIS

The relative importance of various accounts in a company's financial statements for a single year can be highlighted by showing them as a percentage of a key financial statement figure. A financial statement that presents the various account balances as a percentage of a key figure is called a **common-size financial statement**. Sales revenue (or net sales) is the key figure used to construct a common-size income statement, whereas total assets is the key figure used to construct a common-size balance sheet.

LO3 Explain vertical financial statement analysis.

eLecture

MBC

Exhibit 13-2 presents P&G's 2020 and 2019 income statement in dollars and common-size percentages. The common-size percentages show each item in the income statement as a percentage of the company's net sales.

The common-size income statement allows financial statement users to readily compare P&G's ability to manage and control its various expenses while the level of its sales revenue changes over time. For example, P&G's net earnings increased from 5.8 percent of sales in 2019 to 18.4 percent of sales in 2020. We can observe that there are relatively small changes in almost all of the line items as a percentage of net sales with the exception of selling, general, and administrative expense, which decreased from 40.5 percent of sales in 2019 to 28.2 percent of sales in 2020. Common-size income statements are also useful when comparing across firms, especially when the firms are significantly different in size. We would expect firms of different sizes to report different levels of sales revenues and expenses on a dollar basis. But, we would expect far more similarities when the comparison is done on a common-size basis.

Common-size percentages can also be used to analyze balance sheet data. For example, by examining a firm's current assets and long-term assets as a percentage of total assets, we can determine whether a company is becoming more or less liquid over time. Another use of common-size percentages with balance sheet data is to evaluate the changing sources of financing used by a business. For example, the proportion of total assets supplied by short-term creditors, long-term creditors, preferred stockholders, and common stockholders of P&G are shown in **Exhibit 13-3**.

P&G's common-size balance sheets reveal relative stability between 2019 and 2020 with a few minor exceptions. P&G no longer holds short-term investments (although it holds more cash and cash equivalents) and has increased its use of long-term debt from 17.7 percent of total assets in 2019 to 19.5 percent of total assets in 2020.

YOUR TURN! 13.3

GuidedExample

MBC

The solution is on page 13-64.

Hint: When preparing common-size income statements, expenses are expressed as a positive percentage of net sales even though they are subtractions on the income statement.

The Sanford Company reported the following income statement:

SANFORD COMPANY Income Statement For the Year Ended December 31	
Sales revenue.	$13,500
Cost of goods sold	5,400
Gross profit.	8,100
Selling and administrative expenses	1,350
Income from operations	6,750
Interest expense.	675
Other expense	135
Income before income taxes.	5,940
Income tax expense	2,295
Net income.	$ 3,645

Required

Prepare a common-size income statement for Sanford Company.

TAKEAWAY 13.2	**Concept** ➡	**Method** ➡	**Assessment**
	How do the relations within a company's income statement and balance sheet compare to those of prior years?	Income statement and balance sheet for current and prior year. Each income statement item should be presented as a percentage of sales revenue, and each balance sheet item should be presented as a percentage of total assets. Financial statements in this form are called common-size statements.	The percentages should be analyzed for differences between years, and significant changes should be analyzed to determine the reason for any change.

THINKING GLOBALLY

Financial statement analysis is executed in the same way across the world. Common-size financial statements and the financial ratios discussed below are currency neutral and can be effectively used anywhere in the world. Not all ratios are relevant, however, in all countries. For example, in emerging countries that lack the financial infrastructure to support a credit system, ratios involving accounts receivable and accounts payable are likely to be irrelevant since sales transactions in those countries are only executed on a cash basis. Similarly, solvency ratios like the times-interest-earned ratio are irrelevant since bank financing in lesser-developed countries is rare (although it is becoming more prevalent with the advent of micro-finance in these countries).

RATIO ANALYSIS

LO4 **Define** and **discuss** financial ratios for analyzing a firm.

eLecture

MBC

Prior chapters introduced a number of financial ratios. At this juncture, we classify those ratios by their analytical objective and review their analysis and interpretation by calculating them for a single company. P&G's financial statements in **Exhibit 13-2**, **Exhibit 13-3**, and **Exhibit 13-4** provide the data for these calculations (all amounts are in millions). Also, data for industry competitor Colgate-Palmolive are presented for comparison purposes. Some of the financial ratios that are commonly calculated by investment professionals, lenders, and managers are presented and explained in **Exhibit 13-5**.

EXHIBIT 13-5	Key Financial Ratios	
Ratio	**Definition**	**Explanation**
Analyzing Firm Profitability		
• Gross profit percentage	$\dfrac{\text{Gross profit on sales}}{\text{Net sales}}$	Percentage of income generated from sales after deducting the cost of goods sold.
• Return on sales	$\dfrac{\text{Net income}}{\text{Net sales}}$	Percentage of net income remaining from a dollar of sales after subtracting all expenses.
• Asset turnover	$\dfrac{\text{Net sales}}{\text{Average total assets}}$	Amount of sales generated from each dollar invested in assets.
• Return on assets	$\dfrac{\text{Net income}}{\text{Average total assets}}$	Rate of return generated on a company's investment in assets from all sources.
• Return on equity	$\dfrac{\text{Net income}}{\text{Average stockholders' equity}}$	Rate of return generated by a business for its shareholders.
Analyzing Short-Term Firm Liquidity		
• Working capital	Current assets − Current liabilities	The difference between a firm's current assets and its current liabilities.
• Current ratio	$\dfrac{\text{Current assets}}{\text{Current liabilities}}$	Amount of current assets available to service current liabilities.
• Quick ratio	$\dfrac{\text{(Cash and cash equivalents + Short-term investments + Accounts receivable)}}{\text{Current liabilities}}$	Amount of liquid assets available to service current liabilities.
• Operating-cash-flow-to-current-liabilities ratio	$\dfrac{\text{Cash flow from operating activities}}{\text{Average current liabilities}}$	Amount of cash flow from operating activities available to service current liabilities.
• Accounts receivable turnover	$\dfrac{\text{Net sales}}{\text{Average accounts receivable (net)}}$	Number of sales/collection cycles experienced by a firm.
• Average collection period	$\dfrac{365}{\text{Accounts receivable turnover (net)}}$	Number of days required, on average, to collect an outstanding accounts receivable.
• Inventory turnover	$\dfrac{\text{Cost of goods sold}}{\text{Average inventory}}$	Number of production/sales cycles experienced by a firm.
• Days' sales in inventory	$\dfrac{365}{\text{Inventory turnover}}$	Number of days, on average, required to sell the inventory currently on hand.
Analyzing Long-Term Firm Solvency		
• Debt-to-equity ratio	$\dfrac{\text{Total liabilities}}{\text{Total stockholders' equity}}$	Percentage of total assets provided by creditors.
• Times interest earned ratio	$\dfrac{\text{Income before interest expense and income taxes}}{\text{Interest expense}}$	Extent to which current operating income covers current debt service charges.
• Operating-cash-flow-to-capital-expenditures ratio	$\dfrac{\text{Cash flow from operating activities}}{\text{Annual net capital expenditures}}$	The ability of a firm's operations to provide sufficient cash to replace and expand its property, plant, and equipment.
Financial Ratios for Common Stockholders		
• Earnings per share	$\dfrac{\text{(Net income − Preferred stock dividends)}}{\text{Weighted-average number of common shares outstanding}}$	The net income available to common shareholders calculated on a per share basis.
• Price-earnings ratio	$\dfrac{\text{Market price per share}}{\text{Earnings per share}}$	A measure of the price of a share of common stock relative to the share's annual earnings.
• Dividend yield	$\dfrac{\text{Annual dividend per share}}{\text{Market price per share}}$	The earnings on an investment in stock coming from dividends.
• Dividend payout ratio	$\dfrac{\text{Annual dividend per share}}{\text{Earnings per share}}$	The percentage of net income paid out to shareholders as dividends.

Analyzing Firm Profitability

Several ratios assist in evaluating how efficiently a firm has performed in its quest for profits, or what is referred to as firm profitability. These ratios include: (1) gross profit percentage, (2) return on sales, (3) asset turnover, (4) return on assets, and (5) return on equity.

Gross Profit Percentage

The **gross profit percentage** is a closely watched ratio for both retailers and manufacturers, among other industries. The ratio is calculated as:

A.K.A Gross profit is often referred to as *gross margin*.

$$\text{Gross profit percentage} = \frac{\text{Gross profit on sales}}{\text{Net sales}}$$

This ratio shows the effect on firm profitability of changes in a firm's product pricing structure, sales mix, and merchandise costs. **Gross profit**, or **gross profit on sales**, is defined as the difference between net sales and cost of goods sold and reveals the amount of sales revenue remaining after subtracting the cost of products sold.

P&G's common-size income statements (see **Exhibit 13-2**) reveal that its gross profit percentage increased from 48.6 percent in 2019 to 50.3 percent in 2020. These percentages are derived using the following figures:

	2020	2019
Gross profit.	$35,700	$32,916
Net sales.	70,950	67,684
Gross profit percentage	**50.3%**	**48.6%**
Colgate-Palmolive.	60.8%	

In order to gain additional insight into P&G's computed ratios, we compare them to a competitor from the same industry, Colgate-Palmolive, a process known as **benchmarking**. We see that P&G's has a lower gross profit percentage, 55.9 percent to Colgate-Palmolive's 60.8 percent, indicating Colgate-Palmolive has better margins on their product sales.

Return on Sales (Profit Margin)

A.K.A Return on sales is often referred to as *profit margin*.

Another important measure of firm profitability is the **return on sales**. This ratio reveals the percentage of each dollar of net sales that remains as profit after subtracting all operating and nonoperating expenses. The return on sales is calculated as follows:

$$\text{Return on sales} = \frac{\text{Net income}}{\text{Net sales}}$$

When common-size income statements are available, the return on sales equals the net income percentage. P&G's common-size income statements in **Exhibit 13-2** reveal that its return on sales increased from 5.8 percent in 2019 to 18.4 percent in 2020. These percentages are calculated using the following figures:

	2020	2019
Net income.	13,027	3,897
Net sales.	70,950	67,684
Return on sales.	**18.4%**	**5.8%**
Colgate-Palmolive.	17.4%	

The increase in the return on sales for P&G is encouraging, and as noted above, P&G's increase in its return on sales is mostly attributable to the company's cost control. Additionally, P&G's 2020 return on sales exceeds that of Colgate-Palmolive.

The return on sales and gross profit percentages should be used only when analyzing companies from the same industry or when comparing a firm's performance across multiple time periods (as we did above) since the ratio may vary widely across industries. Retail jewelers, for example, have much larger gross profit percentages than do retail grocers. Industry

averages for the asset turnover ratio, discussed next, also would be expected to vary significantly from one industry to another.

Asset Turnover

The **asset turnover ratio** measures how efficiently a firm uses its assets to generate sales
revenue by calculating the amount of sales dollars generated annually for each dollar of assets
invested in the company. This ratio is calculated as follows:

$$\text{Asset turnover} = \frac{\text{Net sales}}{\text{Average total assets}}$$

P&G's asset turnover is calculated as (total assets were $118,310 at year-end 2018):

		2020	2019
Net sales.		$ 70,950	$ 67,684
Total assets			
Beginning of year	(a)	115,095	118,310
End of year	(b)	120,700	115,095
Average [(a + b)/2]		117,898	116,703
Asset turnover		**0.60**	**0.58**
Colgate-Palmolive.		1.06	

P&G's asset turnover increased slightly from 2019 to 2020, indicating that the company is
more effective in using its assets to generate sales revenue. Specifically, the company generated $0.60 in net sales for every dollar invested in total assets in 2020, compared to $0.58 in
2019. This ratio result is, however, below the Colgate-Palmolive's asset turnover of 1.06.

Return on Assets

The rate of return on total assets, called the **return on assets**, is an overall measure of a firm's
profitability. It reveals the rate of profit earned per dollar of assets under a firm's control. The
return on assets is calculated as follows:

$$\text{Return on assets} = \frac{\text{Net income}}{\text{Average total assets}}$$

P&G's return on assets is calculated as:

	2020	2019
Net income	$ 13,027	$ 3,897
Average total assets	117,898	116,703
Return on assets	**11.0%**	**3.3%**
Colgate-Palmolive.	18.5%	

P&G's return on assets increased from 3.3 percent in 2019 to 11.0 percent in 2020; however,
P&G's return on assets is still below Colgate-Palmolive's return on assets of 18.5 percent.

The return on assets ratio summarizes the financial impact of two component ratios: the
return on sales and asset turnover; that is, the return on assets is the multiplicative product of
these latter two ratios, as follows:

Ratio:	Return on sales	×	Asset turnover	=	Return on assets
Ratio calculation:	$\dfrac{\text{Net income}}{\text{Net sales}}$	×	$\dfrac{\text{Net sales}}{\text{Average total assets}}$	=	$\dfrac{\text{Net income}}{\text{Average total assets}}$
P&G:	**18.4 percent**	×	**0.60**	=	**11.0 percent**

Industries that are characterized by low return on sales generally have relatively high asset turnover ratios, and vice versa. Retail grocery chains, for example, typically turn over their assets five to six times per year. By way of contrast, retail jewelers average only one to two asset turnovers per year. These industry differences largely reflect the high cost of products sold by jewelers versus the low cost of products sold by retail grocers.

Return on Equity

The **return on equity** ratio measures the profitability of the ownership interest held by a company's stockholders. The ratio shows the percentage of income available to stockholders for each dollar of stockholder equity invested in a business, as follows:

$$\text{Return on equity} = \frac{\text{Net income}}{\text{Average stockholders' equity}}$$

The return on equity for P&G is calculated as (stockholders' equity was $52,883 at year-end 2018):

		2020	2019
Net income		$13,027	$ 3,897
Stockholders' equity:			
Beginning of year	(a)	47,579	52,883
End of year	(b)	46,878	47,579
Average [(a + b)/2]		47,229	50,231
Return on equity		**27.6%**	**7.8%**
Colgate-Palmolive.		344.8%	

P&G's return on equity increased from 7.8 percent in 2019 to 27.6 percent in 2020. Like the return on assets, P&G's return on equity is well below that of Colgate-Palmolive, a highly leveraged company with very low stockholders' equity compared to its debt financing.

YOUR TURN! 13.4

MBC

The solution is on page 13-64.

The following data were obtained from the current financial statements for Kelly Corporation:

Net sales.	$30,000
Cost of goods sold	10,500
Net income	4,500
Average total assets.	50,000
Average stockholders' equity	35,000

Required

Calculate the following ratios for Kelly Corporation:

a. Gross profit percentage
b. Return on sales
c. Asset turnover

d. Return on assets
e. Return on equity

TAKEAWAY 13.3

Concept	Method	Assessment
How much profit is a company generating relative to the amount of assets invested in the company?	Income statement and balance sheet. Calculate the return on assets by dividing net income by the average total assets for the year.	The higher the return on assets, the better a company is doing in terms of generating profits utilizing the assets under its control.

Analyzing Short-Term Firm Liquidity

A firm's **working capital** is the difference between its current assets and current liabilities. Maintaining adequate working capital enables a firm to repay its current obligations on a timely basis and to take advantage of any available purchase discounts associated with the timely payment of accounts payable. Shortages of working capital, on the other hand, can force a company into borrowing at inopportune times and unfavorable interest rates. As a consequence, many long-term debt contracts contain provisions that require the borrowing firm to maintain a specified working capital position. A firm's working capital is calculated as follows:

Working capital = Current assets – Current liabilities

Analysis of a firm's short-term liquidity utilizes several financial ratios that relate to various aspects of a company's working capital. These ratios are: (1) current ratio, (2) quick ratio, (3) operating-cash-flow-to-current-liabilities ratio, (4) accounts receivable turnover and average collection period, and (5) inventory turnover and days' sales in inventory.

Current Ratio

The **current ratio** is calculated as a firm's current assets divided by its current liabilities:

$$\text{Current ratio} = \frac{\text{Current assets}}{\text{Current liabilities}}$$

This ratio is a widely used measure of a firm's ability to meet its current obligations and to have funds available for use in daily operations. The following calculations reveal that P&G's current ratio increased from 0.75 in 2019 to 0.85 in 2020:

	2020	2019
Current assets	$27,987	$22,473
Current liabilities.	32,976	30,011
Current ratio	**0.85**	**0.75**
Colgate-Palmolive.	0.99	

In essence, P&G had $0.85 in current assets for every $1 in current liabilities at the end of 2020.

In the past, a generally accepted rule of thumb was that a firm's current ratio should be approximately 2, indicating that a company should maintain twice the dollar amount of current assets as needed to satisfy its current liabilities. Improved cash flow management techniques and alternate forms of short-term financing (such as bank lines of credit) have reduced the need for businesses to maintain such a high current ratio. Still, many creditors prefer to see a higher current ratio and consider a low ratio as a potential warning sign of short-term liquidity problems.

Evaluating the adequacy of a firm's current ratio may involve comparing it with the recent past (P&G's current ratio increased from 2019 to 2020) or with an industry peer (P&G's current ratio is below Colgate-Palmolive's current ratio of 0.99). What is considered an appropriate current ratio varies by industry. A service firm with little or no inventory, such as a car wash service, would be expected to have a smaller current ratio than would a firm carrying a large inventory, such as a hardware retailer. The composition (or mix) of a firm's current assets significantly influences any evaluation of a firm's short-term liquidity. The quick ratio, discussed next, explicitly considers the composition of a firm's current assets when evaluating short-term liquidity.

Quick Ratio

The **quick ratio** reveals the relation between a firm's liquid, or quick, assets and its current liabilities. Quick assets include cash and cash equivalents, short-term investments, and accounts receivable. The quick ratio omits a company's inventory and prepaid assets, which may

A.K.A. The quick ratio is also referred to as the *acid-test ratio.*

not be particularly liquid. Consequently, the quick ratio may give a more accurate picture of a company's ability to meet its current obligations.

Comparing the quick ratio and the current ratio indicates the financial impact of a company's inventory on its working capital. For example, a company might have an acceptable current ratio, but if its quick ratio falls to an unacceptable level, a financial analyst is likely to be concerned about the amount of inventory on hand, and consequently, analyze the company's inventory position more thoroughly.

The quick ratio is calculated as follows:

$$\text{Quick ratio} = \frac{\text{(Cash and cash equivalents + Short-term investments + Accounts receivable)}}{\text{Current liabilities}}$$

The quick ratio for P&G is calculated as:

	2020	2019
Cash and cash equivalents, short-term investments, and accounts receivable	$20,359	$15,238
Current liabilities	32,976	30,011
Quick ratio	**0.62**	**0.51**
Colgate-Palmolive	0.49	

P&G's quick ratio increased from 0.51 in 2019 to 0.85 in 2020 and is above the quick ratio of 0.49 reported by Colgate-Palmolive. P&G's increased quick ratio is mainly due to a large increase in cash and cash equivalents in 2020.

Operating-Cash-Flow-to-Current-Liabilities Ratio

Ultimately, cash will be needed to settle a business's current liabilities. Another ratio indicating a firm's ability to pay its current liabilities as they come due focuses on a company's operating cash flow. The **operating-cash-flow-to-current-liabilities ratio** is calculated as follows:

$$\text{Operating-cash-flow-to-current-liabilities ratio} = \frac{\text{Cash flow from operating activities}}{\text{Average current liabilities}}$$

The operating-cash-flow-to-current-liabilities ratio relates the net cash available as a result of operating activities to the average current liabilities outstanding during the period. A higher ratio indicates that a firm has a greater ability to settle its current liabilities using its operating cash flow.

P&G's operating-cash-flow-to-current-liabilities ratio is calculated as (current liabilities at the end of 2018 were $28,237):

		2020	2019
Cash flow from operating activities		$17,403	$15,242
Current liabilities			
Beginning of year	(a)	30,011	28,237
End of year	(b)	32,976	30,011
Average [(a + b)/2]		31,494	29,124
Operating-cash-flow-to-current-liabilities ratio		**0.55**	**0.52**
Colgate-Palmolive		0.88	

P&G's operating-cash-flow-to-current-liabilities ratio increased from 2019 to 2020 due to an increase in cash flow from operating activities. However, this ratio was lower than Colgate-Palmolive's ratio of 0.88.

Accounts Receivable Turnover

The speed with which accounts receivable are collected is of considerable interest to investment professionals when evaluating a firm's short-term liquidity. **Accounts receivable turnover** indicates how many times a year a firm collects its average outstanding accounts receivable, and thus, measures how fast a firm converts its accounts receivable into cash. The quicker a firm is able to convert its accounts receivables into cash, the less cash the company needs to keep on hand to satisfy its current liabilities. Accounts receivable turnover is calculated as follows:

$$\text{Accounts receivable turnover} = \frac{\text{Net sales}}{\text{Average accounts receivable}}$$

Recall from Chapter 8 that accounts receivable less the allowance for doubtful accounts—that is, the net balance of accounts receivable—is the amount of receivables that the company expects to collect from customers. The accounts receivable turnover for P&G is calculated as (accounts receivable, net at the end of 2018 were $4,686):

		2020	2019
Net sales.		$70,950	$67,684
Average accounts receivable (net)			
Beginning of year	(a)	4,951	4,686
End of year	(b)	4,178	4,951
Average [(a + b)/2]		4,565	4,819
Accounts receivable turnover.		**15.54**	**14.05**
Colgate-Palmolive.		12.18	

The higher the accounts receivable turnover, the faster a company is able to convert its accounts receivable into cash. P&G's accounts receivable turnover increased from 14.05 in 2019 to 15.54 in 2020. In addition, P&G's accounts receivable turnover is well above the 12.18 reported by Colgate-Palmolive.

Average Collection Period

An extension of the accounts receivable turnover is the **average collection period**. The average collection period reveals how many days it takes, on average, for a company to collect an account receivable. The ratio is calculated as follows:

A.K.A. The average collection period is also referred to as the days' sales outstanding, or DSO.

$$\text{Average collection period} = \frac{365}{\text{Accounts receivable turnover (net)}}$$

P&G's average collection period is calculated as:

	2020	2019
Days	365	365
Accounts receivable turnover	15.54	14.05
Average collection period	**23.5 days**	**26.0 days**
Colgate-Palmolive.	30.0 days	

P&G's average collection period decreased in 2020. This may have resulted from such actions as P&G tightening the credit standards it applies to its customers or reducing the allowed credit period. Alternatively, it may reflect that P&G's customers have experienced improving cash flows, and thus they are able to pay their accounts more promptly. Knowledge of P&G's credit terms would permit a more complete analysis of these results. If, for example, P&G's credit terms are n/20, then an average collection period of 23.5 days indicates that the company has a problem with slow-paying customers. If, on the other hand, P&G's credit terms are n/30, then the 2020 average collection period shows no particular problem with the company's speed of receivable collection.

Inventory Turnover

An analyst concerned about a company's inventory position is likely to evaluate the company's **inventory turnover**. This ratio indicates whether the inventory on hand is disproportionate to the amount of sales revenue. Excessive inventories not only tie up company funds and increase storage costs but may also lead to subsequent losses if the goods become outdated or unsalable. In general, a higher turnover is preferred to a lower turnover. The calculation of inventory turnover is as follows:

$$\text{Inventory turnover} = \frac{\text{Cost of goods sold}}{\text{Average inventory}}$$

P&G's inventory turnover is calculated as (inventory at the end of 2018 was $4,738):

		2020	2019
Cost of goods sold		$35,250	$34,768
Inventory			
Beginning of year	(a)	5,017	4,738
End of year	(b)	5,498	5,017
Average [(a + b)/2]		5,258	4,878
Inventory turnover		**6.70**	**7.13**
Colgate-Palmolive		4.20	

P&G's inventory turnover decreased from 7.13 in 2019 to 6.70 in 2020, but remains above Colgate-Palmolive's reported inventory turnover of 4.20.

The cost of goods sold is used in the calculation of inventory turnover because the inventory measure in the denominator is a *cost* figure; consequently, it is appropriate to also use a cost figure in the numerator. By way of contrast, accounts receivable turnover uses net sales in the calculation because accounts receivable is based on sales revenue, which includes a markup for the company's expected profit.

A low inventory turnover can result from an overextended inventory position or from inadequate sales volume. For this reason, an appraisal of a firm's inventory turnover should be accompanied by a review of the quick ratio and an analysis of trends in both inventory and sales revenue.

Days' Sales in Inventory

The **days' sales in inventory** ratio is derived from a firm's inventory turnover ratio and reveals how many days it takes, on average, for a firm to sell its inventory on hand. The ratio is calculated as follows:

$$\text{Days' sales in inventory} = \frac{365}{\text{Inventory turnover}}$$

P&G's days' sales in inventory is calculated as:

	2020	2019
Days	365	365
Inventory turnover	6.70	7.13
Days' sales in inventory	**54.5 days**	**51.2 days**
Colgate-Palmolive	86.9 days	

P&G's days' sales in inventory reveals that the average amount of time required to sell its inventory increased by 3.3 days, from 51.2 days in 2019 to 54.5 days in 2020. However, P&G's average length of time to sell its inventory is still much lower than the 86.9 days reported by Colgate-Palmolive.

By combining the days' sales in inventory with the average collection period, it is possible to estimate the average time period from the acquisition of inventory, to the sale of inventory, to the eventual collection of cash. The sum of the days' sales in inventory plus the average collection period measures the length of the company's **operating cycle**. Although operating cycles will naturally vary across different industries, a shorter operating cycle is preferred, as it is an indicator of the operating efficiency and working capital management of the company. In 2020, for example, it took P&G 78.0 days (54.5 days' sales in inventory + 15.5 days average collection period) to sell its average inventory and collect the related cash from its customers. This operating cycle is similar to P&G's 2019 period of 77.2 days (51.2 days + 26.0 days) and significantly better than Colgate-Palmolive's 116.9 days.

YOUR TURN! 13.5

GuidedExample

MBC

The solution is on page 13-64.

The following selected data were obtained from the financial statements of Justin Corporation:

Current assets	$ 60,000
Current liabilities for both current and prior year.	40,000
Cash flow from operating activities.	55,000
Net sales.	100,000
Average accounts receivable	15,000
Cost of goods sold	70,000
Average inventory.	9,000

Required

Calculate the following financial measures and ratios for Justin Corporation:

a. Working capital

b. Current ratio

c. Operating-cash-flow-to-current-liabilities ratio

d. Accounts receivable turnover

e. Days' sales in inventory

Concept	Method	Assessment	TAKEAWAY 13.4
How financially capable is a company to pay its current liabilities as they come due?	Income statement, balance sheet, and statement of cash flows. Calculate the current ratio, the quick ratio, and the operating-cash-flow-to-current-liabilities ratio.	The higher the ratios, the higher the probability that a company will have the ability to pay its current liabilities as they become due.	

Analyzing Long-Term Firm Solvency

The preceding set of ratios examined a firm's short-term liquidity. A separate set of ratios analyzes a firm's long-term solvency, or its long-term debt repayment capability. Ratios in this latter group include: (1) debt-to-equity ratio, (2) times-interest-earned ratio, and (3) operating-cash-flow-to-capital-expenditures ratio.

Debt-to-Equity Ratio

The **debt-to-equity ratio** evaluates the financial structure of a firm by relating a company's total liabilities to its total stockholders' equity. This ratio considers the extent to which a company relies on creditors versus stockholders to provide financing. The debt-to-equity ratio is calculated as follows:

$$\text{Debt-to-equity ratio} = \frac{\text{Total liabilities}}{\text{Total stockholders' equity}}$$

This ratio uses year-end balances for the ratio's components, rather than averages, since we are interested in the firm's capital structure as of a particular point in time. The total stockholders' equity for a business is its total assets minus its total liabilities.

The debt-to-equity ratio gives creditors an indication of the margin of protection available to them (creditors' claims to assets have priority over stockholders' claims). The lower the ratio, the greater the protection being provided to creditors. A firm with a low ratio also has greater flexibility when seeking additional borrowed funds at a low rate of interest than does a firm with a high ratio.

P&G's debt-to-equity ratio is calculated as:

	2020	2019
Total liabilities (year-end)	$73,822	$67,516
Total stockholders' equity (year-end)	46,878	47,579
Debt-to-equity ratio	**1.57**	**1.42**
Colgate-Palmolive	13.46	

P&G's debt-to-equity ratio increased from 1.42 in 2019 to 1.57 in 2020, indicating an increase in reliance on debt to finance its operations. However, the ratio is well below the 13.46 debt-to-equity ratio that Colgate-Palmolive reported in 2020. Colgate-Palmolive is heavily reliant on debt financing.

Times-Interest-Earned Ratio

A.K.A. The times-interest-earned ratio is also referred to as the *interest coverage ratio.*

To evaluate the ability of a company to pay its current interest charges, an analyst may investigate the relation between the company's current interest charges and its operating income available to meet those interest charges. For example, an extremely high debt-to-equity ratio for a company may indicate extensive borrowing by the company; however, if its operating earnings are sufficient to meet the interest charges on the debt several times over, an analyst may regard the situation quite favorably.

Analysts, particularly long-term credit analysts, almost always consider the **times-interest-earned ratio** of a company with interest-bearing debt. This ratio is calculated by dividing the income before interest expense and income taxes by the annual interest expense:

$$\text{Times-interest-earned ratio} = \frac{\text{Income before interest expense and income taxes}}{\text{Interest expense}}$$

P&G's times-interest-earned ratio is calculated as:

	2020	2019
Income before interest expense and income taxes	$16,223	$6,509
Interest expense	465	509
Times-interest-earned ratio	**34.9**	**12.8**
Colgate-Palmolive	23.2	

P&G's income available to meet its interest charges increased significantly from 12.8 in 2019 to 34.9 in 2020, the result of much higher reported earnings in 2020. This ratio indicates that P&G exhibits an exceptionally good margin of safety for creditors. Generally speaking, a company that earns its interest charges several times over is regarded as a satisfactory risk by long-term creditors.

Operating-Cash-Flow-to-Capital-Expenditures Ratio

The ability of a firm's operations to provide sufficient cash to replace and expand its property, plant, and equipment is revealed by the **operating-cash-flow-to-capital-expenditures ratio**. To the extent that acquisitions of plant assets can be financed using cash provided by operating activities, a firm does not have to use other financing sources, such as long-term debt. This ratio is calculated as follows:

$$\text{Operating-cash-flow-to-capital-expenditures ratio} = \frac{\text{Cash flow from operating activities}}{\text{Annual net capital expenditures}}$$

A ratio of 1.0 indicates that a firm's current operating activities provide sufficient cash to fully fund any investment in plant capacity. A ratio in excess of 1.0 indicates that a company has sufficient operating cash flow to fund expansion in its plant capacity.

The operating-cash-flow-to-capital-expenditures ratio for P&G is:

	2020	2019
Cash flow from operating activities.	$17,403	$15,242
Annual net capital expenditures	3,073	3,347
Operating-cash-flow-to-capital-expenditures ratio	**5.7**	**4.6**
Colgate-Palmolive.	9.1	

In 2020, P&G's operating-cash-flow-to capital-expenditures ratio was 5.7, an increase from 4.6 in 2019. Although this is less than the 9.1 operating-cash-flow-to-capital-expenditures ratio reported by Colgate-Palmolive in 2020, it still appears that P&G is generating plenty of operating cash flow to cover its net capital expenditures each year.

YOUR TURN! 13.6

The following selected data were obtained from the financial statements for the Hartford Corporation:

Total liabilities.	$180,000
Total stockholders' equity	600,000
Cash flow from operating activities.	100,000
Annual capital expenditures	30,000
Net income.	55,000
Interest expense.	5,000
Income tax expense	25,000

Guided Example

MBC

The solution is on page 13-64.

Required

Calculate the following ratios for Hartford Corporation:

a. Debt-to-equity ratio

b. Times-interest-earned ratio

c. Operating-cash-flow-to-capital-expenditures ratio

Concept ➡	Method ➡	Assessment	TAKEAWAY 13.5
How solvent is a company?	Income statement, balance sheet, and statement of cash flows. Calculate the debt-to-equity ratio, the times-interest-earned ratio, and the operating-cash-flow-to-capital-expenditures ratio.	The higher the times-interest-earned and the operating-cash-flow-to-capital-expenditures ratios, and the lower the debt-to-equity ratio, the greater is a company's solvency.	

Financial Ratios for Common Stockholders

Present and potential common stockholders share an interest with a business's creditors in analyzing the profitability, short-term liquidity, and long-term solvency of a company. There are also other financial ratios that are primarily of interest to common stockholders. These ratios include: (1) earnings per share, (2) price-earnings ratio, (3) dividend yield, and (4) dividend payout ratio.

Earnings per Share

Because stock market prices are quoted on a per-share basis, the reporting of earnings per share of common stock is useful to investors. **Earnings per share (EPS)** is calculated by dividing the net income available to common stockholders by the weighted average number of common shares outstanding during a year. The net income available to common stockholders is a company's net income less any preferred stock dividends. Preferred stock dividends are subtracted from net income to arrive at the net income available exclusively to a company's common stock stockholders. Thus, earnings per share is calculated as follows:

$$\frac{\text{Earnings}}{\text{per share}} = \frac{\textbf{(Net income – Preferred stock dividends)}}{\textbf{Weighted-average number of common shares outstanding}}$$

Because earnings per share are a required disclosure on a company's income statement, investment professionals do not have to calculate this financial metric. P&G's income statements reveal the following earnings per share (see **Exhibit 13-2**):

	2020	2019
Earnings per share.	**$5.13**	**$1.45**
Colgate-Palmolive.	3.15	

P&G's earnings per share increased from $1.45 in 2019 to $5.13 in 2020, an increase of 254 percent. This is slightly higher than the 234 percent increase in P&G's net income over the same period. The result is due to the increase in P&G's treasury stock, which reduces the number of common shares outstanding.

Price-Earnings Ratio

A.K.A. The price-earnings ratio is also referred to as the *P/E multiple.*

The **price-earnings ratio** is calculated by dividing the market price per share of common stock by a company's earnings per share:

$$\text{Price-earnings ratio} = \frac{\textbf{Market price per share}}{\textbf{Earnings per share}}$$

For many analysts and investors, this ratio is an important tool for assessing a stock's valuation. For example, after evaluating the financial strengths of several comparable companies, an analyst may decide which company to invest in by comparing the price-earnings ratio of each company. Assuming that the companies have equivalent persistent earnings and financial risk profiles, the company with the lowest price-earnings ratio may represent the best investment opportunity.

When calculating the price-earnings ratio, it is customary to use the latest market price per share and the earnings per share for the last four quarters of a company's operations. P&G's price-earnings ratios as of the end of fiscal years 2019 and 2020 are:

	2020	2019
Market price per share (at year-end)	$119.57	$109.65
Earnings per share.	5.13	1.45
Price-earnings ratio	**23.3**	**75.6**
Colgate-Palmolive.	27.1	

The market price of a share of P&G's common stock at year-end 2020 was 23.3 times the company's 2020 earnings per share, which represents a significant improvement from the price-earnings ratio of 75.6 at the end of 2019. P&G's price-earnings ratio at the end of 2020 is somewhat lower than the 27.1 price-earnings reported by Colgate-Palmolive in 2020, suggesting that it may be a better investment opportunity than Colgate-Palmolive.

Dividend Yield

Investor expectations vary greatly with personal economic circumstances and with the overall economic outlook. Some investors are more interested in the potential share price appreciation of a stock than in any dividends that a company may pay on its outstanding shares. Other investors are more concerned with dividends than with stock price appreciation. These investors desire a high **dividend yield** on their investments. Dividend yield is calculated by dividing a company's current annual dividend per share by the current market price per share:

$$\text{Dividend yield} = \frac{\textbf{Annual dividend per share}}{\textbf{Market price per share}}$$

P&G's dividend yield per common share is calculated as (the dividend per share is disclosed in **Exhibit 13-2**):

	2020	2019
Annual dividend per share	$ 3.03	$ 2.9
Market price per share (at year-end)	119.57	109.65
Dividend yield.	**2.5%**	**2.6%**
Colgate-Palmolive.	2.0%	

P&G's dividend yield decreased very slightly from 2.6 percent in 2019 to 2.5 percent in 2020. This dividend yield is still above the 2.0 percent reported in 2020 by Colgate-Palmolive.

Dividend Payout Ratio

Investors who emphasize the yield on their investments may also be interested in a firm's **dividend payout ratio**—that is, the percentage of net income paid out as dividends to stockholders. The payout ratio indicates whether a firm has a conservative or a liberal dividend policy and may also indicate whether a firm is conserving funds for internal financing of its growth. The dividend payout ratio is calculated as follows:

$$\text{Dividend payout ratio} = \frac{\textbf{Annual dividend per share}}{\textbf{Earnings per share}}$$

P&G's dividend payout ratio is calculated as:

	2020	2019
Annual dividends per share	$3.03	$2.90
Earnings per share.	5.13	1.45
Dividend payout ratio.	**59.1%**	**200.0%**
Colgate-Palmolive.	55.6%	

P&G's dividend payout ratio decreased significantly from 200 percent in 2019 to a much more reasonable 59.1 percent in 2020. The 2020 payout ratio is consistent with the payout ratio for most comparable mature U.S. industrial corporations and is slightly higher than the 55.6 percent 2020 dividend payout ratio reported by Colgate-Palmolive.

Payout ratios for mature industrial corporations vary between 40 percent and 60 percent of net income. Many corporations, however, need funds for internal financing of growth and pay out little (if any) of their net income as dividends. At the other extreme, some companies—principally utility companies—may pay out as much as 70 percent of their net income as dividends.

YOUR TURN! 13.7

MBC

The solution is on page 13-64.

The following selected data were obtained from financial statements for Baylor Corporation:

Earnings per share..	$ 4.50
Market price per share of common stock	54.00
Dividends per share of common stock	1.50

Required

Calculate the following ratios for Baylor Corporation:

a. Dividend yield   b. Dividend payout ratio   c. Price-earnings ratio

---

TAKEAWAY 13.6	Concept ➡	Method ➡	Assessment
	How much dividends are common stockholders likely to receive?	Earnings per share, dividends per share, and market price of common stock. Calculate the dividend yield and dividend payout ratio.	The higher the dividend yield and the dividend payout ratio, the more dividends a stockholder can expect to receive.

LIMITATIONS OF FINANCIAL STATEMENT ANALYSIS

LO5 Discuss the limitations of financial statement analysis.

eLecture

MBC

The ratios, percentages, and other relations described in this chapter reflect the analytical techniques used by investment professionals and experienced investors. Nonetheless, they must be interpreted with due consideration of the general economic conditions, the conditions of the industry in which a company operates, and the relative position of individual companies within an industry.

Financial statement users must also be aware of the inherent limitations of financial statement data. Problems of comparability are frequently encountered. Companies within the same industry may use different accounting methods that can cause problems in comparing certain key ratios. For instance, inventory turnover is likely to be quite different for a company using LIFO than for one using FIFO. Inflation may also distort certain financial data and ratios, especially those resulting from horizontal analysis. For example, trend percentages calculated from data unadjusted for inflation may be deceptive.

Financial statement users must also be careful when comparing companies within a particular industry. Factors such as firm size, diversity of product line, and mode of operations can make firms within the same industry dissimilar in their reported results. Moreover, some firms, particularly conglomerates, are difficult to classify by industry. If segment information is available, the financial statement user may compare the statistics for several industries. Often, trade associations prepare industry statistics that are stratified by size of firm or type of product, facilitating financial statement analysis.

FORENSIC ACCOUNTING

It is generally considered more difficult to deter financial statement fraud than it is to deter other types of fraud such as embezzlement. The best approach to fraud deterrence is to put into place a strong set of internal controls. Unfortunately, senior management, such as a firm's CEO and CFO, are the most likely employees to commit financial statement fraud. These individuals are able to use their position of authority to override most internal controls. Thus, it is important to consider alternative approaches to fraud deterrence. Potential alternative approaches are based on the fraud triangle concept, in which fraud is related to the interaction of three factors: (1) pressure, (2) opportunity, and (3) rationalization.

The fraud element of pressure can be reduced by avoiding the practice of setting unachievable financial goals and utilizing compensation systems that are considered fair but which do not create excessive incentives to commit fraud. Although internal controls may be circumvented by senior management, it is still important to maintain a strong system of internal controls and to establish clear and uniform accounting procedures with no exception clauses. In addition, a strong internal control department reporting to the board of directors provides further deterrence. Finally, the creation and promotion of a culture of honesty and integrity throughout an organization make the rationalization of financial statement fraud much more difficult.

COMPREHENSIVE PROBLEM

Knox Instruments, Inc., is a manufacturer of various medical and dental instruments. Financial statement data for the firm follow:

(thousands of dollars, except per-share amount)	2019
Sales revenue.	$200,000
Cost of goods sold	98,000
Net income	10,750
Dividends	4,200
Cash provided by operating activities.	7,800
Earnings per share.	3.07

KNOX INSTRUMENTS, INC.
Balance Sheets

(thousands of dollars)	Current Year	Previous Year
Assets		
Cash.	$ 3,000	$ 2,900
Accounts receivable (net).	28,000	28,800
Inventory.	64,000	44,000
Total current assets.	95,000	75,700
Plant assets (net)	76,000	67,300
Total assets.	$171,000	$143,000
Liabilities and Stockholders' Equity		
Current liabilities.	$ 45,200	$ 39,750
10% bonds payable	20,000	14,000
Total liabilities	65,200	53,750
Common stock, $10 par value	40,000	30,000
Retained earnings	65,800	59,250
Total stockholders' equity	105,800	89,250
Total liabilities and stockholders' equity	$171,000	$143,000

Required

a. Using the given data, calculate the nine financial ratios below. Compare the ratio results for Knox Instruments, Inc., with the following industry medians and comment on its operations.

Median Ratios for the Industry

1.	Current ratio	2.7
2.	Quick ratio	1.6
3.	Average collection period	73 days
4.	Inventory turnover	2.3
5.	Operating-cash-flow-to-current-liabilities ratio	0.22
6.	Debt-to-equity ratio	0.50
7.	Return on assets	4.9 percent
8.	Return on equity	10.2 percent
9.	Return on sales	4.1 percent

b. Calculate the dividends paid per share of common stock. (Use the average number of shares outstanding during the year.) What was the dividend payout ratio?

c. If the year-end market price per share of Knox's common stock is $25, what is the company's (1) price-earnings ratio and (2) dividend yield?

Solution

a.

1. Current ratio = $95,000/$45,200 = 2.10
2. Quick ratio = $31,000/$45,200 = 0.69
3. Average collection period:
   Accounts receivable turnover = $200,000/($28,800 + $28,000)/2 = 7.04
   Average collection period = 365/7.04 = 51.8 days
4. Inventory turnover = $98,000/($44,000 + $64,000)/2 = 1.81
5. Operating-cash-flow-to-current-liabilities ratio = $7,800/($39,750 + $45,200)/2 = 0.18
6. Debt-to-equity ratio = $65,200/$105,800 = 0.62
7. Return on assets = $10,750/($143,000 + $171,000)/2 = 6.8 percent
8. Return on equity = $10,750/($89,250 + $105,800)/2 = 11.0 percent
9. Return on sales = $10,750/$200,000 = 5.4 percent

Although the firm's current ratio of 2.10 is below the industry median, it is still acceptable; however, the quick ratio of 0.69 is well below the industry median. This indicates that Knox's inventory (which is omitted from the quick ratio calculation) is excessive. This is also borne out by the firm's inventory turnover of 1.81 times, which compares with the industry median of 2.3 times. The firm's average collection period of 51.8 days is significantly better than the industry median of 73 days, while the operating-cash-flow-to-current-liabilities ratio is close to the industry median. Knox's debt-to-equity ratio of 0.62 indicates that the firm has proportionately more debt in its capital structure than the median industry firm, which has a debt-to-equity ratio of 0.50. Knox's operations appear efficient as its return on assets, return on equity, and return on sales all exceed the industry medians.

b. Average number of shares outstanding = (4,000,000 + 3,000,000)/2 = 3,500,000 shares.
    $4,200,000 dividends/3,500,000 shares = $1.20 dividend per share.
    Dividend payout ratio = $1.20/$3.07 = 39.1 percent.

c. Price-earnings ratio = $25/$3.07 = 8.1.
    Dividend yield = $1.20/$25 = 4.8 percent.

APPENDIX 13A: Financial Statement Disclosures

LO6   **Describe** financial statement disclosures.

MBC

Disclosures related to a company's financial statements fall into one of three categories: (1) parenthetical disclosures on the face of the financial statements, (2) notes to the financial statements, and (3) supplementary information. Most disclosures amplify or explain aggregated information contained in the financial statements. Some disclosures, however, provide additional information.

Parenthetical Disclosures

Parenthetical disclosures are placed next to an account title or other descriptive label in the financial statements. Their purpose is to provide additional detail regarding the item or account.

An example of parenthetical disclosures indicating the amount of the allowance for doubtful accounts follows:

	2022	2021
Accounts receivable, less allowances for doubtful accounts (2022—$7,545; 2021—$7,098)	$351,538	$300,181

Instead of using a parenthetical disclosure, companies may choose to present the additional detail in the notes to the financial statements.

Notes to the Financial Statements

Although much information is gathered, summarized, and reported in a company's financial statements, the financial statements alone are limited in their ability to convey a complete picture of a company's financial status. *Notes* are added to the financial statements to help fill in these gaps. In fact, over time, accountants have given so much attention to the financial statement notes that the notes now consume more page space in the annual report than the financial statements themselves. Notes may cover a wide variety of topics. Typically, they deal with significant accounting policies, explanations of complex or special transactions, details of reported amounts, commitments, contingencies, business segments, quarterly data, and subsequent material events.

Significant Accounting Policies

GAAP contains a number of instances for which alternative accounting procedures are equally acceptable. For example, there are several generally accepted depreciation and inventory valuation methods. The particular accounting policies selected by a company affect the financial data presented. Knowledge of a firm's specific accounting principles and methods of applying these principles helps users more fully understand a company's financial statements. Accordingly, these principles and methods are disclosed in a **summary of significant accounting policies**, which is typically the first note to the financial statements.

For example, the annual report of the **Columbia Sportswear Company** contains the following description of its inventory policy:

> Inventories consist primarily of finished goods and are carried at the lower of cost or net realizable value. Cost is determined using the first-in, first-out method. The Company periodically reviews its inventories for excess, close-out or slow moving items and makes provisions as necessary to properly reflect inventory value.

Explanations of Complex or Special Transactions

The complexity of certain transactions means that not all important aspects are likely to be reflected in the accounts. Financial statement notes, therefore, report additional relevant details about such transactions. Typical examples include notes discussing the financial aspects of pension plans, profit-sharing plans, acquisitions of other companies, borrowing agreements, stock option and other incentive plans, and income taxes.

Transactions with related parties are special transactions requiring disclosure in the financial statement notes. Related party transactions include transactions between a firm and its (1) principal owners, (2) members of management, (3) subsidiary companies, or (4) affiliate companies.

Details of Reported Amounts

Financial statements often summarize several groups of accounts into a single aggregate dollar amount. For example, a balance sheet may show one asset account labeled *Property, Plant, and Equipment,* or it may list *Long-Term Debt* as a single amount among the liabilities. Notes report more detail, presenting schedules that list the types and amounts of property, plant, and equipment and long-term debt. Other items that may be summarized in the financial statements and detailed in the notes include inventories, other current assets, notes payable, accrued liabilities, stockholders' equity, and a company's income tax expense.

The notes to Columbia Sportswear Company's 2020 annual report contain several examples of financial statement items that are detailed, including revenues (**Note 3**), property, plant, and equipment (**Note 5**), short-term borrowing and credit lines (**Note 7**), accrued liabilities (**Note 8**), income taxes (**Note 10**) , and shareholders' equity (**Note 13**).

Commitments

A firm may have contractual arrangements existing as of a balance sheet date in which both parties to the contract still have acts yet to be completed. If performance under these **commitments** will have a significant financial impact on a firm, the existence and nature of the commitments should be disclosed in the notes to the financial statements. Examples of commitments reported in the notes include contracts to purchase materials or equipment, contracts to construct facilities, salary commitments to executives, commitments to retire or redeem stock, and commitments to deliver goods.

Columbia Sportswear Company reports the following commitments in its annual report:

During its normal course of business, the Company has made certain indemnities, commitments and guarantees under which it may be required to make payments in relation to certain transactions. These include (i) intellectual property indemnities to the Company's customers and licensees in connection with the use, sale and/or license of Company products, (ii) indemnities to various lessors in connection with facility leases for certain claims arising from such facility or lease, (iii) indemnities to customers, vendors and service providers pertaining to claims based on the negligence or willful misconduct of the Company, (iv) executive severance arrangements and (v) indemnities involving the accuracy of representations and warranties in certain contracts. The duration of these indemnities, commitments and guarantees varies, and in certain cases, may be indefinite. The majority of these indemnities, commitments and guarantees do not provide for any limitation of the maximum potential for future payments the Company could be obligated to make. The Company has not recorded any liability for these indemnities, commitments and guarantees in the accompanying Consolidated Balance Sheets.

Contingencies

Contingent liabilities were discussed in Chapter 10. As noted there, if the future event that would turn a contingency into an obligation is not likely to occur, or if the liability cannot be reasonably estimated, the **contingency** is disclosed in a note to the financial statements. Typical contingencies disclosed in the notes include pending lawsuits, environmental cleanup costs, possible income tax assessments, credit guarantees, and discounted notes receivable.

Under Armour, Inc., reports the following regarding contingencies in its annual report:

From time to time, the Company is involved in litigation and other proceedings, including matters related to commercial and intellectual property disputes, as well as trade, regulatory and other claims related to its business. Other than as described below, the Company believes that all current proceedings are routine in nature and incidental to the conduct of its business, and that the ultimate resolution of any such proceedings will not have a material adverse effect on its consolidated financial position, results of operations or cash flows.

Segments

Many firms diversify their business activities and operate in several different industries. A firm's financial statements often combine information from all of a company's operations into aggregate amounts. This complicates the financial statement user's ability to analyze the statements because the interpretation of financial data is influenced by the industry in which a firm operates. Different industries face different types of risk and have different rates of profitability. In making investment and lending decisions, financial statement users evaluate risk and required rates of return. Having financial data available by industry segment is helpful to such evaluations.

The FASB recognizes the usefulness of industry data to investors and lenders. Public companies with significant operations in more than one industry must report certain financial information by industry **segment**. Typically, these disclosures are in the financial statement notes. The major disclosures by industry segment are sales revenue, operating profit or loss, identifiable assets (the assets used by the segment), capital expenditures, and depreciation.

Other types of segment data may also be disclosed. Business operations in different parts of the world are subject to different risks and opportunities for growth. Thus, public companies with significant operations in foreign countries must report selected financial data by foreign geographic area. The required data disclosures include sales revenue, operating profit or loss (or other profitability measure), and identifiable assets. Also, if a firm has export sales or sales revenue to a single customer that are ten percent or more of total sales revenue, the amount of such sales revenue must be separately disclosed.

Note 17 to **Columbia Sportswear's** financial statements in its annual report illustrates segment disclosures by foreign versus domestic segments.

Quarterly Data

Interim financial reports cover periods shorter than one year. Companies that issue interim reports generally do so quarterly. These reports provide financial statement users with more timely information on a firm's progress and are useful in predicting a company's annual financial results. The SEC requires that certain companies disclose selected quarterly financial data in their annual reports to stockholders. Included among the notes, the data reported for each quarter include sales revenue, gross profit, net income, and earnings per share. **Quarterly data** permit financial statement users to analyze such things as the seasonal nature of operations, the impact of diversification on quarterly activity, and whether the firm's activities lead or lag general economic trends.

Subsequent Events

If a company issues a large amount of securities or suffers a casualty loss after the balance sheet date, this information should be reported in a note, even though the situation arose subsequent to the balance sheet date. Firms are responsible for disclosing any significant events that occur between the balance sheet date and the date the financial statements are issued. This guideline recognizes that it takes several weeks for financial statements to be prepared and audited before they are issued. Events occurring during this period may have a material effect on a firm's operations and should be disclosed. Other examples of **subsequent events** requiring disclosure are sales of assets, significant changes in long-term debt, and acquisitions of other companies.

Supplementary Information

Supplementing the financial statements are several additional disclosures—management's discussion and analysis of the financial statements and selected financial data covering a five- to ten-year period along with possible other supplementary disclosures that are either required of certain companies by the SEC or recommended (but not required) by the FASB.

Management Discussion and Analysis

Management may increase the usefulness of financial statements by sharing some of their knowledge about a company's financial condition and operations. This is the purpose of the disclosure devoted to the management discussion and analysis. In this supplement to the financial statements, which is not audited, management identifies and comments on events and trends influencing a company's liquidity, operating results, and financial resources. Management's position within a company not only provides it with insights unavailable to outsiders, but also may introduce certain biases into the analysis. Nonetheless, management's comments, interpretations, and explanations should contribute to a better understanding of a company's financial statements.

A.K.A. The management discussion and analysis are also referred to simply as the *MD&A*.

Comparative Selected Financial Data

The analysis of a company's financial performance is enhanced when financial data for several years are available. By analyzing trends over time, it is possible for a financial statement user to learn much more about a company than would be possible by analyzing only a single year of data. Year-to-year changes may give clues as to a firm's future growth or may highlight areas for concern. Corporate annual reports to stockholders present complete financial statements in comparative form, showing the current year and one or two preceding years. Beyond this, however, the financial statements are supplemented by a summary of selected key financial statistics for a five- or ten-year period. The financial data presented in this historical summary usually include sales revenue, net income, dividends, earnings per share, working capital, and total assets.

SUMMARY OF LEARNING OBJECTIVES

Identify persistent earnings and discuss the content and format of the income statement. (p. 13-3)   **LO1**

- Persistent earnings are earnings that are likely to recur, while transitory earnings are unlikely to recur.
- The continuing income of a business may be reported in a single-step format or in a multiple-step format.
- Gains and losses from discontinued operations are reported in a special income statement section following income from continuing operations.
- The effect of most changes in accounting principle requires restatement of prior financial statements as if the new method had been applied all along.
- Companies are required to report other comprehensive income in addition to regular income in their financial statements.

Identify the sources of financial information used by investment professionals and explain horizontal financial statements analysis. (p. 13-6)   **LO2**

- Data sources for investment professionals include published financial statements, filings with the U.S. Securities and Exchange Commission, and statistics available from financial data services.
- A common form of horizontal analysis involves analyzing dollar and percentage changes in comparative financial statements for two or more years.
- Analyzing trend percentages of key figures, such as sales revenue, net income, and total assets for a number of years, related to a base year, is often useful.

LO3 **Explain vertical financial statement analysis. (p. 13-12)**

- Vertical analysis deals with the relative importance of various accounts in the financial statements for a single year.
- Common-size statements express income statement items as a percentage of sales revenue and balance sheet items as a percentage of total assets.

LO4 **Define and discuss financial ratios for analyzing a firm. (p. 13-13)**

- Ratios for analyzing firm profitability include the gross profit percentage, return on sales, asset turnover, return on assets, and return on equity.
- Ratios for analyzing short-term firm liquidity include the current ratio, quick ratio, operating-cash-flow-to-current-liabilities ratio, accounts receivable turnover, average collection period, inventory turnover, and days' sales in inventory.
- Ratios for analyzing long-term firm solvency include the debt-to-equity ratio, times-interest-earned ratio, and operating-cash-flow-to-capital-expenditures ratio.
- Ratios of particular interest to common stockholders include a company's earnings per share, the price-earnings ratio, dividend yield, and dividend payout ratio.

LO5 **Discuss the limitations of financial statement analysis. (p. 13-27)**

- When analyzing financial statements, financial statement users must be aware of a firm's accounting methods, the effects of inflation, and the difficulty of currently identifying a firm's industry classification.

LO6 **Appendix 13A: Describe financial statement disclosures. (p. 13-29)**

- Parenthetical disclosures on the face of the financial statements provide additional detail regarding the item or account.
- Notes to the financial statements provide information on significant accounting policies, explanations of complex or special transactions, details of reported amounts, commitments, contingencies, segments, quarterly data, and subsequent events.
- Supplemental information includes the management discussion and analysis and comparable selected financial information.

SUMMARY OF FINANCIAL STATEMENT RATIOS

Analyzing Firm Profitability

$$\text{Gross profit percentage} = \frac{\text{Gross profit on sales}}{\text{Net sales}}$$

$$\text{Return on sales} = \frac{\text{Net income}}{\text{Net sales}}$$

$$\text{Asset turnover} = \frac{\text{Net sales}}{\text{Average total assets}}$$

$$\text{Return on assets} = \frac{\text{Net income}}{\text{Average total assets}}$$

$$\text{Return on equity} = \frac{\text{Net income}}{\text{Average stockholders' equity}}$$

Analyzing Short-Term Firm Liquidity

$$\text{Current ratio} = \frac{\text{Current assets}}{\text{Current liabilities}}$$

$$\text{Quick ratio} = \frac{(\text{Cash and cash equivalents} + \text{Short-term investments} + \text{Accounts receivable})}{\text{Current liabilities}}$$

$$\text{Operating-cash-flow-to-current-liabilities ratio} = \frac{\text{Cash flow from operating activities}}{\text{Average current liabilities}}$$

$$\text{Accounts receivable turnover} = \frac{\text{Net sales}}{\text{Average accounts receivable (net)}}$$

$$\text{Average collection period} = \frac{365}{\text{Accounts receivable turnover (net)}}$$

$$\text{Inventory turnover} = \frac{\text{Cost of goods sold}}{\text{Average inventory}}$$

$$\text{Days' sales in inventory} = \frac{365}{\text{Inventory turnover}}$$

Analyzing Long-Term Firm Solvency

$$\text{Debt-to-equity ratio} = \frac{\text{Total liabilities}}{\text{Total stockholders' equity}}$$

$$\text{Times-interest-earned ratio} = \frac{\text{Income before interest expense and income taxes}}{\text{Interest expense}}$$

$$\text{Operating-cash-flow-to-capital-expenditures ratio} = \frac{\text{Cash flow from operating activities}}{\text{Annual net capital expenditures}}$$

Financial Ratios for Common Stockholders

$$\text{Earnings per share} = \frac{\text{(Net income-Preferred stock dividends)}}{\text{Weighted average common shares outstanding}}$$

$$\text{Price-earnings ratio} = \frac{\text{Market price per share}}{\text{Earnings per share}}$$

$$\text{Dividend yield} = \frac{\text{Annual dividend per share}}{\text{Market price per share}}$$

$$\text{Dividend payout ratio} = \frac{\text{Annual dividend per share}}{\text{Earnings per share}}$$

Concept	Method	Assessment	SUMMARY
How does a company's current performance compare with the prior year?	Income statement, balance sheet, and statement of cash flow for current and prior year. The financial statements should be compared using the prior year as the base. Percentage changes in financial statement amounts can be computed as the change between years divided by the base year amount.	Significant changes should be analyzed to determine the reason for any change.	TAKEAWAY 13.1
How do the relations within a company's income statement and balance sheet compare to those of prior years?	Income statement and balance sheet for current and prior year. Each income statement item should be presented as a percentage of sales revenue, and each balance sheet item should be presented as a percentage of total assets. Financial statements in this form are called common-size statements.	The percentages should be analyzed for differences between years, and significant changes should be analyzed to determine the reason for any change.	TAKEAWAY 13.2
How much profit is a company generating relative to the amount of assets invested in the company?	Income statement and balance sheet. Calculate the return on assets by dividing, net income by the average total assets for the year.	The higher the return on assets, the better a company is doing with respect to generating profits utilizing the assets under its control.	TAKEAWAY 13.3
How financially capable is a company to pay its current liabilities as they come due?	Income statement, balance sheet, and statement of cash flows. Calculate the current ratio, the quick ratio, and the operating-cash-flow-to-current-liabilities ratio.	The higher the ratios, the higher the probability that a company will have the ability to pay its current liabilities as they come due.	TAKEAWAY 13.4

continued

continued from previous page

SUMMARY	Concept ⟶	Method ⟶	Assessment
TAKEAWAY 13.5	How solvent is a company?	Income statement, balance sheet, and statement of cash flows. Calculate the debt-to-equity ratio, the times-interest-earned ratio, and the operating-cash-flow-to-capital-expenditures ratio.	The higher the times-interest-earned and the operating-cash-flow-to-capital-expenditures ratios, and the lower the debt-to-equity ratio, the greater is a company's solvency.
TAKEAWAY 13.6	How much dividends are common stockholders likely to receive?	Earnings per share, dividends per share, and market price of common stock. Calculate the dividend yield and dividend payout ratio.	The higher the dividend yield and the dividend payout ratio, the more dividends a stockholder can expect to receive.

KEY TERMS

Accounts receivable turnover (p. 13-20)

Asset turnover ratio (p. 13-16)

Average collection period (days' sales outstanding, or DSO) (p. 13-20)

Benchmarking (p. 13-15)

Change in accounting principle (p. 13-5)

Commitments (p. 13-30)

Common-size financial statement (p. 13-12)

Comparative financial statement analysis (p. 13-7)

Comprehensive income (p. 13-5)

Contingency (p. 13-31)

Current ratio (p. 13-18)

Days' sales in inventory (p. 13-21)

Debt-to-equity ratio (p. 13-22)

Discontinued operations (p. 13-5)

Dividend payout ratio (p. 13-26)

Dividend yield (p. 13-26)

Earnings per share (EPS) (p. 13-4, 13-25)

Gross profit (Gross margin) (p. 13-15)

Gross profit on sales (p. 13-15)

Gross profit percentage (p. 13-15)

Horizontal analysis (p. 13-7)

Inventory turnover (p. 13-21)

MD&A (p. 13-32)

Multiple-step income statement (p. 13-3)

Operating-cash-flow-to-capital-expenditures ratio (p. 13-24)

Operating-cash-flow-to-current-liabilities ratio (p. 13-19)

Operating cycle (p. 13-22)

Persistent earnings (p. 13-3)

Price-earnings ratio (P/E multiple) (p. 13-25)

Quarterly data (p. 13-31)

Quick ratio (acid-test ratio) (p. 13-18)

Return on assets (p. 13-16)

Return on equity (p. 13-17)

Return on sales profit margin (p. 13-15)

Segment (p. 13-31)

Single-step income statement (p. 13-3)

Subsequent events (p. 13-32)

Summary of significant accounting policies (p. 13-30)

Times-interest-earned ratio (interest coverage ratio) (p. 13-23)

Transitory earnings (p. 13-3)

Trend percentages (p. 13-10)

Unusual items (p. 13-3)

Vertical analysis (p. 13-7)

Working capital (p. 13-18)

Assignments with the logo in the margin are available in BusinessCourse.
See the Preface of the book for details.

SELF-STUDY QUESTIONS

(Answers to the Self-Study Questions are at the end of this chapter.)

LO1   1. **Assume that an income statement contains each of the three sections listed below. Which will be the last section presented in the income statement?**

     a.   Gross profit

     b.   Income from continuing operations

     c.   Discontinued operations

LO3   2. **When constructing a common-sized income statement, all amounts are expressed as a percentage of:**

     a.   net income.

     b.   gross profit.

     c.   net sales.

     d.   income from operations.

Questions 3–9 of the Self-Study Questions are based on the following data:

HYDRO COMPANY Balance Sheet December 31			
Cash.........................	$ 40,000	Current liabilities.........................	$ 80,000
Accounts receivable (net)............	80,000	10% bonds payable	120,000
Inventory.......................	130,000	Common stock	200,000
Plant and equipment (net)	250,000	Retained earnings	100,000
Total assets.....................	$500,000	Total liabilities and stockholders' equity	$500,000

Sales revenues were $800,000, gross profit was $320,000, and net income was $36,000. The income tax rate was 40 percent. One year ago, accounts receivable (net) were $76,000, inventory was $110,000, total assets were $460,000, and stockholders' equity was $260,000. The bonds payable were outstanding all year, and the interest expense was $12,000.

3. **The current ratio of Hydro Company at December 31 calculated using the above data was 3.13, and the company's working capital was $170,000. Which of the following would happen if the firm paid off $20,000 of its current liabilities on January 1 of the following year?**
   a. Both the current ratio and the working capital would decrease.
   b. Both the current ratio and the working capital would increase.
   c. The current ratio would increase, but the working capital would remain the same.
   d. The current ratio would increase, but the working capital would decrease.

   LO4

4. **What was the firm's inventory turnover?**
   a. 6.67   *c.* 6
   b. 4   *d.* 3.69

   LO4

5. **What was the firm's return on equity?**
   a. 25.7 percent   *c.* 17.1 percent
   b. 12.9 percent   *d.* 21.4 percent

   LO4

6. **What was the firm's average collection period?**
   a. 36.5 days   *c.* 35.6 days
   b. 37.4 days   *d.* 18.3 days

   LO4

7. **What was the firm's times-interest-earned ratio?**
   a. 4   *c.* 5
   b. 3   *d.* 6

   LO4

8. **What was the firm's return on sales?**
   a. 4.0 percent   *c.* 5.0 percent
   b. 4.5 percent   *d.* 5.5 percent

   LO4

9. **What was the firm's return on assets?**
   a. 6.0 percent   *c.* 7.5 percent
   b. 7.0 percent   *d.* 8.0 percent

   LO4

10. **When performing trend analysis, each line item is expressed as a percentage of:**
    a. net income.   *c.* the prior year amount.
    b. the base year amount. *d.* total assets.

    LO2

11. **Recognized limitations of financial statement analysis include each of the following except:**
    a. companies in the same industry using different accounting methods.
    b. inflation.
    c. different levels of profitability between companies.
    d. difficulty of classifying by industry conglomerates.

    LO5

12. **Financial statement disclosures include each of the following except:**
    a. notes to the financial statements.   *c.* supplementary information.
    b. parenthetical disclosures.   *d.* promotional giveaways.

    LO6
    (Appendix 13A)

QUESTIONS

1. What is the difference between a single-step income statement and a multiple-step income statement?

2. Which of the following amounts would appear only in a multiple-step income statement?
   a. Income from continuing operations.   c. Gross profit on sales.
   b. Income from discontinued operations.   d. Net income.

3. What is a business segment? Why are gains and losses from a discontinued segment reported in a separate section of the income statement?

4. How do horizontal analysis and vertical analysis of financial statements differ?

5. "Financial statement users should focus attention on each item showing a large percentage change from one year to the next." Is this statement correct? Why?

6. What are trend percentages, and how are they calculated? What pitfalls must financial statement users avoid when preparing trend percentages?

7. What are common-size financial statements, and how are they used?

8. What item is the key figure (that is, 100 percent) in a common-size income statement? A common-size balance sheet?

9. During the past year, Lite Company had net income of $5 million, and Scanlon Company had net income of $8 million. Both companies manufacture electrical components for the construction industry. What additional information would you need to compare the profitability of the two companies?

10. Under what circumstances can the return on sales be used to assess the profitability of a company? Can this ratio be used to compare the profitability of companies from different industries? Explain.

11. What is the relationship between asset turnover, return on assets, and return on sales?

12. Blare Company had a return on sales of 6.5 percent and an asset turnover of 2.40. What is Blare's return on assets?

13. What does the return on equity measure?

14. How does the quick ratio differ from the current ratio?

15. For each of the following ratios, is a high ratio or low ratio considered, in general, a positive sign?
    a. Current ratio
    b. Quick ratio
    c. Operating-cash-flow-to-current-liabilities ratio
    d. Accounts receivable turnover
    e. Average collection period
    f. Inventory turnover
    g. Days' sales in inventory

16. What is the significance of the debt-to-equity ratio, and how is it computed?

17. What does the times-interest-earned ratio indicate, and how is it calculated?

18. What does the operating-cash-flow-to-capital-expenditures ratio measure?

19. Clair, Inc., earned $4.50 per share of common stock in the current year and paid dividends of $2.34 per share. The most recent market price per share of the common stock is $46.80. What is the company's (a) price-earnings ratio, (b) dividend yield, and (c) dividend payout ratio?

20. What are two inherent limitations of financial statement data?

SHORT EXERCISES

Use the following financial data for Brenner Instruments to answer Short Exercises 13-1 through 13-10:

(Thousands of Dollars, except Earnings per Share)	
Sales revenue	$210,000
Cost of goods sold	125,000
Net income	8,300
Dividends	2,600
Earnings per share	4.15

BRENNER INSTRUMENTS, INC. Balance Sheets (Thousands of Dollars)	Current Year	Previous Year
Assets		
Cash....	$ 18,300	$ 18,000
Accounts receivable (net)........	46,000	41,000
Inventory.......	39,500	43,700
Total current assets....	103,800	102,700
Plant assets (net)........	52,600	50,500
Other assets........	15,600	13,800
Total assets.....	$172,000	$167,000
Liabilities and Stockholders' Equity		
Notes payable—banks.........	$ 6,000	$ 6,000
Accounts payable.........	22,500	18,700
Accrued liabilities......	16,500	21,000
Total current liabilities......	45,000	45,700
9% bonds payable	40,000	40,000
Total liabilities	85,000	85,700
Common stock, $25 par value (2,000,000 shares).....	50,000	50,000
Retained earnings	37,000	31,300
Total stockholders' equity	87,000	81,300
Total liabilities and stockholders' equity	$172,000	$167,000

Industry Average Ratios for Competitors	
Quick ratio	1.3
Current ratio	2.4
Accounts receivable turnover.....	5.9 times
Inventory turnover.....	3.5 times
Debt-to-equity ratio.....	0.73
Gross profit percentage	42.8 percent
Return on sales	4.5 percent
Return on assets	7.6 percent

SE13-1. **Quick Ratio** Calculate the company's quick ratio for the current year and compare the result to the industry average. **LO4**

SE13-2. **Current Ratio** Calculate the company's current ratio for the current year and compare the result to the industry average. **LO4**

SE13-3. **Accounts Receivable Turnover** Calculate the company's accounts receivable turnover for the current year and compare the result to the industry average. **LO4**

SE13-4. **Inventory Turnover** Calculate the company's inventory turnover for the current year and compare the result to the industry average. **LO4**

SE13-5. **Debit-to-Equity Ratio** Calculate the company's current year debt-to-equity ratio and compare the result to the industry average. **LO4**

SE13-6. **Gross Profit Percentage** Calculate the company's current year gross profit percentage and compare the result to the industry average. **LO4**

SE13-7. **Return on Sales** Calculate the company's return on sales for the current year and compare the result to the industry average. **LO4**

SE13-8. **Return on Assets** Calculate the company's return on assets for the current year and compare the result to the industry average. **LO4**

SE13-9. **Dividends per Share** Calculate the company's dividend paid per share of common stock. What was the dividend payout ratio? **LO4**

SE13-10. **Earnings per Share** If the company's most recent price per share of common stock is $62.25, what is the company's price-earnings ratio and dividend yield? **LO4**

LO1   **SE13-11.   Persistent Earnings** Identify each of the following items as either (P) persistent or (T) transitory.

   a.   Sale of merchandise.   *c.*   Interest income.

   b.   Settlement of a lawsuit.   *d.*   Payment to vendors.

   e.   Loss from expropriations of property by a foreign government.

LO2   **SE13-12.   Horizontal Analysis** Total assets were $1,000,000 in 2022, $900,000 in 2021, and $950,000 in 2020. What was the percentage change from 2020 to 2021 and from 2021 to 2022? Was the change an increase or a decrease?

LO3   **SE13-13.   Common-Size Income Statement** A partial common-size income statement for Jag Company for three years is shown below.

Item	2022	2021	2020
Net sales.	100.0	100.0	100.0
Cost of goods sold	60.5	63.0	62.5
Other expenses	21.0	19.0	20.5

Did Jag's net income as a percentage of net sales increase, remain the same, or decrease over the three-year period?

LO5   **SE13-14.   Financial Statement Analysis Limitations** Which of the following is not considered a limitation of financial statement analysis?

   a.   Firms may use different accounting methods.

   b.   Firms may be audited by different auditing firms.

   c.   Inflation may distort trend analysis.

   d.   It may be difficult to classify large conglomerate firms by industry.

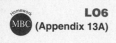

LO6 **(Appendix 13A)**   **SE13-15.   Financial Statement Disclosures** Which of the following is not a common form of financial statement disclosure?

   a.   Notes to financial statements.   *c.*   Parenthetical disclosure.

   b.   Supplemental information.   *d.*   Bullet points.

DATA ANALYTICS

DA13-1.   Critically Analyzing a Visualization in Excel The financial information in the Excel file associated with this exercise was obtained from 10-K reports for **Costco Wholesale Corporation**. In this exercise, we examine how changing the starting point (baseline) of the y-axis from 0.0 impacts the chart that is created. The chart that is created for Costco examines return on equity over a five-year period. The return on equity ratio measures the return of the stockholders' investment in the company. An increase in the ratio generally means that the company is more efficiently using its equity to generate profits.

Required

1. Download Excel file DA13-1 found in myBusinessCourse.

2. Calculate the return on equity for Costco for Year 2 through Year 6 in Excel. Carry your answers to three decimal places.

3. Create a line chart showing the return on equity for Year 2 through Year 6. Note that when you use the default setting, the y-axis starts at point 0.0. *Hint:* Highlight data; click Insert, Line. You may need to edit the data selections. Right-click inside the chart, Select Data. The Series (y-axis) should be the ROE; the Category (x-axis) should be Years 2–6.

4. Create a second line chart showing the return on equity for Year 2 through Year 6. For this second chart, change the scale of the y-axis to start at 0.17 and to end at 0.27. *Hint:* Right-click inside the y-axis scale and select Format Axis. Set Minimum bound as 0.17 and Maximum bound as 0.27 on the column chart icon tab.

5. Indicate which of the following descriptions best depicts the trends in Chart 1 and the description that best depicts the trends in Chart 2:

   a.   Return on equity increased sharply from Year 2 to Year 4, stabilized for a year and dropped more rapidly in Year 5.

   b.   Return on equity gradually increased from Year 2 to Year 4, and remained fairly stable through Year 6.

Return on equity

$$\frac{\text{Net income}}{\text{Average stockholders' equity}}$$

6. Compute the percentage change in ROE from Year 2 to Year 3, Year 3 to Year 4, Year 4 to Year 5, and Year 5 to Year 6 in Excel.

7. Compare Chart 1 to Chart 2.

DA13-2. **Analyzing Trends in the Price-to-Earnings Ratio using Excel** The Excel file associated with this exercise includes market price and ratio information for companies in the S&P 500. (Data obtained from https://datahub.io/core/s-and-p-500-companies#data on August 26, 2021, made available under the Public Domain Dedication and License v1.0 whose full text can be found at: http://opendatacommons.org/licenses/pddl/1.0/.)

For this exercise, we examine trends in the price-to-earnings ratio of S&P 500 companies by industry segment. The price-to-earnings ratio measures the amount an investor is willing to pay per share of stock for each dollar of earnings per share. An increase in this ratio generally means that an investor would have a higher expectation for company profits in the future. In the first analysis, we calculate the average value or mean of the price-to-earnings ratio for each segment. In the second analysis, we calculate the median value of the price-to-earnings ratio for each segment. Lastly, we compare the average and median ratio results and analyze the cause of the differences.

Required

Price-to Earnings Ratio

$$\frac{\text{Market price per share}}{\text{Earnings per share}}$$

1. Download Excel file DA13-2 found in myBusinessCourse.

2. Create a PivotTable (PivotTable 1) showing the average Price/Earnings ratio by sector. *Hint:* With your cursor in your data, select Insert, PivotChart. Add Sector to Rows and Price/Earnings to Values; select Average for the display of Price/Earnings by right-clicking on an amount in the PivotTable, clicking Value Field Settings, and selecting Average.

3. Remove the grand total row (which is irrelevant for this table). *Hint:* Click on the Design tab, Grand totals, Off for rows & columns.

4. Change display of your data to show two decimal places. *Hint:* Right-click on an amount in the PivotTable, click on number format, and make change.

5. Sort your PivotTable in the order of highest to lowest values. *Hint:* Right-click on an amount in the PivotTable; click Sort, Sort Largest to smallest.

6. Indicate which sector has the highest and which sector has the lowest average price/earnings ratio.

7. Copy original PivotTable, paste below the original to create PivotTable 2, change the calculation of price/earnings to now display maximum value, and sort Price/Earnings values from largest to smallest values. *Hint:* Right-click on an amount in the PivotTable, and click Value Field Settings.

8. Indicate which sector has the highest and which sector has the lowest maximum price/earnings ratio.

9. Copy original PivotTable, paste below PivotTable 2 to create PivotTable 3, change the calculation of price/earnings to now display minimum value, and sort Price/Earnings values from largest to smallest values. *Hint:* Click the i button next to Average of Price/Earnings and select Min.

10. Indicate which sector has the highest and which sector has the lowest minimum price/earnings ratio.

11. Read the following article, "Stuck in the Middle—Mean vs. Median," by Dr. Dieter Schremmer found at the following link: https://www.clinfo.eu/mean-median/.

12. Compute the median value of the Price/Earnings ratio for the Energy sector and for the Industrials sector. *Hint:* Median is not a calculation option within the PivotTables. Instead, double-click on the dollar amount in the PivotTable for Energy to open up a new sheet with the underlying data. In a new cell (at least two rows below the table) calculate the median of the Price/Earnings data: =MEDIAN(xx). Repeat steps for the Industrials sector.

13. Compute the difference between the Maximum Price/Earnings (see PivotTable 2) and the Minimum Price/Earnings (see PivotTable 3) for both sectors: Energy and Industrials.

14. Compare the median values obtained in part 12 to the average values listed in PivotTable 1 and answer the following question: What caused the differences between the mean and median values in your calculations?

DA13-3. **Preparing Tableau Visualizations to Analyze the Use of Assets Through Asset Turnover** Refer to PF-26 in Appendix F. This problem uses Tableau to analyze asset utilization of S&P 500 companies in certain segments through the asset turnover ratio.

DA13-4. **Preparing Tableau Visualizations to Decompose Return on Equity Using the Dupont Method: Part 1, Part II, Part III** Refer to PF-29, PF-30, and PF-31 in Appendix F. This three-part problem uses Tableau to decompose the return on equity ratio of S&P 500 companies using the DuPont method. The final part of the problem includes the creation of an interactive dashboard.

DATA VISUALIZATION

Data Visualization Activities are available in myBusinessCourse. These assignments use Tableau Dashboards to expose students to visual depictions of data and introduce students to data analytics through data visualizations. These exercises are easily assignable and auto graded by MBC.

EXERCISES—SET A

LO1   **E13-1A.**   **Income Statement Sections** During the current year, David Corporation sold a segment of its business at a gain of $210,000. Until it was sold, the segment had a current period operating loss of $75,000. The company had $700,000 income from continuing operations for the current year. Prepare the lower part of the income statement, beginning with the $700,000 income from continuing operations. Follow tax allocation procedures, assuming that all changes in income are subject to a 20 percent income tax rate. Disregard earnings per share disclosures.

LO4   **E13-2A.**   **Earnings per Share** Myrtle Corporation began the year with a simple capital structure consisting of 480,000 shares of outstanding common stock. On April 1, 10,000 additional common shares were issued, and another 60,000 common shares were issued on August 1. The company had net income for the year of $589,375. Calculate the earnings per share of common stock.

LO2   **E13-3A.**   **Comparative Income Statements** Consider the following income statement data from the Mono Company:

	Current Year	Previous Year
Sales revenue	$600,000	$450,000
Cost of goods sold	336,000	279,000
Selling expenses	105,000	99,000
Administrative expenses	60,000	50,000
Income tax expense	4,000	3,000

   a.   Prepare a comparative income statement, showing increases and decreases in dollars and in percentages.
   b.   Comment briefly on the changes between the two years.

LO3   **E13-4A.**   **Common-Size Income Statements** Refer to the income statement data given in Exercise E13-3A.

   a.   Prepare common-size income statements for each year.
   b.   Compare the common-size income statements and comment briefly.

LO4   **E13-5A.**   **Ratios Analyzing Firm Profitability** The following information is available for Jay Company:

Annual Data	Current Year	Previous Year
Net sales	$9,000,000	$8,200,000
Gross profit on sales	3,050,000	2,736,000
Net income	567,600	500,000

Year-End Data	Dec. 31, Current Year	Dec. 31, Previous Year
Total assets	$6,500,000	$6,000,000
Stockholders' equity	5,000,000	3,200,000

Calculate the following ratios for the current year:

a.   Gross profit percentage   d.   Return on assets
b.   Return on sales   e.   Return on equity
c.   Asset turnover

E13-6A.   **Working Capital and Short-Term Liquidity Ratios**   Ritter Company has a current ratio of 3.00 on December 31. On that date the company's current assets are as follows:

LO4

Cash.	$ 32,000
Short-term investments	49,300
Accounts receivable (net).	170,000
Inventory.	200,000
Prepaid expenses.	11,600
Current assets	$462,900

Ritter Company's current liabilities at the beginning of the year were $150,000, and during the year its operating activities provided a cash flow of $60,000.

a.   What are the firm's current liabilities on December 31?
b.   What is the firm's working capital on December 31?
c.   What is the quick ratio on December 31?
d.   What is Bell's operating-cash-flow-to-current-liabilities ratio?

E13-7A.   **Accounts Receivable and Inventory Ratios**   Ritter Company, whose current assets at December 31 are shown in Exercise E13-6A, had net sales for the year of $850,000 and cost of goods sold of $550,000. At the beginning of the year, Ritter's accounts receivable (net) were $160,000, and its inventory was $175,000.

LO4

a.   What is the company's accounts receivable turnover for the year?
b.   What is the company's average collection period for the year?
c.   What is the company's inventory turnover for the year?
d.   What is the company's days' sales in inventory for the year?

E13-8A.   **Ratios Analyzing Long-Term Firm Solvency**   The following information is available for Banner Company:

LO4

Annual Data	Current Year	Previous Year
Interest expense.	$ 85,000	$ 82,000
Income tax expense.	200,000	106,000
Net income.	496,500	425,000
Capital expenditures.	320,000	380,000
Cash provided by operating activities.	450,000	390,000

Year-End Data	Dec. 31, Current Year	Dec. 31, Previous Year
Total liabilities.	$2,400,000	$1,900,000
Total stockholders' equity.	4,200,000	3,800,000

Calculate the following:

a.   Current year debt-to-equity ratio.
b.   Current year times-interest-earned ratio.
c.   Current year operating-cash-flow-to-capital-expenditures ratio.

E13-9A.   **Financial Ratios for Common Stockholders**   Morgan Corporation has only common stock outstanding. The firm reported earnings per share of $6.00 for the year. During the year, Morgan paid dividends of $2.10 per share. At year-end the current market price of the stock was $72 per share. Calculate the following:

LO4

a.   Price-earnings ratio   c.   Dividend payout ratio
b.   Dividend yield

LO5 **E13-10A. Financial Statement Limitations** You have been asked to perform financial statement analysis on the Rush Company. The Rush Company is a large chain of retail outlets that sells a wide range of household items. Last year the company introduced its own credit card and is pleased that profit from this financing activity now accounts for over 20 percent of the company's total profit. As part of your analysis you have chosen to compare the Rush Company to Johnson Stores, a much larger chain of stores. Johnson Stores sells household items and groceries, but it does not have its own credit card. Your analysis includes both trend analysis and vertical analysis. Identify some of the limitations from the description above.

LO6 **E13-11A. Financial Statement Notes** The notes to financial statements present information on significant ac-
(Appendix 13A) counting policies, complex or special transactions, details of reported amounts, commitments, contingencies, segments, quarterly data, and subsequent events. Indicate which type of note disclosure is illustrated by each of the following notes:

a. The company has agreed to purchase seven EMB-120 aircraft and related spare parts. The aggregate cost of these aircraft is approximately $52,000,150, subject to a cost escalation provision. The aircraft are scheduled to be delivered over the next two fiscal years.

b. The company has deferred certain costs related to major accounting and information systems enhancements that are anticipated to benefit future years. Upon completion, the related cost is amortized over a period not exceeding five years.

c. The company has guaranteed loans and leases of independent distributors approximating $27,500,000 as of December 31 of the current year.

d. An officer of the company is also a director of a major raw material supplier of the company. The amount of raw material purchases from this supplier approximated $595,000 in the current year.

EXERCISES—SET B

LO1 **E13-1B. Income Statement Sections** During the current year, Ediza Corporation sold a segment of its business at a loss of $175,000. Until it was sold, the segment had a current period operating loss of $200,000. The company has $750,000 income from continuing operations for the current year. Prepare the lower part of the income statement, beginning with the $750,000 income from continuing operations. Follow tax allocation procedures, assuming that all changes in income are subject to a 20 percent income tax rate. Disregard earnings per share disclosures.

LO4 **E13-2B. Earnings per Share** Heart Corporation began the year with a simple capital structure consisting of 35,000 shares of common stock outstanding. On May 1, 5,000 additional common shares were issued, and another 20,000 common shares were issued on September 1. The company had a net income for the year of $468,000. Calculate the earnings per share of common stock.

LO2 **E13-3B. Comparative Balance Sheets** Consider the following balance sheet data for Davis Co., Inc., an electronics and major appliance retailer (amounts in thousands):

	Current Year	Previous Year
Cash and cash equivalents	$ 60,872	$ 7,138
Accounts receivables	52,944	37,968
Merchandise inventories	637,950	249,991
Other current assets	13,844	9,729
Current assets	765,610	304,826
Property and equipment (net)	172,724	126,442
Other assets	15,160	7,774
Total assets	$953,494	$439,042
Current liabilities	$402,028	$186,005
Long-term liabilities	239,022	70,854
Total liabilities	641,050	256,859
Common stock	3,087	1,149
Additional paid-in-capital	224,089	137,151
Retained earnings	85,268	43,883
Total stockholders' equity	312,444	182,183
Total liabilities and stockholders' equity	$953,494	$439,042

     a.   Prepare a comparative balance sheet, showing increases in dollars and percentages.

     b.   Comment briefly on the changes between the two years.

E13-4B.   Common-Size Balance Sheets   Refer to the balance sheet data given in Exercise E13-3B.   **LO3**

     a.   Prepare common-size balance sheets for each year. (Use total assets as the base amount for computing percentages.)

     b.   Compare the common-size balance sheets and comment briefly.

E13-5B.   Ratios Analyzing Firm Profitability   The following information is available for Virginia Company: **LO4**

Annual Data	Current Year	Previous Year
Sales revenue.	$6,600,000	$6,000,000
Cost of goods sold	4,006,400	3,800,000
Net income	325,000	264,000

Year-End Data	Dec. 31, Current Year	Dec. 31, Previous Year
Total assets.	$2,850,000	$2,500,000
Stockholders' equity	1,900,000	1,700,000

Calculate the following ratios for the current year:

a.	Gross profit percentage	*d.*	Return on assets
b.	Return on sales	*e.*	Return on equity
c.	Asset turnover		

E13-6B.   Working Capital and Short-Term Firm Liquidity Ratios   Purple Company has a current ratio of   **LO4**
2.2 on December 31. On that date its current assets are as follows:

Cash and cash equivalents	$ 13,000
Short-term investments	90,000
Accounts receivable (net)	125,000
Inventory.	178,500
Prepaid expenses.	11,500
Current assets	$418,000

Purple Company's current liabilities at the beginning of the year were $195,000, and during the year its operating activities provided a cash flow of $35,000.

     a.   What are the firm's current liabilities at December 31?

     b.   What is the firm's working capital on December 31?

     c.   What is the quick ratio on December 31?

     d.   What is the firm's operating-cash-flow-to-current-liabilities ratio?

E13-7B.   Accounts Receivable and Inventory Ratios   Purple Company, whose current assets at December   **LO4**
31 are shown in Exercise E13-6B, had net sales for the year of $580,000 and cost of goods sold of
$339,000. At the beginning of the year, accounts receivable (net) were $121,000 and inventory was
$160,500.

     a.   What is the company's accounts receivable turnover?

     b.   What is the company's average collection period?

     c.   What is the company's inventory turnover?

     d.   What is the company's days' sales in inventory?

LO4   **E13-8B.**   **Ratios Analyzing Long-Term Firm Solvency** The following information is available for Rae Company:

Annual Data	Current Year	Previous Year
Interest expense.	$170,000	$166,000
Income tax expense	126,000	117,000
Net income	310,000	275,000
Capital expenditures.	435,000	350,000
Cash provided by operating activities.	247,000	220,000

Year-End Data	Dec. 31, Current Year	Dec. 31, Previous Year
Total liabilities	$3,400,000	$2,900,000
Total stockholders' equity	2,200,000	2,000,000

Calculate the following:

a.   Current year debt-to-equity ratio

b.   Current year times-interest-earned ratio

c.   Current year operating-cash-flow-to-capital-expenditures ratio

LO4   **E13-9B.**   **Financial Ratios for Common Stockholders** Jason Corporation has only common stock outstanding. The firm reported earnings per share of $4.00 for the year. During the year, Jason paid dividends of $0.85 per share. At year-end, the current market price of the stock was $70.30 per share.

Calculate the following:

a.   Price-earnings ratio   *c.*   Dividend payout ratio

b.   Dividend yield

LO5   **E13-10B.** **Financial Statement Limitations** You have been asked to perform financial statement analysis on the Ian Company. The Ian Company is a large manufacturer of construction machinery and vehicles. Last year the company closed down a segment of the business that produced mining equipment because it was not providing an adequate return on assets. This segment represented 15 percent of the company's total assets. As part of your analysis you have chosen to compare the Ian Company to Bertran, Inc., a much smaller manufacturer of equipment, although Bertran, Inc., also performs contract repairs for many other brands of equipment. Your analysis includes both trend analysis and vertical analysis. Identify some of the limitations from the description above.

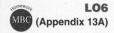

LO6   **E13-11B.** **Financial Statement Notes** Notes to the financial statements present information on significant accounting policies, complex or special transactions, details of reported amounts, commitments, contingencies, segments, quarterly data, and subsequent events. Indicate the type of note disclosure that is illustrated by each of the following notes:

a.   Sales by the Farm and Equipment segment to independent dealers are recorded at the time of shipment to those dealers. Sales through company-owned retail stores are recorded at the time of sale to retail customers.

b.   Members of the board of directors, the advisory board, and employees are not charged the vendor's commission on property sold at auction for their benefit. (From the notes of an auctioneer company.)

c.   Sales to an airline company accounted for approximately 48 percent of the company's net sales in the current year.

d.   The company's product liability insurance coverage with respect to insured events occurring after January 1 of the current year is substantially less than the amount of that insurance available in the recent past. The company is now predominantly self-insured in this area. The reduction in insurance coverage reflects trends in the liability insurance field generally and is not unique to the company.

PROBLEMS—SET A

P13-1A. Income Statement Format The following information from Buchanan Company's current operations is available:

LO1

Administrative expenses	$ 73,000
Cost of goods sold	470,000
Sales revenue	772,000
Selling expenses	87,000
Interest expense	10,000
Loss from operations of discontinued segment	60,000
Gain on disposal of discontinued segment	40,000
Income taxes:	
Amount applicable to ordinary operations	40,000
Reduction applicable to loss from operations of discontinued segment	14,000
Amount applicable to gain on disposal of discontinued segment	8,000

Required
a. Prepare a multiple-step income statement. (Disregard earnings per share.)
b. Prepare a single-step income statement. (Disregard earnings per share.)

P13-2A. Earnings per Share Stanford Corporation began the year with 150,000 shares of common stock outstanding. On March 1, an additional 10,000 shares of common stock were issued. On August 1, another 16,000 shares of common stock were issued. On November 1, 12,000 shares of common stock were acquired as Treasury Stock. Stanford Corporation's net income for the calendar year is $489,000.

LO4

Required
Calculate the company's earnings per share.

P13-3A. Earnings per Share and Multiple-Step Income Statement The following summarized data relate to Robert Corporation's current operations:

LO1, 4

Sales revenue	$800,000
Cost of goods sold	460,000
Selling expenses	65,000
Administrative expenses	72,000
Loss on sale of equipment	4,000
Income tax expense	43,000
Shares of common stock	
Outstanding at January 1	20,000 shares
Additional issued at May 1	7,000 shares
Additional issued at November 1	2,000 shares

Required
Prepare a multiple-step income statement for Robert Corporation for the year. Include earnings per share disclosure at the bottom of the income statement.

P13-4A. Trend Percentages Net sales, net income, and total asset figures for Janice Controls, Inc., for five consecutive years are given below. (Janice manufactures pollution controls.)

LO2, 4

	Annual Amounts (Thousands of Dollars)				
	Year 1	Year 2	Year 3	Year 4	Year 5
Net sales	$72,000	$79,800	$85,275	$88,400	$94,700
Net income	3,200	3,650	4,000	4,250	4,790
Total assets	42,500	45,000	48,700	51,000	54,900

Required
a. Calculate trend percentages, using Year 1 as the base year.
b. Calculate the return on sales for each year. (Rates above 2.8 percent are considered good for manufacturers of pollution controls; rates above 6.5 percent are considered very good.)
c. Comment on the results of your analysis.

LO4   P13-5A.   Changes in Various Ratios Presented below is selected information for Turner Company:

	Current Year	Previous Year
Sales revenue.	$950,000	$850,000
Cost of goods sold	575,000	545,000
Interest expense.	20,000	20,000
Income tax expense	27,000	30,000
Net income.	65,000	55,000
Cash flow from operating activities.	70,000	60,000
Capital expenditures.	45,000	45,000
Accounts receivable (net), December 31	126,000	120,000
Inventory, December 31	196,000	160,000
Stockholders' equity, December 31	450,000	400,000
Total assets, December 31.	750,000	675,000

Required

a. Calculate the following ratios for the current year. The previous year results are given for comparative purposes.

	Previous Year
Gross profit percentage	35.9 percent
Return on assets	8.3 percent
Return on sales	6.5 percent
Return on equity (no preferred stock was outstanding)	13.9 percent
Accounts receivable turnover	8.00
Average collection period	45.6 days
Inventory turnover.	3.61
Times-interest-earned ratio	5.25
Operating-cash-flow-to-capital-expenditures ratio	1.33

b. Comment on the changes between the two years.

LO2, 3, 4   P13-6A. **Ratios from Comparative and Common-Size Data** Consider the following financial statements for Benjamin Company.

During the current year, management obtained additional bond financing to enlarge its production facilities. The company faced higher production costs during the year for such things as fuel, materials, and freight. Because of temporary government price controls, a planned price increase on products was delayed several months.

As a holder of both common and preferred stock, you decide to analyze the financial statements:

BENJAMIN COMPANY Balance Sheets (Thousands of Dollars)	Dec. 31, Current Year	Dec. 31, Previous Year
Assets		
Cash and cash equivalents	$ 21,000	$ 12,000
Accounts receivable (net).	55,000	43,000
Inventory.	120,000	105,000
Prepaid expenses.	20,000	14,000
Plant and other assets (net)	471,000	411,000
Total assets.	$687,000	$585,000
Liabilities and Stockholders' Equity		
Current liabilities.	$ 93,000	$ 82,000
10% bonds payable	225,000	160,000
9% Preferred stock, $50 par value	75,000	75,000
Common stock, $10 par value	200,000	200,000
Retained earnings	94,000	68,000
Total liabilities and stockholders' equity	$687,000	$585,000

BENJAMIN COMPANY Income Statements (Thousands of Dollars)		
	Current Year	**Previous Year**
Sales revenue.	$820,000	$680,000
Cost of goods sold	545,000	433,920
Gross profit on sales.	275,000	246,080
Selling and administrative expenses	175,000	149,200
Income before interest expense and income taxes	100,000	96,880
Interest expense.	23,000	16,000
Income before income taxes.	77,000	80,880
Income tax expense	15,000	19,000
Net income	$ 62,000	$ 61,880
Other financial data (thousands of dollars)		
Cash provided by operating activities	$ 65,200	$ 60,500
Preferred stock dividends	6,750	6,750

Required

a. Calculate the following for each year: current ratio, quick ratio, operating-cash-flow-to-current-liabilities ratio (current liabilities were $77,000,000 at January 1 of the previous year), inventory turnover (inventory was $87,000,000 at January 1, 2018), debt-to-equity ratio, times-interest-earned ratio, return on assets (total assets were $490,000,000 at January 1 of the previous year), and return on equity (stockholders' equity was $235,000,000 at January 1 of the previous year).

b. Calculate common-size percentages for each year's income statement.

c. Comment on the results of your analysis.

P13-7A. **Constructing Statements from Ratio Data** The following are the current year financial statements for Omni Company, with almost all dollar amounts missing: **LO4**

OMNI COMPANY Balance Sheet December 31				
Cash.	$	?	Current liabilities.	$?
Accounts receivable (net)		?	8% bonds payable	?
Inventory.		?	Common stock	?
Equipment (net)		?	Retained earnings	950,000
			Total liabilities and	
Total assets.	$6,500,000		stockholders' equity.	$6,500,000

OMNI COMPANY Income Statement For the Year Ended December 31	
Sales revenue.	$?
Cost of goods sold	?
Gross profit.	?
Selling and administrative expenses	?
Income before interest expense and income taxes	?
Interest expense.	80,000
Income before income taxes.	?
Income tax expense (20%).	?
Net income	$580,000

The following information is available about Omni Company's financial statements:

1. Quick ratio, 0.95.
2. Inventory turnover (inventory at January 1 was $924,000), 5 times.
3. Return on sales, 8.0 percent.

4. Accounts receivable turnover (accounts receivable (net) at January 1 were $860,000), 8 times.

5. Gross profit percentage, 32 percent.

6. Return on equity (stockholders' equity at January 1 was $3,300,000), 16 percent.

7. The interest expense relates to the bonds payable that were outstanding all year.

Required

Compute the missing amounts, and complete the financial statements of Omni Company. *Hint:* Complete the income statement first.

LO4   P13-8A.   Ratios Compared with Industry Averages Because you own the common stock of Jacob Corporation, a paper manufacturer, you decide to analyze the firm's performance for the most recent year. The following data are taken from the firm's latest annual report:

	Dec. 31, Current Year	Dec. 31, Previous Year
Quick assets.	$ 700,000	$ 552,000
Inventory and prepaid expenses.	372,000	312,000
Other assets.	4,788,000	4,200,000
Total assets.	$5,860,000	$5,064,000
Current liabilities.	$ 724,000	$ 564,000
10% bonds payable	1,440,000	1,440,000
8% Preferred stock, $100 par value	480,000	480,000
Common stock, $10 par value	2,700,000	2,160,000
Retained earnings	516,000	420,000
Total liabilities and stockholders' equity	$5,860,000	$5,064,000

For the current year, net sales amount to $12,500,000, net income is $550,000, and preferred stock dividends paid are $50,000.

Required

a. Calculate the following ratios for the current year:

1. Return on sales   4. Quick ratio
2. Return on assets   5. Current ratio
3. Return on equity   6. Debt-to-equity ratio

b. Trade association statistics and information provided by credit agencies reveal the following data on industry norms:

	Median	Upper Quartile
Return on sales	4.2 percent	8.6 percent
Return on assets	6.5 percent	11.2 percent
Return on equity.	10.6 percent	16.3 percent
Quick ratio	1.0	1.8
Current ratio	1.8	3.0
Debt-to-equity-ratio.	1.08	0.66

Compare Jacob Corporation's performance with industry performance.

LO4   P13-9A.   Ratios Compared with Industry Averages Adams Plastics, Inc., manufactures various plastic and synthetic products. Financial statement data for the firm follow:

	Current Year (Thousands of Dollars, except Earnings per Share)
Sales revenue.	$825,000
Cost of goods sold	550,000
Net income	50,500
Dividends	17,500
Earnings per share.	4.04

ADAMS PLASTICS, INC. Balance Sheets (Thousands of Dollars)	Dec. 31, Current Year	Dec. 31, Previous Year
Assets		
Cash..	$ 2,100	$ 2,700
Accounts receivable (net).............................	66,900	60,900
Inventory......................................	148,000	140,000
Total current assets.....................................	217,000	203,600
Plant assets (net).......................................	215,000	194,000
Other assets...	13,900	4,000
Total assets..	$445,900	$401,600
Liabilities and Stockholders' Equity		
Notes payable—banks....................................	$ 31,400	$ 25,000
Accounts payable.......................................	27,600	23,000
Accrued liabilities......................................	25,100	24,800
Total current liabilities.....................	84,100	72,800
10% bonds payable	150,000	150,000
Total liabilities	234,100	222,800
Common stock, $10 par value (12,500,000 shares).............	125,000	125,000
Retained earnings	86,800	53,800
Total stockholders' equity	211,800	178,800
Total liabilities and stockholders' equity	$445,900	$401,600

Required

a. Using the given data, calculate items 1 through 8 below for the current year. Compare the performance of Adams Plastics, Inc., with the following industry averages and comment on its operations.

	Median Ratios for Manufacturers of Plastic and Synthetic Products
Quick ratio	1.2
Current ratio	1.9
Accounts receivable turnover	7.9 times
Inventory turnover.....................................	7.8 times
Debt-to-equity ratio....................................	0.95
Gross profit percentage	32.7 percent
Return on sales	3.5 percent
Return on assets	6.3 percent

b. Calculate the dividends paid per share of common stock. What was the dividend payout ratio?

c. If the most recent price per share of common stock is $51.00, what is the price-earnings ratio? The dividend yield?

P13-10A. Financial Statement Notes: Quarterly Data Quarterly data are presented below for Company A and Company B. One of these companies is Gibson Greetings, Inc., which manufactures and sells greeting cards. The other company is Hon Industries, Inc., which manufactures and sells office furniture. Both companies are on a calendar-year basis.   **LO2**

	First Quarter	Second Quarter	Third Quarter	Fourth Quarter	Year
			(Amounts in Thousands)		
Company A					
Net sales.	$186,111	$177,537	$203,070	$213,608	$780,326
Gross profit	55,457	53,643	64,024	69,374	242,498
Company B					
Net sales.	$ 84,896	$ 83,796	$142,137	$235,336	$546,165
Gross profit	53,900	52,983	66,018	104,961	277,862

Required

a. Compute the percent of annual net sales generated each quarter by Company A. Round to the nearest percent.

b. Compute the percent of annual net sales generated each quarter by Company B. Round to the nearest percent.

c. Which company has the most seasonal business? Briefly explain.

d. Which company is Gibson Greetings, Inc.? Hon Industries, Inc.? Briefly explain.

e. Which company's interim quarterly data are probably most useful for predicting annual results? Briefly explain.

PROBLEMS—SET B

LO1   P13-1B.   Income Statement Format The following information from Jefferson Company's operations is available:

Administrative expenses.	$ 145,000
Cost of goods sold	928,000
Sales revenue.	1,850,000
Selling expenses	174,000
Interest expense.	14,000
Loss from operations of discontinued segment	120,000
Gain on disposal of discontinued segment.	90,000
Income taxes	
Amount applicable to ordinary operations.	125,000
Reduction applicable to loss from operations of discontinued segment	22,000
Amount applicable to gain on disposal of discontinued segment	15,000

Required

a. Prepare a multiple-step income statement. (Disregard earnings per share amounts.)

b. Prepare a single-step income statement. (Disregard earnings per share amounts.)

LO4   P13-2B.   Earnings per Share Lincoln Corporation began the year with 50,000 shares of common stock outstanding. On May 1, an additional 18,000 shares of common stock were issued. On July 1, 20,000 shares of common stock were acquired as treasury stock. On September 1, the 6,000 treasury shares of common stock were reissued. Lincoln Corporation's net income for the calendar year is $229,500.

Required

Compute earnings per share.

LO1, 4   P13-3B.   Earnings per Share and Multiple-Step Income Statement The following summarized data are related to Kennedy Corporation's operations:

Sales revenue.	$2,216,000
Cost of goods sold	1,290,000
Selling expenses	180,000
Administrative expenses.	142,800
Loss from plant strike	95,000
Income tax expense	204,000
Shares of common stock	
Outstanding at January 1	65,000 shares
Additional issued at April 1	17,000 shares
Additional issued at August 1	3,000 shares

Required

Prepare a multiple-step income statement for Kennedy Corporation. Include an earnings per share disclosure at the bottom of the income statement. Kennedy Corporation has no preferred stock.

P13-4B. **Trend Percentages** Sales of automotive products for **Ford Motor Company** and **General Motors Corporation** for a five-year period are:

LO2, 4

	Net Sales of Automotive Products (Millions of Dollars)				
	Year 1	Year 2	Year 3	Year 4	Year 5
Ford Motor Company	$82,879	$81,844	$72,051	$ 84,407	$ 91,568
General Motors Corporation.	99,106	97,312	94,828	103,005	108,027

Net sales for **Pfizer Inc.** and **Abbott Laboratories** for the same five years follow:

	Net Sales (Millions of Dollars)				
	Year 1	Year 2	Year 3	Year 4	Year 5
Pfizer Inc.	$5,672	$6,406	$6,950	$7,230	$7,478
Abbott Laboratories	5,380	6,159	6,877	7,852	8,408

FORD MOTOR
COMPANY

GENERAL MOTORS
CORPORATION

PFIZER INC.

ABBOTT
LABORATORIES

Required

a. Calculate trend percentages for all four companies, using Year 1 as the base year.
b. Comment on the trend percentages of Ford Motor Company and General Motors Corporation.
c. Comment on the trend percentages of Pfizer Inc. and Abbott Laboratories.

P13-5B. **Changes in Various Ratios** Selected information follow for Bush Company:

LO4

	Current Year	Previous Year
Sales revenue.	$700,000	$520,000
Cost of goods sold	407,700	310,000
Interest expense.	22,000	14,000
Income tax expense	6,500	5,100
Net income	30,000	20,300
Cash flow from operating activities.	29,500	26,500
Capital expenditures.	42,000	25,000
Accounts receivable (net), December 31	182,000	128,000
Inventory, December 31	225,000	180,000
Stockholders' equity, December 31	205,000	165,000
Total assets, December 31.	460,000	350,000

Required

a. Calculate the following ratios for the current year. The previous year results are given for comparative purposes.

	Previous Year
Gross profit percentage	40.4 percent
Return on assets	6.5 percent
Return on sales	3.9 percent
Return on equity	14.2 percent
Accounts receivable turnover	4.77
Average collection period	76.5 days
Inventory turnover	2.07
Times-interest-earned ratio	2.81
Operating-cash-flow-to-capital-expenditures ratio	1.06

b. Comment on the changes between the two years.

LO2, 3, 4   P13-6B. **Ratios from Comparative and Common-Size Data** Consider the following financial statements for Nixon Company.

During the year, management obtained additional bond financing to enlarge its production facilities. The plant addition produced a new high-margin product, which is supposed to improve the average rate of gross profit and return on sales.

As a potential investor, you decide to analyze the financial statements:

NIXON COMPANY Balance Sheets (Thousands of Dollars)	Dec. 31, Current Year	Dec. 31, Previous Year
Assets		
Cash	$ 25,000	$ 18,100
Accounts receivable (net)	39,000	21,400
Inventory	105,000	72,000
Prepaid expenses	1,500	4,000
Plant and other assets (net)	463,500	427,500
Total assets	$634,000	$543,000
Liabilities and Stockholders' Equity		
Current liabilities	$ 80,000	$ 48,000
9% bonds payable	187,500	150,000
8% preferred stock, $50 par value	60,000	60,000
Common stock, $10 par value	225,000	225,000
Retained earnings	81,500	60,000
Total liabilities and stockholders' equity	$634,000	$543,000

NIXON COMPANY Income Statements (Thousands of Dollars)	Current Year	Previous Year
Sales revenue	$850,000	$697,500
Cost of goods sold	552,000	465,000
Gross profit on sales	298,000	232,500
Selling and administrative expenses	231,000	174,000
Income before interest expense and income taxes	67,000	58,500
Interest expense	17,000	13,500
Income before income taxes	50,000	45,000
Income tax expense	10,000	9,000
Net income	$ 40,000	$ 36,000
Other financial data (thousands of dollars):		
Cash provided by operating activities	$ 28,000	$ 24,000
Preferred stock dividends	5,000	4,800

Required

a. Calculate the following for each year: current ratio, quick ratio, operating-cash-flow-to-current-liabilities ratio (current liabilities were $40,000,000 at January 1 of the previous year), inventory turnover (inventory was $68,000,000 at January 1 of the previous year), debt-to-equity ratio, times-interest-earned ratio, return on assets (total assets were $490,000,000 at January 1 of the previous year), and return on equity (stockholders' equity was $265,000,000 at January 1 of the previous year).

b. Calculate the common-size percentage for each year's income statement.

c. Comment on the results of your analysis.

P13-7B. **Constructing Statements from Ratio Data** The following are the financial statements for Truman   **LO4** Company, with almost all dollar amounts missing:

TRUMAN COMPANY
Balance Sheet
December 31

Cash..........................	$	?	Current liabilities.................	$?
Accounts receivable (net)..........		?	10% bonds payable	144,000
Inventory......................		?	Common stock	?
Equipment (net)		?	Retained earnings	50,000
			Total liabilities and	
Total assets....................		$576,000	stockholders' equity.............	$576,000

TRUMAN COMPANY
Income Statement
For the Year Ended December 31

Sales revenue..	$?
Cost of goods sold	?
Gross profit on sales..	?
Selling and administrative expenses	?
Income before interest expense and income taxes	?
Interest expense..	?
Income before income taxes..	?
Income tax expense (20%)...	?
Net income	$70,200

The following information is available about Truman Company's financial statements:

1. Quick ratio, 2.5.
2. Current ratio, 3.0.
3. Return on sales, 8.0 percent.
4. Return on equity (stockholders' equity at January 1 was $340,000), 20 percent.
5. Gross profit percentage, 40 percent.
6. Accounts receivable turnover (accounts receivable (net) at January 1 were $97,200), 12 times.
7. The interest expense relates to the bonds payable that were outstanding all year.

Required

Compute the missing amounts, and complete the financial statements of Truman Company. (*Hint:* Complete the income statement first.)

P13-8B. **Ratios Compared with Industry Averages** You are analyzing the performance of Jackson Corpo-   **LO4** ration, a manufacturer of personal care products, for the most recent year. The following data are taken from the firm's latest annual report:

	Dec. 31, Current Year	Dec. 31, Previous Year
Quick assets.	$ 385,000	$ 350,000
Inventory and prepaid expenses.	975,000	820,000
Other assets.	4,165,000	3,700,000
Total assets.	$5,525,000	$4,870,000
Current liabilities.	$ 600,000	$ 500,000
10% bonds payable	1,300,000	1,300,000
7% preferred stock.	900,000	900,000
Common stock, $5 par value	1,925,000	1,800,000
Retained earnings	800,000	370,000
Total liabilities and stockholders' equity	$5,525,000	$4,870,000

In the current year, net sales amount to $8,800,000, net income is $700,000, and preferred stock dividends paid are $70,000.

Required

a. Calculate the following for the current year:

1. Return on sales
2. Return on assets
3. Return on equity

4. Quick ratio
5. Current ratio
6. Debt-to-equity ratio

b. Trade association statistics and information provided by credit agencies reveal the following data on industry norms:

	Median	Upper Quartile
Return on sales	3.7 percent	10.6 percent
Return on assets	5.8 percent	14.2 percent
Return on equity	18.5 percent	34.2 percent
Quick ratio	1.0	1.8
Current ratio	2.2	3.7
Debt-to-equity ratio	1.07	0.37

Compare Jackson Corporation's performance with industry performance.

LO4   **P13-9B.**   **Ratios Compared with Industry Averages** Hardy Instruments, Inc., is a manufacturer of various measuring and controlling instruments. Financial statement data for the firm are as follows:

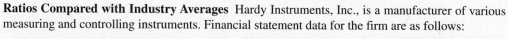

	Current Year (Thousands of Dollars, except Earnings per Share)
Sales revenue.	$220,000
Cost of goods sold	125,000
Net income.	10,000
Dividends.	4,300
Earnings per share.	5.00

HARDY INSTRUMENTS, INC. Balance Sheets (Thousands of Dollars)	Dec. 31, Current Year	Dec. 31, Previous Year
Assets		
Cash..	$ 20,000	$ 19,000
Accounts receivable (net)......................	46,000	43,000
Inventory......................................	39,500	43,700
Total current assets........................	105,500	105,700
Plant assets (net)	52,600	51,500
Other assets..................................	15,600	12,800
Total assets..................................	$173,700	$170,000
Liabilities and Stockholders' Equity		
Notes payable—banks	$ 6,000	$ 6,000
Accounts payable.............................	22,700	18,700
Accrued liabilities	18,000	24,000
Total current liabilities	46,700	48,700
9% bonds payable	40,000	40,000
Total liabilities	86,700	88,700
Common stock, $25 par value (2,000,000 shares)............	50,000	50,000
Retained earnings	37,000	31,300
Total stockholders' equity	87,000	81,300
Total liabilities and stockholders' equity	$173,700	$170,000

Required

a. Using the given data, calculate ratios 1 through 8 for the current year. Compare the performance of Hardy Instruments, Inc., with the following industry averages and comment on its operations.

	Median Ratios for Manufacturers of Measuring and Controlling Instruments
Quick ratio	1.3
Current ratio	2.4
Accounts receivable turnover...................	5.0 times
Inventory turnover............................	3.5 times
Debt-to-equity ratio..........................	0.73
Gross profit percentage	44.3 percent
Return on sales	4.7 percent
Return on assets	7.6 percent

b. Calculate the dividends paid per share of common stock. What was the dividend payout ratio?

c. If the most recent price per share of common stock is $65, what is the price-earnings ratio? The dividend yield?

P13-10B. Financial Statement Notes: Quarterly Data Past quarterly data are presented below for Company C and Company D. One of these companies is a children's specialty retail chain. The company's fiscal year ends on the Saturday nearest to January 31. The other company is a consumer goods company selling branded products worldwide. Their fiscal year ends on December 31.

LO2

		(Amounts in Millions)			
	First Quarter	Second Quarter	Third Quarter	Fourth Quarter	Year
Company C					
Net Sales	$1,216.6	$1,237.3	$1,339.7	$1,617.2	$5,410.8
Gross profit	753.1	773.6	839.0	1,000.8	3,366.5
Company D					
Net Sales	$1,172.5	$1,249.1	$1,345.8	$3,401.8	$7,169.2
Gross profit	362.5	384.6	423.2	1,030.3	2,200.6

Required

a. Compute the percentage of annual net sales generated each quarter by Company C. Round to the nearest percent.

b. Compute the percentage of annual net sales generated each quarter by Company D. Round to the nearest percent.

c. Which company has the most seasonal business? Briefly explain.

d. Which company is the children's specialty retail chain? The branded consumer products company? Briefly explain.

SERIAL PROBLEM: KATE'S CARDS

(Note: This is a continuation of the Serial Problem: Kate's Cards from Chapter 1 through Chapter 12.)

SP13. Kate is very pleased with the results of the first year of operations for Kate's Cards. She ended the year on a high note, with the company's reputation for producing quality cards leading to more business than she can currently manage. Kate is considering expanding and bringing in several employees. In order to do this, she will need to find a larger location and purchase more equipment. All this means additional financing. Kate has asked you to look at her year-end financial statements as if you were a banker considering giving Kate a loan. Comment on your findings and provide calculations to support your comments.

KATE'S CARDS Income Statement Year Ended August 31	
Sales revenue	$185,000
Cost of goods sold	106,000
Gross profit	79,000
Operating expenses	
Wages	18,000
Consulting	11,850
Insurance	1,200
Utilities	2,400
Rent	14,400
Depreciation	3,250
Total operating expenses	51,100
Income from operations	27,900
Interest expense	900
Income before income tax	27,000
Income tax expense	5,400
Net income	$ 21,600

KATE'S CARDS Balance Sheet August 31	
Assets	
Current assets	
Cash..	$17,400
Accounts receivable	11,000
Inventory..	16,000
Prepaid insurance...	1,000
Total current assets	45,400
Equipment	17,500
Accumulated depreciation	3,250
Total assets..	$59,650
Liabilities	
Current liabilities	
Accounts payable...	$ 6,200
Unearned revenue	1,250
Other current liabilities	1,900
Total current liabilities..................................	9,350
Note payable..	15,000
Total liabilities	24,350
Stockholders' equity	
Common stock..	500
Additional paid-in-capital	9,500
Preferred stock..	5,000
Retained earnings	20,300
Total stockholders' equity	35,300
Total liabilities and stockholders' equity	$59,650

KATE'S CARDS Statement of Cash Flows Year Ended August 31	
Cash flow from operating activities	
Net income	$21,600
Add depreciation	3,250
Increase in accounts receivable	(11,000)
Increase in inventory.....................................	(16,000)
Increase in prepaid expenses..........................	(1,000)
Increase in accounts payable	6,200
Increase in unearned revenue	1,250
Increase in other current liabilities	1,900
Cash provided by operating activities................	6,200
Cash flow from investing activities	
Purchase of equipment..................................	(17,500)
Cash used by investing activities	(17,500)
Cash flow from financing activities	
Proceeds from bank note	15,000
Issuance of common stock.............................	10,000
Issuance of preferred stock...........................	5,000
Cash dividends..	(1,300)*
Cash provided by financing activities	28,700
Net increase in cash.....................................	17,400
Cash at beginning of year..............................	0
Cash at end of year	$17,400

*Kate issued cash dividends on both the common stock and the preferred stock. There are 50 preferred shares outstanding and 500 common shares outstanding. The dividends that Kate paid were $6 per share on the preferred shares and $2 per share on the common shares.

EXTENDING YOUR KNOWLEDGE

REPORTING AND ANALYSIS

COLUMBIA
SPORTSWEAR
COMPANY

EYK13-1.   Financial Reporting Problem: Columbia Sportswear Company The financial statements for the Columbia Sportswear Company can be found in Appendix A at the end of this book.

You are considering an investment in Columbia Sportswear after a recent outdoor trip in which you really liked some of the clothes you purchased from the company. You decide to do an analysis of the company's financial statements in order to help you make an informed decision.

Required

a.   Using the five-year selected financial data reported in the annual report, produce a five-year trend analysis, using 2016 as a base year, of (1) net sales, (2) net income, and (3) total assets. Comment on your findings.

b.   Calculate the (1) gross profit percentage, (2) return on sales, and (3) return on assets for 2019 and 2020. Comment on Columbia Sportswear's profitability. (2018 total assets = $2,368,721,000)

c.   Calculate the (1) current ratio, (2) quick ratio, and (3) operating-cash-flow-to-current liabilities ratio for 2019 and 2020 (2018 current liabilities = $572,882,000) Comment on Columbia Sportswear's liquidity.

d.   Calculate the debt-to-equity ratio for 2019 and 2020. Comment on Columbia Sportswear's solvency.

COLUMBIA
SPORTSWEAR
COMPANY

UNDER ARMOUR, INC.

EYK13-2.   Comparative Analysis Problem: Columbia Sportswear Company vs Under Armour, Inc. The financial statements for the Columbia Sportswear Company can be found in Appendix A at the end of this book, and the financial statements of Under Armour, Inc., can be found in Appendix B. (The complete annual report is available on this book's website.)

Required

Based on the information from the financial statements of each company, do the following.

a.   Calculate the percentage change in (1) net sales, (2) net income, (3) cash flow from operating activities, and (4) total assets from 2019 to 2020.

b.   What conclusions can you draw from this analysis?

EYK13-3.   Business Decision Problem Crescent Paints, Inc., a paint manufacturer, has been in business for five years. The company has had modest profits and has experienced few operating difficulties until this year, 2022, when president Alice Becknell discussed her company's working capital problems with you, a loan officer at Granite Bank. Becknell explained that expanding her firm has created difficulties in meeting obligations when they come due and in taking advantage of cash discounts offered by manufacturers for the timely payment of the company's accounts payable. She would like to borrow $50,000 from Granite Bank. At your request, Becknell submits the following financial data for the past two years:

	2022	2021
Sales revenue.	$2,000,000	$1,750,000
Cost of goods sold	1,320,000	1,170,000
Net income	42,000	33,600
Dividends	22,000	18,000
December 31, 2017, data.		
Total assets.	1,100,000	
Accounts receivable (net).	205,000	
Inventory.	350,000	

CRESCENT PAINTS, INC. Balance Sheets	Dec. 31, 2022	Dec. 31, 2021
Assets		
Cash.	$ 31,000	$ 50,000
Accounts receivable (net)	345,000	250,000
Inventory	525,000	425,000
Prepaid expenses	11,000	6,000
Total current assets	912,000	731,000
Plant assets (net)	483,000	444,000
Total assets	$1,395,000	$ 1,175,000
Liabilities and Stockholders' Equity		
Notes payable—banks	$ 100,000	$ 35,000
Accounts payable	244,000	190,000
Accrued liabilities	96,000	85,000
Total current liabilities	440,000	310,000
10% mortgage payable.	190,000	250,000
Total liabilities	630,000	560,000
Common stock	665,000	535,000
Retained earnings	100,000	80,000
Total stockholders' equity	765,000	615,000
Total liabilities and stockholders' equity	$1,395,000	$1,175,000

Calculate the following items for both years from the given data and then compare them with the median ratios for paint manufacturers provided by a commercial credit firm:

	Median Ratios for Paint Manufacturers
Current ratio	2.5
Quick ratio	1.3
Accounts receivable turnover	8.1
Average collection period	44.9 days
Inventory turnover.	4.9
Debt-to-equity ratio	0.78
Return on assets	4.8%
Return on sales	2.4%

Required

Based on your analysis, decide whether and under what circumstances you would grant Becknell's request for a loan. Explain the reasons for your decision.

EYK13-4. **Financial Analysis Problem** Listed below are selected financial data for three corporations: **Honeywell International, Inc.** (environmental controls), **The Dow Chemical Company** (chemicals and plastic products), and **Abbott Laboratories** (health care products). These data cover five years. (Year 5 is the most recent year; net income in thousands.)

	Year 5	Year 4	Year 3	Year 2	Year 1
Honeywell International, Inc.					
Net income	$278,900	$322,200	$246,800	$331,100	$381,900
Earnings per common share	$2.15	$2.40	$1.78	$2.35	$2.52
Dividend per common share.	$1.00	$0.91	$0.84	$0.77	$0.70
The Dow Chemical Company					
Net income	$938,000	$644,000	$276,000	$942,000	$1,384,000
Earnings per common share	$3.88	$2.33	$0.99	$3.46	$5.10
Dividend per common share.	$2.60	$2.60	$2.60	$2.60	$2.60
Abbott Laboratories					
Net income*	$1,399,100	$1,239,100	$1,088,700	$965,800	$859,800
Earnings per common share*	$1.69	$1.47	$1.27	$1.11	$0.96
Dividend per common share.	$0.68	$0.60	$0.50	$0.42	$0.35

*Before accounting change

Required

a.   Calculate the dividend payout ratio for each company for each of the five years.

b.   Companies may differ in their dividend policy; that is, they may differ in whether they emphasize a constant dividend amount per share, a steady growth in dividend amount per share, a target or constant dividend payout ratio, or some other criterion. Based on the data available, identify what appears to be each of the above firm's dividend policy over the five-year period.

CRITICAL THINKING

GENERAL MILLS, INC.

EYK13-5.   Accounting Research Problem: General Mills, Inc.   The fiscal year 2020 annual report of General Mills, Inc., is available on this book's website.

Required

a.   Calculate (or identify) the following financial ratios for 2019 and 2020:
   1.   Gross profit percentage
   2.   Return on sales
   3.   Asset turnover (2018, total assets = $30,624.0 million)
   4.   Return on assets (2018, total assets = $30,624.0 million)
   5.   Return on equity (2018, total stockholders' equity = $6,141.1 million)
   6.   Current ratio
   7.   Quick ratio
   8.   Operating-cash-flow-to-current-liabilities ratio (2018, current liabilities = $7,341.9 million)
   9.   Accounts receivable turnover (2018, accounts receivable = $1,899.1 million)
   10.   Average collection period
   11.   Inventory turnover (2018, inventory = $1,642.2 million)
   12.   Days' sales in inventory
   13.   Debt-to-equity ratio
   14.   Times-interest-earned ratio
   15.   Operating-cash-flow-to-capital-expenditures ratio
   16.   Earnings per share
   17.   Price-earnings ratio (Use year-end adjusted closing stock price of $63.04 for 2020 and $49.44 for 2019.)
   18.   Dividend yield
   19.   Dividend payout ratio

b.   Comment briefly on the changes from fiscal 2019 to fiscal 2020 in the ratios computed above.

EYK13-6.   Accounting Communication Activity   Pete Hollingsworth is currently taking an accounting course and is confused about what his professor told the class about analyzing financial statements. Pete would like you to lead a study session on the topic. In order to help everyone out, you decide to write a short memo describing some of the key points.

Required

Include the following items in your memo:

a.   What is meant by trend analysis, and how is it helpful?

b.   How are common-size statements constructed, and what are their uses?

c.   What are a few common profitability, liquidity, and solvency ratios, and how are they interpreted?

d.   What are some limitations of financial statement analysis?

EYK13-7.   Accounting Ethics Case   Chris Nelson, the new assistant controller for Grand Company, is preparing for the firm's year-end closing procedures. On December 30, 2022, a memorandum from the controller directed Nelson to make a journal entry debiting Cash and crediting Long-Term Advances to Officers for $1,000,000. Not finding the $1,000,000 in the cash deposit prepared for the bank that day, Nelson went to the controller for a further explanation. In response, the controller took from her desk drawer a check for $1,000,000 payable to Grand Company from Jason Grand, chief executive officer of the firm. Attached to the check was a note from Jason Grand saying that if this check were not needed to return it to him next week.

"This check is paying off a $1,000,000 advance the firm made to Jason Grand six years ago," stated the controller. "Mr. Grand has done this every year since the advance; each time we have returned the check to him in January of the following year. We plan to do so again this time. In fact, when Mr. Grand retires in four years, I expect the board of directors will forgive this advance. However, if the firm really needed the cash, we would deposit the check."

"Then why go through this charade each year?" inquired Nelson.

"It dresses up our year-end balance sheet," replied the controller. "Certain financial statement ratios are improved significantly. Further, the notes to the financial statements don't have to reveal a related-party loan. Lots of firms engage in year-end transactions designed to dress up their financial statements."

Required

a. What financial statement ratios are improved by making the journal entry contained in the controller's memorandum?

b. Is the year-end handling of Jason Grand's advance an ethical practice? Discuss.

EYK13-8. Environmental, Social, and Governance Problem The chapter's ESG box highlighted how **Procter & Gamble (P&G)** stands behind its commitment to uphold its responsibility as a good corporate citizen. Go to the P&G website and navigate to th annual citizenship report (under the Our Story tab). The report is broken into four sections: 1) Community Impact; 2) Equality & Inclusion; 3) Environmental Sustainability; and 4) Ethics & Corporate Responsibility. Choose any of these areas and report how P&G demonstrates its commitment to good corporate citizenship.

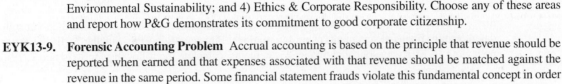

EYK13-9. Forensic Accounting Problem Accrual accounting is based on the principle that revenue should be reported when earned and that expenses associated with that revenue should be matched against the revenue in the same period. Some financial statement frauds violate this fundamental concept in order to overstate net income in the current year. Provide an example of how this may be accomplished.

EYK13-10. Working with the Takeaways Below are income statements and balance sheets for the Peyton Company for 2022 and 2021:

PEYTON COMPANY Income Statement For the Years Ended December 31, 2022 and 2021		
(in millions)	**2022**	**2021**
Sales revenue	$10,000	$9,500
Cost of goods sold	5,500	5,200
Gross profit	4,500	4,300
Selling and administrative expenses	2,800	2,700
Income from operations	1,700	1,600
Interest expense	300	250
Income before income taxes	1,400	1,350
Income tax expense	420	400
Net income	$ 980	$ 950

PEYTON COMPANY Balance Sheet December 31, 2022 and 2021		
(in millions)	**2022**	**2021**
Assets		
Current assets		
Cash and cash equivalents	$ 200	$ 400
Accounts receivable	900	800
Inventory	700	650
Other current assets	400	250
Total current assets	2,200	2,100
Property, plant, & equipment (net)	2,600	2,500
Other assets	5,700	5,900
Total assets	$10,500	$10,500
Liabilities and Stockholders' Equity		
Current liabilities	$ 3,000	$ 2,900
Long-term liabilities	5,000	5,400
Total liabilities	8,000	8,300
Stockholders' equity	2,500	2,200
Total liabilities and stockholders' equity	$10,500	$10,500

Required

Calculate the following ratios for the Peyton Company for 2022 and 2021 and discuss your findings:

1. Profitability
   a. Return on sales
   b. Return on equity (stockholders' equity was $2,000 on December 31, 2020)
2. Liquidity
   a. Current ratio
   b. Accounts receivable turnover (accounts receivable was $780 on December 31, 2020)
   c. Inventory turnover (inventory was $620 on December 31, 2020)
3. Solvency
   a. Debt-to-equity ratio
   b. Times-interest-earned ratio

**LVMH MOET
HENNESSEY-LOUIS
VUITTON S.A.**

EYK13-11. Analyzing IFRS Financial Statements The 2020 financial statements of **LVMH Moet Hennessey-Louis Vuitton S.A.** are presented in Appendix C at the end of this book. LVMH is a Paris-based holding company and one of the world's largest and best-known luxury goods companies. As a member of the European Union, French companies are required to prepare their consolidated (group) financial statements using International Financial Reporting Standards (IFRS). After reviewing LVMH's consolidated financial statements, calculate the following for 2020 and 2019:

a. Current ratio
b. Quick ratio
c. Accounts receivable turnover
d. Inventory turnover
e. Debt-to-equity ratio
f. Times-interest-earned ratio *(Hint: interest expense is called "Cost of net financial debt.")*
g. Return on sales
h. Return on assets
i. Return on equity

ANSWERS TO SELF-STUDY QUESTIONS:

1. c   2. c   3. c   4. b   5. b   6. c   7. d   8. b   9. c   10. b   11. c   12. d

YOUR TURN! SOLUTIONS

Solution 13.1

1. Persistent
2. Transitory
3. Transitory
4. Persistent
5. Transitory
6. Persistent

Solution 13.2

	Change in Current Year	
	Amount	Percent
Sales revenue.	$50,000	6.7 percent [($800,000 – $750,000)/$750,000]
Net income	20,000	20.0 percent [($120,000 – $100,000)/$100,000]
Total assets.	10,000	3.4 percent [($300,000 – $290,000)/$290,000]

Solution 13.3

SANFORD COMPANY Income Statement For the Year Ended December 31	Amount	Percent
Sales revenue.	$13,500	100.0
Cost of goods sold	5,400	40.0
Gross profit.	8,100	60.0
Selling and administrative expenses	1,350	10.0
Income from operations	6,750	50.0
Interest expense.	675	5.0
Other expense	135	1.0
Income before income taxes.	5,940	44.0
Income tax expense	2,295	17.0
Net income	$ 3,645	27.0

Solution 13.4

a. Gross profit percentage = ($30,000 − $10,500)/$30,000 = 65.0 percent

b. Return on sales = $4,500/$30,000 = 15.0 percent

c. Asset turnover = $30,000/$50,000 = 0.60

d. Return on assets = $4,500/$50,000 = 9.0 percent

e. Return on equity = $4,500/$35,000 = 12.9 percent

Solution 13.5

a. Working capital = $60,000 − $40,000 = $20,000

b. Current ratio = $60,000/$40,000 = 1.5

c. Operating-cash-flow-to-current-liabilities ratio = $55,000/$40,000 = 1.375

d. Accounts receivable turnover = $100,000/$15,000 = 6.67 times

e. Days' sales in inventory = 365/($70,000/$9,000) = 46.9 days

Solution 13.6

a. Debt to equity ratio = $180,000/$600,000 = 0.30

b. Times-interest-earned ratio = ($55,000 + $5,000 + $25,000)/$5,000 = 17.0 times

c. Operating-cash-flow-to-capital-expenditures ratio = $100,000/$30,000 = 3.33 times

Solution 13.7

a. Dividend yield = $1.50/$54.00 = 2.8 percent

b. Dividend payout ratio = $1.50/$4.50 = 33.3 percent

c. Price-earnings ratio = $54.00/$4.50 = 12.0

Appendix A
Columbia Sportswear Company

The law requires publicly traded companies to submit an audited annual report to the Securities and Exchange Commission (SEC) within two months of the close of their fiscal year. This annual report is called Form 10-K. Companies also provide their stockholders with an annual report that contains many of the items included in Form 10-K, along with a letter to the shareholders and public relations and marketing material. Although each annual report is different, all annual reports typically include the following elements:

- Letter to the Shareholders
- Management Discussion and Analysis
- Independent Auditor's Report
- Financial Statements
- Notes to Financial Statements
- Report on Internal Control
- Management's Certification of Financial Statements
- Supplemental Information

In addition, many publicly traded companies also provide a voluntary report on their corporate social responsibility commitments. Because this report is voluntary, its content varies to a greater degree from company to company. Most reports, however, discuss the company's commitment in the areas of both social and environmental impact.

The following pages include excerpts from Columbia Sportswear's 2020 Annual Report. The complete 10-K is available on this book's website. Appendix A is organized as follows:

Occasionally, companies restate financial data for previous years, which may cause specific amounts to change in their financial statements. The data in this appendix reflect the most current financial data available at the time this book was written.

REPORT OF INDEPENDENT AUDITORS

Report of Independent Registered Public Accounting Firm

To the Shareholders and the Board of Directors of Columbia Sportswear Company

Opinion on the Financial Statements

We have audited the accompanying consolidated balance sheets of Columbia Sportswear Company and subsidiaries (the "Company") as of December 31, 2020 and 2019, the related consolidated statements of operations, comprehensive income, equity, and cash flows for each of the three years in the period ended December 31, 2020, and the related notes and the schedule listed in the Index at Item 15 (collectively referred to as the "financial statements"). In our opinion, the financial statements present fairly, in all material respects, the financial position of the Company as of December 31, 2020 and 2019, and the results of its operations and its cash flows for each of the three years in the period ended December 31, 2020, in conformity with accounting principles generally accepted in the United States of America.

We have also audited, in accordance with the standards of the Public Company Accounting Oversight Board (United States) (PCAOB), the Company's internal control over financial reporting as of December 31, 2020, based on criteria established in *Internal Control - Integrated Framework (2013)* issued by the Committee of Sponsoring Organizations of the Treadway Commission and our report dated February 25, 2021, expressed an unqualified opinion on the Company's internal control over financial reporting.

Basis for Opinion

These financial statements are the responsibility of the Company's management. Our responsibility is to express an opinion on the Company's financial statements based on our audits. We are a public accounting firm registered with the PCAOB and are required to be independent with respect to the Company in accordance with the U.S. federal securities laws and the applicable rules and regulations of the Securities and Exchange Commission and the PCAOB.

We conducted our audits in accordance with the standards of the PCAOB. Those standards require that we plan and perform the audit to obtain reasonable assurance about whether the financial statements are free of material misstatement, whether due to error or fraud. Our audits included performing procedures to assess the risks of material misstatement of the financial statements, whether due to error or fraud, and performing procedures that respond to those risks. Such procedures included examining, on a test basis, evidence regarding the amounts and disclosures in the financial statements. Our audits also included evaluating the accounting principles used and significant estimates made by management, as well as evaluating the overall presentation of the financial statements. We believe that our audits provide a reasonable basis for our opinion.

Critical Audit Matters

The critical audit matters communicated below are matters arising from the current-period audit of the financial statements that were communicated or required to be communicated to the audit committee and that (1) relate to accounts or disclosures that are material to the financial statements and (2) involved our especially challenging, subjective, or complex judgments. The communication of critical audit matters does not alter in any way our opinion on the financial statements, taken as a whole, and we are not, by communicating the critical audit matters below, providing separate opinions on the critical audit matters or on the accounts or disclosures to which they relate.

Goodwill – prAna Reporting Unit – Refer to Notes 2 and 6 to the Consolidated Financial Statements

Critical Audit Matter Description

The Company's evaluation of goodwill for impairment involves the comparison of the fair value of each reporting unit to its carrying value. The Company uses a combination of discounted cash flow analysis and market-based valuation methods, which requires management to make significant estimates and assumptions related to projected cash flow, discount rates, market-based multiples, and other operating performance measures. Changes in these assumptions could have a significant impact on either the fair value, the amount of any goodwill impairment charge, if any, or both. The goodwill balance was $68.6 million as of December 31, 2020, of which $54.2 million was allocated to the prAna Reporting Unit ("prAna"). The fair value of prAna exceeded its carrying value as of the measurement date and, therefore, no impairment was recognized.

Auditing management's estimates and assumptions related to projected cash flow, discount rates, market-based multiples, and other operating performance measures for prAna involved especially subjective judgment.

How the Critical Audit Matter Was Addressed in the Audit

Our audit procedures related to management's estimates and assumptions related to projected cash flow, discount rates, market-based multiples, and other operating performance measures for the prAna goodwill impairment analysis included the following, among others:

- We tested the effectiveness of internal controls over the prAna goodwill impairment analysis, including those over the forecasts for cash flow and other operating performance measures, and the selection of the discount rate and market-based multiples.
- We evaluated management's ability to accurately forecast cash flow and other operating performance measures by comparing actual results to management's historical forecasts.
- We evaluated the reasonableness of management's cash flow forecasts by comparing the forecasts to:
  ○ Historical cash flow.
  ○ Forecasted information included in Company press releases as well as in analyst and industry reports for the Company and certain of its peer companies.
- We evaluated the impact of changes in management's cash flow forecasts from the October 31, 2020 annual measurement date to December 31, 2020.
- To evaluate the reasonableness of the discount rate, with the assistance of our fair value specialists, we:
  ○ Developed a range of independent estimates of the discount rate and compared those to the discount rate selected by management to assess the appropriateness of the discount rate assumption.
  ○ Tested the inputs and source information underlying the determination of the discount rate by comparing to reputable third-party data or industry information and tested the mathematical accuracy of the calculation.
- With the assistance of our fair value specialists, we evaluated the reasonableness of the selection and application of valuation multiples management applied in i market-based valuation method through comparison to valuation multiples for guideline public companies.

Intangible Assets, Net – prAna Trademark– Refer to Notes 2 and 6 to the Consolidated Financial Statements

Critical Audit Matter Description

The Company has trademarks and trade names ("trademarks") that are indefinite-lived intangible assets. As of December 31, 2020, the carrying value of the intangible assets was $103.6 million, of which $70.5 million was attributed to prAna's trademark, after recognizing $17.5 million of impairment loss in the year ended December 31, 2020. The Company used the relief from royalty method to estimate fair value, which requires management to make significant estimates and assumptions related to projected sales, royalty rates and discount rates to estimate the net present value of future cash flows relating to the prAna trademark.

Auditing management's estimates and assumptions related to projected sales, royalty rates, and discount rates for prAna involved especially subjective judgment.

How the Critical Audit Matter Was Addressed in the Audit

Our audit procedures related to management's estimates and assumptions related to projected sales, royalty rates, and discount rates for the prAna trademark valuation included the following, among others:

- We tested the effectiveness of controls over intangible assets, including those over the forecasts of future sales, and the selection of the discount rate and royalty rate.
- We evaluated management's ability to accurately forecast future sales by comparing actual results to management's historical forecasts.
- We evaluated the reasonableness of management's sales forecasts by comparing the forecasts to:
  ○ Historical sales.
  ○ Forecasted information included in Company press releases as well as in analyst and industry reports for the Company and certain of its peer companies.

- We evaluated the impact of changes in management's forecasts from the October 31, 2020 annual measurement date to December 31, 2020.
- To evaluate the reasonableness of the (1) discount rate and (2) royalty rate, with the assistance of our fair value specialists, we:
  - Developed a range of independent estimates of the discount rate and compared those to the discount rate selected by management to assess the appropriateness of the discount rate assumption.
  - Tested the inputs and source information underlying the determination of the discount rate by comparing to reputable third-party data or industry information and tested the mathematical accuracy of the calculation.
  - Compared the royalty rate selected by management to rates from royalty agreements in the outdoor apparel industry for comparable companies and the Company's own contract royalty rates.

Long-lived Asset Valuation – Refer to Notes 2, 5 and 9 to the Consolidated Financial Statements

Critical Audit Matter Description

The Company evaluates retail location long-lived assets for impairment when events or changes in circumstances exist that may indicate that the carrying amounts of retail location long-lived assets are no longer recoverable. Events that result in an impairment review include plans to close a retail location or a significant decrease in the operating results of the retail location. When such an indicator occurs, the Company evaluates its retail location long-lived assets for impairment by comparing the undiscounted future cash flow expected to be generated by the location to the retail location long-lived asset's carrying amount. If the carrying amount of an asset exceeds the estimated undiscounted future cash flow, an analysis is performed to estimate the fair value of the asset. An impairment is recorded if the fair value of the retail location long-lived asset is less than the carrying amount.

The Company makes significant assumptions to evaluate retail location long-lived assets for possible indications of impairment. Changes in these assumptions could have a significant impact on the retail location long-lived assets identified for further analysis. For the year ended December 31, 2020, impairment charges from underperforming retail location long-lived assets were $7.0 million for lease right-of-use assets and $4.5 million for property, plant, and equipment.

Given the Company's evaluation of possible indications of impairment of retail location long-lived assets requires management to make significant assumptions, performing audit procedures to evaluate whether management appropriately identified events or changes in circumstances indicating that the carrying amounts of retail location long-lived assets may not be recoverable involved especially subjective judgment.

How the Critical Audit Matter Was Addressed in the Audit

Our audit procedures related to the evaluation of retail location long-lived assets for possible indications of impairment included the following, among others:

- We tested the effectiveness of controls over management's identification of possible circumstances that may indicate that the carrying amounts of retail location long-lived assets are no longer recoverable.
- We evaluated management's analysis of long-lived assets for indications of impairment analysis by:
  - Testing retail location long-lived assets for possible indications of impairment, including searching for locations with a history of losses, current period loss, or projected losses.
  - Performing inquiries of management regarding the process and assumptions used to identify potential indicators of impairment and evaluating the consistency of the assumptions with evidence obtained in other areas of the audit.

/s/   DELOITTE & TOUCHE LLP
Portland, Oregon
February 25, 2021

We have served as the Company's auditor since at least 1994; however, an earlier year could not be reliably determined.

FINANCIAL STATEMENTS

COLUMBIA SPORTSWEAR COMPANY

CONSOLIDATED BALANCE SHEETS

(in thousands)	December 31, 2020	December 31, 2019
ASSETS		
Current Assets:		
Cash and cash equivalents	$ 790,725	$ 686,009
Short-term investments	1,224	1,668
Accounts receivable, net of allowance of $ 21,810 and $8,925, respectively	452,945	488,233
Inventories, net	556,530	605,968
Prepaid expenses and other current assets	54,197	93,868
Total current assets	1,855,621	1,875,746
Property, plant and equipment, net	309,792	346,651
Operating lease right-of-use assets	339,244	394,501
Intangible assets, net	103,558	123,595
Goodwill	68,594	68,594
Deferred income taxes	96,126	78,849
Other non-current assets	63,636	43,655
Total assets	$ 2,836,571	$ 2,931,591
LIABILITIES AND EQUITY		
Current Liabilities:		
Accounts payable	$ 206,697	$ 255,372
Accrued liabilities	257,278	295,723
Operating lease liabilities	65,466	64,019
Income taxes payable	23,181	15,801
Total current liabilities	552,622	630,915
Non-current operating lease liabilities	353,181	371,507
Income taxes payable	49,922	48,427
Deferred income taxes	5,205	6,361
Other long-term liabilities	42,870	24,934
Total liabilities	1,003,800	1,082,144
Commitments and contingencies (Note 12)		
Shareholders' Equity:		
Preferred stock; 10,000 shares authorized; none issued and outstanding	—	—
Common stock (no par value); 250,000 shares authorized; 66,252 and 67,561 issued and outstanding, respectively	20,165	4,937
Retained earnings	1,811,800	1,848,935
Accumulated other comprehensive income (loss)	806	(4,425)
Total shareholders' equity	1,832,771	1,849,447
Total liabilities and shareholders' equity	$ 2,836,571	$ 2,931,591

See accompanying notes to consolidated financial statements

COLUMBIA SPORTSWEAR COMPANY

CONSOLIDATED STATEMENTS OF OPERATIONS

		Year Ended December 31,	
(in thousands, except per share amounts)	2020	2019	2018
Net sales	$ 2,501,554	$ 3,042,478	$ 2,802,326
Cost of sales	1,277,665	1,526,808	1,415,978
Gross profit	1,223,889	1,515,670	1,386,348
Selling, general and administrative expenses	1,098,948	1,136,186	1,051,152
Net licensing income	12,108	15,487	15,786
Income from operations	137,049	394,971	350,982
Interest income, net	435	8,302	9,876
Other non-operating income (expense), net	2,039	2,156	(141)
Income before income tax	139,523	405,429	360,717
Income tax expense	(31,510)	(74,940)	(85,769)
Net income	108,013	330,489	274,948
Net income attributable to non-controlling interest	—	—	6,692
Net income attributable to Columbia Sportswear Company	$ 108,013	$ 330,489	$ 268,256
Earnings per share attributable to Columbia Sportswear Company:			
Basic	$ 1.63	$ 4.87	$ 3.85
Diluted	$ 1.62	$ 4.83	$ 3.81
Weighted average shares outstanding:			
Basic	66,376	67,837	69,614
Diluted	66,772	68,493	70,401

See accompanying notes to consolidated financial statements

COLUMBIA SPORTSWEAR COMPANY

CONSOLIDATED STATEMENTS OF CASH FLOWS

	Year Ended December 31,		
(in thousands)	2020	2019	2018
Cash flows from operating activities:			
Net income	$ 108,013	$ 330,489	$ 274,948
Adjustments to reconcile net income to net cash provided by operating activities:			
Depreciation, amortization, and non-cash lease expense	146,601	121,725	58,230
Provision for uncollectible accounts receivable	19,156	(108)	3,908
Loss on disposal or impairment of intangible assets, property, plant and equipment, and right-of-use assets	31,342	5,442	4,208
Deferred income taxes	(11,263)	(1,808)	1,462
Stock-based compensation	17,778	17,832	14,291
Changes in operating assets and liabilities:			
Accounts receivable	22,885	(37,429)	(29,509)
Inventories, net	64,884	(84,058)	(94,716)
Prepaid expenses and other current assets	33,712	(15,068)	(9,771)
Other assets	(21,224)	(3,547)	(12,421)
Accounts payable	(49,275)	(10,419)	19,384
Accrued liabilities	(52,115)	18,863	66,900
Income taxes payable	9,082	(9,402)	(3,958)
Operating lease assets and liabilities	(52,112)	(54,197)	—
Other liabilities	8,613	7,137	(3,387)
Net cash provided by operating activities	276,077	285,452	289,569
Cash flows from investing activities:			
Purchases of short-term investments	(35,044)	(136,257)	(518,755)
Sales and maturities of short-term investments	36,631	400,501	352,127
Capital expenditures	(28,758)	(123,516)	(65,622)
Proceeds from sale of property, plant and equipment	—	—	19
Net cash provided by (used in) investing activities	(27,171)	140,728	(232,231)
Cash flows from financing activities:			
Proceeds from credit facilities	402,422	78,186	70,576
Repayments on credit facilities	(403,146)	(78,186)	(70,576)
Payment of line of credit issuance fees	(3,278)	—	—
Proceeds from issuance of common stock related to stock-based compensation	6,919	19,793	18,484
Tax payments related to stock-based compensation	(4,533)	(5,806)	(4,285)
Repurchase of common stock	(132,889)	(121,702)	(201,600)
Purchase of non-controlling interest	—	(17,880)	—
Cash dividends paid	(17,195)	(65,127)	(62,664)
Cash dividends paid to non-controlling interest	—	—	(19,949)
Net cash used in financing activities	(151,700)	(190,722)	(270,014)
Net effect of exchange rate changes on cash	7,510	(1,244)	(8,695)
Net increase (decrease) in cash and cash equivalents	104,716	234,214	(221,371)
Cash and cash equivalents, beginning of period	686,009	451,795	673,166
Cash and cash equivalents, end of period	$ 790,725	$ 686,009	$ 451,795
Supplemental disclosures of cash flow information:			
Cash paid during the year for income taxes	$ 14,687	$ 99,062	$ 77,408
Supplemental disclosures of non-cash investing and financing activities:			
Property, plant and equipment acquired through increase in liabilities	$ 3,831	$ 9,543	$ 11,831

See accompanying notes to consolidated financial statements

COLUMBIA SPORTSWEAR COMPANY

CONSOLIDATED STATEMENTS OF EQUITY

Columbia Sportswear Company Shareholders' Equity

(in thousands, except per share amounts)	Common Stock Shares Outstanding	Amount	Retained Earnings	Accumulated Other Comprehensive Income (Loss)	Non-Controlling Interest	Total
BALANCE, JANUARY 1, 2018	69,995	$ 45,829	$ 1,585,009	$ (8,887)	$ 30,308	$ 1,652,259
Net income	—	—	268,256	—	6,692	274,948
Other comprehensive income (loss):						
Unrealized holding losses on available-for-sale securities, net	—	—	—	(56)	—	(56)
Unrealized holding gains on derivative transactions, net	—	—	—	23,195	1,067	24,262
Foreign currency translation adjustment, net	—	—	—	(17,800)	(279)	(18,079)
Cash dividends ($0.90 per share)	—	—	(62,664)	—	—	(62,664)
Dividends to non-controlling interest	—	—	—	—	(21,332)	(21,332)
Adoption of new accounting standards	—	—	14,600	(515)	—	14,085
Issuance of common stock related to stock-based compensation, net	600	14,199	—	—	—	14,199
Stock-based compensation expense	—	14,291	—	—	—	14,291
Repurchase of common stock	(2,349)	(74,319)	(127,281)	—	—	(201,600)
BALANCE, DECEMBER 31, 2018	68,246	—	1,677,920	(4,063)	16,456	1,690,313
Net income	—	—	330,489	—	—	330,489
Purchase of non-controlling interest	—	—	—	(99)	(16,456)	(16,555)
Other comprehensive income (loss):						
Unrealized holding gains on available-for-sale securities, net	—	—	—	56	—	56
Unrealized holding losses on derivative transactions, net	—	—	—	(2,383)	—	(2,383)
Foreign currency translation adjustment, net	—	—	—	2,064	—	2,064
Cash dividends ($0.96 per share)	—	—	(65,127)	—	—	(65,127)
Issuance of common stock related to stock-based compensation, net	558	13,987	—	—	—	13,987
Stock-based compensation expense	—	17,832	—	—	—	17,832
Repurchase of common stock	(1,243)	(26,882)	(94,347)	—	—	(121,229)
BALANCE, DECEMBER 31, 2019	67,561	4,937	1,848,935	(4,425)	—	1,849,447
Net income	—	—	108,013	—	—	108,013
Other comprehensive income (loss):						
Unrealized holding gains on available-for-sale securities, net	—	—	—	4	—	4
Unrealized holding losses on derivative transactions, net	—	—	—	(18,851)	—	(18,851)
Foreign currency translation adjustment, net	—	—	—	24,078	—	24,078
Cash dividends ($0.26 per share)	—	—	(17,195)	—	—	(17,195)
Issuance of common stock related to stock-based compensation, net	248	2,386	—	—	—	2,386
Stock-based compensation expense	—	17,778	—	—	—	17,778
Repurchase of common stock	(1,557)	(4,936)	(127,953)	—	—	(132,889)
BALANCE, DECEMBER 31, 2020	66,252	20,165	1,811,800	806	—	1,832,771

See accompanying notes to consolidated financial statements

NOTES TO FINANCIAL STATEMENTS

COLUMBIA SPORTSWEAR COMPANY
NOTES TO CONSOLIDATED FINANCIAL STATEMENTS

NOTE 1—BASIS OF PRESENTATION AND ORGANIZATION

Nature of the Business

Columbia Sportswear Company connects active people with their passions through its four well-known brands, Columbia, SOREL, Mountain Hardwear, and prAna, by designing, developing, marketing, and distributing its outdoor, active and everyday lifestyle apparel, footwear, accessories, and equipment products to meet the diverse needs of its customers and consumers.

Principles of Consolidation

The consolidated financial statements include the accounts of Columbia Sportswear Company, its wholly owned subsidiaries and entities in which it maintained a controlling financial interest (the "Company"). All significant intercompany balances and transactions have been eliminated in consolidation.

Estimates and Assumptions

The preparation of financial statements in conformity with GAAP requires management to make estimates and assumptions that affect the reported amounts of assets and liabilities and disclosure of contingent assets and liabilities at the date of the consolidated financial statements and the reported amounts of revenues and expenses during the reporting period. Actual results may differ from these estimates and assumptions. Some of the more significant estimates relate to revenue recognition, allowance for uncollectible accounts receivable, excess, close-out and slow moving inventory, impairment of long-lived assets, intangible assets and goodwill, and income taxes.

Recently Adopted Accounting Pronouncements

Effective January 1, 2020, the Company adopted Accounting Standards Update ("ASU") No. 2018-15, Intangibles - Goodwill and Other - Internal-Use Software (Subtopic 350-40) issued by the Financial Accounting Standards Board ("FASB") in August 2018, which clarifies certain aspects of accounting for implementation costs incurred in a cloud computing arrangement ("CCA") that is a service contract. Under the ASU, an entity would expense costs incurred in the preliminary-project and post-implementation-operation stages. The entity would also capitalize certain costs incurred during the application-development stage, as well as certain costs related to enhancements. The ASU does not change the accounting for the service component of a CCA. The Company adopted the standard using the prospective method and anticipates an increase in cloud-specific implementation assets as specific cloud initiatives are executed by the Company. These assets will generally be included in *Other non-current assets* in the Consolidated Balance Sheets and will amortize over their assessed useful lives or the term of the underlying cloud computing hosting contract, whichever is shorter. Upon the adoption of the standard, there was no immediate impact to the Company's financial position, results of operations or cash flows.

Effective January 1, 2020, the Company adopted ASU No. 2017-04, Intangibles - Goodwill and Other (Topic 350): Simplifying the Test for Goodwill Impairment issued by the FASB in January 2017, which simplifies the accounting for goodwill impairments by eliminating step two from the goodwill impairment test. Under this guidance, if the carrying amount of a reporting unit exceeds its estimated fair value, an impairment charge shall be recognized in an amount equal to that excess, limited to the total amount of goodwill allocated to that reporting unit. The impact of the new standard will depend on the specific facts and circumstances of future individual goodwill impairments, if any.

Effective January 1, 2020, the Company adopted ASU No. 2016-13, Financial Instruments - Credit Losses (Topic 326): Measurement of Credit Losses on Financial Instruments issued by the FASB in June 2016, as well as the clarifying amendments subsequently issued. The pronouncement changes the impairment model for most financial assets and requires the use of an "expected loss" model for instruments measured at amortized cost. Under this model, entities are required to estimate the lifetime expected credit loss on such instruments and record an allowance to offset the amortized cost basis of the financial asset, resulting in a net presentation of the amount expected to be collected on the financial asset. Upon adoption of the standard, there was no immediate impact to the Company's financial position, results of operations or cash flows. On an ongoing basis, the Company will contemplate forward-looking economic conditions in recording lifetime expected credit losses for the Company's financial assets measured at cost, such as the Company's trade receivables and certain short-term investments.

NOTE 2—SUMMARY OF SIGNIFICANT ACCOUNTING POLICIES

Cash and cash equivalents

Cash and cash equivalents are stated at fair value or at cost, which approximates fair value, and include investments with original maturities of 90 days or less at the date of acquisition. At December 31, 2020, *Cash and cash equivalents* consisted of cash, money

COLUMBIA SPORTSWEAR COMPANY

NOTES TO CONSOLIDATED FINANCIAL STATEMENTS—(Continued)

market funds, and United States government treasury bills. At December 31, 2019, *Cash and cash equivalents* consisted of cash, money market funds, United States government treasury bills, and commercial paper.

Investments

At December 31, 2020, *Short-term investments* consisted of money market funds and mutual fund shares held as part of the Company's deferred compensation plan expected to be distributed in the next twelve months. At December 31, 2019, *Short-term investments* consisted of mutual fund shares held as part of the Company's deferred compensation plan expected to be distributed in the next twelve months. Investments held as part of the Company's deferred compensation plan are classified as trading securities and are recorded at fair value with any unrealized gains and losses included in *SG&A expense*. Realized gains or losses from these trading securities are determined based on the specific identification method and are included in *SG&A expense*.

At December 31, 2020 and 2019, long-term investments included in *Other non-current assets* consisted of money market funds and mutual fund shares held to offset liabilities to participants in the Company's deferred compensation plan. The investments are classified as long-term because the related deferred compensation liabilities are not expected to be paid within the next year. These investments are classified as trading securities and are recorded at fair value with unrealized gains and losses reported as a component of operating income.

Accounts receivable

Accounts receivable have been reduced by an allowance for doubtful accounts. The Company maintains the allowance for estimated losses resulting from the inability of the Company's customers to make required payments. The allowance represents the current estimate of lifetime expected credit losses over the remaining duration of existing accounts receivable considering current market conditions and supportable forecasts when appropriate. The estimate is a result of the Company's ongoing evaluation of collectability, customer creditworthiness, historical levels of credit losses, and future expectations. Write-offs of accounts receivable were $8.0 million and $1.2 million for the years ended December 31, 2020 and 2019, respectively.

Inventories

Inventories consist primarily of finished goods and are carried at the lower of cost or net realizable value. Cost is determined using the first-in, first-out method. The Company periodically reviews its inventories for excess, close-out or slow moving items and makes provisions as necessary to properly reflect inventory value.

Property, plant and equipment

Property, plant and equipment are stated at cost, net of accumulated depreciation. Depreciation is provided using the straight-line method over the estimated useful lives of the assets. The principal estimated useful lives are: land improvements, 15 years; buildings and building improvements, 15-30 years; furniture and fixtures, 3-10 years; and machinery, software and equipment, 3-10 years. Leasehold improvements are depreciated over the lesser of the estimated useful life of the improvement, which is most commonly 7 years, or the remaining term of the underlying lease.

Improvements to property, plant and equipment that substantially extend the useful life of the asset are capitalized. Repair and maintenance costs are expensed as incurred. Internal and external costs directly related to the development of internal-use software during the application development stage, including costs incurred for third party contractors and employee compensation, are capitalized and depreciated over a 3-10 year estimated useful life.

Intangible assets and goodwill

Intangible assets with indefinite useful lives and goodwill are not amortized but are periodically evaluated for impairment. Intangible assets that are determined to have finite lives are amortized using the straight-line method over their estimated useful lives and are measured for impairment only when events or circumstances indicate the carrying value may be impaired. Intangible assets with finite lives include patents, purchased technology and customer relationships and have estimated useful lives which range from approximately 3 to 10 years.

Cloud computing arrangements

The Company's CCAs primarily relate to various enterprise resource planning systems, as well as other supporting systems. These assets are generally included in *Other non-current assets* in the Consolidated Balance Sheets and amortize on a straight-line basis over their assessed useful lives or the term of the underlying cloud computing hosting contract, whichever is shorter. As of December 31, 2020, CCAs in-service have useful lives which range from approximately ten months to five years. As of December 31, 2020, CCA assets consisted of capitalized implementation costs of $24.3 million and associated accumulated amortization of $1.9

COLUMBIA SPORTSWEAR COMPANY

NOTES TO CONSOLIDATED FINANCIAL STATEMENTS—(Continued)

million. Changes in these assets are recorded in *Other assets* within operating activities in the Consolidated Statements of Cash Flows.

Leases

The Company leases, among other things, retail space, office space, warehouse facilities, storage space, vehicles, and equipment. Generally, the base lease terms are between five and 10 years. Certain lease agreements contain scheduled rent escalation clauses and others include rental payments adjusted periodically depending on an index or rate. Certain retail space lease agreements provide for additional rents based on a percentage of annual sales in excess of stipulated minimums ("percentage rent"). Certain lease agreements require the Company to pay real estate taxes, insurance, common area maintenance, and other costs, collectively referred to as operating costs, in addition to base rent.

Certain lease agreements also contain lease incentives, such as tenant improvement allowances and rent holidays. Most leases include one or more options to renew, with renewal terms that can extend the lease term from one to 10 years or more. The exercise of lease renewal options is generally at the Company's sole discretion. The Company's lease agreements do not contain any material residual value guarantees or material restrictive covenants.

The Company determines if an arrangement is or contains a lease at contract inception. The Company recognizes a ROU asset and a lease liability at the lease commencement date. The lease liability is initially measured at the present value of the unpaid lease payments at the lease commencement date. Key estimates and judgments include how the Company determines (1) the discount rate it uses to discount the unpaid lease payments to present value, (2) the lease term and (3) lease payments.

ASC 842 requires a lessee to discount its unpaid lease payments using the interest rate implicit in the lease or, if that rate cannot be readily determined, its incremental borrowing rate. Generally, the Company cannot determine the interest rate implicit in the lease because it does not have access to the lessor's estimated residual value or the amount of the lessor's deferred initial direct costs. Therefore, the Company generally uses its incremental borrowing rate as the discount rate for the lease. The Company's incremental borrowing rate for a lease is the rate of interest it would have to pay on a collateralized basis to borrow an amount equal to the lease payments under similar terms. Because the Company does not generally borrow on a collateralized basis, it uses market-based rates as an input to derive an appropriate incremental borrowing rate, adjusted for the lease term and the effect on that rate of designating specific collateral with a value equal to the unpaid lease payments for that lease. The Company also contemplates adjusting the discount rate for the amount of the lease payments.

The Company's lease contracts may include options to extend the lease following the initial term or terminate the lease prior to the end of the initial term. In most instances, at the commencement of the leases, the Company has determined that it is not reasonably certain to exercise either of these options; accordingly, these options are generally not considered in determining the initial lease term. At the renewal of an expiring lease, the Company reassesses options in the contract that it is reasonably certain to exercise in its measurement of lease term.

For lease agreements entered into or reassessed after the adoption of ASC 842, the Company has elected the practical expedient to account for the lease and non-lease components as a single lease component. Therefore, for those leases, the lease payments used to measure the lease liability include all of the fixed consideration in the contract.

Variable lease payments associated with the Company's leases are recognized upon occurrence of the event, activity, or circumstance in the lease agreement on which those payments are assessed. Variable lease payments are presented in the Company's Consolidated Statements of Operations in the same line item as expense arising from fixed lease payments.

Leases with an initial term of 12 months or less are not recorded on the balance sheet; the Company recognizes lease expense for these leases on a straight-line basis over the lease term.

Concessions

In April 2020, the FASB issued a Staff Q&A, Topic 842 and 840: Accounting for Lease Concessions Related to the Effects of the COVID-19 Pandemic. The FASB staff indicated that it would be acceptable for entities to make an election to account for lease concessions related to the effects of the COVID-19 pandemic consistent with how they would be accounted for as though enforceable rights and obligations for those concessions existed in the original contract. The Company elected to account for lease concessions related to the effects of the COVID-19 pandemic in accordance with the Staff Q&A. For concessions that provide a deferral of payments with no substantive changes to the consideration in the original contract, the Company continues to recognize expense during the deferral period. For concessions in the form of lease abatements, the reduced lease payments are accounted for as reductions to variable lease expense.

COLUMBIA SPORTSWEAR COMPANY

NOTES TO CONSOLIDATED FINANCIAL STATEMENTS—(Continued)

Impairment of long-lived assets, intangible assets and goodwill

Long-lived assets, which include property, plant and equipment, lease right-of-use assets, capitalized implementation costs for cloud computing arrangements, and intangible assets with finite lives, are measured for impairment only when events or circumstances indicate the carrying value may be impaired. In these cases, the Company estimates the future undiscounted cash flows to be derived from the asset or asset group to determine whether a potential impairment exists. If the sum of the estimated undiscounted cash flows is less than the carrying value of the asset, the Company recognizes an impairment loss, measured as the amount by which the carrying value exceeds the estimated fair value of the asset.

The Company reviews and tests its intangible assets with indefinite useful lives and goodwill for impairment in the fourth quarter of each year and when events or changes in circumstances indicate that the carrying amount of such assets may be impaired. The Company's intangible assets with indefinite lives consist of trademarks and trade names. In the impairment test for goodwill, the estimated fair value of the reporting unit is compared with the carrying amount of that reporting unit. In the impairment tests for trademarks and trade names, the Company compares the estimated fair value of each asset to its carrying amount. For goodwill and trademarks and trade names, if the carrying amount exceeds its estimated fair value, the Company calculates an impairment as the excess of carrying amount over the estimate of fair value.

Impairment charges, if any, are classified as a component of *SG&A expense*.

Income taxes

Income taxes are based on amounts of taxes payable or refundable in the current year and on expected future tax consequences of events that are recognized in the financial statements in different periods than they are recognized in tax returns. As a result of timing of recognition and measurement differences between financial accounting standards and income tax laws, temporary differences arise between amounts of pre-tax financial statement income and taxable income and between reported amounts of assets and liabilities in the Consolidated Balance Sheets and their respective tax bases. Deferred income tax assets and liabilities reported in the Consolidated Balance Sheets reflect estimated future tax effects attributable to these temporary differences and to net operating loss and net capital loss carryforwards, based on tax rates expected to be in effect for years in which the differences are expected to be settled or realized. Realization of deferred tax assets is dependent on future taxable income in specific jurisdictions. Valuation allowances are used to reduce deferred tax assets to amounts considered likely to be realized.

Accrued income taxes in the Consolidated Balance Sheets include unrecognized income tax benefits relating to uncertain tax positions, including related interest and penalties, appropriately classified as current or noncurrent. The Company recognizes the tax benefit from an uncertain tax position if it is more likely than not that the tax position will be sustained on examination by the relevant taxing authority based on the technical merits of the position. The tax benefits recognized in the financial statements from such positions are then measured based on the largest benefit that has a greater than 50% likelihood of being realized upon ultimate settlement with the relevant tax authority. In making this determination, the Company assumes that the taxing authority will examine the position and that it will have full knowledge of all relevant information. The provision for income taxes also includes estimates of interest and penalties related to uncertain tax positions.

Derivatives

The effective portion of changes in fair values of outstanding cash flow hedges is recorded in *Other comprehensive income (loss)* until earnings are affected by the hedged transaction, and any ineffective portion is included in current income. In most cases, amounts recorded in *Other comprehensive income (loss)* will be released to earnings after maturity of the related derivative. The Consolidated Statements of Operations classification of effective hedge results is the same as that of the underlying exposure. Results of hedges of product costs are recorded in *Cost of sales* when the underlying hedged transactions affect earnings. Results of hedges of revenue are recorded in *Net sales* when the underlying hedged transactions affect earnings. Unrealized derivative gains and losses, which are recorded in assets and liabilities, respectively, are non-cash items and therefore are taken into account in the preparation of the Consolidated Statements of Cash Flows based on their respective balance sheet classifications.

Foreign currency translation

The assets and liabilities of the Company's foreign subsidiaries have been translated into United States dollars using the exchange rates in effect at period end, and the sales and expenses have been translated into United States dollars using average exchange rates in effect during the period. The foreign currency translation adjustments are included as a separate component of *Accumulated other comprehensive income (loss)* in the Consolidated Balance Sheets.

COLUMBIA SPORTSWEAR COMPANY

NOTES TO CONSOLIDATED FINANCIAL STATEMENTS—(Continued)

Revenue recognition

Revenues are recognized when the Company's performance obligations are satisfied as evidenced by transfer of control of promised goods to customers or consumers, in an amount that reflects the consideration the Company expects to be entitled to receive in exchange for those goods or services. Within the Company's wholesale channel, control generally transfers to the customer upon shipment to, or upon receipt by, the customer depending on the terms of sale with the customer. Within the Company's direct-to-consumer ("DTC") channel, control generally transfers to the consumer at the time of sale within retail stores and concession-based arrangements and upon shipment to the consumer with respect to e-commerce transactions.

The amount of consideration the Company expects to be entitled to receive and recognize as *Net sales* across both wholesale and DTC channels varies with changes in sales returns and other accommodations and incentives offered. The Company estimates expected sales returns and other accommodations, such as chargebacks and markdowns and records a sales reserve to reduce *Net sales.* These estimates are based on historical rates of product returns and claims, as well as events and circumstances that indicate changes to such historical rates. However, actual returns and claims in any future period are inherently uncertain and thus may differ from the estimates. As a result, the Company adjusts estimates of revenue at the earlier of when the most likely amount of consideration the Company expects to receive changes or when the amount of consideration becomes fixed. If actual or expected future returns and claims are significantly greater or lower than the sales reserves established, the Company records an adjustment to *Net sales* in the period in which it made such determination.

Licensing income, which is presented separately as *Net licensing income* on the Consolidated Statements of Operations and represents less than 1% of total revenue, is recognized over time based on the greater of contractual minimum royalty guarantees and actual, or estimated, sales of licensed products by the Company's licensees.

The Company expenses sales commissions when incurred, which is generally at the time of sale, because the amortization period would have been one year or less. These costs are recorded within *SG&A expenses.*

Revenue recognized from contracts with customers is recorded net of sales taxes, value added taxes, or similar taxes that are collected on behalf of local taxing authorities.

Shipping and handling costs

The Company treats shipping and handling activities as fulfillment costs, and as such recognize the costs for these activities at the time related revenue is recognized. The majority of these costs are recorded as *SG&A expenses*, and the direct costs associated with shipping goods to customers and consumers are recorded as *Costs of sales*. Shipping and handling fees billed to customers are recorded as *Net sales*. Shipping and handling costs recorded as a component of *SG&A expenses* and were $98.0 million, $89.2 million and $82.7 million for the years ended December 31, 2020, 2019 and 2018, respectively.

Cost of sales

Cost of sales consists of all direct product costs, including shipping, duties and importation costs, as well as specific provisions for excess, close-out or slow moving inventory. In addition, certain products carry life-time or limited warranty provisions for defects in quality and workmanship. *Cost of sales* includes a warranty reserve established for these provisions at the time of sale to cover estimated costs based on the Company's history of warranty repairs and replacements.

Selling, general and administrative expenses

SG&A expenses consists of personnel-related costs, advertising, depreciation and amortization, occupancy, and other selling and general operating expenses related to the Company's business functions.

Stock-based compensation

Stock-based compensation cost is estimated at the grant date based on the award's fair value and is recorded as expense when recognized. For stock options and service-based restricted units, stock-based compensation cost is recognized over the expected requisite service period using the straight-line attribution method. For performance-based restricted stock units, stock-based compensation cost is recognized based on the Company's assessment of the probability of achieving performance targets in the reporting period. The Company estimates forfeitures for stock-based awards granted, but which are not expected to vest.

Advertising costs

Advertising costs, including marketing and demand creation spending, are expensed in the period incurred and are included in *SG&A expenses*. Total advertising expense, including cooperative advertising costs, were $141.3 million, $166.4 million and $150.4 million for the years ended December 31, 2020, 2019 and 2018, respectively. Cooperative advertising costs are expensed when the related revenues are recognized and included in *SG&A expenses* when the Company receives an identifiable benefit in exchange for the

COLUMBIA SPORTSWEAR COMPANY

NOTES TO CONSOLIDATED FINANCIAL STATEMENTS—(Continued)

cost, the advertising may be obtained from a party other than the customer, and the fair value of the advertising benefit can be reasonably estimated.

Recently issued accounting pronouncements

Effective January 1, 2021, the Company adopted ASU No. 2019-12 , Income Taxes (Topic 740): Simplifying the Accounting for Income Taxes, which, among other things, removes specific exceptions for recognizing deferred taxes for investments, performing intraperiod allocation and calculating income taxes in interim periods, as well as targeted impacts to the accounting for taxes under hybrid tax regimes. At adoption, there was not a material impact to the Company's financial position, results of operations or cash flows.

NOTE 3—REVENUES

Disaggregated revenue

As disclosed below in Note 17, the Company has four geographic reportable segments: United States ("U.S."), Latin America and Asia Pacific ("LAAP"), Europe, Middle East and Africa ("EMEA") and Canada.

The following tables disaggregate our operating segment _Net sales_ by product category and channel, which the Company believes provides a meaningful depiction how the nature, timing, and uncertainty of _Net sales_ are affected by economic factors:

(in thousands)	U.S.		LAAP		EMEA		Canada		Total	
					Year Ended December 31, 2020					
Product category net sales										
Apparel, Accessories and Equipment	$	1,231,835	$	320,616	$	197,052	$	118,116	$	1,867,619
Footwear		371,948		103,873		101,855		56,259		633,935
Total	$	1,603,783	$	424,489	$	298,907	$	174,375	$	2,501,554
Channel net sales										
Wholesale	$	838,388	$	198,083	$	249,161	$	117,628	$	1,403,260
DTC		765,395		226,406		49,746		56,747		1,098,294
Total	$	1,603,783	$	424,489	$	298,907	$	174,375	$	2,501,554

(in thousands)	U.S.		LAAP		EMEA		Canada		Total	
					Year Ended December 31, 2019					
Product category net sales										
Apparel, Accessories and Equipment	$	1,562,487	$	395,002	$	245,381	$	138,292	$	2,341,162
Footwear		380,520		134,280		121,691		64,825		701,316
Total	$	1,943,007	$	529,282	$	367,072	$	203,117	$	3,042,478
Channel net sales										
Wholesale	$	1,049,300	$	272,389	$	312,347	$	148,760	$	1,782,796
DTC		893,707		256,893		54,725		54,357		1,259,682
Total	$	1,943,007	$	529,282	$	367,072	$	203,117	$	3,042,478

COLUMBIA SPORTSWEAR COMPANY

NOTES TO CONSOLIDATED FINANCIAL STATEMENTS—(Continued)

(in thousands)	Year Ended December 31, 2018				
	U.S.	LAAP	EMEA	Canada	Total
Product category net sales					
Apparel, Accessories and Equipment	$ 1,432,711	$ 400,240	$ 226,324	$ 131,783	$ 2,191,058
Footwear	295,765	129,912	124,430	61,161	611,268
Total	$ 1,728,476	$ 530,152	$ 350,754	$ 192,944	$ 2,802,326
Channel net sales					
Wholesale	$ 902,928	$ 267,002	$ 300,626	$ 141,467	$ 1,612,023
DTC	825,548	263,150	50,128	51,477	1,190,303
Total	$ 1,728,476	$ 530,152	$ 350,754	$ 192,944	$ 2,802,326

Performance obligations

For the years ended December 31, 2020 and 2019, *Net sales* recognized from performance obligations related to prior periods were not material. *Net sales* expected to be recognized in any future period related to remaining performance obligations is not material.

Contract balances

As of December 31, 2020 and 2019, contract liabilities included in *Accrued Liabilities* on the Consolidated Balance Sheets, which consisted of obligations associated with the Company's gift card and customer loyalty programs, were not material.

NOTE 4—CONCENTRATIONS

Trade receivables

The Company had one customer that accounted for approximately 14.3% and 13.9% of *Accounts receivable, net* at December 31, 2020 and 2019, respectively. No single customer accounted for 10% or more of *Net sales* for any of the years ended December 31, 2020, 2019 or 2018.

NOTE 5—PROPERTY, PLANT AND EQUIPMENT, NET

Property, plant and equipment, net consisted of the following:

(in thousands)	December 31,	
	2020	2019
Land and improvements	$ 33,231	$ 26,951
Buildings and improvements	209,251	204,077
Machinery, software and equipment	388,808	383,881
Furniture and fixtures	96,521	96,303
Leasehold improvements	152,852	147,760
Construction in progress	3,376	10,771
	884,039	869,743
Less accumulated depreciation	(574,247)	(523,092)
	$ 309,792	$ 346,651

Depreciation expense for property, plant and equipment, net was $ 60.9 million, $59.8 million, and $58.2 million for the years ended December 31, 2020, 2019 and 2018, respectively.

Impairment charges for property, plant and equipment are included in *SG&A expense* and were $5.0 million, $0.4 million and $2.1 million for the years ended December 31, 2020, 2019 and 2018, respectively. Charges during the years ended December 31, 2020, 2019 and 2018 were recorded primarily for certain underperforming retail stores in the U.S., EMEA and LAAP regions.

COLUMBIA SPORTSWEAR COMPANY

NOTES TO CONSOLIDATED FINANCIAL STATEMENTS—(Continued)

NOTE 6—INTANGIBLE ASSETS, NET AND GOODWILL

Intangible assets, net consisted of the following:

(in thousands)	December 31,	
	2020	2019
Intangible assets subject to amortization:		
Patents and purchased technology	$ 14,198	$ 14,198
Customer relationships	23,000	23,000
Gross carrying amount	37,198	37,198
Accumulated amortization:		
Patents and purchased technology	(14,198)	(13,311)
Customer relationships	(17,363)	(15,713)
Accumulated amortization	(31,561)	(29,024)
Net carrying amount	5,637	8,174
Intangible assets not subject to amortization	97,921	115,421
Intangible assets, net	$ 103,558	$ 123,595

Amortization expense for intangible assets subject to amortization was $ 2.5 million for the year ended December 31, 2020, and $ 3.0 million for the years ended December 31, 2020 and 2019.

Impairment charges for the intangible assets not subject to amortization are included in *SG&A expense* and were $17.5 million for the year ended December 31, 2020. The impairment of the prAna trademark and trade name intangible asset was determined as part of the annual impairment test. The fair value was estimated using a relief from royalty method under the income approach. Cash flow projections were developed in part from the Company's annual planning process. The discount rate is the estimated weighted-average costs of capital of the reporting unit from a market-participant perspective. The decline in estimated fair value from the fourth-quarter 2019 impairment test reflects a lower estimated royalty rate and a decline in forecasted revenues. There was no impairment recorded for intangible assets not subject to amortization for the years ended December 31, 2019 and 2018.

Substantially all of the Company's goodwill is recorded in the U.S. segment. The Company determined that goodwill was not impaired for the years ended December 31, 2020, 2019, and 2018.

The following table presents the estimated annual amortization expense for the years 2021 through 2025:

(in thousands)	
2021	$ 1,650
2022	1,650
2023	1,650
2024	688
2025	—

NOTE 7—SHORT-TERM BORROWINGS AND CREDIT LINES

Columbia Sportswear Company Credit Lines

In 2020, the Company entered into a credit agreement, maturing on December 30, 2025, which provides an unsecured, committed revolving credit facility that provides for funding up to $500.0 million. Interest, payable monthly, is based on the Company's option of either LIBOR plus an applicable margin or a base rate. Base rate is defined as the highest of the following, plus an applicable margin:

- the administrative agent's prime rate;
- the higher of the federal funds rate or the overnight bank funding rate set by the Federal Reserve Bank of New York, plus 0.50%; or
- the one-month LIBOR plus 1.00%.

COLUMBIA SPORTSWEAR COMPANY

NOTES TO CONSOLIDATED FINANCIAL STATEMENTS—(Continued)

This credit agreement requires the Company to comply with certain financial covenants covering the Company's funded debt ratio and asset coverage ratio. The credit agreement also includes customary covenants that, among other things, limit or restrict the ability of the Company and its subsidiaries to incur additional indebtedness and liens, engage in mergers, acquisitions and dispositions, and engage in transactions with affiliates, as well as restrict certain payments, including dividends and share buybacks.

At December 31, 2020, the Company was in compliance with all associated covenants and there was no balance outstanding. At December 31, 2019, there was no balance outstanding under the credit agreement in effect for such period.

Columbia Sportswear Company's Subsidiary Credit Lines

At December 21, 2020 and 2019, there was no balance outstanding under the Company's subsidiary credit lines.

The Company's Canadian subsidiary has available an unsecured and uncommitted line of credit, which is payable on demand, guaranteed by the Company, and provides for borrowing up to a maximum of CAD$30.0 million (approximately US$23.5 million) at December 31, 2020. The revolving line accrues interest at the Canadian prime rate for CAD overdraft borrowings or Bankers' Acceptance rate plus 150 basis points for Bankers' Acceptance loans.

The Company's European subsidiary has available two separate unsecured and uncommitted lines of credit, and an unsecured, committed line of credit, which are guaranteed by the Company, and provide for borrowing up to a maximum of €25.8 million, €0.6 million, and €4.4 million, respectively (combined approximately US$37.9 million), at December 31, 2020. Borrowings under the € 25.8 million line accrue interest at a base rate of 185 basis points plus 175 basis points. Borrowings under the €4.4 million and €0.6 million lines each accrue interest at 75 basis points.

The Company's Japanese subsidiary has available two separate unsecured and uncommitted overdraft facilities guaranteed by the Company providing for borrowing up to a maximum of ¥1.5 billion and US$7.0 million, respectively (combined approximately US$ 21.5 million) at December 31, 2020. Borrowings under the ¥1.5 billion overdraft facility accrue interest at the Tokyo Interbank Offered Rate plus 0.50 basis points and borrowings under the US$ 7.0 million overdraft facility accrue interest at 175 basis points.

The Company's Korean subsidiary has available an unsecured and uncommitted overdraft facility guaranteed by the Company providing for borrowing up to a maximum of US$20.0 million at December 31, 2020. Borrowings under the overdraft facility accrue interest at the Korea three month CD rate plus 175 basis points.

The Company's Chinese subsidiary has available an unsecured and uncommitted line of credit providing for borrowings up to a maximum of RMB 140.0 million at December 31, 2020. The Company's Chinese subsidiary also has an unsecured and uncommitted overdraft and clean advance facility, guaranteed by the Company that provides for borrowings of advances or overdrafts up to a maximum of US$20.0 million at December 31, 2020. Borrowings under the RMB 140.0 million line of credit accrue interest at the one year loan prime rate less 10 basis points. Borrowings under the US$20.0 million facility accrue interest on advances of RMB at 4.15%, advances of USD based on LIBOR plus 1.75% per annum or overdrafts of RMB based on 110% of the People's Bank of China rate. The combined available borrowings of the two facilities were approximately US$41.5 million at December 31, 2020.

NOTE 8—ACCRUED LIABILITIES

Accrued liabilities consisted of the following:

(in thousands)	December 31, 2020	December 31, 2019
Sales reserves	$ 83,175	$ 110,758
Accrued salaries, bonus, paid time off and other benefits	80,074	93,887
Accrued import duties	18,522	20,922
Taxes other than income taxes payable	15,002	15,496
Product warranties	14,745	14,466
Other	45,760	40,194
	$ 257,278	$ 295,723

COLUMBIA SPORTSWEAR COMPANY

NOTES TO CONSOLIDATED FINANCIAL STATEMENTS—(Continued)

A reconciliation of product warranties is as follows:

	Year Ended December 31,		
(in thousands)	2020	2019	2018
Balance at beginning of year	$ 14,466	$ 13,186	$ 12,339
Provision for warranty claims	3,033	5,152	5,054
Warranty claims	(3,128)	(3,810)	(3,942)
Other	374	(62)	(265)
Balance at end of year	$ 14,745	$ 14,466	$ 13,186

NOTE 9—LEASES

The components of lease cost consisted of the following:

	Year Ended December 31,	
(in thousands)	2020	2019
Operating lease cost[1]	$ 104,906	$ 78,609
Variable lease cost[1]	58,391	60,085
Short term lease cost[1]	9,600	9,013
	$ 172,897	$ 147,707

[1] For the year ended December 31, 2018, prior to the adoption of ASC 842 on January 1, 2019, rent expenses of $143.9 million and $1.6 million was included in *SG&A expense and Cost of sales, respectively.*

For the year ended December 31, 2020, operating lease cost included $ 16.5 million of accelerated amortization for retail locations that permanently closed during 2020 for which the related lease liabilities have not been extinguished as of December 31, 2020 due to ongoing negotiations with the landlords. In addition, for the year ended December 31, 2020, operating lease cost included $7.0 million of right-of-use asset impairment charges related to underperforming retail locations primarily in the U.S. segment for the year ended December 31, 2020. There was no impairment recorded for the year ended December 31, 2019.

In the periods presented, lease concessions reducing variable lease expense were not material.

The following table presents supplemental cash flow information:

	Year Ended December 31,	
(in thousands)	2020	2019
Cash paid for amounts included in the measurement of operating lease liabilities	$ 82,083	$ 77,350
Operating lease liabilities arising from obtaining ROU assets [1][2]	22,416	471,396
Reductions to ROU assets resulting from reductions to operating lease liabilities	6,400	783

[1] The year ended December 31, 2019 reflects the impact from amount initially capitalized in conjunction with the adoption of ASC 842.
[2] Includes amounts added to the carrying amount of lease liabilities resulting from lease modifications and reassessments.

The following table presents supplemental balance sheet information related to leases:

	Year Ended December 31,	
	2020	2019
Weighted average remaining lease term	6.16 years	6.79 years
Weighted average discount rate	3.72 %	3.82 %

COLUMBIA SPORTSWEAR COMPANY

NOTES TO CONSOLIDATED FINANCIAL STATEMENTS—(Continued)

The following table presents the future maturities of liabilities as of December 31, 2020:

(in thousands)

2021	$	92,756
2022		73,936
2023		66,328
2024		58,726
2025		51,134
Thereafter		130,429
Total lease payments		473,309
Less: imputed interest		(54,662)
Total lease liabilities		418,647
Less: current obligations		(65,466)
Long-term lease obligations	$	353,181

As of December 31, 2020, the Company has additional operating lease commitments that have not yet commenced of $ 3.9 million. These leases will commence in 2021 with lease terms of approximately two to 10 years.

NOTE 10—INCOME TAXES

Income Tax Provision

Consolidated income from continuing operations before income taxes consisted of the following:

(in thousands)	Year Ended December 31,					
		2020		2019		2018
United States operations	$	29,154	$	247,642	$	224,430
Foreign operations		110,369		157,787		136,287
Income before income tax	$	139,523	$	405,429	$	360,717

The components of the provision for income taxes consisted of the following:

(in thousands)	Year Ended December 31,					
		2020		2019		2018
Current:						
Federal	$	18,435	$	41,148	$	59,213
State and local		4,929		7,458		9,959
Non-United States		26,897		30,930		28,700
		50,261		79,536		97,872
Deferred:						
Federal		(14,728)		(7,887)		(10,961)
State and local		(5,097)		(999)		(1,910)
Non-United States		1,074		4,290		768
		(18,751)		(4,596)		(12,103)
Income tax expense	$	31,510	$	74,940	$	85,769

COLUMBIA SPORTSWEAR COMPANY

NOTES TO CONSOLIDATED FINANCIAL STATEMENTS—(Continued)

The following is a reconciliation of the statutory federal income tax rate to the effective rate reported in the financial statements:

	Year Ended December 31,		
(percent of income before tax)	**2020**	**2019**	**2018**
Provision for federal income taxes at the statutory rate	21.0 %	21.0 %	21.0 %
State and local income taxes, net of federal benefit	1.5	1.7	2.0
Non-United States income taxed at different rates	2.1	(0.1)	(0.1)
Foreign tax credits	(0.9)	(0.1)	—
Adjustment to deferred taxes	(1.2)	(2.1)	—
Global Intangible Low-Taxed Income	0.1	—	0.4
Research credits	(1.4)	(0.5)	(0.6)
Withholding taxes	0.5	0.3	0.4
Excess tax benefits from stock plans	(0.8)	(1.6)	(1.4)
Provision for income taxes related to tax reform	—	—	1.4
Other	1.7	(0.1)	0.7
Actual provision for income taxes	22.6 %	18.5 %	23.8 %

Deferred Income Tax Balances

Significant components of the Company's deferred taxes consisted of the following:

	December 31,	
(in thousands)	**2020**	**2019**
Deferred tax assets:		
Accruals and allowances	$ 47,667	$ 38,532
Capitalized inventory costs	38,832	34,389
Stock compensation	6,078	5,013
Net operating loss carryforwards	24,253	23,660
Depreciation and amortization	29,358	32,293
Tax credits	844	2,329
Foreign currency	2,418	—
Other	2,304	2,258
Gross deferred tax assets	151,754	138,474
Valuation allowance	(23,534)	(24,130)
Net deferred tax assets	128,220	114,344
Deferred tax liabilities:		
Depreciation and amortization	(16,206)	(15,738)
Prepaid expenses	(2,085)	(2,661)
Deferred tax liability associated with future repatriations	(19,008)	(19,847)
Foreign currency	—	(3,610)
Gross deferred tax liabilities	(37,299)	(41,856)
Total net deferred taxes	$ 90,921	$ 72,488

The Company has foreign net operating loss carryforwards of $ 89.1 million as of December 31, 2020, of which $ 72.7 million have an unlimited carryforward period and $16.5 million expire between 2025 and 2040. The net operating losses result in deferred tax assets of $ 24.3 million and $23.7 million and were subject to a valuation allowance of $21.2 million and $21.9 million at December 31, 2020 and 2019, respectively.

At December 31, 2020, the Company has accumulated undistributed earnings generated by the Company's foreign subsidiaries of

COLUMBIA SPORTSWEAR COMPANY

NOTES TO CONSOLIDATED FINANCIAL STATEMENTS—(Continued)

$320.8 million. As $100.0 million of such earnings have previously been subject to the one-time transition tax on foreign earnings by the Tax Cuts and Jobs Act, any additional taxes due with respect to such earnings would generally be limited to foreign and state taxes and have been recorded as a deferred tax liability. However, the Company intends to indefinitely reinvest the earnings generated after January 1, 2018 and expects future domestic cash generation to be sufficient to meet future domestic cash needs.

Unrecognized Tax Benefits

The Company conducts business globally, and, as a result, the Company or one or more of its subsidiaries file income tax returns in the United States federal jurisdiction and various state and foreign jurisdictions. The Company is subject to examination by taxing authorities throughout the world, including such major jurisdictions as Canada, China, France, Japan, South Korea, Switzerland, and the United States. The Company has effectively settled Canadian tax examinations of all years through 2012, United States tax examinations of all years through 2013, Japanese tax examinations of all years through 2014, France tax examinations of all years through 2014, Swiss tax examinations of all years through 2014, Italy tax examinations of all years through 2016, and China tax examinations of all years through 2018. The Korean National Tax Service concluded an audit of the Company's 2009 through 2013 corporate income tax returns in 2014, and an audit of the Company's 2014 corporate income tax return in 2016. Due to the nature of the findings in both of these audits, the Company has invoked the Mutual Agreement Procedures outlined in the United States-Korean income tax treaty. The Company does not anticipate that adjustments relative to these findings, or any other ongoing tax audits, will result in material changes to its financial condition, results of operations or cash flows. Other than the findings previously noted, the Company is not currently under examination in any major jurisdiction.

A reconciliation of the beginning and ending amount of gross unrecognized tax benefits is as follows:

(in thousands)	December 31,					
	2020		**2019**		**2018**	
Balance at beginning of year	$	12,478	$	11,064	$	10,512
Increases related to prior year tax positions		1,903		4,374		490
Decreases related to prior year tax positions		(162)		(5,423)		(1,093)
Increases related to current year tax positions		906		4,991		1,818
Settlements		—		(1,464)		319
Expiration of statute of limitations		(632)		(1,064)		(982)
Balance at end of year	$	14,493	$	12,478	$	11,064

Due to the potential for resolution of income tax audits currently in progress, and the expiration of various statutes of limitation, it is reasonably possible that the unrecognized tax benefits balance may change within the twelve months following December 31, 2020 by a range of zero to $5.4 million. Open tax years, including those previously mentioned, contain matters that could be subject to differing interpretations of applicable tax laws and regulations as they relate to the amount, timing, or inclusion of revenue and expenses or the sustainability of income tax credits for a given examination cycle.

Unrecognized tax benefits of $13.6 million, $11.5 million and $9.1 million would affect the effective tax rate if recognized at December 31, 2020, 2019 and 2018, respectively.

The Company recognizes interest expense and penalties related to income tax matters in *Income tax expense*. The Company recognized a net increase of accrued interest and penalties of $0.8 million in 2020, and a net reversal of accrued interest and penalties of $ 0.5 million in 2019 and a net increase of accrued interest and penalties of $0.4 million in 2018, all of which related to uncertain tax positions. The Company had $ 2.3 million and $1.5 million of accrued interest and penalties related to uncertain tax positions at December 31, 2020 and 2019, respectively.

NOTE 11—RETIREMENT SAVINGS PLANS

401(k) Profit-Sharing Plan

The Company has a 401(k) profit-sharing plan, which covers substantially all United States employees. Participation begins the first day of the quarter following completion of 30 days of service. The Company, with approval of the Board of Directors, may elect to make discretionary matching or non-matching contributions. Costs recognized for Company contributions to the plan were $10.1 million, $9.4 million and $8.9 million for the years ended December 31, 2020, 2019 and 2018, respectively.

COLUMBIA SPORTSWEAR COMPANY

NOTES TO CONSOLIDATED FINANCIAL STATEMENTS—(Continued)

Deferred Compensation Plan

The Company sponsors a nonqualified retirement savings plan for certain senior management employees whose contributions to the tax qualified 401(k) plan would be limited by provisions of the Internal Revenue Code. This plan allows participants to defer receipt of a portion of their salary and incentive compensation and to receive matching contributions for a portion of the deferred amounts. Costs recognized for Company matching contributions to the plan totaled $0.4 million, $0.5 million and $0.4 million for the years ended December 31, 2020, 2019 and 2018, respectively. Participants earn a return on their deferred compensation based on investment earnings of participant-selected investments. Deferred compensation, including accumulated earnings on the participant-directed investment selections, is distributable in cash at participant-specified dates or upon retirement, death, disability, or termination of employment.

The Company has purchased specific money market and mutual funds in the same amounts as the participant-directed investment selections underlying the deferred compensation liabilities. These investment securities and earnings thereon, held in an irrevocable trust, are intended to provide a source of funds to meet the deferred compensation obligations, subject to claims of creditors in the event of the Company's insolvency. Changes in the market value of the participants' investment selections are recorded as an adjustment to the investments and as unrealized gains and losses in *SG&A expense*. A corresponding adjustment of an equal amount is made to the deferred compensation liabilities and compensation expense, which is included in *SG&A expense*.

At December 31, 2020, and 2019, the long-term portion of the liability to participants under this plan was $18.7 million and $14.0 million, respectively, and was recorded in *Other long-term liabilities*. At December 31, 2020 and 2019, the current portion of the participant liability was $1.2 million and $1.7 million, respectively, and was recorded in *Accrued liabilities*. At December 31, 2020 and 2019, the fair value of the long-term portion of the investments related to this plan was $18.7 million and $14.0 million, respectively, and was recorded in *Other non-current assets*. At December 31, 2020 and 2019, the current portion of the investments related to this plan was $1.2 million and $1.7 million, respectively, and was recorded in *Short-term investments*.

NOTE 12—COMMITMENTS AND CONTINGENCIES

Litigation

The Company is involved in litigation and various legal matters arising in the normal course of business, including matters related to employment, retail, intellectual property, contractual agreements, and various regulatory compliance activities. Management has considered facts related to legal and regulatory matters and opinions of counsel handling these matters, and does not believe the ultimate resolution of these proceedings will have a material adverse effect on the Company's financial position, results of operations or cash flows.

Indemnities and Guarantees

During its normal course of business, the Company has made certain indemnities, commitments and guarantees under which it may be required to make payments in relation to certain transactions. These include (i) intellectual property indemnities to the Company's customers and licensees in connection with the use, sale or license of Company products, (ii) indemnities to various lessors in connection with facility leases for certain claims arising from such facility or lease, (iii) indemnities to customers, vendors and service providers pertaining to claims based on the negligence or willful misconduct of the Company, (iv) executive severance arrangements, and (v) indemnities involving the accuracy of representations and warranties in certain contracts. The duration of these indemnities, commitments and guarantees varies, and in certain cases, may be indefinite. The majority of these indemnities, commitments and guarantees do not provide for any limitation of the maximum potential for future payments the Company could be obligated to make. The Company has not recorded any liability for these indemnities, commitments and guarantees in the accompanying Consolidated Balance Sheets.

NOTE 13—SHAREHOLDERS' EQUITY

Since the inception of the Company's stock repurchase plan in 2004 through December 31, 2020, the Company's Board of Directors has authorized the repurchase of $1.1 billion of the Company's common stock. Shares of the Company's common stock may be purchased in the open market or through privately negotiated transactions, subject to market conditions, and generally settle subsequent to the trade date. The repurchase program does not obligate the Company to acquire any specific number of shares or to acquire shares over any specified period of time.

Under this program as of December 31, 2020, the Company had repurchased 26.8 million shares at an aggregate purchase price of $1,017.8 million and have $82.2 million remaining available. During the year ended December 31, 2020, the Company purchased an aggregate of $132.9 million of common stock under this program.

COLUMBIA SPORTSWEAR COMPANY

NOTES TO CONSOLIDATED FINANCIAL STATEMENTS—(Continued)

In January 2021, the Company's Board of Directors approved a $ 400.0 million increase in share repurchase authorization.

NOTE 14—STOCK-BASED COMPENSATION

At its Annual Meeting held on June 3, 2020, the Company's shareholders approved the Company's 2020 Stock Incentive Plan (the "2020 Plan"), and the 2020 Plan became effective on that date following such approval. The 2020 Plan replaced the Company's 1997 Stock Incentive Plan (the "Prior Plan") and no new awards will be granted under the Prior Plan. The terms and conditions of the awards granted under the Prior Plan will remain in effect with respect to awards granted under the Prior Plan. The Company has reserved 3.0 million shares of common stock for issuance under the 2020 Plan, plus up to an aggregate of 1.5 million shares of the Company's common stock that were previously authorized and available for issuance under the Prior Plan. At December 31, 2020, 4,169,642 shares were available for future grants under the 2020 Plan and up to 328,486 additional shares that were previously authorized and available for issuance under the Prior Plan may become available for future grants under the 2020 Plan. The 2020 Plan allows for grants of incentive stock options, non-statutory stock options, restricted stock awards, restricted stock units, and other stock-based or cash-based awards. The Company uses original issuance shares to satisfy share-based payments.

Stock Compensation

Stock-based compensation expense consisted of the following:

(in thousands)	Year Ended December 31,		
	2020	2019	2018
Cost of sales	$ 303	$ 278	$ 250
SG&A expense	17,475	17,554	14,041
Pre-tax stock-based compensation expense	17,778	17,832	14,291
Income tax benefits	(4,015)	(4,009)	(3,218)
Total stock-based compensation expense, net of tax	$ 13,763	$ 13,823	$ 11,073

The Company realized a tax benefit for the deduction from stock-based award transactions of $ 4.1 million, $9.9 million and $7.9 million for the years ended December 31, 2020, 2019 and 2018, respectively.

Stock Options

Options to purchase the Company's common stock are granted at exercise prices equal to or greater than the fair market value of the Company's common stock on the date of grant. Options generally vest and become exercisable ratably on an annual basis over a period of four years and expire ten years from the date of the grant.

The fair value of stock options is determined using the Black-Scholes model. Key inputs and assumptions used in the model include the exercise price of the award, the expected option term, the expected stock price volatility of the Company's stock over the option's expected term, the risk-free interest rate over the option's expected term, and the Company's expected annual dividend yield. The option's expected term is derived from historical option exercise behavior and the option's terms and conditions, which the Company believes provide a reasonable basis for estimating an expected term. The expected volatility is estimated based on observations of the Company's historical volatility over the most recent term commensurate with the expected term. The risk-free interest rate is based on the United States Treasury yield approximating the expected term. The dividend yield is based on the expected cash dividend payouts.

The weighted average assumptions for stock options granted and resulting fair value is as follows:

	Year Ended December 31,		
	2020	2019	2018
Expected option term	4.39 years	4.50 years	4.50 years
Expected stock price volatility	21.19%	27.14%	28.39%
Risk-free interest rate	1.14%	2.49%	2.47%
Expected annual dividend yield	1.13%	1.03%	1.15%
Weighted average grant date fair value per share	$14.67	$22.51	$18.86

COLUMBIA SPORTSWEAR COMPANY

NOTES TO CONSOLIDATED FINANCIAL STATEMENTS—(Continued)

The following table summarizes stock option activity under the Plan:

	Number of Shares		Weighted Average Exercise Price	Weighted Average Remaining Contractual Life		Aggregate Intrinsic Value [1] (in thousands)
Options outstanding at January 1, 2018	1,769,887	$	44.22	6.69	$	48,962
Granted	402,010		76.48			
Cancelled	(67,440)		60.75			
Exercised	(499,836)		36.98			
Options outstanding at December 31, 2018	1,604,621		53.86	6.95		48,703
Granted	395,653		93.98			
Cancelled	(68,275)		74.10			
Exercised	(452,325)		43.76			
Options outstanding at December 31, 2019	1,479,674		66.74	7.11		49,930
Granted	660,071		87.25			
Cancelled	(78,163)		83.76			
Exercised	(142,419)		48.58			
Options outstanding at December 31, 2020	1,919,163	$	74.45	7.19	$	29,489
Options vested and expected to vest at December 31, 2020	1,839,590	$	73.88	7.12	$	29,185
Options exercisable at December 31, 2020	806,320	$	60.31	5.53	$	22,620

[1]The aggregate intrinsic value above represents pre-tax intrinsic value that would have been realized if all options had been exercised on the last business day of the period indicated, based on the Company's closing stock price on that day.

Stock option compensation expense for the years ended December 31, 2020, 2019 and 2018 was $ 7.0 million, $6.2 million and $4.9 million, respectively. At December 31, 2020, unrecognized costs related to outstanding stock options totaled $11.5 million, before any related tax benefit. The unrecognized costs related to stock options are being amortized over the related vesting period using the straight-line attribution method. These unrecognized costs related to stock options are being amortized over a weighted average period of 2.33 years. The aggregate intrinsic value of stock options exercised was $ 4.9 million, $26.8 million and $22.4 million for the years ended December 31, 2020, 2019 and 2018, respectively. The total cash received as a result of stock option exercises for the years ended December 31, 2020, 2019 and 2018 was $6.9 million, $19.8 million and $18.5 million, respectively.

Restricted Stock Units

Service-based restricted stock units are granted at no cost to key employees and generally vest over a period of four years. Performance-based restricted stock units are granted at no cost to certain members of the Company's senior executive team, excluding the Chief Executive Officer. Performance-based restricted stock units granted after 2009 generally vest over a performance period of between two and three years. Restricted stock units vest in accordance with the terms and conditions established by the Compensation Committee of the Board of Directors, and are based on continued service and, in some instances, on individual performance or Company performance or both.

The fair value of service-based and performance-based restricted stock units is determined using the Black-Scholes model. Key inputs and assumptions used in the model include the vesting period, the Company's expected annual dividend yield and the closing price of the Company's common stock on the date of grant.

The weighted average assumptions for restricted stock units granted and resulting fair value are as follows:

	Year Ended December 31,		
	2020	**2019**	**2018**
Vesting period	3.79 years	3.76 years	3.77 years
Expected annual dividend yield	1.18%	0.97%	1.15%
Weighted average grant date fair value per restricted stock unit granted	$78.90	$94.58	$73.74

COMPARATIVE SELECTED FINANCIAL DATA

Item 6. *SELECTED FINANCIAL DATA*

Selected Consolidated Financial Data

The selected consolidated financial data presented below for, and as of the end of, each of the years in the five-year period ended December 31, 2020 have been derived from our audited Consolidated Financial Statements. The selected consolidated financial data should be read in conjunction with the Item 7 and Item 8 of this annual report.

(in thousands, except per share amounts)	2020	2019	2018	2017	2016
Statement of Operations Data:					
Net sales	$ 2,501,554	$3,042,478	$ 2,802,326	$ 2,466,105	$ 2,377,045
Gross profit	1,223,889	1,515,670	1,386,348	1,159,962	1,110,348
Gross margin	48.9 %	49.8 %	49.5 %	47.0 %	46.7 %
Income from operations	137,049	394,971	350,982	262,969	256,508
Net income attributable to Columbia Sportswear Company[1]	108,013	330,489	268,256	105,123	191,898
Per Share of Common Stock Data:					
Earnings per share attributable to Columbia Sportswear Company:					
Basic	$ 1.63	$ 4.87	$ 3.85	$ 1.51	$ 2.75
Diluted	1.62	4.83	3.81	1.49	2.72
Cash dividends per share	0.26	0.96	0.90	0.73	0.69
Weighted average shares outstanding:					
Basic	66,376	67,837	69,614	69,759	69,683
Diluted	66,772	68,493	70,401	70,453	70,632
Balance Sheet Data:					
Inventories, net[2]	$ 556,530	$ 605,968	$ 521,827	$ 457,927	$ 457,997
Total assets[2][3]	2,836,571	2,931,591	2,368,721	2,212,902	2,013,894
Non-current operating lease liabilities[3]	353,181	371,507	—	—	—

[1] The year-ended December 31, 2017 reflects the provisional impact from the enactment of the Tax Cuts and Jobs Act in December 2017.
[2] The year-ended December 31, 2018 reflects the impact from adoption of ASU 2014-09, *Revenue from Contracts with Customers.*
[3] The year-ended December 31, 2019 reflects the impact from the adoption of ASU 2016-02, *Leases.*

REPORT ON INTERNAL CONTROL

REPORT OF INDEPENDENT REGISTERED PUBLIC ACCOUNTING FIRM

To the Shareholders and the Board of Directors of Columbia Sportswear Company

Opinion on Internal Control over Financial Reporting

We have audited the internal control over financial reporting of Columbia Sportswear Company and subsidiaries (the "Company") as of December 31, 2020, based on criteria established in *Internal Control - Integrated Framework (2013)* issued by the Committee of Sponsoring Organizations of the Treadway Commission (COSO). In our opinion, the Company maintained, in all material respects, effective internal control over financial reporting as of December 31, 2020, based on criteria established in *Internal Control - Integrated Framework (2013)* issued by COSO.

We have also audited, in accordance with the standards of the Public Company Accounting Oversight Board (United States) (PCAOB), the consolidated financial statements as of and for the year ended December 31, 2020, of the Company and our report dated February 25, 2021, expressed an unqualified opinion on those financial statements.

Basis for Opinion

The Company's management is responsible for maintaining effective internal control over financial reporting and for its assessment of the effectiveness of internal control over financial reporting, included in the accompanying Report of Management. Our responsibility is to express an opinion on the Company's internal control over financial reporting based on our audit. We are a public accounting firm registered with the PCAOB and are required to be independent with respect to the Company in accordance with the U.S. federal securities laws and the applicable rules and regulations of the Securities and Exchange Commission and the PCAOB.

We conducted our audit in accordance with the standards of the PCAOB. Those standards require that we plan and perform the audit to obtain reasonable assurance about whether effective internal control over financial reporting was maintained in all material respects. Our audit included obtaining an understanding of internal control over financial reporting, assessing the risk that a material weakness exists, testing and evaluating the design and operating effectiveness of internal control based on the assessed risk, and performing such other procedures as we considered necessary in the circumstances. We believe that our audit provides a reasonable basis for our opinion.

Definition and Limitations of Internal Control over Financial Reporting

A company's internal control over financial reporting is a process designed to provide reasonable assurance regarding the reliability of financial reporting and the preparation of financial statements for external purposes in accordance with generally accepted accounting principles. A company's internal control over financial reporting includes those policies and procedures that (1) pertain to the maintenance of records that, in reasonable detail, accurately and fairly reflect the transactions and dispositions of the assets of the company; (2) provide reasonable assurance that transactions are recorded as necessary to permit preparation of financial statements in accordance with generally accepted accounting principles, and that receipts and expenditures of the company are being made only in accordance with authorizations of management and directors of the company; and (3) provide reasonable assurance regarding prevention or timely detection of unauthorized acquisition, use, or disposition of the company's assets that could have a material effect on the financial statements.

Because of its inherent limitations, internal control over financial reporting may not prevent or detect misstatements. Also, projections of any evaluation of effectiveness to future periods are subject to the risk that controls may become inadequate because of changes in conditions, or that the degree of compliance with the policies or procedures may deteriorate.

/s/   DELOITTE & TOUCHE LLP
Portland, Oregon
February 25, 2021

Appendix B

Financial Statements for Under Armour

The complete annual report for Under Armour is available on this book's website.

Under Armour, Inc. and Subsidiaries

Consolidated Balance Sheets

(In thousands, except share data)

	December 31, 2019	December 31, 2018
Assets		
Current assets		
Cash and cash equivalents	$ 788,072	$ 557,403
Accounts receivable, net	708,714	652,546
Inventories	892,258	1,019,496
Prepaid expenses and other current assets	313,165	364,183
Total current assets	2,702,209	2,593,628
Property and equipment, net	792,148	826,868
Operating lease right-of-use assets	591,931	—
Goodwill	550,178	546,494
Intangible assets, net	36,345	41,793
Deferred income taxes	82,379	112,420
Other long term assets	88,341	123,819
Total assets	$ 4,843,531	$ 4,245,022
Liabilities and Stockholders' Equity		
Current liabilities		
Accounts payable	$ 618,194	$ 560,884
Accrued expenses	374,694	340,415
Customer refund liabilities	219,424	301,421
Operating lease liabilities	125,900	—
Current maturities of long term debt	—	25,000
Other current liabilities	83,797	88,257
Total current liabilities	1,422,009	1,315,977
Long term debt, net of current maturities	592,687	703,834
Operating lease liabilities, non-current	580,635	—
Other long term liabilities	98,113	208,340
Total liabilities	2,693,444	2,228,151
Commitments and contingencies (see Note 8)		
Stockholders' equity		
Class A Common Stock, $0.0003 1/3 par value; 400,000,000 shares authorized as of December 31, 2019 and 2018; 188,289,680 shares issued and outstanding as of December 31, 2019, and 187,710,319 shares issued and outstanding as of December 31, 2018	62	62
Class B Convertible Common Stock, $0.0003 1/3 par value; 34,450,000 shares authorized, issued and outstanding as of December 31, 2019 and 2018.	11	11
Class C Common Stock, $0.0003 1/3 par value; 400,000,000 shares authorized as of December 31, 2019 and 2018; 229,027,730 shares issued and outstanding as of December 31, 2019, and 226,421,963 shares issued and outstanding as of December 31, 2018.	76	75
Additional paid-in capital	973,717	916,628
Retained earnings	1,226,986	1,139,082
Accumulated other comprehensive loss	(50,765)	(38,987)
Total stockholders' equity	2,150,087	2,016,871
Total liabilities and stockholders' equity	$ 4,843,531	$ 4,245,022

See accompanying notes.

Under Armour, Inc. and Subsidiaries

Consolidated Statements of Operations

(In thousands, except per share amounts)

		Year Ended December 31,	
	2019	2018	2017
Net revenues	$ 5,267,132	$ 5,193,185	$ 4,989,244
Cost of goods sold	2,796,599	2,852,714	2,737,830
Gross profit	2,470,533	2,340,471	2,251,414
Selling, general and administrative expenses	2,233,763	2,182,339	2,099,522
Restructuring and impairment charges	—	183,149	124,049
Income (loss) from operations	236,770	(25,017)	27,843
Interest expense, net	(21,240)	(33,568)	(34,538)
Other expense, net	(5,688)	(9,203)	(3,614)
Income (loss) before income taxes	209,842	(67,788)	(10,309)
Income tax expense (benefit)	70,024	(20,552)	37,951
Income (loss) from equity method investment	(47,679)	934	—
Net income (loss)	$ 92,139	$ (46,302)	$ (48,260)
Basic net income (loss) per share of Class A, B and C common stock	$ 0.20	$ (0.10)	$ (0.11)
Diluted net income (loss) per share of Class A, B and C common stock	$ 0.20	$ (0.10)	$ (0.11)
Weighted average common shares outstanding Class A, B and C common stock			
Basic	450,964	445,815	440,729
Diluted	454,274	445,815	440,729

See accompanying notes.

Under Armour, Inc. and Subsidiaries

Consolidated Statements of Stockholders' Equity
(In thousands)

	Class A Common Stock		Class B Convertible Common Stock		Class C Common Stock		Additional Paid-in-Capital	Retained Earnings	Accumulated Other Comprehensive Income	Total Equity
	Shares	Amount	Shares	Amount	Shares	Amount				
Balance as of December 31, 2016	183,815	61	34,450	11	220,174	73	823,484	1,259,414	(52,143)	$ 2,030,900
Exercise of stock options	609	—	—	—	556	—	3,664	—	—	3,664
Shares withheld in consideration of employee tax obligations relative to stock-based compensation arrangements	(65)	—	—	—	(78)	—	—	(2,781)	—	(2,781)
Issuance of Class A Common Stock, net of forfeitures	898	—	—	—	—	—	—	—	—	—
Issuance of Class C Common Stock, net of forfeitures	—	—	—	—	1,723	1	7,852	—	—	7,853
Impact of adoption of accounting standard updates	—	—	—	—	—	—	(2,666)	(23,932)	—	(26,598)
Stock-based compensation expense	—	—	—	—	—	—	39,932	—	—	39,932
Comprehensive income (loss)	—	—	—	—	—	—	—	(48,260)	13,932	(34,328)
Balance as of December 31, 2017	185,257	$ 61	34,450	$ 11	222,375	$ 74	$ 872,266	$ 1,184,441	$ (38,211)	$ 2,018,642
Exercise of stock options and warrants	2,084	1	—	—	2,127	—	6,747	—	—	6,748
Shares withheld in consideration of employee tax obligations relative to stock-based compensation arrangements	(23)	—	—	—	(140)	—	—	(2,564)	—	(2,564)
Issuance of Class A Common Stock, net of forfeitures	392	—	—	—	—	—	—	—	—	—
Issuance of Class C Common Stock, net of forfeitures	—	—	—	—	2,060	1	(4,168)	—	—	(4,167)
Impact of adoption of accounting standard updates	—	—	—	—	—	—	—	3,507	—	3,507
Stock-based compensation expense	—	—	—	—	—	—	41,783	—	—	41,783
Comprehensive loss	—	—	—	—	—	—	—	(46,302)	(776)	(47,078)
Balance as of December 31, 2018	187,710	$ 62	34,450	$ 11	226,422	$ 75	$ 916,628	$ 1,139,082	$ (38,987)	$ 2,016,871
Exercise of stock options	441	—	—	—	293	—	2,101	—	—	2,101
Shares withheld in consideration of employee tax obligations relative to stock-based compensation arrangements	(15)	—	—	—	(227)	—	—	(4,235)	—	(4,235)
Issuance of Class A Common Stock, net of forfeitures	154	—	—	—	—	—	—	—	—	—
Issuance of Class C Common Stock, net of forfeitures	—	—	—	—	2,540	1	5,370	—	—	5,371
Stock-based compensation expense	—	—	—	—	—	—	49,618	—	—	49,618
Comprehensive income (loss)	—	—	—	—	—	—	—	92,139	(11,778)	80,361
Balance as of December 31, 2019	188,290	$ 62	34,450	$ 11	229,028	$ 76	$ 973,717	$ 1,226,986	$ (50,765)	$ 2,150,087

See accompanying notes.

Under Armour, Inc. and Subsidiaries
Consolidated Statements of Cash Flows
(In thousands)

	Year Ended December 31,		
	2019	2018	2017
Cash flows from operating activities			
Net income (loss)	$ 92,139	$ (46,302)	$ (48,260)
Adjustments to reconcile net income (loss) to net cash provided by operating activities			
Depreciation and amortization	186,425	181,768	173,747
Unrealized foreign currency exchange rate gain (loss)	(2,073)	14,023	(29,247)
Impairment charges	39,000	9,893	71,378
Amortization of bond premium	254	254	254
Loss on disposal of property and equipment	4,640	4,256	2,313
Stock-based compensation	49,618	41,783	39,932
Excess tax benefit (loss) from stock-based compensation arrangements	—	—	(75)
Deferred income taxes	38,132	(38,544)	55,910
Changes in reserves and allowances	(26,096)	(234,998)	108,757
Changes in operating assets and liabilities:			
Accounts receivable	(45,450)	186,834	(79,106)
Inventories	149,519	109,919	(222,391)
Prepaid expenses and other assets	24,334	(107,855)	(52,106)
Other non-current assets	19,966	—	
Accounts payable	59,458	26,413	145,695
Accrued expenses and other liabilities	(18,987)	134,594	109,823
Customer refund liability	(80,710)	305,141	—
Income taxes payable and receivable	18,862	41,051	(39,164)
Net cash provided by operating activities	509,031	628,230	237,460
Cash flows from investing activities			
Purchases of property and equipment	(145,802)	(170,385)	(281,339)
Sale of property and equipment	—	11,285	—
Purchase of equity method investment	—	(39,207)	—
Purchases of other assets	(1,311)	(4,597)	(1,648)
Net cash (used in) provided by investing activities	(147,113)	(202,904)	(282,987)
Cash flows from financing activities			
Proceeds from long term debt and revolving credit facility	25,000	505,000	763,000
Payments on long term debt and revolving credit facility	(162,817)	(695,000)	(665,000)
Employee taxes paid for shares withheld for income taxes	(4,235)	(2,743)	(2,781)
Proceeds from exercise of stock options and other stock issuances	7,472	2,580	11,540
Other financing fees	63	306	—
Payments of debt financing costs	(2,553)	(11)	—
Net cash used in financing activities	(137,070)	(189,868)	106,759
Effect of exchange rate changes on cash, cash equivalents and restricted cash	5,100	12,467	4,178
Net increase in cash, cash equivalents and restricted cash	229,948	247,925	65,410
Cash, cash equivalents and restricted cash			
Beginning of period	566,060	318,135	252,725
End of period	$ 796,008	$ 566,060	$ 318,135
Non-cash investing and financing activities			
Change in accrual for property and equipment	$ (8,084)	$ (14,611)	$ 10,580
Other supplemental information			
Cash paid (received) for income taxes, net of refunds	23,352	(16,738)	36,921
Cash paid for interest, net of capitalized interest	18,031	28,586	29,750

See accompanying notes.

Appendix C

Financial Statements for LVMH Moët Hennessy-Louis Vuitton

The complete annual report for LVMH Moët Hennessy-Louis Vuitton is available on this book's website.

CONSOLIDATED FINANCIAL STATEMENTS

Consolidated income statement

CONSOLIDATED INCOME STATEMENT

(EUR millions, except for earnings per share)	Notes	2020	2019	2018[a]
Revenue	24-25	**44,651**	**53,670**	**46,826**
Cost of sales		(15,871)	(18,123)	(15,625)
Gross margin		**28,780**	**35,547**	**31,201**
Marketing and selling expenses		(16,792)	(20,207)	(17,755)
General and administrative expenses		(3,641)	(3,864)	(3,466)
Income/(loss) from joint ventures and associates	8	(42)	28	23
Profit from recurring operations	24-25	**8,305**	**11,504**	**10,003**
Other operating income and expenses	26	(333)	(231)	(126)
Operating profit		**7,972**	**11,273**	**9,877**
Cost of net financial debt		(35)	(107)	(117)
Interest on lease liabilities		(281)	(290)	-
Other financial income and expenses		(292)	(162)	(271)
Net financial income/(expense)	27	**(608)**	**(559)**	**(388)**
Income taxes	28	(2,409)	(2,932)	(2,499)
Net profit before minority interests		**4,955**	**7,782**	**6,990**
Minority interests	18	(253)	(611)	(636)
Net profit, Group share		**4,702**	**7,171**	**6,354**
Basic Group share of net earnings per share (EUR)	29	**9.33**	**14.25**	**12.64**
Number of shares on which the calculation is based		503,679,272	503,218,851	502,825,461
Diluted Group share of net earnings per share (EUR)	29	**9.32**	**14.23**	**12.61**
Number of shares on which the calculation is based		504,210,133	503,839,542	503,918,140

(a) The financial statements as of December 31, 2018 have not been restated to reflect the application of IFRS 16 Leases. See Note 1.2 to the 2019 consolidated financial statements regarding the impact of the application of IFRS 16.

CONSOLIDATED FINANCIAL STATEMENTS
Consolidated balance sheet

CONSOLIDATED BALANCE SHEET

Assets *(EUR millions)*	Notes	2020	2019	2018[a]
Brands and other intangible assets	3	17,012	17,212	17,254
Goodwill	4	16,042	16,034	13,727
Property, plant and equipment	6	18,224	18,533	15,112
Right-of-use assets	7	12,521	12,409	-
Investments in joint ventures and associates	8	990	1,074	638
Non-current available for sale financial assets	9	739	915	1,100
Other non-current assets	10	845	1,546	986
Deferred tax	28	2,325	2,274	1,932
Non-current assets		**68,698**	**69,997**	**50,749**
Inventories and work in progress	11	13,016	13,717	12,485
Trade accounts receivable	12	2,756	3,450	3,222
Income taxes		392	406	366
Other current assets	13	3,846	3,264	2,868
Cash and cash equivalents	15	19,963	5,673	4,610
Current assets		**39,973**	**26,510**	**23,551**
Total assets		**108,671**	**96,507**	**74,300**

Liabilities and equity *(EUR millions)*	Notes	2020	2019	2018[a]
Equity, Group share	16.1	37,412	36,586	32,293
Minority interests	18	1,417	1,779	1,664
Equity		**38,829**	**38,365**	**33,957**
Long-term borrowings	19	14,065	5,101	6,005
Non-current lease liabilities	7	10,665	10,373	-
Non-current provisions and other liabilities	20	3,322	3,812	3,188
Deferred tax	28	5,481	5,498	5,036
Purchase commitments for minority interests' shares	21	10,991	10,735	9,281
Non-current liabilities		**44,524**	**35,519**	**23,510**
Short-term borrowings	19	10,638	7,610	5,027
Current lease liabilities	7	2,163	2,172	-
Trade accounts payable	22.1	5,098	5,814	5,314
Income taxes		721	722	538
Current provisions and other liabilities	22.2	6,698	6,305	5,954
Current liabilities		**25,318**	**22,623**	**16,833**
Total liabilities and equity		**108,671**	**96,507**	**74,300**

(a) The financial statements as of December 31, 2018 have not been restated to reflect the application of IFRS 16 Leases. See Note 1.2 to the 2019 consolidated financial statements regarding the impact of the application of IFRS 16.

CONSOLIDATED STATEMENT OF CHANGES IN EQUITY

(EUR millions)	Number of shares	Share capital	Share premium account	Treasury shares	Cumulative translation adjustment	Revaluation reserves				Net profit and other reserves	Total equity		
						Available for sale financial assets	Hedges of future foreign currency cash flows and cost of hedging	Vineyard land	Employee benefit commitments		Group share	Minority interests	Total
Notes		16.2	16.2	16.3	16.5							18	
As of Dec. 31, 2017	507,042,596	152	2,614	(530)	354	-	130	1,114	(133)	25,268	28,969	1,408	30,377
Gains and losses recognized in equity					219	-	(259)	3	20		(17)	45	28
Net profit										6,354	6,354	636	6,990
Comprehensive income		-	-	-	219	-	(259)	3	20	6,354	6,337	681	7,018
Bonus share plan-related expenses										78	78	4	82
(Acquisition)/disposal of treasury shares				(256)						(26)	(282)	-	(282)
Exercise of LVMH share subscription options	762,851		49								49		49
Retirement of LVMH shares	(2,775,952)		(365)	365							-	-	-
Capital increase in subsidiaries											-	50	50
Interim and final dividends paid										(2,715)	(2,715)	(345)	(3,060)
Changes in control of consolidated entities										(9)	(9)	41	32
Acquisition and disposal of minority interests' shares										(22)	(22)	(19)	(41)
Purchase commitments for minority interests' shares										(112)	(112)	(156)	(268)
As of Dec. 31, 2018	505,029,495	152	2,298	(421)	573	-	(129)	1,117	(113)	28,816	32,293	1,664	33,957
Impact of changes in accounting standards[a]										(29)	(29)	-	(29)
As of Jan. 1, 2019	505,029,495	152	2,298	(421)	573	-	(129)	1,117	(113)	28,787	32,264	1,664	33,928
Gains and losses recognized in equity					289	-	22	22	(107)		226	17	242
Net profit										7,171	7,171	611	7,783
Comprehensive income		-	-	-	289	-	22	22	(107)	7,171	7,397	628	8,025
Bonus share plan-related expenses										69	69	3	72
(Acquisition)/disposal of treasury shares				18						(44)	(26)	-	(26)
Exercise of LVMH share subscription options	403,946		21								21	-	21
Retirement of LVMH shares	(2,156)										-	-	-
Capital increase in subsidiaries											-	95	95
Interim and final dividends paid										(3,119)	(3,119)	(433)	(3,552)
Changes in control of consolidated entities										2	2	25	27
Acquisition and disposal of minority interests' shares										(17)	(17)	-	(17)
Purchase commitments for minority interests' shares										(5)	(5)	(203)	(208)
As of Dec. 31, 2019	505,431,285	152	2,319	(403)	862	-	(107)	1,139	(220)	32,844	36,586	1,779	38,365
Gains and losses recognized in equity					(1,554)	-	(176)	-	(11)		(1,742)	(91)	(1,833)
Net profit										4,702	4,702	253	4,955
Comprehensive income		-	-	-	(1,554)	-	(176)	-	(11)	4,702	2,960	162	3,122
Bonus share plan-related expenses										60	60	3	63
(Acquisition)/disposal of treasury shares				49						(42)	7	-	7
Exercise of LVMH share subscription options											-	-	-
Retirement of LVMH shares	(673,946)		(94)	94							-	-	-
Capital increase in subsidiaries											-	54	54
Interim and final dividends paid										(2,317)	(2,317)	(376)	(2,693)
Changes in control of consolidated entities										(30)	(30)	7	(23)
Acquisition and disposal of minority interests' shares										(49)	(49)	8	(41)
Purchase commitments for minority interests' shares										193	193	(220)	(27)
As of Dec. 31, 2020	504,757,339	152	2,225	(260)	(692)	-	(283)	1,139	(231)	35,363	37,412	1,417	38,829

(a) The impact of changes in accounting standards arose from the application of IFRS 16 Leases as of January 1, 2019. See Note 1.2 to the 2019 consolidated financial statements.

CONSOLIDATED FINANCIAL STATEMENTS
Consolidated cash flow statement

CONSOLIDATED CASH FLOW STATEMENT

(EUR millions)	Notes	2020	2019	2018(a)
I. OPERATING ACTIVITIES				
Operating profit		7,972	11,273	9,877
(Income)/loss and dividends received from joint ventures and associates	8	64	(10)	5
Net increase in depreciation, amortization and provisions		3,478	2,700	2,302
Depreciation of right-of-use assets	7.1	2,572	2,408	-
Other adjustments and computed expenses		(89)	(266)	(219)
Cash from operations before changes in working capital		**13,997**	**16,105**	**11,965**
Cost of net financial debt: interest paid		(58)	(124)	(113)
Lease liabilities: interest paid		(290)	(239)	-
Tax paid		(2,385)	(2,940)	(2,275)
Change in working capital	15.2	(367)	(1,154)	(1,087)
Net cash from operating activities		**10,897**	**11,648**	**8,490**
II. INVESTING ACTIVITIES				
Operating investments	15.3	(2,478)	(3,294)	(3,038)
Purchase and proceeds from sale of consolidated investments	2.4	(536)	(2,478)	(17)
Dividends received		12	8	18
Tax paid related to non-current available for sale financial assets and consolidated investments		-	(1)	(2)
Purchase and proceeds from sale of non-current available for sale financial assets	9	63	(104)	(400)
Net cash from/(used in) investing activities		**(2,939)**	**(5,869)**	**(3,439)**
III. FINANCING ACTIVITIES				
Interim and final dividends paid	15.4	(2,799)	(3,678)	(3,090)
Purchase and proceeds from sale of minority interests	2.4	(67)	(21)	(236)
Other equity-related transactions	15.4	27	54	(205)
Proceeds from borrowings	19	17,499	2,837	1,529
Repayment of borrowings	19	(5,024)	(1,810)	(2,174)
Repayment of lease liabilities	7.2	(2,302)	(2,187)	-
Purchase and proceeds from sale of current available for sale financial assets	14	69	71	(147)
Net cash from/(used in) financing activities		**7,403**	**(4,734)**	**(4,323)**
IV. EFFECT OF EXCHANGE RATE CHANGES		**(1,052)**	**39**	**67**
Net increase/(decrease) in cash and cash equivalents (I+II+III+IV)		**14,309**	**1,084**	**795**
Cash and cash equivalents at beginning of period	15.1	5,497	4,413	3,618
Cash and cash equivalents at end of period	15.1	19,806	5,497	4,413
Total tax paid		**(2,501)**	**(3,070)**	**(2,314)**

(a) The financial statements as of December 31, 2018 have not been restated to reflect the application of IFRS 16 Leases. See Note 1.2 to the 2019 consolidated financial statements regarding the impact of the application of IFRS 16.

Alternative performance measure

The following table presents the reconciliation between "Net cash from operating activities" and "Operating free cash flow" for the fiscal years presented:

(EUR millions)	2020	2019	2018
Net cash from operating activities	10,897	11,648	8,490
Operating investments	(2,478)	(3,294)	(3,038)
Repayment of lease liabilities	(2,302)	(2,187)	-
Operating free cash flow(a)	**6,117**	**6,167**	**5,452**

(a) Under IFRS 16, fixed lease payments are treated partly as interest payments and partly as principal repayments. For its own operational management purposes, the Group treats all lease payments as components of its "Operating free cash flow", whether the lease payments made are fixed or variable. In addition, for its own operational management purposes, the Group treats operating investments as components of its "Operating free cash flow".

Appendix D

Accounting for Investments and Consolidated Financial Statements

Road Map

LO	Learning Objective	Page	eLecture	Guided Example	Assignments
LO1	Identify and define the investment categories for debt and equity securities.	D-2	D-2	D-1	SS4, SS7, SS13
LO2	Describe the accounting for various kinds of debt security investments.	D-3	D-3	D-2	SS1, SS8, SS11, ED1A, ED2A, ED3A, ED1B, ED2B, ED3B, PD1A, PD2A, PD2B, SS5, SS6
LO3	Describe the accounting for various kinds of equity security investments.	D-8	D-8	D-3	SS2, SS3, SS9, SS10, ED4A, ED5A, ED6A, ED7A, ED8A, ED9A, ED4B, ED5B, ED6B, ED7B, ED8B, ED9B, PD3A, PD4A, PD5A, PD6A, PD1B, PD3B, PD4B, PD5B, PD6B
LO4	Define parent-subsidiary relationships and discuss how their balance sheet data are consolidated.	D-12	D-12		SS12, ED10A, ED10B

INVESTMENTS

Debt and Equity Securities

The assets of a business may include investments in one or more types of debt or equity securities. For some businesses, such as insurance companies, investments in debt and equity securities constitute the major portion of a company's total assets. Investments in various debt and equity securities, for example, represent over 50 percent of the assets of **Prudential Financial, Inc.**, a large diversified insurance company and a Fortune 500 company.

LO1 Identify and define the investment categories for debt and equity securities.

MBC

A **debt security** refers to a financial instrument that creates a creditor relationship for the debtholder. Examples of debt securities include U.S. Treasury bills, notes, and bonds; U.S. government agency bonds, such as Fannie Mae and Ginnie Mae bonds; state and local government bonds; corporate bonds; and commercial paper. Bonds are long-term debt securities and are discussed in detail in Chapter 10. Some bonds may not mature for 30 to 40 years, while others may have short maturity periods. Commercial paper, on the other hand, refers to very short-term (1 to 270 days), unsecured promissory notes issued by large corporations.

An **equity security** is a financial instrument that represents an ownership interest in a company. Shares of stock represent ownership interests in a corporation and are discussed in detail in Chapter 11. Investors owning a company's common stock have the most basic ownership rights, whereas owners of a company's preferred stock have some rights that take preference over the common stockholders, such as preferential treatment in the receipt of dividends and the receipt of assets in the event that a company liquidates.

Debt and equity securities may be acquired directly from the entity that issues the securities or through a secondary market. When corporations or government agencies need to borrow, they offer their debt securities for sale to the general public. This process is called floating an issue. When a corporation initially issues (sells) stock to the general public to raise money, the process is called an initial public offering (IPO). When companies need additional cash to fund their operations after initially going public, they may conduct additional sales of their shares through secondary public offerings.

More frequently, investors acquire debt and equity securities through the secondary capital market. The secondary capital market consists of individual and institutional investors desiring to buy or sell securities. Many debt and equity securities are bought and sold on organized exchanges. Stocks and bonds, for example, may trade on a national exchange such as the New York Stock Exchange or the London Stock Exchange. (Despite their names, both exchanges list both bonds and stocks.) Stocks and bonds may also trade in a less formal market known as the over-the-counter market. Both the buyer and the seller of a security normally use the services of a brokerage firm, such as **Charles Schwab** or **Fidelity Investments**, to facilitate the acquisition and disposition of their investments.

Investment Categories

The accounting for debt and equity securities depends on how the security is categorized. Debt securities are placed in one of three categories: **trading securities**, **available-for-sale securities**, or **held-to-maturity securities**. Equity securities are also placed in one of three categories: **noninfluential securities**, **influential securities**, or **controlling securities**.

For debt securities, the placement of an investment in the proper investment category depends on management's intent with respect to selling the security. For equity securities, the classification depends on the ability to influence or control another entity's activities as a result of the equity investment. Typical evidence of the latter factor is the ownership percentage represented by the equity investment. **Exhibit D-1** defines and explains the six investment categories.

Noninfluential equity securities refer to stock investments that do not permit the investor to exert significant influence over the policies of the investee company (the company whose stock is acquired). Accountants consider stock investments noninfluential if the quantity of stock purchased is less than 20 percent of a company's outstanding voting (common) stock.

An entity that owns 20 percent or more of a company's outstanding voting stock may exert a significant influence on the operating or financial decisions of that company. However, if 50 percent or less of the total voting stock is owned, the investment does not represent a controlling interest. Voting stock investments in the 20 to 50 percent ownership range, therefore, compose the influential securities category.

When more than 50 percent of a corporation's voting stock is owned, the investor is a majority owner and is in a position to control the operating and financial policies of the investee company. These majority-ownership stock investments are classified as controlling securities.[1]

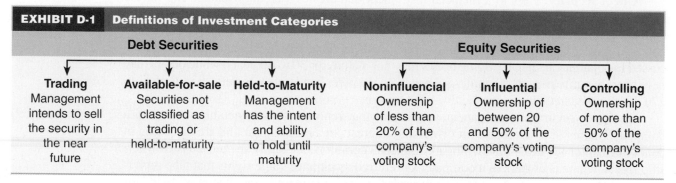

EXHIBIT D-1	**Definitions of Investment Categories**					
	Debt Securities			**Equity Securities**		
	Trading Management intends to sell the security in the near future	**Available-for-sale** Securities not classified as trading or held-to-maturity	**Held-to-Maturity** Management has the intent and ability to hold until maturity	**Noninfluencial** Ownership of less than 20% of the company's voting stock	**Influential** Ownership of between 20 and 50% of the company's voting stock	**Controlling** Ownership of more than 50% of the company's voting stock

Debt and equity investments are placed in one of these categories because accounting guidelines differ among the categories. We now review those accounting guidelines, considering debt securities first, followed by equity securities.

Match the categories of investments from the first column with the descriptions in the second column.

1. Held-to-maturity
2. Noninfluential
3. Controlling
4. Trading
5. Influential
6. Available-for-sale

A. Equity securities that represent an ownership of more than 50 percent of the corporation's voting stock.

B. Debt securities that management intends to hold to maturity.

C. Equity securities where there is not an ability to exercise significant influence over the corporation.

D. Equity securities where there is an ability to exercise significant, but not controlling, influence over the corporation.

E. Debt securities that management neither intends to sell in the near future nor hold to maturity.

F. Debt securities that management buys with the intent to sell in the near future.

Investments in Debt Securities

LO2 Describe the accounting for various kinds of debt security investments.

eLecture

MBC

Investments in debt securities are placed in one of three investment categories: trading securities, available-for-sale securities, or held-to-maturity securities. The major accounting events concerning investments in debt securities are their purchase, the recognition of interest income, their balance sheet valuation, and their sale or redemption at maturity. **Exhibit D-2** summarizes the accounting guidelines for these events.

---

[1] The ownership percentages are guidelines only and may be overcome by other factors. In some cases, a company may own more than 20 percent of the outstanding voting shares of another company and still not be able to significantly influence its operating and financial activities. Or, effective control of another entity may exist with less than 50 percent ownership of its voting stock. For example, ownership of a large minority interest (such as 45 percent), with other owners widely dispersed and unorganized, may provide effective control. The key to proper accounting classification is the presence of significant influence on, or effective control over, another entity.

EXHIBIT D-2	**Accounting Guidelines for Investments in Debt Securities**			
Event/Accounting Guideline		**Trading Securities**	**Available-for-Sale Securities**	**Held-to-Maturity Securities**
1.	**Purchase** Record at cost, which includes any broker's fees.	X	X	X
2.	**Recognition of Interest Income** Interest accrues daily and is usually recorded when payment is received. Premium or discount on purchase price is not amortized.	X		
	Interest accrues daily and is usually recorded when payment is received. Premium or discount on purchase price is amortized as an adjustment of interest income.		X	X
3.	**Balance Sheet Valuation** Measure securities at fair value at balance sheet date. No valuation account to the asset account is used. Changes in fair value are reported in the income statement.	X		
	Measure securities at fair value at balance sheet date. Use a valuation account to the asset account. Changes in fair value are reported in stockholders' equity.		X	
	Measure securities at amortized cost at balance sheet date.			X
4.	**(a) Sale** Sale proceeds less investment's book value is a realized gain or loss.	X		
	Sale proceeds less investment's amortized cost is a realized gain or loss.		X	
	(b) Redemption at Maturity At maturity, the investment's book value will equal the redemption proceeds.			X

Purchase

Assume that Warner Company purchases $300,000 face value of Natco Company 8 percent bonds at 98 on July 1, 2022. (Recall from Chapter 10 that bond prices are quoted as a percentage of face value. Thus, a $1,000 face value bond that is quoted at 98 will sell for $980.) The bonds pay interest on December 31 and June 30 and mature in 10 years. The brokerage commission is $600. Warner's management considers the bond investment to be divided equally between trading securities, available-for-sale securities, and held-to-maturity securities. **Exhibit D-3** shows the entry to record this debt investment. Note that the accounting for the purchase event is the same regardless of the classification of the bond investment.

EXHIBIT D-3	**Purchase of Debt Securities**				

2022							
July	1	Bond investment—Trading (Natco)	98,200		A	= L +	SE
		Bond investment—Available-for-sale (Natco)	98,200		+98,200		
		Bond investment—Held-to-maturity (Natco)	98,200		+98,200		
		Cash		294,600	+98,200		
		To record purchase of $300,000 of Natco Company bonds at 98 plus $600			−294,600		
		commission [($300,000 × 0.98) + $600 = $294,600].					

Recognition of Interest Income

Each $100,000 of Natco Company bonds acquired on July 1, 2022, was purchased at a $1,800 discount ($100,000 − $98,200). This means that the market rate of interest on July 1, 2022, was higher than the 8 percent coupon rate offered on the bonds. For trading securities, any bond discount (or premium) is ignored in accounting for the periodic interest income because management plans to sell the securities in the near future. As such, the effect on net income from ignoring the bond discount (or premium) is immaterial.

PRINCIPLE ALERT	Materiality Concept

Note the role played by the *materiality concept* in determining interest income on trading securities. Because of the short time period that trading securities are held by a company before being sold, accountants do not bother to amortize any discount or premium associated with the debt securities. This simplifies the accounting for these debt securities, yet it causes no significant distortion in the periodic reporting of interest income.

For available-for-sale securities and held-to-maturity securities, any bond discount (or premium) is amortized to interest income. This is done to make periodic interest income more accurately reflect the economic reality of the bond investment. The amortization of bond discount causes the periodic interest income to be higher than the semiannual cash receipt of interest. If the bonds had been purchased at a premium (more than their face value), the premium amortization would cause periodic interest income to be less than the semiannual cash receipt of interest.

Two amortization methods are available for use: the straight-line method and the effective interest method. We use the straight-line method here because the difference in the financial effect between the two methods is immaterial in this case. (See Appendix 10A for a discussion of the effective interest method.) The straight-line method of amortization writes off an equal amount of discount or premium each interest period. The Natco Company bonds, when purchased, had 10 years to maturity, with interest paid semiannually. Consequently, there are 20 interest periods associated with the bonds. During each interest period, $90 ($1,800/20 periods) of discount will be amortized for the available-for-sale securities and the held-to-maturity securities. Each $100,000 (face value) of Natco bonds pays $4,000 interest semiannually (8 percent × $100,000 × ½ year). The entries to record interest income at December 31, 2022, are shown in **Exhibit D-4**.

Balance Sheet Valuation

Debt securities are interest rate sensitive; that is, as market interest rates change, the market values of debt securities also change. Debt securities that management intends to sell (trading securities) or may sell (available-for-sale securities) are reported on the balance sheet at their current fair value. If available, quoted market prices from one of the national bond exchanges provide the best evidence of a bond's fair value. Year-end adjusting entries are made to record these current fair values. Current fair value is not a relevant measure for debt securities that management intends to hold to maturity. Thus, no adjustment to fair value is made for held-to-maturity securities.

Assume that a general decline in market interest rates causes the Natco Company bonds to trade at 99.5 as of December 31, 2022. **Exhibit D-5** shows the adjusting entries made on this date to record the relevant fair values.

EXHIBIT D-4	Recognition of Interest Income on Debt Securities

2022

	Trading Debt Securities			

Dec. 31	Cash	4,000		A = L + SE
	Bond interest income		4,000	+4,000 +4,000
	To record receipt of semiannual interest on $100,000 of trading bonds.			Rev

	Available-for-Sale Debt Securities			

Dec. 31	Cash	4,000		A = L + SE
	Bond investment—Available-for-sale (Natco)	90		+4,000 +4,090
	Bond interest income		4,090	+90 Rev
	To record receipt of semiannual interest and discount amortization on			
	$100,000 of available-for-sale bonds.			

	Held-to-Maturity Debt Securities			

Dec. 31	Cash	4,000		A = L + SE
	Bond investment—Held-to-maturity (Natco)	90		+4,000 +4,090
	Bond Interest income		4,090	+90 Rev
	To record receipt of semiannual interest and discount amortization on			
	$100,000 of held-to-maturity bonds.			

EXHIBIT D-5	Balance Sheet Valuation for Debt Securities

2022

	Trading Debt Securities			

Dec. 31	Bond investment—Trading (Natco)	1,300		A = L + SE
	Unrealized gain on investments (income)		1,300	+1,300 +1,300
	To adjust trading debt securities to year-end fair value			Gain
	($99,500 – $98,200 = $1,300 gain).			

	Available-for-Sale Debt Securities			

Dec. 31	Fair value adjustment to bond investment	1,210		A = L + SE
	Unrealized gain/loss on investments (equity)		1,210	+1,210 +1,210
	To adjust available-for-sale debt securities to year-end fair value			Comprehensive
	($99,500 – $98,290 = $1,210 gain).			Income

Fair value changes in securities that are still owned are called **unrealized gains and losses**. Unrealized gains and losses that relate to trading securities are reported in the income statement. Thus, the $1,300 unrealized gain shown in **Exhibit D-5** is included in Warner's 2022 income statement.

Unrealized gains and losses that relate to available-for-sale securities are excluded from the income statement. Instead, their net amount is reported as a separate component of stockholders' equity called Unrealized Gain/Loss on Investments (Equity). Unrealized Gain/Loss on Investments is included in comprehensive income, which was discussed in Chapter 13 (see page 13-5). Because these unrealized gains and losses are not included in earnings, the investment's cost must be maintained in the accounts so that a total realized gain or loss can be determined when the investment is actually sold. Using the valuation account Fair Value Adjustment to Bond Investment permits the maintenance of the investment's cost in the Bond Investment—Available for Sale account.[2] After the adjustments shown in **Exhibit D-5**, the December 31, 2022, balance sheet reports the bond investments as follows:

Bond investment—Trading (fair value)		$99,500
Bond investment—Available-for-sale (cost)	$98,290	
Add: Fair value adjustment to bond investment	1,210	99,500
Bond investment—Held-to-maturity (cost)		98,290

Hint: Although the accounting for trading securities calls for the recognition of any fair value changes as part of a company's current net income, those unrealized gains or losses are not reported as part of a company's net income for income tax purposes. The IRS does not require the reporting of any gains until they are realized and prohibits the reporting of any losses until realized (when a security is sold).

Sale or Redemption at Maturity

To complete our illustration, assume that the trading and available-for-sale bond investments are both sold on July 1, 2023, for $99,800 each (after recognizing interest income on June 30, 2023). The remaining bond investment is held to maturity (June 30, 2032), at which time the issuer redeems the bonds for their maturity value of $100,000. **Exhibit D-6** shows the appropriate journal entries related to these events.

EXHIBIT D-6	Sale or Redemption at Maturity of Debt Securities

2023

Trading Debt Securities

A = L + SE
+99,800   +300
−99,500   Gain

July	1	Cash	99,800	
		Bond investment—Trading (Natco)		99,500
		Gain on sale of investments		300
		To record sale of trading debt securities for $99,800		
		($99,800 − $99,500 = $300 realized gain).		

Available-for-Sale Debt Securities

A = L + SE
+99,800   +1,420
−98,380   Gain

July	1	Cash	99,800	
		Bond investment—Available-for-sale (Natco)		98,380
		Gain on sale of investments		1,420
		To record sale of available-for-sale debt securities for $99,800		
		($99,800 − $98,380 = $1,420 gain).		

A = L + SE
−1,210   −1,210
    Comprehensive
    Income

Dec.	31	Unrealized gain/loss on investments (equity)	1,210	
		Fair value adjustment to bond investment		1,210
		To adjust these account balances to zero.		

2032

Held-to-Maturity Debt Securities

A = L + SE
+100,000
−100,000

June	30	Cash	100,000	
		Bond investment—Held-to-maturity (Natco)		100,000
		To record redemption of bonds at maturity.		

In **Exhibit D-6**, the $300 gain on the sale of the trading securities is the difference between the $99,800 sales proceeds and the last recorded fair value of $99,500. By July 1, 2023, another $90 of discount amortization would have been recorded on the available-for-sale securities, increasing their amortized cost to $98,380 ($98,290 + $90). The $1,420 gain that is recorded on their sale is the difference between the $99,800 sales proceeds and the amortized cost of $98,380. Because all available-for-sale bonds were sold, the related valuation account and unrealized gain/loss account are adjusted to zero balances at the next financial statement closing date (December 31, 2023). The completion of the discount amortization on the held-to-maturity bonds brings their amortized cost to $100,000 on June 30, 2032. Thus, there is no gain or loss associated with the redemption of the bonds at maturity.

---

[2] The cost of trading securities must be maintained for income tax purposes. A fair value valuation account, therefore, may be used for maintaining the income tax records of trading securities.

YOUR TURN! D-2

On January 1, Juno Company purchased three 10-year, 6 percent bonds, each with a face value of $100,000. Interest is paid semiannually on June 30 and December 31. Bond A was purchased at a premium of 102. Bond B was purchased at face value. Bond C was purchased at a discount of 98. Management intends to sell Bond A in the near future, Bond B will likely be held several years, and Bond C will be held to maturity. On July 1, Bond A is sold for $103,000, and Bond B and Bond C each have a fair market value of $101,000.

    a. Record the purchase of the three bonds on January 1.

    b. Record the receipt of interest on June 30.

    c. Record the sale of Bond A on July 1.

    d. Record any adjustments needed to Bonds B and C on July 1.

The solution is on page D-24.

Investments in Equity Securities

Equity security investments fit into one of three categories: noninfluential securities, influential securities, or controlling securities. The major accounting events associated with investments in equity securities are their purchase, the recognition of investment income, their balance sheet valuation, and their sale. **Exhibit D-7** summarizes the accounting guidelines for these events.

LO3 **Describe** the accounting for various kinds of equity security investments.

EXHIBIT D-7	Accounting Guidelines for Investments in Equity Securities			
	Event/Accounting Guideline	Noninfluential Securities	Influential Securities	Controlling Securities
1.	**Purchase** Record at cost, which includes any broker's fees.	X	X	X
2.	**Recognition of Investment Income** Record dividend income when dividends are received.	X		
	Record equity in investee company's net income as investment income. Decrease investment account for dividends received.		X	X
0.	**Balance Sheet Valuation** Measure securities at fair value at balance sheet date. Changes in fair value are reported in the income statement.	X		
	Report securities at book value (cost plus share of investee net income less dividends).		X	
	Eliminate investment account as part of consolidation procedures.			X
4.	**Sale** Sale proceeds less investment's book value is a realized gain or loss.	X	X	X

Purchase

Assume that Warner Company purchases 1,500 shares of common stock in each of three different companies—Ark, Inc.; Bain, Inc.; and Carr, Inc.—on January 1, 2022. Each investment cost $15,000, including broker's fees. The shares acquired represent 10 percent of Ark's voting stock, 25 percent of Bain's voting stock, and 60 percent of Carr's voting stock.[3] Thus, each of these stock investments is placed in a different category. **Exhibit D-8** presents the journal entry to record the purchase of these investments. Note that each stock investment is recorded at its acquisition cost.

---

[3] We assume that the cost of the investments in Bain and Carr are equal to the book value of the underlying net assets of the investee company. This assumption permits us to simplify the illustration of the accounting for these two investments.

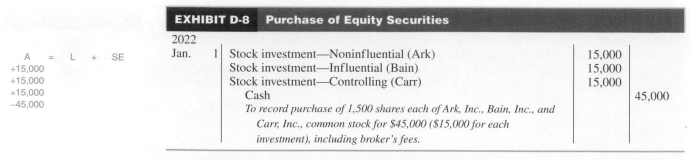

A	=	L	+	SE
+15,000				
+15,000				
+15,000				
−45,000				

Recognition of Investment Income

Now assume that each of the three companies earns net income of $10,000 in 2022 and that each company also declares a cash dividend of $0.50 per share, which is received by Warner on December 31, 2022. **Exhibit D-9** shows the journal entries to record this information.

		EXHIBIT D-9	**Recognition of Investment Income on Equity Securities**		

2022

Noninfluential Equity Securities

		Dec.	31	Cash		750	
				Dividend income			750
				To record receipt of cash dividend from Ark, Inc.			

A = L + SE
+750   +750
              Rev

Influential Equity Securities

		Dec.	31	Stock investment—Influential (Bain)		2,500	
				Income from stock investments			2,500
				To record as income 25% of Bain's 2019 net income of $10,000			
				(investment balance = $17,500).			

A = L + SE
+2,500   +2,500
                Rev

		Dec.	31	Cash		750	
				Stock investment—Influential (Bain)			750
				To record receipt of cash dividend from Bain, Inc.			
				(investment balance = $16,750).			

A = L + SE
+750
−750

Controlling Equity Securities

		Dec.	31	Stock investment—Controlling (Carr)		6,000	
				Income from stock investments			6,000
				To record as income 60% of Carr's 2019 net income of $10,000			
				(investment balance = $21,000).			

A = L + SE
+6,000   +6,000
                Rev

		Dec.	31	Cash		750	
				Stock investment—Controlling (Carr)			750
				To record receipt of cash dividend from Carr, Inc.			
				(investment balance = $20,250).			

A = L + SE
+750
−750

As shown in **Exhibit D-9**, the dividends of $750 received on the Ark investment are reported as Dividend Income. This is the proper treatment for cash dividends received on noninfluential securities.

When the percentage ownership of voting stock reaches 20 percent or more, as is the case with the investment in Bain stock, the **equity method** of accounting is used. Under the equity method, the investor company records as income or loss its proportionate share of the net income or net loss reported for the period by the investee company (Bain), with an offsetting debit or credit going to the Stock Investment account. In addition, the receipt of any cash dividends from the investee company reduces the Stock Investment account. The equity method prevents an investor company from manipulating its own income by the influence it can exercise on the dividend policies of the investee company.

In **Exhibit D-9**, the equity method is used for the Bain stock investment (25 percent ownership) and Carr stock investment (60 percent ownership). At December 31, 2022, the Income from Stock Investments account and the Bain Stock Investment account are increased by 25 percent of Bain's 2022 net income (25 percent × $10,000 = $2,500). The receipt of the $750 cash dividend from Bain reduces the Bain Stock Investment account. Similarly, the equity method causes a $6,000 increase (60 percent × $10,000 net income) in both the Income from Stock Investments account and the Carr Stock Investment account at December 31, 2022. The $750 cash dividend received from Carr decreases the Carr Stock Investment account.

A.K.A. Stock investments involving ownership interests of 20 to 50 percent of the outstanding voting shares are often referred to as **affiliate companies**.

Balance Sheet Valuation

Noninfluential securities are adjusted at year-end to their current fair value, with quoted market prices from established exchanges like the New York and London Stock Exchanges being the best evidence of a stock's current fair value. Assume that at December 31, 2022, the fair value of the 1,500 shares of Ark common stock is $23,000. Exhibit D-10 shows the adjusting entry made on this date to record the relevant fair value. The $8,000 unrealized gain shown in Exhibit D-10 on the noninfluential security (Ark) is reported in Warner's 2022 income statement.

PRINCIPLE ALERT   **Objectivity Principle**

The standard to measure equity noninfluential securities at current fair value applies only to equity securities that have readily determinable fair values. It does not apply to equity investments that would create significant valuation problems, such as equity investments in closely held companies whose shares do not trade on an established stock exchange. This represents an application of the *objectivity principle*, which states that accounting entries should be based on objectively determined evidence.

Stock investments accounted for by the equity method are not measured at year-end fair values. The year-end account balances remain as calculated using the equity method—that is, $16,750 for the Bain investment and $20,250 for the Carr investment. For controlling investments, the financial statements of the investee company are usually consolidated with the statements of the investor company; consequently, the investment account does not appear in the consolidated statements.

EXHIBIT D-10   **Balance Sheet Valuation for Equity Securities**

2022

Noninfluential Equity Securities				
Dec. 31	Stock investment—Noninfluential (Ark)	8,000		A = L + SE
	Unrealized gain on investments (income)		8,000	+8,000 +8,000
	To adjust noninfluential stock securities to year-end fair value of			Gain
	$23,000 ($23,000 − $15,000 = $8,000 gain).			

Sale

To complete our illustration, assume that all three stock investments are sold on July 1, 2023. Each of the stock investments is sold for $22,000. **Exhibit D-11** shows the journal entries related to these events, where each sale generates a different gain or loss. Even though the basic events relating to each of the stock investments were the same, the accounting guidelines result in quite different analyses.

EXHIBIT D-11	Sale of Equity Securities

2023

			Noninfluential Equity Securities		
July	1	Cash		22,000	
		Loss on sale of investments		1,000	
		Stock investment—Noninfluential (Ark)			23,000
		To record sale of noninfluential equity securities for $22,000			
		($22,000 − $23,000 = $1,000 loss).			

A = L + SE
+22,000   −1,000
−23,000   Loss

			Influential Equity Securities		
July	1	Cash		22,000	
		Stock investment—Influential (Bain)			16,750
		Gain on sale of investments			5,250
		To record sale of influential equity securities for $22,000			
		($22,000 − $16,750 = $5,250 gain).			

A = L + SE
+22,000   +5,250
−16,750   Gain

			Controlling Equity Securities		
July	1	Cash		22,000	
		Stock investment—Controlling (Carr)			20,250
		Gain on sale of investments			1,750
		To record sale of controlling equity securities for $22,000			
		($22,000 − $20,250 = $1,750 gain).			

A = L + SE
+22,000   +1,750
−20,250   Gain

THINKING GLOBALLY

In some countries where there are not actively traded markets for debt and equity securities, the balance sheet valuation of debt and equity securities is often at the original acquisition cost of an investment. In other countries, where actively traded markets for securities do exist, a variant of the current fair value approach used under U.S. GAAP, called the lower-of-cost-or-market method, may be used. Under the lower-of-cost-or-market method, a debt or equity security is valued at the lower of two values—its current fair value or its original acquisition cost. When a security's current fair value falls below its acquisition cost, the security's carrying value is written down to the lower amount and an unrealized loss is reported as part of the company's current income.

Current and Noncurrent Classifications

Each investment in debt and equity securities must be classified as either a current asset or a noncurrent asset in the balance sheet. Trading securities are always classified as current assets. Held-to-maturity securities are classified as noncurrent assets until the last year before maturity. Available-for-sale securities and noninfluential securities may be classified as either current or noncurrent assets, depending on management's intentions regarding their sale. Influential investments are usually classified as noncurrent assets, but a current classification is proper if management intends to sell the investments within the next year or operating cycle, whichever is longer. As mentioned earlier, controlling investments do not appear in consolidated financial statements as a separate account but rather are "consolidated" into the accounts of the parent company.

YOUR TURN! D-3

On January 1 Tara Company invests in three equity securities (A, B, and C). Tara purchases a 5 percent stake in Company A for $10,000 and is not able to exercise any significant control of the company. Tara purchases a 25 percent stake in Company B for $50,000 and can exert significant influence, but not control. Tara purchases a 70 percent controlling stake in Company C for $120,000.

continued

continued from previous page

At year-end, the fair value of Tara's stake in each of the companies, the dividends received from each of the companies, and the net income reported by each of the companies are as follows:

Company	Fair Value	Dividends Received	Reported Net Income
A.	$ 12,000	$ 1,000	$70,000
B.	47,000	2,000	80,000
C.	130,000	10,000	(10,000)

a. Record the purchase of the three equity securities on January 1.

b. Record any other adjustments necessary at December 31.

The solution is on page D-25.

PARENT-SUBSIDIARY RELATIONSHIP

A corporation that controls another corporation through ownership of that company's voting stock is known as a **holding company**. Control over another corporation is ensured through ownership of all or a majority of the investee's voting stock. Another name for a holding company is a **parent company**, and the wholly owned or majority-held investees are called **subsidiaries**. The parent company and each subsidiary company are separate legal entities.

LO4 Define parent-subsidiary relationships and **discuss** how their balance sheet data are consolidated.

eLecture

MBC

Consolidated Financial Statements

As separate legal entities, a parent company and its subsidiaries maintain their own accounting records and prepare separate financial statements primarily for internal purposes. In the parent company's separate financial statements, the ownership of a subsidiary's stock is reported as a stock investment accounted for by the equity method. When the parent company prepares financial statements for its stockholders and creditors, however, the financial statements of the parent company and its subsidiaries are combined and reported as a single set of **consolidated financial statements.**

Under consolidated accounting, the individual line item (stock investment – controlling) used to account for an investment in a subsidiary under the equity method is replaced by all the individual asset and liability accounts of the consolidated subsidiary. In other words, the cash account of the subsidiary is combined with the cash account of the parent, the accounts receivable of the subsidiary is combined with the accounts receivable of the parent, the accounts payable of the subsidiary is combined with the accounts payable of the parent, and so on. The financial statements of a parent company and its various subsidiaries are combined using what is known as the acquisition method. When the financial data of these legal entities are consolidated, the resulting statements represent the group as an economic entity, as shown in **Exhibit D-12**.

Consolidated financial statements are prepared to avoid the problem of information overload in which investors and investment professionals receive more financial data than can be reasonably processed. For example, the **General Electric Company** is made up of over 2,000 companies worldwide. A shareholder of General Electric would be overwhelmed to receive 2,000 individual company balance sheets, 2,000 individual company income statements, and 2,000 individual company statements of cash flows. Consolidated financial statements avoid this data problem for financial statement users by providing a single set of financial data for the economic entity.

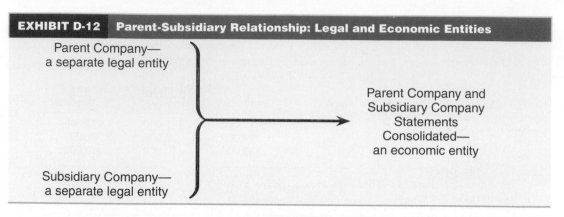

EXHIBIT D-12   Parent-Subsidiary Relationship: Legal and Economic Entities

Consolidated financial statements present both the total assets controlled by a parent company and the aggregate results of the group's operations and cash flows. These amounts are difficult to perceive when viewing only the separate reports of the individual companies. Consolidated statements are particularly valuable to the managers and stockholders of the parent company. In addition, creditors, government agencies, and the general public are informed of the magnitude and scope of an economic enterprise through consolidated statements.

PRINCIPLE ALERT   **Accounting Entity Concept**

The preparation of consolidated financial statements represents an application of the *accounting entity concept*. By viewing the parent company and its subsidiaries as a single economic entity, accountants ignore the legal boundaries of the separate companies. For consolidated financial statements, the overall economic entity is the accounting entity.

Limitations of Consolidated Statements

Consolidated statements have certain limitations. The status or performance of weak subsidiaries in a group can be "masked" through consolidation with more successful subunits. Rates of return, other ratios, and trend percentages calculated from consolidated statements may sometimes prove deceptive because they are really composite calculations. Stockholders and creditors of controlled companies who are interested in their legal rights and prerogatives should examine the separate financial statements of the relevant constituent companies.

Supplemental disclosures do improve the quality of consolidated statements, particularly those of conglomerates—that is, entities with diversified lines of business. U.S. GAAP stipulate that firms disclose information regarding revenues, income from operations, and identifiable assets for significant business segments.

SUMMARY OF LEARNING OBJECTIVES

LO1   **Identify and define the investment categories for debt and equity securities. (p. D-2)**

- Debt and equity security investments are accounted for based on their categorization.
    - a. *Trading security,* a debt security that management buys with the intent to sell in the near future.
    - b. *Held-to-maturity security,* a debt security that management intends to hold to maturity.
    - c. *Available-for-sale security,* a debt security that management neither intends to sell in the near future nor hold to maturity.
    - d. *Noninfluential security*, an equity security that represents a less than 20 percent ownership of a company's voting stock.
    - e. *Influential security,* an equity security that represents a 20 to 50 percent ownership of a company's voting stock.
    - f. *Controlling security,* an equity security that represents an ownership of more than 50 percent of a company's voting stock.

Describe the accounting for various kinds of debt security investments. (p. D-3)   **LO2**

- Debt trading securities are initially recorded at their acquisition cost, and interest income is recorded when received. The securities are reported at current fair value on the balance sheet with fair value changes reported on the income statement. When sold, the difference between the sales proceeds and the investment's book value is a realized gain or loss.

- Debt available-for-sale securities are initially recorded at their acquisition cost. Interest income is recorded when received, with any premium or discount amortized as an adjustment to interest income. The securities are reported at current fair value on the balance sheet with fair value changes reported in stockholders' equity. When sold, the difference between the sales proceeds and the investment's amortized cost is a realized gain or loss.

- Debt held-to-maturity securities are initially recorded at their acquisition cost. Interest income is recorded when received, with any premium or discount amortized as an adjustment to interest income. The securities are reported at amortized cost at the balance sheet date. At maturity, the investment's book value equals the redemption proceeds.

Describe the accounting for various kinds of equity security investments. (p. D-8)   **LO3**

- Equity noninfluential securities are initially recorded at their acquisition cost, and dividend income is recorded when received. The securities are reported at current fair value on the balance sheet with fair value changes reported on the income statement. When sold, the difference between the sales proceeds and the investment's book value is a realized gain or loss.

- Equity influential securities are initially recorded at their acquisition cost. Subsequent accounting uses the equity method: the investment account is increased by a proportionate share of the investee company's net income and decreased by the amount of any dividends received. When sold, the difference between the sales proceeds and the investment's book value is a realized gain or loss.

- Equity controlling securities are initially recorded at their acquisition cost. Subsequent accounting uses the equity method: the investment account is increased by a proportionate share of the investee company's net income and decreased by the amount of any dividends received. For financial reporting, however, the investment account is replaced by a subsidiary's individual assets and liabilities, producing consolidated financial statements. When sold, the difference between the sales proceeds and the investment's book value is a realized gain or loss.

Define parent-subsidiary relationships and discuss how their balance sheet data are consolidated. (p. D-12)   **LO4**

- A corporation that controls another corporation (the investee) by virtue of owning all, or a majority, of the investee's common stock is referred to as the parent company. The wholly owned or majority-owned investee is called the subsidiary.

- When a parent company prepares financial statements for its stockholders, the financial statements of the parent and its subsidiaries are combined and reported as a single set of consolidated financial statements.

KEY TERMS

Affiliate companies (p. D-10)	**Equity method** (p. D-9)	**Noninfluential**
Available-for-sale	**Equity security** (p. D-2)	**securities** (p. D-2)
securities (p. D-2)	**Held-to-maturity**	**Parent company** (p. D-12)
Consolidated financial	**securities** (p. D-2)	**Subsidiaries** (p. D-12)
statements (p. D-12)	**Holding company** (p. D-12)	**Trading securities** (p. D-2)
Controlling securities (p. D-2)	**Influential securities** (p. D-2)	**Unrealized gains and**
Debt security (p. D-2)		**losses** (p. D-6)

Assignments with the logo in the margin are available in BusinessCourse.
See the Preface of the book for details.

SELF-STUDY QUESTIONS

(Answers to the Self-Study Questions are at the end of the chapter.)

1. Julio, Inc., purchased $100,000 of Dane Company's 8 percent, 15-year bonds for $96,400 on January 1. Julio plans to hold the bonds to maturity. Julio records interest and straight-line   **LO2**

amortization on interest dates (June 30 and December 31). At December 31, the bonds have a market value of $97,200. Julio's balance sheet at December 31 should report the bonds at:

a. $96,400.
b. $96,640.
c. $97,200.
d. $96,160.

LO3 2. A firm purchased noninfluential stock investments for $65,000. The firm does not intend to sell the investments in the near future. During the year, the firm received dividends totaling $4,000 from these stock investments. At year-end, the stock portfolio had a quoted market value of $68,000. The increase in net income for the year (ignore income taxes) from these stock investments is:

a. $1,000.
b. $3,000.
c. $4,000.
d. $7,000.

LO3 3. Conway Company purchased 30 percent of the voting stock of Barton Company for $60,000 on January 1. During the year, Barton Company earned $50,000 net income and paid $15,000 in dividends. At the end of the year, Conway Company's account, Stock Investment—Influential (Barton) should have a balance of:

a. $110,000.
b. $70,500.
c. $95,000.
d. $60,000.

LO1 4. The proper category and reporting on the balance sheet to classify an investment in equity securities depend on:

a. management's intentions with regard to when to sell the investment.
b. the size of the investment relative to the purchasing company's total assets.
c. the ability of the purchasing company to influence the investee company.
d. both a and c.

LO2 5. Where would the account unrealized gain/loss on investment appear for trading debt security investment?

a. Income Statement
b. Equity section of the Balance Sheet
c. Statement of Cash Flows
d. It does not appear on any statement.

LO2 6. Where would the account unrealized gain/loss on investment appear for an available-for-sale debt security investment?

a. Income Statement
b. Equity section of the Balance Sheet
c. Statement of Cash Flows
d. It does not appear on any statement.

LO1 7. Controlling securities typically require the investor to acquire what percent of the investee company common stock?

a. Under 20 percent
b. Between 20 and 50 percent
c. Over 50 percent
d. 100 percent

LO2 8. Arlo Company invested in debt securities. Arlo will initially record this investment at:

a. Cost.
b. Cost plus any accrued interest.
c. Cost less any accrued interest.
d. Maturity value.

LO3 9. Francis Co. acquired a 30 percent interest in Esik for $420,000 and appropriately applied the equity method. During the first year, Esik reported net income of $200,000 and paid cash dividends totaling $50,000. What amount will Francis report as it relates to the investment at the end of the first year on its income statement?

a. Investment earnings totaling $60,000
b. Investment earnings totaling $45,000
c. Net investment earnings totaling $150,000
d. Dividend income totaling $15,000

LO3 10. Blanco Co. received dividends from its common stock investments during the year ended December 31 as follows:

• A cash dividend totaling $15,000 from its noninfluential security investment in Fisher Corporation, when the market price of Fisher's shares was $20 per share
• A cash dividend of $10,000 from Myler Corp. in which Blanco Co. owns a 32 percent interest

How much dividend income should Blanco report in its income statement?

a. $25,000
b. $15,000
c. $10,000
d. $ 0

LO2 11. At what value are held-to-maturity debt securities reported on the balance sheet?

a. Acquisition cost
b. Market value

c.   Amortized cost

    d.   Historical cost adjusted for a proportionate share of the affiliate's earnings, losses, and dividends

12. **Doris Travel, Inc., acquired an 80 percent interest in CruisesByBen on December 31 for $870,000. Doris has the ability to exercise significant influence on management decisions. The CruisesByBen stock is publicly traded. During the year, CruisesByBen reported net income of $160,000 and paid cash dividends of $40,000. How should Doris Travel account for its investment in CruisesByBen?**   **LO4**

    a.   Apply the equity method and report the investment at market value at year-end

    b.   Apply the equity method and perform a full consolidation

    c.   Apply mark-to-market accounting and consolidate the statements at year-end

    d.   Account for the investment as a trading security

13. **In classifying investments, how do held-to-maturity securities differ from other marketable securities?**   **LO1**

    a.   The investor plans to hold the securities until they mature.

    b.   The investor has the ability to exercise significant influence over management of the investee.

    c.   The investor has the ability to control the investee.

    d.   These securities have a high degree of liquidity.

QUESTIONS

1. Debt security investments are placed in one of three investment categories. What are these three categories?

2. Equity security investments are placed in one of three investment categories. What are these three categories?

3. Boris Company invests in bonds at a premium. Boris does not intend to sell the bonds in the near future, nor does it intend to hold the bonds to maturity. Should the bond premium be amortized? What measure should be used to report these bonds on the company's year-end balance sheet?

4. What measure should be used to report trading securities on the balance sheet? Available-for-sale securities? Held-to-maturity securities?

5. What is an unrealized gain? Unrealized loss?

6. Where are unrealized gains and losses related to trading securities and noninfluential securities reported in the financial statements? Where are unrealized gains and losses related to available-for-sale securities reported in the financial statements?

7. What is an influential stock investment? Describe the accounting procedures used for such investments.

8. On January 1, Power Company purchased 40 percent of the common stock of Starr Company for $250,000. During the year, Starr reported $80,000 of net income and paid $60,000 in cash dividends. At year-end, what amount should appear on Power's balance sheet for its investment in Starr?

9. What accounting procedures are used when a stock investment represents more than 50 percent of the investee company's voting stock?

10. What is the purpose of consolidated financial statements?

11. What are the inherent limitations of consolidated financial statements?

EXERCISES—SET A

ED-1A. Accounting for Debt Securities—Trading   Green Company had the following transactions and adjustments related to a bond investment: **LO2**

Previous Year

Oct.   1   Purchased $500,000 face value of Skyline, Inc.'s 8 percent bonds at 97 plus a brokerage commission of $2,000. The bonds pay interest on September 30 and March 31 and mature in 20 years. Green expects to sell the bonds in the near future.

Dec.   31   Made the adjusting entry to record interest earned on investment in the Skyline bonds.

      31   Made the adjusting entry to record the current fair value of the Skyline bonds. At December 31, the market value of the Skyline bonds was $490,000.

Current Year

Mar.   31   Received the semiannual interest payment on investment in the Skyline bonds.

Apr.   1   Sold the Skyline bond investment for $492,300 cash.

Record the transactions and adjustments of the Green Company using journal entries.

LO2   ED-2A. Accounting for Debt Securities—Available-for-Sale Hilo Company had the following transactions and adjustments related to a bond investment:

Previous Year

Jan.   1   Purchased $800,000 face value of Cynad, Inc.'s 9 percent bonds at 99 plus a brokerage commission of $1,400. The bonds pay interest on June 30 and December 31 and mature in 20 years. Hilo does not expect to sell the bonds in the near future, nor does it intend to hold the bonds to maturity.

June   30   Received the semiannual interest payment on the Cynad bonds and amortized the bond discount for six months. Hilo uses the straight-line method to amortize bond discounts and premiums.

Dec.   31   Received the semiannual interest payment on the Cynad bonds and amortized the bond discount for six months.

        31   Made the adjusting entry to record the current fair value of the Cynad bonds. At December 31, the market value of the Cynad bonds was $790,000.

Current Year

June   30   Received the semiannual interest payment on the Cynad bonds and amortized the bond discount for six months.

July   1   Sold the Cynad bond investment for $792,500 cash.

Dec.   31   Made the adjusting entry to eliminate balances from the Fair Value Adjustment to Bond Investment account and the Unrealized Gain/Loss on Investments (Equity) account.

Record the transactions and adjustments of Hilo Company using journal entries.

LO2   ED-3A. Accounting for Debt Securities—Held-to-Maturity Burt Company had the following transactions and adjustments related to a bond investment:

2022

Jan.   1   Purchased $750,000 face value of Sphere, Inc.'s 9 percent bonds at 102 plus a brokerage commission of $900. The bonds pay interest on June 30 and December 31 and mature in 10 years. Burt expects to hold the bonds to maturity.

June   30   Received the semiannual interest payment on the Sphere bonds and amortized the bond premium for six months. Burt uses the straight-line method to amortize bond discounts and premiums.

2031

Dec.   31   Received the semiannual interest payment on the Sphere bonds and amortized the bond premium for six months.

        31   Received the principal amount in cash on the maturity date of the Sphere bonds.

Record the transactions and adjustments of Burt Company using journal entries.

LO3   ED-4A. Accounting for Equity Securities—Noninfluential The Durango Company had the following transactions and adjustment related to a stock investment:

Previous Year

Nov.   15   Purchased 6,000 shares of Erie, Inc.'s common stock at $12 per share plus a brokerage commission of $750. Durango expects to sell the stock in the near future. Durango is unable to exercise any significant control over Erie.

Dec.   22   Received a cash dividend of $1.10 per share of common stock from Erie.

        31   Made the adjusting entry to reflect year-end fair value of the stock investment in Erie. The year-end market price of the Erie common stock is $11.25 per share.

Current Year

Jan.   20   Sold all 6,000 shares of the Erie common stock for $63,000.

Record the transactions and adjustment of the Durango Company using journal entries.

LO3   ED-5A. Accounting for Equity Securities—Noninfluential Refer to the data for the Durango Company in ED-4A. Assume that the cash dividend was $1.50 per share and the year-end market price of the Erie common stock was $11.00. Record the transactions and adjustment of the Durango Company using journal entries.

ED-6A. Accounting for Equity Securities—Influential The Bradstreet Company had the following transactions and adjustment related to a stock investment: **LO3**

Previous Year

Jan. 15 Purchased 12,000 shares of Van, Inc.'s common stock at $9 per share plus a brokerage commission of $900. These shares represent a 30 percent ownership of Van's common stock.

Dec. 31 Received a cash dividend of $1.40 per share of common stock from Van.

     31 Made the adjusting entry to reflect income from the Van stock investment. Van's 2019 net income is $95,000.

Current Year

Jan. 20 Sold all 12,000 shares of the Van common stock for $126,000.

Record the transactions and adjustment of the Bradstreet Company using journal entries.

ED-7A. Accounting for Equity Securities On March 15, Katy Corp. purchased 200 shares of common stock of Scott Company for $15 per share. Katy Corp. is not able to exercise significant influence over Scott. On December 31, the market value of the Scott stock was $13.00 per share. Katy Corp. plans to hold the stock for the unforeseeable future.   **LO3**

a. Upon the purchase of the Scott stock, how should Katy Corp. classify the shares on its balance sheet? Justify your answer.

b. Record all transactions necessary for Katy.

ED-8A Recording Influential Securities On January 3, Mahorn Farm purchased 20 percent of the outstanding stock of Flepo Company for $80,000. The purchase gave Mahorn the ability to exercise significant influence over Flepo. During the year, Flepo paid cash dividends totaling $60,000 and reported net income for the year of $120,000.   **LO3**

Record all transactions necessary for Mahorn Farm.

ED-9A. Accounting for Equity Securities Micro, Inc., maintained a large investment in equity securities valued at approximately $39 billion as of the beginning of the year. During the year, the securities produced investment income (dividends and interest income) totaling $2 billion. At year-end, the portfolio of equity securities had appreciated to $43.5 billion.   **LO3**

Calculate the income statement effect of the equity securities if the securities are all considered noninfluential.

ED-10A. Consolidation Accounting Jones Company, a manufacturer of precision mining equipment, acquired 100 percent of the outstanding common stock of Denfork Company, a small mining company.   **LO4**

a. How should Jones account for this acquisition during the year?

b. What adjustments are needed at year-end?

c. What limitations are present in this method of accounting?

EXERCISES—SET B

ED-1B. Accounting for Debt Securities—Trading Flint, Inc., had the following transactions and adjustments related to a bond investment: **LO2**

Previous Year

Nov. 1 Purchased $300,000 face value of Batem, Inc.'s 9 percent bonds at 102 plus a brokerage commission of $800. The bonds pay interest on October 31 and April 30 and mature in 15 years. Flint expects to sell the bonds in the near future.

Dec. 31 Made the adjusting entry to record interest earned on investment in the Batem bonds.

     31 Made the adjusting entry to record the current fair value of the Batem bonds. At December 31, the market value of the Batem bonds was $301,500.

Current Year

Apr. 30 Received the semiannual interest payment on investment in the Batem bonds.

May 1 Sold the Batem bond investment for $300,800 cash.

Record the transactions and adjustments of the Flint Company using journal entries.

LO2   **ED-2B.** **Accounting for Debt Securities—Available-for-Sale** The White Company had the following transactions and adjustments related to a bond investment:

Previous Year

Jan.   1   Purchased $600,000 face value of Chevy, Inc.'s 8 percent bonds at 101 plus a brokerage commission of $1,500. The bonds pay interest on June 30 and December 31 and mature in 10 years. White does not expect to sell the bonds in the near future, nor does it intend to hold the bonds to maturity.

June   30   Received the semiannual interest payment on the Chevy bonds and amortized the bond premium for six months. White uses the straight-line method to amortize bond discounts and premiums.

Dec.   31   Received the semiannual interest payment on the Chevy bonds and amortized the bond premium for six months.

Dec.   31   Made the adjusting entry to record the current fair value of the Chevy bonds. At December 31, the market value of the Chevy bonds was $609,000.

Current Year

June   30   Received the semiannual interest payment on the Chevy bonds and amortized the bond premium for six months.

July   1   Sold the Chevy bond investment for $608,500 cash.

Dec.   31   Made the adjusting entry to eliminate balances from the Fair Value Adjustment to Bond Investment account and the Unrealized Gain/Loss on Investments (Equity) account.

Record the transactions and adjustments of the White Company using journal entries.

LO2   **ED-3B.** **Accounting for Debt Securities—Held-to-Maturity** The Sheppard Company had the following transactions and adjustments related to a bond investment:

2022

Jan.   1   Purchased $250,000 face value of Lowe, Inc.'s 6 percent bonds at 98 plus a brokerage commission of $800. The bonds pay interest on June 30 and December 31 and mature in 15 years. Sheppard expects to hold the bonds to maturity.

June   30   Received the semiannual interest payment on the Lowe bonds and amortized the bond discount for six months. Sheppard uses the straight-line method to amortize bond discounts and premiums.

2036

Dec.   31   Received the semiannual interest payment on the Lowe bonds and amortized the bond discount for six months.

     31   Received the principal amount in cash on the maturity date of the Lowe bonds.

Record the transactions and adjustments of the Sheppard Company using journal entries.

LO3   **ED-4B.** **Accounting for Equity Securities—Noninfluential** The Dole Company had the following transactions and adjustment related to a stock investment:

Previous Year

Nov.   15   Purchased 5,000 shares of Lake, Inc.'s common stock at $16 per share plus a brokerage commission of $900. Dole Company expects to sell the stock in the near future. Dole is unable to exercise any significant control over Lake.

Dec.   22   Received a cash dividend of $1.25 per share of common stock from Lake.

     31   Made the adjusting entry to reflect year-end fair value of the stock investment in Lake. The year-end market price of the Lake common stock is $17.50 per share.

Current Year

Jan.   20   Sold all 5,000 shares of the Lake common stock for $84,500.

Record the transactions and adjustment of the Dole Company using journal entries.

LO3   **ED-5B.** **Accounting for Equity Securities—Noninfluential** Refer to the data for Dole Company in ED-4B. Assume that the cash dividend was $1.20 per share and the year-end market price of the Lake common stock was $17.00. Record the transactions and adjustment of the Dole Company using journal entries.

ED-6B. Accounting for Equity Securities—Influential The Duke Company had the following transactions   **LO3** and adjustment related to a stock investment:

Previous Year
Jan.   15   Purchased 15,000 shares of Park, Inc.'s common stock at $8 per share plus a brokerage commission of $1,000. These shares represent a 25 percent ownership of the Park common stock.
Dec.   31   Received a cash dividend of $1.00 per share of common stock from Park.
       31   Made the adjusting entry to reflect income from the Park stock investment. Park's 2019 net income is $140,000.

Current Year
Jan.   20   Sold all 15,000 shares of the Park common stock for $132,000.

Record the above transactions for the Duke Company using journal entries.

ED-7B. Accounting for Equity Securities On March 15, Morris Corp. purchased 400 shares of common   **LO3** stock of Murat Company for $25 per share. Morris Corp. is not able to exercise significant influence over Murat. On December 31, the market value of the Murat stock was $29.00 per share. Morris Corp. plans to sell the stock soon.

a.   Upon the purchase of the Murat stock, how should Morris Corp. classify the shares on its balance sheet? Justify your answer.
b.   Record all transactions necessary for Morris.

ED-8B. Recording Influential Securities On January 3, Leslie Farm purchased 30 percent of the outstand-   **LO3** ing stock of Philip Company for $90,000. The purchase gave Leslie the ability to exercise significant influence over Philip. During the year, Philip paid cash dividends totaling $80,000 and reported net income for the year of $100,000.
     Record all transactions necessary for Leslie Farm.

ED-9B. Accounting for Equity Securities Macro, Inc., maintained a large investment in marketable securi-   **LO3** ties valued at approximately $60 billion as of the beginning of the year. During the year, the securities produced investment income (dividends and interest income) totaling $5 billion. At year-end, the portfolio of marketable securities had appreciated to $64.5 billion.
     Calculate the income statement effect of the marketable securities if the securities are categorized as noninfluential.

ED-10B. Consolidation Accounting Kali Company, a manufacturer of silicon chips, acquired 100 percent of   **LO4** the outstanding common stock of Visik Company, a small manufacturer of mobile computing devices.

a.   How should Kali account for this acquisition during the year?
b.   What adjustments are needed at year-end?
c.   What limitations are present in this method of accounting?

PROBLEMS—SET A

PD-1A. The Analysis of Bond Investments Gorge Company began operations in January and by year-end (De-   **LO2** cember 31) had made six bond investments. Year-end information on these bond investments follows:

Company	Face Value	Cost or Amortized Cost	Year-End Market Value	Classification
Ling, Inc..	$100,000	$102,400	$106,200	Trading
Wren, Inc..	$250,000	$262,500	$270,000	Trading
Olanamic, Inc..	$200,000	$198,000	$199,000	Available for sale
Fossil, Inc..	$150,000	$154,000	$160,000	Available for sale
Meander, Inc.	$101,000	$101,200	$102,400	Held to maturity
Resin, Inc..	$140,000	$136,000	$137,000	Held to maturity

Required
a.   At what total amount will the trading bond investments be reported on the December 31 balance sheet?

b.   At what total amount will the available-for-sale bond investments be reported on the December 31 balance sheet?

c.   At what total amount will the held-to-maturity bond investments be reported on the December 31 balance sheet?

d.   What total amount of unrealized gains or unrealized losses related to bond investments will appear on the income statement?

e.   What total amount of unrealized gains or unrealized losses related to bond investments will appear in the stockholders' equity section of the December 31 balance sheet?

f.   What total amount of fair value adjustment to bond investments will appear on the December 31 balance sheet? Which category of bond investments does the fair value adjustment relate to? Does the fair value adjustment increase or decrease the financial statement presentation of these bond investments?

LO2   **PD-2A.   Bond Investment Journal Entries**   The following transactions and adjustments relate to bond investments acquired by Bloomington Corporation:

Previous Year

June   30   Purchased $200,000 face value of Dynamo, Inc.'s 20-year, 9 percent bonds dated June 30, 2019, for $215,200 cash. Interest is paid December 31 and June 30. The investment is classified as an available-for-sale security.

Dec.   31   Received the semiannual interest payment from Dynamo and amortized the bond premium (straight-line method).

      31   Purchased $300,000 face value of Link, Inc.'s 10-year, 7 percent bonds dated December 31, 2019, for $297,000 cash. Interest is paid June 30 and December 31. The investment is classified as a held-to-maturity security.

Dec.   31   Made an adjusting entry to record the current fair value of the Dynamo bonds. At December 31, the market value was $216,000.

Current Year

June   30   Received the semiannual interest payment from Dynamo and amortized the bond premium.

      30   Received the semiannual interest payment from Link and amortized the bond discount (straight-line method).

July   1   Sold the Dynamo bonds for $216,500.

Oct.   31   Purchased $60,000 face value of Taxco, Inc.'s 5-year, 8 percent bonds dated October 31, 2020, for $61,000. Interest is paid April 30 and October 31. The investment is classified as a trading security.

Dec.   31   Received the semiannual interest payment from Link and amortized the bond discount.

      31   Made an adjusting entry to record interest earned on the investment in Taxco bonds.

      31   Made an adjusting entry to record the current fair value of the Taxco bonds. At December 31, the market value of the bonds was $59,500.

      31   Made an adjusting entry to eliminate balances in the Fair Value Adjustment to Bond Investment account and the Unrealized Gain/Loss on Investments (Equity) account.

Required

Prepare the journal entries to record these transactions and adjustments.

LO3   **PD-3A.   Stock Investment Journal Entries**   The following transactions and adjustments relate to stock investments made by Stine Corporation:

Previous Year

July   1   Purchased 1,000 shares of Polk, Inc.'s common stock for $66,200 cash. The investment is noninfluential and noncontrolling and is classified as a noninfluential security.

Nov.   9   Received a cash dividend of 90 cents per share on the Polk stock.

Dec.   31   Made an adjusting entry to record the current fair value of the Polk stock. At December 31, the stock had a market value of $63.00 per share.

Current Year

Feb.   1   Sold the Polk stock for $62 per share.

Required

Prepare the journal entries to record these transactions and adjustments.

PD-4A. Contrasting Journal Entries for Stock Investments: Noninfluential and Equity Methods On
January 2, Jeff Corporation purchased 10,000 shares of Forge Company common stock for $15 per
share, including commissions and taxes. On December 31, Forge announced its net income of $80,000
for the year and paid a dividend of $1.10 per share. At December 31, the market value of Forge's stock
was $19 per share. Jeff received its dividend on December 31.

LO3

Required
a. Assume that the stock acquired by Jeff represents 10 percent of Forge's voting stock and is classified as a noninfluential security. Prepare all journal entries appropriate for this investment.
b. Assume that the stock acquired by Jeff represents 35 percent of Forge's voting stock. Prepare all
journal entries appropriate for this investment.

PD-5A. Recording Influential Securities At the beginning of the year, the Carlton and United Brewery
(CUB) of Melbourne, Australia, purchased a 40 percent ownership interest in Icehouse Brewery of
Brisbane, Australia. The investment cost $30 million. At year-end, Icehouse Brewery declared and
paid cash dividends to shareholders totaling $800,000, after reporting earnings of $5 million.

LO3

Required
a. Calculate the income statement effect of CUB's investment in Icehouse Brewery as of year-end.
b. Calculate the book value of CUB's equity investment in Icehouse Brewery at year-end.
c. Calculate the book value of CUB's equity investment in Icehouse Brewery at year-end assuming
that Icehouse reported a loss of $3 million instead of a profit of $5 million and still paid its dividend of $800,000.

PD-6A. Accounting for Equity Securities Susan Company has the following securities in its portfolio that
were purchased in the current year.

LO3

	Cost	Fair Values Dec. 31, 2020
5,000 shares of Answa Corp.	$60,000	$58,000
10,000 shares of Smiler Co.	80,000	85,300

Additional information:

- Susan is not able to exercise significant influence over either of the investments.
- The Smiler Company securities were purchased at the beginning of the following year and appro-
priate year-end adjustments were made at the end of that year.
- The investment in Answa Corp. was in anticipation of a quick sale during February of the follow-
ing year.
- During the current year, Susan received cash dividends of $900 from Smiler Corp.

Required
a. How will each of the two securities be accounted for by Susan Company? Justify your choices.
b. Prepare a partial balance sheet and partial income statement at December 31 of the current year
that reflect the transactions provided.

PROBLEMS—SET B

PD-1B. The Analysis of Stock Investments The Discovery Company began operations in January, and by
year-end (December 31) had made four stock investments. Year-end information on these stock investments follows:

LO3

Company	Cost or Equity (as appropriate)	Year-End Market Value	Classification
Lisle, Inc.	$ 68,000	$ 65,300	Noninfluential
Owl, Inc.	$162,500	$160,000	Noninfluential
Buckley, Inc.	$100,000	$102,400	Influential
Riccer, Inc.	$136,000	$133,200	Influential

Required
a. At what total amount will the noninfluential stock investments be reported on the December 31
balance sheet?

b. At what total amount will the influential stock investments be reported on the December 31 balance sheet?

c. What total amount of unrealized gains or unrealized losses related to stock investments will appear on the income statement?

LO2   **PD-2B.** **Bond Investment Journal Entries** The following transactions and adjustments relate to bond investments acquired by Jeff Corporation:

Previous Year

June   30   Purchased $100,000 face value of Alamo, Inc.'s 20-year, 7 percent bonds dated June 30, 2019, for $97,200 cash. Interest is paid December 31 and June 30. The investment is classified as an available-for-sale security.

Dec.   31   Received the semiannual interest payment from Alamo and amortized the bond discount (straight-line method).

    31   Purchased $300,000 face value of Lyme, Inc.'s 10-year, 8 percent bonds dated December 31, 2019, for $304,000 cash. Interest is paid June 30 and December 31. The investment is classified as a held-to-maturity security.

    31   Made an adjusting entry to record the current fair value of the Alamo bonds. At December 31, the market value was $96,400.

Current Year

June   30   Received the semiannual interest payment from Alamo and amortized the bond discount.

    30   Received the semiannual interest payment from Lyme and amortized the bond premium (straight-line method).

July   1   Sold the Alamo bonds for $96,500.

Oct.   31   Purchased $80,000 face value of Weir, Inc.'s 5-year, 7.5 percent bonds dated October 31, 2020, for $79,000. Interest is paid April 30 and October 31. The investment is classified as a trading security.

Dec.   31   Received the semiannual interest payment from Lyme and amortized the bond premium.

    31   Made an adjusting entry to record interest earned on investment in the Weir bonds.

    31   Made an adjusting entry to record the current fair value of Weir bonds. At December 31, the market value of the bonds was $79,900.

    31   Made an adjusting entry to eliminate balances in the Fair Value Adjustment to Bond Investment account and the Unrealized Gain/Loss on Investments (Equity) account.

Required
Prepare the journal entries to record these transactions and adjustments.

LO3   **PD-3B.** **Stock Investment Journal Entries** The following transactions and adjustments relate to stock investments made by Gerald Corporation:

Previous Year

July   1   Purchased 2,000 shares of Cook, Inc.'s common stock for $96,200 cash. The investment is noninfluential and noncontrolling and is classified as a noninfluential security.

Nov.   9   Received a cash dividend of 70 cents per share on the Cook stock.

Dec.   31   Made an adjusting entry to record the current fair value of the Cook stock. At December 31, the stock has a market value of $50.50 per share.

Current Year

Feb.   1   Sold the Cook stock for $52 per share.

Required
Prepare the journal entries to record these transactions and adjustments.

LO3   **PD-4B.** **Contrasting Journal Entries for Stock Investments: Noninfluential and Equity Methods** On January 2, Rodger, Inc., purchased 30,000 shares of Baer, Inc.'s common stock for $21 per share, including commissions and taxes. On December 31, Baer announced its net income of $280,000 for the year and paid a dividend of 80 cents per share. At December 31, the market value of Baer's stock was $18 per share. Rodger received its dividend on December 31.

Required

a. Assume that the stock acquired by Rodger represents 10 percent of Baer's voting stock and is classified as a noninfluential security. Prepare all journal entries appropriate for this investment.

b. Assume that the stock acquired by Rodger represents 40 percent of Baer's voting stock. Prepare all journal entries appropriate for this investment.

PD-5B. Recording Influential Securities At the beginning of the year, the Frederick and Prince Brewery (FPB) of Auckland, New Zealand, purchased a 45 percent ownership interest in Flanagan Brewery of Belfast, Ireland. The investment cost $40 million. At year-end, Flanagan Brewery declared and paid cash dividends to shareholders totaling $1,200,000, after reporting earnings of $7 million.   **LO3**

Required
a. Calculate the income statement effect of FPB's investment in Flanagan Brewery as of year-end.
b. Calculate the book value of FPB's equity investment in Flanagan Brewery at year-end.
c. Calculate the book value of FPB's equity investment in Flanagan Brewery at year-end assuming that Flanagan reported a loss of $4 million instead of a profit of $7 million and still paid its dividend of $1,200,000.

PD-6B. Accounting for Equity Securities Sally Company has the following securities in its portfolio on December 31:   **LO3**

	Cost	Fair Values Dec. 31, 2020
5,000 shares of Peach Corp.	$ 90,000	$ 90,000
10,000 shares of Gordon Co.	145,000	130,300

Additional information:

- Sally is not able to exercise significant influence over either of the investments.
- The Gordon Company securities were purchased at the beginning of the previous year and the appropriate year-end adjustments were made at the end of that year.
- The investment in Peach Corp. was in anticipation of a quick sale during February of the following year.
- During the current year, Sally received cash dividends of $900 from Peach Corp.

Required
a. How will each of the two securities be accounted for by Sally Company? Justify your choices.
b. Prepare a balance sheet and partial income statement at December 31 that reflect the transactions provided.

ANSWERS TO SELF-STUDY QUESTIONS:

1. b   2. d   3. b   4. d   5. a   6. b   7. c   8. a   9. a   10. b   11. c   12. b   13. a

YOUR TURN! SOLUTIONS

Solution D-1
1. B;   2. C;   3. A;   4. F;   5. D;   6. E.

Solution D-2

a.	Jan. 1	Bond investment—Trading (A)	102,000	
		Bond investment—Available-for-sale (B)	100,000	
		Bond investment—Held-to-maturity (C)	98,000	
		Cash		300,000
		To record purchase of bonds.		
b.	Jun. 30	Cash	9,000	
		Bond investment—Held-to-maturity (C)	100	
		Bond interest income		9,100
		To record $3,000 interest payments on each bond and $100		
		($2,000 discount/20 periods) discount amortization.		

continued

continued from previous page

c.	Jul. 1	Cash	103,000	
		Bond investment—Trading (A)		102,000
		Gain on sale of investments		1,000
		To record sale of trading security at a gain.		
d.	Jul. 1	Fair value adjustment to bond investment	1,000	
		Unrealized gain/loss on investment (equity)		1,000
		To adjust available-for-sale security B to fair value.		

Solution D-3

Jan. 1	Stock investment—Noninfluential (A)	10,000	
	Stock investment—Influential (B)	50,000	
	Stock investment—Controlling (C)	120,000	
	Cash		180,000
	To record the purchase of the three equity securities.		
Dec. 31	Cash	1,000	
	Dividend income		1,000
	To record dividend income from noninfluential security.		
Dec. 31	Stock investment—Noninfluential (A)	2,000	
	Unrealized gain/loss on investments (income)		2,000
	To adjust noninfluential security to fair value.		
Dec. 31	Cash	2,000	
	Stock investment—Influential		2,000
	To record the receipt of dividends from influential security.		
Dec. 31	Stock investment—Influential	20,000	
	Income from stock investments		20,000
	To record as income 25% of Company B's net income of $80,000.		
Dec. 31	Cash	10,000	
	Stock investment—Controlling		10,000
	To record the receipt of dividends from controlling security.		
Dec. 31	Income/loss from stock investments	7,000	
	Stock investment—Controlling		7,000
	To record as income 70% of Company C's net loss of $10,000.		

Appendix E

Accounting and the Time Value of Money

Road Map

LO	Learning Objective	Page	eLecture	Guided Example	Assignments
LO1	**Describe the nature of interest and distinguish between simple and compound interest.**	E-2	E-2	E-1	EE1A, EE1B
LO2	**Calculate future values.**	E-3	E-3	E-2, E-3	SS1, EE2A, EE3A, EE6A, EE8A, EE9A, EE11A, EE12A, EE14A, EE2B, EE3B, EE6B, EE8B, EE9B, EE11B, EE12B, EE14B
LO3	**Calculate present values.**	E-7	E-7	E-4, E-5	SS2, EE4A, EE5A, EE7A, EE10A, EE13A, EE15A, EE4B, EE5B, EE7B, EE10B, EE13B, EE15B

TIME VALUE OF MONEY CONCEPT

LO1 **Describe** the nature of interest and **distinguish** between simple and compound interest.

Would you rather receive a dollar now or a dollar one year from now? Most people would answer "a dollar now." Intuition tells us that a dollar received now is more valuable than the same amount received sometime in the future. Sound reasons exist for choosing the option of receiving the money sooner rather than later, the most obvious of which concerns risk. Because the future is always uncertain, some event may prevent you from receiving the dollar at a later date. To avoid this risk, we choose the earlier date.

A second reason for choosing the earlier date is that the dollar has a **time value**—that is, the dollar received now could be invested such that one year from now, you would have not only the original dollar but also the interest income on the dollar for the past year. **Interest** is a payment for the use of money, much like a rent payment for the use of an apartment. Interest is calculated by multiplying an interest rate, usually stated as an annual rate, by a principal amount for a period of time. The **principal** amount represents the amount to be repaid. The amount of interest can be computed as either a simple interest amount or a compound interest amount.

Time Value of Money: Simple Interest Model

Simple interest calculates interest on only the principal amount owed without considering any interest already earned. Simple interest is calculated using the following formula:

$$\textbf{Interest} = \textbf{p} \times \textbf{i} \times \textbf{n}$$

where

    p = principal
    i = interest rate for one period
    n = number of periods

For example, if you borrow $3,000 for four years at a simple interest rate of 6 percent annually, the amount of simple interest would total $720, calculated as $3,000 × 0.06 × 4.

Time Value of Money: Compound Interest Model

Compound interest differs from simple interest because it is calculated on both the principal and any previously earned interest that has not been paid. In other words, compound interest involves computing interest on interest, along with the principal amount.

As we can see in **Exhibit E-1**, simple interest only uses the original $3,000 principal to compute the annual interest in each of the four years. In contrast, compound interest uses the entire principal balance, including both the original $3,000 principal and the accumulated interest to date, to compute the next year's interest. This results in increasing interest each year, with the result in **Exhibit E-1** for compound interest yielding a larger ending balance by $67.43.

Because almost all businesses use compound interest, we will assume the use of compound interest in all of the illustrations in this appendix. Simple interest is generally only used in short-term credit arrangements, typically lasting less than a year.

EXHIBIT E-1	Illustration Comparing Simple Interest to Compound Interest						
	Simple Interest Model			**Compound Interest Model**			
	Interest Calculation	Simple Interest	Principal Balance	Interest Calculation	Compound Interest	Principal Balance	
Year 1 ..	$3,000.00 × 6%	$180.00	$3,180.00	$3,000.00 × 6%	$180.00	$3,180.00	
Year 2 ..	$3,000.00 × 6%	$180.00	$3,360.00	$3,180.00 × 6%	$190.80	$3,370.80	
Year 3 ..	$3,000.00 × 6%	$180.00	$3,540.00	$3,370.80 × 6%	$202.25	$3,573.05	
Year 4 ..	$3,000.00 × 6%	$180.00	$3,720.00	$3,573.05 × 6%	$214.38	$3,787.43	
		$720.00		→ $67.43 difference ←		$787.43	

Scott Colin invests $100 in the bank for three years. Calculate the amount of interest that Scott will earn at the end of the three years assuming (1) simple interest at the annual rate of 10 percent, and (2) compound interest at the annual rate of 10 percent.

YOUR TURN! E-1

Guided Example MBC

The solution is on page E-15.

FUTURE VALUE OF AN AMOUNT

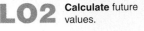 **LO2** Calculate future values.

The **future value** of a single sum is the amount that a specified investment will be worth at a future date if invested at a given rate of compound interest. For example, suppose that we decide to invest $6,000 in a savings account that pays 6 percent annual interest, and that we intend to leave the principal and interest in the account for five years. Assuming that interest is credited to the account at the end of each year, the balance in the account at the end of five years is determined using the following formula:

 eLecture MBC

$$FV = PV \times (1 + i)^n$$

where

FV = future value of an amount
PV = present value (today's value)
 i = interest rate for one period
 n = number of periods

The future value in this case is $8,029, computed as [$6,000 × (1.06)^5] = ($6,000 × 1.33823).

It is often easier to solve time value of money problems with the aid of a time diagram, as illustrated in **Exhibit E-2**. Time diagrams are drawn to show the timing of the various cash inflows and outflows. Note in **Exhibit E-2** that our initial $6,000 cash inflow (the amount deposited in a savings account) allows us to withdraw $8,029 (a cash outflow) at the end of five years.

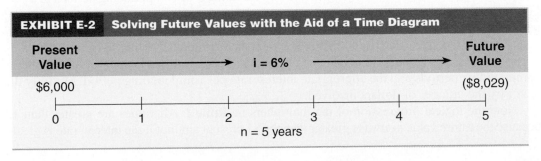

EXHIBIT E-2 Solving Future Values with the Aid of a Time Diagram

We can also calculate the future value of a single amount with the use of a table like **Table I**, which presents the future value of a single dollar after a given number of time periods. Simply stated, future value tables provide a multiplier for many combinations of time periods and interest rates that, when applied to the dollar amount of a present value, determines its future value.

TABLE I	**Future Value of $1**											
Period	**1.0%**	**2.0%**	**3.0%**	**4.0%**	**5.0%**	**6.0%**	**7.0%**	**8.0%**	**9.0%**	**10.0%**	**11.0%**	**12.0%**
1	1.01000	1.02000	1.03000	1.04000	1.05000	1.06000	1.07000	1.08000	1.09000	1.10000	1.11000	1.12000
2	1.02010	1.04040	1.06090	1.08160	1.10250	1.12360	1.14490	1.16640	1.18810	1.21000	1.23210	1.25440
3	1.03030	1.06121	1.09273	1.12486	1.15763	1.19102	1.22504	1.25971	1.29503	1.33100	1.36763	1.40493
4	1.04060	1.08243	1.12551	1.16986	1.21551	1.26248	1.31080	1.36049	1.41158	1.46410	1.51807	1.57352
5	1.05101	1.10408	1.15927	1.21665	1.27628	1.33823	1.40255	1.46933	1.53862	1.61051	1.68506	1.76234
6	1.06152	1.12616	1.19405	1.26532	1.34010	1.41852	1.50073	1.58687	1.67710	1.77156	1.87041	1.97382
7	1.07214	1.14869	1.22987	1.31593	1.40710	1.50363	1.60578	1.71382	1.82804	1.94872	2.07616	2.21068
8	1.08286	1.17166	1.26677	1.36857	1.47746	1.59385	1.71819	1.85093	1.99256	2.14359	2.30454	2.47596
9	1.09369	1.19509	1.30477	1.42331	1.55133	1.68948	1.83846	1.99900	2.17189	2.35795	2.55804	2.77308
10	1.10462	1.21899	1.34392	1.48024	1.62889	1.79085	1.96715	2.15892	2.36736	2.59374	2.83942	3.10585
11	1.11567	1.24337	1.38423	1.53945	1.71034	1.89830	2.10485	2.33164	2.58043	2.85312	3.15176	3.47855
12	1.12683	1.26824	1.42576	1.60103	1.79586	2.01220	2.25219	2.51817	2.81266	3.13843	3.49845	3.89598
13	1.13809	1.29361	1.46853	1.66507	1.88565	2.13293	2.40985	2.71962	3.06580	3.45227	3.88328	4.36349
14	1.14947	1.31948	1.51259	1.73168	1.97993	2.26090	2.57853	2.93719	3.34173	3.79750	4.31044	4.88711
15	1.16097	1.34587	1.55797	1.80094	2.07893	2.39656	2.75903	3.17217	3.64248	4.17725	4.78459	5.47357
16	1.17258	1.37279	1.60471	1.87298	2.18287	2.54035	2.95216	3.42594	3.97031	4.59497	5.31089	6.13039
17	1.18430	1.40024	1.65285	1.94790	2.29202	2.69277	3.15882	3.70002	4.32763	5.05447	5.89509	6.86604
18	1.19615	1.42825	1.70243	2.02582	2.40662	2.85434	3.37993	3.99602	4.71712	5.55992	6.54355	7.68997
19	1.20811	1.45681	1.75351	2.10685	2.52695	3.02560	3.61653	4.31570	5.14166	6.11591	7.26334	8.61276
20	1.22019	1.48595	1.80611	2.19112	2.65330	3.20714	3.86968	4.66096	5.60441	6.72750	8.06231	9.64629
25	1.28243	1.64061	2.09378	2.66584	3.38635	4.29187	5.42743	6.84848	8.62308	10.83471	13.58546	17.00006
30	1.34785	1.81136	2.42726	3.24340	4.32194	5.74349	7.61226	10.06266	13.26768	17.44940	22.89230	29.95992
35	1.41660	1.99989	2.81386	3.94609	5.51602	7.68609	10.67658	14.78534	20.41397	28.10244	38.57485	52.79962
40	1.48886	2.20804	3.26204	4.80102	7.03999	10.28572	14.97446	21.72452	31.40942	45.25926	65.00087	93.05097
50	1.64463	2.69159	4.38391	7.10668	11.46740	18.42015	29.45703	46.90161	74.35752	117.39085	184.56483	289.00219

Future value tables are used as follows. First, determine the number of interest compounding periods involved (five years compounded annually are five periods, five years compounded semiannually are 10 periods, five years compounded quarterly are 20 periods, and so on). The extreme left-hand column indicates the number of periods covered in the table.

Second, determine the interest rate per compounding period. Note that interest rates are usually quoted on an annual or *per year* basis. Therefore, only in the case of annual compounding is the quoted interest rate the interest rate per compounding period. In other cases, the rate per compounding period is the annual rate divided by the number of compounding periods in a year. For example, an interest rate of 10 percent per year would be 10 percent for one compounding period if compounded annually, 5 percent for two compounding periods if compounded semiannually, and 2 ½ percent for four compounding periods if compounded quarterly.

Finally, locate the factor that is in the cell at the intersection of the appropriate number of compounding periods and the appropriate interest rate per compounding period. Multiply this factor by the number of dollars involved.

Note the logical progression of the multipliers in **Table I**. All values are greater than 1.0 because the future value is always greater than the $1 present amount if the interest rate is greater than zero. Also, as the interest rate increases (moving from left to right in the table) or the number of periods increases (moving from top to bottom), the multipliers become larger.

Continuing with our example of calculating the future value of a $6,000 savings account deposit earning 6 percent annual compound interest for five years, and using the multipliers from Table I, we solve for the future value of the deposit as follows:

$$\textbf{Principal} \quad \times \quad \textbf{Factor} \quad = \quad \textbf{Future Value}$$
$$\$6,000 \quad \times \quad 1.33823 \quad = \quad \$8,029$$

The factor 1.33823 is in the row for five periods and the column for 6 percent. Note that this factor is the same as the multiplier we determined using the future value formula in our calculation above.

Suppose, instead, that the interest is credited to the savings account semiannually rather than annually. In this situation, there are 10 compounding periods, and we use a 3 percent rate (one-half the annual rate). The future value calculation using the **Table I** multipliers is as follows:

$$\textbf{Principal} \quad \times \quad \textbf{Factor} \quad = \quad \textbf{Future Value}$$
$$\$6,000 \quad \times \quad 1.34392 \quad = \quad \$8,064$$

Julie Penn invests $5,000 in the bank for four years. How much will be in her account at the end of the four years if the bank pays compound interest at the annual rate of 8 percent?

YOUR TURN! E-2

MBC

The solution is on page E-15.

FUTURE VALUE OF AN ANNUITY

Using future value tables like **Table I**, we can calculate the future value of any single future cash flow or series of future cash flows. One frequent pattern of cash flows, however, is subject to a more convenient calculation. This pattern, known as an **annuity**, can be described as *equal amounts equally spaced over a period.*

For example, assume that $100 is to be deposited at the end of each of the next three years as an annuity into a savings account. When annuity cash flows occur at the *end* of each period, the annuity is called an **ordinary annuity**. As shown below in **Exhibit E-3**, the future value of this ordinary annuity can be calculated from **Table I** by calculating the future value of each of the three individual deposits and summing them (assuming 8 percent annual interest).

EXHIBIT E-3	Future Value of an Ordinary Annuity					
Future Deposits (ordinary annuity)				**FV Multiplier (Table I)**		**Future Value**
Year 1	**Year 2**	**Year 3**				
$100			×	1.16640	=	$116.64
	$100		×	1.08000	=	108.00
		$100	×	1.00000	=	100.00
				3.24640		$324.64

Table II, on the other hand, provides a single multiplier for calculating the future value of a series of future cash flows that reflect an ordinary annuity. Referring to **Table II** in the three periods row and the 8 percent interest column, we see that the multiplier is 3.24640, equal to the sum of the three future value factors in **Exhibit E-3**. When applied to the $100 annuity amount, the multiplier gives a future value of $324.64, or $100 × 3.2464. As shown above, the same future value is derived from the several multipliers of **Table I**. For annuities of 5, 10, or 20 years, numerous calculations are avoided by using annuity tables like **Table II**.

TABLE II	Future Value of an Ordinary Annuity of $1 per Period											
Period	1%	2%	3%	4%	5%	6%	7%	8%	9%	10%	11%	12%
1	1.00000	1.00000	1.00000	1.00000	1.00000	1.00000	1.00000	1.00000	1.00000	1.00000	1.00000	1.00000
2	2.01000	2.02000	2.03000	2.04000	2.05000	2.06000	2.07000	2.08000	2.09000	2.10000	2.11000	2.12000
3	3.03010	3.06040	3.09090	3.12160	3.15250	3.18360	3.21490	3.24640	3.27810	3.31000	3.34210	3.37440
4	4.06040	4.12161	4.18363	4.24646	4.31013	4.37462	4.43994	4.50611	4.57313	4.64100	4.70973	4.77933
5	5.10101	5.20404	5.30914	5.41632	5.52563	5.63709	5.75074	5.86660	5.98471	6.10510	6.22780	6.35285
6	6.15202	6.30812	6.46841	6.63298	6.80191	6.97532	7.15329	7.33593	7.52333	7.71561	7.91286	8.11519
7	7.21354	7.43428	7.66246	7.89829	8.14201	8.39384	8.65402	8.92280	9.20043	9.48717	9.78327	10.08901
8	8.28567	8.58297	8.89234	9.21423	9.54911	9.89747	10.25980	10.63663	11.02847	11.43589	11.85943	12.29969
9	9.36853	9.75463	10.15911	10.58280	11.02656	11.49132	11.97799	12.48756	13.02104	13.57948	14.16397	14.77566
10	10.46221	10.94972	11.46388	12.00611	12.57789	13.18079	13.81645	14.48656	15.19293	15.93742	16.72201	17.54874
11	11.56683	12.16872	12.80780	13.48635	14.20679	14.97164	15.78360	16.64549	17.56029	18.53117	19.56143	20.65458
12	12.68250	13.41209	14.19203	15.02581	15.91713	16.86994	17.88845	18.97713	20.14072	21.38428	22.71319	24.13313
13	13.80933	14.68033	15.61779	16.62684	17.71298	18.88214	20.14064	21.49530	22.95338	24.52271	26.21164	28.02911
14	14.94742	15.97394	17.08632	18.29191	19.59863	21.01507	22.55049	24.21492	26.01919	27.97498	30.09492	32.39260
15	16.09690	17.29342	18.59891	20.02359	21.57856	23.27597	25.12902	27.15211	29.36092	31.77248	34.40536	37.27971
16	17.25786	18.63929	20.15688	21.82453	23.65749	25.67253	27.88805	30.32428	33.00340	35.94973	39.18995	42.75328
17	18.43044	20.01207	21.76159	23.69751	25.84037	28.21288	30.84022	33.75023	36.97370	40.54470	44.50084	48.88367
18	19.61475	21.41231	23.41444	25.64541	28.13238	30.90565	33.99903	37.45024	41.30134	45.59917	50.39594	55.74971
19	20.81090	22.84056	25.11687	27.67123	30.53900	33.75999	37.37896	41.44626	46.01846	51.15909	56.93949	63.43968
20	22.01900	24.29737	26.87037	29.77808	33.06595	36.78559	40.99549	45.76196	51.16012	57.27500	64.20283	72.05244
25	28.24320	32.03030	36.45926	41.64591	47.72710	54.86451	63.24904	73.10594	84.70090	98.34706	114.41331	133.33387
30	34.78489	40.56808	47.57542	56.08494	66.43885	79.05819	94.46079	113.28321	136.30754	164.49402	199.02088	241.33268
35	41.66028	49.99448	60.46208	73.65222	90.32031	111.43478	138.23688	172.31680	215.71075	271.02437	341.58955	431.66350
40	48.88637	60.40198	75.40126	95.02552	120.79977	154.76197	199.63511	259.05652	337.88245	442.59256	581.82607	767.09142
50	64.46318	84.57940	112.79687	152.66708	209.34800	290.33590	406.52893	573.77016	815.08356	1163.90853	1668.77115	2400.01825

As another example, if we decide to invest $50 at the end of each six months for three years at an 8 percent annual rate of return, we would use the factor for six periods at 4 percent, as follows:

Periodic Payment	×	Factor	=	Future Value
$50	×	6.63298	=	$331.65

YOUR TURN! E-3

MBC

The solution is on page E-15.

Kathy Cole invests $100 monthly for 18 months at an annual rate of 12 percent. How much money will Kathy have at the end of the 18 months from her investment?

PRESENT VALUE OF AN AMOUNT

We can generalize that (1) the right to receive an amount of money now—its **present value**—is normally worth more than the right to receive the same amount later—its future value; (2) the longer we must wait to receive an amount, the less attractive the receipt is; and (3) the difference between the present value of an amount and its future value is a function of interest (Principal × Interest Rate × Time). Further, the more risk associated with any situation, the higher the appropriate interest rate.

LO3 Calculate present values.

We support these generalizations with an illustration. What amount should we accept now that would be as valuable as receiving $100 one year from now ($100 represents the future value) if the appropriate interest rate is 10 percent? We recognize intuitively that with a 10 percent interest rate, we should accept less than $100, or approximately $91. We base this estimate on the realization that the $100 received in the future must equal the present value (100 percent) plus 10 percent interest on the present value. Thus, in our example, the $100 future receipt must be 1.10 times the present value. Dividing $100 by 1.10, we obtain a present value of $90.91. In other words, under the given conditions, we would do as well to accept $90.91 now as to wait one year and receive $100. To confirm the equality of a $90.91 payment now with a $100 payment one year later, we calculate the future value of $90.91 at 10 percent for one year as follows:

$$\$90.91 \times 1.10 \times 1 \text{ year} = \$100 \text{ (rounded)}$$

Thus, we calculate the present value of a future receipt by discounting (deducting an interest factor) the future receipt back to the present at an appropriate interest rate. We present this schematically below:

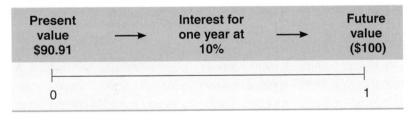

The formula for calculating the present value of a single amount is determined using the following formula:

$$PV = FV \times [1 \div (1 + i)^n]$$

where

PV = present value of an amount
FV = future value
  i = interest rate for one period
  n = number of periods

As can be seen from this formula, if either the number of periods (n) or the interest rate (i) is increased, the resulting present value would decrease. If more than one time period is involved, compound interest calculations are appropriate. **Exhibit E-4** illustrates the calculation of the present value of a single amount.

EXHIBIT E-4	**Present Value of a Single Amount**

How much must be deposited in a savings account today in order to have $1,000 in four years if the savings account pays 12 percent annual interest?

$$PV = \$1,000 \times [1 \div (1.12)^4] = (\$1,000 \times 0.63552) = \$636$$

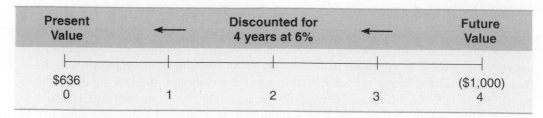

Table III can be used to calculate the present value amounts in a manner similar to the way we previously calculated future values using Table I. As with the future value tables, present value tables provide a multiplier for many combinations of time periods and interest rates that, when applied to the dollar amount of a future cash flow or annuity, determines its present value.

TABLE III	Present Value of $1											
Period	1%	2%	3%	4%	5%	6%	7%	8%	9%	10%	11%	12%
1	0.99010	0.98039	0.97087	0.96154	0.95238	0.94340	0.93458	0.92593	0.91743	0.90909	0.90090	0.89286
2	0.98030	0.96117	0.94260	0.92456	0.90703	0.89000	0.87344	0.85734	0.84168	0.82645	0.81162	0.79719
3	0.97059	0.94232	0.91514	0.88900	0.86384	0.83962	0.81630	0.79383	0.77218	0.75131	0.73119	0.71178
4	0.96098	0.92385	0.88849	0.85480	0.82270	0.79209	0.76290	0.73503	0.70843	0.68301	0.65873	0.63552
5	0.95147	0.90573	0.86261	0.82193	0.78353	0.74726	0.71299	0.68058	0.64993	0.62092	0.59345	0.56743
6	0.94205	0.88797	0.83748	0.79031	0.74622	0.70496	0.66634	0.63017	0.59627	0.56447	0.53464	0.50663
7	0.93272	0.87056	0.81309	0.75992	0.71068	0.66506	0.62275	0.58349	0.54703	0.51316	0.48166	0.45235
8	0.92348	0.85349	0.78941	0.73069	0.67684	0.62741	0.58201	0.54027	0.50187	0.46651	0.43393	0.40388
9	0.91434	0.83676	0.76642	0.70259	0.64461	0.59190	0.54393	0.50025	0.46043	0.42410	0.39092	0.36061
10	0.90529	0.82035	0.74409	0.67556	0.61391	0.55839	0.50835	0.46319	0.42241	0.38554	0.35218	0.32197
11	0.89632	0.80426	0.72242	0.64958	0.58468	0.52679	0.47509	0.42888	0.38753	0.35049	0.31728	0.28748
12	0.88745	0.78849	0.70138	0.62460	0.55684	0.49697	0.44401	0.39711	0.35553	0.31863	0.28584	0.25668
13	0.87866	0.77303	0.68095	0.60057	0.53032	0.46884	0.41496	0.36770	0.32618	0.28966	0.25751	0.22917
14	0.86996	0.75788	0.66112	0.57748	0.50507	0.44230	0.38782	0.34046	0.29925	0.26333	0.23199	0.20462
15	0.86135	0.74301	0.64186	0.55526	0.48102	0.41727	0.36245	0.31524	0.27454	0.23939	0.20900	0.18270
16	0.85282	0.72845	0.62317	0.53391	0.45811	0.39365	0.33873	0.29189	0.25187	0.21763	0.18829	0.16312
17	0.84438	0.71416	0.60502	0.51337	0.43630	0.37136	0.31657	0.27027	0.23107	0.19784	0.16963	0.14564
18	0.83602	0.70016	0.58739	0.49363	0.41552	0.35034	0.29586	0.25025	0.21199	0.17986	0.15282	0.13004
19	0.82774	0.68643	0.57029	0.47464	0.39573	0.33051	0.27651	0.23171	0.19449	0.16351	0.13768	0.11611
20	0.81954	0.67297	0.55368	0.45639	0.37689	0.31180	0.25842	0.21455	0.17843	0.14864	0.12403	0.10367
25	0.77977	0.60953	0.47761	0.37512	0.29530	0.23300	0.18425	0.14602	0.11597	0.09230	0.07361	0.05882
30	0.74192	0.55207	0.41199	0.30832	0.23138	0.17411	0.13137	0.09938	0.07537	0.05731	0.04368	0.03338
35	0.70591	0.50003	0.35538	0.25342	0.18129	0.13011	0.09366	0.06763	0.04899	0.03558	0.02592	0.01894
40	0.67165	0.45289	0.30656	0.20829	0.14205	0.09722	0.06678	0.04603	0.03184	0.02209	0.01538	0.01075
50	0.60804	0.37153	0.22811	0.14071	0.08720	0.05429	0.03395	0.02132	0.01345	0.00852	0.00542	0.00346

Exhibit E-5 illustrates calculations of present values using the factors in Table III. Note the logical progression of the multipliers in Table III. All values are less than 1.0 because the present value is always less than the future amount. Also, as the interest rate increases (moving from left to right in the table), or as the number of periods increases (moving from top to bottom), the multipliers become smaller.

EXHIBIT E-5   Present Value of a Single Amount Using Present Value Tables

Calculate the present value of $1,000 four years hence, at 12 percent interest compounded annually:

Number of periods (one year, annually) = 4
Interest rate per period (12%/1) = 12%
Multiplier = 0.63552
Present value = $1,000 × 0.63552 = $636
(This result agrees with our earlier illustration.)

Calculate the present value of $116.99 two years hence, at 8 percent compounded semiannually:

Number of periods (two years, semiannually) = 4
Interest rate per period (8%/2) = 4%
Multiplier = 0.85480
Present value = $116.99 × 0.85480 = $100 (rounded)

YOUR TURN! E-4

Sabrina Flores wishes to have $2,500 in her bank account in three years. If she can earn 7 percent compounded annually, how much will she need to invest today?

GuidedExample

MBC

The solution is on page E-15.

PRESENT VALUE OF AN ANNUITY

We can use present value tables like **Table III** to calculate the present value of any single future cash flow or series of future cash flows. For example, assume $100 is to be received at the end of each of the next three years as an annuity. As shown in **Exhibit E-6**, the present value of this ordinary annuity can be calculated from **Table III** as the present value of each of the three individual receipts and summing them (assuming 5 percent annual interest).

EXHIBIT E-6   Present Value of an Ordinary Annuity

Future Receipts (ordinary annuity)				PV Multiplier (Table III)		Present Value
Year 1	Year 2	Year 3				
$100			×	0.95238	=	$ 95.24
	$100		×	0.90703	=	90.70
		$100	×	0.86384	=	86.38
				2.72325		$272.32

Table IV, on the other hand, provides a single multiplier for calculating the present value of a series of future cash flows that represent an ordinary annuity. Referring to **Table IV** in the three periods row and the 5 percent interest column, we see that the multiplier is 2.72325, equal to the sum of the three present value factors in **Exhibit E-6**. When applied to the $100 annuity amount, the multiplier gives a present value of $272.33 (with a $0.01 difference due to rounding).

TABLE IV	Present Value of an Ordinary Annuity of $1 per Period											
Period	1%	2%	3%	4%	5%	6%	7%	8%	9%	10%	11%	12%
1	0.99010	0.98039	0.97087	0.96154	0.95238	0.94340	0.93458	0.92593	0.91743	0.90909	0.90090	0.89286
2	1.97040	1.94156	1.91347	1.88609	1.85941	1.83339	1.80802	1.78326	1.75911	1.73554	1.71252	1.69005
3	2.94099	2.88388	2.82861	2.77509	2.72325	2.67301	2.62432	2.57710	2.53129	2.48685	2.44371	2.40183
4	3.90197	3.80773	3.71710	3.62990	3.54595	3.46511	3.38721	3.31213	3.23972	3.16987	3.10245	3.03735
5	4.85343	4.71346	4.57971	4.45182	4.32948	4.21236	4.10020	3.99271	3.88965	3.79079	3.69590	3.60478
6	5.79548	5.60143	5.41719	5.24214	5.07569	4.91732	4.76654	4.62288	4.48592	4.35526	4.23054	4.11141
7	6.72819	6.47199	6.23028	6.00205	5.78637	5.58238	5.38929	5.20637	5.03295	4.86842	4.71220	4.56376
8	7.65168	7.32548	7.01969	6.73274	6.46321	6.20979	5.97130	5.74664	5.53482	5.33493	5.14612	4.96764
9	8.56602	8.16224	7.78611	7.43533	7.10782	6.80169	6.51523	6.24689	5.99525	5.75902	5.53705	5.32825
10	9.47130	8.98259	8.53020	8.11090	7.72173	7.36009	7.02358	6.71008	6.41766	6.14457	5.88923	5.65022
11	10.36763	9.78685	9.25262	8.76048	8.30641	7.88687	7.49867	7.13896	6.80519	6.49506	6.20652	5.93770
12	11.25508	10.57534	9.95400	9.38507	8.86325	8.38384	7.94269	7.53608	7.16073	6.81369	6.49236	6.19437
13	12.13374	11.34837	10.63496	9.98565	9.39357	8.85268	8.35765	7.90378	7.48690	7.10336	6.74987	6.42355
14	13.00370	12.10625	11.29607	10.56312	9.89864	9.29498	8.74547	8.24424	7.78615	7.36669	6.98187	6.62817
15	13.86505	12.84926	11.93794	11.11839	10.37966	9.71225	9.10791	8.55948	8.06069	7.60608	7.19087	6.81086
16	14.71787	13.57771	12.56110	11.65230	10.83777	10.10590	9.44665	8.85137	8.31256	7.82371	7.37916	6.97399
17	15.56225	14.29187	13.16612	12.16567	11.27407	10.47726	9.76322	9.12164	8.54363	8.02155	7.54879	7.11963
18	16.39827	14.99203	13.75351	12.65930	11.68959	10.82760	10.05909	9.37189	8.75563	8.20141	7.70162	7.24967
19	17.22601	15.67846	14.32380	13.13394	12.08532	11.15812	10.33560	9.60360	8.95011	8.36492	7.83929	7.36578
20	18.04555	16.35143	14.87747	13.59033	12.46221	11.46992	10.59401	9.81815	9.12855	8.51356	7.96333	7.46944
25	22.02316	19.52346	17.41315	15.62208	14.09394	12.78336	11.65358	10.67478	9.82258	9.07704	8.42174	7.84314
30	25.80771	22.39646	19.60044	17.29203	15.37245	13.76483	12.40904	11.25778	10.27365	9.42691	8.69379	8.05518
35	29.40858	24.99862	21.48722	18.66461	16.37419	14.49825	12.94767	11.65457	10.56682	9.64416	8.85524	8.17550
40	32.83469	27.35548	23.11477	19.79277	17.15909	15.04630	13.33171	11.92461	10.75736	9.77905	8.95105	8.24378
50	39.19612	31.42361	25.72976	21.48218	18.25593	15.76186	13.80075	12.23348	10.96168	9.91481	9.04165	8.30450

YOUR TURN! E-5

Guided Example

MBC

The solution is on page E-15.

Jamal Turner is planning to attend a four-year university. He hopes to save money from his current job so that he will have enough in the bank account when he starts college to allow him to withdraw $10,000 at the end of each of the four years. He expects to earn 6 percent compounded annually on his investment. How much money will he need in his bank account when he starts college?

CALCULATIONS USING A CALCULATOR AND A SPREADSHEET

While present value tables can provide a handy method to solve some time value of money problems, they are not suitable for many real-world situations. For example, many real-world interest rates are not even integers like those appearing in **Table I** through **Table IV**, nor are many problems limited to the number of time periods appearing in the tables. While it is still possible to solve these problems with the provided formulas, financial calculators and spreadsheet programs provide a much quicker solution. Financial calculators can be distinguished from other calculators by the presence of dedicated keys for present and future values, along with keys for the number of periods, interest rates, and annuity payments. There are many brands of financial calculators; however, all of them work in much the same way.[1] We illustrate the calculation of bond prices using a calculator and a spreadsheet in Appendix 10A at the end of Chapter 10.

---

[1] It is usually necessary to do some preliminary setup on a financial calculator before performing time value of money calculations. For example, the HP 10BII calculator has a default setting of monthly compounding. This may need to be changed if the problem calls for a different number of compounding periods, such as annual. In addition, the calculator assumes annuity payments occur at the end of each period. This will need to be changed if the problem requires beginning of period payments. See your calculator manual to determine how to make these setting changes.

SUMMARY OF LEARNING OBJECTIVES

Describe the nature of interest and distinguish between simple and compound interest. (p. E-2)   **LO1**

- Interest is payment for the use of money over time.
- Simple interest is computed only on the principal.
- Compound interest is computed on the accumulated principal including any earned interest that has not been paid.

Calculate future values. (p. E-3)   **LO2**

- The future value of a single amount is the amount that a specified investment will be worth at a future date if invested at a given rate of compound interest.
- The formula for calculating the future value of a single amount is $FV = PV \times (1 + i)^n$.
- Future value tables provide a multiplier for many combinations of time periods and interest rates that, when applied to the dollar amount of a present value, determines its future value.
- An annuity represents a special case of a pattern of cash flows where the cash flow amounts are of equal amounts and equally spaced over time.
- A separate table is available that provides a multiplier for the future value of an annuity rather than using separate multipliers from the future value of $1 table.

Calculate present values. (p. E-7)   **LO3**

- The right to receive an amount of money now—its present value—is normally worth more than the right to receive the same amount later—its future value.
- The formula for calculating the present value of a single amount is $PV = FV \times [1 \div (1 + i)^n]$.
- A separate table is available that provides a multiplier for the present value of an annuity rather than using separate multipliers from the present value of $1 table.

KEY TERMS

Annuity (p. E-5)	Interest (p. E-2)	Principal (p. E-2)
Compound interest (p. E-2)	Ordinary annuity (p. E-5)	Simple interest (p. E-2)
Future value (p. E-3)	Present value (p. E-7)	Time value (p. E-2)

Assignments with the 🌐 logo in the margin are available in **BusinessCourse**.
See the Preface of the book for details.

SELF-STUDY QUESTIONS

(Answers to Self-Study Questions are at the end of this appendix.)

1. **Calculate the future value of each of the following items.**   **LO2**
   a. $10,000 deposited in a savings account for ten years if the annual interest rate is
      1. Twelve percent compounded annually.
      2. Twelve percent compounded semiannually.
      3. Twelve percent compounded quarterly.
   b. $4,000 received at the end of each year for the next 10 years if the money earns interest at the rate of 4 percent compounded annually.
   c. $2,000 received semiannually for the next five years if the money earns interest at the rate of 8 percent compounded semiannually.
   d. $3,000 deposited each year for the next 10 years plus a single sum of $17,000 deposited today if the interest rate is 10 percent per year compounded annually.

2. **Calculate the present value of each of the following items.**   **LO3**
   a. $75,000 10 years hence if the annual interest rate is
      1. Eight percent compounded annually.
      2. Eight percent compounded semiannually.
      3. Eight percent compounded quarterly.
   b. $2,000 received at the end of each year for the next eight years if money is worth 10 percent per year compounded annually.

    c. $500 received at the end of each six months for the next 15 years if the interest rate is 8 percent per year compounded semiannually.

    d. $200,000 inheritance 10 years hence if money is worth 10 percent per year compounded annually.

    e. $3,000 received each half year for the next 10 years plus a single sum of $60,000 at the end of 10 years if the interest rate is 12 percent per year compounded semiannually.

EXERCISES—SET A

LO1   **EE-1A.** **Simple and Compound Interest**

    a. For each of the following notes, calculate the simple interest due at the end of the term.

Note	Principal	Rate	Term
1	$20,000	2%	6 years
2	$20,000	4%	4 years
3	$20,000	6%	3 years

    b. Compute the amount of interest due at the end of the term for each of the above notes assuming interest is compounded annually.

LO2   **EE-2A.** **Future Value Computation** At the beginning of the year you deposit $5,000 in a savings account. How much will accumulate in three years if you earn 8 percent compounded annually?

LO2   **EE-3A.** **Future Value Computation** You deposit $5,000 at the end of every year for three years. How much will accumulate in three years if you earn 8 percent compounded annually?

LO3   **EE-4A.** **Present Value Computation** You will receive $5,000 in three years. What is the present value if you can earn 8 percent interest compounded annually?

LO3   **EE-5A.** **Present Value Computation** You receive $5,000 at the end of every year for three years. What is the present value of these receipts if you earn 8 percent compounded annually?

LO2   **EE-6A.** **Future Value Computation** What amount will be accumulated in four years if $10,000 is invested today at 6 percent interest compounded annually?

LO3   **EE-7A.** **Present Value Computation** You are scheduled to be paid $10,000 in four years. What amount today is equivalent to the $10,000 to be received in four years assuming interest is compounded annually at 6 percent?

LO2   **EE-8A.** **Future Value Computation** What amount will be accumulated in four years if $10,000 is invested every six months beginning in six months and ending four years from today? Interest will accumulate at an annual rate of 10 percent compounded semiannually.

LO2   **EE-9A.** **Future Value Computation** You are scheduled to receive $10,000 every six months for eight periods beginning in six months. What amount in four years is equivalent to the future series of payments assuming interest compounds at the annual rate of 8 percent compounded semiannually?

LO3   **EE-10A.** **Present Value Computation** Savanna, Inc., believes it will need $150,000 in five years to expand its operations. Savanna can earn 5 percent, compounded annually, if it deposits its money right now. How large of a deposit must Savanna make in order to have the necessary $150,000 in five years?

LO2   **EE-11A.** **Future Value Computation** Kate Company deposited $12,000 in the bank today, earning 8 percent interest. Kate plans to withdraw the money in five years. How much money will be available to withdraw assuming that interest is compounded (a) annually, (b) semiannually, and (c) quarterly?

LO2   **EE-12A.** **Future Value Computation** Stan Smith deposited $5,000 in a savings account today. The deposit will earn interest at the rate of 8 percent. How much will be available for Stan to withdraw in four years, assuming interest is compounded (a) annually, (b) semiannually, and (c) quarterly?

LO3   **EE-13A.** **Present Value Computation** Paul Jefferson made a deposit into his savings account three years ago, and earned interest at an annual rate of 8 percent. The deposit accumulated to $30,000. How much was initially deposited assuming that the interest was compounded (a) annually, (b) semiannually, and (c) quarterly?

EE-14A. Future Value Computation Kendal Jennings has decided to start saving for his daughter's college education by depositing $3,200 at the end of every year for 18 years. He has determined that he will be able to earn 6 percent interest compounded annually. He hopes to have at least $90,000 when his daughter starts college in 18 years. Will his savings plan be successful? **LO2**

EE-15A. Present Value Computation Kershaw Bales won the state lottery and was given four choices for receiving her winnings. **LO3**

1. Receive $500,000 right now.
2. Receive $540,000 in one year.
3. Receive $50,000 at the end of each year for 20 years.
4. Receive $45,000 at the end of each year for 30 years.

Assuming Kershaw can earn interest of 8 percent compounded annually, which option should Kershaw choose?

EXERCISES—SET B

EE-1B. Simple and Compound Interest **LO1**

a. For each of the following notes, calculate the simple interest due at the end of the term.

Note	Principal	Rate	Term
1	$6,000	8%	8 years
2	$6,000	12%	5 years
3	$6,000	4%	2 years

b. Compute the amount of interest due at the end of the term for each of the above notes assuming interest is compounded annually.

EE-2B. Future Value Computation At the beginning of the year you deposit $1,500 in a savings account. How much will accumulate in four years if you earn 6 percent compounded annually? **LO2**

EE-3B. Future Value Computation You deposit $1,500 at the end of every year for four years. How much will accumulate in four years if you earn 6 percent compounded annually? **LO2**

EE-4B. Present Value Computation You will receive $1,500 in four years. What is the present value if you can earn 6 percent interest compounded annually? **LO3**

EE-5B. Present Value Computation You receive $1,500 at the end of every year for four years. What is the present value of these receipts if you earn 6 percent compounded annually? **LO3**

EE-6B. Future Value Computation What amount will be accumulated in six years if $5,000 is invested today at 4 percent interest compounded annually? **LO2**

EE-7B. Present Value Computation You are scheduled to be paid $5,000 in 10 years. What amount today is equivalent to the $5,000 to be received in 10 years assuming interest is compounded annually at 6 percent? **LO3**

EE-8B. Future Value Computation What amount will be accumulated in five years if $4,000 is invested every six months beginning in six months and ending five years from today? Interest will accumulate at an annual rate of 4 percent compounded semiannually. **LO2**

EE-9B. Future Value Computation You are scheduled to receive $5,000 every six months for 12 periods beginning in six months. What amount in six years is equivalent to the future series of payments assuming interest compounds at the annual rate of 8 percent compounded semiannually? **LO2**

EE-10B. Present Value Computation Mimi, Inc., believes it will need $150,000 in 10 years to expand its operations. Mimi can earn 8 percent, compounded annually, if it deposits its money right now. How large of a deposit must Mimi make in order to have the necessary $150,000 in 10 years? **LO3**

EE-11B. Future Value Computation Zeus Company deposited $10,250 in the bank today, earning 8 percent interest. Zeus plans to withdraw the money in five years. How much money will be available to withdraw assuming that interest is compounded (a) annually, (b) semiannually, and (c) quarterly? **LO2**

LO2   **EE-12B. Future Value Computation** Jason Smithton deposited $2,500 in a savings account today. The deposit will earn interest at the rate of 12 percent. How much will be available for Jason to withdraw in three years, assuming interest is compounded (a) annually, (b) semiannually, and (c) quarterly?

LO3   **EE-13B. Present Value Computation** Rose Gomez made a deposit into her savings account four years ago and earned interest at an annual rate of 12 percent. The deposit accumulated to $60,000. How much was initially deposited assuming that the interest was compounded (a) annually, (b) semiannually, and (c) quarterly?

LO2   **EE-14B. Future Value Computation** Herman Lett has decided to start saving for his daughter's college education by depositing $3,000 at the end of every year for 15 years. He has determined that he will be able to earn 6 percent interest compounded annually. He hopes to have at least $65,000 when his daughter starts college in 15 years. Will his savings plan be successful?

LO3   **EE-15B. Present Value Computation** Kelly Fullerton won the state lottery and was given four choices for receiving her winnings.

1. Receive $800,000 right now.
2. Receive $832,000 in one year.
3. Receive $120,000 at the end of each year for eight years.
4. Receive $46,400 at the end of each year for 30 years.

Assuming Kelly can earn interest of 4 percent compounded annually, which option should Kelly choose?

ANSWERS TO SELF-STUDY QUESTIONS:

1. *a.* 1. $10,000 × 3.10585 = $31,059
         2. $10,000 × 3.20714 = $32,071
         3. $10,000 × 3.26204 = $32,620

   b. $ 4,000 × 12.00611 = $48,024

   c. $ 2,000 × 12.00611 = $24,012

   d. $ 3,000 × 15.93742 = $47,812
            $17,000 × 2.59374 = $44,094
                                 $91,906

2. *a.* 1. $ 75,000 × 0.46319 = $34,739
         2. $ 75,000 × 0.45639 = $34,229
         3. $ 75,000 × 0.45289 = $33,967

   b. $ 2,000 × 5.33493 = $10,670

   c. $ 500 × 17.29203 = $ 8,646

   d. $200,000 × 0.38554 = $77,108

   e. $ 3,000 × 11.46992 = $34,410
            $ 60,000 × 0.31180 = $18,708
                                  $53,118

YOUR TURN! SOLUTIONS

Solution E-1

(1)

Year	Calculation	Interest
1	$100 × 0.10 =	$10.00
2	$100 × 0.10 =	$10.00
3	$100 × 0.10 =	$10.00
Total		$30.00

(2)

Year	Calculation	Interest
1	$100 × 0.10 =	$10.00
2	$110 × 0.10 =	$11.00
3	$121 × 0.10 =	$12.10
Total		$33.10

Solution E-2
$5,000 × 1.36049 = $6,802.45

Solution E-3
$100 × 19.61475 = $1,961.48

Solution E-4
$2,500 × 0.81630 = $2,040.75

Solution E-5
$10,000 × 3.46511 = $34,651.10

Appendix F
Data Analytics and Blockchain Technology

Road Map

Learning Objectives		Page	eLecture	Assignments
1	Define big data and describe its four attributes.	F-2	E-1	QF1, EF7, EF8, EF9, EF10, PF15, PF32, PF33, PF34
2	Identify and define the four types of data analytics.	F-3	E-1	QF2, EF7, EF8, EF9, EF10, PF15, PF23, PF24, PF25, PF32, PF33, PF34, PF39, PF40, PF41
3	Describe the use of data analytics within the accounting profession.	F-3	E-2	PF15, PF16, PF17, PF18, PF19, PF20, PF21, PF22, PF23, PF24, PF25, PF26, PF27, PF28, PF29, PF30, PF31, PF35, PF36, PF37, PF38, PF39, PF40, PF41
4	Describe the analytics mindset.	F-5	E-3	QF3, PF16, PF17, PF18, PF19, PF20, PF21, PF22, PF23, PF24, PF25, PF26, PF27, PF28, PF29, PF30, PF31, PF35, PF36, PF37, PF38, PF39, PF41
5	Describe data visualization best practices.	F-7	E-4	QF4, QF5
6	Describe how blockchain technology works and its use within the accounting profession.	F-11	E-5	QF6, EF11, EF12, EF13, EF14

DATA ANALYTICS

Data analytics can broadly be defined as the process of examining sets of data with the goal of discovering useful information from patterns found in the data. Increasingly, this process is aided by computers running programs ranging from basic spreadsheet software, such as **Microsoft Excel** and **Google Sheets**, to specialized software, such as **Tableau** or **Power BI**. This technology can reveal trends and insights that would otherwise be lost in the overwhelming amount of data.

LO1   Define big data and describe its four attributes.

eLecture

MBC

Big Data

The concept of data analytics is intertwined with the concept of **big data**. Although no precise definition exists for big data, a commonly accepted definition is that big data is a collection of data that is both extremely large and also extremely complex, thus making its analysis beyond the scope of traditional tools. Important attributes of big data, commonly referred to as the four V's, are Volume, Variety, Velocity, and Veracity. **Volume** refers to the amount of data. According to IDC (a market intelligence company), there were 33 available zettabytes of data globally in 2018. IDC predicted that the amount of data would increase to 175 zettabytes by 2025. (Just so you know, there are 21 zeros in one zettabyte.) Total amounts of data are growing because we are creating more data (through new technologies) and because we are able to store more data (using cloud storage services like Amazon Web Services [AWS] and Microsoft Azure). Massive datasets can't be managed on a single machine. They must be stored in clusters over multiple physical or virtual machines.

Variety refers to the source of data. Data can be structured, semi-structured, or unstructured. Structured data can be contained in rows and columns and stored in spreadsheets or relational databases. Although most accounting data is structured, it is estimated that less than 20 percent of all data is structured.

Unstructured data cannot be easily contained in rows and columns and is, therefore, difficult to search and analyze. Photos, video and audio files, and social media content are examples of unstructured data.

Semi-structured data has characteristics of both structured and unstructured data. It may include some defining details but doesn't completely conform to a rigid structure. For example, the words in an email are unstructured data. The email date and the addresses of the sender and the recipient are structured data. Artificial intelligence algorithms are used to process unstructured and semi-structured data in a way that makes the information useable.

Velocity refers to the speed at which the data is being produced. The amount of data is not only growing; it's growing exponentially as more people gain internet access, and more technology is created that connects humans to machines and machines to machines. Collecting and translating data (especially unstructured data) into usable information is complicated by how quickly new data is generated.

Veracity refers to the quality of the data. Data quality can be negatively affected by untrustworthy data sources, inconsistent or missing data, statistical biases, and human error. The veracity of unstructured data is especially difficult to determine. Machine learning, a type of artificial intelligence based on the idea that systems can learn from data and can identify patterns, is often used to assess data quality.

In summary, a set of data would be considered "big data" if:

- The dataset is too large to be managed by traditional methods.
- The dataset includes a variety of types of data (structured, semi-structured, and unstructured).
- The amount of data in the dataset is expanding rapidly.
- The accuracy and reliability of the data may be uncertain.

Types of Data Analytics

LO2 Identify and define the four types of data analytics.

eLecture
MBC

Data analytics can be categorized into four main types, ranging in sophistication from relatively straightforward to very complex. The first category is **descriptive analytics**, which describes what has happened over a given period of time. Simple examples include determining sales trends over a period of time and the relative effectiveness of various social media promotions based on click-through rates. Microsoft Excel and other spreadsheet programs include built-in functions that greatly simplify performing descriptive analytics.

Diagnostic analytics focuses more on why something occurred. This data analytics technique is used to monitor changes in data and often includes a certain amount of hypothesizing: Did the marketing campaign lead to the increase in sales? Did changing the beverage items affect food choices? Did the opening of competing restaurants negatively impact sales growth? Diagnostic analytics is useful because past performance is often a reliable predictor of future outcomes and can greatly aid in planning and forecasting.

Whereas descriptive and diagnostic analytics use data to try to understand what happened and why, **predictive analytics** uses data to try to determine what *will* happen. The movie *Moneyball* made the general manager of the **Oakland Athletics**, Billy Beane, famous for using predictive analytics to make personnel decisions in professional baseball. In his evaluation of baseball players, Beane used data to predict player performance so he could assemble the team with the greatest likelihood of winning the World Series. Banks also use predictive analytics to identify and prevent fraudulent transactions by monitoring customer credit card transactions and red flagging those that deviate from a customer behavior profile that was developed from previous transaction and geographic data.

Prescriptive analytics moves beyond what is going to happen to suggesting a course of action for what *should* happen to optimize outcomes. The forecasts created using predictive analytics can be used to make recommendations for future courses of action. For example, if we own a sports bar and determine there is a high likelihood of our local sports team winning the championship this year, we should expand the bar area and add more big-screen televisions to maximize revenues. **Exhibit F-1** summarizes the four types of data analytics.

EXHIBIT F-1	The Four Types of Data Analytics	
Type of Data Analytics	**Purpose**	**Example**
Descriptive	To explain what happened	What were sales by month last year?
Diagnostic	To understand why it happened	Did the new advertising campaign cause sales to increase last quarter?
Predictive	To predict what will happen	Does this credit card charge deviate (amount, location, etc.) from past purchases by this credit card holder?
Prescriptive	To determine what should happen	How many servers should be on the schedule for game nights?

Data Analytics in the Accounting Profession

LO3 Describe the use of data analytics within the accounting profession.

eLecture
MBC

Accountants are already preparing descriptive analytic reports regularly. Comparative income statements, sales reports by location, inventory valuation reports, and ratio calculations (average collection periods, days' sales in inventory, etc.) are all examples of descriptive analytics.

Budget variance reports and segment reports by region or product line prepared by accountants can be used for diagnostic analytics. Accountants may also work with sales and production managers to analyze the reasons behind changes in operating results. A distributor might want to know how much of the increase in overall sales last year was caused by the transfer of two of its representatives to other sales regions. A grocery store manager might want to know if the winter storm last month impacted sales in all or just some of the various departments. A production manager might work with the accounting department to determine any correlation between equipment repair costs and the number of units produced over the last two years.

Data analytics should not be limited to only descriptive and diagnostic analysis. Accountants can provide even more value by employing predictive and prescriptive analytics. Accountants can obtain data from a variety of company sources, including enterprise resource planning systems, customer relationship management systems, and point-of-sale systems, to aid them in obtaining insight into future outcomes and providing guidance for future actions. The area of credit granting provides an example. Predictive analytics can help compute credit scores to predict the likelihood of future payments. As a result, prescriptive analytics can aid in suggesting terms for granting credit. Predictive analytics can also be used to help analyze outstanding accounts receivables and determine estimated credit losses based on how much time has elapsed since the credit sale took place.

Many other opportunities exist for accountants to utilize data analytics. Tax accountants can apply data analysis to unique tax issues to suggest optimal tax strategies. Accountants serving as investment advisors can use big data to find patterns in consumer behavior that others can use to build analytic models for identifying investment opportunities.

Perhaps no area of accounting can benefit more from an understanding of data analytics than auditing. Auditors employ data analytics to shift from the sample-based audit model to one based on continuous modeling of much larger datasets. This allows auditors to identify the riskiest areas of an audit by focusing on outliers and exceptions.

The major accounting firms have fully embraced the power of data analytics. **PricewaterhouseCoopers** (PWC), **Deloitte**, **Ernst & Young** (EY), and **KPMG** all devote significant staffing resources to provide data analytics services to their clients. These firms claim they can help their clients optimize their data assets to aid in faster and better decisions. For example, PWC provides a flowchart starting with the building of a data foundation and applies advanced analytics to improving business performance, ultimately leading to opportunities for innovation.

While computers and software are instrumental in the entire process, the human element is the most critical factor in the success of any data analytics program. One commonality among surveys of top company managers is the value placed on data analytics for the company's future. Another commonality is the need for professionals trained in data analytics to help the company attain its goals.

DATA ANALYTICS IN ACCOUNTING

Benford's Law provides an example of how data analytics has been used to uncover fraud in a national call center. Forensic accountants utilized their knowledge of Benford's Law to form evidence of a problem by observing patterns in the data. According to Benford's Law, in any list of financial transactions, the number one should occur as the first digit 30.1 percent of the time, with each successive number occurring as the first digit in lesser percentages, with the number nine occurring less than 5 percent of the time. Forensic accountants examined issued refunds and noticed an excessively high occurrence of the number four. The forensic accountants learned that the company had a policy that required supervisor approval of refunds that exceeded $50. The accountants were able to identify a small group of operators who had been issuing fraudulent refunds to family, friends, and themselves. These fraudulent $40 refunds totaled several hundred thousand dollars.

Data Analytics

In order to be useful, data needs to be analyzed. Technology has provided the analyst with powerful tools that allow big data to provide insights that would not have been possible in the past. Still, the most important tool in the analytics toolkit comes from the analyst. Without critical thinking and good judgment, the value would remain locked within the data.

The Analytics Mindset[1]

LO4 Describe the analytics mindset.

eLecture

MBC

The analytics mindset consists of a four-step process of (1) asking the right questions; (2) extracting, transforming, and loading the necessary data; (3) applying appropriate data analytics techniques; and (4) interpreting and presenting the results. **Exhibit F-2** summarizes the steps and requirements of an analytics mindset.

EXHIBIT F-2   Steps of an Analytics Mindset

Steps in the Analytics Mindset	Requirements
Ask the right questions	Understand the objectives of the end user Understand the underlying business processes
Extract, transform, and load the data	Know what to ask for Manage the data security Transform the data into the required format Cleanse the data for completeness and accuracy
Apply the appropriate analytics techniques	Determine whether the need is for a confirmatory or an exploratory approach
Interpret and present the results	Use appropriate critical judgment regarding what you see Visually display the results in a format that is easy to understand without unnecessary clutter

Note that while technology is imbedded in this process, the process still begins and ends with the human element of asking the right questions and interpreting the results. Nothing is more critical than the first step of knowing what to ask. The right questions guide the process to find the right data to analyze and interpret.

Asking the right questions requires a few prerequisites. First, you need to know the audience that the analysis is for and what their objectives are. Next, you need to understand the context underlying the problem. For example, to analyze a marketing question you should understand the industry characteristics and the consumer demographics. Without this knowledge, you may not select the correct indicators to analyze.

Along with knowing the right questions to ask, an analytical mindset requires you to form an idea of what to expect from the data. For example, when analyzing inventory salability, you would expect to see certain associated movements in sales and receivables.

After your questions are formed, you need to determine the data needed to aid in finding answers to those questions. This requires a knowledge of the data characteristics of the four V's previously mentioned. With this knowledge you can begin the data extraction process. Here you will need to know what data to ask for, how to manage data security, and what form the data will take.

Once you have the data, you will need to transform it into a format suitable for analysis. This is often referred to as data cleaning. Data is rarely found in the form of a nicely organized Excel spreadsheet. Rather, the data will often need to be converted into a proper format and tested for completeness and accuracy. Further, unnecessary data should be removed from the dataset.

The data should then be loaded into the proper analysis tool, such as **Tableau** or Microsoft's **Power BI**. Once loaded, the data should again be cleansed to be sure it is ready for analysis in the chosen software.

It is necessary to determine the appropriate technique to analyze the data within the analysis tool. There are a multitude of ways that the data can be analyzed. Possible choices include computing ratios between associated measures, identifying trends among various measures,

---

[1] The analytics mindset discussed here is an approach developed by the Ernst & Young Foundation.

creating comparisons between dates, and sorting measures. The proper technique to use will be guided by the questions being asked.

In your interpretation of the data, you should ask yourself what do you see and is this what you expected? In other words, do these results make sense or did the results create new questions that require further analysis?

Eventually, the results must be packaged into a presentation that can be shared with the intended audience. Software such as Tableau, Power BI, or Excel can greatly enhance these presentations through their ability to create **visualizations** and **dashboards**. These visualizations can take many forms, from simple tables to bar or pie charts, to more sophisticated scatter plots, map charts, heat maps, and more. Dashboards are created by combining multiple visualizations. Interactive dashboards allow users to filter out or drill down on content included in the charts and tables, on demand.

Data Analytic Tools

Technologies used by organizations to analyze data and communicate information to users are known as Business Intelligence (BI) tools. Data warehousing (data storage), data mining (extracting usable insights from data), and reporting and querying software are all BI tools.

Excel and Tableau are two popular BI tools that you will be using in the exercises and problems at the end of this Appendix.

Although Excel and Tableau can be used in similar ways, there are some important differences. Excel is a software application that is used for creating, organizing, and analyzing data. Tableau is a data visualization tool. Although calculations can be performed in Tableau, those calculations are made to create new fields for use in visualizations, not as support for accounting transactions. For example, Excel might be used to calculate sales commission amounts, which are then inputted into the accounting system. Tableau would not be used for that purpose.

Users in both Excel[2] and Tableau can

- Connect with different data sources
- Create visualizations and dashboards
- Work with big datasets

Tableau has much stronger interactivity tools and a more comprehensive selection of chart options. Excel generally has more flexibility and more extensive analytics tools.[3]

Python and **R** are popular programming languages that are used for data analysis, particularly when working with big datasets. Although these are programming languages and not application software (Business Intelligence tools), they are relatively easy to code compared to other languages and can be used to write software programs that perform powerful data analyses and visualizations.

ACCESSING EXCEL AND TABLEAU

Excel, if not available to you through your school, can be accessed for free by creating a Microsoft account at https://office.live.com/start/Excel.aspx. A free version of Tableau (Tableau Public) is available to you at https://public.tableau.com/en-us/s/. Tableau Public has most of the functions of Tableau Desktop (the full version). However, you can't save your workbooks locally if you're using Tableau Public. Instead, all workbooks are saved online and are accessible to any Tableau user unless you elect to hide your visualizations. Hiding visualizations is done in Settings after you've registered for Tableau on the Tableau website. Walkthrough videos are available for every exercise and problem at cambridgepub.com. Tableau tutorial videos are available at https://www.tableau.com/learn/training/.

---

[2] Full functionality in Excel is only available if you have Excel 2010 or newer and you are running a 64-bit version of Windows. To determine the version of Windows on your computer, go to Settings>System>About. The version will be listed in the Device specifications section.

[3] Pan and Blankley, Excel vs. Tableau: See your data differently, *Journal of Accountancy*, February 29, 2020.

Data Visualization

LO5 Describe data visualization best practices.

As noted previously, the final step in the analytics mindset is to present your results. This is often done in the form of a visualization. While it is possible to present results as a bunch of tables full of numbers, visualizations with imagery are often a far better means to convey the raw numbers. Visualizations can be thought of as a blending of the art of design with the science of data.

There is an unlimited number of ways that data can be presented; however, certain best practices exist that can serve as a guide when building a visualization. For example, the exact same data on GDP levels are shown in the three charts in **Exhibit F-3**, but each displays the data differently. The table presents the raw data; however, the reader cannot easily rank the different economies. The two bar charts both show the same data; however, the one all in blue makes it far easier to compare economies by showing the data in sorted order. Also, note that adding multiple colors to the other bar chart does nothing to aid the reader; rather it just adds confusion.

Visualizations can be divided into two primary categories, exploratory and explanatory. **Exploratory visualizations** are meant to allow the reader to explore the data presented in order to do additional analysis. Exploratory visualizations would normally include interactive tools like filters that allow the user to change the level of data displayed. This can be useful when the problem is not clearly defined, and the reader wishes to gain a further understanding of the data.

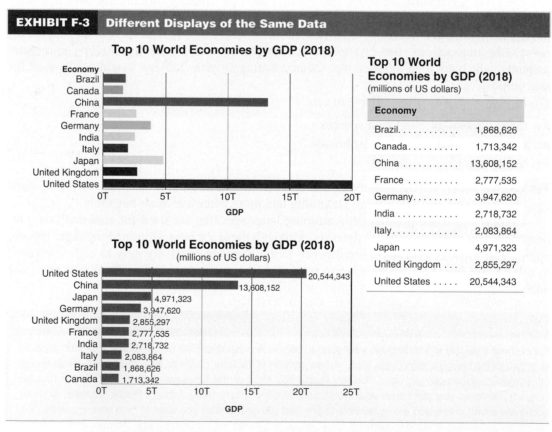

EXHIBIT F-3   Different Displays of the Same Data

Top 10 World Economies by GDP (2018)
(millions of US dollars)

Economy	
Brazil.	1,868,626
Canada.	1,713,342
China	13,608,152
France	2,777,535
Germany.	3,947,620
India	2,718,732
Italy.	2,083,864
Japan	4,971,323
United Kingdom . . .	2,855,297
United States	20,544,343

In contrast to exploratory visualizations, **explanatory visualizations** are used to convey information to the audience. A classic example of such a visualization was prepared in 1854 by the British physician Dr. John Snow. Dr. Snow plotted cholera deaths in central London on a map that also showed the location of water pumps. The visualization identified the relationship between these deaths and the Broad Street water pump and led to a change in the water and waste systems. Dr. Snow's visualization is shown in **Exhibit F-4**.

EXHIBIT F-4   Cholera Deaths in London in 1854

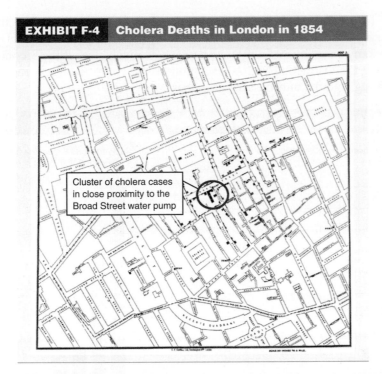

Cluster of cholera cases in close proximity to the Broad Street water pump

Good visualization design can be enhanced by considering how our brains process visual details such as form, position, and color.

For example, items that are different from the rest become the focus of attention as shown in **Exhibit F-5**. An item that is longer, wider, or in a different orientation will stand out, as will an item that is of a different size, shape, in a different position, or has a different hue or intensity of color.

EXHIBIT F-5   Displays That Emphasize How Differences Focus Our Attention

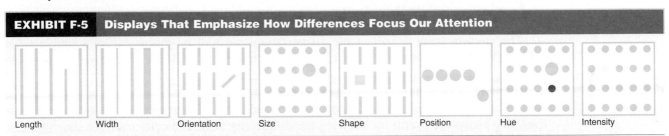

| Length | Width | Orientation | Size | Shape | Position | Hue | Intensity |

While the use of color can help an item to stand out, it is important to use color correctly. The use of too much color can add to visual clutter. And it's important that color is used consistently, such as always representing a certain year or category. The choice of color is also important since color can convey meanings that differ from one culture to another. For example, red may mean good luck, and green may mean jealousy.

Good visualization design requires the removal of items that detract from the message that we are trying to communicate. **Visual clutter** confuses the audience and lessens the chance that they will be able to easily understand the information that is being conveyed. The concept that less is more is the essence of the visualization design principles developed by Edward Tufte, a statistician and professor emeritus at Yale University. Tufte uses the term *chart-junk* to refer to any unnecessary or confusing elements included in information displays. His principles show that "excellence in statistical graphics consists of ideas communicated with clarity, precision and efficiency."[4]

---

[4] E.R. Tufte, *The Visual Display of Quantitative Information* (Graphics Press, Cheshire, CT, 2001).

Exhibit F-6 illustrates **Tufte's principles**. Note in the first visualization all of the visual clutter only serves to distract the audience from seeing the main point that the United States is the largest economy based on its GDP. Now notice how much cleaner the second visualization is after removing the distracting yellow background, the color coding of each economy, the redundant labeling, and the unnecessary grid lines.

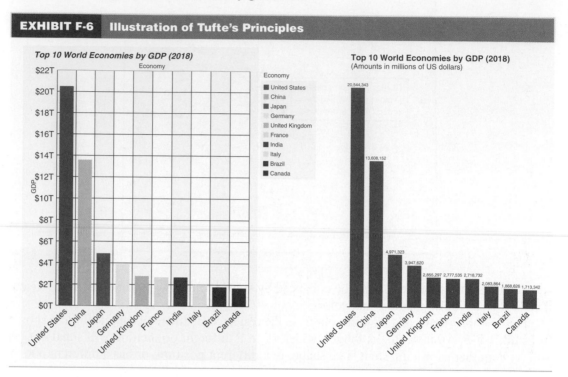

EXHIBIT F-6   Illustration of Tufte's Principles

Good visualization construction also involves choosing the most effective chart type depending on what information is being presented.

The starting point for all of the visualizations we will be discussing is a simple table of data. While the table is excellent for looking up values and can precisely communicate numerical values, visualizations in the form of charts provide the audience an easier method to see what the analyst is attempting to convey.

Among the most used chart types, column and bar charts are best for showing comparisons, line charts are useful for showing trends, pie charts are typically used for showing how individual parts make up a whole, and scatter plots are best for showing relationships and distributions. **Exhibit F-7**, reprinted with permission from the author, provides an excellent tool to help in choosing the correct chart type.[5]

Column (vertical) charts and **bar** (horizontal) charts are best used to compare different categories. Adding labels to the bars rather than just having values showing on the axes makes it easier for the audience to determine these values. Finally, avoid using too many colors that just add to visual clutter.

As a general rule, **line charts** are best for illustrating changes over time and work best with continuous data. Best practices include clearly labeling the axes so the audience knows what is being shown, removing excess clutter such as grid lines and redundant labeling, and avoiding comparing more than five to seven lines.

Pie charts are best used to show parts of a whole. Be sure the parts add up to 100 percent. Pie charts work best when there are just a few categories. If there are many categories of similar size, consider using a bar or column chart instead. Finally, avoid the temptation to get "fancy" with 3-D imagery and tilting the pie chart.

---

[5] Andrew V. Abela, Advanced Presentations by *Design: Creating Communication that Drives Action* (John Wiley & Sons, 2013).

EXHIBIT F-7   **Chart Types**

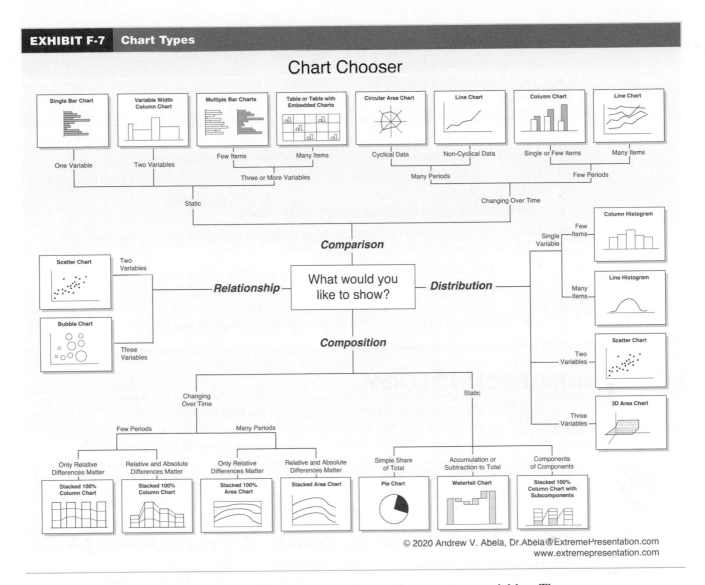

Chart Chooser

© 2020 Andrew V. Abela, Dr.Abela@ExtremePresentation.com
www.extremepresentation.com

Scatter plots are useful if the goal is to show correlations between two variables. They are also useful for showing data distributions and clustering, which can identify anomalies and outliers. A **bubble chart** can extend the capability of a scatter plot by adding an additional dimension through changing the size of each bubble in the scatter plot. The more data that is included in a scatter plot or bubble chart, the better are the comparisons that can be made. If the elements being graphed are distributed over a very wide range, the horizontal axis can be converted from a linear to a logarithmic scale (where the numbers on the horizontal axis increase by multiples of a number). Bubble charts should use only circles rather than other shapes. Bubble charts should be scaled based on the area of the circle and not the diameter.

A **map chart** is a good choice if the data being conveyed in the visualization includes geographic locations. Map charts are best at showing relative differences in numerical values among geographic locations rather than precise differences since the values are usually portrayed as differences in a color gradient.

There are several general rules to follow regardless of the chart type. The following list was found from a search of best practices for data visualization charts.[6]

■   Time axis. When using time in charts, set it on the horizontal axis. Time should run from left to right. Do not skip values (time periods), even if there are no values.

---

[6] https://eazybi.com/blog/data_visualization_and_chart_types/

- Proportional values. The numbers in a chart (displayed as bar, area, bubble, or other physically measured element in the chart) should be directly proportional to the numerical quantities presented.

- Visual clutter. Remove any excess information, lines, colors, and text from a chart that do not add value.

- Sorting. For column and bar charts, to enable easier comparison, sort your data in ascending or descending order by the value, not alphabetically. This applies also to pie charts.

- Legend. You don't need a legend if you have only one data category.

- Labels. Use labels directly on the line, column, bar, pie, etc., whenever possible, to avoid indirect look-up.

- Colors. In any chart, don't use more than six colors.

- Colors. For comparing the same value at different time periods, use the same color in a different intensity (from light to dark).

- Colors. For different categories, use different colors. The most widely used colors are black, white, red, green, blue, and yellow.

- Colors. Keep the same color palette or style for all charts in the series and the same axes and labels for similar charts to make your charts consistent and easy to compare.

BLOCKCHAIN TECHNOLOGY

LO6 Describe how blockchain technology works and its use within the accounting profession.

eLecture

MBC

Blockchain technology differs from the traditional accounting ledger in a fundamental way that has immense implications for the accounting profession. A traditional ledger system is a closed system controlled at a centralized location with individuals at the centralized location responsible for the maintenance and integrity of the ledger. In contrast, a blockchain is an open, decentralized ledger, where the ledger is distributed across multiple computers called **nodes**. The blockchain ledger is managed autonomously by the distributed nodes such that data is authenticated by mass collaboration rather than by a central authority. Each node on the blockchain maintains a complete copy of all past transactions that have been added to the ledger. Thus, by comparing to the other nodes' copies, the ledger is continuously synchronized. Unlike traditional accounting ledgers, none of the nodes has any special rights that differ from those of the other nodes.

Blockchains get their name because new ledger data are periodically bundled into blocks, which are then added to previous blocks to form a chain. Each block can contain a cryptocurrency exchange, as is the case with **Bitcoin**, but other possibilities include sales transactions, equity trades, loan payments, election votes—pretty much any contract transaction. In addition, the block contains a **time stamp** and a **hash #**, which together form a cryptographic signature associated with the previous blocks. This time stamp and hash make the blockchain essentially tamper-proof because the blocks cannot be changed without the change being apparent to all other nodes. While the chain propagates in only a single chronological order, it can be audited in both directions. **Exhibit F-8** is a visual depiction of the blockchain process.

The accounting profession has seen changes arising from a vast array of technological innovations, from computer spreadsheets to general ledger software to enterprise resource systems. Blockchain technology represents another innovation in the way accounting is and will be performed. The invention of double-entry accounting, the bedrock of financial accounting, allowed managers to trust their own financial recordkeeping. Unfortunately, the same level of trust does not exist with outsiders, which is why companies rely on independent auditors for an opinion on the integrity of an entity's financial statements. These audits are often very time consuming and costly.

Accountants working in the traditional centralized-ledger environment are likely to spend a large amount of time reconciling accounts and amounts. This involves comparing balances

EXHIBIT F.8   **Blockchain Process**

How a Blockchain Works

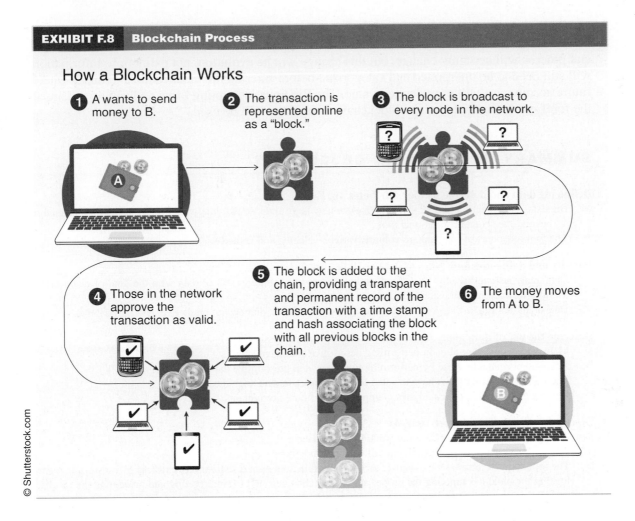

① A wants to send money to B.

② The transaction is represented online as a "block."

③ The block is broadcast to every node in the network.

④ Those in the network approve the transaction as valid.

⑤ The block is added to the chain, providing a transparent and permanent record of the transaction with a time stamp and hash associating the block with all previous blocks in the chain.

⑥ The money moves from A to B.

at their company with external documents from outside entities, including banks, brokerages, and business partners, among others. In addition to the time-consuming process of acquiring all the needed sources of information and performing the comparisons, additional time and effort are often needed to reconcile any differences. In a blockchain's distributed ledger system, all node participants can continually confirm all transactions, greatly reducing the effort involved in periodic reconciliations.

Accountants working in the traditional environment are expected to produce internal, ad hoc reports. This often requires considerable effort reconciling internal documents, perhaps from multiple departments or divisions. In a blockchain environment, accountants spend far less time verifying transactional data, freeing up time for more valuable advisory activities.

As a final example of the many ways blockchain technology will change the way accountants work, consider the traditional closing of the books at the end of each period. Instead of needing to acquire the necessary data, verify its accuracy, and make all the necessary adjustments, one could envision a far more automated process with the use of blockchain technology. Financial statements could be updated continuously from data provided by the blockchain, making the period-ending closing process much less time consuming.

Blockchain technology is widely viewed as the next major step in financial accounting. Instead of keeping separate records documenting each transaction, transactions can be written directly into the decentralized ledger. Thus, each transaction is distributed and cryptographically signed to ensure against later falsification or destruction. This has the potential to allow auditors to automatically verify much of the data in a traditional audit, freeing them to provide value in more important areas, such as the analysis of complex transactions or operational efficiencies.

Some accountants may worry that these evolving technologies will diminish the need for accountants. If history is any indication, the opposite is likely. The accountant's role in the financial process will certainly change, but this change will be evolution, not extinction. Information will still need to be interpreted and categorized before entering the blockchain, and this is where future accountants will provide their value. The Big Four accounting firms realize this and are at the forefront in research on how blockchain technology will be used.

SUMMARY OF LEARNING OBJECTIVES

LO1   Define big data and describe its four attributes. (p. F-2)
- Big data is a collection of data that is both extremely large and also extremely complex, thus making its analysis beyond the scope of traditional tools.
- The four attributes of big data are volume, variety, velocity, and veracity.

LO2   Identify and define the four types of data analytics. (p. F-3)
- Data analytics can broadly be defined as the process of examining sets of data with the goal of discovering useful information from patterns found in the data.
- Data analytics can be categorized into four types: descriptive, diagnostic, predictive, and prescriptive.

LO3   Describe the use of data analytics within the accounting profession. (p. F-3)
- Many accountants are already performing descriptive and diagnostic data analytics.
- Accountants can add value by performing predictive and prescriptive data analytics.
- The large accounting firms have devoted large resources to data analytics.
- Being well trained in data analytics is important for future accountants.

LO4   Describe the analytics mindset. (p. F-4)
- Analytics is the process of deriving value from the data.
- An analytics mindset requires critical thinking and judgment.
- The four steps of the analytics mindset include (1) asking the right questions; (2) extracting, transforming, and loading the data; (3) applying the proper analytics techniques; and (4) interpreting and presenting the results.

LO5   Describe data visualization best practices. (p. F-5)
- Form, position, and color can be used to have elements stand out without any conscious effort by the audience.
- Tufte's principles of design emphasize the elimination of visual clutter that serves to distract from the ability of a visualization to convey its message.
- Use of the proper chart type can help the intended audience to visualize comparisons, compositions, distributions, and relationships in the data.

LO 6   Describe how blockchain technology works and its use within the accounting profession. (p. F-11)
- A blockchain represents a decentralized ledger system and each decentralized computer on the blockchain is called a node.
- Unlike a traditional ledger system where authority for maintenance and integrity rests at a centralized location, each node on the blockchain has the same rights as each other node.
- Each block in the blockchain contains information, such as transaction details, along with a time stamp and a hash linking the block to previous blocks in a chronological order.
- Blockchains are essentially tamperproof because alteration to a block by a node would be apparent to every other node on the blockchain.
- Blockchain technology represents another innovation that will change the way accountants perform their work. Blockchain technology will fundamentally change the way audits are performed, and greatly reduce the time and effort spent on tasks, such as reconciling source documents, producing ad hoc reports, and performing period-ending book closings.

KEY CONCEPTS AND TERMS

Bar charts (p. F-9)	Blockchain technology (p. F-11)	Dashboards (p. F-6)
Benford's Law (p. F-4)	Bubble chart (p. F-10)	Data analytics (p. F-2)
Big data (p. F-2)	Column chart (p. F-9)	Descriptive analytics (p. F-3)

Diagnostic analytics (p. F-3)
Explanatory visualizations (p. F-7)
Exploratory visualizations (p. F-7)
Hash # (p. F-11)
Line charts (p. F-9)

Map chart (p. F-10)
Nodes (p. F-11)
Pie chart (p. F-9)
Predictive analytics (p. F-3)
Prescriptive analytics (p. F-3)
Scatter plots (p. F-10)
Time stamp (p. F-11)

Tufte's principles (p. F-9)
Variety (p. F-2)
Velocity (p. F-2)
Veracity (p. F-2)
Visual clutter (p. F-8)
Visualizations (p. F-6)
Volume (p. F-2)

VIDEO RESOURCES FOR TABLEAU

Many assignments require the use of Tableau. For anyone new to Tableau, the following videos are recommended. In addition to these videos, Tableau offers many more free training videos on its website under the learning tab.

A general introduction to the software. (25 minutes). https://www.tableau.com/learn/tutorials/on-demand/getting-started?playlist=484034

An introduction to the Tableau interface. (4 minutes). https://www.tableau.com/learn/tutorials/on-demand/tableau-interface?playlist=484034

Gaining an understanding of relationships in order to connect to outside data. Stop at 14 minutes and 33 seconds. https://www.tableau.com/learn/tutorials/on-demand/relationships?playlist=484036

A general introduction to visual analytics. (6 minutes). https://www.tableau.com/learn/tutorials/on-demand/getting-started-visual-analytics?playlist=484037

How to use sorting. (5 minutes). https://www.tableau.com/learn/tutorials/on-demand/sorting?playlist=484037

An introduction to filtering. (2 minutes). https://www.tableau.com/learn/tutorials/on-demand/ways-filter?playlist=484037

A deeper look at filtering. (7 minutes). https://www.tableau.com/learn/tutorials/on-demand/using-filter-shelf?playlist=484037

Using interactive filters. (4 minutes). https://www.tableau.com/learn/tutorials/on-demand/interactive-filters?playlist=484037

An introduction to formatting. (7 minutes). https://www.tableau.com/learn/tutorials/on-demand/formatting?playlist=484037

The formatting pane. (7 minutes). https://www.tableau.com/learn/tutorials/on-demand/formatting-pane?playlist=484037

An introduction to calculation in Tableau. (3 minutes). https://www.tableau.com/learn/tutorials/on-demand/getting-started-calculations?playlist=484040

Calculation syntax in Tableau. (4 minutes). https://www.tableau.com/learn/tutorials/on-demand/calculation-syntax?playlist=484040

QUESTIONS

QF-1. **Which of the following are four characteristics of big data?**   **LO 1**

    a.   Volume, variety, vagueness, veracity   *c.*   Volume, validate, velocity, veracity

    b.   Volume, variety, velocity, veracity   *d.*   Volume, variety, velocity, vulnerability

QF-2. **Which of the following are the four categories of data analytics?**   **LO 2**

    a.   Descriptive, diagnostic, predictive, prescriptive   *c.*   Descriptive, analytical, predictive, prescriptive

    b.   Expressive, diagnostic, predictive, prescriptive   *d.*   Descriptive, diagnostic, prognostic, prescriptive

LO 4 **QF-3.** **What is the correct order of the steps in the analytics mindset?**
  a. Extract, transform, and load the data; ask the right questions; apply the proper analytics techniques; interpret and present the results.
  b. Ask the right questions; extract, transform, and load the data; apply the proper analytics techniques; interpret and present the results.
  c. Ask the right questions; extract, transform, and load the data; interpret and present the results; apply the proper analytics techniques.
  d. Ask the right questions; apply the proper analytics techniques; extract, transform, and load the data; interpret and present the results.

LO 5 **QF-4.** **Charts are used in visualizations to convey the following primary types of information:**
  a. comparisons, compositions, distributions, and relationships.
  b. comparisons, historical, distributions, and relationships.
  c. comparisons, compositions, forecasts, and relationships.
  d. geographical, compositions, distributions, and relationships.

LO 5 **QF-5.** **Which of the following statements is not true regarding the use of color in a chart?**
  a. Use at most six different colors in a chart.
  b. To show changes in an item over time use a color gradient rather than different colors.
  c. Always use color in a chart to differentiate items.
  d. Use the same color palette in a chart series.

LO 6 **QF-6.** **The glue that binds blocks in a blockchain consists of what?**
  a. Time stamps
  b. Sequential numbering
  c. Regulatory approval
  d. Hashes
  e. Both *a.* and *d.*

Assignments with the ⓜ logo in the margin are available in ᵐʸBusinessCourse.
See the Preface of the book for details.

EXERCISES

LO 1, 2 **EF-7.** **Public accounting firms and data analytics.**   Go to PWC.com and select "Services" and then "Data and Analytics." Choose a topic and write about how PWC is using data analytics to help its clients.

LO 1, 2 **EF-8.** **Public accounting firms and data analytics.**   Go to KPMG.com and select "Insights." Under "Areas of interest," select "Special Attention" and then "Data and Analytics." Choose a topic and write about how KPMG is using data analytics to help its clients.

LO 1, 2 **EF-9.** **Public accounting firms and data analytics.**   Go to Deloitte.com and select "Services" and then "Analytics." Choose a topic and write about how Deloitte is using data analytics to help its clients.

LO 1, 2 **EF-10.** **Public accounting firms and data analytics.**   Go to EY.com and enter Big data and analytics in the search bar. Choose a topic and write about how Ernst & Young is using data analytics to help its clients.

LO 6 **EF-11.** **Public accounting firms and blockchain technology.**   Go to PWC.com and search for "blockchain." Choose a topic and write about how PWC is using blockchain to help its clients.

LO 6 **EF-12.** **Public accounting firms and blockchain technology.**   Go to KPMG.com and search for "blockchain." Choose a topic and write about how KPMG is using blockchain to help its clients.

LO 6 **EF-13.** **Public accounting firms and blockchain technology.**   Go to Deloitte.com and search for "blockchain." Select "Blockchain—Perspectives, insights, and analysis." Choose a topic and write about how Deloitte is using blockchain to help its clients.

LO 6 **EF-14.** **Public accounting firms and blockchain technology.**   Go to EY.com and search for "blockchain." Choose a topic and write about how Ernst & Young is using blockchain to help its clients.

PROBLEMS

Problems PF-15 through PF-16 use data on employee statistics. The data is contained in the Excel file Employee Data Tableau.xlsx and is accessible in myBusinessCourse.

LO 1, 2, 3 **PF-15.** **Using Tableau to create summary statistics.**   Go to myBusinessCourse and download the Excel file **Employee Data Tableau.xlsx**. Connect Tableau Public to this Excel file. Go to the worksheet and drag the measures "Education," "Jobcat," and "Jobtime" up to Dimensions. Compare the average salaries by gender

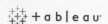

and minority status by dragging "Gender" to Rows and "Minority" to Columns and then "Salary" to the canvas. Change salary from a sum to an average.

   a.   How do average salaries compare by gender and minority status?

Next, explore how education level affects this relation by dragging "Education" to Columns. It may be easier to make this comparison by switching the order of "Minority" and "Education" on the Columns bar.

   b.   Does education level affect how average salaries compare by gender and minority status?

Next, change salary from average to maximum.

   c.   Does education level affect how maximum salaries compare by gender and minority status?

PF-16. **Using Tableau to calculate a visualization.** Starting with the results from PF-16, change salary back to average. Select the side-by-side bar chart (ninth selection) from the "show me" selections.

Based on this visualization of the data, what can you say about relative salaries for males and females and for caucasians and minorities?

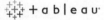

Problems PF-17 through PF-19 use data on executive compensation from S&P 500 companies for the years 2015 through 2019. The data is contained in the Excel file Compensation Data 2015_2019 SP500.xlsx that is available in myBusinessCourse.

PF-17. **Executive Compensation Visualizations with Tableau—Part I.** As a researcher in executive compensation, you desire to learn more about the compensation differences between men and women in the roles of Chief Executive Officer (CEO) and Chief Financial Officer (CFO). Data including salary and total compensation, including salary, bonus, stock option awards, and miscellaneous income, for both men and woman serving as CEOs and CFOs for S&P 500 companies for the five years 2015 through 2019 is contained in the Excel file **Compensation Data 2015_2019 SP500.xlsx**. First connect to this file with Tableau and change the Year field from a number to a date type. Next create the following visualizations:

   a.   A crosstab showing median salary by gender for the entire database. One method to accomplish this is to drag the dimension Gender to the rows shelf and then drag the measure Salary directly to the canvas. Next change the measure of Salary from Sum to Median. Do men or women have a higher median salary and by how much?

   b.   Create a crosstab that separates CEO median total compensation (Measure Comp1) by gender and Sector. Also show how many individual CEOs are shown by gender and sector. One method to accomplish this is to drag the dimension Sector Name to the columns shelf and the dimensions Position and Gender to the rows shelf. Next drag the measures Comp1 and WRDS(Count) directly to the canvas. Finally change the measure of Comp1 to median. In the consumer staples sector, how many men and how many women are CEOs, and what is their median total compensation? Note that the totals shown are combined for all five years.

   c.   Create a separate visualization in the form of a vertical bar chart that displays CEO total compensation by sector, position, and gender. Provide interactive filters for Year, Position, Gender, and Sector Name. Finally, use colors to highlight gender. Within the information technology sector, how much higher is the median compensation for male CEOs than for female CEOs in 2019? What is the name of the highest paid female CEO in this segment and where does she work? One method to accomplish this is to drag the dimensions Sector Name, Position, and Gender to the columns shelf. Next drag the measure Comp1 to the rows shelf and change the measure to Median. Drag Year, Position, Gender, and Sector Name to the filters shelf and then select Show Filter from each dimension pull-down arrow. Select CEO from the Position filter and 2018 from the Year filter. Finally drag Gender to the Color card and WRDS(Count) and Comp1 to the Label card. To see the data behind each of the bars, simply hover over the bar and right-click and then select Full Data.

   d.   Save the file for future use.

PF-18. **Executive Compensation Visualizations with Tableau—Part II.** To further your research in executive compensation, you would like to see the location by state, the level of executive compensation, and also where females hold the position of CFO.

   a.   Create a map visualization that shows the location of companies that employ female CFOs. In 2016, which state had the highest level of median compensation for a female CFO? Who was the CFO, how much was she paid, and what company did she work for? One way to accomplish this is to first create a map by holding the Control key on a Windows machine or the Command key on a Mac and select the measures Latitude and Longitude and then select the map from the Show Me menu. Next drag Total Comp 1 over the Color card and change the measure to Median. Drag the dimension State over the Detail card and the measure WRDS(Count) over the Label card. Drag Gender, Position, Sector Name, and Year to the Filter shelf and select to show these filters. Select 2016 from the Year filter, CFO from the Position filter, and Female from the Gender filter. The state of Washington should appear the darkest indicating the highest median compensation. Click on this state and then click on the View data icon in the top right corner. Select the Full Data tab.

b. Save the file for future use.

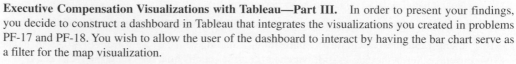

LO 3, 4   **PF-19.** **Executive Compensation Visualizations with Tableau—Part III.**   In order to present your findings, you decide to construct a dashboard in Tableau that integrates the visualizations you created in problems PF-17 and PF-18. You wish to allow the user of the dashboard to interact by having the bar chart serve as a filter for the map visualization.

a. Create a dashboard with the bar chart visualization created in problem PF-17 on the top and the map visualization created in problem PF-18 on the bottom. Make the bar chart serve as a filter for the map. What state had the most female CFOs in 2018 from the financials sector and what companies did they work for? How many male CFOs worked in the financials sector in 2018 in that state? Who was the only female CEO in the real estate sector in 2018, and in what state did she work and for what company? What was her total compensation in 2018? How many male CEOs were there in the real estate sector in 2018 and what state employed the largest number? One way to create this dashboard is to open a new dashboard and drag in the bar chart visualization to the top and the map visualization under it. Next click on the bar chart visualization and click on the funnel icon to turn it on as a filter. In order to see the number of individuals in each bar, you can go back to the bar chart and modify the visualization by dragging WRDS(Count) over the Tooltip card.

b. Save the file for future use.

Problems PF-20 through PF-22 use financial statement data for S&P 500 companies for the years 2015 through 2019. The data is contained in the Excel file Compustat SP500 2015_2019.xlsx that is available in myBusinessCourse.

LO 3, 4   **PF-20.** **Building Basic Tableau Financial Accounting Visualizations.**

a. Connect the Tableau software to the Excel file **Compustat SP500 2015_2019.xlsx**. This file consists of four worksheets. First bring in the Balance sheet worksheets and then join both the cash flow statement and the income statement worksheets to the balance sheet worksheets using both of the fields Company name and Year.

b. What is the sum of net income for all firms in the database for all years combined? One way to determine this is to drag the measure Net income to the canvas.

c. How many unique companies are included in the database? One way to determine this is to drag the dimension Company name to the rows shelf and then select Measure Count(Distinct) from the pull-down menu on the Company name pill.

d. How many distinct firms are there in each segment? One way to determine this is to drag the dimension Segment to the columns shelf in the visualization created in part *c*. The totals for each segment will appear if the Show marks label is checked in the Label card.

e. What is the sum of total assets for all companies in each segment for the year 2018? One way to determine this is to drag the dimension Segment to the columns shelf and then drag the Total Assets measure to the rows shelf. Next drag the Year dimension to the filters shelf, select year as the filter, click Next, and then check 2018. Totals for total assets can be seen in the tool tip by hovering over any bar or by checking Show marks label in the Label card.

f. What firm had the most sales in 2018? What segment was this firm in? One way to determine this is to drag the dimension Company name to the rows shelf and drag the measure Sales to the columns shelf. Next drag the Year dimension to the filters shelf, select year as the filter, click Next, and then check 2018. Segments can be highlighted by dragging the dimension Segment over the color card. Finally sort the Company names by Sales by clicking the sort icon in the tool bar.

g. Save the file for future use.

LO 3, 4   **PF-21.** **Tableau Visualizations to Analyze Accounting Performance Measures.**   You recently joined a firm as a junior financial analyst, and you would like to make a good impression by showing your manager the power of visualizations for analyzing data. In order to get a feel for the Tableau software and the dataset you created of financial statement data for S&P 500 firms, you decided to create a few very basic visualizations.

Two widely used ratios to analyze company performance are gross profit percentage and return on sales. You would like to create a visualization that compares these two ratios by segment and further compares segment performance to the median values of these ratios for the entire database of companies.

a.   Because of the way cost of goods sold is reported for companies in the real estate segment, you decide to exclude this segment from the visualization. After excluding real estate, for the year 2017, which segment reported the highest median value for gross profit percentage and for return on sales?

b.   Did any segment report a higher median return on sales than the upper band of the 95 percent confidence interval of overall median return on sales in 2015?

c.   Which company had the highest gross profit percentage in 2018 for the segment with the highest median gross profit percentage?

PF-22.   Using Tableau to Analyze Inventory.   You have learned of the importance of a company being able to sell its products in a timely fashion, and that the ratio of days sales in inventory provides this useful information. You decide a dashboard would be helpful in seeing whether this ratio is improving or declining in the consumer discretionary and the consumer staples segments between 2017 and 2018. You build two sheets that are included in the dashboard. The first sheet shows the level of the ratio for each segment for the two years in question. The second sheet shows the change in the ratio between the two years.

LO 3, 4

Has the ratio days sales in inventory improved or declined in the consumer discretionary and the consumer staples segments between 2017 and 2018. By how much?

PF-23.   Using Tableau for Accounts Receivable Aging—Hugo Enterprises.   Hugo Enterprises has been performing its aging of accounts receivable manually; however, the task is becoming too time consuming. The company has recently acquired Tableau for some data visualizations; however, it was mentioned that the software could be used for receivables aging. You have been asked to perform Hugo's accounts receivable aging using Tableau.

LO 2, 3, 4

- The Excel file **Hugo Aging Tableau.xlsx** can be found in myBusinessCourse with Hugo's accounts receivable amounts and due dates.
- The first step is to link the Excel file to Tableau. Within Tableau, within the Connect column on the left, select Microsoft Excel. Locate **Hugo Aging Tableau.xlsx** and then click Open.
- If the file needs to be cleaned up for further use, select the checkbox for using the built-in Data Interpreter. This particular file has already been completely cleaned up, so no further work is required here. Now there should appear three columns with customer, amount, and due date data.
- Click on Sheet 1 (this can be renamed) in order to begin creating the aging table.
- A calculated field will need to be created that computes the number of days each invoice is past due. Select Analysis and then select Create Calculated Field. Name this measure Past Due. Next use the formula DateDiff('day',[Due Date],#2023-12-31#). Note the formula is case sensitive and then click OK.
- We now want to put these past due amounts into groupings. We will do this by creating bins and each of the bins will be 30 days. Right-click on the newly created Past Due pill from the Measures shelf on the left of the screen and then select Create and then select Bins. Change the size of the bins to 30 and click OK. A Past Due bin now shows up under Dimensions on the top left of the screen. Double-click the Past Due (bin) in the Dimensions shelf to see a list of the aging groups. To fill in the table with invoice amounts, simply double-click on the Amount measure in the Measures shelf.
- In order to see the data that makes up each total in the aging table, simply click on the amount and then select the view data icon on the top right corner and select Full Data at the bottom of the pop-up window.
- In order to see a visualization of the data, simply select an appropriate chart from the show me selections.

a.   What is Hugo's total dollar value of the invoices that are between 31 and 60 days past due?
b.   What is its largest invoice within the 91- to 120-day grouping?

PF-24.   Using Tableau for Accounts Receivable Aging—Javier Enterprises.   Javier Enterprises has been performing its aging of accounts receivable manually; however, the task is becoming too time consuming. The company has recently acquired Tableau for some data visualizations; however, it was mentioned that the software could be used for receivables aging. You have been asked to perform Javier's accounts receivable aging using Tableau.

LO 2, 3, 4

- The Excel file **Javier Aging Tableau.xlsx** can be found in myBusinessCourse with Javier's accounts receivable amounts and due dates.

- The first step is to link the Excel file to Tableau. Within Tableau, within the Connect column on the left, select Microsoft Excel. Locate **Javier Aging Tableau.xlsx** and then click Open.
- If the file needs to be cleaned up for further use, select the checkbox for using the built-in Data Interpreter. This particular file has already been completely cleaned up, so no further work is required here. Now there should appear three columns with customer, amount, and due date data.
- Click on Sheet 1 (this can be renamed) in order to begin creating the aging table.
- A calculated field will need to be created that computes the number of days each invoice is past due. Select Analysis and then select Create Calculated Field. Name this measure Past Due. Next use the formula DateDiff('day',[Due Date],#2023-12-31#). Note the formula is case sensitive and then click OK.
- We now want to put these past due amounts into groupings. We will do this by creating bins, and each of the bins will be 30 days. Right-click on the newly created Past Due bill from the Measures shelf on the left of the screen and then select Create and then select Bins. Change the size of the bins to 30 and click OK. A Past Due bin now shows up under Dimensions on the top left of the screen. Double-click the Past Due (bin) in the Dimensions shelf to see a list of the aging groups. To fill in the table with invoice amounts, simply double-click on the Amount measure in the Measures shelf.
- In order to see the data that makes up each total in the aging table, simply click on the amount and then select the view data icon on the top right corner and select Full Data at the bottom of the pop-up window.
- In order to see a visualization of the data, simply select an appropriate chart from the show me selections.

a. What is Javier Enterprises' total dollar value of the invoices that are between 31 and 60 days past due?

b. What is its largest invoice within the 91- to 120-day grouping?

LO 2, 3, 4   **PF-25.**   **Using Tableau for Fraud Detection.**   Benford's Law represents a powerful tool in the forensic accountant's toolkit to aid in the detection of fraud. Benford's Law is a mathematical law that recognizes the leading (first) digit in many real-life number sets is distributed in a certain manner, and often not in the manner that a fraudster would expect. Specifically the number 1 occurs as the first digit approximately 30 percent of the time, with each succeeding digit appearing less often as follows: 1–30%, 2–18%, 3–12%, 4–10%, 5–8%, 6–7%, 7–6%, 8–5%, and 9–5%. Fraudsters who are unaware of this natural ordering will often arrange digits in a random order that deviates from Benford's Law.

In Part A of this problem you will use Tableau to show how a natural dataset of GDP by country conforms to Benford's Law and how a random set of numbers does not. In Part B you will use the same data used in an actual court case to convict a fraudster of embezzlement. Finally, in Part C you will use Benford's Law to test a new reimbursement procedure for possible fraud. A video demonstrating the Tableau tools used in this problem is available in myBusinessCourse.

Part A Use Tableau to show how a natural dataset of GDP by country conforms to Benford's Law and how a random set of numbers does not.

- Download the file **GDP Tableau.xlsx** from myBusinessCourse. The file contains World Bank GDP data by country for 2018, along with a separate column of random numbers that was generated in Excel using the command =RAND()*1000.
- After you have uploaded the workbook to Tableau, create two calculated fields.
- The first calculated field will pull the first digit from each country's GDP amount. Choose Analysis > Create Calculated Field and name the calculation First Integer. Then either type or paste the following formula in the formula area: LEFT(STR([GDP]),1)
- Next create a second calculated field named Benfords Law by typing or pasting the following in the formula area: LOG(INT([First Integer])+1)- LOG(INT([First Integer]))
- To create the visualization, drag First Integer from the Dimensions area to Columns and drag Number of Records from the Measures area to Rows. Click Sum(Number of Records) on Rows to show the pull-down menu and choose Quick Table Calculation > Percent of Total. The visualization should now show a bar chart with the bars conforming to Benford's Law.
- While it is relatively easy to see that the data conforms to Benford's Law, with a little more work the visualization can be significantly enhanced. To do this, drag Benfords Law from the Measures area of the Data pane to Detail on the Marks card, and then click Benfords Law on the Marks card and choose Measure > Minimum.

- Next switch from the current Data pane to the Analytics pane and then drag Distribution Band over the chart and drop it on the cell icon in the pop-up. A dialog box will appear. Under computation, change the value to percentages of 90, 100, 110 and select Percent of to be Min(Benfords Law). Choose a fill line as the thick black line and then click OK.
- Finally click on the Label icon in the Marks section and select the Show marks labels box.

a.   Does the GDP data appear to conform to Benford's Law?

Now return to the Data pane and create a new calculated field for the random numbers by naming the calculation Random Values and typing or pasting the following formula in the formula area: LEFT(STR([Random]),1)

- Drag the Min(Benfords Law) pill out of the Marks area to remove the bands and drag Random Values from the Dimensions area on top of First Integer to replace it in the visualization. If both pills remain in the columns section, simply drag First Integer away.

b.   Do the random values appear to conform with Benford's Law?

Part B Use the same data used in an actual court case to convict a fraudster of embezzlement.

In the 1993 court case *State of Arizona v. Wayne James Nelson* Benford's Law was used to convict the defendant of defrauding the state of nearly $2 million by diverting money to a nonexistent vendor. Nelson tried to make the checks appear random; however, he was unaware that these check amounts should actually follow Benford's Law much closer than the random distribution he created. Download the file **Arizona Fraud.xlsx** from myBusinessCourse and follow the same procedure as you did in Part A above and use Tableau to show how the data conforms to Benford's Law.

a.   From a casual observation of the checks, can you detect anything suspect?
b.   After using Benford's Law, does the list of checks appear suspect?

Part C Use Benford's Law to test a new reimbursement procedure for possible fraud.

Wally's Enterprises has been reimbursing its employees for business expenses after the employee submits detailed evidence of the expense, such as paid receipts. Management has recently changed the reimbursement policy because of the time spent checking all the submitted evidence, with an especially high volume of smaller reimbursement requests. The new policy only requires evidence be submitted if the reimbursement request exceeds $50. As the company's internal auditor, you are concerned that this policy change may result in fraudulent reimbursement requests. In order to test the new policy, you have gathered a random sample of 100 reimbursement requests from both before and after the policy change. This data is located in the file **Expense Reimbursement.xlsx** in myBusinessCourse. Download this file and using Tableau, apply Benford's Law to test whether the new policy appears to have resulted in any fraud.

a.   Do the reimbursement requests prior to the policy change appear to follow Benford's Law?
b.   Do the reimbursement requests occurring after the policy change appear to follow Benford's Law?
c.   What, if anything, leads you to believe that fraud may be occurring?

Problems PF-26 through PF-31 use financial statement data for S&P 500 companies for the years 2015 through 2019. The data is contained in the Excel file Compustat SP500 2015_2019.xlsx. The file can be downloaded from myBusinessCourse.

PF-26.   **Using Tableau to Analyze Fixed Assets.**   One of the ratios that provides information on how well a company utilizes its assets is the ratio asset turnover. As part of your analysis of different segments of the S&P 500, you would like to have a visualization that ranks companies within various segments by their asset turnover.

LO 3, 4

a.   For the year 2019 what firm in the consumer discretionary segment had the second highest asset turnover? How did the same firm rank in 2018? Did the segment consumer discretionary or consumer staples have a higher median level of asset turnover in 2017? One way to determine this is to create a visualization by first creating a calculated field of the ratio asset turnover and then dragging the dimensions Segment and Company Name to the rows shelf and the ratio asset turnover to the columns shelf. Using the pull-down arrow of the ratio's pill, change the measure to median. Next sort the horizontal bar chart by Company Name. Drag the dimension Year to the filter shelf and select Show filter. Finally switch from the Data pane to the Analytics pane and drag Median with 95% CI on the canvas and place the distribution band on Pane.
b.   Save the file for future use.

LO 3, 4   **PF-27.**   **Using Tableau to Analyze Liquidity.**   A popular ratio for analyzing a company's short-term liquidity is the current ratio. In your continuing analysis of S&P 500 companies, you have decided to build a simple visualization that uses color highlighting and tooltip labeling to show current ratios by segment over the five-year period 2015 through 2019. You also desire to do some further analysis in Excel, so you will want to export this data as a crosstab to Excel. Finally, you want to include your visualization in a PowerPoint presentation.

a.   What segment has the highest current ratio in each year? One way to create this visualization is to first create the calculated field current ratio. Next drag the dimension Year to the columns shelf and the ratio Current ratio to the rows shelf. Next change the ratio's measure to median. Finally drag the dimension Segment over the Color card. In order to export the data as a crosstab to Excel, click on the worksheet tab in the menu bar and choose Export > Crosstab to Excel. If you would prefer to see the data as a crosstab in Tableau, right-click on the Tableau workbook icon and choose Duplicate as crosstab. Finally, to export the visualization to PowerPoint, select File from the menu bar and choose Export as PowerPoint.

b.   Save the file for future use.

LO 3, 4   **PF-28.**   **Using Tableau to Analyze Dividend Policy.**   Many equity investors are particularly interested in the dividend paying policy of a company. Two ratios that provide information in this regard are the dividend payout ratio and the dividend yield. As an analyst you would like to build a visualization that looks at these two ratios together and in particular which segments outperform the S&P 500 in general.

a.   For the year 2015, did any segment outperform or underperform the median S&P 500 company for both the dividend payout and dividend yield by more than a 95 percent confidence level? One way to determine this is to first create calculated fields for both dividend yield and dividend payout and then build a scatter graph visualization with median dividend payout on the columns shelf and median dividend yield on the rows shelf. Next drag Segment to the Color card to color highlight the segments. Drag Year to the filter shelf in order to filter on Year. Finally, switch to the Analytics pane and drag Median with 95% CI to the canvas.

b.   Save the file for future use.

LO 3, 4   **PF-29.**   **Using Tableau to Study ROE with the Dupont Method—Part I.**   One of the basic tools in any analyst's toolkit is the DuPont method of Return on Equity (ROE) decomposition. You would like to build a series of visualizations to exploit the DuPont method to find value in equities. To do this, you will need visualizations that show, by segment, both ROE and the components of ROE, namely Return on Sales (ROS), Asset Turnover (AT), and Leverage (LEV).

a.   Which segment had the highest ROE in both 2017 and 2018? Which component of ROE was mostly responsible? The first step in determining this is to create calculated fields for ROE, ROS, AT, and LEV. The next step is to create a vertical bar chart visualization by dragging the dimensions Segment and Year to the columns shelf and the median measure of the four new calculated fields to the rows shelf. The dimension Year needs to be dragged to the filter shelf with the years 2017 and 2018 selected. Finally, Segment can be dragged over the Color card to highlight by color.

b.   Which segment showed the largest gain and the largest decline in ROE between 2017 and 2018? This is best shown on a dashboard by combining two separate visualizations. The first visualization in the form of a vertical bar chart can be constructed by dragging the dimensions Segment and Year to the Column shelf and the measure of Median ROE to the rows shelf. The dimension Year should be dragged to the filters shelf and the years 2017 and 2018 selected. To make segments easier to see in the visualization, Segment can be dragged over the Color card to highlight by color. The second visualization, which will show the change in the ratio between 2017 and 2018, can be accomplished by first dragging the dimensions Segment and Year to the columns shelf and also dragging the dimension Year to the filters shelf and selecting the years 2017 and 2018. Next drag the ratio ROE to the rows shelf and change its measure to median. In order to show the change between years, use the pull-down arrow on the ratio's pill and select Quick table calculation and then Difference. Finally, right-click on the year 2017 on the horizontal axis and select Hide. To make segments easier to see in the visualization, Segment can be dragged over the Color card to highlight by color. As the last step, create a new dashboard and drag the two visualizations in.

c.   Save the file for future use.

PF-30. **Using Tableau to Study ROE with the Dupont Method—Part II.**   You wish to continue your analysis of segment ROE by looking at trends within segments and then identifying which companies rank the highest for ROE within those segments.

LO 3, 4

   a. For the period 2015 through 2019, which segments showed the best positive trends in ROE growth? One way to create a line chart visualization showing this trend is to drag the dimensions Segment and Year to the columns shelf and drag the Median measure of ROE to the rows shelf. To make segments easier to see in the visualization, Segment can be dragged over the Color card to highlight by color. Finally, switch to the Analytics pane and drag Trend line to the canvas, selecting "linear."

   b. For the segments identified in part *a*, which firms reported the highest ROE in 2019? A horizontal bar chart visualization can be created by dragging the dimensions Segment and Company name to the rows shelf and the Median measure of ROE to the columns shelf. Segment and Year can be dragged to the filters shelf to allow filtering on these two dimensions. Finally, to aid in the analysis, the company names can be sorted by clicking on the sort icon located on the tool bar.

   c. Save the file for future use.

PF-31. **Using Tableau to Study ROE with the Dupont Method—Part III.**   To complete your analysis of the DuPont method, you would like to have an interactive dashboard that allows the user to select any of the S&P 500 companies and see its segment, its change in ROE between 2017 and 2018, along with the changes in each of the items making up components of ROE.

LO 3, 4

   a. How much did Alphabet's (the parent company of Google) ROE improve between 2017 and 2018 and which component showed the largest increase? Pick any other company and answer the same question. One approach to build this dashboard is to first create five visualizations. The first horizontal bar chart visualization can be created by dragging the dimensions Company name and Year to the rows shelf and the measure ROE to the columns shelf. The dimension Year needs to be dragged to the filters shelf and the years 2017 and 2018 selected. Next drag the dimension Company name to the filters shelf and click on Show filter from the pills pull-down menu. To allow segments to be highlighted by color in the visualization, Segment can be dragged over the Color card. This process can be repeated to create separate visualizations for the components of ROE, namely ROS, AT, and LEV. The fifth visualization, a line chart, can be created by dragging the dimension Year to the columns shelf and the measures Net Income, Stockholders Equity, Sales, and Total Assets to the rows shelf. The dimension Year should be dragged to the filters shelf and the years 2017 and 2018 selected. The dimension Company name should also be dragged to the filters shelf and then have Show filter selected. Finally, to allow segments to be highlighted by color in the visualization, Segment can be dragged over the Color card. Now that each of the visualizations is complete, create a dashboard by dragging the first four visualizations, one under the other, on the left side of the dashboard and drag the fifth visualization to the right side of the dashboard. Convert the filter of Company name to a Single Value drop-down floating filter by selecting those two options and position the filter at the top of the dashboard.

   b. Save the file for future use.

PF-32. **Using Microsoft Excel for descriptive analytics.**   Go to the myBusinessCourse and download the Excel file **Employee Data Excel.xlsx**. You will need to have the Analysis Toolpak add-in installed in Excel. It can be found under the Tools tab. If it does not appear, select Excel Add-ins under the Tools tab, and then check Analysis Toolpak. From the Excel ribbon, select Data and then Data Analysis. From the pop-up window, choose Descriptive Statistics and then click OK. Select the salary column as the input range and check the box for labels in the first row. Choose "New Worksheet" as the output option, click summary statistics, and click OK. Report the following:

LO 1, 2

   a. Mean (average) salary

   b. Median salary

   c. Minimum salary

   d. Maximum salary

   e. Number of salary observations in the database

PF-33. **Using the Microsoft Excel PivotTable function for descriptive analytics.**   Go to myBusinessCourse and download the Excel file **Employee Data Excel.xlsx**. Place your cursor anywhere in the table of data. From the Excel ribbon, select Insert and then Pivot Table. The entire table should be selected automatically along with the choice to output the PivotTable to a new worksheet. Select OK. From the PivotTable Fields section, select and drag "Gender" and "Minority" to the "Rows" box below. Select and drag the variable "Education" to the "Columns" box. Select and drag the variable "Salary" to the "Values" box. Change the

LO 1, 2

sum of salary to the average of salary by clicking the "i" icon to the right of the "Sum of Salary," choosing "Average," and then clicking OK. Report the following:

a. Does additional education appear to be associated with a higher average salary?

b. Do males (1) or females (0) appear to earn higher average salaries?

c. Do minorities (1) or nonminorities (0) appear to earn higher average salaries? Does this hold for both genders?

d. What is the average salary of the entire population? What is the average salary of the entire population of males? What is the average salary of the entire population of females? What is the average salary of the entire population of male minorities? What is the average salary of the entire population of female minorities?

LO 1, 2　**PF-34.**　**Using Microsoft Excel for diagnostic analytics.**　Go to myBusinessCourse and download the Excel file **Employee Data Excel.xlsx**. You will need to have the Analysis Toolpak add-in installed in Excel. It can be found under the Tools tab. If it does not appear, you will need to select Excel Add-ins under the Tools tab and then check Analysis Toolpak. From the Excel ribbon, select Data and then Data Analysis. From the pop-up window, choose "Regression," and then click OK. Select values in the "Salary" column as the Input Y Range and values in the columns for "Gender" through "Education" for the Input X Range. Choose "New Worksheet" as the output option, and then click OK. Report the following:

a. A measure on how well the independent variables gender, minority, and education are able to explain the variation in average salary is the adjusted R Squared. What percentage of the variation in average salaries is described by these variables?

b. The *t* Stat is a measure of how an individual independent variable explains variation in the dependent variable average salary. An absolute value greater than 2 is generally considered a significant value in explaining variation. What do the *t* Stats tell us about the ability of the variables gender, minority, and education to explain average salary?

Problems PF-35 through PF-38 will be using the Excel file Compensation Data 2015_2019 SP500.xlsx that can be downloaded from myBusinessCourse.

LO 3, 4　**PF-35.**　**Building a basic Excel PivotTable.**　You have been tasked by a compensation consulting firm to research compensation amounts being paid to executives in large public companies. In particular you wish to learn more about amounts being paid to CEOs and CFOs within certain industries and how these amounts differ by gender. You have gathered a large database of amounts paid by the S&P 500 companies during the period 2015 through 2019.

a. Your first task is to build a PivotTable that separately shows the average salaries paid to CEOs and CFOs by gender on the rows and these amounts by industry segment on the columns. You do not need to separate the data by year at this time. What was the average salary paid to female CEOs in the healthcare segment? How does this compare to male CEOs in the same segment? Were there more male or female CFOs in the consumer staples segment?

b. What was the total average salary of all CEOs and CFOs in the information technology segment? Did CEOs or CFOs get paid more? Did males or females get paid more?

LO 3, 4　**PF-36.**　**Sorting, grouping, and filtering a basic PivotTable.**　You have been asked to construct a basic PivotTable that shows by position and gender the average salary, average total compensation, and number of executives in each of the industry segments.

a. Construct a PivotTable with Position, Gender, and Sector name on the rows and the average salary, average total compensation, and the count of executives in the columns. To make things easier to read, sort the Sector names by the average of salaries. What sector paid its female CEOs the highest average salary and how many female CEOs made up this calculation? Answer the same question for female CFOs.

b. Rather than combining all five years together, you would like to answer similar questions for a single year. Add the year measure to the filter and select 2017. Repeat the questions from part *a*, but this time report the lowest paying segment.

c. Copy the entire PivotTable to the right on the same worksheet, but this time sort by the count of the executives rather than by the average salary. Again, filter by year, but this time select 2018. Which industry segment employs the second most male CFOs?

d. You would like for the reader of these PivotTables to interact with them so that they can answer specific questions regarding the data within the PivotTables. In order to add interactivity, insert four slicers, one for position and one for gender, one for years and one for segment. Connect each slicer to both of the PivotTables through the report connections. Also, make each slicer multi-select. What was the average salary and number of male CFOs in the consumer staples segment in 2018?

e. Finally, you are interested in how much of an executive's total compensation is from salary. Rather than doing the calculation for each industry segment, you decide to create a calculated field of salary as a percentage of total compensation. What percentage of the female CFOs in the industrials segment during 2016 was from salary?

PF-37. Adding a PivotChart to a PivotTable.   Your audience is having difficulty reading through all the numbers in the PivotTables and would like an easier method to visualize the data. In particular they are interested in seeing the relative salaries among the executives within the various industry segments.

 LO 3, 4

a. Create a PivotTable with position, gender, and sector name in the rows and the average of salary for values. Format the average of salary using number format as currency with zero decimal places. Sort the rows using the field sector name by the value average of salary. Add slicers for gender, year, position, and sector name. Finally, add a PivotChart in the form of a bar chart and give it the title "Salary by position, gender, and industry" and add data labels to the bars. Observe how making selections in the slicers updates both the PivotTable and the PivotChart. Select female CFOs in 2017. What industry segment paid the fifth highest average salary? Answer the same question for male CFOs in 2016.

PF-38. Creating a PivotTable Dashboard.   Your audience was happy with the PivotTable produced in Problem PF-37; however they would like to see several visualizations at one time. Specifically, they would like to see total compensation by industry, number of executives by industry, and the state locations where these executives are employed. You decide to make a dashboard with a bar PivotChart of total compensation by industry, a pie PivotChart for the number of executives by industry, and a column PivotChart with the top five states by number of executives.

 LO 3, 4

a. Create the dashboard described previously. Add slicers for gender, position, and year and link the slicers to all of the PivotTables and PivotCharts. Format the dashboard so as to create a visually pleasing layout that is easy to read. In 2018, for male CEOs, how many executives were there and what was the average salary paid in the information technology segment? Also, in 2018, what state employed the most male CEOs?

PF-39. Using Excel for Accounts Receivable Aging—Bella Co.   Bella Co. has been performing its aging of accounts receivable manually; however, the task is becoming too time consuming. The CFO has heard that the PivotTable function within Microsoft Excel could make the task much easier; however, she has never used this technique before. You have been asked to perform Bella's accounts receivable aging using an Excel PivotTable.

 LO 2, 3, 4

- The Excel file **Bella Aging Pivot.xlsx** can be found in myBusinessCourse with Bella's accounts receivable amounts and due dates.
- Assume that you are performing the aging as of December 31, 2023, the date already entered in cell G1.
- Create new data within column D for the number of days that each invoice is past the due date by entering in cell D2 the formula of cell G1 as an absolute reference minus the cell C2 as a relative reference =$G$1-C2. Next copy this formula down column D to include the entire list of receivables. We now have a list that identifies for each invoice the number of days past due.
- In order to create the PivotTable, simply place the cursor anywhere within columns A through D and select Insert; then select PivotTable. A pop-up should appear with the table range including all the data from columns A through D already selected and the location of the PivotTable being a new worksheet. If this is correct, click OK.
- In the new PivotTable worksheet, locate the PivotTable Fields to the right of the worksheet. Drag the Days Past field down to the rows section and the Amount field down to the values section.
- Finally, in order to do some groupings, place the cursor within the data in column A and right-click and select Group. In the Grouping pop-up, change the starting value to 1, the ending value to 180, and the by value to 30, and click OK. The aging table should appear.
- To add visual impact, a column chart can be added to the worksheet. In order to see all the invoices that make up any grouping, simply place the cursor on the dollar value of the grouping and double-click.

a. What is Bella's total dollar value of the invoices that are between 61 and 90 days past due?

b. What is its largest invoice within the 151- to 180-day grouping?

LO 2, 3 **PF-40.** **Using Excel for Accounts Receivable Aging—Remus Co.**   Remus Co. has been performing its aging of accounts receivable manually; however, the task is becoming too time consuming. The CFO has heard that the PivotTable function within Microsoft Excel could make the task much easier; however, she has never used this technique before. You have been asked to perform Remus' accounts receivable aging using an Excel PivotTable.

- The Excel file **Remus Again Pivot.xlsx** can be found in myBusinessCourse with Remus' accounts receivable amounts and due dates.
- Assume that you are performing the aging as of December 31, 2023, the date already entered in cell G1.
- Create new data within column D for the number of days that each invoice is past the due date by entering in cell D2 the formula of cell G1 as an absolute reference minus the cell C2 as a relative reference =$G$1-C2. Next copy this formula down column D to include the entire list of receivables. We now have a list that identifies for each invoice the number of days past due.
- In order to create the PivotTable, simply place the cursor anywhere within columns A through D and select Insert; then select PivotTable. A pop-up should appear with the table range including all the data from columns A through D already selected and the location of the PivotTable being a new worksheet. If this is correct, click OK.
- In the new PivotTable worksheet, locate the PivotTable Fields to the right of the worksheet. Drag the Days Past field down to the rows section and the Amount field down to the values section.
- Finally, in order to do some groupings, place the cursor within the data in column A and right-click and select Group. In the Grouping pop-up, change the starting value to 1, the ending value to 180, and the by value to 30, and click OK. The aging table should appear.
- To add visual impact, a column chart can be added to the worksheet. In order to see all the invoices that make up any grouping, simply place the cursor on the dollar value of the grouping and double-click.

a. What is Remus' total dollar value of the invoices that are between 61 and 90 days past due?
b. What is its largest invoice within the 151- to 180-day grouping?

LO 2, 3, 4 **PF-41.** **Using Excel for Fraud Detection.**   Benford's Law represents a powerful tool in the forensic accountant's toolkit to aid in the detection of fraud. Benford's Law is a mathematical law that recognizes the leading (first) digit in many real-life number sets is distributed in a certain manner, and often not in the manner that a fraudster would expect. Specifically, the number 1 occurs as the first digit approximately 30 percent of the time, with each succeeding digit appearing less often as follows: 1–30%, 2–18%, 3–12%, 4–10%, 5–8%, 6–7%, 7–6%, 8–5%, and 9–5%. Fraudsters who are unaware of this natural ordering will often arrange digits in a random order that deviates from Benford's Law.

   In Part A of this problem, you will use Microsoft Excel to show how a natural dataset of GDP by country conforms to Benford's Law and how a random set of numbers does not. In Part B you will use the same data used in an actual court case to convict a fraudster of embezzlement. Finally, in Part C you will use Benford's Law to test a new reimbursement procedure for possible fraud.

Part A Use Microsoft Excel to show how a natural dataset of GDP by country conforms to Benford's Law and how a random set of numbers does not.

- Download the Excel file **GDP Excel.xlsx** from in myBusinessCourse. The file contains World Bank GDP data by country for 2018.
- In order to use Benford's Law, you need to first extract the leading digit from each country's GDP amount. To do this, place the cursor in cell C2 and input the formula =Left(B2,1). Copy this formula down column C for each country.
- Next in cells F2 through F-0 input the numbers 1 through 9. In cell G2 input the formula =COUNTIF(c2:$C$205,F2) and copy the formula down for each number 1 through 9. This formula goes through the entire range of extracted first digits in column C and records the count of these digits in the cell if it matches the number in column F.
- Sum the column total in cell G11.
- Next determine the percentage that each leading digit appears by dividing the amount in column G by the total of these amounts in cell G11 and place this figure in column H.
- In column I compute the predicted occurrences of each digit (given above) by placing the formula =Log10(1/F2+1) in cell I2 and copying the formula down the column.
- Finally create a Combo chart to visualize these results by highlighting cells H1:I10 and selecting Combo chart.

   a.   Do the naturally occurring GDP amounts appear to follow Benford's law?

- Next replace the GDP amounts with random numbers to see if random numbers also obey Benford's Law.
- Input the formula =Rand()*1000 in cell B2 and copy this formula down the column.
- Observe the results in the table and the chart. Try to recalculate the spreadsheet several times to obtain different sets of random numbers.

   b.   Do random numbers appear to follow Benford's Law?

Part B Use the same data used in an actual court case to convict a fraudster of embezzlement.

In the 1993 court case *State of Arizona v. Wayne James Nelson* Benford's Law was used to convict the defendant of defrauding the state of nearly $2 million by diverting money to a nonexistent vendor. Nelson tried to make the checks appear random; however, he was unaware that these check amounts should actually follow Benford's Law much closer than the distribution he created. Download the file **Arizona Fraud.xlsx** from myBusinessCourse and follow the same procedure as you did in Part A above to use Excel to show how the data conforms to Benford's Law.

   a.   From a casual observation of the checks, can you detect anything suspect?
   b.   After using Benford's Law, does the list of checks appear suspect?

Part C Use Benford's Law to test a new reimbursement procedure for possible fraud.

Jimmy's Enterprises has been reimbursing its employees for business expenses after the employee submits detailed evidence of the expense, such as paid receipts. Management has recently changed the reimbursement policy because of the time spent checking all the submitted evidence, with an especially high volume of smaller reimbursement requests. The new policy requires evidence be submitted only if the reimbursement request exceeds $50. As the company's internal auditor, you are concerned that this policy change may result in fraudulent reimbursement requests. In order to test the new policy, you have gathered a random sample of 100 reimbursement requests from both before and after the policy change. This data is located in the file **Expense Reimbursement.xlxs** in myBusinessCourse. Download this file and within Excel use Benford's Law to test whether the new policy appears to have resulted in any fraud.

   a.   Do the reimbursement requests prior to the policy change appear to follow Benford's Law?
   b.   Do the reimbursement requests occurring after the policy change appear to follow Benford's Law?
   c.   What, if anything, leads you to believe that fraud may be occurring?

Glossary

10-K The report filed annually with the U.S. Securities and Exchange Commission by publicly held companies that reports the financial position and operating performance of the company. The 10-K contains more detailed information about the company than the annual report to shareholders.

A

Accelerated depreciation method A depreciation method in which the amounts of depreciation expense taken in the early years of an asset's life are greater than the amounts expensed in later years.

Account A record of the additions, deductions, and balances of individual assets, liabilities, stockholders' equity, dividends, revenues, and expenses.

Account form A format of the classified balance sheet in which assets are displayed on the left side and liabilities and stockholders' equity are displayed on the right side.

Accounting The process of measuring the economic activity of a business in money terms and communicating those financial results to interested parties. The purpose of accounting is to provide financial information that is useful in economic decision making.

Accounting cycle A sequence of activities undertaken by company accountants to accumulate and report the financial information of a business.

Accounting entity An economic unit with identifiable boundaries that is the focus for the accumulation and reporting of financial information.

Accounting equation An expression of the equivalency of the economic resources and the claims upon those resources of a business, often stated as Assets = Liabilities + Stockholders' Equity.

Accounting period The time period, usually one year, to which periodic accounting reports are related; also known as the fiscal period.

Accounting transaction An economic event that requires accounting recognition; an event that affects any of the elements of the accounting equation—assets, liabilities, or stockholders' equity.

Accounts receivable A current asset that is created by a sale of merchandise or the provision of a service on a credit basis. It represents the amount owed the seller by a customer.

Accounts receivable aging method A procedure that uses an aging schedule to determine the year-end balance needed in the Allowance for Doubtful Accounts account.

Accounts receivable turnover A ratio calculated as annual net sales divided by the average balance of accounts receivable (net).

Accrual basis of accounting Accounting procedures whereby sales revenue is recorded as goods are transferred to customers or services are performed and expenses are recorded in the period in which they help to generate the sales revenue.

Accruals Adjustments that reflect revenues earned but not received or recorded and expenses incurred but not paid or recorded.

Accrued expense An expense incurred but not yet paid; recognized with an adjusting entry.

Accrued revenue Revenue earned but not yet billed or received; recognized with an adjusting entry.

Accumulated depreciation The cumulative amount of depreciation expense taken in prior periods; subtracted from the related asset account.

Adjusted trial balance A list of general ledger accounts and their balances prepared after all adjustments have been made.

Adjusting entries Entries made at the end of an accounting period under accrual accounting to ensure the proper matching of expenses incurred with revenues earned for the period.

Aging schedule An analysis that shows how long a business's accounts receivable balances have remained unpaid.

Allowance for doubtful accounts A contra-asset account with a normal credit balance shown on the balance sheet as a deduction from accounts receivable to reflect the expected uncollectible amount of accounts receivable.

Allowance method An accounting procedure whereby the amount of bad debts expense is estimated and recorded in the period in which the related credit sales occur.

American Institute of Certified Public Accountants (AICPA) An association representing members of the accounting profession in many areas of practice, including business and industry, public practice, government, education, and consulting.

Amortization The periodic write-off of an intangible asset to expense on a company's income statement.

Annual report A report containing the financial statements that is sent to a company's shareholders.

Annuity A pattern of cash flows in which equal amounts are spaced equally over a number of periods.

Articles of incorporation A document prepared by the founders of a corporation that sets forth the structure and purpose of the corporation and specifics regarding the type and quantity of capital stock to be issued.

Asset turnover ratio Net sales divided by average total assets; it represents a measure of a firm's efficiency in producing sales revenue using its total assets.

Assets The economic resources of a business that can be expressed in money terms.

Auditor's report The report of the independent auditor that describes the activities undertaken by a company's outside auditor and reports the auditor's opinion regarding whether the financial statements fairly present the results of the company's operations and financial health.

Authorized shares The maximum number of shares in a class of stock that a corporation may issue.

Available-for-sale securities Debt securities and noninfluential equity securities that management does not intend to sell in the near future or hold to maturity.

Average collection period A ratio calculated by dividing 365 days by the accounts receivable turnover ratio.

B

Bad debts expense The expense stemming from the inability of a business to collect an amount recorded as receivable. It is normally classified as a selling or administrative expense.

Balance sheet A financial statement showing a business's assets, liabilities, and stockholders' equity as of a specific date.

Bank reconciliation A procedure explaining the various items—such as deposits in transit, checks outstanding, bank charges, and errors—that lead to differences between the balance shown on a bank statement and the related Cash account in a company's general ledger.

Bearer One of the terms that may be used to designate the payee on a promissory note; it means that a note is payable to whoever holds the note.

Benchmarking analysis A technique where the analyst or investor compares a firm's performance, or a ratio like the ROA, to that of the firm's principal competitors or to an industry average.

Betterments Capital expenditures that improve the quality of services rendered by a plant asset or extend the asset's useful life.

Blockchain technology A digital ledger that provides a secure means, for those that have permission, to view recorded transactions.

Bond A long-term debt instrument that promises to pay interest periodically and a principal amount at maturity. Bonds may incorporate a variety of provisions relating to security for the debt involved, methods of paying the periodic interest, and retirement provisions.

Book value The dollar amount carried in the accounts for a particular asset. For example, the book value of a depreciable asset is derived by deducting the contra account Accumulated Depreciation from the balance in the depreciable asset account.

Budget A planning device that forecasts a business's future operating activities using financial data. The budget serves as an internal control device by providing a benchmark to compare actual performance against so that material deviations can be investigated.

C

Calendar year A fiscal year that ends on December 31.

Call provision A feature associated with bonds or preferred stock that allows the issuing corporation to redeem (call in) the bonds or preferred stock at a prespecified price.

Capital expenditures An expenditure that increases the book value of long-term assets.

Cash An asset category representing the amount of a firm's paper money, coins, checks, money orders, traveler's checks, and funds on deposit at a bank in a company's checking accounts and savings accounts.

Cash basis of accounting Accounting procedures whereby sales revenue is recorded when cash is received from operating activities and expenses are recorded when cash payments related to operating activities are made.

Cash discount An amount that a purchaser of merchandise may deduct from the purchase price for paying within the allowed discount period.

Cash equivalents Short-term, highly liquid investments that firms acquire with temporarily idle cash to earn interest on these funds. To qualify as a cash equivalent, an investment must be readily convertible into cash and be close enough to maturity so that its market value is not sensitive to interest rate changes. Examples are U.S. Treasury bills and money market funds.

Cash management Management's efforts to determine cash needs and maintain the proper amount of cash for the company's needs.

Certificate of deposit (CD) An investment security offering a fixed rate of return for a specified period of time.

Certified public accountant (CPA) A professional designation given to an accountant who has fulfilled stringent licensing requirements.

Change in accounting principle A switch from one generally accepted accounting method to another generally accepted method, such as changing depreciation methods.

Chart of accounts A list of all of the general ledger account titles and their numerical code.

Check A written order signed by a checking account owner directing the bank to pay a specified amount of money to the person or company named on the check.

Classified balance sheet A balance sheet in which items are classified into subgroups to facilitate financial analysis and management decision making.

Classified income statement An income statement in which items are classified into subgroups to facilitate financial analysis and management decision making.

Closing process A step in the accounting cycle in which the balances of all temporary accounts are transferred to the Retained Earnings account, leaving the temporary accounts with zero balances.

Commitments A contractual arrangement in which both parties to the contract still have acts yet to perform.

Common stock The basic ownership class of capital stock, carrying the right to vote, share in earnings, participate in future share issues, and share in any liquidation proceeds after all more senior claims have been settled.

Common-size financial statement A financial statement in which each item is presented as a percentage of a key statement item.

Comparability The qualitative characteristic that enables users to determine similarities and differences among items.

Comparative financial statement analysis A form of horizontal analysis involving a comparison of two or more periods of financial statement data showing dollar and/or percentage changes.

Compensating balance A minimum amount that a financial institution requires a firm to maintain in its bank account as a condition of a borrowing arrangement.

Compound interest Interest that is computed on the accumulated principal balance plus any interest that has been earned but not yet paid.

Compound journal entry A journal entry containing more than one debit and one credit.

Comprehensive income A broader definition of a company's income that includes net income plus any changes in the market value of certain marketable securities and any unrealized gains and losses from translating foreign currency denominated financial statements into U.S. dollars.

Conceptual framework A cohesive set of interrelated objectives, elements, and recognition and measurement criteria for the GAAP developed by the FASB.

Conservatism principle An accounting principle stating that judgmental determinations should tend toward understatement rather than overstatement of assets and net income.

Consignment goods Items held for sale by parties other than the item's owner.

Consistency An accounting principle stating that accounting reports should be prepared on a basis consistent with the prior periods.

Consolidated financial statements Financial statements prepared to portray the financial position, results of operations, and cash flows of two or more affiliated companies as a single economic entity.

Contingency A possible future event; significant contingent liabilities must be disclosed in the notes to the financial statements.

Contingent liabilities A potential obligation, the eventual occurrence of which usually depends on some future event beyond the control of the firm. Contingent liabilities may originate from such things as lawsuits, credit guarantees, and contested income tax assessments.

Contra account An account related to, and deducted from, another account when financial statements are prepared or when book values are computed.

Contributed capital The capital contributed to a company by stockholders when they purchase shares of stock from the company.

Control numbers Preprinted numbers on documents such as purchase orders, invoices, credit memos, and checks used to provide an internal control that all documents are accounted for.

Controlling securities Equity securities that represent an ownership of more than 50 percent of a corporation's voting stock.

Convertible A feature associated with bonds or preferred stock allowing for the conversion into common stock at a specified conversion rate.

Copyright An exclusive right that protects an owner against the unauthorized reproduction of a specific written work or artwork.

Corporate social responsibility The practice that considers how a corporation's behavior affects its various stakeholders to ensure an adherence to ethical standards.

Corporation A legal entity created under the laws of a state or the federal government. The owners of a corporation receive shares of stock as evidence of their ownership interest in the company.

Cost flow The actual or assumed assignment of costs to goods sold and to ending inventory.

Cost of goods available for sale An amount that represents the inventory available to be sold, consisting of the beginning inventory plus purchases during the period.

Cost of goods sold The total cost of merchandise sold to customers during the accounting period; often abbreviated as COGS.

Cost of goods sold percentage The ratio of cost of goods sold divided by net sales.

Cost principle An accounting principle stating that asset measures should be based on the price paid to acquire an asset.

Cost-benefit constraint Requires that the benefits derived from accounting information are greater than the cost of providing the information.

Coupon rate The rate of interest stated on a bond certificate.

Credit (entry) An entry on the right side (or in the credit column) of an account.

Credit card fee A fee charged to retailers for credit card services provided by a financial institution. The fee is usually stated as a percentage of credit card sales.

Credit guarantee A guarantee of another company's debt by cosigning a note payable; a guarantor's contingent liability must be disclosed in a balance sheet footnote.

Credit period The maximum time period, stated in days, that a purchaser of merchandise has to pay a seller.

Credit-collection policy A policy establishing the amount of time that customers are allowed before they must pay their outstanding accounts receivable.

Credit-granting policy A policy to determine which customers to grant credit and how much credit to grant those customers.

Creditor An individual or financial institution that lends money or services to a company with the expectation of receiving repayment in the future.

Cumulative A feature associated with preferred stock whereby any dividends-in-arrears must be paid before any dividends may be paid on common stock.

Current assets Cash and other assets that will be converted to cash or used up during the normal operating cycle of a business or one year, whichever is longer.

Current liabilities Liabilities that must be settled within the normal operating cycle or one year, whichever is longer.

Current ratio A measure of a firm's liquidity, calculated as current assets divided by current liabilities.

D

Data analytics The process of examining sets of data with the goal of discovering useful information from patterns found in the data.

Days' sales in inventory A ratio computed by dividing 365 by Inventory Turnover; this ratio indicates the number of days it takes, on average, for a company to sell its inventory.

Debenture bond A bond that has no specific property pledged as security (or collateral) for the repayment of the borrowed funds.

Debit (entry) An entry on the left side (or in the debit column) of an account.

Debt financing A source of financing for a company involving the use of debt, such as a bank loan or the issuance of bonds.

Debt security A security that creates, for the holder, a creditor relationship with an entity.

Debt-to-equity ratio A firm's total liabilities divided by its total stockholders' equity.

Debt-to-total-assets ratio A measure of a firm's solvency, calculated as total liabilities divided by total assets.

Declining-balance method An accelerated depreciation method that allocates depreciation expense to each year by applying a constant depreciation percentage to the declining book value of a long-lived asset.

Deferrals Adjustments that allocate various assets and revenues received in advance to the proper accounting periods as expenses and revenues.

Deferred revenue A liability representing revenues received in advance; also called *unearned revenue*.

Depletion The process of allocating a portion of a natural resource's cost to expense on the income statement to reflect the consumption of the asset as it produces revenue for a business.

Deposits in transit Cash deposits made to a bank account near the end of a month that do not appear on that month's bank statement.

Depreciation The process of allocating the cost of buildings, equipment, and vehicles to expense over the time periods benefiting from their use.

Depreciation accounting The process of allocating the cost of long-lived assets (less salvage value) to expense in a systematic and rational manner over the time period benefitting from their use.

Descriptive analytics A form of data analytics that describes what has happened over a given period of time.

Detection control An internal control designed to discover problems soon after they arise.

Diagnostic analytics A form of data analytics that focuses on why something occurred.

Direct method A presentation of the cash flow from operating activities in a statement of cash flows that shows the major categories of operating cash receipts and payments.

Direct write-off method An accounting procedure whereby the amount of bad debts expense is not recorded until specific uncollectible customer accounts are identified.

Discontinued operations Operating segments of a company that have been sold, abandoned, or disposed of during the accounting period. Related operating income (or loss) and related gains and losses on disposal are reported separately on the income statement.

Discount period The maximum amount of time, stated in days, that a purchaser of merchandise has to pay a seller if the purchaser wants to claim any available cash discount.

Discounting Selling a note receivable for cash at a financial institution.

Dividend payout ratio A financial ratio showing the percentage of net income available to common stockholders that is paid out as dividends; calculated as the annual dividend per share divided by earnings per share.

Dividend yield Annual dividend per share divided by the market price per share.

Dividends Distributions of assets (usually cash) or stock from a corporation to its stockholders.

Dividends in arrears Dividends omitted in past years on cumulative preferred stock.

Double-entry accounting A method of accounting that results in the recording of equal amounts of debits and credits.

E

Earned capital Capital that is earned by a company and not distributed to its stockholders as a dividend; referred to as retained earnings.

Earnings per share (EPS) A financial ratio computed as net income less preferred stock dividends divided by the weighted average number of common shares outstanding for the period.

Earnings quality The degree to which reported financial results reflect the actual financial condition and performance of the reporting company.

Effective interest method A method to amortize a bond discount or premium where the amount amortized as interest expense each period is a constant percentage of the bond.

Effective interest rate The current rate of interest in the market for a bond or other debt instrument. When issued, a bond is priced to yield the market rate of interest at the date of issuance.

Electronic funds transfer Sending an electronic message from one computer to another to cause a transfer of money from one financial institution to another.

Employee collusion When one or more employees work together to circumvent an internal control.

Equity financing A source of financing for a company involving the sale of shares of common stock.

Equity method A method of accounting by a parent company for investments in affiliate companies by which the parent's share of subsidiary income or loss is periodically recorded in the parent company's investment account.

Equity security A security that represents an ownership interest in an entity.

Ethics An area of inquiry dealing with the values, rules, and justifications that govern an individual's way of life or a corporation's behavior.

Expense recognition (matching) principle An accounting guideline that states that net income is determined by relating expenses to the sales revenues generated by the expenses.

Expenses Decreases in stockholders' equity incurred by a firm during the process of generating its sales revenues.

F

F.O.B. destination Free-on-board destination indicates that the items being shipped are owned by the seller while the items are in transit.

F.O.B. shipping point Free-on-board shipping point indicates that the items being shipped are owned by the buyer while the items are in transit.

Factoring Selling an account receivable for cash to a financial institution.

Factors Finance companies and financial institutions that buy receivables.

Faithful representation The fundamental qualitative characteristic that requires a depiction to be complete, neutral, and free from error such that it depicts the phenomena it purports to represent.

Federal Insurance Contributions Act (FICA) Under this act, the income of an individual is taxed to support the national social security program providing retirement income, medical care, and death benefits. Employers pay a matching amount of tax on their eligible employees.

Fidelity bond An insurance policy that provides financial compensation for theft by employees specifically covered by the insurance.

Finance lease A lease that transfers to the lessee substantially all of the usual benefits and risks related to ownership of the property. The lessee records the leased property as an asset and establishes a liability for the lease obligation.

Financial accounting The area of accounting dealing with the preparation of financial statements showing a business's results of operations, financial position, and cash flow.

Financial Accounting Standards Board (FASB) A private, not-for-profit organization whose task is to develop generally accepted accounting principles in the United States.

Financial flexibility A firm's ability to generate sufficient amounts of cash to respond to unanticipated business needs and opportunities.

Financial reporting objectives A component of the conceptual framework which specifies that financial statements should provide information that is (1) useful for investment and credit decisions, (2) helpful in assessing an entity's ability to generate future cash flows, and (3) about an entity's resources, claims on those resources, and the effects of events causing changes in these items.

Financial statement audit An examination of a company's financial statements by a firm of independent certified public accountants.

Financial statement elements A component of the conceptual framework that identifies the significant components—assets, liabilities, stockholders' equity, revenues, and expenses—used to prepare financial statements.

Financing activities A section in the statement of cash flows that reports cash flows associated with obtaining cash from owners and creditors, returning cash to owners, and repaying amounts borrowed.

Finished goods inventory A manufacturer's inventory that includes all products that have been completed and are ready for sale to customers.

First-in, first-out (FIFO) method An inventory costing method that assumes that the oldest (earliest purchased) goods are sold first.

Fiscal year The annual accounting period used by a business.

Forensic accounting A branch of accounting that involves investigations that result from actual or anticipated disputes such as criminal activity.

Forward stock split Additional shares of capital stock issued by a corporation to its current stockholders in proportion to their current ownership interests without changing the balances in the related stockholders' equity accounts. A forward stock split increases the number of shares outstanding and reduces proportionately the stock's par value per share.

Franchise An exclusive right to operate or sell a specific brand of products in a given geographic area.

Fraud Any act by the management or employees of a business involving an intentional deception for personal gain.

Fraud triangle The three elements of fraud, consisting of (1) pressure, (2) rationalization, and (3) opportunity.

Free cash flow (FCF) A measure of a firm's cash flow health, calculated as cash provided by operating activities less cash expenditures for property, plant, and equipment. Free cash flow is a measure of a firm's operating cash flow available for general corporate purposes such as debt retirement or dividend payment.

Free on board A term for determining ownership for items in transit.

Full disclosure principle An accounting principle stipulating that all facts necessary to make financial statements useful should be disclosed in a firm's annual report.

Future value The amount that a specified investment (or series of investments) will be worth at a future date if invested at a given rate of compound interest.

G

General journal An accounting record with enough flexibility so that any type of business transaction may be recorded in it; a diary of a business's accounting transactions.

General ledger A grouping of all of a business's accounts that are used to prepare the basic financial statements.

Generally accepted accounting principles (GAAP) A set of standards and procedures that guide the preparation of financial statements.

Going concern concept An accounting principle that assumes that, in the absence of evidence to the contrary, a business enterprise will have an indefinite life.

Goods flow The actual physical movement of inventory through a business.

Goods in transit Items that are being shipped by a common carrier.

Goodwill The value of all attributes acquired in an acquisition that are not otherwise associated with other specific assets; calculated as the purchase price of the acquired company less the fair market value of the identifiable net assets.

Gross pay The amount an employee earns before any withholdings or deductions.

Gross profit The difference between net sales and cost of goods sold; also called gross margin.

Gross profit percentage Gross profit on sales divided by net sales.

H

Hash A cryptographic signature linking separate blocks in a blockchain.

Held-to-maturity securities Debt securities that management intends to hold to maturity.

Holding company A corporation that controls another corporation through ownership of the latter's stock.

Horizontal analysis The analysis of a firm's financial statements that covers two or more years.

I

Impairment loss A loss recognized on an impaired asset equal to the difference between its book value and its current fair value.

Income statement A financial statement reporting a business's sales revenue and expenses for a given period of time.

Indirect method A presentation of cash flow from operating activities in a statement of cash flows that begins with net income and applies a series of adjustments to convert the net income to a cash basis amount.

Influential securities Equity securities that represent a 20 to 50 percent ownership of a corporation's voting stock.

Institute of Management Accountants An association representing members who work in management accounting, including jobs in decision support, planning and control positions.

Intangible asset An asset lacking a physical presence; examples of intangible assets include patents, copyrights, and brand names.

Interest A payment for the use of money.

Internal auditing A company function that provides independent appraisals of the company's financial statements, its internal control, and its operations.

Internal controls The measures undertaken by a company to ensure the reliability of its accounting data, protect its assets from theft or unauthorized use, insure that employees follow the company's policies and procedures, and evaluate the performance of employees, departments, divisions, and the company as a whole.

International Accounting Standards Board (IASB) An independent accounting standard-setting agency whose purpose is to develop international financial reporting standards.

International Financial Reporting Standards (IFRS) An international set of accounting standards, interpretations, and the framework for the preparation and presentation of financial statements used in many countries.

Inventory carrying costs Costs created by just-in-case inventories, including casualty insurance, building usage costs, and the cost of capital invested in the inventory.

Inventory overage The increase in the inventory account that occurs when the physical inventory count is greater than the inventory account balance.

Inventory shrinkage The decrease in the inventory account that occurs when the physical inventory count is less than the inventory account balance.

Inventory turnover ratio A ratio computed by dividing cost of goods sold by the average ending inventory.

Investing activities A section in the statement of cash flows that reports cash flows involving (1) the purchase and sale of plant assets and intangible assets, (2) the purchase and sale of stocks, bonds, and other securities (other than cash equivalents), and (3) the lending and subsequent collection of money.

Invoice price The price that a seller charges a purchaser for merchandise.

Issued shares Shares of stock that have been sold and issued to stockholders; issued stock may be either outstanding or held in the treasury.

J

Journal A tabular record in which business transactions are analyzed in debit and credit terms and recorded in chronological order.

Journal entry An entry of accounting information into a journal.

Just-in-case inventory The extra quantity of inventory that a firm carries just in case suppliers do not deliver when scheduled or just in case the company decides to make previously unplanned quantities of product for sale to customers.

Just-in-time (JIT) manufacturing A manufacturing philosophy that seeks to minimize or eliminate just-in-case inventory quantities through careful planning of raw material purchases and manufacturing management.

L

Land improvements Improvements with limited useful lives made to land sites, such as paved parking lots and driveways.

Last-in, first-out (LIFO) method An inventory costing method that assumes that the newest (most recently purchased) goods are sold first.

Lawsuit A prosecution of a claim in a court of law; may lead to a financial statement footnote disclosure by the defendant as a contingent liability.

Lease A contract between a lessor (owner) and lessee (tenant) for the rental of property.

Leasehold The rights transferred from the lessor to the lessee by a lease.

Leasehold improvements Expenditures made by a lessee to alter or improve leased property.

Lessee The party acquiring the right to the use of property by a lease.

Lessor The owner of property who transfers the right to use the property to another party by a lease.

Leverage The use of borrowed funds to finance the assets or operations of a firm.

Liabilities The obligations or debts that a business must pay in money or services at some time in the future as a consequence of past transactions or events.

LIFO conformity rule A section of the Internal Revenue Code requiring that any company that selects LIFO for income tax reporting must also use LIFO for financial reporting to stockholders.

LIFO inventory reserve The difference between the value of ending inventory reported under LIFO and what the inventory would have been valued at under FIFO.

Liquidity A measure of a company's ability to pay its obligations expected to come due in the next year.

List price The suggested price or reference price of merchandise in a catalog or price list.

Long-term liabilities Debt obligations not due to be repaid within the normal operating cycle or one year, whichever is longer.

Lower-of-cost-or-market (LCM) A measurement method that, when applied to inventory, provides for ending inventory to be valued on the balance sheet at the lower of its acquisition cost or current replacement cost.

Lower-of-cost-or-net realizable value (LCNRV) A measurement method that provides for the recognition of an inventory write-down loss when the inventory's net realizable value declines below its recorded acquisition cost.

M

Maker The signer of a promissory note.

Management Discussion and Analysis (MD&A) Part of the 10-K report that contains management's interpretation of the company's recent past performance along with discussion of possible future opportunities and risks.

Managerial accounting The accounting activities carried out by a firm's accounting staff primarily to provide management with accounting data for decisions related to a firm's operations.

Manufacturer A company that converts raw materials and components into finished goods through the application of skilled labor and machine operations.

Market rate of interest The rate of interest in the market for a bond or other debt instrument.

Materiality An accounting guideline that states that insignificant data that would not affect a financial statement user's decisions may be recorded in the most expedient manner.

Maturity date The date on which a note or bond matures.

Merchandise inventory A stock of goods that a company buys from another company and makes available for sale to its customers.

Merchandising firm A company that buys finished goods, stores the goods for varying periods of time, and then resells the goods.

Modified accelerated cost recovery system (MACRS) A system of accelerated depreciation for U.S. income tax purposes; it prescribes depreciation rates by asset-life classification.

Monetary unit concept An accounting guideline that reports assets, liabilities and stockholders' equity in the basic unit of money.

Multiple-step income statement An income statement in which one or more intermediate performance measures, such as gross profit on sales, are derived before the continuing income is reported.

N

Natural resource Resources supplied by nature, such as timber stands, mineral deposits, and oil and gas deposits.

Net assets The difference between a business's assets and liabilities. Net assets are equal to stockholders' equity.

Net income The excess of a business's sales revenues over its expenses.

Net pay The amount of an employee's paycheck, after subtracting withheld amounts.

Net realizable value An asset measure calculated by subtracting the expected disposal cost from an asset's expected selling price.

Net sales The total revenue generated by a company through merchandise sales less the revenue given up through sales returns and allowances and less the revenue given up through sales discounts.

New York Stock Exchange (NYSE) A marketplace, located in New York City, for the buying and selling of corporate shares.

No-par value stock Stock that does not have a par value.

Node A decentralized computer separated from other computers on a blockchain.

Noncash expenses Expenses that do not involve any current period cash outflows and that are deducted in the process of calculating a company's accrual basis net income.

Noncash investing and financing activities Investing activities and financing activities that do not affect current cash flows; information about these events must be reported as a supplement to the statement of cash flows.

Normal balance The side on which increases to the account are recorded.

Normal operating cycle The average period of time between the use of cash to buy goods for resale or to provide services and the subsequent collection of cash from customers.

Not-sufficient-funds check A check from an individual or company that had an insufficient cash balance in the bank when the holder of the check presented it to the bank for payment.

Note receivable A promissory note held by the note's payee.

Notes to the financial statements The annual report section following the four financial statements that includes a description of the assumptions and estimates that were used in preparing the statements, the measurement procedures that were followed, and the details behind the summary numbers.

O

Objectivity An accounting notion requiring that, whenever possible, accounting data should be based on objectively determined evidence.

Off-balance-sheet financing The structuring of a financing arrangement such that no liability is recorded on the borrower's balance sheet.

Open account A charge account provided by a retailer for its customers.

Operating activities A section in the statement of cash flows that reports cash flows from all activities that are not classified as investing or financing activities.

Operating cycle For a particular business, the average period of time between the use of cash in its typical operating activity and the subsequent collection of cash from customers.

Operating lease A lease by which the lessor retains the usual risks and rewards of owning the property.

Operating-cash-flow-to-capital-expenditures ratio A financial ratio calculated by dividing a firm's cash flow from operating activities by its annual capital expenditures.

Operating-cash-flow-to-current-liabilities ratio A financial ratio calculated by dividing cash flow from operating activities by the average current liabilities for the year.

Operational audit An evaluation of activities, systems, and internal controls within a company to determine their efficiency, effectiveness, and economy.

Ordinary annuity An annuity where the payments occur at the end of each period.

Outstanding checks Checks issued by a firm that have not yet been presented to its bank for payment.

Outstanding shares Shares of stock that are currently held by stockholders.

P

Paid-in capital The amount of capital contributed to a corporation by its stockholders in excess of its par value or stated value.

Par value An amount specified in the corporate charter for each class of stock and imprinted on the face of each stock certificate; often determines the legal capital of a corporation.

Parent company A company holding all, or a majority, of the voting stock of another company, called a subsidiary.

Participating A feature associated with preferred stock whereby the preferred stock can share any special dividend distribution with common stock beyond the regular preferred stock dividend rate.

Partnership A voluntary association of two or more persons for the purpose of conducting a business.

Password A string of characters that a user enters into a device to prove that the user is actually the user that is allowed to use the device.

Patent An exclusive privilege granted for 20 years to an inventor that gives the patent holder the right to exclude others from making, using, or selling the invention.

Payee The company or individual to whom a promissory note is made payable.

Percentage of net sales method A procedure that determines the bad debts expense for the year by multiplying net credit sales by an estimated uncollectible percentage.

Period-in-time statement A financial statement accumulating information for a specific period of time; examples include the income statement, the statement of stockholders' equity, the statement of retained earnings, and the statement of cash flows.

Periodic inventory system A system that records merchandise transactions in a variety of accounts; the Inventory account and Cost of Goods Sold account are not updated until the end of the period when a physical count of the inventory is taken.

Permanent account An account used to prepare the balance sheet—that is, an asset, liability, or stockholders' equity account; any balance in a permanent account at the end of an accounting period is carried forward to the following accounting period.

Perpetual inventory system A system that records the cost of merchandise inventory in the Inventory account at the time of purchase and updates the Inventory account for subsequent purchases and sales of merchandise as they occur.

Persistent earnings Earnings that are expected to recur over time. Also known as sustainable earnings or permanent earnings.

Petty cash fund A special, relatively small cash fund established for making minor cash disbursements in the operation of a business.

Physical count of inventory The counting of inventory used to verify the balance of inventory.

Plant assets A firm's property, plant, and equipment; also called fixed assets.

Point-in-time statement A financial statement presenting information as of a particular date; the balance sheet is a point-in-time statement.

Post-closing trial balance A list of general ledger accounts and their balances after closing entries have been recorded and posted.

Postdated check A check from another person or company with a calendar date that is later than the current date. A postdated check does not become cash until the calendar date of the check.

Posting The transfer of information from the journal to the general ledger accounts.

Posting references A series of abbreviations used in posting to indicate to where or from where a journal entry is posted.

Predictive analytics A form of data analytics that aids in predicting what is going to happen in the future.

Preemptive right The right of a stockholder to maintain his or her proportionate ownership interest in a corporation by having the right to purchase an appropriate quantity of shares in any new share issue.

Preferred stock A class of capital stock with priority over common stock in dividend payments and in the distribution of assets in the event of a corporation liquidation.

Prescriptive analytics A form of data analytics that helps suggest a course of action for what should occur in the future.

Present value The current worth of amounts to be paid (or received) in the future; calculated by discounting the future payments (or receipts) at a specified interest rate.

Prevention control An internal control designed to discover problems before they arise.

Price-earnings ratio The current market price per common share divided by a company's earnings per share.

Principal As it relates to debt financing, the amount initially borrowed from the creditor.

Product warranties Guarantees against product defects for a designated period of time following product sale.

Promissory note A written promise to pay a certain sum of money on demand or at a determinable future time.

Property, plant, and equipment The land, buildings, equipment, vehicles, furniture, and fixtures that a firm uses in its operations; often referred to as PP&E.

Public Company Accounting Oversight Board (PCAOB) A quasi-governmental agency established by the Sarbanes-Oxley Act to overhaul auditing standards, inspect the work of accounting firms, and discipline independent auditors that fail to meet and maintain acceptable standards of audit performance.

Purchase allowance A reduction in the selling price of merchandise granted by a seller due to dissatisfaction by the purchaser.

Purchase return Shipping unsatisfactory merchandise from a purchaser back to the seller for a purchase allowance.

Q

Qualitative characteristics of accounting information The characteristics of accounting information that contribute to decision usefulness; the primary qualities are relevance and faithful representation.

Quarterly data Selected quarterly financial information that is reported in the annual report to stockholders.

Quick ratio Quick assets (that is, cash and cash equivalents, short-term investments, and accounts receivable) divided by current liabilities.

Quick response system A system used with a point-of-sale system that is designed to insure that a retailer quickly orders more of the items that are selling and quickly eliminates those items that are not selling.

R

Ratio analysis The process of expressing the relationship of one accounting number to another accounting number through the process of division.

Raw materials inventory A manufacturer's inventory that includes raw materials and components that have been purchased for use in the factory but have not yet been placed into production.

Recognition and measurement criteria The criteria that must be met before a financial statement element may be recorded in the accounts. Essentially, the item must meet the definition of an element and must be measurable, and the resultant information about the item must be relevant and reliable.

Relevance A qualitative characteristic of accounting information; relevant information contributes to the predictive and evaluative decisions made by financial statement users.

Reliability A qualitative characteristic of accounting information; reliable information contains no bias or error and faithfully portrays what it intends to represent.

Remittance advice A form that accompanies a check to inform the person receiving the check about the purpose of the check.

Remittance list A list of the checks received from customers to pay their accounts receivable.

Report form A format of the classified balance sheet where assets are displayed on the top and liabilities and stockholders' equity are displayed below the assets.

Research and development costs Expenditures for the research and development of products or processes. These costs are almost always expensed rather than capitalized.

Restricted cash Cash that is restricted for a specific use and not available for general use.

Retailer A company that buys goods from wholesale distributors and sells the goods to individual customers.

Retained earnings The earnings of a corporation that have been retained in the corporation (have not been paid out as a dividend) for future corporate use.

Return on assets (ROA) A measure of profitability; defined as net income divided by average total assets (or period-end assets).

Return on common stockholders' equity (ROE) A financial ratio computed as (net income − preferred stock dividends) divided by average common stockholders' equity.

Return on sales (ROS) ratio A measure of a firm's profitability, calculated as net income divided by net sales. Also called profit margin.

Revenue expenditures An expenditure related to plant assets that is expensed when incurred.

Revenue recognition principle An accounting principle requiring that sales revenues be recognized when services are performed or goods are sold.

S

Sale on account (sale on credit) A sale of merchandise made on a credit basis.

Sales discounts An account used by a seller to record cash discounts taken by a buyer when payment is made during the allowed discount period.

Sales returns and allowances An account used by a seller to record either the return of merchandise by a buyer or an allowance given to the buyer in lieu of a return.

Sales revenue Increases in stockholders' equity that result when a firm provides goods or services to its customers.

Salvage value The expected net recovery when a plant asset is sold or removed from service; also called residual value.

Sarbanes-Oxley Act (SOX) A set of legislative rules enacted in 2002 to provide stricter guidance over corporate behavior.

The legislation was a reaction to the infamous accounting scandals at Enron and WorldCom.

Secured bond A bond that pledges specific property as security (or collateral) for meeting the terms of a bond agreement.

Segment A subdivision of a firm for which supplemental financial information is disclosed.

Segregation of duties An internal control principle that requires that duties should be allocated to separate individuals.

Serial bond A bond issue that staggers the bond maturity dates over a series of years.

Service company A firm whose primary revenue source is from providing services to a customer rather than manufacturing or selling a physical product.

Simple interest Interest that is calculated only on the initial principal and not on any unpaid interest.

Single-step income statement A simple format of the income statement where net income is computed in a single step; subtracting total expenses from total revenues.

Sinking fund provision A bond feature that requires the borrower to retire a portion of the outstanding bonds each year or, in some cases, to make payments each year to a trustee who is responsible for managing the resources needed to retire the bonds at maturity.

Socially responsible investing (SRI) An investment strategy that considers not just financial performance but also the social concepts of environmental stewardship, consumer protection, human rights, and diversity.

Sole proprietorship A form of business organization in which one person owns the business.

Solvency A measure of a company's ability to repay its debts in the long term.

Source document Any written document or computer record evidencing an accounting transaction, such as a bank check, deposit slip, sales invoice, or cash register tape.

Specific identification method An inventory costing method involving the physical identification of goods sold and goods remaining and costing these amounts at their actual costs.

Stated value A nominal amount that may be assigned to each share of no-par value stock and accounted for much as if it were a par value.

Statement of cash flows A financial statement showing a firm's cash inflows and cash outflows for a specific period, classified into operating, investing, and financing activity categories.

Statement of retained earnings A financial statement showing the financial changes that occurred in retained earnings during the accounting period.

Statement of stockholders' equity A financial statement presenting information regarding the events that cause a change in stockholders' equity during a period. The statement presents the beginning balance, additions to, deductions from, and the ending balance of stockholders' equity for the period.

Stock dividends Additional shares of capital stock issued by a corporation to its current stockholders in proportion to their existing ownership interest.

Stockholder An owner of a corporation as a result of the purchase of the corporation's shares of stock; also known as a shareholder.

Stockholders' equity The residual interest in the assets of a business after all liabilities have been paid off; stockholders' equity is equal to a firm's net assets, or total assets less total liabilities.

Straight-line depreciation A depreciation procedure that allocates uniform amounts of depreciation expense to each period of an asset's useful life.

Straight-line interest method A method to amortize a bond discount or premium where the amount amortized as interest each period is a constant dollar amount.

Subsequent events Events occurring shortly after a fiscal year-end that are reported as supplemental information to the financial statements of the year just ended.

Subsidiaries Corporations that have at least a majority of their voting stock owned by another company.

Summary of significant accounting policies A financial statement disclosure, usually the initial note to the financial statements, which identifies the major accounting policies and procedures used by a firm.

T

T-account An abbreviated form of the formal account in the shape of a T.

Temporary account An account used to gather information for an accounting period; revenue, expense, and dividend accounts are temporary accounts.

Term loan A long-term borrowing, evidenced by a note payable, that is arranged with a single lender.

Time value of money The concept that money can be invested at a positive interest rate and grow to a larger sum in the future.

Timeliness Having information available in time to be capable of influencing a decision.

Times-interest-earned ratio Income before interest expense and income taxes divided by interest expense.

Timestamp A date and time associated with a block on a blockchain.

Trade name (trademark) An exclusive and continuing right to use a certain term or name to identify a brand or family of products.

Trading securities Debt securities and noninfluential equity securities that management buys with the intent to sell in the near future.

Transitory earnings Single-period events such as special items, restructuring charges, changes in accounting principle, and discontinued operations, that are not expected to recur in the future.

Treasury stock Shares of a corporation that have been acquired for purposes other than retiring (cancelling) the stock. Treasury stock is a contra account recorded at cost and is deducted from stockholders' equity on the balance sheet.

Trend analysis A process in which an analyst or investor compares a company's results, or the results of a ratio, over time.

Trend percentages A comparison of the same financial item over two or more years stated as a percentage of a base-year amount.

Trial balance A list of the account titles in the general ledger, their respective debit or credit balances, and the totals of the debit and credit balances.

Triple bottom line A form of reporting that captures an expanded set of measures in addition to traditional financial reporting. The three bottom lines include economic, ecological, and social.

U

U.S. Securities and Exchange Commission (SEC) An independent agency of the U.S. federal government responsible for enforcing the federal securities laws, proposing securities rules, and regulating the securities industry.

Unadjusted trial balance A list of general ledger accounts and their balances taken before adjustments have been made.

Unearned revenue A liability representing revenues received in advance; also called deferred revenue.

Units-of-production method A depreciation method that allocates depreciation expense to each operating period in proportion to the amount of the asset's total expected productive capacity used each period.

Unusual items Items that display a high degree of abnormality and/or are unrelated, or only incidentally related, to the normal activities of a business.

Useful life The period of time that an asset is used by a business, running from the date of acquisition to the date of disposal (or removal from service).

V

Verifiability Different individuals can independently reach a consensus that the reported amounts represent a faithful representation.

Vertical analysis Analysis of a firm's financial statements that focuses on the statements of a single year.

W

Weighted-average cost method An inventory costing method that calculates an average unit purchase cost, weighted by the number of units purchased at each price, and uses that weighted-average unit cost to determine the cost of goods sold for all sales.

Wholesaler A company that buys finished products from manufacturing firms in large quantities and resells the products to retailers.

Work-in-process inventory A manufacturer's inventory that consists of units of product that have been entered into production in the factory but have not been completed.

Worksheet An informal accounting document used to facilitate the preparation of financial statements.

Z

Zero-coupon bond A bond that offers no periodic interest payments and that is issued at a substantial discount from its face value.

Index

Exhibits and notes are included in the index with a corresponding e or n following the page numbers.

Exhibits and notes are included in the index with a corresponding e or n following the page numbers.

Exhibits and notes are included in the index with a corresponding e or n following the page numbers.

Exhibits and notes are included in the index with a corresponding e or n following the page numbers.

Exhibits and notes are included in the index with a corresponding e or n following the page numbers.

Exhibits and notes are included in the index with a corresponding e or n following the page numbers.

Exhibits and notes are included in the index with a corresponding e or n following the page numbers.

Exhibits and notes are included in the index with a corresponding e or n following the page numbers.

Exhibits and notes are included in the index with a corresponding e or n following the page numbers.

Exhibits and notes are included in the index with a corresponding e or n following the page numbers.

Exhibits and notes are included in the index with a corresponding e or n following the page numbers.

transactions, recording, *(continued)*
  posting journal entries to general ledger, 2-15–2-16
  provided services for cash and on account, 2-18
  provided services to customers, 2-18
  purchased equipment, 2-17
  purchased office supplies on account, 2-17
  received customer prepayment, 2-18
  received payment, 2-19
  recording process, 2-16–2-19
  signed bank note, 2-17
transferability of ownership, 11-4
transitory earnings, 13-3
transportation costs
  incurred by buyer, 5-6–5-7
  incurred by seller, 5-7
  periodic inventory system, 5-17
transpositions, 7-21
treasury stock, 11-7, 11-13–11-14
trend analysis, 4-11, 13-10–13-12
trend percentages, 13-10
trial balance, 2-22–2-23
  post-closing, 3-20, 3-21e, 3-26
triple bottom line, 1-15
Tucker Enterprises, 6-12
Tufte's principles, F-8
TurboTax, 2-16
Turner Company, 8-7
Turner, Jamal, E-10
Twitter, 2-4
Tyler Company, 7-24–7-25, 10-25

U

unadjusted trial balance, 3-7
  Balke Laboratory, 3-23
  worksheet, 3-31
uncollectible accounts, balance sheet for, 8-6
Under Armour, Inc., 13-31
understandability, 1-25
unearned revenue, 2-7, 3-10, 10-5–10-6
  to revenue, 3-10–3-11
UNICEF, 13-6
United Parcel Service, 1-6
units-of-production method, 9-10–9-11

unrealized gains and losses, D-6
unrecorded expenses, 3-11–3-12
unrecorded revenues, 3-12–3-13
unusual items, 13-3
useful life, 9-7
U.S. Securities and Exchange Commission (SEC), 1-9

V

variety, F-2
velocity, F-2
veracity, F-2
vertical analysis, 13-7, 13-12–13-13
vice pressure, 7-3
virtuous cycle, 1-14
Visa, 5-5
visual clutter, f-8
visualizations, F-5
volume, F-2

W

wages payable, 1-11
Walmart Corporation, 1-6, 5-14
  bond certificate, 10-12
  gross profit percentage for, 5-14e
  return on sales ratios for, 5-14e
Warner Company, D-4, D-8
wasting assets (*see* natural resources)
WebWork, Inc.
  accounting equation, transactions and, 2-5–2-10
  accrued fees, 3-13
  accrued interest, 3-12, 3-13
  accrued wages, 3-11–3-12
  adjusted trial balance for, 3-16e
  adjusting entries, 3-14
  cash T-account, 2-13
  chart of accounts for, 2-11
  closing process, 3-20
  closing revenue and expense accounts, 3-27–3-28
  deferred service revenue, 3-10–3-11
  depreciation, 3-9–3-10
  financial statements, preparing, 3-16–3-18
  general journal for, 2-20e

  general ledger for, 2-21e
  income statement, 4-10c
  office supplies, 3-8–3-9
  post-closing trial balance, 3-21e, 3-29e
  prepaid rent, 3-9
  recording transactions, 2-14–2-21
  statement of cash flows for, 7-21–7-22, 7-22e
  trial balance, 2-22
  unadjusted trial balance, 2-22e, 3-7e
  worksheet, 3-30–3-32
weighted-average cost method, 6-11
  selection of, 6-14
  perpetual inventory system and, 6-24, 6-24e
Wells Fargo & Company, 1-6, 1-7
Weyerhaeuser Company, 9-22
  balance sheet, 9-22e
Whirlpool, 1-6
wholesale EFT, 7-16
wholesalers, 5-3
Williams Distributing Company, 5-16
Wilson Corporation
  bank statement of, 7-18e
  bank reconciliation process, 7-19–7-21, 7-32e
Wirecard AG, 1-7, 7-3
working capital, 10-22, 13-18
work-in-process inventory, 6-3
worksheet, 3-30
  adjusted trial balance, 3-31–3-32
  adjustments, 3-31
  balancing, 3-32
  extension of adjusted trial balance, 3-32
  heading, 3-30–3-31
  preparing, 3-30–3-32
  unadjusted trial balance, 3-31
WorldCom, 2-23, 7-9, 9-16
Worthington Industries, 11-20

Y

year-end adjustments, 10-16

Z

Zales, 6-19
zero-coupon bonds, 10-15

Exhibits and notes are included in the index with a corresponding e or n following the page numbers.